Encyclopedia of
ANCIENT EGYPT

THIRD EDITION

Encyclopedia of
ANCIENT EGYPT

THIRD EDITION

Margaret R. Bunson

An Infobase Learning Company

Encyclopedia of Ancient Egypt, Third Edition

Facts On File, Inc.
An Imprint of Infobase Learning
132 West 31st Street
New York NY 10001

Library of Congress Cataloging-in-Publication Data

Bunson, Margaret.
Encyclopedia of ancient Egypt / Margaret R. Bunson. — 3rd ed.
p. cm.
Includes bibliographical references and index.
ISBN 978-0-8160-8216-2 (alk. paper)
1. Egypt—Civilization—To 332 B.C.—Dictionaries. 2. Egypt—
Antiquities—Dictionaries. I. Title.
DT58.B96 2011
932.003—dc23   2011026433

Facts On File books are available at special discounts when purchased
in bulk quantities for businesses, associations, institutions, or sales
promotions. Please call our Special Sales Department in New York at
(212) 967-8800 or (800) 322-8755.

You can find Facts On File on the World Wide Web at
http://www.infobaselearning.com

Text design by Joan Toro
Maps and genealogies by Dale Williams and Patricia Meschino
Composition by Hermitage Publishing Services
Cover printed by Yurchak Printing, Landisville, Pa.
Book printed and bound by Yurchak Printing, Landisville, Pa.
Date printed: January 2012
Printed in the United States of America

10 9 8 7 6 5 4 3 2 1

This book is printed on acid-free paper.

Dedicated to the memory of
Dr. Rafael Zamora of Aguadilla, Puerto Rico

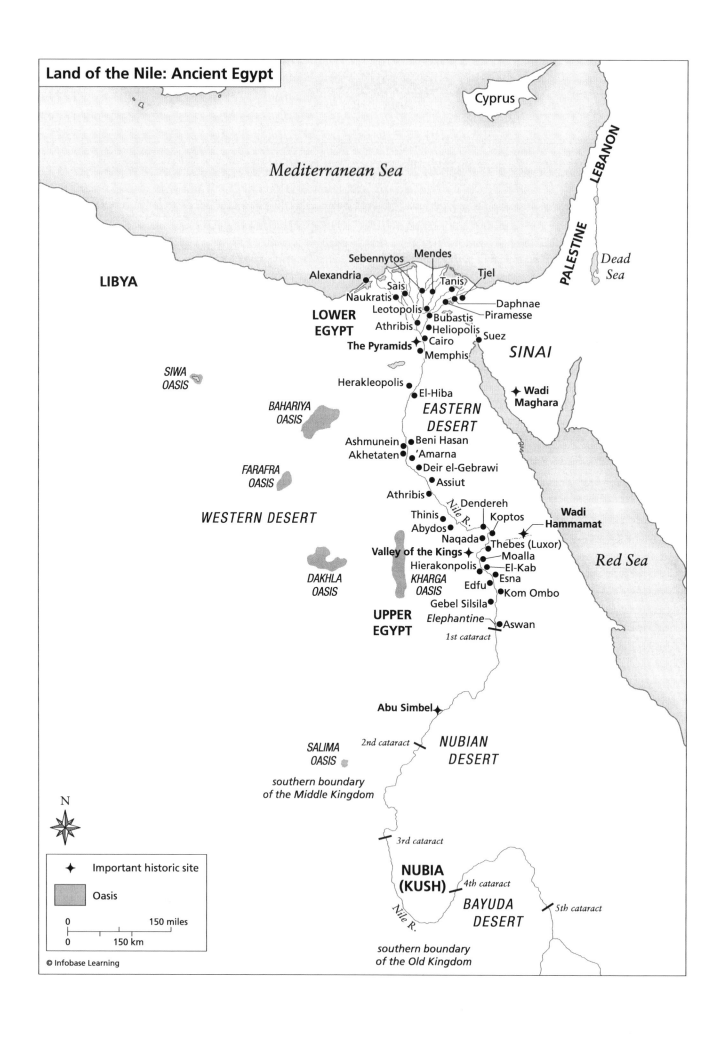

Land of the Nile: Ancient Egypt

Cyprus

Mediterranean Sea

LEBANON

PALESTINE

Dead Sea

LIBYA

Sebennytos · Mendes
Alexandria
Sais · Tanis · Tjel
Naukratis
Daphnae
Leotopolis · Bubastis · Piramesse
Athribis · Heliopolis
Cairo
The Pyramids ✦ Memphis
Suez

LOWER EGYPT

SINAI

Herakleopolis
El-Hiba

SIWA OASIS

BAHARIYA OASIS

EASTERN DESERT

✦ **Wadi Maghara**

Ashmunein · Beni Hasan
Akhetaten · 'Amarna
Deir el-Gebrawi
Assiut

FARAFRA OASIS

Athribis

Dendereh
Thinis · Koptos
Abydos
Naqada
Valley of the Kings ✦ Thebes (Luxor)
Moalla
Hierakonpolis · El-Kab
Esna
Edfu
Kom Ombo
Gebel Silsila
Elephantine · Aswan
1st cataract

Wadi Hammamat

Red Sea

WESTERN DESERT

DAKHLA OASIS

KHARGA OASIS

UPPER EGYPT

N

Abu Simbel ✦

2nd cataract
SALIMA OASIS

NUBIAN DESERT

southern boundary
of the Middle Kingdom

3rd cataract

✦ Important historic site

Oasis

NUBIA (KUSH)
4th cataract

BAYUDA DESERT

5th cataract

Nile R.

0   150 miles
0   150 km

© Infobase Learning

southern boundary
of the Old Kingdom

CONTENTS

LIST OF ILLUSTRATIONS AND MAPS

Photographs and Illustrations

Maps

INTRODUCTION

The study of an ancient civilization can be an educational and fulfilling activity that makes one aware of elements of culture and civilization that have been blurred in the modern era. A nation such as Egypt, which has survived as a united people for more than 3,000 years through countless wars, natural disasters, and changing political scenes, offers a dazzling array of vibrant personalities, artistic heights, and profound spiritual realities.

The royals of the ancient Nile, the men and women who ruled over the Land of the Two Kingdoms, had an unprecedented awareness of their own destinies. Their reigns were dominated by vigor and daring because they knew that the people of the Nile Valley shared and supported their vision of the nation and the rule of the gods.

Charting the night skies, the first astronomers of Egypt named the various constellations of the stars and recognized that human beings on earth were linked to these heavenly bodies not only during their brief life spans but in eternal realms after death. At the same time, the Nile River, streaming northward on its journey out of the heart of Africa, taught the Egyptians the necessity of cooperation, moderation, and dedication in order to survive the floods that arrived with Sirius, the Dog Star, in the night skies.

When first published by Facts On File in 1991, *The Encyclopedia of Ancient Egypt* was the first comprehensive A-to-Z reference to the more than 5,000-year period of ancient Egyptian civilization. A new edition was released in 2002 that was marked by extensive revisions and updating, but the encyclopedia remained faithful to its essential purpose of offering the reader a comprehensive reference to the personalities, topics, issues, and important sites constituting the remarkable civilization that developed and flourished along the Nile.

It is one of the realities of reference publishing—especially when covering a topic that is subject to ongoing research and fieldwork by archaeologists—that over time there is a need to update titles by integrating new discoveries and research results. This is what this third edition of *The Encyclopedia of Ancient Egypt* sets out to accomplish.

The third edition of *The Encyclopedia of Ancient Egypt* compiles around 2,000 entries on every aspect of ancient Egyptian life and civilization spanning literally thousands of years of history. The entries have been updated with the most recent scholarship. They are written and organized in a way that makes the material easily accessible and beneficial both to students and to other readers who have an interest in Egyptian history.

The front matter now includes a historical overview, a geographical overview, and a chronology of major events. At the end of the book the reader will find a glossary, a revised reading list, and a new guide on How to Study Ancient Egypt.

These introductory materials serve as the first bridge to the entries, which receive more detailed treatment in the A-to-Z section. Every entry, especially the major ones, has been updated to reflect the recent discoveries, the return of artifacts to Egypt, and the progress made in research around the world. Key overview entries, such as those on administration, law, art and architecture, family life, health and sickness, science, and warfare, have been significantly expanded. The entries also offer revised reading lists at the end. As with previous editions, the volumes chosen for both the suggested readings at the end of entries and the book list in the back matter are intended for the general reader and are deliberately restricted to English-language editions. Nevertheless, the volumes chosen represent some of the most up-to-date works available for the specific topics, and all of them are recommended. New maps and illustrations are sprinkled throughout.

As with earlier editions, in keeping with the preferred method of dating for modern historical works, the system of dates according to B.C. (before Christ) and A.D. (*anno Domini*, "in the year of the Lord") has been changed to B.C.E. (before the common era) and C.E. (of the common era). The intention is to make this book consistent with other works on the subject and for purposes of consistent dating in the Facts On File database. The editorial revision of the dating system is undertaken despite the personal preferences of the author.

The introductory sections to the front matter are ideal for the reader who wants first to have an overview of the extensive timeline of ancient Egyptian history. Once familiar with the general outline of the civilization's history, the entries on general topics (such as administration, religion, etc.) are good places to turn to next, followed by the biographical entries. The latter will also be helpful in introducing other topics and areas of interest that are related to the efforts and achievements of these pharaohs and queens.

Researching this remarkable ancient civilization and reading the works it produced has been a privilege and a lifelong adventure. It would be impossible to describe my gratitude for this experience without thanking two people from Facts On File: Claudia Schaab, executive editor, and Melissa Cullen-DuPont, associate editor. I am genuinely grateful for their dedication and patience as I labored to bring the work on this new edition to its completion. With the encouragement and dedication of these individuals, I am delighted to be able to offer the splendors and the mysteries of ancient Egypt to another generation of readers.

HISTORICAL OVERVIEW

Called the "gift of the Nile," Egypt evolved in isolation on the northeastern section of the African continent. The name Egypt is the modern version of Aigyptos, the Greek word derived from the Egyptian for the city of Memphis (Hiku Ptah, which translates to the "Mansion of the Soul.") Egyptians call their land Msr today, and in Pharaonic times it was designated Khem or Khemet, which translates to the "Black Land" between the Deshret, the red Deserts.

Because of its geographical position on the African continent, and because of its relative isolation, Egypt developed in a unique fashion. The natural defenses of the cataracts of the Nile and the eastern and western deserts kept the land comparatively free of foreign domination in the early stages of growth and confederation. The Nile was the primary factor in this development, as the region offered no other rivers and little rainfall. The annual inundation provided a bountiful agricultural economy and also prompted a remarkable sense of cooperation among the Egyptians. This spirit illuminated much of their religious and political thinking and left an imprint on their lives and on their future.

PREDYNASTIC PERIOD

The Predynastic Period was the era in which hunters and gatherers abandoned the heights and plateaus to enter the lush valley of the Nile, where they discovered both safety and abundant resources, the combination of which induced them to begin settlements. These first settlements were not uniform throughout Egypt, and a list of Predynastic Period cultural sequences has been developed to trace the development of cultural achievements in Upper and Lower Egypt.

Evolution and development took place in the Nile Valley as early as ca. 120,000 B.C.E. The Achulean culture appeared in the region, extending their range until ca. 90,000 B.C.E. *Homo erectus* gave way to *Homo sapiens* ca. 10,000 B.C.E., and the Mousterian culture was active by ca. 50,000 B.C.E. The last periods of the Achulean cul-

ture in Egypt were marked by the development of technological advances, including the use of flake tools.

The Asterian culture, associated with the Mousterian, used bows and arrows and was widespread in Maghreb and in the southern Sahara. Then, the Khormoussan culture, named for the Khor Musa, near Wadi Halfa (a site located near modern-day Sudan), appeared ca. 45,000 B.C.E. The Khormoussans, who in earlier times lived in the deserts, encamped in river valleys and followed wild herds.

From ca. 15,000 to 10,000 B.C.E., what is known as the Qadan phase moved to the Neolithic stage of development at Wadi Halfa; at Elkab, a site located on the east bank of the Nile; and in the Faiyum, a natural depression extending along the western bank. The Qadan phase was marked by hunting and gathering that included grains, as well as the creation of stone tools. Along with several others near Helwan, which serves as a southern suburb of modern-day Cairo, these settlements developed improved weaponry and used agricultural plots alongside the usual hunting and fishing routines. Pottery and baskets appeared, and people began to use necropolises, or burial sites, as well as other funerary practices.

By 3500 B.C.E. the Naqada III, or Gerzean B, cultures were in place in the Nile Valley alongside the Ma'adi, or so-called Dynasty 0, cultures. In both of these cultures regional kingdoms had been established, and people of this time used slate palettes for burials.

The Neolithic cultures of the Badarian, Tassan, and Faiyum A and B were at Badari, Hemania, Merimda Beni Salami, and in the Faiyum by 5540 B.C.E. These were followed by the Faiyum A and B cultures, the Naqada I (or Amratian) cultures, and the Fassan cultures. A dual ceramic development took place, with people using theriomorphic (animal-shaped) vessels for burial. People of this period also used copper in architecture, along with mined gold and tin, which were discovered in the Eastern Desert. Settlements started quarries, and flint was commonly used in the manufacture of weaponry. The first architectural forms appeared in this age, and settlements planned and erected towns.

The Naqada II, or Gerzean A, Period began ca. 4000 B.C.E., along with the Omari B culture. Settlements at el-Gerze and elsewhere displayed ceramic changes in this development, with style, motifs, and the use of natural images emerging. People of the time used boats and adopted standards as clan or regional totems, fashioned palettes out of schist, and produced funerary items. Small slates used for cosmetics became popular in the Nile Valley, and large and elaborate grave sites were developing.

The Naqada II, or Gerzean A, Period signaled a turning point in Predynastic Period Egypt. One of the aspects of this cultural event was contact with other nations beyond Egypt's borders. Trade was conducted with the Sinai region on Egypt's eastern border and with southern Palestine. Cultural aspects also included the rise of the nome (province) families, the use of stone figures both as art and in burial rituals, and the centralization of power.

Two cities dominated in this era: Buto in the north and Hierakonpolis in the south. In these cities, clans were in place, the members of which built temples and developed a priesthood for the worship of such deities as Horus. Other cities, such as Tell Edfu, were rising, and the system of nomes, or provinces, was in place.

LOWER EGYPT
Faiyum A (4400–3900 B.C.E.)

Faiyum A was a cultural sequence that emerged on the northern and northeastern shores of an ancient lake in the Faiyum district, possibly seasonal in habitation. The site was occupied by agriculturalists, but it is evident that they depended upon fishing and hunting and may have moved with the changes of the yearly migrations of large mammals. People of this sequence caught fish with harpoons and beveled points, but they did not use fishhooks.

People of this time erected mat or reed huts on the sheltered sides of mounds beside fertile grounds. There were underground granaries, removed from the houses to higher ground, no doubt to protect the stored materials from flooding. Archaeologists have gathered some evidence at these sites to indicate that the people kept sheep, goats, and possibly domesticated cattle. The granaries also showed remains of emmer wheat and a form of barley.

The stone tools used by the people of Faiyum A were large, with notches and denticulates. People of this sequence set flints into wooden handles and used arrowheads. They also wove baskets for the granaries and for daily needs and manufactured a variety of rough linen. Pottery in the Faiyum A sites was made out of coarse clay, normally in the form of flat dishes and bag-shaped vessels. Some were plain and some had red slip.

The people of this era appear to have lived in microbands, single and extended family groups, with chieftains who provided them with leadership. The sequence indicates the beginning of communities in the north.

Merimda (4300–3700 B.C.E.),

Merimda, a site on the western edge of the Delta, covered a vast territory with layers of cultural debris that give indications of up to 600 years of habitation. The people of this cultural sequence lived in pole-framed huts with windbreaks, and some used semisubterranean residences, building the walls high enough to stand above ground. The small habitations were laid out in rows, possibly part of a circular pattern. Granaries were composed of clay jars or baskets, buried up to the neck in the ground. People of the Merimda sequence probably buried the dead on the sites, but little evidence of grave goods has been recovered.

El-Omari (3700–3400 B.C.E.)

El-Omari is a site between modern Cairo and Helwan. The pottery from this sequence was red or black and unadorned, as revealed by the vases and lipped vessels archaeologists have discovered. People of this area made flake and blade tools, as well as millstones. They constructed oval shelters, with poles and woven mats, and probably had granaries.

Ma'adi (3400–3000 B.C.E.)

Ma'adi, a site located to the northwest of the El-Omari sequence location, contained a large area that was once occupied by the people of this sequence. People here constructed oval huts and windbreaks, with wooden posts placed in the ground to support red and wattle walls, sometimes covered with mud. Archaelogists discovered jars and grindstones beside the houses. There were also two rectangular buildings there, with subterranean chambers, stairs, hearths, and roof poles.

People of this site used three cemeteries, including one at Wadi Digla, although archaeologists have found remains of some unborn children in the settlement. Animals were also buried there. The Ma'adi sequence people were more sedentary in their lifestyle, probably involved in agriculture and in some herding activities. A copper ax head and the remains of copper ore (the oldest dated find of this nature in Egypt) were also discovered. There is some evidence of Naqada II influences from Upper Egypt, and there are some imported objects from the Palestinian culture on the Mediterranean, probably the result of trade.

UPPER EGYPT
Badarian (4500–4000 B.C.E.)

Badarian was one of the cultural groups living in the Nile region in the areas of el-Hammamiya, el-Matmar, el-Mostagedda, and at the foot of the cliffs at el-Badari. Archaeologists have discovered some Badarian artifacts at Erment, Hierankopolis, and in the Wadi Hammamat. A semisedentary people, the Badarians lived in tents made of skins, or in huts of reeds hung on poles. They cultivated wheat and barley and collected fruits and herbs, using the castor bean for oil. The people of this sequence wove cloth and used animal skins as furs and as leather. The bones of cattle, sheep, and goats were found on the sites, and people of time time buried domesticated and wild animals in the necropolis areas.

Weapons and tools included flint arrowheads, throwing sticks, push planes, and sickle stones. These were found in the gravesites, discovered on the edge of the desert on the eastern side of the Nile between el-Matmar and el-Etmantieh. The graves were oval or rectangular and were roofed. People placed food offerings in the graves and covered the corpses with hides or reed matting. Rectangular stone palettes were part of the grave offerings, along with ivory and stone objects. The manufactured pottery of the Badarians demonstrates sophistication and artistry, with semicircular bowls dominating the styles. Vessels that people used for daily life were normally brown and of either a smooth or rough texture. The quality pottery was thinner than any other forms manufactured in the Predynastic Period, combed and burnished before firing. The most unique type was a pottery painted red with a black interior and a lip, formed while the vessel was cooling.

Naqada I (4000–3500 B.C.E.)

Naqada I (Amratian) was located from Deir Tasa to Nubia, including Hierakonpolis and Naqada, with a large concentration of sites evident between Naqada and Abydos. The people of this sequence erected oval huts (a type used in Naqada II as well), containing hearths, and were wattled and daubed. There were no windows evident, but these could have been placed in the upper levels. Archaeologists have also found windbreaks and cooking pots.

The tools of the people were bifacial flint knives with cutting edges and rhomboidal knives. Basalt vases were found, along with mace heads, slate palettes, and ivory carvings. People of the time carved ritual figures depicting animals and humans out of ivory or molded them in clay. A black-topped pottery gave way to red wares in this sequence, some with white cross designs or scenes. Metal was very rare.

Naqada II (3500–3000 B.C.E.)

Naqada II (Gerzean A) was a cultural sequence that existed in sites from the Delta to the Nubian border, with most of the habitation centers located south of Abydos. This sequence is marked by the changes brought about in contacts with other peoples and other lands. The period also indicates growing institutions and traditions.

Accelerated trade brought advances in the artistic skills of the people of this era, and Palestinian influences are evident in the pottery, which began to include tilted spouts and handles. A light-colored pottery emerged in Naqada II, composed of clay and calcium carbonate. Originally the vessels had red patterns, changing later on to scenes of animals, boats, and trees. It is probable that such pottery was mass-produced at certain settlements for trading purposes. Copper was evident in weapons and in jewelry. The people of this sequence used gold foil and silver. Flint blades were sophisticated, and people made beads and amulets out of metals and lapis lazuli.

Funerary pottery indicates advanced mortuary cults. People built brick houses to form settlements; these small single-chambered residences had their own enclosed courtyards. A settlement erected a temple with battered walls at Hierakonpolis. Graves erected in this period were also lined with wooden planks and contained small niches for offerings. Some were built with plastered walls, which were painted.

The Predynastic Period

The cultural sequences just discussed were particular aspects of a growing civilization along the Nile, prompted to cooperate with one another by that great waterway. The Nile, the most vital factor in the lives of the Egyptians, was not always bountiful. It could be a raging source of destruction if allowed to surge uncontrolled. Irrigation and diverting projects were necessary to tame the river and to provide water throughout the agricultural seasons. The river, its bounty, and the rich soil it deposited gave birth to a nation.

Sometime in the late part of the Predynastic Period, leaders from Upper Egypt made attempts to conquer the northern territories. Upper Egypt probably was united by that time, but Lower Egypt's political condition is not known for certain. Rulers such as Scorpion I, Narmer, Hierakonpolis, and Thinis have been documented, but scholars have not determined their individual efforts and successes. There was, however, a renaissance of the arts, a force that would come to flower in the Early Dynastic Period (also called the Archaic Period), or Dynasty 0.

THE EARLY DYNASTIC PERIOD (ARCHAIC)
2920–2575 B.C.E.

The era of the founding of the Egyptian state and the start of its ruling dynasties was dynamic and prolonged. The First Dynasty, begun at Memphis by Aha (Menes), who was responsible for organizing a project to change the course of the Nile in order to drain a plain for the capital, was marked by significant cultural achievements. Aha probably cemented his claims to the throne by marrying a Memphite heiress and by instituting or reinforcing the previous modes of governmental and religious traditions that would become unique aspects of Egypt's heritage. Papyrus, writing, and a calendar were in use, and linear measurements, mathematics, and astronomy were practiced. A census, tax assessments, the reestablishment of boundaries after the yearly Nile inundations, and the development of new astronomical instruments improved Egyptian life and furthered scholarship. The rulers of the Early Dynastic Period raided Libya and the Sinai and began the exploitation of vital natural resources. These rulers also conducted some punitive expeditions in Nubia, as well as the annexation of land around Aswan.

It cannot be verified that the first rulers of this period accomplished the actual unification of Egypt. They ruled portions of the land and tried to gain control of the nomes (provinces) that were still independent. Regions such as the northeastern Delta remained outside of their domination for a long period, as did other territories. It is assumed that Kha'Sekhemwy, the last king of the Second Dynasty (ca. 2649 B.C.E.), was responsible for the unification of Upper and Lower Egypt. Kha'sekhemwy also started a settlement at Buhen in Nubia. Religious texts permeated Egyptian society during this period, and elaborate tomb complexes based upon religious beliefs were constructed by the rulers, who also built secondary tombs called cenotaphs. Egypt was governed firmly by these pharaohs, with the aid of nome officials and dedicated administrators.

Art and architecture, especially the forms associated with mortuary rituals, showed an increased degree of innovation and skill. The first evidence of the use of stone in large monuments dates to this period, and the conventions of Egyptian art developed at the same time. Cities flourished, and temples were raised for the local cults and for the emerging national deities. The achievements of the Early Dynastic Period culminated in the splendid mortuary complex erected for Djoser (r. 2630–2611 B.C.E.) by Imhotep, the chancellor, or vizier, of the pharaoh.

The Egyptians believed in material comforts and enjoyed amusements and pleasures, tempered by the ideals of moderation, quietude, and a respect for the wisdom of elders. While they were obedient to superiors, the Egyptians firmly acknowledged an unprecedented awareness of human freewill. They translated this aspect of freewill into personal responsibility for one's actions, summarized by the concept of *ma'at*. Sages such as Ptah-Hotep (2), who is reported as having lived in this era, wrote didactic literature extolling the virtues to the nation.

THE OLD KINGDOM (2575–2134 B.C.E.)

The great pyramid builders of the Fourth Dynasty (2575–2465 B.C.E.) erected monuments, which rise from the sands of Giza as eternal testaments to the vigor and dynamism of this age, and sent exploratory and punitive expeditions into Libya, Syria, and Nubia. A navy came into use in this era and land-based forces were frequently engaged. Quarries and mines were opened. New

expeditions ventured as far south as northern modern Sudan and to the shores of the Red Sea. Mining operations and other activities for extracting foreign natural resources demanded a military presence and a commitment of men and materials. By the close of the Old Kingdom the defensive posture of the Egyptian military was altered by General Weni (fl. 23rd century B.C.E), who began aggressive campaigns using veteran troops and mercenaries.

The last two dynasties of this historical period were unable to resist the growing independence of the provinces. The Seventh Dynasty was short-lived (having no real power), and the Eighth Dynasty could not maintain its grip on the various nomes and territories that were rebelling against this last line of kings in an effort to establish political alliances.

It is now known that changes taking place within the Delta Nile channels left some areas stranded as arid wastelands, with people in these regions suffering through severe drought. Riots as a result of anger on the part of the displaced and hurting brought about the deaths of the local ruling aristocrats.

THE FIRST INTERMEDIATE PERIOD
(2134–2040 B.C.E.)

The First Intermediate Period was an age of turmoil and chaos that began with the collapse of the Old Kingdom and ended with the military campaigns of Mentuhotep II (2061–2010 B.C.E.) of the Eleventh Dynasty. Following the Seventh and Eighth Dynasties, the capital shifted to the south to Herakleopolis, in the Faiyum. This city was the home of the rulers of the Ninth and Tenth Dynasties (called Khety by some and Aktoy by others), and 18 rulers of this line are listed in part or in whole in the Turin Canon—12 papyrus pages, formed as a roll, describing the finest chronological list of Egyptian rulers. The first of the royal line, Khety (fl. 22nd century B.C.E) was so ferocious in attempting to gain control of the nomes surrounding his capital that he earned a reputation for cruelty.

This was also the period in which the *Instructions for Merikaré* and the advice of the "Eloquent Peasant" were written. *Instructions for Merikaré* is believed to be the work of Khety III (r. ca. 2100 B.C.E.), who designed it as a moral treatise for his son, Merikaré, who in turn succeeded on the throne at Hierakonpolis during this turbulent time of rival kingdoms. The "Eloquent Peasant" was a popular rags-to-riches account of eloquent commoner Khunianupu's adventures and sayings. (The account is included in four New Kingdom [1550–1070 B.C.E.] papyri, today housed in Berlin and London.)

The end of the First Intermediate Period came when the Inyotef line, which ruled the southern nomes in Thebes, began an assault on Herakleopolis. The last ruler of the Tenth Dynasty lost his capital to Mentuhotep II, an Inyotef, in 2040 B.C.E.

THE MIDDLE KINGDOM PERIOD
(2040–1640 B.C.E.)

This historical period, an era of great artistic gains and stability in Egypt, began with the fall of Herakleopolis to Mentuhotep II. A strong government fostered a climate in which a great deal of creative activity took place. The greatest monument of this period was on the western bank of the Nile, at a site called Deir el-Bahri, within the city of Thebes. There Mentuhotep II erected his vast mortuary complex, a structure that would later influence the architects of the New Kingdom (1550–1070 B.C.E.).

The Mentuhotep royal line encouraged all forms of art and relied upon military prowess to establish new boundaries and new mining operations. The Mentuhoteps, like their ancestors the Inyotefs, were fierce competitors on the battlefield. They campaigned in Nubia, Libya, the Sinai, Palestine, and perhaps even visited Syria on a punitive campaign. The Mentuhoteps were followed by a royal line that was started by a usurper, Amenemhet I. Having served as a vizier and military commander for Egypt, Amenemhet took the throne and then sailed a fleet of 40 galleys up and down the Nile to put down rebellious nomes. He built his new capital at Itj-Tawy, south of Giza and Saqqara. He also established a "Wall of the Prince," a series of fortresses on Egypt's eastern and western borders. Both Amenemhet I and the Wall of the Prince were supposedly foretold by a sage named Nefer Rohu (Neferti), who was reported to have lived in the Fourth Dynasty and promised that a savior would appear to help Egypt in a time of need.

The Twelfth Dynasty pharaohs raided Syria and Palestine and marched to the third cataract of the Nile to establish fortified posts. They sent expeditions to the Red Sea, using the overland route to the coast and the path through the Wadi Timulat and the Bitter Lakes. To stimulate the national economy, these rulers also began vast irrigation and hydraulic projects in the Faiyum to reclaim the lush fields there. The agricultural lands made available by these systems revitalized Egyptian life.

The rulers built vast pyramids at Itj-tawy and at Dashur, including the multichambered Labyrinth, which was an administrative center. Prompted by the leadership of the royal family, it was an age of cultural and literary achievement on the Nile that was later revered by Egyptians as the nation's golden age. By 1799 B.C.E., however, the royal line had waned. Amenemhet IV ruled for a decade, followed by Sobekneferu, the first woman to appropriate all the royal names of a pharaoh. Her reign lasted only four years, and the Thirteenth Dynasty came to power in a futile effort to retain a grip on the nation. This royal line was listed in the Turin Canon, which credited between 50 and 60 rulers to a period of 140 or more years. The rulers of this dynasty continued to conduct building projects and governmental administration, but they were increasingly harassed by the growing number of Asiatics in the northeastern Delta, and in time the Thirteenth Dynasty collapsed and its rulers served as vassals to the new foreign regime of the Hyrsos.

In Xois, in the western Delta, the Fourteenth Dynasty, which was a contemporary of the Thirteenth Dynasty, maintained independence of a sort and promulgated a long line of kings (76 according to the third century B.C.E. Egyptian historian Manetho). Scarcely any evidence remains of this royal line, but its rulers are mentioned in the Turin Canon.

THE SECOND INTERMEDIATE PERIOD
(1640–1550 B.C.E.)

The Second Intermediate Period was an era of struggle and confusion, marked by the presence of the Hyksos, the Asiatics who conquered the northeastern territories of Egypt. The historian Manetho stated that the Asiatics, whom he called the Hyksos, arrived in a whirlwind of devastation to conquer the land. The Hyksos did come to the Nile and did assume kingly roles, but in actuality their introduction into the land was gradual and dependent upon many factors.

Slavery had been introduced as an institution into Egypt during the Middle Kingdom, whose last rulers held their power from Memphis or Thebes. While Egypt's military powers declined, the clamor for slaves increased, especially for the feudal and priestly estates of the Delta and the Faiyum.

The Asiatics, called the A'amu, Seteyu, or Hikau-Khoswet (Manetho's Hyksos), came willingly into Egypt as mercenary border guards or as indentured servants, because Egypt offered them opportunities. As their numbers increased, they began to insinuate themselves into various positions of power. The Ipuwer Papyrus's complaints about the presence in Egypt of the "Desert," a reference to the Hyksos, provides an image of the changes taking place. The Desert, the coarse nomads, consolidated their gains and opened Egypt to more and more migrations from the Mediterranean region.

The Fifteenth Dynasty, ruling from Avaris in the eastern Delta, was the royal line of the Hyksos. These kings ruled from 1640 to 1532 B.C.E. A second group of Hyksos kings ruled contemporaneously as the Sixteenth Dynasty but exercised less political control and held limited territory. Both Asiatic royal lines ruled at the same time as the Seventeenth Dynasty, the kings of Thebes, who maintained a tight grip on Upper Egypt. The Seventeenth Dynasty is dated from ca. 1640 to 1550 B.C.E. and was entirely Egyptian.

When the Hyksos and their allies were entrenched in the eastern Delta and were constructing their capital at Avaris, the Thebans maintained somewhat cordial relations with them. The Hyksos sailed past Thebes on their way to the lands below the cataracts of the Nile in order to trade there, and the Theban cattle barons grazed their herds in the Delta marshlands without incident. The cordiality vanished after a time, however, and the Hyksos had to abandon all hopes of penetrating deep into Theban territories. They remained ensconced with their forces at Cusae, a city on the border of Hyskos-controlled land, unable to maintain their dominance of more southerly lands.

Then Apophis of Avaris sent an insulting message to Ta'o II, the second to last ruler of Thebes, the content of which was recorded in the *Quarrel of Apophis and Sekenenré* (Ta'o II). The messenger related Apophis's complaint that the snoring hippopotami in the sacred pool at Thebes were keeping the Hyksos ruler awake at night. Considering the fact that Apophis's royal residence was about 400 miles to the northeast, the Thebans, upon hearing the complaint, were stupefied. The Thebans declared war on the Hyksos ca. 1570 B.C.E., and Ta'o II mobilized his armies and struck at the Asiatic outposts. He died in battle or as a result of an ambush, but his son, Kamose, took up the war with equal vigor.

Kamose, the last king of the Seventeenth Dynasty, used the famed Medjay troops and other military strategies and was approaching the defenses of Avaris when he died. His brother, 'Ahmose, the founder of the Eighteenth Dynasty and the New Kingdom, laid siege to the city and ran the Asiatics out of Egypt, pursuing them to Sharuhen and then into Syria.

The arts and architecture of Egypt waned during the Second Intermediate Period, although the tombs of the nomarchs in the outlying provinces were adorned with vivacious scenes that reflected the continuity of life in areas untouched by Egypt's warring dynasties. The Second Intermediate Period did have one lasting effect, however. Egypt came to understand the military and political realities of the age. The Thebans, watching the domination of the Asiatics in the northeast section of the nation, resolved to oust them from the Nile and to seal the borders once again.

THE NEW KINGDOM (1550–1070 B.C.E.)

The era following the departure of the Asiatics, the New Kingdom became a period of empire, prestige, and military prowess. The New Kingdom was actually a combination of three separate historical periods: the beginning of the empire, the 'Amarna era, and the age of the Ramessids. 'Ahmose destroyed Avaris and put down rebellions within Egypt and Nubia, and then he set about conducting the affairs of state with a keen and energetic mind. He reduced the status of the hereditary princes and counts of the various nomes, thus putting an end to the petty rivalries that had plagued the nation in the past. He established the viceroyalty of Nubia and conducted all other government affairs through a series of judges and governors, who were sworn to serve him

and the cause of his dynasty. This early part of the New Kingdom was particularly graced by talented Egyptians who brought loyalty and dedication to their tasks as officials of the court. Amun, the god of Thebes, honored by the Mentuhoteps of the Eleventh Dynasty, became the supreme deity of Egypt and the occupied territories. Costly offerings and gifts were presented to the god at Karnak and the Luxor temples, which were expanded during this era.

Amenhotep I (r. 1525–1504 B.C.E.), the second king of the New Kingdom period, followed in his father's footsteps, but it was his successor, Tuthmosis I, who began the empire in earnest. He fought against enemies in far-flung lands and conquered territories all the way to the Euphrates River, where he put up a stela of victory to commemorate his success. His grandson, Tuthmosis III, called the "Napoleon of Egypt," would be one of the greatest warrior-kings in Egypt's history.

Tuthmosis III (r. 1479–1425 B.C.E.) was named as heir to the throne by his father, Tuthmosis II, but he was unable to assume the throne because Queen Hatshepsut usurped the titles and roles of pharaoh. She ruled Egypt from 1473 to 1458 B.C.E., and her reign was a time of comparative peace and stability. It was also a period of intense building in the northern and southern regions of Egypt. Hatshepsut remained powerful with the support of the priests of Amun and her able courtiers until Senenmut, one of her lead advisors, and Neferu-Ré, her daughter, died. Then the forces of Tuthmosis III began to press for her abdication. She disappeared while Tuthmosis was on his first major military campaign at Ar-Megiddo.

Tuthmosis III not only conquered vast territories but set in place an imperial system. He placed his own officials in the palaces of vassal rulers and brought back the young nobles of other lands to be educated as Egyptians so that they could return to rule in his name. Treaties, tributes, a standing army, a vast naval force, and garrisons installed throughout the Mediterranean consolidated his military conquests. Tuthmosis's son, Amenhotep II (1427–1401 B.C.E.), maintained the same firm hold on the territories. His son, Tuthmosis IV, did not undertake many military campaigns, as the lands won by his ancestors remained firmly in Egyptian hands. He is, however, remembered for his restoration of the Sphinx at Giza.

Amenhotep III came to the throne in 1391 B.C.E., when Egypt's empire was at its height. He was not particularly martial or attentive to his duties, but his commoner wife, Queen Tiye, worked with government officials to keep the government stable. Amenhotep III also cemented ties with other lands by marrying their royal princesses, including one from Babylon. His son Amenhotep IV (Akhenaten) (r. 1353–1335 B.C.E.) abandoned Thebes and the god Amun and initiated the 'Amarna Period, a time of great artistic innovation and political disaster. He remained isolated in Akhetaten, a city he constructed as the new Egyptian capital, where he worshiped the god Aten, and the empire almost collapsed around him. When he died in 1335 B.C.E., Egypt had lost its imperial territories, and its allies had suffered severe military setbacks. After the brief reigns of King Smenkhare', King Tut'Ankhamun, and King Aya, General Horemhab (r. 1319–1307 B.C.E.) came to the throne. He worked to restore lost lands and to bring cohesion and order to the government of the nation. His laws were stern and effective, and he managed to lift Egypt to greatness again. Horemhab died childless and left the throne to a military companion, Ramesses I.

The Ramessid Period began in 1307 B.C.E. and lasted until 1070 B.C.E. to the Nineteenth and Twentieth Dynasties. Ramesses I did not rule more than a year, but his son, Seti I (r. 1306–1290 B.C.E.), was a trained military commander who was eager to see the empire fully restored. He and his son, Ramesses II (r. 1290–1224 B.C.E.), called the Great, took the field against Near Eastern powers, gaining territories and securing Egypt's prominence. Ramesses II also endowed Egypt with a multitude of monuments honoring his reign. The kings following Ramesses II were not as vigorous or talented, although Merenptah (r. 1224–1214 B.C.E.) stopped an invasion in the Delta of the Sea Peoples, a confederation of various groups who were active as pirates and marauders during this period. The Nineteenth Dynasty came to a close with the reign of the widow of Seti II, Twosret. She had served as regent for the young ruler Siptah and had usurped the throne with the aid of Bay, her foreign-born counselor.

The Twentieth Dynasty began with Sethnakhte, who started his royal line in 1196 B.C.E. Ramesses III (r. 1194–1163 B.C.E.), another military giant, managed to maintain the empire and restored Egypt's artistic and cultural traditions. Ramesses III was followed, however, by eight additional rulers named Ramesses, each one having little military or administrative competence. The Twentieth Dynasty and the New Kingdom were destroyed when the powerful priests of Amun divided the nation and usurped the throne.

The New Kingdom was a time of flowering, both militarily and artistically. Egypt received tribute from lands from the Sudan to the Euphrates, and vassal kings waited upon the pharaoh in his palace. The original capital of the New Kingdom was Thebes, but the Ramessids had come from Avaris, the former Asiatic capital in the Delta, and returned there to build a splendid new city called Per-Ramesses.

Thebes was a wondrous site, and the Greeks, coming upon it centuries later, sang the praises of the ancient capital. The Greek epic poet Homer (850–750 B.C.E.), in fact, spoke of its hundred gates and of its eternal charms. Other magnificent sites, such as Abu Simbel, Medinet Habu, Abydos, Deir el-Bahri, and countless shrines and temples up and down the Nile stand as reminders of the glories of this age.

THIRD INTERMEDIATE PERIOD (1070–712 B.C.E.)

After the fall of the New Kingdom, Egypt entered a period of decline and foreign domination. This era was marked by the rise of the Amunite priests, who usurped the power of the ruler even before the death of Ramesses XI (r. 1100–1070 B.C.E.). These priests acknowledged the Twenty-first Dynasty kings of Tanis in Lower Egypt and married into that royal family but ruled Upper Egypt from Thebes. The Libyans had also intervened in Egyptian affairs and had come to hold certain territories, in time becoming the Twenty-second Dynasty. Military campaigns were conducted, especially by Shoshenq I (r. 945–924 B.C.E.) in Palestine, and trade was revived, bringing new prosperity. By the end of the eighth century B.C.E., however, there were many kings in Egypt, each holding a small area. A Twenty-fifth Dynasty king, Piankhi (r. 750–712 B.C.E.), set out from Nubia to subjugate other rulers of Egypt and inspired other Nubians to follow him.

LATE PERIOD (712–332 B.C.E.)

Starting in 712 B.C.E. with the reign of Shabaka, the Late Period was fraught with civil wars. The Nubians inhabited the Nile Valley, eventually taking Memphis and making it their capital. The Nubians did not actually dispossess local rulers but rather allowed them to continue their rule as vassals. Throughout their tenure the Nubians built massive structures and brought about a certain renaissance of the arts. Another priest of Amun, Mentuemhat, rose up in Thebes and controlled much of Upper Egypt. In 671 B.C.E. the Assyrians took Memphis, destroying the Nubian hold, and forced all of Egypt to pay tribute. Egypt, no longer isolated, was thus engaged in the struggles of the Mediterranean.

Greek mercenaries, used by the Egyptian rulers in their unification struggles, had set up their own communities on the Nile and by the fourth century B.C.E. had influenced much of the nation through their skill in trade and warfare. Reunification was eventually accomplished by a new royal line, recorded as the Twenty-sixth Dynasty (664–525 B.C.E.), and Egypt prospered under a central authority. The era of prosperity was not long lived, however. In 567 B.C.E. the Babylonians attempted an invasion. The Egyptians defeated the Babylonians, only to face a growing Persian menace. The Persians attacked during the reign of Psammetichus III (r. 526–525 B.C.E.), successfully defeating the armies of Egypt. A line of Persians ruled Egypt until 404 B.C.E., when Amyrtaios of Sais freed the Delta from the foreigners. Amyrtaios was listed as the sole ruler of the Twenty-eighth Dynasty. The Twenty-ninth and Thirtieth Dynasties presided over troubled times until 343 B.C.E., when the Persians once again gained control of the land. This decade-long period of occupation, listed in historical accounts as the Thirty-first Dynasty, was the Second Persian Period.

GRECO-PTOLEMAIC PERIOD (332–30 B.C.E.)

In 332 B.C.E., Alexander III the Great, having defeated the Persian forces of Darius III Codoman (r. 336–330 B.C.E.) in a series of military campaigns, took control of Egypt and founded the city of Alexandria. At his death the nation became the property of Ptolemy I Soter (r. 304–284 B.C.E.), one of his generals. For the next 250 years the Greeks successfully ruled Egypt, imbuing the land with the Hellenic traditions in the capital but not affecting rural Nile areas. It was a time of economic and artistic prosperity, but by the second century B.C.E. there was a marked decline. Family feuds and external forces took their toll, even though the Ptolemaic line remained in power. This royal house died with Cleopatra VII (r. 51–30 B.C.E.) and her short-lived corulers. Octavian (the future emperor Augustus) took control and began the period of Roman occupation, ca. 30 B.C.E., which Egypt endured for the next 500 years.

See also ADMINISTRATION; ART AND ARCHITECTURE; DYNASTY HISTORIES; LITERATURE; RELIGION AND COSMOGONY; SOCIAL EVOLUTION IN EGYPT.

GEOGRAPHICAL OVERVIEW

Modern Egypt, called the Arab Republic of Egypt, is located on the eastern edge of North Africa. It sits at the meeting point of two continents, Africa and Asia, and thus it has long served as the gateway for trade and travel from Africa to Palestine and the Near East, as well as for access to the waterways of the Red Sea, which lead into the Arabian Sea and Indian Ocean. Egypt's borders have been remarkably stable since the time it was founded in 2920 B.C.E., largely due to the natural geographic boundaries that surround it: the Libyan and Nubian Deserts to the west and southeast; cataracts, or rapids, on the Nile to the south; the Mediterranean to the north; and the Red Sea and Sinai Peninsula to the east. (Though part of the Arab Republic of Egypt, the Sinai Peninsula is separated geographically from the Egyptian mainland.) Its neighbors are Libya to the west and Sudan (called Nubia by the ancient Egyptians) to the south.

As today, ancient Egypt's defining geographical feature was the Nile Valley, stretching from several miles below Aswan and the first cataract of the Nile (an area that was called Upper Egypt) to the Delta region that opens into the Mediterranean Sea (a region called Lower Egypt). The terms *Upper* and *Lower* stem from the fact that the Nile flows from south to north. The ancient Egyptians knew that the source of this vast stream of water was somewhere far to the south. The area called Upper Egypt was considered closest to that source, hence the name.

The longest river in the world, the Nile cuts across the Western (Libyan) and Nubian deserts, creating a belt of abundance and fertile land along its two banks several miles into the arid land. The river stands in rather stark contrast to the Tigris and Euphrates rivers in the Fertile Crescent, where another people, the Mesopotamians, built a thriving civilization around the same time: While the Mesopotamians had to find a way to control the unpredictable and dangerous flooding of the two rivers, the Egyptians benefited from the fact that the Nile flood rose in predictable fashion. The summer rains in central Africa caused the waters to rise in Egypt in September and October. The result of the flooding was beneficial, as the water left rich amounts of silt that nourished the soil and added to the fertility of the strips of land along the banks. The "Hymn to the Nile," which was sung by the Egyptians, proclaimed:

> Hail to thee, O Nile, that issues from the earth and
>   comes to keep Egypt alive! . . .
> He that makes to drink the desert . . .
> He who makes barley and brings emmer [wheat] into
>   being . . .
> He who brings grass into being for the cattle . . .
> He who makes every beloved tree to grow . . .
> O Nile, verdant art thou, who makest man and cattle
>   to live.

The Nile was the chief lifeline of the country and the primary source for national and cultural cohesion. The Egyptians built their cities and towns all along the line of the river, which facilitated communication between settlements. Abundant in natural resources such as stone, clay, and gold, Egypt needed little from beyond its borders, but the resources it possessed gave it immense opportunities for trade with other places. Egypt traded with Mesopotamia, the states along the Mediterranean, Nubia, and Punt (modern Ethiopia). It was with good reason that Herodotus, the Greek historian of the fifth century B.C.E., referred to Egypt as the "gift of the Nile."

The stability of the Nile and the relative geographic isolation of Egypt had a profound effect on the outlook of the Egyptian people. Egyptians prized order and unity, as reflected in the concept of *ma'at*—meaning order, justice, and harmony—which was central to their philosophical system. The stars, sun, and moon followed a systematic and orderly progression in the heavens; the Nile rose and fell each year; and the Egyptians embraced this pattern of existence and the promise of continuity that it offered. Aided by long periods of peace and

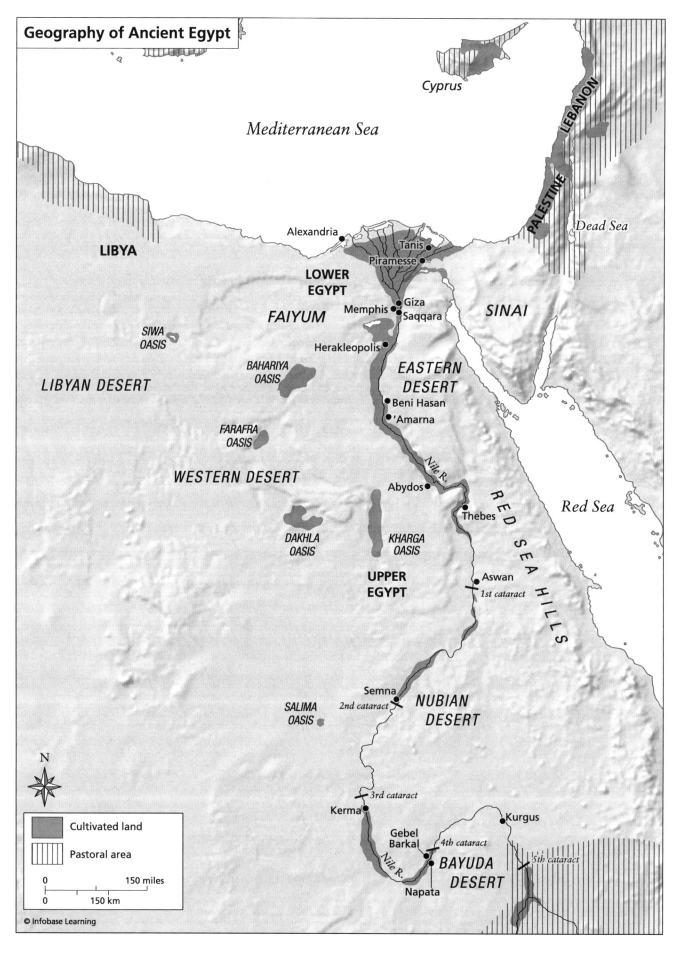

Geography of Ancient Egypt

Cyprus

Mediterranean Sea

PALESTINE

LEBANON

Dead Sea

LIBYA

Alexandria

Tanis

Piramesse

LOWER EGYPT

FAIYUM

Memphis

Giza

Saqqara

SINAI

SIWA OASIS

Herakleopolis

BAHARIYA OASIS

EASTERN DESERT

LIBYAN DESERT

Beni Hasan

'Amarna

FARAFRA OASIS

WESTERN DESERT

Nile R.

Abydos

Thebes

Red Sea

DAKHLA OASIS

KHARGA OASIS

R E D   S E A   H I L L S

UPPER EGYPT

Aswan

1st cataract

Semna

2nd cataract

SALIMA OASIS

NUBIAN DESERT

N

3rd cataract

Kerma

Kurgus

Gebel Barkal

4th cataract

5th cataract

Cultivated land

Pastoral area

Nile R.

BAYUDA DESERT

0   150 miles

0   150 km

Napata

© Infobase Learning

tranquility, the other central feature of Egyptian philosophy was a well-developed notion of eternity, which gave rise to elaborate mortuary rituals.

THE NILE VALLEY

The longest river on Earth, the Nile flows more than 4,000 miles northward from twin sources: the White Nile, which forms in Lake Victoria, Uganda; and the Blue Nile, which originates in the Ethiopian highlands. The two Niles meet at Atbara, near modern Khartoum in Sudan. From Atbara, the river continues its journey for some 660 miles through the trench-like depression that is termed the Nile Valley until it reaches the Uat-Ur (the Great Green), the Mediterranean Sea. The northerly flow of the Nile caused amazement for the Egyptians visiting foreign lands on military campaigns or trade expeditions, as every foreign river that they encountered flowed southward.

In Upper Egypt, the Nile Valley, which is lined by deserts and fertile land on either side, cuts through sandstone cliffs and massive outcroppings of granite. These cliffs, sometimes set back from the shore and sometimes coming close to the river's edge, once included river terraces and areas of continued moisture. The remains of trees and vegetation indicate that the region was once part of the monsoon region of Predynastic Period times. The first settlers of the region built their sites there, on the edges of the desert, to lessen damage to their settlements during the floods.

Lower Egypt, located in the north, is believed to have encompassed the land from the Mediterranean Sea to Itj-tawy (Lisht) or possibly to modern Assiut. It is bordered by the Western (Libyan) Desert, the Eastern Desert, and the Sinai Peninsula. Lower Egypt has always been dominated by the Delta, which was originally formed by perennial swamps and lakes. This triangular-shaped region became the dividing line between Lower Egypt and Upper Egypt, and many of the greatest cities in Egypt arose at the tip of the Delta, as it afforded Egyptians access to both the Delta and to the Upper Nile.

The Nile spread across the Delta along main or lesser branches. These were not always stable or permanently in place; some moved or disappeared entirely. Aha (Menes), the first pharaoh of Egypt, founded the nation and a new capital, Memphis (modern Mit Rahinah), in 2920 B.C.E. by moving a channel of the river to expose a flat plain that could be developed. Dams, dikes, and earthen walls were erected to divert the Nile and to open the land to urban construction. As the Nile flooded Lower Egypt each year, irrigation systems put the Delta channels to good use.

FAIYUM

The Faiyum is a region composed of rich farmlands and orchards located in the central area of the nation, approximately 80 miles south of the modern capital of Cairo. It served as a foundation for ancient Egypt's economy for 3,000 years. The Faiyum was well irrigated by an offshoot of the Nile called Bahr Yusef; area workers put up barriers in the region to keep the water from draining away. The area supported a vast variety of crops, and growing seasons could be altered with rotation of fields and crops.

The Faiyum was well occupied, and in time temple plantations arose there. Crocodiles roamed the region, and during the New Kingdom (1550–1070 B.C.E.) there was a large mansion at Miwer that served as a retirement place for the royal women of the various dynasties.

HABITATION

Sometime around 6000 B.C.E., herdsmen and farming clans from the desert regions to the west settled in the Nile Valley. Prior to 6000 B.C.E., monsoons had made the Western (Libyan) Desert habitable and turned the Nile Valley into damp marshlands. The monsoons ceased sometime around the seventh millennium B.C.E., forcing the herdsmen and farmers of the desert to migrate into the river valley and the Faiyum. The lush farmlands and grazing plains offered a lasting refuge to these early humans.

Upper Egypt was an area of plains, rocky outcroppings, and dry scrub territories. The first inhabitants learned how to use the available soil deposits and the grazing areas, and discovered which crops would prosper in their particular regions. They used irrigation canals to divert water from the river, dug wells, and made use of the oases that were hidden in the deserts.

Lower Egypt was supplied with the channels of the Nile that provided continual resources. Settlers developed extensive farming regions, orchards, and gardens. More dependent on the various channels, or branches, of the Nile, the settlers in the Delta region were at times victims of the changing river patterns. When a channel dried up or changed course, entire communities found themselves surrounded by deserts. These communities often moved everything they owned to a nearby channel and started life over again.

Cities began to form both in Upper Egypt and Lower Egypt—among the earliest are Hierakonpolis and Edfu in the south and Buto in the Delta—and the people traded the different products of their regions in order to prosper. The land of Egypt was called Khemet (the Black Land), possibly in reference to the dark soil of the fertile valley. The surrounding deserts were called the Deshret (the Red Land).

CLIMATE

The landscape and climate of Egypt profoundly affected the development of Egyptian civilization. About 95 percent of the modern territory of Egypt is covered by desert. Thus the country's agriculture was entirely dependent on the annual inundation of the Nile.

The Nile Valley offered a stable climate and temperate seasons. Modern Egypt receives about 80 millimeters of rainfall each year, although the coastal region can receive more. The capital, Cairo, receives one centimeter of rain annually. Ancient Egypt enjoyed three basic seasons each year, each consisting of four months. The year began with the time of the inundation, *akhet,* in the third week of modern July. Following *akhet* was Proyet, the time of sowing, and Shomu, the harvest time. Throughout the year the climate was temperate, although rare cold spells could endanger the crops, as could prolonged high temperatures.

There are fierce sandstorms in modern Egypt, called the *khamsin,* a lasting storm of sand that blots out the sun. These storms start in February or March and last about two months. There is no historical documentation as to whether or not these storms came yearly in ancient times.

The ancient Egyptians recognized the effect that natural forces had on their survival, and they honored these forces in their religion and daily rituals. The sun provided the warmth, energy, and light needed to sustain a civilization, and the sun god Ré was one of the most important deities. (Horus, the protector of the nation's rulers, was another.) Astronomers mapped the night skies and learned early on that the appearance of the star Sirius, called Sopdu or Sothis by the Egyptians, signaled the rising of the Nile waters. They studied the sun with similar intensity and developed solar cults. Rather early in their cultural evolution the Egyptians designated the sunrise and sunset as events of particular meaning. They celebrated life on the eastern shore of the river and honored death on the western shore. Records of these observances are especially evident in the southern regions.

DESERTS

Deserts, called "the Red Lands," or Deshret, by the Egyptians, surrounded the narrow, fertile strip of rich black soil along the Nile. The Deshret served as a natural barrier for Egypt in the early historic periods, failing only in the late Middle Kingdom (2040–1640 B.C.E.), when the eastern borders were overcome and the Asiatics, or Hyksos, entered the Nile Valley. The desert is very much visible in the land today, especially in Thebes, where the red cliffs stand as spectacular guardians on the western shore of the Nile, a stark contrast to the lush green and black fields below.

The deserts of Egypt have always been viewed as dangerous places of death and normally served as necropolis sites. The Eastern Desert is formed by the Red Sea hills and in the north is an extension of the Sinai Peninsula. The Western Desert, or Libyan Desert, covers two-thirds of Egypt and was believed to contain the entrance to Tuat, the Underworld. The area contains the oldest human settlement in Egypt, and records there

indicate the use of domesticated animals as early as 9000 B.C.E. This desert has plateaus, sandy depressions, and fertile oases.

OASES

The oases of Egypt are the lush, habitable depressions found in the Western (Libyan) Desert, which were inhabited from the earliest times. They connected the Nile Valley with Libya and with the domains beyond the first cataract of the Nile, and served as rest stops for caravans traveling the vast trade network. Called *wehat* and *wake,* terms that denote a fertile region or garden, the oases produced a variety of crops, especially grapes and dates. They also functioned as havens in the early trade routes across the land, as expeditions followed a route that enabled them to camp in the oases that they encountered. The Theban military units hid in the oases and used them as equipment depots in the campaigns to oust the Hyksos from Lower Egypt, ca. 1540 B.C.E. Other oases were used as military outposts against the Libyans in the west. The great Siwa Oasis was used as a shrine for the god Amun, and the oracle there welcomed Alexander the Great when he conquered the land in 332 B.C.E. In some periods the oases were also places of exile for those banished from Egypt by the various rulers. The major oases were Baharia, Dailah, Dakla, Dunqul, Farafra, Kurkur, and Siwa.

LIBYA

Beyond the narrow strip of fertile land along the western Nile, the geography of Egypt transforms into the inhospitable desert that is part of the truly enormous Sahara Desert, which itself covers some 3,630,000 square miles and technically encompasses the deserts of Egypt. To the south of the Mediterranean coast in Libya is the Qattara Depression, a desert basin some 7,000 square miles in size that, after Lake Assal in Djibouti, is the lowest spot in Africa. South of the Qattara Depression is the Western (Libyan) Desert.

The Western Desert had to be guarded at all times against invading Libyan tribes. In the Middle Kingdom (2040–1640 B.C.E.) the so-called Wall of the Prince, a series of fortresses and garrisons that protected the Delta from attacks and invasions, was erected in many northern border regions.

NUBIA

South of Aswan, in Upper Egypt, the flow of the Nile River is disrupted by a series of six cataracts, rapids produced by rocky outcroppings that are located at various positions between modern Khartoum, northern Sudan, and Aswan, Egypt. The first cataract, at Aswan, formed the southern border of Egypt until the Middle Kingdom (2040–1640 B.C.E.), although the armies of the Early Dynastic Period (2920–2575 B.C.E.) and Old Kingdom (2575–2134 B.C.E.) conducted trading and punitive expeditions and even erected fortified settlements and centers south of Aswan.

The land south of Aswan and the first cataract was Nubia (modern Sudan). In ancient times the region was called Kush, with various areas designated as Wawat or Yam. The Kermeh culture was prominent by 1900 B.C.E. and in later eras a dynasty developed at Meroë and Napata.

The present geography of Nubia is different from ancient times, chiefly because of the Aswan High Dam, which was built in the 1960s and has changed forever the flow of the Nile. Part of the northern territories of modern Sudan is under water from Lake Nasser, which was created by the dam. Some 90,000 people had to be relocated and countless ancient monuments were submerged by the lake; some 20 monuments, including Abu Simbel, were moved to higher ground to preserve them.

Nubia was traditionally divided into three regions. Lower Nubia comprised what is modern southern Egypt and occupied the territory between the first and second cataracts on the Nile. South of Lower Nubia was Upper Nubia, located between the second and sixth cataracts on the Nile. Farther downriver was southern Nubia. Both Upper Nubia and southern Nubia are found today in Sudan, north of Khartoum.

As with Egypt, both ancient Nubia and modern Sudan were much influenced by the Nile. The Blue Nile and White Nile meet at Khartoum, and the life of the country clung to the narrow, fertile strip on the banks of the greatest of rivers. The Blue Nile stretches for some 800 miles through Sudan, and on either side were two significant deserts: the Western (Libyan) Desert to the west and the Nubian Desert to the east.

While arid, Nubia was a territory of great natural resources and a varied animal population. The Egyptians began to claim the natural resources of the region during the Early Dynastic Period, and they built fortresses to control traffic on the Nile and to beat back the Nubians.

The development of quarries and mines brought gold, copper, gemstones, and other metals into Egypt, along with ivory, exotic animals, oils, skins, feathers, and harvested crops. The Egyptians sailed southward with trade or military campaigns and made canals alongside the cataract rapids in order to continue safely. Early on, they recruited mercenary warriors from Nubia. An elite group called the Medjay, these mercenaries served in military campaigns and in times of peace composed the metropolitan police forces. The Medjay were part of the army of General Weni, who served Pepi I (2289–2255 B.C.E.) when he began punitive raids in the Sinai Peninsula.

The Egyptians also erected temples in Nubia promoting the Egyptian gods and, in particular, devotion to the deity Amun. The Nubians became very devout and maintained their Amunite rituals into the Third Intermediate Period (1070–712 B.C.E.). The Nubians invaded Egypt in 750 B.C.E. and briefly established a ruling dynasty that revived the worship of Amun on the Nile. Nubia was a vital territory for Egypt throughout the centuries, offering a vast array of products that strengthened the Egyptian trade systems and enriched the Egyptians' day-to-day lifestyles.

THE SINAI

To the northeast of Egypt, the Sinai Peninsula achieved importance to the Egyptians early on as a link to the Levant (the areas adjoining the Mediterranean Sea to its east) and to the Near East. The Sinai comprises 23,500 square miles and was occupied from a very early time by local tribes of the Bedouins. Today, it is separated from the rest of Egypt by the Suez Canal, but 20 million years ago it was geographically part of Egypt and the Saudi Arabian Peninsula; at some point the land was separated by tectonic shifting. It remains part of the Great Rift Valley that extends across East Africa into the Red Sea and the Gulf of Aqaba and the Jordan Valley. Its valuable position is made obvious by what surrounds it: the Gulf of Suez to the southwest, the Gulf of Aqaba to the southeast, the Mediterranean coast (called the Via Maris in the Roman period) to the north, and Palestine to the east.

The northern part of the peninsula is noted for its deserts, with the sand broken by limestone hills. The central area is marked by the Tih Plateau, reaching in an arc southward to the more mountainous south famed especially for Mount Sinai.

The peninsula was chiefly valued as the bridge between Egypt and the rest of Palestine and the Near East, but it also possessed valuable natural resources, including minerals such as turquoise, copper, and malachite.

Mines and quarries used by the Egyptians were in operation during the Early Dynastic Period (2920–2575 B.C.E.) This land was not an uninhabited wasteland, however, and the Egyptians had to suppress the Bedouin tribes who tried to halt their construction of various Egyptian developments, especially Serabit Khadim, the prized turquoise mine that was dedicated to the goddess Hathor. The Egyptians had to go on the offensive during the reign of Pepi I, and a campaign led by General Weni subdued the Bedouins.

Likewise, the Sinai Peninsula was the area by which Egypt built its empire across parts of the Near East. It was also the area by which foreign peoples and civilizations like the Hyksos and Persians penetrated Egypt during such eras of instability as the Second Intermediate Period (1640–1550 B.C.E.), when hordes of Asiatics entered the Nile region freely.

THE RED SEA

The Egyptians were aware from an early time of the value of the Red Sea. They established shipbuilding compounds there and sent expeditions south along the Red Sea to Punt, which is believed to be the area of modern Ethiopia. The Egyptians are thought to have been able to navigate and sail along the Mediterranean and the Red Sea as early as the Old Kingdom (2575–2134 B.C.E.) or perhaps even before.

The Red Sea is part of the Great Rift Valley. It has a surface of 170,000 square miles and is almost 1,400 miles long and more than 220 miles wide. In the north, the sea is marked by the coastal edges of the Sinai Peninsula, with the Gulf of Suez (reaching the Suez Canal) in the west and the Gulf of Aqaba in the east. In the south, the sea provides access to the Indian Ocean through the Bab el Mandeb Strait into the Gulf of Aden.

THE NEAR EAST

The development of the Egyptian Empire brought the Egyptians into direct contact with the wider world to the south, north, and east of the Nile Valley. The greatest extent of the empire was achieved through a series of campaigns waged by the rulers of the Eighteenth Dynasty, especially Tuthmosis I (r. 1504–1492 B.C.E.), who extended Egypt's reach all the way to the Euphrates River. Tuthmosis III (r. 1479–1425 B.C.E.) conducted campaigns into southern Palestine, along the Mediterranean coast of the Levant (the areas adjoining the Mediterranean Sea to its east), and again reached the Euphrates. At its peak, the empire received tribute from Babylon, Assyria, Cyprus, Crete, and all of the small city-states of the Mediterranean region. Tuthmosis III's son, Amenhotep II (r. 1427–1401 B.C.E.), dominated the city-states of Syria, and his son, Amenhotep III (r. 1391–1353 B.C.E.), ruled over a sizable Egyptian Empire for the last time. The empire at the time stretched across much of the Near East and into Palestine and included Nubia as far south as modern Khartoum.

The Near East includes the Asian portion of modern Turkey, the Levant, and Mesopotamia, the land between the Tigris and Euphrates rivers. It also claims in its area the Fertile Crescent, an enormous arc of land that reaches from the Mediterranean Sea to the Persian Gulf and from the north of the Sinai Peninsula to the Zagros Mountains along modern Iran. Also called the cradle of civilization, this fertile stretch of land is irrigated by several rivers, notably the Tigris and Euphrates, and was the site of many of the earliest human settlements.

The Egyptians were able to extend their political and military reach to the Euphrates River, but they were only one among several players that vied for domination in the region, the Mitanni and the Hittites being two of the other notable forces. A primary battleground for these empires was the area that is today Palestine and Syria—the stretch of territory between the Euphrates in the east, the Mediterranean coast to the west, the Taurus Mountains to the north, and the Arabian Desert to the south. The cities and trading centers that dotted this area benefited not only from their location along the Mediterranean coast and strategic access to Mesopotamia, but also from the fertile strip of land extending along the coastal plain from the Jordan to the Orontes rivers and the Taurus Mountains.

By the middle of the 17th century B.C.E., this area was dotted with city-states made up of Canaanites and Semitic Amorites who were active traders and merchants. Thus the area became a tempting target for the Hittites, Mitanni, and Egyptians. Significant cities included Ebla (which was sacked by the Amorites around 2000 B.C.E.), Byblos, Ugarit, and Yamkhad (Aleppo). The Egyptians lost their hold over the Near East in the 15th century and were supplanted by the Hittites, who then seemed to disappear from history after the onslaught of the Sea Peoples. In the succeeding centuries new empires vied for supremacy, a struggle that endured into the 20th century.

See also AGRICULTURE; BAHARIA OASIS; BEKHEN QUARRY MAP; DAKHLA; DELTA; ELEPHANTINE; FAIYUM; FARAFRA OASIS; GIZA; *KHAMSIN*; LAKES; LIBYA; LIBYAN DESERT; NATURAL RESOURCES; NILE; NUBIA; NUBIAN DESERT; OASES; SINAI; SIWA; QUARRIES..

CHRONOLOGY OF MAJOR EVENTS

Egypt	Near East and Mediterranean

3000 B.C.E.–2700 B.C.E.

Narmer captures Lower Egypt	Sumerian cities flourish
'Aha (Menes) founds Memphis	Troy is founded
Irrigation projects are employed	Towns in Syria and Palestine
Writing and calendar are in use	Malta megaliths are erected
Royal tombs at Abydos and Saqqara	The Minoans build on Crete
Egypt is fully united	Gilgamesh at Uruk

2600 B.C.E.–2100 B.C.E.

Step Pyramid at Saqqara	Megaliths appear in Europe
Pyramids at Giza	Royal graves are used in Ur
Nubian lands are dominated	The Minoans open trade routes
Copper mines are used in Sinai	Ziggurat is built at Sumer
Heliopolis is a powerful Ré center	
Pyramid Texts are used	
Expeditions are sent to Punt	
Pepi II reigns for almost a century	
Coffin Texts are adopted	

2000 B.C.E.–1600 B.C.E.

Mentuhotep II unifies Egypt	Babylon is a regional power
Deir el-Bahri becomes a shrine	Greece is occupied
Art and architecture are revived	Stonehenge is erected
Tale of Sinuhe the Sailor is introduced	Sumer is revitalized
Faiyum is restored with hydraulics	Hammurabi in Babylon
Forts in Nubia are built to the third cataract	The Persian Empire begins
The Wall of the Prince guards Egypt's borders	Knossus on Crete becomes a vast city
Hyksos begin incursions into Egypt	
Karnak is formed as a shrine	
Avaris becomes the Hyksos capital	

1500 B.C.E.–1300 B.C.E.

The Thebans oust the Hyksos	The Hittites destroy Babylon
Tuthmosis I reaches the Euphrates	The Minoan civilization collapses
The Valley of the Kings started	The Mitanni people are ascendant
Karnak is embellished	The Myceneans establish citadels
Deir el-Bahri temples are expanded	The Assyrians begin a recovery after a time of decline
Akhenaten reigns at 'Amarna	
Thebes is the capital of Egypt	

CHRONOLOGY OF MAJOR EVENTS (*continued*)

Egypt	Near East and Mediterranean

1200 B.C.E.–1000 B.C.E.

Egypt	Near East and Mediterranean
Ramessids regain lands lost in the 'Amarna Period	Babylon is restored after a time of decline
Abu Simbel is opened	The Sea Peoples destroy the power of the Hittites
Per-Ramesses becomes the capital of Egypt	The Iron Age commences in the Mediterranean
Treaty is established with the Hittites	
The Sea Peoples are defeated	
The Egyptian Empire is eroded by internal and external pressures	
Amunite priests reach their ascendancy	
Medinet Habu is completed	

1000 B.C.E.–700 B.C.E.

Egypt	Near East and Mediterranean
Third Interim Period	The Phoenicians establish the city of Carthage
Egypt is divided between Tanis and Thebes	The Etruscans settle in the Italian Peninsula
Libya assumes control of Egypt	Assyria collapses as the major power in the Tigris-Euphrates region
Shoshenq I conducts campaigns against the invaders	Babylon regains its ancient power
Egypt is splintered	The first Olympic Games are held in Greece
The Nubians take control of part of Egypt under the leadership of Piankhi	Homer writes the *Iliad*
The Assyrians assault the Nile	
Egypt undergoes a cultural renaissance	

600 B.C.E.–300 B.C.E.

Egypt	Near East and Mediterranean
Trade and commerce are revived under Saites	Cyrus the Great of Persia conquers Babylon
The Persian Empire conquers Egypt	The Persian capital of Persepolis is founded
Egyptians briefly reclaim control	The first war between Greece and Persia is fought
The Persians reconquer Egypt	Athens emerges as the chief political power in Greece
Darius I of Persia codifies laws for Egypt	Philosophy and art flourish in Greece
The last flowering of Egyptian art	Rome begins its rise to power in the Italian Peninsula
Alexander the Great enters Egypt during his campaign against the Persian Empire	The Gauls sack Rome
Alexandria is founded by Alexander the Great	Alexander the Great becomes king of Macedon and conquers the Persian Empire

300 B.C.E.–30 B.C.E.

Egypt	Near East and Mediterranean
Rise of the Ptolemaic dynasty	Rome and Carthage fight the Punic Wars, leaving Rome master of the Mediterranean
A leap year is added to the calendar	Rome conquers Greece
Manetho writes his history	Pompey the Great campaigns in the East
Eratosthenes, Archimedes, and Euclid are in Egypt	Rome conquers Gaul
The Ptolemaic Empire begins its steady decline	Julius Caesar defeats his rivals in the Roman Civil War
The Rosetta Stone is erected	The Augustan Age begins with the birth of the Roman Empire
Cleopatra VII ascends to the throne and begins the last reign of the Ptolemies	
Julius Caesar comes to Alexandria	
Antony and Cleopatra are defeated at the battle of Actium	
Egypt falls to the legions of Octavian (Augustus)	
The end of the Ptolemaic dynasty and beginning of the Roman occupation of Egypt	

ENTRIES A TO Z

Aa A mysterious and ancient being worshipped in Egypt from the earliest eras of settlement and best known from cultic ceremonies conducted in the Old Kingdom (2575–2134 B.C.E.), Aa's cult was popular in the city of HELIOPOLIS, possibly predating NARMER (ca. 3000 B.C.E.), who attempted to unite Upper and Lower Egypt. Aa was revered as "the Lord of the PRIMEVAL ISLAND OF TRAMPLING," a mystical site associated with the moment of creation in Egyptian lore. In time this divine being became part of the cult of the god RÉ, the solar deity that was joined to the traditions of the god AMUN in some periods.

The moment of creation remained a vital aspect of Egyptian religion, renewed in each temple in daily ceremonies. The daily journeys of Ré across the heavens, as the sun, and the confrontation of the god with the dreaded terror of the TUAT, or Underworld, kept creation as a pertinent aspect of Egyptian mythology. In this constant renewal of creation, Aa was revered as the "COMPANIONS OF THE DIVINE HEART," a designation that he shared with the divine being WA. *See also* RELIGION AND COSMOLOGY; RÉ.

A'ah (A'oh) A moon deity of Egypt, also called A'oh in some records, identified before ca. 3000 B.C.E., when NARMER attacked the north to unite the Upper and Lower Kingdoms. A'ah was associated with the popular god THOTH, the divinity of wisdom, who was a patron of the rites of the dead. In the Fifth Dynasty (2465–2323 B.C.E.) A'ah was absorbed into the cult of OSIRIS, the god of the dead. A'ah is depicted in The LAMENTATIONS OF ISIS AND NEPHTHYS, a document of Osirian devotion, as sailing in Osiris's *ma'atet* boat, a spiritual vessel of power. In some versions of the BOOK OF THE DEAD (the spells and prayers provided to deceased Egyptians to aid them in their journeys through the Underworld), Osiris is praised as the god who shines forth in the splendor of A'ah, the Moon.

A'ah was also included in the religious ceremonies honoring the god HORUS, the son of ISIS and Osiris. The moon was believed to serve as a final resting place for all "just" Egyptians. Some of the more pious or holy deceased went to A'ah's domain, while others became polar stars.

A'ahset (fl. 15th century B.C.E.) *royal woman of the Eighteenth Dynasty*
A'ahset was a lesser ranked wife or concubine of TUTHMOSIS III (r. 1479–1425 B.C.E.). Her tomb has not been discovered, but a funerary offering bearing her name was found at THEBES. Such an offering indicates a rank in the court, although her name on the offering bears no title. It is possible that A'ahset was a foreign noble woman, given to Tuthmosis III as tribute or as a cementing element of a treaty between Egypt and another land. Such women received elaborate burial rites and regalia in keeping with their station in the royal court.

a'akh (a'akhu; akh) A spirit or soul freed from the bonds of the flesh, *a'akh* means "useful efficiency." The name was also translated as "glorious" or "beneficial." The *a'akh*, had particular significance in Egyptian mortuary rituals. It was considered a being that would have an effective personality beyond the grave because it was liberated from the body. The *a'akh* could assume human form to visit the earth at will.

It was represented in the tomb in the portrait of a crested IBIS. The spirit also used the SHABTI, the statue used to respond to required labors in paradise, a factor endorsed in cultic beliefs about the afterlife.

See also MORTUARY RITUALS.

A'ametju (fl. 15th century B.C.E.) *Eighteenth Dynasty court official*
He served Queen-Pharaoh HATSHEPSUT (r. 1473–1458 B.C.E.) as VIZIER or ranking governor. A'ametju belonged to a powerful family of THEBES (modern Luxor). A'ametju's father, Neferuben, was governor (or vizier) of Lower Egypt and his uncle, Userman, served TUTHMOSIS III (r. 1479–1425 B.C.E.) in the same position. Userman's tomb at Thebes contains wall paintings that depict the installation of government officials in quite elaborate ceremonies.

The most famous member of A'ametju's family was REKHMIRÉ, who replaced Userman as vizier for Tuthmosis III. Rekhmiré's vast tomb at Thebes contains historically vital scenes and texts concerning the requirements and obligations of government service in Egypt. Some of these texts were reportedly dictated to Rekhmiré by Tuthmosis III himself. Another family that displayed the same sort of dedicated performers is the clan of the Amenemopets.

See ADMINISTRATION.

A'amu (Troglodytes) This was a term used by the Egyptians to denote the Asiatics who tried to invade the Nile Valley in several historical periods. AMENEMHET I (r. 1991–1962 B.C.E.) described his military campaigns on the eastern border as a time of "smiting the A'amu." He also built or refurbished the WALL OF THE PRINCE, a series of fortresses or garrisoned outposts on the east and west that had been started centuries before to protect Egypt's borders. One campaign in the Sinai resulted in more than 1,000 A'amu prisoners.

The HYKSOS were called the A'amu in records concerning the Second Intermediate Period (1640–1532 B.C.E.) and 'AHMOSE (NEBPEHTIRÉ) (r. 1550–1525 B.C.E.), the founder of the New Kingdom. RAMESSES II (r. 1290–1224 B.C.E.) used the term to designate the lands of Syria and Palestine. In time the A'amu were designated as the inhabitants of western Asia. In some eras they were also called the Troglodytes.

See also WARFARE.

A'a Nefer (Onouphis) A sacred bull venerated in religious rites conducted in ERMENT (Hermonthis), south of THEBES (modern Luxor). The animal was associated with the god MONTU and with the BUCHIS bull in cultic ceremonies and was sometimes called Onouphis. The

A'a Nefer bull was chosen by priests for purity of breed, distinctive coloring, strength, and mystical marks. The name A'a Nefer is translated as "Beautiful in Appearing." In rituals, the bull was attired in a lavish cape, with a necklace and a crown. During the Assyrian and Persian periods of occupation (ca. 671 and 525–404/343–332 B.C.E.), the sacred bulls of Egypt were sometimes destroyed by foreign rulers or honored as religious symbols.

ALEXANDER III THE GREAT, arriving in Egypt in 332 B.C.E., restored the sacred bulls to the nation's temples after the Persian occupation. The Ptolemaic rulers (304–30 B.C.E.) encouraged the display of the bulls as THEOPHANIES of the Nile deities, following Alexander's example. The Romans, already familiar with such animals in the Mithraic cult, did not suppress them when Egypt became a province of the empire in 30 B.C.E.

A'aru A mystical site related to Egyptian funerary cults and described as a field or garden in Amenti, the West, it was the legendary paradise awaiting the Egyptian dead found worthy of such an existence beyond the grave. The West was another term for Amenti, a spiritual destination. A'aru was a vision of eternal bliss as a watery site, "blessed with breezes," and filled with lush flowers and other delights. Several paradises awaited the Egyptians beyond the grave if they were found worthy of such destinies. The MORTUARY RITUALS were provided to the deceased to enable them to earn such eternal rewards.

A'at (fl. 19th century B.C.E.) *royal woman of the Twelfth Dynasty*
The ranking consort of AMENEMHET III (r. 1844–1797 B.C.E.), A'at died at the age of 35 without producing an heir and was buried at DASHUR, an area near MEMPHIS, along with other royal women of Amenemhet III's household. This pharaoh constructed a necropolis, or cemetery, at Dashur, also erecting a pyramid that was doomed to become a cenotaph, or symbolic gravesite, instead of his tomb. The pyramid displayed structural weaknesses and was abandoned after being named "Amenemhet Is Beautiful." Despite the instability of the pyramid, A'at and other royal women were buried in secondary chambers of the structure that remained undamaged by structural faults. Amenemhet built another pyramid, "Amenemhet Lives," at HAWARA in the FAIYUM district, the verdant marsh area in the central part of the nation. He was buried there with Princess NEFERU-PTAH (1), his daughter or sister.

A'ata (fl. 16th century B.C.E.) *ruler of Kermeh, in Nubia*
KERMEH, an area of NUBIA, modern Sudan, was in Egyptian control from the Old Kingdom Period (2575–2134 B.C.E.), but during the Second Intermediate Period (1640–1532 B.C.E.), when the HYKSOS ruled much of

Egypt's Delta region, A'ata's people forged an alliance with these Asiatic invaders. A'ata's predecessor, Nedjeh, had established his capital at BUHEN, formerly an Egyptian fortress on the Nile, displaying the richness of the Kermeh culture, which lasted from ca. 1990 to 1550 B.C.E. This court was quite Egyptian in style, using similar architecture, cultic ceremonies, ranks, and government agencies.

When A'ata came to the throne of Kermeh, he decided to test the mettle of 'AHMOSE (NEBPEHTIRÉ) (r. 1550–1525 B.C.E.), who had just assumed the throne and was conducting a campaign by land and by sea against AVARIS, the capital of the Hyksos invaders. Seeing the Egyptians directing their resources and energies against Avaris, A'ata decided to move northward, toward ELEPHANTINE Island at modern ASWAN. 'Ahmose is believed to have left the siege at Avaris in the hands of others to respond to the challenge of A'ata's campaign. He may have delayed until the fall of Avaris before sailing southward, but A'ata faced a large armada of Egyptian ships, filled with veteran warriors from elite units. The details of this campaign are written on the walls of the tomb of 'Ahmose, son of Ebana, at THEBES (modern Luxor). The text states that 'Ahmose found A'ata at a site called Tent-aa, below modern Aswan. The Egyptian warriors crushed A'ata's forces, taking him and hundreds more as prisoners. A'ata was hung from the prow of 'Ahmose's vessel for the return journey to Thebes, where he was probably executed publicly. The Egyptians received A'ata's men as slaves. 'Ahmose, son of Ebana, took two prisoners and received five more slaves as well.

An Egyptian ally of A'ata tried to regroup the Kermeh forces. 'Ahmose, son of Ebana, received three more slaves when this rebel and his forces were crushed as a result of new campaigns. Buhen, the great fortress near the first cataract of the Nile River, became the administrative center of the Nubian region for Egypt as a result of the war, ending the Kermeh dominance there. The culture continued, however, until the New Kingdom collapsed. A military commander named Turi was installed as viceroy of Kush, or Nubia, under 'Ahmose's son and heir, AMENHOTEP I.

Aazehre *See* AHMOSE (NEBPEHTIRÉ); BUHEN; NUBIA.

ab The spiritual heart that existed on earth within an individual human and then served as an advocate in the JUDGMENT HALLS OF OSIRIS for the deceased. The Egyptians believed that human emotions, ideals, and beliefs resided in both the spiritual heart and in the organic physical heart, called the *hat*. Believed to be essentially useless, the human brain was discarded during the mortuary rituals, but the heart was preserved in a CANOPIC JAR or box. An AMULET that was buried in the linen wrappings of the deceased begged the spiritual heart to testify to Osiris and the judges of the dead that the deceased had righteous intentions and good thoughts throughout life.

Abar (fl. seventh century B.C.E.) *royal woman from Napata, in Nubia*
She was the mother of TAHARQA (r. 690–664 B.C.E.) of the Nubian Twenty-fifth Dynasty of Egypt and the daughter of KASHTA and Queen PEBATMA. Abar was the wife of PIANKHI (1) (750–712 B.C.E.). It is not known if Abar traveled northward to see her son's coronation upon the death of his predecessor, SHEBITKU, but Taharqa visited NAPATA to build new religious sanctuaries, strengthening his original base there. In 671 B.C.E., he returned as an exile when ESSARHADDON, the Assyrian king (r. 681–668 B.C.E.), overcame the Egyptian defenses on his second attempt to conquer the Land of the Nile.

Abbott Papyrus A historical document used as a record of the Twentieth Dynasty (1196–1070 B.C.E.) in conjunction with the AMHERST PAPYRUS and accounts of court proceedings of the era. Serious breaches of the religious and civil codes were taking place at this time, as royal tombs were being plundered and mummies mutilated or destroyed. Such acts were viewed as sacrilege rather than mere criminal adventures. Grave robbers were thus condemned on religious as well as state levels. The Abbott Papyrus documents the series of interrogations and trials held in an effort to stem these criminal activities. In the British Museum, London, the Abbott Papyrus now offers detailed accounts of the trials and the uncovered network of thieves.

See also PASER (3); PAWERO; TOMB ROBBERY TRIAL.

Abdiashirta (fl. 14th century B.C.E.) *ruler of Amurru, modern Syria*
Abdiashirta reigned over Amurru, known today as a region of Syria, and was a vassal of AMENHOTEP III (r. 1391–1353 B.C.E.). His son and successor was AZIRU. Abdiashirta made an alliance with the HITTITES, joining SUPPILULIUMAS I against the empire of the MITANNIS, the loyal allies of Egypt. Abdiashirta and Amurru epitomize the political problems of Egypt that would arise in the reign of AKHENATEN (r. 1353–1335 B.C.E.) and in the Ramessid Period (1307–1070 B.C.E.).

Abdi-Milkuti (fl. seventh century B.C.E.) *ruler of the city of Sidon in Phoenicia, modern Lebanon*
He was active during the reign of TAHARQA (r. 690–664 B.C.E.) of the Twenty-fifth Dynasty and faced the armies of ASSYRIANS led by ESSARHADDON. An ally of Taharqa, Abdi-Milkuti was unable to withstand the Assyrian assault, which was actually a reckless adventure on the part of Essarhaddon. Sidon was captured easily by Assyria's highly disciplined forces. Abdi-Milkuti was made a prisoner, probably dying with his family.

Abdu Heba (fl. 14th century B.C.E.) *prince of Jerusalem, in modern Israel*
He corresponded with AKHENATEN (r. 1353–1335 B.C.E.) of the Eighteenth Dynasty concerning the troubled events of the era. The messages sent by Abdu Heba are included in the collection of letters found in the capital, 'AMARNA, a remarkable accumulation of correspondence that clearly delineates the life and political upheavals of that historical period. This prince of Jerusalem appears to have maintained uneasy relations with neighboring rulers, all vassals of the Egyptian Empire. Shuwardata, the prince of Hebron, complained about Abdu Heba, claiming that he raided other cities' lands and allied himself with a vigorous nomadic tribe called the Apiru.

When Abdu-Heba heard of Shuwardata's complaints, he wrote Akhenaten to proclaim his innocence. He also urged the Egyptian pharaoh to take steps to safeguard the region because of growing unrest and migrations from the north. In one letter, Abdu Heba strongly protested against the continued presence of Egyptian troops in Jerusalem. He called them dangerous and related how these soldiers went on a drunken spree, robbing his palace and almost killing him in the process.

See also 'AMARNA LETTERS.

Abgig   A site in the fertile FAIYUM region, south of the Giza plateau. Vast estates and plantations were located here, and a large STELA of SENWOSRET I (r. 1971–1926 B.C.E.) was discovered as well. The stela is now at Medinet el-Faiyum. Abgig was maintained in all periods of Egypt's history as the agricultural resources of the area warranted pharaonic attention. The rulers of the Twelfth Dynasty, of which Senwosret I was a member, revitalized ABGIG and other sites, introducing hydraulic and irrigation systems that provided more arable lands and larger harvests. The TRADE systems of Egypt at the time were also expanding and needed products for new markets.

Abibaal (fl. 10th century B.C.E.) *ruler in Phoenicia, modern Lebanon*
Abibaal was active during the reign of SHOSHENQ I (r. 945–924 B.C.E.) of the Twenty-second Dynasty. Shoshenq I, of Libyan descent, ruled Egypt from the city of TANIS (modern San el-Hagar) and was known as a vigorous military campaigner. Shoshenq I also fostered TRADE with other nations, and Abibaal signed a treaty with him. The PHOENICIANS had earned a reputation for sailing to far-flung markets in the Aegean and Mediterranean Seas, going even to the British Isles in search of copper. As a result, Abibaal and his merchants served as valuable sources of trade goods for their neighboring states. Abibaal insured Shoshenq I's continued goodwill by erecting a monumental statue of him in a Phoenician temple, an act guaranteed to cement relations.

Abisko   A site south of the first cataract of the Nile, near modern ASWAN. Inscriptions dating to MENTUHOTEP II (r. 2061–2010 B.C.E.) were discovered at Abisko. These inscriptions detailed Mentuhotep II's Nubian campaigns, part of his efforts to unify and strengthen Egypt after the First Intermediate Period (2134–2040 B.C.E.) and to defeat local southern rulers who could threaten the nation's borders. During Mentuhotep II's reign and those of his Middle Kingdom successors, the area south of Aswan was conquered and garrisoned for TRADE systems and the reaping of the vast natural resources available in the region. Canals, fortresses, and storage areas were put into place at strategic locales.

See also NUBIA.

Abu Gerida   A site in the eastern desert of Egypt used as a gold mining center in some historical periods. The area was originally explored and claimed by the Egyptians, then enhanced by the Romans as a gold production region.

See also NATURAL RESOURCES.

Abu Ghurob   A site north of ABUSIR and south of GIZA, containing two sun temples dating to the Fifth Dynasty (2465–2323 B.C.E.). The better preserved temple is the northern one, erected by NIUSERRÉ (Izi) (r. 2416–2392 B.C.E.), and dedicated to RÉ, the solar deity of HELIOPOLIS. An OBELISK was once part of the site, and inscriptions of the royal *heb-sed* (*see* SED) ceremonies honoring the ruler's three-decade reign were removed from the site in the past. The temple has a causeway, vestibule, and a large courtyard for sacrifices. A chapel and a "Chamber of the Seasons" are also part of the complex, and the remains of a SOLAR BOAT, made of brick, were also found. The complex was once called "the Pyramid of Righa." The sun temple of USERKHAF (r. 2465–2458 B.C.E.) is also in Abu Ghurob but is in ruins.

Abu Rowash (Abu Rawash)   A site five miles north of GIZA, containing the "Lost Pyramid" of the Fourth Dynasty pharaoh RA'DJEDEF (r. 2528–ca.2520 B.C.E.). The presence of this pyramid at Abu Rowash puts into question the dates of his reign because of the time required to construct such a monument (around two decades). Because the construction of this royal burial site and the adjoining structures were completed before Ra'djedef's death, the formerly accepted details about his life have also been dismissed.

It was once believed that Ra'djedef, a son of KHUFU (Cheops) (r. 2551–2528 B.C.E.), murdered the rightful heir, his brother, Prince KEWAB, and was then assassinated in return. However, this line of events no longer appears credible. One objection to this theory is that Ra'djedef's mortuary rituals were continued long after his death, which, along with the construction of the vast pyramid at Abu Rowash, indicates that he was an accepted and popular ruler and therefore an unlikely candidate for assassination.

Abu Rowash is now part of an Egyptian military complex, but when excavations began there in the late 1990s it was discovered that the pyramid was vandalized by later rulers who used its materials for their own building projects.

Ra'djedef chose the site deliberately because of its elevation. Erected in the traditional fashion, the pyramid had a causeway that is over a mile long. A nearby quarry, still in use, provided the materials for the pyramid's construction, which would have lasted more than a decade. The base of the pyramid was composed of granite brought by barge from Aswan. The harbor site at Abu Rowash is still visible.

The pyramid rose 225 feet from this base, originally encased in costly electrum, an alloy of gold and silver. Corridors in the ancient palace style were completed within the structure, as was an elaborate complex for the workers. (The ruins of this complex still remain.) The burial chamber was surrounded by stone blocks.

A MORTUARY TEMPLE is on the eastern side of the pyramid and a VALLEY TEMPLE was designated as part of the complex. A boat pit on the southern side of the pyramid contained statues of Ra'djedef, the lower part a

statue of Queen Khentetka, and a SPHINX form, the first such sphinx form found in a royal tomb. In the valley temple of the complex a statue of ARSINOE (2), the consort of PTOLEMY II PHILADELPHUS (285–246 B.C.E.), was discovered. Also found were personal objects of AHA (Menes), the founder of Egypt's First Dynasty in 2920 B.C.E., and DEN (fl. ca. 2850 B.C.E.), the First Dynasty's fourth ruler. A newly discovered mud-brick pyramid on the site has not been identified, but an Old Kingdom (2575–2134 B.C.E.) necropolis is evident. Today signs of robbery and plundering are also visible throughout the complex.

Abu Simbel   A temple complex on the west bank of the Nile, above WADI HALFA in NUBIA (modern Sudan), Abu Simbel was erected by RAMESSES II (r. 1290–1224 B.C.E.) early in his reign. The structures on the site honor the state gods RÉ-HARAKHTY, AMUN, PTAH, and the deified Ramesses II. The site is famous around the world, not only for its main temple, but also for a second, smaller temple, dedicated to Queen Nefertari Merymut. During the construction of the temples and after their dedication, Abu Simbel employed vast numbers of priests and workers. Some records indicate that an earthquake in the region damaged the temples shortly after they were opened, and Setau, the viceroy of Nubia,

The mortuary temple of Ramesses II at Abu Simbel, moved to higher ground when the Aswan Dam flooded the original site *(Courtesy Steve Beikirch)*

conducted repairs to restore the complex to its original splendor. The archaeological work done in Abu Simbel reveals details regarding the arts, political life, and religious sensibilities of the era.

SITE DESCRIPTION AND CONSTRUCTION

A gateway leads to the forecourt and terrace of the Great Temple of Abu Simbel, presenting a unique rock-cut facade and four seated colossi of Ramesses II, each around 65 feet in height, showing him wearing the war helmet of southern (Upper) Egypt and the wicker crown of the "Bee King" of northern (Lower) Egypt, respectively. The symbol of the NINE BOWS, the ancient enemies of Egypt, is under his feet. Statues of Ré and Ma'at are also in the facade area. Smaller figures of Nefertari Merymut, Ramesses II's favorite queen, and of his elder sons, as well as his mother, Queen TUYA, are depicted standing beside the legs of the colossi. A niche above the temple entry displays the god RÉ, as a falcon, and baboons saluting the rising sun. At the north end of the terrace there is a covered court that depicts Ramesses II worshipping the sun as well. A large number of stelae are part of this court, including the Marriage Stela, which announces the arrival of a HITTITE bride.

The interior HYPOSTYLE HALL of this temple was designed with three aisles and six pillars. Hathor and Set are depicted on the walls, as well as ANKET, the patron goddess of the first cataract of the Nile. Also shown are Nefertari Merymut and Princess MERYATMUN, the daughter of Ramesses and Nefertari Merymut. Princess Meryatmun attended the opening ceremonies of Abu Simbel, while Nefertari reportedly was not present.

The original temple was designed to allow the sunlight appearing on the eastern bank of the Nile to penetrate the halls and sanctuary on two designated dates in February and October (which never varied over the centuries). On these days, the rays of the rising sun entered the entrance doorway and penetrated the dark interior to illuminate the figures of the deified Ramesses II and the three deities commemorated by the temple, all seated along the rear wall of the temple, deep within the rock foundation.

During the 31st year of Ramesses' reign an earthquake struck the site, causing severe damage. The pillars of the interior hypostyle hall were cracked and one collapsed. One of the colossal statues at the front was also damaged. The viceroy of Kush (Nubia, modern Sudan), named Paser, began the reconstructions, which were completed by his successor, Sethu. The fallen head of Ramesses dates to this earthquake. For some reason, Paser's work crews did not reattach the head, perhaps because the break was too severe. Modern visitors to Abu Simbel can still see the head in its ancient fallen state.

Entering the main temple there is a series of pillared halls, and a large hall is located just inside the entrance. As the temple recedes, the scale of the inner rooms becomes progressively smaller, and the level of the floor rises. These architectural conventions, common in most Egyptian temples, focus the structural axis toward the sanctuary, where the god resides. The first pillared hall, however, is on a grand scale, with eight Osiride statues of Ramesses forming roof support or pillars. The walls are covered with battle scenes commemorating Ramesses II's military prowess, including the slaughter of captives and the BATTLE OF KADESH. A second hall has four large pillars and presents religious scenes of offerings. Side rooms are attached for cultic storage areas, and the entire suite leads to the sanctuary. Within this chamber an ALTAR is still evident as are four statues, seated against the back wall and representing the deities Ré-Harakty, Amun, Ptah, and the deified Ramesses II.

Beyond the Great Temple at Abu Simbel lies a small chapel dedicated to the god THOTH and, beyond that, a temple to HATHOR. This temple glorifies Nefertari Merymut. At the entrance to the temple, she is depicted between two standing colossi of the pharaoh. Past the opening is a hall containing six pillars with sistrum-style capitals. A vestibule is beyond the hall, and then a sanctuary completes the traditional format. In the sanctuary, the goddess Hathor is shown as the protector of Ramesses II. She appears with symbols of the sistrum, the musical instrument used especially in temple ceremonies; Hathor was identified with the sistrum and with turquoise.

ARCHAEOLOGY

When the Swiss traveler Jean-Louis Burckhardt (d. 1817) discovered Abu Simbel in 1813, it was buried in the sands up to the heads of the colossal statues in its facade; the site had gone unnoticed for centuries. The Venetian explorer Giovanni Belzoni (1778–1823) arrived about four years after its discovery. Having heard about Abu Simbel, Belzoni hired local workers to remove the sand. The temples were opened before him, and word of the site soon spread to Europe.

Between 1964 and 1968, the temples of Abu Simbel, endangered because of their placement near the ASWAN Dam, were relocated to a more elevated position on the Nile. The temples had to be cut into movable sections and lifted on cranes from their vulnerable positions to a cliff site. The fallen head of Ramesses was not repaired during the move, as it was believed that the earlier repairs after the earthquake should be honored. (In the new position, the facade of the Great Temple has a colossal head of Ramesses II on the ground.) The remarkable feat of relocating the temples was a worldwide effort, costing some $40 million, much of the funds raised by international donations and sponsored by the United Nations Economic, Scientific and Cultural Organization (UNESCO) and member states. Notably, the move carefully replicated the solar phenomenon that takes place in the temple in February and October.

Further reading: Choukry, Nermine. *Abu Simbel.* Cairo: American University of Cairo Press, 2008; Hawass, Zahi, and Farouk Hosni. *The Mysteries of Abu Simbel: Ramesses II and the Temples of the Rising Sun.* Cairo: American University in Cairo Press, 2001; Siliotti, Alberto. *Abu Simbel and the Nubian Temples.* Cairo: American University in Cairo Press, 2001; Williams, Bruce. *Excavations Between Abu Simbel and the Sudan Frontier, Part Seven: 25th Dynasty and Napatan Remains at Qustul Cemeteries W and V.* Chicago: Oriental Institute of the University of Chicago, 1990.

Abusir A site south of GIZA dating to the Fifth Dynasty (2465–2323 B.C.E.) and containing a vast cemetery and pyramidal complexes. The large pyramid of SAHURÉ (r. 2458–2446 B.C.E.) dominates the site that once contained 14 such structures, most now reduced to cores of rubble or stone. Sahuré's pyramid has a causeway, VALLEY TEMPLE, and a canal intact. The portico of the valley temple has eight columns as well as a large hall provided with wall reliefs and a black basalt pavement. A temple area dedicated to the goddess SEKHMET appears to have been refurbished as a shrine in later eras, aiding in its preservation. Storerooms, corridors, and niches form two levels, and red granite papyrus columns support the upper floor. Cultic chambers, a sanctuary with an altar, and a granite false door were also found there. An elaborate drainage system was incorporated into the complex, using lion-headed gargoyles and open channels. Copper-lined basins were connected to underground copper pipes in this system. These are still visible. Called "the Soul of Sahuré Glistens" at its dedication, this pyramid has a limestone core as the foundation, filled with sand and rubble and faced with fine stone.

The mastaba of the nobleman PTAHSHEPSES (2), a relative of NIUSERRÉ (r. 2416–2392 B.C.E.) and a court official, is a fully developed structure to the north of

The sun temple of Niuserré at Abusir as reconstructed

Niuserré unfinished monument. Ptahshepses' tomb has a colonnaded court with 20 pillars, a portico, a hall, and a chamber depicting family portraits.

Niuserré's pyramidal complex was dedicated as "the Places of Niuserré are Enduring." In erecting his valley temple, Niuserré usurped part of KAKAI's original structure. The core was made of limestone and included a colonnaded court and cultic chamber.

The pyramid of Kakai (Neferirkaré; r. 2446–2426 B.C.E.) was built out of mud brick and completed by his successor. It was dedicated as "Kakai Has Become a Soul" or as "the Pyramid of the *Ba*-spirit." Local limestone formed the core, and the facing was a fine limestone and red granite.

The pyramid of NEFEREFRÉ (r. 2419–2416 B.C.E.) is also located on the site of Abusir. It was dedicated as "the Pyramid which is Divine of the *Ba*-spirits" but was never completed. It was a low mound of limestone, with no causeway or temple. Another ruin at Abusir is associated with Queen KHENTAKAWES (1), the consort of SHEPSESKHAF (r. 2472–2467 B.C.E.).

A new tomb was recently discovered at Abusir, dating to the Sixth Dynasty (2323–2150 B.C.E.) and built for a judge named Inti. Large, with ground and subterranean levels, the tomb is part of a complex of sites belonging to Inti's family. Elaborate decorations and statues have also been found.

Abydos Abydos was a necropolis located on the western shore of the Nile just north of DENDEREH, capital of the Thinite NOME, or district. Called Abdju by the Egyptians, Abydos was considered home to the god OSIRIS and revered as Egypt's holiest site in all of the dynastic periods. The kings of the Predynastic Period, including SCORPION I, were buried here, as were the pharaohs of the early dynastic periods. In some instances the rulers had cenotaphs interred there, symbolic burials to express their devotion to the god Osiris, the patron of Abydos. The commoners of the Nile Valley, unable to give their relatives tombs or elaborate grave sites, carried the remains of the deceased for miles in order to find a small spot of land at Abydos. Burying the deceased in that holy site was an act of generosity.

SITE DESCRIPTION AND CONSTRUCTION

Abydos was in use from the earliest times and benefited from royal patronage throughout its history. The earliest tombs at Abydos were erected at a site known as UMM EL-QA'AB (the Mother of Pots)—so called because of the large quantity of vessels discovered on the surface, particularly jars used for funerary offerings at the graves. The First Dynasty grave sites were large and are next to the Predynastic area sites. Aha (Menes) (r. ca. 2920 B.C.E.), the founder of Egypt, had a cenotaph tomb there, as did his ranking consort, Queen BERENIB.

Temple remains from Seti I's cenotaph at Abydos, displaying a truly ancient form of architecture *(Courtesy Steve Beikirch)*

As the ceremonies of the god Osiris grew in popularity, the temple of Osiris, called Kom el-Sultan by the Egyptians, developed in the north. Egyptians brought stelae and other commemoratives to leave as symbols of their devotion. Pilgrimages to Abydos were made by people from all over the valley.

Of the royal monuments erected in Abydos, the temple of SETI I (r. 1306–1290 B.C.E.) is the largest, built of fine white limestone and containing splendid reliefs. The first two courts of the temple, as well as the portico, were probably completed by RAMESSES II (r. 1290–1224 B.C.E.) after Seti I's death. One scene in the temple depicts Ramesses II adoring the gods Isis and Osiris as well as deified Seti I. Ramesses II is also credited with the decoration in the first HYPOSTYLE HALL of the temple, which has seven doors leading to chapels beyond a second hypostyle hall. The second hypostyle hall serves as a vestibule for the seven chapels incorporated into its west wall. False vaults cover the chapels, and all have reliefs. The chapels honored six gods and the deified Seti I.

A KING LIST was discovered in a gallery in the shrine; the shrine shows Seti I and Ramesses II, as a prince, offering honors to their royal predecessors. Beside the gallery, known as the Gallery of Lists, there are halls for the preservation of the BARKS OF THE GODS, butchers' quarters, and magazines. Immediately behind the temple is an area called the OSIREION, actually a CENOTAPH, or false tomb, built by Seti I but probably completed by MERENPTAH (r. 1224–1214 B.C.E.), his grandson. A feature in this shrine is an island, formed by canals of water that were kept filled at all times, upon which the sarcophagus and canopic chests were maintained.

The temple of Ramesses II, located to the northeast of the shrine of Seti I, is noted for its delicate reliefs, which provide a description of the BATTLE OF KADESH, carved into limestone. A red granite doorway leads to a pillared open court, and more reliefs depict a procession of offerings for the king. A portico on the west side of the temple opens onto small chapels honoring various gods and Seti I as a deified being. Some of the deities have been provided with suites of rooms, and there is a humanoid DJED pillar in one of the apartment chambers. Granite statues honor Ramesses II, Seti I, the god AMUN, and two other goddesses. The temple of Osiris in Abydos is located in the northeast of Ramesses II's temple. Now called Kom el-Sultan, the region has only a few remains of a limestone portico and ramparts. Cenotaphs dedicated to individuals were erected in the area.

The Shunet el-Zabib, or "Storehouse of Dates," an enclosure dating to the Second Dynasty (2770–2649 B.C.E.), is in the northwestern desert. Two actual complexes, designed with massive inner walls and outer mud-brick walls, had main ramparts. The cenotaphs of the royal personages are located farther out in the desert.

To the south, cenotaphs of the Middle Kingdom and early New Kingdom were also discovered. A temple of Senwosret III (r. 1878–1841 B.C.E.) stands at the edge of the desert. The ruler's cenotaph is located near the face of the nearby cliffs. A pyramid, possibly erected by 'Ahmose (Nebpehtiré) (r. 1550–1525 B.C.E.), is located near the temple. A mortuary complex of Tetisheri, the grandmother of 'Ahmose and a leader in the Theban campaigns against the Hyksos and the start of the New Kingdom, is also in the area.

Abydos, as the seat of the Osirian cult, was a large city and was much revered during all eras of ancient Egypt. The city's standing as Osiris's main cult center demanded industries and structures that promoted the devotion. The city's original deity was apparently a black dog-headed creature known as KHENTIAMENTIU, the "Chief of the Dwellers of the West," a title assumed by Osiris when his cult grew popular among the Nile. The west, AMENTI, was always a territory of death in the nation's religious and mythological texts.

Two stelae were discovered in Abydos. One measuring six feet by three feet was from the Thirteenth Dynasty, placed there by NEFERHOTEP I (r. ca. 1741–1730 B.C.E.). The second records the plans of TUTHMOSIS I (r. 1504–1492 B.C.E.) to honor Osiris by endowing the god's temple with gifts. Neferhotep I and other rulers had to limit the number of individual burials taking place within the city limits and in the necropolis areas. People from other regions brought their loved ones to Abydos to bury them beside the god Osiris.

A recently discovered temple founded by TUTHMOSIS III (r. 1479–1425 B.C.E.) was built to the southwest of the Osiris enclosure in the northern section of the site. Tuthmosis III erected the temple to honor Osiris and included colossal Osiride statues of himself in the precincts. Ramesses II later built in the same area, at the Portal Temple.

In the southern part of Abydos, Senwosret III built a mortuary temple as well as channels to provide water to the site for rituals. The cenotaph tomb has a pole roof chamber, corridors, and a burial room with a concealed sarcophagus and canopic box of red granite set into niches concealed by masonry. The limestone mortuary temple has an enclosed wall and a pylon gate. Colonnades, courts, and cultic chambers were discovered in fragmented condition in the complex.

The commoners of Egypt also held Abydos in great esteem, believing it to be the only truly sacred necropolis of the nation. Families came from all across the nation, bringing the mummified remains of their loved ones to be buried in the holy ground. Abydos was considered the gateway to the eternal realms of the dead and was the capital of the Osiris cult. A gap in the nearby mountains was believed to lead to the Tuat, the land of the dead. The reenactment of the rituals of Osiris, each one called a "mystery," depicted the god's life, death, and resurrection; thousands attended these celebrations.

ARCHAEOLOGY

Despite the importance of the site, even after it was discovered by archaeologists Abydos was long overshadowed by other sites in Egypt, including KARNAK and the GIZA plateau. Nevertheless, its value was not lost on tomb robbers who looted it and sold their discoveries.

One of the realities about the excavations and digs at Abydos is the degree to which the vast legacy of this site has been scattered around the world, especially after the groundbreaking labors of legendary Egyptologists such as Auguste Mariette (1821–1881) and Sir William Matthew Flinders Petrie (1853–1942). Petrie, in particular, was crucial in helping archaeologists realize that the site of Abydos was significantly older than had been previously thought. Further work was undertaken by the Swiss Egyptologist Édouard Naville (1844–1926).

Excavations since 1967 carried out by the American Abydos Expedition under codirectors William Kelly Simpson and David B. O'Connor have done much to place earlier discoveries in perspective. In 1991 the Abydos Expedition discovered 14 boats on the site, each buried in separate mounds and each protected by a pit enclosure. These royal SOLAR BOATS were buried outside of the walls of the main tomb enclosure, which dates to the earliest dynastic periods. The mounds are topped with symbols of an anchor, designed to moor the ships in the eternal realms. Each boat measures 90 feet by 10½ feet and is made of cedarwood planks, some two to three inches wide. They resemble the famous boat of KHUFU (Cheops) (r. 2551–2528 B.C.E.) found at the Great Pyramid at Giza, with ropes and painted surfaces. These vessels were part of the mortuary rituals, designed to carry the pharaohs to the western shore of the spiritual Nile and into the blessed eternal realms.

Further reading: David, A. R. *A Guide to Religious Ritual at Abydos.* London: Warminster, 1981; Grimal, Nicholas. *A History of Ancient Egypt.* Oxford, U.K.: Blackwell, 1995; O'Connor, David B. *Abydos: Egypt's First Pharaohs and the Cult of Osiris.* London: Thames & Hudson, 2009; Shaw, Ian. *The Oxford History of Ancient Egypt.* Oxford, U.K.: Oxford University Press, 2000.

Abydos Fleet An armada of greater than 12 royal vessels discovered buried near ABYDOS, some eight miles from the Nile. Each vessel, from 50 to 60 feet in length, was encased in a mud-brick coffin and pit. They date to the earliest eras of Egypt. Shorter, less elaborate vessels have been found at SAQQARA and HELWAN. Like the vessel found at the Great PYRAMID of KHUFU (Cheops) (r. 2551–2528 B.C.E.), these ships were part of the MORTUARY RITUALS of the early eras. The deceased pharaohs were provided with such vessels in order to sail on the spiritual Nile into eternity. Excavations at the site give indications that more vessels may be part of the necropolis treasures of Abydos.

Abydos List   *See* KING LISTS.

Achaemenes (d. ca. 460 B.C.E.) *prince of Persia slain by an Egyptian rebel*
He was the son of DARIUS I (r. 521–486 B.C.E.). The prince was appointed satrap, or governor, of the Nile by his brother XERXES I (r. 486–466 B.C.E.), Darius I's heir. In 481 B.C.E., Achaemenes led a military force composed of conscripted Egyptians amassed to conduct various military campaigns, including assaults on the Greeks. These units were defeated at the battle of SALAMIS by the Greeks. Returning to Egypt, Achaemenes carried out the harsh ruling policies of Xerxes, enslaving Egypt as a Persian province with little value. Such a policy stemmed from Persian disdain for the Egyptian religious or philosophical heritage and a firm belief in the unique revelations concerning human affairs that had been bestowed upon the Persian people. The confiscation of temple wealth was carried out at least in one instance, and Xerxes did not endear himself to the conquered Egyptians by assuming ancient titles or roles in keeping with Nile traditions.

In 460 B.C.E., INAROS, a native Egyptian and a prince of HELIOPOLIS, started a full-scale insurrection. Inaros, listed in some records as a son of PSAMMETICHUS III (Psamtik) (r. 526–525 B.C.E.), set up an independent capital at MEMPHIS. Achaemenes led an army against Inaros, confronting him at Papremis, a Delta site. There the Persian prince died on the field. His death prompted the terrible punitive campaign conducted against Inaros by a veteran Persian general, MEGABYZUS. Queen Atossa, Prince Achaemenes' mother, demanded that Inaros be crucified, an act protested by General Megabyzus.

Achaemenians (Achaemenids; Hakhamanishiya)
A royal house of Persia. This dynasty of Persia (modern Iran) ruled Egypt as the Twenty-seventh Dynasty (525–404 B.C.E.) and as the Thirty-first Dynasty (343–332 B.C.E.). The Achaemenians were descendants of Achaemenes, the ruler of a vassal kingdom in the Median Empire (858–550 B.C.E.). Cyrus the Great (ca. 590–529 B.C.E.), a descendant of the dynasty's founder, overthrew the Median line ruling Persia and expanded his control of neighboring lands. His son, CAMBYSES, took Egypt in 525 B.C.E. The Achaemenians included: DARIUS I, who came from a collateral branch of the royal line; XERXES I; ARTAXERXES I Longimanus; Xerxes II; DARIUS II Nothus;

ARTAXERXES II Memnon; ARTAXERXES III OCHUS; ARSES; and DARIUS III CODOMAN, who fell before the armies of ALEXANDER III THE GREAT in 330 B.C.E.

Achillas (d. ca. 47 B.C.E.) *military officer of Egypt*
He served PTOLEMY XIII (r. 51–47 B.C.E.) and was possibly present when the murder of POMPEY the Great took place. Pompey had fled to Egypt for safety but was assassinated on September 28, 48 B.C.E. His head was reportedly preserved and presented as an offering to Julius CAESAR. When Caesar occupied ALEXANDRIA, Achillas was involved in a siege of that capital, an offensive that proved unsuccessful.

A veteran of many battles, esteemed by other military figures, even among his political foes, Achillas ran afoul of ARSINOE (4), the royal sister of CLEOPATRA VII. Arsinoe was an enemy of Cleopatra and Caesar, wanting the throne of Egypt for herself. She raised an army to depose her sister and her Roman allies, and she asked Achillas to serve as her commanding general. Not skilled in court intrigues or in the murderous ways of Arsinoe and her predecessors, Achillas managed to confront and infuriate the princess, who had him executed.

Achoris   A site just south of the FAIYUM and north of modern Tihna el Gebel. The famed Fraser Tombs, rock-cut grave enclosures, are in Tihna el-Gebel and date to the Old Kingdom (2575–2134 B.C.E.). The other ruins at Achoris contain three small temples and a Greco-Roman necropolis. Achoris was used by NOMARCHS of the Fifth Dynasty (2465–2323 B.C.E.).

Actium   This promontory on the western coast of GREECE at the entrance to the Ambracian Gulf is where a decisive battle for control of Egypt and the Roman empire took place in 31 B.C.E. Octavian, the future AUGUSTUS, met Marc ANTONY and CLEOPATRA VII (51–30 B.C.E.) at Actium. Antony was camped on the site, and the naval battle that took place outside of the gulf provided the name for the battle. Octavian's 400 ships defeated the 500 vessels of Marc Antony and Cleopatra VII, and they fled to ALEXANDRIA. Antony committed suicide outside of Alexandria, and Cleopatra VII, facing imprisonment and humiliation, killed herself when the Roman forces took up residence in the city soon after the battle. Octavian (Emperor Augustus) initiated an Olympic-style series of games at Actium to commemorate his victory there.

Adea-Eurydice (fl. fourth century B.C.E.) *royal woman of the Greeks*
She was the wife of PHILIP III ARRHIDAEUS (r. 323–316 B.C.E.), the half brother of ALEXANDER III THE GREAT. Adea-Eurydice was a half niece of Philip and joined in the plot to slay him. She died in a similar purge conducted by the heirs of Alexander the Great. Her ambitions and criminal activities contributed to the dis-

integration of Alexander's empire, as his former companions fought to build their own respective states. PTOLEMY I SOTER, the founder of the Ptolemaic Dynasty (304–30 B.C.E.), was thus able to use the decline to his advantage, claiming Egypt as his own.

Adicran (fl. sixth century B.C.E.) *Libyan ruler*
He was partially responsible for the fall of APRIES (r. 589–570 B.C.E.) of the Twenty-sixth Dynasty. An ally of Egypt, Adicran faced a Greek invasion and appealed to Apries for aid in repelling the foe. The Greeks had established the colony of CYRENE on the Libyan coast and were now threatening the Libyan ruler. Apries sent several units of Egyptian veteran troops to Adicran's aid, and they suffered a stinging defeat at the hands of the Greeks. The Egyptian troops returned home and mutinied because of the incident. When Apries sent his general, AMASIS (r. 570–526 B.C.E.) to mediate the mutiny, Amasis sided with the troops and was proclaimed the rightful ruler of Egypt.

Adicran faced the Cyrene King Battus II the Lucky, who overcame the Libyans and Egyptians in ca. 570 B.C.E. He founded new colonies and Hellenized the hump of eastern Libya, calling it Cyrenaica. In 525 B.C.E., the internal feuds between rival Egyptian families seeking the throne ended when the Persians arrived with the army of CAMBYSES.

'Adjib (Merpubia; Enezib; Anedjib) (fl. ca. 2700 B.C.E.) *fifth ruler of the First Dynasty*
His name meant "Strong of Heart" or "Safe Is His Heart." 'Adjib was the first Egyptian ruler in the Saqqara KING LIST. MANETHO, the Ptolemaic Period historian, credits 'Adjib with a reign of 26 years, but he is now believed to have ruled only 14 years. 'Adjib is probably the first ruler to be recognized by most areas of Lower and Upper Egypt as the ruler of united Egypt. He conducted military campaigns to gain territories and to consolidate his position. His principal wife was TARSET, or Betresh, the mother of his heir, SEMERKHET.

He built two tomb complexes, one at SAQQARA and one in ABYDOS, the holy city of OSIRIS, the god of the dead. His Abydos tomb, small and poorly constructed, had stone vessels bearing his name. Semerkhet usurped some pieces after succeeding him on the throne. 'Adjib's Saqqara tomb was decorated in the palace facade style, a unique design of recessed panels.

administration   In 2920 B.C.E., when AHA (Menes) founded MEMPHIS and began the First Dynasty (2920–2770 B.C.E.), the administrative system of the Nile Valley was already well defined by the traditions and governing entities of the cities of HIERAKONPOLIS and then THINIS. The concepts, beliefs, and practices that formed the foundation for the system of government in Egypt distinguished it from every other state in existence at the time. These included a sense of individual responsibility, the sharing of labors, patriotism, and a belief that nations on earth had to mirror the order, beauty, and harmony of the universe.

DIVISION OF POWER
The Pharaoh
The pharaoh, the ruler of the land, was considered destined by the gods to serve as an intermediary for the people. The pharaohs were considered semidivine and their titles were written as *neter nefer*. A *neter* was a god, and the word *nefer* meant good and beautiful. The *neter* was compromised, meaning the pharaoh was not a spectacular, all-powerful deity but a human chosen to serve as a shield for his people. The people, therefore, had to serve at the pharaoh's side if Egypt was to survive and prosper. The administration of the pharaoh relied heavily upon the dedication, intelligence, and loyalty of hundreds of public servants. Furthermore, any Egyptian demonstrating the attributes of a leader could attain political power and hold the highest offices in the land. When Aha began the First Dynasty in 2920 B.C.E., this philosophy prevailed.

Not all Predynastic Period rulers have been documented, but SCORPION I is considered to have been the pioneer in administrative endeavors. He is dated to around 3000 B.C.E., in the cities of Hierakonpolis and Thinis. One of his descendants, NARMER, is documented as the warrior-king set on uniting the Two Kingdoms, Upper and Lower Egypt, and Aha is believed to have been Narmer's son. The administrative traditions that Aha brought to his reign were successfully imposed on the emerging government. These traditions included loyalty to one's NOME, or province, and equality of men and women under the law, a unique concept in that historical period. The ever-present court scribes of the first dynasties, devoted to keeping records of all events, composed volumes of data on the pharaoh's duties and appearances, and there is consistency in their roles from the earliest days of Egypt.

The basic tenets and autocratic traditions of Egypt provided a uniquely competent level of rule. The pharaoh, a manifestation of the god RÉ while he lived and a form of the god OSIRIS beyond the grave, was the absolute monarch of Egypt in stable eras. He/she relied upon non-divine officials, the NOMARCHS, or ruling clans of the nomes, to muster troops for defense and to safeguard the NATURAL RESOURCES of each region. Such nomarchs, who were also given official standing in the administration, controlled the vast bureaucracy. The pharaoh relied upon the priests to conduct ceremonies in the temples as his representatives.

Nomarchs
Under the rule of the pharaohs the various regions of Egypt were grouped into nomes, or provinces, called

sepat. These nomes had been designated in the Early Dynastic Period (2920–2575 B.C.E.), and each one had its own deity, totems, and lists of venerated ancestors. There were 20 nomes in Lower Egypt and 22 in Upper Egypt. Each was ruled by a *heri-tep a'a,* called "the great over-lord" or nomarch. The power of such men was modified in the reigns of strong pharaohs, but generally they served the central government, accepting the traditional role of "Being First Under the King." This rank denoted an official's right to administer a particular nome or province on behalf of the pharaoh. Such officials were in charge of the region's courts, treasury, land offices, militia, archives, and storehouses. They reported to the vizier and to the royal treasury on affairs within their jurisdiction.

Viziers

A prime minister, or vizier, reigned in the ruler's name in most ages. Beginning in the New Kingdom (1550–1070 B.C.E.) or earlier, there were two such officials, one each for Upper Egypt and Lower Egypt, though in some dynasties the office was held by one person. The role started early in the form of chancellor. Viziers in the Old Kingdom (2575–2134 B.C.E.) were normally related to the royal house. One exception was IMHOTEP, the com-moner who became high priest of the temple of PTAH and vizier of DJOSER (r. 2630–2611 B.C.E.) in the Third Dynasty. The viziers heard all territorial disputes within Egypt's borders, maintained a cattle census, controlled the various reservoirs and food supplies, collected taxes, supervised industries and conservation projects, and managed repairs of all dikes. The viziers were also required to keep accurate records of rainfall (as minimal as it was) and to maintain current information about the expected levels of the Nile's inundations. All documents had to have the vizier's seal in order to be considered authentic. The ideals of the office were clearly stated by TUTHMOSIS III (r. 1479–1425 B.C.E.) in his "Instructions for the Vizier Rekhmire."

Each vizier was normally assisted by members of the royal family or by aristocrats. This office was con-sidered an excellent training ground for the young princes of each dynasty. Tax records, storehouse receipts, crop assessments, and a census of the human inhabitants of the Nile Valley were constantly updated in the vizier's office by a small army of SCRIBES. These scribes aided the vizier in his secondary role in some periods, that of the official mayor of THEBES (modern Luxor). In the New Kingdom the mayor of Thebes's western side, normally the necropolis area, served as an aide, maintaining the burial sites on that side of the Nile, and reported back to the vizier (the mayor of Thebes's eastern side was the vizier himself, in his sec-ondary role as the official mayor of Thebes.). The viziers of both Upper and Lower Egypt saw the ruler each day or communicated with him on a daily basis. Both served as the chief justices of the Egyptian courts, giving all

decisions in keeping with the traditional judgments and penalties.

As with the position of vizier, the other administra-tive offices of the central government were in most eras doubled, one for Upper Egypt and one for Lower Egypt. The nation viewed itself as a whole, but there were cer-tain traditions dating back to the legendary northern and southern ancestors and the concept of symmetry that were reflected in the government system. In general, the admin-istrative offices of the central government were exact duplicates of the traditional provincial agencies; dupli-cate central government offices included those for foreign affairs, military affairs, treasury and tax, departments of public works, granaries, armories, mortuary cults of deceased pharaohs, and regulators of temple priesthood.

The Royal Treasurer and the Chancellor

The royal treasurer, normally called the treasurer of the god, had two assistants, one each for Upper and Lower Egypt. In most ages this official was also the keeper of the royal seal placed on all official documents, although that position was sometimes given to the chancellor. The trea-surer presided over the religious and temporal economic affairs of the nation. He was responsible for mines, quar-ries, and national shrines. The treasurer paid workers on all royal estates and served as the paymaster for both the Egyptian army and navy. The chancellor of Egypt was assisted by other officials and maintained administrative staffs for the operation of the capital and royal projects. The judicial system and the priesthood served as counter-balances to the royal officials and ensured representation of one and all in most dynastic periods.

Viceroyalty of Nubia and Governors of the Northlands

In the Eighteenth Dynasty, 'AHMOSE (NEBPEHTIRÉ) (r. 1550–1525 B.C.E.) established the viceroyalty of NUBIA (modern Sudan), an office bearing the title of "King's Son of Kush." Many officials of previous dynasties had served in the same capacity at the ELEPHANTINE ISLAND at ASWAN, but 'Ahmose made it a high-level rank. This offi-cer controlled the affairs of the lands below the cataracts of the Nile, which extended in some eras hundreds of miles to the south. Certain governors of the northlands were also appointed during the New Kingdom Period in order to maintain control of Asiatic lands under Egypt's control, as well as to govern the eastern and western bor-ders. Some officials served also as resident governors of occupied territories, risking the loss of their lives when caught in rebellions by the conquered states.

SPLINTERING AND DECLINE OF TRADITIONAL GOVERNMENT

The government of ancient Egypt was dependent upon the competence and goodwill of thousands of officials. In general, the rulers appear to have been able to inspire capable individuals to serve in various capacities with dedication and a keen sense of responsibility. Some families involved in various levels of government agencies, such as the Amenemopet clan, served for generations. During certain ages, particularly in the waning years of the Ramessids of the Twentieth Dynasty (1196–1070 B.C.E.), officials became self-serving and corrupt, with serious consequences for Egypt.

During the Third Intermediate Period (1070–712 B.C.E.), the government of Egypt was divided between the royal court and the religious leaders at Thebes. Women were given unique roles in Thebes in the office of GOD'S WIFE OF AMUN, or the Divine Adoratrices of Amun. This office became part of the political rivalry of competing dynasties. PIANKHI (r. 750–712 B.C.E.) marched out of Nubia to conquer Egypt in order to put an end to such fractured government and to restore the unity of the older traditions.

The Twenty-sixth Dynasty (664–525 B.C.E.) tried to restore the standards of government in Egypt but was faced with the Persians led by CAMBYSES (r. 525–522 B.C.E.). The Persians placed Egypt under the control of a satrap, or governor, and Egyptian institutions were subject to the demands of the conquerors. The Twenty-eighth Dynasty (404–393 B.C.E.) and the longer-lived Twenty-ninth Dynasty (393–380 B.C.E.) and Thirtieth Dynasty (380–343 B.C.E.) attempted to revive the old ways. The Persians returned in 343 B.C.E., only to be ousted by ALEXANDER III THE GREAT in 332 B.C.E.

The Ptolemaic Period (304–30 B.C.E.) restored the government of Egypt, bringing Hellenic concepts to the older forms and centralizing many aspects of rule. The internal feuds of the Ptolemies, and their refusal to accept Egyptians in their court or in their royal families, however, led to an isolation that made these rulers somewhat distant and alien to the average people on the Nile. Also, the laws were not the same for native Egyptians and the Greeks residing in the Nile Valley. The old Egyptian ways, including the unabashed dedication of entire families to government service, were strained if not obliterated by the new political realities. The suicide of Egyptian queen-pharaoh CLEOPATRA VII in 30 B.C.E. put an end to the traditional Egyptian government, as the nation became a territory of Rome.

Further reading: David, Rosalie. *Handbook to Life in Ancient Egypt, Revised Edition.* New York: Facts On File, 2003; Kemp, Barry J. *Ancient Egypt: Anatomy of a Civilization.* London: Routledge, 1989; Spencer, A. J. *Early Egypt: The Rise of Civilization in the Nile Valley.* London: British Museum Press, 1993; Tyldesley, Joyce. *Judgement of the Pharoah: Crime and Punishment in Ancient Egypt.* London: Orion, 2001.

Admonitions of Ipuwer   This is a remarkable literary relic dating to the First Intermediate Period (2134–2040 B.C.E.), or perhaps later. Egypt, bereft of a strong royal house, suffered a series of rival kingdoms during this time and a reversal of the traditional social customs. The *Admonitions* are profoundly pessimistic for this reason, questioning the cosmic implications of Egypt's fallen state. The text was discovered in the Leiden Papyrus 344, having been copied from an earlier version by Nineteenth Dynasty scribes (1307–1196 B.C.E.). Ipuwer calls for a strong pharaoh to restore the spirit of MA'AT, justice, piety, and peace to the Nile kingdoms. Such didactic literature was always popular in Egypt.

See also LITERATURE.

Adule   A site on the Red Sea near Massawa, Adule was used as a hunting ground for wild elephants by PTOLEMY II PHILADELPHUS (r. 285–246 B.C.E.) and PTOLEMY III EUERGETES (r. 246–221 B.C.E.). Adule and other nearby areas on the shores of the Red Sea were occupied by the Egyptians over the centuries, eventually becoming trade centers for goods imported from many distant lands and linked to well-known TRADE routes leading to the Nile.

afnet   A head covering shown on the goddesses SELKET and ISIS and on a statue of TUT'ANKHAMUN (r. 1333–1323 B.C.E.), discovered in his tomb. The *afnet* resembled the NEMES, the royal headdress, but was not striped and lacked the front panels. Its use was probably restricted to royalty or to the images of divine beings, although commoners and nobles alike wore a similar head covering. The headdress dates to the Predynastic Period (before 3000 B.C.E.) in HIERAKONPOLIS.

See also CROWNS.

Agatharchides (fl. second century B.C.E.) *chronicler and trade expert*
He served PTOLEMY VIII EUERGETES II (r. 170–163, 145–116 B.C.E.) in the capital of ALEXANDRIA. Born a Greek in Cnidus, a city on the coast of Anatolia (modern Turkey), Agatharchides went to Egypt's capital to study the monumental archives in the LIBRARY OF ALEXANDRIA. As a result of his scholarly reputation, he was commissioned by Ptolemy's officials to prepare a comprehensive report on the city's trade and commerce. Agatharchides produced *On The Red Sea,* a work that used testimony from contemporary merchants and traders. Their accounts provide historical authenticity to the report and offer vivid insights into the wide-ranging TRADE efforts of that time. Agatharchides is considered one of the most significant scholars of the second century B.C.E. He also wrote *Events in Asia* and *Events in Europe,* now lost.

Agathocles (1) (fl. third century B.C.E.) *prince of Thales*
This prince fell victim to the political intrigues of ARSINOE (2), the sister of PTOLEMY II PHILADELPHUS (r. 285–246 B.C.E.). The son of King LYSIMACHUS, he was the ranking heir to the throne of Thrace, a region in

the modern southeastern Balkans. Agathocles faced the political cunning of Arsinoe. She married Lysimachus and bore him two children, viewing Agathocles as an obstacle to the throne. He became the object of ridicule and rumors in the court of Thrace, all designed to isolate him and to alienate him from his father. Arsinoe and her followers then accused him of treason, claiming he was bent on murdering Lysimachus and taking the throne. Lysimachus believed the accusation and executed Agathocles. Arsinoe did not benefit from the death, however. When Lysimachus died, she faced her own tragic consequences seeing her sons barred from inheriting and having to flee to her half brother. The governor of Pergamum (modern Bergama in Turkey), so horrified by the unjust treatment of the Thracian prince, started a campaign of military retribution against Lysimachus. Thrace fell to the Seleucids of Syria as a result.

Agathocles (2) (d. ca. 205 B.C.E.) *court official and conspirator of the Ptolemaic Period*
He became powerful in the court during the reign of PTOLEMY V EPIPHANES (r. 205–180 B.C.E.). Agathocles joined forces with a courtier named SOSIBIUS in a palace coup in ALEXANDRIA, the capital of Egypt. Ambitious and eager to control Ptolemy V, who was quite young, Agathocles and Sosibius murdered the king's mother, ARSINOE (3). Agathocles served as regent for the orphaned king, but he was unable to hold power.

Governor TLEPOLEMUS of the city of PELUSIUM (near modern Port Said in Egypt) was so enraged by the murder of Queen Arsinoe that he marched on Alexandria with his frontier army. Along the way, Tlepolemus announced his intentions to the Egyptian people, who left their villages to swell the ranks of his forces. An angry horde of Egyptians thus faced Agathocles at the palace in the capital. He resigned on the spot and hurried home to prepare for a flight out of the city. Ptolemy V was carried to a large arena in Alexandria, surrounded by Tlepolemustroops. There the Egyptians bowed before the young king, swearing their loyalty. The governor then demanded retribution for the death of Queen Arsinoe, and Ptolemy V agreed. A crowd raced to Agathocles' home, where they beat him to death along with his entire family.

Agesilaus (d. 360 B.C.E.) *king of Sparta in Greece*
Agesilaus was critically involved in Egyptian affairs in the reign of TEOS (r. 365–360 B.C.E.) of the Thirtieth Dynasty. The son of Archidamus and half brother of Agis II, Agesilaus was a great military commander and a master of the siege. He had a varied military career, campaigning throughout his reign despite ill health. He was eventually humiliated militarily and forced to add to state revenues by hiring out as a mercenary for other rulers, such as Teos.

The Egyptians, involved in a campaign against Palestine, asked Agesilaus to aid in invasion plans. The Spartans sailed to Palestine to join the Egyptians there. Teos was beginning a series of expansion campaigns, hoping to take Syria and oppose PERSIA on all fronts. Having the veteran Spartans in his service promised success. Agesilaus, however, found Teos to be militarily naive and quarrelsome. The two argued about troop placements, making the veteran Spartan warrior uneasy at the thought of continuing the alliance. When he received word that Teos was taxing the temples of Egypt to pay for his military adventures, Agesilaus realized that the Egyptian ruler would be short-lived on the throne. The Spartans decided to abandon Teos, an act that greatly handicapped the Egyptians and made the campaign extremely doubtful.

Agesilaus returned to SPARTA. There he received the Egyptian delegates of NECTANEBO II (r. 360–343 B.C.E.), who was a nephew of Teos. Agesilaus agreed that Teos would not remain on the throne because of his ill-advised policies and his unfit temperament. In order to hold on to their power, Teos's relatives proposed to depose him. Agesilaus agreed to the overthrow and aided Nectanebo's cause, standing at his side at his coronation. Agesilaus died at the age of 84 while journeying home to Sparta from the coronation.

agriculture   Agriculture was the bountiful occupation of ancient Egyptians from the Predynastic Period (before 3000 B.C.E.) that enabled them to transform an expanse of semiarid land into rich fields after each inundation of the NILE. Agriculture in Egypt always depended upon the pooling of resources and labor so that the mineral-rich waters of the Nile could be introduced inland for fertilization of lands.

DEVELOPMENT OF EGYPTIAN AGRICULTURE
Early farmers dug trenches from the Nile shore to the farmlands, using draw wells, crude irrigation tools, and later the SHADUF, a primitive machine that allowed them to raise levels of water from the Nile into canals. The *shaduf* was introduced into Egypt by the HYKSOS, or Asiatics, ca. 1600–1500 B.C.E. Fields thus irrigated produced abundant annual crops.

From the Predynastic Period, agriculture was the mainstay of the Egyptian economy. Most Egyptians were employed in agricultural labors, either on their own lands or on the estates of the temples or nobles. Control of irrigation became a major concern, and provincial officials were held responsible for the regulation of water. The storage of crops occurred at the local level and at royal granaries in the capital, and assessors were sent from the capital to the provinces to collect taxes in the form of grain. The local temples of the gods also had vast fields, with their own irrigation needs. The temples had storage units and were subject to taxes in most eras, unless exempted for a particular reason or favor.

Agriculture began in the FAIYUM and in the DELTA regions well before the start of the Dynastic Period, ca. 2920 B.C.E. Normally the Egyptians plowed the fields with oxen, and teams of two men each worked to form shallow furrows for the seeds. One man guided the plow, and the other led the oxen through the designated pattern. Some tomb reliefs depict the activity and show a second plow being dragged behind the first one. The second implement turned up the earth between the furrows. If the farmers wanted only the top layer of soil tilled in any season, they used lighter plows, normally pushed by the farm workers. In any case, the furrows had to be broken up after the initial plowing. Men and women entered the fields with simple wooden hoes to break up the clumps of earth. The sowing of the fields was a two-part activity in most areas. The farmers put the seed in the earth and then drove herds of sheep or swine into the fields to trample the seeds deep into the furrows. Normally crops were harvested with sickles.

Barley, emmer, and other grains were gathered with such tools and taken to the local threshing areas, where again animals were employed. The harvest was carried on the backs of donkeys or asses, and at the storage areas the crops were ground by oxen.

The first fruits of each harvest were reserved for the local gods and the temples. The deity MIN (1), popular throughout Egypt, was offered praise for each crop drawn from the earth. Sometimes ALTARS were erected to provide adequate rituals, and granary officials, priests, or government representatives were on hand for all harvests, measuring the crops for tax assessments. These harvest celebrations were attended by the entire populations of the nearby districts, and the people gave thanks to the Nile and to the agricultural patrons for the abundance of another year.

EGYPTIAN CROPS AND PRODUCTS

The Egyptians used the main cereal crops of their fields for the staples of their daily diets: emmer for bread and barley for beer. Wheat was not known along the Nile

A tomb display of agriculture, dating to the New Kingdom Period and portraying harvesters in the fields *(Hulton Archive)*

until the Ptolemaic Period (304–30 B.C.E.). Early Egyptians also raised chickpeas and lentils, pomegranates, lettuce (of various varieties), onions, carob, garlic, and plants used for oils, such as sesame. Honey collected from hives was used as a sweetener, and there were condiments, spices, and oils, including sesame and olive. Most commoners did not enjoy the luxury of meat as part of their daily diets. Herds of cattle were large in many eras, however, and the Egyptians liked beef, mutton, pork—which was restricted in some eras—and goat. It is probable that certain species of antelope supplemented diets as well.

The Nile provided a variety of fish for the table, and the Egyptians became skilled at catching them. Fish were netted or caught in baskets, while spearfishing and angling were done from small rafts made of papyrus. There appear to have been some religious restrictions regarding the eating of at least one particular type of fish in particular districts. This custom was observed by priests and by the upper classes, while commoners gathered whatever came their way.

The Nile also provided a variety of waterfowl, which were caught in clap nets and taken to poultry yards for slaughter. The two halves of the net were spread over an area and then snapped shut to ensnare the fowl. These fowl, however, were probably reserved for the upper classes. Pigeons were as common in ancient times as now and were used as a food source, perhaps even raised for that purpose. Ducks and geese were also plentiful, and during the New Kingdom (1550–1070 B.C.E.) chickens were introduced into the Nile Valley.

Grapes were grown in the western Delta and in the oases, and the BAHARIA OASIS was famous for its quality wines. The Egyptians drank both red and white wines, and the vineyards labeled them according to quality and variety. The favorite beverage of both poor and rich alike, however, was barley beer, made everywhere and kept in vats. Pomegranate and date wines were also available. Other useful crops were the papyrus, date palm, and flax. Such plants produced sources of fibers and other materials.

HYDRAULIC SYSTEMS OF THE FAIYUM

One of the first necessities for the evolving Egyptian nation was to control the Nile River, which inundated the land throughout its valley each year with deposits of silt and mud. In the Faiyum, where Predynastic Period inhabitants had discovered the ease with which they could turn to agricultural pursuits, efforts were made to channel the water coming through the BAHR YUSEF into the region. Dikes, canals, and ditches were dug in the Old Kingdom (2575–2134 B.C.E.), but the major renovations were accomplished by the pharaohs of the Twelfth Dynasty, especially by AMENEMHET III (1844–1797 B.C.E.).

The purpose of the irrigation systems and hydraulic projects was to extend the time during which the Nile

waters could be made available to fields in the western Delta and the Faiyum. The Nile had formed Lake MOERIS there in the Predynastic Period, and the Egyptians started building a retaining wall some 27 miles long, a construction that provided them with 27,000 acres of farmland. During the flood period, the Nile provided new water for the lake, and the water was carefully channeled into depressions that were dug from the soil by hand. Regulators, such as matted covers and wooden slats, provided control over the flow of the water. It has been estimated that Lake Moeris doubled in size during inundations, and most of its water was directed into other depressions or into channels that led to a vast irrigation-ditch complex.

Sluices and narrow ravines were devised for regulating irrigation, and gullies were cut into the natural banks or placed in the retaining walls at various points so that water could be stored or used as the seasons and the crops demanded. These sluices were covered with the same reed mats and kept under constant supervision by a unit of trained irrigation experts. The mats were lowered or raised according to the requirements of distant fields that were connected to the water reserve by channels. All of the hydraulic system components required constant vigilance and repairs, and these were carried out throughout the year. When the *shaduf* was introduced by the Hyksos in the Second Intermediate Period (1640–1532 B.C.E.), the movement of water was greatly improved. Crops could be rotated and an additional growing season coaxed from the Faiyum because of the ability of crews to transfer water efficiently.

Though the Egyptians had a skillfully designed hydraulic system, they did not have earthmoving equipment. Instead, hundreds of able-bodied men came into an area and simply dug out the ground in a desired region. The earth was put into baskets, which were carried away to a particular point where a wall was needed or where mounds could protect various crops or estates. The assembly line of diggers, basket carriers, and mound builders worked ceaselessly until the new reservoir was completed and filled. Such a feat was accomplished in the reign of AMENHOTEP III (1391–1353 B.C.E.). Amenhotep III built a vast resort, MALKATA, on the western shore of the Nile at THEBES, including a lake for the royal barges dug out of the ground by crews of workmen who accomplished the ruler's will in just over two weeks.

The fall of the New Kingdom in 1070 B.C.E. did not hinder agriculture in Egypt. The farmers simply turned to local NOME, or province, administrators and continued their seasonal routines. Some dynasties, ruling a century or two, made efforts to reclaim the Faiyum, and the Ptolemies (r. 304–30 B.C.E.) added royal residences and new innovations to the fields, introducing advanced systems of irrigation and crop controls. The Greek methods supplemented the traditional ones, adding to the fertility of the Nile Valley. During the Ptolemaic Period agriculture was a state-controlled industry. Seeds, grains, and textile plants, as well as tools, were lent to the farmers by the state-operated agricultural offices, and designated crops were grown throughout the Nile Valley according to the seasons and the schedules mandated. The crops were repayments to the state and had to be delivered to the same agencies. The Ptolemies coordinated the agricultural output of Egypt with current trade systems.

The Romans, aware of Egypt as "the breadbasket of the world," took over in 30 B.C.E. and maintained regimented improvements in the important agricultural districts. Other farmers, isolated and unconcerned about political rivalries or changes, continued tilling the land, irrigating their fields, and reaping bountiful harvests.

THE IMPORTANCE OF EGYPTIAN AGRICULTURE

For centuries, Egypt was considered the world's richest agricultural prize. Rising nations looked to the Nile Valley as a vital ally in trade and exchange, and many states became vassals of the pharaohs in order to receive grain and other agricultural products. In time, the very crops that sustained Egypt made it a target for other powers. Rome had long sought to dominate the Nile Valley in order to maintain its own resources of necessary FOODS. In 30 B.C.E., Egypt became a protected province of the Roman Empire.

Throughout the centuries, however, no matter what the political situation was in the land, Egypt's farmers and orchard owners stayed on the land and maintained the routines that ensured healthy crops. The inundations of the Nile ended with the completion of the Aswan High Dam in 1970, and secure irrigation practices became steady and uninterrupted.

Further reading: Baines, John, and Jaromir Malek. *Atlas of Ancient Egypt.* New York: Facts On File, 1985; James, T. G. H. *Pharaoh's People: Scenes from Life in Imperial Egypt.* Oxford, U.K.: Oxford University Press, 1984; Kemp, Barry J. *Ancient Egypt: Anatomy of a Civilization.* London: Routledge, 1989; Spencer, A. J. *Early Egypt: The Rise of Civilization in the Nile Valley.* London: British Museum Press, 1993.

Agrippa, Marcus Vipsanius (d. 12 B.C.E.) *friend and adviser to Octavian (later Augustus)*
Agrippa was largely responsible for the military campaign that resulted in the crushing defeat of the combined army and fleet of Egypt under Marc ANTONY and Queen CLEOPATRA VII in 31 B.C.E. at the battle of ACTIUM. A commoner born in 63 B.C.E., Agrippa was a constant companion to Octavian, nephew to Julius CAESAR and the future Emperor AUGUSTUS. When Octavian entered into military training in 45 B.C.E., Agrippa accompanied him. He subsequently stood at Octavian's side at Caesar's funeral in 44 B.C.E. and was a formi-

dable representative of Octavian in the period after Caesar's assassination, during which his friend came into possession of extensive wealth and consolidated his political power. Agrippa was also instrumental in arranging the union of Octavian and Antony in the extermination of the Liberators, Caesar's assassins, in particular Brutus.

After the defeat of the Liberators, Agrippa was Octavian's chief lieutenant, defeating Antony's brother, Lucius, in the Perusine War in 40 B.C.E. and suppressing a rebellion in Gaul. Returning in triumph to Rome, Agrippa was elected consul and then, in 37, was appointed admiral. He spent the next six years cleansing parts of the Mediterranean of pirates, including Sextus Pompey, the son of Pompey the Great, who had been reduced to pirating after the defeat of his father by Julius Caesar.

In 31 B.C.E., Agrippa joined Octavian at Actium where the Romans faced the fleet and army of Cleopatra and Marc Antony. Agrippa commanded the left wing, but just as important as his tactical skill was his invention of the *harpax*, a grappling hook fired by a catapult at an enemy vessel, which then permitted the vessel's capture by the superior Roman marines. The *harpax* was pivotal to the success of the Romans at Actium and the defeat of both the fleet and the ambitions of Cleopatra VII and her lover, Marc Antony.

When Octavian became Augustus, Agrippa conducted a census of the provinces, from 29 to 28 B.C.E. He found life in Rome, with its intrigue and competition for the favor of Augustus, not to his taste, however. At his request, he was posted to the eastern provinces. There he added to his reputation for administrative talent. Recalled to Rome, he rebuilt much of the Eternal City, including the Panthera, and founded colonies in Phoenicia (modern Lebanon).

He wed Caecillia, the daughter of Pomponius Atticus, divorcing her to marry Marcella, the wealthy niece of Augustus. That marriage resulted in the birth of Vipsania Agrippina, the first wife of Emperor Tiberius. In 21 B.C.E., when he was recalled to Rome, he married Julia, Augustus's daughter. She bore him three sons and a daughter.

A-Group An independent people in Upper NUBIA (modern Sudan) from ca. 3100–2800 B.C.E., the A-Group were also designated as being from "the LAND OF THE BOW." The rulers of these people had considerable local power and resources. Their graves contained gold jewelry and finely made pottery. Egyptian and other foreign items found in these graves indicate a trade system that reached into the Mediterranean. Other groups in the area became enemies of the A-Group, but the B-Group appears partially related. Egypt's pharaohs of the First Dynasty (2920–2770 B.C.E.) annexed part of Nubia and the A-Group people formed the new colony.

Aha (Hor-Aha; Menes) (d. ca. 2900 B.C.E.) *first ruler of the First Dynasty (2920–2575 B.C.E.)*

The origins of Aha can be traced to the development of Upper Egypt, the southern region where the cities of HIERAKONPOLIS and Edfu were highly developed and powerful. Narmer, the reported father of Aha, moved northward in his efforts to unify the land, and Aha began a nation in the Delta as a result. The first dynastic ruler of ancient Egypt, Aha was called Hor-Aha, "the Fighting Hawk."

BIOGRAPHY

A ruler who could trace his lineage to Hierakonpolis and THINIS in Upper Egypt, Aha is believed to be the legendary MENES, as the name Menes appears as one of his ROYAL NAMES. In the tomb of his mother, NEITHOTEP, however, a small ivory tablet was discovered that depicted Aha and Menes side by side. Aha's relationship to NARMER, a descendant of SCORPION I, is also open to speculation. Neithotep is believed to have been a consort of Narmer, given to him to seal alliances with local Delta clans, including those of the powerful city of Buto. Narmer, who had marched out of Thinis to unite the Upper and Lower Kingdoms, was probably the father of Aha.

Aha is the ruler recorded as founding the city of Memphis, known as Ineb Hedj, "the White Walled." The capital was formed by Aha when he erected a series of levees and dams on a Nile channel in the Delta and deflected the course of that river with a dam south of the present city's site. A small army of workers built the dams and kept them in repair. The city of Memphis, which was built by the people, was located south of modern Cairo at the apex of the Delta, thus raised in a position of power. This plain, on the western side of the Nile, was some four miles wide, with sloping cliffs at the western end.

Memphis was originally called Ankh-tawy, "Life of the Two Lands," the two lands being Upper and Lower Egypt. Made of mud brick, plastered and painted white, the walls of the city prompted the new name. Ineb Hedj derives from the era of the Sixth Dynasty (2323–2150 B.C.E.), when Pepi I, the second ruler of that dynasty, built his pyramid in SAQQARA. The capital was soon Men-Nefer and then Menti, and the Greeks changed it to Memphis. The old capital is today the site of a town called Mit-Rahina.

Although Aha did not control all of Egypt, he consolidated his power in Memphis and began a central government. To his capital Aha brought officials from Thinis, and perhaps Hierakonpolis, who put into place the offices and administrative courts and agencies for Memphis's government. The nation was given an administrative foundation that would last until the Greco-Roman Period beginning in 332 B.C.E. Aha even managed to claim land in Nubia (modern Sudan), conducting a campaign there and commemorating the event with a wooden label found in Abydos.

Aha established trade with Palestine and Syria while campaigning to bring more of Egypt under his control. A temple honoring the god PTAH was erected at Memphis in Aha's reign, and he built a shrine to the goddess NEITH in SAIS in the eastern Delta. Aha also established the cult of the Apis bulls in the capital.

The Egyptian historian MANETHO (fl. ca. 280 B.C.E.) credits Aha with about 63 years on the throne, mentioning that, according to legend, he was slain by a hippopotamus. Another legend claims that he was saved from enemies by riding on the back of a crocodile. Aha built a temple in the Faiyum to SOBEK, the crocodile deity.

Queen BERENIB, her name meaning "Sweet of Heart," was his consort, or the ranking queen; however, she was not the mother of the heir. Aha's son and heir, DJER, was the child of a lesser-ranked queen, HENT (1); Aha also wed TEY. Djer was raised to take Aha's place in the governing of Egypt. (At this time, the royal cult as the deification of the pharaoh was already to some degree in place.) Aha's three wives probably were buried beside Aha in Saqqara, the necropolis of Memphis. Aha's CENOTAPH tomb at Abydos erected at Umm el-Ga'ab is the largest in the area. It is a brick-lined structure, rectangular in form and adorned with corner bastions and towers. A subterranean chamber was designed for burial, and wooden poles were used in the construction. Servants and courtiers were slain or died willingly in order to accompany Aha into the next world.

His tomb in Saqqara is a pit cut into the rock, with 27 magazines on the ground level and five subterranean chambers. Made of mud brick, this tomb was decorated in the palace facade style. A boat pit on the north side of the tomb contained a SOLAR BOAT. There were enclosure walls provided as well. Along with the remains of young Egyptian men who were obviously slain or died by their own hand to accompany Aha into eternity, there were also seven young lions buried in subsidiary graves in the complex of Aha, the animals representing royal strength.

HISTORICAL IMPACT

Aha was the founder of Egypt; the name Egypt was derived from a name later given to Memphis, his capital. Through the rule of Aha, Egypt assumed many of the chief characteristics of pharaonic rule that marked Egyptian civilization until the final fall of the kingdom to the Romans in 30 B.C.E. He consolidated his power in Memphis and began a central government. He also instituted the tradition of having educated, trained commoners in positions of power, a tradition that would serve Egypt well for centuries.

In addition, during Aha's reign Egypt assumed an international presence both by trading with surrounding cultures, such as Palestine and Syria, and pursuing military ventures against Nubia. One of the most striking signs of Aha's rule are the pyramids in the southern, Nubian region of Africa, in modern Sudan.

Further reading: Breasted, James. *Ancient Records of Egypt: The First Through the Seventeenth Dynasties,* Vol. 1. Chicago: University of Illinois Press, 2001; Clayton, Peter. *Chronicle of the Pharaohs: The Reign-by-Reign Record of the Rulers and Dynasties of Ancient Egypt.* New York: Thames & Hudson, 1994; Midant-Reynes, Beatrix. *The Prehistory of Egypt: From the First Egyptians to the First Pharaohs.* London: Wiley-Blackwell, 2000; Wenk, Robert. *The Ancient Egyptian State: The Origins of Egyptian Culture (c. 8000–2000 B.C.).* Cambridge: Cambridge University Press, 2009; Wilkinson, Toby. *Early Dynastic Egypt.* London: Routledge, 1999.

Ahenobarbus, Gnaeus Domitius (d. ca. 31 B.C.E.)
Roman general and supporter of the various Roman factions in Egypt
Ahenobarbus aided Marc ANTONY in his effort to become master of the Roman world. The son of a prominent family that wielded much influence in the Roman Senate, he bore the name Ahenobarbus, or "red beard," because of the traditional tale that a distant ancestor had his beard turned that color by the gods Castor and Pollux. He was also noted as the grandfather of the future emperor Nero.

Originally Ahenobarbus backed Brutus and the Liberators who had assassinated Julius CAESAR, calling for the continuation of the Roman Republic. Following the defeat of the Republicans after Caesar's assassination in 44 B.C.E., Ahenobarbus fled Rome and was forced to survive by working as a pirate in the Mediterranean. In 40 B.C.E., he was reconciled with Marc Antony (who had declared himself against the Liberators), serving him as the governor of Anatolia (modern Turkey) until 35 B.C.E. He was a consul of Rome when Marc Antony and OCTAVIAN, the future Augustus and first emperor of Rome, proved unable to remain political allies. Ahenobarbus went with Antony to ALEXANDRIA, Egypt, but soon found CLEOPATRA VII (51–30 B.C.E.), Antony's famed lover, to be an evil influence. He charged that she was opposed to traditional Roman values and, when Antony declined to heed his counsel, Ahenobarbus deserted Antony's cause just before the battle of ACTIUM in 31 B.C.E. He died soon after, supposedly of remorse, but probably from a terminal illness. His foul temper was legendary.

Ah'hotep (1) (fl. 16th century B.C.E.) *royal woman of the Seventeenth Dynasty*
She was the consort of Sekenenré TA'O II (ca. 1560 B.C.E.) and the mother of the founder of the New Kingdom, 'AHMOSE (NEBPEHTIRÉ) (r. 1550–1525 B.C.E.). The daughter of Senakhtenre TA'O I and Queen TETISHERI, Ah'hotep was raised in DEIR EL-BAAS, just north of Thebes, during

the period in which the HYKSOS, or Asiatics, ruled the northern terri tories. She bore two sons, KAMOSE and 'Ahmose, and two daughters, 'AHMOSE-NEFERTARI and 'AHMOSE-HETEMPET.

When Ta'o II began the war of unification, Ah'hotep stood as guardian of the Theban throne. She received Ta'o's body when he was slain and then sent her first-born son, Kamose, on the same crusade. Kamose died in 1550, and 'Ahmose became the new ruler. Ah'hotep served as regent for this young son, marrying him to his sister, 'Ahmose-Nefertari, who was possibly Kamose's widow. For almost 10 years, Ah'hotep ruled the Theban lands of southern Egypt, maintaining an uneasy peace with the Hyksos. When 'Ahmose began his spectacular campaign against the Asiatics, Ah'hotep maintained order and recruited more and more units for the army. Her name was linked with that of 'Ahmose in inscriptions, as in the fortress of BUHEN, south of ASWAN on the Nile.

She died at the age of 90 after the nation was unified, and she was given a vast mortuary complex at THEBES, being buried near Kamose. Magnificent offerings were provided for her burial, including a ceremonial ax (a military honor) and a golden boat mounted on a wooden chariot with bronze wheels. 'Ahmose praised her on a stela at KARNAK, saying: "She is the one who performed the rites and cared for Egypt." The immense coffin of Ah'hotep was found in 1881, used for PINUDJEM (1). Her mummified remains were discovered in a small tomb near the entrance to the VALLEY OF THE KINGS. No original tomb has been identified.

Ah'hotep (2) (fl. 16th century B.C.E.) *royal woman of the Eighteenth Dynasty*
She was the consort of AMENHOTEP I (r. 1525–1504 B.C.E.). The daughter of 'AHMOSE (NEBPEHTIRÉ) and Queen 'AHMOSE-NEFERTARI, Ah'hotep married her brother and is listed on her tomb as "King's Daughter, King's Wife, King's Mother." Amenhotep I, however, died without an heir. The son born to him by Ah'hotep died in infancy. This baby, AMUNEMHET (1), was discovered in a cache of mummies alongside his aunt 'AHMOSE-MERYTAMON, in DEIR EL-BAHRI, having been rewrapped and reburied by priests of the Twentieth Dynasty, when his original tomb was plundered. The child died in the first or second year of his life. Ah'hotep was buried in THEBES.

'Ahmose (fl. 16th century B.C.E.) *royal woman of the Eighteenth Dynasty*
She was the Great Wife, or ranking consort, of TUTHMOSIS I (r. 1504–1492 B.C.E.). Although she is sometimes mentioned as a daughter of 'AHMOSE and sister of AMENHOTEP I, in her titles she is called "King's Sister" but not "King's Daughter." She may have been the daughter of Prince 'AHMOSE-ANKH.

She was given in marriage to Tuthmosis I when he was designated as the heir of Amenhotep I. 'Ahmose bore four children: her sons AMENMOSE and WADJMOSE, and her daughters NEFERUKHEB and HATSHEPSUT. Neither of 'Ahmose's sons was designated as heir to the throne, probably because they died before their father. Neferukheb died young, and Hatshepsut became a queen-pharaoh of Egypt.

'Ahmose was celebrated in the temple reliefs erected by Hatshepsut, who ruled from 1473 to 1458 B.C.E. The temple is at DEIR EL-BAHRI on the western shore of the Nile at Thebes. These inscriptions and a portrait were designed to validate Hatshepsut's usurpation of the throne. 'Ahmose is described as having been visited by the god AMUN, who fathered Hatshepsut in a shower of gold. She did not live to see her daughter raised to the throne, as she died at a young age. The portraits of Queen 'Ahmose depict a vigorous, handsome woman.

See also HATSHEPSUT'S BIRTH RECORDS.

'Ahmose (Nebpehtiré) (d. 1525 B.C.E.) *founder of the Eighteenth Dynasty and the New Kingdom*

'Ahmose, whose name means "the Moon Arises," reigned from 1550 B.C.E. until his death. He founded the New Kingdom (1550–1070 B.C.E.).

BIOGRAPHY

'Ahmose was the son of TA'O II (Sekenenré) and Queen AH'HOTEP (1) of THEBES, and the younger brother of KAMOSE, the last ruler of the Seventeenth Dynasty. Kamose and Ta'o II had waged war against the HYKSOS, or Asiatics, who had usurped the northeastern regions of Egypt, and both perished in the attempt. 'Ahmose succeeded to the throne of Thebes when Kamose died in 1550 B.C.E.

The war had come to a halt around the time of Kamose's death, as the Hyksos ruler, Apophis, also died soon after. Hyksos governors controlled the northern lands as far south as CUSAE and held firmly there. Young at the time, 'Ahmose was unable to take advantage of Kamose's gains, and the Hyksos regrouped and captured HELIOPOLIS. For perhaps a decade 'Ahmose was trained by his mother, who served Egypt as the throne regent. TETISHERI, his grandmother, counseled him in his early years as well. Queen Ah'hotep earned the respect and gratitude of Upper Egyptians as she consolidated the southern holdings and prepared her son to lead an army northward. Eventually, 'Ahmose moved against AVARIS, the Hyksos capital in the eastern DELTA, using land forces and ships that were able to navigate the eastern branches of the Nile. Placing Avaris under siege, 'Ahmose put down a rebellion of priests in another area, taking a small fleet and several units of the army to accomplish that campaign. 'AHMOSE, SON OF EBANA, present at these military campaigns, detailed the activities in his funerary hieroglyphs. Other details are available from the tomb of 'AHMOSE-PEN NEKHEBET, another contemporary who served in the military.

After a long period, Avaris surrendered, and the Hyksos fled into Sharuhen, a fortress in southwestern Palestine. The Egyptians followed them there and placed Sharuhen under siege. While the army kept the Hyksos sealed inside their fortress in Palestine, 'Ahmose faced another revolt. This rebellion was instituted by A'ATA, a ruler of KERMEH, a region south of ASWAN, in NUBIA (modern Sudan). 'Ahmose put down this rebellion and and took A'ata captive. 'Ahmose then established the viceroyalty, or governorship, of Kush, or Nubia, with the administrative offices located on the ELEPHANTINE Island at Aswan. A trusted companion, 'AHMOSE SITAYET, was named to this position. A second Nubian campaign settled the region.

Meanwhile, the Hyksos sealed in Sharuhen surrendered after three, or possibly six, years, and the Egyptians followed them all the way into modern Syria. They fought battles there to rid themselves of Hyksos survivors, and when that campaign ended, 'Ahmose turned to the matter of a national government.

'Ahmose's chief consort was 'Ahmose-Nefertari, and they had several children: AMENHOTEP I (his heir), 'AHMOSE-SIPAIR, SIAMUN (2), and Ramose. His daughters were 'AHMOSE-MERYTAMON and AH'HOTEP (2). 'Ahmose's other consorts were 'AHMOSE-IN-HAPI and Thent Hep, the mother of Princess Hent Temehu. A unique BUILDING INSCRIPTION depicts 'Ahmose and 'Ahmose-Nefertari seated together in the royal residence. This ABYDOS commemorative, a stela six and a half feet high and three feet wide, describes how the royal couple planned the great mortuary memorials for his mother, Ah'hotep, and his grandmother, Tetisheri.

'Ahmose returned to the campaign in Palestine and on the Mediterranean coast in his later years. He was about 35 years old when he died in 1525 B.C.E. His tomb was erected at DRA-ABU' EL-NAGA on the western shore of Thebes, and a second false tomb was erected in Abydos with a terraced temple. The false tomb was a true pyramid with scenes of his expulsion of the Hyksos. 'Ahmose's remains were removed from Dra-abu' el-Naga by priests of the Twenty-Second Dynasty for safety. They were found in DEIR EL-BAHRI in 1881, wreathed in pale blue delphiniums and protected by a covering of tough black resin. He was buried in a large cedar coffin. After 'Ahmose's death, the pharaoh TUTHMOSIS I (r. 1504–1492 B.C.E.) erected a stela in honor of 'Ahmose on the Euphrates River in modern Iraq. Forensic studies indicate that 'Ahmose was of medium height, somewhat thin, with a firm chin and good teeth. He suffered from arthritis and scoliosis, both diseases prominent in the dynasty. 'Ahmose was not circumcised, although circumcision was a custom of the time.

HISTORICAL IMPACT

'Ahmose was not only the founder of the Eighteenth Dynasty (1550–1307 B.C.E.), but also the founder of the

New Kingdom (1550–1070 B.C.E.), the most powerful historical period of the nation.

'Ahmose brought a unique administrative prowess to his era, putting into place programs of retribution and favor. After defeating the Hyksos and thus ending their dominance of Egypt, 'Ahmose rebuilt canals and irrigation systems and rewarded his loyal followers with land grants. Mines and QUARRIES were opened and foreign trade resumed. An inscription at MASARA states that in his 22nd year of rule, 'Ahmose opened the quarry there for limestone to be used at Heliopolis and for the Theban god AMUN's temple at OPET, in THEBES, now part of modern Luxor. The MASARA STELA, erected by an official named NEFERPERET, states that captured Hyksos oxen were used to drag the quarried stones to the barges on the Nile.

'Ahmose attributed his military success over the Hyksos to the god Amun, an attribution that elevated the god's importance to the nation. Throughout the Eighteenth Dynasty, the pharaohs succeeding 'Ahmose also credited their victories to Amun, who, by the end of this dynasty, was a preeminent deity worshipped by all of Egypt. Amun received considerable support from the ruling clan, and Thebes, the site of Amun's religious complex, became the deity's cult center. The Tuthmossids of the Eighteenth Dynasty (1550–1307 B.C.E.) lavished care and wealth upon Thebes, which soon replaced Memphis as the capital.

Further reading: Desroches-Noblecourt, Christiane. *Ancient Egypt: The New Kingdom and the Amarna Period.* New York: New York Graphic Society, 1960; Spalinger, Anthony. *War in Ancient Egypt: The New Kingdom.* London: Wiley-Blackwell, 2005; Tyldesley, Joyce. *The Pharaohs.* London: Quercus, 2009.

'Ahmose, son of Ebana (fl. 16th century B.C.E.) *military and court official of the Eighteenth Dynasty*
'Ahmose, son of Ebana, served the dynastic founder, 'AHMOSE (NEBPEHTIRÉ) (r. 1550–1525 B.C.E.), and then AMENHOTEP I (r. 1525–1504 B.C.E.) and later rulers. A noble of Nekheb (modern ELKAB), he was involved in military campaigns of Egypt which he described on the walls of his tomb (as did 'AHMOSE-PEN NEKHEBET). Personalized and dramatic, these accounts provide a rare insight into the military procedures of the era and the religious and social processes.

He was in the campaign against A'ATA, in the Nubian area (modern Sudan), receiving slaves and lands as his share in the victory of the Egyptians under 'Ahmose. 'Ahmose, son of Ebana, was the grandfather of PAHERI.

'Ahmose II *See* AMASIS.

'Ahmose-ankh (fl. 16th century B.C.E.) *prince of the Eighteenth Dynasty*

The son of 'AHMOSE (NEBPEHTIRÉ) (r. 1550–1525 B.C.E.), this prince is an obscure figure but is reported in some lists to have been the original heir to the throne. When 'Ahmose-ankh died, 'AHMOSE-SIPAIR became the heir and possibly co-regent, also dying before 'Ahmose. AMENHOTEP I became the second king of the dynasty. It is possible that Queen 'AHMOSE, the consort of TUTHMOSIS I (1504–1492 B.C.E.), was a daughter of Prince 'Ahmose-ankh.

'Ahmose-Hetempet (fl. 16th century B.C.E.) *royal woman of the Seventeenth Dynasty*
'Ahmose-Hetempet was a daughter of Sekenenré TA'O II (ca. 1560 B.C.E.) and Queen AH'HOTEP (1). Her mummified remains were discovered in DEIR EL-BAHRI in 1881. 'Ahmose-Hetempet had dark hair and was discovered in a sycamore coffin. Her original tomb has not been located. No details about her personal life have been documented.

'Ahmose-Hettinehu (fl. 16th century B.C.E.) *royal woman of the Seventeenth Dynasty*
She was a daughter of Sekenenré TA'O II (ca. 1560 B.C.E.) and Queen 'AHMOSE-IN-HAPI. Her remains were found at DEIR EL-BAHRI, damaged and refurbished. 'Ahmose-Hettinehu's coffin was made of acacia and saved from her original vandalized tomb.

'Ahmose-In-Hapi (fl. 16th century B.C.E.) *royal woman of the Seventeenth Dynasty*
She was a secondary consort of Sekenenré TA'O II (ca. 1560 B.C.E.) and the mother of Princess 'AHMOSE-HETTINEHU. 'Ahmose-In-Hapi's remains, found at DEIR EL-BAHRI, are those of a strong woman, and her dark hair was in plaits. She was a daughter of Senakhtenré TA'O I.

'Ahmose-Merytamon (fl. 16th century B.C.E.) *royal woman of the Eighteenth Dynasty*
She was a lesser-ranked consort of AMENHOTEP I (1525–1504 B.C.E.) and the daughter of 'AHMOSE (NEBPEHTIRÉ) and the half sister of Amenhotep I. Little is known of her life, but her remains provide extensive evidence of arthritis and scoliosis, diseases prominent in her royal line. Her mummy was discovered in a cache of royal remains at DEIR EL-BAHRI, moved from her original tomb on the west bank of the Nile at Thebes. The mummy of an infant prince, AMUNEMHET (1), her nephew, was found beside her remains. 'Ahmose-Merytamon's body was badly damaged, and her arms were broken off her body.

'Ahmose-Nefertari (fl. 16th century B.C.E.) *royal woman of the Eighteenth Dynasty*
She was the daughter of Sekenenré TA'O II and Queen AH'HOTEP (1) and the wife of 'AHMOSE (NEBPEHTIRÉ) (r. 1550–1525 B.C.E.). 'Ahmose-Nefertari probably married her brother, KAMOSE, the last ruler of the Seventeenth

Dynasty, who died in 1550 B.C.E. while engaged in a war with the HYKSOS, or Asiatics, in the northeastern DELTA. When 'Ahmose came to the throne at a young age, she became his Great Wife, or ranking queen. She was 'Ahmose's sister.

'Ahmose-Nefertari played a unique role in founding the Eighteenth Dynasty and the New Kingdom historical period with her husband. She was visible to Egyptian society in all phases of rebuilding the nation after the expulsion of the Hyksos by 'Ahmose and his forces. Inscriptions in the SINAI Peninsula and on SAL ISLAND at the third cataract of the Nile, in modern Sudan, include her name and rank. The "BUILDING INSCRIPTION" erected in ABYDOS relates how 'Ahmose and 'Ahmose-Nefertari sat together to plan the great mortuary complexes for their mother, Ah'hotep (1), and their grandmother, Queen TETISHERI. Their recorded conversation is tenderly described, concerned with fulfilling obligations to these deceased women who had guided Egypt during the Hyksos crisis.

'Ahmose-Nefertari bore the heir, AMENHOTEP I; Prince 'AHMOSE-SIPAIR (one of the original heirs); Prince Ramose; Princess AH'HOTEP (2); and other daughters. She survived 'Ahmose and counseled Amenhotep I (r. 1525–1504 B.C.E.) during the early years of his reign, having the title "Female Chieftain of Upper and Lower Egypt." Many honors were bestowed upon 'Ahmose-Nefertari by the court because of her prior role as queen regent. When she died at the age of 70, she was given a portion of Amenhotep's mortuary temple on the western shore of the Nile at THEBES. Her mortuary cult—the daily offerings and ceremonies made at her tomb—remained popular for almost a century.

'Ahmose-Nefertari was the first Egyptian royal woman to be designated the "GOD'S WIFE OF AMUN." This title, associated with the deity AMUN, assumed powerful attributes in later eras, providing dynasties with unique political powers. Some lists indicate that she was alive when TUTHMOSIS I came to the throne as Amenhotep I's heir. At the death of Amenhotep I in 1504 B.C.E., he and 'Ahmose-Nefertari were deified as the patrons of Thebes. 'Ahmose-Nefertari also founded an order of upper-class women, called the "Divine Votaresses of Karnak." The unusual depictions of 'Ahmose-Nefertari in blue-black tones of deification reflect her status and cult, which remained popular for centuries. The mummified remains of 'Ahmose-Nefertari were discovered in DEIR EL-BAHRI in damaged condition. She was almost bald and had on a human-hair wig. Her front teeth were prominent, a physical trait inherited from her line, and her right hand had been removed.

See also DEIFICATION.

'Ahmose-Pen Nekhebet (fl. 16th century B.C.E.) *courtier and military officer of the Eighteenth Dynasty*

He served in the reign of 'AHMOSE (NEBPEHTIRÉ) (r. 1550–1525 B.C.E.), and, like 'AHMOSE, SON OF EBANA, another military chronicler of the era, 'Ahmose-Pen Nekhebet was a noble from Nekheb (modern ELKAB). The military campaigns that led to the expulsion of the HYKSOS, or Asiatics, from Egypt by 'Ahmose are clearly recorded in 'Ahmose-Pen Nekhebet's tomb. On the walls of the tomb in Elkab, he chronicles 'Ahmose's campaigns, including the battle with A'ATA and the Nubian forces south of Aswan in modern Sudan.

He lived to take part in at least one campaign conducted by AMENHOTEP I (r. 1525–1504 B.C.E.). 'Ahmose-Pen Nekhebet received many honors during his lifetime, and his tomb chronicles have served succeeding generations by providing a precise and clear firsthand account of his tumultuous era. Some records indicate that he lived until the reign of HATSHEPSUT (r. 1473–1458 B.C.E.)

'Ahmose-Sipair (fl. 16th century B.C.E.) *prince and possible coruler of the Eighteenth Dynasty*

He was the son of 'AHMOSE (NEBPEHTIRÉ) (r. 1550–1525 B.C.E.) and Queen 'AHMOSE-NEFERTARI, and possibly served as coruler with his father. His tomb, which was erected on the western shore of THEBES, displays insignias reserved for kings. 'Ahmose-Sipair died before he could inherit the throne, and AMENHOTEP I, his brother, became the second ruler of the New Kingdom Period. Another brother, Prince 'AHMOSE-ANKH, had been the original heir but had died young. The mummified remains of Prince 'Ahmose-Sipair were found in DEIR EL-BAHRI, tied to a stick and in a sycamore coffin, having been recovered from his vandalized tomb.

'Ahmose Sitayet (fl. 16th century B.C.E.) *vizier of the Eighteenth Dynasty*

'Ahmose Sitayet was appointed by 'AHMOSE (r. 1550–1525 B.C.E.) as the viceroy of Kush, or NUBIA, the territory south of ASWAN (in modern Sudan). He accompanied 'Ahmose in the military campaigns against A'ATA and the Nubian rebellion, and after the Egyptian victory he was appointed VIZIER, or governor, of the region, a post that carried the title "King's Son of Kush." In this capacity 'Ahmose Sitayet lived at Aswan on the ELEPHANTINE Island. There he administered the mines and quarries of the region and supervised the extensive trade campaigns conducted by the Egyptians from forts extending southward on the Nile, outposts dating to the Middle Kingdom era (2040–1640 B.C.E.). His son, Tjuroy, succeeded him in the post.

'Ahmose Tumerisy (fl. 16th century B.C.E.) *royal woman of the Eighteenth Dynasty*

She was the daughter of AMENHOTEP I (r. 1525–1504 B.C.E.) and Queen AH'HOTEP (2). During the reign of TUTHMOSIS I (1504–1492 B.C.E.), 'Ahmose Tumerisy lived in the royal residence of THEBES, serving perhaps as an "auntie" to the royal children or being married to an official. A favorite of the court, she was honored by the pharaoh and his family. 'Ahmose Tumerisy was buried in a platform at DEIR EL-BAHRI, on the Theban shore of the Nile, in the complex erected by MENTUHOTEP II (r. 2061–2010 B.C.E.). Some records indicate that she was originally buried in DRA-ABU' EL-NAGA.

Aion A deity of the Greco-Roman Period in Egypt from 332 B.C.E. to 395 C.E., he was believed to be a personification of Time. A solar deity, associated with SERAPIS and the Roman deity Mithras, the god was depicted in a relief found in OXYRRHYNCHUS (1) (modern el-Bahnasa). The panel shows a winged creature with the head of a lion, the torso of a human, and the legs of a goat. An aura or nimbus surrounds the god's head. He holds keys, a torch, and a bolt of lightning. His cult was popular only in local areas.

Aker An ancient deity of Egypt in the form of a lion, usually depicted in pairs, back to back, and called Akeru in the plural, Aker was originally an earth god but became involved in the cult of RÉ, which was solar in origin. He represented the eastern and western horizons of the Underworld, or TUAT, and faced both the sunrise and the sunset. The Akeru guarded the solar bark of Ré on his daily sojourns across the sky. A lion cult in Aker's honor was started at To Remu or LEONTOPOLIS (the modern Tel Migdam). Akeru were depicted in the tomb of Queen NEFERTARI, the Great Wife, or first consort, of RAMESSES II (r. 1290–1224 B.C.E.).

Akhenaten (Amenhotep IV; Neferkheperure' Wa'en're) (d. 1335 B.C.E.) *ninth ruler of the Eighteenth Dynasty, called the "heretic pharaoh"*
He reigned from 1353 B.C.E. until his death. Akhenaten has been called the first monotheist or the "heretic pharaoh" in some lists, because of his denial of the divine pantheons of Egypt. His throne name was Neferkheperuré (translated as "Ré's transformations are perfect"), to which he added Wa'en're (the unique one of Ré).

Akhenaten served as co-regent with his father, AMENHOTEP III (r. 1391–1353 B.C.E.), maintaining the usual cultic rituals until he married NEFERTITI, perhaps a cousin, and possibly a daughter of AYA (2) and Tiye, commoners. Alternatively, Nefertiti might have been a commoner granddaughter of YUYA and Tuya, the parents of Queen TIYE (1). The marriage was politically advantageous because Nefertiti's family came from AKHMIN, a stronghold of aristocratic power needed by the pharaohs.

In the second year of his reign, Akhenaten began his worship of the solar god ATEN, a deity that had been evident in the royal structures of TUTHMOSIS IV (r. 1401–1391 B.C.E.), his grandfather, and AMENHOTEP III. Aten was a SOLAR DISK that shone on the Nile River,

believed by some scholars to be a form of Re'-Harakhte. The young pharaoh renounced the name Amenhotep and called himself Akhenaten, the "Horizon of the Sun Disk" or "He Who is of the Service to Aten." Nefertiti became Nefer-Nefru-Aten, meaning "Beautiful is the Beauty of Aten."

In the fourth year of his reign, Akhenaten and Nefertiti visited a site on the Nile south of modern MALLAWI. There a new capital was constructed, called Akhetaten, "the Horizon of the Sun Disk." This site is now known as el-'AMARNA, in honor of a tribe of Bedouins who settled there in the 1700's C.E. Vast and marked by 14 perimeter stelae, the new capital was six miles long, centering on the royal residence and the temple of Aten. There were well-planned urban districts, pools, gardens, and a royal avenue that ran parallel to the Nile. An innovative brick bridge, designed to connect two separate buildings and containing an opening called the WINDOW OF APPEARANCE, where the ruler and his consort addressed guests and bestowed honors upon courtiers who had served with distinction, graced the royal avenue. The beautiful and unique "Amarna style" was used in decorating the capital, demonstrating a natural and free unison of the arts. Akhetaten was completed in the fifth or sixth year of Akhenaten's reign.

Religious services in the capital were reserved for Akhenaten alone, although he appointed a high priest in the later years. Few others had access to the sacred precincts; even Nefertiti was relegated to minor roles in the daily rituals. Many ceremonies were held in the open sunlight, a custom that brought about complaints from foreign dignitaries. These ambassadors and legates from other lands attended the ceremonies in honor of Aten and suffered heatstrokes as a result.

Outside of the capital, however, the old gods of Egypt held sway. Akhenaten closed down some temples, confiscating the vast plantations of the priests. He also viewed himself as the lone mediator with Aten, thus injuring the great bureaucratic machinery that maintained Egypt's vast government agencies. His destruction of temple plantations, sources of valuable food products, led Egypt toward economic ruin. Abuses by lesser officials and the weakening of established distribution processes started early in his reign.

In his eighth year, Akhenaten welcomed his mother, Queen Tiye, and his sister, BAKETAMUN, to the capital. They accepted a villa there and remained at Akhenaten's side. He was still militarily active at the time, not having established his reclusive ways or his abandonment of Egypt as a nation. During this period he conducted a campaign south of ASWAN (in modern Sudan) and sent troops to Egyptian vassal states in the Mediterranean region. Mercenary troops maintained garrisons in vassal cities. The collection of correspondence from this era is called the 'AMARNA LETTERS. They demonstrate his military activities.

His family life was deteriorating, however. A second wife, KIYA, possibly a MITANNI princess originally named TADUKHIPA, bore him two sons and a daughter but then fell out of favor. A daughter by Nefertiti, MEKET-ATEN, is reported to have died bearing Akhenaten's child, and by the 12th year of his reign, Nefertiti was no longer at his side. She was replaced by another one of her daughters, MERYT-AMUN (1). Nefertiti remained in the capital but resided in a separate villa, removed from religious and social affairs. Her demise is not documented. Some historical accounts state that she lived to counsel TUT'ANKHAMUN when he took the throne in 1333 B.C.E.

After Nefertiti's exit from the palace, Akhenaten became even more involved in the service of Aten. He spoke of the god as a celestial pharaoh, using the sun disks and its illuminating rays as symbols of creation. Akhenaten's hymn to Aten, discovered in the tomb of Aya in 'Amarna, provides the universal theme of worship that he tried to promote throughout the land. His agents, however, began a program of destruction that violated the other temples and shrines of Egypt, dismaying the common populace and making Aten unpopular.

SMENKHARÉ, a relative of Akhenaten, and the husband of Meryt-Amun, is believed by some scholars to have been Nefertiti in assumed guise, serving for a time as co-regent. He succeeded Akhenaten in 1335 B.C.E. but ruled only two years, dying at the age of 20. Akhenaten died in his 18th year of reign, 1335 B.C.E., and was buried in 'Amarna. His remains were moved by priests when Tut'ankhamun was entombed and placed somewhere in THEBES. His capital was abandoned, and later rulers, such as HOREMHAB (1319–1307 B.C.E.), removed stones called TALATATS for other projects. Some 12,000 blocks from Akhenaten's capital at 'Amarna have been gathered from a pylon built by Horemhab at KARNAK.

Akhenaten's portraits intrigue modern scholars, depicting a grotesque figure with a sagging torso and elongated features. Some of these images indicate a disease, such as Fröhlich's Syndrome. It is possible, however, that these statues were Osirian in style, portraying the god of death in the stages of decomposition, a popular artistic device in certain eras. The statues correlate to other innovations of the 'Amarna style of art, a wondrously free and gifted method of expressing Egyptian metaphysical ideals. Egyptian LITERATURE of this time demonstrates the same creativity and limitless exploration of ideas. During Akhenaten's reign the spoken language of Egypt was used in written texts, replacing the formal, classical language of former periods. 'Amarna is also famous for its potent beer, which has survived to this day. Using the recipe discovered in the ruins of the capital, breweries in Scotland and elsewhere are marketing that era's refreshment.

Akhenaten has been called the world's first monotheist, but he allowed other solar deities to be displayed in his capital at 'Amarna. He also declared himself a god, the son of Aten, and had a high priest dedicated to his cult, sharing his jubilee ceremonies with Aten. Akhenaten has been recorded as being a pacifist, oblivious to the needs of the empire. However, wall scenes at 'Amarna depict him and Nefertiti smiting Egypt's enemies, and he did maintain garrisons in his territories.

The fact that Egypt entered a period of turmoil during his reign can be attributed to his attempt at religious reformation, a concept quite beyond the comprehension of the average Egyptian at the time. His choice of lesser ranked individuals, newcomers to power in his court, led to a dismal inability to grasp foreign affairs in their full context and to maintain the vast bureaucratic machinery that guided Egypt over the centuries, leading to chaotic abuses and confusion. Akhenaten was a recluse in 'Amarna for too long a period and was unable to communicate his own religious vision to the Egyptian people as a whole.

Further reading: Montserrat, Dominic. *Akhenaten: History, Fantasy and Ancient Egypt*. New York: Routledge, 2000; Redford, Donald. *Akhenaten*. Princeton, N.J.: Princeton Univ. Press, 1987; Weigall, Arthur. *The Life and Times of Akhnaton*. New York: Cooper Square Press, 2000.

akhet The season of inundation in the ancient Egyptian calendar, the rising of Sirius, the dogstar, called SOPDU by the Egyptians and Sothis by the Greeks, signaled the beginning of the annual flooding of the Nile. When this sign appeared in the heavens the river was set to spread over the fields and orchards along the banks, revitalizing the land with silt and effluvium from Africa's core. *Akhet* was the first season of the year, starting as it did with the rising of the Nile, a factor that all Egyptians understood as basic to the nation's vitality. *Akhet* was one of the three major seasons of the Egyptian calendar year, with a duration of four 30-day months. *Akhet* was followed on the calendar by the seasons PROYET and SHOMU.

See also CALENDAR; SEASONS.

Akhetaten *See* 'AMARNA, EL-.

Akhethotep (fl. 24th century B.C.E.) *official of the Fifth Dynasty and the son of the vizier Ptah-hotep*
Akhethotep served NIUSERRÉ (r. 2416–2392 B.C.E.) as VIZIER, a position also held by his father before him. He also served as a judge and as an overseer of priests involved in the MORTUARY RITUALS conducted at the pyramids of deceased pharaohs. His grandson, PTAH-HOTEP (2), the great sage famous for his *Maxims*, was buried in an alcove of Akhethotep's tomb. Elaborate paintings testify to the wealth and prestige of this distinguished family. Akhethotep's tomb was discovered in SAQQARA, near modern Cairo.

Akhlane (Akhlamu) An ancient Semitic nomadic group in northern Syria, called "the enemies of the ASSYRIANS." In the reign of AKHENATEN (Amenhotep IV, r. 1353–1335 B.C.E.), the Akhlane appear in the Egyptian correspondence known today as the 'AMARNA LETTERS. They are described as a vigorous clan on the Euphrates River and in the area of the Persian Gulf. The Assyrians, who found them a formidable foe, called them the "Akhlamu-Aramaeans." The Akhlane disappeared soon after Akhenaten's reign, possibly absorbed into other cultures or renamed in later historical periods.

Akhmin (Khent Menu; Apu; Panopolis; Khemmis) A site almost 300 miles south of modern Cairo, called Khent Menu, or Apu by the Egyptians and Panopolis by the Greeks. Another name, Khemmis, was derived from the Greeks. Akhmin served as the capital of the ninth NOME and the cultic center for the worship of the god MIN (1). A temple discovered at Akhmin is being studied, as it is one of the finest ever erected on the Nile.

The goddess TAIT was also honored in the city. A necropolis dating to the Sixth Dynasty (2323–2150 B.C.E.) is on the site. Construction on this site in 1981 uncovered a statue base of immense proportions. The statue is a monument of RAMESSES II (r. 1290–1224 B.C.E.). A second statue, the largest depiction of a royal woman ever seen on the Nile, is of Ramesses II's daughter, Queen MERYAMUN. A temple dating to Egypt's Eighteenth Dynasty was also uncovered there. The dimensions of this capital, now buried under the city, indicate that this too was immense in size. Egypt's linen industry was fostered in Akhmin in late eras. The Greek scholar Strabo visited Akhmin in the Ptolemaic Period (304–30 B.C.E.).

Akhtoy *See* KHETY.

Akkadians The dynasty founded by Sargon in northern Mesopotamia ca. 2371 B.C.E. also used to designate groups in the area who shared the Semitic languages, the Akkadians adopted the Sumerian cuneiform writing system and were represented culturally in Assyria and Babylon. The Akkadian language became the lingua franca of Egypt's vast empire in the New Kingdom Period (1550–1070 B.C.E.). The 'AMARNA LETTERS were written in Babylonian, a late form of the Akkadian language.

Alara (fl. ca. 780 B.C.E.) *powerful ruler of Napata, in Nubia*
The kingdom of NAPATA, located in NUBIA, modern Sudan, maintained Egyptian traditions in religious, social, and governmental affairs. Alara was the brother of KASHTA, who founded the Twenty-fifth Dynasty of Egypt, ruling from 770 to 750 B.C.E. Kashta and his successor, PIANKHI (1), ruled only a part of Egypt in their lifetimes. The Napatans would later claim all of Egypt when SHABAKA marched northward in 712 B.C.E.

and conquered the entire Nile Valley. Alara's daughter, TABIRY, the mother of Shabaka, married Piankhi. Alara's wife was a noblewoman named Kassaga.

Alexander II *See* PTOLEMY XI.

Alexander III the Great (d. 323 B.C.E.) *conqueror of Egypt in 332 B.C.E. and the ruler of the known world in his era*
One of the greatest conquerors in world history, Alexander ended Persian rule on the Nile and founded the legendary city of ALEXANDRIA.

BIOGRAPHY

He was the third king in Macedonia named Alexander and was the son of Philip of Macedonia and Queen OLYMPIAS of Epirus. Born in Philip's capital, Pellas, in 356 B.C.E., Alexander was tutored for three years, from the ages of 13 to 16, by Aristotle, who was at Alexander's side when the young prince assumed the Macedonian throne in 336 B.C.E. Alexander had also been trained in military arts, in keeping with Macedonian tradition

Two years after his coronation, Alexander started a campaign against the Persian Empire, and in November 333 B.C.E. the Macedonian king and his superbly trained army defeated the Persians under King DARIUS III CODOMAN at GRANICUS and ISSUS. The Persians held a superior tactical position, but Macedonian resolve and Alexander's military acumen ensured the victory for the Greeks. Darius III tried to make peace, but Alexander refused and went with his forces to Phoenicia, where he conquered the city of Tyre in 332 B.C.E. His capture of this key site ended Persia's power on the Mediterranean coast. Alexander then conquered Palestine and entered the Nile Valley in the fall of 332 B.C.E. The Persian satrap on the Nile resisted for a time but then surrendered Egypt to the young conqueror.

The Egyptians were thus free of the Persians, but now the Greeks laid claim to the nation. Egyptian officials wanted to welcome Alexander, the most talked-about conqueror in the world, but the Egyptian people and the priests of the cultic temples had reservations. Aware of the fact that the Egyptians saw him as yet another foreign tyrant, Alexander courted them by using their own religious mechanisms. He went to the famed SIWA Oasis in the LIBYAN DESERT, where he visited the ORACLE of AMUN. This was a shrine dedicated to the god Amun, who Egyptians believed spoke to worshippers and gave responses to questions about religious and state affairs. Alexander was reportedly declared at Siwa Oasis to be the true ruler of Egypt, and word of Amun's recognition spread quickly throughout the land.

Believed by many to be divine or semidivine, and having already been declared the true ruler by Amun, the Egyptian people largely began to welcome his arrival. Alexander cemented this acclamation by going to MEMPHIS, the ancient capital, to be crowned in the traditional manner, including receiving the seal of approval of the SOULS OF PE and the SOULS OF NEKHEN. These were Predynastic Period figures, remembered and honored in every historical period on the Nile. Throughout Egypt, rumors spread that Alexander was the son of NECTANEBO II, the ruler of Egypt from 360 to 343 B.C.E. Queen Olympias was depicted as having had an affair with Nectanebo II, with Alexander resulting from their love. Alexander's Egyptian throne name was Meryamun-Setepenre, translated as "Beloved of Amun, Chosen by Ré."

Alexander also founded a new capital for the Land of the Two Kingdoms at the site of a small village called Rakhotis, on the shore of the Mediterranean Sea. This city, ALEXANDRIA, would become one of the major cultural centers of the world during the Ptolemaic and Roman periods. Alexandria was located in the western Nile Delta and was provided with an offshore causeway that connected to a small island, which provided safe harbor for trading ships.

In the spring of 331 B.C.E., Alexander marched out of Egypt, leaving two Greek governors in command, Ptolemy and Cleomenes. CLEOMENES OF NAUKRATIS, a Greek resident of Egypt, soon took charge of affairs, completing the construction of Alexandria. Ptolemy, the son of Lagus, bided his time but had his own ambitions for Egypt and became Ptolemy I SOTER. As they consolidated Macedonian control over Egypt, Alexander met Darius III at GAUGAMELA and defeated him once again. Darius fled but was assassinated by a former ally.

Alexander conquered the great Persian cities of Babylon, Ecbatana, Persepolis, and Susa, and then marched on Medea. He took the title of Basileus, "the Great King," and entered India in 326 B.C.E. His advance was effectively blocked at the battle of Hydaspes by the Indians under King Porus. His troops were demoralized and exhausted, and they were open in their criticism of his leadership and excessive ambition. Alexander returned to Babylon, where he died on June 10, 323 B.C.E. Many studies have been made about his demise, as symptoms noted at the time provided suspicions about the actual nature of his last illness. Charges of political assassination have been raised, but the most recent study of his death provides a different perspective.

Alexander had lost a close companion, Hephaestion, and was depressed about the death. Physicians in that era normally treated depression with a medicine made partly from hemlock, which is a dangerous poison. The idea that one of his close friends or advisors would have killed him is dismissed by historians who know the customs and traditions of the time. The fact that hemlock was used as an antidepressant makes it far more likely that his physician, hoping to restore him to mental stability, did not grasp the lethal qualities of the drug. Alexander was also spending his nights and days in bouts of drinking, a factor that would lessen his ability to take the hemlock without doing damage to himself.

The sudden and unexpected death of the young conqueror started a titanic struggle for control of his vast empire. In a bold stroke, Ptolemy I, who had claimed Egypt for himself, picked a cohort of veterans and rode hard to the north to intercept the massive funeral procession of Alexander's remains. Alexander had been embalmed in honey and placed in a large mausoleum on wheels so that his body could be seen and publicly venerated by the people of his conquered domain as he progressed toward the royal burial ground in Macedonia. Ptolemy I and his men captured the body and set off for Egypt. The dead king was buried at first in Memphis, but Ptolemy II transferred the remains to Alexandria. The initial sarcophagus was made of gold and was placed inside a larger gold outer sarcophagus. Both sarcophagi were reportedly removed by order of Ptolemy IX in the early first century B.C.E., and the body was placed in a glass or crystal coffin. The sarcophagi were then supposedly sold by the king. Various personages visited the tomb over the centuries, including Julius Caesar and Emperor Augustus. The body was later removed from public display and has never been found.

HISTORICAL IMPACT

Alexander the Great was one of the most significant figures in the history of the ancient world. At the head of the armies of Macedonia and an alliance of Greek states, he completed the work of his father, Philip, in waging a final, devastating war upon the Persian Empire. Alexander's conquests literally changed the course of ancient history. By toppling the Persian Empire he placed many different people around the Mediterranean and in southern Asia under the direct influence of Greek culture and institutions. Alexander thus paved the way for the triumph of Hellenism in the centuries after his death. In his own marriage to Roxane (d. 313 B.C.E.), a princess of Bactria (which was then part of the Persian Empire), and the encouragement he gave his own generals and soldiers to wed Persians, Alexander sought harmony between the cultures.

The sudden death of Alexander left the colossal empire without an heir, except for Alexander's intellectually challenged brother and a son born posthumously to Roxane. The claims of the infant were thrust aside by Alexander's generals and satraps. After 40 years of open warfare, the generals founded four dynasties that carved up Alexander's empire. One of these empires included in its territory Egypt and parts of the Middle East and was under the rule of General Ptolemy, who started the Ptolemaic Dynasty, which lasted until 30 B.C.E. The empires fought with each other for the next several centuries, but no one dynasty ever reestablished a global empire from the ashes of Alexander's realm.

Nevertheless, the dynasties were crucial in deepening the roots of Hellenic culture that Alexander first planted. They did so by making Greek institutions a permanent feature of life for their subjects by building major Hellenic cities and promoting extensive trade systems that united the Near East and Mediterranean into a wide Hellenic cultural entity. The Greek metropolises boasted temples, theatres, and schools, and all socially prominent or ambitious people cultivated a Greek spirit, spoke Greek (the common Greek tongue called koine became the lingua franca, or common language, of the ancient world), sent their children to Greek schools, and exported these ideals to other cities. The preeminent city for this process was Alexandria in Egypt. Under the Ptolemies, the city became the center of commerce and culture for the Hellenistic world and was renowned for its harbor, the tomb of Alexander, the great LIGHT-HOUSE OF ALEXANDRIA (one of the Seven Wonders of the Ancient World), and the famed Library of Alexandria, which was a repository for virtually all of the knowledge of the known world with some half a million volumes.

Further reading: Fox, Robin Lane. *Alexander the Great.* New York: Penguin, 1994; Gergel, Tania. *Alexander the Great: The Brief Life and Towering Exploits of History's Greatest Conqueror as Told by His Original Biographers.* New York: Penguin, 2004; Green, Peter. *Alexander of Macedon 356–323 B.C.: A Historical Biography.* Berkeley: University of California Press, 1992; Wood, Michael. *In the Footsteps of Alexander the Great: A Journey from Greece to Asia.* Berkeley: University of California Press, 1997.

Alexander III the Great enters Egypt (332 B.C.E.) In the fall of 332 B.C.E., the king of Macedonia, ALEX-ANDER III THE GREAT (r. 336–332 B.C.E.), entered the Nile Valley with his victorious army, having recently triumphed over the Persian army in Asia Minor. At this time Egypt was under the control of the second Persian occupation, listed historically as the Thirty-first Dynasty (343–332 B.C.E.).

CONTEXT

Although they were under Persian rule, the Second Persian Period was not particularly difficult for the Egyptian people, as the Persians were absentee rulers who were never at home on the Nile and were seemingly too engaged with problems in their homeland to visit distant provinces. Instead, satraps, governors appointed by the Persians, ruled Egypt, and attempted to do so without involving themselves in the day-to-day affairs of the Egyptians. However, when Persia first conquered Egypt in 525 B.C.E., the Persian king Cambyses (r. 525–522 B.C.E.) did visit the Nile Valley, and records of his stay in Egypt contain the Egyptian judgment that he was a "criminal lunatic." This judgment was possibly due to the fact that Cambyses had the mummified remains

of the pharaoh AMASIS (r. 570–526 B.C.E.) taken from his tomb and desecrated and burned. Cambyses also stabbed a sacred Apis bull in a rage and whipped the priests of the APIS CULT. Thus the Egyptians were not sorry to see Cambyses return to Persia to put down a rebellion by the Medes. (Cambyses would die during this campaign, either by murder or suicide.)

By 398 B.C.E., the Persians had been expelled from Egypt completely, not to return again until 343 B.C.E. This next occupation was not a peaceful one, as the Egyptians had by now grown tired of Persian rule, no matter how unobtrusive it was.

EVENT

Emperor DARIUS III CODOMAN was the last Persian who would claim Egypt. He was attacked several times by Alexander III the Great, and his forces suffered a series of setbacks, including at the battles of Granicus and Issus. The Persians, even the famed Immortals, an elite unit, fought each war with the military logistics of previous campaigns. Facing the army of Alexander, however, they were up against new techniques, new military maneuvers, and a flexibility in the field that brought about Persian defeat. Darius III Codoman had fled from the scene of the battle of Issus, and the Macedonian triumph opened the way for further campaigns in Palestine. In 332 B.C.E., Alexander waged a bitter siege of the major city of Tyre on the Mediterranean coast of Phoenicia (modern Lebanon); at its end, he slaughtered the surviving men of the city and sold the women and children into slavery. The rest of Palestine, including Jerusalem, surrendered. After capturing the Persian fortress at Gaza, Alexander traveled to Egypt to claim the land.

There were Persian military units still in Egypt at the time, but the Persian satrap Mazeus, who was in full control of the land and troops, feared his troops would suffer huge losses and sent messengers to every Persian encampment and garrison, demanding that they surrender peacefully to the Macedonians. Mazeus then formally surrendered Egypt to Alexander. Alexander rode across the desert to the Siwa Oasis, located 524 miles northwest of modern Cairo, where the Oracle of Amun received him in the main temple. Alexander was proclaimed a true son of the god Amun and a true pharaoh.

After being crowned in the traditional ceremonies at Memphis, the original capital of ancient Egypt, Alexander set about establishing a new capital, Alexandria. For his capital, Alexander chose the site of Rhakotis in the western Delta of the Nile. Rhakotis was an ancient town, dating to the New Kingdom (1550–1070 B.C.E.), and was located on the westernmost Nile tributary, a location Alexander thought was an ideal crossroad between Egypt and Greece. Two limestone ridges run parallel to the coast of Alexandria, the outer one breaking the waves and the inner ridge protecting the city against shifting alluvium. Alexander ordered a causeway, called the Heptastadion, "seven stades long," to link the two ridges. Two ancient harbors were on either side: the Eunostos, or "Harbor of Safe Return," on the west, and the Great Harbor on the east. A third harbor, on Lake Mareotis, linked the city to the Nile. The city, planned by Dinocrates, a Greek city planner from Rhodes, and constructed under Alexander's viceroy, Cleomenes of Naukratis, was ideally situated for trade and commerce. Alexander's plans included royal residences, marketplaces, temples, streets, and courts. Alexandria expanded rapidly and soon became the main commercial hub of the entire eastern Mediterranean.

Alexander did not remain in Egypt, however, and continued invading various lands, including India, where the people repulsed his attempts and gave him a serious wound in a battle. Alexander's companions convinced the young conqueror to return to Babylon, where he died, on June 10, 323 B.C.E., just before his 33rd birthday. Alexander never saw the city that was being constructed in his name.

IMPACT

Alexander transformed Egypt when he added it to his empire, which then stretched approximately 2 million square miles. His city of Alexandria would become the marvel of the world, and the Egyptian economy would soar as new trade markets opened and relations with other parts of the empire improved. Alexander's entrance into the Nile Valley would thus have lasting consequences for the Egyptian people.

Although there were already some Greek influences in Egypt at the time of Alexander due to the Greek trading merchant community based in Naukratis in the Delta, Alexander spread Greek culture throughout Egyptian society. He replaced Egypt's finance, tax, and bureaucratic systems with ones based on Greek models. For instance, the city of Alexandria itself, which was based on a Greek model, was intended to serve as a crowning achievement of architecture, demonstrating the skills of the finest Greek architects.

After it was built, Alexandria evolved into an important economic hub in the region, as it started taking over the trade previously conducted in the city of Tyre. With the construction of the Library of Alexandria, which would eventually house some 700,000 papyri, Alexandria also became the center of learning for the known world of that historical period. Alexandria was a major Mediterranean port both in ancient times and still today. Under the wealthy Ptolemy dynasty that followed Alexander, the city soon surpassed Athens as the cultural center of the Greek world.

Further reading: Fox, Robin Lane. *Alexander the Great.* New York: Penguin, 1994; Gergel, Tania. *Alexander the Great: The Brief Life and Towering Exploits of History's Greatest Conqueror as Told by His Original Biographers.*
New York: Penguin, 2004; Green, Peter. *Alexander of Macedon 356–323 B.C.: A Historical Biography.* Berkeley: University of California Press, 1992; Wood, Michael. *In the Footsteps of Alexander the Great: A Journey from Greece to Asia.* Berkeley: University of California Press, 1997.

Alexander IV (Ha'a-ibre Setep-en-Amun) (d. 304 B.C.E.) *ruler of Egypt and son of Alexander III the Great*
He was the son of ALEXANDER III THE GREAT and Roxanne and ruled Egypt from 316 B.C.E. until his death. Alexander IV took the throne name Ha'a-ibre Setep-en-Amun, translated as "Ré's Heart Rejoices, Chosen of Amun." Alexander IV was born after the death of his father in 323 B.C.E. His uncle PHILIP III ARRHIDAEUS, reportedly a somewhat challenged half brother of Alexander the Great, ruled from 323 to 316 B.C.E., when he was murdered.

PTOLEMY I served as satrap or governor of Egypt for both Philip and Alexander. Roxanne, as queen, probably held the post of regent for her son. In 304 B.C.E., Cassander, the Macedonian "General of Europe," murdered Alexander and Roxanne. Queen OLYMPIAS, the mother of Alexander the Great, fell to the henchmen of Cassander at the same time. The royal house of Macedonia had been destroyed.

Alexander Aetolus (fl. third century B.C.E.) *Greek poet of Alexandria*
PTOLEMY II PHILADELPHUS (r. 285–246 B.C.E.) appointed Alexander Aetolus as an official of the great LIBRARY OF ALEXANDRIA. The library was an institution known for its vast archives that included centuries of world history and the cultural achievement of many peoples. His task was to list and catalog the tragic dramas housed in the library. Alexander Aetolus's writings are lost, although the title of one of his plays, *Astragalistae,* or "The Dice Throwers," has survived. Alexander's shorter poetic works are known in modern times only by fragments that have survived over the centuries.

Alexander Balas (Ephiphanes) (fl. second century B.C.E.) *king of Syria and Pergamum, modern Turkey*
He asked PTOLEMY VI PHILOMETOR (r. 180–164/163–145 B.C.E.) to aid him in ruling the remains of the crumbled Macedonian Empire. Alexander Balas slew Demetrius I Soter, the heir of the Syrian Seleucid Dynasty. When DEMETRIUS II NICATOR, the son of Demetrius I, met Alexander Balas in battle, he avenged his father's death. Alexander Balas had maintained Egyptian support and the approval of the Senate of Rome until the fateful battle that ended his life.

Alexander Helios (fl. first century B.C.E.) *son of Cleopatra VII (51–30 B.C.E.) and Marc Antony*
He was born in 40 B.C.E., the twin of CLEOPATRA SELENE. Alexander Helios was designated the ruler of "Farther Asia," an area that included Armenia, Medea, and the

unconquered realms of the Parthians. He vanishes from the scene after the battle of ACTIUM and the suicides of CLEOPATRA VII and Marc ANTONY.

Alexandria The capital of Egypt in the Ptolemaic Period, Alexandria was founded in 331 B.C.E. by ALEXANDER III THE GREAT. Today, Alexandria is the second-largest city in Egypt, occupying some 20 miles along the Mediterranean coast, with a population of more than 4 million.

HISTORY

The arrival of Alexander the Great in Egypt put an end to the Persian occupation and revitalized many areas of life in the NILE Valley. Alexander did not remain on the Nile for long, but he did establish a new capital in the Delta, the city of Alexandria. Greek historian Arrian (first century C.E.) recorded that Alexander personally laid out the site, including marketplaces, temples, palaces and administration offices. He even designated the deities that were to be honored in the city and set the foundations for the city's defensive structures.

The conqueror chose the site of Rhakotis in the western Delta of the Nile as the site for his new capital. Rhakotis was an ancient town, dating to the New Kingdom (1550–1070 B.C.E.), and was located on the westernmost Nile tributary. Two limestone ridges run parallel to the coast of Alexandria, the outer one breaking the waves and the inner ridge protecting the city against shifting alluvium. Alexander ordered a causeway, called the Heptastadion, "seven stades long," to link the ridges. Two ancient harbors were on either side: the Eunostos, or "Harbor of Safe Return," on the west, and the Great Harbor on the east. A third harbor, on Lake MAREOTIS, linked the city to the Nile.

Two suburban areas, Neopolis and the island of PHAROS, were included in Alexander's original plans. He did not remain in Egypt, however, and never saw the city being constructed in his name. Alexander's viceroy, CLEOMENES OF NAUKRATIS, was thus the actual creator of Egypt's new capital, which was ideally situated for trade and commerce, and expanded rapidly. Dinocrates, the Greek city planner from Rhodes, supervised the actual construction. Cleomenes had served Alexander as finance minister and was the assistant satrap of the city. However, he was later found to be corrupt and was executed by PTOLEMY I SOTER (r. 304–284 B.C.E.), after the Ptolemaic Dynasty (304–30 B.C.E.) was founded.

Ptolemy I took Egypt as his own domain after the death of Alexander the Great in 323 B.C.E. When news came of the conqueror's passing, Ptolemy I set out with an army from Egypt to interrupt the journey of Alexander's remains. Alexander's corpse was in an immense sarcophagus, drawn by oxen, and was being taken to Macedonia through various conquered regions. Ptolemy I stole the sarcophagus and took it to Alexandria, stating that the young conqueror had requested to be buried on the Nile. Ptolemy claimed Egypt as his domain at

Sphinxes and other monuments displayed in Old Alexandria *(Hulton Archive)*

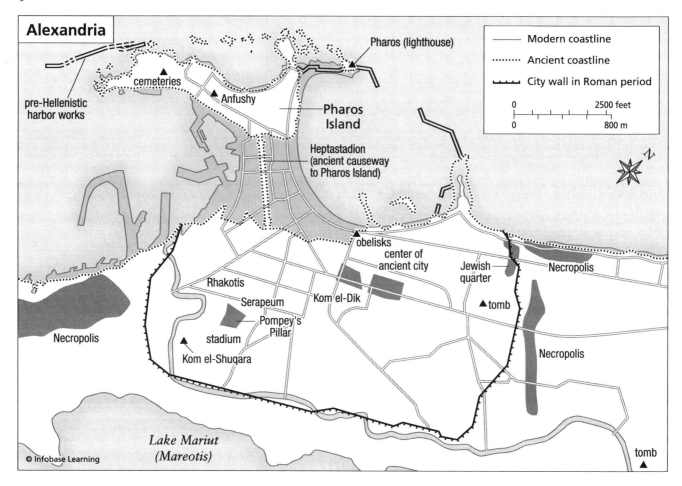

the same time. The remains of Alexander the Great were reportedly placed in the Soma, a mausoleum, of the city after being restored to the capital by Ptolemy I later that year. Ptolemaic mausoleums, including the tombs of the Roman general Marc ANTONY (83–30 B.C.E.) and the last Ptolemic queen, CLEOPATRA VII (r. 51–30 B.C.E.), have disappeared over the centuries, along with Alexander's body.

Ptolemy I was energetic and quick in building his realm. He erected palaces, temples, a museum, a library, and houses of study, inviting scholars from other lands to take up residence in his capital. He also invented a new deity, Serapis, while promoting the cult of Osiris, in hopes of uniting with the Egyptian people. Although the Ptolemaic rulers and their families constructed temples throughout the valley, they never left the capital personally.

The center of Alexandria included markets, residences, sunken courts, and even catacombs. The SERA-PEUM (2), the sacred burial site and shrine of the sacred APIS bulls, was built on the hill of Rhakotis in the city's oldest section. Royal residences, municipal buildings, and government seats were also built. Two structures brought special acclaim to the new capital: the LIBRARY OF ALEXANDRIA and the LIGHTHOUSE OF ALEXANDRIA,

both erected on the island of Pharos. The Lighthouse of Alexandria would become one of the Seven Wonders of the Ancient World. Started by Ptolemy I Soter, it was completed by PTOLEMY II PHILADELPHUS (r. 285–246 B.C.E.). Standing some 400 feet, with a light that could be seen 23 miles out to sea, the lighthouse was constructed in three tiers and was topped by a gold statue. The lighthouse survived until 1477, although at that time it was already in a ruined state.

The Library of Alexandria, another project of Ptolemy I, was served by some of the greatest philosophers and scholars of that historical period. The agents of the Ptolemies were relentless in finding papyri, books, and manuscripts. It has been reported that within 200 years, the Library of Alexandria owned 500,000 to 700,000 separate papyri. The Library of Alexandria had zoological gardens and scientific facilities as well for the study of anatomy, biology, and astronomy. City officials confiscated any books or papyri that new arrivals and visitors had in their possession. Copies were made of these works and such copies were returned to the original owners. (The library kept the originals.)

The city prospered over the centuries, despite the violence, degradation, and weaknesses of the various Ptolemaic rulers, who became more and more dependent upon Rome in times of crisis. When Cleopatra VII and Marc Antony faced the Romans at ACTIUM and were defeated, Octavian, the future Emperor AUGUSTUS, occupied Egypt. Arrius Diudymus, a companion of Octavian, became the savior of Alexandria, as he stopped the Roman troops from destroying the city.

Since 1994, archaeologists have been rediscovering the sections of Alexandria that were submerged in an earthquake that struck the region centuries ago. Divers are recovering monuments and architectural structures, such as obelisks and columns. The city of Alexandria was a true Hellenic site, as the Ptolemaic rulers preserved their Greek and Macedonian traditions and laws. The Egyptians were allowed to carry on their vast traditional court system, while the Greeks were judged by their own standards. Alexandria remained the capital of Egypt after the death of Cleopatra VII, but the nation was reduced to the status of a Roman province.

POPULATION

From the start of the city in the fourth century B.C.E., Alexandria attracted a large population that included Egyptians, Greeks, Jews, Nubians, and people from all over the Mediterranean. Thousands of new residents flocked to Alexandria, and grants of property, called *cleruchies,* were given to foreign mercenaries who resided in the city and made themselves available for military service. Greek elite moved from NAUKRATIS (el-Nibeira), the original Hellenic outpost, and special laws and regulations were passed to protect their unique status.

Alexandria became a key trading center, which spurred the continued growth of its population, and by the first century B.C.E. there were more than 180,000 inhabitants. This number continued to increase during the Roman period in the city until it reached more than 300,000 by the late second century C.E. This made Alexandria the second-largest city in the Roman Empire, and it stood as the artistic and economic rival to Rome itself. Entire fleets of traders and merchants sailed to its ports, just as massive caravans entered the gates to do business. Many of these merchants and travelers stayed.

The diversity of the city was a testament to its place as one of the economic metropolises of the ancient Mediterranean. Alexandria's population was multiethnic, even as it then possessed the largest Jewish population in the world from the time of the Diaspora. The Jews in the city lived in their own quarter, a development permitted by the early Ptolemies in order to allow them to be separate from the pagans elsewhere in Alexandria; there they had their own local administration under an ethnarch.

ECONOMY

Much as the population of Alexandria was both diverse and grew rapidly in size, so too did the economy of the city emerge as one of the greatest in the ancient world. Its wealth was the result of its favorable location on the coast of Egypt, its natural port, and the rich natural resources of grain, minerals, and vegetables that were found along the Nile. The city was built literally at the crossroads of the ancient trade routes, including sea-lanes and caravan lines.

The economy was built around several major pillars. The first was trade. As the produce and grain of Egypt was brought to Alexandria for export, vast merchant fleets carried it off to all of the corners of the Mediterranean to feed other cities. One of the primary reasons for the importance of Alexandria in the Roman world was the steady flow of grain from Egypt to Rome. Rome depended on grain from Egypt, and the Senate and the Roman emperors greeted any disruption of that flow with great alarm. Enormous warehouses and granaries were built near the ports to hold the produce and grain for distribution.

SIGNIFICANCE

Built under the influence of the campaigns and vision of Alexander the Great, Alexandria became the foremost expression of Hellenism in the time before the final ascendancy of Rome. For centuries, it was the largest city in the Mediterranean and the most prosperous trading center in the world. Its schools, markets, and library lured people from across the ancient world, and it enticed traders of wares and services to come and make a fortune on its streets.

The city was also a model for Alexander's vision of a grand and unified Hellenic civilization. While Alexander's empire fell apart almost immediately after his death, the city of Alexandria came the closest to bringing to life what he had hoped would be created in the aftermath of his conquests. The Ptolemies profited from this prosperity, and their administration was unobtrusive so as not to interrupt their source of economic power. The city survived the fall of the Ptolemies and remained one of the most important cities in the entire Roman Empire. Its importance continued as an economic center and then from the fourth century C.E. as a major place of learning for Christian theology.

Further reading: Empereur, Jean-Yves. *Alexandria Rediscovered.* Trans. Margaret Moehler. New York: George Braziller, 1998; Fraser, P. M. *Ptolemaic Alexandria: Text, Notes, Indexes.* London: Clarendon Press, 1985; La Riche, William. *Alexandria: The Sunken City.* London: Weidenfeld & Nicolson, 1996; Vrettos, Theodore. *Alexandria: City of the Western Mind.* New York: Free Press, 2001.

Alexandria, battle of The military campaigns between Julius CAESAR and the forces supporting PTOLEMY XIII (r. 51–47 B.C.E.) in Egypt's capital. Caesar was under siege in Alexandria from August 48 B.C.E. to February 47 B.C.E. after placing CLEOPATRA VII on the throne and exiling Ptolemy to the desert. The Romans defended the royal residence at ALEXANDRIA from land forces and an Egyptian naval force. Setting fire to these ships, Caesar inadvertently engulfed the LIBRARY OF ALEXANDRIA in flames as well. Caesar also took Pharos Island, the site of the LIGHTHOUSE of Alexandria, one of the Seven Wonders of the World.

By January 47 B.C.E., Caesar was thoroughly surrounded by Egyptians, but Mithridates of Pergamum arrived with 20,000 men. Caesar had sent for him at the start of the campaign. When the new allies entered the conflict, Caesar went out to confront Ptolemy XIII in the desert region. The BATTLE OF THE NILE ensued, with Caesar victorious.

altar   Called a *khat* by Egyptians, this was a table of offerings in temples and tomb chapels, in use from the earliest eras on the Nile. An altar fashioned out of travertine alabaster was included in the sun temple of NIUSERRÉ (r. 2416–2392 B.C.E.) at ABU GHUROB. TUTHMOSIS III (r. 1479–1425 B.C.E.) presented the great religious complex of KARNAK at THEBES with a pink granite altar. The New Kingdom (1550–1070 B.C.E.) altars had evolved into vast stone tables with ramps and steps that added to their dominance. The limestone altar of the god Ré-Horakhte at DEIR EL-BAHRI, on the western shore of Thebes, had ten steps leading to its dais. The ATEN altars at 'AMARNA were designed with ramps and courtyards. In the Late Period (712–332 B.C.E.), altars with horned designs were used, made of stone or brick blocks with raised corners.

See also TEMPLES.

Amada   A site in NUBIA, modern Sudan, Amada was where a temple dedicated to the gods AMUN and Ré Horakhte was started by TUTHMOSIS IV (r. 1401–1391 B.C.E.) and decorated by AMENHOTEP III (r. 1391–1353 B.C.E.). Tuthmosis IV extended the shrine during his reign. The shrine is noted for fine reliefs in color and for images of MESSUY, the viceroy of Kush, as Nubia was called. MERENPTAH's cartouches are also preserved there. Messuy's depiction at Amada led to his identification in some eras with Amunmesses, a usurper following Merenptah's reign (1224–1214 B.C.E.).

The great temple at Amada was erected by RAMESSES II (r. 1290–1224 B.C.E.) with pillared halls and Osiride statues of that pharaoh. Two stelae, one dedicated to Amun-Ré and the other announcing the arrival of a HITTITE princess as Ramesses II's bride, were found there. Elaborate paintings, vestibules, a sanctuary, and a chapel to the god THOTH complete the temple design. Two more stelae, honoring various officials of the eras, were also discovered on the site. The temple of Amada was moved when the ASWAN High Dam was constructed.

Amara   A fortified site near WADI HALFA on the Nile in NUBIA, modern Sudan, Amara was founded by SETI I (r. 1306–1290 B.C.E.). There are two settlements involved in Amara, on the eastern and western banks of the river. Amara West was a vast FORTRESS complex with enclosing walls and defenses. Amara East dates to the Meroitic Period (ca. 300 B.C.E.–350 A.D.). The remains of a Ramessid temple, probably erected by RAMESSES II (r. 1290–1224 B.C.E.), and a necropolis were discovered here.

'Amarna (el-'Amarna; Akhetaten Tell el-'Armana)   The Arabic name of the site that served as the capital, Akhetaten, "The Horizon of ATEN," it was built by AKHENATEN (Amenhotep IV of the Eighteenth Dynasty, r. 1353–1335 B.C.E.) as his capital and destroyed by HOREMHAB a few decades later. Erected on a level plain between the Nile and the eastern cliffs north of Assiut, 'Amarna was six miles long and marked by boundary stelae. The districts of the city were well planned and laid out with geometric precision and artistry. All of the regions of 'Amarna were designed to focus on the royal residence and on the temple of the god Aten.

Officials and courtiers lived in the principal districts, and the homes provided for them were large and lavish. Most contained gardens, pools, and summer villas, as well as reception areas. The temple and the palace were located on the royal avenue, which was designed to run parallel to the Nile. This thoroughfare was spanned by an immense brick bridge, which was not only a startling architectural innovation but achieved an artistic unity that became the hallmark of the god's abode. The bridge joined two separate wings of the royal residence and contained the famed WINDOW OF APPEARANCE, which was discovered in reliefs of the area. Akhenaten and NEFERTITI greeted the faithful of the city in the window and honored officials, military leaders, and artisans, forming an appealing portrait of regal splendor in this setting.

The palace did not serve as a royal residence but as a site for rituals and ceremonies. The royal family occupied limited space in separate apartments. The remaining parts of the structure were designed as altar sites, halls, stables, gardens, pools, throne rooms, and ceremonial chambers. The entire palace was decorated with painting in the 'Amarna style. Waterfowl and marsh scenes graced the walls, adding a natural pastoral quality to the residence. The main throne room for official ceremonies in honor of Aten was set between pillared chambers and halls, one with 30 rows of 17 pillars each. Adjacent to the palace was the temple of the god. This site had a rectangular wall that measured 2,600 by 900 feet. The temple was adapted, as many of the structures in 'Amarna were, to the Nile climate and designed for outdoor services. There were few roofs evident in the architectural planning of the complexes. The homes of the 'Amarna artisans were in the southeast section of the city, surrounded by another wall. Six blocks of such residences were laid out in this area, between five parallel streets.

Akhetaten, also called "the City of the SOLAR DISK," is supposedly named 'Amarna or Tell el-'Amarna today to commemorate a tribe of Bedouins that settled on the site approximately two centuries ago. A vast cliff cemetery was established nearby, linked to 'Amarna by the ROYAL WADI.

See also ART AND ARCHITECTURE; TALATAT.

'Amarna Letters A collection of correspondence spanning the reigns of AMENHOTEP III (r. 1391–1353 B.C.E.), AKHENATEN (r. 1353–1335 B.C.E.), and into the first year of TUT'ANKHAMUN's reign (r. 1333–1323 B.C.E.), these were discovered in the ruins of Akhenaten's capital of 'AMARNA in 1887, taken from a site called "the Place of the Letters of the Pharaohs." Some 382 cuneiform tablets constitute the body of the collection, written in the old Babylonian dialect of the AKKADIANS, the lingua franca of the territory at the time. This adopted language used altered Egyptian and Syrian terms as well. The letters contain diplomatic texts that reflect the changing trade and military exploits of the era. They are actually representations of correspondence between known kingdoms, providing insights into allegiances, protocol, pacts, vassal status, and the ever-changing realms of competing empires.

Amasis (Khnemibré) (d. 526 B.C.E.) *sixth ruler of the Twenty-sixth Dynasty*
Amasis usurped the throne of APRIES and ruled from 570 B.C.E. until his death. He was a general of Egypt's armies, having served PSAMMETICHUS II (r. 595–589 B.C.E.) as commander of an expedition to NUBIA, modern Sudan. He served Apries (r. 589–570 B.C.E.) in the same capacity until Egypt was drawn into a war between Libya's ruler, ADICRAN, and the Greek colony of CYRENE. Apries sent troops to aid Libya in freeing itself from the Greek colonists, but they were badly defeated by the superior Greek military. The Egyptian troops promptly mutinied, and Amasis was sent to their camp in the Delta to mediate a truce. He sided with the soldiers and was hailed as the new ruler of Egypt.

Apries, forced into exile, returned in 567 B.C.E. with Greek mercenaries who had little enthusiasm for the civil war that ensued. Apries met Amasis at MOMEMPHIS (probably a site near Terana on the Canopic branch of the Nile) in the Delta region and was quickly routed. He was then handed over to a mob and was slain but was buried with considerable pomp. A red granite STELA was erected on the site of the battle.

Amasis, secure on the throne, proved a capable ruler. Being a commoner by birth, he brought a unique perspective to the throne, one that earned him a reputation for amiability, demonstrating a good nature, unpretentious attitudes, and a rare understanding of life among the common castes on the Nile. He started his reign in SAIS in the eastern Delta by assigning

Apries's Greek troops to MEMPHIS, where they formed a bodyguard. Amasis earned the title of "Philhellene," or "He who loves the Greeks," because of his concern about Greek resistance to the growing Persian imperial domain. He limited the TRADE activities of the Greeks in Egypt to the city of NAUKRATIS, which provided them with a haven but protected Egyptian merchants from competition at the same time. He married LADICE, a Cyrenian woman, and so came to control parts of Cyprus, including the vast Cyprian fleet. A friend of Polycrates, the tyrant of Samos, Amasis donated funds, about 11,000 talents, for the restoration of the temple of Apollo at Delphi after its ruination in 548 B.C.E. When CROESUS of Lydia asked for aid in repelling the Persians, Amasis proved a generous ally.

Amasis's mother was TAKHEREDENESET, a commoner. He also married Queen NAKHSEBASTERU, who bore a son named 'Ahmose, and Queen KHEDEBNEITHERET, who was possibly the daughter of Apries. His daughter, Princess NITOCRIS (1), was officially "adopted" by ANKHESNE-FERIBRÉ, a sister of the slain Apries, as a GOD'S WIFE OF AMUN, or a Divine Adoratrice of Amun.

He built monuments at Sais, BUTO, Memphis, and ABYDOS, and a temple to the god Amun in the SIWA Oasis of the LIBYAN DESERT. Only a few statues of Amasis survive, as the Persian conqueror CAMBYSES (ruling Egypt from 525 to 522 B.C.E.) destroyed those he could find. Amasis was buried in Sais in a stone structure with double doors and pillars. SHABTIS, or tomb statues, were found on the site. His son PSAMMETICHUS III succeeded him in 526 B.C.E. but faced a Persian invasion a year later. CAMBYSES (r. 525–522 B.C.E.) had Amasis's body exhumed and ravaged, possibly because of Amasis's support for the Greeks.

Amaunet (Amunet) The divine consort of the god AMUN, worshipped in THEBES in the early Middle Kingdom (2020–1640 B.C.E.), her name meant "the hidden one." Amaunet was also included in the OGDOAD, the eight deities of HERMOPOLIS. Self-created, she was depicted as a woman wearing the crown of Lower Egypt. Amaunet was popular throughout Egyptian historical periods.

Am Duat (Am Tuat) A mortuary text depicted on the walls in the tomb of TUTHMOSIS III (r. 1479–1425 B.C.E.) in the VALLEY OF THE KINGS in THEBES, the Am Duat (Book of that which is in the underworld), shows the nightly journey of the god Ré, a prototype of the sojourn required of the deceased. The Am Duat is divided into 12 sections, representing fields or caverns, and traces the pathway into the earth that starts at the gateway of the western horizon. The text contains many adventures and torments but ends in spiritual redemption and the attainment of paradise.

See also BOOK OF THE DEAD; TOMB TEXTS.

Amemait A ferocious divine being associated with Egyptian MORTUARY RITUALS and traditions, the creature possessed the head of a CROCODILE, the foreparts of a large CAT, and the rear of a HIPPOPOTAMUS. Called "the Great of Death" or "the Devourer," Amemait was female. The illustrations of the beast in the BOOK OF THE DEAD depict Amemait waiting beside the scales in the JUDGMENT HALLS OF OSIRIS, where the god OSIRIS weighed the hearts of the deceased against the feather of the goddess MA'AT. The hearts of those who were evil in life were given to Amemait as food. The NEGATIVE CONFESSIONS, claims of not committing various crimes or sins, were designed to protect the deceased from Amemait, who was clearly a dispenser of justice, not of mindless terror. AMULETS and spells were also employed to keep this divine being from devouring the dead. The horror involved in Amemait's dining on the dead derived from the Egyptian's fear of going into "nothingness," or the endless void.

Amenemhab (fl. 15th century B.C.E.) *military general of the Eighteenth Dynasty*
Amenemhab served TUTHMOSIS III (r. 1479–1425 B.C.E.) and AMENHOTEP II (r. 1425–1401 B.C.E.) and had a long and distinguished military career. His wife served as a nurse for the royal family, and she probably introduced him to Tuthmosis III. His tomb on the western shore of the Nile at THEBES provides elaborate autobiographical inscriptions that contain detailed accounts of Tuthmosis III's vigorous campaigns. Amenemhab followed this warrior pharaoh across many lands as Egypt forged an empire. On one occasion, when Tuthmosis III recklessly started elephant hunting, Amenemhab cut off the trunk of a maddened bull elephant that charged the pharaoh. He received the third "Gold of Valor" award for this feat.

On another battlefield, Amenemhab saw the enemy release a young mare into the ranks of the oncoming Egyptian cavalry. Such a mare was designed to bring about a mating frenzy among the Egyptian stallions. Amenemhab slit open the belly of the mare, thus reducing the animal's allure. He dismembered it at the same time, using the stench of blood and gore to further enrage the Egyptian steeds in their charge. Ever at the side of Tuthmosis III, Amenemhab outlived that pharaoh and served his son and heir, Amenhotep II, a man who delighted in military life and in hand-to-hand combat in the field.

Amenemhet (1) (fl. 14th century B.C.E.) *prince of the Eighteenth Dynasty*
Amenemhet's mummy was found standing upright, propped against the wall of TUTHMOSIS IV's (1401–1391 B.C.E.) tomb. He was the son of Tuthmosis IV, but not an heir. Limestone CANOPIC JARS (containers for the vital organs) were found nearby, bearing his name. He obviously predeceased his father and was buried in a secondary chamber of Tuthmosis IV's tomb in the VALLEY OF THE KINGS on the western shore of the Nile at THEBES.

This tomb was robbed soon after the death of Tuthmosis IV and then restored in the reign of HOREMHAB (1319–1307 B.C.E.). Tuthmosis IV's body was removed by priests of a later era and placed in the tomb of AMENHOTEP II. The mummy of prince Amenemhet was probably recovered and prepared for a similar relocation but somehow overlooked in the process. Well preserved, Amenemhet stood stiffly against the wall through the centuries prior to his discovery.

Amenemhet (2) (fl. 20th century B.C.E.) *nobleman of Beni Hasan*
He served his nome, BENI HASAN, and the state in the reign of SENWOSRET I (1971–1926 B.C.E.). This noble typifies the NOMARCHS, or provincial aristocrats of Egypt, individuals who inherited titles of prince or count in each separate nome of the land. Part of Amenemhet's inherited province was called MENET-KHUFU, revered as the birthplace of KHUFU (Cheops) (r. 2551–2528 B.C.E.), the builder of the Great Pyramid at GIZA. Amenemhet was the son of KHNUMHOTEP (1), inheriting the Oryx nome, a region always known as demonstrating strong support for the ruling pharaohs of Egypt.

A military commander, probably leading army units from his own territory, Amenemhet served Senwosret I in Nubian campaigns, the region below ASWAN (now modern Sudan). He led expeditions for TRADE and handled operations in the royal quarries and mines. For his services he received golden collars (symbols of honor) and 3,000 head of cattle. Amenemhet served the throne of Egypt for more than a quarter of a century.

Amenemhet (3) (fl. 19th century B.C.E.) *official of the Twelfth Dynasty*
Amenemhet served AMENEMHET III (r. 1844–1797 B.C.E.) as superintendent of repairs conducted at WADI HAMMAMAT, an important TRADE route from KOPTOS to the Red Sea. Amenemhet led a large military force to Wadi Hammamat to escort workers assigned to quarry blocks of basaltic stone in the area. Numbering 2,000, Amenemhet's force not only quarried the stones but also refurbished the site and added new conveniences that promoted settlements.

Amenemhet (4) (fl. 15th century B.C.E.) *temple official of the Eighteenth Dynasty*
He served Queen-Pharaoh HATSHEPSUT (r. 1473–1458 B.C.E.). Amenemhet was also a priest of the temple of AMUN. Once believed to have been the brother of SENENMUT, a favorite of Hatshepsut, Amenemhet served as a supervisor of the bark of the deity Amun and a leader in the festivals on which Amun was paraded

through the streets or carried to the western shore of THEBES. He was buried in Thebes.

Amenemhet I (Sehetepibré) (d. 1962 B.C.E.) *founder of the Twelfth Dynasty*

He reigned from 1991 B.C.E. until his death. His name meant "AMUN is foremost," and he served as the VIZIER of Upper Egypt (the southern territories) in the reign of MENTUHOTEP IV (r. 1998–1991 B.C.E.), the last pharaoh of the Eleventh Dynasty, who died without an heir. Amenemhet I led an expedition for the pharaoh to the WADI HAMMAMAT, a dried river gully near KOPTOS, where the Nile swerves closest to the Red Sea. There he obtained the stone used for the sarcophagus of Mentuhotep IV.

Amenemhet I was a commoner, the son of one Senwosret and a woman named NEFRET, listed as prominent members of a family from ELEPHANTINE Island. Amenemhet I portrayed himself as the true unifier of Egypt after years of decline and partial separation. Various prophecies, including the famous one written by Nefer-rohu, were made public to guarantee authenticity for the new pharaoh's claims. The prophecy of Nefer-rohu, also called Neferti, describes Amenemhet I as the son of "a woman of NUBIA" (or of the Elephantine area in modern Aswan).

Having had years of experience as a vizier, Amenemhet knew how to force the Egyptians to accept his rule. He commanded a fleet of ships and sailed throughout the land to demand obeisance from his people. On one such voyage, Amenemhet I was accompanied by KHNUMHOTEP (1), a prince and undisputed leader of the Oryx nome (or province) at BENI HASAN. There were 20 ships in this armada, and Amenemhet I was displaying the political support of a nome aristocrat alongside military might. He also moved the capital from Thebes to ITJ-TAWY, "the Seizer of the Two Lands," near the modern town of Lisht. The capital was originally called Amenemhet-Ity-tawy and was shortened over the years. He married NEFRU-TOTENEN, who is believed to have borne SENWOSRET I, the heir. A second queen, SIT-HATHOR, gave birth to Princess DEDYET and Princess Nensebdjebet. Later in his reign a woman named NEFRU-SOBEK (2) became his queen. He had two daughters: Nefrusheri and Nyetneb.

Amenemhet I proved an efficient administrator and militarily astute ruler. He established his new capital between the boundaries of Upper and Lower Egypt in order to have increased control of the DELTA. He also erected the WALL OF THE PRINCE, a series of forts that safeguarded Egypt's eastern and western borders. He founded SEMNA fort in Nubia and routed the Bedouins on the SINAI Peninsula, using the genius of General Nysumontu. Within the palace, however, Amenemhet I faced harem revolts, one unsuccessful attempt on his life, and a last murderous assault.

In 1979 B.C.E., Amenemhet I named his son, Senwosret I, as his co-regent, thus discouraging attempts by others to take the throne. Senwosret also received a set of "*Instructions*" from Amenemhet I. This document was also called the *Testament of Amenemhet*. In it the pharaoh declares that a ruler must avoid all intimacy with lesser courtiers, and these "*Instructions*" clearly define royal obligations based upon the needs of the people, including personal sacrifices and loneliness. Possibly the INSTRUCTIONS OF AMENEMHET I was written after the second assault on the pharaoh's life, a palace feud that was successful in bringing Amenemhet I's reign to an end.

Senwosret I, who campaigned militarily in his father's name, was in the desert region when word came of the assassination. He raced back to the capital with a large force and routed the enemies of his inheritance. Amenemhet was buried in a pyramid in LISHT, called "Horus of Repeating Births," now in ruins. The assassination of Amenemhet is a key element in the plot of the tale of "SINUHE THE SAILOR." The hero of the tale is involved in some way in the harem struggles, and he flees Egypt when Senwosret I receives word of the royal death.

See also NEFER-ROHU'S PROPHECY.

Amenemhet II (Nubkauré) (d. 1892 B.C.E.) *third ruler of the Twelfth Dynasty*

He reigned from 1929 B.C.E. until his death. Amenemhet II was the son of SENWOSRET I and Queen NEFRUSHERI. Serving three years as co-regent with his father, AMENEMHET II conducted two military campaigns, a foray into NUBIA, modern Sudan, and one to rout the BEDOUINS on the SINAI Peninsula. He also made trade pacts with Syria and Levantine cities. His reign was highlighted by internal difficulties as the various NOMARCHS (provincial aristocrats) attempted to overthrow a centralized system of government in order to exercise independence. Beginning under Senwosret, Amenemhet II reclaimed the FAIYUM territory of Egypt, the lush marshland fed by the BAHR YUSUF (a small river that leads into the region from the Nile between modern el-Ashmunein and old Meir). The Faiyum, called Ta-she by the Egyptians, "the Land of the Lakes," or Payuum, became an agricultural base for the country. At various times, the Faiyum extended over 4,000 square miles and included Lake MOERIS. The cult of SOBEK, the crocodile god, was established in Shedet, the capital of the region. Amenemhet II's CARTOUCHE was discovered in Lebanon, and other seals were found in the temple of MONTU at Thebes. He sent expeditions to the Red Sea and to PUNT and used the local gold mines.

Amenemhet II married Queen MERYET (2), the mother of the heir, SENWOSRET II and Queens TEO and KEMANWEB. His daughters were Ata, Atuart, Khnumt, Sit Hathor, Sit Hathor Hormeret, and Sit Hathor Meryt. Senwosret II served as his co-regent for five years before Amenemhet II died.

Amenemhet II was buried in DASHUR, near MEMPHIS, in a white pyramid originally some 263 feet square, called "the Soul of Amenemhet." The tombs of the princesses of the reign contained a vast collection of jewelry, now prized by the modern world. A queen, KEMINIBU, from the Thirteenth Dynasty (1784–1640 B.C.E.) was found buried there also.

Amenemhet III (Nima'atré) (d. 1797 B.C.E.) *sixth ruler of the Twelfth Dynasty*

He reigned from 1844 B.C.E. until his death. Amenemhet was the son of SENWOSRET III and Queen NEFERHENT (2) and is considered one of the outstanding pharaohs of the Middle Kingdom (2040–1640 B.C.E.). Egypt enjoyed a period of economic growth during his reign. In an era of peace, Amenemhet III developed the FAIYUM region in Middle Egypt and used the mines and quarries of the SINAI and southern Egyptian regions to good advantage. Amenemhet III also held the government of Egypt in tight rein. In the Sinai, 49 texts concerning the era were discovered at SERABIT EL-KHADIM, with others found at WADI MAGHARA and WADI NASB. Originally the Egyptians set up seasonal camps at such mining sites, but in Amenemhet III's reign permanent settlements were established, complete with residences, defensive fortifications, wells, and cemeteries. The temple of HATHOR at Serabit el-Khadim, designed to honor that goddess, was enlarged, and military units

The warrior pharaoh Amenemhet III of the Middle Kingdom's Twelfth Dynasty *(Hulton Archive)*

were assigned to the mines for protection of workers gathering gems.

In the south, Amenemhet III fortified the great trading post at SEMNA, at the southern end of the second cataract. Most of Amenemhet III's efforts were aimed at the Faiyum region, however, as he reclaimed the dense marshlands and furthered the irrigation projects and dikes started by other pharaohs of his line. He was honored in the Greco-Roman eras for his reclamation of the Faiyum and worshipped under the name Lamares. Two colossal statues of Amenemhet III made of granite on limestone bases were discovered at BIAHMU, a site northeast of HAWARA. He decorated the temple of the god SOBEK at Kiman Fares and built a chapel for RENENUTET, the Egyptian goddess of the harvest.

Amenemhet III's queen was A'AT, the mother of AMENEMHET IV, who was buried at DASHUR in a southwest corridor. The pyramid there, called "Amenemhet Is Beautiful," was faulty, and the pharaoh abandoned it and built a second one at Hawara, in the southeastern Faiyum, called "Amenemhet Lives." This second pyramid is called a LABYRINTH because of its intricate chambers, trapdoors, dead-end passages, and sliding panels. The burial chamber is a vast block of quartzite, hollowed out and sunk into the foundation of the pyramid. Amenemhet III's SARCOPHAGUS, also of quartzite, and a smaller one for princess Neferu-ptah, his daughter, were found in the chamber. This burial site was sealed by a single slab of stone that weighed an estimated 45 tons.

Amenemhet IV (Ma'akheruré) (d. 1787 B.C.E.) *seventh ruler of the Twelfth Dynasty*

He reigned from 1799 B.C.E. until his death. The son of AMENEMHET III and probably Queen A'at, he served as co-regent with his father for two years and carried on the family's projects in the FAIYUM, the lush region in middle Egypt. He is believed to have erected the temple of QASR EL-SAGHAH, just north of Lake QARUN. He also completed Amenemhet III's temple at Medinet MA'ADI, and he sent an expedition to the SINAI and maintained TRADE pacts. SOBEKNEFERU, the sister of Amenemhet IV, whom he had married, assumed the throne when he died after a brief reign. Sobekneferu thus became a woman pharaoh, the only woman holding that title in the Middle Kingdom (2040–1640 B.C.E.). The two pyramids at MAZGHUNA, in the southern part of DASHUR, are ascribed to this royal pair, the last rulers of the Twelfth Dynasty, bringing to an end this royal line and an entire historical period.

Amenemhet V (Ameny Intef IV; Sekhemkaré; Sankhibré; Hornedjheritef) (fl. ca. 1760 B.C.E.) *fourth ruler of the Thirteenth Dynasty*

His throne name meant "the Heart of Ré lives." He was also called Ameny Intef IV and by the throne name Hornedjheritef, "Horus, Avenger of His Father," in some monuments. The HYKSOS, or Asiatics, were in the DELTA during his reign, establishing their hold on the northern and eastern territories, but there are no records of conflict between the two royal houses. He is credited with receiving tribute from BYBLOS (in modern Lebanon). The Thirteenth Dynasty in the Second Intermediate Period is a shadowy royal line, reportedly composed of 50 pharaohs, most unidentified.

Amenemhet VI (fl. 18th century B.C.E.) *obscure ruler of the Thirteenth Dynasty*
His actual date of reign is unknown. Amenemhet VI was called "the Asiatic" and his mortuary pyramid is reportedly in DASHUR.

Amenemhet VII (Sedjefakaré) (fl. 18th century B.C.E.) *fifteenth ruler of the Thirteenth Dynasty*
He ruled ca. 1740 B.C.E. Amenemhet VII's name was discovered on monuments in TANIS, the ELEPHANTINE Island (at modern Aswan), and in MEDAMUD. Nothing else is known about his reign.

Amenemhet's Instructions   See INSTRUCTIONS OF AMENEMHET I.

Amenemnisu (Neferkaré) (d. 1040 B.C.E.) *co-regent of the second ruler of the Twenty-first Dynasty*
Amenemnisu held this rank during the last four years of the reign of SMENDES (1) on the throne from 1044 B.C.E. until his death. He was probably the son of HERIHOR, the high priest of AMUN at Thebes, and a woman named NODJMET. Smendes allowed Amenemnisu to serve in this capacity at the new capital of TANIS, in the eastern Delta, in order to unite efforts with Thebes.

Amenemnisu, whose name meant "Amun Is King," had served Menkheperresenb (2), another high priest in Thebes. During the civil war in the Theban region, Amenemnisu exiled his opponents to the LIBYAN DESERT for a time but then pardoned them, supposedly in a decree dictated by an oracle of the god Amun. The burial site of Amenemnisu was unknown until recent excavations in Tanis revealed his tomb there. He made PSUSENNES I his co-regent before his death.

Amenemope (Userma'atré Setepenamun) (d. 984 B.C.E.) *fourth ruler of the Twenty-first Dynasty*
Amenemope reigned from 993 B.C.E. until his death. He was the successor and probable son of PSUSENNES I and Queen MUTNODJMET (2), having served as a co-regent for two years. He built a tomb for himself at TANIS, but his mummy was placed in Mutnodjmet's tomb for some reason unexplained. His name meant "Amun in Opet," a section of the old capital of Thebes. Amenemope buried Psusennes I with rich offerings, whereas his own funerary regalia was small. He had a yellow quartzite SARCOPHAGUS, which had a lid fashioned out of a block of stone usurped from an Old Kingdom site but had a gilded CARTONNAGE mummy mask. The sarcophagus was in his tomb, but his mummy, found intact, was discovered in his mother's burial chamber near the temple of Tanis.

Amenemope (1) (fl. 12th century B.C.E.) *high priest of Amun in the Twentieth Dynasty*
He served in the reign of RAMESSES IX (r. 1131–1112 B.C.E.). Amenemope was the son of RAMESSESNAKHT and the brother of Mesamun, his predecessors. His son was the usurper HERIHOR. Amenemope began to assert his religious powers in the 10th year of Ramesses IX's reign. He was depicted in temple reliefs as equal to the pharaoh, a violation of the Egyptian artistic canon. He was buried in THEBES.

Amenemope (2) (fl. 14th century B.C.E.) *a sage of the New Kingdom*
He lived probably during the reign of AMENHOTEP III (r. 1391–1353 B.C.E.) and was the author of the *Instructions of Amenemope*. This text was found in a papyrus now in the British Museum in London. He was a resident of AKHMIN, and described himself as an agricultural official who set up the royal titles to land uncovered by the lowering of the Nile water each year. Amenemope, whose wife was Twasoret, also served as the overseer for taxes for the Akhmin area and administered the distribution of crops locally.

He wrote his *Instructions* for his son, and this work reflects the spirit of MA'AT, nurtured on the Nile over the centuries. His work was composed of more than 80 sections and was written in short lines. Amenemope translated the ideals of Egypt into everyday tasks of a common person's life. *The Maxims of Ptah-hotep* is another example of this type of literature. Such didactic LITERATURE was popular in the Nile Valley. Amenemope was buried in a pyramid in Akhmin. Amenemope's work was discovered on various writing boards, on an ostracon (see OSTRACA), and in a fragmentary papyrus.

Amenemopet A remarkable family of THEBES, serving the pharaohs of the New Kingdom (1550–1070 B.C.E.), some held positions in the temple of AMUN at Thebes and others headed bureaucratic offices. The third prophet of Amun in the reign of RAMESSES III (1194–1163 B.C.E.) was a member of this family. Another individual named Amenemope served as the viceroy of Kush or NUBIA, the area south of Aswan in modern Sudan, for SETI I (r. 1306–1290 B.C.E.). BAKENKHONSU, the high priest of Amun in the reign of RAMESSES II (1290–1224 B.C.E.), was also a family member. These public servants were aristocrats, or NOMARCHS, from a southern province. Their efforts, and those of other large clans involved in various bureaucratic offices, allowed the government of Egypt to continue, decade after decade, without interruption.

Amenhirkhopshef (1) (fl. 12th century B.C.E.) *prince of the Twentieth Dynasty*
Amenhirkhopshef was the son of RAMESSES III (r. 1194–1163 B.C.E.) and Queen ISET (2). The prince died at the age of nine. Queen Iset is reported to have miscarried a baby when she heard of Amenhirkhopshef's death, and the unborn infant was mummified and entombed in the prince's own crypt. In Amenhirkhopshef's burial chamber, Ramesses III is depicted leading his son to the god ANUBIS, the jackal-headed deity associated with OSIRIS and funerary rituals. The prince served as a royal scribe during his brief life. He was buried in the VALLEY OF THE QUEENS on the western shore of the Nile at THEBES, the site used for the tombs of princes in the New Kingdom (1550–1070 B.C.E.). The walls of some chambers of this tomb are exquisitely painted.

Amenhirkhopshef (2) (fl. 13th century B.C.E.) *prince of the Nineteenth Dynasty*
The son of RAMESSES II (1290–1224 B.C.E.) and Queen NEFERTARI MERYMUT, he was called Amenhirwonmef ("Amun is at his right hand") originally and then Amenhirkhopshef ("Amun wields his sword"). This prince is shown in the procession of Ramessid royal heirs in LUXOR Temple, and in ABU SIMBEL, the site of his father's great monument. He is also depicted in KV5, the recently opened tomb of the sons of Ramesses II. This tomb, the largest ever found in Egypt, was designed to house the remains of more than 100 of Ramesses II's sons in the valley. There is another lavish tomb bearing his name in the VALLEY OF THE QUEENS on the western shore of the Nile at THEBES.

Amenhirkhopshef was the commanding general of Egypt's armies and heir apparent of the throne. He was active in Ramesses II's campaigns, punishing city-states such as Moab that had accepted the protection of the HITTITES, the enemies of Egypt at the time. When a treaty was signed between the Hittites and the Egyptians, Amenhirkhopshef was mentioned in royal correspondence. The Hittite king HATTUSILIS III and his queen, PEDUKHIPA, sent greetings to Nefertari Merymut and the crown prince Amenhirkhopshef. He died in the 20th year of Ramesses II's reign. Eleven other brothers would precede their father in death. MERENPTAH, his eventual heir, was 13th in the line of succession.

Amenhotep, son of Hapu (Huy) (fl. 14th century B.C.E.) *court official of the Eighteenth Dynasty*
A revered sage and scholar, he served in the reign of AMENHOTEP III (r. 1391–1353 B.C.E.). Amenhotep, son of Hapu, was one of only a few commoners to be deified in ancient Egypt. Also called Huy, he was from the Delta area of ATHRIBIS, born around 1460 B.C.E. He rose through the ranks of government service, including the office of scribe of the military, and then served as a commander, and eventually as a general. Amenhotep also supervised

A statue of the famed sage Amenhotep, Son of Hapu; he is distinctive because of his flowing hair; now in the Egyptian Museum, Cairo. *(S. M. Bunson)*

the building projects of Amenhotep III. When he died around 1380 B.C.E., at the age of 80, a funerary chapel was erected for him beside Amenhotep III's temple.

Amenhotep, Son of Hapu, was depicted in many statues placed in KARNAK temple, a royal favor in that age. He is shown usually with long wavy hair instead of a formal wig. His association with the god AMUN brought about a claim by the temple priests of the Twenty-first Dynasty (1070–945 B.C.E.) that Amenhotep had divine origins. He was deified alongside IMHOTEP, the architect of the STEP PYRAMID of DJOSER (r. 2630–2611 B.C.E.). Clinics or shrines were developed for their cults, and ceremonies were conducted in their memory throughout Egypt.

Amenhotep I (Djeserkaré) (d. 1504 B.C.E.) *second ruler of the Eighteenth Dynasty*
Amenhotep I was one of the most handsome and popular of the ancient pharaohs, whose name meant "Amun is Content." He reigned from 1525 B.C.E. until his death and was the son of 'AHMOSE and Queen 'AHMOSE-NEFERTARI, who possibly served as regent at the start of Amenhotep I's reign. He was not the original heir. Records indicate that he outlived two older brothers to inherit the throne from 'Ahmose.

In his first regnal year, or perhaps during the time of 'Ahmose-Nefertari's regency, Egypt faced an invasion and had to defeat a confederation of Libyan tribes on the nation's western borders. A royal army, probably led by Amenhotep I personally, went south to halt expansion of the Nubians in the area below ASWAN, in modern Sudan. Amenhotep restored and refurbished the FORTRESSES on the Nile south of the first cataract, bastions dating in some instances to the Middle Kingdom (2040–1640 B.C.E.). He also installed a governor for that region, a noble named Turi, who was entrusted with the duties of maintaining order, promoting trade, and gathering tribute for the throne.

Within Egypt, Amenhotep I initiated building projects at the temple of KARNAK in THEBES. This temple, one of the most remarkable religious complexes in the world, covered 250 acres. The building programs of Amenhotep I added to the original shrine, begun in the Middle Kingdom, and set the standard for later pharaohs of the New Kingdom (1550–1070 B.C.E.), who continued the work there for centuries. Because of his military defenses and his building programs, Amenhotep was very popular during his lifetime. He also used the SINAI mines and the various quarries. Egypt, unified and free of the Asiatic HYKSOS (defeated by 'Ahmose), prospered. His popularity only increased after his death in 1504 B.C.E. He and Queen 'Ahmose-Nefertari were proclaimed the patron deities of Thebes. A shrine was dedicated to them on the western shore of the Nile at the capital, Thebes.

AH'HOTEP (2), a sister of Amenhotep I, was his Great Wife, or ranking queen. Secondary consorts were 'AHMOSE MERYTAMON and SATKAMOSE. Ah'hotep bore the son and heir, but the child died in infancy. Because there was no one to succeed him, Amenhotep chose TUTHMOSIS I from among his military officials. Tuthmosis was probably from a secondary royal line. A relative named 'Ahmose was given to Tuthmosis as consort to consolidate his claims and to link him in yet another fashion to the royal family.

Amenhotep I was the first pharaoh to separate his tomb from his mortuary temple and burial complex. Normally the MORTUARY TEMPLES of the pharaohs were erected at the gravesites to allow priests to make daily offerings and to conduct rituals of eternal rest for the deceased. Looters reached the burial chambers of such complexes, tearing apart the mummies and sometimes burning them. Amenhotep wanted to escape destruction at the hands of such grave robbers, who were possibly given aid by the priests themselves, in return for a share in the goods. His original tomb is now unknown but was listed in the inspection done by RAMESSES IX (1131–1112 B.C.E.) as being located at Dra Abu el-Nuga. Amenhotep I's mummy was rewrapped by priests of the Twenty-first Dynasty (1070–945 B.C.E.) after his original tomb was vandalized, taken to DEIR EL-BAHRI, and placed in the mummy cache there. During this second burial, delphiniums were used to adorn his remains, along with other red, yellow, and blue flowers. A wasp settled onto one of the flowers and died there, keeping the pharaoh company through the centuries.

Amenhotep I was five and one-half feet tall, with a long, oval skull and sloping forehead. His strong jaw marks him as the son of 'Ahmose. Statues of him were carried through the streets of Thebes as an oracle, or prophet, called "the judge of the living and the dead." The cult of Amenhotep I continued through the Twentieth Dynasty (1196–1070 B.C.E.).

Amenhotep II (Akhepruré) (d. 1401 B.C.E.) *seventh ruler of the Eighteenth Dynasty*

The son of TUTHMOSIS III and Queen MERYT-RÉ-HATSHEPSUT, Amenhotep II reigned from 1427 B.C.E. until his death. He was reportedly not the original heir. A brother, Amenemhet, believed to be the son of Tuthmosis III and Queen NEFERU-RÉ, died before he could inherit the throne. Amenhotep II was handsome, tall, and athletic. He was a warrior delighting in hand-to-hand combat, executing prisoners personally in elaborate ceremonies. When he was made co-regent, Amenhotep added Hegaiunu to his name, meaning "the ruler of Iunu," HELIOPOLIS.

His entire life was spent preparing for his reign as he underwent the usual education for princes and heirs. He excelled in archery and horsemanship, and he commanded the vast Egyptian naval base at PERU-NEFER near Memphis. Experienced in war, Amenhotep II moved quickly in the second year of his reign against the cities on the Mediterranean Sea that were in open revolt. He marched into Palestine to Shemesh-Edom and subdued each city-state all the way to the Orontes River, to modern Lebanon and Syria. At Tikishi he captured seven princes and brought them to Egypt. Amenhotep moved on to the Euphrates River in modern Iraq, where he erected a stela alongside the ones raised up there by his father and great grandfather (TUTHMOSIS I) (r. 1504–1492 B.C.E.), the founders of the empire. He also rescued Egyptian troops surrounded at another battle site in the area. Returning to Egypt, Amenhotep brought prisoners and considerable booty to THEBES.

In Egypt, Amenhotep II left monuments at DENDEREH, HELIOPOLIS, GEBEL EL-SILSILEH, TOD, ELKAB, GIZA, ERMENT, and MEDAMUD with the help of many, including Amunemhet, a temple official of the Eighteenth Dynasty. Amunemhet was a high priest of the god AMUN, but he served the court in other capacities as well, as did most of the Amunite priests of that period. An accomplished architect, he supervised royal building projects.

In his third year, Nubian rebellions brought Amenhotep to ASWAN and the ELEPHANTINE Island. The princes captured in the region of the Orontes River the year before accompanied Amenhotep on this voyage. All seven of them hung head downward from the prow of his ship. The bodies were later displayed in prominent sites. Amenhotep II reportedly delighted in the slaughter of his enemies. In his seventh year he went to CARCHEMISH, in Syria, to subdue another revolt.

Amenhotep II's consorts were SITAMON and then MERYT-AMUN (2), his sister, but another consort, Queen TEO, bore his heir, TUTHMOSIS IV. His mother, Meryt-Ré-Hatshepsut, however, remained the Great Wife, or ranking queen. Amenhotep II had several sons and daughters. One of his sons, 'Ahmose, served as the high priest of the god at HELIOPOLIS. A burial stela at the cemetery of the Mnevis bulls, the THEOPHANIES of the god RÉ in some eras, was discovered bearing his name. (His own burial site remains undiscovered.)

Amenhotep's mummy was discovered in his tomb in the VALLEY OF THE KINGS on the western shore of the Nile at Thebes. He had wavy brown hair, graying at the temples. His mummified skin was studded with small tubercules, possibly the result of embalming. Believed to have died at the age of 45, Amenhotep suffered from rheumatism and some sort of systemic disease, no doubt from tooth problems. Signs of severe dental decay are evident in his mummy.

His tomb in the Valley of the Kings proved to be a treasure house of Egyptian history. The AM DUAT prayers are depicted on the walls in compelling reliefs. The burial chamber of his tomb, found undisturbed, was used by priests of later dynasties as a storehouse for other rescued mummies of the New Kingdom (1550–1070 B.C.E.). This tomb had an early styled entry stairwell, corridors, antechambers, pillared halls, and a decorated sunken burial chamber. Magazines and well shafts were included in the design. One of Amenhotep II's sons shared the tomb.

See also MUMMY CACHES.

Amenhotep III (Nebma'atré) (d. 1353 B.C.E.) *ninth pharaoh of the Eighteenth Dynasty*

The son of TUTHMOSIS IV and Queen MUTEMWIYA, Amenhotep III reigned from 1391 B.C.E. until his death. As a young man, Amenhotep III married TIYE (1), the daughter of Hurrian master of horse at THEBES. Together they ruled an empire that extended from northern Sudan to the Euphrates River. His mother, Mutemwiya, is believed by some scholars to have been the daughter of ARTATAMA, the MITANNI king, given to Egypt as part of Tuthmosis IV's treaties with that nation. Amenhotep III's birth was recorded in the temple in LUXOR, given divine intervention and divine patronage. Tiye, whom he had married before ascending the throne, bore him AKHENATEN (Amenhotep IV), and princesses SITAMUN (2), BAKETAMUN, HENUTTANEB, NEBETAH, ISET (3), and other children. Amenhotep III married Iset, Henuttaneb, and Sitamun when they came of age.

A vast series of commemorative scarabs issued by the pharaoh provide a portrait of his first 12 years on the throne. One SCARAB memorializes the arrival of GILUKIPA

(or Khirgipa), a Mitanni princess who came with an entourage of more than 300 Mitannis to be his wife. Her niece, TADUKHIPA, arrived at the end of Amenhotep's reign and possibly married Akhenaten. These Mitanni royal women were sent to Egypt by King Shuttarna II, who was their relative.

The addition of such women to AMENHOTEP III's harem led to the construction of a new palace to the south of MEDINET HABU, on the western shore of the Nile at THEBES, called MALKATA, or "the Place Where Things Are Picked Up," by modern Egyptians. This palace was actually a miniature city with several royal compounds, an artificial lake reportedly dug and filled within a matter of weeks, and a harbor. Shrines and temples, as well as bureaucratic offices, were part of the complexes.

Tributes and trade profits provided Amenhotep III with unending wealth as he built many shrines and monuments, many of which have not survived. Among these monuments are the COLOSSI OF MEMNON, two gigantic statues of Amenhotep III that were part of his mortuary temple. The Greeks named the statues after Memnon, the Trojan hero slain by Achilles. Strabo, the historian, reported that the northern statue of Amenhotep III emitted a soft bell-like sound at each dawn. In the early third century B.C.E. the Roman emperor Septimius Severus ordered repairs on the upper part of that statue, which were performed crudely, and as a result the singing sound stopped forever.

Amenhotep III celebrated three *heb-sed* (see SED), normally used to denote 30 years of rule. He constructed a palace, Per-Hay, "the Mansion of Rejoicing," for this event. Queen Tiye and the massive bureaucracy of Egypt maintained foreign and domestic affairs, while Amenhotep lolled in Malkata, and the military might of Egypt suppressed any rebellions against the empire. The pharaoh could spend his time building on the Nile and erecting monuments in his honor at his leisure.

He was quite obese in his later years. His portraits, already sculpted in the style that would blossom in the 'Amarna Period, depict him as having a snub nose, full lips, and almond-shaped eyes. Troubled with severe tooth decay, a dynastic period condition, Amenhotep became ill. An ally, King TUSHRATTA of Babylon, sent him a statue of Ishtar—the Babylonian goddess of healing—to restore his vigor and to demonstrate friendly concern.

Amenhotep III's tomb in the VALLEY OF THE KINGS, on the western shore of Thebes, has three main corridors. The tomb chamber has a pillared hall, and the various chambers are all highly decorated. The red granite lid used on the sarcophagus for the burial of Amenhotep III was usurped by SETI I (1306–1290 B.C.E.) of the Nineteenth Dynasty. Amenhotep III's mummy was discovered in the tomb of AMENHOTEP II. Modern scholars, however, do not believe that this embalmed body is truly Amenhotep III. There is considerable debate about the actual identity of several recovered remains.

Further reading: Fletcher, J. *Chronicle of a Pharaoh: The Intimate Life of Amenhotep III.* Oxford, U.K.: Oxford University Press, 2000; O'Connor, D., and E. Cline, eds. *Amenhotep III, Perspectives on His Reign.* Ann Arbor: University of Michigan Press, 1998.

Amenhotep IV *See* AKHENATEN.

Amenia (fl. 14th century B.C.E.) *woman of the court in the Eighteenth Dynasty*
She was the commoner wife of HOREMHAB (r. 1319–1307 B.C.E.). Amenia married Horemhab when he was a military man, serving in Egypt's army and attaining the rank of chief of the forces and king's deputy in the reign of TUT'ANKHAMUN (r. 1333–1323 B.C.E.). Horemhab was also decorated for valor by AKHENATEN (r. 1353–1335 B.C.E.) in 'AMARNA.

Horemhab built a vast tomb for himself and Amenia in SAQQARA, the MEMPHIS necropolis, while he was a military officer. This tomb, recently uncovered, depicts Horemhab as a commoner, although the URAEUS, the symbol of royalty, was added to some of his figures there during his reign. Amenia was buried in Saqqara, probably dying before Horemhab took the throne of Egypt. Queen MUTNODJMET (1), who became Horemhab's Great Wife, or *hemet,* was buried beside Amenia in Saqqara rather than having a tomb in the royal necropolis at THEBES.

Ameni-A'amu (fl. 19th century B.C.E.) *mysterious royal personage in the Thirteenth Dynasty*
He is historically associated with AMENEMHET III (r. 1844–1797 B.C.E.). A small pyramid at DASHUR is inscribed with his name and royal insignias. These inscriptions appear to place him in the reign of Amenemhet III, perhaps as the designated heir to the throne.

Amenirdis (1) (fl. eighth century B.C.E.) *royal woman of the Twenty-fifth Dynasty*
She was the sister of PIANKHI (1) (750–712 B.C.E.) and the daughter of KASHTA and Queen PEBATMA. As a royal princess, Amenirdis was adopted by SHEPENWEPET (1) as her successor in the role of GOD'S WIFE OF AMUN or Divine Adoratrice of Amun, the office of high priestess and political representative of the ruling family. This role, carried out in THEBES, descended over the years from the title of God's Wife held by New Kingdom queens starting with 'AHMOSE-NEFERTARI, the wife of 'AHMOSE (NEBPEHTIRÉ) (r. 1550–1525 B.C.E.). The high priestess presided over a harem of Amun's devotees and conducted ceremonies.

Amenirdis could not marry while serving as Divine Adoratrice of Amun, adopting her successor, SHEPEN-WEPET (2). When she retired, however, she married her brother, SHEBITKU (r. 698–690 B.C.E.) and bore Shepenwepet III. Statues have been recovered depicting Amenirdis in royal regalia. Like other high priestesses, she built a tomb in KARNAK. Some priestesses were buried in a necropolis called "the vineyard of Anubis." Such women held considerable political power over Upper Egypt, the southern territories, serving as a "voice" of the god Amun and thus able to dictate many policies. They were recruited mostly from the ranks of the royal families of Egypt and wore the crowns and ornaments of queens.

Amenirdis (2) (fl. seventh century B.C.E.) *royal woman of the Twenty-sixth Dynasty*
Amenirdis was destined to become a GOD'S WIFE OF AMUN or a Divine Adoratrice of Amun, a high priestess of the deity at THEBES. She was designated as the successor of the high priestess SHEPENWEPET (2). When PSAMMATI-CHUS I (r. 664–610 B.C.E.) came to power, however, he sent a large fleet of ships to Thebes, bearing his daughter NITOCRIS (2), who then assumed the role of Divine Adoratrice, an act that overthrew the Nubian control of Egypt. Amenirdis, a member of the overthrown family of NECHO I (r. 672–664 B.C.E.), was ousted from Thebes. Her role was ended because she no longer had the political base necessary to influence Egypt's affairs.

Amenken (fl. 15th century B.C.E.) *financial official of the Eighteenth Dynasty*
He served AMENHOTEP II (r. 1427–1401 B.C.E.) as a high official in the royal treasury of Egypt, concerned with the tabulation and the distribution of gifts to court favorites and NOME officials. The pharaohs presented outstanding servants with golden collars and other costly insignias of honor on feast days. Amenken was buried in THEBES.

Amenmesses (Menmiré) (fl. ca. 1214 B.C.E.) *sixth ruler of the Nineteenth Dynasty, recorded as a usurper*
He took the throne of SETI II (r. 1214–ca. 1204 B.C.E.). His name, Amenmesses, meant "Fashioned by Amun, God of Thebes." He ruled only four years, possibly as an interlude ruler between MERENPTAH and Seti II, who was the crown prince and designated heir. Amenmesses was possibly the son of MERENPTAH and Queen TAKHAT (1). Records give her only the title of "King's Mother," not that of a royal wife of rank. He is believed to have married BAKETWEREL, but no documentation supports this. Three bodies discovered in Amenmesses' tomb in the VALLEY OF THE KINGS on the western shore of Thebes have not been identified. He is also recorded as marrying TIA (2), the mother of SIPTAH. Amenmesses did not rule in the north, where Seti II controlled the Delta and the dynastic capital of PER-RAMESSES.

He had the backing of the Theban priests, including the high priest, Roma-Ray, who had considerable power in the name of the god AMUN. Amenmesses also controlled NUBIA, modern Sudan. How he died at the end of four years is unknown. He simply disappeared from the scene, and Seti II usurped his statues and monuments. Some cartouches were even removed from his tomb in Thebes, at BIBAN EL-MOLUK, and some chambers were vandalized. The tomb has three corridors, a square chamber, and four pillared halls.

Amenmose (fl. 16th century B.C.E.) *prince of the Eighteenth Dynasty*
He was the son of TUTHMOSIS I (r. 1504–1492 B.C.E.) and Queen 'AHMOSE (1), and an older brother of Queen-Pharaoh HATSHEPSUT (r. 1473–1458 B.C.E.). Records indicate that he was general of Egypt's armies. He predeceased Tuthmosis I. Amenmose had a brother, WADJMOSE, who also died before he could inherit the throne from his father. Amenmose was buried in the royal necropolis on the western shore of THEBES.

Amennakht (fl. 12th century B.C.E.) *official of the Twentieth Dynasty*
Amennakht served RAMESSES III (r. 1194–1163 B.C.E.) as a supervisor of tomb artists and craftsmen. These artists resided in a special community near the VALLEY OF THE KINGS on the western shore of the Nile at THEBES (modern Luxor). The community was called DEIR EL-MEDINA, once known as "the Place of the Servitors of Truth." Amennakht was a trained scribe who served as an overseer for the workers in the royal tombs. He and his fellow SERVANTS OF THE PLACE OF TRUTH were able to build personal tombs of unusual size, ornately decorated. They donated their skills in providing one another with exquisitely painted gravesites.

Amenpanefer (fl. 11th century B.C.E.) *tomb robber of the Twentieth Dynasty*
Amenpanefer committed his crimes in the reign of RAMESSES XI (r. 1100–1070 B.C.E.) in THEBES. A stone carver who labored in the tombs of the VALLEY OF THE KINGS at Thebes, he was arrested by authorities and taken in for questioning after a rash of tomb robberies. Amenpanefer confessed to being part of a nefarious gang that preyed upon the mummies of Egypt's dead pharaohs. He described how he and eight coconspirators dug a tunnel and broke into the tomb of SOBEKEMSAF III (a Seventeenth Dynasty ruler). They stole jewels and then set fire to the royal mummy. Queen NUBKHAS (2) (Seventeenth Dynasty) received the same destructive treatment from Amenpanefer and his fellow criminals. Amenpanefer and his cohorts faced harsh sentences when condemned. Most grave robbers were executed, not just for stealing and vandalism, but also for the crimes of blasphemy and impiety.
See also TOMB ROBBERY TRIAL.

Amenwah (fl. 12th century B.C.E.) *tomb robber of the Twentieth Dynasty*
Amenwah reportedly invaded the tomb of RAMESSES III (r. 1194–1163 B.C.E.). The desecration came in a troubled era following the pharaoh's death, in which temple priests and entire villages plundered gravesites. Amenwah was associated with DEIR EL-MEDINA, an ancient village housing artisans who worked in the tombs in the VALLEY OF THE KINGS on the western shore of the Nile at THEBES. He was rounded up in a sweeping raid on tomb robbers of that era. Pleading innocent to all charges brought against him, he was eventually released for lack of evidence. Modern excavations of Amenwah's tomb established his guilt. He not only robbed Ramesses III's tomb but also placed his ill-gotten goods in his own burial chamber for all eternity.
See also TOMB ROBBERY TRIAL.

ames The ancient Egyptian name for the SCEPTER in the form of a club or mace that was used as a royal insignia in most eras, the *ames* dates back to the early period of Egypt (ca. 3000 B.C.E.), when the warriors of the south invaded the Delta, subduing the Bee King's armies and unifying the nation. The kings maintained the insignias of ancient times and incorporated them into the newer rituals of office. The mummies of the pharaohs were always arranged so that one arm was folded over the chest, indicating that the deceased once carried the AMES as the symbol of royal power.

Amherst Papyrus This was a document from THEBES that contained an account of the Ramessid-Period TOMB ROBBERY TRIALS. With the ABBOTT PAPYRUS, which includes an account of the same event, this text provides detailed information and insight into the Twentieth Dynasty (1196–1070 B.C.E.), a period of declining royal authority and law and order in the Nile Valley. The Amherst Papyrus was owned originally by the first baron Amherst of Hockney, England, and consisted of the lower half of a document concerning Twentieth Dynasty robberies. The upper portion of the papyrus, now called the Leopold II Papyrus, was discovered in Brussels. The two sections were joined by scholars and photographed for translation purposes.

Ami-ut A dog-headed deity of ancient Egypt, concerned with funerary elements, he was probably a forerunner of OSIRIS and became overshadowed by that deity. A headless BULL's skin attached to a rod was the symbol of Ami-ut, an insignia used in some funerary rituals.
See also TEKENU.

Amorites An ancient Semitic people called the *Amurru* or *Martu* in records from Sumeria, they dominated the region of Mesopotamia, Syria, and Palestine from ca. 2000 to ca. 1600 B.C.E., bringing them into conflict with Egypt. Their homeland is believed to have been Arabia, and they are credited with bringing the fall of the city of Ur.

The Amorites migrated into the region in the 21st century B.C.E., assimilating to the Sumerian-Akkadian culture in time. Almost all of the kings of Babylon could trace their ancestry to this stock. The Amorites had a capital at Meri, modern Tell al-Hariri, Syria, and at

Halab, now called Aleppo. The region called Amurru was located in northern Palestine and in the Syrian desert region. Inscriptions from the era of Egypt's First Intermediate Period (2134–2040 B.C.E.) indicate that the Amorites controlled Phoenicia, modern Lebanon, disrupting TRADE with Egypt. AMENEMHET I (r. 1991–1962 B.C.E.) restored such trade during his reign.

Amratian   The name given to the first Predynastic phase, NAGADA I, this phase was centered in el-'Amirah, near ABYDOS, in Upper Egypt. Sites dating to ca. 3600 B.C.E. give evidence of Badarian (a prior phase) influences, improved and adapted to advance techniques. The pottery from this Amratian period includes black topped red ocher ware, with linear designs in white, including figures. MACEHEADS, vases, and ivory carving were also recovered from Amratian sites.

Amtes (Yamtes)   (fl. 23rd century B.C.E.) *royal woman of the Sixth Dynasty*
She was a consort of PEPI I (r. 2289–2555 B.C.E.). Some records indicate that Amtes was involved in a HAREM (1) plot to overthrow Pepi I. The conspiracy was unsuccessful, and an official named WENI was called upon to investigate the charges against Amtes and her fellow conspirators. No record is available to give an account of the verdict of the trial, but Amtes disappeared from the court, perhaps as a result of Weni's decision.

amulet   This was a decoratively carved item that was worn by ancient Egyptians in keeping with their religious traditions. Called the *wedjau,* such an amulet was normally fashioned out of metal, wood, FAIENCE, terracotta, or stone and was believed to contain magical powers, providing the wearer with supernatural benefits and charms. The potential power of the amulet was determined by the material, color, shape, or spell of its origin. Living Egyptians wore amulets as pendants, and the deceased had amulets placed in their linen wrappings in their coffins. Various styles of amulets were employed at different times for different purposes. Some were carved as sacred symbols in order to demonstrate devotion to a particular deity, thus ensuring the god's intercession and intervention on behalf of the wearer.

The DJED, for example, was the symbol of stability that was associated with the god OSIRIS. This was normally worn on the chest, on a cord or necklace. The amulet was placed on the neck of the deceased, in order to protect that part of the anatomy in the afterlife. The *djed* was normally fashioned out of glazed faience, gold, gilded wood, LAPIS LAZULI, or some other semiprecious stone. The *djed* as a national symbol was used in festivals and celebrations.

The ANKH, the EYE OF RÉ, the Amulet of the Heart, the PAPYRUS SCEPTER, and images of the vulture were popular among the faithful. The favored, and most enduring, amulet, however, appears to be the SCARAB, the sacred beetle symbol that represented all of the mystical connotations of the solar cults and eternal life. The scarabs were normally fashioned out of stone, wood, metal, schist, steatite, and bronze (discovered in a Twentieth Dynasty site), and could be small in size or large. They were worn by the living and buried with the dead and were considered more powerful if they were carved with the name of a popular pharaoh.

The BOOK OF THE DEAD, the mortuary text used throughout Egypt's later eras, contained a list of amulets required for the proper preparation of a corpse. One amulet placed in almost every mummy was the *djed.* The scarab and other amulets were placed according to tradition and fashioned out of specific materials, colored red or green normally. Incanted with spells these symbols supposedly were inspired by the god THOTH in HERMOPOLIS in the Old Kingdom (2575–2134 B.C.E.).

Other forms of amulets served specific purposes for the living and the dead. The amulet of the heart, for example, implored the heart of the deceased to defend him or her in the JUDGMENT HALLS OF OSIRIS, where the eternal destination of the deceased was decided by rituals.

The *menat* was an elaborately carved stone hung at the back of the elaborate royal collars to bring good fortune and to balance the weight of the collar. The *thet,* the Girdle of Isis, protected the living and the dead. The *uatcht,* any green stone, alerted the wearer to the presence of magic.

See also MAGIC.

Amun (Amon)   The full name of this god was Sankh-Amun'sekem'tawy, which meant "Amun, the Most Powerful God of the Two Lands Who Sustains Life." A god of ancient Egypt known in early eras but attaining dominance in the New Kingdom at THEBES, Amun (which means "hidden"), figured in the Hermopolitan myths associated with the dynamic force of life. The deity and his female counterpart, AMAUNET, were mentioned in the PYRAMID TEXTS in the Fifth Dynasty (2465–2323 B.C.E.) and Sixth Dynasty (2323–2150 B.C.E.). The first evidence locating the god in Thebes is an inscription of the NOMARCH Rehuy, also of the Sixth Dynasty, who claimed to have performed services for Amun.

When the Thebans began to exert influence over Egypt's political scene, Amun's cult started its ascendancy. During the New Kingdom (1550–1070 B.C.E.) the god was elevated in status and infused with many attributes of other divine beings. Amun was declared to have given birth to himself, and it was stressed that no other gods had such power. All of the other deities in Egypt's pantheon traced their being to his self-creation. Amun was included in the OGDOAD of HERMOPOLIS, then at the PRIMEVAL MOUND of MEMPHIS, at which time he was supposed to have formed all the other gods. He then left the earth to abide as RÉ in the heavens, taking the form of a divine child revealed in the LOTUS.

In statues, Amun was normally depicted as a handsome, virile young man or as a ram with curled horns. The rulers of the New Kingdom carried his banners everywhere in their establishment of the empire, and the temple in Thebes received tributes from many lands. Amun was "the Greatest of Heaven, Eldest of Earth," and the priests of his temple wrote tender hymns in his honor.

The generosity of 'AHMOSE (NEBPEHTIRÉ) (r. 1550–1525 B.C.E.), who made donations to the temple of Amun in thanksgiving for his victories, set a pattern in the New Kingdom, and the god was showered with gifts by 'Ahmose's successors. Both the temples at KARNAK and LUXOR benefited from royal patronage. In time, Amun was revered throughout Egypt, as the Amunite priests assumed more and more political control. In some historical periods, the deity was addressed as Amun-Ré. A shrine was erected for Amun in the SIWA OASIS, which was later called Jupiter Ammon by the Romans, and pilgrimages were undertaken in every era to worship the god there.

At Thebes, Amun was provided with a consort, the goddess MUT, and with a son, KHONS (1) or Khonsu. The ram, the symbol of the god's true spiritual power, was kept at Thebes for religious ceremonies, embodying the energies of the deity and his beauty. During the 'AMARNA Period the temples of Amun were attacked and closed by order of AKHENATEN (r. 1353–1335 B.C.E.). When TUT'ANKHAMUN came to the throne in 1333 B.C.E., he restored the god's primacy over Egypt. This restoration of Amun as the paramount deity of Egypt was calculated to appease the priests of Amun and to settle the unrest caused in the land by the heretical actions of Akhenaten.

Many FESTIVALS were celebrated in honor of Amun. One of these, the "Beautiful Feast of the Valley," was especially popular. The god's statue was taken across the Nile to the western shore of Thebes, where people waited to greet the retinue of priests and devotees. Ritual meals and mortuary offerings were set before the tombs of the dead, while people held picnics in the various mortuary chambers and courts. Amun's priests visited each tomb or grave site, and special Bouquets of the God were placed at the tombs as mementos. Singers and dancers, accompanied by lively bands, followed the priests and conducted rituals. The festivals of Amun were popular throughout Egypt in the New Kingdom.

Further reading: Ashby, Muata Abhaya. *The Hymns of Amun: Ancient Egyptian Mystical Psychology.* New York: Cruzian Mystic, 1997; Assman, Jan, and Anthony Alcock, trans. *Egyptian Solar Religion in the New Kingdom: Re, Amun and the Crisis of Polytheism.* New York: Routledge, 1995.

Amun-dyek'het (fl. seventh century B.C.E.) *queen of the Twenty-fifth Dynasty enslaved by the Assyrians*
The consort of TAHARQA (r. 690–664 B.C.E.), she fell into the hands of ESSARHADDON of Assyria when he invaded Egypt in 671 B.C.E. Taharqa had been routed by Assyrian forces and had fled southward. Taharqa's son and heir, USHANAHURU, as well as the consort, Queen Amun-dyek-'het, and the entire Egyptian court were taken by Essarhaddon to his capital at NINEVEH as slaves and were never seen again in Egypt.

Amunet (Amuniet) (fl. 21st century B.C.E.) *royal woman of the Eleventh Dynasty*
She was a consort of MENTUHOTEP II (r. 2061–2010 B.C.E.), called Amuniet in some records. Amunet was buried in the royal mortuary complex at DEIR EL-BAHRI, a site located on the western shore of the Nile at THEBES. Mentuhotep and his other female companions were entombed beside Amunet. Her sarcophagus listed her as the "King's Sole Favorite," a designation shared by every woman buried in this mortuary complex.

Amunnakhte's Instructions A text written by a scribe of the PER-ANKH, the House of Life, a medical educational institute in THEBES. *Amunnakhte's Instructions* date to the Eighteenth Dynasty (1550–1070 B.C.E.). A copy of the original was discovered in the Chester BEATTY PAPYRUS IV. The *Instructions* were addressed to an assistant, urging the young man to take up the noble profession of scribe, an important position in Egyptian society. The Egyptians revered such didactic LITERATURE, seeking wisdom and purpose in texts that explained the roles of life and the opportunities of service.

Amun's Bark A vessel called Userhetamun, or "the Mighty Brow Is Amun," a floating temple for the god Amun at THEBES, the bark was supposedly a gift presented by 'AHMOSE (NEBPEHTIRÉ) (r. 1550–1525 B.C.E.) in thanksgiving for his successful military campaigns. The vessel was a divine ark, and special STATIONS OF THE GODS were erected throughout Thebes to greet it on its holiday rounds. The bark was viewed as a potent symbol of Amun's power and was refurbished or rebuilt in almost every era of the empire period. On the feast of OPET, the Bark of Amun was moved from KARNAK to LUXOR and back. On other feasts the floating temple sailed on the Nile or on the sacred lake of the shrine. It was covered with gold from the waterline up and filled with cabins, obelisks, niches, and elaborate adornments.

See also BARKS OF THE GODS.

Amun's Wives A title assumed by high-ranking royal women who took part in religious ceremonies at KARNAK and LUXOR during the New Kingdom, Queens AH'HOTEP (1) and 'AHMOSE-NEFERTARI in the reign of 'AHMOSE (1550–1525 B.C.E.) were the first such women to assume the role, serving as patronesses for the festivals and cultic rites. A princess of the royal house was consecrated as the god's spouse, served by virgins in the harem of

Amun. In time this group became the GOD'S WIVES OF AMUN, or the Divine Adoratrices of Amun.

Amun-wosret (15th century B.C.E.) *vizier of the Eighteenth Dynasty*
He served TUTHMOSIS III (r. 1479–1425 B.C.E.) and was active in the latter part of Tuthmosis III's lengthy reign, named VIZIER of Egypt. Amun-wosret served in a time of imperial expansion and military campaigns. His Theban tomb provides details of his office.

Amyrtaios (1) (fl. fifth century B.C.E.) *rebel Egyptian who fought against the Persian occupation of the Nile*
He is associated in some records with the revolt of an individual named INAROS, who threatened the rule of the Persian ARTAXERXES I (r. 465–424 B.C.E.). When Inaros was betrayed, captured, and executed, Amyrtaios continued to hold sway in the western DELTA, unchallenged by the Persians. No documentation is available concerning his length of supremacy in this region.
See also REBELS OF EGYPT.

Amyrtaios (2) (d. 393 B.C.E.) *founder and sole known ruler of the Twenty-eighth Dynasty of Egypt*
Amyrtaios reigned from SAIS originally and then over much of the entire nation from 404 to 393 B.C.E. He probably proclaimed himself pharaoh after the death of DARIUS II in 404 B.C.E. He was possibly a descendant of AMYRTAIOS (1), a rebel of the land. Amyrtaios was the prince of Sais. No documented successors are recorded. One tradition states that Amyrtaios offended "the Law" in some heinous fashion, and because of his transgression could not bequeath the throne to his son. The dynasty ended with his death. Other dynasties flourished in the same era on local levels. Reportedly NEPHRITES I (r. 399–393 B.C.E.) captured Amyrtaios and executed him.

Ana (fl. 18th century B.C.E.) *royal woman of the Thirteenth Dynasty*
She was a consort of SOBEKHOTEP III (r. ca. 1745 B.C.E.). Ana is listed in some records as the mother of Princesses Ankhetitat and Fent-Ankhnet. The rulers and the consorts of this dynasty remain obscure.

Anastasi Papyri This is a collection of Egyptian documents collected from various sources by the Swedish consul to Egypt. This diplomat was on the Nile during the time when extensive exploration was beginning in the ruins of the ancient civilized areas. Some of the papyri date to the Ramessid Period (1307–1070 B.C.E.) and contain hymns to the god AMUN and accounts from that era of Egyptian history.

Anath (Anat) A goddess of the Canaanites, patroness of both love and war, Anath, always depicted as a beautiful young woman and called "the Virgin," was the sister of the Semitic god Baal. Anath was honored as a goddess of war and military campaigns and was adopted by RAMESSES II (r. 1290–1224 B.C.E.) as one of his patrons. In Egypt, Anath was portrayed nude, standing on a lion and carrying flowers. In the Ptolemaic Period (304–30 B.C.E.) Anath was merged with ASTARTE, assuming the name Astargatis. In other eras she was given RESHEF and Baal as consorts in rituals.

Anather (d. ca. 1600 B.C.E.) *Ruler of the Sixteenth Dynasty, a lesser Hyksos line*
His dynasty was contemporary with the Great HYKSOS of the Fifteenth Dynasty at AVARIS (ca. 1640–1532 B.C.E.). Anather was called "the Ruler of the Desert Lands." His dynasty came to an end when the Thebans began their relentless war to remove the Hyksos from the Delta region. SCARABS bearing Anather's name have been found in the Delta region and in southern Palestine.

ancestor cult letters Messages written on clay vessels, strips of linen, or stelae and left in or near tombs. These letters were of two types: friendly, or designed to placate the dead to avoid being haunted. The first type of letters inquired about life "in the West," the land beyond the grave. They also asked for intercessions from the deceased, who were requested to act as patrons in legel procedures on earth or in the judgment courts of the dead. The second asked the dead to rest in peace.
    Some ancestors addressed by the ancestor cult letters were called the *akh-iker-en-Ré,* "the excellent spirit (departed) of Ré." Shrines were erected in households in the New Kingdom Period (1550–1070 B.C.E.), and offerings were made to the *akh-iker-en-Ré.* Some clay figures of these spirits were used in later eras, and an industry emerged for their manufacture. A cache of 17,000 such figures was found in KARNAK.
    See also ANCESTOR WORSHIP.

ancestor worship A cultic tradition of Egypt, associated with the gods OSIRIS and Ré, the dead ancestors were called the *akh-iker-en-Ré,* "the excellent spirit (departed) of Ré" and were the deceased parents of a nonroyal family. In the New Kingdom (1550–1070 B.C.E.) such worship ceremonies employed busts and stelae commemorating the *akh-iker-en-Ré.* Some 150 red effigies made out of stone were found in DEIR EL-MEDINA, the artisan enclave near the VALLEY OF THE KINGS at Thebes. Some 55 stelae were also recovered there. The *akh-iker-en-Ré* traveled endlessly in the bark of Ré and were sometimes portrayed as the rays of the sun in commemoratives. Offerings and prayers were provided for these ancestors at their tombs.

Andjeti He was a very ancient deity of Egypt who was absorbed into the cult of OSIRIS. A shepherd god originally, Andjeti's symbol was the CROOK, called the *AWET*, which was used as a royal insignia of the pharaohs, along with the flail. An ivory crook was discovered in the tomb of the Predynastic Period (before 3000 B.C.E.) ruler SCORPION I, which possibly documents the worship of Andjeti in that era.

Andreas (fl. 3rd century B.C.E.) *medical official of the Ptolemaic Period*
He served as court physician to PTOLEMY IV PHILOMETOR (r. 221–205 B.C.E.). Andreas was skilled in pharmaceuticals and tried to direct the physicians of his era to divorce themselves from the magical or superstitious traditions of the past. He wrote books on the pharmaceuticals available and the effect of serpent bites, but these survive only in fragmented forms.

See also MEDICINE.

Anen (fl. 14th century B.C.E.) *priestly official of the Eighteenth Dynasty*
He served in the reign of AMENHOTEP III (r. 1391–1353 B.C.E.). Anen was the high priest of the temple of HELIOPOLIS, now a suburb of modern Cairo, and the brother of Queen TIYE (1). YUYA and TUYA were his parents. A statue of him in his priestly attire is in the Turin Museum.

Anhai Papyrus This is one of the most elaborately illustrated papyri of the BOOK OF THE DEAD, the ancient Egyptian mortuary texts that evolved over the centuries. Discovered in THEBES, the work depicts the rites of burial and the judgments of the dead. The Anhai Papyrus measures 14 feet six inches and is now in the British Museum, London.

See also TOMB TEXTS.

Anhur A god of ancient Egypt, called Onouris by the Greeks, his name meant "the Sky-Bearer," and he was worshipped in conjunction with the god SHU, another solar deity. The lion goddess Mehit was the consort of Anhur. Anhur was believed to be the warrior aspect of Ré, but he also represented the creative aspects of humans. He was portrayed as a muscular man with an embroidered robe and a headdress of four plumes. Sometimes he had a beard and carried a spear. He was particularly popular in the New Kingdom Period (1550–1070 B.C.E.), when he was addressed as "the Savior" because of his martial powers and his solar connection. Mock battles were conducted at his festival, and he was a patron against enemies and pests. Anhur remained popular in later eras, after the fall of the New Kingdom, especially in ABYDOS. He was also honored at THINIS. NECTANEBO II (r. 360–343 B.C.E.) built a temple for Anhur and in later eras the god was called "the Lord of the Lance." He then was portrayed as an avenger of the god Ré.

Aniba The site of a New Kingdom (1550–1070 B.C.E.) FORTRESS, located between the first and second cataracts in NUBIA, or Kush (modern Sudan), the fort was originally surrounded by three walls and contained the remains of a temple and storage facilities dating to the Middle Kingdom (2040–1640 B.C.E.). The newer structures date to the Eighteenth Dynasty (1550–1307 B.C.E.). A necropolis near Aniba was used for New Kingdom tombs and pyramids. Rock chapels were discovered on the western shore of the Nile, opposite the site, as well as an ancient cemetery plot. In one era, Aniba served as the administrative center for the region. HUY (1), the viceroy of Kush, serving TUT'ANKHAMUN (r. 1333–1323 B.C.E.), resided at Aniba.

Ani Papyrus A document that is one of the surviving BOOKS OF THE DEAD, it measures 178 feet three inches and contains mortuary texts from the New Kingdom (1550–1070 B.C.E.). The Ani Papyrus is noted for its illustrations and its tales and legends, some of which are included in other available papyri of that nature. The LITANY OF OSIRIS and a treatise on the origins of the gods and the union of RÉ and Osiris distinguish the papyrus as well. A feature of the Ani Papyrus is a section that contains the opinions of the various priestly colleges in existence in the New Kingdom.

See also MORTUARY RITUALS; TOMB TEXTS.

ankh The symbol of eternal life in ancient Egypt, as well as the word for physical life, the *ankh* resembled a cross with a loop at the top and represented eternity when positioned in the hands of deities. The symbol dates to the establishment of the cults of the deities ISIS and OSIRIS in the Early Dynastic Period (2920–2575 B.C.E.). The original meaning of the symbol was lost in later periods, but it remained a constant hieroglyphic insignia for life. The *ankh* was used in rituals, especially in those involving the royal cults, and it had special significance when used in various temple ceremonies.

See also AMULET; ETERNITY.

Ankhefenmut (fl. 11th century B.C.E.) *prince of the Twenty-first Dynasty*
He was the son of PSUSENNES I (r. 1040–992 B.C.E.) and Queen MUTNODJMET (2) but did not succeed his father, perhaps because he was a younger son or died early. Ankhefenmut's tomb was prepared for him by Psusennes I in southern TANIS.

Ankhesenamon (Ankhesenpa'aten) (fl. 14th century B.C.E.) *royal woman of the Eighteenth Dynasty*
A daughter of AKHENATEN (r. 1353–1335 B.C.E.) and Queen NEFERTITI, she was born to the royal family in the city of 'AMARNA. Ankhesenamon was married to TUT'ANKHAMUN and became queen when he succeeded SMENKHARÉ in 1333 B.C.E. The royal couple ruled only 10

years. Tut'ankhamun was eight years old when he took the throne and Ankhesenamon was 13. At 'Amarna she was called Ankhesenpa'aten. During her marriage to Tut'ankhamun, she gave birth to two stillborn babies who were buried with the young pharaoh.

Perhaps fearful of the priests and the growing power of HOREMHAB, a general of the armies who had stirred opposition to 'Amarna and the worship of the god ATEN, Ankhesenamon took a drastic step when Tut'ankhamun died. She wrote to King SUPPILULIUMAS I of the HITTITES, an emerging power on the northern Mediterranean, offering herself and the throne to one of his royal sons. A prince, ZANNANZA, set out for Egypt and the wedding but was murdered at the border of Egypt.

AYA (2), a master of the horse in THEBES, was chosen to succeed Tut'ankhamun. As the royal widow, Ankhesenamon was given to him as his bride. Some question has been raised as to the possibility that Aya was the father of Nefertiti, which would have made him Ankhesenamon's grandfather. The couple assumed the throne before the burial of Tut'ankhamun, thus performing the required ritual that each successor had to provide for the deceased pharaoh in the tomb. Aya died in 1319 B.C.E., but Ankhesenamon disappeared from the scene before that, giving way to Aya's wife, TEY, also a commoner.

Ankhesneferibré (fl. sixth century B.C.E.) *royal woman of the Twenty-sixth Dynasty, a God's Wife of Amun*
She was a daughter of PSAMMETICHUS II (r. 595–589 B.C.E.) and Queen TAKHAT (3) adopted by the Divine Adoratrice Nitocris and succeeding her as the GOD'S WIFE OF AMUN in Thebes. Ankhesneferibré served in the office for almost 60 years. Her SARCOPHAGUS, made of basalt, is now in the British Museum in London. A schist statuette of her was also recovered in KARNAK.

Ankh-Hor (fl. sixth century B.C.E.) *vizier and temple official of the Twenty-sixth Dynasty*
He served PSAMMETICHUS II (r. 595–589 B.C.E.) as the VIZIER of Upper Egypt, the overseer of the priests of AMUN, the mayor of MEMPHIS, and the steward of the Divine Adoratrice NITOCRIS (2). Ankh-Hor also served APRIES (r. 589–570 B.C.E.). His tomb at DRA-ABU' EL-NAGA in Thebes is large. The tomb contains PYLONS, courts, pillared halls, and subterranean burial chambers.

Ankhkhaf (fl. 26th century B.C.E.) *princely vizier of the Fourth Dynasty*
He was a son of SNEFRU (r. 2575–2551 B.C.E.), serving the royal family as a VIZIER. This royal line maintained control by using only family members in high positions of trust and authority. Ankhkhaf's statue, actually a bust of exquisite artistry, is in the Museum of Fine Arts in Boston. He married HETEPHERES (2) and predeceased her. His tomb was the largest MASTABA in the eastern cemetery in GIZA.

Ankh-ma-hor (Sheshi) (fl. 23rd century B.C.E.) *medical official of the Sixth Dynasty, noted for his tomb in Saqqara*
Ankh-ma-hor was a VIZIER and physician in the court of PEPI II (r. 2246–2152 B.C.E.). He was buried in SAQQARA in a site called "the street of tombs," and his gravesite is called "the Doctor's Tomb" because of the medical scenes painted on its walls. The tomb has six chambers, including a SERDAB, a room designed to allow a statue of the deceased to watch the daily rituals being offered on his or her behalf. Portraits of Ankh-ma-hor and scenes, including animals and daily activities, are also present. In some records he is listed as Sheshi.

Ankhnesmery-Ré (1) (fl. 23rd century B.C.E.) *royal woman of the Sixth Dynasty*
She was a consort of PEPI I (r. 2289–2255 B.C.E.). The daughter of an official named Khui, and the sister of Djau and ANKHNESMERY-RÉ (2), she became the mother of MERENRÉ. Ankhnesmery-Ré is reported as having died giving birth to this son or dying soon afterward. She was also the mother of Princess NEITH (2), who married PEPI II.

Ankhnesmery-Ré (2) (fl. 23rd century B.C.E.) *royal woman of the Sixth Dynasty*
She was a consort of PEPI I. The daughter of an official named Khui, and the sister of Djau and ANKHNESMERY-RÉ (1), she became the mother of PEPI II. When the young Pepi II succeeded his brother MERENRÉ (I), Ankhnesmery-Ré served as regent for her child. She was aided by Djau, her brother, who served as VIZIER during the regency. They raised the young heir and kept Egypt stable until he reached his majority. The story of the two sisters Ankhnesmery-Ré was discovered on a tablet in ABYDOS.

Ankhnes-Pepi (fl. 22nd century B.C.E.) *royal woman of the Sixth Dynasty*
She was a lesser consort of PEPI II (r. 2246–2152 B.C.E.). Ankhnes-Pepi lived to see her son or grandson, NEFERKURÉ, become the founder of the Eighth Dynasty in 2150 B.C.E. She was buried in a storage chamber and entombed in a sarcophagus borrowed for the occasion from a family friend who had prepared it for his own funeral. Her remains were placed in SAQQARA, in the tomb pyramid of Queen IPUT (2). The tomb of Ankhnes-Pepi was formed by adding a FALSE DOOR to the original burial chamber area of Iput.

Ankhsheshongy (fl. first century B.C.E.) *Egyptian sage who wrote his Instructions ca. 100 B.C.E.*
Preserved on papyrus, this literary work is written in the demotic style and discusses the moral precepts of the age. Traditionally it is believed that Ankhsheshongy wrote his *Instructions* while in prison for some crime, ca. 100 B.C.E. This didactic text was popular, as it echoed the centuries' old spirit of the traditional aspirations of

the Egyptians in a period of Greek dominance and Hellenic literary forms.

Ankh-tawy   The ancient name for the city of MEMPHIS or part of its environs, meaning "Life of the Two Lands." The city's name was changed to Men-nefer-Maré in the Sixth Dynasty in the reign of PEPI I (r. 2289–2255 B.C.E.). He built his pyramid nearby, called by that name. The Greeks translated Men-nefer-Maré as Memphis. Many cities in the Nile Valley were called Ankh-tawy, designating their value to the nation.

Ankhtify (fl. ca. 2100 B.C.E.) *powerful aristocratic rebel*
He was the ranking noble of HIERAKONPOLIS, who resided in el-MOALLA, south of THEBES in the Ninth Dynasty (2134–? B.C.E.). Ankhtify led an army against THEBES and was defeated in his efforts to establish an independent southern kingdom. His tomb in el-Moalla has six chambers and is decorated with paintings depicting various activities and portraits of him and his wife. The biographical hieroglyphs of his tomb reliefs relate the horrors of the First Intermediate Period (2134–2040 B.C.E.), a time of severe drought and chaos. Ankhtify distributed food to the local Egyptians and hoped to better stabilize the area by assuming control of Thebes.

Ankhu (fl. 18th century B.C.E.) *court official and a family of public servants*
Ankhu and his clan served during the Thirteenth Dynasty (1784–ca. 1640 B.C.E.) at el-LISHT and at THEBES. Two of his memorial statues are in the Louvre in Paris. He recorded extensive restorations in ABYDOS. Several generations of the Ankhu family conducted official business for the crown. One Ankhu was in the service of KHENDJER (ca. 1740 B.C.E.) and SOBEKHOTEP III (ca. 1745 B.C.E.).

Ankhwennofre (fl. second century B.C.E.) *rebel of Egypt in the reign of Ptolemy V Epiphanes*
He ruled many areas of the Nile Valley, prompted by the death of PTOLEMY IV PHILOPATOR and the intervention of the Seleucid king ANTIOCHUS III THE GREAT. The Ptolemaic army was defeated by Antiochus III at Panion, resulting in the loss of Egypt's Asiatic possessions. PTOLEMY V focused on Ankhwennofre and defeated him, putting an end to the rebellion and to the threatened succession of Upper Egypt.
   See also REBELS OF EGYPT.

Antefoker (fl. 20th century B.C.E.) *official of the Twelfth Dynasty*
He served SENWOSRET I (r. 1971–1926 B.C.E.) as VIZIER. Antefoker's tomb at SHEIK ABD' EL-QURNA contains long corridors that lead to the burial chamber. These corridors are decorated with vibrant scenes of hunts, agricultural practices, musicians, and a pilgrimage to ABYDOS.

The tomb contained a statue and shrine for Antefoker's wife. A FALSE DOOR was included in the design.

Anti   An ancient Egyptian war god, worshiped in Upper Egypt, having a cult center at DEIR EL-GEBRAWI, near old ASSIUT. The deity was a patron of MERENRÉ I of the Sixth Dynasty (r. 2255–2246 B.C.E.). Honoring Anti was probably part of Merenré's efforts to influence supporters in the southern region. The symbol of Anti was the falcon.

Antigonus I Monophthalmus (Antigonus I Cyclops) (d. 301 B.C.E.) *founder of the Antigonids and an enemy of Egypt*
He was a general under ALEXANDER III THE GREAT (332–323 B.C.E.) and a Macedonian by birth, also called Antigonus I Cyclops (One-Eyed). Antigonus I founded the Macedonian dynasty of Antigonids (306–168 B.C.E.) after Alexander's death. A brilliant military leader, Antigonus served as satrap, or provincial governor, in Phrygia (now part of Turkey), establishing control over Asia Minor and defeating other rivals of the region.
   PTOLEMY SOTER I (r. 304–284 B.C.E.) of Egypt was a competitor for power, and Antigonus clashed with him, defeating the Egyptian forces at SALAMIS in a naval battle that took place in 306. Antigonus was aided in this battle by his son, DEMETRIUS I POLIOCRETES. The two soon attacked Egypt but were unable to overcome Ptolemy's defenses in battle. Ptolemy I then went to the aid of the island of Rhodes, held by Antigonus, and was given the title of *soter,* or "savior," by the grateful populace when he freed them. Antigonus faced a coalition of his rivals at the battle of Ipsus, in Phrygia, and he was slain there in 301 B.C.E.

Antigonus II Gonatas (d. 239 B.C.E.) *ruler of Macedonia and an enemy of Egypt*
He was the son of DEMETRIUS I POLIOCRETES and the grandson of ANTIGONUS I, ruling from 276 to 239 B.C.E. He forced a rival of ANTIOCHUS I, a Seleucid, to renounce claims on Macedonia and slowly gained control of Greece. In 261 B.C.E., during the Chremonidean War, he also managed to keep Egyptian forces out of the Aegean Sea. PTOLEMY II PHILADELPHUS (285–246 B.C.E.) had started the feud and saw his influences weakened as a result. In the Second Syrian War (ca. 260–253 B.C.E.), Antigonus and Antiochus I allied against Ptolemy II. The Egyptian ruler talked Antigonus into a peace treaty and then into marrying his daughter, BERENICE (2), the Egyptian princess.

Antiochus I (d. 29 B.C.E.) *ruler of Commagene involved with Marc Antony*
Antiochus I came from the Seleucid line and ruled Commagene, a city-state on the Euphrates River. His rule was sanctioned by POMPEY in 63 B.C.E., making Antiochus a

figurehead. During Marc ANTONY's Parthian campaign (36 B.C.E.), retreating Parthians sought refuge at Samosata. Antony's lieutenant, Bassus Ventidius, followed them there but was bribed by Antiochus to delay prosecutions. Antony arrived and deposed Antiochus, replacing him with Mithridates II. When AUGUSTUS (formerly Octavian) came to the throne and sent an envoy to Mithridates, Antiochus slew him. Antiochus was captured, taken to Rome, and executed in 29 B.C.E.

Antiochus I Soter (d. 262 B.C.E.) *king of the Seleucid Kingdom of ancient Syria*
He was born in 324 B.C.E. Anointed king of the Seleucid Kingdom in 292 B.C.E., he had to battle against nomads who destroyed his eastern possessions between the Caspian Sea and Aral Sea and the Indian Ocean. In 299 B.C.E., due to PTOLEMY II PHILADELPHUS of Egypt (r. 285–246 B.C.E.), he lost Miletus in southwest Asia Minor, and the Egyptians invaded northern Syria in 276. Antiochus defeated the Egyptians, however, and secured alliances. He died in 262 B.C.E.

Antiochus II (Theos) (d. 246 B.C.E.) *Seleucid king of Syrian territories*
Antiochus II was born ca. 287 B.C.E. He avenged his father, ANTIOCHUS I SOTER, by making war on Egypt. He then found an ally in ANTIGONUS I MONOPHTHALMUS and waged war against PTOLEMY II PHILADELPHUS (r. 285–246 B.C.E.). Successful at first, Antiochus II regained Miletus and Ephesus. In 253, he deposed his queen to marry Ptolemy's daughter, BERENICE (2).

Antiochus III the Great (d. 187 B.C.E.) *Seleucid king of ancient Syria*
He was born in 242 B.C.E., becoming the ruler in 283 B.C.E. Antiochus III fought PTOLEMY IV PHILOPATOR (r. 221–205 B.C.E.) in the Fourth Syrian War and was defeated at RAPHIA. Advancing into India through Parthia, he set up new vassal states. In 192 B.C.E., he invaded Greece but was defeated by the Romans at the battle of Magnesia. In the peace settlement, the Seleucid Kingdom was divided into three parts. He gave his daughter, CLEOPATRA (1), to PTOLEMY V EPIPHANES (205–180 B.C.E.).

Antiochus IV (d. 164 B.C.E.) *Seleucid king who invaded Egypt*
He attacked the Nile in 170 B.C.E., in the reign of PTOLEMY VI PHILOMETER (180–164, 163–145 B.C.E.) and established a "protectorate" over the young king. In 169 B.C.E. Antiochus's renewed invasion again put the government in Memphis in danger. A Roman contingent under Papillius Laenas arrived and set up a display of power at Antiochus's camp. Antiochus was told to withdraw but he asked to be allowed to consider the move. Laenas drew a line in the sand around Antiochus and told

him to give his answer before he stepped outside of the circle. Antiochus withdrew from Egypt. Having been a hostage of Rome as a lad, Antiochus IV was called Epiphane. Other records list him as "the Mad." Forced out of Egypt, he unsuccessfully attacked Jerusalem and died.

Antiochus Hierax (d. 226 B.C.E.) *prince of the Seleucid empire of ancient Syria*
He was the brother of Seleucus II, and the son of ANTIOCHUS II and Queen Laodice. When Seleucus II was involved in the Third Syrian War (246–241 B.C.E.) with PTOLEMY II PHILADELPHUS (r. 285–246 B.C.E.), Antiochus was sent to Asia Minor to become the ruler there. He sent an army into Syria perhaps to overthrow Seleucus. The appearance of Antiochus's troops, however, brought peace between Egypt and Seleucus, who invaded Asia Minor instead. "The War of the Brothers" resulted, lasting from 239 to 236. Antiochus allied himself with the Galatians (Celts) and others to defeat Seleucus at Ancyra in 236.

He found himself thrown out of Asia Minor, however, by an army from Pergamum (aroused by the presence of the Galatians in their area). Antiochus tried other rebellions and was exiled to Thrace (modern Balkans, Greece) in 227 B.C.E. He escaped, fled into the mountains, and tried to raise an army but was killed by a band of the Galatian allies.

Antipater of Idumea (d. 43 B.C.E.) *ruler of Idumea and ally of Egypt*
As an adviser to Queen Alexandra Salome, ruler of Palestine and Judea, Antipater was responsible for bringing Romans into the region by involving King Aretas III in the succession dispute of the queen's sons upon her death in 67 B.C.E. Antipater became minister of the state of Hyrcanus, who was placed on the throne by POMPEY.

In 57 B.C.E., Antipater was given control of the kingdom of Idumea by Aulus GABINUS, the local Roman authority. He joined Gabinus in a campaign to restore PTOLEMY XII NEOS DIONYSIUS (r. 80–58, 55–51 B.C.E.) in Egypt. When CAESAR fought at Pharsalus in 48 B.C.E., Antipater marched to his aid in ALEXANDRIA. Named chief minister in Judea, he was given Roman citizenship. His son Phaesael became governor of Jerusalem, and his other son, Herod the Great, was governor of Galilee. Antipater was poisoned in 43 B.C.E.

Antony, Marc (Marcus Antonius) (ca. 83–30 B.C.E.) *famed Roman general, consul, and lover of Cleopatra VII*
Antony was the son of Antonius Creticus, an unsuccessful admiral, and Julia. His father died early in Antony's childhood, and P. Cornelius Lentulus raised him after marrying Julia. In 63 B.C.E., his adoptive father was strangled on Cicero's order for involvement in the famed Catiline Affair, an act that Antony did not forget and that sparked one of the most bitter feuds in the late years

of the Roman Republic. As he grew to manhood and beyond, Antony earned the reputation for being an insatiable womanizer.

In 58 or 57 B.C.E., he traveled to Syria, joining the army of Gabinius, where as a cavalry commander he served in Egypt and Palestine with distinction. He was in Gaul in 54 B.C.E. as a staff member for Julius CAESAR. This connection proved useful, for in 52 B.C.E., Marc Antony became a quaestor and the most ardent and determined member of the inner circle of Caesar. In 49 B.C.E., while serving as Caesar's tribune in Rome, Antony vetoed the Senate decree stripping Caesar of his command and then joined him in Gaul. The Senate's actions launched the Roman civil war. Returning to Rome, Antony watched over Caesar's interests during the general's Spanish campaign and then commanded the left wing of Caesar's forces at the famous battle of Pharsalus in 48 B.C.E. There Caesar's great enemy, POMPEY the Great, was defeated and forced to flee to what he believed to be sanctuary in Egypt. For his courage and loyalty Antony was made Caesar's coconsul in 44 B.C.E.

Whatever plans Caesar had for Antony died with his assassination at the hands of conspirators on March 15, 44 B.C.E. Antony seized the dead general's papers, read his will, gave the funeral oration, and occupied Caesar's property, representing himself to the people as Caesar's heir.

In the confused and highly charged days that followed, Antony gained control of Cisalpine Gaul and faced the forces of Brutus and Caesar's other assassins, who were joined by Cicero and the Roman Senate and Octavian (the future emperor AUGUSTUS), Caesar's heir. Antony was defeated in April 43 B.C.E., suffering setbacks at Forum Gallorum and especially at Mutina. He retreated into Gallia Narbonensis and there gathered assorted allies and supporters.

The Second Triumvirate, a coalition of political leaders, was established in November of 43 B.C.E., comprising Antony, Octavian, and Lepidus. These men and their forces faced the Republicans (Caesar's assassins) at Philippi in 42 B.C.E., where the last of them fell in battle. Antony took control of the East, with plans to carry out Caesar's planned campaign against Parthia. He was delayed by a meeting with CLEOPATRA VII of Egypt, in Tarsus in 41 B.C.E. The growing rift between Antony and Octavian was furthered in the Perusine War when Fulvia, Antony's wife, and Lucius, his brother, also opposed Octavian in the conflict.

Fulvia's death ended the dispute, and peace was made between Octavian and Antony in 40 B.C.E., at Brundisium. As part of the political settlement, Octavian gave his sister OCTAVIA to Antony in marriage, receiving in return Cisalpine Gaul.

The long-awaited Parthian Campaign of 36 B.C.E. was intended to cement Antony's position in the Roman world, but it proved less than successful. Antony repulsed King Phraates IV of Parthia around Phraaspa but was forced to retreat because of the heat and the clever use of cavalry by the enemy. Antony thus failed to make himself the military equal of the murdered Caesar. He subsequently proved inadequate in replacing Caesar in the realm of politics as well.

Around the same time as his ill-fated campaigns, the weakest member of the triumvirate, Marcus Lepidus, fell from power, leaving mastery of the Roman world to only two combatants. Octavian in effect ruled the western half of the empire and Antony the East. The East tempted Antony with dreams of unlimited power, and he succumbed completely.

Key to Antony's attraction to the East was his legendary affair with Cleopatra VII. She and the vast wealth of Egypt became his principal allies, but as a result, Antony drifted further from Rome and the base of his political power. A final split with Octavian came in 33 B.C.E., followed by a divorce from Octavia. Sensing that universal support would be crucial, Octavian swayed public opinion in Rome by publishing Antony's will, which left large gifts to his illegitimate children by Cleopatra. Antony was stripped of his authority by the Senate, and war was declared upon Cleopatra.

The war climaxed at the battle of ACTIUM, off the west coast of Greece, on September 2, 31 B.C.E. It proved a disaster for Antony, whose personal courage and determination were not enough to overcome the precision of Octavian's fleet or the halfhearted support of the Romans who served Antony's cause. Following the battle, Antony joined Cleopatra in ALEXANDRIA. After a brief effort to stem the Roman advance into Egypt, Antony and Cleopatra killed themselves in August of 30 B.C.E..

Anubis (Anpu; Anup)   The Greek rendering of the Egyptian Anpu or Anup, called the "Opener of the Way" for the dead, Anubis was the guide of the afterlife. From the earliest time Anubis presided over the embalming rituals of the deceased and received many pleas in the mortuary prayers recited on behalf of souls making their way to TUAT, or the Underworld.

Anubis was normally depicted as a black JACKAL with a bushy tail or as a man with the head of a jackal or a DOG. In the PYRAMID TEXTS Anubis was described as the son of Ré and given a daughter, a goddess of freshness. In time he lost both of those attributes and became part of the Osirian cultic tradition, the son of NEPHTYS, abandoned by his mother, who had borne him to OSIRIS. ISIS raised him and when he was grown he accompanied Osiris. He aided Isis when SET slew Osiris and dismembered his corpse. Anubis invented the mortuary rites at this time, taking on the title of "Lord of the Mummy Wrappings." He was also called Khenty-seh-netjer, "the Foremost of the Divine Place" (the burial chamber). He was called as well Neb-ta-djeser, "the Lord of the Sacred Land," the necropolis.

Anubis henceforth ushered in the deceased to the JUDGMENT HALLS OF OSIRIS. The deity remained popular in all periods of Egyptian history and even in the time of foreign domination. Anubis took over the cult of KHEN-TIAMENTIU, an early canine deity in ABYDOS. There he was addressed as Tepiy-dju-ef, "He Who Is on His Mountain." Anubis guarded the scales upon which the souls of the dead were weighed at judgment. He was a member of the ENNEAD of Heliopolis, in that city. Anubeion, a shrine in SAQQARA, was erected to honor Anubis. The deity was also honored with the construction in the galleries of the shrine of a necropolis for canines.

Anukis (Anuket; Anqet) A female deity of Egypt, she was the goddess of the first cataract of the Nile, probably Nubian (modern Sudanese) in origin. She formed a triad with the gods of KHNUM and SATET and was depicted as a woman with a plumed CROWN carrying a PAPYRUS or a SCEPTER. A daughter of the god Ré, Anukis was revered as early as the Old Kingdom (2575–2134 B.C.E.). Her entrance into the divine triad on ELEPHANTINE Island with Khnum and Satet dates to the New Kingdom (1550–1070 B.C.E.). SEHEL ISLAND was one of her cult centers, and she had a temple there. Anukis was considered a female personification of the NILE, as the inundator of the land. She also had a temple at PHILAE and a shrine at ABU SIMBEL.

Aoh (Yah) (fl. 21st century B.C.E.) *royal woman of the Eleventh Dynasty*
She was the consort of INYOTEF III (r. 2069–2061 B.C.E.). The mother of MENTUHOTEP II (r. 2061–2010 B.C.E.), she is sometimes listed as Yah. Aoh was depicted in the company of her royal son on a STELA from his reign. It is not known if Aoh lived long enough to see her son's crusade to unite the Two Kingdoms of Egypt by marching against the KHETY clan in Herakleopolis.

Apedemak A Nubian (modern Sudanese) deity worshipped at MEROË and in some Upper Egypt sites, Apedemak was depicted as a lion. The inscriptions at the deity's shrine on the sixth cataract of the Nile are in Egyptian hieroglyphs.

Apis The sacred BULL of the Ptah-Sokar-Osiris cult in MEMPHIS. The PALERMO STONE and other records give an account of the FESTIVALS held to honor this animal. The ceremonies date to the First Dynasty (ca. 2900 B.C.E.) and were normally called "the Running of APIS." The animal was also garbed in the robes of the Nile god, HAPI (1). The name Apis is Greek for the Egyptian term Hep or Hapi. The sacred bull of Apis was required to have a white crescent on one side of its body or a white triangle on its forehead, signifying its unique character and its acceptance by the gods. A flying VULTURE patch on the back of the animal was also considered a sign that it was eligible for ceremonies. A black lump under its tongue was enough to qualify if all other signs were absent. Each bull was believed to have been conceived in a blaze of fire, according to HERODOTUS.

When a bull of Apis died, an immediate search was begun for another animal with at least one of the markings required. Such animals were dressed in elaborate golden robes and paraded in the ceremonies of PTAH. It is believed that the bull was born of a virgin cow, impregnated by Ptah for a life of service in the temple. The bulls were also used as ORACLES on festival days. In a special chamber in Memphis the animal was turned loose to decide which gate it would enter to seek its food. The gates held symbols as to the positive or negative response to the questions put to the animal by believers.

Each bull was cared for by the priests for a period of 15 to 20 years and then was drowned. Various parts of the animal were then eaten in a sacramental meal in the temple, and the remains were embalmed and placed in the SERAPEUM (1) or in another bull necropolis structure. An alabaster table was used there for embalming procedures, and other tables were found at MIT RAHINAH and Memphis. In the Eighteenth Dynasty (1550–1070 B.C.E.), the bulls were buried in SAQQARA in chapels, then in a catacomb. This developed into the Serapeum. Prince KHA'EMWESET (1), a son of RAMESSES II (r. 1290–1224 B.C.E.), was involved in the Apis liturgies. In time SERAPIS became the human form of Apis, called Osarapis.

King CAMBYSES, who ruled Egypt from 525–522 B.C.E., reportedly stabbed an Apis bull and whipped the Apis priests in a fit of rage. This Persian ruler also presided over the burial of an Apis bull. He was listed by the Egyptians as a "criminal lunatic" because of his sacrilege in dealing with the sacred bulls of Apis.

Apollonius of Rhodes (fl. third century B.C.E.) *director of the Library of Alexandria and a noted poet*
He was born ca. 295 B.C.E. and served as director of the LIBRARY OF ALEXANDRIA, in the reign of PTOLEMY II PHILADELPHUS (r. 285–246 B.C.E.). Apollonius was famous for his *Argonautica*, "the Voyage of Argo," a four-volume epic on the adventures of Jason. The character of Medea, Jason's love, is clearly defined in the work, serving as the first epic in the classical period to employ a woman's viewpoint for dramatic purposes. Apollonius succeeded ZENODOTUS as director of the Library of Alexandria from 260 B.C.E.

Apophis (1) (Apep; Apepi) A giant serpent with mystical powers who was the enemy of the god RÉ. Apophis lived in the waters of NUN, the cosmological area of chaos, or in the celestial waters of the Nile, the spiritual entity envisioned in Egyptian religious texts. He attempted each day to stop Ré from his appointed passage through the sky. In some traditions, Apophis was a previous form of Ré that had been discarded, a myth that accounted for the strength of the creature. Apophis was deemed to be a legitimate threat to Ré by the

Egyptians. On sunless days, especially on stormy days, the people took the lack of sunshine as a sign that Apophis had swallowed Ré and his SOLAR BOAT. Apophis never gained a lasting victory, however, because of the prayers of the priests and the faithful. The ritual document, "the Book of OVERTHROWING APOPHIS," and "the Book of Knowing How Ré Came into Being and How to Overthrow Apophis" were discovered in KARNAK, and in the Papyrus Bremner-Rhind, and contained a list of the serpent's secret names that would wound him if recited aloud and a selection of hymns to be sung to celebrate Ré's victories. A series of terrible assaults were committed upon Apophis each time the serpent was defeated, but he rose in strength that following morning, an image of evil always prepared to attack the righteous. Apophis was the personification of darkness and evil.

Apophis (2) ('Awoserré) (d. 1542 B.C.E.) *ruler of the Fifteenth Dynasty (Hyksos), called "the Great"*
He reigned from ca. 1585 B.C.E. until his death. Apophis ruled over the DELTA region from AVARIS while the Seventeenth Dynasty (ca. 1585–1542 B.C.E.) ruled Upper Egypt from THEBES. He was mentioned in the SALLIER PAPYRI and the RHIND PAPYRUS and on the KARNAK Stelae. His contemporaries were Sekenenré TA'O II and Wadj-Kheperré KAMOSE (r. 1555–1550 B.C.E.) in Thebes. These Theban rulers began to reclaim land during his reign, forcing the HYKSOS to retreat northward.

Apophis sent word to Sekenenré Ta'o II that the snoring hippopotami in the sacred pool at Thebes kept him awake at night with their unseemly noises. This was perhaps a sheer literary device used by the Thebans to justify their cause, but Sekenenré Ta'o II, receiving the message, decreed that it was insult, because Apophis's bedchamber was more than 400 miles away. He promptly declared official war on Avaris and began the campaign to drive them out of Egypt. He was slain in battle or in an ambush, and KAMOSE, his eldest son, took up the crusade with renewed vengeance.

The Hyksos gave way up and down the Nile, and Apophis died in Avaris, possibly from old age or from the stress of seeing the Thebans' victorious advance into his kingdom. He had ruled northern Egypt down to CUSAE. Apophis usurped the colossal sphinxes of AMENEMHET III (r. 1844–1797 B.C.E.). His daughter was HERIT. Her name was found in the tomb of AMENHOTEP I (r. 1525–1504 B.C.E.).

Apries (Wa'a ibré) (d. 570 B.C.E.) *fifth ruler of the Twenty-sixth Dynasty*
He reigned from 589 B.C.E. until his death, the son of PSAMMETICHUS II and probably Queen TAKHAT (3). An active builder, he added sphinxes to the shrine at HELIOPOLIS and aided the revival of the cult of OSIRIS in ABYDOS. He also supported the Palestinian states in their revolt against Babylon, although records indicate that at

one point he withdrew his aid. NEBUCHADNEZZER was on the throne of Babylon during Apries's reign.

Apries then involved Egypt in a dispute between the Libyans and the Greeks. Sending an Egyptian army to aid the Libyans, he saw his units destroyed and faced a mutiny among his native troops. Apries sent his general AMASIS to put down the revolt. Amasis sided with the Egyptian troops and was declared the ruler. Apries, exiled as a result, went to Babylon and returned to Egypt in 567 B.C.E. to face Amasis at the battle of MOMEMPHIS, aided by Babylonian troops, a battle recorded on a massive red stela.

Having only mercenaries in his command, Apries lost the battle. Some records indicate that he was taken as a prisoner to his former palace. After a time he was turned over to the irate Egyptian troops that he had formerly commanded and was slain by them. Apries was given a solemn state funeral by Amasis (r. 570–526 B.C.E.) and buried in SAIS. The tomb of Apries was vandalized by CAMBYSES (r. 525–522 B.C.E.), who dug up his body and had it dismembered. A magnificent black granite heart-shaped vase, dedicated to the god THOTH by Apries, is now in the Egyptian Museum in Cairo. Apries was honored by an invitation to conduct the Olympic games in Greece. He also had a personal bodyguard of Greeks and Carians. His sister, ANKHESNEFERIBRÉ, became a GOD'S WIFE OF AMUN at THEBES.

Arabian Desert The eastern desert of Egypt, mountainous and rutted with deep wadis or dry riverbeds, this hostile region protected Egypt from invaders crossing the Red Sea or the SINAI. The sandy terrain is marked by a chain of hills, from north to south, which rises in some places to a height of 7,000 feet above sea level. The hills provided Egypt with vast quarries and mining areas that yielded granite, diorite, and other stones.

See also NATURAL RESOURCES.

Aramaeans A people from the Syrian desert region who built enclaves in the area and in the modern Levant, by 1069 B.C.E., the Aramaeans were a power, blocking Assyrian advances to the Mediterranean and trading with Egypt and other nations. The language of the Aramaeans was Aramaic, which remained in use until 700 C.E., when Arabic was adopted. In 1069 B.C.E., Adad-apla-iddina was on the throne of Babylon. The last of the true pharaohs, RAMESSES XI (r. 1100–1070 B.C.E.), had just ended his reign on the Nile.

Archelaus Sisines (fl. first century B.C.E.) *last king of Cappadocia (modern Turkey)*
Archelaus was given his realm by Octavian, the future Emperor AUGUSTUS of Rome, in 36 B.C.E. He had been an ally of Marc ANTONY and had made peace with Octa-

vian after recognizing that Rome would prove successful in the confrontation of military might. Ruling until 17 C.E., Archelaus was removed from power by the emperor Tiberius.

Archimedes (d. 212 B.C.E.) *famous Greek scientist who studied in Egypt*
He was born ca. 287 B.C.E. in Syracuse, Greece. Archimedes studied in ALEXANDRIA and then returned to the service of King Hiero II. He was a pioneer in geometry and mechanics, inventing the Archimedean screw and developing the principle concerning displacement of water. He also devised war machines and discovered the relation between the volume of a sphere and its circumscribing cylinder. Archimedes, enthused by his discovery about water displacement, is recorded as stating: "Eureka," which is translated as "I have found it." He also boasted that he, "given a place to stand, could move the earth."

Archimedes was killed in 212 B.C.E. when the Romans conquered Syracuse. He designed his own tomb, forming a sphere inside a cylinder, to demonstrate his theories.

Aristarchus of Samothrace (fl. second century B.C.E.) *director of the Library of Alexandria*
Aristarchus was appointed to that office in 153 B.C.E. in the reign of PTOLEMY VI PHILOMETOR (180–164, 163–145 B.C.E.). He was a Greek critic and grammarian who had studied with ARISTOPHANES OF BYZANTIUM. After serving as director of the famed Alexandrian institution, he retired to Cyprus. Aristarchus was known for his critical studies of Homer, Pindar, Sophocles, Aeschylus, and Herodotus.
See also LIBRARY OF ALEXANDRIA.

Aristophanes of Byzantium (fl. third century B.C.E.) *director of the Library of Alexandria and the founder of the Alexandrian Canon*
Aristophanes was born ca. 257 B.C.E. and became famous for his critical editions of the works of Homer and Hesiod. He also annotated the odes of Pindar and the comedies of the Athenian playwright Aristophanes. His system of accents is still used in modern Greek.

In ca. 195 B.C.E., he was named director of the LIBRARY OF ALEXANDRIA in the reign of PTOLEMY V EPIPHANES (205–180 B.C.E.). He established the Alexandrian Canon, a selection in each genre of LITERATURE that set standards for excellence. He also founded a grammarian school and gained worldwide fame for arranging the Dialogues of Plato.

Arius Didymus (fl. 1st century B.C.E.) *savior of Alexandria after the fall of Marc Antony and Cleopatra VII (d. 30 B.C.E.)*
Arius was a student of Antiochus of Askalon and during that scholastic period became a friend of Octavian (the future emperor AUGUSTUS of Rome). Arius went to ALEXANDRIA with Octavian after the battle of ACTIUM. A stoic philosopher who was enraptured by the intellectual status of Alexandria, Arius convinced Octavian to keep his troops from harming the city.

Arkamani (d. ca. 200 B.C.E.) *ruler of Merok, the Nubian cultural capital*
He ruled in his capital south of ASWAN on the Nile (in modern Sudan) from ca. 218 B.C.E. until his death. Arkamani had good relations with PTOLEMY IV PHILOPATOR (r. 221–205 B.C.E.) and conducted TRADE and building projects with Egypt. He is recorded as having sponsored construction at DAKKA in the period. He is also mentioned on the temple of ARSENUPHIS at Philae.

Ar-Megiddo *See* AR-MEGIDDO, BATTLE OF

Ar-Megiddo, battle of One of the most pivotal battles in the history of ancient Egypt took place at Ar-Megiddo, a fortress on Mount Carmel, in modern Israel. TUTHMOSIS III (r. 1479–1425 B.C.E.), a young and untested pharaoh, started his long military exploits there, routing an army of rebellious city-states.

CONTEXT
Tuthmosis III, who would later be called the Napoleon of Egypt, had been crowned as the young heir to his father, TUTHMOSIS II (r. 1492–1479 B.C.E.), but was in the care of HATSHEPSUT (r.1473–1458 B.C.E.), his stepmother, who served as regent. Hatshepsut took the throne in her own right and became a pharaoh; she proved to be a capable ruler, and had the support of the court and the priests of Amun as she assumed the throne. Tuthmosis III was appointed the commander of Peru-Nefer, the vast naval base near Memphis, but maintained the rank of a pharaoh.

At this time several nations, including Egypt, were interested in Ar-Megiddo, an important site commanding the Euphrates Valley and trade routes of the region. The king of Kadesh ruled there, and he rebelled against Egypt's control of the region. A fortress at Ar-Megiddo was located on a ridge and served as a barrier to any military force coming from the south.

EVENT
Although Hatshepsut was a queen-pharaoh, and may have led some military campaigns or had them conducted in her name, it was believed that no woman could command the Egyptian army in such a vast and critical undertaking. In addition, Hatshepsut's future was already in doubt, as she was at this time very ill from both a systemic infection caused by an abscessed tooth and a cancerous tumor, and kept to her own royal suite. Tuthmosis III was thus designated as the full commander and rightful pharaoh.

Egypt had a standing army and other special military units at the time. In the earlier eras, each pharaoh would summon the military units from the various nomes, or provinces, and they would march under their own banners and follow the king to war. However, with the coming of the New Kingdom Period (1550–1070 B.C.E.) and the beginning of the empire, Egypt needed, and so established, standing armies and trained regiments. Tuthmosis reportedly led some 30,000 troops toward Mount Carmel, leaving Egypt on April 19 and reaching the mountain on May 10.

Some of the troops Tuthmosis III led were the famous Medjay, Nubian (modern Sudanese) warriors and berserkers who were known for appearing unaffected by any wounds they received until after the enemy was dead. The Medjay had served Egypt from the earliest eras and acted as metropolitan police in times of peace. Tuthmosis III's main forces, meanwhile, consisted of cavalry units and infantry, and they moved swiftly on the Way of Horus, a military highway maintained over the decades. It is probable that a large number of the troops were transported by ship and united with Tuthmosis somewhere on the Mediterranean coast. Scouts, probably the Medjay, moved ahead of the Egyptian forces and reported to Tuthmosis that Kadesh and his allies were positioned for battle on the main road leading to the village of Aruna in front of Mount Carmel, far from Ar-Megiddo.

Nearing the Aruna road, where Kadesh and his allies waited, Tuthmosis III made a startling decision. He told his commanders that they would divert from the main road and use a pathway over Mount Carmel that the scouts had discovered. His veteran officers protested because the path was narrow, steep, and some 40 miles long. Tuthmosis gave the command despite the counsel of his veteran officers, and the Egyptians adandoned the main advance to lead horses, chariots, and units up a path over the mountain itself. For 40 miles the army traveled single file up the side of Mount Carmel. Reaching the top after hours of climbing, Tuthmosis had his men scout for a place to rest.

The Egyptians camped just north of Ar-Megiddo, using the banks of the river Kina to hide their position. The troops rested and waited, and then Tuthmosis and his cavalry attacked the enemy. The Egyptians were behind enemy lines, blocking retreat. Kadesh and his fellow rebels, panicking at the sight, abandoned their chariots and weapons and fled to the fortress of Ar-Megiddo, scrambling up cliffs and hills to reach the safety of the fortified structure. Some reached the fort, but many died at the hands of the Egyptians. The rebels who were slow in reaching the fort found the gates blocked against them, and they climbed up the walls using ropes made out of linens and clothing.

The Egyptians troops stopped attacking the enemy in order to gather weapons and other possessions left by the retreating enemy. In the resulting lull, Kadesh escaped. Tuthmosis III was furious and began scolding the troops. The battle had ended, and the rebels within the fortress wept with relief. Then they heard the sound of the Egyptians outside of their fortress walls. Another wall was being built around Ar-Megiddo. In typical Egyptian fashion, this wall was called "Menkheperre (Tuthmosis's throne name) Is the Surrounder of the Asiatics."

Tuthmosis III built the first documented siege wall in history. Seeing it secure, he left a small unit on the wall to kill anyone trying to escape, and with his main force marched on to ravage the city-states that had opposed him. Instituting a new policy that proved successful, Tuthmosis III gathered up the young aristocratic and royal men and women of the conquered city-states and sent them back to THEBES (modern Luxor) to be educated as Egyptians so that they could go back to become vassal rulers of their native lands.

Siege warfare was common in the historical period, but actual walls around cities under attack have not been recorded. Within the Ar-Megiddo fortress, people died in agony, their cries heard by their captors patrolling the area. Water and food disappeared, and cholera and other diseases claimed new victims each day. Tuthmosis and the main army units later returned back to the fortress when the surrender took place.

As the surrendered inhabitants walked out of the front gate of the fortress, Egyptian officers designated each individual's fate. The leaders of the rebel forces died at the hands of their captors. The common soldiers, minor officers, and all noncombatants were given water and food and granted their freedom.

Afterward Tuthmosis returned to Thebes to celebrate the feast of Opet, during which he received praise for his military prowess. He would spend his life in military campaigns, and the Ramessid clan that followed his dynasty to the throne would carry Egypt's banners forward with renewed ferocity. During the Eighteenth and Nineteenth Dynasties (1550–1307 B.C.E.) the Egyptian Empire reached its zenith. Egypt ruled over an estimated 400,000 square miles of the Middle East, from modern Khartoum in the Sudan to Carchemish on the Euphrates River and westward to the Siwa Oasis.

IMPACT

News of the fall of Ar-Megiddo resounded throughout the world. Survivors returning to their homelands described the horrors they had endured, and their words were carried along in trade caravans and in diplomatic missions.

Egypt and Tuthmosis III were suddenly known to the wider world, as word of the siege and particularly the siege wall itself, an innovation that brought dread, was spread along with descriptions of the Egyptian ascent of Mount Carmel to other nations. The survivors of Ar-Megiddo had called the event "the end of the world," with the name of the site literally translating in English to "Armageddon," a term that has lived on through modern times.

The siege and victory for Tuthmosis III signaled that Egypt had truly reached a position of political and military ascendancy over the Near East and Palestine and that Egypt was about to enjoy its greatest extent as an empire. Moreover, the triumph allowed Egyptian cultural ascendancy as well. Tuthmosis III demanded that the vanquished enemies send a son to the Egyptian court. There, the youths were trained in Egyptian language and culture; this effectively created vassals not merely familiar with Egyptian customs, but vassals predisposed toward Egyptian policies and accepting of the concept of Egyptian hegemony.

Arsamis (fl. fifth century B.C.E.) *Persian satrap of Egypt in the reign of Darius II (424–404 B.C.E.)*
He was away from Egypt at the time when the priests of the god KHNUM at the ELEPHANTINE Island, at modern ASWAN, decided to harass the Jewish community there. The priests bribed the local military commander, VIDA RANAG, and destroyed the Jewish temple on the Elephantine. Arsamis punished Vidaranag, but no effort was made to rebuild the temple. A petition was sent to Bago as, the governor of Judah, asking that the temple be restored. That request was ultimately granted.

Arsenuphis (Harsenuphis) A Nubian deity associated with the goddess ISIS, Arsenuphis wore a plumed CROWN. He received tributes from pharaohs of the New Kingdom (1550–1070 B.C.E.) and had a cult center at MEROË. He was addressed as "Iry-hemes-nefer" (the Good Companion)" and was worshipped at DENDEREH. In the reign of PTOLEMY IV PHILOPATOR (221–205 B.C.E.), a shrine to Arsenuphis was built at the PHILAE temple of ISIS. The Meroë ruler, Arkamani (r. ca. 218 B.C.E.–200 B.C.E.), aided Ptolemy IV in this project.
See also GODS AND GODDESSES.

Arses (d. 336 B.C.E.) *ruler of Persia and Egypt, who was murdered*
He reigned only from 338 B.C.E. until his untimely death. The youngest son of ARTAXERXES III OCHUS and Queen Atossa, Arses came to the throne when a eunuch court official, BAGOAS, murdered the king and his eldest sons. Arses witnessed an invasion of Asia Minor (modern Turkey) by Philip of Macedonia. Alert to the treacheries of Bagoas, Arses tried to poison the eunuch but was slain with his children. His successor was DARIUS III CODOMAN.

Arsinoe (1) (fl. third century B.C.E.) *royal woman of the Ptolemaic Period*
She was the consort of PTOLEMY II PHILADELPHUS (r. 285–246 B.C.E.). The daughter of LYSIMACHUS, the king of Thrace, she became the ranking queen of "Great Wife" of the ruler. Arsinoe bore him three children, including PTOLEMY III EUERGETES, his heir. The marriage, which took place ca. 282 B.C.E., was part of an alliance between Thrace and Egypt against Syria.

Despite producing an heir, Arsinoe was repudiated when Ptolemy Philadelphus's sister, another ARSINOE (2), came to the court. She was accused of trying to assassinate Ptolemy Philadelphus and was banished to the city of KOPTOS in Upper Egypt. Ptolemy's sister married the king and adopted Arsinoe (1)'s children.

Arsinoe (2) (fl. third century B.C.E.) *royal woman of the Ptolemaic Period*
She was the daughter of PTOLEMY I SOTER (r. 304–284 B.C.E.) and Queen BERENICE (1). A sister of PTOLEMY II PHILADELPHUS (r. 285–246 B.C.E.), Arsinoe was married to LYSIMACHUS, the king of Thrace. She received three cities on the Black Sea and another one in northern Greece upon her marriage. To gain access to the Thracian throne for her own children, Arsinoe charged the heir to the throne, AGATHOCLES (1), of attempting to murder Lysimachus. The result of Lysimachus's decision to execute his son was a war between Thrace and the Seleucid Kingdom.

Lysimachus died in 281, and Arsinoe fled to her half brother, Ptolemy Ceraunus. When she entered Cassandria, a city in northern Greece, Ptolemy Ceraunus executed her two younger sons. She fled to ALEXANDRIA and arrived ca. 279 B.C.E.

Charges were made against Ptolemy II Philadelphus's wife, ARSINOE (1) of Thrace, and she was sent to KOPTOS in Upper Egypt, in exile. Arsinoe married her brother, and he received the title "Brother Loving," Philadelphus, as a result. Arsinoe aided Ptolemy II in his war against the Syrians (274–271 B.C.E.). She was given many titles and honors, including the Arsinoeion, a great shrine in Alexandria. A part of the FAIYUM region was also dedicated to her name. At her death she became the goddess Philadelphus.

Arsinoe (3) (fl. third century B.C.E.) *royal woman of the Ptolemaic Period*
She was the consort of PTOLEMY IV PHILOPATOR (221–205 B.C.E.). They were brother and sister, as she was the daughter of PTOLEMY III EUERGETES and Queen BERENICE (3). In 217, Arsinoe accompanied her husband to the Egyptian army camp in Palestine, where she encouraged the troops to win against the Seleucids in a battle there. She gave birth to the heir, PTOLEMY V EPIPHANUS, in 210 B.C.E.

The court under Ptolemy IV Philopator was quite depraved. Arsinoe tried to stem the debauchery and made many enemies among the courtiers. When Ptolemy IV Philopator died in 205, these courtiers plotted to murder Arsinoe, accomplishing that deed in 204 B.C.E. The heir was protected by the courtiers who did not announce the death of Ptolemy IV or Arsinoe until Ptolemy V Epiphanus was crowned. Rioting resulted from word of her murder.

Arsinoe (4) (fl. first century B.C.E.) *royal woman of the Ptolemaic Period*

She was the daughter of PTOLEMY XII Neos Dionysius (80–58, 55–51 B.C.E.) and sister of the famed CLEOPATRA VII (51–30 B.C.E.). Arsinoe attempted to rouse the Egyptians against Cleopatra VII and Julius CAESAR. When Caesar rounded up the Egyptians aligned against him, Arsinoe escaped. Her patron, Ganymedes, aided her in her flight and she joined the army led by ACHILLAS, intent on destroying the Romans and her sister. When Achillas argued with her, Arsinoe ordered him executed.

In a treaty with Caesar, Ganymedes exchanged Arsinoe for the captive PTOLEMY XIII. When the Romans conquered the Egyptian forces, Arsinoe was taken to Rome, where she was led through the streets as part of Caesar's triumph. After this humiliation, Arsinoe went to Ephesus in Asia Minor and took refuge in the temple of Artemis there. In 41 B.C.E., however, she was hunted down by Marc ANTONY's agents and slain because she posed a threat to Cleopatra VII. Her death caused a scandal in Egypt and in Rome because it involved the violation of religious sanctuary. The tomb of Arsinoe at Ephesus was later opened, and her skull and bones were removed for forensic testing. Using the genetic results, experts reproduced the face of Arsinoe, creating her first known portrait.

Arsinoe (5) (fl. third century B.C.E.) *royal woman of the Ptolemaic Period*

She was the wife of LAGUS, a general of the army of ALEXANDER III THE GREAT (332–323 B.C.E.). Arsinoe bore PTOLEMY I SOTER (304–284 B.C.E.), who became the satrap of Egypt under Alexander the Great and the founder of the Ptolemaic Dynasty.

Arsinoe (6) A site erected by PTOLEMY II PHILADELPHUS (285–246 B.C.E.) near Crocodilopolis in his efforts to restore the FAIYUM region of Egypt, many papyri were discovered in the ruins of Arsinoe.

Arsinoe (7) A site erected by PTOLEMY II PHILADELPHUS (285–246 B.C.E.) near modern Ardscherud, beside Suez at the northern end of the gulf, the city was the terminal point for a canal that dated back centuries. In time Arsinoe became a port for Red Sea trade wares.

Artabanus (Ardahan) (fl. fifth century B.C.E.) *commander of the palace guard and the slayer of Xerxes I (486–466 B.C.E.)*

Also called Ardahan, he is credited with killing Xerxes I's son Darius, either before or after killing XERXES I. Artabanus was in control of Persia for seven months and was recognized by Egypt as king. He was slain by ARTAXERXES I (465–424 B.C.E.), Xerxes' son, after the Persian general MEGABYZUS turned on him in 464/465 B.C.E.

art and architecture The art of ancient Egypt, including the architectural splendors, has transcended the passage of time and the political realities of evolving civilization and has been the focus of study and examination for centuries. Art in Egypt was not a part-time or simple occupation. The people of the Nile Valley were imbued with spiritual visions and regulations concerning the representation of the life around them. This adherence to tradition made Egyptian art and architecture enduring.

The art and architecture of the ancient people of the Nile illuminate the national concern with the worship of the gods and the cultic beliefs in eternal life. Such images arose early in the Nile Valley and assumed new dimensions as the national culture developed.

PREDYNASTIC PERIOD (BEFORE 3000 B.C.E.)

Art

The people of the Nile Valley began producing art as early as the seventh millennium B.C.E. Decorative patterns consisted of geometric designs of varying shapes and sizes and obscure symbols representing totems or cultic priorities. Direct representational drawings, mainly of animals and hunters, came at a slightly later date. Evidence of these sorts of artistic advances among the Neolithic cultures in Upper Egypt and NUBIA (modern Sudan) is provided by the drawings of boats and domesticated animals, most notably at HIERAKONPOLIS, where some elements of the Mesopotamian and Saharan styles are evident.

Pottery of the Predynastic Period, as well as figures fashioned out of bone and ivory, initiated the artistic motifs that would be influential for many centuries. Vessels and palettes accompanied fine black-topped pottery, leading to red polished ware decorated with cream-colored paint. The light-on-dark painting technique made pottery of this period distinctive. While geometric designs were developed first, artisans began to experiment with human, plant, and animal forms as well. An excellent example is the bottom of a bowl with entwining hippopotami. Such bowls can be dated to the NAGADA I Period (4000–3500 B.C.E.), also called Amratian (from el-'Amra). The ultimate achievement of this period was the mastering of Egypt's most famous artistic medium: stone.

In the NAGADA II Period (3500–3000 B.C.E.), also called the Gerzean (from Girza), stone pieces were being fashioned with regularity. Some of the most notable examples of these were discovered in a cemetery in the Girza district, the Thinite nome of Upper Egypt. Ivory and stone figures were carved in cylindrical form, crude in detail but remarkable for their size. Reliefs in stone and statuary were also used by the cult of the god MIN (1). Technical advances were evident in the pieces recovered in Hierakonpolis (both in stone and faience), and in ABYDOS and HALWAN.

Stone PALETTES and MACEHEADS appeared at the end of the Predynastic Period but with a clarified sense of composition. The Oxford palette from Hierakonpolis is probably the earliest example of this form, along with the Louvre fragment and the macehead of SCORPION I. Of primary importance in the development of composition was the NARMER PALETTE, a green slate slab from Hierakonpolis intended to serve as a tablet on which cosmetics were blended. The palette, utilitarian in purpose, was crucial nevertheless from an artistic standpoint. The style of later Egyptian art is also remarkably visible in the depiction on these pieces of the military campaigns in the Delta. Vitality, power, and a certain sense of drama are incorporated into the carvings. The palette thus was a model for later generations of artists. Increased regulation of human representation came later with the canon of Egyptian art.

Architecture

Architecture in the Predynastic Period evolved at the same pace as reliefs, painting, and sculpture. Writing and the construction of tombs and temples were the almost immediate result of the rise of political centralization in the late Nagada II (or Gerzean A) Period. The few remaining examples of architecture in this era point to the use of mud brick, demonstrated in the painted chamber, Decorated Tomb 100, at Hierakonpolis. Cities were being erected with walls, projecting towers, and gates, the designs of which were preserved on the palettes of this time and thus survived to influence later historical periods.

Of particular interest architecturally are the average dwellings of the Egyptians. The earliest abodes were probably versions of tents or roofless areas protected from the wind and rain by walls or thickets. Eventually mud was utilized to make walls, thus providing the models for the first actual residences. The mud, daubed at first onto thatched walls, was later turned into bricks, sun dried and considerably more durable. Buildings were circular or oval in design, but innovations in wall constructions, such as battering (the process of sloping walls to provide sturdier bases), provided artistic flair and balance. Windows and doors were employed at the same time. The windows were set into walls at high levels, and both portals were trimmed with wood, a material that became scarce in later periods.

In Upper Egypt there were definite advances, but generally speaking, one of three basic plans was followed in construction. The first was a rectangular structure with paneled sides and a hooped roof. The second was a rectangular pavilion with a vaulted roof. The third was the SEREKH (1) design. This was a large system of elaborately paneled facings and niches. Flax chalk lines (lines drawn in chalk after being measured with taut ropes) were used early for construction measurements.

EARLY DYNASTIC PERIOD (2920–2575 B.C.E.) AND THE OLD KINGDOM (2575–2134 B.C.E.)

Art

Although the Early Dynastic Period and the Old Kingdom are noted for the rapid and impressive development of architecture, as evidenced in tombs, TEMPLES, the evolving MASTABA, and the PYRAMID, the decorative arts flourished as well. Craftsmen produced exceptional pieces of statuary, painting, furniture, jewelry, and household instruments, which all benefited from experimentation.

Sculpture in the round (freestanding statues) fulfilled a ceremonial need for display in religious matters and provided representation of the royal lines. Most statues were made of limestone or granite. Sometimes wood, clay, or even bronze was used, but such materials were rare. Sculpture followed the same convention as painting and relief, displaying a stylistic similarity. Statues were

A statue of the Old Kingdom Period pyramid builder Khafre displays the flowering of art in the early eras of Egypt. *(Hulton Archive)*

compact and solid, notable for the air of serenity and idealized features that they imparted to their subjects. Such idealization was a key element in the art of the time, formalized into powerful conventions. Portraiture was not practiced on the elite, but realism emerged in the statues of the commoners or lesser-known individuals. The eyes of the statues were sometimes brought to life by the insertion of stones into the eye sockets. Paint-

THE CANON OF THE HUMAN FIGURE

The set of artistic regulations called the canon of the human figure evolved in the Early Dynastic Period and was used by the ancient Egyptians as a model for representing the human figure in reliefs and paintings. This evolved within the parameters of cultic traditions. The Predynastic Period Egyptians, already deeply concerned with spiritual matters, had a need to communicate ideas and ideals through the representation of divine beings, human personages, and events. From the beginning, the Egyptians understood the propagandistic aspects of art and formulated ways in which artistic representations could serve a didactic purpose. Art was meant to convey information.

The canon of the human figure was the result of such concerns, and it was a convention by which representations could convey metaphysical concepts while at the same time bringing a vision of the material world to the viewer. The canon dealt mainly with paintings and reliefs as they were used in mortuary structures and cultic shrines, and it governed the representation of three-dimensional elements on a two-dimensional surface, which demanded anatomical knowledge, perspective, and idealized composition.

Early examples demonstrate an increasing sophistication in such compositions, represented by the NARMER PALETTE of the Predynastic Period. The Narmer Palette integrated all of the earlier artistic elements while displaying a unique energy and vitality. With the start of the Old Kingdom (2575 B.C.E.), artistic conventions were being codified to provide generations of artists with formal guidelines on the proper positioning of the human figures within a scene or a pictorial narrative, or a framework of hieroglyphs and cultic symbols. According to the canon, the human figure was to be composed in a prescribed manner. To facilitate execution in reliefs and paintings, a surface was divided into 18 rows of squares (the 19th reserved for the hair). In later historical periods more rows were added.

The human figure, when sketched or traced onto a surface, was depicted from a dual perspective. The head was always shown in profile, but the human eye and eyebrow were depicted in full view. The shoulders and upper torso were also shown in full view, so that the arms, hands, and fingers were visible. The abdomen from armpit to the waist was shown in profile and the navel was normally placed on the side of the figure, directly on the edge. The legs and feet were also shown in profile, balancing the head, and until the mid-Eighteenth Dynasty (ca. 1400 B.C.E.) the inside of the feet was preferred over the outside in human representations.

The canon of the human figure, the artistic standard introduced in the Old Kingdom Period and demonstrated in this mortuary relief of the official Hesiré *(Hulton Archive)*

The canon was strictly observed when artists portrayed the ruling class of Egypt. The formality allowed by the canon and its idealized conception lent grace and authority, deemed critical to royal portraits. While one might expect rigidity and a certain staleness to result from this type of regimentation, the canon provided a framework for continual elaboration, and the teams of artists who worked together to adorn the private and public shrines found a common ground for individual expression.

Artistic quality was maintained, and the needs of each generation were incorporated into the standards regulating fine art.

ings and reliefs displayed a religious orientation. As part of the decoration of mortuary complexes they depicted architectural and hunting scenes, paradise scenes, and depictions of everyday life, with references to the Nile River and its marshlands. One remarkable tomb at MEIDUM depicts uniquely beautiful paintings of geese, portrayed with engaging naturalism.

At the close of the Fourth Dynasty (2465 B.C.E.) the art of depicting figures and scenes in shrunken reliefs was started. The outline of the form was cut sharply into the surfaces of the walls, leaving enough space to emphasize the figure. Shadows thus emerged, accentuating line and movement while protecting the forms from wear. In this era the solar temples (designed to honor RÉ, the sun god, and to catch the sun's rays at dawn) were being erected along the Nile, and artists began to depict the natural loveliness of the landscape and the changing seasons, as well as the heavenly bodies.

Wall surfaces were marked by red and black lines in the first stage of painting, allowing the artists to develop scope and perspective. Once the carvings were completed, the walls were given a light coat of stucco, and some were touched by paints of various hues. The figures were outlined one last time so that they would come to life against the neutral backgrounds.

Furniture from this period shows the same remarkable craftsmanship and fine details, as evidenced by the funerary objects of Queen HETEPHERES (1), the mother of KHUFU (Cheops) (r. 2551–2528 B.C.E.). Wooden furniture inlaid with semiprecious stones graced the palaces of that era, and Hetepheres was buried with chairs, beds, a canopy, and gold-covered boxes. She had silver bracelets and other jewelry pieces of turquoise, lapis lazuli, and carnelian. CROWNS and necklaces, all of great beauty, adorned the royal mother while she lived and were placed in her tomb to adorn her throughout eternity.

Architecture

By the time the Early Dynastic Period was established in MEMPHIS, experimentation and the demands of the mortuary rituals challenged the architects of Egypt to provide suitable places for the dead. The mastaba, the rectangular building erected with battered walls and subterranean chambers and shafts, became more and more elaborate. Small temples were fashioned out of stone, and one such place of worship constructed at the end of the Second Dynasty (2649 B.C.E.) was composed of granite. Stelae began to appear. They were round-topped stone slabs designed to hold inscriptions commemorating great events and personages, religious and secular. SAQQARA became an elaborate necropolis for Memphis, and other mortuary complexes were erected in ABYDOS, the city dedicated to the god OSIRIS.

The turning point in such complexes came during the reign of DJOSER (2630–2611 B.C.E.) when IMHOTEP, his vizier, fashioned the STEP PYRAMID on the Saqqara plain. This structure, composed of mastabas placed one on top of the other, became the link between the original tomb designs and the true pyramids of the next dynasty. The pyramid complexes that emerged in the Fifth Dynasty (2465–2323 B.C.E.) consisted of VALLEY TEMPLES, causeways, MORTUARY TEMPLES, and accompanying subsidiary buildings. In time, they became the eternal symbol of Egypt itself and were included in the Seven Wonders of the Ancient World.

These pyramids reflected not only mathematical and construction skills but other aspects of Egyptian civilization. Rising from the plain of GIZA and at other locations, the structures were no longer simple tombs but stages for elaborate ceremonies where priests offered continual prayers and gifts as part of an ongoing mortuary cult. Later pharaohs were forced to reduce the size of their pyramids, eventually abandoning the form entirely because of a lack of resources, but the Giza monuments remained vivid examples of Egypt's architectural glories.

MIDDLE KINGDOM (2040–1640 B.C.E.)

Art

At the close of the Old Kingdom, the authority of Egypt's rulers had eroded, bringing about severe civil unrest. One of the consequences was a decline in both art and architecture. The Eleventh Dynasty (2040–1991 B.C.E.) reunited Upper and Lower Egypt and resumed patronage of the arts and the building of monuments. The art of this new age was marked by realism and by a new degree of classical motifs that were revived from the Old Kingdom. An elegant and elaborate style was popular and detail became paramount, as evidenced in the head of SENWOSRET III (r. 1878–1841 B.C.E.) of the Twelfth Dynasty, in which a portrait of his age and weariness are realistically depicted.

The jewelry of this period is famous in modern times because of a cache of necklaces, bracelets, and pectorals discovered in DASHUR, the mortuary site of the Twelfth Dynasty. Beautifully crafted of enameled gold and semiprecious stones, it attests to the artistic skill of the era. Another treasure found at el-LAHUN yielded golden wire diadems with jeweled flowers, as well as a dazzling variety of bracelets, collars, and pectorals of semiprecious stones set in gold.

Architecture

Under the nomarchs—the rulers of the nomes, or provinces, in outlying districts who were able to maintain their authority amid general unrest—architecture survived the fall of the Old Kingdom, resulting in such sites as BENI HASAN, with its rock-carved tombs and large chapels, complete with porticoes and painted walls. The Eleventh Dynasty, however, resumed royal sponsorship of architectural projects, symbolized by the mortuary complex of MENTUHOTEP II (r. 2061–2010 B.C.E.), at DEIR EL-BAHRI on the western shore of THEBES. The temple there influenced later architects and was the first complex set on terraces of varying height with a columned portico at the rear, forming a facade of the tomb. The tomb area was recessed into a cliff.

During the Middle Kingdom most of the temples were built with columned courts, halls, and chambers for rituals. The sanctuaries of these shrines were elaborate, and most had small lakes within the precincts. KARNAK was begun in this era, and in time the temple would become the largest religious complex in the history of the world. The famed temple of LUXOR would be linked to Karnak with an avenue of ram-headed SPHINXES.

Residences of the upper classes and some of the common abodes began to assume architectural distinction as well. Made of sun-dried brick and wood, most villas or mansions had two or three floors, connected by staircases. Storehouses, a separate kitchen area, high ceilings, and vast gardens were parts of the residential designs. Some had air vents for circulation, and all of these houses, whether owned by aristocrats or commoners, had gently sloping roofs on which Egyptian families slept in warm weather. Made of vulnerable materials, no physical examples of domestic architecture from this era survive.

Little is known of the palaces or royal residences of this period because they too were fashioned out of brick and wood. It is clear that the palaces (PERO or per-a'a) always contained two gateways, two main halls, and two administrative sections to reflect the upper and lower regions of the nation. FLAGSTAFFS were used at the gates, as they were placed before temples. The remains of the Seventeenth Dynasty (1640–1550 B.C.E.) palace at DEIR EL-BALLAS, on the western shore north of Thebes, indicate somewhat luxurious surroundings and innovative decoration, following the "double" scheme. In some instances the walls and floors were designed to portray pools of fish and vast tracts of flowering shrubs.

The Second Intermediate Period (1640–1532 B.C.E.) and the domination of the north by the HYKSOS curtailed artistic endeavors along the Nile, although the arts did not vanish. A renaissance took place, however, with the arrival of the New Kingdom after the Hyksos were driven from the land.

NEW KINGDOM (1550–1070 B.C.E.)

The New Kingdom is recognized as a period of great artistic horizon, with art and architecture evolving in three separate and quite distinct eras: the Tuthmossid Period, from the start of the New Kingdom (1550 B.C.E.) to the end of the reign of AMENHOTEP III (1353 B.C.E.), the 'AMARNA Period (1353–1335 B.C.E.), and the Ramessid Period (1307–1070 B.C.E.).

Art
Tuthmossid Period

With the expulsion of the Hyksos and the reunification of Upper and Lower Egypt, the pharaohs of the Eighteenth Dynasty, called the Tuthmossids, began elaborate rebuilding programs in order to reflect the spirit of the new age. Sculpture in the round and painting bore traces of Middle Kingdom standards while exhibiting innovations such as polychromatics and the application of a simplified cubic form.

Osiride figures, depictions of Osiris or of royal personages assuming the deity's divine attire of this time, were discovered at Deir el-Bahri in Thebes and are of painted limestone, with blue eyebrows and beards and red or yellow skin tones. Such color was even used on black granite statues in some instances. Cubic forms popular in the era are evidenced by the statues of the chief steward SENENMUT and Princess NEFERU-RÉ, his charge, encased in granite cubes. These stark forms are nonetheless touching portraits, enhanced by hieroglyphs that interpret their rank, relationship, and affection for one another. Other statues, such as one fashioned in granite as a portrait of TUTHMOSIS III (r. 1479–1425 B.C.E.), demonstrate both the cubist and polychromatic styles.

Sculpture was one aspect of New Kingdom art where innovations were forged freely. In painting, artists adhered to the canon established in earlier eras, but incorporated changes in their work. Egypt's military successes, which resulted in an empire and made vassals of many Mediterranean nations, were commemorated in pictorial narratives of battles or in processions of tribute-bearers from other lands. A grace and quiet elegance permeated the works, a sureness borne out of prosperity and success. The surviving tomb paintings of the era display banquets and other trappings of power, while the figures are softer, almost lyrical. The reign of AMENHOTEP III (r. 1391–1353 B.C.E.) brought this new style of art to its greatest heights.

'Amarna

The city of Akhetaten at 'AMARNA was erected by AKHENATEN (r. 1353–1335 B.C.E.) in honor of the god ATEN, and it became the source of an artistic revolution that upset many of the old conventions. The rigid grandeur of the earlier periods was abandoned in favor of a more naturalistic style. Royal personages were no longer made to appear remote or godlike. In many scenes, in fact, Akhenaten and his queen, NEFERTITI, are depicted as a loving couple surrounded by their offspring. Physical deformities are frankly portrayed, or possibly imposed upon the figures, and the royal household is painted with protruding bellies, enlarged heads, and peculiar limbs.

The famed painted bust of Nefertiti, however, demonstrates a mastery that was also reflected in the mag-

Figures at Abu Simbel display the Egyptian sense of sureness with stone in monumental art. *(Courtesy Thierry Ailleret)*

nificent pastoral scenes adorning the palace. Only fragments remain, but they provide a wondrous range of animals, plants, and water scenes that stand unrivaled for anatomical sureness, color, and vitality. The palaces and temples of 'Amarna were destroyed in later reigns by pharaohs such as HOREMHAB (r. 1319–1307 B.C.E.), who razed the site in order to use the materials for personal projects of his reign.

Ramessid Period (1307–1070 B.C.E.)

From the reign of RAMESSES I (1307–1306 B.C.E.) until the end of the New Kingdom, art once again followed the established canon, but the influences from the Tuthmossid and 'Amarna periods were evident. The terminal years of the Twentieth Dynasty brought about a degeneration in artistic achievement, but until that time the Ramessid accomplishments were masterful. RAMESSES II (r. 1290–1224 B.C.E.) embarked upon a building program unrivaled by any previous Egyptian ruler.

Ramesses II and his military units were involved in martial exploits, and the campaign narratives popular during the reign of Tuthmosis III (r. 1479–1425 B.C.E.) became the dominant subject of temple reliefs once again. Dramatic battle scenes were carved into the temple walls and depicted in the paintings in the royal tombs. Queen NEFERTARI, the consort of Ramesses II, was buried in a tomb that offers stunning glimpses of life on the Nile. The campaign scenes of RAMESSES III (r. 1194–1163 B.C.E.) at MEDINET HABU are of equal merit and are significant because they rank among the major artistic achievements of the Ramessid Period.

Architecture
Tuthmossid Period

Architecture at the start of the New Kingdom reflected the new vitality of a unified land. Its focus shifted from the tomb to the temple, especially those honoring the god AMUN and those designed as mortuary shrines. The mortuary temple of HATSHEPSUT (r. 1473–1458 B.C.E.) at Deir el-Bahri in Thebes allowed the architects of her reign the opportunity to erect a masterpiece. Three ascending colonnades and terraces were set into the cliffs on the western shore and were reached by two unusual ramps providing stunning visual impact at the site. The temples of the other pharaohs of this era are less grand but equally elegant. The great temple and recreational complex of AMENHOTEP III (r. 1391–1353 B.C.E.), which included chapels, shrines, and residences set into a manmade lake, was a masterpiece of architectural design. This is known as MALKATA. Karnak and Luxor, both massive in scale, reflected the enthusiasm for building of the Tuthmossids. Although several stages of construction took place at the sites, the architects were able to integrate them into powerful monuments of cultic designs.

'Amarna

The entire city of el-'Amarna was laid out with precision and care, leading to the temple of the god ATEN. The distinctive aspect of these buildings was the absence of a roof. The rays of the divine sun, a manifestation of Aten, were allowed to reach into every corner, providing light and inspiration. The WINDOW OF APPEARANCE was displayed there, and the actual grid layouts of the city were masterful and innovative interpretations of earlier architectural styles.

Ramessid Period

The period of Ramessid architecture, which can be said to include Horemhab's tomb in Saqqara, was marked by construction on a gigantic scale. Three of the greatest builders in Egyptian history, SETI I (r. 1306–1290 B.C.E.) and Ramesses II (r. 1290–1224 B.C.E.) of the Nineteenth Dynasty and RAMESSES III (r. 1194–1163 B.C.E.) of the Twentieth Dynasty, reigned during this age.

Seti began work on the second and third pylons of Karnak and instituted the Great Hall, completed by his son, Ramesses II. Ramesses II also built the RAMESSEUM in Thebes. He left an architectural legacy as well at PER-RAMESSES, the new capital in the eastern Delta. Medinet Habu, Ramesses III's mortuary temple complex, which included a brick palace, displays the same architectural grandeur. This was the last great work of the Ramessid era of the New Kingdom.

The most famous of the Ramessid monuments, other than the great mortuary temples at Abydos, was ABU SIMBEL, completed on the 30th anniversary of Ramesses' reign. The rock-carved temple was hewn out of pink limestone. With the fall of the Ramessids in 1070 B.C.E., Egypt entered into a period of decline.

THIRD INTERMEDIATE PERIOD (1070–712 B.C.E.)

The division of Egypt into two separate domains, one dominating politically in the Delta and the other held by the high priests of Amun in the south, resulted in a collapse of artistic endeavors in the Third Intermediate Period. The rulers of the Twenty-first (1070–945 B.C.E.) and Twenty-second (945–712 B.C.E.) Dynasties had few resources for advanced monumental construction. At times they had even less approval or cooperation from the Egyptian people.

Art and Architecture

The modest royal tombs of this period, mostly constructed at Tanis, were built in the courtyards of existing temples. They are not elaborately built and have mediocre decorations. The funerary regalia used to bury the rulers of these royal lines were often usurped from the previous burial sites of older pharaonic complexes. Gold was scarce, and silver became the dominant metal used.

The Twenty-third Dynasty (828–712 B.C.E.) and Twenty-fourth Dynasty (724–712 B.C.E.) were even less capable of restoring artistic horizons to the nation. No monuments of note resulted from these rulers, who governed limited areas and were contemporaries. They barely maintained existing structures and did not advance the artistic endeavors to a notable level.

THE LATE PERIOD (712–332 B.C.E.)

The artistic horizons of Egypt would be revived by the Twenty-fifth Dynasty (712–657 B.C.E.), whose rulers came from Napata at the fourth cataract of the Nile in Nubia (modern Sudan). Their own cultural advances at Napata and other sites in Nubia were based on the cultic traditions of ancient Egypt. They moved north, in fact, to restore the old ways to Egypt and imprint realism and a new vitality on old forms.

Art

The Twenty-sixth Dynasty (664–525 B.C.E.), once again composed of native Egyptians, despite its brevity continued the renaissance and added refinements and elegance. This royal line left a deep impression in the land and restored the artistic vision.

The Twenty-sixth Dynasty rulers used large-scale bronze commemoratives, many inlaid. The jewelry of the period was finely done, and furniture was high level in design and construction. The tomb of Queen TAKHAT (3), the consort of PSAMMETICHUS II (r. 595–589 B.C.E.), discovered at Tell Atrib, contained many articles of exquisite beauty, including golden sandals. The portrait of a priest of the era, called the Green Head, has fine details and charm. The ATHRIBIS treasure, which dates to this dynasty, contained golden sheets belonging to AMASIS (r. 570–526 B.C.E.). The surviving architectural innovation of this time is associated with the high mounds of sand, supported by bricks, that formed the funerary structures of the age. No significant monuments arose, however, as Egypt was engaged in regional wars that drained resources and led to an invasion by the Persians.

Architecture

The temple of MENDES, built in this dynastic era, and the additions made at Karnak—the temple complex in Thebes—and at Medinet Habu demonstrate the revival of art and architecture.

The Persians, led by CAMBYSES (r. 525–522 B.C.E.), ruled Egypt as the Twenty-seventh Dynasty (525–404

COLUMNS IN EGYPTIAN ARCHITECTURE

One of the most appealing and awe-inspiring aspects of Egyptian temple architecture are the spectacular columns, resembling groves of stone trees. These columns, especially at Karnak and Luxor, dwarf human beings and bear inscriptions, carved reliefs, and a weighty majesty unequaled anywhere else in the world.

Columns held special significance for the Egyptians, representing as they did the expanses of nature. Columns alluded to the times when vast forests dotted the land, forests that disappeared as the climate changed and civilization took its toll upon the Egyptian environment. They also represented the Nile reed marshes. The columns were introduced in order to simulate nature, and to identify man again with the earth. The first tentative columns are still visible in the STEP PYRAMID of SAQQARA, but they are engaged columns, attached to walls for support and unable to stand on their own. Imhotep designed rows of such pillars at the entrance to various buildings and incorporated them into corridors for DJOSER's shrine (2600 B.C.E.).

In the Fourth Dynasty (2575–2465 B.C.E.) masons experimented with columns as a separate architectural entity. In one royal tomb built in GIZA in the reign of KHUFU (2551–2465 B.C.E.) limestone columns were used effectively. In the tomb of SAHURÉ (2458–2446 B.C.E.) of the Fifth Dynasty, the columns were made of granite, evincing a more assured style and level of skill.

Wooden columns graced a site in the reign of KAKAI (2446–2426 B.C.E.) in that same dynasty, and another king of the royal line, NIUSERRÉ (2416–2392 B.C.E.), had limestone columns installed in his ABUSIR necropolis complex. At BENI HASAN in the Eleventh Dynasty (2134–2140 B.C.E.) local nomarchs, or provincial chiefs, built their own tombs with wooden columns. The same type of columns was installed in tombs in the Twelfth Dynasty (1991–1773 B.C.E.), but they were made of wood set into stone bases. With the coming of the New Kingdom (1550–1070 B.C.E.) the columns become part of the architectural splendor that marked the capital at Thebes and at the later capital of PER-RAMESSES in the eastern Delta. Extensive colonnades stood on terraces, or in the recesses of temples, opening onto courts and shrines.

B.C.E.). While recorded by contemporary Egyptians as a royal line that was cruel, even insane and criminal in some instances, the Persians erected a temple to Amun at KHARGA OASIS.

The final renaissance of architecture before the Ptolemaic Period came in the Thirtieth Dynasty. The rulers of this royal line revived the Saite form and engaged in massive building projects, led by NECTANEBO I (r. 380–362 B.C.E.). All of the arts of Egypt were revived in his reign. Nectanebo I built in Philae, Karnak, Bubastis, Dendereh, and throughout the Delta. He also added an avenue of finely carved sphinxes at Luxor. In Dendereh he erected a *mammisi,* or birth house. Much of the architectural work accomplished in this dynastic era reflected the growing Greek presence in Egypt, but the traditional canon was respected and used in reliefs and portraits.

THE PTOLEMAIC PERIOD (332–30 B.C.E.)

Art

Ptolemaic artists continued the Egyptian styles, but added fluidity and Hellenic influences in statuary, jewelry, and crafts. In ALEXANDRIA, such art was transformed into Greek designs. In Egyptian territories outside of the capital, the old jewelry, amulets, pendants, and wares remained traditional.

Architecture

The arrival of ALEXANDER III THE GREAT (r. 332–323 B.C.E.) and the subsequent Ptolemaic Period (304–30 B.C.E.) changed Egyptian architecture forever. The Ptolemies, however, conducted a dual approach to their architectural aspirations. The artistic endeavors of the city of Alexandria, the new capital, were purely Greek or Hellenic. The artistic projects conducted throughout Egypt were based solely upon the traditional canon and the cultic imperatives of the past.

Alexandria was intended to serve as a crowning achievement of architecture, with the LIBRARY OF ALEXANDRIA and the Pharos (the LIGHTHOUSE OF ALEXANDRIA) demonstrating the skills of the finest Greek architects.

The massive temple columns, supports used at a shrine of Horus, display different capital designs and architectural innovations. *(Courtesy Steve Beikirch)*

Even the tombs, such as the famed site erected for Petosiris, combined Egyptian and Greek designs. Outside of Alexandria, however, the Ptolemaic rulers used the traditional centuries-old styles. At PHILAE, Dendereh, ESNA, KOM OMBO, and throughout the Nile Valley, the canon reverberated once again in new temples and in designs for statues, stelae, and other monumental commemoratives. The temple at Esna, dedicated to Khnum-Horus, was erected by PTOLEMY III EUERGETES (r. 246–221 B.C.E.) and completed by PTOLEMY XII NEOS DIONYSIUS (r. 80–58, 55–51 B.C.E.). The Dendereh temple, dedicated to Hathor, used the traditional column forms but added a carved screen. Reliefs in these houses of cultic worship were traditional, but Greek anatomical corrections, softer forms, and draped garments displayed the Hellenic advances. The Egyptian form had survived over the centuries on the Nile, as it triumphed in the restored monuments displayed in modern times.

Further reading: Aldred, Cyril. *Egyptian Art in the Days of the Pharaohs, 3100–320 B.C.* New York: Thames & Hudson, 1985; Arnold, Dorothea, Christiane Ziegler, and James P. Allen, eds. *Egyptian Art in the Age of the Pyramids.* New Haven, Conn.: Yale University Press, 1999; D'Avennes, E. Prisse. *Atlas of Egyptian Art.* Cairo: American University in Cairo, 2008; Fazzini, Richard, James F. Romano, and Madeleine E. Cody. *Art for Eternity: Masterworks from Ancient Egypt.* New York: Scala Books, 1999; Malek, J. *Egypt: 4,000 Years of Art.* New York: Phaidon Press, 2003; Robins, Gay. *The Art of Ancient Egypt: Revised Edition.* Cambridge: Harvard University Press, 2008; Smith, William Stevenson, and William Kelly Simpson. *The Art and Architecture of Ancient Egypt.* New Haven, Conn.: Yale University Press, 1999; Stevenson Smith, W., rev. by W. Simpson. *Art and Architecture of Ancient Egypt.* New Haven, Conn.: Yale University Press, 1998; Tierney, Tom. *Ancient Egyptian Fashions.* Mineola, N.Y.: Dover, 1999; Wilkinson, Richard H., and Richard Wilk. *Symbol & Magic in Egyptian Art.* New York: Thames & Hudson, 1999.

Artatama (fl. 14th century B.C.E.) *Mitanni ruler allied to Egypt*
He was the head of the MITANNI state during the reign of TUTHMOSIS IV (1401–1391 B.C.E.), living in Washukanni, the capital, in northern Syria. Tuthmosis IV wrote to Artatama seven times, asking for the hand of his daughter. Such a marriage would cement relations and strengthen the alliance in the face of the growing HITTITE empire. Tuthmosis IV's pact with Artatama would have serious repercussions in the Ramessid Period because the Hittites overcame the Mittanis and viewed Egypt as an enemy.

Artavasdes III (d. 34 B.C.E.) *king of Armenia, executed by Cleopatra VII*
The son and successor of Tigranes the Great, Artavasdes was an ally of Rome. He had supported Marc ANT-ONY until the Parthians, enemies of Rome under Orodes I, invaded Armenia. Artavasdes then gave his sister to Pacorus, Orodes' son. In 36 B.C.E., Marc Antony invaded Armenia and captured Artavasdes. The king was sent to ALEXANDRIA, where CLEOPATRA VII (51–30 B.C.E.) ordered his death.

Artaxerxes I (Macrocheir) (d. 424 B.C.E.) *fourth ruler of the Twenty-seventh Dynasty*
A Persian of the royal Achaemenid line, he reigned from 465 B.C.E. until his death. Called "the Long Handed," Artaxerxes was the son of XERXES I and Queen AMESTRIS. He was raised to the throne when ARTABANUS murdered Xerxes I. To revenge his father, Artaxerxes slew Artabanus in hand-to-hand combat. A brother rebelled against Artaxerxes and was defeated just before an Egyptian, INAROS, rose up on the Nile and killed General ACHAEMENES, Artaxerxes I's uncle and a beloved Persian general.

General MEGABYZUS was sent to Egypt to halt Inaros's revolt and to restore Persian control. Inaros was executed and Megabyzus protested this punishment as a blot on his personal code of honor. Artaxerxes I, however, was not unpopular in Egypt because he was generous to various native groups. He completed a vast memorial throne chamber in Persepolis, his capital, before he died at Susa. He was buried in Nagh-e-Rostam.

Artaxerxes II (d. ca. 358 B.C.E.) *Persian ruler who tried to regain Egypt*
He made this attempt in the reign of NECTANEBO II (360–343 B.C.E.). Artaxerxes II was the successor of DARIUS II and the father of ARTAXERXES III OCHUS. He led two expeditions against Egypt but could not reclaim the region because of Nectanebo II's strong defenses. Artaxerxes ruled Persia from 404 to 359/358 B.C.E.

Artaxerxes III Ochus (d. 338 B.C.E.) *Persian ruler who subjugated Egypt and started the Second Persian War (343–332 B.C.E.)*
He attacked the Nile Valley originally in the reign of NECTANEBO II (360–343 B.C.E.). The successor of ARTAXERXES II, he put relatives to death when he inherited the throne and was described by contemporaries as cruel and energetic. His first attempt at regaining Egypt took place in 351 B.C.E., but Egyptian defenses held, and Phoenicia and Cyprus distracted him by rebelling.

Artaxerxes III met Nectanebo II on the Nile in 343, winning the battle of PELUSIUM. He ravaged the northern part of the land and killed the sacred APIS bull with his own hands in vengeance against Egyptian resistance. Artaxerxes III returned to Persia and was poisoned with most of his children by the eunuch official of the court, BAGOAS, in 338 B.C.E. His wife, Atossa, survived, and her son, ARSES, inherited the throne.

Asasif   This is a depression on the western shore of the Nile near DEIR EL-BAHRI, across from the city of THEBES. Located near the KHOKHA hills, the area was used as a necropolis. Tombs of the Saite or Twenty-sixth Dynasty (664–525 B.C.E.) were discovered in the region, as well as mortuary complexes from the Eleventh Dynasty (2134–1991 B.C.E.). RAMESSES IV (1163–1156 B.C.E.) also started a temple on the site.

Ashait   (fl. 21st century B.C.E.) *royal woman of the Eleventh Dynasty*
She was a lesser-ranked consort of MENTUHOTEP II (r. 2061–2010 B.C.E.). Ashait was buried in the elaborate mortuary complex at DEIR EL-BAHRI, on the western shore of the Nile at THEBES. Her tomb reliefs supposedly identified her as an Ethiopian or Nubian. Ashait's coffin contained an enchanting hymn about the four winds, delineating the sort of weather and abundance that came from the four cardinal points of the earth, all brought to Egypt by mythical beings. Her sarcophagus contained a depiction indicating her as the "King's Sole Favorite" (Ashait was not the only woman with this depiction).

Ashmunien, el   *See* HERMOPOLIS MAGNA.

Ashoka (Asoka)   (d. ca. 238 B.C.E.) *emperor of India*
A vigorous patron of the Buddhist religion, Ashoka sent an embassy to ALEXANDRIA and received one from PTOLEMY II PHILADELPHUS (r. 285–246 B.C.E.). He invited Ptolemy to become a Buddhist. Buddhist monks lived in Alexandria, and there was a great procession in the city in 270 B.C.E. of Indian women, pets, and cattle, all religious and social symbols of India at the time. Ashoka sent Buddhist books to the LIBRARY OF ALEXANDRIA as well.

Ashur-uballit I   (d. ca. 1330 B.C.E.) *Assyrian ruler who created the First Assyrian Empire*
Ashur-uballit I created the first Assyrian empire, threatening the Hittites and Hurrians of the era as he ruled all of Babylonia. He also aided the HITTITES in destroying the MITANNI Empire. Ashur-uballit I served as an ally of Egypt in the reign of AKHENATEN (1335–1353 B.C.E.). He sent AMENHOTEP III, Akhenaten's father, a statue of Ishtar.

Assiut (Lykopolis; Lyconpolis; Zawty; Syut)   A city located south of HERMOPOLIS MAGNA on the eastern side of the Nile, Assiut was dedicated to the god WEPWAWET, the wolf deity. The city was important because it was the terminus of the caravan route from the KHARGA OASIS and the lands below the first cataract. Assiut also served as a center for a trade route, called the "FORTY DAY ROUTE," from Darfur to the Libyan OASES. The nomarchs of Assiut were famous in many eras of Egyptian history for their military prowess and were enlisted to aid some rulers during periods of unrest.

Inscriptions carved into the tombs of the necropolis that was hewn out of the cliffs overlooking Assiut indicate the power and independent status of these locals. Most of the tombs date from the period of the Ninth (ca. 2134 B.C.E.) and Tenth (2134 B.C.E.) Dynasties when the Herakleopolitan kings looked to the Assiut warriors to defend the land against the encroaching Thebans. Attacking Thebans on behalf of the Ninth and Tenth Dynasties, the warriors of Assiut started the war that would bring about their downfall and unite all of Egypt. At that time Mentuhotep II (r. 2061–2010 B.C.E.) ruled in Thebes. When the Assiut forces attacked a Theban necropolis, vandalizing graves and corpses, all Egyptians were horrified, as such an act was sacrilege. Mentuhotep II called up his Upper Egyptian troops, called the "Followers of Horus," and marched against Assiut and Heraklepolis, destroying the Khety (Aktoy) rulers.

One interesting relief among those discovered in the tombs of Assiut is that of a female nomarch named Sitré, who served as regent and kept the hereditary land intact until her son reached his majority. Two Ramessid (1307–1070 B.C.E.) tombs were also found there.

Assurbanipal   (d. ca. 627 B.C.E.) *ruler of Assyria who attacked Egypt*
He reigned from 669 B.C.E. until his death and succeeded his father, ESSARHADDON. Upon gaining the throne, Assurbanipal renewed his campaign against Egypt. He used the ruler of SAIS, NECHO I (r. 672–664 B.C.E.), and then PSAMMETICHUS I (r. 664–610 B.C.E.), to gain an Assyrian foothold on the Nile. In 663, he led a campaign against TANUTAMUN (r. 664–657 B.C.E.), the successor to TAHARQA (r. 690–664 B.C.E.), but Babylonian affairs caused him to halt his Egyptian efforts. His wife was Anhursharrat, and he ruled from NINEVEH (opposite modern Mosul, in Iraq).

Assyrians   The people living on the right bank of the Tigris River at Assur, modern Kileh Shergat, in northern Iraq. The Assyrian Empire began at Assur, possibly by a ruler called Nemrod, spread into the mountains of Niphates ca. 1270 B.C.E., and lasted until 740 B.C.E. Babylon fell to the Assyrians ca. 1260 B.C.E., and northern Syria felt the Assyrian presence. The first known true king was Bel-bani. About 1450 B.C.E., after Egyptian supremacy, Assyria began a second period of advancement, entering Zagros and Armenia. Syria fell to their advance, as well as Phoenicia, Damascus, and Israel. The third period, ca. 1100 B.C.E., was a time of further expansion. The Assyrians conquered Egypt, Susiana, Cyprus, and the Mediterranean and Persian Gulf regions. The expansion was halted by the Scythian invasion, by Median resistance, and by the power of Babylon. Nineveh, the last Assyrian capital, fell ca. 612 B.C.E.

Astarte   This was a goddess originating in Syria and brought into Egypt in the New Kingdom (1550–1070 B.C.E.). AMENHOTEP II (r. 1427–1401 B.C.E.) erected a STELA honoring her in GIZA. She was given the rank of a daughter of the god RÉ and was made a consort of SET. Astarte served as the patroness of the pharaoh's chariots in military campaigns. She was depicted as a naked woman wearing the *atef,* or bull's horns. She had served as a war goddess in Syria.

Asten (Astes)   A deity who served as a companion of the god THOTH, the patron of wisdom; in some lists he is addressed as Astes. Thoth remained popular throughout all eras, and the concept of a companion for a deity was appreciated by the Egyptians as a way of honoring older gods who no longer had an effect on society.

astrology   A practice attributed to the ancient Egyptians, highly dramatized in the modern world. The Egyptians practiced a form of astrology, but it had little in common with that of later eras. The Egyptians practiced astral-theology, a form of divination that responded to the astronomical observances of their day but held no independent value.

The Egyptians were always anxious to equate human endeavors with cosmic events as observed in the night sky, and much of their writings and teachings about the spirit of MA'AT were concerned with a need to mirror the divine order demonstrated by the heavenly bodies. Horoscopes, in the modern sense of the word, were not known by the Egyptians before the fall of the New Kingdom. They did not have the traditional signs of the zodiac or the concept of planetary houses. When the Egyptians did learn about horoscopes and the attendant lore, it was from Mesopotamian and Hellenistic sources late in the Ptolemaic Period. The Egyptians had other methods of divination and fortune-telling, such as the mythological CALENDARS that dealt with lucky and unlucky days, especially as they pertained to births.

The true horoscope arrived on the Nile with the Ptolemaic Period (304–30 B.C.E.). The Babylonian zodiac and Greek interpretations replaced the Egyptian concept of the heavens. The *dekans* associated with astrological computations, however, had been depicted in the tomb of SENENMUT in the reign of HATSHEPSUT (1473–1458 B.C.E.) but had not been universally regarded.

Astronomical Room   *See* RAMESSEUM.

astronomy   The ancient Egyptian science of the stars was prompted in the early eras by the demands of agriculture. Because the harvest seasons and the fertilization of the fields and orchards depended upon the annual inundation of the Nile, the priests of the formative years of Egypt's history began to chart the heavenly bodies and to incorporate them into a religious tradition that would provide information about the Nile and its patterns of inundation.

There was a fascination with celestial activities, as evidenced by tomb inscriptions of the Old Kingdom (2575–2134 B.C.E.) and the First Intermediate Period (2134–2040 B.C.E.), which continued into later eras and was elaborated in the Ptolemaic time. These inscriptions contained lists of the divisions of the sky, called *dekans* by the Greeks. The *dekans* were the so-called 12 hours of the night, represented by pictures. Each *dekan* was personified and given a divine attribute. NUT, an important sky goddess of Egypt, was associated with the inscriptions and their depictions. As the goddess of the heavens, the celestial bodies were incorporated into her body.

Certain priests, designated as the "Keepers of Time," watched the nightly movement of the stars. They were required to memorize the order of the fixed stars, the movements of the moon and the planets, the rising of the moon and the sun, as well as their setting times, and the orbits of the various celestial bodies. Such learned individuals were then ready to recite this information in counsel and to provide details about the changes taking place in the sky in any given season.

One set of stars known to the temple astronomers was called the Ikhemu-Seku, the "Stars That Never Fail." These were the polar stars that remained fixed in the night sky and were much venerated as special souls having attained true bliss. The second set of stars, actually planets, were the Ikhemu-Weredu, the "Never Resting Stars," which followed distinct orbits in the night sky. There is no information as to whether the Egyptians made a true distinction between the planets or the stars. Both sets of "stars" were believed to accompany the SOLAR BOAT on its nightly voyage.

The stars noted were Sirius the Dogstar, called SOPDU or Sopdet, considered the true symbol of the coming inundation of the Nile, signaling the rising of the river; Orion, called Sah, the "Fleet-Footed, Long-Strider"; Ursa Major (Great Bear or Big Dipper), called Meskhetiu. Also noted were Cygnus, Cassiopeia, the Dragon, Scorpio, and the Ram. There is no evidence that the Egyptians charted the Pleiades until the Ptolemaic Period (304–30 B.C.E.).

The planets noted were Hor-tash-tawy (Jupiter), called "Horus Who Binds the Two Lands"; Hor-ka-Pet (Saturn), called "Horus the Bull of Heaven"; Horus-Desher (Mars), the "Red Horus"; Sebeg (Mercury), meaning unknown; Seba-Djai (Venus), the "Star that Crosses." The sun was preeminent in Egyptian religion from Predynastic times, represented as the SCARAB beetle, Khepri, rising in the morning, RÉ at noon (overhead), and ATUM at night. The sun became important to Egyptian astronomy in the Twenty-sixth Dynasty. The Egyptians had no special interest in the stars and planets in themselves. It was enough for them to recognize the astral bodies as part of the cosmic harmony that had to be maintained by mankind so that the world could prosper and survive.

Aswan The most southern city of ancient Egypt, Aswan was located just above the first cataract of the Nile. Modern Aswan is on the first cataract, on the eastern shore of the Nile, and is a busy commercial and tourist center, with a population of approximately 275,000 inhabitants. It is also the seat of one of the governorates of the Republic of Egypt. Called "the Southern Gate," or *swenet,* Aswan became known as Syrene in the Greek era. The city served as a provincial headquarters for the territories below the cataract, as viceroys of NUBIA (modern Sudan) used the ELEPHANTINE Island at Aswan as a residence in some reigns. The area is famous for red granite, called syrenite.

Always one of the most prosperous cities in the Nile Valley, Aswan was composed of three main regions: the city, the temple sites, and the granite quarries. Next to the city is the Elephantine Island, which served as a shrine to the god KHNUM, as a military garrison, and as a trade administration center.

HISTORY

Settlements at Aswan date to Predynastic Period times, before the unification of Egypt ca. 3000 B.C.E. From the earliest periods of Egyptian history, Aswan was a strategic site for defense and trade industries. It also represented the southern frontier of Egypt. The lords of the local NOMES, or provinces, were called the "Magnates of the Southern Gate"; the "gate" led to Nubia (modern Sudan). Also called Kush, Nubia was a vast region along the cataracts of the Nile with a remarkable variety of natural resources, including gold. As the Egyptians explored and established trade with Nubia, Aswan developed into a trade center. Customs officers on Elephantine Island located in the Nile River next to Aswan met expeditions and extracted tolls and custom taxes. In the early periods, Elephantine Island was called Abu or Yabu, words for elephant. The Greeks translated the name of the island to Elephus. Reportedly, the island resembled an elephant swimming, hence the name. The very early trade of elephant tusks, made of desirable ivory, probably served as the suggestion of the modern name.

The city of Aswan was one of the most sophisticated and cosmopolitan metropolises of ancient Egypt. A trade, expedition, and military hub, Aswan was home to people from many lands and cultures, including Nubians (modern Sudanese), PHOENICIANS (modern Lebanese), and Greeks. Unlike the Egyptians to the north, the traders, military personnel, and officials of Aswan were exposed to many languages. The city would remain a powerful military and trade center into the era of Roman occupation.

ECONOMY

Aswan and the Elephantine shared marketplaces for the goods and resources that entered the country from Nubia and the Red Sea. Gold, oils, incense, ivory, animals, and hides were among the valuables arriving by ship or by caravan. One powerful woman by the name of NEBT was commemorated on a local stela. She was the heiress of the Elephantine and the ranking nomarch during the Eleventh Dynasty. She had her own offices, libraries, and a bevy of scribes to keep her accounts and correspondence. Nebt was considered a patroness of the arts and was revered by Mentuhotep II (r. 2061–2010 B.C.E.), who made her daughter one of his queens.

In time, the pharaohs of the Middle Kingdom built canals beside the cataracts so that their ships could voyage south conveniently. Thus the products of Nubia increased as trade items. The shipbuilding efforts on the Red Sea, mainly at a site called Kuser, also widened the scope of trade markets. Egyptian ships sailed to PUNT, which has not been identified but is believed to have been modern Ethiopia, and provided myrrh trees, spices, rare animals, and other exotic trade goods.

The quarries of Aswan also expanded. The granite rock called syrenite was particularly prized. Obelisks were fashioned out of this sturdy stone. A remnant of the quarrying is visible at Aswan, where a granite piece, called the Broken Obelisk, still remains in the quarry.

SIGNIFICANCE

Located strategically on the southern border with Nubia, Aswan and the Elephantine Island were active sites in every historical period of Egypt. The warrior-pharaohs campaigning in Nubia used the area for preparations and assembly of troops and then rested there before making the voyage back to their capitals. Traders and adventurers located and then exploited resources, including gold, precious stones, and electrum, found south of the kingdom.

The tombs at Aswan include Sixth Dynasty (2323–2150 B.C.E.) sites. Of particular note are the tombs of Mekhu and Sabni, father and son, who conducted expeditions to find resources and to garrison positions along the Nile cataracts. Mekhu died south of Aswan, and Sabni recovered his father's body and brought it to Egypt for burial. PEPI II (r. 2246–2152 B.C.E.) gave mortuary gifts for the tomb, which contains rock pillared chambers and frescoes. HARKHUF, the faithful servant of Pepi II, is also buried there. The Middle Kingdom (2040–1640 B.C.E.) tombs of local NOMARCHS, most equipped with long passages and ornamented with frescoes and reliefs, are also in the Aswan necropolis.

Aswan was the abode of the deities KHNUM, SATET, and ANUKET. The Nile god, HAPI (1), resided in a cave in the region, and one site was reserved as the grave of OSIRIS. Many built at the sites to honor the local deities. HATSHEPSUT (r. 1473–1458 B.C.E.) erected a temple to the goddess

Satet, featuring reliefs and a granite niche. RAMESSES II (r. 1290–1224 B.C.E.) and NEC TANEBO II (r. 360–343 B.C.E.) added to the temple of Khnum. PHILAE temple, which was moved in the 1970s to the island of Agilkia to save it from the waters of Lake Nasser (caused by the Aswan High Dam), fell under the jurisdiction of the city.

Further reading: Haag, Michael. *Luxor Illustrated: With Aswan, Abu Simbel, and the Nile.* Cairo: American University of Cairo Press, 2010; Kamil, Jill, and Michael Stock, photographer. *Aswan and Abu Simbel: History and Guide.* New York: Columbia University Press, 1999; Siliotti, Albert. *Aswan.* Cairo: American University in Cairo Press, 2001.

Aten A deity introduced into Egypt during the New Kingdom (1550–1070 B.C.E.), Aten was also known as "Aten of the Day," the SOLAR DISK that shone upon the river, possibly a form of Ré-Harakhte. AKHENATEN (r. 1353–1335 B.C.E.), upon ascending the throne in THEBES, proclaimed a great religious reformation and decreed worship of Aten as the only true religion of the land. Aten was not an invention of Akhenaten, having been known in the reigns of his predecessors TUTHMOSIS IV and AMENHOTEP III.

He established a new capital in honor of the god, a site called Akhetaten, "the Horizon of Aten," now known as el-'AMARNA, north of Thebes. Vast temple complexes arose on the shore of the Nile, but there were no statues of the god. This deity was represented by a great red disk, from which long rays, complete with hands, extended to the faithful. Akhenaten and his queen, NEFERTITI, accompanied by their daughters, conducted cultic ceremonies of the god. Until the last years of his reign, Akhenaten was the only priest of the cult.

Ceremonies to Aten consisted mainly of the offering of cakes and fruit and the recitation of lovely hymns composed in his honor. Aten was lauded as the creator of man and the nurturing spirit of the world. He was a solar god, possibly a form of RÉ. A distinct strain of brotherhood and equality of all races and peoples was expressed in the hymns. Aten's worship was a modified form of monotheism, and as long as Akhenaten was alive the deity was the official god of Egypt. Akhenaten associated himself to Aten, however, sharing feasts as a being united to Aten. Stern measures were taken against the temple of AMUN in particular and against the veneration of most other deities as well. Even the cartouche of Akhenaten's father, Amenhotep III, was damaged because the name of the god Amun was part of it. When Akhenaten died in 1335 B.C.E., 'Amarna fell victim to the many enemies of the new deity and Aten was banished forever.

Atet (Itet) (fl. 26th century B.C.E.) *royal woman of the Fourth Dynasty*
She was a wife of Prince NEFERMA'AT, son of SNEFRU (2575–2551 B.C.E.) and Princess NEFERKAU. She was pos-

sibly related to Neferma'at by birth. Their son, HEMIUNU, was vizier for KHUFU (Cheops) (r. 2551–2528 B.C.E.). She was buried with Prince Neferma'at in MEIDUM. The famous beautiful reliefs depicting geese were discovered in Atet's tomb. Other paintings portrayed pets, sacred birds, and children. In some lists she is called Itet.

Athenaeus (fl. fourth century B.C.E.) *general in the army of Antigonus I Monophthalmus who opposed Egypt*
He was a rival of PTOLEMY I SOTER (304–284 B.C.E.) and competed with him for domination after the death of ALEXANDER III THE GREAT. In 312 B.C.E., Athenaeus led 4,600 men into the region of the Nabataeans to impose an economic blockade against Egypt and to halt their flow of bitumen, used in mummification. Athenaeus raided Nabataea during a festival in which the men gathered at a place called "the Rock," believed to be Petra. He captured or killed many attending the festival and made off with hundreds of camels, silver, frankincense, and myrrh. The Greeks, however, were attacked by the Nabataeans soon after, and Athenaeus lost his infantry and several cavalry units. When the Nabataeans wrote ANTIGONUS I MONOPHTHALMUS to protest the Greek invasion, he declared that General Athenaeus had acted on his own.

Athribis (Sohag; Tell Atrib) A site in the western Delta, northeast of BENHA on the Damietta branch of the Nile, now Tell Atrib, the Egyptians called the city Huthery-ib, the cult center of Kem-wer, "the Great Black One," a BULL deity. Khenti-kheti, or Horus-Khentikheti, was worshipped at Athribis. The city was probably founded in the Fourth Dynasty (2575–2465 B.C.E.) and maintained by later royal lines. Monuments from the Twelfth Dynasty (1991–1783 B.C.E.) are at Athribis, as well as a temple erected by AMENHOTEP III (r. 1391–1353 B.C.E.) and another by AMASIS (r. 570–526 B.C.E.). The tomb of Queen TAKHAT (3), consort of PSAMMETICHUS II (r. 595–589 B.C.E.), was also discovered at the site. One of the city's priests, AMENHOTEP, SON OF HAPU, achieved lasting fame in Egypt.

Athribis Stela A monument erected in the reign of MERENPTAH (1224–1214 B.C.E.), the son and heir of RAMESSES II, this stela, along with the Cairo Column and an inscription discovered in KARNAK, recounts the military challenges facing Merenptah when he took the throne of Egypt. The Libyans and their allies, who hoped to invade Egypt, were defeated by Merenptah at Per-yer in the Delta.

Atum (Tem; Tum) One of the earliest deities in Egypt, an earth god also called Tem and Tum, Atum existed alone in the beginning of time, floating inert in the watery chaos of NUN or Nu. A self-generating deity, capable also of self-impregnation, his name meant

"Completed One." Atum rose alone on the site of his temple at HELIOPOLIS.

A Twentieth Dynasty (1196–1070 B.C.E.) papyrus that was copied in the Ptolemaic Period (332–30 B.C.E.) states that Atum evolved alone, coming out of the chaos of Nun. He sired the deities SHU and TEFNUT. They created GEB and NUT, who begat OSIRIS, ISIS, SET, and NEPHTHYS. These gods formed the ENNEAD of Heliopolis, joined by HORUS or RÉ. For this reason Atum was called "the plural of the plural."

During the Old Kingdom (2575–2134 B.C.E.), Atum was associated with the cult of Ré, worshipped as Atum-Ré. He was depicted as a man wearing the double crown of Egypt and carrying a royal scepter and the ANKH. Atum was a form of the god Ré as the setting sun, and he also appeared as a mongoose. The creator of all of the Nile deities, Atum was later associated with cults of PTAH and then Osiris.

Augustus (Octavian) (d. 14 C.E.) *first emperor of the Roman Empire and the first to rule over Egypt*

He held Egypt as a special province from 30 B.C.E. until his death. He was born Gaius Julius Caesar Octavianus in 63 B.C.E. and was the great nephew and adopted son and heir of Julius CAESAR. When Caesar was assassinated in 44 B.C.E., Octavian, as he was called then, allied himself with Marc ANTONY and Lepidus in the ensuing civil war against his uncle's murderers, Brutus, Cassius, and the so-called Liberators.

The political alliance between Octavian and Antony collapsed in 31 B.C.E., and Octavian, aided by Marcus AGRIPPA and others, set out to destroy Marc Antony and CLEOPATRA VII (51–30 B.C.E.). Winning the battle of ACTIUM, Octavian occupied ALEXANDRIA and watched the suicides of Egypt's last queen-pharaoh, Cleopatra VII, and Marc Antony. He refused to honor the APIS BULL in SAQQARA and the mummies of ancient pharaohs. Reportedly he did touch the body of ALEXANDER III THE GREAT, causing a piece of the preserved nose to fall off the body. Augustus did tour the Nile Valley, and he started programs of repair on the irrigation system, using Roman troops to make the necessary changes.

Augustus made Egypt an imperial estate of Rome and set out to rule the largest empire in that historical period. He brought peace and prosperity to Rome and maintained the provinces securely. The Altar of Peace, erected in 13 B.C.E. in Rome's Campus Martius, and the Monument Ancyranum, erected in Ankara (modern Turkey), provide evidence of his robust vision and his careful rebuilding and administration of the empire. Octavian, as Augustus, died in Rome in 14 C.E.

Augustus's annexation of Egypt was a necessary move, and he handled the Roman occupation of the Nile Valley with tact and with an awareness of the land's history and potential prosperity. Giving Egypt the status of an imperial estate, a personal possession of the reigning

A silver denarius struck to celebrate the victory of Octavian (Augustus) and his conquest of Egypt in 30 B.C.E. *(Courtesy Historical Coins, Inc.)*

emperor, he applied a prefect to govern in his name. This prefecture was open only to members of the Equestrian Knighthood. He also decreed that no Roman of the Senatorial or Equestrian classes could enter Egypt without the emperor's personal permission. The Egyptians reconciled themselves to the political changes and turned inward again, forming stable NOMES and leaders that endured the Roman presence, the taxes, and the obligations.

Ausim (Hem; Letopolis)
A site north of modern Cairo in Egypt's Delta territory, called Hem by the Egyptians and Letopolis by the Greeks. The site was a cult center for the falcon deity, HORUS, in the forms of Khenty-Khem or Khenty-Irty. Monuments honoring Horus were erected at Ausim by NECHO II (r. 610–596 B.C.E.), PSAMMETICHUS II (r. 595–589 B.C.E.), HAKORIS (r. 393–380 B.C.E.), and NECTANEBO I (r. 380–362 B.C.E.)

Avaris (Hut-Waret)
A site located in the eastern Delta, northeast of BUBASTIS, in the region of Khatana and Qantir, the site of the PER-RAMESSES, the residence of the Nineteenth Dynasty (1307–1196 B.C.E.) rulers. Avaris dates to ancient times and was considered a shrine city of the god OSIRIS; a piece of the god's body was supposed to be buried there as a holy relic. The city was called Hut-Waret by the Egyptians. Avaris became the capital of the HYKSOS, the Asiatics, who dominated northern territories during the Second Intermediate Period (1640–1532 B.C.E.) and was probably founded ca. 1720–1700 B.C.E. They used distinctly Canaanite architecture and displayed alien cultural symbols.

The Hyksos provided the city with walls, causeways, and various defenses to protect the inhabitants against sieges and missile attacks. KAMOSE tried to reach Avaris with his southern army in ca. 1500 B.C.E. in order to expel the Hyksos, but the task fell to his brother, 'AHMOSE (NEBPEHTIRÉ) (r. 1550–1525 B.C.E.), founder of the Eighteenth Dynasty. He used both land and sea forces to assault the capital. Avaris endured the siege, and the withdrawal of the Hyksos appears to have been the result of negotiations, although the Egyptian army pursued them even beyond the border. The surrender of Avaris in 1532 B.C.E. ended the Hyksos domination and the division of Egypt.

In the Ramessid Period the site would become a spectacular metropolis again. Avaris appears to have been the home of the first RAMESSES (r. 1307–1306 B.C.E.), and his successors transformed the city into a vast complex of temples, palaces, shrines, and military encampments.

awet The ancient CROOK and FLAIL, the royal symbol of the pharaohs, adopted from the god OSIRIS and the ancient shepherd deity ANDJETI. The crook denoted the pharaoh's role as the guardian of the people of the Nile. The crook and the flail were used in all royal ceremonies and were part of the mortuary regalia of all rulers. A crook fashioned out of ivory was found in the tomb of SCORPION I, the Predynastic Period ruler of HIERANKOPOLIS and THINIS. The value of such symbols, therefore, was recognized before Egypt was founded as a nation in 2920 B.C.E.

Awibré Hor (fl. 19th century B.C.E.) *mysterious royal personage of Egypt in the Twelfth Dynasty*
He was possibly the son and heir, perhaps even coregent, of AMENEMHET III (r. 1844–1797 B.C.E.). No records of his coregency survive, but his tomb, located in the funerary complex of Amenemhet III at DASHUR, contained royal insignias. A rare wooden statue of this young man was discovered there, as well as a gilded mask and a sarcophagus, made out of a single square of sandstone. The tomb of a princess, NWEBHOTEP-KHRED, is located beside that of Awibré Hor. She was possibly his consort, as she was buried wearing a silver crown and a golden URAEUS, the symbol of the rulers of Egypt. The wooden statues of Hor depict him as a KA, an astral being that rises at death. He possibly served as co-regent for only seven months.

Axe of Ah'hotep A New Kingdom military emblem discovered in the tomb of Queen AH'HOTEP (1), the mother of 'AHMOSE (NEBPEHTIRÉ) (r. 1550–1525 B.C.E.). The axe symbolized the emblem of honor in MILITARY events. A common form of the axe was used in all parades. The blade of the weapon displays the SPHINX, the Nile, and various goddesses and is made of copper, gold, semiprecious stones, and glass paste. This blade was secured to the handle with leather thongs.

Aya (1) (Merneferré) (d. 1690 B.C.E.) *ruler of the Thirteenth Dynasty*
He reigned from 1704 B.C.E. until his death. His throne name meant "Beautiful Is the Desire of Ré." This ruler is believed to have been a native of AVARIS and a vassal of the HYKSOS, the Asiatics who dominated the northern territories at the time. A diorite capstone from his tomb was found in the eastern Delta, and other monuments were found throughout the Nile Valley. His tomb, however, is unidentified. The eastern Delta rebelled at the end of Aya's reign.

Aya (2) (Kheperkheprure) (d. 1319 B.C.E.) *ruler of the Eighteenth Dynasty*
He reigned from 1323 B.C.E. until his death. Aya ascended the throne upon the death of TUT'ANKHAMUN and apparently married ANKHESENAMON, the boy king's widow. She does not appear after the initial succession of Aya, however. The queen who is shown in all surviving texts is TEY, a commoner who had served as a nurse to NEFERTITI and had married Aya before his accession to the throne.

Aya, also a commoner, had been the "Master of the Horse" and Fan Bearer and then vizier and chancellor for AKHENATEN (r. 1353–1335 B.C.E.) at 'AMARNA, but he followed the process of reorganizing the government and the aggrandizement of the god AMUN during his brief reign. His portraits depict a man with a narrow, bony face and a long, slender nose. Aya erected KARNAK's colonnade and a rock-cut shrine at AKHMIN. He built a mortuary temple at MEDINET HABU in western Thebes but did not provide himself with a tomb there. In the VALLEY OF THE KINGS a tomb was decorated for him and for Tey, but his remains have never been found. His tomb is long and straight in design, with four corridors. An elaborate passage leads to a burial chamber, which was decorated with the text of the AM DUAT. Aya's burial site included a red granite sarcophagus. He also had an unfinished tomb in 'Amarna. Aya designated NAKHTMIN (1), possibly a relative and a military commander, as his heir, but HOREMHAB put him aside and became the last pharaoh of the dynasty.

Aziru (fl. 14th century B.C.E.) *ruler of Amurru, successor of Abdiashirta*
He had political dealings with AKHENATEN (r. 1353–1335 B.C.E.) and TUT'ANKHAMUN (r. 1333–1323 B.C.E.). Aziru maintained an alliance with the HITTITES and began seizing the prosperous port cities on the Mediterranean coast, claiming that his actions were based on Egyptian needs. In time, however, Aziru lost the support of Egypt and became a vassal of SUPPILULIUMAS I and the Hittites.

See also PAWARA.

B

ba (1) The human-headed bird representing the soul or the vital essence of human beings, the *ba* appears at the moment of union between the KA and the body, leaving the mortal remains at death with the *ka*. The *ba* can survive in the afterlife only if it remains in close proximity to the *ka,* whose servant it appears to be at that time. The *ba* was originally written with the symbol of the Nile Jabiru bird and was thought to be an attribute of the god king. The symbol for the *ba* was then changed to that of a human-headed hawk.

The translation of the actual name *ba* is possibly "manifestation," and supposedly it was spoken "in words of weeping." The literal translation is "power." Humans had only one *ba,* but the gods had many. The *ba* was also considered a "divine essence." In many eras it was listed as the soul of the *ka*. For human affairs, the *ba* played the role of moral sense or a conscience. Great care was taken that the *ba* was not led astray after death by evil influences, as it appears to have had mobility. Rituals were designed to lead the *ba* to the *ka* and the mortal remains of the deceased after wandering. When the *bas* were destined for eternal joy, they were called the *baiu menkhu*. When damned according to the Egyptian moral codes, they were termed *baiu mitu*. The *ba* was also equipped with spiritual weapons, such as spells and AMULETS, and was then termed the *ba'apur*.

Ba (2) This was a name used for the ram god of MENDES, BA'EB DJET, a cult translated into a popular devotion in the first dynasties.

Ba (3) A deity associated with the soul, this god had many specific functions in the eternal paradise in Amenti, the mythological domain of the dead. Considered to be the residence of the god OSIRIS, Amenti was a luxurious paradise of lakes, trees, and flowers, an abode of peace for all eternity for those deemed worthy of such rewards. The goddess Bait served as Ba's consort.

Bab el-Gusus A tomb at DEIR EL-BAHRI, it was on the western shore of the Nile in THEBES, dating to the Twenty-first Dynasty (1070–945 B.C.E.). Translated as "the Door of the Priests," Bab el-Gusus contains an entrance to a deep vertical shaft that leads to subterranean corridors and chambers and extends 300 feet under the forecourt of the temple of HATSHEPSUT (r. 1473–1458 B.C.E.). Within the lower chamber 153 sets of COFFINS were discovered, aligned side by side, containing remains of the personnel of the temples of the god AMUN. Funerary regalia, stelae, and other objects were also recovered on the site.

Bab el-Hosan The name given to a tomb under the pyramidal complex of MENTUHOTEP II (r. 2061–2010 B.C.E.) of the Eleventh Dynasty at DEIR EL-BAHRI, the burial site is actually below a forecourt of the Deir el-Bahri complex on the western shore of THEBES, near the kiosk of TUTHMOSIS III (r. 1479–1425 B.C.E.). It appears to have been a cenotaph structure, a symbolic tomb that was never used. No mummified remains were discovered there.

baboon Originally called Hedjerew, or "the Great White One," the dog-headed variety, *Papio cymocephalus,* is a theophany of the gods THOTH and KHONS (1). A baboon sat in the JUDGMENT HALLS OF OSIRIS, erect upon the scales used to weigh souls. The animal informed the gods when the balance was achieved upon the scale between the symbol of righteousness and the soul. Some temples kept baboons as mascots. Quartzite colossal statues of baboons were found in HERMOPOLIS MAGNA, and they were depicted in a relief at ABU SIMBEL.

See also BAIN-A'ABTIU; BAKHAU.

Bacchias (Bakchis; Bakkhis) A site in the FAIYUM region, near KARANIS, dating to the Late Period (712–332 B.C.E.). The site was built on two rises and was a sister city to Hephaistias. A temple to the obscure deity SOKNOKNONNEUS is nearby.

Badari, el- A site near Matmar, in Upper Egypt, serving as a Predynastic necropolis, it adjoins the necropolises of Mostagedda, Deir Tasa, and Hammamia. El-Badari is the source of all data concerning the Badarian culture.

Ba'eb Djet (Banaded; Mendes) This is the ancient Egyptian name for the sacred ram of MENDES. Depicted with elaborate horns surmounted by the URAEUS, the animal was carefully sought and tested for signs of its fitness to serve as a manifestation of RÉ, OSIRIS, and PTAH. In some eras the ram was believed to house Osiris's soul. Ba'eb Djet was altered to Banaded in time, which the Greeks translated as MENDES. A living ram was kept in the temple at Mendes to ward off misfortunes. THOTH, the god of wisdom, is supposed to have recommended this practice in ancient times. The ram was a popular subject for statues and reliefs. In later eras the animal stood as a symbol of the great god AMUN. In this form the ram had great curved horns and an elaborate crown.

Bagoas (fl. fourth century B.C.E.) *Eunuch chamberlain of the Persian Empire and a notorious slayer*
He was a confidential friend of ARTAXERXES III OCHUS who ruled Egypt 343–332 B.C.E., after defeating NECTANEBO II (r. 360–343 B.C.E.) at PELUSIUM. Bagoas's name is the Greek form of the Persian word for eunuch.

When Artaxerxes III conquered Egypt, Bagoas was commander in chief of the Achaemenid forces. He looted the Egyptian temples and sold the sacred papyri back to the priests at exorbitant prices, thus amassing considerable wealth. Bagoas also worked with Mentor of Rhodes and consolidated his power in court. Bagoas poisoned Artaxerxes III and all of his sons, except ARSES, whom he placed on the throne. Two years later, Arses was also poisoned by the eunuch to make way for DARIUS III CODOMAN. Bagoas made an attempt at a court gathering to slay Darius III but was forced to drink from the royal cup that he offered the king and promptly died.

Baharia Oasis This site is located in the LIBYAN DESERT, southwest of HERAKLEOPOLIS MAGNA, considered one of the most important of the ancient Egyptian oases. KAMOSE, the last ruler of the Seventeenth Dynasty (r. 1555–1550 B.C.E.) rested at this oasis with his troops while campaigning against the Hyksos (Asiatics) in the northern territories. The Baharia Oasis, hidden in an expanse of sand and wilderness, served as a sanctuary for Egyptians in this era. The oasis was also a starting point for desert caravans to the Nile. The wines of the region were popular in ancient times and were considered an important tribute from the area.

El-Qasr is now the capital of the Baharia Oasis, which has become a modern archaeological focus because of the VALLEY OF THE GILDED MUMMIES, a Greco-Roman necropolis. Also on the site are tombs and monuments from various historical periods. Amenhotep Huy, a governor of the oasis during the New Kingdom (1550–1070 B.C.E.) is buried in a site at Qarat Heluwat. The IBIS catacomb and tombs of the Twenty-sixth Dynasty (664–525 B.C.E.) are at el-Qasr and at el-Bawiti, along with the chapel of APRIES (r. 589–570 B.C.E.). At Qasr Allam there is a stone chapel of ALEXANDER III THE GREAT (r. 332–323 B.C.E.).

Baharia Oasis also served as a cult center for the god BES. A temple was erected for the deity there, complete with a causeway, halls, magazines, and shafts. A statue of Bes was also recovered on the site.

The oasis has received world attention in recent years, as the Valley of the Golden Mummies was discovered there. These mummified remains, buried in family groups and wearing golden masks and other gilded adornments, date to the Roman Period (32 B.C.E.–395 C.E.) These mummies are being studied and protected, and it is estimated that thousands of such groupings will be found.

Bahnasa, el- *See* OXYRRYNCHUS (1).

ba **house** A small house-type container, fashioned out of pottery in most eras and placed in the TOMBS of commoners who could not afford the elaborate offertory chapels of the larger pyramids or mastabas, the *ba* house was fashioned as part of the MORTUARY RITUAL and was designed to offer the *ka* a resting place and a proper receptacle for funerary offerings. Some houses contained clay images of food and gifts to imitate the costly offerings given in the tombs and chambers of the royal family and the aristocrats. This custom was started in the Middle Kingdom (2040–1640 B.C.E.), when the priests wanted to provide ordinary Egyptians with as many mortuary rituals and magical implements as possible to ensure their eternal bliss.

See also OSIRIS BEDS; OSIRIS GARDENS.

Bahr Libeini This was a waterway through MEMPHIS dating to the Early Dynastic Period. Legend stated that

AHA (r. 2920–? B.C.E.) altered the course of the Nile in order to reclaim the region of land constituting the city of Memphis as the site of Egypt's first capital.

Bahr Yusef (Hau-wereh)   A natural canal connecting the Nile to the FAIYUM between HERMOPOLIS and MEIR, originally called Hau-wereh, the stream was allowed to enter the Faiyum region but was trapped there, forming a lake and an area for agriculture. The name, translated as "Joseph's River," is not of biblical origin but honors a local hero of Islam. The canal is supposed to have been regulated by AMENEMHET III (r. 1844–1797 B.C.E.) of the Twelfth Dynasty during the reclamation and irrigation projects conducted at that time. The Bahr Yusef paralleled the Nile for hundreds of miles, and is fed in modern times by a canal at ASSIUT.

bain-a'abtiu   These were the deities of the souls in ancient Egypt that were transformed into BABOONS at each new dawn. In this form, the deities performed spiritual concerts in adoration of RÉ as the god emerged as the sun. In some eras, the term *bain-a'abtiu* identified the Morning Star.

Bakenkhonsu (fl. 13th century B.C.E.) *official of the Nineteenth Dynasty*
He served RAMESSES II (r. 1290–1224 B.C.E.) as the high priest of AMUN. Bakenkhonsu was a member of the AMENEMOPET clan of that era, and he supervised the building of one of Ramesses' temples and erected sacred barks for the gods of THEBES. Bakenkhonsu also served in the Egyptian court system. He was mentioned in the BERLIN PAPYRUS and memorialized on some statues now in the possession of the Egyptian Museum in Cairo. His name is associated with Queen NEFERTARI also, as some lists place her as a member of his family.

Bakenkhonsu was a temple PRIEST who entered the service of the deity as a young man. He spent 12 years as a devotee in the temple, before being named the Third Prophet of Amun, an office that he held for 15 years. Becoming the Second Prophet of Amun, Bakenkhonsu became the high priest and is recorded as serving in that exalted capacity for more than a quarter of a century. A second Bakenkhonsu followed him into the same priestly office.

Bakenrenef (Wahka-ré, Bocchoris) (d. 712 B.C.E.) *ruler of the city of Sais in the Twenty-fourth Dynasty*
He reigned from 717 B.C.E. until his death. Bakenrenef succeeded TEFNAKHTE, his reported brother. Joining in the alliance against PIANKHI (1), the Nubian conqueror, the Egyptians, including Tefnakhte and Bakenrenef, were defeated. He was eventually allowed to remain in SAIS. However, when SHABAKA (r. 712–698 B.C.E.) entered Egypt to found the Kushite, or Nubian, Dynasty, the Twenty-fifth, he put Bakenrenef to death by burning him alive.

Baketamun (Baketaten) (fl. 14th century B.C.E.) *princess of the Eighteenth Dynasty*
She was a daughter of AMENHOTEP III (r. 1391–1353 B.C.E.) and Queen TIYE (1). Baketamun was a sister of AKHENATEN (Amenhotep IV) and witnessed the 'AMARNA era of Akhenaten's reign in living there with her mother for a time. She bore the name Baketaten in 'Amarna and was depicted in tomb reliefs. A limestone bust was identified as Baketamun in 'Amarna.

In 2010 the mummified remains of a young woman with a badly damaged face were discovered. DNA tests indicate that these remains are of a daughter of Queen TIYE (1), a sister of AKHENATEN, and the mother of TUT'ANKHAMUN (r. 1333–1323 B.C.E.). These may be the remains of Princess Baketamun.

Baketwerel (fl. 13th century B.C.E.) *royal woman of the Twentieth Dynasty*
She is believed to have been the consort of AMENMESSES, a usurper in the reign of SETI II (1214–1204 B.C.E.). Her remains have not been identified but possibly have been found in Amenmesses' tomb, alongside his mother, TAKHAT (1). Baketwerel has also been identified as the consort of RAMESSES IX. If she were the consort of Ramesses IX, she would have been the mother of RAMESSES X. It is possible that a second Baketwerel was named after an ancestral member.

See also QUEENS.

Bakhau   A spiritual site called "the Land of the Sunrise," and part of the cult of the god RÉ, Bakhau was the setting of the cosmic battle between Ré and the god SET, who was defeated. The site was called the spiritual "Mountain of Sunrise" and was associated with solar rituals. BABOONS greeted the dawn at Bakhau as part of the solar rituals. Manu was the spiritual "Mountain of Sunset."

Bakht (Baqet) (fl. 21st century B.C.E.) *official and nomarch of the Eleventh Dynasty (2040–1991 B.C.E.)*
He served as governor of the Oryx nome. He was buried in his clan necropolis in BENI HASAN. Bakht's tomb contains a rectangular chapel with two columns and seven shafts. Elaborate wall murals depict Bakht and his wife in everyday activities, and paintings of gazelles, a unicorn hunt, and winged monsters are also preserved. Bakht's son was Kheti, who inherited the office and titles of the nome. He was buried nearby. Bakht was the third member of his clan to bear that name.

Balakros (fl. fourth century B.C.E.) *Greek satrap of Egypt, appointed by Alexander the Great (332–323 B.C.E.)*
Balakros was the son of Amyntos, a member of Alexander's military command. When the conqueror left Egypt, Balakros was given partial control of the Nile region, sharing powers with PEUKESTAS. His term in office and the length of his satrapy are not documented well.

Ba'lu-shipti (fl. 14th century B.C.E.) *prince of Gezer, in modern Palestine*

He succeeded Miliku as Gezer's ruler in the reign of AKHENATEN (1353–1335 B.C.E.). Ba'lu-shipti wrote to the pharaoh to complain about the commander of the Egyptian forces in Palestine, a man named Maya, and his correspondence is included in the 'AMARNA LETTERS. Upon arriving in the area to offer assistance, Maya and his troops reportedly commandeered Ba'lu-shipti's palace, and the prince expressed his outrage to Akhenaten.

baptism This spiritual ritual was depicted in the temple of Hermonthis (modern ERMENT) portraying TUTHMOSIS III (r. 1479–1425 B.C.E.). Another baptism is portrayed on the walls of KARNAK, showing SETI I (r. 1306–1290 B.C.E.) and RAMESSES II (r. 1290–1224 B.C.E.) performing the rite. HATSHEPSUT (r. 1473–1458 B.C.E.) was also portrayed receiving baptism in her shrine in THEBES. The temples at ABYDOS, AMADA, and HELIOPOLIS depicted the same ceremony.

Egyptian baptism was a solemn cleansing by means of water. The rite was often connected with coronations, and at that time called the *hes* purification. In baptismal ceremonies the deities of Egypt saluted the PHARAOH and welcomed him into the sacred circle of kingship. Water and the *ankh,* the ansate cross symbol of life, were shown. Some references to baptism as part of the daily morning rituals of the pharaoh are evident.

barks of the gods Sacred boats, either in miniature form or full-size, used as part of ancient Egyptian religious ceremonies, these vessels were important because they accentuated the nurturing role of the Nile in Egyptian life through the centuries. The religious significance of the barks can be traced to the belief in the spirit ual Nile, which carried the dead to the various levels of eternal paradise and bliss. The spiritual Nile led the deceased out of the mortal world if they were worthy.

RÉ sailed across the heavens on solar barks, using the MANDET to ascend the sky each morning and the MESEKET to descend at twilight. He also employed a bark for his nightly voyage through the TUAT, or the Underworld. The bark of OSIRIS was mentioned in PYRAMID TEXTS. An elaborate vessel, this bark had a cabin for a shrine and was decorated with gold and other precious metals and stones. In the New Kingdom, the bark of Osiris was called the *neshmet* or the *KHA'EMHET,* and was refurbished or replaced by each pharaoh. The bark of the god PTAH was the *neb-heh.*

AMUN's bark, called the *userhetamun,* or the *weseghatamun,* "Mighty of Brow Is Amun," was Egypt's most famous ritual boat. Made of cedar wood and about 200 feet in length, the bark was entirely gilded and dec-

The bark of Amun, from a temple relief in Thebes; such vessels sailed on the Nile and on temple lakes or were carried in gala processions.

orated with gems. The rams' heads were fashioned out of gold. The vessel was replaced or redecorated almost every year and was used for special Amunite ceremonies in and around THEBES. A special lake was built for certain rites, and a temple was designed to house the bark when it was not in use.

Most barks followed a similar design. They were fashioned as floating temples, fronted by miniature obelisks, with flagstaffs and highly ordained cabins, which served as the sanctuary of the god. The major deities had barks covered in gold. Other Egyptian deities sailed in their own barks on feast days, with priests rowing the vessels on sacred lakes or on the Nile. KHONS'S (1) bark was called "Brilliant of Brow" in some eras. The god MIN'S (1) boat was named "Great of Love." The HENNU BOAT of SOKAR was kept in MEDINET HABU and was paraded around the walls of the capital on feast days. This bark was highly ornamented and esteemed as a cultic object. The barks could be actual sailing vessels or be carried on poles in festivals. The gods normally had both types of barks for different rituals. A fleet of such barks was discovered in ABYDOS.

See also ABYDOS FLEET.

Barramiyeh A site on the eastern desert near EDFU, this was a rich mining area for the ancient Egyptians. SETI I (r. 1306–1290 B.C.E.) of the Nineteenth Dynasty recorded his efforts to dig wells for the benefit of the local miners there. Such projects were royal obligations throughout Egypt's history. A temple at the WADI MI'AH celebrated his concerns and care also.

See also NATURAL RESOURCES.

Bastet A goddess of ancient Egypt, whose THEOPHANY was the cat, Bastet's cult center was at BUBASTIS. She was the protector of pregnant women and was a pleasure loving goddess who served as the patroness of music and dance. Bastet was also believed to protect men from diseases and demons. The goddess was considered the personification of the warming rays of the sun on the Nile. She was normally depicted as a woman with a cat's head, holding a SISTRUM and the symbol of life, the *ANKH*.

The goddess remained popular throughout Egypt even to Roman times. Her festivals at Bubastis were among the most well-attended celebrations in Egypt. People set out in festooned barges, and music accompanied all who made the pilgrimage to her shrine. The festival was a time of pranks as well as another designated period of intoxication. A gigantic parade culminated the celebration, and on that day few Egyptians were sober. Shrines of the gods were erected in Rome, Ostia, Nemi, and Pompeii.

Bata (1) A bull's tail, the symbol of a truly ancient deity. Bata, usually depicted as a ram, was used in the anniversary celebrations of the pharaoh, the *heb-sed,* and dates to Predynastic eras. The pharaoh wore a bull's tail as he performed the rituals of the celebration. It is documented that SCORPION I (fl. ca. 31st century B.C.E.) wore the tail in ceremonies at HIERAKONPOLIS and THINIS.

Bata (2) A character in the ancient Egyptian work *TALE OF TWO BROTHERS,* preserved in the Papyrus ORBINEY in the British Museum, the character is believed to represent BATA (1), or Batu, the deity, who quarrels with Anup (a possible representation of the god ANUBIS). Anup's wife, repulsed by Bata when she tries to seduce him, accuses him of assault. Anup learns the truth and slays her, while Bata goes on many adventures. In the end, he sires the first pharaoh of Egypt, AHA (Menes) (r. 2920–? B.C.E.). The tale, much loved in Egypt, was in the library of SETI II (r. 1214–1204 B.C.E.) of the Nineteenth Dynasty.

See also LITERATURE.

Batn el-Hagar Called "the Belly of Stone" by the local inhabitants, a site near the second cataract, Batn el-Hagar is a desolate region extending more than 100 miles, filled with white-water rapids, eddies, and hidden rocks surrounded by harsh wastelands. Such stark landscapes were part of the natural defenses of ancient Egypt throughout its history. The kings normally fortified areas such as Batn el-Hagar, using them to control the movements of the Nubians, modern Sudanese, in the region.

battle of the Nile This was a naval and land engagement that took place in 47 B.C.E. between Julius CAESAR and PTOLEMY XIII (r. 51–47 B.C.E.) on the Nile near ALEXANDRIA. Caesar, who had been under attack in the palace of CLEOPATRA VII (r. 51–30 B.C.E.) after ousting Ptolemy XIII from the throne, faced an Egyptian army opposed to his decision. The Roman leader, however, had summoned an ally, Mithridates of Pergamum, who had arrived with a large military force.

Ptolemy XIII tried to halt Mithridates but saw his units swept aside. He then waited for Caesar to join his ally but was taken by surprise when the Romans sailed around his encamped forces to link up with Mithridates. The Egyptians were routed, and in the effort to retreat, Ptolemy XIII drowned in the Nile. Cleopatra VII became the sole ruler of Egypt.

Bauerdat (Bauerded) (fl. 24th century B.C.E.) *official of the Fifth Dynasty*
Bauerdat served IZEZI (Djedkaré) (r. 2388–2356 B.C.E.) as a leader of expeditions to the regions below the CATARACTS of the Nile. Bauerdat and his companions journeyed as far south as NUBIA, modern Sudan, in the service of the pharaoh. He is supposed to have returned to court with a DWARF, probably of the Deneg variety.

Dwarfs were highly prized in the Egyptian royal households in every period. Bauerdat recorded his honors and service on a mortuary stela.

See also HARKHUF; PEPI II.

Baufré (fl. 26th century B.C.E.) *prince of the Fourth Dynasty*

He was a son of KHUFU (Cheops) (r. 2551–2528 B.C.E.) who is listed in older studies on Egypt as the successor of KHAFRE (Chephren). Baufré was the brother of DJEDEFHOR, a renowned sage. His role in dynastic affairs, however, remains obscure, and there is no evidence that he assumed the throne at any time. Baufré was mentioned in the WESTCAR PAPYRUS and was depicted at WADI HAMMAMAT. His name meant "Ré is his soul." He has also been identified as Nebka. His unfinished pyramid was found in ZAWIET EL-ARYAN.

Bay (Irsu) (fl. 12th century B.C.E.) *official of the Nineteenth Dynasty*

Bay served both SIPTAH and Queen-Pharaoh TWOSRET (r. 1204–1196 B.C.E.). He was supposedly of Syrian descent, a fact that irritated many Egyptian aristocrats of his era. A confidant of Twosret, he began his usurpation of power while she was regent for the young Siptah.

When Twosret served as queen-pharaoh in her own right, Bay was her chancellor. He is listed in Siptah's mortuary texts. The official was much disliked by his contemporaries, however, and he has been recorded as a usurper and interloper during the days of failing pharaonic power. His mortuary graffiti lists him as the one "who establishes the king upon the seat of his father," a phrase denoting his role. He built himself a smaller gravesite in the VALLEY OF THE KINGS.

The Papyrus Harris I described Bay as "the Syrian who made himself chief." The name Irsu translates as a "self-made usurper." His attempt to rule after Twosret died brought SETHNAKHTE, the founder of the Twentieth Dynasty, to action in Thebes. Bay's Egyptian name was Ramesse-kha'emnetjeru. Bay's tomb was taken over by RAMESSES III for the burial of one of his family members, and his remains are unidentified. The tomb was vast and filled with reliefs.

beards   Sacred symbols in the early eras of Egypt, the first conquerors, such as NARMER and the SCORPION King, were depicted as having beards. Reliefs of the Early Dynastic Period (2920–2575 B.C.E.) display beards as well. References to the kings and gods even in later periods noted that these divine beings wore "beards like lapis lazuli." These beards were affectations, however, as the Egyptians normally were clean-shaven or wore only mustaches.

Beatty Papyrus IV, Chester   A document that dates to the Ramessid Period, the Nineteenth and Twenti-eth Dynasties (1307–1070 B.C.E.), the papyrus contains medical diagnoses and prescriptions for the treatment of diseases of the anus. The breast, heart, and bladder are also discussed, indicating an advanced knowledge about the human anatomy concerning organ functions and symptoms. Such papyri have offered modern scholars an insight into the sophisticated medical knowledge and practices of the ancient Egyptians, a science that was not attributed to them in the past.

See also MEDICINE.

Bedouins (Badu; Bedu; Bedwi; Bedawi; Bedway)   The Asiatic, nomadic tribes of the southern SINAI, on Egypt's eastern border, the tribes threatened Egyptian mining interests in the region. The Bedouins tried to hold their ground against the many expeditions sent by the Egyptians in the early eras of the nation. Such expeditions were designed to locate quarries, mines, and other NATURAL RESOURCES. In time full operations were conducted in Bedouin territories, resulting in military campaigns and the eventual displacement of the tribes. The *Bedwi* were sometimes recorded as the *Shashi*, and they were believed to have been members of the Khabiri clan of the Sinai, active in that historical period.

beer   Called *heneket* or *booza*, a popular drink in ancient Egypt, the brew was made of barley and home-brewed in some areas. Pieces of barley bread were soaked in water, and the beer was drained off after a period of fermentation. Beer was kept in vats in cellars and storehouses and was consumed by rich and poor alike. Modern excavations of Egyptian brewery sites indicate that the beer was usually potent. A brewery in HIERAKONPOLIS was recently discovered. Dating to Predynastic eras, this brewery provided 300 gallons of beer a day for local consumption. Another brewery was discovered on the GIZA plateau near the pyramids and is believed to have been used by those working on the monuments. Various brews were served to the local work crews at least three or four times a day. There were five types of beer available, stored in jars. Some were made of barley, emmer, or both grains, and dates, honey, and spices were added for flavors. The Egyptian beer was nutritious and was used as a staple in the diets of commoners in all historical periods. A recipe for beer was discovered in the ruins of 'AMARNA, and when a sample was made from the recipe, the brew was found to be much stronger than modern varieties.

See also AGRICULTURE; FOODS.

bees   A favored insect of the Egyptians, used as a source of honey from the earliest years in the Nile Valley, the bee products resulting from the keeping of hives were taxed by the state in the Ptolemaic Period (304–30 B.C.E.). Beekeeping methods and breeding programs were instituted at this time in the Nile Valley, as honey was a staple in the diets of the people. Honey was used in every era of ancient Egypt as a sweetener, but it was associated with medical practices as well. Honey was a symbol of resurrection and was deemed a poison for ghosts, the dead, demons, and evil spirits; it was used as a warning to any ghosts attempting to steal a baby. A New Kingdom (1550–1070 B.C.E.) lullaby lists the fatal qualities of the substance.

See also FOODS.

Behbeit el-Hagar (Per-hebyt; Iseum) This was a site in the north central territory of the Delta, near SEBENNYTOS (modern Sammanud). A temple dedicated to the goddess ISIS was built in Behbeit el-Hagar. Reliefs were placed in the temple by NECTANEBO I (r. 380–362 B.C.E.) and NECTANEBO II (r. 360–343 B.C.E.). PTOLEMY II PHILADELPHUS (r. 285–246 B.C.E.) completed the temple, and PTOLEMY III EUERGETES (r. 246–221 B.C.E.) added other reliefs. The temple of Isis was plundered in a later era by the Romans, and parts of it were taken to Rome for the observances of the Isis cult there.

Behnesa *See* OXYRRYNCHUS (1).

Beit el-Wali This was a temple site south of ASWAN, erected by RAMESSES II (r. 1290–1224 B.C.E.) of the Nineteenth Dynasty. A detailed account of the pharaoh's military campaigns was inscribed on the walls of this temple. A narrow court, adorned with reliefs and scenes, led to the interior chambers. This temple was moved to another island to save it from the waters of the High Aswan Dam.

Beit Khallaf A site on the western shore of Nile near AKHMIN, Old Kingdom (2575–2134 B.C.E.), Beit Khallaf contains famous tombs, as well as seals and mortuary effects bearing the names of DJOSER (r. 2630–2611 B.C.E.) and NEBKA (r. 2649–2630 B.C.E.). The territory was a necropolis for the Third Dynasty (2649–2575 B.C.E.). A brick MASTABA was also found on the site, with ground-level and subterranean chambers. The seals of KHUFU (Cheops) (r. 2551–2520 B.C.E.) were discovered in the lower sections.

Bekhen Quarry Map This is a remarkable geological document that dates to the reign of RAMESSES IV (1163–1156 B.C.E.), called the oldest surviving geological map in the world. A scribe, Amennakhte, was the author of this text, which is contained in a papyrus scroll that is at least six feet long and 16 inches wide. Interior segments are missing, as well as segments at one end.

This quarry map was found at DEIR EL-MEDINA and is in the Egyptian Museum at Turin, Italy. The map traces routes through the desert to the WADI HAMMAMAT and delineates wells and temples. The map also describes the types of stone available in the region, such as schist and pink granite. The Bekhen area was mountainous and had seams of gold as well. Two sites are listed as "mountains of gold." Wadi Hammamat began at Kaptan and was a dried riverbed. Recent comparisons of the map and the actual geological formations in the Eastern Desert document the map's accuracy.

See also NATURAL RESOURCES; QUARRIES.

Bekhtan's Princess *See* BENTRESH STELA.

benben **(pyramidion)** The ancient Egyptian insignia kept in the shrine of the god RÉ at HELIOPOLIS and incorporating the pyramidal symbol with the rays of the sun, this sign evoked the concept of resurrection and was also considered the personification of the god ATUM. Ré was associated with the *benben* in his cultic rites, and the symbol was an influence on the builders of the massive pyramids of the Old Kingdom. As such, the pyramids, gigantic *benbens,* served as stages of resurrection rituals and commemorative ceremonies that inspired Egyptians in all periods. The *benben* was the PRIMEVAL MOUND, the first to catch the rays of the sun as caps on pyramids. Formed out of precious metals, the *benbens* were the first part of the pyramids plundered by later rulers.

Beni Hasan (Menat-Khufu) A site north of HERMOPOLIS MAGNA which was a NOME stronghold in the First Intermediate Period (2134–2040 B.C.E.) and in the Twelfth Dynasty (1991–1783 B.C.E.), the tombs of the nomarchs of the Middle Kingdom (2040–1640 B.C.E.) were discovered in the upper range of the Oryx nome necropolis area there, all having elaborate chambers, columns, and offering chapels, with elegant vestibules. Some 39 tombs were found. Almost 900 burials from the Sixth Dynasty (2323–2150 B.C.E.) to the First Intermediate Period (2134–2040 B.C.E.) are in the lower cemetery, now stripped of decorations. Thirty-nine Middle Kingdom TOMBS were also erected on a bluff at Beni Hasan, but only 12 were decorated. The style of this age employed a false door and lotus bud columns. Some burial shafts were also used, as well as columned ante chambers. Paintings depict the gods ANUBIS and OSIRIS in the tombs, as well as military events, mythical animals, and daily routines.

Noted tombs include those of Kheti, BAKHT, KHNUMHOTEP (1), and others. These are famous for paintings of historical events in the area and provide biographical details of these Middle Kingdom officials. HATSHEPSUT (r. 1473–1458 B.C.E.) started the unique shrine located just to the south of Beni Hasan. The Greeks named it the SPEOS ARTEMIDOS and it is now called *stabl antar,* the Stable of Antar. The temple on the site was completed by SETI I (r. 1306–1290 B.C.E.), and it was dedicated to PAKHET, the lion goddess. The modern name of the site, Beni Hasan al-Shurruq, is derived from an Arabic tribe that settled in the region in the 18th century. Quality limestone is plentiful in the cliffs of the area.

Benimeryt (fl. 15th century B.C.E.) *official of the Eighteenth Dynasty*
He served TUTHMOSIS III (r. 1479–1425 B.C.E.) as the royal architect and a director of public works. Benimeryt was involved in Tuthmosis III's building projects in Upper and Lower Egypt, and especially at THEBES. He also served as an overseer of the royal treasury. Much honored for his skills, this official was given the title of Tutor of Princess Merit-Amun, an honorary post held by outstanding officials in the capital.

Bennu (Bnr, Bnrt)   The PHOENIX-like bird of ancient Egyptian legends and religious mythology that was sheltered in the PERSEA TREE in HELIOPOLIS, the solar and Osirian cults used the bird in their cultic ceremonies as a symbol of resurrection. The eggs of the Bennu bird, actually created by priests out of precious spices, were entombed at Heliopolis as part of the rites there. Images of the Bennu were found on tomb walls from the earliest eras. A date palm on the Nile bore the same name. The Bennu was depicted as a heron and was the incarnation of the sun, creating itself out of a fire at the top of the Persea Tree. The creature originally sprang from the heart of OSIRIS, but it was a form of the god ATUM. The name translates as "to rise in brilliance."

Bent Pyramid   This curious mortuary monument was erected by SNEFRU (r. 2575–2551 B.C.E.) at Dashur. Also called the Rhomboidal Pyramid, it was an attempt to perfect the pyramidal form. Constructed out of local limestone, the structure had several severe angles that caused instability. The original angle of the walls could not be completed as a result and had to be altered, which led to the pyramid's unique appearance. A descending passage inside the pyramid has a corbelled roof and cedar beam; a mud-brick wall originally surrounded the pyramid, flanked by two stelae; and a valley temple was also included in the design. Snefru's son, KHUFU (Cheops) (r. 2551–2528 B.C.E.), built the Great Pyramid at Giza. Khufu kept building pyramids until his architects and construction engineers perfected the form for the Giza mortuary monuments.

Bentresh   *See* TARSET.

Bentresh Stela   This is a stela dating to 300 B.C.E., relating a story concerning RAMESSES II (r. 1290–1224 B.C.E.) at THEBES. The story details the arrival of the princess of Bekhtan (identified as the land of the HITTITES). She was given to Ramesses as a wife and her name is listed in the stela as Bentresh, although she was probably MA'AT HORNEFRURÉ. In the legend promoted by the Bentresh Stela, the princess was possessed by a demon when she arrived in Egypt. She was so lovely that the pharaoh made an effort to free her of her evil spell. Finally, when all else failed, an image of the god KHONS was brought into her presence and the demon fled. The story appears to have been a commemorative fancy concerning the marriage of Ramesses II to a Hittite princess during his reign. The legend appeared in other variations as well and was probably fostered by the priests of Khons in an attempt to bolster the reputation of their god, by linking him with the glories of Ramesses II.

   See also HITTITE ALLIANCE.

Berenib (Berner-ib) (fl. 30th century B.C.E.) *royal woman of the First Dynasty*
Berenib was supposedly the *hemet,* or ranking consort of AHA (Menes) (r. 2920–? B.C.E.), although she was not the mother of the heir. When she married Aha, she was probably the Memphite clan heiress of the period: the woman bearing the aristocratic titles and privileges. Her marriage to Aha would have provided legitimacy to his claims and stabilized the reign. Her name meant "Sweet of Heart." She was provided with a tomb in ABYDOS, and her name was found on articles discovered in NEITHHOTEP's tomb as well.

Berenice (Berenike) (d. 275 B.C.E.) *royal woman of the Ptolemaic Period*
She was the consort of PTOLEMY I SOTER (r. 304–284 B.C.E.) and the mother of PTOLEMY II PHILADELPHUS and ARSINOE (2). A widow from Macedonia, Berenice was also the mother of MAGAS of Cyrene and a daughter who became the wife of Pyrrhus of Epirus. She was reportedly a stepsister of Ptolemy I and arrived in Egypt in the entourage of Queen EURYDICE, the daughter of King Antipater of Macedonia, given to Ptolemy I as part of an alliance. Ptolemy I married Berenice around 317 B.C.E., deposing Eurydice and inventing a legendary royal genealogy to support his choice. Berenice gave birth to the heir in 308 B.C.E. Eurydice's children were removed from the lines of succession as a result. Berenice died ca. 275 B.C.E. and was posthumously deified by Ptolemy I.

Berenice (2) (Berenike Syra) (fl. third century B.C.E.) *royal woman of the Ptolemaic Period*
The daughter of PTOLEMY II PHILADELPHUS (r. 285–246 B.C.E.) and ARSINOE (2), she was given to the Seleucid ruler ANTIOCHUS II (Theos) in marriage. Antiochus renounced his queen, Laodice, and established Berenice's court at Antioch. When Antiochus II died, Berenice and her son were killed by Queen Laodice to clear the way for her offspring. PTOLEMY III EUERGETES (r. 246–221 B.C.E.), her brother, started the Third Syrian War to avenge Berenice and invaded the lands of Laodice and her son, Seleucus II Callinicus.

Berenice (3) (Berenike) (fl. third century B.C.E.) *royal woman of the Ptolemaic Period*
She was the consort of PTOLEMY III EUERGETES (r. 246–221 B.C.E.) and the daughter of King Magas of Cyrene (modern Libya) who married Ptolemy III as part of an alliance. When Demetrius of Farr, a Macedonian prince, was brought in by some Cyrenian courtiers to thwart the marriage, Berenice arranged his murder. She became Ptolemy III's queen in 246 B.C.E.

When Ptolemy set out to avenge the death of his sister Berenice (2) in Syria, Berenice dedicated a lock of her hair for his safe return. This lock was transferred to heaven, according to court astronomical priests, and became the new constellation, *coma berenices,* "the Hair of Berenice." She gave birth to four children: PTOLEMY IV PHILOPATOR, MAGAS, ARSINOE (3), and BERENICE (6), who died as a child. After Ptolemy III died, Berenice served as regent for five years but was linked to a plot to regain prominence. Ptolemy IV had her poisoned at the insistence of the courtier Sosibius. Magas was scalded to death.

Berenice (4) (Berenike) (d. ca. 80 B.C.E.) *royal woman of the Ptolemaic Period*
Berenice was the daughter of PTOLEMY IX SOTER II (r. 116–110, 109–107, 88–80 B.C.E.) and Queen CLEOPATRA SELENE. She married her uncle, PTOLEMY X ALEXANDER I (r. 107–88 B.C.E.), and became the queen of Egypt. Ptolemy X was forced to flee from Egypt because the people believed that he had killed Queen CLEOPATRA (3). Recruiting a mercenary army, Ptolemy X retook Egypt and plundered the golden coffin of ALEXANDER III THE GREAT in order to cover his expenses.

Expelled again, Ptolemy X was accompanied to Lycia by Berenice. He was killed in exile, and she returned to Egypt in 88 B.C.E. By 80 B.C.E. she was sole ruler of Egypt, but she was murdered soon after by Ptolemy Alexander, the son of Ptolemy X.

Berenice (5) (Berenike) (fl. first century B.C.E.) *royal woman of the Ptolemaic Period*
Berenice was the eldest daughter of PTOLEMY XII NEOS DIONYSIUS (r. 76–51 B.C.E.) and the sister of CLEOPATRA VII. When her father was forced to leave Egypt, Berenice ruled the land in his absence. She also married Archelaus of Pontus. When Ptolemy XII returned to Alexandria, he executed Berenice on the charge of treason.

Berenice (6) (Berenike) (d. ca. 240 B.C.E.) *royal woman of the Ptolemaic Period*
Berenice was the daughter of PTOLEMY III EUERGETES (r. 246–221 B.C.E.) and Queen BERENICE (3). She died at a very young age but achieved a remarkable posthumous status in Egypt. After 240 B.C.E., she was identified with the god OSIRIS. Rites and shrines were devoted to her cult, and she was served by a special group of priests established to maintain the cult of the royal family, living or dead.

Berenice (7) A site on the Red Sea, near modern Ras Benas, founded by PTOLEMY II PHILADELPHUS (r. 285–246 B.C.E.). The town was linked to KOPTOS by TRADE routes and became a chief trading port for wares from Arabia, eastern Africa, and India in the early Roman Period (after 30 B.C.E.).

Berlin Papyri A series of documents now in the Egyptian Museum, Berlin. Some date to the Middle Kingdom (2040–1640 B.C.E.) and others to the Ramessid Period (1307–1070 B.C.E.). One of the papyri, discovered in SAQQARA, contains 204 separate paragraphs and discusses medical conditions and treatments. The papyrus repeats much of the Eber and Hearst texts but is believed to be a copy of a papyrus of the Old Kingdom dynasties (2575–2134 B.C.E.). Diagnoses and treatises on rheumatism, ear problems, fertility, and the conditions of the heart are treated in this document. Another papyrus contains literary and popular mythological works. Also included in the texts are the tale of *SINUHE THE SAILOR,* the story of *Khufu and the Magicians,* and "THE ELOQUENT PEASANT" OF HERAKLEOPOLIS, all valued for their demonstrations of Egyptian LITERATURE.

Bersha (Deir al-Bersha) This was a site north of 'AMARNA, where AMENHOTEP III (r. 1391–1353 B.C.E.) reopened a mining site near the famous TUREH quarry, valued for its high-quality limestone. TOMBS of local NOMARCHS were discovered in Bersha, rock-cut in the cliffs of the valley. Some of the tombs date to the Twelfth Dynasty (1991–1783 B.C.E.) or earlier. The most noted of the tombs was constructed for DJEHUTIHOTEP, called "the Great Overlord of the Hare Nome." The chapel was designed as a portico with two columns and a niched inner chamber. The west wall of the interior room contained the famous scenes depicting Djehutihotep directing the transport of a colossal statue from the HATNUB quarries.

Bes An ancient Egyptian god in the shape of a grotesque DWARF who was the patron of women and childbirth, he probably was a Babylonian deity originally. Bes was also the patron of war and the protector of hunters. His cultic home was supposedly PUNT. The god was depicted in reliefs and statues as a dwarf, with a leonine head and a protruding tongue. His legs were bowed, and his ears were large. He was clad in animal skins, bore a tail, and wore a fashioned diadem. Appealing mostly to commoners, the god was popular in the New Kingdom (1550–1070 B.C.E.). In the Ptolemaic Period (304–30 B.C.E.) his portrait adorned the walls of "the birthing places" erected at the time. His consort was Beset. Bes carried the *sa* symbol of protection.

Beset *See* BES.

Biahmu (Byahmu) A site northeast of HAWARA and near MEDINET AL-FAIYUM in central Egypt. The remains of two colossal statues of AMENEMHET III (r. 1844–1797 B.C.E.) were discovered there. The bases of the two fallen statues are the remains of a temple complex believed to have been erected at Hawara or Biahmu on the nearby dried lake. The statues were originally the size of the surviving colossi of AMENHOTEP III (r. 1391–1353 B.C.E.). Amenemhet III and his dynastic rulers were patrons of the Faiyum area in their own period. These statues have been compared to the COLOSSI OF MEMNON.

Biga An island near Philae, called the home of "the PURE MOUND" by ancient Egyptians, or Abaton, the mound was associated with Egypt's creation traditions. Biga was also revered as a site of OSIRIS's tomb. A temple was erected on the island.

Bint-Anath (Batau'anth) (fl. 13th century B.C.E.) *royal woman of the Nineteenth Dynasty*
She was the daughter of RAMESSES II (r. 1290–1224 B.C.E.) and Queen ISETNOFRET (1). Bint-Anath became Ramesses II's consort when Queen NEFERTARI and Iset-nofret died or retired. She is depicted in ABU SIMBEL on a pillar in the main hall, offering a SISTRUM and flowers to the goddess ANUKIS. Also called Bent-Anta, she was honored with a colossal statue in a temple at Ipu, near Akhmin.

bird symbols The representation of divine powers used by the ancient Egyptians in religious reliefs and ceremonies concerning certain deities. Bird THEOPHANIES were honored throughout Egypt's history. In some eras the birds were mummified and revered in temples. The ability of birds to fly gave them special significance for the Egyptians because in that activity they reflected the spiritual aspirations of the people and engendered many funerary beliefs. The BA, the soul, was always depicted as a winged being.

The hawk was the insignia for HORUS and RÉ, the falcon identified as Ré-Harakhte, Horus, MONTU and KHONS (1). The IBIS represented the god THOTH, and the GOOSE symbolized GEB, known as the Great Cackler and in some later eras was associated with AMUN. The swallow represented ISIS and the owl was a hieroglyphic character. The sparrow was an omen of bad tidings in some periods of Egyptian history, and the sight of a dead bird, called a *zent*, was considered a particularly ominous sign of disaster by various groups. Because the gods sometimes were depicted as physical representations of birds, various temples raised flocks of sacred species for the delight of the people. These hawks, falcons, or other varieties performed on special platforms at the gateways to the temples.

Biridiya (fl. 14th century B.C.E.) *prince of Ar-Megiddo, the Canaanite site on Mount Carmel*
Biridiya was in power during the reign of AKHENATEN (1353–1335 B.C.E.) and wrote to complain about the withdrawal of Egyptian forces from his area. Ar-Megiddo, which had been in Egyptian control since the reign of TUTHMOSIS III, was apparently under siege as Biridiya made his complaint. The prince's communication, which was included in the 'AMARNA LETTERS, demonstrates the chaos resulting from Akhenaten's policies in the empire.

Bir Tarfawi This is a site in the LIBYAN DESERT, along with Bir Sahara, where evidence was found concerning the Prehistoric Period called Saharan Mousterian. This dated to 80,000–150,000 years ago in the Egyptian Paleolithic Period. Side scrapers, points, and denticules were discovered at Bir Tarfawi.

Bitter Lakes A region stretching from the Nile to the WADI TIMULAT in the Egyptian Delta, the lakes became popular in the Late Period (712–332 B.C.E.) and in the Ptolemaic Period (304–30 B.C.E.), when the CANAL OF NECHO II was developed to connect the lakes to the Red Sea.

Blemmyes A Nubian (modern Sudanese) group that served as mercenary warriors for Egypt, the Blemmyes were associated with the famous MEDJAY troops. A nomadic people, the Blemmyes served in military campaigns and as capital police. During the Roman Period, following the suicide of CLEOPATRA VII in 30 B.C.E., the Blemmyes took over KOPTOS and had to be removed by Roman forces. The city was almost destroyed as a result.

board games These were a recreation popular in all historical periods of ancient Egypt. The people of the Nile Valley were delighted by all types of amusements or diversions, and a variety of table games were played in the palace and in humbler abodes. Mortuary reliefs in the tombs of royalty and nobles depict personages engaged in such games. FAIENCE and ivory inland boxes were designed for the game of *senet* and were discovered in tombs. These boxes were fashioned with 30 squares and had places for position games, much like the modern Parcheesi.

Senet and the game called *tjau* were possibly of Asiatic origin. "Robbers," another game, was played with five or more pieces. The moves were determined by the toss of knucklebones or by wooden or ivory wands. The game boxes had drawers held in place by ivory pieces, which were shaped like cones or spools. Another game, "Serpent," was played on a circular board with small balls inscribed with the names of the early Egyptian rulers. "Jackals and Hounds," one of the most popular of the board amusements, used wands to determine moves.

boats From the earliest eras the Egyptians treasured the BARKS OF THE GODS, elaborate vessels carrying images of the deities in festival processions. The Nile was a true highway, and the Egyptians learned to use large and small vessels to conduct their daily affairs. Boats and barges throughout Egyptian history carried trade goods and military units to both local and far-flung destinations.

The people of the Nile Valley were at home on the water. The earliest rulers and their courts were provided boats for their celebrations and their military campaigns. The historical expeditions into NUBIA (modern Sudan) during the Middle Kingdom (2040–1640 B.C.E.) brought about the construction of efficient canals at the sites of the Nile rapids. In Nubia, in the Nile Valley and along the Mediterranean Sea, called the Uat-ur (the Great Green), military or trade expeditions used both land units and naval vessels.

Boats had specific religious connotations as well, especially in the mortuary rituals of every age. Souls were carried to the western shores, the abode of the dead. The magnificent boat of KHUFU (Cheops) (r. 2551–2528 B.C.E.), discovered at the Great Pyramid at GIZA, showcases the skills of the ship builders of the Old Kingdom. Now on public display, Khufu's wooden boat stands 13 stories tall. Some 1,200 beams of wood form the hull, held in place by an elaborate system of ropes and knots. At the necropolis of ABYDOS, the earliest royal burial site, an entire fleet of boats associated with the mortuary rituals has been discovered, skillfully preserved in individual burial mounds.

The earliest boats were made of bundles of papyrus lashed together, probably in the Predynastic Period (before 3000 B.C.E.), but shipbuilding flourished as the Egyptians moved through the Delta and understood the presence of enemies on the borders. The campaigns to conquer Nubia during the Middle Kingdom led to an increased number of naval forces, with pharaohs such as SENWOSRET III (r. 1878–1841 B.C.E.) using large fleets and canals to build a chain of garrisons on the Nile in Nubia.

In the New Kingdom Period, 'AHMOSE (NEBPEHTIRÉ) (r. 1550–1525 B.C.E.) used the Nile effectively in his campaign against the HYKSOS and the Nubians. TUTHMOSIS I (r. 1504–1492 B.C.E.), who began the Egyptian Empire, employed naval forces with skill. The pharaohs that followed Tuthmosis I perfected the transfer of troops by sea and expanded the number of naval units. A great naval station was also built near Memphis, at Peru-Nefer.

After the SEA PEOPLES destroyed the HITTITES and city-states, they then attacked Egypt during the reign of RAMESSES III (r. 1194–1163 B.C.E.), but the Egyptian naval forces destroyed the Sea Peoples by trapping them in Nile channels and defeating them in land battles with the Egyptian cavalry. The collapse of the New Kingdom and the empire, however, brought about military weakness because the land was not united but under the rule of local, petty kings. Egypt's naval forces were not employed again until foreign nations invaded the Nile Valley and conquered Egypt. One development of the Ptolemaic Dynasty was the use of massive royal barges, a custom adopted by the Roman emperors. CLEOPATRA VII (r. 51–30 B.C.E.) possessed a remarkable barge during her reign.

Book of Caverns A form of the traditional funerary texts on tomb walls or enclosed in burials on papyri providing spells and incantations to safeguard the deceased beyond the grave, the *Book of Caverns* illustrated RÉ on his six-stage journey through Tuat, or the Underworld. The moral imperatives of the various episodes in the land beyond the grave are quite striking. The *Book of Caverns* mirrors the traditional didactic LITERATURE of Egypt and guides the dead to moral enlightenment and eternal bliss.

See also TOMB TEXTS.

Book of Overthrowing Apophis *See* OVERTHROWING APOPHIS.

Book of the Dead A loose collection of magical spells and incantations that were normally written on papyrus and sometimes illustrated, and which were popular in Egypt as early as the New Kingdom (1550–1070 B.C.E.). The original writings were on the walls of the TOMBS in SAQQARA. Middle Kingdom (2040–1640 B.C.E.) coffins also contained early versions. An important element of the mortuary rituals, the Book of the Dead was transformed over the centuries and provided guidance for the deceased on his or her journey to paradise. During the New Kingdom, the Book of the Dead was buried with the mummified remains.

The Book of the Dead was later called the *pert em hru* (Chapters of the Coming Forth by Day). The Am Duat, or Am Tuat, another version, was designed to instruct the deceased on how to overcome the dangers of the afterlife by enabling them to assume the form of several mythical creatures, and to give them the passwords necessary for admittance to certain stages of the Underworld. The spells also allowed the deceased to proclaim themselves as bearing the identity of many gods. It is estimated that there were approximately 190 independent "chapters," or sections, of the Book of the Dead, although there is no single extant papyrus containing all of them.

The spells and passwords were placed in the tombs of the ancient Egyptians from about 1600 B.C.E. onward, although there are indications that they were included in the sections called chapters as early as the Twelfth Dynasty (1900 B.C.E.). These spells and passwords were not part of a ritual but were fashioned for the deceased, to be recited in the afterlife. Egyptians believed in the efficacy of MAGIC and in the cultic powers of the gods.

An illustration of everyday life, from the mortuary text of the Book of the Dead, used in all eras of Egypt *(Hulton Archive)*

At the same time, they had considerable faith in life after death, a belief that included specific paradises and activities. The abundance of their material world was something cherished by the Egyptians, who translated paradise into similar terms, with the same fertile fields, light, and sacred waters.

In the early periods the funerary texts were reserved for the reigning families and other aristocrats. In time, however, these texts became more and more available to the commoners. The Book of the Dead became a normal item of manufacturing, and the individual could decide the number of chapters to be included, the types of illustrations, and the quality of the papyrus used. The individual was limited only by his or her financial resources.

During the New Kingdom (1550–1070 B.C.E.), the papyri were lengthy and involved whole collections of spells and passwords, some magnificently illustrated in color. The versions of the Theban RECENSIONS Book of the Dead, a form adopted at the time, averaged between 15 and 90 feet in length and about 13 inches in width. Some papyri were made to order for special clients, but great stocks of the Book of the Dead were available for those who could afford them, and individual names were put into them when purchased.

The extant papyri of the Book of the Dead were written in hieroglyphic script, called the hieratic. They contained vignettes, protests of innocence, spells, and magic words to provide comfort and security in Tuat. Three of the most famous versions of the Book of the Dead, discovered in the tombs of Egyptians, called ANI PAPYRUS, ANHAI PAPYRUS, and HUNEFER, are now in the British Museum, London.

The *Book of the Pylons,* called the *Shat en Sebau,* was another version of the Book of the Dead. This work was written to provide the dead with detailed descriptions of the Underworld. Another funerary text, called alternately the *Deliverance of Mankind* or the *Destruction of Mankind,* was discovered in the tomb of SETI I (r. 1306–1290 B.C.E.) of the Nineteenth Dynasty. Yet other versions of the Book of the Dead included the *Book of Breathing,* the *Book of Traversing in Eternity,* and the *Book of Being* in Tuat. The various religious or funerary texts called the Book of the Dead evolved over the centuries as mortuary rituals became broader and more sophisticated in their appeal. New versions appeared in the New Kingdom, and another appeared after the fall of the pharaonic dynasties. These were recensions, formulated in HELIOPOLIS, THEBES, and SAIS.

The ancient Egyptians did not fear death as the end of human existence. Rather, they believed that they were part of the cosmos and would thus continue to exist beyond the grave, in one form or another. Copies of the Book of the Dead were given to children by their parents as gifts, and parents also provided tombs for their offspring, if they were able to do so.

Further reading: Ellis, Normandi, Gary Robertson, and Robert Kelley. *Awakening Osiris: The Egyptian Book of the Dead.* New York: Phanes, 1991; Goelet, Ogden, ed.; Raymond, Faulkner, trans. *The Egyptian Book of the Dead: The Book of Going Forth by Day.* New York: Chronicle Books, 2000; Seleem, Ramses. *Illustrated Egyptian Book of the Dead.* New York: Sterling, 2001; Wallis Budge, A. E. *The Book of the Dead: The Hieroglyphic Transcript and Translation into English of the Papyrus of Ani.* New York: Gramercy, 1995; Winston, Robert. *The Egyptian Book of the Dead.* New York: Penguin Classics, 2008.

Book of the Gates See BOOK OF THE DEAD.

Book of Thoth See THOTH, BOOK OF.

Bubastis This was a site 50 miles north of modern Cairo, now called Zapgazig, the capital of the eighteenth nome of the Lower Kingdom and the cult center for the goddess BASTET. A vast temple was erected in the Ramessid Period (1306–1070 B.C.E.), and some statues from this structure survive. A Sixth Dynasty (2323–2150 B.C.E.) shrine was also discovered, with architectural seals belonging to KHUFU (Cheops) (r. 2551–2528 B.C.E.) and KHAFRE (Chephren) (r. 2575–2134 B.C.E.) of the Fourth Dynasty. A seal of PEPI I (r. 2289–2255 B.C.E.) was also found on the site, which contained Tell Basta. A great

A burial site for animals under the protection of the goddess Bastet in Bubastis *(Erich Lessing / Art Resource, NY)*

catacomb containing the remains of mummified cats was found in Bubastis, which was a popular destination for pilgrims attending the lavish festivals in honor of Bastet, and AMENHOTEP III (r. 1391–1353 B.C.E.) celebrated an anniversary of his coronation there. He left an inscription at Bubastis to commemorate the event and to announce his military campaign in NUBIA. Bubastis is recorded as having suffered an earthquake ca. 2700.

The city was a thriving community before the Fourth Dynasty and was abandoned in the first century C.E. Egypt's largest festival was held there, with as many as 700,000 celebrators spending days in the vicinity. At the close of the New Kingdom (1070 B.C.E.), Bubastis became an even more important site. The city straddled one of the major TRADE routes connecting MEMPHIS to the Mediterranean and SINAI regions. OSORKON II (r. 883–855 B.C.E.) erected a temple there, and NECTANEBO II (r. 360–343 B.C.E.) built a sanctuary.

Bubastite Portal This was a gateway to a court of the temple of AMUN at KARNAK in THEBES, erected by SHOSHENQ I (r. 945–924 B.C.E.). He had planned to renovate the entire court but died before the rest of the architectural work could be accomplished. The elaborate gateway, covered in detailed reliefs, celebrates Shoshenq I's campaigns in Palestine.

Bucheum A site at ERMENT (Hermonthis), on the edge of the desert, south of THEBES, serving as a necropolis for the BUCHIS bulls, the Egyptians called it *bakhbekh*. Extensive, the necropolis also contained the graves of cows, called "the Mothers of BUCHIS." NECTANEBO II (r. 360–343 B.C.E.) built on the site. Thirty-six Buchis bulls were buried there, with their mothers interred nearby.

Buchis (Bukhe) The ancient Egyptian sacred bull residing in ERMENT (Hermonthis) and buried at the necropolis of the center, Buchis was considered a THEOPHANY or early form of the god MONTU, and then designated as a manifestation of the Theban deity AMUN. Any bull selected for the temple ceremonies had to have a white body and a black head from birth. A cemetery provided for these animals was called the BUCHEUM and contained COFFINS with lids weighing up to 15 tons for the remains. Other tombs were carved out of walls to receive the animals' bodies. The Buchis bull was called "the Bull of the Mountains of Sunrise and Sunset."

Buhen Buhen, a fortress between the second and first cataracts of the Nile near Wadi Halfa, was settled as an outpost as early as the Second Dynasty (2770–2649 B.C.E.). Military fortresses were a basic element of Egyptian defenses from the earliest eras and were refurbished and garrisoned by each new royal line. As Nubia's products and natural resources—particularly the gold mines—were considered vital to the Egyptian economy,

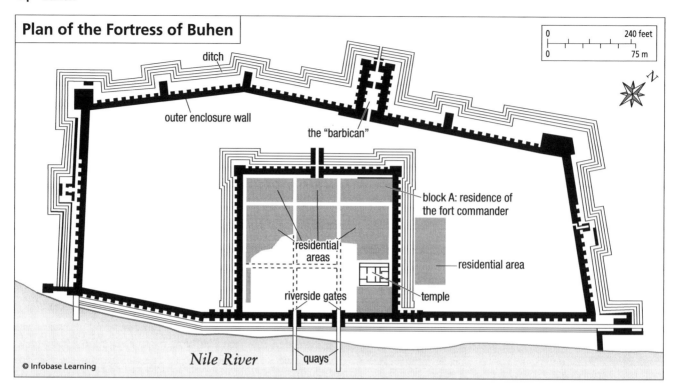

Plan of the Fortress of Buhen

0 ────── 240 feet
0 ────── 75 m

ditch

outer enclosure wall

the "barbican"

block A: residence of the fort commander

residential areas

residential area

riverside gates

temple

© Infobase Learning

Nile River   quays

---

the military outpost at Buhen was considered vital in defending the ability to exploit these resources.

SITE DESCRIPTION

Erected just north of the second cataract, the great fortress of Buhen was built to serve both as a military garrison and caravan stop and transfer center. Buhen, the most northerly of a series of forts in Nubia, was designed to house self-sufficient military units and to provide residences, administrative offices, and storage facilities for trade expeditions. Copper brought from the southern mines could be processed in a smelt at Buhen. Safe boxes were also on the site in order to protect particular treasures being transported to Aswan.

The architectural design of Buhen was reportedly approved by SENWOSRET III (r. 1878–1841 B.C.E.). The forts further south were also apparently built according to the Buhen design. These forts, however, varied in size and some lacked Buhen's extensive accommodations.

The fortress itself was built on a rise so that it dominated the local Nubian landscape. It extended over 500 feet (150 meters) along the bank of the river and occupied some 42,500 feet (13,000 square meters) of land. The structure was designed to house the military units and their families. A battalion of the Egyptian army at the time numbered some 500 men, so it is possible that an entire battalion was on duty there. The "King's Son of Kush," the VICEROY who governed the territory, also resided there at times. Buhen was not just a fortress, but a miniature Egyptian city.

The sentry station at Gebel Turob, located on a hill, had men on duty night and day. They watched for the approach of Nubians, and if boats appeared on the southern horizon, they ran to the fort. Buhen would stand on alert and would meet the Nubians with a large unit, denying them access to the river north of the fort. Another sentry station was added to the defenses at modern Gebel Sheikh Suleiman.

The interior of Buhen contained religious temples, chapels, and administrative offices. The main compound was large enough for a general assembly of troops. Bakeries, breweries, laundries, magazines, warehouses, armories, mess halls, barracks, family housing, and resource processing areas were located within the complex.

CONSTRUCTION

The cataracts of the Nile served as effective sites upon which to erect garrisons and fortresses. Ships sailing on the Nile were unable to maneuver the rapids and the large granite boulders that caused them. The Egyptians built canals that could be used as detours around the cataracts, and they used the land areas beside the cataracts as logistical sites for controlling all traffic on the river.

Buhen, which displayed remarkable military innovations in defensive architecture, was constructed as a garrison overlooking the Nile. The purpose of Buhen was to ensure the safety of the caravans coming into Egypt that carried Nubian goods (animal and agricultural products as well as gold and other metals) and to halt any

Nubian incursions marching northward. It was seen also as a staging area for possible campaigns southward into Nubia. Constructed out of a rock base, Buhen was surrounded by multilayered mud-brick walls that were reinforced with timber. An outer ditch, guarded by ramparts with loop holes (or stone slits) for the firing of arrows, was smoothed on a sloping wall, descending to the base in order to deter scaling by the enemy. If an enemy force succeeded in getting past this first defense, there was a second wall, similar in thickness, and positioned so that the area between the first and the succeeding wall formed a killing field. Defenders had multiple slots in their levels from which they could aim at the individuals trapped below. Buhen had two entrances, a water gate and a narrower gate, flanked by towers. A drawbridge defended this narrower entrance. External buttresses faced south and east.

Begun in the Old Kingdom (2575–2134 B.C.E.), Buhen was not maintained when that dynastic line failed. During the First Intermediate Period (2134–2040 B.C.E.), a time of chaos, the site was probably deserted. However, the warrior-pharaohs of the Middle Kingdom (2040–1640 B.C.E.) established the fort in its defensive and monumental splendor. It took thousands of laborers to construct the site. These pharaohs added the canals at the Nile cataracts and established a line of forts as they penetrated deeper into the southern regions. Buhen was occupied by the Nubians, probably during the Second Intermediate Period (1640–1550 B.C.E.). Not until the Nubian chief A'ata was defeated late in the reign of 'Ahmose (Nebpehtiré) (d. 1525 B.C.E.) and taken back to Thebes (modern Luxor) was Buhen once again an Egyptian outpost. Pharaohs such as TUTHMOSIS III (r. 1479–1425 B.C.E.) refurbished the fort while establishing the Egyptian Empire.

The Ramesids of the Nineteenth Dynasty (1307–1196 B.C.E.) and Twentieth Dynasty (1196–1070 B.C.E.) maintained Buhen with vigor. When the New Kingdom collapsed, however, the strengthened Nubians retook the fortress.

ARCHAEOLOGY

Buhen no longer exists: The site was covered by Lake Nasser, created by the Aswan High Dam, in 1964. The size and complexity of Buhen attracted teams of archaeologists prior to the site's inundation. As early as 1819, the ruins were studied, and more extensive excavations were made between 1956 and 1964 by British Egyptologist Walter Bryan Emery (1902–1971).

Further reading: Caminos, R. A. *The New Kingdom Temples of Buhen,* Vol. 1. *Egypt Exploration Society,* 1974; Emery, W. B., et al. *The Fortress of Buhen: The Archaeological Report.* Egypt Exploration Society, 1979; Smith, H. S. *The Fortress of Buhen: The Inscriptions.* Egypt Exploration Society, 1976.

"Building Inscription" A unique text discovered in ABYDOS and dating to the reign of 'AHMOSE (NEBPEHTIRÉ) (r. 1550–1525 B.C.E.), this document provides a charming and romantic scene between 'Ahmose and his consort, 'AHMOSE-NEFERTARI. They are depicted in intimate and loving conversation, deciding the mortuary arrangements to be made for their grandmother, Queen TETISHERI, and their mother, Queen AH'HOTEP (1). Both of these royal women served Egypt faithfully and held leadership positions during the campaigns to oust the HYKSOS from the land.

Building Text A document provided for every TEMPLE in ancient Egypt, these texts were engraved in a prominent place and provided the name of the temple, the nature of its cultic rituals, and the special significance of its sanctuaries. Building Texts linked the temple to the original time of creation, following the established traditions of the cults of the "PRIMEVAL MOUNDS." The temple thus became more than a material demonstration of the spiritual truths. Because of the documentation added, the shrine was part of the original "Appearance" of the god in Egypt. Even the particular decorative aspects of the temple were included in the Building Text, as well as such aspects related to a specific deity.

See also "APPEARING."

bulls These animals were used as THEOPHANIES of certain Egyptian deities and as symbols of power and resurrection. The APIS bull, the most popular and longest lasting bull cult, was called Hap. The MNEVIS bull was sacred to the god RÉ, and was called Merur. The Buchis bull was sacred to MONTU and then to AMUN.

Bull hides were also worn by some chiefs of nomes and by pharaohs, who chose to be buried in them. These hides, called *meska,* were insignias of power as well as rebirth signs. The early warrior-kings, such as SCORPION and NARMER (ca. 3000 B.C.E.) were depicted as bulls in commemorative wares. In some ceremonies the pharaohs wore bull tails to designate their rank and might. Royal titles sometimes referred to pharaohs and princes as "the Bull of his mother."

Burna-Buriash II (d. 1333 B.C.E.) *Kassite king of Babylon, ruling from 1359 B.C.E. until his death*
He sent a communication to AMENHOTEP III (r. 1391–1353 B.C.E.) about protocol. The Egyptian delegation sent by Amenhotep III to escort Burna-Buriash's daughter was deemed inadequate by the Babylonian court, and the king complained. This Kassite princess was to marry the pharaoh, and only five carriages were included in the royal procession. Burna-Buriash did not consider that number of carriages proper for a woman of the Kassite royal family. The Kassites had founded the Second Dynasty of Babylon.

Burullus   This was one of the four great salt LAKES in the Delta of Egypt.

Busiris   A central Delta town originally called *Djedu,* the Per-Usiré, House of OSIRIS, Busiris was dedicated originally to the local vegetation god, ANDJETI. The Osirian cult, however, became popular, and Osiris assumed the titles and ceremonies of the elder deity. The god SOBEK was also honored in the town. Busiris was originally inhabited by shepherd tribes in the Predynastic eras. The town never became politically powerful but remained an important shrine center for Osiris.

Buto (the goddess)   *See* WADJET.

Buto (Tell el-Fara'un)   A site south of TANIS in the Delta, Buto—called Pe, or Per-Wadjet (the House of WADJET)—was the capital of Lower Egypt in Predynastic times. Predynastic tombs and some dating to the First Dynasty (2900–2770 B.C.E.) were discovered in Buto, which remained popular as the seat of power for the legendary kings of Egypt's Predynastic Period (before 3000 B.C.E.). In all major festivals these rulers were portrayed as the SOULS OF PE in Lower Egypt, and as the SOULS OF NEKHEN (HIERAKONPOLIS) of Upper Egypt. These legendary kings greeted each new claimant to the throne during the coronation rituals and were called upon to serve as the guardians of the land in each new generation.

Buto was divided into Pe and Dep. Three mounds remain on the site, two from the town and one a ruined temple. RAMESSES II (r. 1290–1224 B.C.E.) donated various objects as offerings, and SHOSHENQ V (r. 773–735 B.C.E.) erected a stela there. The ruined mounds provide the modern name of Buto, Tell el-Fara'un, "the Mound of the Pharaohs."

See also MUU DANCERS.

Byblos (Kubna; Gubla)   A city of Phoenicia, an ancient seaport of modern Lebanon, that was allied to Egypt throughout its history and was a vassal city-state for a time. Egyptian records indicate that trade between the two nations started as early as ca. 2700 B.C.E. SNEFRU (r. 2575–2551 B.C.E.) had 40 ships built to sail to Byblos

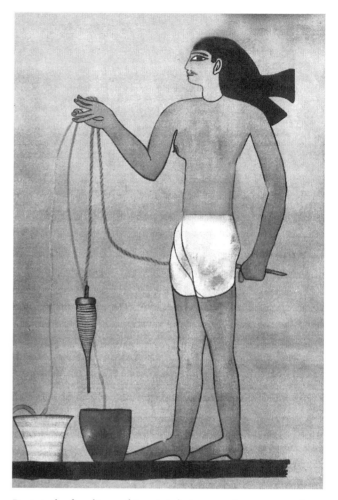

Byssus, the fine linen of Egypt, is being spun by a woman in a relief in the tomb of Khnumhotep *(Hulton Archive)*

to collect cedar logs. In the Twelfth Dynasty (1991–1783 B.C.E.) the city became a dependency of the pharaohs, and TRADE increased. Byblos was an allied state of Egypt during the New Kingdom (1550–1070 B.C.E.).

byssus   This was the name given to fine linen products developed in certain regions in Egypt, especially in AKHMIN. Originally believed to be of cotton, the byssus products have been found to contain quality linen.

Caesar, Julius (d. 44 B.C.E.) *Roman military and political leader who was one of the most powerful men in the world*

He established CLEOPATRA VII as sole ruler of Egypt ca. 48 B.C.E. while in ALEXANDRIA and altered the course of Egyptian history. Julius Caesar was born in 100 B.C.E. and rose steadily in Rome, becoming a hero because of his military successes in the Gallic Wars.

A rival of POMPEY the Great, Caesar followed him to Egypt after defeating Pompey's legions at the battle of Pharsalus in 48. Once in Egypt, Caesar extricated himself from a precarious military position in Alexandria and then conducted campaigns against PTOLEMY XIII and the Alexandrians in the BATTLE OF THE NILE. He placed Cleopatra VII on the throne as sole ruler and recognized her child, PTOLEMY XV CAESARION, as his own son.

Leaving Egypt, Caesar continued to hunt down Pompey's allies and returned victorious to Rome. There he became dictator and held consulships. He also instituted a new calendar. Marc ANTONY, one of his companions, offered him a crown, but he refused it. Republicans, however, conspired against him and assassinated him on the Ides of March 44 B.C.E.

One of the finest orators of Rome, Caesar also wrote commentaries on his wars, as well as poetry and works on grammar. Caesar laid the foundation for the Roman Empire. His heir was his nephew, Gaius Octavian, whom he adopted and who became the first emperor of Rome, AUGUSTUS.

Further reading: Bradford, Ernle. *Julius Caesar: The Pursuit of Power.* London: H. Hamilton, 1984; Dodge, Theodore. *Caesar: A History of the Art of War Among the Romans Down to the End of the Roman Empire, With a Detailed Account of the Campaigns of Gaius Julius Caesar.* New York: Da Capo Press, 1997; Ferrero, Guglielmo. *The Life of Caesar.* Trans. A. E. Zimmern. New York: G. P. Putnam's Sons, 1933; Gelzer, Matthias, and Needham, Peter, trans. *Caesar: Politician and Statesman.* Cambridge, Mass.: Harvard Univ. Press, 1985; Grant, Michael. *Caesar.* London: Weidenfeld and Nicolson, 1974; Grant, Michael. *The Twelve Caesars.* London: Weidenfeld and Nicolson, 1975; Julius Caesar. *The Civil War.* New York: Penguin, 1967; Julius Caesar. *The Conquest of Gaul.* New York: Penguin, 1982; Meier, Christian. *Caesar.* New York: HarperCollins, 1997; Suetonius. *The Twelve Caesars.* Trans. Robert Graves. New York: Penguin, 1979.

Caesareum A shrine in ALEXANDRIA, erected by CLEOPATRA VII (r. 51–30 B.C.E.), starting with an ALTAR for cultic ceremonies honoring Marc ANTONY, who became her lover, the historian Philo visited the shrine in 40 B.C.E. A great sanctuary was part of the design, and two OBELISKS of TUTHMOSIS III (r. 1479–1425 B.C.E.) were brought from HELIOPOLIS to adorn the site. When Cleopatra VII committed suicide after the battle of ACTIUM, Octavian (later the first emperor of Rome, AUGUSTUS), completed the Caesareum for his own cultic ceremonies as the new ruler of Egypt.

Caesarion *See* PTOLEMY XV.

Cairo Calendar An astrological text that dates to the reign of RAMESSES II (1290–1224 B.C.E.) of the Nineteenth Dynasty, this was a calendar of lucky and unlucky days of the year. The good or bad potential fortune of a single day was determined by past events connected to that particular date, mainly concerning the gods, omens, battles, or prophecies recorded for that specific time period.

The start of a journey, the planning of a marriage or business transaction, and especially days of birth were studied in relationship to the calendar and its lucky or unlucky connotations. People born on unlucky days were doomed to a bad end according to Egyptian traditions. In the case of royal princes, children on whom the fate of Egypt depended, such birth dates were critical. If such a royal heir was born on a day of ill fortune, the SEVEN HATHORS, divine beings, arrived on the scene and changed the child, substituting one born on a propitious day. In that way calamities were avoided, not only for the royal family but for the nation. In time the Seven Hathors were thought to provide that service for all children, even commoners. The calendar was used by the literate or upper-class Egyptians in much the same way that horoscopes are used in modern times. This calendar bears the name of Egypt's capital, Cairo, but that city was not founded until decades after Rome assumed power in 30 B.C.E.

calcite   An opaque, white stone commonly called alabaster, calcite was popular in all building programs throughout Egyptian history. The stone was quarried at a remote site called HATNUB, to the east of 'AMARNA, and was believed to have solar connections in a mythical sense. The calcite was revered as part of the solar traditions of Egypt, as the stone was deemed an essential part of the universe. Vessels and SARCOPHAGI were made out of calcite for royal or aristocratic tombs, but it was never used as a common building material.

See also NATURAL RESOURCES; SOLAR CULT.

calendar   A timekeeping system of annual designations in use in Egypt as far back as the Predynastic Period (before 3000 B.C.E.). Lunar in origin, the calendar was designed to meet the agricultural demands of the nation and evolved over the centuries until recognized as inaccurate in real time. The calendar that developed in the Early Dynastic Period (2920–2575 B.C.E.) had 12 months of 30 days. The inaccuracy of this calendar was self-evident almost immediately. The lunar calculations made by the priests and the actual rotation of the earth around the sun did not coincide, and very rapidly Egyptians found themselves celebrating festivals out of season. The calendar was then revised by adding five days at the end of each year, called EPAGOMENAL DAYS (connected to the goddess NUT), which provided some stability to the calendar calculations.

The calendar contained three seasons of four months each. *AKHET* was the season of the inundation, the first third of a year, starting at the end of modern August and followed by *PROYET* and *SHOMU*. *Proyet* was

the time in which the land emerged from the floodwaters, and *shomu* was the time of harvest.

As the calendar veered from the true year, the Egyptians invented a corrected calendar and used it side by side with the one dating to Predynastic times. They would not set aside something so venerable, preferring to adjust their enterprises to the new calendar, while maintaining the old.

In the reign of Djer (ca. 2900 B.C.E.) a formative calendar was inscribed on an ivory tablet, that included the image of Sirius. The goddess SOPDU, depicted as a sacred cow bearing the symbol of the year (a young plant) between her horns, is also portrayed. Egyptian astronomers had established the link between the helical rising and the beginning of a year: the solar calendar.

The rising of a star called Sopdu or Sopdet by the Egyptians, and known in modern times as Sirius, the Dog Star, started each new year on the revised calendar around July 19th. The arrival of Sopdu at a given time was due to the fact that the star appears just above the horizon at dawn about the same time of year that *akhet* began. This calendar was inaccurate, as the solar year was longer than the calendar year.

PRIESTS used their own measurements, based on lunar months of around 29.5 days, to conduct feasts. In the Ptolemaic Period (304–30 B.C.E.) a leap year was added, along with astrological aspects, planetary houses, and other innovations used by the Greeks and Romans.

See also SOTHIC CYCLE.

Callias of Sphetlus   (d. ca. 265 B.C.E.) *Greek military commander who served Ptolemy I Soter (r. 304–284 B.C.E.)* Callias entered PTOLEMY I's service after being exiled from Athens. He was from Sphetlus and was involved in political affairs. In 287 B.C.E., Callias returned to Athens with Egyptian mercenaries to aid his brother, Phaedrus, in bringing in a harvest and represented Athens in negotiations with other states, remaining, however, in the service of Ptolemy I. As a result of his role in the negotiations, Athens voted Callias full civic honors before he died ca. 265 B.C.E.

Callimachus of Cyrene   (fl. third century B.C.E.) *poet deemed a master of the Alexandrian style* Callimachus achieved his fame in the reign of PTOLEMY II PHILADELPHUS (285–246 B.C.E.). He aided in the evolution of the traditional epics, defending the form against criticism by APOLLONIUS OF RHODES. He also provided ALEXANDRIA with remarkable examples of the epic form and wrote 120 books, giving biographical details about literary figures. Callimachus may have served briefly as the director of the LIBRARY OF ALEXANDRIA.

He was born in Cyrene but was welcomed by the Ptolemaic court, where he wrote the *Aelia,* "Causes," a narrative in four books. Callimachus was also famous for his *Iambi,* a compilation of 13 short poems, for his *Hecole,* a narrative poem, and for *Hymns* and epigrams.

Cambyses (d. 522 B.C.E.) *Persian king who ruled Egypt from 525 to 522 B.C.E.*

The Persian Empire was founded by Cyrus the Great (r. 559–530 B.C.E.), who died in 530 B.C.E. The death of Cyrus brought a crisis to Persia in the form of a rivalry between his sons, who fought each other for the throne. Cambyses, who had been charged by Cyrus with the conquest of Egypt, emerged the victor, reportedly through the murder of his brother. The empire, though, remained unsettled.

Cambyses would rule over Egypt for three years, extending the power of the Persian Empire into the Nile Valley. However, the period of his reign was the cause of great unhappiness in Egypt. Although he adopted the dress and titles of a pharaoh, Cambyses failed to expand Persian rule to areas outside of the Egyptian territory, despite his efforts to do so. In the end, his reign was ended under mysterious circumstances and failed in part because of the unsettled political situation in the wider empire.

BIOGRAPHY

According to the Greek historian Herodotus (fl. fifth century B.C.E.), called the Father of History, who mentioned Cambyses in his writings, this Persian ruler was the target of a rumor circulating through the royal court since Cambyses was a child. The rumor stated that Cambyses was actually the son of Cyrus the Great by a Saite princess of Egypt. How this union took place was not recorded, but Herodotus insists that Cambyses was labeled Cyrus's illegitimate son. Despite this rumor, historians believe that Cambyses was the legitimate son of Persian king Cyrus the Great and probably Queen AMYTIS in 538 B.C.E., although one record proposes Cassandane, another wife of Cyrus, as the mother of Cambyses.

Cambyses was named the ruler of Babylon by his father but was dethroned a year later because of his behavior. He returned to the throne as coruler in 530 B.C.E., shortly before the death of Cyrus the Great. After Cyrus's death in 530 B.C.E., Cambyses went on to conquer Egypt as his father had charged, defeating the Egyptian ruler PSAMMETICHUS III (r. 526–525 B.C.E.) at the battle of PELUSIUM, starting the Twenty-seventh Dynasty in 526 B.C.E. Once ruler of Egypt, Cambyses allowed his name to be translated into Egyptian hieroglyphs and displayed within a cartouche, the emblem of the pharaohs. The consort of Cambyses was his sister, Queen Atossa.

Cambyses also planned campaigns against Carthage, Ethiopia, and the SIWA Oasis in the Libyan Desert. The Persian expedition to Siwa, a shrine area for the Egyptian god AMUN, was a disaster and a mystery. Cambyses sent out a large unit of Persians, hoping to plunder the temples in the oasis, a site reported to be made

The meeting of Cambyses II and Psammetichus III after the battle of Pelusium, 525 B.C.E. *(Réunion des Musées Nationaux / Art Resource, NY)*

of gold, but all of his troops vanished. Not one soldier escaped the desert to describe the calamity that must have overtaken the forces. The Carthage expedition was delayed as a result of this disaster.

Egyptian records call Cambyses a "criminal lunatic," but not all of the charges leveled against him are substantiated. For example, Egyptians claimed that when Cambyses conquered Egypt, he officiated over the burial of a sacred APIS bull in 526 B.C.E. and then honored the goddess NEITH (1) at SAIS. Cambyses also forged links with NOMARCHS, or clan chiefs, of the Egyptian provinces and adopted ceremonial titles and rituals. The Egyptians also claimed that he struck at an Apis bull, wounding the sacred animal in the thigh and then slaying the animal in an act of sacrilege. He also reportedly whipped the Apis cult priests. Cambyses did have the mummy of Amasis (r. 570–526 B.C.E.), who had aided the enemies of the Persians during his reign, dug up and mutilated; the remains were torn apart and the mummy was burned before a crowd of horrified Egyptians. According to Egyptian tradition, destroying the body of Amasis would deprive him of an eternal life. The Egyptians would have been outraged by such sacrilege.

Cambyses and the Persian rulers who succeeded him were not comfortable in Egypt. After Cambyses, in fact, most of the Persian kings governed the Nile Valley from a distance, using satraps, governors, and military units to enforce Persian demands.

Within the Persian Empire, there were groups of people who rebelled against conquerors on a regular basis. The Magi, a remarkable clan suppressed by Cambyses in a region of modern Syria, revolted against Persian rule, and he made his way to that area to put down the rebel forces. He died there in the summer of 522 B.C.E., either by accident or by his own hand, and was buried in Takt-i-Rustan, near Persepolis (modern Iran). When Cambyses departed from Egypt, an aide, ARYANDES, was left in control of the Nile Valley as governor. Within a year, however, Aryandes was executed on charges of treason by Cambyses' successor, DARIUS I.

HISTORICAL IMPACT

By defeating Psammetichus III at the battle of Pelusium, Cambyses conquered Egypt and established the Twenty-seventh Dynasty. Although he adopted some Egyptian customs, including allowing his name to be translated into Egyptian hieroglyphs (he took the name Mesut-Ré, meaning "offspring of Ré") and displayed within a cartouche, the emblem of the pharaohs, Cambyses' brief three-year reign was marred by outrageous acts that labeled him a criminal and a despot. He was not a good representative of the empire forged by his father, Cyrus the Great, who was noted for the tolerance and generosity with which he treated those he conquered. He lacked his father's grand vision for an international empire ruled by the Persians in an enlightened manner and displayed instead a lack of world leadership, compassion, and diplomacy.

Further reading: Herodotus. *The Histories.* New York: Penguin, 2003.

Canaan The name applied by the Egyptians to the entire western region of Syria and Palestine, it was actually "the Land of the Purple," a name resulting from the popularity of a rich purple dye used in the territory in the manufacture of materials. Canaan extended from Acre northward on the coast. Egypt had control of Canaanite cities from ca. 1550 to 1200 B.C.E.

Canal of Necho II A connective waterway leading from the NILE to the Red Sea, through the WADI TIMULAT to the BITTER LAKES and then into the sea and called "the Sweet Water Canal" by the Egyptians, this canal was opened by NECHO II (r. 610–595 B.C.E.) and maintained by later dynasties. The Persians of the Twenty-seventh (525–404 B.C.E.) and the Thirty-first (343–332 B.C.E.) Dynasties repaired and deepened the canal. During the Ptolemaic Period (304–30 B.C.E.), the canal was maintained yearly.

Canal of Sehel This was a passage on the NILE River that dates to the Sixth Dynasty (2323–2150 B.C.E.), dug alongside the first cataract of the Nile at the island of SEHEL in order to allow Egyptians easy access to the territories below. In the Twelfth Dynasty (1991–1783 B.C.E.), SENWOSRET II (r. 1897–1878 B.C.E.) cleared the canal and mounted an inscription on the rocks of the island to commemorate the event. He claimed that he was in the process of making a new entranceway into NUBIA and returned several years later to repair it. The goddess ANUKIS was the patroness of Sehel, serving as well as part of KHNUM's triad at ASWAN. Later pharaohs maintained the canal throughout many eras.

Cannibal Hymn A text used as part of the PYRAMID TEXTS in the pyramid of UNIS (2356–2323 B.C.E.) in SAQQARA, in this funerary utterance, Unis is described as rising from the grave in a divine form to feast upon his ancestors and the gods themselves. He was aided by other divine beings, including KHONS (1), in catching his victims and slaying them. SHESHMU, an ancient deity of the olive and grape presses, then proceeded to cook them and to resurrect Unis. As with most forms of archaic cannibalism, Unis performed these terrible acts to gain the *HEKA*, the magical powers innate to the gods.

canon of the human figure *See* ART AND ARCHITECTURE.

canopic jars Containers used in funerary rituals to preserve the viscera of the deceased Egyptians after embalming, the jars varied in style over the centuries but were useful throughout Egypt's history, considered a vital part of the elaborate mortuary processes. The name given to the vessels is Greek, not Egyptian, because the shape resembled the tributes made to the Greek hero Canopus in early periods. The vessels were made out of wood, pottery, faience, cartonnage, or stone.

In the Middle Kingdom (2040–1640 B.C.E.), the canopic jars were squat in design, with plain lids and seals. By the time of the New Kingdom (1550–1070 B.C.E.), the stoppers had been designed to represent the specific patrons of the dead, the sons of HORUS involved in the protection of a specific human organ. The jar containing the liver was under the protection of the god IMSETY, and the stopper was carved into the shape of a human head with a beard.

The jar protecting the lungs used HAPI (2) as a patron, and the stopper on this vessel was shaped to represent the head of a baboon. The canopic jar containing the embalmed stomach was protected by DUA-MUTEF, and his form was the JACKAL. The intestines, protected by QEBEHSENNUF, had a stopper in the form of a hawk's head. The canopic jars were enclosed within elaborately designed cabinets and kept separate from the mummified corpse. Various protective deities were used to guard the cabinet. In CANOPUS, OSIRIS was worshipped as well in the form of a canopic jar. The use of jars declined in the Twenty-first Dynasty (1070–945 B.C.E.), as the mummification process was reformed and employed a method of returning the viscera to the body.

In 2007 the canopic box of Queen-Pharaoh HATSHEP-SUT (r. 1473–1458 B.C.E.) was discovered as the officials of the Egyptian Museum of Antiquities at Cairo were conducting studies and tests to identify her mummified remains. The box held a broken tooth that was discovered to match the mouth of one of the mummies being studied, and the remains were identified as Hatshepsut.

See also MORTUARY RITUALS.

Canopus A site on the western coast of the Nile Delta, near Abu Qir, on the Canopic branch of the river, now silted over, the city was called Pe Gewat in early times and was a cult center for the god OSIRIS. A temple was maintained there, and Canopus was the center of Egypt's ointment industry. In time, the Greeks of the Ptolemaic Period (304–30 B.C.E.) initiated shrines of the god SERA-PIS at Canopus. The name Canopus is derived from Osirian cultic rites and Greek mythology. In his shrines, OSIRIS was worshipped under the form of a human-headed vessel, the CANOPIC JAR, named by the Greeks after their hero.

Canopus Decree Also called the Table of Tanis, a trilingual text dating to March 7, 238 B.C.E., the decree honored PTOLEMY III EUERGETES (r. 246–221 B.C.E.) and his consort BERENICE (3). Two copies of the decree were found in TANIS in 1886, inscribed in Greek and in the Egyptian language forms called demotic and hieroglyphic. The Canopus Decree aided modern scholars in deciphering the ancient language.

Carchemish, battle of The military confrontation between NEBUCHADNEZZER of Babylon and NECHO II (r. 610–595 B.C.E.) of Egypt's Twenty-sixth Dynasty. Carchemish, once located on the Euphrates River, near modern Jarblus, Syria, had been part of Egypt's empire carved out by the New Kingdom Period rulers (1550–1070 B.C.E.). Nebuchadnezzer assaulted the Egyptians as the military commander of his father, Nabopolassar, king of Babylon. He defeated Necho II's forces and made Carchemish and the surrounding areas part of Babylon's holdings.

Carmel, Mount In northwestern modern Israel, at Haifa, called "Antelope Nose" by the Egyptians. Mount Carmel divides the Plain of Esdraelon and Galilee from the Plain of Sharon. The mountain covers 95 square miles and rises about 1,791 feet at its highest peak. The Egyptians revered Mount Carmel as a holy site, and TUTHMOSIS III (r. 1479–1425 B.C.E.) led an army across the mountain's heights single file, to fall upon the ruler of Kadesh and his allies at Ar-Megiddo, a fortress in the pass. The Canaanites faced a formidable force of Egyptian archers and the dreaded cavalry units and fled into Ar-Megiddo, where they were surrounded by a siege wall and starved into submission by Tuthmosis III. Ar-Megiddo is modern Armageddon.

See also TUTHMOSIS III'S MILITARY CAMPAIGNS.

cartonnage This was a unique form of funerary wrappings composed of a combination of plaster, linen, papyrus, and other pliable materials used for the manufacture of SARCOPHAGI and mummy masks, starting in the First Intermediate Period (2134–2040 B.C.E.). Linen sheets were glued together with gums or resins and covered with plaster in order to shape the masks to the contours of the head and shoulders of the mummies. The masks were then gilded and painted to provide a realistic portrait of the deceased. By the end of the Middle Kingdom (1640 B.C.E.), however, the cartonnage was extended to cover the entire mummified form.

See also COFFINS.

cartouche The modern French word designating the original Egyptian symbol called the *shenu* or *shennu*, "that which encircles," a cartouche is an ellipse found in reliefs, paintings, sculpture, and papyri encircling certain royal names of the ancient pharaohs, starting in the Fourth Dynasty (2575–2465 B.C.E.). The form evolved from the hieroglyph for ETERNITY, a circle called the *shen* and symbolizing the course of the sun. In time, the form was elongated and used as a frame for the names of the pharaohs. The double knot used in the symbol is an amulet of power. A stela depicting the royal name of DJET (Wadj; r. ca. 2300 B.C.E.) was discovered at ABYDOS.

cat An animal associated in ancient Egyptian cultic rituals with the goddess BASTET and in some eras considered a manifestation of the god RÉ as well, in funerary legends the cat took up residence in the PERSEA TREE in HELIOPOLIS. The word for cat in Egyptian is *miu,* the feminine being *mut* (translated by some as "kitty"). There is evidence of the domestication of cats in the Predynastic Period (before 3000 B.C.E.), as burial sites in HIERAKONPOLIS contained cat bones, sometimes alongside human bones. Cats were used in hunting, particularly of rats, as the Egyptians instituted rat-control programs in early eras. Cats, however, were not represented in tomb paintings until the Middle Kingdom (2040–1640 B.C.E.) and were very popular in the New Kingdom (1550–1070 B.C.E.). They were depicted as sitting under the chair or on the lap of the deceased. Cats were also featured in dream books, and the SATIRICAL PAPYRUS uses them for ironic effects. MORTUARY RITUALS warned against cat-shaped demons in TUAT, or the Underworld.

cataracts The white-water falls or rapids of the NILE River, six in number, these dangerous regions of the Nile extended from ASWAN to just above modern Khartoum in the Sudan. The first cataract, south of Aswan, served as the natural barrier along the original southern border of Egypt. The rulers of the various dynasties began exploring the territories to the south, and the region between the first and second cataract was always important as a trading area. The Egyptian settlements and fortresses in the cataract regions during the Fourth and Fifth Dynasties (2575–2465; 2465–2323 B.C.E.) indicate that the Egyptians had started a process of incorporation. The unsettled period following the Sixth Dynasty (ca. 2150 B.C.E.) caused the Egyptians of the area to withdraw from the region to some extent, but in the Eleventh Dynasty (2040–1991 B.C.E.) control was established once again. The Eighteenth Dynasty pharaohs (1550–1070 B.C.E.) pushed as far south as KURGUS. During the periods in which the territories below the first cataract were held by the Egyptians, the administration of the territory was conducted at ELEPHANTINE Island at ASWAN or at another southern post by a special VICEROY.

See also CANAL OF SEHEL.

cenotaphs The mortuary complexes or simple tombs built to provide a religiously motivated burial site that remained empty, the cenotaphs contained no bodies but were ceremonial in nature. Much debate is in progress concerning cenotaph sites and purposes. In the Early Dynastic Period (2920–2575 B.C.E.), the rulers normally erected cenotaphs in ABYDOS, the cultic center of the god OSIRIS.

C-Group A people of NUBIA (modern Sudan), who lived in a region called WAWAT by the Egyptians (ca. 2100–1500 B.C.E.), they are noted as early as the Sixth Dynasty (2323–2150 B.C.E.). By the reign of SENWOSRET I (1971–1926 B.C.E.), the C-Group people were considered a threat to Egypt. Senwosret I constructed FORTRESSES at the second cataract to control them. Troops were stationed there to monitor the movement of the C-Group on the Nile, and the forts served as centers for trade and gold-mining activities in the deserts of the area.

Chaldeans They were a people living in the alluvial plains at the head of the modern Persian Gulf. A kingdom was formed there as early as 2000 B.C.E. Hebrew records credit Nimrod as the founder of the Chaldean Dynasty that lasted from 2000 to 1543 B.C.E. The Chaldeans founded Babylon, Erech, Akkad, and Calneh, as well as Ur. Trade and art were important to the Chaldeans, with land and sea routes employed. The so-called Ships of Ur were prominent in the ancient world and dealt with Egyptian merchants.

chancellor A court administrative position in ancient Egypt that evolved over the centuries into the role of VIZIER. The first recorded chancellor, serving Lower Egypt in the reign of DEN (ca. 2820 B.C.E.), was HEMAKA. The first recorded chancellor for Upper Egypt appears in the reign of PERIBSEN (ca. 2600 B.C.E.). The chancellors were responsible for the annual census, supervising irrigation projects, land registration, taxation, and the distribution of goods among the temple and court workers.

chariots Vehicles employed in military and processional events in ancient Egypt, becoming a dreaded war symbol of the feared cavalry units, the chariot was not an Egyptian invention but was introduced into the Nile Valley by the HYKSOS, or Asiatics, during the Second Intermediate Period (1640–1532 B.C.E.). Egyptian innovations, however, made the Asiatic chariot lighter, faster, and easier to maneuver. Egyptian chariots were fashioned out of wood, with the frames built well forward of the axle for increased stability. The sides of the chariots were normally made of stretched canvas, reinforced by stucco. The floors were made of leather thongs, interlaced to provide an elastic but firm foundation for the riders.

A single pole, positioned at the center and shaped while still damp, ran from the axle to a yoke that was attached to the saddles of the horses. A girth strap and breast harness kept the pole secure while the vehicle was in motion. Originally, the two wheels of the chariot each had four spokes; later six were introduced. These were made of separate pieces of wood glued together and then bound in leather straps.

KAMOSE (r. 1555–1550 B.C.E.) was the first Egyptian ruler to use the chariot and cavalry units successfully. The Hyksos, dominating the northern territories at the time,

A chariot design from a New Kingdom Period temple relief; the relief depicts a pharaoh in combat.

were startled when the first chariots appeared against them on the field at NEFRUSY, led by Kamose. The horses of the period, also introduced to Egypt by the Asiatics, were probably not strong enough to carry the weight of a man over long distances, a situation remedied by the Egyptians within a short time. The horses did pull chariots, however, and they were well trained by the Egyptian military units, especially in the reigns of TUTHMOSIS I, TUTHMOSIS III, RAMESSES II, and RAMESSES III. These warrior pharaohs made the chariot cavalry units famed throughout the region as they built or maintained the empire.

Charonnophis (fl. third century B.C.E.) *native ruler of Thebes during the reign of Ptolemy IV Philopator (221–205 B.C.E.)*
He rebelled against ALEXANDRIA. Theban rebels attempted to oust the Ptolemaic Period rulers but were unsuccessful.
See also REBELS OF EGYPT.

Chemmis This was the legendary sacred floating island in the western Delta, near BUTO, that was the mythological site of the lovely legend concerning the goddess ISIS and her infant son, HORUS. Isis, impregnated by the corpse of the god OSIRIS, whom she buried, retired to the sacred island to give birth to the child who would avenge Osiris's assassination. SET, the murderous brother of Osiris, also a god, sought Isis and Horus, but at Chemmis the mother and child remained in hiding. The goddess WADJET was in attendance, arranging reeds and foliage to keep Isis and Horus out of sight. The legend, recounted each year in Egypt, was one of the greatest examples of the maternal and wifely instincts of Isis, who embodied the ever-faithful spouse and the mother ready to sacrifice herself for her offspring. Isis was beloved in Egypt and throughout much of the inhabited world because of this and other tales of her suffering and endurance.

Cheops   *See* KHUFU.

Chephren   *See* KHAFRE.

Chremonides (fl. third century B.C.E.) *Athenian politician aided by Ptolemy II Philadelphus (285–246 B.C.E.)*
Chremonides studied philosophy with Zeno of Citium and entered Greek politics. Around 266 B.C.E., he was accredited with starting a war over an anti-Macedonian alliance. As a result of Athens's surrender, Chremonides fled to ALEXANDRIA. He served as an admiral of the Egyptians during the Second Syrian War and was defeated in battle by ANTIOCHUS II THEOS, the Seleucid ruler.

Chronicle of Prince Osorkon   This is a mysterious text dating to the reign of SHOSHENQ III (835–783 B.C.E.) that describes a civil war in Egypt, situated in the Upper Egyptian regions. Shoshenq III lost control of many southern areas as a result. Another crisis caused his kingship to be divided, giving rise to the Twenty-third Dynasty.
    See also OSORKON III.

Cippus of Horus   A form of STELA popular in the Ptolemaic Period (304–30 B.C.E.) featuring the god Harpocrates (HORUS as a child) standing on a crocodile and holding scorpions and other dangerous creatures, magical texts accompanied the image and provided protection against the beasts displayed. Water was poured over the Cippus, and by drinking the water a person was rendered invulnerable. The Cippus was reportedly created by an Egyptian named Psammeticus-Ankh, and it stood in prominent sites throughout the Nile Valley. Originally the Cippus was a protective monument with powers to repel SET and the beast APOPHIS (1).

circumcision   The surgical removal of part of the male prepuce, practiced by the Egyptians as part of their methods of hygiene and called *sebi*, male circumcision was not performed at birth but during adolescence. 'AHMOSE (NEBPEHTIRÉ) (r. 1550–1525 B.C.E.) was not circumcised, as his mummified remains demonstrate. He was frail as a youngster, and the procedure may have been considered too rigorous for him. Scenes of a circumcision were discovered in a SAQQARA tomb and in a relief in the temple of MUT in KARNAK. These depictions show that circumcision was performed on young Egyptian males, usually in their teens. A First Intermediate Period (2134–2040 B.C.E.) stela shows 120 young boys enduring circumcision. A curved flint knife was used for the operation.
    See also HEALTH AND DISEASE; PRIESTS.

Claudius Ptolemy (fl. second century B.C.E.) *Greek geographer and astronomer of Alexandria*
He achieved his status as a scientist in the reign of PTOLEMY VI PHILOMETOR (180–164, 163–145 B.C.E.) and became famous for his *Geography,* an atlas in eight volumes. Claudius Ptolemy also wrote on mathematics, astronomy, and music. His *Geography,* erroneous because of his miscalculations of the earth's circumference and lack of astronomical calculation, was the standard work until the 16th century C.E.

Cleomenes of Naukratis (fl. third century B.C.E.) *counselor of Alexander III the Great (332–323 B.C.E.)*
He was instrumental in building the city of ALEXANDRIA. Cleomenes was a Greek merchant who lived in NAUKRATIS, the Hellenic site founded in the Nile Delta by AMASIS (r. 570–526 B.C.E.) to serve as a center for Egyptian Greek trade. Cleomenes had knowledge of the NILE, Egypt's markets, and trade routes. He became a finance minister under ALEXANDER III THE GREAT and supervised aspects of Alexandria's growth. He also conducted an international TRADE monopoly and reportedly started extorting funds from Egyptian temples. Cleomenes was made assistant satrap of Egypt as well, aided by Pete'ese and Dolopsis. He was, however, executed by PTOLEMY I SOTER (304–284 B.C.E.) for his crimes.

Cleopatra (1) (d. 176 B.C.E.) *royal woman of the Ptolemaic Period*
She was the consort of PTOLEMY V EPIPHANES (205–180 B.C.E.) and the daughter of the Seleucid king ANTIOCHUS III THE GREAT, who had defeated Ptolemy at the battle of Panion, stripping Egypt of its Asiatic holdings. Cleopatra married Ptolemy V in 195 B.C.E. and bore him two sons, including PTOLEMY VI PHILOMETOR, and a daughter, CLEOPATRA (2). When Ptolemy V died in 180 B.C.E., she became regent for the heir, Ptolemy VI Philometor. As a result she received the right to display her name as a CARTOUCHE and the use of a Horus name in her title. Cleopatra proved an able regent until her death.

Cleopatra (2) (fl. second century B.C.E.) *royal woman of the Ptolemaic Period*
She was the daughter of PTOLEMY V EPIPHANES and Queen CLEOPATRA (1) and became the consort of her brother, PTOLEMY VI PHILOMETOR (r. 180–164, 163–145 B.C.E.). They ruled Egypt and CYPRUS. Their reign was marred by an invasion by ANTIOCHUS IV of Syria and interventions by Rome. Ptolemy VI's younger brother, Ptolemy VIII, also rebelled against the couple and was given Cyprus as a placating gesture.
    Ptolemy VI Philometor died in 145 B.C.E. after a fall from his horse. PTOLEMY VIII PHYSKON returned to Egypt and married CLEOPATRA (2), assuming the name Euergetes II. She was the mother of PTOLEMY VII NEOS PHILOPATOR (Memphites), who was born during the coronation rites at MEMPHIS in 144 B.C.E. Three years later, Ptolemy VIII married his niece and stepdaughter, CLEOPATRA (3), which led to his expulsion from ALEX-

ANDRIA. Cleopatra served as regent for Ptolemy VII, but he was lured to Cyprus, where Ptolemy VIII killed him and sent his dismembered body back to his mother as an anniversary present. Cleopatra is remembered for her benevolence to the Jewish community of Egypt. She authorized the building of a temple at Tell el-Yahudiya Leratopolis in the eastern Delta. She was deposed by Ptolemy VIII in 124 B.C.E. but remained on the scene until PTOLEMY IX SOTER II was crowned.

Cleopatra (3) (fl. first century B.C.E.) *royal woman of the Ptolemaic Period*

The daughter of PTOLEMY VI PHILOMETOR and Queen CLEOPATRA (2), Cleopatra married her uncle and step-father, PTOLEMY VIII EUERGETES II (r. 170–163, 140–116 B.C.E.). She bore him several children, including two sons, and began to work against her mother, Cleopatra (2), who was Ptolemy VIII's ranking wife. In 132 B.C.E., Ptolemy VIII and Cleopatra (3) were exiled and took refuge on CYPRUS. There her brother was slain, dismembered, and sent to Cleopatra (2) in 124 B.C.E.

When Ptolemy VIII died at the age of 68 in 116 B.C.E., Cleopatra (3) became regent for her son PTOLEMY IX SOTER II (r. 116–107, 88–81 B.C.E.), granting him Cyprus when he reached his majority. However, she preferred her son PTOLEMY X ALEXANDER I, and in 107 B.C.E. she named him pharaoh, deposing Ptolemy IX Soter II. When the deposed pharaoh invaded Egypt, Cleopatra (3) sent out a military force and pushed Ptolemy IX Soter II back to Cyprus. Ptolemy X Alexander I assassinated Cleopatra (3) shortly after, having grown tired of her dominance.

Cleopatra (4) (fl. first century B.C.E.) *royal woman of the Ptolemaic Period*

She was the daughter of PTOLEMY VIII EUERGETES II and Queen CLEOPATRA (3), and she married her brother, PTOLEMY IX SOTER II (r. 116–107, 88–81 B.C.E.). This marriage was quickly declared invalid by her mother, Cleopatra (3), and Cleopatra (4) was deposed.

Cleopatra (5) Selene (fl. first century B.C.E.) *royal woman of the Ptolemaic Period*

A daughter of PTOLEMY VIII EUERGETES II and Queen CLEOPATRA (3), she married PTOLEMY IX SOTER II (r. 116–107, 88–81 B.C.E.). He had wed CLEOPATRA (4), his sister, but was forced to put her aside for CLEOPATRA (5) Selene, also his sibling. She endured Ptolemy's exile in CYPRUS and his restorations.

Cleopatra (6) Tryphaina (fl. first century B.C.E.) *royal woman of the Ptolemaic Period*

She was an illegitimate daughter of PTOLEMY IX SOTER II and married her brother, PTOLEMY XII NEOS DIONYSIUS (r. 80–58, 55–51 B.C.E.). Raised to the throne by the courtiers and councilors, the royal couple was hailed throughout Egypt. Ptolemy XII, however, was also called Auletes, the Flutist. He was dedicated to the arts and ecstasy and was a mere pawn of Rome. A younger brother of the royal couple had been made king of CYPRUS, but he was deposed in 58 B.C.E., when the Roman Cato took Cyprus for Rome. The brother killed himself, sparking riots in ALEXANDRIA. Ptolemy XII fled from Egypt, leaving Cleopatra (6) Tryphaina with their children. Cleopatra (6) Tryphaina had been removed from her royal rank in 69 B.C.E. and welcomed her return to the throne but died soon after. She was the mother of CLEOPATRA VII and PTOLEMY XIII and XIV.

Cleopatra VII (d. 30 B.C.E.) *last ruler of the Ptolemaic Period*

Cleopatra ruled Egypt from 51 to 30 B.C.E. Her reign brought an end to the rule of Egypt by the Ptolemies and the start of the Roman era's influence over Egyptian life.

BIOGRAPHY

Cleopatra was the daughter of PTOLEMY XII NEOS DIONYSIUS, called Auletes, and Queen CLEOPATRA (6) TRYPHAINA. Cleopatra VII married her brother, PTOLEMY XIII (r. 55–47 B.C.E.), whom she had learned to despise for his weaknesses. She served as co-regent with her father from 88 to 51 B.C.E. and then ruled with her brother, who exiled her from ALEXANDRIA in 48 B.C.E.

That same year, POMPEY THE GREAT, who had served as a guardian for the siblings, arrived unexpectedly in Egypt. One of the two most powerful figures in the Roman Empire, Pompey had fought a civil war with General Julius CAESAR (100–44 B.C.E.) and had suffered a crushing defeat at the battle of Pharsalus in 49 B.C.E. He fled the field and made his way to Egypt, where he believed he would be safe with the ruling Ptolemies. Pompey was slain by Ptolemy XIII's courtiers, however, who believed the murder would placate Julius Caesar, who was known to be hunting his enemy. Caesar arrived soon after and was aghast at receiving the head of Pompey; he soon restored Cleopatra VII to the throne. Caesar then became involved in the BATTLE OF THE NILE, which resulted in Ptolemy XIII's death by drowning. The Roman general remained in Alexandria, and, in 47 B.C.E., Cleopatra VII bore him a son, PTOLEMY XV CAESARION. This affair made Cleopatra a subject of much gossip in Rome and began speculation about her feminine lures. Caesar, on the other hand, was noted for his dalliances. However, Cleopatra's position in Egypt—which was a valuable resource for Rome—along with her remarkable education and ambitions, were charms she possessed in addition to those of the physical variety.

Called the "Goddess Beloved by the Father" by the Egyptians, Cleopatra was thoroughly educated by Greek scholars in alchemy, arts, geography, astronomy, languages, military science, and physics—subjects not normally taught to women in that historical period. She

A relief depicting Cleopatra VII, the last ruler of the Ptolemaic Period, who committed suicide in 30 B.C.E. *(Hulton Archive)*

was the only member of the Ptolemaic Dynasty to speak the ancient Egyptian language. Greek or Macedonian in origin, the Ptolemies lived separately from their subjects and traditionally spoke Greek. They generally never learned the Egyptian language, written or spoken.

In 46 B.C.E., Cleopatra VII visited Caesar in Rome, and when he was assassinated she fled to Egypt. Her younger brother, PTOLEMY XIV (r. 47–44 B.C.E.), served for a time there as Cleopatra VII's regent, but she had him killed in 44 B.C.E. and put her son, Ptolemy XV, on

the throne in his place. Together they ruled Egypt, and the Roman Senate recognized the royal pair in 42 B.C.E.

Marc Antony, in an alliance with Octavian (the future Emperor Augustus), had defeated the assassins of Julius Caesar and had put an end to the supporters of the Roman Republic. Needing financial backing for his future political aspirations, Marc Antony demanded a meeting with Cleopatra. The two embarked on a famous romance, and after she bore him twins, ALEXANDER HELIOS and CLEOPATRA SELENE, in 41 B.C.E., Cleopatra VII and Marc Antony were wed. A traditional Egyptian wedding, their marriage alarmed Antony's Roman friends and allies, who saw it as a rejection of Roman customs and a sign that he had fallen completely under Cleopatra's spell. Cleopatra VII gave birth to another son, PTOLEMY PHILADELPHOS, in 36 B.C.E.

Two other events also raised alarms throughout the Roman world. The first involved King Artavasdes II of Armenia. King of Armenia since 53 B.C.E., Artavasdes was an ally of Rome, but he proved unreliable. He was forced to side with the Parthians when Orodes II of Parthia invaded Armenia in 53 B.C.E., rejoined the Romans with Antony's invasion of Armenia in 36 B.C.E., and betrayed Rome again a mere two years later. Antony responded to this second betrayal by besieging the Armenian capital Artaxata, capturing Artavasdes, and bringing him to Alexandria. There, Artavasdes was harshly treated by Cleopatra and beheaded; his head was sent as a gift to the ruler of Media Atropatene, an enemy of Artavasdes, as an inducement to enter into an alliance with Antony and Cleopatra. The treatment of a king and a onetime ally of Rome caused much controversy in Rome.

Even more damaging to the couple's reputation in Rome was their decision to draft a document called "the Donation of Alexandria," which divided the eastern parts of the Roman Empire between Cleopatra VII and her children. A religious and political document, the donation was intended to place Cleopatra's children in seats of power across the East, and it also sought from the Roman Senate recognition that Caesarion, the son of Julius Caesar by Cleopatra, should be declared Caesar's legitimate heir and thus next in line for the throne after Antony. This request was rejected by the Senate, but the act was seen as a direct attack upon the legally recognized claims of Octavian as Caesar's heir. These actions made another war in the region inevitable.

Octavian declared war on Cleopatra VII in 32 B.C.E. The battle of ACTIUM ensued the next year. After being overwhelmed in battle by Octavian's forces, Cleopatra retreated and sailed to Alexandria. Antony soon followed but, realizing all was lost, committed suicide before he could be taken captive. Desperate to find a means of escape, Cleopatra decided to join Antony in death and killed herself with the sting of an asp, a deadly reptile. Some debate has taken place over the centuries as to how she managed this, and some scholars believe she used a simple poison instead. However she died, Octavian found her body dressed in royal robes, lying on a bier. He possibly took her corpse to Rome and displayed it in his parade. Her children were put to death by the Romans to prevent any possible claimants, the line of the Ptolemies came to an end, and Egypt became a Roman province. Octavian departed Egypt to become sole ruler of the Roman world as Emperor Augustus.

HISTORICAL IMPACT

Cleopatra VII was a brilliant woman who was skilled in political rule. Fluent in many languages, she also learned to speak ancient Egyptian, the only Ptolemaic ruler to have knowledge of the tongue. A Greek marble portrays her as beautiful, a contradiction to the depiction of her on her own coins. She was memorialized in PHILAE and in a colossal carving at DENDEREH, where she is shown with Ptolemy XV Caesarion. Skilled in statecraft and history, Cleopatra VII received a gift of 200,000 volumes for the LIBRARY OF ALEXANDRIA from the ruler of Pergamum, which was occupied at the time by Marc Antony.

The reign of Cleopatra brought with it the brief reemergence of Ptolemaic Egypt into the wider political affairs of the Mediterranean. Since the end of the third century, Egypt had a direct involvement in the struggle for control over the Hellenistic world, although its position was always a precarious one and was based on its rulers maintaining close political and even personal relations with the greatest leaders of the Roman Republic. Cleopatra was able to entice both Julius Caesar and Marc Antony into political alliances that stemmed in large part from their personal relationships with her.

While celebrated in history for her feminine charms, Cleopatra was a shrewd and capable ruler who had great ambitions for Egypt and came close to achieving her dreams of a Pan-Mediterranean empire ruled jointly with Antony. The last heir of the Ptolemaic Dynasty, she was also a final heir to the Macedonian ruler ALEXANDER III THE GREAT, whose campaigns in the fourth century made possible the rise of the Ptolemies. She sought to emulate Alexander's vision of a united Mediterranean Empire ruled from the East but encompassing the whole of Hellenistic civilization. These plans were undone by her inability to create a fighting force capable of defeating the Roman war machine. In addition, she and Antony were politically outmaneuvered by Octavian. In the final battle for supremacy at Actium, the largely Egyptian fleet was no match for Rome.

Further reading: Chauveau, Michel, and David Lorton, transl. *Egypt in the Age of Cleopatra: History and Society Under the Ptolemies.* Ithaca, N.Y.: Cornell University Press, 2000; Grant, Michael. *Cleopatra.* London: Phoenix Press, 2000; Holbl, Gunther, and Tina Saavedra, transl. *A History of the Ptolemaic Empire.* New York: Routledge, 2000; Mysliwiec, Karol, and David Lorton, transl. *The Twilight of Ancient Egypt: 1st Millennium B.C.* Ithaca, N.Y.: Cornell University Press, 2000; Rowlandson, Jane, and Roger Bagnall, eds. *Women and Society in Greek and Roman Egypt: A Sourcebook.* Cambridge, U.K.: Cambridge University Press, 1998; Walker, Susan, and Peter Higgs, eds. *Cleopatra of Egypt: From History to Myth.* Princeton, N.J.: Princeton University Press, 2001.

clocks The time indicators used in ancient Egypt, introduced around 3500 B.C.E. Known as a gnomon, this measure of time was formed by a vertical pillar used to cast a shadow and so indicate the time of day. The sundial, invented by the 8th century B.C.E., is represented by an Egyptian green schist form, the earliest such device surviving. The sundial had a straight base with a raised crosspiece at one end. Inscribed time divisions were intersected by the shadow of the crosspiece.

Water clocks also date to the New Kingdom Period in Egypt. AMENHOTEP III (r. 1391–1353 B.C.E.) used them, and the Greeks adopted the timepieces, calling them *clepsydras* (from *kleptein,* "to steal," and *hydor,* "water"). The water clocks were fashioned out of sloping vats, filled with water and containing a small hole. Pressure reduced as water escaped, but it still served its purpose in darkness.

coffins The mortuary regalia that appeared in Egypt in the Old Kingdom (2575–2134 B.C.E.), designed to protect the remains of the deceased, such boxes were placed inside of MASTABAS, which were large enough to provide chapels and chambers for offerings. The coffins were painted on their sides to make them resemble the walls of the royal palaces, and doors, windows, and even patterns of hanging reed mats were fashioned as designs for these receptacles.

Illustrations of TUAT, or the Underworld, were often painted inside the coffins for the benefit of the deceased, and other maps, mortuary texts, and symbols were placed on the outside, with magical spells included for protection. Anthropoid coffins appeared in the Seventeenth Dynasty (1640–1550 B.C.E.) as large, wooden boxes. The CARTONNAGE style used the external pattern of bandages with prayers and the name of the deceased. Collars and AMULETS were part of the design. By the Twentieth Dynasty (1196–1070 B.C.E.) the coffins had a yellow base coat with painted designs. Some had low reliefs that included headdresses, carved wooden hands, head collars, and braces.

Cartonnage masks were developed in the First Intermediate Period (2134–2040 B.C.E.) but were extended in later dynasties to cover the entire mummified remains. Both the inner and outer coffins were fashioned in cartonnage, with idealized masks of the deceased along with the usual mortuary incantations. The anthropoidal coffins were elaborately painted, dressed in the robes of HORUS or in the feathers of the goddess NEKHEBET. The RISHI PATTERN or feather design was popular in the Seventeenth and early Eighteenth Dynasties (1640–1400 B.C.E.).

See also MORTUARY RITUALS.

Coffin Texts These were inscriptions placed inside the coffins of Egyptians, containing spells and incantations intended to help the deceased on their journeys to the hereafter. Developed in HERAKLEOPOLIS MAGNA in the First Intermediate Period (2134–2040 B.C.E.), these texts evolved from the Twelfth Dynasty (1991–1783 B.C.E.) mortuary formulas. The Coffin Texts were composed of the PYRAMID TEXTS, which had been placed only in royal tombs in the Fifth and Sixth Dynasties (2465–2150 B.C.E.), and they were used by all Egyptians. Such texts had to be transferred to the coffins as the tombs became smaller, no longer offering wall space for inscriptions.

See also TOMB TEXTS.

coinage A monetary system was not in use in Egypt until the New Kingdom (1550–1070 B.C.E.), possibly brought into the Nile Valley by TUTHMOSIS III (r. 1479–1425 B.C.E.). No actual coins were minted in Egypt until the Thirtieth Dynasty (380–343 B.C.E.), as foreign monetary units were imported to serve the financial needs before that time. Prior to the introduction of coins, Egyptians relied on simple bartering, using copper, barley, or other commodities of exchange. The *deben* was a designated weight employed in such barters. By the reign of Tuthmosis III, units of gold or silver were used to measure monetary value. There were also metal tokens of fixed weight used for barters, called *shet, shena, shenat,* or *siniu.*

During the Ptolemaic Period (304–30 B.C.E.), coins from Greece were in use in Egypt, and the nation had a sophisticated banking system. The Ptolemies established public banking institutions in all of the major cities, with smaller agencies serving the rural areas as well. The central bank was in ALEXANDRIA, but agencies in other areas collected government revenues and handled loans to farmers and businessmen. Thousands of Egyptians were reportedly employed by these banks in order to keep them functioning in diverse regions.

colors Often symbolic in nature, the various hues used in ancient Egypt were derived from mineral and vegetable sources. The great monuments, including temple pillars, and sphinxes and other statues, were always painted in vivid colors. These colors lent a realistic, natural value in reliefs and other forms of art. Artisans began to observe the natural occurrence of colors in their surroundings and pulverized various oxides and other materials to develop the hues they desired.

COLORS

Color	Symbolism	Source
White *(hedj)*	Used to represent limestone, sandstone, silver, milk, fat, honey, vegetables, teeth, bones, moonlight, some crowns. Symbolized baboon (associated with THOTH), the crown of Upper Egypt, joy, luxury, and white bread (in offerings to the dead).	Made from powdered limestone.
Black *(kem)*	Used to represent ebony, emmer wheat, cattle, hair, eyes, Nubians. In tombs used to represent mascara. Symbolized the Underworld, the dead, OSIRIS, fertility (from the Nile mud), the HEART, ANUBIS, and the IBIS.	Made from carbonized materials, such as burnt wood and lampblack, at times from manganese oxide found in the Sinai.
Red *(deshier)* **Blood-red** *(yenes)* **Blue-red** *(tjemes)*	Used to represent male skin color, NATRON, fruits, myrrh, woods, animals, blood, fire, the red crown of Lower Egypt, hair, baboons, foreigners, some clothing, and sometimes the dead. Anything bad in the calendars or bad days were written in red at times. Symbolized anger, rage, disorder, or brutality, or, on the contrary, positive aspects.	Made from anhydritic iron oxide.
Blue *(khesbed)*	Skin color of the solar gods, wigs and BEARDS of the gods, popular in faience.	Made from powdered azurite, lapis, or copper carbonate.
Green *(wadj)*	Associated with WADJET, the cobra goddess. Name *(wadj)* means healthy, flourishing, etc. Green represented the fertile fields, the respected Osiris. Heart scarabs were made out of green nephrite. Green was popular color for AMULETS. FAIENCE could be either blue or green and was favored in amulets. The "Eye" amulet was called the *wadjet,* "that which is healthy."	Made from malachite.
Yellow *(ketj)*	Represented vegetal matter, some foods, and skin color of females in some eras. Gold represented sunlight, the disc, the rays of the sun, and metal.	Made from hydrated iron oxide.

The gigantic mortuary statues of Amenemhotep III, called the Colossi of Memnon by the Greeks *(Courtesy of Steve Beikirch)*

Colossi of Memnon Sandstone statues that are still standing on the western shore of the Nile at THEBES, they were once part of the mortuary complex of AMENHOTEP III (r. 1391–1353 B.C.E.) of the Eighteenth Dynasty. The statues stand 65 feet high, including their bases, and depict the ruler in a seated position, allowing his figure to dominate the landscape. The Greeks, coming upon them in later eras, decided the statues honored their hero, Memnon, who fought at Troy, and named them accordingly. In the past the northernmost statue was said to have made musical sounds at dawn, amazing visitors and bringing it world fame until the Romans made crude repairs and silenced the statue. An earlier collection of stone statues, dating to the Middle Kingdom (2040–1640 B.C.E.) are in ruins in BIAHMU, erected by AMENEMHET I (r. 1991–1962 B.C.E.).

Companions of the Divine Heart Two deities called WA and AA, they made their home on the "PRIMEVAL ISLAND OF TRAMPLING," as depicted on the walls of the EDFU temple. They are called the Lords of the Island of Trampling and are associated with the god RÉ.

Contending of Ré and Set A mythological text found at THEBES in the Chester Beatty Papyrus I, the long account was written in the reign of RAMESSES V (r. 1156–1151 B.C.E.) and relates the confrontations between the child god HORUS and the deity SET. The gods of Egypt who were called upon to settle the dispute debated for about 80 years but then made Horus the true ruler of Egypt. Set, banished from the abodes of the gods, was given lightning in order to allow him to frighten mortals.

Coptos *See* KOPTOS.

Corners of the Earth The four cardinal points recognized by the ancient Egyptians and honored in the construction of the pyramids and other monuments, the gods of the four corners were SOPDU, HORUS, SET, and THOTH. Queen ASHAIT, a lesser ranked consort of MENTUHOTEP II (r. 2061–2010 B.C.E.), had a hymn to the spirits of the four corners of the earth in her tomb. This hymn remarkably categorized the physical aspects of the winds that came from each corner and was beautifully written.

coronation rituals An ancient Egyptian ceremony that evolved from the Predynastic Period, before 3000 B.C.E., and was used upon the accession of each new ruler to the throne. The ruler was shown to the people in opening rites as the heir to Upper and Lower Egypt. In some dynasties the ceremony took place while the old ruler was still on the throne, elevating his successor to a coregency that ensured an orderly succession. Another aspect of succession, not involved in the actual ceremonies of coronation but vital to the elevation of the new ruler, was the mortuary rite. Each new ruler had to be present at the burial of his predecessor.

Wearing the white CROWN, the *hedjet,* of Upper Egypt, the heir to the throne was led out to the people. He then put on the red wicker basket crown, the *deshret,* of Lower Egypt's Bee Kings. When the crowns were united as the pachent, or *pschent,* upon the head of the pharaoh, a great celebration took place. At this point the ruler entered the hall of the NOME gods of Upper Egypt, wearing only the white crown. When these divinities welcomed him he repeated the same ceremony in the hall of the nome gods of Lower Egypt, wearing the red crown only. The SOULS OF PE and the SOULS OF NEKHEN had to approve the new ruler. A stake was then put into the ground, entwined with the LOTUS and PAPYRUS symbols of both kingdoms. The monogram or CARTOUCHE of the new ruler was worked in gold and precious stones alongside the stake. The CROOK and the FLAIL, the symbols of Egyptian royalty traditionally handed down from the agricultural beginnings of the nation, were placed in the hands of the new ruler, who was then led in procession around the walls of the capital.

A ceremony called "the placing of the diadem in the hall" started in the Early Dynastic Period (2920–2575 B.C.E.). By the time of the New Kingdom (1550–1070 B.C.E.), the rituals had become more sophisticated and elaborate. The inscriptions detailing the coronation of Queen-Pharaoh HATSHEPSUT (r. 1473–1458 B.C.E.) describe purifying rites and a journey from THEBES to HELIOPOLIS (at modern Cairo), where the god ATUM offered her the crown. AMENHOTEP III (r. 1391–1353 B.C.E.) also made the trip down the Nile for his accession.

A proclamation of the pharaonic role was then announced in Thebes, supposedly by the god AMUN, and the new ruler was led before the courtiers and the people. Purified once again and robed, the heir received the crowns and was honored by the gods, portrayed by priests in masks serving as attendants. The concluding ceremonies and festivals lasted for several days and were occasions of immense joy for the nation. It was also believed that the gods and goddesses took part in the celebrations as the ruler's name was inscribed mystically on the PERSEA TREE upon coronation.

corvée A French word used to designate a unique form of labor used in Egypt: the king, as the living god of the land, had the right to ask his people to assume staggering burdens of labor. This privilege of the Egyptian ruler has been viewed both as a form of slavery and as a unique method of civil responsibility. The corvée was not slavery, although that particular system was formally introduced into Egypt in the Middle Kingdom (2040–1640 B.C.E.). The massive constructions along the Nile were possible only because of the seasonal enlistment of the Egyptian people.

Vast armies of workers left their fields and orchards and took up their construction tasks with enthusiasm because of the spiritual rewards of their labors, especially at royal mortuary sites. Each man called to the scene of royal projects worked his allotted hours and went home carrying beer and bread. Work was seasonal and carried out in shifts, depending upon the Nile's inundations and the readiness of the land for sowing or harvesting. Elaborate camps were established on the sites of building projects, and entertainment and medical care were provided for the workers during rest periods. Women were also drafted to aid in some large projects. They cooked, cared for the sick, wove clothes, and aided the workers. In return they were sent home with ample supplies and honor. The corvée was possible

The Great Pyramid stands at Giza, the result of voluntary labors by thousands of Egyptians who answered pharaoh's demand for corvée, his right to ask for their unending toil on behalf of his mortuary site. *(Courtesy Thierry Ailleret)*

only in times of dynastic strength and stable government. When a dynasty failed, as in the First (2134–2040 B.C.E.) and Second (1640–1550 B.C.E.) Intermediate Periods, volunteer labor was not only impractical but impossible.

cosmetics These were the beautifying materials of ancient Egypt. From the earliest times Egyptian women employed creams and powders to brighten or color their faces. They were particularly concerned with mascara, which was used to recreate the sacred EYE OF RÉ symbol on their own eyes, at once both a religious and a fashion statement. This mascara was made of malachite, or copper ore, used in the Early Dynastic Period (2920–2575 B.C.E.) and probably used for the same purpose in the Predynastic Period (before 3000 B.C.E.). During the Old and Middle Kingdom (2575–2134 B.C.E. and 2040–1640 B.C.E.) galena was used as mascara, and then a form of kohl (like the modern cosmetic) was popular. Mascara was either imported or obtained from a natural source near KOPTOS. Various red pigments were used to adorn the face, mostly ochres and natural dyes. Scents from cedar and sandalwood, barks, flowers, and plants were fashionable, and perfumes were composed of rarefied fats and alcohol or oils.

Most royal or noble women took care not to allow the sun to darken their faces, and in funerary paintings they were depicted as fair-skinned. The cosmetics of the women were kept in beautifully carved boxes, or in chests made out of ivory or other precious materials. Spoons, palettes for grinding powders, brushes for mascara, and small tubes for ointments to adorn the lips have been found, as well as combs, mirrors, and various trinkets for wigs and hair.

Council of Ten An essential unit of government for the territory of Upper Egypt, working with "the Officials of Nekhen," this council, which had a counterpart in the Delta area of Lower Egypt, handled NOME affairs and served as the crown's liaison to the *djadjet,* an assembly of nomarchs, or hereditary lords, of the provinces. When the land was in turmoil because of a failed dynasty, the Council of Ten and other local authorities maintained stability and calm in the various regions. When the Ptolemies lived under Greek law and allowed the Egyptians to use their traditional legal systems, the Council of Ten and other legal units held full authority.

See also ADMINISTRATION.

crocodile This was an animal revered by the ancient Egyptians as a THEOPHANY of the god SOBEK. Sobek was worshipped in GEBELEIN, DENDEREH, and SAIS. Particular honor was given to the crocodile in the FAIYUM. Crocodiles eventually were kept in pools or in small lakes, where priests tended to their daily needs. Some of the animals wore crystal or golden earrings, and some had bracelets on their forepaws. When they died they were embalmed with care.

Crocodiles were plentiful in the early period. A legend stated that AHA (Menes) of the First Dynasty (r. 2920–? B.C.E.) was befriended by one of them when attacked by enemies in the Faiyum. The embalmed remains of these animals were discovered in the tomb of AMENEMHET III (r. 1844–1797 B.C.E.) and elsewhere. KOM OMBO was an important center for the crocodile cult in later times. At CROCODILOPOLIS, renamed Arsinoe in the Ptolemaic Period (304–30 B.C.E.), crocodiles were displayed for religious ceremonies and as attractions for visitors.

Crocodilopolis An ancient Egyptian site, originally called Shedet, then Arsinoe, and now Medinet el-Faiyum. A tradition states that AHA (Menes) (the founder of Egypt's First Dynasty in 2920 B.C.E.) founded Crocodilopolis. The city served as the capital of the FAIYUM and was the cultic center for the crocodile deity SOBEK. An agricultural center watered by the BAHR YUSEF (the Joseph River, honoring a local hero of Islam), the city also had a shrine honoring the goddess RENENET. A temple discovered on this site dates to the reign of AMENEMHET III (1844–1797 B.C.E.), but it was probably finished by him, having been started by SENWOSRET I (r. 1971–1926 B.C.E.). There is some speculation that the red granite OBELISK at ABGIG (a site in the fertile FAIYUM region, south of the GIZA plateau) was once part of this temple. RAMESSES II (r. 1290–1224 B.C.E.) restored the temple of Sobek. During the Ptolemaic Period (304–30 B.C.E.), the city was named for Queen ARSINOE and served as an important cultic center for Sobek. Visitors to the city fed crocodiles nurtured there. There were various mines in the area of Crocodilopolis, exploited throughout Egypt's history. The site also had a sacred lake and baths.

Croesus (d. 546 B.C.E.) *king of Lydia (modern Turkey)*
He ruled from ca. 560 B.C.E. until his death. A member of the Mermnad line, Croesus conquered mainland Ionia of Greece and then faced the Persian king, Cyrus II the Great. Retreating to his capital of Sardis, Croesus was besieged there by Cyrus II and sentenced to death by burning. However, having been spared, he entered the service of Cyrus II and was made the governor of Barene in Media. He also accompanied CAMBYSES (r. 525–522 B.C.E.) when that Persian ruler entered Egypt.

crook A royal symbol, the *awet,* carried by the rulers of ancient Egypt, representing the early shepherds, the scepter had magical powers and represented traditions of the past and the government. The crook was carried with the flail, called the *nekhakha,* which represented the gods OSIRIS and MIN.

An ivory crook was discovered in the tomb of SCORPION I (fl. ca. 3000 B.C.E.), who ruled at HIERAKONPOLIS

and then at THINIS as a member of Dynasty 0. The crook possibly represented the herdsmen who entered the Nile Valley from the western desert in the Predynastic Period. Some truly ancient deity probably used the crook as an insignia as well.

crowns These were the various royal headdresses used by the rulers of ancient Egypt for specific ceremonies or rituals. The white war crown of Upper Egypt, the *hedjet,* was combined with the *deshret,* the red wicker basket crown of Lower Egypt, to form the *wereret,* the double crown of Upper and Lower Egypt. Called *pachent* or *pschent* by the Greeks, the crowns represented the *paekhemty,* the double magic of the pharaohs. The rulers also wore the *seshed,* the crown covered with a filet of ribbon with a bow at the back and fluttering pennants. A cobra, WADJET, was used as an insignia in the front of a circlet, which had bows shaped like the timbrels of the PAPYRUS plant.

The ram's horn crown, called both the *atef* and the *hemhemet,* depending upon their style and use, was a ritual head covering and was worn only on solemn occasions when the ruler wished to be connected with OSIRIS and RÉ in rituals. The *nemes,* the striped head cloth designed with panels extended on the front, was worn only by the pharaohs. The *khephresh,* the military crown, was made of ELECTRUM and was blue in color, worn on campaigns or in triumphal processions.

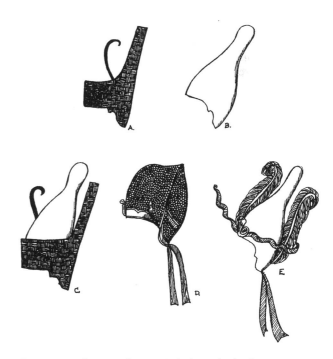

The crowns of Egypt's kings: (a) *deshret,* the basket crown of Lower Egypt; (b) *hedjet,* the white war helmet of Upper Egypt; (c) *pschent* or *wereret,* the double crown of Upper and Lower Egypt; (d) *khepresh,* the electrum war helmet; (e) *atef* or *hemhemet,* ram's horn crown

cult centers   These were the ancient Egyptian sites where the gods were honored with special rites or ceremonies, and where temples were erected for their devotion. Each town had its own particular deity, but these were the centers of the major gods:

CENTER	GOD
Abydos	Osiris
Assiut	Wepwawet
Bubastis	Bastet
Busiris	Osiris
Buto	Bubastis
Crocodilopolis	Sobek
Dendereh	Hathor
Edfu	Horus
Elephantine	Khnum
Elkab	Nekhebet
Koptos	Min
Heliopolis	Ré and Atum
Herakleopolis	Harsaphes
Hermopolis Magna	Thoth and the Ogdoad
Hierakonpolis	Horus
Leratopolis	Lions (Akeru)
Letopolis	Horus
Memphis	Ptah and Sekhmet
Ombo	Set
Sais	Neith
Tanis	Set
Thebes	Amun
Thinis	Anhur (Onouris)

cults   These were Egyptian religious practices embraced throughout all historical periods, related to the "TIME OF THE GODS," the Predynastic Period before 3000 B.C.E. The deities traditionally preceded the first pharaohs, and GEB, OSIRIS, SUTEKH, HORUS, THOTH, and MA'AT were among them. The symbolism of every cultic ceremony was twofold: the rite was celebrated so that divine grace could enter Egypt's social and religious life, and every rite was reenacted to repeat a divine event from "the Time of the Gods." At the close of the day's services in the temples, for example, the priests raised up a statue of Ma'at, to denote the fact that right and truth had been established by the ceremonies, reenacting the eras in which right and truth were originally proclaimed on the Nile.

Such cults were unique in human history. They were based on celestial observations of the ancient Egyptians. The animal THEOPHANIES represented in the cultic rituals were chosen for their particular strengths or virtues. The BULL and the ram, for example, symbolized physical powers and virility. The lion, crocodile, and leopard displayed muscular agility and savagery. The goose and cow depicted fertility, the jackal cunning, the cobra and scorpion lethal power, the baboon wisdom, and the scarab rebirth.

Cusae   The ancient Egyptian site named el-Qusiya in modern times, this was the main city of the fourteenth NOME of Upper Egypt, located just south of 'Amarna. Cusae was at one time the southern area of the HYKSOS domain during the Second Intermediate Period (1640–1532 B.C.E.). A FORTRESS was erected on the site, taken by KAMOSE (r. 1555–1550 B.C.E.) of the Seventeenth Dynasty during Egypt's war of independence. The nearby necropolis of MEIR (Mir) contained rock-carved tombs of the nomarchs of the region, some dating to the Old (2575–2134 B.C.E.) and Middle Kingdom (2040–1640 B.C.E.) Periods.

cylinder seals   Carved seals originating in Sumeria and entering Egypt in the Predynastic Period (before 3000 B.C.E.), or in the Early Dynastic Period (2920–2575 B.C.E.), the cylinder seals were used to imprint titles on clay objects. Some were attached to metal handles, while others, specifically those of the early dynasties, were handheld in the form of a scarab. Fragments of such seals were found at Khafr Tarkhan and elsewhere. These carried the insignias of NARMER and AHA (Menes) (r. 2920–? B.C.E.). Queen NEITHOTEP's seals were also discovered from the same period. Cylinder seals were made of black steatite, serpentine, ivory, and wood. Officials suspended the seals from cords around their necks and then impressed symbols or cartouches into damp clay or other substances to mark items as reserved for royal use. By the Middle Kingdom (2040–1640 B.C.E.) the cylinder seals were discarded in favor of SCARABS.

Cyprus (Alashya)   An island in the eastern Mediterranean, called Alashya by the Egyptians, noted for its copper resources and Greek in origin, the island was controlled briefly by Assyria and then by Egypt. The Persians ruled Cyprus 525–333 B.C.E., and ALEXANDER III THE GREAT assumed control when he defeated the Persians. PTOLEMY I SOTER (r. 304–284 B.C.E.) captured Cyprus in a naval battle. He bequeathed it to the Ptolemaic government, and Egypt ruled there until Rome made it part of the province of Cilicia in 58 B.C.E.

TUTHMOSIS III (r. 1479–1425 B.C.E.) brought minerals and wood from Cyprus to Egypt during his reign. Lion hunting SCARABS of AMENHOTEP III (r. 1391–1353 B.C.E.) were found in a Cyprus tomb.

Cyrene   A Libyan city founded by the local king Battus and Greeks from Thera ca. 630 B.C.E., the successor of Battus ruled the city until ca. 440 B.C.E., with a brief period of Persian control (525–475 B.C.E.). A democratic system of government flourished on Cyrene after 440 B.C.E., but ALEXANDER III THE GREAT assumed control and gave the area to the Ptolemies. In ca. 74 B.C.E. the Roman province of Cyrenaica was formed, and Cyrene became part of the empire. Cyrene possessed a medical school and other academic institutions and attracted outstanding scholars, such as Aristippus, the philosopher, and Erasthenes, the geographer.

D

Dabá, Tell-el *See* AVARIS.

Dagi (Dagy) (fl. 21st century B.C.E.) *official of the Twenty-first Dynasty*

He served MENTUHOTEP II (r. 2061–2010 B.C.E.) at DEIR EL-BAHRI on the western shore of the Nile. Dagi was the superintendent of the southern domains of THEBES, which was used as an administrative center for the rulers of the Middle Kingdom (2040–1640 B.C.E.). He was buried in Thebes, having erected a tomb on the western shore near the royal necropolis area.

daily royal rites The ceremonies of the divine royal cult that were listed on the TEMPLE walls at ABYDOS and recounted in Egyptian papyri, these were rites dedicated to the god AMUN and date from the New Kingdom Period (1550–1070 B.C.E.). The deity was honored by the ruler or by his priestly representative in the great Theban temples each day. The god Amun was offered unguents, wine, incense, and articles of fine clothing and jewelry at the start of the services. Lavish care was taken of the statues of Amun in the temple, reserved in sanctuaries and hidden from the view of the noninitiated commoners. Only the highest-ranking priests and members of the royal family could enter the sealed chambers of Amun to perform the morning greetings, the washing rituals, and the clothing ceremonies. Each priest knew that he was acting solely as a substitute for the ruler. It was only in the name of the pharaoh that such ceremonies could be performed, because the pharaoh alone was the official representative who could fulfill the royal obligation designed to bring about the grace of office in return.

Most New Kingdom (1550–1070 B.C.E.) rulers performed the rites personally when they were in Thebes. In other temples the same ceremonies were conducted before other deities. Again, the cult priests were aware that they were substitutes for the ruler. The pharaoh went to the temple to "visit his father" each day, a poetic form for the ceremony. When the pharaoh, or his high-ranking representative, arrived in the shrine, he was greeted by a priest wearing a costume representing the god. The double crown of Egypt was offered to the king as part of the ceremony, and a masked priest embraced the royal person in a fatherly manner.

Dating back to the ancient times, the ritual was believed to impart to the king the SA-ANKH, the "Life-Giving Waters," sometimes called the "Fluids of Life." The original concept of the *sa-ankh* was part of the cult of OSIRIS and RÉ, although the HORUS rituals at EDFU used the same tradition. On some occasions the ruler nursed from the breasts of a statue of HATHOR, ISIS, or SEKHMET. In this manner he received divine life, a grace that he was able to extend to the people in turn. MAGIC was thus achieved, and a pact was acknowledged between the deity and the ruler and the people. In some eras it was believed that these ceremonies allowed the ruler not only to receive divine life but to transmit it back to the god in return, thus providing a daily mystical communion. Such rites were designed to give an outward and visible sign of something spiritually experienced.

See also GODS AND GODDESSES; TEMPLES.

Dakhla One of Egypt's major OASES in the western, or LIBYAN DESERT, the oasis of Dakhla was called "the Inner

Oasis" from archaic times and was located directly west of the region of KHARGA OASIS. The capital was Balat in the historical period of the Old Kingdom (2575–2134 B.C.E.), and there was a necropolis. Mut is the newest capital. The necropolis at Dakhla has yielded 80 mummies, some displaying symptoms of leprosy, a disease found in Egypt in the very late eras. A shrine at the oasis was discovered, and representations of 47 deities were displayed within the structure. There were Sixth Dynasty (2323–2150 B.C.E.) mastabas near Balat. There are also tombs from the First Intermediate Period (2134–2040 B.C.E.) and a temple of MUT from the Ramessid Period (1196–1070 B.C.E.) at Dakhla. Sites uncovered at Dakhla include MASARA, Bashendi, and Sheikh Mufta. Prehistoric documentation of habitation is also available there.

Dakka A site in NUBIA (modern Sudan), on the west side of the modern High Aswan Dam, started by the Meroitic ruler ARKAMANI (r. ca. 220 B.C.E.–ca. 200 B.C.E.). The Ptolemaic Period (304–30 B.C.E.) rulers completed temples on the site. Dakka was a cultic center for the deities THOTH and ISIS. The temples honoring these gods were elaborate.

Dal Island A site overlooking the second cataract of the Nile, where it enters the gorge called BATN EL-HAGAR, or "the Belly of Stones." SENWOSRET III and other members of the Twelfth Dynasty (1991–1783 B.C.E.) maintained canals near the site. Such waterways provided safe passage for military and trade vessels. Later pharaohs, such as TUTHMOSIS III (r. 1479–1425 B.C.E.), reopened the canals and improved them for rapid descent to the Nubian territories (modern Sudan).

See also MILITARY.

Damanhur (Timinhor) A site in the western Nile Delta, no longer standing but in ruins. The Egyptians called the site Timinhor, the City of HORUS. In the Ptolemaic Period (304–30 B.C.E.) the site was called Damanhur Hermopolis Parva.

Damietta A site located on a narrow strip of land between the Phatnitic arm of the NILE and Lake Manzala, Damietta thrived in early Egyptian times as a port city. Damietta is also the modern name given to the branch of the Nile River on the eastern side of the Delta.

Danaus The legendary clan leader and son of Belus, Danaus was supposedly a ruler of Egypt and brother of the legendary Aegyptus. Driven out of Egypt by his brother, Danaus took his 50 daughters, the Danaids, to Argo in Greece. The 50 sons of Aegyptus followed and wed Danaus's daughters. He had commanded these women to slay their husbands, and all obeyed, except Hypermesta, who spared her spouse, Lycneus. The Dan-

aids were punished for their cruelty by eternally having to fill bottomless vats with water.

Darius I (Selutré) (d. 486 B.C.E.) *Persian emperor and ruler of Egypt in the Twenty-seventh Dynasty*
Darius I reigned from 521 B.C.E. until his death, with the throne name of Selutré, which meant "the Likeness of Ré." Egypt was part of the Sixth Persian Satrapy, along with the Libyan Oases and Cyrenaica. Darius I was the successor and probably the son of CAMBYSES and had to put down rivals who vied for the throne. One historical document states that Darius avenged his father's murder at the hands of a Magi named Gaumata before visiting Egypt. His favorite wife was Artystone, who bore him two sons.

Darius I was militarily trained, having campaigned in India and Syria. His reign was beneficial to Egypt because of his administrative concerns. He used the CARTOUCHE of Egypt and other pharaonic traditions to keep peace, and he was firm about the authority of his officials and about maintaining a mercenary garrison on the ELEPHANTINE Island. He also aided the temples, restoring their annual incomes and coded laws. Darius I erected a temple to HIBIS in the KHARGA OASIS and completed NECHO II's canal linking the Red Sea and the Nile. In 490 B.C.E., the Greeks defeated the Persians at Marathon, prompting an Egyptian revolt as well. Darius I set out to put down the rebels but died and was buried in the cliff site of Nagh-i-Rustam at Persepolis (in modern Iran) and was succeeded on the throne by XERXES I.

He is mentioned in the Petition of Pete'ese. An Egyptian style statue of Darius I was discovered in Susa, in western Iraq.

Darius II (Ochus) (d. 405 B.C.E.) *Persian emperor and ruler of Egypt in the Twenty-seventh Dynasty*
He was the successor of ARTAXERXES I as the Persian emperor and as a ruler of Egypt, reigning from 423 B.C.E. until his death. Darius II was the son of Artaxerxes I by a Babylonian concubine, thus considered illegitimate in matters concerning the throne. When Artaxerxes I died in 424 B.C.E., Darius II, then called Ochus, was a satrap in a remote part of the empire.

He was married to his half sister PARASITES, an ambitious and energetic woman with a personal fortune. Darius II usurped the throne of Persia from the rightful heir, his brother Xerxes, and then faced other relatives who rebelled against him. He killed aristocratic clans and maintained control, earning a reputation for cruelty and the name Nothus, or "bastard."

Egypt, meanwhile, showed some resistance in the region of SAIS. The Nile Delta was far enough removed from Persian intrigues to function in a semi-independent fashion. Darius II completed the temple of HIBIS in the KHARGA Oasis and installed Persian style tunnels

Darius I, Persian emperor from 521 B.C.E. until his death in 486 B.C.E. and ruler of Egypt in the Twenty-seventh Dynasty, is shown on his throne. A Median officer is paying homage, with two Persian guards standing behind him. *(The Art Archive / Gianni Dagli Orti)*

and pipes for delivering water. Darius II also added to the codified laws of Egypt. During his reign, the Jewish temple on ELEPHANTINE Island was razed. Darius II's satrap, or governor, one ARSAMIS, investigated and discovered that the priests of the Egyptian god KHNUM had arranged the devastation by bribing the local commander of the Persian forces.

Darius II continued his efforts to stem the rising Greek ambitions and to put down sporadic revolts throughout the empire. He was on a campaign north of Media when he became ill and died. His successor was ARTAXERXES II.

Darius III Codoman (d. ca. 332 B.C.E.) *Persian emperor and ruler of Egypt in the Thirty-first Dynasty*
He ruled Egypt from 335 B.C.E. until his death. A cousin of ARSES (Artaxerxes IV), Darius III was installed on the throne when BAGOAS, the murdering eunuch of the court, killed the rightful heir, a prince of the line. Darius III, however, forced Bagoas to drink his own poison, ridding the empire of the slayer.

MAZEUS was the Persian satrap of Egypt appointed by Darius III. Darius ruled only three years in Egypt before he faced ALEXANDER III THE GREAT at ISSUS. He fled from the field, abandoning his mother, wife, and children to the Greeks. Darius III then tried to make peace and to ransom his family, but his efforts were in vain, as the Greeks continued to conquer former Persian areas, including Egypt. He faced Alexander again at GAUGAMELA and once again fled from the battle. The satrap of Bactria, Bessus, murdered Darius III. This last Persian ruler of Egypt was buried at Persepolis. Mazeus, Darius III's Egyptian satrap, welcomed Alexander into Egypt.

Dashur A site on the Libyan Plateau, south of SAQQARA, that served as a necropolis for early Egyptian royal clans, two massive stone pyramids of SNEFRU (r. 2575–2551 B.C.E.) of the Fourth Dynasty are at Dashur, as well as the pyramidal complexes of SENWOSRET III (r. 1878–1841 B.C.E.), AMENEMHET II (r. 1929–1892 B.C.E.), and AMENEMHET III (r. 1844–1797 B.C.E.) of the Twelfth Dynasty.

The northern pyramid of Snefru, called "Snefru Gleams," was built out of local limestone and enclosed with the higher grade Tureh limestone. Once higher than the famed PYRAMID of KHUFU at GIZA, this is the Red Pyramid, considered the first successful structure of its type. The square of the pyramid was 721 feet and it was designed to stand 341 feet in height. There are three chambers within, all with corbelled roofs, but there are no signs of a royal burial present. The valley and mortuary complex have not been uncovered.

The southern pyramid complex of Snefru is called the Bent Pyramid or Rhomboidal Pyramid. It was constructed out of local limestone and encased with Tura limestone, laid in sloping courses. Many theories have evolved concerning the change in angle evident in the mortuary structure. The pyramid's original angle was obviously too steep and had to be altered. There is a descending passage inside, with a corbelled roof and lower chambers in which cedar beams were used. A mortuary complex was found beside Snefru's southern pyramid, consisting of a small shrine, a limestone slab, and an elaborate offering table. Two large stelae flanked the temple, which was surrounded by a mud-brick wall. The VALLEY TEMPLE, part of the complex, is a rectangular building with sculpted friezes and a temenos wall.

The pyramidal complex of Senwosret III has a MORTUARY TEMPLE and a valley temple, linked by a causeway. The complex, now in ruins, was built of mud brick and encased with bonded limestone blocks. The interior burial chamber was lined with red granite, and the sarcophagus was made of the same stone. A gallery on the northeast side leads to the royal tombs of family members. There are four ruined MASTABAS on the northern side and three on the southern side. Individual burial chambers provided a cache of jewelry from Senwosret III's female relatives. Three cedar boats were also uncovered, and a stone wall surrounded the site.

The pyramidal complex of AMENEMHET II was built of brick, designed with a foundation of compartments that were filled with sand. There is a vast causeway and a mortuary temple that contains slabs inscribed with the name of the god AMUN. The pyramid was once covered with limestone, and a sandstone sarcophagus was found in the interior burial chamber. To the west are the pyramids of Amenemhet II's queen and four princesses.

The pyramidal complex of AMENEMHET III, called "Amenemhet Is Beautiful" by the Egyptians and now listed as the Black Pyramid, is the last major structure in Dashur. The pyramid was made out of mud brick with a black basalt pyramidion. A causeway paved with limestone slabs, a valley temple, and a residence for mortuary priest officials complete the complex. The pyramid, a cenotaph, was originally 26 and a half feet in height and 344 feet square. This complex was also the burial site of the mysterious AWIBRÉ HOR.

death   *See* ETERNITY.

"Debate of a Man with His Soul"   A didactic text found in the BERLIN PAPYRI sometimes called "The Man Who Tired of Life," "Debate of a Man with His Soul" is dated probably to the Twelfth Dynasty (1991–1783 B.C.E.) and authored by an unknown sage.

The work, part of the Berlin Papyri, a series of documents now in the Egyptian Museum, Berlin, may be a copy of an earlier original. The text is not complete but clearly delineates the troubles of an Egyptian of that period who fears death but wants to exit from his world. The ancient Egyptians invented the word "soul," calling it the *ba*. The soul was depicted as a winged bird that could take flight. The ancient Egyptians also invented the concept of eternity, and this literary work examines a human encounter with the soul and eternity.

Not every Egyptian of the ancient historical periods thought in lofty terms or promoted spiritual well-being. Most of the commoners, especially the farmers and fisher-folk, had to work night and day in order to feed their families and did not have leisure hours in which to contemplate the spiritual aspects of their existence. Festivals, however, brought commoners and aristocrats alike into contact with ideals, traditions, and spiritual aspirations. The religious practices of Egypt were designed to accomplish such contact, and in some eras there were as many as 15 religious festivals each month. The people learned to sense their own spiritual destinies and to prepare for their ultimate deaths. The periods in which dynasties collapsed or invaders had control of the Delta regions were thus ordeals for the average individual in the Nile Valley, who understood that life on the earth was supposed to mirror the order, beauty, and harmony evident in the universe, not the disorder and national chaos in which they found themselves. "The Debate of a Man with His Soul" illustrates such a confrontation with disorder and national chaos.

The contrast between the terrors of death and the consolations of the world beyond the grave are beautifully demonstrated in the text. The man complains about what he sees in life, and the soul calmly identifies the wonderful elements of existence, both on earth and in the afterlife. The man uses a simple refrain: "Death is in my sight today!" He is alluding to the possibility of suicide, but he is also declaring that he is witnessing the destruction of everything that he thought stable and lasting. A society that is crumbling or disoriented because of the collapse of a ruling house can bring about such despair. The soul, however, gives the man an eternal view of both life and death, and when the man persists in his morbid preoccupation with suicide, the soul threatens to abandon him. As the Egyptians believed that no one without a soul could exist in paradise, such a threat alarms the man and brings him to his senses. The soul then becomes reconciled with the man and promises that they will be together in life and in paradise, if he has courage enough to fulfill his destiny as a mortal upon the earth.

Declarations of Innocence *See* NEGATIVE CONFESSIONS.

Dedi (fl. 26th century B.C.E.) *seer of the Fourth Dynasty and a court official*
He served KHUFU (Cheops) (r. 2551–2528 B.C.E.) in the dynastic court. Mentioned in the WESTCAR PAPYRUS, Dedi is considered to be the prophet who predicted the birth of the rulers of the Fifth Dynasty, a royal clan aided by the deity RÉ.

Dedu (fl. 15th century B.C.E.) *official of the Eighteenth Dynasty*
Serving in the reign of TUTHMOSIS III (1497–1425 B.C.E.), Dedu was a chief of the famed MEDJAY troops in the New Kingdom Period (1550–1070 B.C.E.). These Nubian warriors distinguished themselves in Egypt's battles against the Asiatic invaders during the Second Intermediate Period (1640–1532 B.C.E.) and in the early stages of the New Kingdom, aiding both KAMOSE and 'AHMOSE (NEB-PEHTIRÉ) as they fought the HYKSOS in the Delta. When the country returned to peace, the Medjay assumed the role of state police, along with the BLEMMYES. Dedu served as the superintendent of the LIBYAN DESERT and as a royal envoy to the tribes living there. He commanded police units in strategic locations and maintained the peace. Dedu was buried in THEBES, on the western shore.

Dedumose II (Djedneferré) (fl. ca. 1640 B.C.E.) *ruler of the Thirteenth Dynasty*
Dedumose II was a vassal of the HYKSOS, listed by MANETHO, the Ptolemaic historian. The Hyksos had taken control of MEMPHIS at the time. "The Great Hyksos," the rulers of the Fifteenth Dynasty (1640–1532 B.C.E.), expanded into the region held by Dedumose II's line, and he had to rule in their name. He left monuments in THEBES, DEIR EL-BAHRI, and GEBELEIN.

Dedun A deity who was honored by TUTHMOSIS III (r. 1479–1425 B.C.E.) of the Eighteenth Dynasty, Tuthmosis built a temple at SEMNA for the worship of Dedun, obviously designated as a tribute to pacify the local inhabitants and to establish a rapport with the region. The temple also served as a monument to the troops of the famous MEDJAY during the struggle with the Asiatics in the Delta. Dedun was the presiding god of NUBIA (modern Sudan) at the time.

Dedyet (fl. 20th century B.C.E.) *royal woman of the Twelfth Dynasty*
She was the sister and wife of AMENEMHET I (r. 1991–1962 B.C.E.). Both Amenemhet I and his sister were com-

moners and reportedly of partial Nubian descent. Dedyet was not the ranking queen consort, or "the Great Wife," of the pharaoh. Queen NEFRU-TOTENEN was the ranking woman of the reign.

Defufa A site in the area of the third cataract of the Nile in NUBIA (modern Sudan), where twin brick FORTRESSES were erected in the Old Kingdom Period (2575–2134 B.C.E.). The rulers of Egypt's early dynasties used the area for TRADE and constructed fortified outposts to protect their settlements and their wares. The fortress at Defufa was in operation in the reign of PEPI II (2246–2152 B.C.E.) in the Sixth Dynasty. Later rulers refurbished and strengthened the fortress and maintained it for defensive purposes during periods of Nubian expansion.

deification This was the process of designating human beings as divine, a practice that was part of the cultic environs throughout Egyptian history and was made official in the New Kingdom (1550–1070 B.C.E.). The pharaohs were deified in this period, and in the case of AMENHOTEP I (r. 1525–1504 B.C.E.), his mother, Queen 'AHMOSE-NEFERTARI, received the same divine status. RAMESSES II (r. 1290–1224 B.C.E.) was deified while still alive, considered a manifestation of the god Ré.

IMHOTEP, the Old Kingdom VIZIER and PRIEST who designed the STEP PYRAMID for DJOSER (2630–2611 B.C.E.), was deified with AMENHOTEP, SON OF HAPU, an official of the Eighteenth Dynasty (1550–1307 B.C.E.). A clinic and a sanitarium were operated at DEIR EL-BAHRI, on the western shore of THEBES, in his honor. Cultic shrines appeared elsewhere as part of the cultic traditions that honored both Imhotep and Amenhotep, Son of Hapu. They were deemed inspired sages worthy of deification.

Some individuals were deified in local communities and had shrines erected for them in their nomes or in the territories that they served. HEKAIB, an official serving PEPI II (r. 2246–2152 B.C.E.), was murdered on an expedition to the Red Sea. When his son returned his body to the ELEPHANTINE Island at ASWAN, the priests erected a cult and shrine in the martyr's honor.

Deinokrates (fl. fourth century B.C.E.) *Greek architect employed by Alexander III the Great (332–323 B.C.E.)*
He was instrumental in erecting the city of ALEXANDRIA. Deinokrates labored under satraps, or governors, when ALEXANDER III THE GREAT left Egypt to march into Asia. The architect arrived on the scene in 231 B.C.E., but the city was not completed until the reign of PTOLEMY II PHILADELPHUS (285–246 B.C.E.). Deinokrates came from Rhodes and was one of four advisers used by Alexander. He proposed laying the city on an east-to-west plane, using a main avenue and a grid. He also assisted in connecting Alexandria to the PHAROS Island with a causeway called the Heptastadium.

Deir el-Bahri (Djeseru-Djeseru)   A large complex of mortuary temples and tombs on the western shore of the Nile opposite the city of THEBES, Deir el-Bahri was called Djeseru-Djeseru (the Holy of Holies) by the Egyptians. The present name of the site is from the Arabic, meaning "Monastery of the North," to denote an early community of Coptic Christian monks who established a religious house there. The great unifier of Egypt, MENTUHOTEP II (r. 2061–2010 B.C.E.) of the Eleventh Dynasty was the first to build his mortuary complex at Deir el-Bahri. AMEHNHOTEP I and HATSHEPSUT of the Eighteenth Dynasty also built extensively at the site.

SITE DESCRIPTION AND CONSTRUCTION

Mentuhotep II was a member of the famed Inyotef clan of Thebes and returned home for his burial. His temple was pyramidal in design, with terraces, walled courts, ramps, porticos, and colonnaded walkways. The roof of the tomb was supported by 140 separate columns. Mentuhotep's royal female companions were buried at the rear of the complex in elaborate tombs. The entire structure was carved out of a cliff, and a vast burial chamber was fashioned under a pyramid, called BAB EL-HOSAN in modern times. (Today Bab el-Hosan is a terrace that houses a replica of the mythical primeval mound, and a cenotaph-style tomb is located in the main structure.) Shrines, chapels, and companion tombs were part of the original complex. Some 60 soldiers who served in the army of Mentuhotep II and died during his campaign to reunite Egypt were entombed at the TOMB OF THE WARRIORS. The warriors' remains were embalmed and wrapped in linens bearing the seals and cartouches of Mentuhotep.

Queen-Pharaoh Hatshepsut of the Eighteenth Dynasty built a complex north of Mentuhotep II's tomb, called "the Gardens of My Father Amun." Her temple

The temple complex at Deir el-Bahri *(Courtesy Steve Beikirch)*

is considered one of the finest architectural structures in the ancient world. Elaborate reliefs and designs display the accomplishments of Hatshepsut, including the announcement of her divine birth as the daughter of Amun. These reliefs, along with her statues, were mutilated years after her death. (Hatshepsut was not buried in the complex; her mummified remains were identified in 2007 at the Egyptian Museum in Cairo laboratory by a team of forensic experts.)

Hatshepsut's structure, started in the seventh year of her reign, was built with terraces similar to those of Mentuhotep II's mortuary complex and, also like that complex, was hewn out of cliffs; SENENMUT and other architects of that time were influenced by the splendor of Mentuhotep II's designs. In Hatsheput's structure, a walled courtyard led to a ramp and a series of raised terraces. A portico on the first level had 22 pillars and a series of reliefs depicting an expedition to PUNT. A chapel dedicated to HATHOR and a shrine in honor of the god ANUBIS were graced with HYPOSTYLE HALLS. Another columned portico completed that section, while a ramp led to another court enclosed with columns and then to another portico. The sanctuary on the highest level of the complex contained a solar chapel and a shrine to the royal cult. Gardens of flowers and myrrh trees flourished at the shrine, and terraces resembled an oasis against the red cliffs. Osiride statues of Hatshepsut, fountains, lion statues, and reliefs added splendor to the site.

Deir el-Bahri also contained the famed cache of mummies found in a shaft in 1881 and another cache at a location named BAB EL-GUSUS (the Door of the Priests). Considerable excavation and restoration has resulted in the maintenance of the site in modern times.

ARCHAEOLOGY

The first major excavations of the complex were started in 1881. The primary motivation for the effort was the discovery that mummies from the site were being sold

Hatshepsut's mortuary temple at Deir el-Bahri on the western shore of the Nile at Thebes *(Courtesy Steve Beikirch)*

to interested buyers. French Egyptologist Gaston Maspero (1846–1916) led the effort to bring an end to the practice. Studies and digging at the temple complex commenced at the end of the century by the Swiss archaeologist Édouard Naville (1844–1926).

These excavation efforts led to the discovery of a cache of mummies, including those of a large number of great pharaohs. Because of recurring grave robberies during the Twenty-first Dynasty (1070–945 B.C.E.) the priests of Amun had gathered up the mummified remains of the pharaohs in the VALLEY OF THE KINGS and placed them in a hidden sanctuary at Deir el-Bahri; reports from that historical period describe the repeated efforts of these priests to safeguard the remains. An inscription in the tomb declares that the pharaoh mummies were reburied there in "the twentieth day of the fourth day of winter in the tenth year of PINUDJEM (1), the High Priest of AMUN." The cache contained the coffins and mummies of the official Nebseni, 'AHMOSE-IN-HAPI, Duathathor-HENUTTAWY, SETI I, TUTHMOSIS I (now in dispute), AMENHOTEP I, and TUTHMOSIS II. Also discovered in the cache were the mummies of TUTHMOSIS III, RAMESSES II, RAMESSES III, RAMESSES IX, TA'O II (Sekenenré), SIAMUN (2), and 'AHMOSE and the remains of the queens 'AHMOSE HETTINEHU, 'AHMOSE MERTAMON, 'AHMOSE NEFERTARI, 'Ahmose Sitkamose, MA'AT KARÉ, NESKHONS, NODJMET, and TAWERET. The princes and princesses found in the cache include 'AHMOSE HETEMPET, 'AHMOSE SIPAIR, NESITANEBTISHRU (2), and SITAMUN (1). Also discovered were Djedptahaufankh, MASAHARTA, PINUDJEM I, PINUDJEM II, and RAI, along with anonymous remains.

Six sarcophagi were discovered on the site of the temple of Mentuhotep II, belonging to his queens. Each sarcophagus describes the remains of the mummified queen within as "the Favorite of the King." One, the sarcophagus of Queen ASHAIT, depicted in her tomb as a Nubian (a modern Sudanese), contains a hymn to the four winds, composed of remarkable images of the four corners of the earth. A very young girl was entombed in one of the sarcophagi also. The tomb of Queen Kawait, the ranking queen, or *hemet,* is beautifully decorated. The young girl may have been Mentuhotep II's daughter or a relative. Dying young, she was probably given the burial rights of the ranking women of the court.

Also discovered in Deir el-Bahri was a cache at a location named Bab el-Gusus. This site contains an entrance to a deep vertical shaft that leads to subterranean corridors and chambers and extends 300 feet under the forecourt of the temple of Hatshepsut. Within the lower chambers, 153 sets of coffins were aligned side by side, containing remains of the personnel of the temples of the god Amun. Funerary regalia, stelae, and other objects were also recovered, as was a cache of mummies in a Deir el-Bahri grave of Queen 'Ahmose In-Hapi, a member of the Eighteenth Dynasty (1550–1307 B.C.E.).

Édouard Naville was succeeded by the American Herbert Winlock (d. 1950), who later served as director of the Metropolitan Museum of Art. His excavation team discovered and reconstructed the statues of Hatshepsut that once decorated the queen's temple at Deir el-Bahri.

Further reading: Brugsch-Bey, Emil, G. Maspero, and C. N. Reeves. *The Royal Mummies of Deir El-Bahri.* London: Kegan Paul, 1990; Winlock, H. E. *Excavations of Deir El-Bahri,* 1911–1931. London: Kegan Paul, 2000.

Deir el-Balah A remarkable Egyptian site located on the Gaza Strip in modern Israel, an outpost of the Egyptian Empire of the New Kingdom (1550–1070 B.C.E.), the site had several levels of occupation evident, starting with one dating to the mid 14th century B.C.E., and displaying 'AMARNA decorative motifs. The next level also has Egyptian influences, as does level four. The Philistine occupation is revealed in level three, with Israelite and Byzantine remains denoting levels two and three.

Egyptian burials were also found in the Deir el-Balah necropolis. Exquisite funerary items were discovered in the graves, including jewelry, carnelian seals, and other personal objects. On level five there are remains of an Egyptian fortress.

Deir el-Balah was the farthest outpost in the line of garrisoned fortresses that composed Egypt's "WAY OF HORUS." These FORTRESSES, with six such sites discovered, stretched along the Mediterranean coast from Egypt, through the SINAI, to Deir el-Balah. The Egyptians residing in these outposts used their own architectural designs, artistic styles, and mortuary rituals.

Deir el-Ballas A site some 30 miles north of THEBES, where the palace complex of the Seventeenth Dynasty was discovered. TA'O I (r. ca. 1640 B.C.E.), or perhaps one

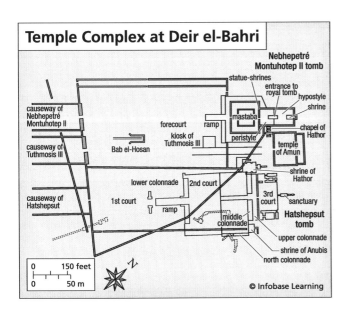

Temple Complex at Deir el-Bahri

Nebhepetré Montuhotep II tomb

statue-shrines
entrance to royal tomb
hypostyle
shrine

causeway of Nebhepetré Montuhotep II

mastaba

forecourt
kiosk of Tuthmosis III

ramp

peristyle

chapel of Hathor

causeway of Tuthmosis III

Bab el-Hosan

temple of Amun

shrine of Hathor

lower colonnade
2nd court

3rd court
sanctuary

causeway of Hatshepsut

1st court

ramp

middle colonnade

Hatshepsut tomb

upper colonnade
shrine of Anubis
north colonnade

0   150 feet
0   50 m

© Infobase Learning

of the earlier rulers, constructed the double palace there. It was used by his successors, TA'O II and KAMOSE, but the rulers of the New Kingdom (1550–1070 B.C.E.) abandoned the site.

An enclosing wall, measuring some 900 by 400 feet, surrounded a complex of columned halls, courts, audience chambers, suites, and royal apartments at Deir el-Ballas. Also included in the complex were silos and stables, indicating the agricultural interests of the royal family. The northern palace seems to have served as the actual royal residence, while the southern building was used as an administrative center. The southern palace had a second floor and a remarkable staircase in place. A village for staff members, workers, and artisans was part of the northern enclave. Some New Kingdom graves were also found in Deir el-Ballas. The Seventeenth Dynasty (1640–1550 B.C.E.) ruled in Thebes as contemporaries of the HYKSOS, or Asiatics, who dominated the Delta. Ta'o II was the Egyptian king who began the war to achieve Egyptian independence from all alien invaders.

Deir el-Bersha A site located north of ASSIUT, opposite MALLAWI at the Wadi el-Nakhla. A necropolis area, Deir el-Bersha contains rock-cut tombs of the Twelfth Dynasty (1991–1783 B.C.E.). The most famous tomb was built for DJEHUTIHOTEP, who served the rulers of the Twelfth Dynasty. The tomb contained a columned chapel and a painted scene of the delivery of a colossal statue from the nearby HATNUB quarry.

See also NATURAL RESOURCES.

Deir el-Durunka A site south of ASSIUT in ancient Egypt where tombs of NOMARCHS from the Nineteenth Dynasty (1307–1196 B.C.E.) were discovered. The tombs were noted for their charming reliefs, which depict lush pastoral scenes, and elaborate statues, all indications of the high standards of mortuary art during the Ramessid Period.

Deir el-Gebrawi The site of an Old Kingdom (2575–2134 B.C.E.) NOMARCH necropolis located near ASSIUT in Upper Egypt. Deir el-Gebrawi was some distance from the Nile, which makes its location typical for that era, when the southern clans used the desert fringes as necropolis regions. Some 100 tombs were discovered there, several containing funerary chambers of offerings, part of the evolving mortuary rituals of the period. Two groups of rock-cut tombs from the Sixth Dynasty (2323–2150 B.C.E.) were also found at Deir el-Gebrawi.

Deir el-Medina A village of ancient Egyptian artisans attached to the New Kingdom (1550–1070 B.C.E.) necropolis at THEBES. It is located on the west bank between the RAMESSEUM and MEDINET HABU. The site was called *Set-Ma'at* when founded by TUTHMO-

The ruins of the settlement of the "Servants of the Place of Truth" at Deir el-Medina, the Valley of the Kings *(Courtesy Thierry Ailleret)*

SIS I (r. 1504–1492 B.C.E.) near the original Eleventh Dynasty (2040–1991 B.C.E.) necropolis. The artisans were formerly known as "the SERVANTS OF THE PLACE OF TRUTH," the laborers of the tombs in the VALLEYS OF THE KINGS and QUEENS. Such workers were valued for their skills and imaginative artistry. In some records these workers were called "the Servitors of the Place of Truth."

The homes of these artisans had several rooms, with the workers of higher rank enjoying vestibules and various architectural adornments. They also erected elaborate funerary sites for themselves and their families, imitations of the royal tombs upon which they labored throughout their entire lives. Small pyramids were fashioned out of bricks, and the interior walls were covered with splendid paintings and reliefs. The site has provided scholars with inscribed papyri, ostraka, and elaborate depictions of everyday life.

AMENHOTEP I (r. 1525–1504 B.C.E.) was an early patron of the region. A temple erected on the site by AMENHOTEP III (r. 1359–1353 B.C.E.) was refurbished by PTOLEMY IV PHILOPATOR (r. 186–164, 163–145 B.C.E.). SETI I (1306–1290 B.C.E.) erected temples to HATHOR and AMUN on the site. TAHARQA (r. 690–664 B.C.E.) also built an Osirian chapel there.

Further reading: Bomann, Ann H. *The Private Chapel in Ancient Egypt: A Study of the Chapels in the Workmen's Village at El Amarna with Special Reference to Deir El Medina.* New York: Routledge, 1991; Lesko, Leonard, ed. *Pharaoh's Workers: The Village of Deir El Medina.* Ithaca, N.Y.: Cornell University Press, 1994.

Delta The area of Lower Egypt formed by the Nile River tributaries located north of MEMPHIS, the region is now intersected by the Damietta and Rosetta branches of the Nile River. At one time there were five such tributaries. The Canopic, Sebennytic, and Pelusiac branches have dried up over the centuries. The Delta played a major role in many eras of Egypt's history. It is actually a triangle of some 8,500 square miles. The coastal areas of the Delta have lakes, wetlands, lagoons, and sand dunes.

Demetrius I Poliorcetes (d. 283 B.C.E.) *king of Macedonia*
Born ca. 336 B.C.E., he was the son of ANTIGONUS I MONOPHTHALMUS and a sworn enemy of PTOLEMY I SOTER (304–284 B.C.E.). Demetrius fought Ptolemy I at Gaza in 312 B.C.E., losing the battle, but he defeated the Egyptian naval forces at Cypriot SALAMIS in 306 B.C.E. He became ruler of Macedonia in 294 B.C.E. Nine years later he was captured by SELEUCUS I Nicator and died from drinking in captivity in the city of Rhodes. Called "the City Sacker" or "the Beseiger," Demetrius attacked the Nabataean city of Petra in 312 B.C.E. He was trying to obtain a monopoly on bitumen, a substance vital to the embalming rituals of the Egyptians. Demetrius was not successful in this venture.

Demetrius II Nicator (fl. second century B.C.E.) *Seleucid king who aided Ptolemy VI Philometor (r. 180–164, 163–145 B.C.E.)*
He married a daughter of PTOLEMY VI PHILOMETOR but faced his own political problems. In 144 B.C.E., Demetrius had to share his throne with a rival, Diodotus Tryphon, and he was deposed by a pretender, who was backed decades later by PTOLEMY VIII EUERGETES II (r. 170–163, 140–116 B.C.E.).

Demetrius of Phalerum (fl. fourth century B.C.E.) *Greek orator and philosopher trained by Aristotle*
Born ca. 350 B.C.E., Demetrius served as the governor of Athens in 318–317 B.C.E. but was exiled from GREECE by DEMETRIUS I POLIORCETES. Going to ALEXANDRIA, he received a welcome from PTOLEMY I SOTER (304–284 B.C.E.). Demetrius also received a mandate from Ptolemy: to collect all the books available in the world. A large amount of financial backing was also provided, and the LIBRARY OF ALEXANDRIA took shape. A tale from this era states that a visitor to Alexandria arrived with a book not in the library, and the volume was immediately confiscated and added to the collection. Demetrius was also a prolific writer, providing Alexandria with a philosophical history and moral treatises.

Democritus (b. 460 B.C.E.) *"Laughing Philosopher" of Greece*
He traveled extensively in Egypt and was a noted encyclopedist. Democritus was honored for his humor as well as his abilities. Some 60 titles are attributed to him.

Democritus supported the atomic theories popular in his age.

Demotic Chronicle A papyrus dating to the reign of PTOLEMY I SOTER (304–284 B.C.E.) and concerning the Late Period (712–332 B.C.E.). The historical records of the last dynasties before the arrival of ALEXANDER III THE GREAT (r. 332–323 B.C.E.) are obscure, and the Demotic Chronicle provides political information as well as pseudo-prophetic dates. The Demotic Chronicle is Papyrus 215 in the Bibliothèque National, Paris.

See also PAPYRUS.

Den (Udimu) (fl. ca. 2850 B.C.E.) *fourth ruler of the First Dynasty*
Reigning ca. 2850 B.C.E., he was called "the Horus Who Attacks." Den received the throne from his father, DJET, while still an infant, and his mother, MERNEITH, stood as his regent. During this regency, Merneith limited the powers of court officials and raised Den in the old traditions.

Upon reaching his majority, Den married Queen HERNEITH (2). He began vigorous military campaigns and fought in the eastern desert. A plaque from ABYDOS shows him striking an Asiatic and states that this was "the first occasion of smiting the East." Den used the name Khasty, meaning "man of the desert." During his campaigns he overran an enemy encampment and brought a harem of females back to Egypt.

Den wrote spells for funerary manuals and recorded medical lore. He is listed as celebrating rites in honor of the deities APIS and ATUM. Den also instituted a national census, recorded in the PALERMO STONE, and was depicted on a hippopotamus hunt on this monument. During his reign, HEMAKA, a courtier, was appointed the chancellor of Lower Egypt, a new position in the government.

Den had a tomb in SAQQARA and another in ABYDOS. The Saqqara tomb is uncertain, however, as the site is now known to belong to Hemaka. The Abydos tomb is the first known example of stone architecture, displayed in the form of a granite pavement. This tomb was large, with a stairway and vast burial chambers, as well as a wooden roof. There are 174 satellite burials on the site. A patron of the arts and a trained medical practitioner, Den is mentioned in the Ebers and Berlin Medical Papyri. An object bearing his name was found at ABU ROWASH, where RA'DJEDEF (r. 2528–2520 B.C.E.) built his pyramidal complex. He is also listed on the Abydos KING LIST.

Dendereh (Dendera; Inuit; Tantere) A site north of THEBES, the capital of the sixth nome of Upper Egypt and the cultic center of the goddess HATHOR. The city was called Inuit or Tantere by the Egyptians. The goddess ISIS was also honored in the region, and the

Egyptians maintained a CROCODILE sanctuary there. In the early periods, Dendereh was on the trade route from Qena to the Red Sea.

The main chapel, dedicated to Hathor, dates to the reign of KHUFU (Cheops) (r. 2551–2528 B.C.E.), and another from the Eleventh Dynasty (2134–1991 B.C.E.) was discovered near a sacred lake at Dendereh. The main temple was fashioned out of a stone platform on a sand foundation with a mud-brick enclosure wall. A propylon entrance leads to a transverse hypostyle hall with 24 columns. A second hall has six columns and a short ramp. Also included in the temple are the Hall of Offerings, an inner vestibule, and the Hall of the Cycle of the Gods. Several chapels are also in the complex, the Per-Ur, dedicated to the start of the new year; Per-Nu, honoring the journey of the goddess to Edfu; Per-Neser, dedicated to the goddess as a lioness. Below, there are 32 treasure crypts. The main temple reliefs at Dendereh also mention PEPI I (r. 2289–2255 B.C.E.), TUTHMOSIS III (r. 1479–1425 B.C.E.), and PTOLEMY XII Auletes (r. 88–58, 55–51 B.C.E.). Pepi I decorated this shrine, and Tuthmosis III refurbished it. This structure also had a "Dendereh Zodiac" relief and a sanitarium where Egyptians were reportedly cured of illness through Hathor's intercessions.

The temple complex dates to the Sixth Dynasty (2323–2150 B.C.E.), attributed to "the FOLLOWERS OF HORUS" of that time. The present form dates to the Ptolemaic Period (304–30 B.C.E.). The chapel of OSIRIS and the temple reliefs of CLEOPATRA VII (r. 51–30 B.C.E.) and PTOLEMY XV CAESARION (r. 44–30 B.C.E.) attest to the Ptolemaic influences. Three birth houses, called MAMMISI, and a temple of Isis complete the religious complex. The founder of the Roman Empire, Augustus, who conquered Egypt in 30 B.C.E., provided funds for the restoration of this temple. A temple dedicated to the goddess Min, a popular deity of the region, and another

shrine, dedicated to HORUS of Edfu, were also erected in the area.

The necropolis of Dendereh included tombs from the Early Dynastic Period (2920–2575 B.C.E.) as well as a number of mastabas belonging to local NOMARCHS. On the western side of the cemetery there are brick-vaulted catacombs in which birds, cows, and dogs were entombed in mummified form. A small chapel from MENTUHOTEP II (r. 2061–2010 B.C.E.) was also discovered in Denderch and now is in the Egyptian Museum in Cairo. The building commemorated the royal cult and had inscriptions from MERENPTAH (r. 1224–1214 B.C.E.) of the Nineteenth Dynasty. Extensive building continued in Dendereh throughout ancient historical eras.

Derr A site south of AMADA in NUBIA (modern Sudan), where a rock-carved temple was discovered, dating to the reign of RAMESSES II (1290–1224 B.C.E.) of the Nineteenth Dynasty. This shrine was dedicated to the god RÉ-HORAKHTE and was designed with hypostyle halls and three sanctuaries. There were painted reliefs within the temple.

Deshasha A territory of ancient Egypt that served as a necropolis for the southeastern part of the FAIYUM. The tombs discovered there date to the Old Kingdom (2575–2134 B.C.E.) and provide documentation of that period of Egyptian history. Some 100 tombs were fashioned on the site of Deshasha, which is located on the west bank of the Nile.

Diadoche A council that served as the successor of ALEXANDER III THE GREAT (r. 332–323 B.C.E.), lasting until the battle of IPSUS in 301 B.C.E. The original membership of this council included Antipater, Craterus, Eumenes of Cardia, and PERDICCAS, who died soon after Alexander. The remaining members were PTOLEMY I SOTER (304–284 B.C.E.), ANTIGONUS I MONOPHTHALMUS, Cassander, LYSIMACHUS, and SELEUCUS I Nicator. All became rivals for power in the division of Alexander's empire.

Dimeh el-Siba An island site in the FAIYUM, near the modern village of Shakhshouk, called Soknopaiou-Mesos, the Island of Soknapaiou, the area was dedicated to the deity SOKNOKNONNEUS, a form of SOBEK. The temple of the deity, also dedicated to ISIS, contains reliefs of PTOLEMY II PHILADELPHUS (r. 285–246 B.C.E.). Made of limestone with high walls, the site also served as a garrisoned caravan station.

See also BACCHIAS.

Dionyseas (Qasr Qarun) A site on the western shore of Lake QARUN, dating to the Ptolemaic Period (304–30 B.C.E.) and earlier. A Ptolemaic temple to SOBEK is located there. This temple has secret chambers once used for oracle ceremonies and a sun chapel positioned

The opening to the shrine of Hathor at Dendereh, the cult center of the goddess *(Courtesy Steve Beikirch)*

on the roof. The temple was actually a maze of corridors and chambers related to cultic rites.

Diospolis Parva (Hiw; Hut-sekhem) A site south of ABYDOS, called Hiw or Hut-sekhem in the Middle Kingdom (2040–1640 B.C.E.), it was originally an estate of SENWOSRET I (r. 1971–1926 B.C.E.) and was called "Kheperkaré the Justified Is Mighty," and "the Mansion of the SISTRUM." A temple on the site during this period is now gone, probably dating to a refurbished form of the Ptolemaic Period (304–30 B.C.E.) as well. A necropolis area is part of Diospolis Parva, containing human and sacred animal burials from the Greco-Roman Periods.

District of Tekhenu-Aten A tract of land on the western shore of THEBES, once part of AMENHOTEP III's (r. 1391–1353 B.C.E.) vast palace complex, the territory, known in modern times as MALKATA, was called the District of Tekhenu-Aten in the Ramessid Period (1307–1070 B.C.E.) and was listed as a royal tract in throne records.

Divine Adoratrice *See* GOD'S WIFE OF AMUN.

Divine Companions A group of ancient Egyptian deities who were considered protectors of the temples and the throne, these gods date to Predynastic (before 3000 B.C.E.) or Early Dynastic (2920–2575 B.C.E.) times. The Divine Companions were four in number, but each had 14 attendants of spiritual aides. They were magical, supernatural, and powerful. The Divine Companions were: the Hawk, "the Lord of the Spear," accompanied by 14 hawks; the Lion, "the Lord of the Knife," accompanied by 14 lions; the Snake, "the Lord Greatly Feared," accompanied by 14 snakes; and the Bull, "the Lordly Great Roarer," accompanied by 14 bulls.

Djar (fl. 21st century B.C.E.) *official of the Eleventh Dynasty*
He served MENTUHOTEP II (r. ca. 2061–2010 B.C.E.) as the overseer of the royal HAREM (1), an important position in his time. Mentuhotep II maintained a large harem and buried several of his royal female companions at DEIR EL-BAHRI in his mortuary complex. Djar was provided with a tomb near Mentuhotep II on the western shore of Thebes, indicating his reputation and rank.

djeba An ancient Egyptian name for the sacred perch or reed that was associated with the creation tales. The reed, split in two at the moment of creation, rose out of the waters of chaos to serve the emerging deity. It was a popular symbol throughout Egyptian history. The *djeba* was the perch upon which the god landed. Several Egyptian deities were involved with this reed in their cultic rites. The god HORUS, called the Falcon, was called the "Lord of the Djeba" in some rituals.

See also "FIRST OCCASION"; PAY LANDS; TEMPLES.

djed (djet, tjet) The ancient Egyptian symbol of stability, the *djed* was a pillar, crossed by bars and depicted with inscriptions and reliefs to serve as an amulet in mortuary rituals. It was the sacred sign of the god OSIRIS, actually considered the deity's backbone, a powerful symbol of magic for all deceased Egyptians, considered necessary to aid in the transformation of the human flesh into the spiritual form assumed by the dead in eternity.

The Djed Pillar Festival, a cultic celebration of the symbol and its powers, was held annually in Egypt and was a time of great enthusiasm and spiritual refreshment for the people. The priests raised up the *djed* pillar on the first day of SHOMU, the season of harvesting on the Nile. The people paid homage to the symbol and then conducted a mock battle between good and evil. Oxen were then driven around the walls of the capital, honoring the founding of the original capital Memphis by AHA (Menes) (r. 2920 B.C.E.). Various reliefs in early tombs depict the procession that was celebrated in early times. AMENHOTEP III (r. 1391–1353 B.C.E.) of the Eighteenth Dynasty took part in the Djed Pillar Festival during his reign and had an inscription commemorating his royal presence. Amenhotep III concluded the festival by sailing in his royal bark on his sacred lake, at MALKATA in THEBES.

Djedefhapi (fl. ca. 19th century B.C.E.) *nomarch, or provincial leader, of Lyconpolis, modern Assiut*
He governed the Lyconpolis territory (modern ASSIUT) during the Twelfth Dynasty (1991–1783 B.C.E.). Djedefhapi was a devotee of the wolf god, WEPWAWET, a deity considered a companion of the god ANUBIS, and very popular in certain regions of the Nile Valley. Djedefhap's tomb, later discovered in the Assiut area, contained a detailed legal text of endowment and was used locally as a Wepwawet cult center.

Djedefhor (fl. 26th century B.C.E.) *prince of the Fourth Dynasty*
A son of KHUFU (r. 2551–2528 B.C.E.) and Queen MERITITES (1), he was the heir after the death of his brother Prince KEWAB. Djedefhor was the father of Queen KHENTAKAWES (1). When Kewab died, Khufu's family became involved in a struggle for the throne. One side supported RA'DJEDEF, who was crowned. Djedefhor and another brother, Baufré, were passed over.

Djedefhor's mastaba tomb at GIZA was unfinished and appears to have been vandalized. He was a scholar, famed for his *Instructions*, a work quoted by later generations of scribes and intended for his son, Prince AUIBRE. The young prince was urged to marry and to "raise up stout sons for Egypt." He was also involved in an occult episode, much repeated in later times. Djedefhor sought the god THOTH's Book of the Dead, a magical work, and he came across four chapters of the book in HERMOPO-LIS. He is also credited with bringing the magician Djedi to his father's court. The WESTCAR PAPYRUS relates that episode. Djedefhor lived to see KHAFRE (Chephren) on the throne of Egypt. His name also appeared at WADI HAMMAMAT.

Djedefptah (fl. 25th century B.C.E.) *mysterious royal personage of the Fourth Dynasty*
He was possibly the son of SHEPSESKHAF (r. 2472–2467 B.C.E.) and Queen KHENTAKAWES (1). The TURIN CANON lists Djedefptah as succeeding Shepseskhaf and ruling only two years. MANETHO also credits him with a reign, but no documentation is available.

Djedhorbes (fl. fifth century B.C.E.) *prince of the Persian Twenty-seventh Dynasty (525–404 B.C.E.)*
He was the son of Artjam, a Persian royal official. A funerary STELA erected for Djedhorbes was inscribed in hieroglyphs. On the stela, Djedhorbes is depicted with the god ANUBIS and a sun disk. Such mortuary symbols represent the adoption of Egyptian funerary rituals by this foreign family.

Djedi (Djedamankh) (fl. 26th century B.C.E.) *official magician of the Fourth Dynasty*
He served SNEFRU (r. 2575–2551 B.C.E.) and KHUFU (Cheops) (r. 2551–2528 B.C.E.) as court physician and as a magician of some note. Djedi apparently was introduced to these rulers by Prince Djedefhor, who had some skills in magic. The magician reached the age of 101. His diet was recorded as the daily consumption of 500 loaves of bread, a side of beef, and 100 jugs of beer. Djedi predicted the rulers of the Fifth Dynasty. He reportedly could replace the decapitated heads of animals and refused to attempt the same feat on a human. While sailing with the court on the Nile, Djedi parted the waters so that the servants could retrieve a bracelet from the riverbed.

Djedji (Tjetji) (fl. 21st century B.C.E.) *courtier of the Eleventh Dynasty*
He served INYOTEF II (r. 2118–2069 B.C.E.) of that royal line. Djedji's mortuary STELA, found at THEBES, is one of the ancient world's most complete biographical texts. The inscriptions include complimentary accounts of his life but also provide in-depth descriptions of the Theban royal affairs.

Djedmutesankh (fl. ninth century B.C.E.) *royal woman of the Twenty-second Dynasty*
She was a consort of OSORKON II (r. 883–855 B.C.E.) and the mother of TAKELOT II and Prince NIMLOT (3). Queen KAROMANA (4) was also the daughter of Djedmutesankh.

Djehor (fl. fourth century B.C.E.) *famous healer of Athribis*
He lived in the reign of PHILIP III ARRHIDAEUS (333–316 B.C.E.). Djehor was able to cure people of the effects of scorpion stings and snake bites. He made a statue and endowed it with magical spells. Victims poured water or wine on the statue, let the liquid run off into a cup, and then drank it. The spells, thus absorbed, reportedly cured everyone. Djehor's statue is now in the Egyptian Museum in Cairo.

Djehuti (fl. 15th century B.C.E.) *military commander of the Eighteenth Dynasty*
Djehuti served TUTHMOSIS III (r. 1479–1425 B.C.E.) in campaigns founding the vast empire. He is famous for his role in the Egyptian assault on the city of JOPPA in modern Palestine, serving in one of Tuthmosis III's campaigns. A captain, Djehuti was sent with a small force to take the ancient site. He met with a Joppa chief and promised to defect. Loading troops into panniers placed on donkeys, Djehuti gained entrance into Joppa. His men sprang from the panniers and opened the gates to more waiting Egyptians. Djehuti received a golden collar from Tuthmosis III for this victory. The collar is in the Louvre in Paris. The tale was possibly the model for the story of Ali Baba and the Forty Thieves in the *Tales of the Arabian Nights.*

Djehutihotep (fl. 19th century B.C.E.) *official of the Twelfth Dynasty*
He served in the reigns of AMENEMHET II (1929–1892 B.C.E.) and SENWOSRET II (1897–1878 B.C.E.). Djehutihotep was a NOMARCH of the Hare nome, with considerable prestige. He accompanied Senwosret II on a military campaign in Syria and performed other services for the royal family. He is best remembered, however, for the reliefs in his tomb at el-BERSHA. These reliefs depict the transportation of a colossal statue from the quarry at HATNUB. The details of the relief provided insight into the architectural and construction methods of his period, a time of vast building projects on the Nile. The statue weighed more than 60 tons and was hauled on a gigantic sledge by the Egyptians as part of their CORVÉE obligations. Other reliefs depict his daughter in elaborate ceremonial attire.

Djehutnufe (fl. 15th century B.C.E.) *official of the Eighteenth Dynasty*
He served TUTHMOSIS III (r. 1479–1425 B.C.E.) and AMEN-HOTEP II (r. 1427–1401 B.C.E.) as a royal scribe and as overseer of the royal treasury. Djehutnufe erected two separate tombs on the western shore of THEBES. One TOMB, quite modest, was probably built in the early stages of his career. The second, the result of his success, was elaborate, with depictions of his villa and wealth.

Djer (Athothis, Iti) (d. 2870 B.C.E.) *second ruler of the First Dynasty, ruling from 2920 B.C.E. until his death*
He was the successor and son of AHA (Menes) and a lesser wife, Queen HENT, also called Khenthap. Djer is translated as "Horus Who Nurtures." He married HER-NEITH (1) and sired a daughter and a son, DJET, the royal heir. A physician who wrote medical and anatomical works, Djer also conducted military campaigns. He led forces against the Libyans and went as far south as WADI HALFA. An inscription recounts his capture of a local chief there. Djer also initiated economic and religious organizations for Egypt and established a palace at MEM-PHIS. He conducted religious celebrations at SAQQARA and visited BUTO and SAIS.

Djer's tomb at ABYDOS is large and is located near Aha's gravesite. The tomb is fashioned out of a rectangular pit with magazines on either side. It was roofed with timber. Within the tomb an arm was discovered in a wall crevice. It was believed to have been part of the remains of Djer's queen. The limb had bracelets of gold, turquoise, lapis lazuli, and amethyst as ornaments. Djer's Saqqara tomb was larger than the Abydos gravesite, having subterranean chambers and seven magazines. The Abydos tomb had 338 subsidiary graves, possibly sacrificed courtiers and servants. A SER-EKH (1) was used for Djer's royal names and power. The tomb also took on a religious significance well beyond the throne. It was identified in later eras as the actual burial site of the god OSIRIS. KHENDJER (r. ca. 1740 B.C.E.) of the Thirteenth Dynasty installed an "OSIRIS BED" in Djer's burial chamber, depicting the deity lying on a bier formed by the bodies of carved lions. Pilgrims attended festivals at the tomb, which remained popular for centuries.

Djet (Wadj; Wadji; Iterty; Uadj) (fl. ca. 2850 B.C.E.) *third ruler of the First Dynasty*
He was the son of DJER and probably Queen HERNEITH (2). His wife was MERNEITH, who stood as regent for their son, DEN. Djet died at a young age and was provided with two tombs, at SAQQARA and ABYDOS. The Saqqara tomb, once believed to have been Djet's, is now known to belong to the noble SEKHEM-KHA. Another site is probably Djet's, and it has 62 satellite burials. The Abydos tomb has 174 satellite burials and a wooden burial chamber in a large pit, surrounded by brick chambers. A STELA discovered there, among some 20 such monuments, complete with a SEREKH (1), is preserved in the Louvre at Paris. An inscription bearing his name was also discovered in EDFU.

Djoser (Netjerykhet) (d. 2611 B.C.E.) *second ruler of the Third Dynasty*
He reigned from 2630 B.C.E. until his death. Inheriting the throne as the son of KHA'SEKHEMWY and a lesser ranked royal woman, Queen NIMA'ATHAP or Hapnyma'at,

he ruled during an age that witnessed advances in civilization on the Nile. The construction of architectural monuments, agricultural developments, trade, and the rise of cities were all evident on the Nile at the time. Djoser ruled for almost two decades, and during his reign territories were consolidated and nomes subdued. He is remembered, however, for the great architectural achievement of his reign, the STEP PYRAMID at SAQQARA. His chancellor or VIZIER, IMHOTEP, was the architect who directed the building of the great complex, which was Djoser's tomb.

Djoser fought the nomads on Egypt's eastern border and the Libyans in the west, as the nation strove to evolve without foreign interference. A statue discovered near his pyramid depicts him as standing on foreigners, identified as the "NINE BOWS," and on the opposing clans of native Egyptians called the Lapwings or REKHET. He was also involved in an event that assumed legendary importance in Egyptian records, being recorded in the famed FAMINE STELA at SEHEL ISLAND, which may date to the Ptolemaic Period (304–30 B.C.E.). A famine lasted in Egypt for a period of seven years, and Djoser counseled with Im hotep and with his governor of the south, a man named MEDIR. Both advised him to sail to the ELEPHAN-TINE Island at ASWAN, where the cult of the god KHNUM was centered. Khnum was believed to control the annual flow of the Nile, and Djoser had dreamed that the god appeared to him and complained about the sorry state of his shrine. He arrived at the Elephantine Island and erected a new temple on the site to honor Khnum, which brought about a miraculous end to the famine. The PHI-LAE priestesses of ISIS claimed that Djoser gave them their island at the same time.

Djoser's queen was HETEPHERNEBTY, thought to be a daughter of Kha'sekhemwy. Djoser used the throne name of Netjerykhet on all monuments, including the Step Pyramid. A mummified left foot, parts of the spine and chest, and an upper right arm and shoulders recovered in Saqqara are believed to be all that is left of Djoser's remains. Relatives of this pharaoh were interred in the pyramid's shafts and tunnels. A life-size statue was found in the SERDAB of the pyramid, depicting Djoser in a *heb-sed* (*see* SED) cloak. He is listed in the Turin KING LIST, and inscriptions record his invasion of the SINAI for turquoise. Djoser's daughters were Hetephernebty and Intkaes. His successor was SEKHEMKHET, possibly a relative.

dogs   Domesticated animals used in hunting, in agricultural systems, and as pets as early as the Predynastic Period (before 3000 B.C.E.). The bones of dogs dating to this era were found in tombs at HIERAKONPOLIS, sometimes buried alongside human remains. The canines of the Nile Valley developed from two distinct historic genetic lines: *Canis familiaris Leineri,* known for greyhounds and sight hounds, and *Canis familiaris inter-*

medius, known for Egyptians' smaller house dogs. The Saluki-type breed, the hounds, and the short-legged terriers were well established by the Middle Kingdom (2040–1640 B.C.E.). Nomarchs were buried with their dogs, and funerary stelas represent certain breeds. The custom of keeping dogs as pets faded between the Middle Kingdom and the New Kingdom (1550–1070 B.C.E.), but Queen-Pharaoh Hatshepsut (r. 1473–1458 B.C.E.), revived the popularity of the various breeds.

Dra-abu' el-Naga The oldest section of the Theban necropolis on the western shore of the Nile opposite the New Kingdom (1550–1070 B.C.E.) capital, now modern LUXOR. Tombs dating to the Eleventh Dynasty (2134–2040 B.C.E.) were discovered there.

The tombs found in the area included those of INYOTEF V, INYOTEF VI, INYOTEF VII, SOBEKEMZAF II, and KAMOSE, all rulers of the Seventeenth Dynasty (1640–1550 B.C.E.). Queen HENUTEMPET, a consort of Senakht-enré TA'O I, was also buried there. Other royal women interred in Dra-abu' el-Naga are Queen Mentuhotep, an unknown consort, whose diadem was recovered at the site, and Queen NUBKHAS (2), the consort of Sobekemzaf I. The site is in a range of hills north of DEIR EL-BAHRI. The ABBOTT PAPYRUS lists an inspection of the tombs there in ca. 1080 B.C.E. Some mortuary complexes in Dra-abu' el-Naga have small pyramids.

Dream Stela A monument erected in the reign of TANUTAMUN (664–657 B.C.E.) at GEBEL BARKAL, the stela commemorates a dream experience by Tanutamun, a member of the Twenty-fifth Dynasty, a Nubian royal line. He dreamed of two serpents that allowed him to hold them without striking. The serpents represented Upper and Lower Egypt, the Two Kingdoms. Tanutamun moved forward with confidence to punish evildoers who opposed his reign, but he faced an implacable enemy in ASSURBANIPAL, who entered Egypt with a large Assyrian force.

dress These were the various styles of apparel used throughout Egyptian history. As the warm climate of Egypt dictated the agricultural seasons, so it influenced the style of dress. There were seasons, and on some evenings the temperature was cold because of the surrounding deserts, but normally the climate remained consistently warm and dry. In accordance with the temperature, the Egyptians devised simple styles and comfortable materials in which to dress from the earliest eras. Cotton was a major crop put to good use, and linen, especially the special material called BYSSUS, became the basis for clothing for upper classes.

In the Predynastic Periods (before 3000 B.C.E.), both men and women wore kilts, skirts that hung in simple folds or were adorned with narrow belts made of rope, fibers, and leathers. In time women wore an empire-type long skirt that hung just below their uncovered breasts. Men kept to the simple kilts. These could be dyed in exotic colors or designs, although white was probably the color used in religious rituals or by court elite.

In the Early Dynastic Period (2920–2575 B.C.E.), both men and women wore their hair short, adorned with various bands or flowers. Then the women of Memphis began to appear in long cotton gowns with sleeves. Others adopted the empire style with a band over the shoulders. Men added simple cotton tops to their kilts when the weather cooled. That style remained consistent throughout the Old Kingdom (2575–2134 B.C.E.) and Middle Kingdom (2040–1640 B.C.E.), although an extra panel, sometimes goffered, sometimes stiffened, was attached to the kilts for special occasions. Furs were used in cold weather, and the Egyptians probably had capes and shawls.

Wigs were used, and various types of head coverings were worn to protect the hair or bare scalp from dust and the heat of the sun. During the Old and Middle Kingdoms, wigs were made of fiber or human hair and were adapted for use by the upper classes. Such wigs were often long, with great masses of hair pulled together in a stiff design. In such instances beads were woven into the hair at set intervals to form an intricate pattern.

Styles expanded with the coming of the New Kingdom (1550–1070 B.C.E.), as the Egyptians were exposed to foreign elements. During that period, red girdles, clearly visible under the sheer cotton fabrics, were considered stylish. Also popular were dresses with patterned beadwork set into the material, and elaborate designs made out of bits of shell and small stones that were embroidered along the length of women's gowns.

The capelet, made of sheer linen, was the fashion innovation of the New Kingdom, a time in which men wore kilts and sheer blouses with elaborately pleated sleeves. Great panels of woven materials hung from the waist, and intricate folds were visible under sheer overskirts.

VIZIERS kept to a simple skirt of white cotton, and PRIESTS used white for all temple functions, placing animal skins or colored sashes and pectorals on their costumes to signify their rank and function. Priests wore shaved heads, and some wore the lock of youth as part of their insignia. This lock was also affected by the royal princes, who shaved their heads but maintained a single lock of hair on the side of the skull, normally entwined with beads and bits of metal.

After the death of the last Ramesses, RAMESSES XI, in 1070 B.C.E., the nation became vulnerable to outside influences. The Libyan, Nubian (modern Sudanese), Persian, and Greek cultures advanced in the Nile Valley, bringing about a change in styles. The 300-year Hellenization of Egypt during the Ptolemaic Period (304–30

B.C.E.) was actually confined to ALEXANDRIA, the Delta capital. Even there the traditional pharaonic court styles continued, as evidence of a link between the Greek conquerors and the first rulers of the Nile. Throughout the land the styles of clothing remained static because of the demands of the climate and the inherent tendency of the Egyptians to maintain traditions. Such dress codes faded, of course, as the Romans and other cultures arrived in the Nile Valley. Softer styles prevailed, and elaborate collars and jewels were popular, as well as intricate wigs and hairstyles.

"Drunkards of Menkauré" The name of the gang of laborers who helped build the pyramids of MENKAURÉ (Mycerinus, r. 2490–2472 B.C.E.) of the Fourth Dynasty in Giza, these laborers were part of the CORVÉE system employed to erect monuments of that era. "The Drunkards," their chosen name, worked in five groups, each composed of 10 to 20 men. They were housed in barracks on the site, alongside as many as 4,000 other laborers. Granaries, breweries, bakeries, medical clinics, and other supportive institutions are still evident in the ruins of Giza. There was also a structure designed for mortuary and embalming processes.

Duamutef One of the four divine sons of HORUS who guarded the internal organs of the deceased. Duamutef protected the stomach. The Sons of Horus were the patrons of CANOPIC JARS, the containers used in funerary rituals to preserve the viscera after embalming and placed in Egyptian tombs. The stoppers on Duamutef's jars were shaped in the heads of JACKALS.

Duat *See* TUAT.

Duauf's Instructions A didactic text included in the PYRAMID TEXTS that date to the Old Kingdom (2575–2134 B.C.E.) in ancient Egypt, the *Instructions* include adages about morality and the true purpose of human life. Duauf urged his fellow Egyptians to love books and learning and to aspire to the honorable and prosperous career of a scribe.

dwarf Called *deneg, nem,* or *hua,* in various ages, several dwarfs in Egypt attained high positions and honors, usually marrying normal-sized mates and raising families. They had roles in government offices and in festival rites. Records from the reign of NIUSERRÉ (2416–2392 B.C.E.) of the Fifth Dynasty indicate that a particular dwarf, called a *deneg,* was brought to the king to dance with royal princesses in rituals. A particularly touching incident involving a dwarf (or pygmy) took place in the reign of PEPI II (2246–2152 B.C.E.) of the Sixth Dynasty. Pepi II was a child when one of his officials, a man named HARKHUF, sent word from the cataracts that he was bringing a dwarf back to MEMPHIS. The small pharaoh wrote a letter giving explicit details about the care of the dwarf and even alerted the governors of the cities along the way to extend special hospitality to the dwarf and his companions.

dynasties The royal houses of ancient Egypt from the beginning of the Early Dynastic Period (2920 B.C.E.) to the end of the Ptolemaic Period (30 B.C.E.), the rulers of each royal line exemplified a particular era in Egyptian history, some serving as victims of change and political upheaval, and others leaving a profound imprint upon the life of the land. The rulers listed below are also found in their own entries. Each ruler is listed below with his or her prenomen (first cartouche name) in parentheses.

See also DYNASTY HISTORIES.

LATE PREDYNASTIC PERIOD CA. 3000 *B.C.E.*
Scorpion
Narmer

EARLY DYNASTIC PERIOD 2920–2575 *B.C.E.*

First Dynasty 2920–2770 *B.C.E.*
Aha (Menes)
Djer
Djet (Wadj)
Den
'Adjib (Anedjib)
Semerkhet
Qa'a

Second Dynasty 2770–2649 *b.c.e.*
Hotepsekhemwy
Re'neb
Ninetjer
Weneg
Peribsen
Sendji
Neterka
Neferkara
Kha'sekhemwy

Third Dynasty 2649–2575 *b.c.e.*
Nebka (Zanakht) 2649–2630
Djoser (Netjerykhet) 2630–2611
Sekhemkhet 2611–2601
Kha'ba 2603–2599
Huni 2599–2575

OLD KINGDOM PERIOD 2575–2134 *B.C.E.*

Fourth Dynasty 2575–2465 *B.C.E.*
Snefru 2575–2551
Khufu (Cheops) 2551–2528
Ra'djedef 2528–2520
Khafre (Chephren) 2520–2494

Menkauré (Mycerinus) 2490–2472
Shepseskhaf 2472–2467

Fifth Dynasty 2465–2323 B.C.E.
Userkhaf 2465–2458
Sahuré 2458–2446
Kakai (Neferirkaré) 2446–2426
Shepseskaré (Ini) 2426–2419
Neferefré (Ra'neferef) 2419–2416
Niuserré (Izi) 2416–2392
Menkauhor 2396–2388
Izezi (Djedkaré) 2388–2356
Unis (Weni) 2356–2323

Sixth Dynasty 2323–2150 B.C.E.
Teti 2323–2291
Userkaré 2291
Pepi I (Meryré) 2289–2255
Merenré I (Nemtyemzaf) 2255–2246
Pepi II (Neferkaré) 2246–2152
Merenré II date unknown
Nitocris (1) (Q.) date unknown

Seventh Dynasty
Dates unknown

Eighth Dynasty 2150–2134 B.C.E.
Neferkuré 2150–?
Qakaré Iby date unknown
Wadjkaré date unknown
Nakare-Aba date unknown
Neferku-Hor date unknown
Neferku-Min date unknown

FIRST INTERMEDIATE PERIOD 2134–2040 B.C.E.

Ninth Dynasty 2134–? B.C.E.
Khetys date unknown
Merikaré date unknown
Kaneferré date unknown
Ity date unknown

Tenth Dynasty ?–2040 B.C.E.

Eleventh Dynasty (at Thebes) 2134–2040 B.C.E.
Mentuhotep I ?–2134
Inyotef I (Sehertawy) 2134–2118
Inyotef II (Wah'ankh) 2118–2069
Inyotef III (Nakhtnebtepnufer) 2069–2061

MIDDLE KINGDOM PERIOD 2040–1640 B.C.E.

Eleventh Dynasty (all Egypt) 2040–1991 B.C.E.
Mentuhotep II (Nebhepetré) 2061–2010
Mentuhotep III (S'ankharé) 2010–1998
Mentuhotep IV (Nebtawyré) 1998–1991

Twelfth Dynasty 1991–1783 B.C.E.
Amenemhet I (Sehetepibré) 1991–1962
Senwosret I (Kheperkaré) 1971–1926
Amenemhet II (Nubkauré) 1929–1892
Senwosret II (Kha'kheperré) 1897–1878
Senwosret III (Kha'kauré) 1878–1841
Amenemhet III (Nima'atré) 1844–1797
Amenemhet IV (Ma'akheruré) 1799–1787
Sobekneferu (Sebekkaré) (Q.) 1787–1783

Thirteenth Dynasty 1783–after 1640 B.C.E.
Wegaf (Khutawyré) 1783–1779
Amenemhet V (Sekhemkaré) c. 1760
Amenemhet VI date unknown
Harnedjheriotef (Hetepibré) ca. 1760
Hor Awibré date unknown
Amenemhet VII (Sedjefakaré) ca. 1740
Sobekhotep I (Kha'ankhré) date unknown
Sobekhotep II (Sekhemré-khutawy) date unknown
Khendjer (Userkaré) date unknown
Sobekhotep III (Sekhemré-swadjtawy) ca. 1745
Neferhotep I (Kha'sekhemré) ca. 1741–1730
Sahathor ca. 1730
Sobekhotep IV (Kha'neferré) ca. 1730–1720
Sobekhotep V (Kha'hotepré) ca. 1720–1715
Aya (Merneferré) 1704–1690
Mentuemzaf (Djed'ankhré) date unknown
Dedumose II (Djedneferré) ca. 1640
Neferhotep III (Sekhemré-s'ankhtawy) date unknown

Fourteenth Dynasty Contemporary with the Thirteenth Dynasty at Xois

SECOND INTERMEDIATE PERIOD 1640–1550 B.C.E.

Fifteenth Dynasty (Hyksos) 1640–1532 B.C.E.
Salitis ca. 1640
Sheshi date unknown
Yaqub-Hor date unknown
Khian (Swoserenré) date unknown
Apophis (Awoserré) ca. 1585–1553
Khamudi ca. 1550–1540

Sixteenth Dynasty ca. 1640–1532 B.C.E. (Minor Hyksos rulers, contemporary with the Fifteenth Dynasty)
Sekhaen-Ré date unknown
Anather date unknown
Yakoba'am date unknown

Seventeenth Dynasty (Theban) 1640–1550 B.C.E.
Sekhemré-Wahkhau Rahotep date unknown
Inyotef V (Nubkheperré) ca. 1640–1635
Sobekemsaf I (Sekhemré-wadjka'u) date unknown
Nebireyeraw (Swadjenré) date unknown
Sobekemsaf II (Sekhemré-shedtawy) date unknown
Inyotef VII ca. 1570

Ta'o I (or Djehuti'o) (Senakhentenré) date unknown
Ta'o II (or Djehuti'o) (Sekenenré) date unknown
Kamose (Wadjkheperré) ca. 1555–1550

NEW KINGDOM PERIOD 1550–1070 B.C.E.

Eighteenth Dynasty 1550–1307 B.C.E.

'Ahmose (Nebpehitré) 1550–1525
Amenhotep I (Djeserkaré) 1525–1504
Tuthmosis I (Akheperkaré) 1504–1492
Tuthmosis II (Akhderneré) 1492–1479
Tuthmosis III (Menkheperré) 1479–1425
Hatshepsut (Q.) (Ma'atkaré) 1473–1458
Amenhotep II (Akheprué) 1427–1401
Tuthmosis IV (Menkheprué) 1401–1391
Amenhotep III (Nebma'atré) 1391–1353
Amenhotep IV (Akhenaten) 1353–1335
Smenkharé (Ankheprué) 1335–1333
Tut'ankhamun (Nebkheprué) 1333–1323
Aya (2) (Kheperkheprué) 1323–1319
Horemhab (Djeserkhepuré) 1319–1307

Nineteenth Dynasty 1307–1196 B.C.E.

Ramesses I (Menpehtiré) 1307–1306
Seti I (Menma'atré) 1306–1290
Ramesses II (Userma'atre'setepenré) 1290–1224
Merenptah (Baenre'hotephirma'at) 1224–1214
Seti II (Userkheprure'setepenré) 1214–1204
Amenmesses (Menmiré), usurper during reign of
    Seti II
Siptah (Akhenre'setepenré') 1204–1198
Twosret (Q.) (Sitre'meritamun) 1198–1196

Twentieth Dynasty 1196–1070 B.C.E.

Sethnakhte (Userkha'ure'meryamun) 1196–1194
Ramesses III (Userma'atre'meryamun) 1194–1163
Ramesses IV (Heqama'atre'setepenamun) 1163–1156
Ramesses V (Userma'atre'sekhepenré) 1156–1151
Ramesses VI (Nebma'atre'meryamun) 1151–1143
Ramesses VII (Userma'atre'meryamun) 1143–1136
Ramesses VIII (Userma'atre'akhenamun) 1136–1131
Ramesses IX (Neferkare'setenré) 1131–1112
Ramesses X (Kheperma'atre'setepenre') 1112–1100
Ramesses XI (Menma'atre'setepenptah) 1100–1070

THIRD INTERMEDIATE PERIOD 1070–712 B.C.E.

Twenty-first Dynasty 1070–945 B.C.E.

Smendes (Hedjkheperre'setepenré') 1070–1044
Amenemnisu (Neferkaré) 1044–1040
Psusennes I (Akheperre'setepenamun) 1040–992
Amenemope (Userma'atre' Setepenatnun) 993–984
Osochor (Akheperre' setepenré) 984–978
Siamun (Netjerkheperre'setepenamun) 978–959
Psusennes II (Titkhepure'setepenré) 959–945

Twenty-second Dynasty 945–712 B.C.E.

Shoshenq I (Hedjkheperre'setepenré) 945–924
Osorkon I (Sekhemkheperre'setepenré) 924–909
Takelot I (Userma'atre'setepenamun) 909–883
Shoshenq II (Hegakheperre'setepenré) 883
Osorkon II (Userma'atre'setepenamun) 883–855
Takelot II (Hedjkheperre'setepenré) 860–835
Shoshenq III (Userma'atre'setepenréamun) 835–783
Pami (Userma'atre'setepenre'amun) 783–773
Shoshenq V (Akheperré) 773–735
Osorkon IV (Akheperre'setepenamun) 735–712

Twenty-third Dynasty ca. 828–712 B.C.E.

Various contemporary lines of kings recognized in
    Thebes, Hermopolis, Herakleopolis, Leontopolis,
    and Tanis; precise arrangement and order are still
    disputed.
Pedubaste I 828–803
Iuput I date unknown
Shoshenq IV date unknown
Osorkon III 777–749
Takelot III date unknown
Rudamon date unknown
Iuput II date unknown
Nimlot date unknown
Peftjau'abast (Neferkaré) 740–725

Twenty-fourth Dynasty (Sais) 724–712 B.C.E.

Tefnakhte (Shepsesré) 724–717
Bakenrenef (Boccharis) (Wahkaré) 717–712

Twenty-fifth Dynasty 770–712 B.C.E. (Nubia and Theban area)

Kashta (Nima'atré) 770–750
Piankhi (Piye) (Userma'atré) 750–712

LATE PERIOD 712–332 B.C.E.

Twenty-fifth Dynasty 712–657 B.C.E. (Nubia and all Egypt)

Shabaka (Neferkaré) 712–698
Shebitku (Djedkauré) 698–690
Taharqa (Khure'nefertem) 690–664
Tanutamun (Bakaré) 664–657 (possibly later in Nubia)

Twenty-sixth Dynasty 664–525 B.C.E.

Necho I 672–664
Psammetichus I (Wahibré) 664–610
Necho II (Wehemibré) 610–595
Psammetichus II (Neferibré) 595–589
Apries (Wa'a'ibré) 589–570
Amasis (Khnemibré) 570–526
Psammetichus III (Ankhkaenré) 526–525

Twenty-seventh Dynasty 525–404 B.C.E. (First Persian Period)

Cambyses 525–522
Darius I 521–486

Xerxes I 486–466
Artaxerxes I 465–424
Darius II 423–405

Twenty-eighth Dynasty 404–393 B.C.E.
Amyrtaois 404–393

Twenty-ninth Dynasty 393–380 B.C.E.
Nephrites I (Baenre'merynetjeru) 399–393
Psammuthis (Userre'setenptah) 393
Hakoris (Khnemma'atré) 393–380
Nephrites II 380

Thirtieth Dynasty 380–343 B.C.E.
Nectanebo I (Kheperkaré) 380–362
Teos (Irma'atenré) 365–360
Nectanebo II (Senedjemibre'setepenahur) 360–343
Nakhthoreb ca. 343

Thirty-first Dynasty (Second Persian Period) 343–332 B.C.E.
Artaxerxes III Ochus 343–338
Arses 338–336
Darius III Codoman 335–332
Period interrupted by a native ruler, Khababash (Senentanen-setepenptah)

GRECO-ROMAN PERIOD 332 B.C.E.–395 C.E.

Macedonian (Thirty-second) Dynasty 332–304 B.C.E.
Alexander III the Great 332–323
Philip III Arrhidaeus 323–316
Alexander IV 316–304

Ptolemaic Period 304–30 B.C.E.
Ptolemy I Soter 304–284
Ptolemy II Philadelphus 285–246
Ptolemy III Euergetes I 246–221
Ptolemy IV Philopator 221–205
Ptolemy V Epiphanes 205–180
Ptolemy VI Philometor 180–164, 163–145
Ptolemy VII Neos Philopator 145
Ptolemy VIII Euergetes II (Physcon) 170–163, 145–116
Cleopatra (3) (Q.) and Ptolemy IX Soter II (Lathyros) 116–107, 88–81
Cleopatra (3) (Q.) and Ptolemy X Alexander I 107–88
Cleopatra Berenice (Q.) 81–80
Ptolemy XI Alexander II 80
Ptolemy XII Neos Dionysius (Auletes) 80–58, 55–51
Berenice (4) (Q.) 58–55
Cleopatra VII (Q.) 51–30
Ptolemy XIII 51–47
Ptolemy XIV 47–44
Ptolemy XV Caesarion 44–30

dynasty histories These recounted the achievements of the various royal lines throughout Egypt's history.

Each dynasty faced difficulties and challenges, and some remained strong and vibrant while others were consumed by events of the eras or were faced with overwhelming enemies. The destiny of Egypt rested in the hands of these royal families, and most had a unique vision of the nation as a "gift of the gods." The following summarizes the accomplishments of these royals of the NILE.

EARLY DYNASTIC PERIOD (2920–2575 B.C.E.)
First Dynasty (2920–2770 B.C.E.)
The Predynastic warrior-kings from Upper Egypt, SCORPION I, NARMER, and others, established the traditions of the royal cult and built the first temples and tombs at HIERAKONPOLIS and at THINIS, thus establishing the foundations of the nation. Narmer began the great campaigns to subdue the areas of the Delta in Lower Egypt. The process was slow and costly, as the people of Lower Egypt had developed their own culture and had fortified cities throughout the Delta. When AHA, the legendary Menes, took the throne as the probable heir to Narmer, the unification of the Two Kingdoms was well advanced. Aha could rely on the support of many nomes, or provinces, when he founded the capital city of MEMPHIS and continued pacifying the clans that had stood apart from the merging efforts.

His successors continued the campaigns aimed at unification and began expeditions into the SINAI and the surrounding deserts to claim the NATURAL RESOURCES of the area. These forays into the deserts led to confrontations with the native BEDOUIN tribes, and the Egyptians began to amass military units to defend the mines and QUARRIES that they acquired. The nome aristocrats responded to the pharaoh's call and marched at the head of troops from their provinces. DEN, a ruler of the earliest historical periods, was depicted on an ivory label as smiting the Asiatics, the dwellers in the eastern desert, also called the Troglodytes.

In Egypt, the pharaohs of the first royal line erected monuments and mortuary structures, demonstrating a maturity in vision and form. The massive tombs at ABYDOS, startling architectural structures, decorated with paneling that also distinguished the palace facades in MEMPHIS, stand as silent portraits of a nation on the path of a unique destiny on the Nile.

Second Dynasty (2770–2649 B.C.E.)
The rulers of this royal line had to continue to subdue areas in the Nile Valley that resisted unification and the authority of the pharaoh in Memphis, "the White Walled" capital. Religious debates raged across Egypt as well, as the various cults vied for the dominance and the status of a particular deity. It is probable that actual confrontations took place as the cults of SET and HORUS competed for dominance. The southern city of HIERAKONPOLIS witnessed royal mortuary complexes and perhaps even battles within its domain. Victory was hard

won, but KHA'SEKHEMWY appears to have defeated the last of the rebel clans and returned to Memphis. He built his mortuary complex not in SAQQARA, where earlier Second Dynasty rulers had been laid to rest, but at ABYDOS.

As part of the religious expansion and cultic evolution, a number of theophanies, animal representations of the gods, were introduced in shrines and temples. The city of MENDES displayed its sacred ram. The APIS bull was at Memphis, and the MNEVIS bull achieved popularity. Within the court and the nomes, a generation of trained officials had Egypt's administrative structures in place and operated with efficiency. The land was poised to enter one of the truly magnificent periods of Egypt's history, the Old Kingdom.

Third Dynasty (2649–2575 B.C.E.)

The pharaoh NEBKA opened this royal line with comparative calm in Egypt. Nebka was a warrior, and he led military units into the SINAI to claim new mines and quarries and to garrison those already in operation. He also extended the authority of the throne as far south as ASWAN. Nebka's successor, his brother DJOSER, would cement Egypt's hold on the area around the first cataract of the Nile and Aswan.

Artistically, Djoser's reign was pivotal in the Nile Valley, as IMHOTEP, his vizier, designed and supervised the building of the STEP PYRAMID. The monument declared that the god-kings of Egypt were powerful and capable of uniting the people in a single envisioned act of creation. The Step Pyramid also solidified the spiritual aspirations of the Nile Valley as it soared over the plain of Saqqara.

Djoser also saved Egypt from a famine by sailing to ELEPHANTINE Island at Aswan where the god KHNUM dwelled, the controller of the Nile's inundations. One of his successors, KHA'BA, built a layered pyramid at Zawiet el-Aryan and Huni erected the MEIDUM pyramid complex.

OLD KINGDOM (2575–2134 B.C.E.)
Fourth Dynasty (2575–2465 B.C.E.)

This royal line and the Old Kingdom opened with an innovative pharaoh, SNEFRU. He built an Egyptian navy, sending a fleet of 40 ships on the Mediterranean Sea to Phoenicia, modern Lebanon. He was seeking wood, a rare commodity in the Nile Valley. Snefru also started the Pyramid Age by building the Bent Pyramid and the Red Pyramid at Dashur.

KHUFU, his son and heir, erected a Wonder of the World, the Great Pyramid at GIZA. KHAFRE and MENKAURÉ, successors in the line, erected two more pyramidal complexes on the same site, and the Great SPHINX was created to keep eternal watch on the horizon.

Magical tales of women clad only in fishnets, the parting of the waters of a lake, and a prophecy about future pharaohs were part of this dynasty's events. Khufu's family had rivalries, dissension, perhaps a royal murder, and it ended with SHEPSESKHAF, who could not command another grand pyramid. He erected "the Pharaoh's Bench," the MASTABAT EL-FARA'UN, in southern Saqqara.

This dynasty used only royal family members in positions of power, relying on princes to safeguard the throne and the nation. This would change when the next royal line, the sun kings, came to Egypt's throne.

Fifth Dynasty (2465–2323 B.C.E.)

This was the age of SOLAR CULTS, the traditions dated to the earliest eras in Egypt and embodied by the god RÉ and his divine associated beings. This royal line had been foretold a century before, and USERKHAF began the nation's new historical period. He was possibly the grandson of RA'DJEDEF, the heir to Khufu and a shadowy figure. Userkhaf did not seek the shadows. His portraits depict a powerful, determined individual who understood the reins of power.

The new bureaucracy of the court was composed of both commoners and nobles. Ability and dedication were necessary requirements for high office, and a series of intelligent, hardworking individuals served Egypt during this dynasty. They sent expeditions to PUNT and expanded Egypt's military and trade systems. These "Sun Kings" built solar pyramid complexes in Saqqara and Abydos.

Sixth Dynasty (2323–2150 B.C.E.)

This royal line was opened by TETI (1), who appears to have been murdered by his own bodyguard. After USERKARÉ, PEPI I inherited the throne and began a series of campaigns that revolutionized Egyptian warfare. Using the skills of a general named WENI, Pepi I had Nubian mercenary units in his army as he attacked the Sinai and part of southern Palestine. The HAREM (1) of Pepi I was involved in an attack on his person, but he survived and saw the guilty punished. He then married sisters, the ANKHNESMERY-RÉS, who bore his heirs.

His son, MERENRÉ, ruled briefly, followed by PEPI II, who was on the throne for about 94 years. A touching royal dispatch from the small ruler's earlier years displays his concern for a petite DWARF who was captured by HARKHUF during an expedition to NUBIA. Major building projects took place during Pepi II's reign. Officials were also opening trade routes to the Red Sea and deep into Nubia. MERENRÉ II followed Pepi II, but his reign was short-lived, and his consort, Queen NITOCRIS (1), appears to have ruled briefly. HERODOTUS assigns a fearful massacre to this queen-pharaoh.

Seventh Dynasty (dates unknown)

This royal line was actually a series of "70 rulers in 70 days," according to MANETHO. The dynasty list contains few names, known only by surviving decrees issued by the rulers.

Eighth Dynasty (2150–2134 B.C.E.)

A ruler named NEFERKURÉ founded this dynastic line, which recorded several rulers who could not maintain the throne or call upon the allegiance of the Egyptian people. An exemption decree was issued by WADJKARÉ, and a small pyramid by QAKARÉ IBY is all that remains of that line.

FIRST INTERMEDIATE PERIOD (2134–2040 B.C.E.)

Ninth Dynasty (2134–? B.C.E.), Tenth Dynasty (?–2040 B.C.E.), and Eleventh Dynasty (at Thebes, 2134–2040)

The two royal families of the Ninth and Tenth Dynasties were usurpers from the city of HERAKLEOPOLIS who ruled the northern domains but not the lands south of Abydos. Called the KHETYS or the Aktoys, their rule was unstable, but some interesting documentation of their eras has survived. "THE ELOQUENT PEASANT" OF HERAKLEOPOLIS, an individual named KHUNIANUPU, was welcomed by one of the rulers of this line, and *THE INSTRUCTIONS FOR MERIKARÉ* dates to their rule.

During the continuing battle against the rulers of THEBES, the Eleventh Dynasty, the Herakleopolitan rulers allowed an assault on a southern region by their allies in ASSIUT. In this attack, tombs and corpses were vandalized, an act of sacrilege that empowered a Theban, MENTUHOTEP II, and led to their ruin.

MIDDLE KINGDOM (2040–1640 B.C.E.)

Eleventh Dynasty (All Egypt 2040–1991 B.C.E.)

The royal lines of INYOTEFS in THEBES, having ruled only Thebes for a time, mounted a new campaign to unify all Egypt in the reign of Mentuhotep II (2061–2010 B.C.E.). He defeated the Herakleopolitans and campaigned throughout the Nile Valley to suppress nomes and individuals who opposed his rule. He buried some 60 warriors, veterans of these military ventures, to honor their sacrifice on behalf of the nation.

Mentuhotep II regained lost land, penetrated into NUBIA and the Sinai, and built extensively. He erected a massive mortuary complex at DEIR EL-BAHRI, on the western shore of the Nile at Thebes, and this became a model for later temples on the site.

His successors were not as successful in their reigns, and the last ruler of this dynasty, MENTUHOTEP IV, was succeeded by a usurper, AMENEMHET I, in 1991 B.C.E.

Twelfth Dynasty (1991–1783 B.C.E.)

Amenemhet I founded this royal line of rulers by usurping the throne, and he brought administrative and military skills to the throne. His successors, the Amenemhets and Senwosrets, were fierce warriors who defended Egypt from Libyan invasions and built a series of fortresses to protect the eastern and western borders, called the WALL OF THE PRINCE. The FAIYUM was refurbished and aided by vast irrigation projects. FORTRESSES were erected at key military and trade centers in Nubia, with canals dug to allow the passage of Egyptian vessels through the cataracts of the Nile.

Amenemhet I was slain by a harem cabal, but his son, SENWOSRET I, carried on his traditions. SENWOSRET III was revered as the ultimate warrior. The Twelfth Dynasty, along with the line of the Mentuhoteps before them, was honored in Egypt as the rulers of a Golden Age. Vast pyramidal complexes, which included elaborate burial sites for family members, were erected by these pharaohs at DASHUR, HAWARA, el-LISHT, and el-LAHUN. The dynasty closed with the brief rule of another woman, SOBEKNEFERU. She and AMENEMHET IV are believed to have erected their tombs at MAZGHUNA, south of Dashur.

Thirteenth Dynasty (1784–after 1640? B.C.E.)

A royal line of briefly reigning pharaohs, lasting only about a century and a half, this dynasty usurped the former capital of ITJ-TAWY near the FAIYUM. Some of these rulers are mentioned in the official lists, but they are known only by fragmentary papyri, seals, or inscriptions. They erected four pyramids, but the dynasty faced a steady decline of power. Some Delta cities opted for independence, and these rulers had to withdraw from these eastern and Nubian territories. The HYKSOS were already in the Delta, amassing lands and consolidating their influence.

Fourteenth Dynasty (1640? B.C.E.)

These rulers were located at XOIS in the Delta and had little impact on the rest of Egypt. They reigned for about 57 years and are relatively obscure.

SECOND INTERMEDIATE PERIOD (1640–1550 B.C.E.)

Fifteenth Dynasty (1640–1532 B.C.E.)

This royal line is remembered as the Great HYKSOS, the Asiatics who entered Egypt over the decades and built AVARIS in the Delta. They sacked Memphis and opened Egypt's borders to the east, welcoming Canaanites and others. Fortified structures were erected by the Hyksos in their domains, and certain Cretan influences are evident. The Hyksos ruled Egypt as far south as CUSAE, blocked there by the Seventeenth Dynasty at Thebes.

Several rulers are known by papyri and seals, and one, APOPHIS, became famous because of his quarrel with TA'O II, a ruler in Thebes. The Hyksos were attacked and driven out of Egypt by the armies of 'AHMOSE (NEBPEHTIRÉ), the founder of the New Kingdom (1550–1070 B.C.E.), chasing them to Saruhen and then into Syria.

Sixteenth Dynasty (Contemporaries of the Fifteenth Dynasty)

This royal line served as vassals of the Great Hyksos and were also Asiatics. Obscure because of their limited scope of power, the rulers of this dynasty left no lasting monuments. Three are known: SEKHAEN-RÉ, ANATHER, and YAKOBA'AM.

Seventeenth Dynasty (1640–1550 B.C.E.)

Sekenenré TA'O II, one of the Theban rulers who had maintained tense relations with the Hyksos, was a pivotal figure in Egypt's history. Like the Inyotefs and his father, Senakhentenré TA'O I, before him, he was the master of Upper Egypt and content to allow the Hyksos, the Asiatics, to dominate the Delta. For decades the two groups had lived side by side, keeping a relative calm on the Nile.

APOPHIS, the ruler of the Hyksos capital at Avaris, stepped over the bounds, however, by sending Ta'o II an insulting message. Before Apophis could recant his words or explain, the Thebans were gathered to oust the foreigners from the land. Ta'o II died soon after, the victim of an ambush and hideous head wounds, and the war appeared to be ended for a time.

KAMOSE, however, as the heir to the throne of Thebes, brushed aside councils of peace and started the battles in earnest. The last ruler of the dynasty, Kamose adapted the Hyksos CHARIOT and attacked the Asiatic southern site. He rolled the Hyksos force back toward Avaris before he died. Apophis had been dead for months and his heir, KHAMUDI, faced a renewed campaign in the reign of another son of Ta'o II. This young warrior, imbued with Kamose's rage, was 'Ahmose, the founder of the New Kingdom (1550–1070 B.C.E.).

NEW KINGDOM (1550–1070 B.C.E.)

Eighteenth Dynasty (1550–1307 B.C.E.)

Some of the most popular pharaohs of Egypt were part of this royal line, and these warriors carved out an empire by warring against other lands and peoples. 'Ahmose inherited the throne at a very young age, and his mother, Queen AH'HOTEP (1), stood as regent for almost a decade. Peace was restored on the Nile, but the Thebans were armed and ready. When 'Ahmose reached his majority, he led an army northward and put Avaris under siege by land and by sea. The Asiatics fled, and 'Ahmose dealt a smashing blow to the Nubians in the south and then punished the northerners who had collaborated with the Hyksos at Avaris.

His son, AMENHOTEP I, was a warrior also, but Amenhotep I's successor, TUTHMOSIS I, was the first pharaoh to march on his enemies in the name of Amun and begin the great empire. TUTHMOSIS III, his grandson, ruled from Khartoum in modern Sudan to the Euphrates River. He is called the "Napoleon of Egypt." AMENHOTEP II, his son and heir, loved hand-to-hand combat and expanded the imperial cause.

By the time AMENHOTEP III came to the throne, he was the most powerful and wealthiest human being in the known world of the time. His son, AKHENATEN, living in seclusion in 'AMARNA and worshiping a deity named ATEN, brought the empire perilously close to an end. TUT'ANKHAMUN, who returned the court to Thebes and the nation's devotion to the god AMUN, did not live long enough to distinguish himself. That task would fall to the last pharaoh of the dynasty, HOREMHAB. When Horemhab knew that he was dying without an heir, he passed the fate of the nation into the hands of a trusted military commander: RAMESSES I.

Nineteenth Dynasty (1307–1196 B.C.E.)

Ruling only one year, Ramesses I could go to his tomb content that he had raised up a family of warriors to defend Egypt and to adorn the holy cities on the Nile. His son and heir was SETI I, a military man and an administrator who understood the needs of the people. His campaigns, the monuments at Thebes, KARNAK, and Abydos, and his concern for idle mines and quarries set the pace for the royal line that would be called the Ramessids.

His son and heir, RAMESSES II, the Great, reigned 66 years. His Syrian campaigns, his battle at KADESH, and his treaty with the HITTITES restored Egypt's power. His monuments, appearing at ABU SIMBEL and in Upper and Lower Egypt, bequeathed a legacy of aristocracy on the Nile.

MERENPTAH, the 13th of his sons, was named the heir. He outlived Ramesses II and took the throne at an advanced age. He campaigned in Libya and Syria and defeated a contingent of the SEA PEOPLES. His son, SETI II, was unable to keep the throne, which was taken by a usurper, AMENMESSES. In time he secured the throne, but he was weakened.

This royal line ended with the reign of another queen-pharaoh, TWOSRET, who ruled a short time before disappearing. Her chancellor, BAY, a foreigner and ambitious, made his own plans, but a true Ramessid ended the dynasty.

Twentieth Dynasty (1196–1070 B.C.E.)

SETHNAKHTE, probably a grandson of Ramesses II, rose up and began campaigns to undo the chaos of the closing days of the previous reign and secured the throne against the ambitions of others. His son, RAMESSES III, the last truly great pharaoh of Egypt, had to defeat the Libyans and the Sea Peoples. These wandering nomads had conquered the Hittites. Ramesses III defeated them when they invaded the Delta. He built MEDINET HABU and other monuments and then received apparently mortal wounds in a harem revolt.

His son, RAMESSES IV, restored order and punished the guilty. He sent trade expeditions to Sinai and Nubia and started monuments, but he only lived a few years. Other Ramesses followed, but difficult times and a devastating smallpox epidemic took a tragic toll in the royal family. Tomb robberies and trials took place in the period, and the criminals were prosecuted during the reign of RAMESSES IX. RAMESSES XI, a recluse, faced problems in Thebes and left the administration of Egypt to his courtiers. Two of these, SMENDES (1) and HERIHOR, divided Egypt and set the pattern for the dynasty that followed.

THIRD INTERMEDIATE PERIOD (1070–712 B.C.E.)

Twenty-first Dynasty (1070–945 B.C.E.)

This royal line opened the Third Intermediate Period of Egypt. Smendes ruled in TANIS in the Delta, and PINUDJEM (1) assumed the pharaonic role in Thebes. The Tanis and Theban families intermarried, and eventually Thebes sent PSUSENNES I to Tanis as the ruler.

The monuments and records of the nation in that historical period indicate an era of calm and prosperity, but the Thebans rebelled, being open to many southern influences that Tanis could not control from a distance. The high priests of Amun had to assume military as well as temple roles, defeating rebel groups and exiling the leaders for a time to the western oases.

Psusennes I adorned TANIS as a capital, and his mortuary regalia, as well as those of some of his successors, are masterpieces of gold and silver. These rulers, however, could not hold on to power in an era of political and religious change. The Libyans who had settled in the city of BUBASTIS were ready to launch their own dynastic claims.

Twenty-second Dynasty (945–712 B.C.E.)

The Libyan rulers who reigned during this dynasty could trace their ancestry back to OSOCHOR, one of the pharaohs of the previous line. SHOSHENQ I, a direct descendant, opened the Libyan period and began military campaigns recorded in the Bible. He also took the precaution of installing his own sons in the highest offices of the priesthood of Amun in Thebes. An increase in trade, lands, and artistic projects demonstrated a revitalization of Egypt during Shoshenq I's reign.

Some rather obscure successors to Shoshenq I maintained the throne, and Egypt remained a power in the region. The reign of TAKELOT II of this line, however, witnessed the first signs of decline. HARSIESE, a prince, assumed pharaonic titles and fostered a Theban rebellion that endangered Upper Egypt for decades. SHOSHENQ III was another usurper, setting aside the true heir, his brother. The division between Thebes and Tanis widened, and other cities and nomes began to seek ways in which they could gain independence.

Twenty-third Dynasty (ca. 828–712 B.C.E.)

A prince named PEDUBASTE I, who controlled LEONTOPOLIS, started this royal line, and another family opened a Tanis royal line, contemporaries and rivals for the allegiance of the people. There were other petty rulers at HERMOPOLIS and Herakleopolis as well. Holding such limited areas, these rulers were vulnerable to the powerful Nubians, who had already begun their march into Egypt.

As the Nubians posed a real threat, the rulers of Tanis, Leontopolis, Herakleopolis, and Hermopolis joined a confederation led by TEFNAKHTE of Sais and confronted the Nubian armies. They were swept aside as the Nubians moved northward to restore the old traditions and beliefs.

Twenty-fourth Dynasty (724–712 B.C.E.)

Tefnakhte and BAKENRENEF are the only rulers of this royal line at Tanis. They were contemporaries of the city-states and faced the Nubian threat. Tefnakhte organized a confederation of self-appointed "kings" to meet the army marching out of Nubia, led by a warrior named PIANKHI (1).

At Herakleopolis, Tefnakhte's coalition was routed. His allies surrendered to Piankhi and were allowed to rule their own former domains as vassal governors, and Tefnakhte eventually endured the same humiliation. Bakenenref's reign was that of a vassal and was very brief. There were too many Nubians in Egypt by then, and they were intent on restoring the old traditions and the faith-based society of the past.

LATE PERIOD (712–332 B.C.E.)

Twenty-fifth Dynasty (Nubia and Thebes 770–750 B.C.E.; All Egypt 712–657 B.C.E.)

The Late Period of Egypt began with this Nubian Dynasty, a royal family that marched northward along the Nile to restore faith and the purity of the god Amun to the people of the Two Kingdoms. Coming out of the capital at Napata, the Nubians controlled much of the Theban domain and then, led by Piankhi, moved to capture the ancient capital of Memphis. Tefnakhte, who ruled in Sais, formed a coalition of petty rulers, and they met Piankhi's army and suffered a severe defeat. Piankhi celebrated his victory with a stela and retired to Nubia.

SHABAKA, his brother, mounted another campaign and took control of Egypt personally. He was followed on the throne of Egypt by his heir, SHEBITKU, and then by TAHARQA, all members of the same line. King ESSARHADDON of Assyria entered Egypt in Taharqa's reign, taking the abandoned Nubian queen and one of Taharqa's sons back to Nineveh as slaves. Taharqa fought back, and his successor, TANUTAMUN, tried to maintain power, but the Saite-Arthribis royal line that had served as allies of the Assyrians would be the ones to free the nation from foreign rule.

Twenty-sixth Dynasty (664–525 B.C.E.)

While the Nubians fled from the Assyrians and then regrouped to oust the Assyrians, NECHO I and PSAMMETICHUS I adapted and secured their holdings. Necho I was slain by the Nubians, but his son, Psammetichus I, united Egypt and amassed a mercenary and native army. He ousted the Assyrians and began his royal line. All that Piankhi had hoped for Egypt's rebirth was realized by this dynasty. Old traditions of faith and the skills and vision of the past flourished on the Nile. NECHO II, the son of Psammetichus, followed in his stead, and the land flourished. Necho II even connected the Nile and the Red Sea with a canal.

APRIES came to the throne and introduced a program of intervention in Palestine, increasing trade and the use of Greek mercenaries. His involvement in Libya, however, led to a mutiny in the Egyptian army and the rise of AMASIS, his general. Apries died in an attempt to regain his throne. Amasis was Hellenic in his outlook and was recorded as aiding Delphi in returning the oracle and the temple of Apollo. The city of NAUKRATIS, ceded to the Greeks in the Delta, was started in this historical period.

PSAMMETICHUS III, the last ruler of this dynasty, faced CAMBYSES and the invading Persian army. Psammetichus was taken prisoner and sent to Susa, the Persian capital.

Twenty-seventh Dynasty—
The First Persian Period (525–404 B.C.E.)

This was not a dynasty of native Egyptians but a period of foreign occupation, also recorded as the First Persian Period. Egypt survived under foreign rule, prospering under some of the satraps and Persian kings, as the ACHAEMENIANS had problems in their own land. A court eunuch murdered some of the rulers, along with their sons, and the survivors had to endure political complications.

The Egyptians categorized CAMBYSES as a criminal lunatic, but he treated the nation with a certain discretion in most instances. A large unit of the Persian army, sent by Cambyses to loot the Oasis of SIWA in the Western Desert, disappeared to a man. DARIUS I, XERXES I, ARTAXERXES I, and DARIUS II followed Cambyses, but they faced rebellions and political intrigues at home as well as rebellions on the Nile. Darius II reigned over the Nile Valley from Persia and was viewed as tolerable as far as the Egyptians were concerned.

Twenty-eighth Dynasty (404–393 B.C.E.)

AMYRTAIOS (2) was a rebel in the Delta, holding the rank of prince in Sais. Egyptians felt loyal to him, and he exerted influence even as far south as ASWAN. His dynasty was doomed, however, because he was judged a violator of the laws of Egypt and was not allowed to name his son as heir to the throne. NEPHRITES I, the founder of the Twenty-ninth Dynasty, captured and killed him.

Twenty-ninth Dynasty (393–380 B.C.E.)

NEPHRITES I founded this line of rulers at MENDES and began to rebuild in many areas of Egypt. He maintained the APIS cult and regulated trade and government in the land. Nephrites I was followed by PSAMMUTHIS, whose brief reign was cut short by the usurper HAKORIS, who expanded the dynasty's building programs. NEPHRITES II, Hakoris's son and heir, did not succeed him, as NECTANEBO I took the throne.

Thirtieth Dynasty (380–343 B.C.E.)

This royal line was founded from Sebennytos, and Nectanebo I faced a Persian army, using Greek mercenaries. The Persians bypassed a strategic fortress at Pelusium, and Nectanebo I launched a counterattack and defeated the invaders. He had a stable, prosperous reign in which he restored temples and sites and built at PHILAE. His son and heir, TEOS, began wars to regain lost imperial lands but took temple treasures to pay for his military campaigns. He was ousted from the throne by his own royal family after only two years and fled to Susa. NECTANEBO II, chosen to replace Teos, faced the Persian ARTAXERXES III, who came with a vast army and reoccupied the Nile Valley.

Thirty-first Dynasty—
The Second Persian Period (343–332 B.C.E.)

Artaxerxes III lasted only about five years and was poisoned in his own court by the eunuch BAGOAS. ARSES, his heir, reigned only two years before meeting the same fate. DARIUS III CODOMAN, wise to the machinations of Bagoas, made him drink the cup that he was offering to the king, and Bagoas died as a result. Darius III faced ALEXANDER III THE GREAT, however, and he was defeated in three separate battles and then slain by one of his own associates. Alexander the Great now ruled Egypt.

GRECO-ROMAN PERIOD (332 B.C.E.–395 C.E.)
Thirty-second Dynasty—
Ptolemaic Period (304–30 B.C.E.)

The brief period of Macedonian rule (332–304 B.C.E.) was ended by PTOLEMY I SOTER, the Macedonian general of Alexander the Great, who stole the body of Alexander and declared himself and his heirs the rulers of Egypt. The Ptolemies modernized and Hellenized much of Egypt's agricultural and governmental agencies but also instituted a dual system in the land.

They did not relate to the native Egyptians, did not intermarry with nome heiresses, and imported their consorts from other Greek city-states. The Ptolemaic rulers also did not speak the ancient language and seldom traveled out of ALEXANDRIA. They were warrior-kings in the Greek world, but at home they maintained the traditions of the god-kings of the Nile. Greek citizens were treated according to Greek laws, while the traditional courts of Egypt served the natives.

The land prospered under their rule, particularly the agricultural bases, and the Egyptians were allowed to exist in peace, despite the rivalries within the Ptolemaic family and the alliances made with other Greek states. The Ptolemies were not remarkable for their reigns, and queens were politically powerful and at times murdered. Such activities, however, did not impact on the daily lives of the Egyptians beyond Alexandria.

The dynasty was fatally wounded in the reign of CLEOPATRA VII, who killed herself to escape the inevitable humiliation at the hands of Octavian (Emperor AUGUSTUS) in 30 B.C.E. Her son was slain as well to halt the Ptolemaic influence. Egypt became a special territory of Rome, closely guarded by the emperor as a province with unique assets and unique needs.

E

Ebers Papyrus One of the longest papyri from ancient Egypt, dating to the reign of AMENHOTEP I (r. 1525–1504 B.C.E.) of the Eighteenth Dynasty, discovered by George Ebers, a German Egyptologist in 1873, the PAPYRUS is a medical text measuring 65 feet with 108 separate pages. The document is one of the modern world's major sources for information concerning the medical knowledge and techniques of Egypt's priest-physicians. These medical practitioners gained a considerable reputation throughout the ancient world. Sections on digestive diseases, worm infestations, eye ailments, skin problems, burns, fractures, rheumatism, and anatomy are included in the texts, as well as discussions of the treatment of tumors and abscesses. Cardiac and circulatory illnesses, as well as mental disorders, are given special focus. More than 900 diagnoses and prescriptions are listed in this papyrus. They indicate the fact that the priest-physicians understood pain and recognized the pulse and the problems related to the main artery. These priests also displayed a remarkable awareness of the circulation of the blood in the human body. The Ebers Papyrus is now in Berlin.

See also MEDICINE.

economy Egypt has been called the "gift of the Nile," and from the earliest eras that river provided renewal and life. Around 6000 B.C.E., the herdsmen and hunters who had prospered in the Western (Libyan) Desert migrated into the Nile Valley and began settlements. They were hunters, gatherers, and farmers who used a barter system to trade.

THE EARLY ECONOMY

Communities developed on the banks of the river, and over time the Two Kingdoms of Upper and Lower Egypt emerged. The oldest city in Upper Egypt, between modern ESNA and EDFU, was the city of HIERAKONPOLIS, called NEKHEN by the Egyptians in honor of the local deity, Nekheny. The original settlements of Hierakonpolis, which date to 5000 to 4400 B.C.E. and are small in size, were joined by the migrating herdsmen clans. The city established breweries, bakeries, metallurgy industries, animal husbandry, and farming. The patron deity of Hierakonpolis was HORUS, who became the symbol of the living pharaohs. The Horus cult absorbed Nekheny. A metal Horus, represented by a statue of a falcon, was discovered recently in new excavations in Hierakonpolis. The bird dates to around 3800 B.C.E. and indicates that metallurgy and other skills were evident in the valley even before the migrants arrived to bolster the population and the productivity.

A succession of kings, called Dynasty 0, ruled the city. These kings and their people called the river Hopi, a god of abundance. Some depictions of Hopi contained two identical figures, representing the Blue Nile and the White Nile, which join just before entering Egypt. Because they were so dependent upon Hopi, the Nile, for their economic growth, the people of Hierakonpolis and other enclaves sacrificed a young maiden to the river each year. Egyptian legend has it that the god Osiris scolded the people for such an activity, and that young maidens from that point forward were no longer tied to posts and left to be swallowed up by the rising Nile.

A well-documented king of Hierakonpolis, SCORPION I (fl. ca. 3000 B.C.E.), made war on surrounding areas in order to forge a nation in the valley. Labels in his tomb indicate that a trade system was in place, involving both Upper and Lower Egyptian sites. The Egyptian artistic styles, so distinct, became popular among neighboring peoples.

When AHA (Menes) founded the city of MEMPHIS in 2920 B.C.E., the nation of Egypt had already developed a basic economy capable of sustaining the population. The Egyptians knew that when Sirius, the Dog Star, appeared in the night sky, the waters of the Nile would rush over the fields and orchards, depositing rich silt and nutrients. The Egyptians could plant multiple harvests each year, with lush results in many regions. They raised emmer and barley wheat, vegetables, and fruits, and panned salt and tended hives of bees. The Nile also preserved the lush grazing fields for cattle and provided a stable avenue for the ships that the people built out of wood and ropes. Fishing became another way of making a living on the Nile.

These early Egyptians also discovered the FAIYUM, also known as Ta-she, the Land of the Lakes. They called this natural depression extending along the Nile a national treasure and took steps to preserve it. Faiyum A and Faiyum B cultures date to ca. 4500 B.C.E. The BAHR YUSUF, a subsidiary stream of the river beginning at ASSIUT, was allowed to flow into the Faiyum but prevented from draining away. AGRICULTURE and animal husbandry became two vital components of the nation's economy as a result.

NATURAL RESOURCES

After the early pharaohs united Egypt, their administrators assessed the natural resources of the nation and put them to use. The government inspected and regulated mines and stone quarries and allotted products for national consumption or export. Many of the lands on the Mediterranean Sea had fleets of ships that scoured ports for products, and peoples such as the PHOENICIANS sailed into the Nile Delta to carry away the goods provided. The natural resources of Egypt included agate, alabaster, amethyst, beryl, carnelian, chalcedony, copper, diorite, electrum, feldspar, garnet, gold, hematite, jasper, limestone, malachite, mica, obsidian, olivine, onyx, peridot, porphyry, quartz, rock crystal, silver, and turquoise.

One area that was especially rich in natural resources, including stone, minerals, and gold, was NUBIA (modern Sudan), and Egypt occupied the territory south of modern Aswan as early as the Archaic Period when the Egyptians annexed the area around Elephantine Island. During the New Kingdom (1550–1070 B.C.E.) Egypt extended all the way to modern Khartoum.

Military forces were used to defend mines and quarries, and trade routes, which used oases as havens, were developed along the Nile. As production increased, all of these resources, alongside the harvests of the agricultural base, provided the materials for builders, artisans, and other ambitious endeavors. The increase in production also allowed the administration of Egypt to conduct biannual censuses.

TAX COLLECTION

Tax collectors went into the various NOMES, or provinces, to measure the lands being cultivated, the crops, the artistic products, the mineral deposits recovered, and the bales of precious grains. The Egyptians were taxed for such wealth and paid in kind. Scribes would beat recalcitrant citizens for back taxes. In some eras, however, groups protested the harsh demands being made and refused to continue their labors. SETI I (r. 1306–1290 B.C.E.), who was building his mortuary monument in ABYDOS, faced such a protest. In danger of seeing his monument delayed he issued the Nauri Decree, an exemption declaration that allowed the workers on his project to be free of taxation for the duration of their labors.

WEIGHTS AND MEASURES

Weights and measurements were used throughout a kingdom. These weights and measures were standardized when the royal administration was in place. The length of an object was determined by the royal cubit of 20 inches. The royal palm width was three inches, and the finger width three-quarters of an inch. The *khet* was the measure of 110 square cubits, or two-thirds of an acre. Liquid measurements were also used. A *deben* was a measure of weight that equaled 32 ounces or 91 grams and a *kite* was equivalent to one-tenth of a *deben*. Special measurements were used for the construction of pyramids, allowing remarkable accuracy. TUTHMOSIS III (r. 1479–1425 B.C.E.) brought coins to Egypt after a military campaign, but the system of monetary usage was not employed at the time. Bartering had proven successful in trade and it continued to serve the nation.

TRADE AND EXCHANGE

Although domestic trade seems to have been limited, commerce with foreign lands was always actively pursued and controlled by the central government. The Egyptians traveled by land and sea to Nubia, the Near East, and Punt to obtain commodities, primarily raw materials. They exported many products, including salt, beads of glass, papyrus, baskets, and jewelry. Textiles were also developed during the Middle Kingdom and New Kingdom. Linens, especially the elegant byssus style, were as popular in the world's courts as modern Egyptian cotton is today.

Great trade centers and garrisoned fortresses were established alongside the cataracts of the Nile. These forts and centers, erected with mud-brick walls, moats, courts, towers, and other defensive elements, maintained peace and promoted explorations of mines and quarries.

During the Eighteenth and Nineteenth Dynasties (1550–1307 B.C.E., 1307–1196 B.C.E.), when the Egyptian Empire was at its zenith, Egypt ruled from Khartoum in modern Sudan to the Tigris and Euphrates rivers and westward to the Siwa Oasis. The conquered lands became vassal states and found themselves open to new trade markets with the entire Nile Valley.

THE LATER ECONOMY

With the collapse of the New Kingdom and the lack of sturdy pharaonic dynasties and a united nation, Egypt's economy was splintered but not destroyed. The great holdings of the empire on the Mediterranean coast were lost, as were the enclaves in Nubia.

The nome, or province, system prevailed, however. The NOMARCHS, or hereditary lords of the provinces, promoted agriculture, mining, quarries, and trade, as well as managed the economy of their domain. The foreign occupation of Egypt did not destroy economic affairs either. When the Persians ruled the Nile (525–404 B.C.E. and 343–332 B.C.E.), life and the economy went on as usual, in part because the Persians tended to be absentee rulers. The arrival of ALEXANDER III THE GREAT (r. 332–323 B.C.E.) revitalized Egypt. He built the grand city of ALEXANDRIA, and upon his death, PTOLEMY I SOTER (r. 304–284 B.C.E.) founded the Ptolemaic Period.

The economy of Egypt was renowned during the early Ptolemaic Period thanks to the wealth of the trading centers of Alexandria and Naukratis, and Egypt was considered a great source of grain and a perpetual gold mine. From a historical perspective, trade and economic growth was rather astounding during the Ptolemaic Period (304–30 B.C.E.). The Phoenicians (the modern Lebanese) were the navy of the world at the time. They built warships to guard their own fleets of trading ships against pirates and hired them to other lands that sought to protect their fleets. The ports of Egypt were crowded with visiting trade fleets, and the products of Egypt were in demand everywhere.

This prosperity made Egypt a target of the Romans, who defeated CLEOPATRA VII (r. 51–30 B.C.E.) at the battle of ACTIUM. Thus, Egypt became a Roman imperial province and was tied closely to the wider Roman economy.

Further reading: David, Rosalie. *Handbook to Life in Ancient Egypt, Revised Edition.* New York: Facts On File, 2003; Kemp, Barry J. *Ancient Egypt: Anatomy of a Civilization.* London: Routledge, 1989; Mark, Samuel. *From Egypt to Mesopotamia: A Study of Predynastic Trade Routes.* Austin: Texas Monthly Press, 1997; Price, Betsy. *Ancient*

Economic Thought. London: Routledge, 1997; Zingarelli, Andrea Paula. *Trade and Market in New Kingdom Egypt: Internal Socio-economic Processes and Transformations.* London: British Archaeological Reports, 2010.

Edfu (Behdet) A site on the Nile 72 miles south of THEBES, Edfu was the capital of the second nome of Upper Egypt and the HORUS cultic site from early times. The city was called "the Exaltation of Horus" in some eras. Tombs dating to the Sixth Dynasty (2323–2150 B.C.E.) and erected by the local NOMARCHS were discovered in the city's necropolis, as well as a step pyramid dating to the Third Dynasty (2649–2575 B.C.E.). MASTABAS and reliefs were also discovered there. In the Ptolemaic Period (304–30 B.C.E.) a great temple was erected on the site. The city was always considered militarily strategic for the defense of the nation and was fortified against assaults by the Nubians (the modern Sudanese). During the Second Intermediate Period (1640–1550 B.C.E.) when the Asiatics (HYKSOS) ruled the northern Delta territories, Edfu was fortified by the Theban dynasties.

The great temple of Horus, located at Edfu, was started by PTOLEMY III EUERGETES I (r. 246–221 B.C.E.) and probably erected on an earlier established foundation. More than 451 feet long, the temple honored Horus of the Winged Disk, called Behdet by the Egyptians and revered as the consort of HATHOR of Denderah. Hathor's effigy was brought annually to the temple on a boat for a ceremonial visit. Fronted by a PYLON, the temple opened onto a court with columns and elaborate wall reliefs. Granite falcons were also built to serve as divine patrons of this area. The dedication ceremony took place there in 142 B.C.E., and the temple was completed in 57 B.C.E.

A processional way, a MAMMISI (a birthing room), and a colonnade continue the architectural splendor of Edfu's temple, with columns and northern and southern wings. Horus statues adorn the courts, and a relief of the "Feast of the Beautiful Meeting," the annual reunion of Horus and Hathor, depicts the joy of that religious event. Other chambers honor "the Triumph of Horus," an annual celebration. Two HYPOSTYLE HALLS open onto an eastern library and robing rooms and lead to a sanctuary containing a pedestal for the sacred bark of Horus. The halls also lead to reliefs depicting PTOLEMY IV PHILOPATOR (r. 221–205 B.C.E.) offering devotion to Horus and Hathor. A relief in the New Year Chapel shows the goddess NUT.

The sanctuary is a monolithic shrine with an ALTAR and is illuminated by an aperture in the roof. A staircase leads to the roof, as at Denderah; the granite *naos,* a part of the design, was installed by NECTANEBO II (r. 360–343 B.C.E.). Other sections of the temple include the chamber of linens and the throne of the god. A double chapel of KHONS (1) and Hathor is located alongside the chapel of the throne of RÉ and the chapel of "the Spread Wings," a

Horus cultic sign. Another chamber also honors the god MIN.

The temple of Horus at Edfu holds the cosmological records of "the Adoration of the Sanctified Deity Who Came into Being at the First Occasion." PTAH was also worshiped there as the SCARAB, the "Divine Beetle." Other reliefs show "the Stretching of the Cord over the Temple," "the Foundation of the Great Seat," a procession of the Builder Gods, and seated figures representing the Ogdoad. Another relief depicts 30 deities in "the Adoration of the Great Seat." Temple services recorded in the book were supposedly dictated by the god THOTH to the SAGES OF MEHWERET, the ancient scholars and devotees. Building texts displayed include "the Sacred Book of the Primeval Age of the Gods" and the "Coming of Ré into His Mansion of Ms-nht."

See also FESTIVALS; TEMPLES.

Edku   This was a salt lake in Egypt's Delta region.

education   In ancient Egypt, the administrative and economic systems depended on the written language and on the enforcement of basic legal concepts. Although education was prized in every era, no efforts were made to give every resident in the Nile Valley a scholarly foundation.

A COMMONER EDUCATION

Among the farmers and trade people the process of providing knowledge depended mainly upon fathers training their sons. Fathers would take their sons into the field as children and train them in the seasonal needs of producing crops, protecting the irrigational structures, and caring for the crops and animals. This father-son relationship would have also been practiced among the fisher-folk. Daughters were seldom provided with classes in any subjects not related to the home.

The tradesmen and the artisans, socially above the farmers and fisher-folk, had varying educations dependent upon the success of the family business or the artistic positions available. Almost every town had a school of sorts, operated by SCRIBES, where young boys sat reciting the texts of ancient eras and making copies of the didactic maxims or adages of the sages of the era. The students sat cross-legged on mats, reciting or copying texts, and they advanced into higher learning programs according to their abilities.

EDUCATION FOR THE ADMINISTRATIVE CLASS

In the nomes, children who were members of various clans holding administrative powers and, in early eras, military obligations, were normally educated by priests of the various cultic temples or by scribes hired by the nomarchs, the provincial hereditary lords.

It is now documented that a written language was in use in Egypt at the same time (or perhaps earlier) as in Mesopotamian cities. The Egyptians were obsessed with record keeping, and a bevy of scribes was necessary to write down events or decrees from leaders. These scribes resided not only in the court of the pharaohs but in the various nome clan villas and offices. The famous SCHOOL BOY TEXTS, written materials used as exercises in copying for students, demonstrate the type of records kept. The vast bureaucracy of Egypt also demanded the presence of scribes for recording events, speeches, edicts, products, and taxes. For instance, no tax collector made his rounds without record keepers and scribes keeping a tally of taxes received.

The profession of scribe was considered the gateway to appointments and ultimate security. One sage wrote a treatise on being a scribe in which he urged his countrymen to advance themselves. All of the scribes were men; however, there were exceptions within the nomes. In addition to holding occasionally the role of scribe in the nomes, some women inherited the position of nomarch. Those women were educated and literate and held great power. The 21st century B.C.E. noblewoman NEBT, the ranking aristocrat of the ELEPHANTINE ISLAND, was one such powerful woman.

EDUCATION OF THE ROYAL FAMILY

Above the nomarchs were the members of the royal family: the pharaoh, his family and his wives, and his harem. The heirs to the throne attended the Kap, the royal school that was conducted almost daily by learned sages, priests, and scribes. Outsiders, young men who had attracted attention because of their abilities or intellect, were in attendance as well, and this membership in the Kap led them to secure posts within the government.

Lessons were conducted in the memorization of revered didactic works from the past, called texts "written in the time of the gods," as well as the study of language, writing, mathematics, military structures, legal traditions, and religious tenets. The protocol of courts and diplomatic training were also offered to young men in this facility, to introduce them to the social standing routines of high offices.

The pharaohs of the New Kingdom Period also used education as a political tool. When TUTHMOSIS III (r. 1479–1425 B.C.E.) attacked the rebel king of KADESH and his allies at AR-MEGIDDO, in modern Israel, the enemy fled into the fort. Tuthmosis III erected a wall around the fort and left a unit there to prevent any enemy escape. He then marched on Kadesh and every other city-state involved in the rebellion and crushed them. Choosing the best and brightest of the vanquished enemy's noble men and women, he sent them to Egypt as honored guests. There they were taught Egyptian traditions, beliefs, and language. When these young people embraced the ways of Egypt, they were escorted back to their homelands to rule their city-states as loyal vassals of the pharaohs. When the SEA PEOPLES attacked Egypt during the reign of RAMESSES III (r. 1194–1163 B.C.E.), the pharaoh defeated them and then pressed the experienced sailors and navigators into the Egyptian naval school. There the Sea Peoples taught the Egyptians their maritime secrets, which had brought havoc and destruction across much of the Aegean and Mediterranean, including to the great Hittite empire.

Some queens were also educated by private tutors and sages. HATSHEPSUT (r. 1473–1458 B.C.E.) was given an education by her father and eventually assumed the throne as pharaoh. Queen TIYE (1), the Great Wife of AMENHOTEP III (r. 1391–1333 B.C.E.), received correspondence from foreign rulers and conducted the nation's affairs as her royal husband spent much of his time with his harem. Queen CLEOPATRA VII (r. 51–30 B.C.E.) was one of the most educated women in her historical period. Gifted in languages, she was the only royal of the Ptolemaic Dynasty (304–30 B.C.E.) to speak, read, and write the ancient Egyptian language. (The Ptolemies spoke Greek almost exclusively.)

EDUCATION OF SERVANTS OF THE PLACE OF TRUTH AND PRIESTS

In the New Kingdom Period (1550–1070 B.C.E.) the SERVANTS OF THE PLACE OF TRUTH, the artists and workers who prepared the tombs of the pharaoh in the VALLEY OF THE KINGS and lived at DEIR EL-MEDINA, also received training and considerable education. Ostraca, or fragments of clay slabs and tablets, as well as the walls of their tombs, demonstrate that the workers at Deir el-Medina could read and write.

The priests of the various temples also received an education, particularly in the cults of AMUN, RÉ, PTAH, and THOTH. Many served as physicians and maintained a PER-ANKH, a House of Life, in all of the major cities. The *per-ankh* was an institution that served as a library, a research center, and a school for apprentices. Classes at the *per-ankh,* which were rigidly observed in courts and temples, did not restrict its students to those of privilege. Any Egyptian, from any social standing, could advance as a priest, a scribe, or as an official if the student demonstrated loyalty, intellect, and honor.

After the collapse of the New Kingdom and the rise of less powerful dynasties the various royal families set their own standards of education, but Egyptians as a whole maintained the practices of the past.

The ancient Egyptians viewed education as a means to an end (another "necessary art," as they termed the science of medicine), in that certain topics were expected to be known by one and all. Those included the work of sages and scholars, whose writings were read aloud by priests or town leaders and memorized. Wisdom literature was remembered, word for word, by all classes of people. The remarkable "THE ELOQUENT PEASANT" OF HERAKLEOPOLIS who showed up in the royal courts during the First Intermediate Period (2134–2040 B.C.E.) and was able to recite the honored sages as he scolded corrupt officials, proved the worth of traditional Egyptian knowledge.

Edwin Smith Papyrus   A text called "the Secret Book of Physicians," dating to the Third Dynasty (2649–2575 B.C.E.) and containing 38 sections, this document is also called the Edwin Smith Surgical Papyrus.

Probably the most important medical document from ancient Egypt, the papyrus was found positioned between the legs of a deceased physician buried at ASA-SIF, a necropolis near modern Luxor. The Edwin Smith Papyrus is studied in conjunction with the EBERS PAPYRUS, which describes numerous medical conditions but focuses most closely on cardiac and circulatory illnesses, as well as mental disorders. The Edwin Smith Papyrus was written in the hieratic style. Each of the sections of the work is accompanied by possible diagnoses, medical treatments, and procedures. The sections are presented with five headings: title, symptoms, diagnosis, opinion, and treatment. The "opinion" phase of medical care is related to the physician's ability to state: "This is an infection with which I shall or shall not attempt treatment."

Some 800 medical procedures are offered, demonstrating that the document was a reliable medical text. Such a text would have been available to physicians and priests at the *per-ankh,* the House of Life, an academy and library in use in almost every city. The *per-ankh* was also established in large temple complexes.

The present form of the Edwin Smith Papyrus was a copy made in the period of the New Kingdom (1550–1070 B.C.E.). It opens with a section on the heart and pulse, but the main sections concern general trauma and orthopedic surgical procedures. There are specific detailed references to organs, with anatomical awareness evident. There are even references to depressed skull injuries and fractures of the vertebrae, dislocation of the jaw, and traumatic paraplegia. These sections establish clear relationships between symptoms and trauma. The priests early on in Egypt understood relationships between injuries and movements and encouraged observations and patient care. The use of *hemayet* (Arabic *helbah* oil) was prescribed for the preservation of the skin of geriatric patients.

The priest-physicians of ancient Egypt conducted clinics throughout the Nile Valley and at the site of monuments as well. The pyramids were built by the common Egyptians who came at the call of the pharaoh, in the institution called CORVÉE. (The builders of the pyramids were not slave workers, and they were provided with food, clothing, bread, beer, festivals, beds, and medical care.) The scope of the physicians' knowledge was enhanced with the building of every monument on the Nile because as the work involved towering heights and the use of incredibly heavy stones, and because there were hundreds of workmen on the sites of monuments, accidents were inevitable. Workers also arrived with diseases and illnesses that had to be treated. The physicians at these sites had to have a reliable text to guide them in a hands-on approach when various traumatic injuries or illnesses were presented to them. Because of the continuing education of these medical professionals, and because of the availability of documents like the Edwin Smith Papyrus, the physicians of ancient Egypt were held in high esteem by the rulers of Egypt's neighboring lands.

See also HEALTH AND DISEASE; *PER-ANKH.*

Egypt, 'Amarna and the Restoration of   The 'Amarna Interlude is the tumultuous period of the New Kingdom during the brief reign of AKHENATEN (Amenhotep IV) (r. 1353–1335 B.C.E.), when the capital of Egypt was the city called Akhetaten (the Horizon of Aten). Called the "heretic pharaoh," Akhenaten built the capital of 'Amarna shortly after his coronation, and he took his consort Nefertiti (r. 1379–1362 B.C.E.), whose name meant "the Beautiful Woman Has Come," to live with him there.

At this time the insignia of the solar god Aten was comparatively new to Egypt. Still, Akhenaten felt transformed by this deity, and he dedicated his reign and life solely to acts of worship honoring the god, and focusing on his own role as Aten's chief worshipper. Akhenaten's new capital opened an entire artistic period in ancient Egypt, with courts, kiosks, and broad avenues, all decorated with depictions of nature. It also resulted in the demolition of the temples of the traditional gods of the Nile. The new site was itself was later methodically destroyed by HOREMHAB (r. 1310–1307 B.C.E.) after Akhenaten's death in 1335 B.C.E.

CONTEXT

In the second year of his reign, Akhenaten began his worship of the solar god Aten, a deity that had been evident in the royal structures of his grandfather, TUTHMOSIS IV (r. 1401–1391 B.C.E.), as well as in the sails of the ships of his father, AMENHOTEP III (r. 1391–1353 B.C.E.). Akhenaten had also seen signs of the god displayed by his father at his palace of Malkata. (No documentation has been discovered explaining why these two pharaohs honored this particular deity.) Akhenaten's preference for Aten became increasingly evident and led to the falling from favor of the god Amun and other ancient deities.

Aten's symbol was a solar disk, believed by some scholars to be a form of Re-Harakhte. The young pharaoh renounced the name Amenhotep and called himself Akhenaten, "the Horizon of the Sun Disk" or "He Who Is of the Service to Aten." Akhenaten's consort Nefertiti also had her name changed and became Nefer-Nefru-Aten, meaning "Beautiful Is the Beauty of Aten."

In the fourth year of his reign, Akhenaten and Nefertiti visited a site on the Nile south of modern Malawi. There the new capital was constructed. Erected on a level plain between the Nile and the eastern cliffs north of Assiut, 'Amarna was six miles long and marked by boundary stelae. The districts of the city were laid out with geometric precision and artistry. All of the regions of 'Amarna were designed to draw attention to the royal residence and to the temple of the god Aten.

EVENT

Akhenaten allowed only the temple of the god Aten in 'Amarna. Called Per-Aten en Akhetaten, the temple, as many of the structures built in 'Amarna, was adapted to the Nile climate and designed for outdoor services, a custom that brought about complaints from foreign dignitaries, as some ambassadors and legates from other lands attending the ceremonies in honor of Aten suffered heatstroke as a result.

Endless ceremonies were conducted in the capital for Aten, but eventually Akhenaten decided to put an end to them. He closed down temples, confiscating the vast plantations of the priests. He also viewed himself as the lone mediator with Aten, thus injuring the great bureaucratic machinery that maintained Egypt's vast religious programs, which were responsible for the care of the poor and the ill. The worship services in the capital were reserved for Akhenaten alone, with only Nefertiti in attendance. There was a priesthood of Aten established after a time, but only Akhenaten presided, as he had assumed a divine status and became more and more absorbed in worship. Few others had access to the sacred precincts; even Nefertiti was relegated to minor roles in the daily rituals.

Soon Akhenaten became even more involved in the service of Aten. He spoke of the god as a celestial pharaoh, using the sun disk and its illuminating rays as symbols of creation. Akhenaten's hymn to Aten, discovered in a tomb in 'Amarna, provides the universal theme of worship that he tried to promote throughout the land. His agents, however, began a program of destruction that violated the other temples and shrines of Egypt, dismaying the common populace and making Aten unpopular. In addition, the administration of the state, and the protection of vassal states of the empire, was ignored by the pharaoh as he became a recluse absorbed in worship. His destruction of temple plantations, which were sources of valuable food products, led Egypt toward economic ruin.

Egypt was in turmoil by the end of Akhenaten's reign, and General Horemhab and other state officials tried to rouse the pharaoh to action on domestic and foreign concerns. Even Queen TIYE, Akhenaten's mother, arrived in the capital to meet with her son about the chaotic state of the nation but was unable to rouse him to action. Thousands of human lives were affected by Akhenaten's refusal to protect the vassal city-states of the empire. As a result, most of the Egyptian people, including the priests and military officials, welcomed the death of Akhenaten.

Akhenaten's son and heir, Smenkhare (r. 1335–1333 B.C.E.), began immediate reconciliation programs with the temple priesthoods and the military, but the young man came to the throne with severe health problems due to congenital disorders and died before he could bring about a genuine restoration of the traditions and cultic life of the people.

After Smenkhare's death, the "Boy King" Tut'ankhamun (r. 1333–1323 B.C.E.) came to the throne and was a symbol of hope and renewal after the 'Amarna Interlude. He returned Egypt's capital to THEBES and issued restoration commands for all temples and priesthoods. After ruling for only a decade, what appeared to be the sudden and unexpected death of Tut'ankhamun came as a profound shock to Egypt. (Few knew about the state of the pharaoh's physical conditions, specifically his bouts with malaria tropica, as the priest-physicians and court officials would not have disclosed such things to the public.)

The counselor Aya (r. 1323–1319 B.C.E.) next took the throne, possibly because he was a blood relative of Queen Nefertiti. Aya is depicted on the wall of Tut'ankhamun's tomb as presiding over the young pharaoh's burial ceremonies, a required duty of every successor to the throne. Because he was so young, and had such a short reign, Tut'ankhamun's tomb had to be fashioned quickly, and the funerary objects in the 'Amarna graves were used to adorn his burial site. The coffins and funerary goods, along with the mummified remains of Akhenaten, Tiye, and Tiye's daughter (Akhenaten's sister) were also included in Tut'ankhamun's tomb.

Aya was prudent and promoted the glorification of Amun and the old gods, but he was elderly and did not enjoy a long reign. Although Aya declared that his child was his heir and successor, the military commander Horemhab (r. 1319–1307 B.C.E.) became the next to take the throne. Horemhab was popular with the Egyptian people and the priesthoods because of his efforts to persuade Akhenaten to act to save the land and the empire. He had risen through the ranks of the military, serving in 'Amarna and then becoming the general of Egypt's army under Tut'ankhamun.

Assuming the throne, Horemhab married MUT-NODJMET (1), who was reportedly a sister of Queen Nefertiti. Intent upon destroying any vestiges of the 'Amarna Interlude, Horemhab officially dated the start of his reign to the death of Amenhotep III and set about destroying the tombs and buildings of the period. It was reported that Horemhab wanted to destroy Tut'ankhamun's tomb also, but MAYA, Horemhab's trusted treasurer, intervened and saved the tomb from obliteration. The city of 'Amarna, however, was destroyed, and it is presumed that Horemhab gave the order. Horemhab did set about expunging any cult wor-

ship of the god Aten and demolishing the Aten chapels that had been erected in the temple of Karnak in Thebes, however.

Horemhab distinguished his reign with extensive programs designed to bring order, to defend the nation's borders, and to rebuild Egypt's religious institutions. He sent military units to reclaim lost territories and reopened mines and quarries. He also issued a series of laws that stopped corruption by officials and protected the poor. Although he had been honored at 'Amarna, and possibly bore the name Pa'atenemhab in that court, Horemhab nevertheless continued to allow the city to be steadily dismantled. He ultimately demolished 'Amarna and dismantled Aya's tomb and mortuary temple, erasing all names and faces recorded in these monuments. From the Delta to Nubia (modern Sudan) he destroyed all traces of the god Aten. He especially targeted an individual named HUY (1), who was the viceroy during the 'Amarna Interlude, and punished the city of AKHMIN, which was allied with Akhenaten.

Restoring Egypt's military, Horemhab once again nurtured vassal states and received delegates and tributes. He moved Egypt's capital back to MEMPHIS (which had been the capital in the Early Dynastic Period [2920–2575 B.C.E.]) and set about restoring temple properties by building and rebuilding sections of KARNAK and Nubian shrines. Horemhab erected statues of the god Amun everywhere, to promote the cult and the morale of the people. At Karnak he began construction on a hypostyle hall and on two PYLONS, the ninth and tenth.

IMPACT

Absorbed in worshipping the god Aten, Akhenaten ignored matters pertaining to the administration and protection of his kingdom, which resulted in social disorder, legal abuses, and economic ruin. Akhenaten's decision to close the temples of the ancient gods added to the devastation. For thousands of years the Egyptians had honored the old deities and planned to spend eternity in the blissful realms of such divine protectors. By closing the temples of these ancient gods, Akhenaten was not only ending their earthly worship but was denying the afterlife for his people. Tombs emblazoned with the Book of the Dead (the guides for the journey beyond the grave), temples and shrines of ancient deities, and monuments and stelae honoring the spiritual pilgrimages were violated and destroyed, dismaying Egypt's populace. His disbanding of religious programs that provided social services only furthered the Egyptians' dismay. Akhenaten also destroyed the temple plantations, thus destroying critical and valuable sources of food products. Akhenaten died leaving his city vulnerable and in turmoil.

Akhenaten left Egypt in such dire crisis that after two short-reigning pharoahs it is reported the people of Egypt ignored Pharoah Aya's declaration that his child was his heir and successor and accepted the reign of General Horemhab. His famous edict reestablishing various laws was found on a fragmented stela in Karnak. This edict concerned itself with legal abuses taking place because of the laxity of Akhenaten's rule.

A champion of civil rights, in the edict Horemhab declared that officials of the state and provinces would be held accountable for cheating the poor, for pocketing funds, and for misappropriating the use of slaves, ships, and other properties. The ruler singled out higher-ranked officials, promising swift judgments and even the death penalty for offenses. The edict also announced the appointment of responsible men as viziers and gave information about the division of the standing army into two main units, one in Upper Egypt and one in Lower Egypt. Horemhab not only published his edict throughout the land but also took inspection tours to make sure that all of the provisions were being carried out in the remote regions as well as in the cities.

The laws put into effect included an enactment against the poor being robbed of wood by royal breweries and royal kitchens; an enactment against robbing a poor man by collecting heavy taxes; an enactment against the robbing of the poor by harem or palace soldiers; an enactment against unlawful use of slave laborers; an enactment against the stealing of hides from the poor by soldiers; and an enactment against stealing vegetables from the poor and calling such theft a form of taxation. The forms of punishment for wrongdoers violating these laws were swift and severe. These enactments, prominently placed and made public on a stela at Karnak, were popular with the common people, who had previously been vulnerable to such injustices. Horemhab's throne name was Djoserkheperrare-Setpenre Horemhab Meriamun, which meant "Holy Are the Manifestations of Ré, Chosen of Ré, Horus in Jubilation, Beloved of Amun."

Further reading: Dodson, Aidan. *Amarna Sunset: Nefertiti, Tutankhamun, Ay, Horemheb, and the Egyptian Counter-Reformation.* Cairo: American University Press, 2009; Moran, William. *The Amarna Letters.* Baltimore: The Johns Hopkins University Press, 2000; Silverman, David P., et al. *Akhenaten and Tutankhamun: Revolution and Restoration.* Philadelphia: University of Pennsylvania Museum of Archaeology and Anthropology, 2006.

Egypt, fall of (30 B.C.E.) The final demise of pharaonic Egypt occurred in 30 B.C.E. in the aftermath of the battle of Actium the year before, which saw the defeat of Queen CLEOPATRA VII (r. 51–30 B.C.E.) and Marc ANTONY (83–30 B.C.E.) by Octavian (the future Emperor Augustus) (63 B.C.E.–14 C.E.). Historians have placed the burden for the final decline and fall of Egypt and its subsequent seizure by Rome on the shoulders of Cleopatra VII, but many believe Egypt's demise was chiefly the result of two major developments. The first was the

internal deterioration of Ptolemaic Egypt, and the second was the end of the Hellenistic kingdoms brought about by the ascendancy of Rome, the preeminent power in the Mediterranean world.

CONTEXT

In 334 B.C.E., ALEXANDER III THE GREAT of Macedonia defeated the Persian forces of DARIUS III CODOMAN (r. 336–330 B.C.E.) at the battle of Granicus in northwest Asia Minor. This was followed by a triumph in 333 B.C.E. at the battle of Issus, where Alexander forced Darius to flee for his life. Alexander next captured Miletus and Tyre (332 B.C.E.), followed by Syria, Palestine, and Egypt (331 B.C.E.). In Egypt, he embraced the title of pharaoh, was proclaimed the son of the god Amun (the equivalent in the Greek mind to their own god Zeus), and began construction of the first in a number of cities named in his honor. Alexander cultivated his place as a conqueror and the logical successor to the pharaohs. He founded the city of Alexandria and embraced the continuation of Egyptian religious practices as part of his wider vision of a pan-Hellenistic civilization diverse in its religious outlook but united by a commitment to a common Hellenistic culture.

The sudden death of Alexander in 323 B.C.E. left the colossal empire without an heir, save for a half brother and a son born posthumously to his wife Roxane (d. 313 B.C.E.). The claims of the infant were thrust aside by Alexander's generals and satraps. They soon fell to squabbling and then to 40 years of open warfare. Eventually, the generals carved up Alexander's empire into four territories. Syria and the remnants of the Persian Empire passed to General Seleucus, beginning the Seleucid Empire. Macedonia, Thrace, and parts of northern Asia Minor fell under the rule of Antigonus and his son Demetrius (the Antigonid Kingdom). The Attalid Kingdom was formed around Pergamum in eastern Asia Minor. Meanwhile, PTOLEMY I SOTER (r. 304–284 B.C.E.), another of Alexander's generals, secured control of Egypt and established the Ptolemaic Dynasty, which ruled Egypt for the next 250 years.

The Ptolemies, rulers of Alexandria who were Greek in origin and committed to their culture, completed the flowering of Alexandria as one of the greatest cities in human history, and nurtured their capital as a leading center for Hellenistic culture. Under the Ptolemies, the city became the center of commerce and culture for the Hellenistic world and was renowned for its harbor, the tomb of Alexander, the Lighthouse of Alexandria (one of the Seven Wonders of the Ancient World), and the famed Library of Alexandria, which was a repository for virtually all of the knowledge of the known world with some half a million volumes.

The Ptolemies proved capable administrators and assumed in a smooth transition control over the rural Nile areas that were also some of the most important agricultural centers in the Mediterranean world. The result was that the first century of Ptolemaic Egypt was a time of economic and artistic prosperity. By the second century B.C.E., however, there was a marked decline in all segments of society. Family feuds and external forces began to take their toll, even though the Ptolemaic line remained in power.

The four empires divided up after Alexander's death fought with each other for the next several centuries, but no one dynasty ever reestablished a sole empire from the ashes of Alexander's realm. Each suffered from its own internal problems, challenges that were partly endemic to the Hellenistic civilization first established by Alexander.

First, the Hellenistic kings squandered their resources on wars with each other and allowed a serious gulf to open between themselves and the vast majority of their subjects. Political, cultural, and dynastic stagnation crippled the Seleucid, Antigonid, and Ptolemaic Kingdoms and made them easy targets for the next great and lasting power in the Mediterranean and Near East: Rome.

Internally, the Hellenistic Kingdoms remained even to the end essentially foreign regimes that ruled over subjects far removed from their own Greek and Macedonian origins. This was especially true in Egypt. The Ptolemies were Greeks, imbued with Hellenistic principles and committed to speaking only Greek in the royal court, living under Greek laws that were different from those that governed the rest of the Egyptian population, and marrying strictly to other Greek dynasties. As a result, the Egyptian people viewed the Ptolemies as foreigners in power and continued to live under the traditional laws and customs of the Nile. The Ptolemies were perceived as distant rulers, a view only exacerbated by the fact that the Ptolemies—while assuming many of the pharoanic rituals and costumes—seldom appeared outside of Alexandria. Thus, the Egyptians maintained their normal traditions and customs, ignoring to some degree the presence of the foreign pharaohs. Still, the Ptolemies were difficult at times to ignore, as the royal line was inclined to quarrels, degenerate behavior, dysfunction, and even murder.

EVENT

The primary event that signaled the irreversible decline of the Ptolemies was the rise of Rome as a major power in the Mediterranean. With the defeat and destruction of Carthage—a major trading rival of the Ptolemies—by the Romans in the Punic Wars (264–146 B.C.E.), Rome was able to turn its attention to the East. Philip V of Macedonia's alliance with Carthage had awakened the Romans to the presence and threat of the Hellenistic Kingdoms, and new wars were waged to bring the successor states of Alexander under Roman dominion.

The Romans defeated the ambitions of the Seleucid Empire under ANTIOCHUS III THE GREAT (241–187 B.C.E.).

Antiochus had sought to expand the Seleucid Empire at the expense of the Ptolemaic Empire following the death of Ptolemy IV. This raised the concerns of Rome that the Seleucids might interfere in the Mediterranean and in the trading interests of Rome in Africa. After bitter fighting, Antiochus was beaten at the battles of Thermopylae and Magnesia in 190 B.C.E. and forced to sue for peace at Apamea in 188 B.C.E. The treaty included a severe indemnity and the pledge never to attempt to expand Seleucid holdings beyond the Taurus Mountains. Antiochus was killed the following year in battle against tribesmen in his eastern territory. His death marked the end of Seleucid ambitions in the East and hastened the ascendancy of the Roman Republic in the affairs of Asia Minor, Palestine, and Egypt.

Roman armies routed the Macedonians and declared the Greek cities to be free by 196 B.C.E. In 148 B.C.E., Macedonia was made a province. The Greek states soon revolted against Roman interference. The city of Corinth was destroyed in 146 B.C.E., and Greece fell under Roman rule. In 133 B.C.E., the king of Pergamum left his kingdom to Rome, which meant the Romans now possessed territory in Asia Minor.

Further Roman interference took place from ca. 63 B.C.E. as a result of Rome's war with Mithridates VI of Pontus (r. 120–63 B.C.E.) in Asia Minor. His final defeat and the arrival of the Roman general Pompey the Great brought a general reorganization of the East along lines that best served the strategic interests of Rome.

By the time of Pompey's destruction of the Hellenistic Kingdoms and subsequent restructuring of the East, the Ptolemies had already assumed the position of being essentially vassals to the Roman Republic. This situation was necessitated by the presence of Rome as an arbiter to settle the often bloody dynastic squabbles among Ptolemaic claimants and the simple reality that the Ptolemies and Egyptians could not long resist the Romans in the event of a war.

The Ptolemies had established diplomatic dealings with Rome from at least the reign of Ptolemy II Philadelphus (284–246 B.C.E.), and from the time that Rome had defeated Carthage and began involving itself actively in the affairs of the Hellenistic states, the Ptolemies had turned to them as a means of securing political stability and also as a buffer against the Seleucids and, later, Pontus.

Thus, when the Seleucid king Antiochus IV effectively conquered Egypt in 170 B.C.E., he permitted Ptolemy VI to remain on the throne as a kind of puppet until the people of Alexandria chose a new king. Their choice ended up being one of Ptolemy's brothers, Ptolemy VIII Euergetes Physcon (r. 145–116), and the two brothers participated in joint rule of the kingdom. Antiochus IV eventually withdrew but in 168 B.C.E. launched a new attack on Egypt. On the road to Alexandria, however, he was met by the Roman ambassador Gaius Popillius Laenas, who delivered the famous message of the Roman Senate: The ambassador drew a circle in the sand around Antiochus IV, essentially implying that if the Seleucid crossed the circle he would be at war with Rome. Antiochus abandoned his plans and withdrew.

From the reign of Ptolemy VIII Euergetes the involvement of Rome increased, not only because of a Roman desire to extend its influence, but also because the internal strife of the dynasty made the Ptolemies vulnerable to threats by the Seleucids, thus forcing Rome to prop up the ailing kingdom in an effort to defend its interests.

In 80 B.C.E., for example, the young PTOLEMY XI ALEXANDER II was installed on the Egyptian throne at the command of the Roman dictator Sulla. Ptolemy XI proved young and unpredictable and began his reign by murdering his stepmother, Cleopatra Berenice III, whom he had been forced to marry that same year. As she was immensely popular in the city, Ptolemy XI was hanged by a mob. In his will, the king had bequeathed the kingdom to Rome, but the Romans, taken up with their own social problems in Italy, chose not to press the matter and permitted the accession of PTOLEMY XII NEOS DIONYSIUS AULETES (d. 51 B.C.E.), the son of Ptolemy IX. His reigns from 80 to 58 B.C.E. and from 55 B.C.E. until his death signaled the final phase of Ptolemaic Egypt.

Called Neos Dionysius, "the New Dionysius," or Nothos, "the Bastard," and also termed Auletes, "the Flute Player," Ptolemy XII ordered construction at DENDEREH and EDFU and refurbished PHILAE. But if the Ptolemies were foreigners in many ways to the Egyptians, Ptolemy XII was even more so, as much of his life had been spent in the court of Mithridates VI of Pontus at Sinope. His reign was troubled even further by the unpopular taxes that he levied chiefly to fund his projects but also to continue paying bribes and tribute money to the Romans. He cultivated a political relationship with Pompey the Great.

Such was his unpopular rule that in 58 B.C.E. Ptolemy XII was forced to flee the country, and his daughter Berenice IV was installed as co-regent with Cleopatra VI Tryphaena (who died the following year). Ptolemy made his way to Rome, where he paid further bribes to secure the blessings of Rome for his enforced return. He lived in Rome as a guest of Pompey, and included in his retinue was his young daughter, Cleopatra VII. To circumvent a return by Ptolemy XII, the Egyptians sent a delegation to Rome to plead for Rome to stay out of an internal Egyptian matter.

In the end, Ptolemy secured Roman support by paying 10,000 talents to General Aulus Gabinius to march on Egypt. The campaign was swift and ended with Ptolemy's return to power in 55 B.C.E. He lived for another four years and reigned with the military backing of several thousand Roman soldiers serving as mercenaries. For the Romans, the restoration provided them with a puppet ruler, which more easily allowed Roman creditors to pursue relentlessly the repayment of Egyptian loans. To oversee the finances of the kingdom, Ptolemy appointed Gaius Rabirius Postumus, a Roman. The appointee proved so severe in his administration that the king had him arrested before permitting him to leave the country. By the time of Ptolemy's death in 51 B.C.E., Egyptian currency had been severely debased in the effort to repay Roman creditors.

Ptolemy deposited his will in Rome's public treasury, and upon his death Pompey became the temporary guardian of Egypt until the instructions of Ptolemy's will could be fulfilled. Those instructions stated that Cleopatra should reign with her brother, Ptolemy XIII (d. 47 B.C.E.). Cleopatra married her brother and then ruled with him until their sister, Arsinoe, sided with him and persuaded him to exile Cleopatra from Alexandria in 48 B.C.E. In the midst of this upheaval the Romans themselves waged their own civil war, a conflict that soon embroiled Egypt and brought Cleopatra onto the world stage.

Pompey the Great arrived in Egypt when he fled from Julius Caesar after his defeat at the battle of Pharsalus in 49 B.C.E. Knowing that Caesar would pursue Pompey to Egypt, Ptolemy XIII's courtiers ordered the great Roman general murdered in the mistaken belief that presenting Pompey's severed head to Caesar would win favor with the new master of the Roman world. Caesar was far from pleased with the manner of Pompey's death, and soon after his arrival in Alexandria he restored Cleopatra to the throne. Caesar then became involved in the BATTLE OF THE NILE, which resulted in Ptolemy XIII's death by drowning. The Roman general remained in Alexandria, and in 47 B.C.E. Cleopatra VII bore him a son, PTOLEMY XV CAESARION. This affair made Cleopatra a subject of much gossip in Rome and prompted speculations about her feminine lures (although Caesar was noted for his affairs with women). However, Cleopatra's position in Egypt, which was a valuable resource for Rome, and her remarkable education and ambitions, granted her an attractiveness apart from her physical charms. Called the "Goddess Beloved of Her Father" by the Egyptians, Cleopatra was thoroughly educated by Greek scholars in alchemy, the arts, geography, astronomy, languages, military campaigns, and physics, which were subjects not normally taught to women in that historical period. She was unique in being the only member of the Ptolemaic Dynasty to speak the ancient language of Egypt.

In 46 B.C.E. Cleopatra visited Caesar in Rome, causing a stir in the city and setting into motion the political ambitions of other Roman officials. Caesar was assassinated during her stay in Rome in 44 B.C.E., and Cleopatra fled to her ship and returned to Egypt. Her younger brother, PTOLEMY XIV (r. 47–44 B.C.E.), had served for a time as Cleopatra VII's regent, but she had him killed in 44 B.C.E. and put her son, Ptolemy XV, on the throne in his place. Together they ruled Egypt, and the Roman Senate recognized the royal pair in 42 B.C.E.

A year later the Roman general Marc Antony met with Cleopatra and established a political and personal alliance with her. She soon bore him twins, ALEXANDER HELIOS and CLEOPATRA SELENE in 40 B.C.E., and another son, PTOLEMY PHILADELPHOS, in 36 B.C.E., long after Antony's marriage for political purposes to Octavia (the sister of Octavian, Caesar's nephew and heir and Antony's partner [with Lepidus] in the Second Triumvirate). With this alliance, Cleopatra agreed to help fund Antony's campaigns in the East, particularly against Parthia and Armenia, and in return she was permitted to expand Egypt's influence in a way that had not been enjoyed for many decades. This new assertion of power was formalized in the document called the "Donations of Alexandria" in 34 B.C.E., which divided parts of the Roman Empire among Cleopatra VII and her children. This claim, combined with Antony's union with Cleopatra (and possibly marriage to her), caused immense consternation in Rome and hastened the inevitable war between Octavian and the combined forces of Antony and Cleopatra. The result was a clash over control of the Roman world, and it was decided at the battle of ACTIUM in 31 B.C.E.

Octavian set sail for Alexandria with a Roman fleet and the valuable support of his military advisor, MARCUS AGRIPPA. The two fleets and armies clashed off the western coast of Greece at the entrance to the Ambracian Gulf, at Actium. Agrippa commanded the left wing of the fleet, bringing to bear his tactical genius and the weapon that he had invented, the harpax. The harpax was composed of grappling hooks fixed to a catapult. Shot at an enemy vessel, the weapon held the enemy fast or drew the ship close enough for the Romans to board at will. The Egyptians had 500 ships, the Romans 400. The Egyptians, however, were overwhelmed by the Romans. Cleopatra gave orders to retreat and withdrew to her palace, and Marc Antony found himself stranded alone in the battle. He committed suicide on the shore of Alexandria after attempting to follow Cleopatra. When the Romans entered the royal residence, she knew all was lost. Ptolemy XV, her son by Caesar, had been sent away. He was found by the Romans and slain.

Cleopatra had defended Egypt all of her life and knew the ways of her enemies. She had killed those who opposed her, including her sister Arsinoe. (After the defeat of the Egyptian forces in the battle of the Nile in Alexandria, Julius Caesar had taken Arsinoe to Rome, parading her in a victory celebration. She had then fled to the city of Ephesus, in Asia Minor, where the temple of the goddess Artemis served as a haven for political exiles. Marc Antony's men hunted Arsinoe down in the temple and killed her as retribution for her opposition to Cleopatra's rise to power. The entire world was shocked at this sacrilege.) Cleopatra knew that she could expect the same sort of treatment from Octavian, after he humiliated her in his own victory parade. She killed herself with the sting of an asp, a deadly reptile. Some debate has taken place over the centuries as to how she managed this, and some scholars believe she used a simple poison instead. However she died, Octavian found her body dressed in royal robes, lying on a bier. He possibly took her corpse to Rome and displayed it in his parade. Egypt became a province of Rome as Octavian became the first emperor.

HISTORICAL IMPACT

The battle of Actium brought to an end the Ptolemaic Dynasty, and Egypt became a province reserved for the emperor. The Romans, experienced in dealing with various conquered areas and adept at keeping the peace, assumed control of Egypt, and they ruled it with two simple objectives: to attach Egypt to the wider imperial world and to exploit its natural resources of grain on which much of the empire relied for food. This meant bringing an end to the ancient traditions of rule in the Nile Valley, including the pharaonic system, and instituting Roman provincial administration. Egypt's importance to Rome was made clear by the fact that the province was under the direction of the prefect of Egypt, a member of the Roman equestrian class, who answered directly to the emperor. The Romans also kept garrisons in strategic places and maintained the Faiyum and trade routes.

The people of Egypt in the nomes, or provinces, complained about Roman rule and taxes, but their daily lives continued as normal and with added security. Egypt had been brought into a new historical period as a key province of the most powerful empire on the earth at the time.

The Romans living among the Egyptians were also brought into the ways of Egypt. At the Bahariya Oasis, thousands of Romans were buried with the mortuary rituals of ancient times. The "Valley of the Gilded Mummies" at Baharia contains such Roman-era remains, buried in family groups, with proper wrappings and golden masks.

Roman rule in Egypt endured for the next six centuries. It ended in the early seventh century with the Persian invasions and finally the Arab Muslim invasion that captured Alexandria in 641.

Further reading: Chauveau, Michel, and David Lorton, transl. *Egypt in the Age of Cleopatra: History and Society Under the Ptolemies.* Ithaca, N.Y.: Cornell University Press, 2000; Grant, Michael. *Cleopatra.* London: Phoenix Press, 2000; Hawass, Zahi. *Cleopatra: The Search for the Last Queen of Egypt.* New York: National Geographic, 2010; Holbl, Gunther, and Tina Saavedra, transl. *A History of the Ptolemaic Empire.* New York: Routledge, 2000;

Mysliwiec, Karol, and David Lorton, transl. *The Twilight of Ancient Egypt: 1st Millennium B.C.* Ithaca, N.Y.: Cornell University Press, 2000; Rowlandson, Jane, and Roger Bagnall, eds. *Women and Society in Greek and Roman Egypt: A Sourcebook.* Cambridge, U.K.: Cambridge University Press, 1998; Schiff, Stacy. *Cleopatra: A Biography.* New York: Little, Brown, 2010; Walker, Susan, and Peter Higgs, eds. *Cleopatra of Egypt: From History to Myth.* Princeton, N.J.: Princeton University Press, 2001.

Egypt, founding of (ca. 2900 B.C.E.)

The founding of Egypt was the culmination of centuries of vigorous growth and development along the Nile. Aha (Menes) (r. ca. 2920 B.C.E.), credited as the founder of Egypt, was the product of a line of Predynastic Period rulers, sometimes called Dynasty 0, who reigned in the southern cities of HIERAKONPOLIS (near the modern city of EDFU) and THINIS (just north of ABYDOS). 'Aha's mother was reportedly NEITHOTEP, the heiress of the Delta nomes, and his father was reportedly NARMER of Thinis, who had first conquered parts of the Delta region in an effort to unite Upper and Lower Egypt. 'Aha established the First Dynasty (2920–2575 B.C.E.), building a new capital city in the north, later known as Memphis. The actual unification of all the nomes, or provinces, of Egypt came at a later time.

CONTEXT

Hierakonpolis was one of the largest cities in Predynastic Egypt and the capital of the southern kingdom. During the Predynastic Period (before 3000 B.C.E.) settled communities had gradually grown into larger geographical units, which later developed into nomes, and small cities had sprung up across the land. Each geographical unit had its own capital, chieftain, and major deity. Based on archaeological evidence it appears that the southern part had formed a common culture by ca. 4000 B.C.E. during the NAGADA Period. Burial sites indicate that by 3000 B.C.E. Egyptian society was organized hierarchically, led by an elite class called nomarchs. Traditions state that eventually two independent kingdoms were established, the southern Upper Kingdom and the northern Lower Kingdom. However, there is evidence that Lower Egypt, based in the Delta, was not actually a kingdom but rather a territory loosely joined in alliance with the Delta city of Buto.

EVENT

When 'Aha founded ancient Egypt, his warriors marched under the banner of HORUS, the falcon god worshiped in Hierankopolis. 'Aha was not the first southern leader to attempt conquest of the north. He followed in the footsteps of his father, Narmer, as well as in those of SCORPION I (fl. ca. 3000 B.C.E.), an Upper Egyptian ruler who began the process of unification as early as ca. 3050 B.C.E. 'Aha was not successful in bringing all of the Delta

nome clans under his control, and many of his successors continued the military and diplomatic efforts to unite the land. KHA'SEKHEMWY, the last ruler of the Second Dynasty (2770–2549 B.C.E.), reportedly succeeded in uniting all of Egypt.

After conquering a large portion of the Delta region, 'Aha built the first capital of the new nation, a city called "the White Walled" (later known as Memphis), in the Delta. The founding of the capital established for much of the Nile Valley an enduring administration that remained intact and powerful even when Egypt was occupied by foreign armies. 'Aha brought officials from Thinis and perhaps Hierakonpolis, who instituted the offices, administrative courts, and agencies for government. The founding of Memphis and the nation not only centralized authority but also facilitated massive administrative, architectural, irrigation, and defense projects.

'Aha built his new capital at the apex of the Delta south of modern Cairo. Tradition states that 'Aha altered the course of the Nile in order to clear a nearby plain for his capital. This plain, on the western side of the Nile, was some four miles wide, and its western end sloped upward to the cliffs of the LIBYAN DESERT. At the apex of the Nile Delta, this site provided prestige and political distinction.

Other areas were developed at the same time to serve as necropolis sites or burial grounds for the new nation. Abydos, considered in time to be the true resting place of the god OSIRIS, had served as a site of royal burials since the time of Scorpion I and became the most sacred repository for the remains of all Egyptians. SAQQARA, GIZA, ABUSIR, and DASHUR also served as necropolis sites or cemeteries.

Originally, Memphis was called Ankh-tawy, the "Life of the Two Lands" (the two lands being Upper and Lower Egypt). Made of mud brick, plastered and painted white, the walls of the city prompted a new name, Heb-hadj, "the White-Walled." The modern name derives from the era of the Sixth Dynasty (2323–2150 B.C.E.), when Pepi I built his pyramid in Saqqara. The capital was soon called Men-nefer and then Menti, and the Greeks changed this to Memphis. The old capital is today the site of a town called Mit-Rahina.

IMPACT

Although neither the first nor the last attempt at unifying Egypt, 'Aha's conquest of large parts of the Delta region, the founding of Memphis, and establishment of a central administration laid the foundations for Egyptian society for the coming centuries. By the time of the Old Kingdom Egypt had become a highly centralized theocracy that brought forth the unique hieroglyphic writing system, the solar calendar, and the Pyramids and Great Sphinx. Memphis remained the administrative and religious center for most of Egypt's long history. Today, the city has all but disappeared, with only limited

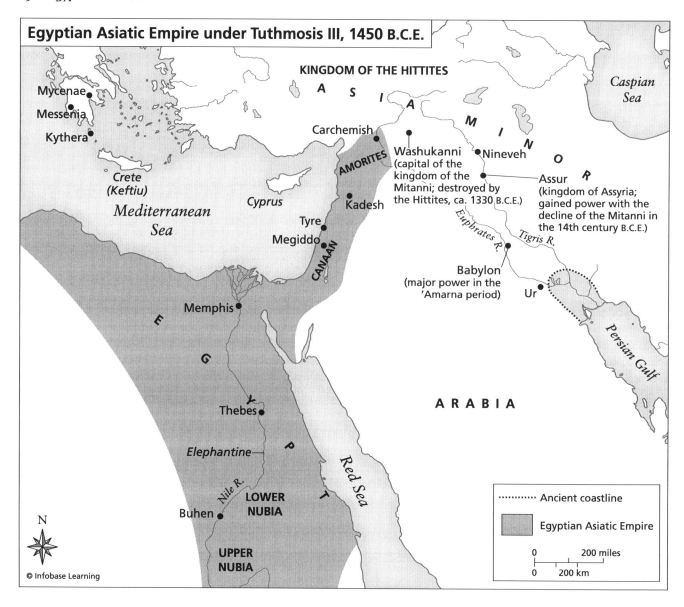

Egyptian Asiatic Empire under Tuthmosis III, 1450 B.C.E.

KINGDOM OF THE HITTITES

Caspian Sea

A S I A M I N O R

Mycenae

Messenia

Kythera

Carchemish

Washukanni (capital of the kingdom of the Mitanni; destroyed by the Hittites, ca. 1330 B.C.E.)

Nineveh

Assur (kingdom of Assyria; gained power with the decline of the Mitanni in the 14th century B.C.E.)

Crete (Keftiu)

Mediterranean Sea

Cyprus

AMORITES

Kadesh

Euphrates R.

Tigris R.

Tyre

Megiddo

CANAAN

Babylon (major power in the 'Amarna period)

Ur

Memphis

E

G

Y

P

T

Persian Gulf

ARABIA

Thebes

Elephantine

Red Sea

Nile R.

LOWER NUBIA

Buhen

N

UPPER NUBIA

© Infobase Learning

.... Ancient coastline

Egyptian Asiatic Empire

0   200 miles

0   200 km

---

archaeological remains hinting of the once extensive city complex.

Further reading: Bard, Kathryn. *An Introduction to the Archaeology of Ancient Egypt.* London: Wiley, 2007; Martin, Geoffrey. *The Hidden Tombs of Memphis: New Discoveries from the Time of Tutankhamun and Ramesses the Great.* London: Thames & Hudson, 1992; Wilkinson, Toby. *Early Dynastic Egypt.* London: Routledge, 1999.

Egypt and the East   The relationship between the Nile Valley and Mediterranean states was complex and subject to many historical factors, including dynastic vitality and foreign leadership. From the Early Dynastic Period (2920–2575 B.C.E.), Egypt guarded its borders, especially those that faced eastward, as Egyptians had ventured into the SINAI and opened copper and turquoise mines in that area, repulsing the Asiatics and

staking their own claims. The Egyptians maintained camps and fortresses in the area to protect this valuable fount of NATURAL RESOURCES. In the Old Kingdom (2575–2134 B.C.E.), the Egyptians led punitive raids against their rebellious eastern vassals and defended their borders furiously. In the Sixth Dynasty (2323–2150 B.C.E.), the leadership of General WENI ushered in a new period of Egyptian military expansion, and the people of southern Palestine began to look toward the Nile uneasily. Weni and his Nubian mercenaries and conscripts raided the lands and the natural resources of much of southern Palestine.

During the First Intermediate Period (2134–2040 B.C.E.), Egyptians held onto limited powers until Middle Kingdom (2040–1640 B.C.E.) pharaohs secured Egypt's borders again and established a firm rule. The Mentuhoteps, Amenemhets, and Senwosrets were warrior pharaohs who conquered entire city-states, establishing vassals and trade partners while controlling the people of Nubia. This relationship with other states lasted until the Second Intermediate Period (1640–1550 B.C.E.), at which time vast hordes of Asiatics entered the Nile region with ease. In this era it appears as if no border existed on the eastern side of the nation, and many peoples in southern Palestine viewed themselves as Egyptians and lived under the rule of the HYKSOS kings of the eastern Delta. The Eighteenth Dynasty changed that condition abruptly. 'AHMOSE (NEBPEHTIRÉ) (r. 1550–1525 B.C.E.) chased the Asiatics from Egypt and sealed its borders, reestablishing the series of fortresses called the WALL OF THE PRINCE erected during the Middle Kingdom period.

AMENHOTEP I (r. 1525–1504 B.C.E.) maintained this firm rule, but it was his successor, TUTHMOSIS I (r. 1504–1492 B.C.E.), who defeated the MITANNIS, once Egypt's principal Asiatic enemies, and marched to the Euphrates River with a large army. The Mitannis remained firm allies of Egypt from that time onward, and many treaties and pacts maintained the partitioning of vast territories between them. Mitanni princesses also entered Egypt as wives of the pharaohs. The Mitanni people flowered as an empire, having started their invasion of neighboring lands during Tuthmosis I's era. In time they controlled city-states and kingdoms from the Zagros Mountains to Lake Van and even to Assur, proving to be loyal allies of Egypt. They suffered during the 'AMARNA Period (1353–1335 B.C.E.), when AKHENATEN failed to meet the challenge of the emerging HITTITES and their cohorts and the roving bands of barbarians who were migrating throughout the Mediterranean region. The Ramessids, coming to power later, could not protect the Mitannis either. By that time the Mitanni Kingdom had already been subjugated by the warriors of the hittites. When TUTHMOSIS III came to the throne in 1479 B.C.E., the Mitannis were still in power, and the Hittites were consumed by their own internal problems and by wars with their immediate neighbors.

He began campaigns in southern Palestine and in the city-states on the Mediterranean Coast, eventually reaching the Euphrates. Palestine and the Sinai had been under Egypt's control since Tuthmosis I. A confederation of states threatened by Egypt, or in the process of seeking total independence, banded under the leadership of the king of KADESH. Tuthmosis III met them at AR-MEGIDDO, near Mount Carmel, and laid siege. He then attacked Phoenicia (modern Lebanon) and fortified the coastal cities there, placing them all under Egyptian control. Egypt, as a result, received gifts and tribute from Babylon, Assyria, CYPRUS, Crete, and all of the small city-states of the Mediterranean region. Even the Hittites were anxious to send offerings and diplomats to the Egyptian court at THEBES.

Tuthmosis III's son, AMENHOTEP II (r. 1427–1401 B.C.E.) conducted ruthless campaigns in Syria and governed the provinces with a firm hand. His heir, TUTHMOSIS IV (r. 1401–1391 B.C.E.), did not have to exert himself, because the tributary nations were not anxious to provoke another Egyptian invasion. AMENHOTEP III (r. 1391–1353 B.C.E.) came to power in an era of Egyptian supremacy, and he too did not have difficulty maintaining the wealth or status of the nation. His son, Akhenaten (r. 1353–1335 B.C.E.), however, lost control of many territories, ignoring the pleas of his vassal kings and allies when they were threatened by hostile forces instigated by the Hittites.

The Hittites had arrived at the city of Hattus sometime ca. 1400 B.C.E. and renamed it Hattusa. This capital became a sophisticated metropolis in time, with vast fortified walls complete with stone lions and a sphinx gate. The Hittites conquered vast regions of Asia Minor and Syria. They worshipped a storm god and conducted administrative, legislative, and legal affairs ably. They worked silver, gold, and electrum skillfully, maintained three separate languages within their main territories, kept vast records, and protected the individual rights of their own citizens. Their legal code, like the Hammurabic code before it, was harsh but just. The Hittites were warriors, but they were also capable of statecraft and diplomacy.

The son of Hittite king SUPPILULIUMAS I was offered the Egyptian throne by TUT'ANKHAMUN's young widow, ANKHESENAMON, ca. 1323 B.C.E. Prince ZANNANZA, however, was slain as he approached Egypt's border. HOREMHAB (ca. 1319–1307 B.C.E.) who became the last pharaoh of the Eighteenth Dynasty, was probably the one who ordered the death of the Hittite prince, but when he came to power he was able to arrange a truce between the two nations. He needed to maintain such a pact in order to restore Egypt's internal affairs, greatly deteriorated by Akhenaten's reign.

The first Ramessid kings, all military veterans, were anxious to restore the empire again, and they began to assault Egypt's former provinces. They watched the Hittites begin their own attacks on new territories with growing annoyance. The Hittites had conducted a great Syrian campaign, defeating the Mitanni king and attacking that empire's vassal states as a result. The city-state of Amurru also rose to prominence as the Amurrian king and his heir conducted diplomatic maneuvers and statecraft skillfully as agents of the Hittites. Many loyal Egyptian states fell to them.

The Hittites next assaulted the Hurrian region, taking the city of CARCHEMISH. The Hurrians had come into this territory from an unknown land, bringing skills in war, horses, and chariot attacks. In time the Egyptians were the beneficiaries of the Hurrian skills, as many of them entered the Nile Valley to conduct training sessions and programs.

When the Hittites began to invade Egyptian territories, SETI I (r. 1306–1290 B.C.E.) started a counteroffensive. He easily overcame Palestine and Lebanon with his vast and skilled army. He then advanced on Kadesh, a Hittite ally, and consolidated his victories by reaching an agreement with the Hittites over the division of lands and spoils. The Hittites and the Egyptians thus shared most of the Near East with Egypt, maintaining the whole of Palestine and the Syrian coastal regions to the Litani River.

Seti's son, RAMESSES II, faced a reinvigorated Hittite nation, however, one that was not eager to allow Egypt to keep its fabled domain. The battles displayed on Ramesses II's war memorials and on temple walls, especially the celebrated Poem of PENTAUR, depict the clash between the Hittites and the Egyptians. Ramesses II and his army were caught in a cleverly devised ambush, but he led his troops out of the trap and managed an effective delaying effort until reinforcements arrived. This, the battle of KADESH, resulting in heavy losses on both sides, led to the HITTITE ALLIANCE.

From that point on, the Hittites and the Egyptians maintained cordial relations. Both were suffering from the changing arenas of power in the world, and both were experiencing internal problems. It is significant that the successors of Ramesses II fought against invasions of Egypt as the Hittites faced attacks from enemies of their own. The SEA PEOPLES, the SHERDEN PIRATES, and others were challenging the might and will of these great empires. Men like WENAMUN, traveling in the last stages of Egyptian decline, faced hostility and contempt in the very regions once firmly within the Egyptian camp.

With the decline and fall of the Ramessid line in 1070 B.C.E., the imperial designs of Egypt faded. The internal rivalries between Thebes and the Delta rulers factionalized the military and political power of the nation. City-states arose, and the nomarchs once again fortified their holdings. TANIS, SAIS, BUBASTIS, and THEBES became centers of power, but little effort was made to hold on to the imperial territories, and Egypt settled for trade pacts and cordial relations with surrounding lands.

When the Libyans came to power in 945 B.C.E., however, SHOSHENQ I made successful campaigns in Palestine and amassed vassal states. Others in that dynasty were unable to sustain the momentum, however, and Egypt did not affect the Near East but stood vulnerable and partitioned by local clans. The Twenty-third Dynasty (ca. 828–712 B.C.E.) and the nation witnessed the disintegration. The Twenty-fourth Dynasty (724–712 B.C.E.), a contemporary line of rulers, joined with their counterparts in facing the Nubian army, led into the various cities of Egypt by PIANKHI (r. 750–712 B.C.E.).

Egypt was entering the historical era called the Late Period (712–332 B.C.E.), a time of conquest by newly emerging groups in the region. The ASSYRIANS, expanding and taking older imperial territories, arrived in Egypt in the reign of TAHARQA (690–664 B.C.E.), led by ESSARHADDON. The Assyrian conquest of Egypt was short, but other rising powers recognized that the Nile Valley was now vulnerable.

The presence of large numbers of Greeks in Egypt added to the relationship of the Nile Valley and the Near East. The Greeks had NAKROTIS, a city in the Delta, and were firmly entrenched in Egypt by the Twenty-sixth Dynasty (664–525 B.C.E.). NECHO I, PSAMMETICHUS I, APRIES, and AMASIS, all rulers of this line, used other city-states and mercenaries to aid their own causes. They joined confederacies and alliances to keep the Assyrians, Persians, and other military powers at bay.

In 525 B.C.E., however, CAMBYSES, the Persian king, marched into Egypt and began a period of occupation that would last until 404 B.C.E. The Persians faced only sporadic resistance during this period. In 404 B.C.E., AMYRTAIOS ruled as the lone member of the Twenty-eighth Dynasty (404–393 B.C.E.), and the Twenty-ninth Dynasty (393–380 B.C.E.) arose as another native Egyptian royal line.

The Persians returned in 343 B.C.E. and ruled in Egypt until DARIUS III CODOMAN (335–332 B.C.E.) was defeated by ALEXANDER III THE GREAT. Egypt then became part of Alexander's empire, and PTOLEMY I SOTER (r. 304–284 B.C.E.) claimed the land and started the Ptolemaic Period that lasted until the suicide of CLEOPATRA VII. Throughout the period, the Ptolemaic rulers aligned themselves with many Greek city-states and conducted wars over Hellenic affairs. In 30 B.C.E., Egypt became a holding of the Roman Empire.

Egyptian Empire   During the Eighteenth and Nineteenth Dynasties (1550–1307 B.C.E., 1307–1196 B.C.E.), when the empire was at its zenith, Egypt ruled over an estimated 400,000 square miles of the Middle East, from Khartoum in modern Sudan to CARCHEMISH on the Euphrates River and westward to the SIWA OASIS. By the Twentieth Dynasty (1196–1070 B.C.E.), however, the empire was failing as new and vigorous nations challenged Egypt's domain.

The rulers of the Eighteenth Dynasty (1550–1307 B.C.E.), inspired by TUTHMOSIS I (r. 1504–1492 B.C.E.), began the conquest and modernized the military machine of Egypt. KAMOSE (r. 1555–1550 B.C.E.) had continued his father's war on the HYKSOS invaders of the Delta with a standing army. In the earlier times, the various nomes of the nation had answered the call of their pharaohs and had gathered small armies to join in military campaigns. Such armies, however, marched behind nomarchs and clan totems and disbanded when the crises were over. Kamose and his successor, 'AHMOSE (NEBPEHTIRÉ) (r. 1550–1525 B.C.E.), had professional soldiers, a corps of trained officers, and an army composed of regular troops. Instantly, Egypt became a first-class military power with innovative weapons and various units that terrorized neighboring states. From the start, Egypt's foreign policy was based on a firm control of Palestine, NUBIA, and Syria.

Pharaoh normally led campaigns in the field, with the Tuthmossids and the Ramessids rising to the occasion and accepting each challenge. If a pharaoh did commit himself to participation in battle, he could rely on trusted generals, veterans of previous campaigns. The fielded army was organized into divisions, each consisting of charioteers and infantry and numbering around 5,000 men or more.

The chaotic conditions of the Middle East at this time aided the single-minded Egyptians in their quest for power. The city of Babylon was in the hands of the Kassites, the warrior clans from the eastern highlands. To the north, the MITANNI Empire stretched across Iraq and Syria as far as the Euphrates (c. 1500–1370 B.C.E.). The Mitannis were Indo-European invaders who came in the wave of the migrating peoples from the Caucasus. The Mitannis were enemies of Egypt and Egypt's allies until accommodations were reached.

The HITTITES, Indo-Europeans who crossed the Taurus Mountains to found the city of Hatti, were beginning their migratory conquests. In time they would destroy the Mitanni and then become an uneasy neighbor of Egypt. The Eighteenth Dynasty cleared the Nile Valley of the Hyksos and started the era of the greatest imperial achievements. The political and military gains made during the reigns of these pharaohs were never equaled.

The Nubians south of the first cataract had responded to the Hyksos' offer of alliance and had threatened Upper Egypt. 'Ahmose (Nebpehtiré) (r. 1550–1525 B.C.E.) subdued Nubia and maintained new defenses along the Nile, refurbishing the FORTRESSES started centuries before. These fortresses were sustained by his successors, and new bastions were added. With the expulsion of the Hyksos and the subjugation of NUBIA, the Egyptians developed a consciousness of the nation's destiny as the greatest land on earth. The centuries of priests and sages had assured the Egyptians of such a destiny, and now the conquests were establishing such a future as a reality.

Tuthmosis I, the third ruler of the Eighteenth Dynasty, carved Egypt's empire out of the Near East, conquering Mediterranean lands all the way to the Euphrates River. His grandson, TUTHMOSIS III (r. 1479–1425 B.C.E.), called "the Napoleon of Egypt," was the actual architect of the empire. He recruited retaliatory military units and established garrisons and administrative policies that kept other potential powers away from Egypt's holdings and vassal states.

AKHENATEN (r. 1353–1335 B.C.E.) imperiled the empire, as the 'Amarna Period correspondence illustrates. HOREMHAB (r. 1319–1307 B.C.E.), however, began the restoration and then named RAMESSES I (r. 1307–1306 B.C.E.) as his heir. Ramesses I's son, SETI I (r.

1306–1290 B.C.E.), a trained general, and RAMESSES II (r. 1290–1224 B.C.E.), called the Great, as well as MERENPTAH (r. 1224–1214 B.C.E.), all maintained the empire, stretching for a long time from Khartoum in modern Sudan to the Euphrates River. As the SEA PEOPLES destroyed the Hittites and other cultures, Egypt remained secure. The last imperial pharaoh was RAMESSES III (r. 1194–1163 B.C.E.) of the Twentieth Dynasty. After his death, the Ramessid line collapsed slowly, and Egypt faced internal divisions and the growing menace of merging military powers.

In the Third Intermediate Period, SHOSHENQ I (r. 945–924 B.C.E.) conquered parts of Palestine once again, but these city-states broke free or were overcome by other empires. Egypt was invaded by the Syrians, Nubians, Persians, and then by ALEXANDER III THE GREAT. The Ptolemaic Period (304–30 B.C.E.) that followed ushered in a new imperial period, but these gains were part of the grand Hellenic scheme and did not provide the nation with a true empire carved out by Egypt's armies. The Romans put an end to Egypt as an independent nation in 30 B.C.E.

Egyptian language   *See* LANGUAGE.

Elephantine (Abu; Yebu)   An island at the northern end of the first cataract of the Nile near ASWAN, called Abu or Yebu by the ancient Egyptians. One mile long and one-third of a mile wide, Elephantine contained inscriptions dating to the Old Kingdom (2575–2134 B.C.E.). The name Elephantine probably was derived from the vast ivory trade conducted there, as the Nubians (modern Sudanese) brought tusks to Egypt for trade. The island and that part of Aswan served as the capital of the first nome (province) of Upper Egypt and the cult center of the god KHNUM. DJOSER (r. 2630–2611 B.C.E.) of the Third Dynasty visited the shrine of Khnum to put an end to seven years of famine in Egypt. His visit was commemorated in a Ptolemaic Period (304–30 B.C.E.) stela, the famed FAMINE STELA at SEHEL. The temple personnel of PHILAE also claimed that Djoser gave them the island for their cult center.

A NILOMETER was placed on the Elephantine Island, and others were established in the southern territories and in the Delta, to determine the height of the annual inundations. This Nilometer was a large stone building equipped with measuring devices and a staff of priests who kept records of the Nile's water levels.

Ruins from a Twelfth Dynasty (1991–1783 B.C.E.) structure and others from the Eighteenth Dynasty (1550–1307 B.C.E.) were discovered on the island. When 'AHMOSE (NEBPEHTIRÉ) of the Eighteenth Dynasty established the viceroyalty of NUBIA, the administrative offices of the agency were located on the Elephantine Island. Similar officials, given other names in various eras, had served in the same capacity in the region. The

The deities of the Elephantine and the first cataract of the Nile—Khnum, Satet, and Atet

Elephantine Island was always considered militarily strategic.

A small pyramid dating to the Old Kingdom was also discovered on the island, and the Elephantine was supposedly noted for two nearby mountains, called Tor Hapi and Mut Hapi, or Krophi and Mophi. They were venerated in early times as "the Cavern of Hopi" and the "Water of Hopi." The territory was considered "the Storehouse of the Nile" and had great religious significance, especially in connection with the god Khnum and with celestial rituals. The temple of Khnum was erected on a quay of the island and was endowed by many pharaohs.

A CALENDAR was discovered in fragmented form on the Elephantine Island, dating to the reign of TUTHMOSIS III (1479–1425 B.C.E.) of the Eighteenth Dynasty. The calendar was inscribed on a block of stone. This unique document was called the Elephantine Calendar. Another inscription was discovered on a STELA at the Elephantine. This commemorated the repairs made on a fortress of the Twelfth Dynasty and honors SENWOSRET III (r. 1878–1841 B.C.E.). The fortress dominated the island in that era, giving it a commanding sweep of the Nile at that location.

The Elephantine Papyrus, found on the island, is a document dating to the Thirteenth Dynasty (1783–1640 B.C.E.). The papyrus gives an account of that historical period. The Elephantine temple and all of its priestly

inhabitants were free of government services and taxes. The area was called "the Door to the South" and was a starting point for trade with Nubia.

Elkab (Nekheb)   A site called Nekheb by the Egyptians and one of the nation's earliest settlements, dating to c. 6000 B.C.E. Elkab is on the east bank of the Nile, 20 miles south of ESNA. The site is across the river from HIERAKONPOLIS and is related to nearby Nekhen (modern Kom el-Ahmar). Predynastic palaces, garrisoned ramparts, and other interior defenses attest to the age of the site, which was sacred to the goddess NEKHEBET, the patroness of Upper Egypt.

Elkab's citizens rose up against 'AHMOSE (NEBPEHTIRÉ) (r. 1550–1525 B.C.E.) when he started the Eighteenth Dynasty, and he interrupted the siege of the HYKSOS capital of AVARIS to put down the rebellion. The nomarchs of the area were energetic and independent. Their rock-cut tombs are in the northeast section of the city and display their vivacious approach to life and death. TUTHMOSIS III (r. 1479–1425 B.C.E.) erected the first chapel to Nekhebet, finished by his successor AMENHOTEP II. The temple of Nekhebet had a series of smaller temples attached as well as a sacred lake and a necropolis. A temple honoring the god THOTH was started by RAMESSES II (r. 1290–1224 B.C.E.). The present Nekhebet shrine dates to the Late Period (712–332 B.C.E.). In the valley of Elkab shrines of Nubian deities were discovered, and in distant wadis a shrine to a deity named SHESMETET and a temple of HATHOR and Nekhebet stand in ruins. The rock-cut tombs of 'AHMOSE-PEN NEKHEBET; 'AHMOSE, SON OF EBANA; and PAHERI are also on the site. Elkab also contains El-Hammam, called "the Bath," which was dated to the reign of Ramesses II. His stela is still evident there. AMENHOTEP III (r. 1391–1353 B.C.E.) also erected a chapel there for the sacred Bark of Nekhebet.

El-Kula   A site on the western shore of the Nile north of HIERAKONPOLIS and ELKAB, the remains of a step pyramid were discovered there, but no temple or offertory chapel was connected to the shrine. The pyramid dates to the Old Kingdom (2575–2134 B.C.E.).

El-Lisht   *See* LISHT, EL-.

"The Eloquent Peasant" of Herakleopolis   This popular account of the adventures and sayings of a commoner named KHUNIANUPU was recorded in the Twelfth Dynasty (1991–1783 B.C.E.) and is included in four New Kingdom (1550–1070 B.C.E.) papyri, now in Berlin and London. It is a classic in ancient Egyptian literature. The tale tells the story of Khunianupu who farmed land in the WADI NATRUN, in the desert territory beyond the western Delta, probably in the reign of KHETY II (Aktoy) of the Ninth Dynasty (r. 2134–2040 B.C.E.). Khunianupu decided to take his produce to market one day and entered the district called Perfefi. There he ran afoul of Djehutinakhte or Nemtynakhte, the son of a high-ranking court official, Meri. Djehutinakhte stole Khunianupu's donkeys and produce and then beat him. The peasant took his complaints to Rensi, the chief steward of the ruler, when local officials would not aid him. Taken before a special regional court, Khunianupu pleaded eloquently, using traditional moral values as arguments. Rensi was so impressed that he gave the transcript of the testimony to the ruler. The court and ruler promptly punished Djehutinakhte by taking all his lands and personal possessions and awarding them to Khunianupu.

Called "the Eloquent Peasant," announcing to the court officials the fact that "righteousness is for eternity," Khunianupu eventually made his way into the royal court, where he was applauded and honored. The ruler supposedly invited Khunianupu to address his officials and to recite on state occasions. Such tales delighted the Egyptians, who appreciated the didactic texts of their literature and especially admired the independence and courage of the commoners, whether or not they were real people or fictitious characters.

embalming *See* MORTUARY RITUALS.

Ennead A system of nine deities worshipped at HELIOPOLIS during the Early Dynastic Period (2920–2575 B.C.E.), the Ennead was part of the cosmogonic or creation myths of the region. The Ennead varies according to ancient records, but the usual deities involved were Ré-ATUM, SHU, TEFNUT, GEB, NUT, ISIS, SET, NEPHTHYS, and OSIRIS. In some lists Thoth or Horus are included. PTAH was given an Ennead in MEMPHIS also. The Ennead gathered at Heliopolis and influenced human affairs. All Enneads were called "Companies of Gods."

epagomenal days The five days at the end of the Egyptian CALENDAR that were used to commemorate the birthdays of the gods with gala festivals and ceremonies, the epagomenal days were officially added to the Egyptian calendar by IMHOTEP, the vizier of DJOSER (r. 2630–2611 B.C.E.) in the Third Dynasty. Imhotep also designed the STEP PYRAMID. He used the additional time to correct the calendar, which had been in use since the Early Dynastic Period (2920–2575 B.C.E.). The original lunar calendar did not correspond to the actual rotation of the earth around the sun, thus veering steadily away from real time. The epagomenal days were added to make the necessary adjustments, although the traditional calendar was never accurate. The birthdays celebrated on these additional periods of time were: the first day, OSIRIS; second, HORUS; third, SET; fourth, ISIS; and the fifth, NEPHTHYS. The days were actually called "the God's Birthdays."

The cosmological tradition associated with the epagomenal days concerns NUT, the sky goddess, and GEB, the earth god. ATUM, the creator, discovered that Nut and Geb were lovers and had Nut raised up to form the sky. Discovering that the goddess was pregnant, Atum said that she could give birth, but not on the traditional days of the known calendar. The god THOTH, taking pity on Nut, gambled with the other deities of Egypt and won five extra days for Nut. Nut gave birth on those days, bringing Osiris, Horus, Set, Isis, and Nephthys into the world.

Eratosthenes of Cyrene (d. 194 B.C.E.) *Greek scientist, astronomer, and poet*
He was born ca. 276 B.C.E. in CYRENE, Libya. He became the chief of the LIBRARY OF ALEXANDRIA ca. 255 B.C.E. and wrote about poetry, philosophy, literary criticism, geography, mathematics, and astronomy. His *Geographica* and *On the Measurement of the Earth* were instant classics.

Eratosthenes was reportedly the first person to measure the earth's circumference. He stated that the earth was round and assessed the circumference using geometric calculation. The length of the shadows measured at noon on the summer solstice in ALEXANDRIA and ASWAN started the calculations. Eratosthenes also mapped the world in lines of latitude and longitude. As the head of the Library of Alexandria, he tried to reform the calendar and to fix the historical dates in literature. When he went blind, Eratosthenes committed suicide by voluntary starvation ca. 194 B.C.E. He died in Alexandria.

Erment (Hermonthis; Iun-Mut; Iun-Montu; Armant) This was a site south of Thebes, called Iun-Mut, "the Pillar of Mut," or Iun-Montu, "the Pillar of Montu," in Egyptian; Hermonthis in Greek; also Armant in some lists. Erment was once the capital of the fourth nome of Upper Egypt but was replaced by Thebes as early as the Middle Kingdom (2040–1640 B.C.E.). The god MONTU had a cult center at Erment, associated with the sacred bull BUCHIS. Remains of an Eleventh Dynasty (2040–1991 B.C.E.) palace were discovered on the site. A temple from the Eighteenth Dynasty, built by Queen-Pharaoh HATSHEPSUT (r. 1473–1458 B.C.E.) and restored by TUTHMOSIS III (r. 1479–1425 B.C.E.), was also found in Erment. The BUCHEUM, the bull necropolis, is also on the site.

A major temple at Erment dates to the Middle Kingdom with later additions. NECTANEBO II (r. 363–343? B.C.E.) started a similar shrine that was completed by the Ptolemies (304–30 B.C.E.). CLEOPATRA VII (r. 51–30 B.C.E.) and PTOLEMY XV CAESARION (r. 44–30 B.C.E.) built a MAMMISI, or birth house there, with a sacred lake.

Ernutet She was an Egyptian goddess revered in the FAIYUM, near modern Medinet el-Faiyum (CROCODILOPOLIS). A temple honoring Ernutet, SOBEK, and HORUS was erected there by AMENEMHET III (r. 1844–1797 B.C.E.) and completed by AMENEMHET IV (r. 1799–1787 B.C.E.).

Esna (Iunit; Enit; Letopolis)

A site 34 miles south of LUXOR in the Upper Kingdom. Tombs from the Middle Kingdom (2040–1640 B.C.E.). Second Intermediate Period (1640–1550 B.C.E.), and New Kingdom (1550–1070 B.C.E.) were discovered there. Esna is noted, however, for the Ptolemaic Period (304–30 B.C.E.) temple. It served as a cult center for the god KHNUM and the goddess Nebtu'u. There was also a necropolis for the sacred Nile perch (*Lates niloticus*) at Esna.

The temple stood at a crossroads of oasis caravans from the Nubian (modern Sudanese) region. Construction began in the reign of PTOLEMY III EUERGETES (246–221 B.C.E.) and was completed in the mid-first century. Twenty-four columns, with various capitals, designed as imitation palms and other plants, form a stone forest in the shrine. Highly decorated, the temple of Khnum and NEITH (1) was adorned with Ptolemaic symbols and architectural styles. The ceilings have astronomical decorations, and CROCODILES and rams figure prominently. Predynastic sites, dated to ca. 13,000–10,000 B.C.E., were also found in Esna.

Essarhaddon (Assur-Akh-Iddina) (d. 669 B.C.E.) *king of Assyria and ruler of Egypt*

He reigned from 681 B.C.E. until his death. His Assyrian name was *Assur-Akh-Iddina*, which was Persian for "the God Ashur Has Given Me a Brother." He was named the heir by King Sennacherib and inherited when Sennacherib was slain. Essarhaddon marched on the rebels who had assassinated the king and then was crowned in NINEVEH. In 657 B.C.E., he attacked the frontier outposts of Egypt and took the northern capital of MEMPHIS. In 671 B.C.E., TAHARQA, the Egyptian ruler of the time, fled to NUBIA, abandoning his wife, AMUN-DYEK'HET, and their son, USHANAHURU, who were taken as slaves by the Assyrians. Two years later, Taharqa returned to Egypt to regain his throne. Essarhaddon died on his way to defeat Taharqa and was succeeded by his son ASSURBANIPAL.

eternity

This ancient Egyptian concept gave impetus to the mortuary rituals and to the religious philosophy of every period on the Nile. Early in their history the people of the Nile Valley determined that the earth reflected the cosmos, a vision glimpsed nightly by the astronomer-priests and incorporated into spiritual ideals. This led to the concept of timeless order called eternity. Two basic concepts were involved in this awareness of eternity: (1) that eternity was changeless existence and (2) that eternity was continued renewal. Time was thus viewed in terms both linear and cyclical, an important element in the reenactment of ancient ceremonies. The deity AMUN represented changeless existence, and OSIRIS depicted daily renewal, thus uniting the concepts in cultic terms.

Egyptians feared eternal darkness and unconsciousness in the afterlife because both of these conditions belied the orderly transmission of light and movement evident in the universe. They understood that death was in reality the gateway to eternity. The Egyptians thus esteemed the act of dying and venerated the structures and the rituals involved in such human adventure. HEH, called Huh in some eras, the god of eternity, was one of the original gods of the OGDOAD at HERMOPOLIS and represented eternity—the goal and destiny of all human life in Egyptian religious beliefs, a stage of existence in which mortals could achieve eternal bliss.

Eternity was an endless period of existence that was not feared by any Egyptian because it carried with it everlasting renewal. One ancient name for it was *nuheh*, but eternity was also called the *shenu*, which meant round, hence everlasting or unending, and became the form of the royal cartouches. The astral term "Going to One's *ka*," a reference to the astral being that accompanied humans through earthly life, was used in each age to express dying. The hieroglyph for a corpse was translated as "participating in eternal life." The tomb was "the Mansion of Eternity" and the deceased was an *akh*, a transformed spirit. The PYRAMID TEXTS from the Old Kingdom Period (2575–2134 B.C.E.) proclaimed that the *akh* went to the sky as the mortal remains went into the earth.

While the concept of eternity provided the impetus for the rituals and ceremonies of the mortuary rites, the arts and architecture benefited from the same vision of the afterlife. The surviving monuments of Egypt are mostly related to MORTUARY RITUALS because they were made of stone and raised as insignias of the Egyptian contemplation of eternity. The PYRAMIDS rising out of the sand at GIZA were symbols of everlasting power and transformation in death. The elaborate TOMBS and TEMPLES were introductions into the supernatural ways of the realm beyond the grave, called TUAT in passage. This concept was also the foundation of the role of the rulers of Egypt. Each pharaoh was the god RÉ while he lived upon the earth. At his death, however, he became OSIRIS, "the First of the Westerners," "the Lord of the Dead." Thus rulers were divine and destined for eternal happiness. UNIS (r. 2356–2323 B.C.E.), of the Fifth Dynasty, declared in his tomb in SAQQARA that "the stars would tremble when he dawned as a soul." Eternity was the common destination of each man, woman, and child in Egypt. Such a belief infused the vision of the people, challenging their artists to produce soaring masterpieces and providing them with a certain exuberance for life, unmatched anywhere in the ancient world.

Euclid (fl. third century B.C.E.) *"Father of Mathematics"*

Euclid was an Alexandrian scholar who served in the reign of PTOLEMY I SOTER (304–284 B.C.E.). He is best known for his *Elements of Geometry,* which he presented to Ptolemy. When the ruler declared that the work was too long and too difficult, Euclid stated that the pharaohs had "royal roads" in Egypt but that geometry could not be reached with speed or ease. Euclid systematized the entire body of mathematics, developing axiomatic proofs. He founded mathematical schools in ALEXANDRIA and was esteemed internationally.

Eurydice (fl. third century B.C.E.) *royal woman of the Ptolemaic Period*
She was the consort of PTOLEMY I SOTER (r. 304–284 B.C.E.) and the daughter of King Antipater of Macedonia. In her retinue, however, was a woman named BERENICE (1), reportedly a half sister of Ptolemy I. He set Eurydice aside and disinherited her children, Ptolemy Ceraunus, Ptolemais, Lysander, and Meleager, in favor of Berenice (1)'s offspring.

execration This was the ritualized destruction of objects or depictions of individuals, especially in Egyptian tombs or MORTUARY TEMPLES and cultic shrines. By demolishing or damaging such depictions or texts, the power of the deceased portrayed was diminished or destroyed. There are many surviving examples of execration in tombs, especially in the New Kingdom Period (1550–1070 B.C.E.). The images of Queen-Pharaoh HATSHEPSUT (r. 1473–1458 B.C.E.) were destroyed or vandalized at DEIR EL-BAHRI and in other shrines. The entire capital of AKHENATEN (r. 1353–1335 B.C.E.) was razed. The tomb of AYA (2) (1323–1319 B.C.E.) was savaged. The deceased's power in the afterlife was traditionally thought to be destroyed by such vandalism.

Execration texts were inscribed as well on pottery or figurines and listed cities and individuals in Palestine and southern Syria as enemies. Some 1,000 execration texts survive, dating from the Old Kingdom (2575–2134 B.C.E.) to CLEOPATRA VII (r. 51–30 B.C.E.). One discovered dates to ca. 1900 B.C.E. and curses Askalon, Rehab, and Jerusalem. Two other such texts, made perhaps a century later, curse the cities of Acshaf, Acre, Ashtaroth, Hazor, Myon, Laish, Mishal, Qanah, Qederesh, and Jerusalem.

exemption decrees Documents used in various eras of ancient Egypt to exempt designated temple complexes from taxes, CORVÉE labor, and other civic responsibilities, the most famous of these decrees were issued in KOPTOS.

extradition A clause included in the HITTITE ALLIANCE between RAMESSES II (r. 1290–1224 B.C.E.) of the Nineteenth Dynasty and the HITTITES, it provided that persons of rank or importance would be returned to their own rulers if they tried to flee from one territory to the other to escape punishment for their crimes. This clause, sophisticated and remarkably advanced for this period, exemplified the complex judicial aspects of Egyptian law in that period.

Eye of Horus *See* HORUS EYE.

Eye of Ré This was a complex tradition concerning the eye of the sun deity, viewed as a physical component of the god and functioning as well as a separate spiritual entity. The goddess ISIS, along with HATHOR and SEKHMET, were associated with this tradition, and the cobra, WADJET, was also part of the symbolism. AMULETS and other mystical ornaments employed the eye of Ré as a powerful insignia of protection.

F

Fag el-Gamous A necropolis site in the FAIYUM, used from 300 B.C.E., the start of the Ptolemaic Period (304–30 B.C.E.) to 400 C.E., this burial ground contains multiple burials in single graves, all containing commoners of the era. The reason for the multiple burials is being studied; it is considered likely that an epidemic, or outbreak of a disease, would have prompted such graves.

faience A glassy manufactured substance of the ancient Egyptians, the process developed by the artisans of the Nile Valley may have been prompted by a desire to imitate highly prized turquoise, or lapis lazuli, although there was a great diversity of color in the faience manufactured. The usual Egyptian faience was composed of a quartz or crystal base, covered with a vitreous, alkaline compound with calcium silicates made of lime, ash, and natron, to provide the colors and glassy finish. The Egyptians called faience *tjehenet,* which translates as "brilliant." It was used in sacred and royal insignias, AMULETS and jewelry, as well as inlay.

See also NATURAL RESOURCES.

Faiyum (Ta-she; Pa-yuum; Pa-yom) The region of Egypt once called Ta-she, "the Land of the Lakes," and used in many eras as an agricultural center, the Faiyum was also called Pa-yuum and Pa-yom. The area was settled in Paleolithic times when hunters and gatherers, attracted by the abundant game and grasses, came down from the arid plateaus of the region.

A natural depression extending along the western side of the NILE River, the Faiyum had distinct Predynastic cultures, including Faiyum A and B. These cultures date to ca. 4500 B.C.E. The BAHR YUSEF, an Arabic name meaning "Joseph's River" (not a biblical reference but one honoring an Islamic hero), left the Nile at ASSIUT, becoming a subsidiary stream. The Bahr Yusef was allowed by natural forces to enter the Faiyum but was not provided with a natural route of exit, thus inundating the area and transforming it into lush fields, gardens, and marshes. The site of CROCODILOPOLIS was the capital for the territory and served as a cult center for the god SOBEK. Located on Lake QARUN, called Me-Wer by the Egyptians, Crocodilopolis was also a haven for aquatic life forms, such as crocodiles, which were plentiful.

The rulers of the Twelfth Dynasty (1991–1783 B.C.E.) began reconstruction of this area. Seeing the need for increased agricultural output, these pharaohs started a series of hydraulic systems to reclaim acres of land. AMENEMHET I (r. 1991–1962 B.C.E.) widened and deepened the channels, bringing water to various parts of the Faiyum and establishing a true reservoir. During the annual inundations of the Nile, regulators installed at el-LAHUN controlled the Faiyum water levels. Every January the sluices at el-Lahun were closed to enable repairs to be made on bridges and walkways. AMENEMHET III (r. 1844–1797 B.C.E.) erected dikes and retaining walls, with sluices and canals that regulated the flow of water. In the process he provided Egypt with vast tracts of arable land, all of which strengthened the economic base of the nation. The Faiyum, adapted with such regulators, thus served as an emergency reservoir in periods of great floods.

One of the most beautiful regions in the Nile Valley, the Faiyum was reclaimed again and again as an agricultural site. In the Ptolemaic Period (304–30 B.C.E.)

the rulers developed the region and made it a major agricultural and population center. Olive production was encouraged as the Greek Ptolemies deemed the Faiyum olive the tastiest of all. At various times the territory extended over 4,000 square miles. PTOLEMY II PHILADELPHUS (r. 285–246 B.C.E.) renamed the nome containing the Faiyum Arsinoe, after his relative ARSINOE (2).

KARANIS, located in the Faiyum, was founded by the Ptolemies and endowed with two limestone temples. A SOBEK shrine, called Dineh el-Giba or Soknopaiou Neos, was also erected there. The famed statues of Amenemhet III graced the area as well. Medinet el-Faiyum is the modern capital of the region.

Further reading: Doxiadis, Euphrosyne, and Dorothy J. Thompson. *The Mysterious Faiyum Portraits: Faces from Ancient Egypt.* New York: Harry Abrams, 1995.

false door A TOMB element dating to the Old Kingdom (2575–2134 B.C.E.), normally fashioned out of wood or stone and serving as a monument to the deceased, false doors appeared early in MASTABAS and tombs and were designed to allow the KA of the deceased to move from the burial chamber to the chapel or shrine room, where offerings were made during MORTUARY RITUALS. Sometimes called the *ka* door, the false door was also believed to link the human deceased with TUAT, or the Underworld. This door was elaborately designed or was only a simple STELA encased in a wall. Most were narrow, stepped niches with stone slabs depicting figures of the deceased or life statues of the dead, sometimes portrayed as returning from Tuat in a resurrected state.

An example of this architectural device, a large red granite false door, was discovered in 2010 in the tomb of User, a powerful advisor to HATSHEPSUT (r. 1473–1458 B.C.E.). The door was found near KARNAK, in modern Luxor. At five feet seven inches high and 19 inches thick, the door was decorated with User's titles and with religious themes. The door had been removed from User's tomb during the Roman occupation and used in another structure.

family The ancient Egyptians placed great emphasis on the role of the family. The family was a small, independent unit consisting of father, mother, and children, although it was sometimes extended to include unmarried or widowed female relatives. The financial position of women and children was protected by law, and even after marriage women retained ownership of their own property. Commoners and aristocrats outside of the royal family did not practice polygamy.

MARRIAGE

Marriage brought official status to the individual in the local societies. Though they likely occurred, there are no records of marriage in the earlier periods of Egyptian history; the first documents of marriages appear only after the fall of the New Kingdom (1550–1070 B.C.E.) Until the Twenty-sixth Dynasty (664–525 B.C.E.), a groom asked permission to marry a woman, and the father had to give such permission; no arrangement was made concerning a "bride's price." In the Late Period (712–332 B.C.E.), however, the grooms or the families of the grooms offered silver or heads of cattle when a proposal was made.

The lack of documentation about rituals or arrangements does not mean that marriage was not held in high esteem. Couples apparently appeared before friends, family members, and neighbors and made promises to one another. In some instances, in the later eras, men and women did sign prenuptial agreements of a sort, many of which concerned the dowry in case the marriage ended in divorce.

Under the law and tradition, women had equal rights in marriage as they had under the law of the land. The status of women, however, was essentially secondary to men. Even the tomb paintings and mortuary stelae depict women as smaller than the males. An unusual aspect of such depictions is the fact that women are shown in the tombs as young and lovely, even if they died at the age of 70 or 80, often shown standing as diminutive, exquisite dolls beside their husbands' knees. NEFERTARI MERYMUT, the Great Wife of RAMESSES II (r. 1290–1224 B.C.E.), was an exception, as she had her own temple at ABU SIMBEL.

The average married couple in ancient Egypt married for love, whereas aristocrats entered into arranged matrimony in order to link powerful clan families, secure estates, or consolidate nome alliances. As they were not involved in clan politics, commoners, farmers, laborers, and fisher-folk had certain levels of freedom in choosing mates.

The average Egyptian, including the aristocracy in the nomes (provinces), did not marry their siblings but looked to partners outside of their families. The royal family, however, often intermarried in order to strengthen the position of the pharaoh and keep rivals at bay. In the earlier eras, the firstborn princess of a royal line was called "the princess with the throne in her loins." She guarded the throne, and any male wanting to mount the throne had to accept her in marriage. The disastrous genetic effects of such inbreeding naturally could have brought dynasties to ruin. However, sisters serving as wives normally did not provide the male heirs. These were borne by the lesser wives or even harem women.

One husband, one wife was the normal marriage arrangement. Commoner couples met one another, asked for permission for the marriage, arranged dowry affairs (though sometimes not), and vowed eternal fidelity as lovers. Most commoners began life together with the groom's parents on the farm or in the orchard; normally the couple would not have been able to afford a separate residence, and normally the son inherited the farm and therefore he would want to reside there. The bride learned how to run a successful household under the watchful eye of a mother-in-law and the village matriarchs. Customarily, the bride would be from the same village or city neighborhood as the groom's family; if she was not, her mother-in-law would introduce her to the local officials and to the other women of the town.

Some marriages ended in divorce, and families were broken as a result. Divorces could be started by husbands or by wives, depending upon the circumstances. In divorce settlements, it was mandated the couple had to share equally, so partners were normally cooperative in dividing up properties and assets. The dowry, however, was returned to the wife, unless she had been charged with adultery. The husband also had to give up one-third of the profits earned during the marriage. In some regions a form of alimony was also paid. The children were given into the care of the mother, unless she had disgraced herself before the community. Divorces were rare in commoner marriages both because commoners could not afford them and because relatives of the couple intervened. Egyptians were realists, despite their passionate love songs and poems. If a husband disappeared or departed, the wife stayed on the farm, aided by her brothers, and raised the family.

CHILDREN

For families on farms or engaged in fishing or hunting, offspring were vital to the survival of the family. For the artisan groups, children could carry on the traditions of the various crafts. Entire clans of officials raised their sons to carry on the same levels of service to the throne or the nome. Girls were prized as coworkers on farms or as prizes for aristocratic alliance marriages.

FAMILY LIFE

The routines of the Egyptian families were stable, especially in those expansive areas devoted almost exclusively to farming. The demands of maintaining fields and orchards, as well as caring for the domesticated animals, took up the days of the average Egyptian. The evenings, however, were usually times of visiting neighbors, going to temples, or gathering around the courtyards with one another. The upper class nome leaders, scribes, bureaucrats, and servants did not labor in the fields but handled the administrative aspects of provincial life. The courtiers residing in the PERO, the palace, also had specific duties and had to attend functions of the state or temple.

A large collection of board games was available, many of which were homemade because of economic reasons. Children played such games with their par-

ents and with one other. One member of every family also played an important role in the nightly pasttimes: That family member memorized the words of the sages of Egypt and recited the words to the family. Such texts, called didactic texts, were the most popular literary forms in every historical period of Egypt. The sages spoke of the earlier periods of Egypt, called "the time of the gods," and urged their fellow Egyptians to be models of cooperation, moderation, and courtesy. The children memorized the texts in time and carried them into the next generation.

One element present in every Egyptian home (whether that of farmers, fisher-folk, nome aristocrats, or royalty) was a shrine to their ancestors. Even if they were not fond of their relatives while they lived, deceased family members became "beloved Osirises" in death and were recognized as powerful allies of the living. A festival was held every year in the necropolis areas, and tombs were blessed by priests of the dominant regional cult. The families held picnics at the tombs and left letters there for the deceased.

When SIRIUS, the Dog Star, called Sopdu by the Egyptians, appeared in the night sky, however, married couples in the commoner caste knew that life was about to change for them and their children. The Egyptian astronomers had charted Sirius over the decades and recognized that the presence of this celestial orb signaled the beginning of the Nile floods, a period in which fields and orchards were covered with water and with the rich soil brought out of central Africa by the river. Every Egyptian was involved in some way with the irrigation projects made necessary by the floods, as dams and sluices were built to try to control the rising waters. At ASWAN, a Nilometer, installed in a large structure and staffed with hydraulic experts, measured the height of the water. The keepers of such records took notes and estimated the extent of the flooding throughout the Nile Valley. Communities were warned, and preparations, including evacuations of some areas, were made.

ROYAL SERVICE

In the Old Kingdom, starting probably with the reign of DJOSER (r. 2630–2611 B.C.E.), who built the STEP PYRAMID at SAQQARA, the average Egyptian, both men and women, obeyed the summons of the pharaoh and left their flooded lands to work on monument construction sites. The summons was part of a system called *corvée*, a French term denoting the right of the ruler to demand periods of labor from the citizens of the nation. Entire cities of people and service areas came to these construction sites, each of which helped to raise such monuments as the Pyramids. (The Step Pyramid at Saqqara and the later Pyramids at the GIZA plateau involved thousands of workers.) Egypt did not have slaves in that historical period; instead, paid labor gangs were used year-round and, in the time of the floods, the commoners who arrived ready to help build the pharaoh's tombs. When performing this royal service, couples would leave their homesteads and take their children to trusted relatives or friends.

Recent excavations at Giza have unearthed bakeries, breweries, kitchens, dining areas, dormitories, and burial sites. The men labored on the building of the pyramids, and the women worked to provide food, drink, and other necessities. At night, festivals and other entertainments were held on the site. The Egyptians bedded down as musicians serenaded them, and the days of corvée became a continual reunion of old friends and a celebration of Egypt's destiny.

When the waters began to ebb, and the corvée was over, couples were given rations of bread, beer, and other foods, and gathered their children and returned to their own fields, which were by that time ready for the hard work of planting; the Nile floods had done their job of leaving the soil enriched with vital nutrients, and the river returned to its normal patterns of flow. Days later, the Egyptians would celebrate the renourished fields and orchards in festivals.

DIET

The families of Egypt usually had diets that were varied and plentiful, especially when compared to contemporary nations or city-states. The fields yielded grains for daily loaves of bread and for porridge. Vegetables were plentiful and remarkably varied. Spices such as cinnamon and garlic were available, and orchards were rich in fruits. The Nile marshes offered fowls and more than 50 varieties of fish. Other wild birds were also available, and the herds raised across the land made meats accessible. The commoners did not dine on rich meats often, however.

DEATH

When a family member died, the common families took the corpse to the mortuary priests and brought "yesterday's linens" for mummification wrappings. That expression denotes the fact that such families could not afford new, fresh linen wrappings, so they often gathered up used cloths to provide the deceased with ample wrappings. If the family could afford them, tombs were erected in the local necropolis. The poorer families buried their loved ones in the desert areas or carried the mummified remains to Abydos or some other holy necropolis to bury them there. There was a great festival honoring the deceased, and families went to the grave sites and stayed there for the night, having picnics, watching the priests bless the graves, and listening to musicians who serenaded them under the stars.

THE EGYPTIAN MIDDLE CLASS

By the New Kingdom Period (1550–1070 B.C.E.) a distinct middle class, composed of artists, craftsmen, tavern owners, traders, and vendors, had emerged. Not tied to fields or orchards, and not sailing on the Nile as fisher-folk, these families lived in cities or towns and tended to be urbanized and a bit more sophisticated than commoners. Having shops or galleries, bakeries or breweries, they worked together to serve customers and to expand their interests.

Middle-class Egyptians were socially active and involved often in local affairs. Middle-class businessmen sometimes served also as part-time priests in the local cult temples and/or received government appointments. As their occupations demanded a certain acumen and literary awareness, these men were normally educated in temple schools or by scribes. Middle-class families built two-storied residences with slightly sloping roofs and staircases. These villas often had gardens and pools, although Egyptians did not swim in pools but instead used the area around the pools for social gatherings.

ARISTOCRATS

The nomarchs, the lords of the various provinces, led family lives that involved administration, politics, and service to the pharaoh's courts. Most held hereditary titles that dated to the earliest eras of the nation. Some were counts or barons in rank, but there were hereditary princes of aristocratic clans in the nomes, related to the present or past dynasties.

These noble families resided in one- or two-story villas, and most had pools of sparkling water in extensive gardens on large estates, surrounded by walls. Egyptians did not swim in the pools but gathered around them and dined there on occasions. In some eras, the lords of nomes had to reside at the palace of the pharaoh as the guest of the ruler. The nomarch and his wife would live well at the court, but they knew they were hostages for the cooperation and loyalty of their nome.

Entire families of aristocrats served in the administration of the nation. Some families had three or more generations of offspring holding positions of authority. REKHMIRÉ, the vizier of Tuthmosis III (r. 1479–1525 B.C.E.), belonged to such a dedicated line.

Marriages among the nomarchs and aristocrats were seldom borne out of love. Nome lords had to maintain alliances with others of their standing. As women could inherit titles, rank, properties, and assets, and as they could hold primary positions in the nomes, they were bargaining prizes for their family and were married to the candidate who brought equal or better propositions for the future.

ROYAL FAMILIES

Family life in the *pero,* or palace, of the pharaoh was regulated by the royal cult and by the need to produce an heir to the throne. Couples of royal rank did not have the freedom of the commoners to choose someone for marriage; instead, they were involved in the dynastic ambitions and realities. The throne princess, the ranking daughter of the pharaoh, had an obligation to the throne. She normally married her brother or half brother but did not usually produce the heir. The lives of the royals were always on display and always held to certain standards of education and behavior.

The palace was filled with servants, guests, diplomats, priests, and bureaucrats. Some pharaohs had a large harem and several queens. The *hemet,* or Great Wife, ruled over the other women, and she was easily recognized by the size and magnificence of her attire. The wigs worn by most Egyptians were strictly designed to signal the rank of the individual. Such Great Wives controlled populations within the palace walls. RAMESSES II (r. 1290–1224 B.C.E.) had 150 sons and an unknown number of daughters. Each of the wives or concubines had ambitions for themselves and their offspring.

See also WOMEN'S ROLE.

Further reading: Allen, Troy. *The Ancient Egyptian Family: Kinship and Social Structure.* London: Routledge, 2008; McDowell, A. G. *Village Life in Ancient Egypt: Laundry Lists and Love Songs.* Oxford, U.K.: Oxford University Press, 2002; Mertz, Barbara. *Red Land, Black Land: Daily Life in Ancient Egypt.* New York: Harper, 2007; Szpakowska, Kasia. *Daily Life in Ancient Egypt.* London: Wiley-Blackwell, 2007; Romer, John. *Ancient Lives: Daily Life in Egypt of the Pharaohs.* New York: Henry Holt, 1997; Tyldesley, Joyce. *Daughters of Isis: Women of Ancient Egypt.* New York: Penguin History, 1995.

Famine Stela   A monument located on SEHEL ISLAND south of ASWAN, where dynasties throughout Egypt's history left records, the Famine Stela dates to the Ptolemaic Period (304–30 B.C.E.) but relates a tale about a famine that took place in the reign of DJOSER (2630–2611 B.C.E.) of the Third Dynasty. The Nile had not flooded for several years, and Djoser, informed that the inundations were the prerogatives of the god KHNUM, erected a temple on ELEPHANTINE Island to appease the deity. He had a dream in which the god berated him for not taking care of the sacred on Elephantine Island. When Djoser repaired the shrine, the Nile resumed its normal inundation levels.

Farafra Oasis   A site in a vast depression in the western desert of Egypt, located south of the BAHARIA OASIS, Farafra was once called the Land of the Cow and has a modern capital named Qasr el-Farafra. The monuments from ancient eras are mostly in ruins.

Faras   This was a site near ABU SIMBEL, in NUBIA (modern Sudan), which contained temples and a rock chapel from the New Kingdom Period (1550–1070 B.C.E.). Also on the site is a temple of TUT'ANKHAMUN (r. 1333–1323 B.C.E.) from the Eighteenth Dynasty. This temple had a stylish

portico and HYPOSTYLE HALLS. The shrine originally measured 81 by 182 feet.

fate   Called *shoy* or *shai* by the ancient Egyptians, who put great stock in the appointed destiny of each individual, *shoy* was the good or ill destiny laid down for each Egyptian at the moment of his or her birth by the divine beings called the SEVEN HATHORS. If the fate was good, it was called RENENET, or Renenutet, after the goddess of generation. In the case of royal princes, the Seven Hathors always guaranteed a favorable fate. They arrived at the crib of any prince born on an unlucky day and put a lucky child in his place to avoid disaster for the individual and the nation. The CAIRO CALENDAR reflects this belief among the ancient Egyptians.

Fatieh el-Beida   A site in the Eastern Desert that was used as a QUARRY in many ages of Egyptian history, the ruins of the settlement and a temple dating to the Roman Period (after 30 B.C.E.) were discovered there.

Festival of Entering a Temple   A unique celebration associated with the cult of the god RÉ. The deity was saluted by another god, Ptah-Tenen, during the ceremonies, while priests chanted hymns and formed processions. The ritual was formally called the Testimony of Entering the House of the God, and every divine being was represented. The festival was reenacted wherever Ré's cult flourished and remained popular over the centuries.

festivals   The celebrations of ancient Egypt were normally religious in nature and held in conjunction with the lunar calendar in temples. Some festivals, mortuary or funerary in nature, were held as well in the royal and private tombs. The Egyptians liked visible manifestations of their beliefs and used festivals to make spiritual concepts meaningful. Most of the cultic celebrations were part of the calendar and were based on local temple traditions. In some periods of Egypt there were as many as 75 such celebrations observed throughout the nation annually.

Starting in the Old Kingdom (2575–2134 B.C.E.), the first, sixth, and 15th day of every month were festivals associated with the lunar CALENDAR. The seventh and 23rd days had similar significance each month. The festival of the first day was a celebration of a new moon. Such festivals and the first day were both called *pese djentiu.* The most common name for a festival was *heb,* taken from the hieroglyph for an alabaster bowl.

Festivals were designed to commemorate certain specific events in the daily lives of the people as well, particularly agriculturally oriented events. The DJJED Pillar Festival, for example, depicted growth and the movement of the sap in the trees as part of rebirth. In two separate times of the year the Festival of Wepet or

Wall paintings portraying Egyptians enjoying one of the many religious festivals held throughout each year *(Hulton Archive)*

Wepet-renpet, the New Year, was celebrated. Other festivals honored the NILE, and on those occasions elaborate shrines were floated onto the river, with flowers and hymns saluting the nurturer of all life in the land. In the fall, the death and resurrection of OSIRIS was staged at ABYDOS, and the Festival of the Sowing and Planting followed.

The purpose of most of the festivals was to allow the people to behold the gods with their own eyes and to make mythic traditions assume material reality. Particular images of the gods, sometimes carried in portable shrines, were taken out of the temple sanctuaries and carried through the streets or sailed on the Nile. STATIONS OF THE GODS were erected throughout the various cities in order to provide stages for the processions. ORACLES were contacted during these celebrations, as the images of the deities moved in certain directions to indicate negative or positive responses to the questions posed by the faithful.

One of the major Osirian festivals displayed a golden ox clad in a coat of fine black linen. The sacred animal was exhibited to the people during the season of the falling Nile, a time in which the Egyptians symbolically mourned the coming death of Osiris, a sign that the growing season was ending. When the river rose again, rituals were conducted on the banks of the Nile to greet Osiris's return. The priests used precious spices and incense to honor the god in his rejuvenated form.

The Beautiful Feast of the Valley, held in honor of the god AMUN, was staged in THEBES for the dead and celebrated with processions of the barks of the gods, as well as music and flowers. The feast of HATHOR, celebrated in DENDEREH, was a time of pleasure and intoxication, in keeping with the goddess's cult. The feast of the goddess ISIS and the ceremonies honoring BASTET at BUBASTIS were also times of revelry and intoxication. Another Theban celebration was held on the nineteenth of Paophi, the feast of OPET, during the Ramessid Period (1307–1070 B.C.E.). The feast lasted 24 days and honored AMUN and other deities of the territory. In the New Kingdom Period (1550–1070 B.C.E.), some 60 annual feasts were enjoyed in Thebes, some lasting weeks. The Feast of the Beautiful Meeting was held at EDFU at the New Moon in the third month of summer. Statues of the gods HORUS and Hathor were placed in a temple shrine and stayed there until the full moon.

The festivals honoring Isis were also distinguished by elaborate decorations, including a temporary shrine built out of tamarisk and reeds, with floral bouquets and charms fashioned out of lilies. The HARRIS PAPYRUS also attests to the fact that the tens of thousands attending the Isis celebrations were given beer, wine, oils, fruits, meats, fowls, geese, and waterbirds, as well as salt and vegetables.

These ceremonies served as manifestations of the divine in human existence, and as such they wove a pattern of life for the Egyptian people. The festivals associated with the river itself date back to primitive times and remained popular throughout the nation's history. At the first cataract there were many shrines constructed to show devotion to the great waterway. The people decorated such shrines with linens, fruits, flowers, and golden insignias.

The PALERMO STONE and other pharaonic records list festivals in honor of deities no longer known, and in honor of the nation's unification. The *heb-sed* (*see* SED) celebrations of the rulers, usually marking the 30th year of the reign, remained a vital festival throughout Egypt's history. Calendars of festivals adorned the walls of the temples at Abydos, Dendereh, Edfu, MEDINET HABU, and elsewhere in the Nile Valley.

"First Occasion"   A term used in ancient Egypt to designate the primeval times involved in cosmological traditions. Such times were called *pat, paut,* or *paut-taui.* The First Occasion denoted the appearance of the god RÉ on earth, commemorating the emergence of the deity in the PRIMEVAL MOUND. Other deities had their own First Occasions, explaining their roles as primal beings in the creative phases of human existence.

"First Under the King"   This was an Egyptian court title, denoting a particular rank and the right to rule a certain district in the ruler's name. In Upper Egypt the senior officials were also called MAGNATES OF THE SOUTHERN TEN. This affirmed their hereditary or acquired rights as an elite group of governors and judges. Most areas of Egypt had courts of law, treasuries, and land offices for settling boundary disputes after the inundations, conservation bureaus for irrigation and dike control, scribes, militias, and storage facilities for harvest. Tax assessors were normally attached to the storage offices, which were temple-operated in many provinces. The governors of the NOMES and the judges of these regional courts bore the titles of privilege and rank and reported directly to the VIZIER and to the royal treasurer in the capital. In some periods there were viziers for both the Upper and Lower Kingdoms as well as Kush, or NUBIA (modern Sudan).

flagstaffs   The symbolic poles used in the front of the PYLONS (entrance gates) at all major temples and shrines. Originally the cult centers had two insignias of the god visible in the court of the shrine. Called *senut,* the flagstaffs in their original form were adorned with religious symbols and perhaps even with clan and NOME totems. When the rulers began their massive building programs along the Nile, they copied the original cultic design pioneered in temples and in the first capital of MEMPHIS and erected tall poles upon which the particular pendant of the temple or the god could be displayed. The poles were made of pine or cedar and tipped with electrum caps.

flail A royal symbol of Egypt, used with the CROOK to represent the majesty of the rulers of the Two Lands, the flail, carried originally by the god OSIRIS, is normally displayed in the hands of deceased rulers. It was once described as a whip but now is believed to represent the *labdanisterion*, the instrument used by early goatherds in the Near East. Such a symbol, dating back to ancient times, would have had magical connotations. Agricultural workers used the flail to gather labdanum, an aromatic shrub that yielded gum and resin. The crook and the flail were both identified with the god OSIRIS's patronage of vegetation and eternal life. It associated each new ruler with the past traditions and with Osiris, thus providing the people with a clear image of an unbroken line of divinely inspired pharaohs.

Flies of Valor An Egyptian military decoration composed of golden fly forms attached to a chain, the decoration was given to Queen AH'HOTEP (1) by her son 'AHMOSE (NEBPEHTIRÉ) (r. 1550–1525 B.C.E.) during the struggle with the HYKSOS (ca. 1555–1532 B.C.E.). Queen Ah'hotep provided strong leadership as regent during 'Ahmose's first decade and made vital resources available throughout Egypt's rebellion against Hyksos domination. The actual reason for choosing the fly as a symbol of bravery is no longer understood.

Followers of Horus These were three distinct groups of ancient Egyptians, each with a unique role in the life of the nation. The first group, the supernatural, hence magical company bearing this name, were creatures who supposedly followed the god HORUS, the son of ISIS and OSIRIS, in his Predynastic battles at EDFU and in the Delta. Such companions were called *heru-shemsu* and were honored in all Horus temples. They are depicted in the tomb of KHERUEF, an official in the reign of AMENHOTEP III (1391–1353 B.C.E.). These Followers of Horus were portrayed as bearing clubs and other weapons. They served as veteran forces in the Predynastic wars, especially at Edfu. In the mortuary texts, the Followers assume even more dramatic roles. They purify the deceased on their journeys and are described in some documents as Predynastic rulers who welcome the dead into their domains of eternal bliss.

The second group of Followers is associated with the SOULS OF PE and the SOULS OF NEKHEN, the legendary godlike kings before the Early Dynastic Period (2920–2575 B.C.E.). At the various Osirian and Horus festivals, a third group called the Followers of Horus conducted mock battles with others called the FOLLOWERS OF SET. The Horus Companions always won those "wars."

The Followers of Horus, deemed both mythical companions and Predynastic rulers of legend, may have been the confederation of nome warriors who followed the Thinite ruler NARMER north in his quest to overcome the Delta and unify Egypt. They may also have been members of the ruler's retinue, accompanying him when he conducted his biennial tours of inspections along the NILE. The mock battles, in which the Followers of Horus always proved victorious, commemorated the traditions and religious commitments of earlier eras and concretized the Horus cult.

Followers of Set A group of Egyptians who participated in staged mock battles in the ceremonies honoring OSIRIS and HORUS, the Followers of Set were always overcome by the opposing members of the FOLLOWERS OF HORUS in these mock struggles because the Horus associates represented good. They were called *mesu-betesht*, or *desheru*, the red ones, and they were believed to be troublemakers who followed "the Bringer of Chaos," the god Set. They were called "the red ones" because they supposedly had red faces and red hair. The Followers of Set appeared prominently in the later part of the Nineteenth Dynasty (1307–1196 B.C.E.). They were recorded as drunkards, womanizers, and rebels who threatened the spirit of MA'AT on the Nile. Such evildoers were cursed as ones who could not reach paradise in the West (Amenti) but would rot in the desert wastes as food for the birds and rodents.

foods The dietary products of the Egyptians were among the most diverse and plentiful in ancient times. Egypt was always called "the breadbasket of the world" by contemporary nations, and the rich annual agricultural harvests in the Nile Valley were envied by the rulers of other lands. The Romans, especially, recognized the value of Egypt, and after the suicide of CLEOPATRA VII in 30 B.C.E. they guarded the land as a unique provider of the empire.

Barley and emmer were the earliest cereal crops harvested in Egypt. Emmer was used to make bread, and barley was the basis for the extensive brewing of beer. In the Ptolemaic Period (304–30 B.C.E.) wheat was introduced to the Nile fields and prospered. These fields also provided chickpeas, lentils, garlic, squashes, leeks, beans, lettuce, radishes, cabbages, cucumbers, onions, and other vegetables. Other farm products included cinnamon, carob, olives, melons, dates, figs, raisins, dom nuts, cactus figs, *seneb* berries, pomegranates, apples, grapes, and palm tree materials for eating and weaving.

Because of the herding techniques used, the Egyptians of various classes feasted on beef often or occasionally and used milk products to make cheeses and yogurts. They also ate sheep and goats and hunted for other meats. A type of oryx was prized, as were gazelles, although they were cherished as pets. Hyenas were used as hunting animals, and the deceased received their meat as offerings. When eating oxen or bulls, the Egyptians preferred the loins. Meat was grilled or stewed. Swine were regarded as contaminants

A relief of workers caging wild geese from the Nile marshes, a constant food supply for the Egyptians *(Hulton Archive)*

in many ages and forbidden as food. They were, however, raised as food or as temple offerings in ABYDOS and elsewhere.

The Nile offered more than 50 varieties of fish in its waters, and the shore marshlands provided a vast quantity of fowls. Partridges, quails, pigeons, cranes, herons, storks, ducks, geese, and doves were served as food. Chickens were introduced into the land in a later era, possibly as late as the fourth century B.C.E. The Egyptians prized eggs of other birds also. Oils were also essential ingredients, and the Egyptians used the oils from olives, sesame, and safflowers, as well as a type of butter fat. All of these foods were enjoyed in elaborate home feasts or on picnics during certain Nile festivals. Such picnics included 30 types of bread, some used as desserts. HONEY sweetened cakes and bread, and fruits accompanied indoor and outdoor meals. The wines served, as well as the beers, were flavored and graded according to strength, flavor, and quality.

fortresses A series of remarkable military installations known as *mennu* was designed to provide garrisons for troops and defensive measures on frontiers or in occupied territories. Egypt maintained such garrisons on the eastern and western territories of the Delta and in NUBIA (modern Sudan). Other fortresses were built and subsidized throughout the empire period of the New Kingdom (1550–1070 B.C.E.) and then were abandoned to other political powers along the Mediterranean Sea. Traces of fortifications at ABYDOS and HIERAKONPOLIS indicate the use of such defensive installations within the Nile Valley as well, especially in the Predynastic periods (before 3000 B.C.E.) or in times of civil unrest.

The WALL OF THE PRINCE, a series of fortresses and garrisons on the eastern and western boundaries of Egypt, dates to the reign of AMENEMHET I (1991–1962 B.C.E.), although he may have strengthened older military structures to form the defense system. Such fortresses, especially in Nubia, were directly connected to Egypt's pursuit of NATURAL RESOURCES in mines and quarries and the regulation of the active trade routes. The fortresses built in conquered lands were defensive structures that stabilized entire regions during the imperial era. The collapse of these encampments in the Levant and in other Near East regions was reported in letters from the 'AMARNA Period (1353–1335 B.C.E.), and their loss was viewed as catastrophic by allied rulers of the various territories involved.

The Nubian fortresses, the ones documented and studied in recent times, provide the modern information about Egyptian military prowess because they are still available, in ruined form, for study. Erected on rocky pinnacles overlooking the Nile and stretching south from below the first CATARACT, these structures date to the Twelfth Dynasty (1991–1783 B.C.E.) or possibly earlier in primitive forms, and they guarded the Nile between the ELEPHANTINE at ASWAN and the second cataract. A cluster of such fortresses protected Egypt's southern border.

Among them was the famed fortress at BUHEN, originally an Old Kingdom (2575–2134 B.C.E.) settlement, located on the western shore of the Nile opposite WADI HALFA. This defense worked in conjunction with Gebel Turob, a hill where Egyptians kept watch on all native movements. During the Twelfth Dynasty (1991–1783 B.C.E.) the Nubians were not allowed to move northward without permission, and the sentries on Gebel Turob were stationed in strategic positions to enforce this royal policy. Watchers ran down the hill to the fortress the instant they saw large groups of Nubians in the vicinity. The watchers were provided shelters, and several men remained on duty at all times. They were required to send detailed reports on the day's activities to the BUHEN commander and to the commander of the fort at SEMNA. A similar sentry operation was undertaken at Gebel Sheikh Suleiman, also beside Buhen.

Buhen fortress itself was fashioned out of the rocky point on which it was located and was surrounded by temples and administrative offices, a pattern used for most forts in Nubia. It was constructed of large sundried bricks, laced with granite gravel for support. A wall with external buttresses followed the contours of the ledge and then swept downward to the river. This main wall was protected by other walls and by a ditch carved out of rock and sloped with smooth sides to protect against enemy footholds. The fortress also held a garrison and storage area. Towns sometimes grew inside these garrisons.

Such fortresses were built southward into Nubia when the Egyptians expanded both their territories and their interests in the region's natural resources. The garrison outposts as erected by the ancient Egyptians included walls and towers and were positioned in strategic locations so that southern forts could signal the ones to the north in times of emergency. It is estimated that these fortresses each contained from 200 to 300 men and their families. Most of these troops were veteran units with conscripts.

Another important Middle Kingdom fort was at Semna, designated as the Middle Kingdom southern border. SENWOSRET I (r. 1971–1926 B.C.E.) started the garrison at Semna, and it was completed by SENWOSRET III (r. 1878–1841 B.C.E.). A fortress at Kumma was constructed in the normal rectangular pattern. Just below that another fortress was at URONARTI, triangular in shape. At Shalfak, on the western bank opposite the town of Sarras, another garrison was erected, and at MIRGISSA a fort built in the style of Buhen was put up to command a strategic position.

At Dabnati a fortress dominated an island, complete with towers and ramparts. Another garrison was located at the second cataract, opposite the island of Mayanarti. Buhen was at Wadi Halfa, and two more compounds were erected between that site and ANIBA, where a vast garrison was manned year round. At Kubban, Ikkur, and BIGA there were fortresses that guarded the last approach to the interior of Egypt.

BETWEEN THE ELEPHANTINE AND THE SECOND CATARACT

Ikkur	Amada
Sabaqura	Qasr Ibrim
Kuban	Armanna
Korosko	

BETWEEN THE SECOND CATARACT AND SEMNA

Buhen	Sarras
Mayanarti	Uronarti
Dorgaynarti	Semna el-Sharq
Matuka	Semna el-Gharb
Dabnarti (Tabai)	Semna el-Ganuub
Kumma	

"Forty Day Route" A trail used by the Egyptian trade caravans from the earliest periods, the route went from the KHARGA OASIS to the south, using Selima as a destination, or left from Kharga and arrived in the DAKHLA Oasis. Such caravans brought vital minerals and luxury items, such as furs, ivory, and gems, into Egypt. When the New Kingdom ended in 1070 B.C.E., the caravans were exposed to dangers on the way. The Ptolemaic Period (304–30 B.C.E.) reopened the "Forty Day Route."

Forty-two Judges Divine beings who greeted deceased Egyptians in the JUDGMENT HALLS OF OSIRIS. There the dead were called upon to give an account of their lives upon earth and to receive judgments of their worthiness to take part in eternal bliss. Each of the judges sat in council with the god OSIRIS to evaluate the mortals in their presence. The Forty-two Judges were awesome creatures, some bearing titles indicating their ferocity and purpose, such as "Long of Stride," "Eater of Shades," "Stinking Face," "Crusher of Bones," "Eater of Entrails," and "Double Lion." Some of the judges assumed other roles in the mortuary mythology, such as Hraf-hef, "HE-WHO-LOOKS-BEHIND-HIMSELF." This creature was the ancient, cranky ferryman who had to be placated by the deceased in order for him to row them to the sites of eternal bliss across the spiritual Nile.

Foundation Deposits Collections of significant spiritual symbols that were buried during the construction of a monument or royal TOMB, these objects were placed into the ground on a corner of a site or in another area deemed appropriate as the base blocks were installed. The tools bearing the names of the era's rulers were often included in the deposits.

"Friend of the King" This rank was popular in the Old Kingdom (2575–2134 B.C.E.) and conferred through out all historical periods. An honorary position, the title was used to distinguish officials who had access to the ruler as a counselor or attendant. Courtiers could also be styled as "Well-Beloved Friends" or "Nearest to the King," as in the reign of PEPI II (2246–2152 B.C.E.) of the Sixth Dynasty. These titles gave the bearer prestige in the court and were often inscribed on mor tuary stelae in the tomb complexes of the deceased honorees.

frog A symbol of generation, rebirth, and fertility in ancient Egyptian lore, the frog goddess was HEKET, depicted as a creature or as frog-headed woman. The four male gods of the OGDOAD of HERMOPOLIS were also frog-headed, a symbol of their role in the rejuvenation and fertilization of Egypt at the creation and at the annual inundation periods. Frog AMULETS were used to ensure rebirth for the deceased in the tomb.

funerals *See* MORTUARY RITUALS.

funerary cones These were small monuments fashioned out of clay and placed at the entrance of tombs, particularly in the necropolis areas of THEBES. Most popular in the Eighteenth Dynasty (1550–1307 B.C.E.) these cones were used from the Middle Kingdom (2040–1640 B.C.E.) to the Late Period (712–332 B.C.E.). The cones were stamped with the name of the deceased tomb owner. These hieroglyphic inscriptions sometimes included biographical details as well. Some 300 were placed in various tombs in the Theban necropolises, set in plaster. They possibly symbolized the sun and rebirth.

G

Gabinus, Aulus (d. 47 B.C.E.) *Roman political ally of Pompey the Great*
His loyalty to POMPEY the Great made Aulus Gabinus a political enemy of Julius CAESAR. While a tribune in 67 B.C.E., Gabinus gave Pompey unlimited command of the Roman forces handling the pirates marauding the Mediterranean at the time. He served as Pompey's representative in Egypt from 66 to 63 B.C.E. during the troubled reign of PTOLEMY XII NEOS DIONYSIUS (Auletes) (r. 80–58, 55–51 B.C.E.) and was governor of Syria 57–54 B.C.E. Aulus Gabinus died in Illyricum (the modern Adriatic area).

Gallus, Gaius Cornelius (d. 26 B.C.E.) *first Roman prefect of Egypt after the Roman occupation of the Nile Valley*
He was appointed after the suicide of CLEOPATRA VII (30 B.C.E.). An ally of Octavian, the future emperor AUGUSTUS, Gallus was renowned in Rome as a poet. He modeled his verse forms on the Alexandrian love poems popular at the time. He was also a friend of Catullus and Virgil. A manuscript in Gallus's own hand was discovered in Primio (modern Qasr Ibrim), dating to ca. 30 B.C.E. Gallus also inscribed his own name on a pyramid at GIZA. When he lost Augustus's trust and friendship in 26 B.C.E. he committed suicide.

Games *See* BOARD GAMES.

Garf Hussein This was a site south of the first cataract of the Nile that was dedicated to the MEMPHIS god PTAH. Located near WADI ALAKI, Garf Hussein had a temple dedicated to Ptah, erected by RAMESSES II (r. 1290–1224 B.C.E.) of the Nineteenth Dynasty. This shrine was built into a rocky cliff. A PYLON led to a court area, where three porticos were highly decorated. A subterranean level of the TEMPLE contained a pillared hall and five sanctuaries in the form of crosses.

Geb An Egyptian deity worshipped throughout the nation as the father of OSIRIS and the representation of the earth, he was the brother-husband of the goddess NUT, the sky, fashioned by the creator ATUM, and the son of SHU and TEFNUT. Geb was also called "the Great Cackler," a reference to the cosmic egg that contained the sun, the symbol of creation. In some temple reliefs, Geb was depicted as a man with a GOOSE on his head.

When Atum discovered that Geb and Nut had become lovers, he commanded the god Shu to separate them by raising Nut into the heavens as the sky. Geb was inconsolable, and as he wept over his loss his tears formed the oceans and seas on the earth. In reliefs he was shown in a prone position, weeping for Nut, and in his physical form representing earth's mountains and valleys. Geb was a member of the ENNEAD of HELIOPOLIS and the father of Osiris, ISIS, SET, and NEPHTHYS, given birth by Nut on the EPAGOMENAL DAYS of the calendar year along with Horus. He gave Lower Egypt to Osiris and Upper Egypt to Set after centuries of ruling alone. Geb was worshipped in Bata, a shrine in HELIOPOLIS. He was the keeper of the throne and the wise speaker of the gods. As the earth, he was sometimes colored green. In funerary texts, Geb could be an enemy of the deceased. Earthquakes were considered the result of Geb's laughter.

Gebel Abu Rowash *See* ABU ROWASH.

Gebel Adda   A site north of FARAS in NUBIA (modern Sudan), HOREMHAB (r. 1319–1307 B.C.E.) of the Eighteenth Dynasty built a temple there honoring the deities AMUN and THOTH. This shrine complex, part of the royal building programs in the territory, was graced with columned halls, a staircase, and three altar chambers for ceremonies. The Adda Stone, a worn fragment of a stela, was discovered at Gebel Adda, inscribed with demotic and Meroitic hieratic scripts. Despite lapses, the Adda Stone provided keys to the translation of Meroitic, the language of the Nubian culture that dominated that region from ca. 270 B.C.E. until 360 C.E.

Gebel Barkal   This was a site in NUBIA (modern Sudan) near the fourth cataract of the Nile. A temple honoring the god AMUN was started at Gebel Barkal by pharaohs of the Eighteenth Dynasty (1550–1307 B.C.E.) and refurbished by SETI I (r. 1306–1290 B.C.E.) of the Nineteenth Dynasty. Gebel Barkal was one of the southernmost frontiers of Egypt during the imperial period, but it was not maintained by the less powerful rulers of the later eras. TAHARQA (r. 690–664 B.C.E.) erected a temple at Gebel Barkal, which was designated as a "Holy Mountain." This temple had a rock formation in the form of a sacred cobra, as tradition states that a giant cobra emerged from a cave in the mountain to witness the religious rites conducted there.

The "Holy Mountain" promoted the cult of the god Amun through the centuries. In 750 B.C.E., PIANKHI, the heir to the Nubian throne as the son of KASHTA, led a large army into Egypt and established the Twenty-fifth Dynasty. He claimed that he had invaded Egypt because the people had forgotten Amun and were no longer worthy of the god's patronage.

Gebelein (Pi-Hathor, Pathyris)   This is the modern name for a site on the western shore of the Nile River, located south of ERMENT. The city was originally called Pi-Hathor by the Egyptians, and then named Pathyris by the Greeks. Gebelein was a center for the goddess HATHOR from ancient times. Temples were discovered there from the Eleventh and Twelfth Dynasties (2040–1783 B.C.E.), all dedicated to this popular female deity. The necropolis area of the city also contained tombs from the First Intermediate Period (2134–2040 B.C.E.). Fragments from the Gebelein temple include inscriptions from the reign of MENTUHOTEP II (2061–2010 B.C.E.), commemorating the ruler's victories. The inscriptions do not specify whether the defeated enemies were Egyptians or foreign, and they possibly refer to Mentuhotep II's victory over the city of HERAKLEOPOLIS in 2040 B.C.E.

Gebel el-Ahmar   A site called "the Red Mountain," located south of modern Cairo, where quartzite was produced for monuments, the stone in this QUARRY was reddish in color and one of the most beautiful and durable materials available to the Egyptians over the centuries. TUTHMOSIS III (r. 1479–1425 B.C.E.) fashioned a shrine out of the highly prized stone at HELIOPOLIS. Limestone was also mined in the region.

See also NATURAL RESOURCES.

Gebel el-Sidmant   This is a site south of MEIDUM, located near HIERAKONPOLIS. A large necropolis, the graves found there date to the Old Kingdom (2575–2134 B.C.E.) and the First Intermediate Period (2134–2040 B.C.E.). Gebel el-Sidmant served the city of Herakleopolis as a burial setting for the local nomarchs and the rulers of the Ninth and Tenth Dynasties.

Gebel el-Silsileh (Khenw, Khenyt, Chenu)   A quarry site south of EDFU on the western shore of the Nile called Khenw, Khenyt, or Chenu by the Egyptians, sandstone was plentiful at Gebel el-Silsileh and was mined in many periods in Egypt's history, particularly in the New Kingdom (1550–1070 B.C.E.). Three shrines were erected on the site by pharaohs of the New Kingdom: SETI I (r. 1306–1290 B.C.E.), RAMESSES II (r. 1290–1224 B.C.E.), and MERENPTAH (r. 1224–1214 B.C.E.). A stela of Ramesses II was discovered as well, and monuments of RAMESSES III (r. 1194–1163 B.C.E.), RAMESSES V (r. 1156–1151 B.C.E.), and SHOSHENQ I (r. 945–924 B.C.E.) were found there. HOREMHAB (r. 1319–1307 B.C.E.) built a temple at Gebel el-Silsileh to commemorate his victory over the Nubians (modern Sudanese) to the south. The temple of Horemhab was designed with pillared halls, a rectangular vestibule, and a sanctuary. Reliefs throughout the temple depict Horemhab's military prowess. Ceremonies of devotion to the god KHNUM were also performed in the temple. Grottoes, ruined chapels, sphinxes, and other stelae were discovered at Gebel el-Silsileh, and to the northwest there are Greco-Roman ruins.

Gebel el-Zebara   A mining area in the Eastern Desert near EDFU. SETI I (r. 1306–1290 B.C.E.) sent expeditions to dig wells in the region to provide water for local workers. He also provided other accommodations for the well-being of the territory's inhabitants. Such mines were maintained throughout the nation's history.

Gebel Mokattem   This was a limestone quarry located near modern Cairo that provided Tureh stone for royal building projects from the Early Dynastic Period (2920–2575 B.C.E.) until the collapse of the New Kingdom in 1070 B.C.E. The pyramids at GIZA and other monuments made use of the Gebel Mokattem stone, which was highly prized for its beauty and endurance in monumental sites.

See also QUARRIES.

Gebel Tingar   *See* QUARRIES.

genitals The male reproductive organs received special attention from the Egyptian embalmers in some eras. During the Nineteenth (1307–1196 B.C.E.) and Twentieth (1196–1070 B.C.E.) Dynasties, the genitals of the mummified rulers were often surgically removed. They were then embalmed and placed in separate wooden receptacles fashioned in the image of the god OSIRIS. Obviously this was done to commemorate the loss of Osiris's genitals when he was slain by the god SET. RAMESSES III (r. 1193–1163 B.C.E.) was definitely embalmed in this fashion. The Ramessids were from AVARIS, an area dedicated to the god Set, as the names of some of the rulers indicate, and it may have been in tribute to Set that the genitals were embalmed separately.

Gerze This is a site in the FAIYUM region, called the Lower Valley. A large necropolis was discovered at Gerze, dating to the Predynastic Period (before 3000 B.C.E.). A distinct Predynastic era, the Gerzean Period (also called Naqada II), stems from this region. The graves in this necropolis were oval in shape, normally fashioned out of brick or wood.

Gilukipa (fl. 14th century B.C.E.) *royal woman of the Eighteenth Dynasty*
She was the daughter of King Shuttarna or Shutama of the MITANNIS, who arrived in THEBES as part of an alliance between her father and AMENHOTEP III (r. 1391–1353 B.C.E.). When she entered Thebes in a wedding procession, Gilukipa had 317 serving women in her retinue. She entered Amenhotep III's HAREM and resided at MALKATA, on the western shore of Thebes. SCARABS were produced and distributed throughout Egypt by the royal court to commemorate her arrival on the Nile in Amenhotep III's 10th regnal year.
See also TADUKHIPA.

"Ginger" A mummified Egyptian now on display in the Egyptian Antiquities Department of the British Museum in London and dating to ca. 3300 B.C.E. or earlier, the mummified remains were named "Ginger" because of the reddish brown color of his hair. "Ginger" was not embalmed but mummified by the hot sands of his original grave on the edge of the desert. His fingernails and toenails are perfectly preserved. He was buried lying on his left side, face down, with his hands positioned under his head. His remains were covered with sand and then with rocks.

Girdle of Isis An Egyptian AMULET, called the *thet* and shaped in the form of an *ankh,* with drooping lateral arms, the Girdle of Isis was usually fashioned out of jasper, carnelian, or some other red material. The amulet was believed to confer strength upon the living and the dead. When used in funerary ceremonies, the Girdle of Isis was made of gold and was dipped in a bowl of flowers and water and then placed on the corpse.

Giza Southwest of modern Cairo, the Giza plateau served as a necropolis for the royal families of the Fourth Dynasty (2575–2465 B.C.E.). The Great Pyramid, erected on the Giza plateau in the reign of KHUFU (Cheops) (r. 2551–2528 B.C.E.), is the only surviving Wonder of the Ancient World. In addition to this pyramid, Giza offers a series of monuments and grave sites that attract thousands of visitors each year.

There are other funerary monuments or relics that predate the Fourth Dynasty at Giza, and later pharaohs erected or converted existing ones. A MASTABA at Giza, dating to the reign of DJET (r. ca. 2850 B.C.E.) in the First Dynasty, is surrounded by the graves of more than 50 servants, which denotes that the individual buried in the mastaba (as yet unidentified) was a person of considerable rank. Jar seals inscribed with the name of NINETJER (r. ca. 2670 B.C.E.), a ruler of the Second Dynasty, were found in an area south of the main necropolis. In the early eras, Giza was called Rostau and was believed to be the domain of the god Osiris, and therefore considered holy ground.

SITE DESCRIPTION

The Giza plateau was located in the Western Desert on a branch of the Nile. Such a waterway was essential for the valley rituals of the pharaohs. Boats designed to carry their mummified remains in decorated coffins arrived at Giza, and mortuary rituals were completed at a mortuary temple at Giza's shore. Causeways between the shore and the pyramids allowed for the processions of these mummies, then called "Beloved Osirises."

The three pyramids of the Fourth Dynasty (2575–2465 B.C.E.) dominate the plateau. The first, the pyramid of Khufu, known as the Great Pyramid, inspired two of his heirs, KHAFRE (Chephren) (r. 2520–2494 B.C.E.) and MENKAURÉ (Mycerinus) (r. 2490–2472 B.C.E.), to erect their tombs (the second and third dominating Fourth Dynasty pyramids) in the same fashion. Menkauré's pyramid was called the "Divine Pyramid," and the tomb contains a remarkable piece of ancient graffiti from the time of its construction, in which one of the permanent labor teams, competing with fellow workers, declared that their work was completed. The name of the team, the "DRUNKARDS OF MENKAURÉ," is clearly visible. The Great SPHINX stands in front of Khafre's pyramid, with possibly that pharaoh's features imposed upon its own. The sphinx is an image of a mythical beast with the body of a lion and the head of a man wearing the *nemes,* the royal head covering. The position of the sphinx adds to the debate about which came first, the pyramid or the sphinx, as the causeway leading to the river temple on the original shore had to be angled to move past the sphinx.

Layout of the Giza Plateau

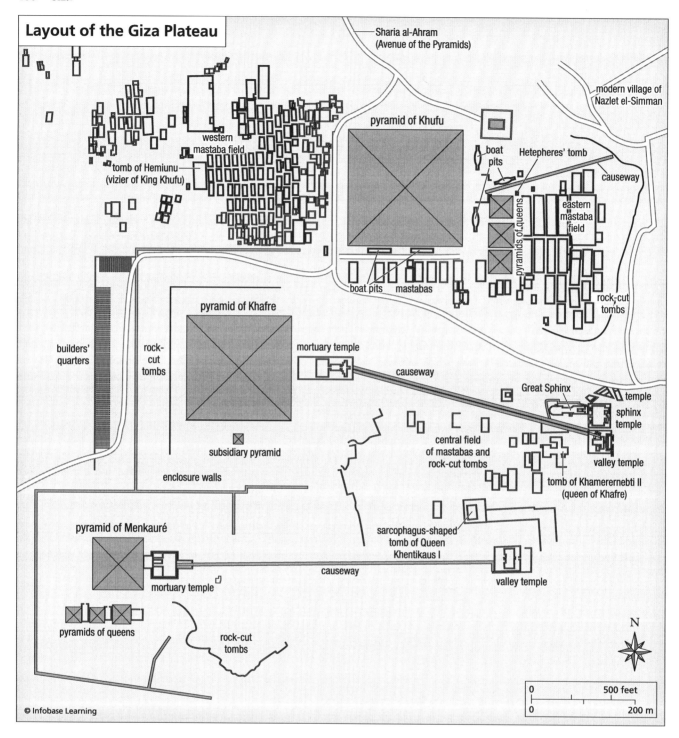

The immediate successor to Khufu, his son RA'DJEDEF (r. 2528–2520 B.C.E.), also built an immense pyramid near the plateau, at a site now called ABU ROW-ASH; his pyramid was dismantled by later pharaohs. (An expedition sent to study the site, called the "Lost Pyramid," verified the original magnificence of this tomb.)

Khufu's Great Pyramid is now called the "Stone Pyramid of Giza." In ancient times, it was referred to as the "Place of Sunrise and Sunset." The *benben*, the pyramidion, or the unique cap placed on the top of the pyramid,

was designed to catch the sun's rays the instant they appeared in the sky. Subsidiary pyramids were placed near the Great Pyramid, one belonging to Queen HET-EPHERES (1), the second to Queen MERITITES (1), and another belonging to Queen HENUTSEN. This last pyramid was provided with a mortuary chapel on the eastern side. A fourth finished pyramid has not been identified, and two other tombs were not completed. Another subsidiary pyramid was situated at the southeastern corner of the Great Pyramid. This was probably designed for

Khufu's *KA* or for his *HEB-SED* memorial, the commemoration of the decades of his reign.

Five boat pits have been discovered around the Great Pyramid, two of which contained Khufu's barks. Seventy mastabas, containing Khufu's servants, were situated nearby. There was also a harbor, linking the complex to the Nile. This harbor has now disappeared, but a half-mile wall remains to mark the perimeter. This border is called Heit el-Ghurab, "the Wall of the Crow."

The private necropolis of Giza lies east and west of the pyramids; some later burials disrupted the orderly layout of the Fourth Dynasty complex. Of particular interest is the tomb of Queen MERYSANKH (3), the consort of Khafre and the daughter of Prince KEWAB and Queen HETEPHERES (2). Remarkable scenes and a row of statues of the royal family fill this vast burial site. The tomb was originally made for Queen Hetepheres (2), who gave it to Merysankh (3) when she died young. The plateau of Giza also contains the ruins of a temple honoring HORUS of the Horizon, a local variation of the deity. This shrine was erected near the Great Sphinx by AMENHOTEP II (r. 1427–1401 B.C.E.) of the Eighteenth Dynasty. A temple of ISIS was also built in one of the subsidiary pyramids of Giza by a later dynasty.

CONSTRUCTION

There are still many questions as to the building methods used to construct the pyramids at Giza. The Egyptians did not have levers, pulleys, or wheels, yet they were able to manipulate stones weighing tons. It has been estimated that the Great Pyramid is composed of more than three million stone blocks, each weighing two and one-half tons.

It is known, however, that the pharaohs who commissioned these structures did not need to raise money to pay the workers. Egypt had no monetary system at the time, and bartering was the manner in which goods and services were obtained. It is also known that the pyramids were not constructed by slaves, as Egypt did not have slaves until the end of the Middle Kingdom (2040–1640 B.C.E.). Instead, a system called CORVÉE was in place, in which a ruler could demand the service of commoners for a period of time. Khufu and his successors would have had around 4,000 workers available during the inundation period, when men and women left their homes and went to royal construction sites to participate in the mass building projects. In addition to these citizens, there were also architects, stonemasons, engineers, and professionally trained workers laboring on these structures. It took more than 20 years to build the Great Pyramid. Bakeries, breweries, cooking areas, medical clinics, and cloth makers were located in Giza as amenities to this construction workforce.

The Great Pyramid, called "the Horizon of Khufu," originally stood 480 feet high on a 755-foot base. The pyramid was built using 3.2 million blocks of limestone, each weighing 2.5 tons. The pyramid was covered in Tureh limestone and capped with a gold pyramidion. Inside the structure, the King's Chamber was built to ease pressure from the slanted architectural design. A Grand Gallery extends through the edifice, and there is a Queen's Chamber and an Ascending Gallery. A descending corridor leads to a bedrock burial chamber, which appears to have been abandoned early in the construction. An enclosure wall was also provided for the pyramid, and a mortuary temple was erected on its eastern side. This temple is a rectangular building with a basalt pavement and an interior courtyard. A causeway originally 2,630 feet long extended from the temple, but it is now buried under the modern settlement of Nazlet el-Simman. The valley temple had a black-green basalt pavement 180 feet long and mud-brick walls 26 feet wide.

The pyramid of Khafre is smaller than Khufu's, but it was erected on a rise and appears almost the same height. Khafre's pyramid originally rose to a height of 471 feet, on a 705-foot base. There are two entrances, descending passages, an ascending corridor, and a burial chamber containing a red granite SARCOPHAGUS. One subsidiary pyramid rests beside Khafre's monument, probably the tomb of an unidentified queen. Five boat pits were also installed on the site. Khafre's mortuary temple is made of limestone and has a pillared hall, two chambers, and an open courtyard. Magazines and statuary niches completed the design. A causeway, some 1,600 feet in length, was attached to the mortuary temple. The valley temple was built as a square structure with two entrances. Magnificent statues of Khafre, protected by Horus, were discovered there.

The pyramid erected as the resting place of Menkauré is the smallest of the great pyramids of Giza and was unfinished when Menkauré died. This pyramid, however, was completed by Menkauré's son and heir, SHEPSESKHAF. Originally 240 feet high, the pyramid was erected on a 357-foot base. An unusual feature of this monument is the use of reliefs depicting the palace walls of the period on interior walls. Mycerinus's mortuary temple was made of mud bricks. The causeway that was attached to the temple was 1,995 feet in length, and another mud-brick valley temple contained fine triad statues. Three subsidiary pyramids were erected beside Menkauré's main tomb. It is believed that Queen KHAMERERNEBTY (2) was buried in one of these, but they were never finished.

The Great Sphinx was carved out of a knoll of poor-grade limestone and is 150 feet long and 75 feet high from base to crown. The modern name is a Greek version of the Egyptian *shesep-ankh,* "the living image." The sphinx is believed to represent Khafre, as Horus of the Horizon. Originally the carving was faced with Tureh limestone, and a beard extended from the chin, almost to the center of the breast. A stela dating from the reign of TUTHMOSIS IV (r. 1401–1391 B.C.E.) rests between its paws. The stela concerns a dream in which Tuthmosis IV was told to clear the monument of sand. In return, he would become pharaoh, a prediction that proved accurate.

Scholars still debate the origins of the sphinx and the identification of the face of the monument. A temple stood beside the sphinx in truly ancient times, and a document, the INVENTORY STELA, dating to the reign of Khufu, declares that Isis, Hathor, and Osiris were honored on the plateau long before the pyramids were built. The current consensus among scholars is that the head of the sphinx is that of Khafre.

ARCHAEOLOGY

The most prominent site in Egypt, the Giza plateau has been of immense interest to archaeologists from the time they first arrived with the conquering troops of French emperor Napoleon Bonaparte (1769–1821) in 1798. Archaeologists have worked almost ceaselessly at Giza since then. Italian adventurer and archaeologist Giovanni Belzoni (d. 1823) began to systematically excavate the site. He was succeeded by Italian Egyptologist Giovanni Caviglia (d. 1845) and British Egyptologists Richard Vyse (d. 1853) and John Perring (d. 1865). Caviglia is noteworthy for focusing especially on the Great Pyramid. Vyse is remembered in part for his extreme archaeological methods, including the use of explosives to secure entry into Menkauré's pyramid and the pyramid of Khafre. Auguste Mariette (d. 1881) is given a special place of honor for his work at Saqqara, but he also did important work at the sphinx site and other spots at Giza during his time in Egypt.

A vast area containing the ruins of living quarters, clinics, bakeries, breweries, and other structures has been discovered at Giza in recent years and since then archaeologists have paid particular attention to the workers' village. In 2002, the University of Chicago/Harvard University Giza Plateau Mapping Project, under Dr.

The watcher on the horizon, the Great Sphinx, the mysterious monument at Giza (Courtesy Thierry Ailleret)

Mark Lehner, discovered that some of the workers were buried on the plateau, perhaps the victims of accidents. The discoveries confirm the fact that able-bodied Egyptians provided free labor throughout the building process of the Giza plateau complexes. Dr. Zahi Hawass, director of the Supreme Council of Egyptian Antiquities, and teams of archaeologists continue to explore the Giza plateau in order to bring to light the details of the vast construction projects there.

gods and goddesses The supernatural beings who constituted the great pantheon of deities in ancient Egypt, some surviving throughout the history of the nation. These deities served as the focal points for Egyptian cultic rites and personal spiritual aspirations. The deities associated with creation and cosmological roles were worshiped throughout the Nile Valley, and others evolved from local fetish symbols and particular geographic traditions. Still others were associated with mortuary and funerary rites and were beloved throughout the land.

The Predynastic Egyptians, those living in Egypt before 3000 B.C.E., practiced animism, the spiritual and philosophical system that was mirrored in other aboriginal peoples in the region. Through animism, the belief that all objects on earth have consciousness and a personality, the earliest Egyptians sought to explain natural forces and the role human beings played in the patterns of existence. Animism defined "spirits" in creatures and in nature and included awareness of the power of the dead. Animists felt compelled to placate such spirits and to cooperate with immaterial entities that they believed populated the world.

The concerns for such "spirits" in the realm of the dead led to elaborate funerary rituals and a sophisticated belief system concerning existence beyond the grave. Animism also concerned the "spirits" of all natural things as well. The Egyptians lived with forces that they did not understand. Storms, earthquakes, floods, and dry periods all seemed inexplicable, yet the people realized acutely that natural forces had an impact on human affairs. The "spirits" of nature were thus deemed powerful, in view of the damage they could inflict on humans. It was also believed that the "spirits" of nature could inhabit human bodies.

Two other forms of worship coexisted with animism: fetishism and totemism. Fetishism recognized a spirit in an object (as in animism) but treated the object as if it had a conscious awareness of life around it and could bring to bear certain magical influences. Fetishes had two significant aspects: first as the object in which a "spirit" was present and, second, as an object used by a "spirit" for a specific purpose (such as amulets or talismans). Totems evolved out of nome emblems, a particular animal portrait or sign that signified the province's spirit. Such totems appeared on the nome staffs used in battle, and each nome unit marched behind its own leader and its own insignias in the early historical periods.

Several ancient gods and goddesses of Egypt were associated with these totems. NEITH, HATHOR, MONTU, and MIN, for example, were early examples of fertility, hunting, pleasure, and war. Fetishes appeared early in amulet form as well. The DJED pillar, which was associated with the god OSIRIS, became the nation's symbol for stability. The GIRDLE OF ISIS represented the virtues of that goddess as a wife and divine mother. As the Predynastic Period drew to a close, certain fetishes and totems were given human traits and characteristics, a process called anthropomorphism. The Egyptian gods evolved during this era, particularly Osiris, who represented not only the death of the earth at the end of the growing season but the regeneration of plant life as well. At that time, animals became objects of cultic devotion because of their particular abilities, natures, or roles on earth. Some were made divine because of the dangers they posed to humans, in an effort to constitute what is called sympathetic magic. In time, others were used as THEOPHANIES, manifestations of the gods, because of their familiar traits or characteristics.

Although the Egyptians were polytheists, they displayed a remarkable henotheism: the act of worshiping one god while not denying the existence of others. This is particularly evident in the hymns, didactic literature, and tales of Egyptians, where the devoted addressed one god as the self-created supreme being. The Egyptians had no problem with a multitude of gods, and they seldom shelved old deities in favor of new ones. The characteristics and roles of older deities were syncretized to reconcile changes or differences in beliefs, customs, and ideals of particular eras. It has been argued by some scholars, in fact, that the Egyptians were actual monotheists who viewed all other deities as *avatars*, or representations of one, self-begotten, created god. Whatever intent prompted the pantheon of gods in Egypt, some of these supernatural beings interjected remarkable concepts into the human experience. The cult of PTAH, for example, based traditions upon the use of the *logos*, and the deity AMUN, the unseen creator of life, represented profound recognition of the spiritual aspirations of humans.

FOREIGN GODS

Over the centuries alien deities were brought to Egypt and more or less welcomed. Most of these gods were introduced by conquering alien forces, which limited their appeal to the Nile population. Some came as representatives of other cultures that were eager to share their spiritual visions. Only a few of these deities attained universal appeal on their own merits. The Egyptians normally attached the deity to an existing one of long standing. The APIS bull, for example, became SERAPIS in

The opening to the temple of Isis at Philae and dating to the Ptolemaic Period (304–30 B.C.E.), displaying the favored goddess, Isis *(Courtesy Steve Beikirch)*

the Ptolemaic Period (304–30 B.C.E.) and SOKAR became part of the Ptah-Osiris cult. The major foreign gods introduced into Egypt are included in the preceding list of major deities of the nation.

Animal deities were also part of the cultic panorama of Egypt, serving as divine entities or as manifestations of a more popular god or goddess. The animals and birds so designated, and other creatures, are as follows:

ANIMALS

Creatures were believed by the Egyptians to represent certain aspects, characteristics, roles, or strengths of the various gods. Sacred bulls were manifestations of power in Egypt in every era. The gods were called "bulls" of their reign, and even the king called himself the "bull" of his mother in proclaiming his rank and claims to the throne. The bull image was used widely in Predynastic times and can be seen on maces and palettes from that period. The bulls A'A NEFER, APIS, BUCHIS, and MNEVIS were worshipped in shrines on the Nile.

Rams were also considered a symbol of power and fertility. The ram of MENDES was an ancient divine being, and AMUN of THEBES was depicted as a ram in his temples in the New Kingdom. In some instances they were also theophanies of other deities, such as KHNUM.

DEITIES OF EGYPT

Most of the major deities of Egypt are provided with individual entries because of the complex roles, cultic ramifications, and titular designations associated with their worship. The major deities of Egypt are:

AA a companion of the heart of the god Ré.

A'AH a moon deity associated with Osiris.

A'A NEFER the sacred bull of Hermonthis, associated with Montu.

AION a Greek-introduced personification of time.

AKER a lion deity associated with mortuary rituals.

AMAUNET the consort of the god Amun in the Ogdoad.

AMEMAIT a mortuary creature that devoured the unworthy dead.

AMI-UT a canine god of death, associated with Osiris.

AMUN the Theban deity who assumed national dominance, associated with Ré.

ANATH a Canaanite goddess of love and war.

ANDJETI a shepherd deity associated with Osiris.

ANHUR a solar deity of the Nile Valley.

ANI a moon deity, a form of Khons.

ANIT the consort of the god Ani.

ANTI an ancient war god of Egypt.

ANUBIS a deity of the dead, associated with Osiris.

ANUKIS the goddess of the first cataract of the Nile.

APEDEMAK a Nubian lion deity worshiped in Egypt.

APIS the sacred bull of the Ptah-Sokar-Osiris cult.

APOPHIS (1) the serpent enemy of the god Ré.

ARSENUPHIS the "Good Companion" from Nubia.

ASTARTE a Syrian war goddess adopted in the New Kingdom era in Egypt.

ASTEN a patron of wisdom and a companion of the god Thoth.

ATEN a solar deity, the solar disk.

ATUM a deity of creation.

BA a deity of the eternal paradise.

BA'EB DJET the sacred ram of Mendes.

BAIN-A'ABTIU the deities of souls transformed into baboons at dawn.

BAIT the consort of Ba.

BASTET the feline patroness of the arts and pregnant women.

BATA (1) an ancient bull deity.

BES the dwarf patron of women, childbirth, and war.

BESET the consort of Bes.

BUCHIS the sacred bull representing the deity Montu.

DEDUN the patron of Nubia, adopted by Egypt.

DOUAO the patron of diseases of the eye.

DUAMUTEF a son of Horus, patron of canopic jars.

ERNUTET a patroness of the Faiyum area.

ESYE a deity of wisdom, associated with the god Thoth.

FORTY-TWO JUDGES the patrons of the Judgment Halls of Osiris.

GEB an earth deity, husband of Nut.

HA a fertility deity, patron of deserts.

HAPI (1) the Nile god.

HAPI (2) a son of Horus, patron of the canopic jars.

HARSAPHES the creator ram deity.

HARSOMTUS a divine being from the union of Hathor and Horus.

HATHOR a solar goddess, patroness of the sky and a popular deity.

HAT-MEHIT the patroness of Mendes.

HEH the god of eternity, consort of Hauket.

HEKET the frog-headed goddess, consort of Hek.

HEMETCH the serpent demon of Tuat, or the Underworld.

HENEB an ancient deity of agriculture.

HEPTET a protectoress associated with Osiris.

HETEPHAKEF an ancient deity of Memphis.

HORUS a major solar deity, assuming many roles.

HRAF-HEF the divine ferryman of the dead.

HU a Heliopolis god of taste.

HUDET a divine, winged form of the god Ré.

IMSETY a son of Horus, guardian of the canopic jars.

INUET a consort of the god Montu.

ISIS the mother of the gods, consort of Osiris, mother of Horus.

IUSAS a consort of the god Tem.

KAMUTEF a creator deity associated with Amun.

KEBAWET an ancient goddess of eternal paradises.

KHAFTET-HIR-NEBES a protector goddess of Thebes.

KHATRU the mongoose deity (ICHNEUMON).

KHENTIAMENTIU an early funerary deity, obscured by Osiris.

KHEPER a solar deity, the form of the sun at dawn.

KHNUM a creator deity called the "Molder," patron of Elephantine Island.

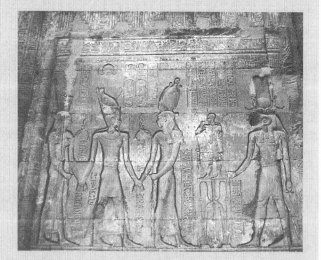

Renditions of the god Sobek and other deities attending the pharaoh shown in the center, as carved onto a temple wall *(Courtesy Steve Beikirch)*

Khons the moon deity of the Theban triad, patron of childbirth.

Ma'ahes a lion god, probably originating in Nubia.

Ma'at the goddess of cosmic awareness and order, associated with Osiris.

Mafdet a feline goddess associated with solar cults.

Mandulis a Nubian deity honored in Egypt.

Matit a lion goddess associated with the god Ré.

Mau a symbol of Bast, associated with the Persea Tree.

Mau-Taui a mortuary deity who aided Osiris.

Mehen the serpent associated with the divine bark of Ré.

Mehurt a celestial cow deity associated with the waters of heaven.

Menyu a warrior bull god called the Lord of the Desert.

Meresger a cobra goddess of the necropolis of Thebes, the Lover of Silence.

Merit the goddess of the inundation of the Nile.

Meskhent the goddess of childbirth, associated with Hathor.

Min a fertility deity, patron of desert travels and crop harvests.

Mnevis a bull god of Heliopolis.

Montu a war deity, represented by the Buchis bull.

Mut the patroness of the pharaohs.

Nebertcher a divine personification of the god Ré.

Nebetu'u a form of Hathor, worshiped in Esna.

Nefer-hor a form of the god Ptah at Memphis.

Nehah-ré a serpent associated with the solar cults.

Nehem-awit a divine form of Hathor.

Nehes a divine form of Ré.

Neith a patroness of the Delta and a war goddess.

Nekhebet a vulture goddess, patroness of Upper Egypt.

Neper a grain god associated with harvests.

Nephthys the patroness of the dead, consort of Set and mother of Anubis.

Neser a fish deity.

Nun the deity of chaos and the primordial age.

Nut the goddess of the heavens and consort of Geb.

Osiris the beloved patron of Egypt and judge of the dead.

Pakhet a lioness deity, patroness of the living and the dead.

Par a form of the god Amun, an agricultural deity.

Pneb-tawy a deity of Kom Ombo, called the Lord of the Two Lands.

Ptah the cosmogonic creator deity of all eras.

Qebehsennuf a divine son of the god Horus, and guardian of the canopic jars.

Qebhet the personification of cool water, associated with paradise.

Qebhui the god of the north wind.

Ré major solar deity of Egypt.

Renenet a goddess of good fortune.

Renpet a goddess of the calendrical year.

Repyt a lioness goddess of Egypt.

Ret an ancient solar goddess of Heliopolis.

A procession of divine beings welcoming a royal deceased (the central figure) into paradise, on a temple wall at Abydos *(Courtesy Steve Beikirch)*

Satet the patroness of the Nile and a goddess of Elephantine Island.

Sefer-t a winged lion associated with the Pyramid Texts.

Sekhmet a lioness goddess of war and consort of Ptah.

Selket a scorpion goddess associated with Isis.

Sept a deity of the twentieth nome and associated with Horus.

Shai a goddess of fate.

Sheshat a patroness of learning and records.

Shesmetet a lioness goddess, a form of Bastet.

Shu a deity of the air, associated with Atum.

Sobek a crocodile deity of the Faiyum area.

Sokar a deity of the Memphite necropolis.

Soknoknonneus a Greek deity introduced in the Ptolemaic Period.

Sutekh a canine god associated with Set.

Tait a goddess of linen, associated with Akhmin.

Tasenetnofret a goddess of Kom Ombo, called the Good Sister.

Tatenen an earth god, called the Risen Land.

Tawaret the hippopotamus goddess, patroness of childbirth.

Tchesertep a serpent demon who threatens the dead.

Tefnut the consort of Shu, a goddess representing rain, dew, and moisture.

Tem a solar deity of the setting sun.

Thoth the ancient god of learning and wisdom.

Tjet the god of Busiris and Mendes, associated with Osiris.

Typhonean animal a form of the god Set.

Unu the hare deity of Egypt.

Wa a companion of the Divine Heart of Ré.

Wadjet the cobra patroness of Lower Egypt, associated with Isis.

Wenut the rabbit goddess of Thebes.

Wepwawet the wolf god, associated with Anubis.

Weret the deity of the sky, associated with Thoth and Horus.

A pantheon of divine beings in Egypt, as displayed in the White Chapel at Karnak, including Amun and Min *(Courtesy Thierry Ailleret)*

The lion was viewed as a THEOPHANY, as was the cat, and the deities SHU, BASTET, SEKHMET, and the SPHINX were represented by one of these forms. The hare was a divine creature called Weni, or Wen-nefer. The hare was an insignia of RE's rising as the sun and also of the resurrective powers of OSIRIS. The jackal was ANUBIS, the prowler of the graves who became the patron of the dead. As WEPWAWET, the jackal was associated with the mortuary rituals at ASSIUT (or Lykonpolis) and in some regions identified with Anubis. Wepwawet was sometimes depicted as a wolf as well.

The pig, Shai, was considered a form of the god SET and appeared in some versions of the BOOK OF THE DEAD, where it was slain by the deceased. The ass or the donkey, A'a, was also vilified in the mortuary texts. The mongoose or ICHNEUMON, was called Khatru and was considered a theophany of RE as the setting sun. The mouse, Penu, was considered an incarnation of HORUS.

The leopard had no cultic shrines or rites, but its skin was used by priests of certain rank. The BABOON, Yan, was a theophany of THOTH, who greeted RE each dawn, howling at the morning sun in the deserts. The elephant, Abu, was certainly known in Egypt but is not often shown in Egyptian art or inscriptions. Ivory was prized and came from NUBIA. The HIPPOPOTAMUS, a manifestation of the god Set, was vilified. As TAWARET, however, she also had characteristics of a CROCODILE and a lion. The bat was a sign of fertility, but no cultic evidence remains to signify that it was honored. The oryx, Maliedj, was considered a theophany of the god Set.

BIRDS

The BENNU bird, a type of heron, was considered an incarnation of the sun and was believed to dwell in the sacred PERSEA TREE in HELIOPOLIS, called the soul of the gods. The PHOENIX, similar to the Bennu, was a symbol of resurrection and was honored in shrines of the Delta. The falcon (or HAWK) was associated with Horus, who had important cultic shrines at EDFU and at HIERAKON-POLIS. The vulture was NEKHEBET, the guardian of Upper Egypt. The goose was sacred to the gods GEB and AMUN and called Khenken-ur. The IBIS was sacred to the god Thoth and was found at many shrines. The ostrich was considered sacred and its unbroken eggs were preserved in temples.

See also BIRD SYMBOLS.

REPTILES

The turtle, Shetiu, was considered a manifestation of the harmful deities and was represented throughout Egyptian history as the enemy of the god Ré. The crocodile was sacred to the god SOBEK, worshiped in temples in the FAIYUM and at KOM OMBO in Upper Egypt. The cobra, WADJET, was considered an emblem of royalty and throne power. The cobra was also the guardian of Lower Egypt, with a special shrine at BUTO.

Snakes were symbols of new life and resurrection because they shed their skins. One giant snake, METHEN, guarded the sacred boat of Ré each night, as the god journeyed endlessly through the Underworld. APOPHIS, another magical serpent, attacked Ré each night. Frogs were symbols of fertility and resurrection and were members of the OGDOAD at HELIOPOLIS. The scorpion was considered a helper of the goddess Isis and was deified as SELKET.

FISH

The OXYRRHYNCHUS (2) was reviled because it ate the phallus of the god Osiris after his brother, Set, dismembered his body.

INSECTS

The BEE was a symbol of Lower Egypt. The royal titulary "King of Upper and Lower Egypt" included the hieroglyph for the bee. The SCARAB beetle in its form of Khephri, was considered a theophany of the god Ré. The image of a beetle pushing a ball of dung reminded the Egyptians of the rising sun, thus the hieroglyph of a beetle came to mean "to come into being." The scarab beetle was one of the most popular artistic images used in Egypt.

SACRED TREES

The tamarisk, called the *asher*, was the home of sacred creatures, and the coffin of the god Osiris was supposedly made of its wood. The PERSEA, at the site called Shub, was a sacred mythological tree where Ré rose each morning at HELIOPOLIS and the tree upon which the king's name was written at his coronation. The Persea was guarded by the cat goddess, and in some legends was the home of the Bennu bird. The ISHED was a sacred

The *saget*, a mythical creature found on a tomb wall in Beni Hasan and dating to the Twelfth Dynasty

tree of life upon which the names and deeds of the kings were written by the god Thoth and the goddess SESHAT.

The SYCAMORE, *nehet*, was the abode of the goddess Hathor and was mentioned in the love songs of the New Kingdom. According to legends, the LOTUS, *seshen*, was the site of the first creation when the god Ré rose from its heart. The god NEFERTEM was associated with the lotus as well. The flower of the lotus became the symbol of beginnings. Another tree was the TREE OF HEAVEN, a mystic symbol.

MYTHICAL ANIMALS

The *saget* was a mythical creature of uncertain composition, with the front part of a lion and a hawk's head. Its tail ended in a lotus flower. A painting of the creature was found in BENI HASAN, dating to the Middle Kingdom (2040–1640 B.C.E.).

AMEMAIT, the animal that waited to pounce upon condemned humans in the JUDGMENT HALLS OF OSIRIS, had the head of a crocodile, the front paws of a lion, and the rear end of a hippopotamus. Other legendary animals were displayed in Egyptian tombs, representing the peculiar nightmares of local regions. One such animal gained national prominence. This was the TYPHONEAN animal associated with the god Set, depicted throughout all periods of Egypt.

Further reading: Armour, Robert A. *Gods and Myths of Ancient Egypt.* Cairo: American University of Cairo, 2001; Frankfurter, David. *Religion in Roman Egypt.* Princeton, N.J.: Princeton University Press, 2000; Gah lin, Lucia. *Egypt: Gods, Myths and Religion.* New York: Lorenz, 2001; Hornung, Erik, and John Baines, transl. *Conceptions of God in Ancient Egypt: The One and the Many.* Ithaca, N.Y.: Cornell University Press, 1996; Kong, S. *The Books of Thoth: The Adventure that Unveiled the Mysteries of Ancient Egypt.* Victoria, B.C., Canada: Evergreen Press Pty. Ltd., 1998; Lesko, B. *The Great Goddesses of Egypt.* Norman: University of Oklahoma Press, 1999; Meeks, Dimitri. *Daily Life of the Egyptian Gods.* Ithaca, N.Y.: Cornell University Press, 1996; Quirke, Stephen. *The Cult of Ra: Sun-Worship in Ancient Egypt.* London: Thames & Hudson, 2001; Sauneron, Serge, and David Lorton, trans. *The Priests of Ancient Egypt.* New edition. Ithaca, N.Y.: Cornell University Press, 2000; Vernus, Pascal. *The Gods of Ancient Egypt.* New York: George Braziller, 1998.

God's Wife of Amun   A mysterious and powerful form of temple service that started in the first years of the Eighteenth Dynasty (1550–1307 B.C.E.) and lasted until later eras. Queen 'AHMOSE-NEFERTARI, the consort of 'AHMOSE (NEBPEHTIRÉ) (r. 1550–1525 B.C.E.), started the office of God's Wife when she served as a priestess in the cult of AMUN. The office had its predecessor in the Middle Kingdom (2040–1640 B.C.E.) when queens conducted some temple rites.

HATSHEPSUT (r. 1473–1458 B.C.E.) not only assumed this role while a queen but as pharaoh groomed her daughter, NEFERU-RÉ, to perform the same powerful office. During the time of the Eighteenth Dynasty, the God's Wife was one of the chief servants of Amun at THEBES. A relief at KARNAK depicts such a woman as destroying the enemies of "the God's Father," a male religious leader. The God's Wife also held the title of "Chieftainess of the HAREM," designating her as the superior of the vast number of women serving the temple as adoratrices, chantresses, singers, dancers, and ritual priestesses. In Karnak the God's Wife was called "the God's Mother" or "the Prophetess."

Following the fall of the New Kingdom (1070 B.C.E.), the role of God's Wife of Amun took on new political imperatives, especially in Thebes. Sharing power with the self-styled "pharaohs" in the north, the Theban high priests of Amun needed additional accreditation in order to control their realms. The women were thus elevated to prominence and given unlimited power in the name of cultic traditions.

The daughters of the high priests of Amun, such as the offspring of PINUDJEM (2), were highly educated and provided with pomp, wealth, and titles. In the Twenty-first Dynasty (1070–945 B.C.E.) the God's Wife of Amun ruled all the religious females in Egypt. AMENIRDIS, NITOCRIS, SHEPENWEPET, and others held great estates, had their names enshrined in royal cartouches, lived as celebrities, and adopted their successors. By the era of the Twenty-fifth Dynasty (712–657 B.C.E.) such women were symbolically married to the god in elaborate ceremonies. All were deified after death. The role of God's Wife of Amun did not fare well in the face of foreign invasions and subsequently lost power and faded from the scene. Before that, however, the office was a political weapon, and some God's Wives were removed from office, supplanted by new women who were members of an emerging dynastic line. The best known God's Wives, or Divine Adoratrices of Amun, were Amenirdis I and II, Nitocris, Shepenwepet I and II, and ANKHESNEFERIBRÉ. Many were buried at MEDINET HABU, and some were given royal honors in death as well as deification.

Golden Horus Name   *See* ROYAL NAMES.

goose   It was the symbol of GEB, who was called the great cackler, the legendary layer of the cosmic egg that contained the sun. The priests of AMUN also adopted the goose as a theophany of Amun in the New Kingdom. The bird was sometimes called *kenken-ur,* the Great Cackler.

government   *See* ADMINISTRATION.

granite   A stone called *mat* by the Egyptians, much prized from the earliest dynasties and quarried in almost every historical period, hard granite was *mat-rudjet.* Black granite was *mat-kemet,* and the red quarried at ASWAN was called *mat-en-Abu.* Other important mines were established periodically, and granite was commonly used in sculptures and in reliefs. It served as a basic building material for Egyptian MORTUARY TEMPLES and shrines. Made into gravel, the stone was even used as mortar for fortresses, designed to strengthen the sun-dried bricks used in the construction process. The "Lost Pyramid" of Ra'djedeef (r. 2526–2520? B.C.E.) at ABU ROWASH (near the GIZA plateau) had a base made of granite. This use of granite was extraordinary in his era.

Greatest of Seers   A title used for some of the prelates of the cultic temples at KARNAK, MEMPHIS, and HELIOPOLIS, the name refers to rituals involving ORACLES, record-keeping, and probably astronomical lore.

Greece   This ancient peninsula on the Aegean Sea was invaded around 2100 B.C.E. by a nomadic people from the north, probably the Danube Basin. The original inhabitants of the Greek mainland were farmers, seamen, and stone workers. These native populations were overcome, and the invaders merged with them to form the Greek nation, sharing mutual skills and developing city-states. The nearby Minoan culture, on Crete, added other dimensions to the evolving nation.

By 1600 B.C.E., the Greeks were consolidated enough to demonstrate a remarkable genius in the arts and in government. Democracy or democratic rule was one of the first products of the Greeks. The Greeks also promoted political theories, philosophy, architecture, sciences, and sports and fostered an alphabet and biological studies. The Greeks traveled everywhere to set up trade routes and to spread their concepts about human existence. The Romans were themselves influenced by Greek art and thought and began to conquer individual Greek city-states. By 146 B.C.E., Greece became a Roman province.

In Egypt, the Greeks were in the city of NAUKRATIS, developed during the Twenty-sixth Dynasty (664–525 B.C.E.). Naukratis was a port city, offering trade goods from around the known world and pleasures that enticed visitors. The brother of the Greek poetess Sappho lost his fortune and his health while residing in Naukratis and courting a well-known courtesan there. During the Persian occupation of the Nile (525–404 B.C.E. and 343–332 B.C.E.), Naukratis and the Greek traders did not fare well. When ALEXANDER III THE GREAT (r. 332–323 B.C.E.) defeated the Persians and founded Alexandria, Naukratis suffered economically and politically. The last dynasty in Egypt, however, was Greek, founded by PTOLEMY I SOTER (304–284 B.C.E.) and ended with CLEOPATRA VII (51–30 B.C.E.).

griffin (gryphen)   A mystical winged lion with an eagle head, used as a symbol of royal power in Egypt. NIUSERRÉ, (Izi) (r. 2416–2392 B.C.E.), of the Fifth Dynasty used the griffin in his sun temple at ABU GHUROB. The pharaoh is depicted in a relief as a griffin destroying Egypt's enemies.

H

Ha He was an ancient deity of fertility, the patron of Egypt's DESERT regions. In various historical eras, Ha was worshipped as a guardian of the nation's borders and as a protector of the pharaoh and the throne. The seventh NOME of Lower Egypt conducted cultic rituals in Ha's honor. It is possible that Ha dates to the Predynastic Period (before 3000 B.C.E.) and was worshipped by the nomadic herdsmen and their families as they entered the Nile Valley and began the first settlements on the banks of the river.

Hakoris (Khnemma'atré; Achoris) (d. 380 B.C.E.) *third ruler of the Twenty-ninth Dynasty*
He reigned from 393 until his death. Hakoris was not related to the royal family of NEPHRITES I, but upon the death of that ruler, he rose up against the designated son and heir of Nephrites I, Psammetichus. Nephrites I, originally from SAIS, had established his capital at MENDES. Hakoris took the throne there after a year of struggle and dated his reign from Nephrites I's death. He also named his own son, another Nephrites, as his successor and set out to maintain the ideals of the dynasty.

Hakoris's reign witnessed considerable rebuilding and restoration within Egypt, and he kept the Persians at bay while he lived. Concluding a treaty with Athens, Hakoris was able to field a mercenary army with Greek veterans in times of peril. The Athenian general, KHABRIAS, aided him, and the Egyptian general, Nabktnenef (NECTANEBO I) headed native troops. In Hakoris's eighth regnal year, Nabktnenef put down a troublesome revolt.

ARTAXERXES II of Persia had been struggling with GREECE but made peace in 386 and turned his attention to Egypt. In 385 and 383 B.C.E. the Persians attempted to subdue Hakoris but were stopped by the renewed Egyptian navy. Hakoris died in 380 B.C.E. and was succeeded by his son, NEPHRITES II, but General Nabktnenef overthrew the heir and took the throne as Nectanebo I, starting the Thirtieth Dynasty.

Halicarnassus A city now called Bodrum on the modern Bay of Gokova in Turkey, during the reign of XERXES I (486–466 B.C.E.), the city was ruled by Artemisia, a woman, who served also as a naval tactician. She also aided Xerxes as a counselor. HERODOTUS was a native of Halicarnassus, and Mausolas was a ruler of the city. ALEXANDER III THE GREAT took Halicarnassus, and the Ptolemaic Dynasty of Egypt (304–30 B.C.E.) ruled it during the second century B.C.E., losing it eventually to the Romans.

Hammamat *See* WADI HAMMAMAT.

"Hanging Tomb" Called Bab el-Muallaq and located south of DEIR EL-BAHRI on the western shore of THEBES. The site might be "the High Place of Inhapi" of legend, reportedly a safe haven used originally for the royal mummies in the Deir el-Bahri cache. It was so named because of its position in the cliffs.

Although many of the tombs of the pharaohs in the Valley of the Kings had been robbed and even vandalized, "Hanging Tomb" was undisturbed and was used temporarily to safeguard the mummified remains that were later moved to Deir el-Bahri.

Hapi (1) (Hopi, Hap, Hep) A personification of the NILE and a patron of the annual inundation, Hapi was the bearer of the fertile lands, nourishing both humans and the gods of Egypt. The husband of the goddess NEKHEBET, Hapi was particularly honored at the first CATARACT of the Nile. In reliefs he is depicted as a bearded man, normally painted blue or green, with full breasts for nurturing. Hapi sometimes is shown with water plants growing out of his head. He is pictured often as a double figure, representing the Blue and White Nile. Hymns in honor of Hapi speak of the Nile in cosmic terms, provoking images of the river as the spiritual stream that carried souls to Tuat, or the Underworld. These hymns express the nation's gratitude for the annual flood times and the lush fields that resulted from the deposited effluvium and mud. Annual FESTIVALS were dedicated to Hapi's inundation.

Hapi (2) A divine son of the god HORUS who is associated with the funerary rites of Egypt, he was one of the four guardians of the vital organs of the deceased in the CANOPIC JARS in tombs. Hapi was guardian of the lungs, and on the canopic jars this deity was represented by the head of a baboon. The other sons of Horus involved in canopic rituals were DUAMUTEF, QEBEHSENNUF, and IMSETY.

Hapuseneb (fl. 15th century B.C.E.) *temple official of the Eighteenth Dynasty*
He served TUTHMOSIS II (r. 1492–1479 B.C.E.) and HATSHEPSUT, the queen-pharaoh (r. 1473–1458 B.C.E.). Hapuseneb was the first prophet of AMUN at THEBES and the overseer of all of the Amunite priests of Egypt. In his era the cult of Amun was elevated to the supreme rank as Egypt's commanding deity. A noble by birth, and related to the royal clans through his mother Ah'hotep, Hap useneb supported Queen Hatshepsut when she took the throne from the heir, Tuthmosis III (1479–1425 B.C.E.). His aid pledged the Amunite temples to her cause and served as a buffer against her enemies. He directed many of her building projects and served as her counselor. Hapuseneb owned a great deal of land in both Upper and Lower Egypt. He was buried on the western shore at THEBES, and after his death was honored as well with a shrine at GEBEL EL-SILSILEH.

harem (1) This was the household of lesser wives of the king, called the *per-khenret* in ancient Egypt, a highly organized bureaucracy, functioning primarily to supply male heirs to the throne, particularly when a male heir was not born to the ranking queen. The earliest evidence for a harem dates to the Early Dynastic Period (2920–2575 B.C.E.) and to the tombs of several women found beside that of DJER (r. 2900 B.C.E.) in ABYDOS. These women were obviously lesser ranked wives who provided additional birthing opportunities. Some of these wives were also given to the pharaohs by NOME clans, as a sign of alliance. These lower ranked

wives and concubines lived in the harem. By the Sixth Dynasty (2323–2150 B.C.E.), the institution was presided over by a queen and included educational facilities for the children of the royal family and those of important officials.

In the reign of AMENHOTEP III (1391–1353 B.C.E.) of the Eighteenth Dynasty, the harem was located at MALKATA, his pleasure domain on the western bank at THEBES. AKHENATEN had a harem at 'AMARNA (1353–1335 B.C.E.) and the administration of this enclave has been well documented. Harems of this period had overseers, cattle farms, and weaving centers, which served as training facilities and as a source for materials. Harems employed SCRIBES, inspectors, and craftsmen as well as dancers and musicians to provide entertainment for royal visits. Foreign princesses were given in marriage to the Egyptian rulers as part of military or trade agreements, and they normally resided in the harem. In some eras, harem complexes were built in pastoral settings, and older queens, or those out of favor, retired there. In RAMESSES II's reign (1290–1224 B.C.E.) such a harem retirement estate was located near the FAIYUM, in MI-WER (near Kom Medinet Ghurob), started by TUTHMOSIS III (r. 1479–1425 B.C.E.).

The harem could also be a source of conspiracy. The first such recorded plot dates to the Old Kingdom and the reign of PEPI I (2289–2255 B.C.E.). An official named WENI was commissioned to conduct an investigation of a queen, probably AMTES. Because the matter was so confidential, Weni left no details as to the circumstances surrounding the investigation. A second harem intrigue occurred in the reign of AMENEMHET I (1991–1962 B.C.E.) of the Twelfth Dynasty. Amenemhet had usurped the throne, and an attempt was made on his life, as he recorded himself in his INSTRUCTIONS (also called *The Testament of Amenemhet*). The ruler fought hand to hand with the attackers, later stating that the plot to kill him stemmed from the harem before he named SENWOSRET I (the son to whom he addressed his advice) his coruler. Amenemhet died while Senwosret was away from the capital, giving rise to the speculation that he was finally assassinated by another group of plotters. There is no evidence proving that he was murdered, but the *Tale of SINUHE THE SAILOR,* dating to that period, makes such a premeditated death a key element.

The third harem plot, the best documented, took place in the reign of RAMESSES III (1194–1163 B.C.E.) of the Twentieth Dynasty. The conspiracy was recorded in the JUDICIAL PAPYRUS OF TURIN and in other papyri. TIYE (2), a minor wife of Ramesses III, plotted with 28 high-ranking court and military officials and an unknown number of lesser wives of the pharaoh to put her son, PENTAWERET, on the throne. A revolt by the military and the police was planned for the moment of Ramesses III's assassination. With so many people involved, however, it was inevitable that the plot should be exposed.

The coup was perhaps successful in its purpose. Ramesses III is believed to have died soon after. He commissioned a trial but took no part in the subsequent proceedings. The court was composed of 12 administrators and military officials. Five of the judges made the error of holding parties with the accused women and one of the men indicted during the proceedings, and they found themselves facing charges for aiding the original criminals.

There were four separate prosecutions. Tiye, who had plotted in favor of her son, Pentaweret, was executed in the first proceeding with 20 others, members of the police, military, and palace units that were supposed to rise up in support of Pentaweret when Ramesses III died. In the second prosecution, six more were found guilty and were forced to commit suicide in the courtroom. Pentaweret and three others had to commit suicide as a result of the third prosecution. During the final episode, several judges and two officers were convicted. Three of these judges lost their ears and noses. One was forced to commit suicide and one was released after a stern reprimand.

harem (2) This was the name given to the women who served in the temples of KARNAK and LUXOR as Dedicated Adoratrices of the deity Amun. Taking roles as chanters, adorers, priestesses, etc., these women were in full-time employment or served as volunteers. The GOD'S WIFE OF AMUN, a rank reserved for princesses, headed the god's vast "harem," thus regulating such service. The women were involved in such duties as officials of the temple until the end of the Third Intermediate Period (1070–712 B.C.E.). Many continued in the roles throughout the remaining historical periods of the nation.

Harkhuf (fl. 23rd century B.C.E.) *trade official of the Sixth Dynasty*
He served PEPI I (r. 2289–2255 B.C.E.), MERENRÉ (r. 2255–2246 B.C.E.), and PEPI II (r. 2246–2152 B.C.E.). Harkhuf was a leader of expeditions below the first CATARACT of the Nile. Eventually he was named the overseer of foreign soldiers in the service of the throne and the governor of the region south of ASWAN. On one such journey he captured a dancing DWARF and sent word to the ruler, Pepi II, who was a child at the time. Harkhuf informed Pepi II that he was bringing home the little one as a gift. Pepi II responded with a letter detailing the care and comfort to be extended to the dwarf. He stated that the official would be handsomely rewarded if the dwarf arrived "alive, prosperous and healthy." The governors of the various territories on the Nile were also notified by Pepi II to offer hospitality to Harkhuf and his cherished traveling companion. The text of Pepi II's letter is on a wall of Harkhuf's tomb at QUBBET EL-HAWWA at Aswan.

Harmachis (fl. eighth century B.C.E.) *prince of the Twenty-fifth Dynasty*
He was the son of SHABAKA (r. 712–698 B.C.E.) and served as the first prophet of AMUN during his father's reign. The presence of a royal prince in the Amunite temple in THEBES unified the religious and political aspects of Shabaka's claim to the throne. A quartzite statue of Harmachis was found in KARNAK.

Harnakhte (1) (fl. 10th century B.C.E.) *prince of the Twenty-second Dynasty*
He was the son of SHOSHENQ I (r. 945–924 B.C.E.). Little is known of Harnakhte's life or duties in the court of his father, but his tomb was discovered at TANIS. The burial site had been plundered, but Harnakhte's mummy was intact.

Harnakhte (2) (fl. 10th century B.C.E.) *prince of the Twenty-second Dynasty*
He was the son of OSORKON II (r. 883–855 B.C.E.). The prince was named high priest of AMUN but died young. Buried at TANIS with his father, Harnakhte was placed in a coffin that dated to the reign of RAMESSES II (1290–1224 B.C.E.). Unfortunately, the SARCOPHAGUS was too small, so Harnakhte's legs and feet reportedly were amputated to make him fit into the funerary container. Both his tomb and that of Osorkno II were despoiled by robbers.

Harnedjheriotef (fl. ca. 1760 B.C.E.) *ruler of the Thirteenth Dynasty, probably succeeding Amenemhet V*
Harnedjheriotef resided in ITJ-TAWY, the dynastic capital near the FAIYUM. His origins are undocumented, and in some lists he is called "the Asiatic," which would attest to a Canaanite ancestry. A statue and a STELA bearing his name were found in the Delta, and a commemorative stela was discovered in the city of Jericho.

Haronophis (fl. second century B.C.E.) *Egyptian who led a revolt against Ptolemy V Epiphanes (205–180 B.C.E.)*
He was a Theban who tried to restore a native dynasty in the former capital of THEBES and enlisted the aid of Upper Egypt's NOMARCHS. His rebellion, aided by the ruler CHARONNOPHIS, was short-lived and confined to the southern territory.

See also REBELS OF EGYPT.

Harpson (fl. eighth century B.C.E.) *official and sage of the Twenty-second Dynasty*
He served SHOSHENQ V (r. 773–735 B.C.E.) as a counselor at court. Harpson could trace his lineage to the reign of SHOSHENQ I and was a Libyan. He served as a prophet of the goddess NEITH (1) in the Delta. Harpson was revered for his prophecies and piety.

Harris Papyrus Called the Great, this is a document discovered in a cliff tomb at DEIR EL-MEDINA under a pile of mummies and dated to the reign of RAMESSES IV (1163–1156 B.C.E.). The most elaborate of extant papyri, this document measures some 133 feet and contains 117 columns. The Harris Papyrus provides a detailed account of the donations made to temples in Egypt by RAMESSES III (1194–1163 B.C.E.) and was deposited by Ramesses IV, his son, as part of the MORTUARY RITUALS involved in the burial of the ruler. By making such donations, Ramesses IV provided the world with a lasting tribute to his father. The largest papyrus surviving in the modern age, the Harris Papyrus provides information about three decades of Ramesses III's reign. It was written by three scribes and contains sections concerning Ramesses III's patronage of the cities THEBES, HELIOPOLIS, and MEMPHIS. Providing colorful details of the life of the assassinated Ramesses III, descriptions of the festivals celebrated by the pharaoh add historical insight to the era. The document was dated "the Sixth of Epiphi," the day of Ramesses III's death. It is now in the British Museum, in London. The papyrus was purchased by Mr. A. C. Harris of Alexandria, hence its name.

Harsaphes   A sacred ram deity bearing the Greek derivation of the original god, Her-shef, the cult center of Harsaphes was at HERAKLEOPOLIS MAGNA since ancient times. A shrine was erected in his honor as early as the First Dynasty (2920–2770 B.C.E.). His Egyptian name meant "He Who Is on His Lake," and traditions of his cult depict him as a creator god who arose out of the primeval waters. He is mentioned in the PALERMO STONE and was associated with the cults of the gods RÉ and OSIRIS.

Harsiese   (fl. ninth century B.C.E.) *prince of the Twenty-second Dynasty*
He was the son of SHOSHENQ II (r. 883 B.C.E.) and Queen NESITANEBETASHRU (I) and was made the high priest of AMUN. Harsiese also served SHOSHENQ III (r. 835–783 B.C.E.) until PEDUBASTE I (r. 828–803 B.C.E.) founded the Twenty-third Dynasty. The prince sided with Pedubaste and then tried to establish himself as the ruler. Ambitious and popular because of his lineage, he caused difficulties for the royal family in control of Egypt, but he died without having won his cause. He was buried at MEDINET HABU, at THEBES.

Harsiese's mummified skull has a hole in the forehead, made some years before his death and signaling the fact that the medical treatment that he received allowed him to survive the trauma. He was buried in a granite COFFIN taken from the tomb of HENUTMIRÉ, the sister of RAMESSES II (r. 1290–1224 B.C.E.). This coffin had a hawk-headed lid.

Harsomtus   He was a divine being resulting from the mystical union of the deities HATHOR and HORUS. A MAM-MISI, or birth house, was erected for Harsomtus at Edfu by PTOLEMY VIII EUERGETES II (r. 170–163, 145–116 B.C.E.).

Hat-Aten   This was the title of the villa of the god ATEN in the city of AKHETATEN, the 'AMARNA site founded by AKHENATEN (Amenhotep IV; r. 1353–1335 B.C.E.). Queen NEFERTITI is recorded as living in the Hat-Aten when she moved out of the royal residence after the death of one of her daughters.

Hathor   A major Egyptian deity whose name meant "the House of HORUS," in the Early Dynastic Period (2920–2575 B.C.E.), she was esteemed as the consort of a necropolis god called "the Bull of Amenti." She then became associated with Egypt's SOLAR CULT and was worshipped as the daughter of RÉ and the consort of HORUS. HARSOMTUS, popular in the Ptolemaic Period (304–30 B.C.E.) was the result of the divine union between Hathor and Horus.

This goddess was associated with the sky and with the DESERT. She also served as "the mother" of the pharaohs in early historic periods. Her titles included: Lady of the Sky, Lady of Byblos, Lady of Turquoise, Lady of Faience, Lady of the Sycamore, and Lady of the West. When the sun set at night, Hathor protected it from the evils of the darkness and sent it on its path each dawn. In this role she assumed the image of the celestial cow.

Columns honoring the goddess Hathor at Dendereh
(Courtesy Steve Beikirch)

The Dendereh temple of the goddess Hathor, once a thriving cult center *(Courtesy Steve Beikirch)*

She was depicted as a cow or as wearing a crown of horns.

Her earliest cultic traditions describe Hathor as Sekhat-Hor, an ancient forest deity who nursed the child Horus and kept him safe from the god Set. She turned herself into a cow to offer the young god better protection. A reference to her forest origins was reflected in a temple of her cult near modern DAMANHUR in the western Delta. The temple was called "the House of the Lady of the Palm Trees." As the daughter of Ré, Hathor became a lioness who slew humans until she was tricked into a drunken stupor and awoke benevolent again.

The SISTRUM, or *seses*, was her favorite instrument, and the goddess played it to drive evil from the land. The protectress of women, Hathor was also the patron of love and joy. She was a mistress of song and dance and a source of royal strength. In the DAILY ROYAL RITES, as shown on temple reliefs, Hathor nursed the ruler or his priestly representative from her breasts, thus giving him the grace of office and the supernatural powers to protect Egypt. She had a mortuary role as well that made her the protectress of the necropolis regions of the Nile. Many New Kingdom (1550–1070 B.C.E.)

shrines were erected for her cult, and her most important temple was at DENDEREH. The inscriptions there give lavish accounts of this goddess, dating to the late periods.

Hathor was associated with several minor goddesses, who were also represented as cows. She was called the mother of Ré in some rites because she carried the sun between her horns. Hathor was called the daughter of Ré because she was assimilated with the stars, which were Ré's children. She is sometimes seen in tomb paintings as a cow with stars in her belly. In every way Hathor was the benefactress of the nation, and the Egyptians celebrated her annual reunion with Horus by taking her image from Dendereh to EDFU, where the divine couple was placed in a chamber for a night. Associated with Hathor's cult was a group of divine beings called the SEVEN HATHORS. These deities dwelt in the TREE OF HEAVEN and supplied the blessed deceased with celestial food in paradise.

Hatnofer (fl. 15th century B.C.E.) *courtier of the Eighteenth Dynasty*
She was the mother of SENENMUT, a counselor of Queen-Pharaoh HATSHEPSUT (r. 1473–1458 B.C.E.). Hatnofer was married to Ramose and was possibly the mother of Amenemhet, Minhotep, and Pairy. She also had two daughters, 'Ah'hotep and Nofrethor. The mummy of Hatnofer was adorned with a scarab inscribed with the name of Hatshepsut as "the God's Wife." Two amphorae bearing the queen-pharaoh's throne name, Ma'atkaré, were also found in the tomb. Hatnofer was buried in western Thebes, in the seventh regnal year of TUTHMOSIS III (1479–1425 B.C.E.).

Hatnub A quarry for travertine, called "Egyptian alabaster," near 'AMARNA in Upper Egypt. The name meant "House of Gold." The quality of the stone and the yield of the site made Hatnub popular in all dynasties. An inscription dates quarrying activities at Hatnub to the reign of SNEFRU (2575–2551 B.C.E.), and it was active throughout the centuries and in the Roman Period. There were three main quarries at Hatnub. Also on the site are remains of enclosure walls, stoneware, and a worker's necropolis. The alabaster mined here was used for royal monuments and temples.

Hatshepsut (Ma'atkaré) (d. 1458 B.C.E.) *most successful queen-pharaoh in Egypt's history, the fifth ruler of the Eighteenth Dynasty*
She reigned as pharaoh from 1473 B.C.E. until retiring or dying. Her name meant "Foremost of the Noble Ones," and she was the surviving daughter of TUTHMOSIS I and Queen 'AHMOSE (1). She married her half brother, TUTHMOSIS II, and gave birth to a daughter, NEFERU-RÉ. Tuthmosis II's heir, TUTHMOSIS III, was the child of a lesser harem lady, ISET (1).

BIOGRAPHY

Hatshepsut was not the original heiress of the royal family; her older sister died when she was still very young, placing Hatshepsut in the royal line. Two older brothers had also been born to Tuthmosis I and Queen 'Ahmose, but they both died before they could inherit the throne.

Hatshepsut's marriage to Tuthmosis II came when she was only 20 years old. When Tuthmosis II died in 1479 B.C.E. from a severe systemic illness, Hatshepsut stood as regent for Tuthmosis III, the heir, who was very young. Contemporary records state that she "managed affairs of the land." (She had already managed court and governmental affairs for her husband, who was frail and ill for most of his life.) A few years later, however, she put aside Tuthmosis III (r. 1479–1425 B.C.E.) and declared herself pharaoh, adopting masculine attire and assuming traditional titles. Her throne name, Ma'at-Ka-Ré, meant "Truth Is the Soul of Ré." It is possible that she assumed pharaonic titles as early as Tuthmosis III's second regnal year; a tablet in the Red Chapel dates her assumption of titles to "Year Two, 2 Perit 29, Third Day of the Festival of AMUN." She had the full support of the Amunite priests and the court officials and was accepted by the people as "Beautiful to Behold." This was a complimentary salutation often given to royal women, but in her case it appears that it had physical foundations. The statues of her, even in the Osiride pose, which depicts her as a mummified goddess, portray a woman with beautiful features; all of the statues are in conformity in portraying her finely featured face.

Hatshepsut was well educated and skilled in imperial administration. It is possible that she led military campaigns in NUBIA and Palestine, and she sent a famous expedition to PUNT (probably modern Ethiopia). In Egypt, Hatshepsut renovated large sections of KARNAK and maintained an apartment there. She also erected within the temple of Amun the Red Chapel, a pair of granite OBELISKS, a formal route for religious processions, and the eighth PYLON in the southern axis of the complex. Near BENI HASAN, Hatshepsut and Tuthmosis III erected the SPEOS ARTEMIDOS, later called "the Stable of Antar" (after a warrior-poet of modern Islam). This was a rock-cut temple of the goddess PAKHET. Her CARTOUCHES at the Speos were hammered out by SETI I (r. 1306–1290 B.C.E.) and replaced with his own.

Hatshepsut also erected her major monument at DEIR EL-BAHRI on the western shore in THEBES. This is a temple with low, broad porticos and ramps within three terraces. The upper terrace has square pillars that were originally faced with Osiride statues of Hatshepsut. In the middle terrace she constructed chapels for the gods Hathor and Anubis. This terrace also contains reliefs concerning the expedition that was sent to Punt. Hatshepsut's divine birth legend is depicted here as well. In the temple reliefs her mother, 'Ahmose, is celebrated

The reserved area for Queen Hatshepsut in the complex of Karnak *(S. M. Bunson)*

through inscriptions and a portrait, designed to validate Hatshepsut's usurpation of the throne. 'Ahmose is described as having been visited by the god AMUN, who then fathered Hatshepsut in a shower of gold. The bottom terrace of this temple has bas-reliefs heralding the raising of Hatshepsut's obelisks at Karnak, and the court in front of the terraces were once believed to be two pools and MYRRH trees in ceramic pots. Deir el-Bahri was called Djeseru-Djeseru, "the Holy of Holies," and was dedicated to the gods Amun-Ré, Ré-Horakhty, HATHOR, and ANUBIS.

Hatshepsut's tomb in the VALLEY OF THE KINGS, KV20, was one of the largest in that necropolis. Corridors form half circles from the entrance to the burial chamber. The tomb was not decorated, but limestone slabs, inscribed in red, are featured. A quartzite SARCOPHAGUS was part of the funerary material. Tuthmosis I (1504–1492 B.C.E.) was also buried in Hatshepsut's tomb for a time.

Neferu-Ré, her daughter, was groomed as Hatshepsut's successor and as a GOD'S WIFE OF AMUN. Some scholars believe that Neferu-Ré married Tuthmosis III and bore him a son. Neferu-Ré's presence provided considerable support to Hatshepsut in her reign. But when Neferu-Ré died in Hatshepsut's 11th regnal year, followed by the death or disgrace of SENENMUT, who was a trusted ally and tutor to Princess Neferu-Ré, the queen-pharaoh became vulnerable.

During Hatshepsut's reign, Egypt remained secure, and she initiated many building projects. Although she professed hatred for the Asiatics in her reliefs, Hatshepsut apparently did not sponsor punitive campaigns against them. When KADESH and its allies started a revolt ca. 1458 B.C.E., Tuthmosis III led the army out of Egypt.

Toward the end of her life, Hatshepsut suffered from a tumor in her abdomen, a malignant bone disorder, arthritis, osteoporosis, and diabetes. Her gum at the site of a broken tooth contained signs of a severe abscess, which indicates that she was probably unable to eat solid foods. An infection from the abscess probably penetrated her bloodstream.

Hatshepsut's remains had been found along with another female mummy in 1903 but were not identified, and were left in a protected area. Among the funerary articles found over the years was a CANOPIC BOX containing a broken tooth, wrapped in linen. Her mummified liver was reportedly found in a quartzite box in 1881. A tomb found in Wadi Siqqet Taga el-Zeid contains her crystalline limestone SARCOPHAGUS, but there is no evidence of burial there. Today Hatshepsut is on permanent display in the Eyptian Museum in Cairo, having been identified 2007 by Dr. Zahi Hawass of the Supreme Council of Egyptian Antiquities. Dr. Hawass established laboratories in the museum to undertake DNA and other forensic studies on all mummified remains. While examining Hatshepsut's remains, the authorities discovered a broken tooth in her mouth. They were able to fit the broken tooth from the canopic box into place in her mouth and were able to make forensic diagnoses about the cause of her death.

After Hatshepsut's death, the monuments of Hatshepsut began to show signs of vandalism and desecration. Her obelisk at Karnak was plastered over (which actually protected the inscriptions over the centuries), and her figure in reliefs was also scratched away. The idea that there was a feud between Hatshepsut and Tuthmosis III, and that he was the one responsible for the damage, has been exaggerated over the centuries. The destruction of Hatshepsut's images did not take place until the 10th regnal year of Tuthmosis III, and the desecration was possibly an Amunite rejection of female rule. Hatshepsut's own chapel depicts Tuthmosis III paying honors to her upon her death.

HISTORICAL IMPACT

In her era, Hatshepsut was one of the most powerful women on earth. She brought a competence to the throne that benefited Egypt and held its enemies at bay. Her reign is of interest to scholars as a model of effective administration that was reminiscent of the pharaonic administrations of the Middle Kingdom (2040–1640 B.C.E.). Several women in ancient Egypt went on to became sole rulers of Egypt, including Sobekneferu of the Twelfth Dynasty, who ruled for only a few months before losing power, and Twosret of the Nineteenth Dynasty, who was said to have ruled for seven years but whose independent reign lasted only a little over a year. CLEOPATRA VII was coruler of Egypt for 21 years—though her corulers were believed to be in name only, as she appointed them and murdered at least one to suit her political aims—and was sole ruler for more than a decade. Unlike these women, whose reigns ended when they were forcibly removed from power, Hatshepsut ruled independently for 15 years and left Egypt stable, peaceful, and prosperous at the end of her reign.

Further reading: Greenblatt, Miriam. *Hatshepsut and Ancient Egypt.* New York: Marshall Cavendish, 2000; Tyldesley, Joyce A. *Hatchepsut: The Female Pharaoh.* London: Penguin, 1998; Whitman, Ruth. *Hatshepsut, Speak to Me.* Detroit, Mich.: Wayne State University Press, 1992.

Hatshepsut's Birth Records Hatshepsut's Birth Records is a remarkable public relations document employed by the queen-pharaoh Hatshepsut (Ma'atkaré) (r. 1473–1458 B.C.E.). Hatshepsut's name meant "Foremost of the Noble Ones," and she was the surviving daughter of TUTHMOSIS I and Queen 'AHMOSE. Hatshepsut married her half brother, TUTHMOSIS II, and gave birth to a daughter, NEFERU-RÉ. Tuthmosis II's heir, TUTHMOSIS III, was the child of a lesser harem lady, ISET (1). When Tuthmosis II died in 1479 B.C.E. from a severe systemic illness, Hatshepsut stood as regent for the heir, who was very young. Contemporary records state that she "managed affairs of the land." Approximately six years later, however, she bypassed Tuthmosis III (r. 1479–1425 B.C.E.) and declared herself PHARAOH, adopting masculine attire on occasions and assuming the traditional titles. It is possible that she assumed pharaonic titles as early as Tuthmosis III's second regnal year. (A tablet in the Red Chapel dates the assumption of these titles to "Year Two, 2 Perit 29, Third Day of the Festival of AMUN.") She had the full support of the Amunite priests and the court officials and was accepted by the people as a ruler called "Beautiful to Behold."

Hatshepsut was well educated and skilled in imperial administration. It is possible that she led military campaigns in NUBIA (modern Sudan) and Palestine, and she sent a famous expedition to PUNT (probably modern Ethiopia). During her reign, Egypt was prosperous and secure, and the people welcomed her at festivals and ceremonies. Nevertheless, her coronation mocked the traditions of the male pharaohs and made her vulnerable. When her daughter, Neferu-Ré, and her architect and supporter, SENENMUT, died, she was alone in making her claims to the throne. Early on, Hatshepsut set about making herself worthy of the throne, announcing her divine birth, a factor that would insure her acceptance and deter any opposition.

The divine birth announcement of Hatshepsut was placed firmly on the wall of her magnificent mortuary temple at DEIR EL-BAHRI, on the western shore of the Nile at THEBES (modern Luxor). There she had inscribed a message purportedly from the god Amun to the ENNEAD, a powerful group of deities. In the message, Hatshepsut claims Amun declared to the Ennead and to the people that he had long loved Queen 'AHMOSE. The biographical details of Queen 'Ahmose are scant. She was given to TUTHMOSIS I as a wife and queen by AMNHOTEP I (r. 1525–1504 B.C.E.). As Tuthmosis I was the designated heir, Queen 'Ahmose must have had rank and power on her own, according to the traditions of the royal cult. She may have been a sister of Amenhotep I or some other ranking relative. Her portraits in monuments depict a vigorous, attractive woman.

The words purportedly from Amun continue, declaring in the wall reliefs that in the beginning of his courtship of 'Ahmose he assumed the features of her pharaoh-husband but then revealed himself to her. He sired Hatshepsut and protected her when she assumed the throne. He announces: "She (Hatshepsut) is my beloved daughter, out of my own seed." The birth record thus elevated Hatshepsut far above the average Egyptian. Some pharaohs had been deified at their death, but she assumed full divine status while she lived.

By propagating this myth, Hatshepsut was ruling as wisely as any man. Queen 'Ahmose had died much earlier, so her views of the affair were irrelevant. In addition, there was a precedent in history. IMHOTEP, the vizier, architect, and physician of the reign of Djoser (r. 2630–2611 B.C.E.), as well as the designer of the Step Pyramid, was deified when he died. As High Priest of PTAH in HELIOPOLIS (On), he was called "the son of Ptah." This title was taken seriously, and Imhotep's mother was revered as having been the object of the god Ptah's affections.

Hatshepsut's Birth Records served its purpose until the king of KADESH and his allies rebelled against Egypt. Tuthmosis III marched toward the enemy with thousands of troops, and Hatshepsut, ill and elderly, disappeared from view.

Further reading: Greenblatt, Miriam. *Hatshepsut and Ancient Egypt.* New York: Marshall Cavendish, 2000; Tyldesley, Joyce A. *Hatchepsut: The Female Pharaoh.* London: Penguin, 1998; Whitman, Ruth. *Hatshepsut, Speak to Me.* Detroit, Mich.: Wayne State University Press, 1992.

Hattusilis I (Labarnas II) (d. ca. 1620 B.C.E.) *Hittite ruler and rival of Egypt*
His name meant "Man of Hattusas." He came to power ca. 1650 B.C.E. during Egypt's Second Intermediate Period (1640–1550 B.C.E.). Hattusilis started his empire by conquering various states around Hattusas, the HITTITE capital. During a battle at Aleppo, he received a fatal wound and died. He was succeeded on the Hittite throne by his grandson, MURSILIS I.

Hattusilis III (Khattushilish) (d. ca. 1250 B.C.E.) *Hittite ruler and ally of Egypt in the Nineteenth Dynasty*
He was a usurper who overthrew his nephew, Mursilus III. Involved in wars with Assyria and Egypt, Hattusilis III signed a treaty with RAMESSES II (r. 1290–1224 B.C.E.), a document that included an EXTRADITION clause. HITTITE royal women were sent to Egypt as part of

this treaty, and Egyptian priest-physicians, respected throughout the region, were provided to Hattusilis III. His wife was Queen PEDUKHIPA, who carried out a long correspondence with NEFERTARI, the consort of Ramesses II. MA'AT HORNEFRURÉ, probably the daughter of Hattusilis, married Ramesses II.

See also BENTRESH STELA.

Haukhet *See* OGDOAD.

Hawara This was a royal necropolis in the southern region of the FAIYUM used by the Twelfth Dynasty. The pyramidal complex of AMENEMHET III (r. 1844–1797 B.C.E.), a monument called the LABYRINTH that served as the MORTUARY TEMPLE of the PYRAMID, was erected on the site. The temple reportedly contained 3,000 chambers connected by winding passages, shafts, and corridors on subterranean levels. The burial chamber was fashioned out of a single piece of quartzite, estimated by HERODOTUS (in Egypt ca. 450 B.C.E.) as weighing several tons.

The Labyrinth had 12 covered courts, facing south and north. Herodotus toured the upper and lower levels and named the complex. All of the walls were decorated with reliefs, and white marble pillars were used throughout. No causeway or valley temple was erected. SOBEKNEFERU (r. 1787–1783 B.C.E.), a possible daughter of Amenemhet III, completed the pyramid for her father. Little remains of the structure. A nearby necropolis contained wax portraits and graves dating to the later Greco-Roman Periods.

hawk A symbol of the incarnation of the Spirit of Heaven in ancient Egypt, associated in most periods with the god HORUS. The eyes of the hawk were viewed as the sun and the moon, and the creature was deemed the offspring of the god TEM (1). The hawk was worshipped as a divine soul in Tema-en-Hor (modern DAMANHUR) in Lower Egypt and in HIERAKONPOLIS in Upper Egypt.

headrests The ancient Egyptian wooden or stone form used as a pillow, headrests were sometimes padded for comfort, as were the formal chairs of court ceremonies. The earliest surviving headrest dates to the Third Dynasty (2649–2575 B.C.E.), although they were used from the earliest times in the Nile Valley. Pillows were not thought to have been used in Egypt until the later dynastic periods; however, found in the newest tomb, KV63, opened in the VALLEY OF THE KINGS in 2006 and associated with TUT'ANKHAMUN (r. 1333–1323 B.C.E.), was a collection of pillows, proving the fact that at sometime in the New Kingdom era, and perhaps earlier, pillows were used.

health and disease The ancient Egyptians enjoyed a varied and plentiful diet, no matter what their status was in life. They also had access to medical care that was extraordinary for their historical periods. Their diseases and physical ailments are much like modern health problems, despite medical advances over the centuries. Hygiene was a tradition in Egypt, especially among the higher social classes. The famous wigs of Egypt developed when the aristocrats shaved their heads for the sake of cleanliness. It is considered likely that royals and nobles bathed as many as seven times a day in some seasons. The contemporaries of the Egyptians noted this sense of cleanliness, along with the Egyptian capacity for enjoying life on the Nile. Medical documents that have provided information on the medical practices include the EBERS, EDWIN SMITH, Chester BEATTY IV, and HEARST papyri.

DIET

The dietary products of the Egyptians were among the most diverse and plentiful in ancient times. Loaves of bread came out of Egyptian ovens, some spiced or sweetened. Beer foamed in jugs, and as a surviving recipe for beer clearly indicates, the varieties of beer and wine that were available contained ample alcoholic levels. Beer was a staple beverage for young and old, rich and poor. Egyptian farmers also grew chickpeas, lentils, carob, garlic, squashes, leeks, onions, beans, radishes, cucumbers, cabbage, olives, melons, dates, figs, raisins, nuts, berries, pomegranates, apples, and grapes. Raising cattle, sheep, pigs, and goats, the Egyptians made a large variety of cheeses, as well as yogurts. The upper classes enjoyed lamb and beef, and all Egyptians caught a variety of fish from the Nile. The river marshes also provided ducks, partridges, geese, quail, pigeons, and doves, and chickens were introduced into the Nile Valley. Cakes were made with honey and spices, and foods were fried in oil. The variety of cakes was remarkable, and nomes bakers vied with one another, especially at festivals.

MEDICINE AND AVAILABLE CARE

The science of medicine was called "the necessary art" in Egypt. It was supported by the *per-ankh,* "the House of Life," and by schools of training and research. Most general practitioners of Egyptian medicine were priests educated in medical techniques ranging from trauma to gynecology, and many specialized in particular fields. The Egyptian medical practitioners understood the purpose of the pulse, blood, tears, mucus, urine, and semen, and their anatomical derivations from the earliest periods.

Because of the mythological and magical aspects attributed to the practice of medicine in Egypt by the Greek historians, scholars have not bestowed honor upon the practices fostered in the Nile Valley. The Greeks honored many of the early Egyptian priest-physicians, however, especially IMHOTEP (fl. ca. 27th century B.C.E.) of the Third Dynasty, whom they equated with their god Asclepius. When they recorded the Egyptian medical customs and procedures as history, the Greeks included the magic and incantations used by the PRIESTS, which made medicine appear trivial or a superstitious aspect of Egyptian life. Magical spells were indeed a part of Egyptian medicine, thus the Greeks' disdain was not totally unfounded. Nevertheless, scholars have long recognized that the Egyptians carefully observed various ailments, injuries, and physical deformities and offered many prescriptions for their relief.

Generally speaking, the citizens of Egypt were a vigorous and resilient people. They faced many illnesses, however, all of which can be studied in the forensic examination of mummified remains. In most of the older royal mummies, for example, definite signs of bone damage, scoliosis, osteoporosis, and arthritis are present. If such royal individuals suffered bone diseases, one can assume that the commoners, involved in the endless labors of farms and orchards, would have greater damage. The physicians of Egypt, however, were able to provide sedatives and other medicines for such bone wear. More than 8,000 pharmaceutical prescriptions were available. When bones were broken, splints, casts, and bandages aided recovery. Mummies do carry indications of the healing of bones during their lifetimes.

DIAGNOSIS

Diagnostic procedures for injuries and diseases were common and extensive in Egyptian medical practice. The physicians consulted texts and made their own observations. Each physician listed the symptoms present in a patient and then decided whether he had the skill to treat that condition. If a priest determined that a cure was possible, he reconsidered the procedures, medicines, or therapeutic remedies available and acted accordingly. The physicians understood that the pulse was "the Speaker of the HEART," and they interpreted the condition known as angina. They were also aware of the relationship between the nervous system and voluntary movements. The physicians could identify lesions of the head, fractures of the vertebrae, and other complex conditions. Operations were performed on the brain, and skulls recovered from graves and tombs indicate that the Egyptian patients lived through such operations and survived for years afterward. The human brain was not saved during the embalming process, however, deemed unworthy of protection in the canopic jars. Brains of the deceased were normally destroyed or savaged in the actual embalming procedure.

TRAUMA CARE

The priest-physicians were experts in trauma care, taking part in the construction sites of monuments and treating accident victims on the site. Medical clinics were opened in cities and towns, and some physicians made the rounds of farm regions, often caring for both people and animals. In the early eras such physicians had little medical science to offer, but that was later remedied by great physicians such as Imhotep, the builder of the STEP PYRAMID for DJOSER (r. 2630–2611 B.C.E.), who also wrote about symptoms, diagnoses, and treatments.

Trauma care in Egypt included the treatment of various bone injuries, with cranial fractures frequent. Surgical procedures were provided, including the insertion of rolled linens for fractured noses and the splinting of bones with bark, wood, linen, and vegetable fibers. Amputations were performed successfully, and trephination, including the removal of pieces of bone from the brain, was also provided to patients. Gags and wooden tubes were inserted into the mouths of patients being treated for jaw injuries. The tubes were used to provide nourishment conveniently and to drain fluids. Brick supports and body casts were employed to keep patients still and upright, and other materials were molded to their bodies to supply clean, sturdy foundations for recovery. Flax and other materials were used in the clinics or medical establishments to pack wounds as well as in the treatment of sores or surgical incisions. Bandages were normally made of linen and were applied with hygienic standards adopted in the nation. Priests also used poultices, adhesive strips, and cleansing agents. Other therapeutic procedures included cauterization of wounds using fire drills or heated scalpels.

DENTISTRY

The Ebers Papyrus, dating to the New Kingdom (1550–1070 B.C.E.), details the care of periodontal diseases, including dental caries. The Egyptians of all historical periods had terrible teeth and periodontal problems. By the New Kingdom (1550–1070 B.C.E.), however, dental care was critical. It appears that Egyptians suffered an enormous amount of tooth decay, a condition that can be fatal under some circumstances. The cause of such damage can be traced to the fresh loaves of bread served every day. The grinding stones for the grain used in breads were made of a soft stone that chipped or turned into a dust when used too long, and the stone entered the dough of the bread, subsequently damaging teeth.

Sand was ever-present in the Nile Valley, as it lies between two large desert regions. In modern times, the *khamsin*, a sandstorm, strikes Egypt in the early part of every year. There is no documentation to prove that the *khamsin* was active in ancient Egypt, but if it did strike the area then it would have left deposits of sand in homes, palaces, temples, and stores. In any case, loaves of bread found in excavation activities indicate that sand was another major ingredient in that cherished food product.

Teeth that are decayed and plagued with abscesses can infect the gums; this infection can then enter the bloodstream. There were trained dentists in ancient Egypt, but when abscesses formed, they had no antibiotics to stem infections. Hatshepsut (r. 1473–1458 B.C.E.),

who was recently identified in her mummified form, died of an abscessed tooth that had caused a fatal infection.

Physicians packed some teeth with honey and herbs, perhaps to stem infection or to ease pain. Some mummies were also provided with bridges and gold teeth. It is not known if these dental aids were used by the wearers while alive or were inserted into the mouths of the deceased during the embalming process.

EYE CARE

Egyptian doctors specializing in the care of the eyes labored as devotees of the god Douao, the patron of medicine. The deity Wer, or WERET, who was believed to suffer blindness on moonless nights, was another patron of eye specialists. Green malachite, called *wadju*, and a galena mixture, called *mesdemet*, were used to aid blindness and trachoma. The Ebers Papyrus advises such procedures.

GYNECOLOGY AND CHILDBIRTH

Physicians treated women with medical problems and provided an accurate pregnancy test. Infant mortality was high in some periods, and women did die in childbirth. Giving birth was called "sitting on the bricks," as small stools were made of bricks to aid in labor. Children were born at times with spina bifida, cleft palettes, and clubbed feet. Leprosy and sexually transmitted diseases were not present in Egypt until Roman times.

PARASITES AND PESTS

With reptiles and Nile parasites, the Egyptians of ancient eras suffered many ailments that are recognizable in the modern age. Hippopotami and crocodiles inhabited the river until the later historical periods, and both were aggressively territorial. Such dangers could be avoided, but other perils faced the Nile people every day. The most common diseases afflicting Egyptians included the illness caused by *Schistosoma haematobium*, a parasitic worm still present in standing Nile waters, an infection of which may result in bilharziasis. Another parasitic infection was caused by *Dracunculus medinensis*, found in Nile drinking water.

In addition, the ancient Egyptians faced a menacing condition carried by the mosquitoes in the Nile marshes. These insects carried malaria, a debilitating condition that can lead to death. Malaria is still a worldwide problem, now accompanied by West Nile virus. King TUT'ANKHAMUN (r. 1333–1323 B.C.E.) died of malaria tropica, an extremely dangerous type, as it attacks the human brain.

Lice caused a form of dermatitis, epidemics, and fevers. Rats added to the spread of disease and were recognized as creatures that had to be controlled. A rat trap from the early historical periods was discovered at Kahun. Each community also had a "snake charmer," an individual who cornered cobras and other reptiles and took them away.

EPIDEMICS

Smallpox epidemics appeared at times, including the period of the Twentieth Dynasty (1196–1070 B.C.E.) when the succession to the throne was imperiled by the deadly toll of the disease. Tuberculosis was present in both bovine and human forms. Pott's disease, spinal tuberculosis (leading to humpbacks, emaciation, and exhaustion), arteriosclerosis, scoliosis, and poliomyelitis were known in Egypt as well. Two fetuses discovered in the tomb of Tut'ankhamun (r. 1333–1323 B.C.E.) also depict spina bifida and Sprengel's disease. SIPTAH (r. 1204–1198 B.C.E.) had talipes equinovarus, or clubfoot. That condition was also recorded in the tombs of the Middle Kingdom Period (2040–1640 B.C.E.).

OTHER AILMENTS

The Ebers Papyrus details the treatment of worm infestations, burns, fractures, rheumatism, tumors, and abscesses. There are 900 diagnostic instructions in the papyrus, with remedies for the alleviation of pain.

Tumors were recognized as early as the Fifth Dynasty (2465–2323 B.C.E.), and in the same historical period Egyptians suffered from nasopharyngeal cancer. Hernias were treated, and Graves disease was recorded on a statue in the Old Kingdom (2575–2134 B.C.E.). Rheumatoid arthritis was also depicted in a Fifth Dynasty tomb. Leprosy (*Mycobacterium leprae*) did not appear until the Ptolemaic Period (304–30 B.C.E.). A Ptolemaic cemetery at DAKHLA Oasis contained lepers. Egyptians on average suffered many diseases, including high blood pressure, heart ailments, bronchitis, pneumonia, kidney stones, abscesses, and gynecological problems.

CHANGES IN HEALTHCARE

The arrival of the Greeks in Egypt, and the subsequent occupation of the country under ALEXANDER III THE GREAT (r. 332–323 B.C.E.) and the Ptolemies, brought about changes in medical studies and procedures, as the Greek scientific approaches, especially the medical advances proposed by Galen and other Greek physicians, impacted upon the Egyptian practitioners, at least in ALEXANDRIA and other major centers. Preserved texts from the medical specialists of the Ptolemaic Period (304–30 B.C.E.) include pleas for modernization of methods and the abandonment of the magical aspects of medicine as practiced in prior generations. The Egyptians adapted to the new concepts and improvements to some extent, but they maintained their time-honored services in the old ways at the same time.

When the Romans entered the Nile Valley, they respected much of what they saw in the functioning medical clinics and brought their own scientific systems into play. Egypt was a prized provincial territory under Emperor AUGUSTUS, after Octavian defeated CLEOPATRA VII and Marc ANTONY in 30 B.C.E. The Egyptians accepted the changes and continued honoring the past.

The pharmaceutical resources of the ancient Egyptian priest-physicians included antacids, copper salts, turpentine, alum, astringents, alkaline laxatives, diuretics, sedatives, antispasmodics, calcium carbonates, and magnesia. They also employed many exotic herbs. The dispensing of medicines was carefully stipulated in the medical papyri, with explicit instructions as to the exact dosage, the manner in which the medicine was to be taken internally (as with food or wine), and external applications. Some of the prescriptions contained strange and exotic ingredients, and the dosage sometimes included magical spells or incantations as accompanying remedies.

Further reading: Allen, James P., et al. *The Art of Medicine in Ancient Egypt.* New York: Metropolitan Museum of Art, 2005; Estes, J. Worth. *The Medical Skills of Egypt.* New York: Watson Publishing International, 1993; Nunn, John F. *Ancient Egyptian Medicine.* Norman: Red River Books, 2002.

Hearst Papyrus A medical document discovered in DEIR EL-BALLAS, a Seventeenth Dynasty complex, several miles north of THEBES, the text dates to the Seventeenth (1640–1550 B.C.E.) or Eighteenth Dynasty (1550–1307 B.C.E.) and repeats much of what was found in the EBERS PAPYRUS. A section on the treatment of injured bones is especially interesting. Bites, ailments of the fingers, and other medical matters were discussed in the document. The Hearst Papyrus is now in the possession of the University of California at Berkeley.

heart *See* AB.

heb The ancient Egyptian word for festival. The hieroglyph for *heb* is a primitive reed hut on a bowl, depicting vegetation or reed growth in the hut and purity in the bowl. All festivals contained two distinct aspects in Egypt. They were reenactments of past events in history or in traditions, and they were channels for divine graces and aspects of spiritual existence that were manifested in the lives of the participants.

Hebenu This was a site in Upper Egypt, probably the foundation for the modern village of Zawiet el-Meiten, that served as a cult center for the falcon, worshipped as the soul of HORUS. Called *bik* in Egyptian, the falcon was revered especially in Hierakonpolis as the hawk. The falcon or hawk was an important pharaonic insignia. Hebenu was one of the oldest settlements on the Nile. An unidentified pyramid was erected in Hebenu's necropolis.

Hecataeus of Abdera (fl. fourth century B.C.E.) *Greek historian who authored an Egyptian history ca. 300 B.C.E.*
He was in Egypt in the reign of PTOLEMY I SOTER (304–284 B.C.E.). Hecataeus visited the mortuary complex called the RAMESSEUM at THEBES and translated the inscriptions on the remains of a colossal seated statue of RAMESSES II (r. 1290–1224 B.C.E.). He wrote the name of Ramesses as Ozymandias. The statue was originally 66 feet high and weighed 1,000 tons. Diodorus Siculus copied a great deal from Hecataeus's history when he composed his work in the mid-first century B.C.E.

Heh   The god of eternity, one of the deities of the OGDOAD of HELIOPOLIS. The consort of HAUKHET, he was depicted as a man kneeling and holding notched palm ribs, the symbol of years. An *ANKH*, the life sign, sometimes hangs on his arm. The word *heh* meant millions. Heh's cult center was at HERMOPOLIS MAGNA, and he was the protector of the pharaohs. In some depictions he is shown holding a SOLAR BOAT.

Hekaib (fl. 22nd century B.C.E.) *official of the Sixth Dynasty and a commander of Egyptian military forces*
He served PEPI II (r. 2246–2152 B.C.E.) as a military adviser and as a commander of troops. He also led expeditions to the Red Sea, where Egypt maintained shipyards that constructed seagoing vessels. Hekaib was murdered while on an expedition to the port of KUSER on the Red Sea. His body was recovered by his son and returned to ELEPHANTINE Island in ASWAN. Hekaib was

Heh, the god of eternity, is shown seated on a sacred *djeba*, or perch, carrying rods of life and the *ankh*, the symbol of life. He wears a solar disk, surmounted by cobras, the protectors of Lower Egypt and the kings of Egypt.

declared a god by the priests of the temples of Aswan after his death, and a series of small brick shrines were erected with a sanctuary in his honor. A statue recovered depicts Hekaib in the robes of a court official. He was also called "He Who Is Master of His Heart," a reference to his dignified, stately decorum and his public service.

heker   This was the hieroglyph for "decoration" that was used as a vivid border design in the tomb of TUTHMOSIS III (r. 1479–1425 B.C.E.) in the VALLEY OF THE KINGS of THEBES. A ceiling of stars completed the adornments in the tomb, along with figures of the AM DUAT, a version of the BOOK OF THE DEAD. The black stick-like figures on the walls of the tomb of TUTHMOSIS III are unique and stark and cast a somber note not present in other tombs.

Heket   A FROG goddess of Egypt, the symbol of new life, this deity is mentioned in the PYRAMID TEXTS as assisting the dead pharaohs in their ascent to the heavens. PETOSIRIS's tomb in the TUNA EL-GEBEL (ca. 300 B.C.E.) contains a text in her honor. The cultic center of Heket was at QUS. In the Middle Kingdom (2040–1640 B.C.E.) she was a protector of households and pregnant women, fashioning children in the womb. In some eras she was associated with the god KHNUM and with OSIRIS. SETI I (r. 1306–1290 B.C.E.) was depicted making offerings to Heket in his ABYDOS temple. The frog aspects of the Heket cult relate to the fact that these amphibians appeared each year as the Nile floods began. As such, frogs heralded the rebirth and regeneration of Egypt when the nation received the Nile waters. She was the consort of another frog deity, Hek, or Hakut.

Heliopolis (On; Iunu; Iunet Mehet)   This city was called On in ancient times and now serves as a suburb of modern Cairo, the cult center of RÉ-Atum. Heliopolis was a thriving shrine site throughout ancient Egyptian historical periods, and, economically, it was influential even when the cult of the god AMUN at THEBES dominated.

PITHOM (2), the Estate of ATUM, was erected on the site, making Heliopolis a religious and political power center. The original name was Iunu, "the Pillar," or Iunet Mehet, "the Northern Pillar." The temple dominating Heliopolis was called "Atum the Complete One" and was a lavish complex. The priests serving the cult of Ré-Atum were learned and politically active. They also conducted shrines for the BENNU, the phoenixlike bird that sheltered in the Persea Tree; Ré-Horakhte, a sunrise-oriented aspect of the god Horus; and the MNEVIS bull, considered to be a true oracle. The symbol of Heliopolis in all eras was the Bennu.

The ENNEAD, the pantheon of the nine deities of creation, evolved out of the cosmological traditions of

Heliopolis and was revered throughout Egypt. Heliopolis, in its association with Atum, was also known as the PRIMEVAL MOUND. The cosmogonic teachings of the city remained influential for many centuries, and the rulers began to assume their royal titles from Ré and his divine powers early in Egypt's history.

Only a single OBELISK, taken from the temple of SENWOSRET I (r. 1971–1926 B.C.E.) at Heliopolis, now marks the site of the once famed center of religion and learning. A STELA discovered at Heliopolis commemorated offerings also made by TUTHMOSIS III (r. 1479–1425 B.C.E.). He provided gifts for the temple of Ré and renovated the city complex with red quartzite from GEBEL EL-AHMAR. Another stela gave an account of RAMESSES II (r. 1290–1224 B.C.E.) of the Nineteenth Dynasty, who also honored the city. Temple inscriptions dating to the Twelfth Dynasty (1991–1783 B.C.E.), or a copy from one of that era, were also discovered inscribed on leather there.

A secondary temple was built at Heliopolis by AMENHOTEP III (r. 1391–1353 B.C.E.), and black granite column fragments remain on the site. SETHNAKHTE (r. 1196–1194 B.C.E.) and MERENPTAH (r. 1224–1214 B.C.E.) added to this shrine. The inscriptions on these fragments are in the form of a poem and praise Senwosret I for the restoration of a temple there. A Predynastic Period (before 3000 B.C.E.) necropolis was found on the site. An unknown goddess, Iusáasit, was once worshipped there.

Helwan A site near SAQQARA in the el-Saff territory, which is located on a plateau above the Nile River and serves as a southern suburb of modern Cairo, Helwan has been inhabited since the Predynastic Period (before 3000 B.C.E.) and has cemeteries containing First Dynasty (2920–2700 B.C.E.) tombs as well. The tombs have walls manufactured out of brick and hard stone, and they are considered examples of the first use of such stone in monumental architecture on the Nile. Magazines for storage and staircases demonstrate a skilled architectural design. The ceilings were fashioned with wooden beams and stone slabs. The Helwan culture is classified as part of the Neolithic Age of Egypt. There were 10,000 graves at Helwan, and signs of mummification processes, all performed in a rudimentary manner, are evident. Stelae, statues, and linen bandages were also found on various sites in the area.

Hemaka (fl. 28th century B.C.E.) *chancellor and vizier of the First Dynasty*
He served DEN (r. 2850 B.C.E.) in a variety of court roles and then as CHANCELLOR of Lower Egypt. Hemaka was the first to conduct affairs as a VIZIER, as Den instituted that office. His tomb in SAQQARA contained rich funerary offerings and a stela bearing the name of Den, as well as a description of the mummification process. Den is depicted as a seated mummified form in Hemaka's tomb. Hemaka's name was also found on jar sealings and labels at ABYDOS and Saqqara. The tomb contained 42 storage chambers, an ivory label of DJER (r. ca. 2900 B.C.E.), alabaster and pottery vases, flints, adzes, and arrows. A famous Hennu Boat of SOKAR was made for Hemaka.

Hemamiyeh This was a Predynastic Period (before 3000 B.C.E.) settlement in the central part of the Nile Valley that testifies to community life in Egypt's earliest historic times. There are remains of circular residential structures at Hemamiyeh, which date to the Badarian cultural sequence (4500–4000 B.C.E.).

Hemetch A serpent demon concerned with the deceased in their journey through TUAT, or the Underworld. Hemetch was depicted in the PYRAMID of UNIS (r. 2356–2323 B.C.E.) of the Fifth Dynasty. The supernatural creature was one of many perils faced by the newly dead, but spells and incantations provided by the various mortuary cults allowed the deceased to placate Hemetch and to assure their safe arrival in OSIRIS's paradises.

See also BOOK OF THE DEAD.

Hemiunu (fl. 26th century B.C.E.) *prince of the Fourth Dynasty*
He was the son of Prince NEFERMA'AT and Princess ATET, and a nephew of KHUFU (Cheops) (r. 2551–2528 B.C.E.). Serving as the VIZIER and seal bearer for Khufu, he was also in charge of the construction of the Great PYRAMID at GIZA. His tomb was built at the base of that famed monument. Hemiunu was the only private individual allowed to place a self-portrait statue within his tomb, which is of the mastaba design. Such a statue, now in Hildesheim, Germany, depicts Hemiunu as a robust, heavyset man.

Hemiunu was also the courtier involved in the reburial of the mortuary regalia of Queen HETEPHERES (1), Khufu's royal mother. Her original tomb had been robbed, and her mummified remains were missing. Hemiunu reburied a cache of magnificent furniture and personal effects belonging to Queen Hetepheres.

Heneb An ancient deity of Egypt, associated with AGRICULTURE in the earliest eras. One of his cultic symbols was grain. In time the god OSIRIS became popular in the land, assuming the role of patron of harvests and grains. As a result, Heneb's cult disappeared into the new Osirian rituals.

Henenu (fl. 21st century B.C.E.) *agricultural official of the Eleventh Dynasty*
He served MENTUHOTEP II (r. 2061–2010 B.C.E.) as a steward and overseer of the royal herds. This position required him to collect taxes and serve as the pharaoh's legate in some territories of the country. Henenu

was buried at DEIR EL-BAHRI, on the western shore of THEBES. Mentuhotep II built an elaborate mortuary complex there and honored Henenu by providing him burial space within the complex.

Henhenit (fl. 21st century B.C.E.) *royal woman of the Eleventh Dynasty*
She was a consort of MENTUHOTEP II (r. 2061–2010 B.C.E.) but not the mother of the heir. Henhenit was buried in the vast mortuary complex of Mentuhotep II at DEIR EL-BAHRI, on the western shore of THEBES. Her mummified remains were found intact in 1911. Her SARCOPHAGUS was made of limestone blocks. Like the others buried in Mentuhotep's complex, Henhenit's sarcophagus bore the inscription "Sole Favorite of the King."

Hennu Boat *See* BARKS OF THE GODS; SOKAR.

Hent (1) (fl. 30th century B.C.E.) *royal woman of the First Dynasty*
She was a consort of AHA (r. ca. 2920 B.C.E.). Aha is the legendary Menes, the founder of Egypt's First Dynasty. Hent, a lesser-ranked wife in Aha's court, gave birth to the heir, DJER.

Hent (2) (fl. 19th century B.C.E.) *royal woman of the Twelfth Dynasty*
She was a consort of SENWOSRET II (r. 1897–1878 B.C.E.) but was not the mother of the heir. Hent was buried near Senwosret II at LAHUN in the FAIYUM.

Henu (fl. 20th century B.C.E.) *expedition leader of the Eleventh Dynasty*
He served MENTUHOTEP III (r. 2010–1998 B.C.E.) as an expedition leader in the Mediterranean region. His achievements were inscribed on the rocks of WADI HAMMAMAT, dated to Mentuhotep III's eighth year of reign. Henu was governor of Upper Egypt's southern domain. He led an army from OXYRRHYNCUS (1) and GEBELEIN to the Wadi Hammamat to quarry stone for royal statues of the pharaoh. He also outfitted a ship for an expedition to PUNT, probably modern Ethiopia.

See also NUBIA; TRADE.

Henutempet (fl. 16th century B.C.E.) *royal woman of the Seventeenth Dynasty*
She was a consort of Sekenenré TA'O II (r. ca. 1560 B.C.E.). Henutempet was buried in Dra-abz el-Naga, near Thebes. She served as a lesser-ranked wife.

Henutmiré (fl. 13th century B.C.E.) *royal woman of the Nineteenth Dynasty*
She was a consort of RAMESSES II (r. 1290–1224 B.C.E.) and a daughter of SETI I. Henutmiré was buried in the VALLEY OF QUEENS, but the location of her tomb is now unknown. Part of Henutmiré's funerary regalia was taken by HARSIESE, a prince of the Twenty-second Dynasty, and used in his tomb at MEDINET HABU. Henutmiré's granite SARCOPHAGUS, a funerary piece prepared for her burial, was also usurped by Harsiese.

Henutsen (fl. 26th century B.C.E.) *royal woman of the Fourth Dynasty*
She was a consort of KHUFU (Cheops) (r. 2551–2528 B.C.E.) and the mother of Prince Khufu-Khaf and possibly the heir, Khafre (Chephren). She was buried in a small pyramid beside Khufu's Great PYRAMID at GIZA. Her tomb was listed in the INVENTORY STELA.

Henuttaneb (fl. 14th century B.C.E.) *royal woman of the Eighteenth Dynasty*
She was a daughter of AMENHOTEP III (r. 1391–1353 B.C.E.) and Queen TIYE (1). Henuttaneb is identified on a limestone relief celebrating Amenhotep III's *heb-sed* (*see* SED) festival. Her name also appears on ceramic vessels in tombs in the VALLEY OF THE KINGS at THEBES.

Henuttawy (Duathathor Hennuttawy) (fl. 11th century b.c.e.) *royal woman of the Twentieth and the Twenty-first Dynasties*
She was the wife of PINUDJEM (1), a priest of THEBES, and the daughter of RAMESSES XI (r. 1100–1070 B.C.E.) and Queen TANTAMUN (1). She was the mother of PSUSENNES I, MASAHARTA, MA'ATKARÉ (1), MENKHEPERRESENB, and MUT NODJMET (2). Henuttawy is famous because of her mummified face, which was overpacked during embalming. Her limbs were also packed and enlarged. The face of Henuttawy's mummy was recently restored to normal size. A form of butter, soda, and sawdust was used in the first embalming process. Her mummy was in the DEIR EL-BAHRI cache, discovered in 1881, and her original mirror box was discovered in her mummy wrappings.

Hepdjefau (fl. 19th century B.C.E.) *nobleman and religious leader of the Twelfth Dynasty (1991–1783 B.C.E.)*
He was called the "Superior of Priests" and probably served several pharaohs of the Twelfth Dynasty. Hepdjefau is also known for his personal funerary contracts, which arranged for priests to offer food and prayers to him in his tomb on the first day of every season and on a special feast of OSIRIS, the 18th day of the first month of the year.

Heptet An ancient goddess associated with the cult of OSIRIS throughout all periods of Egyptian history, Heptet was revered as one of the cow nurses attending Osiris during reenactments of his resurrection. Heptet was often pictured as a woman with the head of a bearded snake. She was also part of the cult of the goddess HATHOR.

Hepu (fl. 14th century B.C.E.) *vizier of the Eighteenth Dynasty*
He served TUTHMOSIS IV (r. 1401–1391 B.C.E.). Hepu's tomb in THEBES is noted for the relief containing the text known as the INSTALLATION OF THE VIZIER, which notes the requirements of a vizier and the duties of the office, as well as the ideals expected of such an appointed person.

Hepzefa (fl. 20th century B.C.E.) *official of the Twelfth Dynasty and a nomarch of the province of Assiut*
He served SENWOSRET I (r. 1971–1926 B.C.E.) as a regional supporter. Hepzefa's tomb at ASSIUT contains a mortuary contract concerning the continuance of cultic rituals. His wife was Princess SENNUWY, who was immortalized by a beautiful statue found in a fort in KERMEH, NUBIA (modern Sudan), and now in the Museum of Fine Arts in Boston.

Herakleopolis Magna (Ihnasiyah el-Medineh; Nennesut; Nenen-nesut; Ninsu) A site south of MEIDUM at the entrance to the FAIYUM, now Ihnasiyah el-Medineh, originally called Nen-nesut, Nenen-nesut, or Ninsu by the Egyptians, Herakleopolis was the capital of the twentieth nome of Upper Egypt and the cult center for HARSAPHES (Her-shef). The site was settled as early as the First Dynasty (2920–2770 B.C.E.) but rose to prominence in the First Intermediate Period (2134–2040 B.C.E.). The name Herakleopolis Magna was bestowed upon the site by the rulers of the Ptolemaic Period (304–30 B.C.E.). In the First Intermediate Period, Herakleopolis was the home of the KHETY (Aktoy) clan. During the Khety period of rule (2134–2040 B.C.E.), a canal linked Herakleopolis Magna to Memphis. Mentuhotep II attacked the site in 2040 B.C.E. when he started his campaign to reunify Egypt.

The temple of Harsaphes, a ram-headed deity, was restored at Herakleopolis Magna by RAMESSES II (r. 1290–1224 B.C.E.). A granite monument of Ramesses II, PTAH, and Harsaphes was also erected in Herakleopolis Magna. An Old Kingdom (2575–2134 B.C.E.) shrine and a necropolis, GEBEL EL-SIDMANT, are on the site.

Herihor (fl. 11th century B.C.E.) *high Priest of Amun at Thebes, who usurped pharaonic powers*
He began his career in the reign of RAMESSES XI (1100–1070 B.C.E.). Possibly of Libyan descent, Herihor served as a general and as the VICEROY of Kush after being sent to THEBES to put down rebellions there. He ousted the local high priest, RAMESSESNAKHT, and the viceroy, PIANKHI (2) and then assumed their offices himself. He married NODJMET. Assuming pharaonic titles and dress, Herihor ruled in Thebes, while SMENDES administered the northern territories for the reclusive Ramesses XI. Both he and Nodjmet used CARTOUCHES on their funerary regalia, and Herihor was depicted in a relief in KARNAK's temple of Khonsu. Elsewhere he was portrayed wearing the double crowns of Egypt. A statue of him and one of his commemorative stelae also survived. Herihor was the official who sent WENAMUN on his misadventures in Syria. Herihor preceded Ramesses XI in death. Smendes, starting the Twenty-first Dynasty (1070–945 B.C.E.), succeeded Ramesses XI in the north, but the Theban priests maintained their powers.

Herit (fl. 16th century B.C.E.) *royal woman of the Fifteenth Dynasty, the Great Hyksos royal line*
She was the daughter of APOPHIS (r. 1585–1553 B.C.E.). Fragments of a vase bearing her name and royal rank were found in a Theban tomb. Nothing is known of her life. She lived during the time when the HYKSOS were ousted from Egypt by 'AHMOSE (NEBPEHTIRÉ) (r. 1550–1525 B.C.E.).

Hermes Trismegistos The Greek version of the Egyptian deity of wisdom, THOTH, the adaptation involved the identification of Thoth as Hermes, and Trismegistos meant "Thrice Greatest." The Egyptians called Thoth "A'a, A'a, A'a," "Great, Great, Great," in cultic rituals. An occult system emerged out of this designation both academic and popular. The theological and philosophical writings that developed as part of the cult were included in the 17 works of the *Corpus Hermeticum*. They were composed in Greek. The popular Hermetic works included astrological and esoteric scientific pieces that mirrored occult or mythical views of the era. They were also an evolution of the Egyptian system of magic.

Hermonthis *See* ERMENT.

Hermopolis Magna (Khnum Khemenu; Ashmun; Per-Djehuty) This was a site on the west bank of the Nile near MALLAWI and el-Ashmunien in central Egypt. Originally called Khnum Khemenu, or Ashmun, "the Eight Town" (in honor of the OGDOAD), the site was also revered as Per-Djehuty, "the House of THOTH." A giant statue of Thoth as a BABOON was erected there, as well as a temple for the god's cult. NECTANEBO I (r. 380–362 B.C.E.) restored that temple, but it is now destroyed.

Hermopolis Magna was the capital of the fifteenth nome of Upper Egypt and was traditionally recorded as having been erected on a primal hill of creation. AMENHOTEP III (r. 1391–1353 B.C.E.) erected a temple to Thoth on the site (rebuilt by Nectanebo I). A temple of AMUN made of limestone was started in Hermopolis Magna by MERENPTAH (r. 1224–1214 B.C.E.) and finished by SETI II (r. 1214–1204 B.C.E.). A PYLON and a HYPOSTYLE HALL have survived. Ruins of an Old Kingdom (2575–2134 B.C.E.) shrine and a devotional center restored by HATSHEPSUT (r. 1473–1458 B.C.E.) are also on the site, as well as two seated colossi statues of RAMESSES II (r. 1290–1224 B.C.E.). The Ramessid structure at Hermopolis Magna used stones, called TALATAT, taken from

'AMARNA, the razed capital of AKHENATEN (r. 1353–1335 B.C.E.), and contained many important reliefs. TUNA EL-GEBEL was the necropolis for Hermopolis Magna. The famous tomb of PETOSIRIS is located there. Three documents from the Twelfth Dynasty (1991–1783 B.C.E.) were also found on the site, as well as Ptolemaic Period (304–30 B.C.E.) statues.

Hermopolis Parva   This was a site south of modern El-Bagliya, called Ba'h in ancient times. Built on three mounds, Hermopolis Parva had three major monuments. The first was at Tell el-Nagus and was a temple to the god THOTH. The remains of the temple have bell-shaped ruins and are called "the Mounds of the Bell." The second mound was used as a cemetery of ibises at Tell el-Zereiki. The third monument, located at TELL EL-RUB'A, was a shrine to Thoth, erected by APRIES (r. 589–570 B.C.E.). A torso of NECTANEBO I (r. 380–362 B.C.E.) was also found there, as well as blocks of stone from PSAMMETICHUS I (r. 664–610 B.C.E.).

Herneith (1) (fl. 30th century B.C.E.) *royal woman of the First Dynasty*
She was the consort of DJER (r. ca. 2900 B.C.E.). Herneith was buried in SAQQARA, probably in the reign of Djer's successor, DJET. His jar sealings were found in her tomb, which had a stairway and a burial pit as well as surface chambers. She was the mother of Djet.

Herneith (2) (fl. 28th century B.C.E.) *royal woman of the First Dynasty*
She was the consort of DEN (r. ca. 2700 B.C.E.). Herneith was probably not the mother of the successor, ADJIB, but was a descendant of HERNEITH (1).

Herophilus of Chalcedon (d. 280 B.C.E.) *Alexandrian physician who practiced "new medicine"*
The "new medicine" was the name applied to forensics and the dissection of human cadavers. He was born ca. 335 B.C.E. in Chalcedon (modern Kadiköy, Turkey) and went to ALEXANDRIA to study under the new regulations that allowed human dissection. His awareness of the workings of the human brain and his careful accounts of his studies of various organs won praise in the later medical fields in Greece. Galen and others detailed his accomplishments.
See also PER-ANKH.

Hesira (fl. 27th century B.C.E.) *official of the Third Dynasty, called the "greatest of physicians and dentists"*
He served DJOSER (r. 2630–2611 B.C.E.) and is famous for the tomb decorations that he commissioned, works that demonstrate the human canon of ART. Hesira was the overseer of royal scribes and called "the greatest of physicians and dentists," and he was honored with a mastaba in SAQQARA. His tomb has a corridor chapel that contains carved panels depicting Hesira in epic poses, representing the artistic gains of his time. He was buried in a subterranean chamber connected to the tomb by a shaft. The chapel contains a SERDAB, a statue chamber like the one found in the STEP PYRAMID. Traditional palace facade panels also adorn the tomb, which was made out of mud bricks.
See also ART AND ARCHITECTURE.

***hes* purification**   *See* BAPTISM.

Hesseb (el-Hesseb Island)   This site near the first cataract of the Nile, south of ASWAN, served as a boundary fortress in some periods. The site contained a stela from the Sixth Dynasty (2323–2150 B.C.E.). Egypt was already involved in TRADE with NUBIA (modern Sudan) at that time.

Hetephakef   An obscure deity of Egypt, associated with the city of MEMPHIS. A life-sized statue of the god was made out of schist and contained the CARTOUCHE of RAMESSES II (r. 1290–1224 B.C.E.). No cultic temples of Hetephakef remain.

Hetepheres (1) (fl. 26th century B.C.E.) *royal woman of the Third and Fourth Dynasties of Egypt*
She was the daughter of HUNI (r. 2599–2575 B.C.E.) and the consort of SNEFRU (r. 2575–2551 B.C.E.). Hetepheres was the mother of KHUFU (r. 2551–2528 B.C.E.), also called Cheops. Her tomb regalia, discovered in a shaft without her mummified remains, reflect the tragedy of tomb robberies and vandalism in that age and throughout all of Egypt's historical periods.
HEMIUNU, a prince nephew who served as Khufu's VIZIER, discovered Hetepheres' tomb in shambles and removed the mortuary furniture and personal goods from the original DASHUR burial site to GIZA. These items included bedroom furnishings, gold casings, toiletries, and a statue of Hetepheres in a sheath gown, tripartite wig, and bracelets. Her vital organs had been placed in CANOPIC JARS with a natron solution but had decayed. Her COFFIN was fashioned out of calcite, a white translucent alabaster. This was placed in the shaft at Giza without her mummy, which was probably destroyed by the thieves. The 90-foot shaft was filled with stones after her regalia was deposited.

Hetepheres (2) (fl. 26th century B.C.E.) *royal woman of the Fourth Dynasty*
She was the daughter of KHUFU (Cheops) (r. 2551–2528 B.C.E.) and possibly Queen MERITITES (1). Hetepheres married Prince KEWAB, the heir to Khufu's throne and bore him MERYSANKH (3) and others. Kewab died on an expedition, and she was given to RA'DJEDEF (r. 2528–2520 B.C.E.). When Ra'djedef died, Hetepheres married ANKHKHAF, a powerful vizier serving KHAFRE (r. 2520–

2494 B.C.E.). Prince Kewab had fashioned a magnificent tomb for Hetepheres in GIZA. A MASTABA design, sumptuously adorned, the tomb was used to bury Hetepheres' daughter Merysankh (3) when she died. Hetepheres provided this site for her daughter and built another tomb in the eastern portion of the eastern plateau of Giza. There she was buried in a black granite sarcophagus. She is believed to have reached the age of 70.

Hetephernebty (fl. 27th century B.C.E.) *royal woman of the Third Dynasty who was much honored with her sister, Intakaes*
Hetephernebty was possibly a consort of DJOSER (r. 2630–2611 B.C.E.). Hetephernebty also appears in some accounts. Hetephernebty and Intakaes were possibly the daughters of KHA'SEKHEMWY (r. ca. 2649 B.C.E.), the last king of the Second Dynasty. The two sisters were popular in the court of Djoser. They are probably buried in SAQQARA, in Djoser's STEP PYRAMID complex.

"He-Who-Looks-Behind-Himself" A divine being associated with Egyptian burial rituals, named Hraf-hef, he was also called the Great Fowler. Hraf-hef, "He-Who-Looks-Behind-Himself," was the ferryman on the celestial lake of TUAT, or the Underworld. He also served as one of the 42 judges in the JUDGMENT HALLS OF OSIRIS, where the deceased had to prove their worthiness. Hraf-hef had to be placated with funerary litanies and with magical ointments. The NET SPELLS included in some versions of the BOOK OF THE DEAD were intended to soothe "He-Who-Looks-Behind-Himself" and to persuade him to ferry the deceased to paradise.

Hiba, el- (Tendjai) A site between HERAKLEOPOLIS MAGNA and HERMOPOLIS MAGNA, called Tendjai originally, el-Hiba was a frontier fortress and residence. A temple of AMUN was erected on the site by SHOSHENQ I (r. 945–924 B.C.E.), and inscriptions of the Twenty-first Dynasty (1070–945 B.C.E.) high priests of Amun, PINUDJEM (1) and MENKHEPERRESENB (2), were also discovered there. The fortress was revived ca. 305 B.C.E., in the reign of PTOLEMY I SOTER, as Ankyronpolis. El-Hiba dates probably to the New Kingdom (1550–1070 B.C.E.) or slightly earlier.

Hibis (Hebet) The ancient capital of the KHARGA OASIS, located south of ASSIUT in the western desert, also called Hebet, Hibis contained a temple started by DARIUS I (r. 521–486 B.C.E.) or DARIUS II (r. 424–404 B.C.E.) and completed by NECTANEBO II (r. 360–343 B.C.E.). The rulers of the Ptolemaic Period (304–30 B.C.E.) added decorations and chambers. The temple was constructed in a grove and had vivid reliefs and a rooftop shrine dedicated to the god OSIRIS. A winged figure of SET, the fertility deity of the oasis, is also displayed. A Roman temple was built on a nearby hill.

Hierakonpolis (Nekhen; Al-Kom el-Ahmar) A major site in Upper Egypt and the largest city in both the Predynastic Period and the Early Dynastic Period, Hierakonpolis is situated south of THEBES (modern Luxor), between Esna and Edfu, across the NILE from Nekheb (modern Elkab). Originally called Nekhen, it was named Hierakonpolis, "the City of the Falcon," by the Greeks. The falcon was the symbol of the god HORUS, and Hierakonpolis was the cult center for the worship of that god. Earlier, a deity named Nekheny was worshiped in the area, hence the Egyptian designation of the site as Nekhen; Nekheny was absorbed into the Horus cult. Hierakonpolis is ranked among the most important archaeological sites in all of Egypt. At its peak it was a vibrant, prosperous metropolis that served as the model for the development of Egyptian cities along the Nile.

SITE DESCRIPTION
Hierakonpolis was approximately two miles long and located on the edge of the eastern desert. It was a center of trade and administration in Upper Egypt, a role played in Lower Egypt by the city of BUTO. The city had residential districts, an immense temple, and a large necropolis, or cemetery area. There is also a freestanding mud-brick monument structure that archaeologists call the "fort," which was probably the ceremonial enclosure of Pharaoh KHA'SEKHEMWY (r. ca. 2600 B.C.E.).

The residential areas of the city were similar to modern Egyptian neighborhoods. Bakers, brewers, artisans, priests, potters, and bureaucrats lived along city streets or on neighboring farms. The potters, needing large kilns, built firing sheds and studios according to their needs; some 300,000 pieces of pottery were found in the neighborhood by modern archaeologists. The weavers and other manufacturers carved out their own spaces as well. On the northern side of Hierakonpolis, brewers had enormous vats in which they used wheat to make a staple of Egyptian life, beer, called *booza*. A recipe for brewing beer was discovered in 'AMARNA, and a sample was made according to the hieroglyphic instructions. Tasters of the beer found it to be of high quality, but it was also noted that the beer was stronger than modern varieties. Egyptians drank beer with all meals and preferred it to wine. The brewery discovered at Hierakonpolis produced 300 gallons of beer a day. (Egyptians are credited with inventing the tavern, or saloon.)

The temple complex of Hierakonpolis, dating to the Old Kingdom (2575–2134 B.C.E.), was a symbol of power and prosperity. A massive wall that surrounds an opening oval compound has survived over the centuries despite the fact that it was built of mud brick, not stone. The ruler SCORPION I probably presided over sacrificial ceremonies in this courtyard. The courtyard was also the site of production areas, where artisans made jewelry, symbols, and other religious mementos for the people.

Egyptologists believe that the priests were as educated as scribes and were able to read and write. The ranking priests came from the aristocracy, but commoners were able to serve within the temple on a rotating, part-time basis. Most probably, this temple offered services to the community, including the primitive elements of medical care. Such care, at this stage of development on the Nile, would have consisted of amulets, magic spells, and the use of dead animals. In time, the physicians of ancient Egypt would assume scientific methods and become the most revered medical practitioners in the ancient world. On feast days, the temple at Hierakonpolis, like the one at Edfu, displayed as manifestations of Horus the falcons or other raptor birds that were raised within the temple grounds.

The central area of the temple comprised three separate chambers. The facade of this structure, made of mud bricks and designed with niches, had four wooden poles standing 20 feet high. The gateway to the temple dominated the site. It was 35 feet thick and contained design elements that are similar to Mesopotamian shrines.

The city of Hierakonpolis benefited from contact with other cultures and expanded its dominance. In a vast mound within the city as well as in the temple areas, stunning manifestations of Hierakonpolis's artistic advances were discovered. Maceheads, palettes, cylinder seals, and a magnificent golden Horus statue with a crown were found in the city. These artistic items recount the exploits of Scorpion I and NARMER.

It has been estimated that at its zenith, Hierakonpolis had a population of 5,000 to 10,000. A necropolis near the site contains more than 60 burials, dating to the NAQADA II culture. Petroglyphs were also discovered as well as a decorated tomb made of brick. This tomb contained Early Dynastic Period (2920–2575 B.C.E.) reliefs. Several other tombs that are rock-cut have also been found. The tombs in Hierakonpolis contain both human and animal remains. It is obvious that at this historical period humans owned and prized domesticated cats, dogs, and donkeys, and many of the people were prosperous enough to be buried with animals as companions in the afterlife; remains of baboons and even a young elephant have been found.

ARCHAEOLOGY

One of the largest and most significant Predynastic Period centers on the Nile, Hierakonpolis has provided archaeologists with a treasure trove of artifacts and knowledge regarding early Egypt. For more than a century, Egyptologists have labored to uncover the secrets and the legacy of Hierakonpolis. Important discoveries were made at the site, including the NARMER PALETTE, the ceremonial enclosure of Kha'sekhemwy, a Scorpion macehead, and

copper statues of PEPI I (r. 2289–2255 B.C.E.) and his son MERENRÉ (r. 2255–2246 B.C.E.). One of the masterpieces of Hierakonpolis is a golden-crowned hawk's head, a symbol of Horus.

The first significant expedition was started in 1898, when two English archaeologists studied the city and its burial sites. These Egyptologists, John Quibell and Frederick Green, made excavations of the royal residences of some of the early Egyptian kings. In doing so, they discovered the Narmer Palette, which is considered not only a depiction of the unification of Upper and Lower Egypt, but the earliest political document in Egyptian history. They also uncovered the famed macehead of Scorpion I. Quibell and Green also reported the discovery of a "Painted Tomb," the grave site of an aristocrat, filled with wall paintings that had the designation of "Tomb 100." One of these paintings depicted ships arriving on the Nile. The archaeologists, however, did not keep records to document the contents or decorations of each tomb; they also did not number the tombs in their observations and did not try to preserve a visible record of the paintings. As a result, the Painted Tomb remains lost.

New excavations started in 1967 under American archaeologist Dr. Walter Fairservis, who was joined by another American archaeologist, Dr. Michael Hoffman, in 1969. In the period from 1979 to 1985, Fairservis and Hoffman discovered 12 tombs of NOMARCHS, or nobles, from the Nagada II Period (3500–3200 B.C.E.). All 12 of these grave sites had been moved in ancient times and were then restored sometime in the modern era. It was also discovered that cedarwood was used in the necropolis, which meant that at some point the city of Hierakonpolis traded with Phoenicia, an area that roughly corresponds to modern-day Lebanon.

Direction of this expedition was passed in 1996 to American Egyptologist Dr. Renee Friedman and British Egyptologist Barbara Adams. Their ongoing work has led to extensive discoveries, including dozens of tombs and large numbers of artifacts, that have expanded the world's knowledge of the culture and economic life of Hierakonpolis. In 2009, excavations revealed remains of the oldest known zoo, dating to 3500 B.C.E., a park area that held baboons, elephants, and hippos.

Further reading: Green, Frederick, et al. *Hierakonpolis.* Charleston, N.C.: BiblioBazaar, 2009. Midant-Reynes, Beatrix. *The Prehistory of Egypt: From the First Egyptians to the First Pharaohs.* London: Wiley, 2000. Wilkinson, Toby. *Early Dynastic Egypt.* London: Routledge, 1999.

hieratic   *See* LANGUAGE AND WRITING.

hieroglyphs   *See* LANGUAGE AND WRITING.

High Gates of Medinet Habu   Crenelated towers added a distinctive touch to MEDINET HABU, the *migdal-*

style fortified temple complex erected by RAMESSES III (r. 1194–1163 B.C.E.) on the western shore of the Nile at Thebes. The gates provided an immense entranceway and contained upper chambers. These suites, beautifully decorated, were used by Ramesses III and his harem. It was here that Ramesses III was attacked and mortally wounded, living only long enough to set a trial of his attackers in motion.

hippopotamus A former denizen of the NILE in ancient Egypt, associated with religious and cultic traditions, the hippopotamus was viewed in two forms, as Herpest and TAWARET. Herpest was a symbol of HORUS's victory and an emblem displayed in the temple of EDFU. Tawaret was the protector of women in childbirth. In some eras, the hippopotamus was viewed as SET, the slayer of OSIRIS. This resulted in the animal being hunted in some regions and honored in others. Snoring hippopotami were the cause of a quarrel between Sekenenré TA'O II (r. ca. 1560 B.C.E.) and the HYKSOS ruler APOPHIS (r. ca. 1585–1553 B.C.E.), commemorated in the *QUARREL OF APOPHIS AND SEKENENRÉ* (TA'O II). The quarrel led to the Theban advance on Apophis's domains in the eastern Delta and the eventual expulsion of the Hyksos from Egypt.

Hittite Alliance An Egyptian text translated from the cuneiform, describing the pact between Egypt and the HITTITES and recorded on the walls of temples of KARNAK and at the RAMESSEUM, the alliance was formed between RAMESSES II (r. 1290–1224 B.C.E.) and the ruler of the Hittite empire, HATTUSILIS III (d. ca. 1250 B.C.E.). It was the result of a series of military confrontations over decades. Written in Akkadian and signed by Ramesses II, the treaty forged a reasonable approach to the division of territories and vassal nations. An unusual extradition clause was part of the alliance. A silver tablet was sent to Egypt by the Hittites, requesting this truce. Ramesses II played host to a delegation from that land for the occasion. Three versions of the treaty are still in existence. One was inscribed on the wall of KARNAK, and one was kept at PER-RAMESSES. The Hittites kept one at Hattusas. The treaty ended years of military confrontations and also served as a pact of alliance in times of danger. This event was also commemorated in a legendary manner in the BENTRESH STELA.

Further reading: MacQueen, J. G. *The Hittites: And Their Contemporaries in Asia Minor.* London: Thames & Hudson, 1996; Bryce, Trevor. *Kingdom of the Hittites.* Oxford, U.K.: Oxford University Press, 1999.

Hittites They were a people called the Great Kheta (Khenta) from Anatolia (modern Turkey) who arrived on the scene as a military power around 2000 B.C.E. Called also "the Sons of Heth," the Hittites had a tomb complex at Alaca Hüyük in Anatolia in 2500 B.C.E. They came originally from the Anatolian Lake District of the area once called Lydia. They were in Hattusas, their capital near the Kizilirmak River, by ca. 1800 B.C.E., remaining as a power until ca. 1200 B.C.E.

The Hittites spoke an Indo-European language and wrote in the Hittite-Luwian script, uncovered at Hattusas, Boghazkoy in central Anatolia. Coming into the area from their original homeland in the lower Danube, from the Black Sea to the Caucasus, this group arrived in central Anatolia ca. 1840 B.C.E., destroying a native culture of the region, Karum II. Evidence of the Hittite migration from the Caucasus has been documented. At times they were accompanied by other groups, such as the Luwians, who disappeared after their arrival in the region. Hattusas was originally the center of the Hattic peoples, who vanished.

The Hittite ruler Anitta of Kussara had warned his people not to enter Hattusas, but the capital was founded by HATTUSILIS I and strengthened. The Hittites began their reign, which they called "the kingdom of thousands of gods." In ca. 1610 B.C.E., MURSILIS I attacked the city of Aleppo in northern Syria and then took Babylon. He was murdered on his return to Hattusas, and Babylon and other cities were freed. The succeeding kings, however, started the Hittite empire.

When the Hittites threatened the MITANNIS, Egypt responded as an ally. TUTHMOSIS IV (r. 1401–1391 B.C.E.) sided with the Mitannis, forcing the Hittites to assume the role of the enemy. The growing enmity between Egypt and the Hittites was fueled as well in the days following the death of TUT'ANKHAMUN (r. 1333–1323 B.C.E.). His widow, ANKHESENAMON, offered herself and her throne to Hittite ruler SUPPILULIUMAS I. He sent his son, Prince ZANNANZA, to marry the young queen, but the son was slain at the border.

RAMESSES II (r. 1290–1224 B.C.E.) had to fight the Hittites led by King MUWATALLIS at KADESH on the Orontes River. Both sides claimed victory after a series of conflicts, including spies and ambushes, but the Egyptians and the Hittites recognized a stalemate. The battle of Kadesh is documented in Egyptian reliefs and in Hittite Akkadian language cuneiform tablets. After more years of conflict, both sides agreed to a treaty, sealed by the marriage of Ramesses II to a Hittite princess, the daughter of HATTUSILIS III (d. ca. 1250 B.C.E.) and Queen PEDUKHIPA.

The Hittites are described in historical contemporary records as a people skilled in the forging of iron. They were fierce warriors who wore heavy coats and boots with upturned toes. Their capital had a double wall fortification that spanned a deep gorge. They worshipped Heput, the mother goddess, and Teshub, a god of weather. The capital also had a natural rock sanctuary. The eventual destruction of the Hittite capital, Hattusas, and the Hittite empire was brought about during the reign of RAMESSES III (1194–1163 B.C.E.) by the SEA PEOPLES, who were later defeated in Egypt. The capital collapsed, replaced by Neo-Hittite sites that were conquered by the Assyrians.

Hiwa Semaina   This is a Predynastic Period (before 3000 B.C.E.) site on the eastern bank of the Nile, stretching from Hiwa to Semaina and depicting Naqada I and II cultures. An ancient mine and a Predynastic necropolis were discovered there, as well as graves dating to the Old Kingdom (2575–2134 B.C.E.). Settlement remains on the site have also been cataloged.

Hor Awibré (fl. ca. 1760 B.C.E.) *ruler of the Thirteenth Dynasty, who reigned only a few months*
He is mentioned in the Royal TURIN CANON, and his name appears on monuments from TANIS in the north to the ELEPHANTINE Island in ASWAN. Hor Awibré was buried in the pyramidal complex of AMENEMHET III (r. 1844–1797 B.C.E.) at DASHUR, probably as a measure of security in a troubled period. A remarkable wooden statue of Hor Awibré as a KA was discovered at his burial site. The statue, bearing the outstretched arms of the *ka* on his head, depicts the youthful ruler completely naked.

Horemhab (Djeserkhepruré) (d. 1307 B.C.E.) *fourteenth and last ruler of the Eighteenth Dynasty*
He reigned from 1319 B.C.E. until his death. His name meant "HORUS in Celebration." Horemhab came from HERAKLEOPOLIS and claimed a noble title, although no ancestral records document this. A military man, Horemhab rose through the ranks, serving in 'AMARNA and then becoming the general of Egypt's army under TUT'ANKHAMUN (r. 1333–1323 B.C.E.). He remained in power during the reign of Tut'ankhamun's successor, AYA (2) (1323–1319 B.C.E.), and then assumed the throne, marrying MUTNODJMET (1), possibly a sister of Queen NEFERTITI. Intent upon destroying any vestiges of the 'Amarna Period, Horemhab officially dated the start of his reign to the death of AMENHOTEP III (r. 1391–1353 B.C.E.) and set about destroying the tombs and buildings of the 'Amarna episode. The tomb of Tut'ankhamun was saved by the intervention of MAYA, Horemhab's trusted official.

Horemhab distinguished his reign with extensive programs designed to bring order, to defend the nation's borders, and to rebuild Egypt's religious institutions. Although he had been honored by AKHENATEN (r. 1353–1335 B.C.E.) at 'Amarna, and possibly bore the name Pa'atenemhab in that court, Horemhab continued to erase all trace of the Atenists.

He finally demolished 'Amarna and dismantled Aya's tomb and mortuary temple, erasing all names and faces recorded in these monuments. From the Delta to Nubia (modern Sudan) he destroyed all traces of the god ATEN.

He especially focused on HUY (1), the viceroy during the 'Amarna Interlude, and attacked the city of AKHMIN, the allies of Akhenaten.

Restoring Egypt's military, Horemhab once again nurtured vassal states and received delegates and tributes. He moved Egypt's capital back to MEMPHIS and set about restoring temple properties, building and rebuilding sections of KARNAK and Nubian shrines. When the tombs of TUTHMOSIS IV (r. 1401–1391 B.C.E.) and Tut'ankhamun were invaded by robbers and vandalized, he restored them.

His most ambitious and beneficial act was the reestablishment of law and order in the Nile Valley. His famous edict reestablishing various laws was found on a fragmented stela in Karnak. The edict concerned itself with legal abuses taking place because of the laxity of Akhenaten's rule. Horemhab declared that officials of the state and provinces would be held accountable for cheating the poor, for pocketing funds, and for misappropriating the use of slaves, ships, and other properties. The ruler singled out higher ranked officials, promising swift judgments and even the death penalty for offenses. The edict also announced the appointment of responsible men as viziers and gave information about the division of the standing army into two main units, one in Upper Egypt and one in Lower Egypt. Horemhab not only published his edict throughout the land but also took inspection tours to make sure that all of the provisions were being carried out in the remote regions as well as in the cities.

When Horemhab approached his death without an heir, he appointed a military companion to succeed him, RAMESSES I. He built two tombs, one in SAQQARA (Memphis) and one in the Theban necropolis, the VALLEY OF THE KINGS. He was buried in THEBES. The Memphis tomb was erected before his ascent to the throne, and it became the burial place for Mutnodjmet and his first wife, AMENIA, a commoner.

His tomb in the Valley of the Kings is long and straight but unfinished. It begins with a steep descent through undecorated corridors to a false burial chamber with pillars. The inner rooms are elaborately decorated, and a red granite sarcophagus was provided for burial. The remains of four other individuals were also discovered in the tomb, possibly members of Horemhab's family. The tomb in Saqqara (Memphis) has magnificent reliefs and sumptuous remains of funerary regalia. His mummy was not found in either tomb.

Horhirwonmef (fl. 13th century B.C.E.) *prince of the Nineteenth Dynasty*
He was a son of RAMESSES II (r. 1290–1224 B.C.E.), the 12th son designated as the heir to the throne, but he died before his father. Horhirwonmef was depicted in LUXOR Temple reliefs as leading prisoners at the battle of KADESH. He was probably buried in the massive structure called the Tomb of the Sons of Ramesses II, in the

VALLEY OF THE KINGS. This tomb contains greater than 100 chambers.

horizon A spiritual symbol, the *akhet* was a metaphysical term used to describe shrines and other religious objects. The horizon was the universe, both in the past and in the present. Temples and shrines were considered the actual land of glory in which the gods resided through time. The actual plots of land upon which temples stood were called the PRIMEVAL MOUNDS of creation. The *akhet* symbol depicted two mounds side by side with a space in which the sun appeared at dawn.

The AKER lions guarded the horizon, which was called the home of HORUS. The pylons and gates of temples reproduced the image of the two mounds side by side, framing the light, thus serving as true images of the horizon. The WINDOW OF APPEARANCE used in temples and capital cities by the royal families was associated with the horizon.

The god RÉ was at times depicted as a winged creature that studied the horizon, seeking the enemies of Egypt. The Great Sphinx at GIZA was called Horemku and saluted as "the Watcher on the Horizon."

Hor of Sebennytos (fl. second century B.C.E.) *prophet of the Ptolemaic Period known for his ability to foresee the future*
He had an audience with PTOLEMY VI PHILOMETOR (r. 180–164, 163–145 B.C.E.) in ALEXANDRIA, on August 29, 168 B.C.E. During this court session Hor predicted that the hated Seleucid king ANTIOCHUS IV would leave Egypt in peace. Antiochus had invaded the Nile area in 170 B.C.E., taking control of the child ruler. A Seleucid governor remained in Alexandria when Antiochus left, administrating Egypt until Antiochus's return in 168 B.C.E.

The Romans, already a power in the Mediterranean world, sent Papillius Laenas to Antiochus's camp in PELUSIUM in the Delta to announce that Rome wanted the Seleucids out of Egypt, drawing a line in the sand to demonstrate the threat that Rome's legions offered. Antiochus and his people left the region within a month, and Hor achieved considerable recognition for predicting this. He may have been a true seer or may have had advance word of the Roman intentions. Hor was the administrator of the sacred IBIS cult in MEMPHIS. The ibis was a symbol of the god THOTH.

horse A domesticated animal introduced into Egypt in the Second Intermediate Period (1640–1532 B.C.E.), probably by the invading HYKSOS, there was a burial site for a horse at the fortress of BUHEN in NUBIA (modern Sudan) that dates to the Middle Kingdom (2040–1640 B.C.E.), but the animal was not seen extensively at that time. The Hyksos left a horse burial at Deir el-Dab'a in the Delta.

The horse was used by the Hyksos in CHARIOT forces. The Egyptians under KAMOSE (r. 1555–1550 B.C.E.) and then 'AHMOSE (NEBPEHTIRÉ) (r. 1550–1525 B.C.E.) adopted the chariots and bred the available horses in order to campaign against the Hyksos outposts. The original horses introduced did not carry human riders, but the Egyptians adapted them over time. By the middle of the Eighteenth Dynasty (ca. 1391) horses became valued gifts sent by the Egyptian pharaohs to neighboring vassal kings and allies.

The Egyptian adaptation of the animal, and the formation of the dreaded cavalry units of the Nile forces, enabled the pharaohs to achieve their vast empire. RAMESSES II (r. 1290–1224 B.C.E.) had a pair of favorite horses that pulled his royal chariot and helped him escape the HITTITE ambush by Muwatallis and his forces at KADESH. The horses were named "Victory in Thebes" and "Mut Is Pleased." These steeds were well cared for and stabled at the royal residence. Other pharaohs employed Hurrians, well known for their skills with horses, and the cavalry of the empire period was well supplied with new horses from the ongoing breeding programs.

When the Nubian warrior-king Piankhi (r. 750–712 B.C.E.) invaded Egypt to restore the cult of the god Amun, the defeated Egyptian rulers sent him women from their court as gifts. Piankhi is recorded as thanking them for the women but said that he would have preferred Egyptian horses.

Horurre (fl. 19th century B.C.E.) *expedition leader and mining official of the Twelfth Dynasty*
Horurre served AMENEMHET III (r. 1844–1797 B.C.E.) as seal-bearer, director of gangs (work groups), friend of the Great House (the palace), and expedition leader. He left a STELA inscribed with his biographical details in SERABIT EL-KHADIM, a turquoise mine in the SINAI. He dedicated a temple altar and two other stelae to the goddess HATHOR on the site. A temple had been erected at a cave, invoking Hathor as "the Lady of Turquoise."

Horus The Greek name for the Egyptian Hor, one of the oldest deities of the nation. The original form of Horus was that of a falcon or HAWK. He was a solar deity, considered a manifestation of the pharaoh in the afterlife. Early inscriptions depict Horus with his wings outstretched as a protector of the nation's rulers. In the Early Dynastic Period (2920–2575 B.C.E.) and into the Old Kingdom (2575–2134 B.C.E.) the rulers used the god's name as part of their royal titles. The SEREKH (1), the earliest of the pharaoh's symbols, depicted a falcon, or hawk, on a perch for DJER (ca. 2850 B.C.E.). As a result, devotion to Horus spread throughout Egypt, but in various locales the forms, traditions, and rituals honoring the god varied. In each nome cult center Horus was known by a different epithet.

In the form of Horus the Elder, the god's eyes were the sun and the moon, and his battle with the god SET

Horus, the great deity of Egypt, depicted as a hawk or falcon in a temple sanctuary *(Courtesy Steve Beikirch)*

epitomized the eternal struggle between darkness and light, good and evil. Horus was called Haroeris by the Greeks when they came to Egypt. As Horus of Gold, Hor Nubti, the god was the destroyer of Set. The Egyptian name Harakhte meant "Horus of the Horizon," who merged with Ré at Heliopolis, gradually losing identity and becoming Ré-Harakhte.

Horus the Behdetite was a celestial falcon god with a great shrine at Edfu. When his father was attacked by Set and his fellow demons, this Horus soared up into the air to scout the terrain for demons. He was called Horus Netj-Hor-Atef, Horus the Avenger of His Father. Turning into a winged sun disk, he attacked Set's forces and battled them, on the earth and in TUAT, the Underworld. The war was almost endless, but Horus proved victorious. As a result, the emblem of the sun disk became a popular symbol in Egypt. This Horus was also depicted in reliefs as the protector of Egypt's dynasties. One of the most famous Horus images can be found in the statue of KHAFRE (r. 2520–2494 B.C.E.) in the Egyptian Museum in Cairo. The falcon protects the head and shoulders of the seated pharaoh.

Hor-sa-iset, or the Greek Harsiesis, was one of the most popular forms of Horus in Egypt. This was the Horus, Son of ISIS. As a child the god was called Harpocrates by the Greeks and Horpakhered by the Egyptians and was a much-loved deity. The Horus, Son of

Isis, had been sired by the dead OSIRIS and hidden on the island of CHEMMIS by his goddess mother. The goddess WADJET, the protector of Lower Egypt, stayed on the island as a serpent to keep watch over the child and his mother. While Set's henchmen sought the divine pair, Wadjet kept them covered with reeds and papyrus. This Horus suffered many assaults while still a child but survived to attack Set in vengeance for the death of Osiris. Victorious at last, having suffered the loss of one eye in combat with Set, Horus became Horu-Semai-Taui, the Horus, Unifier of the Two Lands. He reestablished the authority of Osiris over the eternal realms and began the solar cycles of life on the Nile. In the New Kingdom (1550–1070 B.C.E.), both Horus and Set were depicted as the gods who brought the double crowns of Upper and Lower Egypt to the ruler. The Set-Horus-Osiris legends continued throughout Egyptian history, varying with each new generation.

Originally, Horus was called "the far one," depicted as a man or as a falcon-headed man. He was also revered as Hor-a'akhuti (Horakhte), the sun god on two horizons, part of his cult as Harmakhis. As Hor-Khentikhati, he was Horus in the Womb, as Hor-sa-Aset, he was the son of Isis. The blind Horus, representing night sky without a moon, was Hor-Khenti-an-ma'ati. The god's other titles included Hor-Hekenu, the Horus of Praises; Hor-Merti, the Hawk Headed; and Horus-An-Mutef, Horus, the Pillar of His Mother.

The Horus Eye was an occult symbol associated with the deity HORUS, representing the eye lost in his battle to avenge his father, OSIRIS. After SET caused this wound, ISIS restored the eye, which was called "the healthy eye" ever after. It was considered a powerful symbol. The AMULET depicting the Horus Eye was fashioned out of blue or green faience or from semiprecious stones.

Horus Eye   *See* HORUS.

Horus's Four Sons   *See* CANOPIC JARS.

Hor-wen-nefer (fl. 3rd century B.C.E.) *native Egyptian who tried to establish an independent state at Thebes*
Hor-wen-nefer rebelled in 206 B.C.E. against the reign of PTOLEMY IV PHILOPATOR (221–205 B.C.E.). The Ptolemaic military confronted Hor-wen-nefer immediately, ending his attempts and routing confederates and allies.
See also REBELS OF EGYPT.

Hotepiriaket (fl. 23rd century B.C.E.) *fifth Dynasty priest noted for his tomb text*
He served as a mortuary attendant in the temple of KAKAI (Neferirkaré; r. 2446–2426 B.C.E.) at ABUSIR. Hotepiriaket's tomb contained a remarkable text in which he implored visitors to donate mortuary gifts of bread, beer, clothing, ointments, grains, and other items "in great quantity." He also offered to intercede for all generous donors in the afterlife.

Hotepsekhemwy (Boethos; Buzau) (fl. ca. 2770 B.C.E.) *founder of the Second Dynasty of Egypt*
He may have been related to QA'A, the last ruler of the First Dynasty who died ca. 2575 B.C.E. His name meant "Pleasing in Might." A Thinite, Hotepsekhemwy was listed as Boethos by MANETHO and Buzau in other accounts. He did not erect a tomb at ABYDOS, preferring southern Saqqara, but he did build a temple there. His SEREKH (1) designs were discovered near the pyramid of UNIS (r. 2356–2323 B.C.E.). Various speculations have been made concerning the actual site of Hotep sekhem-wy's tomb. The burial place, a site in SAQQARA, may have been obscured or demolished when Unis erected his own complex.

House of Adorers   An institution associated with the temple of Amun during the New Kingdom (1550–1070 B.C.E.), also called the House of the Adoratrices, the institution was part of the evolving roles of women as the GOD'S WIFE OF AMUN. The services and practices of this religious organization were absorbed into the God's Wife of Amun after the New Kingdom collapsed. Then the office, restricted to women of royal rank, assumed political as well as cultic powers.

House of Life   *See PER-ANKH.*

Hraf-hef   *See "HE-WHO-LOOKS-BEHIND-HIMSELF."*

Hreré (fl. 10th century B.C.E.) *royal woman of the Twenty-first Dynasty (1070–945 B.C.E.)*
She was the wife of one of the high priests of AMUN, who ruled at THEBES, in Upper Egypt. Hreré married the high priest PIANKHI (2) and bore PINUDJEM (1). Piankhi had to put down rebels during his term of office. There is some evidence that Hreré possibly was a daughter of HERIHOR.

Hu   An Egyptian deity associated with the sensation of taste, the god was worshipped in early eras of the nation and was mentioned in a document in a temple of HELIOPOLIS, dating to the reign of SENWOSRET I (1971–1926 B.C.E.). No cultic shrines dedicated to Hu have survived.

Hua   A mountain or high mound in the region of the NILE below the first cataract, Hua was a landmark used by the New Kingdom (1550–1070 B.C.E.) pharaohs in their campaigns in NUBIA (modern Sudan). The mountain was a navigational point for Egyptian ships and a southern measuring site for both military and TRADE expeditions.
   See also GEBEL BARKAL.

Hudet   *See RÉ.*

Hunefer Papyrus   A copy of the BOOK OF THE DEAD dating to the reign of SETI I (1306–1290 B.C.E.) in the Nineteenth Dynasty, the text was either composed in that reign or copied from an earlier version. Beautifully illustrated, the Hunefer Papyrus is in the British Museum, London.

Huni (d. 2575 B.C.E.) *fifth and last ruler of the Third Dynasty, called "the Smiter"*
He was the successor of KHA'BA, reigning from 2599 B.C.E. until his death, but no relationship has been documented. He married MERYSANKH (1), probably an heiress of the royal clan, and she bore him a son, SNEFRU. He also had a daughter, HETEPHERES (1).
   Huni built a pyramid at MEIDUM, on the edge of the FAIYUM, using a square ground plan. Step styled, the PYRAMID was covered with Tureh limestone. Three steps remain, as the limestone covering collapsed. A burial chamber was carved out of the bedrock, and a causeway and temple were erected. He may have been buried in the site, which was completed by Snefru. MASTABA tombs of courtiers and nobles were built around the pyramid. One such tomb, the resting place of NEFERMA'AT and his wife ATET, contained the famous relief paintings of geese. The statues of Prince RAHOTEP (1) and NOFRET (1), his wife, were discovered in another mastaba.
   Huni reportedly erected a brick pyramidal tomb in ABU ROWASH, south of SAQQARA. This layered tomb is badly damaged. A red granite head of Huni is in the British Museum. Huni is also credited with a fortress on the ELEPHANTINE Island in some records. During his reign, KAGEMNI, the famous sage, served as his VIZIER.

Hurbeit   A site in the Nile Delta, northeast of BUBASTIS, where the remains of a temple were uncovered. The seals of RAMESSES II (r. 1290–1224 B.C.E.) were found on building blocks of the temple. Sacred BULLS were buried at Hurbeit in some periods. The Greeks renamed the site Pharbaites.

Hurrians   A people whose homeland was originally near Lake Urmia, in northern Mesopotamia (modern Iraq), in the reign of AMENEMHET III (1844–1797 B.C.E.), the Hurrians invaded the lands east of the Tigris River. By 2200 B.C.E., they were thriving at their capital, Urkesh, and building the Temple of the Lion. They used the Hurrian and Akkadian languages and worshipped a pantheon of gods. By 1780 B.C.E., the Hurrians had achieved military and political power on the upper Tigris and Euphrates Rivers and on the border of Anatolia (modern Turkey). Urkesh had an estimated population of 10,000 to 20,000 at its height. The capital was abandoned, however, ca. 1500 because of climatic changes and failing water supplies.
   The HITTITES admired the Hurrians and feared their military prowess. When the Hurrians approached Syria and Palestine, local city-states learned to appreciate their martial abilities. Egyptians respected the Hurrians as expert horsemen and used their talents during the New Kingdom (1550–1070 B.C.E.). The Hurrians also had

access to metals and used stone effectively. They excelled at mining and trade. Reportedly, Queen TIYE, the powerful consort of AMENHOTEP III (r. 1391–1353 B.C.E.), was of Hurrian descent.

Huy (1) (Amenhotep) (fl. 14th century B.C.E.) *officials and viceroy of the Eighteenth Dynasty*

He served TUT'ANKHAMUN (r. 1333–1323 B.C.E.) as the VICEROY of Nubia (modern Sudan). Huy, called Amenhotep in some records, was buried in QURNET MURAI, on the western shore of THEBES. His tomb contained elaborate paintings depicting Tut'ankhamun receiving Nubian subjects and accepting tributes.

Huy (2) (Amenhotep) (fl. 14th century B.C.E.) *governor of the Eighteenth Dynasty*

He served AKHENATEN (r. 1353–1335 B.C.E.) as the governor of the BAHARIA OASIS. He was also listed as Amenhotep in some records. Huy's tomb at Baharia was discovered previously but not identified until 1986.

Huya (fl. 14th century B.C.E.) *harem official of the Eighteenth Dynasty*

He served in the reign of AMENHOTEP III (1391–1353 B.C.E.) as a steward of Queen TIYE (1) and the superintendent of the royal HAREM. He followed Queen Tiye to 'AMARNA after Amenhotep III's death and served the entire royal family, including AKHENATEN and NEFERTITI.

Huya's tomb in 'Amarna contains pillared chambers and an inner room with a burial shaft and a shrine. Reliefs depict him at a royal banquet, court ceremonies, and having honors bestowed upon him by Akhenaten. A statue of Huya, unfinished, was also recovered. Queen Tiye and Princess BAKETAMUN (Baketaten) are also depicted in the tomb.

Hyksos   A nomadic group that swept over Syria, Palestine, and Egypt ca. 1750 B.C.E., the earliest recorded Hyksos had Canaanite names, associating them with the Amorites of the same period. A STELA found at TANIS states that they took the area of AVARIS ca. 1640 B.C.E. From Avaris they moved into Memphis. These Asiatics, called the *Hikau-Khoswet, Amu, A'am,* or *Setetyu* by the Egyptians, were recorded by the Ptolemaic Period historian MANETHO as having suddenly appeared in the Nile Valley. He wrote that they rode their horse-drawn chariots to establish a tyranny in the land. They did enter Egypt, but they did not appear suddenly, with what Manetho termed "a blast of God."

The Hyksos entered the Nile region gradually over a series of decades until the Egyptians realized the danger they posed in their midst. Most of the Asiatics came across Egypt's borders without causing much of a stir. Some had distinguished themselves as leaders of vast trading caravans that kept Egypt's economy secure. Others were supposedly veterans of the various border

police, started in the Middle Kingdom when AMENEMHET I (r. 1991–1962 B.C.E.) constructed the WALL OF THE PRINCE, the series of fortresses that guarded the eastern and western borders of the land.

If there was a single factor that increased the Asiatic population in Egypt, it was slavery, introduced officially as an institution in the Middle Kingdom (2040–1640 B.C.E.). Asiatics came either as captives or as immigrants eager for employment. As workers they were assimilated into Egyptian society. During the Second Intermediate Period (1640–1550 B.C.E.), when several rival dynasties competed in the land, the Asiatics gained control of the eastern Delta. Moving steadily southward and making treaties with nomes or subjecting them with the aid of Egyptian allies, the Asiatics established themselves firmly. Only THEBES, the capital of the south, stood resolute against their expansion, and the Hyksos were denied most of Upper Egypt. Their hold on the western Delta is poorly documented. For a time the nome clan of XOIS stood independent. The Xois Dynasty, the Fourteenth Dynasty, was contemporaneous with the Fifteenth Dynasty (1640–1532 B.C.E.). While these rulers remained independent, the Asiatics moved around them and built their domain at AVARIS, a site in the eastern Delta, as their capital.

In the beginning, Thebes and Avaris managed to conduct their affairs with a certain tolerance. The Hyksos sailed to the southern cataracts of the Nile to conduct trade without being hindered, and the Theban cattle barons grazed their herds in the Delta without incident. There were two separate royal lines of Hyksos in the Delta, the Fifteenth, called "the Great Hyksos," and a contemporaneous Sixteenth Dynasty, ruling over minor holdings.

The Thebans were soon contesting the Asiatic control, and the Theban Seventeenth Dynasty (1640–1550 B.C.E.) began to harass their caravans and ships. APOPHIS (2), the Hyksos ruler who came to the throne in 1585 B.C.E., then sent an insult to Sekenenré TA'O II of Thebes and found himself in the middle of a full scale war as a result. KAMOSE took up the battle when Sekenenré Ta'o died, using the desert oases as hiding places for his army. The young Egyptian was in striking distance of Avaris when he died or was slain. Apophis died a short time before him. 'AHMOSE, (NEBPEHTIRÉ) the founder of the Eighteenth Dynasty and the father of the New Kingdom (1550–1070 B.C.E.), took up the battle of his father and brother and laid siege to Avaris. The city fell to him in c. 1532 B.C.E., and the Asiatics fled to Sharuhen in Palestine, with the Egyptians in hot pursuit. When Sharuhen fell to the same Egyptian armies, the Hyksos ran to Syria. Thus the Hyksos domination of Egypt was ended.

Building at Tell ed-Dab'a, or Lisht, the Hyksos founded Avaris as a fortified city with palaces and enclosed tombs. The population was mixed, and heavy trade in oil and wine flourished. A Minoan influence is evident at Avaris, and some 500 pieces of Cyprian pottery, containing oils and perfumes, were discovered. Minoan inscriptions were also found on Cypriot spindle-shaped bottles. Hyksos styled vessels called *bilbils* and poppy-shaped as well as spindle style jugs held perfumes, HONEY, and opium.

As the Middle Kingdom declined and fell, the Hyksos rose at TELL ED-DAB'A, Tell Hiba, and TANIS. Avaris flourished with fortified citadels, gardens, and vineyards. The paintings in the residences were Minoan in style. The Hyksos worshiped SET, uniting him with the Canaanite Baal-Reshef. Several of the Hyksos rulers opened Egypt's eastern borders, welcoming Canaanites and other groups into the Nile Valley.

The Asiatics had come to the Nile to absorb the material benefits of Egyptian civilization. In turn, the Hyksos introduced the HORSE and CHARIOT, the *SHADUF* (the irrigational implement that revolutionized the farming techniques), and military weapons that transformed the armies of the Nile into formidable forces. The Hyksos episode also brought an awareness to the Egyptians that they could not remain in isolation. That realization served as an impetus for later expansion. The Tuthmossid rulers would march in cycles of conquest to the Euphrates River areas as declared instruments of vengeance for the Asiatic dominance of Egypt for more than a century.

See also QUARREL OF APOPHIS AND SEKENENRÉ (TA'O II).

Further reading: Oren, Eliezer D. *The Hyksos: New Historical and Archaeological Perspectives.* University Museum Monograph 96. Philadelphia: University of Pennsylvania Press, 1997.

Hyksos, expulsion of the   The location of Egypt had always deterred invasion, as it was bordered by the two deserts and sheltered by cliffs that created the Nile Valley. At the close of the Middle Kingdom in ca. 1640 B.C.E., however, nomadic clans appeared on the banks of the Nile. Egypt's barriers had failed to deter these clans from entering the valley, and soon they were not only within Egypt's borders but in positions of power in the Delta. Consisting of Asiatic clans called the Hikau-Khoswet, Aam, Amu, or Setetyu, this group was collectively called the Hyksos and was probably associated with the Amorite peoples of the same era, as the Hyksos people had Canaanite names.

CONTEXT

The Hyksos were able fighters, and utilizing their horse-drawn chariots, they had brought destruction to other lands; they swept over Syria, Palestine, and other regions around 1750 B.C.E. Although the Egyptian historian Manetho (fl. 3rd century B.C.E.) claimed that the Hyksos arrived in a sudden attack that he called "a blast from god," many Asiatics actually came to Egypt as captives during the Middle Kingdom Period (2040–1640 B.C.E.), when slavery was introduced officially as an institution. It was during this period that the temple priesthoods began operating vast plantations for agricultural products and demanded that workers be made available; Egyptian rulers met this need with the vast number of prisoners brought back to Egypt from their endless wars.

Not all Hyksos arrived to Egypt enslaved, however. Some also came as immigrants eager for employment. While as workers they were assimilated into Egyptian society, they were looked down upon by the Egyptians; the Hyksos were unhygienic, according to Egyptian standards. The Egyptian upper classes, who mostly wore linen, shaved their heads for the sake of cleanliness, bathed as many as seven times a day, and were fastidious in their personal hygiene; the Hyksos generally wore heavy woven robes and cared little about bathing. Further contributing to their alienation from the Egyptians, some Hyksos had red hair. (The only creatures with red hair in the Nile Valley before the Hyksos arrived were donkeys.)

During the Second Intermediate Period (1640–1550 B.C.E.), when several rival dynasties competed in the northern lands, the Asiatics allied themselves with Egyptian nomarchs and aristocrats and gained political control of the eastern Delta. Moving steadily southward and making treaties with nomes or subjecting them with the aid of Egyptian allies, the Asiatics firmly established themselves. Although they had been living in Egypt and slowly raising their status in society since the Middle Kingdom, it was not until the Second Intermediate Period that the Egyptians living in the Delta began to feel the Hyksos's now-powerful presence. Only THEBES, the capital of the south, ultimately stood resolute against their expansion and remained independent, though for a time the nome clan of XOIS, a site in the Delta, stood independent as well. While these rulers remained autonomous, they were limited in their powers, as the Hyksos surrounded them and built their domain at AVARIS, a site in the eastern Delta, as their capital. Though powerful in the Delta, the Hyksos were denied most of Upper Egypt and were able to move only as far south as CUSAE.

EVENT

For a time, Thebes and Avaris managed to conduct their affairs with a certain tolerance. The Hyksos sailed to the southern cataracts of the Nile to conduct trade without being hindered, and the Theban cattle barons grazed their herds in the Delta without incident. Soon, however, Thebans were contesting Asiatic control. The Thebans, during the reign of the ruler TA'O II (Sekenenré; Djehuti'o), began to harass Hyksos caravans and ships and reclaimed land, forcing the Hyksos to retreat northward.

Then Ta'o II received a message, allegedly from the Hyksos ruler at Avaris, Apophis (who had come to the throne in 1585 B.C.E.). A Hyksos official arrived at the Theban court and announced that his master Apophis was upset because the snoring hippopotami in the sacred pool at Thebes were keeping him awake at night with their unseemly noises. The message, contained in the SALLIER PAPYRI and called the QUARREL OF APOPHIS AND SEKENENRÉ (Ta'o II), was somewhat of a shock to the Thebans, since Apophis's bedchamber was more than 400 miles north of the sacred pool. Ta'o II, receiving the message, declared that it was an insult. Ta'o promptly declared official war on Avaris and began the campaign to drive the Hyksos out of Egypt, who at that time ruled Lower Egypt as far south as Cusae.

The Hyksos tried to halt the Theban campaigns, ambushing Ta'o II and his advancing forces with axes, spears, and possibly arrows. Ta'o then met a violent death, probably at the hands of enemy attackers. He suffered five major wounds, including two axe cuts that caused a skull fracture, a blow to the bridge of his nose, a blow to the left cheek, and another to the right side of his head. Studies of Ta'o II's mummy show that his ribs and vertebrae were also damaged. The mummy had no wounds on the arms or hands, indicating that Ta'o II was disabled by a blow from behind him and then slain viciously. He was attacked some distance from Thebes, apparently, because his remains were not given mortuary rituals early enough to stop bodily decay. (The mummy to this day has a pungent odor, indicating a delay in the mummification and purification processes.)

After being slain, KAMOSE, Ta'o II's eldest son and heir to the throne of Thebes, took up the crusade with renewed vengeance. Kamose carried on the military confrontations against the Hyksos, using the desert oases as hiding places for his army, and was approaching Avaris when he too died. Apophis did not live long after Kamose's death, and the war between Thebes and Avaris temporarily came to a halt.

Kamose's younger brother, 'AHMOSE (NEBPEHTIRÉ), the founder of the Eighteenth Dynasty and the father of the New Kingdom (1550–1070 B.C.E.), was the last son and heir of Ta'o II. As he was too young to conduct a campaign, the Thebans and Hyksos kept an uneasy truce for a decade. Reaching his majority, however, 'Ahmose took up the battle of his late father and brother and laid siege to Avaris. The city fell to him in ca. 1532 B.C.E., and the Asiatics fled to Sharuhen, in Palestine, with the Egyptians in hot pursuit. When Sharuhen fell to the same Egyptian armies, the Hyksos retreated to Syria. Thus the Hyksos's domination of Egypt was ended. 'Ahmose punished all of the aristocrats of the Delta who had supported the Hyksos, and he then routed the Nubians (modern Sudanese), who were planning to invade Egypt from the south. 'Ahmose attributed his military success to the god Amun.

IMPACT

The god Amun had been worshiped by Thebans since Egypt's earliest times, but once 'Ahmose credited his victory over the Hyksos—as well as all of his future victories—to the god, he elevated Amun's importance to the nation. The pharaohs succeeding 'Ahmose throughout the Eighteenth Dynasty also credited their victories to Amun, who, by the end of this dynasty, was a preeminent, all-powerful deity worshipped by the nation.

Amun received considerable support from the ruling clan, especially at KARNAK, an ancient religious complex erected in Thebes, and the city became the deity's cult center. The Tuthmossids of the Eighteenth Dynasty (1550–1307 B.C.E.) lavished care and wealth upon Thebes, making it the nation's new capital, although the previous capital, Memphis, remained an administrative center of government and a temporary residence of the royal clan. During the period of AKHENATEN (r. 1353–1335 B.C.E.), Thebes was abandoned for el-'Amarna, to the north. Akhenaten's death, however, signaled a return to Thebes and a resumption of the building projects and adornment of the temples, shrines, and royal residences. The western shore of Thebes became a vast and beautiful necropolis, as stunning mortuary complexes were built at Deir el-Bahri (where MENTUHOTEP II had erected his mortuary temple in the Eleventh Dynasty) and in the Valley of the Kings and the Valley of the Queens. The shrines, temples, and buildings erected in Thebes gave it a reputation for splendor and beauty that lasted for centuries. All other cities were judged after the pattern of Thebes.

"Hymn of Rising" A ceremony conducted each morning in the palaces of ancient Egypt. Courtiers and priests wakened the pharaoh and the gods with songs and hymns of praise. The lyrics of the songs were dedicated to NEKHEBET and WADJET, the protectors of Upper and Lower Egypt.

hypostyle hall A Greek term for a room or chamber that has many columns. The architectural innova-

Hypostyle columns displayed in the temple of Luxor in the papyrus bundle design (*Courtesy Steve Beikirch*)

tion developed gradually in Egypt, starting with the first attached pillars placed by IMHOTEP in the courtyard of the STEP PYRAMID of DJOSER (r. 2630–2611 B.C.E.) in SAQQARA. Such halls became a feature of Egyptian architecture, a reference to the reeds of the primordial marsh of creation or to the forests that had vanished on the Nile.

See also ART AND ARCHITECTURE.

I

Ibhet A site near the second cataract of the Nile, located in NUBIA (modern Sudan), Ibhet contains a QUARRY of black granite. The Egyptians discovered the mine in the Sixth Dynasty Period (2323–2150 B.C.E.) or perhaps earlier. By the Middle Kingdom (2040–1640 B.C.E.) expeditions were active at the site. AMENEMHET III (r. 1844–1797 B.C.E.) led a campaign against the local inhabitants of Ibhet in his first regnal year. The Egyptians prized the stone and maintained fortified operations in Ibhet.

See also NATURAL RESOURCES.

Ibi (fl. 22nd century B.C.E.) *official of the Sixth Dynasty*
He was the son of Djau, the brother of Queens ANKHNESMERY-RÉ (1) and ANKHNESMERY-RÉ (2), and a cousin of PEPI II (r. 2246–2152 B.C.E.). Ibi was trained for government service and became the VIZIER of the southern region, Upper Egypt. He was buried in DEIR EL-GEBRAWI near ASSIUT, and in his tomb he promises to "pounce" on anyone who enters his tomb with evil intentions. Ibi married a nome heiress and served as nomarch of THINIS for a time. His son, Djau (Zau) Shemai, succeeded him and in turn ruled as "the Keeper of the Door to the South," an ELEPHANTINE Island noble position.

ibis This bird was considered sacred to the Egyptian god of wisdom, THOTH. The ibis was considered a theophany of Thoth and was praised for its purification practices. The city of HERMOPOLIS MAGNA was the cult center for ibises. Another ibis shrine, called the Ikheum, was located north of the city and attracted many wor-shippers. The mummified remains of ibises have been recovered in several areas.

ibu The mortuary site where mummified corpses were purified and prepared for the journey into Tuat, or the Underworld. These were sometimes part of the royal pyramidal complexes, mainly the VALLEY TEMPLES. In some records this mortuary site was called the *PERNEFER*, or House of Beauty. Monuments such as the pyramids at GIZA had *ibus* in the form of valley temples as part of the main complex.

Ichneumon (Shet, Seshet) The mongoose deity of Egypt, called Khatru as an animal and Shet or Seshet as a god. The Greeks identified the deity as Ichneumon. Statues of the mongoose, standing erect, were attired in the sun disk. The Ichneumon, revered because it could slay evil serpents, was considered a theophany of the god ATUM of HELIOPOLIS. Because it ate crocodile eggs, it was associated with the god RÉ. In some depictions the Ichneumon brandished weapons of war.

Idu (fl. 23rd century B.C.E.) *mortuary official of the Sixth Dynasty*
He served PEPI I (r. 2289–2255 B.C.E.) as a supervisor of mortuary priests and ceremonies at the pyramidal complexes of KHUFU (Cheops) and KHAFRE (Chephren) at GIZA. Idu and others maintained daily MORTUARY RITUALS at such funerary sites, as the cults of the deceased pharaohs continued for decades. The number of cultic personnel involved normally led to the building of small

cities alongside the pyramids and to the appointment of officials and urban service agencies.

Ihy (fl. 20th century B.C.E.) *innovative courtier of the Twelfth Dynasty*
He served AMENEMHET I (r. 1991–1962 B.C.E.) as a mortuary ritual official. Ihy joined a coworker named Hetep in preparing a tomb as part of the mortuary complex of TETI (2323–2291 B.C.E.). They were servants of the funerary cult of Teti's PYRAMID complex in SAQQARA, erected during the Sixth Dynasty (2323–2150 B.C.E.), and they constructed twin tombs that had visible chapels on the outer boundaries of Teti's pyramid.

However, the two courtiers tunneled 15 feet down and 21 feet across the pyramidal boundaries in order to build their actual burial chambers as part of Teti's mortuary site. This, they believed, would entitle them to share in the pharaoh's heavenly rewards. The tombs built at the end of the tunnels were small but insured a prosperous afterlife for both men.

Ikhernofret (fl. 19th century B.C.E.) *mining official and treasurer of the Twelfth Dynasty*
He served SENWOSRET III (r. 1878–1841 B.C.E.) and was part of the campaigns to conquer NUBIA (modern Sudan). Ikhernofret was sent to ABYDOS to adorn the temple of the god OSIRIS there. An official named SISATET accompanied Ikhernofret to Abydos, where both men erected commemorative stelae. A supervisor of mining operations and the chief royal artisan, Ikhernofret prepared a portable shrine for Osiris and refurbished the Abydos temple complexes. His stela at Abydos lists these royal assignments as well as details of Senwosret III's campaigns in his 19th regnal year. Ikhernofret also performed treasury duties in Nubia.

Ikudidy (fl. 20th century B.C.E.) *expeditionary official of the Twelfth Dynasty*
He served SENWOSRET I (r. 1971–1926 B.C.E.) as a leader of expeditions in the western or LIBYAN DESERT. These military probes were momentous because the western desert regions had not been explored. Ikudidy mapped the OASES and the natural resources of the territory. He was buried in ABYDOS after long and faithful service to the throne. A STELA erected in Abydos provided biographical data about his exploits.

Imhotep (fl. 27th century B.C.E.) *priest-physician, vizier, and designer of the Step Pyramid at Saqqara*
Imhotep was an official of the Third Dynasty (2649–2575 B.C.E.) who served four pharaohs of Egypt. He was best known as the vizier and high priest of the god PTAH—a creator deity, worshipped since the earliest time on the Nile and popular for centuries—in the reign of DJOSER (2630–2611 B.C.E.). Imhotep designed and supervised the building of the STEP PYRAMID at SAQQARA as Djoser's mortuary complex.

BIOGRAPHY

Imhotep was a commoner by birth, born to Kaneferu and Ankh-Kherdu. Both parents are listed in an inscription found at WADI HAMMAMAT. Rising through the ranks in the court and in the temple, Imhotep became treasurer of Lower Egypt and was called "the First After the King." He also served as the administrator of the Great Palace, as the high priest of PTAH (called "the Son of Ptah"), and as the ruler's chief architect. He was known as "the wise counselor," as listed in the TURIN CANON.

The greatest achievement of Imhotep, the one that stands as a living monument to his genius, was the Step Pyramid at Saqqara. He built the complex as a mortuary shrine for Djoser, but it became a stage and an architectural model for the spiritual ideals of the Egyptian people. The Step Pyramid was not just a single pyramidal tomb but a collection of temples, chapels, pavilions, corridors, storerooms, and halls. Fluted columns engaged, or attached to, the limestone walls that emerged from the stone walls, according to his plan. Yet in the end he made the walls of the complex conform to those of the palace of Djoser, according to ancient styles of architecture, thus preserving a link to the past. The walls of the complex stretch a mile long and stand more than 30 feet high.

Djoser, knowing that he had to build his mortuary monuments, described his vision of them as a stage of resurrection, a dramatic symbol of faith in the afterlife. Most burials, even of royalty at the time, took place in underground chambers covered by a mastaba, the Arabic word for "bench," as the tomb coverings resembled benches. Djoser realized that there was nothing inspiring in a bench. He also wanted to place his tomb in a spectacular miniature city that the people could visit and where they could pray for his soul. (The Egyptian people are credited for inventing the concept of the soul and depicted it as a winged bird called the *ba*.)

Imhotep studied the site chosen by Djoser. The first thing that he had constructed was a mastaba made of mud bricks. With that base positioned, Imhotep's laborers added another mastaba, slightly smaller in size. The layering of mastabas continued until the six separate tiers rose above the plain. Through this design, a basic bench became a towering pyramid that dominated the area. The Step Pyramid could be seen for miles.

Imhotep also provided Djoser with a unique tomb addition: a chamber called the *serdab*, an Arabic word for cellar. The *serdab* held a statue of Djoser, positioned in front of a slot in the wall. The slot enables the eyes of the statue to look into the main area where priests conducted daily rituals honoring Djoser as a risen being. Thus, the deceased could witness the liturgies that kept him vital beyond the grave. The *serdab* was originally called "the House of the Eyes of Ka." The *ka* was an astral being that accompanied every human being on earth and led the deceased to paradise beyond the grave.

Imhotep also studied medicine, becoming "the Father of Medicine" on the Nile. When a famine struck Egypt, caused by low levels of Nile water, Imhotep advised Pharaoh Djoser to visit the shrine of the god KHNUM on the ELEPHANTINE Island at ASWAN. Djoser also claimed that he had a dream about Khnum. Djoser made the pilgrimage, and the floods reappeared and the crops grew. Thus, Imhotep became the "wise counselor" mentioned in the Turin Canon. Imhotep was also a renowned poet and priest-physician, equated with Asclepios, the Greek god of medicine and healing.

Imhotep's didactic texts were well known in later times, as were his medical writings. The Greeks honored him, and during the Roman Period the emperors Tiberius (r. 14–37 C.E.) and Claudius (r. 41–54 C.E.) inscribed their praises of Imhotep on the walls of Egyptian temples. He was deified with AMENHOTEP, a rare occurrence in Egypt, as commoners were normally not eligible for such honors. In the days following his deification, Imhotep's mother was given the status of a semidivine woman. Shrines and clinics were erected throughout the Nile Valley in his memory, and he was worshipped as far south as KALABSHA in NUBIA (modern Sudan). A temple of his cult was erected in PHILAE. Imhotep reportedly lived to the end of the reign of HUNI (r. 2599–2575 B.C.E.) and was believed to have been buried in Saqqara, but his tomb has not been identified.

HISTORICAL IMPACT

Imhotep was the most famous figure in the entire history of ancient Egypt who was not a member of a royal house or one of the dynasties. His fame has endured into modern times. He was arguably the most varied and multifaceted public servant in the long history of the Nile Valley and his contributions to society influenced generations to come.

"The Father of Medicine" on the Nile, Imhotep was one of the pioneers who introduced the traditions of giving diagnoses, procedures, prescriptions, and therapeutic care. He dismissed the magical spells of the past and provided physicians with methods for dealing with diseases, wounds, and disabilities that came with advanced age. Although no copy of the work has been preserved, Imhotep's medical primer, serving as a textbook for beginning physicians, was quoted widely by generations of Egyptians. (He is also the reputed author

of other medical texts, such as the EDWIN SMITH PAPYRUS.) Medical clinics and shrines were opened in his name all across the nation and many of those on the Nile remained opened for centuries.

Imhotep was also honored as a sage. In some cities, Egyptians would go to a shrine dedicated in Imhotep's name and sleep there for a night or two, attended by priests and servants. The overnight stays were prompted by the hope that Imhotep would appear to them in a dream and offer advice.

As an architect, the Step Pyramid was his masterpiece, as it unlocked religious, artistic, and architectural aspirations on the Nile. Few pharaohs could leave behind the great insignia of power that Imhotep had given to Djoser. This legacy makes Imhotep the first architect in history whose name has endured into modern times. He was honored not only with a host of inscriptions but statues that show him as a man of wisdom and learning, as well as humility. One such statue has survived, showing a somewhat small, refined individual, wearing a simple robe and a cultic priest's cap.

The completion of the Step Pyramid began the Egyptian obsession with pyramids and inspired future rulers and architects, such as SNEFRU (r. 2575–2551 B.C.E.), to keep erecting pyramids until they achieved what is now referred to as a "true" form. One such surviving pyramid, the Great Pyramid at Giza, was completed during the reign of Snefru's son and heir, KHUFU (Cheops) (r. 2551–2528 B.C.E.), and is the only surviving Wonder of the Ancient World.

The architectural mastery and diversity of the entire complex of the Step Pyramid spurred other visionaries to utilize materials and designs to make spiritual visions come to life. The semi-columns used by Imhotep, the first attempt at a true, freestanding pillar, led to the great colonnades and hypostyle halls at Karnak and other sacred sites.

A statue of Pharaoh Djoser contains an inscription on the base that clearly explains the position of Imhotep in the nation. The inscription states:

> The Chancellor of the King of Lower Egypt,
> the First Under the ruler of Upper Egypt,
> Administrator of the Great House, Hereditary
> Lord, the High Priest of Heliopolis, Imhotep,
> the builder, the sculptor.

Further reading: Allen, James, et al. *The Art of Medicine in Ancient Egypt.* New York: Metropolitan Museum of Art, 2000; Hurry, Jamieson. *Imhotep: The Vizier and Physician of King Zoser.* Oxford, U.K.: Oxford University Press, 2000.

Imi (Yem) (fl. 20th century B.C.E.) *royal woman of the Eleventh Dynasty*
She was the consort of MENTUHOTEP III (r. 2010–1998 B.C.E.) but not the Great Wife or ranking queen. Imi was

the mother of MENTUHOTEP IV. An inscription in WADI HAMMAMAT praises her as a royal mother.

Imsety He was one of the four "Sons of HORUS" associated with the mortuary rituals of Egypt. The Sons of Horus assisted with the mummification process and served as patrons of the deceased as the guardians of the CANOPIC JARS used to store the vital organs removed from the mummified remains. Imsety was the guardian of the liver. The stoppers on his canopic vessels were carved to portray a human head.

Imu (Kom el-Hisn) This was a site in the western Delta of Egypt, south of NAUKRATIS, modern Kom el-Hisn. A temple that was dedicated to the cults of the deities SEKHMET and HATHOR was erected at Imu by SENWOSRET I (r. 1971–1926 B.C.E.). A rectangular structure, the temple also contained statues of AMENEMHET III (r. 1844–1797 B.C.E.) and RAMESSES II (r. 1290–1224 B.C.E.), installed in later dynasties. Imu became the capital of the third nome of Lower Egypt. The necropolis associated with the site contains tombs from the First Intermediate Period (2134–2040 B.C.E.) to the New Kingdom (1550–1070 B.C.E.).

Inaros (fl. fifth century B.C.E.) *Egyptian rebel in the Persian Period*
Inaros was from the southwestern Delta, possibly the son of a commoner named Psammetichus. He is also listed as a prince of HELIOPOLIS, the son of PSAMMETICHUS III. Inaros established his headquarters near modern ALEXANDRIA and rebelled against the rule of ARTAXERXES I (r. 465–424 B.C.E.), a Persian of the royal Achaemenid line. He clashed with Persian forces at Papremis, a site in the northwestern Delta. Achaemenes, a prince and the brother of the Persian king, XERXES I, was slain in the battle, and the Persians were forced to retreat to MEMPHIS.

The Persian general MEGABYZUS was sent to put down the revolt as a result of this defeat, and Inaros and his companions were driven to an island in the Nile marshes. Inaros was betrayed by a fellow rebel and was captured. The queen mother, Amastris, of Persia demanded his crucifixion, despite the arguments from General Mega byzus, who had given Inaros a pledge of safety. Inaros was crucified in 454 B.C.E. His ally, however, an Egyptian named AMYRTAIOS (1), remained undefeated in the Delta. Another AMYRTAIOS (2) founded the Twenty-eighth Dynasty in 404 B.C.E.

incense An important material for religious and royal rites in Egypt, called *senetjer,* several types of incense were used in rituals in the temples and at royal cult celebrations. Myrrh, a red form of incense imported from PUNT, was considered the most sacred and was used for the most solemn of rituals. Frankincense, or *olibanum,* was also favored. Incense was a purifying element in all of the Egyptian observances and was the substance used to bestow honor upon the gods and the dead or living rulers. Myrrh incense was offered in the temples at noon. At sunset the compound called *kyphi* was used. The pellets of the chosen resins were put in a bronze censer pan with a long wooden handle. A pottery bowl heated with charcoal was used to burn the incense and the sanctuary was perfumed.

Ineni (fl. 15th century B.C.E.) *overseer of the granary of Amun and an architect of the Eighteenth Dynasty*
Ineni served TUTHMOSIS I (r. 1504–1492 B.C.E.) and continued in the court through the reign of HATSHEPSUT (1473–1458 B.C.E.). He may have entered service at the court of THEBES, in the reign of Amenhotep I (1524–1504 B.C.E.). Ineni was one of the most revered architects of his age, supervising various projects at KARNAK.

He built the original tombs, one large, one small, of Tuthmosis I and transported and erected OBELISKS for that ruler. As overseer of the Granary of AMUN, Ineni erected a protective wall around the deity's Theban shrine. PYLONS were added, as well as doors made of copper and gold. Ineni also designed flagstaffs, called *senut* by the Egyptians, at Karnak. These flagstaffs were fashioned out of cedar and electrum.

An aristocrat of his nome, Ineni was buried in an elaborate tomb at KHOKHA on the western shore of THEBES with his wife, Ah'hotep. This tomb contained paintings and vivid reliefs of funerary rituals and everyday life. Statues of Ineni and his family are in the tomb. He is believed to have died during the reign of TUTHMOSIS III (1479–1425 B.C.E.).

Inhapi (fl. 21st century B.C.E.) *royal woman of the Eleventh Dynasty*
She was a lesser consort of MENTUHOTEP II (r. 2061–2010 B.C.E.) who was buried in a shaft at the southern end of DEIR EL-BAHRI in the great complex on the western shore of THEBES. Queen Inhapi's tomb is listed in some accounts as containing the cache of royal mummies that was transferred there when their original tombs were found plundered. The royal remains discovered on the site in 1881 include those of Sekenenré TA'O II, 'AHMOSE (NEBPEHTIRÉ), TUTHMOSIS I, II, and III, SETI I, RAMESSES II, III, and IX, PINUDJEM I and II, and SIAMUN (1). This collection is called the Deir el-Bahri cache.

See also MUMMY CACHES.

Installation of the Vizier A text discovered in the tomb of REKHMIRÉ, serving TUTHMOSIS III (r. 1479–1425 B.C.E.), another version was found in the tomb of Userman, Rekhmiré's uncle, and yet another in the chambers of the tomb of Hepu, who served TUTHMOSIS IV (r. 1401–1391 B.C.E.). Other viziers, such as PASER (2) serving RAMESSES II (r. 1290–1224 B.C.E.), used parts of the text for their own mortuary reliefs.

In each text, the vizier was admonished sternly by the ruler that he had served to perform the prescribed duties with honor. The ceremony probably dates to the Middle Kingdom (2040–1640 B.C.E.), possibly in the reign of Senwosret III (1878–1841 B.C.E.).

A similar text, the *Duties of the Vizier,* was also displayed in Rekhmiré's tomb, a detailed itemization of protocol, attitudes, and demands on viziers. All such officials were deemed responsible for the agents and representatives conducting government affairs in their terms of office, and the vizier had to be responsive to requests and the needs of individual citizens.

Instructions for Merikaré

A didactic text that dates to the First Intermediate Period and is believed to be the work of KHETY III (r. ca. 2100 B.C.E.), designed as a moral treatise for his son, MERIKARÉ, who succeeded on the throne at HIERAKONPOLIS, the *Instructions* offer a remarkable documentation of that historical period, a time of rival kingdoms.

In the *Instructions* Khety III cites a raid on THINIS conducted by his allies from ASSIUT. That assault ravaged Thinis and desecrated the graves in the local necropolis, resulting in a general outrage in the land and a Theban military campaign that led to the ruin of the Khety line. The text clearly outlines the duties of a wise ruler as well and echoes the moral precepts of earlier dynasties on the Nile. Khety III bade his son and heir to imitate the great pharaohs of the past and to promote equal justice, compassion, and prudence in military campaigns, expressing regret that such a devastation of Thinis had come about in his name. The text is included in a papyrus in St. Petersburg, Russia, and dates in its surviving form to the New Kingdom (1550–1070 B.C.E.) when it was obviously copied by a scribe.

Instructions of Amenemhet I

A classic text that is reportedly from the reign of AMENEMHET I (r. 1991–1962 B.C.E.) serving as a last testament for his son and heir, SENWOSRET I (r. 1971–1926 B.C.E.), the actual text was probably composed by a scribe named Aktoy, who served Senwosret I. The *Instructions* warn against trusting anyone while holding royal powers. Senwosret I was co-regent when Amenemhet I was assassinated by a harem revolt. Amenemhet I was speaking posthumously, in this text, describing his ordeal and listing his accomplishments. There are some 70 copies of the *Instructions of Amenemhet* surviving, particularly in the Milligen Papyrus and the Papyrus Sallier II.

Instructions of Prince Djedefhor

This is a text probably dating to the Fourth Dynasty. Djedefhor was the son of KHUFU (Cheops) (r. 2551–2528 B.C.E.) and one of the most respected sages of the Old Kingdom. This document is the earliest recorded *Instruction* from Egyptian literature. Only part of the original has survived on a wooden tablet and ostraca. Djedefhor wrote the *Instruction* for his son, Awibré. In it he urges Awibré to marry and "raise a stout son." He also states that "the house of death is for life . . ." a spiritual admonition concerning eternal anticipations.

Instructions of Ptah-hotep   *See MAXIMS OF PTAH-HOTEP.*

Instructions to the Vizier Rekhmiré

A text on the tomb wall at THEBES of REKHMIRÉ, the vizier of TUTHMOSIS III (r. 1479–1425 B.C.E.), the *Instructions* reiterate the commands given to Rekhmiré and clearly define the obligations of the vizier, who is called "the First Man." A vizier was an official (in time the post could be held even by a commoner) who was to serve as an intermediary between the god-king and the people of Egypt. The text reiterates the traditions and ideals of Egypt, in operation since "the time of the gods," the beginning of all things, when RÉ emerged out of the chaos on the primeval mound.

Rekhmiré was the son of A'AMETJU, who had served as vizier for HATSHEPSUT (r. 1475–1458 B.C.E.), and the nephew of Useramun, who had served Tuthmosis III as vizier in his early years of his reign. Like his father and uncle, Rekhmiré went on to hold the highest nonroyal office in ancient Egypt. Called a *djat* or *tjat,* the vizier served as the prime minister of the nation in all periods. In the Old Kingdom Period of Egypt the viziers were normally kinsmen of the ruler, members of the royal clan, and thus trusted with the affairs of the court. An exception to this tradition, however, was the best-known vizier of the Old Kingdom, a commoner named IMHOTEP, who was revered as a high priest and as a physician. He built the STEP PYRAMID for DJOSER (r. 2630–2611 B.C.E.) of the Third Dynasty.

Rekhmiré was the most famous vizier of the New Kingdom. This able official was buried at Thebes, and on his tomb walls he gave an account of Tuthmosis III's instructions concerning the duties and obligations of a righteous vizier. The commands or instructions are remarkable for their detailed description of the workings of all levels of government. They include a description of the vizier's palace office, the type of reports deemed necessary to maintain communications with other government bureaus, and 30 separate activities that were part of his position. Again and again stress is placed on service to the oppressed or the weak, a theme that dates back to the sages of the Old Kingdom Period and to "THE ELOQUENT PEASANT" of the Tenth Dynasty. The words of Tuthmosis III appear on the wall. They read: "Behold the regulations laid upon you."

Normally the vizier of Egypt was astute, well-trained, and entirely dedicated to the service of rich and poor alike, in an ideal expression of the spirit of MA'AT, the ethical and moral principal guiding the nation. The role of vizier was maintained to some degree in the later historical periods of Egypt, but the strength of the vizier depended upon the vigor and energies of the pharaoh of the time.

Gradually the office of vizier was divided, with one vizier serving as the director of affairs for Lower Egypt and the other assuming the same responsibilities for Upper Egypt. The vizier of Upper Egypt ruled from the ELEPHANTINE to ASSIUT, and the other governed all the lands above Assiut. Viziers heard all domestic territorial disputes, maintained a cattle and herd census, controlled the reservoirs and the food supply, supervised industries and conservation programs, and repaired all dikes. The biannual census of the population came under their purview, as did the records of rainfall and the varying levels of the Nile during its inundation. All government documents used in ancient Egypt had to have the seal of the vizier in order to be considered authentic and binding. Tax records, storehouse receipts, crop assessments, and other necessary agricultural statistics were kept in the offices of the viziers.

Members of the royal family normally served as assistants to the viziers in every era. The office was considered an excellent training ground for the young princes of each royal line, although many queens and princesses also received extensive training and undertook a period of service with the vizier and his staff. Queen-Pharaoh Hatshepsut and Queen TIYE (1), the consort of AMENHOTEP III (r. 1391–1353 B.C.E.), are New Kingdom Period examples of royal women involved in the day-to-day administration of the nation.

The vizier of Upper Egypt lived at Thebes, the capital, and also served as mayor of the city. Normally, the vizier was assisted in his duties by the mayor of the western shore, as the vast necropolis sites and the artisans' villages there demanded supervision. The viziers of Upper and Lower Egypt saw the ruler on a daily basis and/or communicated with him frequently. Both served as the chief justices of the Egyptian courts and listened to appeals or decisions from the NOME justices. Other state officials, such as the treasurer, CHANCELLOR, keeper of the seal, etc., served under the viziers in a tight-knit and efficient bureaucracy. 'AHMOSE (NEBPEHTIRÉ) (r. 1550–1525 B.C.E.) of the Eighteenth Dynasty established the viceroyalty of Nubia in order to maintain order in the rapidly expanding territories below the cataracts. This viceroy was called "the King's Son of Kush."

Intef (1) (fl. 20th century B.C.E.) *priest and mining expedition leader of the Twelfth Dynasty*
He served AMENEMHET I (r. 1991–1962 B.C.E.) as a prophet of the god MIN (1) and as a leader of expeditions for the crown. Intef led expeditions to WADI HAMMAMAT and other desert sites, seeking quarries and mines. The Egyptians were expanding their control of natural resources in the Middle Kingdom Period (2040–1640 B.C.E.).

Intef (2) (fl. 15th century B.C.E.) *governor and military official of the Eighteenth Dynasty*
He served TUTHMOSIS III (1479–1425 B.C.E.) as a military aide. Originally from THINIS, Intef accompanied Tuthmosis III on military campaigns as a personal attendant. In time, Intef became the royal herald and governor of the OASES in the western or LIBYAN DESERT. His biographical account is on a stela in the Louvre in Paris.

Intef I–IV *See* INYOTEF.

Intefoker (Inyotefoker) (fl. 20th century B.C.E.) *vizier of the Twelfth Dynasty*
He served AMENEMHET I (r. 1991–1962 B.C.E.) as VIZIER. He was buried with his wife, Senet, at el-LISHT, the royal necropolis. Sometimes listed as Inyotefoker, he also served SENWOSRET I as the governor of the pyramidal complex of Amenemhet I. His tomb was a long corridor dug into the hillside, and it contained a shaft leading to a burial chamber. Senet, who outlived Intefoker, was buried farther up the hill. There is a possibility that Intefoker was considered a suspect in the murder of Amenemhet I. His tomb was mutilated, and his portrait was removed from the painted scenes of paradise on the walls.

Inventory Stela The Inventory Stela is a commemorative tablet discovered in an excavation of the Great SPHINX at the plateau of GIZA. It was found in a temple of ISIS on the site and is dedicated to the goddess as "the Mistress of the Pyramid."

The stela was discovered by French Egyptologist Auguste Mariette (1821–1881) during his labors on the Giza plateau, which started in 1853. The document concerns monuments at Giza and dates to the reign of Khufu (Cheops) (r. 2551–2528 B.C.E.), the builder of the Great Pyramid, the only surviving Wonder of the Ancient World. The Inventory Stela poses questions about the Sphinx, which was a shrine dedicated to Isis and Osiris of Rostau, and the plateau. Divided into two sections, the document refers to a temple that stood beside the Sphinx.

The Inventory Stela identifies this temple as existing before the portal to the causeway of KHAFRE (Chephren) (r. 2520–2494 B.C.E.) was built. The stela indicates that the Isis temple, east of the Great Pyramid, was on the Giza plateau before the pyramids were constructed. References to the Great Sphinx are equally enigmatic. The stela was sunken into the ground when discovered. On one section of it, the following was written:

> He [Khufu] made [it] for his mother, Isis, Divine Mother, Hathor, Mistress of Nun. The investigation was placed on a stela. He gave to her an offering anew, and he built her temple of stone again. He

found three gods in the place. The district of the Sphinx of Hormachis is on the south of the House of Isis, Mistress of the Pyramid, on the north of Osiris of Rostau. The writings of the goddess of Hormachis were brought, in order to investigate . . . [May] he [Khufu] grow, may he live forever and ever, looking toward the east.

The lower half of the stela has reliefs of the deities involved with the plateau. Yet other reliefs on the stela declare:

> Live the Horus, Mezer King of Upper and Lower Egypt, Khufu who is given life. He found the house of Isis, Mistress of the pyramid. Behind the house of the Sphinx of Hormachis, on the northwest of the house of Osiris, Lord of Rostau. He built his pyramid, beside the temple of this goddess and he built a pyramid for the king's daughter, Henutsen, beside this temple.

It is possible that the Inventory Stela was a copy of an earlier document, assumed by Khufu for his reign. The use of the word *investigation* refers to documents and records of the three deities on the plateau from earlier eras. Some devotions to Osiris allude to the area called Rostau in older records and appear to testify that the area was the god's "resting place" since the earliest historical periods. Statues found there were also subjects of the "investigation." The reference to the Sphinx, called "Hormachis (Horemkhu), the Watcher on the Horizon," adds impetus to certain speculations and debates about the age of the monument and the position it maintains. Auguste Mariette reportedly discovered the temple of Osiris of Rostau when he labored on the plateau. Another debate centers on the face of the Sphinx and the individual ruler who fashioned it as a pharaoh. The Inventory Stela was often overlooked as a component of the Giza plateau, but because of these and other debates, it has become a greater topic of discussion.

Inyotef I (Sehertawy) (d. 2118 B.C.E.) *founder of the Eleventh Dynasty*

Called the Elder, he reigned from 2134 B.C.E. until his death. Inyotef I was the son of MENTUHOTEP I, inheriting military problems in a time of unrest. With his capital at THEBES, Inyotef I began to attack neighboring nomes and the cities of KOPTOS, DENDEREH, and HERAKLEOPOLIS, the holdings of rival clans. Uniting the nomes of Upper Egypt, he remained independent of the Ninth and Tenth Dynasties, contemporaries that held limited realms in the north. Inyotef I was buried at DRA-ABU' EL-NAGA, Saff el-Dawaba, in Thebes. His mortuary cult was conducted by his successors.

Inyotef II (Wah'ankh) (d. 2069 B.C.E.) *second ruler of the Theban Eleventh Dynasty*

He was the brother of INYOTEF I, whom he succeeded, and ruled from 2118 B.C.E. until his death. Inyotef II was militarily active, leading an army against Herakleopolis's allies at ASSIUT. The army of Assiut attacked the city of THINIS, desecrating the tombs in the local necropolis, bringing shame upon the northerners, and motivating the Theban clans to assault them.

Inyotef II also faced a famine in Upper Egypt and had to import produce and regulate the distribution of needed rations. He erected temples for SATET and KHNUM on the ELEPHANTINE Island for famine relief. His queen was NEFERU-KHAYET (1), the mother of his heir, INYOTEF III. Inyotef II was depicted on a tomb STELA with his five DOGS. That monument was found at el-TARIF and is now in the Egyptian Museum of Cairo. He is mentioned as well in the WESTCAR PAPYRUS. Inyotef was buried at Saff el-Kisiya, el-Tarif, at Thebes.

Inyotef III (Nakhtnebtepnufer) (d. 2061 B.C.E.) *third ruler of the Theban Eleventh Dynasty*

He reigned from 2069 B.C.E. until his death. Inyotef III was the father of MENTUHOTEP II, the unifier of Egypt. Militarily active, Inyotef III pushed the Theban domain to ASSIUT. He also defended ABYDOS and other Upper Egyptian cities from northern assaults. A truce with HIERAKONPOLIS brought a period of calm to the region. Called Inyotef the Great, his name was inscribed on the walls of GEBEL EL-SILSILEH. His queen was AOH (or Yah), the mother of Mentuhotep II. His secondary queen was Henite. Inyotef III was elderly when he assumed the Theban throne. He was the son of INYOTEF II and Queen NEFERU-KHAYET. He was buried in DRA-ABÚ EL-NAGA, Saff el-Bagar, and is depicted in reliefs near ASWAN. Inyotef III is listed in the TURIN CANON.

Inyotef IV (fl. 16th century B.C.E.) *ruler of the Seventeenth Dynasty at Thebes whose date of rule is unknown*

He reigned at THEBES and controlled much of Upper Egypt as part of this royal line.

Inyotef V (Nubkheperré) (d. ca. 1635 B.C.E.) *ruler of the second group of the Seventeenth Dynasty*

Called "the Old," he ruled at THEBES from ca. 1640 B.C.E. until his death. Militarily active, Inyotef V campaigned in ABYDOS, KOPTOS, and other sites. He is noted for the KOPTOS DECREE, a legal document issued to punish a nobleman named Teti, who was charged and convicted of stealing temple goods. His anthropoid coffin is in the British Museum in London, and his royal diadem is in Leiden, Netherlands. Inyotef V was buried in DRA-ABU' EL-NAGA at Thebes.

Inyotef VI (fl. 16th century B.C.E.) *ruler of Thebes in the Seventeenth Dynasty, whose reign is undated*
He was the son of SOBEKEMSAF I. Inyotef VI was buried at DRA-ABU' EL-NAGA at THEBES with his ancestors.

Inyotef VII (Nubkheperre) (fl. 16th century b.c.e.) *ruler of the Theban Seventeenth Dynasty, dates of reign unclear*
He was the father of TA'O I and a contemporary of the HYKSOS ruler APOPHIS (2) (1585–1553 B.C.E.). Inyotef VII was a warrior who defended the Theban lands from the Hyksos assaults and built at ABYDOS, ELKAB, KARNAK, and KOPTOS. He also issued a decree concerning the temple of MIN. Inyotef VII was mentioned in the TURIN CANON. He was buried at DRA-ABU' EL-NAGA at THEBES with his weapons. His wife was SOBEKEMSAF, the mother of Ta'o I.

Inyotefoker SEE INTEFOKER.

Ipsus The site of a major battle between the members of the Diadoche, the council of Greek warriors who struggled for power following the death of Alexander III the Great (323 b.c.e.), Ipsus was located in Phrygia, modern Turkey, and there a coalition of Ptolemy I Soter (304–284 b.c.e.), Cassander, Lysimachus, and Seleucus I Nicator faced Antigonus I Monophthalmus and his son Demetrius I Poliorcetes. Antigonus was defeated and slain at Ipsus. His death put an end to the aspirations of restoring a Seleucid-Alexandrian empire. The domains of Antigonus I were assumed by the victors of this battle.

Ipuki (fl. 15th century B.C.E.) *famed sculptor of the Eighteenth Dynasty*
He served AMENHOTEP III (r. 1391–1353 B.C.E.). Ipuki was a famous sculptor involved in the royal building programs of the period. He was buried at THEBES on the western shore near DEIR EL-BAHRI. A fellow artist named NEBAMUN (2) shared Ipuki's tomb.

Iput (1) (fl. 24th century B.C.E.) *royal woman of the Sixth Dynasty*
She was a daughter of UNIS (r. 2356–2323 B.C.E.) and became the consort of TETI (r. 2323–2291 B.C.E.). Iput was the mother of PEPI I (r. 2289–2255 B.C.E.) and served as his regent during his infancy. Her tomb in SAQQARA, near Teti's pyramid, contained a limestone SARCOPHAGUS, and her mummy was interred in a cedar coffin. There is evidence of a robbery soon after her burial, but a necklace and bracelet were discovered in her tomb. Her mortuary temple, now in ruins, contained a limestone FALSE DOOR with her name and titles and an offering table of red granite.

Iput (2) (fl. 23rd century B.C.E.) *royal woman of the Sixth Dynasty*
The daughter of PEPI I (r. 2289–2255 B.C.E.) or MERENRÉ (r. 2255–2246 B.C.E.), she was a lesser ranked queen of PEPI II (r. 2246–2152 B.C.E.). Her tomb at SAQQARA was decorated with a version of the PYRAMID TEXTS.

Iput-isut An Egyptian term translated as "the most revered place," used to designate the original core of the temple of AMUN at KARNAK, in THEBES, the Iput-isut stood between the festival hall erected by TUTHMOSIS III (r. 1479–1425 B.C.E.) and the PYLON erected by MENTUHOTEP II (r. 2061–2010 B.C.E.). The origins or foundations of temples were esteemed over the centuries because they had spiritual connotations of dating to "the time of the gods," the moment of creation.
See also FOUNDATION DEPOSITS.

Ipuwer *See* ADMONITIONS OF IPUWER.

Irbast'udjefru (fl. eighth century B.C.E.) *royal woman of the Twenty-third Dynasty*
She was the consort of PEFTJAU'ABAST (r. 740–725 B.C.E.), the daughter of RUDAMON, and a niece of TAKELOT III. Peftjau'abast was defeated by the Nubian (modern Sudanese) armies of PIANKHI (1) and was reduced to the status of governor for his former capital, HERAKLEOPOLIS.

Irukaptah (fl. 24th century B.C.E.) *official of the royal kitchens during the Fifth Dynasty*
He was "the Chief of Butchers" during the reign of several pharaohs and was buried in the royal complex of SAQQARA as a sign of his rank and faithful service. Irukaptah's elegant burial site contained reliefs and paintings depicting the butchering of animals. He also commissioned KA statues for his burial site.

Irunefer (fl. 13th century B.C.E.) *Nineteenth Dynasty artist and official of the Valley of the Kings*
He served several rulers in royal burial projects in the VALLEY OF THE KINGS on the west bank of the NILE at THEBES. His tomb at DEIR EL-MEDINA, the community erected for the artisans, who were called the "SERVANTS OF THE PLACE OF TRUTH," identifies him and his family. A rock-cut chamber, originally capped with a brick pyramid, the burial site contained portraits of his father, Siwozet, and his mother, Tauret. They are depicted wearing white wigs.

Iry Hor (fl. before 3000 B.C.E.) *Predynastic Period ruler who reigned before the unification of Upper and Lower Egypt*
His burial site is reportedly at ABYDOS, where he was venerated as a warrior from "the time of the gods." Details about the actual lives of such Predynastic Period figures are interwoven with mythical lore.

Iset (1) (fl. 15th century B.C.E.) *royal woman of the Eighteenth Dynasty, the mother of Tuthmosis III (1479–1425 B.C.E.)*

She was not a princess by birth but a concubine of TUTHMOSIS II (r. 1492–1479 B.C.E.), bearing the heir to the throne. As the mother of a pharaoh, Iset rose to a high rank in the Theban court and was buried with honors in THEBES. A statue of Iset was discovered in the Karnak Cache. She is portrayed in a seated position, carved out of black granite.

Iset (2) (Iset Takemdjert) (fl. 12th century B.C.E.) *royal woman of the Twentieth Dynasty*

She was the ranking queen of RAMESSES III (r. 1194–1163 B.C.E.). She was the mother of RAMESSES IV, and probably RAMESSES VI, RAMESSES VIII, and Princes KHA'EMWESET (2), AMENHIRKHOPSHEF (1), and MERYAMEN. Her large tomb was the last one erected in the VALLEY OF THE QUEENS on the western shore of THEBES. When Prince Amenhirkhopshef died at the age of nine, Queen Iset miscarried the child that she was carrying at the news of his demise.

Iset (3) (fl. 14th century B.C.E.) *royal woman of the Eighteenth Dynasty*

She was the daughter of AMENHOTEP III (r. 1391–1353 B.C.E.) and Queen TIYE (1). Like her royal sister, SITAMUN (2), Iset married her father. A CARTOUCHE discovered on a cosmetic case commemorates this marriage.

Isetnofret (1) (fl. 13th century B.C.E.) *royal woman of the Nineteenth Dynasty*

She was the ranking consort of RAMESSES II (r. 1290–1224 B.C.E.). Isetnofret replaced Queen NEFERTARI MERYMUT as the Great Wife, or *hemet*, sometime after the dedication of ABU SIMBEL by the pharaoh. She was the mother of Ramesses II's successor, MERENPTAH (r. 1224–1214 B.C.E.), and she bore several other sons and daughters, including Prince Kha'emweset and Queen BINT-ANATH. Isetnofret died or retired to MI-WER, the harem enclosure in the FAIYUM a decade after replacing Nefertari. There is some indication that she may have been buried in the SERAPEUM (1) alongside her son, Prince Kha'em weset (1).

Isetnofret (2) (fl. 13th century B.C.E.) *royal woman of the Nineteenth Dynasty*

She was the ranking consort of MERENPTAH (r. 1224–1214 B.C.E.), also his sister. Isetnofret was the mother of SETI II (r. 1214–1204 B.C.E.), Prince Kha'emweset, and Princess Isetnofret.

Ished Tree A sacred tree in Egypt, thought to be the *Balanites aegyptiaca,* the Ished Tree was used as a symbol throughout the nation's history, dating to the earliest periods. Like the PERSEA TREE, the Ished Tree was associated with life and destiny. The god THOTH and the goddess SESHAT wrote the names of the newly appointed pharaohs on the leaves of the Ished Tree.

Ishtar *See* ASTARTE.

Isis (Eset; Iset; Weret-Hikau; Mut-netjer) The most enduring and beloved goddess of Egypt, whose name was translated as "the seat," she was also addressed as Weret-Hikau, "the Great of Magic," and as Mut-netjer, "the Mother of the Gods." Her cult started in the Delta, and she was praised in the PYRAMID TEXTS of the Old Kingdom (2575–2134 B.C.E.) as "the Great One." She was hailed as the wife of the god OSIRIS and was credited with civilizing Egypt with her husband and institutionalizing marriage.

The traditions concerning her cult state that when Osiris was slain by the god SET, Isis began a journey to discover his remains. Osiris's coffin was eventually engulfed by a fragrant tamarisk tree, and Isis soon found the box and the corpse in BYBLOS, where it floated on the Mediterranean Sea. Many adventures accompanied this search. Returning to the swamplands of BUTO, Isis hid the coffin of Osiris, but Set discovered it and dismembered the body into 14 pieces. Isis persisted and began to look for the parts of her husband. She found all of his remains except for his phallus, which had been devoured by a Nile fish, called OXYRRYNCHUS (2) by the Greeks.

Fashioning the body together and reanimating it, Isis became pregnant from the corpse. She then fled to the mythical island of CHEMMIS, where WADJET, the goddess protector of Lower Egypt, kept her and her newborn son, HORUS, safe from the agents of Set. In time, however, Set attacked Horus as a serpent, and Isis had to call upon the god RÉ for aid. Ré sent THOTH to be her ally. He was able to exorcise the poison from the child by reciting the cosmic disasters that would occur if the baby did not recover. Horus was cured and then given to local inhabitants to be cared for in safety. He also became their leader, thus uniting the cultic myth to the real populace of the Delta.

In another adventure, the goddess Isis discovered the secret name of the god Ré, viewed always as the most potent of magical weapons. She thus provided herself with additional powers, all of which she dedicated to the service of humankind. Isis was the epitome of the selfless woman, the charmer, the endurer, and the loyal spouse. To the Egyptians of every generation she was "the fertile plain, the arbor and the gentle pool of living waters." The cult of Isis endured because she fostered honor, courage, and loyalty in people, while evoking sympathy, admiration, and a recognition of injustice.

In the Middle Kingdom (2040–1640 B.C.E.) there were passion plays featuring the dramatic events of Isis's legends. In the New Kingdom (1550–1070 B.C.E.)

Columns forming a hall leading to an interior chamber in the temple of Isis, the Mother Goddess, at Philae *(Courtesy Steve Beikirch)*

in the various versions of the BOOK OF THE DEAD, Isis was hailed as the Divine Mother of Horus, the Widow of Osiris, clever and energetic and ever true. She is listed in the WESTCAR PAPYRUS as the protective deity of Egypt's royals.

Queen ARSINOE (1) Philadelphus introduced Isis to the Ptolemaic court (ca. 280 B.C.E.), and cult centers appeared in BUBASTIS, BUSIRIS, DENDEREH, ALEXANDRIA, TEBTYNIS, Medinet Ma'adi, MEMPHIS, and elsewhere. As Isis Pelagia, the goddess was the patroness of the capital, ALEXANDRIA. PHILAE, the great monument of Isis, was adorned by all of the Ptolemaic Period rulers. Many hymns to Isis were intoned in the Ptolemaic Period as well, and she was identified with an array of Greek goddesses. By the fourth century B.C.E., Athens honored Isis with a temple, and she was worshipped in Italy in the second century B.C.E. The "Isia" was a Roman festival held in honor of her search for Osiris. A temple complex called the Iseion was erected by PTOLEMY II PHILADELPHUS (r. 285–246 B.C.E.) in the DAMIETTA region of the Nile in Egypt, and shrines for her cult were popu-

lar in Tyre, Gaza, Crete, Thessaly, Chios, Lesbos, Delos, Cyprus, Epirus, Megara, Corinth, Argos, Malta, Castanio, Reggio, Pompeii, Herculaneum, Rome, Marseilles, and then in Spain, Germany, Gaul, Switzerland (Helvetia), and North Africa.

Despite efforts to eradicate Isis's cult in certain periods in Rome, the cult continued until the reign of the Emperor Justinian. The Greeks and the Romans were entranced by the mysteries of her rituals and by the exotic, charming image that she conveyed. The goddess was normally portrayed as a woman with a throne on her head, the spelling of her name in Egyptian, and a symbol connected to Osirian ceremonies. In many periods she was depicted as wearing the sun disk, set between the horns of a cow. In this representation, she was sometimes associated with the goddess HATHOR.

Island of Trampling   A spiritual site called Geswaret that appeared at the moment of creation in Egypt's cosmological texts, WA and AA, the COMPANIONS OF THE DIVINE HEART, landed there. The Island of Trampling was depicted in reliefs in the temple of EDFU. PTAH was also honored as part of this devotion, as well as HORUS.

See also PRIMEVAL MOUND.

Issus   This was an ancient battle site near Alexandretta, on the Gulf of Issus in modern Syria, where ALEXANDER III THE GREAT (r. 332–323 B.C.E.) inflicted his second major defeat on the army of DARIUS III CODOMAN (r. 335–332 B.C.E.). After his victory at the GRANICUS River, Alexander conquered Asia Minor and moved toward PHOENICIA (modern Lebanon) and Egypt. The Persian cavalry raced to intercept him, vastly outnumbering the Greeks. The Persian force was routed, along with Darius III's infantry. The mother and wife of Darius III were captured in this confrontation. Alexander refused the Persian overtures of peace and proceeded toward Egypt.

Istemkhebe (1) (fl. 11th century B.C.E.) *royal woman of the Twenty-first Dynasty*
She was the wife of PINUDJEM (1), the high priest of AMUN, at THEBES, and the mother of MASAHARTA and Djedkhonsufankh.

Istemkhebe (2) (fl. 11th century B.C.E.) *royal woman of the Twenty-first Dynasty*
She was the wife of MENKHEPERRESENB (2), the high priest of AMUN at THEBES, and the mother of SMENDES (2).

Istemkhebe (3) (fl. 11th century B.C.E.) *royal woman of the Twenty-first Dynasty*
She was the wife of PINUDJEM (2), the high priest of AMUN in THEBES. She was the mother of PSUSENNES II (r. 959–945 B.C.E.) and MA'ATKARÉ (2).

Ita (fl. 19th century B.C.E.) *royal woman of the Twelfth Dynasty*

She was a daughter of AMENEMHET II (r. 1929–1892 B.C.E.). Ita was buried in DASHUR beside her father's pyramid with her sister, KHNUMT. Her burial chamber contained a bronze ceremonial dagger, a ceremonial mace, and jewelry, including loose carnelian pieces and glazed beads. Her tomb was enclosed by a trap door and contained a limestone SARCOPHAGUS. Ita's mummy had a bitumen-soaked covering under a thin layer of plaster. Her funerary mask had gold trim and silver mounted eyes.

Itaweret (fl. 19th century B.C.E.) *royal woman of the Twelfth Dynasty*

She was a daughter of AMENEMHET II (r. 1929–1892 B.C.E.). Itaweret was buried at DASHUR near her father, and her tomb contained a rose granite SARCOPHAGUS. Gold and stone bracelets, a collar of gold and beads, a crown, and a statue of a swan were discovered in her burial chamber. No details of Itaweret's personal life are available.

Itj-tawy This was the capital of the Twelfth Dynasty (1991–1783 B.C.E.), started by AMENEMHET I (r. 1991–1962 B.C.E.). He called the site Amenemhet-Itj-tawy, "It Is Amenemhet Who Has Conquered the Two Lands." The name was shortened to Itj-tawy, "Seizer-of-the-Two-Lands." The capital was near modern el-LISHT. The actual site has not been determined, and no excavations have been conducted in the area.

Ity (fl. 22nd century B.C.E.) *ruler of the Ninth Dynasty, date of reign unknown*

His capital was at HERAKLEOPOLIS, and he was the successor of Kháneferré. Ity's brief reign is obscure, and his burial site is unknown.

Iuni (fl. 14th century B.C.E.) *viceroy of the Nineteenth Dynasty*

He served both SETI I (r. 1306–1290 B.C.E.) and RAMESSES II (r. 1290–1224 B.C.E.) as the viceroy of NUBIA (modern Sudan). Originally from the FAIYUM, Iuni followed Amenemopet as vizier for the Ramessid rulers, regulating trade and overseeing the military installations guarding the Nile and ASWAN.

Iuput (fl. 10th century B.C.E.) *prince of the Twenty-second Dynasty*

The son of SHOSHENQ I (r. 945–924 B.C.E.) and Queen KAROMANA (1), Iuput was appointed the high priest of Amun at THEBES in order to consolidate the nation. He then became involved in a massive effort to preserve royal mummies from further desecration in tomb robberies. Iuput also served as the governor of Upper Egypt and the commander of the regional armies. He was not the heir to the throne. Iuput aided in the erection of the BUBASTITE PORTAL in KARNAK. His tomb at ABYDOS is a long narrow pit with a granite burial chamber, never used.

Iuput I (d. ca. 805 B.C.E.) *coruler of the Twenty-third Dynasty*

He was the son and co-regent of PEDUBASTE I (r. 828–803 B.C.E.). They ruled in LEONTOPOLIS, but Iuput I died about two years after being named co-regent with his father.

Iuput II (fl. eighth century B.C.E.) *ruler of the Twenty-third Dynasty*

He was the successor to RUDAMON. The actual dates of his reign are unknown. He ruled at LEONTOPOLIS and then joined TEFNAKHTE of SAIS in opposing the invasion of PIANKHI (1) (r. 750–712 B.C.E.) and the Nubian (modern Sudanese) armies. Defeated at HERAKLEOPOLIS by Piankhi, Iuput II was made a vassal governor of Leontopolis.

Iusas (Nebhethotep) A goddess of Egypt, sometimes worshipped as Nebhethotep, she was a consort of the god TEM (1), depicted in some periods as the sole parent of the deities SHU and TEFNUT. Portrayed as a woman holding a scepter and an *ankh,* she is shown wearing a vulture headdress and a horned disk. Iusas was a female aspect of Tem.

Iuwelot A royal estate was located at Lake MOERIS, refurbished in all eras of Egypt's history. This estate was called "the Great Lake" and was watered by the BAHR YUSEF (named for a local Muslim hero), the river that branched from the Nile into the FAIYUM. A series of dikes and sluices was erected and maintained by all of the royal dynasties there.

ivory A substance highly prized by the ancient Egyptians and called *abu.* The Egyptians had to import ivory, receiving most of it on ELEPHANTINE Island, brought northward from NUBIA (modern Sudan). During the New Kingdom (1550–1070 B.C.E.), ivory was imported also from PUNT and Syria, carved into rings and scarabs and used as materials for inlays.

Iwntyw-Seti They were a Nubian (modern Sudanese) people, called "the Troglodytes" in Egyptian records, and inhabiting a site called "the Holy Mountain" at GEBEL BARKAL near the fourth cataract of the Nile. The Holy Mountain contained a rock formation in the shape of a *wadjet,* a cobra. The barbarians faced an Egyptian army led by 'AHMOSE (NEBPEHTIRÉ) (r. 1550–1525 B.C.E.) and a second assault by AMENHOTEP I (r. 1525–1504 B.C.E.). Amenhotep I caused the Nubians to flee to Khnemetheru, a site called the "Highest Well," located in the desert. The Egyptians built a fort at Gebel Barkal and started trade with the region. TUTHMOSIS I (r. 1504–1492 B.C.E.) attacked again at an area between the fourth and fifth cataracts. He left a STELA at KURGUS to commemorate his victories.

Iymery (Iumeri) (fl. 24th century B.C.E.) *royal scribe and mortuary official of the Fifth Dynasty*
He served NIUSERRÉ (Izi) (r. 2416–2392 B.C.E.) as a royal SCRIBE in the archives of the court. Iymery rose through the ranks of the court and became a steward of royal lands. He ended his career as a prophet of the mortuary cult of KHUFU (Cheops), conducted at the Great Pyramid in GIZA. Iymery's tomb at Giza contained elaborate reliefs and paintings of processions, banquets, agricultural scenes, and various industries.

Izezi (Djedkaré) (d. 2356 B.C.E.) *eighth ruler of the Fifth Dynasty*
He reigned from 2388 B.C.E. until his death. He adopted the god RÉ as his patron and honored the sage PTAH-HOTEP (2). Izezi exploited Egypt's NATURAL RESOURCES, using the quarries and mines at WADI HAMMAMAT and the SINAI. His name was also inscribed at WADI MAGHARA and WADI HALFA, and he is listed in the TURIN CANON. Izezi mined at ABU SIMBEL as well and sent trade expeditions to BYBLOS and PUNT. A royal son, RE'EMKUY, was the designated heir but died before he could assume the throne.

Izezi ruled for more than 30 years and celebrated his *heb-sed* (*see* SED). During his reign, the viziers and nobles became powerful. Izezi was buried in a pyramid with a mortuary temple at southern SAQQARA, and his queens were interred nearby. His tomb has fine reliefs and a black basalt SARCOPHAGUS, demolished by thieves.

Izi *See* NIUSERRÉ.

J

jackal This animal, called *auau* or *a'asha,* was associated with MORTUARY RITUALS and the cults of the gods ANUBIS and DUAMUTEF. The jackal was viewed as a strong, cunning, and persistent hunter and was also known to destroy early Egyptian gravesites. The DOG and the wolf were both revered. Anubis is depicted as a jackal in mortuary reliefs, and priests wore jackal masks in ceremonies. Duamutef, one of the Sons of Horus serving as guardians of the vital organs of the deceased, was illustrated as a jackal's head on the CANOPIC JARS. The jackal cult had its origins in the area of ABYDOS early in Egyptian history. The PYRAMID TEXTS of the Old Kingdom Period (2575–2134 B.C.E.) attested that a dead pharaoh would assume the face of a jackal. In time the jackal was called KHENTIAMENTIU, "the Prince or Lord of the West," or "the Prince of the Divine Hall." OSIRIS assumed these titles when his cult achieved national prominence.

Joppa This was a site on the coast of southern Israel located at modern Tel Aviv-Yafo. DJEHUTI, a trusted Egyptian officer of TUTHMOSIS III (r. 1479–1425 B.C.E.), took over the ancient city of Joppa. This officer used a ruse that has become a plot element in literature. The event was celebrated in Egypt and recorded in the HARRIS PAPYRUS 500, now in the British Museum in London. This military deceit was also transformed into an Arabic tale of later centuries.

According to this literary tradition, Djehuti met with an official of Joppa outside the city gates and declared that he and his family hoped to defect to Joppa and the Hurrian troops that served as the city's allies. The Joppa official was thrilled to hear of the proposed defection and anticipated caravans of loot and spoils of war that Djehuti promised to deliver. He also allowed a unit of Egyptian cavalry to enter the city, followed by troops and donkeys carrying more than 200 baskets. Once inside the gates of Joppa, the fully armed Egyptian soldiers leaped from the baskets, and the charioteers and escort troops joined in taking the defenseless city. Djehuti was able to send an immediate message of victory to Tuthmosis III.

Djehuti was buried on the western shore of Thebes, and his mortuary regalia is now on display in various European collections. The best known of these grave objects, a golden bowl, is in the Louvre in Paris. The capture of Joppa was retold in the story of "Ali Baba and the Forty Thieves" in the *Tales of the Arabian Nights.* The story of the Trojan Horse in the later Greek epic is also similar.

Judgment Halls of Osiris Also called the Judgment Halls of the Dead, a mythical site located in TUAT, or the Underworld, the destination of all Egyptians beyond the grave. OSIRIS, as the Lord of the Underworld, sat in judgment of all souls, aided by the goddess MA'AT, the FORTY-TWO JUDGES, and other mortuary deities. The site and the rituals of the halls are depicted in various mortuary papyri. In some of these papyri, the site is called "the Hall of the Two Ma'at Goddesses." When the goddess Ma'at was in attendance at these judgments of the deceased, she often appeared in double form, hence the name. The entrance to the area was called Kersek-shu, and the entire edifice was in the shape of a coffin. Two pools were normally included in the setting, both of which were mentioned in various versions of the BOOK

OF THE DEAD in the New Kingdom (1550–1070 B.C.E.) and later.

Osiris, accompanied by the Forty-two Judges, demon-like creatures, reviewed the lives of the deceased Egyptians and absolved them or condemned them. Mortuary texts and the priests provided the deceased with the Declarations of Innocence, also known as the NEGATIVE CONFESSIONS. The names of the individual Forty-two Judges were provided to the deceased by priests as well, so that the corpse could effectively plead its case. In addition, AMULETS, spells, and incantations were also available.

The deceased who appeared before the Forty-two Judges and Osiris understood the guiding principles of the ritual. The dead whose good deeds outweighed evil were deemed pure and eligible to enter Amenti, the western paradise. Those who had committed equally good and bad deeds were allowed to become part of the retinue of Osiris in many forms. The deceased who had committed more evil deeds than good were given to AMEMAIT, the fabulous beast that dined not only on their flesh but also on their souls. This last fate was the most dreaded because it resulted in total annihilation.

Gigantic scales were present in the hall, and there divine beings helped THOTH in keeping an account of the deceased's heart, which determined his or her worthiness to enter the realms of eternal bliss. While the weighing of the heart took place, the corpse addressed a series of prayers and commands to its heart and recited various mortuary formulas. The effort resulted in an exact balance between the heart and the Feather of Ma'at, the symbol of righteousness.

Additional aspects of the ritual in the Judgment Halls of Osiris included naming of the stones and bolts of the doors, so that they could open onto the realms of eternal happiness. The deceased was then faced with performing bargaining rituals with the ferryman, who rowed the dead to the domain of Osiris. "HE-WHO-LOOKS-BEHIND-HIMSELF," Hraf-hef, was the ferryman, a testy individual. All of the rites conducted in the hall and in the ceremonies indicated a remarkable recognition of human free will and personal responsibility for moral actions during one's life on earth. Such recognition, however, was immediately countered by the use of magic, which the Egyptians believed would guarantee a quick passage to the eternal fields of happiness. This ritual of death and judgment remained firm in Egyptian religious beliefs, as eternity remained the goal of Egyptians throughout their history. The tribunal in the Judgment Halls of Osiris and its everlasting consequences were part of the framework upon which the Egyptians based their continual spiritual aspirations.

Further reading: Antelme, Ruth, and Stephane Rossini. *Becoming Osiris: The Ancient Egyptian Death Experience.* Rochester, Vt.: Inner Traditions Intl. Ltd., 1998; Hare, Tom. *Remembering Osiris: Number, Gender, and the Word in Ancient Egyptian Representational Systems.* Stanford, Calif.: Stanford University Press, 1999; Houston, Jean. *The Passion of Isis and Osiris: A Union of Two Souls.* New York: Ballantine, 1998.

Judicial Papyrus of Turin A text dating to the reign of RAMESSES III (1194–1163 B.C.E.) or soon after, the Judicial Papyrus of Turin concerns the HAREM conspiracy against Ramesses III and the resulting uncovering of the judicial conspiracies of the event.

The plot was initiated by Queen TIYE (2), a lesser consort of Ramesses III, who wanted to put her son, PENTAWERET, on the throne instead of RAMESSES IV (r. 1163–1156 B.C.E.). The proceedings of several court sessions are also contained in Papyrus Lee and Papyrus Rollin. The Judical Papyrus of Turin is about 20 inches high and was published in 1865 and then in a revised version in 1868.

In ancient Egypt, the harem was the household of lesser wives of the king. Called the *per-khenret*, it was a highly organized bureaucracy, functioning primarily to supply male heirs to the throne, particularly when a male heir was not born to the ranking queen. The earliest evidence for a harem dates to the Early Dynastic Period (2920–2575 B.C.E.) and to the tombs of several women found beside that of DJER (r. 2900 B.C.E.) in ABYDOS. These women were lesser-ranked wives who provided additional birthing opportunities. Some of these

A Spirit Boat, the vessel used to ferry the dead Egyptians to the paradise of eternity after being found worthy in the Judgment Halls of Osiris *(Hulton Archive)*

wives were also given to the pharaohs by NOME clans, as a sign of alliance. These lower-ranked wives and concubines lived in the harem.

Harems employed SCRIBES, inspectors, and craftsmen, as well as dancers and musicians, to provide entertainment for royal visits. Foreign princesses were given in marriage to the Egyptian rulers as part of military or trade agreements, and they normally resided in the harem. In some eras, harem complexes were built in pastoral settings, and older queens, or those out of favor, retired there. In RAMESSES II's reign (1290–1224 B.C.E.) such a harem retirement estate was located near the FAIYUM, in MI-WER (near Kom Medinet Ghurob), started by TUTHMOSIS III (r. 1479–1425 B.C.E.).

The plot, directed at RAMESSES III in MEDINET HABU, proved to be quite complex. Queen Tiye plotted with 28 high-ranking court and military officials and an unknown number of lesser wives of the pharaoh to put her son, PENTAWERET, on the throne. A revolt by the military and the police was planned for the moment of Ramesses III's assassination. With so many people involved, however, the plot was exposed.

The coup was perhaps successful in its purpose. Ramesses III is believed to have died soon after. He commissioned a trial before he died but took no part in the subsequent proceedings. The court was composed of 12 administrators and military officials, with several foreigners included in the court, a sign of dynastic weakness. (The presence of foreign advisors was seen as a deterioration of Egyptian autonomy.) Five of the judges made the error of associating with the accused women and one of the men indicted during the proceedings. These officials found themselves facing charges for aiding the accused. Some of the accused also faced charges of using magic while conducting the assassination. This was a serious matter in that era, especially when magic was directed against a pharaoh, as the use of spells, images, or incantations would be considered blasphemous.

There were four separate prosecutions after the first scandalous efforts, conducted by the rightful heir, RAMESSES IV. Tiye was convicted in the first proceeding with 20 others, who included members of the police, military, and palace units that were supposed to rise up in support of Pentaweret when Ramesses III died. This group faced executions by various means. In the second prosecution, six more were found guilty and were forced to commit suicide in the courtroom. Pentaweret and three others also had to commit suicide as a result of the third prosecution. During the final episode, several judges and two officers were convicted. Three of these judges lost their ears and noses. One was forced to commit suicide and one was released after a stern reprimand.

A mystery, called "Prince Unknown" or "Man E," may be connected to this harem plot. The embalmed remains of a royal young man were discovered in DEIR EL-BAHRI, buried in a white case with no inscriptions. The mummy was wrapped in a sheepskin, a material considered unclean and forbidden in ancient Egypt. Anyone buried in such a garment would not be welcomed in paradise. The face of this mummy was found distorted, as if by agony, and its limbs were twisted and the stomach was distended. No wounds were evident, providing evidence that the young prince had died of internal causes, most likely poison. Prince Pentaweret had been forced to kill himself when convicted.

Julius Caesar, Gaius　*See* CAESAR, JULIUS.

Jupiter Ammon　*See* SIWA.

K

ka The ancient Egyptian term for a spiritual essence that existed alongside the human form and yet maintained individuality throughout the earthly sojourns, the *ka* was an astral being, yet considered the guiding force for all human life. The Egyptians recognized "the double" aspects of the *ka,* and in some statues the pharaohs were depicted as having an identical image at their sides. While existing with the human being during his or her mortal life, the *ka* was the superior power in the realms beyond the grave. The term for death was "go to one's KA" or "go to one's *ka* in the sky."

Kas resided in the divine beings as well, and pious Egyptians placated the *kas* of the gods in order to receive favors. Some deities combined their *kas* and *bas,* their souls, in cosmological traditions, and they entered as guardians of places at the same time. OSIRIS was always called the *ka* of the PYRAMIDS. The *ka* entered eternity before its human host, having served its purpose by walking at the human's side on earth to urge kindness, quietude, honor, and compassion. Throughout the life of the human, the *ka* was the conscience, the guardian, the guide. After death, however, the *ka* became supreme. Rulers thus laid claim to multiple *kas.* RAMESSES II (r. 1290–1224 B.C.E.) of the Nineteenth Dynasty declared that he had more than 20 such astral beings at his side.

The *ka* was also viewed as part of the divine essence that nurtured all existence on the earth and in the heavens. KHNUM, the god who molded humankind from clay in each generation, was depicted on many occasions as forming identical figures on his pottery wheel—one, the human, and the other the *ka,* which was the vital element of eternal life in Egyptian beliefs. For this reason,

the BA was supposed to stay close beside the *ka* in the grave. The rituals of embalming were performed in order to prepare the corpse for the arrival of the *ka,* as well as for resurrection. The *ka* came to visit the mummy of the deceased, and the union of the *ba* and the *ka* forms the A'AKH in death. For those commoners who could not afford the elaborate embalming processes, simple statues of themselves in the mummified form were provided by the mortuary priests. Such statues were supposed to attract the *kas* to their gravesites. The *ka* assimilated the life force of all mortuary offerings presented to the deceased in the tomb and put them to use in TUAT, or the the Underworld.

See also RESERVE HEADS.

Ka (fl. before 3000 B.C.E.) *Predynastic Period ruler of Egypt*
His reign remains obscure and legendary and is listed as taking place before the campaigns of the first unifier of Egypt, NARMER. Ka was probably a Thinite or Hierakonopolitan warrior who campaigned militarily against the local Delta holdings. He was buried in ABYDOS and honored as a SOUL OF NEKHEN by later generations of Egyptians.

Ka'a *See* QA'A.

Ka'aper statue This is a rare wooden life-sized statue of an ancient Egyptian official discovered in a MASTABA tomb at SAQQARA. Ka'aper was a high priest and lector in a Memphite temple, serving MENKAURÉ (r. 2490–2472 B.C.E.), and his career probably continued in the reign of NIUSERRÉ (r. 2416–2392), as Ka'aper lived a long time.

His wooden statue, made out of sycamore, had inlaid eyes, rimmed in copper. The whites of the eyes were fashioned out of opaque quartz, with corners of rock crystals and pupils composed of black resin. The statue depicts a thickset man in a straight skirt, holding a SEKHEM (2) scepter. When the Ka'aper statue was taken out of the mastaba, the modern Egyptian workmen on the site announced that it was a portrait of Sheikh el-Beled, their local mayor. A second statue depicting Ka'aper as a young man was also found in SAQQARA.

Kab, El   *See* ELKAB.

Kadesh

A city-state near Lake Homs in modern Syria, commanding the upper valley of the Orontes River, it was the key to the massive TRADE route to Asia, stretching between the Lebanon land ridges to the Euphrates River and Assyrian domains. In the reign of TUTHMOSIS III (1479–1425 B.C.E.), Kadesh rebelled against Egyptian domination and gathered an army of allies at AR-MEGIDDO on Mount Carmel's northern slope. Tuthmosis III led his army across Mount Carmel, single file, and came down behind the enemy.

When the foe entered the Ar-Megiddo fortress, Tuthmosis erected a siege wall and starved the besieged. Kadesh's ruler, however, escaped, and Tuthmosis had to campaign again and again in order to put an end to the rebellion. The city-state had water defenses composed of a moat and a canal. RAMESSES II (r. 1290–1224 B.C.E.) would also campaign against Kadesh.

Kadesh, battle of

A famous confrontation between RAMESSES II (Ramesses the Great) (r. 1290–1224 B.C.E.) and MUWATALLIS of the HITTITES, the battle of Kadesh took place ca. 1285 B.C.E. on the Orontes River in modern Syria. The battle was recounted in 10 inscriptions, including bulletins, reliefs on temple walls, and a poetic form. Since the battle ended in a truce, with each side relieved that they had not been vanquished, the overwhelming publicity about the confrontation was, in truth, a public relations campaign that worked marvelously in Egypt and elevated the status of Ramesses II.

CONTEXT

To understand the origins of the battle of Kadesh, it is necessary to consider the remarkable recovery of Egypt in the aftermath of the HYKSOS invasion at the end of the Second Intermediate Period around 1700 B.C.E., which had witnessed the conquest of Lower Egypt, the installation of the Hyksos as rulers from their capital at AVARIS, and the payment of tribute from Upper Egypt. The defeat and expulsion of the Hyksos was achieved through the campaigns of King KAMOSE and completed by his brother 'AHMOSE (NEBPEHTIRÉ) when he captured Avaris in 1590 B.C.E.and drove the last of the Hyksos from Egyptian lands. This victory marked the rise of the New Kingdom (1550–1070 B.C.E.) and a startling period of Egyptian resurgence.

Under the succeeding Egyptian pharaohs, the Egyptian Empire expanded rapidly. TUTHMOSIS I (r. 1525–1512 B.C.E.) waged a campaign into Syria, and TUTHMOSIS III (r. 1479–1425 B.C.E.) won a great triumph at the Battle of AR-MEGIDDO in 1483 at Kadesh. The city-state of Kadesh had rebelled against Egyptian domination and gathered an army of allies at Ar-Megiddo on Mount Carmel's northern slope. Tuthmosis III led his army across Mount Carmel, single file, and came down behind the enemy. When the foe retreated to the Ar-Megiddo fortress, Tuthmosis erected a siege wall and starved the enemy troops. Kadesh's ruler, however, escaped. As the city-state was well protected with water defenses composed of a moat and a canal, Tuthmosis campaigned and put an end to the rebellion.

The challenge for Egypt in the aftermath of these campaigns was to hold the recently acquired lands. This proved strategically difficult, and in the weak reign of AKHENATEN (r. 1372–1354 B.C.E.) at the end of the Eighteenth Dynasty, a new threat emerged in Syria in the form of the Hittites (called the Great Kheta by the Egyptians). A Bronze Age Anatolian people, the Hittites established a kingdom at their chief city of Hattusas in the 18th century and reached their zenith in the 14th century under King Suppiluliumas I, when they controlled much of Asia Minor, Syria, and parts of Mesopotamia. This expansion was achieved at the expense of Egypt's empire.

During the reign of TUTHMOSIS IV (r. 1401–1391 B.C.E.), the Hittites threatened the powerful MITANNI people, who were expanding their own imperial domain, forcing the Mitanni to form an alliance with Egypt, an alliance that enraged the Hittites. The strength of the people of Hattusas and the weakness of Egypt was revealed in the aftermath of King TUT'ANKHAMUN's death in 1323. His widow, Ankhesenamun, offered herself and the throne of Egypt to Suppiluliumas if he sent a son to wed her. The Hittite prince Zannanza traveled to Egypt as a result and was murdered at the border, probably at the command of Horemhab, who was the general of Egypt's army at the time. The murder earned the lasting enmity of the Hittites, and with the formal end of the Eighteenth Dynasty and the start of the Ramessid line, the Hittite rulers made new inroads into Egyptian holdings.

The second pharaoh of the Nineteenth Dynasty, SETI I, campaigned to restrict the Hittite expansion. Seti I enjoyed only a brief success as the Hittites again expanded, and their next attack secured control of Kadesh, which meant they had control over a significant trading center that commanded a strategic position on the Orontes in Syria. To stave off an immediate Egyptian response, however, they paid tribute to the Egyptians and bought time to prepare for what was an inevitable clash. This clash came during the reigns of two ambitious rulers: Seti I's successor, Ramesses II (r. 1290–1224 B.C.E.) and the Hittite king MUWUTALLIS.

EVENT

Ramesses II is reported to have marched out of Egypt on the ninth day of the second month of summer, stopping at Tjel, an Egyptian outpost. He had the Regiment of Amun and three other major units with him, as well as the Sherden infantry, which comprised 20,000 men. Reaching Ramesses-Meryamen, an Egyptian fortress in the Valley of the Cedars in modern Lebanon, Ramesses II saw no sign of the Hittites. Tricked by two "Shoshu," Hittite spies posing as local inhabitants, Ramesses II stretched his forces 30 miles into the enemy territory, divided his troops, and then made camp. When Muwatallis began a series of raids and ambushes, Ramesses II beat the Shoshu and received confirmation of the Hittite trap and his peril.

The Hittites reportedly had 3,500 chariots, each manned by three men, and an infantry of 18,000 to 19,000 with auxiliary units and escorts totaling 47,500. Apparently alarmed, Ramesses II sent for the Regiment of Ptah. While this was happening, however, the Hittites broke through the Regiment of Ré, sealing the trap. Hundreds of Egyptians began to arrive at Ramesses II's camp in headlong flight, with the Hittite cavalry close behind, followed by some 2,500 chariots. The Regiment of Amun was overwhelmed by the panicking soldiers and began to retreat northward.

According to records, Ramesses II, despite the chaos, began to fight his way through the enemy in order to reach his southern forces. With only his household troops, a few officers, and followers, and with the rabble of the defeated units standing by, he mounted his chariot, drawn by his favorite horses, "Victory of Thebes" and "Mut Is Content." Ramesses II then charged and broke through the east wing of the assembled force, allowing the Egyptians to escape the net that Muwatallis had cast and pushing the Hittites and their allies into the river, where they drowned. The brother of the Hittite king was also believed to have been killed in this charge.

While the enemy soldiers were looting the abandoned Egyptian camp, they were surprised by a group of Ramesses II's soldiers and slain. Ramesses II gathered up his unit and held his position at the camp. The Hittite king, in turn, ordered his reserves of 1,000 chariots to attack, but the Egyptians were able to hold off the charge. The Regiment of Ptah soon after arrived, and the Hittite cavalry was driven into the city, took terrible losses, and eventually withdrew by the order of Muwatallis.

IMPACT

Although Muwatallis withdrew, Ramesses II did not capture Kadesh, and the Hittite king claimed a Hittite victory and the acquisition of the city of Apa (modern Damascus). Ramesses II also claimed victory and executed all of the Egyptians who had not rushed to his aid. Ramesses had suffered serious casualties, had committed a major tactical error, and had been duped. He conducted personally the execution of those commanders who had failed to come to his rescue, and their families were forced to witness the executions and then stripped of their holdings and estates. As for the Hittites, they too had many casualties, but Kadesh was still in their possession and their chariot corps had not been destroyed.

Muwutallis died soon after the battle and future Hittite attacks were repulsed by Ramesses, who, in turn, made further raids into Hittite territory. In the 16th year of Ramesses' reign, Muwutallis's heir, Mursilis III, was deposed and replaced by HATTUSILIS III. Banished from his city, Mursilis made his way to Egypt, where he sought asylum from the enraged members of his family. The Hittites demanded extradition and were refused. Both nations thus contemplated another war, but the emergence of the Assyrians, called "the mad dogs," who were becoming the next major force in the Near East, posed a threat to both the Hittites and the Egyptians. Because of this, a rapprochement was finally reached between the Hittites and Egyptians. A diplomatic initiative was launched, and in 1280 B.C.E., Ramesses and Hattusilis III signed what is recognized as the oldest known international agreement, the so-called Hittite Alliance. This alliance was later cemented by the marriage of Ramesses to one of Hattusilis's daughters. Several texts of the Egyptian-Hittite peace treaty have been discovered. The treaty brought an end to decades of Egyptian-Hittite conflict and contained a remarkable extradition clause that allowed both countries to demand the return of anyone fleeing a charge. The resulting peace was honored until the Hittite Empire's collapse around 1180 B.C.E., during the reign of Ramesses III (r. 1191–1163), when the Sea Peoples attacked the Hittite capital of Hattusas and destroyed it. Rivalries among the ruling Hittite class also brought about political instability, and the Hittites disintegrated.

Further reading: Healy, Mark. *The Warrior Pharaoh: Ramesses II and the Battle of Quadesh.* London: Osprey Publishing, 2000; Kitchen, K. A. *Ramesside Inscriptions: Ramesses II, His Contemporaries.* London: Blackwell, 2000; Menu, Bernadette. *Ramesses II: Greatest of the Pharaohs.* New York: Harry N. Abrams, 1999; Montet, Pierre. *Everyday Life in the Days of Ramesses the Great.* Philadelphia: University of Pennsylvania, 1998; *Road to Kadesh: A Historical Interpretation of the Battle Reliefs of King Sety I at Karnak.* Chicago: Oriental Institute of the University of Chicago, 1990; Tyldesley, Joyce A. *Ramesses: Egypt's Greatest Pharaoh.* New York: Penguin, 2001.

Kagemni (fl. 26th century B.C.E.) *famed sage and vizier of the Old Kingdom*
Kagemni served the rulers of both the Third (2649–2575 B.C.E.) and Fourth (2575–2465 B.C.E.) Dynasties of Egypt. He acted as the mayor of the capital of MEMPHIS for HUNI (r. 2599–2575 B.C.E.) and as a vizier for SNEFRU (r. 2575–2551 B.C.E.). Kagemni, however, is famous for his *Instructions,* written for him by a scribe named Kaires, a didactic text concerned with proper attitudes of service and dedication on the part of high-ranking officials. Kagemni's tomb at SAQQARA, near the pyramid of TETI, was L-shaped and depicted dancers, acrobats, hunting, scribes, and agricultural scenes in beautiful reliefs. There were pits included in the tomb for spirit boats as well.

Kagemni's Instructions A didactic text contained in the PRISSE PAPYRUS. The author, a scribe named Kaires, wrote the *Instructions* intending to advise the vizier KAGEMNI (fl. 26th century B.C.E.) in matters of deportment and justice befitting a high official of the PHARAOH. Much of the text available is concerned with manners and social attitudes, attributes of the high-ranked individual in any organized society. For the Egyptian, however, such moderated, courteous behavior symbolized the spirit of MA'AT, the orderly behavior that mirrors celestial harmony.

Kahun A community structure at el-LAHUN, started by SENWOSRET II (r. 1897–1878 B.C.E.) of the Twelfth Dynasty (1991–1783 B.C.E.), Kahun was the abode of the workers and artisans involved in royal mortuary monuments. The site was surrounded by a gated mud-brick wall and divided into three residential areas. A temple of ANUBIS was also found on the site, and a cache of varied papyri was discovered in the temple. Called Hotep-Senwosret, "Senwosret Is Satisfied," and located at the opening of the FAIYUM, the site is famous for a cache of jewelry found in the tombs of Princess (or possibly queen) SIT-HATHOR YUNET and other family members buried in the complex. The site was divided into three sections, including a necropolis area for nobles and officials and a residential area on the east and on the west. Vast granaries served the entire region. The treasury of papyri at Kahun contained hundreds of texts concerning legal matters, literature, mathematics, medicine, temple affairs, and veterinarian information. The site was abandoned abruptly in a later historical period, perhaps as a result of an earthquake or some other natural disaster.

Kahun Papyrus A document discovered in Kahun, the worker's settlement at el-LAHUN in the FAIYUM, the papyrus dates to the reign of AMENEMHET II (1929–1892 B.C.E.). One section of the text is devoted to medical procedures. Another is concerned with veterinary MEDICINE, and a third deals with mathematics.

Kai (fl. 26th century B.C.E.) *mortuary priest of the Fourth Dynasty*
He served as a member of the mortuary cult of KHUFU (Cheops) (r. 2551–2528 B.C.E.) at GIZA. Vast numbers of priests resided in the pyramidal complex of Khufu after his death, as his mortuary cult remained popular. Kai was buried in western Giza, and his tomb is called "the Nefertari of Giza," "the beautiful one." He is depicted in reliefs with his wife in the tomb chambers, and there are a FALSE DOOR and raised, elaborate carvings. A statue of Kai was also recovered.

Kakai (Neferirkaré) (d. 2426 B.C.E.) *third ruler of the Fifth Dynasty*
He reigned from 2446 B.C.E. until his death and was probably the brother of SAHURÉ. Kakai is mentioned in the PALERMO STONE and in the tomb of an official named WESTPTAH. He was militarily active but left no monuments other than his tomb complex at ABUSIR. That structure was not completed, but the temple on the site provided an important cache of papyri, dating from the reigns of NIUSERRÉ (2416–2392 B.C.E.) through PEPI II (2246–2152 B.C.E.). One papyrus deals with a legacy bequeathed to his mother, Queen KHENTAKAWES (1). These papyri display the use of the Egyptian hieratic script. Kakai's mortuary causeway at Abusir was eventually usurped by Niuserré, a later ruler who made the structure part of his own mortuary shrine.

Kalabsha A site in northern NUBIA (modern Sudan), famed for a fortress and temple that were erected by TUTHMOSIS III (r. 1479–1425 B.C.E.) in the Eighteenth Dynasty era, the temple complex was fashioned out of sandstone and contained a PYLON, forecourt, HYPOSTYLE HALL, vestibules, and an elaborate sanctuary. The shrine was dedicated to MANDULIS, a Nubian deity adopted by the Egyptians. AMENHOTEP II, the son and heir of Tuthmosis III, was depicted there in reliefs. Kalabsha was expanded in Greco-Roman times. The Ptolemaic rulers (304–30 B.C.E.) refurbished the temple and added shrines to the complex with the cooperation of King ARKAMANI of Nubia. The Roman emperor AUGUSTUS erected a temple of OSIRIS, ISIS, and Mandulis. The temple was moved north when the Aswan dam was opened.

Kamose (Wadjkheperré) (d. 1550 B.C.E.) *fifteenth and last king of the Seventeenth Dynasty of Thebes*
He reigned from ca. 1555 B.C.E. until his death, possibly in battle. Kamose was the son of Sekenenré TA'O II and Queen AH'HOTEP (1) and the brother of 'AHMOSE. He was raised at DEIR EL-BALLAS, north of THEBES, where the rulers of this dynasty had a royal residence. During his youth he was also trained in royal and court matters by his grandmother, Queen TETISHERI.

The Thebans went to war with the HYKSOS when APOPHIS (a Hyksos ruler of the contemporary Fifteenth

Dynasty at AVARIS) insulted Sekenenré Ta'o II. The Thebans gathered an army and set out to rid Egypt of foreigners and their allies. Kamose came to the throne when Sekenenré Ta'o II died suddenly, and he took up the war with enthusiasm. It is possible that he married his sister, 'AHMOSE-NEFERTARI, who became the wife of 'Ahmose when Kamose died. The elders of Thebes counseled against the war, stressing the fact that Avaris and Thebes had been at peace for decades. Kamose rebuked them, however, declaring that he did not intend "to sit between an Asiatic and a Nubian" (the Hyksos in Avaris and the Nubians in modern Sudan below the first cataract). He vowed to renew the war and to rid Egypt of all alien elements.

The Thebans made use of the HORSE and CHARIOT, introduced into the Nile Delta by the Hyksos when they began to swarm into Egypt in the waning days of the Middle Kingdom (2040–1640 B.C.E.) and in the Second Intermediate Period (1640–1550 B.C.E.). The Thebans had lightened the chariots for maneuverability and had trained troops in their use. At the same time, Kamose had enlisted a famous fighting machine for his cause. When he went into battle, the MEDJAY Nubian troops were at his side. These Nubians loved hand-to-hand combat and served as scouts and as light infantry units, racing to the front lines of battle and striking terror into the hearts of enemies. Kamose caught the Hyksos off guard at NEFRUSY, a city north of HERMOPOLIS, with a cavalry charge. After his first victory, he moved his troops into the Oasis of BAHARIA, on the Libyan or Western Desert, and struck at the Hyksos territories south of the Faiyum with impunity.

At the same time he sailed up and down the Nile in Upper Egypt to punish those who had been traitorous to the Egyptian cause. One military man was singled out for particularly harsh treatment, and Kamose was proud that he left the man's wife to mourn him on the banks of the Nile. Some documents state that Kamose was within striking distance of Avaris when he died of natural causes or battle wounds. Apophis had died just a short time before. A stela discovered in KARNAK provides much information about this era.

The mummy of Kamose was discovered in a painted wooden coffin at DRA-ABU' EL-NAGA, but it was so poorly embalmed that it disintegrated when it was taken out of the coffin. The state of the body indicates that Kamose died in the field or in an encampment some distance from Thebes and the mortuary establishment. This warrior-king left no heirs and was succeeded by his brother, 'Ahmose, of the famed Eighteenth Dynasty (1550–1307 B.C.E.) and the New Kingdom (1550–1070 B.C.E.).

Kamutef (Kemutef) An ancient Egyptian creator deity, considered a form of the god Amun. A temple was erected on the west bank of THEBES to honor Kamutef. The temple was designed as a replica of the PRIMEVAL MOUND of creation. An image of Kamutef was displayed, called "the Amun of the Sacred Place." Every 10 days or so, this temple was visited by a statue of AMUN from Thebes. Kamutef was a serpentine figure in some periods.

Kaneferré (d. ca. 2040 B.C.E.) *ruler of the Ninth Dynasty* His name translates as "Beautiful Is the Soul of Ré." Kaneferré's reign is not well documented, but the famed ANKHTIFY served him, and he is mentioned in a tomb at MOALLA. His burial site is unknown.

Kap *See* EDUCATION.

Kapes (fl. 10th century B.C.E.) *royal woman of the Twenty-second Dynasty* She was the consort of TAKELOT I (r. 909–883 B.C.E.) and probably of Libyan or MESHWESH descent. Kapes was an aristocrat from BUBASTIS. She was the mother of OSORKON II (r. 883–855 B.C.E.).

Karanis A site in the FAIYUM region founded in the Ptolemaic Period (304–30 B.C.E.), Karanis had a population of about 3,000 on the banks of Lake MOERIS. Two limestone temples were erected on the site, dedicated to the crocodile gods Pnepheros and Petesouchus. A smaller temple honoring ISIS and SOBEK was also discovered at Karanis.

Karaotjet (fl. ninth century B.C.E.) *royal woman of the Twenty-second Dynasty* She was the consort of OSORKON III (r. 777–749 B.C.E.). Karaotjet bore a daughter, SHEPENWEPET (1), who became a GOD'S WIFE OF AMUN at THEBES, TAKELOT III, and RUDAMON.

Karnak Karnak is the modern name for an ancient religious complex erected at THEBES (modern Luxor) in Upper Egypt. Called Nesut-Tawii, "the Throne of the Two Lands," or Ipet-Iset, "the Finest of Seats," Karnak was the site of the temple of the god AMUN. Amun had been worshipped as a creator deity since the earliest historical periods in Upper Egypt, and the rulers of many dynasties supported his Karnak shrine. The complex remains one of the most remarkable religious sites ever constructed. Karnak's 250 acres of temples and chapels, obelisks, columns, and statues, built during a period of more than 2,000 years, incorporated the finest aspects of Egyptian art and architecture and transformed the original small shrines into a great historical monument of stone.

SITE DESCRIPTION

Karnak was originally the site of a shrine erected in the Middle Kingdom (2040–1640 B.C.E.), but many rulers of the New Kingdom (1550–1070 B.C.E.) repaired or refurbished the structure (as did those of the Ptolemaic Dynasty, 304–30 B.C.E.). It was designed in three sections: The first one extended from the northwest to the southwest, with the second part at right angles to the original shrine; the third section was added by later rulers and completed the complex. Used as a place of worship, Karnak was enormous even by modern standards. It contained a worship space in the main temple of Amun that was more than 60 acres, large enough to accommodate St. Peter's Basilica in Rome, Notre Dame Cathedral in Paris, and the Duomo of Milan.

The plan of the temple dedicated to the god Amun, evident even in its ruined state, contained a series of well-coordinated structures and architectural innovations, all designed to maximize the strength of the stone and the monumental aspects of the complex. Karnak, as all other major temples of Egypt, was graced with a ramp and a canal leading to the Nile.

The unfinished entrance to Karnak is a gigantic pylon, 370 feet wide, which dates to a period after the fall of the New Kingdom. Just inside this pylon is a three-chambered shrine erected by SETI I (r. 1306–1290 B.C.E.) of the Nineteenth Dynasty for the barks of the gods Amun, Mut, and Khonsu (1). The gate opens onto a court that includes the temple compound of RAMESSES III (r. 1194–1163 B.C.E.) of the Twentieth Dynasty, as well as stations of the gods, daises (raised platforms), and small buildings to offer hospitable rest to statues or barks of the various deities visiting the premises. The shrine of Ramesses III is actually a miniature festival hall, complete with pillars and elaborate reliefs. The so-called Bubastite portal, built in the Third Intermediate Period (1070–712 B.C.E.), is next to the shrine. The court of Ramesses III was eventually completed by the addition of a colonnade, and a portico was installed by HOREMHAB (r. 1319–1307 B.C.E.), the last ruler of the Eighteenth Dynasty.

The second pylon in the structure, probably dating to the same dynastic era and refurbished by the pharaohs of the Nineteenth Dynasty, is graced by two colossi of RAMESSES II (r. 1290–1224 B.C.E.), and a third statue of that king and his queen-consort stands nearby. This second pylon leads to a great hypostyle hall, the work of Seti I and Ramesses II, where 134 center columns are surrounded by more than 120 papyrus bundle-type pillars. Stone slabs served as the roof, with carved stone windows allowing light to penetrate the area. The Ramessid rulers decorated this hall with elaborate reliefs. At one time there were many statues in the area as well, all removed or lost now. Of particular interest are the reliefs discovered in this hall of the Poem of Pentaur, concerning military campaigns and cultic ceremonies of Egypt during its imperial period, including the battle of Kadesh. The Hittite alliance text is part of the decorative reliefs.

The third pylon of Karnak was erected by AMENHOTEP III (r. 1391–1353 B.C.E.) of the Eighteenth Dynasty. The porch in front of the pylon was decorated by Seti I

and Ramesses II. At one time four obelisks stood beside this massive gateway. One remains, dating to the reigns of TUTHMOSIS I (1504–1492 B.C.E.) and TUTHMOSIS III (1479–1425 B.C.E.), both of the Eighteenth Dynasty. A small area between the third and fourth pylons leads to precincts dedicated to lesser deities. The fourth pylon, erected by Tuthmosis I, opens into a court with Osiride statues and an obelisk erected by Hatshepsut (r. 1473–1458 B.C.E.). Originally part of a pair, the obelisk now stands alone; the second was discovered lying on its side near the sacred lake of the temple complex. Tuthmosis I also erected the fifth pylon, followed by the sixth such gateway, built by Tuthmosis III.

These open onto a courtyard and a Middle Kingdom sanctuary, the Deir el-Bahri, the holy of holies. Statues and symbolic insignias mark this as the core of the temple. The sanctuary now visible was built in a late period, replacing the original one. A unique feature of this part of Karnak is the sandstone apartment structure designed by Hatshepsut. She occupied these chambers on occasion and provided the walls with reliefs. Tuthmosis III added a protective outer wall, which was inscribed with the annals of his military campaigns. This is the oldest part of Karnak, and much of it has been destroyed. The memorial chapel of Tuthmosis III is located just behind the court and contains chambers, halls, magazines, and shrines. A special chapel of Amun is part of this com-

An impressive nighttime image of the great temple complex at Karnak *(Courtesy Thierry Ailleret)*

plex, and the walls of the area are covered with elaborate reliefs that depict exotic plants and animals, duplicates in stone of the flora and fauna that Tuthmosis III came upon in his Syrian and Palestinian military campaigns and called "the Botanical Garden."

A number of lesser shrines were originally built beyond the limits of the sanctuary, dedicated to Ptah, Osiris, Khonsu (1), and other deities. To the south of the sixth pylon was the sacred lake, where the barks of the god floated during festivals. A seventh pylon, built by Tuthmosis III, opened onto a court, which has yielded vast amounts of statues and other relics from the New Kingdom. Three more pylons complete the structure at this stage, all on the north–south axis. Some of these pylons were built by Horemhab, who used materials from Akhenaten's destroyed temple complex at 'Amarna. A shrine for Khonsu dominates this section, alongside other monuments from later eras. A lovely temple built by Senwosret I (r. 1971–1926 B.C.E.) of the Twelfth Dynasty was discovered hidden in Karnak and has been restored. A shrine for the goddess Mut, with its own lake, is also of interest.

The Karnak obelisks vary in age and some are no longer on the site, having been moved to distant capitals. Those that remain provide insight into the massive quarrying operations conducted by the Egyptians during the New Kingdom (1550–1070 B.C.E.). The Karnak pylon inscriptions include details about the New Kingdom and later eras and provide scholars with information concerning the rituals and religious practices, as well as the military campaigns, of the warrior-kings of that period. One Karnak stela records the gifts given to the god Amun at Karnak by 'Ahmose (r. 1550–1525 B.C.E.), presumably in thanks for a victory in the war to oust the Asiatics. The list includes golden caplets, lapis lazuli, gold and silver vases, tables, necklaces, plates of gold and silver, ebony harps, a gold and silver sacred bark, and other offerings. The Karnak king list, also discovered in the temple site, was created by Tuthmosis III. The document contains the names of more than 60 of ancient Egypt's rulers, not placed in chronological order.

The magnificent complex of Karnak was always open. A select group of priests served in the temples on a permanent basis, and hundreds of others served at scheduled intervals. Some areas dedicated to worship were restricted to the initiates of the cult. A statue of the deity Amun was kept in a golden sanctuary, positioned far back in the temple and carefully guarded. Sections of the complex were designed for business affairs as well. Artisans created jewelry for sale to visitors. Others processed gold or fashioned pottery and dishes for use within Karnak's residential areas. Cooks, farmers, and servants were part of the complex staff, and scribes were on hand every day. At its height under Ramesses III, the serving population of the temple is believed to have been close to 100,000 people.

By the fourth century C.E., Karnak was largely abandoned as a spiritual center. The Christian community in the area adopted a part of the space and started a church in the Festival Hall of Tuthmosis III.

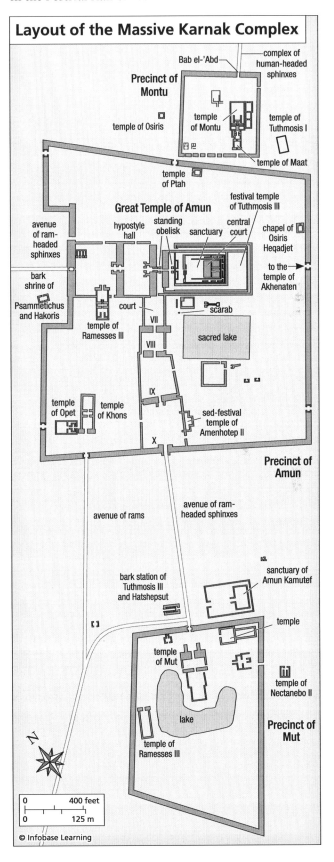

Layout of the Massive Karnak Complex

© Infobase Learning

ARCHAEOLOGY

The Karnak temple complex was visited by travelers from Europe as early as the end of the 16th century when an unknown Venetian wrote an account of his visit, although he had no name for the complex. Karnak was named for the first time in 1668 by two members of the Capuchin Franciscans. More accounts were composed in the next century, including a colorful and unreliable account by Paul Lucas in *Voyage du Sieur Paul Lucas au Levant* (1704). Detailed descriptions were made by members of the expedition of Napoleon Bonaparte in 1798–1799. The temple complex was also photographed in 1856 by the English photographer Francis Frith.

Early excavations were undertaken by Giuseppe Belzoni (d. 1823) and Jean-François Champollion (d. 1832). A treasure trove, called the KARNAK CACHE, was discovered in the main complex between 1903 and 1905 by Georges Legraine, under the direction of Gaston Maspero. As the cache was primarily found in areas of water deposits, archaeologists believe that the statues and other valuable works were hidden along a sacred lake in a time of crisis, perhaps during an occupation of the area by foreign troops.

In addition to looking for such artifacts, archaeological teams are focused on restoring structures that once added to the religious impact of Karnak, such as Hatshepsut's White Chapel, which was reconstructed beginning in 1924. This small but well-designed house of worship was erected by Senwosret I (r. 1971–1926 B.C.E.). A marvel of finely cut reliefs, the chapel demonstrated the artistic skills of the Middle Kingdom and the devotion of the pharaohs of that historical period. One wall relief depicts Senwosret I being greeted by Amun, Atum, Ptah, and Horus. In 2001 archaeologists completed reconstruction of the Red Chapel, another of Hatehpsut's building projects.

Construction of Karnak took place over many centuries and involved multiple deities, presenting a challenge to the restoration process as archaeologists try to place each stone in its original context. To add to the challenge are the *talatal*, the stones bearing the unique artistic designs and reliefs from the period of 'Amarna (1353–1335 B.C.E.), the capital of Akhenaten, which were incorporated into structures by later pharaohs. 'Amarna was largely demolished after the death of Akhenaten.

Further reading: Amer, Amin. *The Gateway of Ramesses IX in the Temple of Amun at Karnak*. New York: Aris & Phillips, 1999; Blyth, Elizabeth. *Karnak: Evolution of a Temple*. New York: Routledge, 2006; De Lubicz, Schwaller. *The Temples of Karnak: A Contribution to the Study of Pharaonic Thought*. Rochester, Vt.: Inner Traditions, 1999; Murname, William J. *The Road to Kadesh: A Historical Interpretation of the Battle Reliefs of King Sety I at Karnak*. Chicago: Oriental Institute of the University of Chicago, 1990.

A section of the great religious complex at Thebes, dating to the Ramessid era, dedicated to the god Amun and other members of Egypt's pantheon of deities *(Courtesy Steve Beikirch)*

Karnak cache   A group of statues, vast in number, that were discovered in the courtyard of the seventh pylon of that religious complex. These statues, now in the Egyptian Museum of Cairo, probably were buried during a time of crisis for security reasons. They span many eras of Egyptian religious endeavors at the great temple of Karnak at THEBES.

Karnak Stelae of Kamose   Remarkable documents that date to the reign of the last ruler of the Seventeenth Dynasty, the Karnak Stelae are different from the formal royal proclamations of other periods. The Karnak Stelae are records of the passionate outbursts of a vigorous, young ruler intent on uniting the Two Kingdoms and ridding the Nile Valley of a hated enemy. This young ruler, Kamose (also known as Waqdjkheperre), ruled from ca. 1555–1550 B.C.E. in THEBES. He was the son of ruler Sekenenré TA'O II the Brave and Queen AH'HOTEP (1), and the brother of 'AHMOSE (NEBPEHTIRÉ), the founder of the New Kingdom (1550–1070 B.C.E.). Kamose may have died in battle.

The Thebans had been at war with the HYKSOS after APOPHIS (a Hyksos ruler of the contemporary Fifteenth Dynasty at AVARIS) insulted Sekenenré Ta'o II. The Thebans gathered an army and set out to rid Egypt of foreigners and their allies. When Sekenenré Ta'o II died suddenly and brutally, his son Kamose came to the throne and took up the war with a renewed enthusiasm. It is possible that Kamose married his sister, 'AHMOSE-NEFERTARI, who became the wife of 'Ahmose when Kamose died.

The elders of Thebes counseled against the war, stressing the fact that Avaris and Thebes had been at peace for decades. Kamose rebuked them, however, declaring that he did not intend to accept a broken and divided Egypt. (The Hyksos in Avaris and the Nubians below the first cataract of the Nile [modern Sudan] had formed a union and were intent on dividing up the

Nile Valley.) Kamose vowed to renew the war and to rid Egypt of all alien elements.

The young ruler's responses to the advisory council in Thebes were recorded and appear on the Karnak Stelae, adding a new dimension to the role of the pharaohs of the land. They read:

> His Majesty spoke in his palace to the council of nobles who were in his suite: 'I should like to know what serves this strength of mine when a chieftain is in Avaris and another in Kush [Nubia], and I sit united with an Asiatic [Hyksos] and a Nubian, each man in possession of his slice of Egypt . . . I will grapple with him [Apophis] and I shall slit his belly. My desire is to deliver Egypt and to smite the Asiatics.

In their war with Avaris, the Thebans made use of the HORSE and CHARIOT, introduced into the Nile Delta by the Hyksos when they began to swarm into Egypt in the waning days of the Middle Kingdom (2040–1640 B.C.E.) and in the Second Intermediate Period (1640–1550 B.C.E.). The Thebans had lightened the chariots for maneuverability and had trained troops in their use. At the same time, Kamose had enlisted the MEDJAY Nubian troops for his cause. When he went into battle, the Medjay Nubian troops were at his side. These Nubians excelled at hand-to-hand combat and served as scouts and as light infantry units. Kamose caught the Hyksos off guard at NEFRUSY, a city north of HERMOPOLIS, with a cavalry charge. After his first victory, he moved his troops into the BAHARIA Oasis, on the Libyan, or Western, Desert, and struck with impunity at the Hyksos territories south of the Faiyum.

At the same time Kamose sailed up and down the Nile in Upper Egypt to punish those who had been traitorous to the Egyptian cause. Records indicate the harsh treatment he inflicted upon those who were disloyal. Written on a second stela discovered in Karnak is Kamose's warning to Apophis:

> Look behind you! My army has your rear in difficulties. The ladies of Avaris will not conceive, their hearts will not stir in their bellies when they hear the war whoops of my troops . . . Behold! I am come, and . . . my time is opportune. As the mighty Amun endures, I shall not leave you alone, I shall not let you walk in the fields, even when I am not here with you . . .

Placing Avaris under siege, Kamose died while with his troops. Some documents state that he was within striking distance of Avaris when he died. (It is unclear whether Kamose died of natural causes or battle wounds.) Kamose's body was taken back to Thebes, where his mother and his grandmother, TETISHERI, conducted the royal mortuary ceremonies. Apophis had died just before Kamose, and the war ended abruptly and settled into a cautious truce. Kamose left no heirs.

Queen Ah'hotep served as regent for 'Ahmose until he achieved his majority and picked up the torch of his fallen brother, destroying the Hyksos for all time and ending Nubian dreams of invading Egypt.

The mummy of Kamose was discovered in a painted wooden coffin at DRA-ABU' EL-NAGA, but it was so poorly embalmed that it disintegrated when it was taken out of the coffin. The state of the body indicates that Kamose died in the field or in an encampment some distance from Thebes and the mortuary establishment.

Karomana (1) (Karomama; Kamama; Karomet) (fl. 10th century B.C.E.) *royal woman of the Twenty-second Dynasty*
She was the consort of SHOSHENQ I (r. 945–924 B.C.E.). Karomana was the mother of two sons, OSORKON I (though some records indicate MAÁTKARE (2) was actually Osorkon's mother) and Prince IUPUT, and probably a daughter, Karomana (2). This Karomana was the consort to her brother Osorkon I, during his reign from 924–909 B.C.E., and the mother of Takelot I.

Karomana (2) (Karomama) (fl. 10th century B.C.E.) *royal woman of the Twenty-second Dynasty*
She was the consort of OSORKON I during his reign from 924–909 B.C.E., and was probably also his sister. Karomana was the mother of TAKELOT I.

Karomana (3) (fl. ninth century B.C.E.) *royal woman of the Twenty-second Dynasty*
She was the consort of SHOSHENQ II (r. 883 B.C.E.). Karomana was buried in LEONTOPOLIS.

Karomana (4) (fl. ninth century B.C.E.) *royal woman of the Twenty-second Dynasty*
The consort of OSORKON II (r. 883–855 B.C.E.), Karomana (4) was the mother of TAKELOT II (r. 860–835 B.C.E.), who took KAROMANA (5) as consort.

Karomana (5) (Karomana-Merymut) (fl. ninth century B.C.E.) *royal woman of the Twenty-second Dynasty*
She was the consort of TAKELOT II (r. 860–835 B.C.E.) and the mother of OSORKON III. Karomana may have been the mother of SHOSHENQ III as well and was reportedly a GOD'S WIFE OF AMUN for a time.

Karomana (6) (fl. eighth century B.C.E.) *royal woman of the Twenty-second Dynasty*
She was probably the consort of SHOSHENQ IV and the mother of OSORKON IV (735–712 B.C.E.). Karomana was buried at To-Remu, LEONTOPOLIS.

***ka* servant** The mortuary priest contracted by the deceased and his or her heirs to perform services on a daily basis for the *ka*. Such priests were normally paid by a prearranged endowment, sometimes recorded in "tomb balls" placed at the gravesite. The MORTUARY TEMPLES in the complexes of royal tombs had ALTARS for the services of these *ka* servants. A *SERDAB*, a chamber containing statues of the deceased and designed so that the eyes of each statue could witness the daily rituals, were included in the tombs from an early period. The Egyptian dread of nothingness predicated the services of the *ka* servants. They said the names of the deceased aloud as they conducted rituals, thus insuring that the dead continued to live in the hearts and minds of the living and therefore maintained existence.

Kashta (Nima'atré) (d. 750 B.C.E.) *founder of the Twenty-fifth Dynasty*
He reigned from 770 B.C.E. until his death in GEBEL BARKAL in NUBIA (modern Sudan), but he was accepted in much of Upper Egypt. Kashta's queen was PEBATMA, probably the mother of his sons, PIANKHI (1) (Piye) and SHABAKA. His sister or daughter, AMENIRDIS (1), was named GOD'S WIFE OF AMUN, or "Divine Adoratrice of Amun," at Thebes, and was adopted by SHEPENWEPET (1). Piankhi succeeded Kashta, who during his reign erected a stela to the god KHNUM on ELEPHANTINE Island. The reign of OSORKON III (777–749 B.C.E.) in the Delta's Twenty-third Dynasty, a contemporary royal line, was threatened by Kashta's move into Upper Egypt.

Kassites   A people that are recorded as originating in Central Asia, taking the city of Babylon ca. 1595 B.C.E. The Kassites ruled Babylon for almost three centuries, restoring temples at Ur, Uruk, and Isin, as well as at Dur-Kurigalzu, modern Agar Quf in Iraq. By the 13th century B.C.E., the Kassite Empire covered most of Mesopotamia, but it was overrun by the Elamites ca. 1159 B.C.E. Several Kassite rulers had dealings with Egypt, and some are mentioned in the 'AMARNA correspondence. Burna-Buriash II (1359–1333 B.C.E.), Kurigalzu I (ca. 1390 B.C.E.), and Kurigalzu II (1332–1308 B.C.E.) are among those kings.

Kawit (1) (Khawait; Kawait) (fl. 24th century B.C.E.) *royal woman of the Sixth Dynasty*
She was the consort of TETI (r. 2323–2291 B.C.E.). Her pyramidal complex in SAQQARA has been eroded over the centuries.

Kawit (2) (Khawait; Kawait) (fl. 21st century B.C.E.) *royal companion of the Eleventh Dynasty*
She was a member of the HAREM of MENTUHOTEP II (2061–2010 B.C.E.). Her burial chamber was part of Mentuhotep II's vast complex at DEIR EL-BAHRI on the western shore of THEBES. This tomb contained elaborate and stylish scenes of her cosmetic rituals. Kawit had a SARCOPHAGUS that designated her as "the Sole Favorite of the King," a distinction often repeated in other female burials in Deir el-Bahri.

Kay (fl. 25th century B.C.E.) *priest of the Fourth Dynasty (2575–2465 B.C.E.) who was beloved by many rulers of Egypt*
Kay served the rulers SNEFRU, KHUFU (Cheops), RA'DJEDEF, and KHAFRE (Chephren). Revered for his years of faithful service, Kay was buried in GIZA beside the Great PYRAMID of Khufu. His TOMB contains beautiful depictions of daily life, funerary scenes, and human experiences. Kay's tomb was probably provided by one of the rulers that he served.

Kebawet   An early goddess in Egypt, worshipped only locally and disappearing as the deities of the land assumed roles in the government and in daily life, Kebawet was called the goddess of "cold water libations," an element considered vital for paradise. She was thus part of the MORTUARY RITUALS, representing desired attributes of the mythological domain of the dead called Amenti.

Kebir (Qaw el-Kebir)   A necropolis on the eastern shore of the Nile at ASSIUT. Tombs of the Middle Kingdom (2040–1640 B.C.E.) nomarchs were discovered there. Three elaborate mortuary complexes at Kebir contained sophisticated architectural elements, including corridors, porticos, shrines, and terraces.

"Keeper of the Door to the South"   This was the title given to the viceroys of Kush (Nubia, now modern Sudan). The governors of ASWAN carried the same title. The rulers of the Eleventh Dynasty (2040–1991 B.C.E.) and the Seventeenth Dynasty (1640–1550 B.C.E.), the lines of Inyotefs and the Ta'os at THEBES, assumed the same role in their own eras. Controlling Upper Egypt as contemporaries of the Delta or northern dynasties, these Thebans ruled as far south as the first cataract of the Nile or beyond.

Keepers of Time   *See* ASTRONOMY.

Kemanweb (Kemanub) (fl. 19th century B.C.E.) *royal woman of the Twelfth Dynasty*
She was probably the consort of AMENEMHET II (r. 1929–1892 B.C.E.). Kemanweb was buried in Amenemhet II's mortuary temple at DASHUR, entombed in the main structure there. Her coffin was a single trunk of a tree, hollowed out and inscribed.

Kemenibu (fl. 17th century B.C.E.) *mysterious royal woman of the Thirteenth Dynasty*
A queen, she was a consort of one of the rulers of the Thirteenth Dynasty. Kemenibu's tomb was discovered in the complex of AMENEMHET II (r. 1929–1892 B.C.E.) of the Twelfth Dynasty at DASHUR.

Kem-wer   This was a bull, called the "Great Black One," established at ATHRIBIS in the earliest eras of Egyptian history. Obscure observances were conducted in honor of this animal in the city, and Kem-wer remained popular for centuries.

See also APIS; BULLS.

Kemyt   A scholar's text cited in the *SATIRE ON TRADES*, dating to the Twelfth Dynasty (1991–1783 B.C.E.) or possibly earlier. Surviving copies were found in 'AMARNA and in other New Kingdom sites. The *Kemyt* was a standard school text in use by the Twelfth Dynasty, particularly for scribes. In vertical columns, the text provided basic training in the hieratic script. Students had to copy such texts to demonstrate their knowledge of the language and their writing abilities.

Kenamun (1) (fl. 15th century B.C.E.) *military naval superintendent of the Eighteenth Dynasty*
Kenamun started his career by serving as the chief steward of AMENHOTEP II (r. 1427–1401 B.C.E.) and then was appointed the superintendent of PERU-NEFER, the naval base near MEMPHIS. Kenamun's mother, Amenenopet, was a royal nurse. Kenamun had a special glass *SHABTI* given to him by the pharaoh.

Kenamun (2) (fl. 14th century B.C.E.) *mayor of Thebes in the Eighteenth Dynasty*
He held this important office during the reign of AMENHOTEP III (1391–1353 B.C.E.). THEBES was a powerful city in this era, serving as the capital of the Egyptian Empire. Kenamun was buried on the western shore of Thebes.

kenbet   The local and national courts of Egypt that evolved from the original court called the *seru,* a council of nome elders who rendered judicial opinions on cases brought before them, the *kenbet* replaced the former council, the *djadjat,* of the Old Kingdom (2575–2134 B.C.E.) and made legally binding decisions and imposed penalties on the nome level. The great *kenbet,* the national equivalent of modern supreme courts, heard appeals and rendered legal decisions on all cases except those involving treason or any other capital offense. These matters were not within the jurisdiction of any legal institution but were reserved to the ruler alone.

See also "THE ELOQUENT PEASANT" OF HERAKLEOPOLIS; LAW.

Keper (fl. 12th century B.C.E.) *ruler of the land of Libya in the reign of Ramesses III (1194–1163 B.C.E.)*
He faced an invasion of his domain and then united with his enemies to assault Egypt. The MESHWESH, a tribe living deep in the Libyan Desert, allied themselves with Keper and his son, Meshesher, when they entered his territory. In turn, Keper and the Meshwesh invaded Egypt. They entered the canal called "the Water of Ré," in the western Delta. Ramesses III attacked the invading force and routed them, chasing the enemy some 12 miles into the Libyan Desert. Meshesher was captured along with 2,052 prisoners, while 2,175 Libyans were slain. A wall text and a relief at MEDINET HABU document Keper's pleas for his own life, apparently in vain.

See also SEA PEOPLES, DEFEAT OF THE

Kermeh (Kerma)   A site and culture at the second cataract of the Nile in Kush, or NUBIA (modern Sudan), The region was somewhat controlled by Egypt as early as the Middle Kingdom (2048–1640 B.C.E.). AMENEMHET I (r. 1991–1962 B.C.E.) of the Twelfth Dynasty erected a fortress at Kermeh. In time the people of Kermeh became a powerful state, ruled by kings who used the traditions of Egypt for their religious and national priorities. These royals were buried in circular mounds, accompanied by slain courtiers and servants. During the Second Intermediate Period (1640–1550 B.C.E.), the Kermeh people allied themselves with the HYKSOS, the Asiatics who ruled from AVARIS in the Delta. Taking over the Egyptian fortresses on the Nile, the people of Kermeh advanced toward Egypt. One group led by A'ATA was halted by 'AHMOSE (NEBPEHTIRÉ) (r. 1550–1525 B.C.E.) and slain. Egypt maintained control of Kermeh for centuries afterward.

Kewab (fl. 26th century B.C.E.) *prince of the Fourth Dynasty, possibly murdered by a rival heir to the throne*
He was a son of KHUFU (Cheops) (r. 2551–2528 B.C.E.) and Queen MERITITES (1) and the designated heir to the throne. Kewab married HETEPHERES (2), a royal heiress. They had a daughter, MERYSANKH (3, and other children. Kewab died while on an expedition outside of Egypt possibly a victim of murder.

He was depicted as a portly man in Queen Merysankh's tomb, a site at GIZA prepared for her mother and given to her when she died at a relatively young age. Kewab was buried in a MASTABA near the Great PYRAMID of Khufu. His mortuary cult was popular in MEMPHIS, and in the New Kingdom (1550–1070 B.C.E.), Prince KHA'EMWESET (1), a son of Ramesses II, restored Kewab's statue.

Kha (fl. 15th century B.C.E.) *official of the Eighteenth Dynasty*
He served AMENHOTEP II (r. 1427–1401 B.C.E.) and his two successors, TUTHMOSIS IV (r. 1401–1391 B.C.E.) and AMENHOTEP III (r. 1391–1353 B.C.E.). Kha was an architect involved in mortuary complexes for the royal families. He was buried at THEBES, probably in a tomb provided for him by one of the pharaohs that he served.

Kha'ba (Tety) (d. 2599 B.C.E.) *fourth ruler of the Third Dynasty*
He reigned from 2603 B.C.E. until his death. His name meant "the Soul Appears," and he was the successor of SEKHEMKHET on the throne. Kha'ba was listed on stone vessels in SAQQARA and in the tomb of SAHURÉ (r. 2458–2446 B.C.E.). He built the pyramid at ZAWIET EL-ARYAN, between GIZA and ABUSIR. A layered pyramid, originally

with seven steps, Kha'ba's tomb contained a SARCOPHA-GUS of alabaster. The pyramid was never completed and apparently was not used. MASTABA tombs were erected near his pyramid, probably for his royal family members and high-ranking courtiers.

Khababash (fl. ca. 338 B.C.E.) *Egyptian rebel mentioned in the Satrap Stela*
Considered a successor to NECTANEBO II (r. ca. 360–343 B.C.E.), Khababash led a revolt against the Persians sometime around 338 B.C.E. PTOLEMY I SOTER (r. 304–284 B.C.E.) was the satrap (provincial governor) of Egypt for PHILIP III ARRHIDAEUS (r. 333–316 B.C.E.) and ALEXANDER IV (r. 316–304 B.C.E.) when he issued the stela to link his own rule to that of Khababash, who was a national hero. Khababash ruled over a small region of Egypt, during the Persian occupation of the Nile Valley. He had the throne name of Senentanen-setepenptah.

See also REBELS OF EGYPT.

Khabrias (fl. fourth century B.C.E.) *Greek mercenary general*
He commanded the mercenary forces serving HAKORIS (r. 393–380 B.C.E.) of the Twenty-ninth Dynasty. An Athenian, Khabrias resided in Egypt, and his daughter, PTOLEMAIS (1), married an Egyptian general named Nakhtnebef. Nakhtnebef became the founder of the Thirtieth Dynasty, as NECTANEBO I. General Khabrias was recalled to Athens ca. 373 B.C.E.

Kha'emhet (fl. 14th century B.C.E.) *scribe and overseer of the Eighteenth Dynasty*
He served AMENHOTEP III (r. 1391–1353 B.C.E.). Kha'emhet was a court SCRIBE and an overseer of the royal granaries of THEBES. He was buried in a necropolis on the western shore at Thebes. His tomb has fine low reliefs that depict Amenhotep III as a SPHINX. Also portrayed are Osirian funeral rituals, scenes of daily life, and court ceremonies.

Kha'emweset (1) (fl. 13th century B.C.E.) *prince of the Nineteenth Dynasty, called "the First Egyptologist"*
He was a son of RAMESSES II (r. 1290–1224 B.C.E.) and Queen ISETNOFRET (1), becoming the heir to the throne upon the death of three older brothers. Kha'emweset served as the high priest of PTAH and as the overseer of the interment of the sacred APIS bull in SAQQARA. He devoted countless hours to restoring monuments and was revered for his magical skills.

Prince Kha'emweset was depicted in the relief of a battle scene as accompanying Ramesses II on an expedition to NUBIA (modern Sudan). In that scene Ramesses II was identified as a prince, not having succeeded SETI I at the time. Training in battle and in administrative affairs in the royal court was followed by further education in sacred matters in the temple of the god Ptah in MEMPHIS.

When Kha'emweset was named heir to the throne in regnal year ca. 43 of Ramesses II, he was already at an advanced age and died in regnal year 55. His tomb has not been identified, but a mummy found in the granite tomb of APIS Bull XIV has raised possibilities as to the prince's final resting place. A golden mask believed to belong to Kha'emweset was discovered in the catacombs of the SERAPEUM in Saqqara. The prince and his mother, Queen Isetnofret, were possibly buried nearby.

Kha'emweset (2) (fl. 12th century B.C.E.) *prince of the Twentieth Dynasty*
He was a son of RAMESSES III (r. 1194–1163 B.C.E.). Kha'emweset was depicted on the walls of MEDINET HABU with 19 of his brothers. His service to Egypt was conducted as a priest of the god PTAH. The prince's tomb was built in the VALLEY OF THE QUEENS, on the western shore of THEBES, and has a square burial chamber with side chapels. Paintings in the tomb depict Ramesses III introducing Kha'emweset to the deities of TUAT, or the Underworld.

Khafre (Chephren; Ra'kha'ef) (d. 2494 B.C.E.) *fourth ruler of the Fourth Dynasty*
He reigned from 2520 B.C.E. until his death. Khafre was the builder of the second pyramid at GIZA and was the son of KHUFU (Cheops) (r. 2551–2528 B.C.E.) and probably Queen HENUTSEN. He married Queens KHAMERERNEBTY (1) and MERYSANKH (3) and raised Prince MENKAURÉ (Mycerinus), Prince Nekuré, Princess KHAMERERNEBTY (2), and others. Another son, Baefré, is listed in some records as having succeeded him briefly, but Menkauré is normally identified as the actual heir. When his brother pharaoh, RA'DJEDEF, died in 2520 B.C.E., Khafre put aside his sons: Setka, Baka, and 'Ahanet.

Khafre's pyramid in GIZA was 702 feet square and originally 470 feet high. Encased in TUREH limestone, the structure was completed by mortuary and valley temples. A causeway, 430 feet in length, connected the complex structures and was carved out of the rock. In the burial chamber a red granite SARCOPHAGUS awaited the mummified remains, and five boat pits were found in the complex, without boats.

Khafre's accession to the throne demonstrated the revived dominance of the older faction of Khufu's divided family. Khafre's pyramid at Giza restored the plateau as the royal necropolis, and the Great SPHINX, bearing his facial likeness, provided Giza with another insignia of pharaonic power. However, there is debate about the face of the Sphinx. The likeness appears to resemble Khufu more than Khafre, and certain logistical arrangements of Khafre's causeway has brought about new ideas regarding the Sphinx and the role pharaoh Ra'djedef (r. 2528–ca. 2520) played in the building of the plateau.

Khafre's heir and successor was Menkauré (Mycerinus), his son by Queen Khamerernebty (1). Queen

Merysankh (3) bore him Prince Nebemakht, Queen Nedjhekenu bore Prince Sekhemkaré, and Queen PERSENTI bore NEKAURÉ, who became famous because of his will. Khafre's reign spanned over a quarter of a century, and he was popular with his people.

Khaftet-hir-nebes She was a goddess of the city of THEBES (modern Luxor), serving as a protector of the local area of the capital. TUTHMOSIS III (r. 1479–1425 B.C.E.) depicted her on a black granite tablet called "the Hymn of Victory." The tablet was discovered in KARNAK at Thebes.

khaibit This was the Egyptian word for the shadow of a soul, viewed as the spiritual essence that was released from the confines of the human body at death. No particular role or purpose has been clearly defined for the *khaibit* in surviving texts, but the Egyptians anticipated the liberation of the shadow beyond the grave.

Khakheperresonbe's Complaints A literary work compiled in the Twelfth Dynasty (1991–1783 B.C.E.) or in the Second Intermediate Period (1640–1550 B.C.E.), the surviving copy, dating to the New Kingdom (1550–1070 B.C.E.), is now in the British Museum in London. Khakheperresonbe was a priest in HELIOPOLIS and wrote on the popular theme of a nation in distress. He carries on a conversation with his heart and receives counsel for silent courage in the face of adversity. The *Complaints* develops a dolorous cadence and is similar to, or perhaps a version of, the "DEBATE OF A MAN WITH HIS SOUL." The work became the staple of schools and survived as a lesson board. Egyptians appreciated didactic LITERATURE as well as poetry and religious works.

Khama'at (Ma'atkha) (fl. 25th century B.C.E.) *princess of the Fifth Dynasty*
She was a daughter of SHEPSESKHAF (r. 2472–2467 B.C.E.) and Queen KHENTAKAWES (1) and is also called Ma'atkha in some records. Khama'at married PTAHSHEPSES (1) the high priest of MEMPHIS, who had been raised and educated in the royal palace as a companion of MENKAURÉ (Mycerinus; r. 2490–2472 B.C.E.) and Shepseskhaf.

Khamerernebty (1) (fl. 25th century B.C.E.) *royal woman of the Fourth Dynasty*
She was the consort of KHAFRE (Chephren) (r. 2520–2494 B.C.E.) and probably the mother of MENKAURÉ (Mycerinus, the heir), and Princess KHAMERERNEBTY (2). Khamerernebty was a daughter of KHUFU. She was buried in a large tomb east of Khafre's pyramid at GIZA.

Khamerernebty (2) (fl. 25th century B.C.E.) *royal woman of the Fourth Dynasty*
She was a daughter of KHAFRE (Chephren) (2520–2494 B.C.E.) and probably Queen KHAMERERNEBTY (1). The consort of MENKAURÉ (Mycerinus; r. 2490–2472 B.C.E.),

she was the mother of Prince Khuneré, who died young. A statue of her was discovered in Menkauré's mortuary complex. Khamerernebty was also the mother of the heir, SHEPSESKHAF. She was not buried near her husband but within her father's mortuary complex.

Khamet (fl. 14th century B.C.E.) *Eighteenth Dynasty treasury official*
He served TUTHMOSIS IV (r. 1401–1391 B.C.E.) and AMENHOTEP III (r. 1391–1353 B.C.E.) as a treasurer and superintendent of royal building projects of the dynasty. Khamet was buried on the western shore of the Nile at THEBES, and his tomb has reliefs depict the military campaigns of Egypt during his term of service.

khamsin An Arabic name for a seasonal storm condition in the Nile Valley arising in February or March and lasting about two months, the *khamsin* is composed of southerly or southwesterly winds, sometimes reaching intense velocities. Diurnal, meaning that the wind speeds increase throughout the daylight hours, the *khamsin* brings sand into the populated territories. The storm season was viewed as a time of contagion and disease, ending with "the sweet breath of the north wind" that brought welcome relief. How early the *khamsin* appeared in the Nile is not clearly documented. Climatic changes may have brought the storm season into Egypt in pharaonic times, or it may be a relatively modern phenomenon.

Khamudi (Swoserenré; Asseth; A'azekhre) (d. ca. 1523 B.C.E.) *last ruler of the HYKSOS Fifteenth Dynasty, called the Great Hyksos*
Khamudi reigned from ca. 1550 B.C.E. until his death. He is listed in the TURIN CANON and was called Asseth by MANETHO, the Ptolemaic Period (304–30 B.C.E.) historian. In other lists he is named A'azekhre. Khamudi's OBELISK was discovered at the abandoned capital of AVARIS in the eastern Delta. He had the misfortune of ascending to power when 'AHMOSE (NEBPEHTIRÉ) (r. 1550–1525 B.C.E.) became the founder of the Eighteenth Dynasty at THEBES. There was a period of comparative calm for the first decade of 'Ahmose's reign, but upon reaching majority he renewed Thebes's assault on the Hyksos, ultimately ousting them from power and forcing them to flee from Egypt.

Kharga Oasis A miniature jewel in the LIBYAN DESERT, called Uakt-rest, the Outer or Southern Oasis, Kharga was also part of "the OASES ROUTE." Located some 77 miles southwest of ASSIUT, Kharga contains temples and towns, including HIBIS. A temple to AMUN was established there in the reign of DARIUS I (521–486 B.C.E.) and refurbished in later periods. This temple had an elaborate sacred lake and an avenue of sphinxes. Other temples were built in honor of ISIS, MUT, KHONS (2), and SERAPIS. Kharga, the largest of the oases, was a vital TRADE outpost. With the other oases it served as an agricultural resource, a haven for fugitives, and in some historical periods, a place of exile for individuals banned by the pharaoh.

See also OASES.

Kha'sekhemwy (Kheneres) (fl. ca. 2640 B.C.E.) *final ruler of the Second Dynasty, the actual unifier of Egypt*
He reigned ca. 2640 and was called Kheneres by MANETHO, the Ptolemaic historian. Kha'sekhemwy is credited with the actual completion of Egypt's unification, changing his name from Kha'sekhem to Kha'sekhemwy as a result. His name after the unification meant "the Two Kingdoms Are at Peace in Him."

The task was not an easy one, and his three-decade rule was turbulent. He might not have been the direct successor to PERIBSEN. The names of the pharaohs Sendji, Neterka, and Neferkara appear as interlopers in some king lists, or they may have been the rebels subdued by Kha'sekhemwy. He is recorded as campaigning in DENDEREH, Minya, ELKAB, the FAIYUM, and in some northern regions that rebelled against his rule. The bases of his statuary announced that 47,209 rebels died in battle. Another stone vase records: "Year of Fighting the Northern Enemy."

Kha'sekhemwy's consort was NIMA'ATHAP (Hapnima'at or Nema'athop), and she was designated as "King Bearer," being the mother probably of NEBKA and DJOSER. His mortuary complex at ABYDOS is called SHUNET EL-ZABIB, "the Storehouse of Dates." A rectangular mud-brick structure surrounded by thick walls, the tomb was decorated with paneled walls. His second tomb in HIERAKONPOLIS was actually a fortress that was abandoned. The Abydos site has a central corridor opening onto 33 magazines on either side of a burial chamber of limestone. Vast quantities of tools, vessels, beads, sealings, and gold were discovered there. A scepter of gold and sard was also found there.

Khemsit (Khemsait, Kemsiyet) (fl. 21st century B.C.E.) *royal companion of the Eleventh Dynasty*
She was a member of the HAREM of MENTUHOTEP II (r. 2061–2010 B.C.E.) of the Eleventh Dynasty. Khemsit was buried in the king's vast mortuary complex in DEIR EL-BAHRI on the western shore of THEBES. Her SARCOPHAGUS designated her as yet another "Sole Favorite of the King."

Khendjer (Userkaré) (fl. ca. 1740 B.C.E.) *Thirteenth Dynasty ruler*
An obscure ruler of this relatively undocumented dynasty, he came to power ca. 1740 B.C.E. Khendjer is listed in the TURIN CANON. He is famed for adorning the tomb of DJER, the second pharaoh of the First Dynasty, at ABYDOS. Djer's tomb was thought to be the actual grave of the god OSIRIS. Khendjer's act of piety in providing the tomb with an OSIRIS BED, a votive memo-

rial, was recorded in his records. He also commissioned the cleaning and refurbishing of the temple of Osiris at Abydos. Ruling only about four years, Khendjer built his tomb in southern SAQQARA. The pyramidal complex, made of a mud-brick core with a limestone facing, was graced with quartzite portcullises and corridors that led to a burial chamber, also made of black quartzite. The MORTUARY CHAPEL of the tomb had palm columns. The limestone facing used on the complex structures of Khendjer was later removed by RAMESSES II (r. 1290–1224 B.C.E.) for his own monuments. There is evidence of robbery on the site, but Khendjer does not appear to have used the pyramid. His name was erased in some areas of the complex.

Khenemsu (Khentikhety-hotep) (fl. 19th century B.C.E.) *official and mining leader of the Twelfth Dynasty*
He served SENWOSRET III (r. 1878–1841 B.C.E.) as the royal treasurer and the leader of the various mining expeditions conducted in that era. The utilization of Egypt's natural resources was a vital aspect of Senwosret III's reign. Khenemsu was in charge of the SINAI territory and had to defend Egypt's holdings from BEDOUIN (*bedwi*) raids while mining copper and malachite. While inspecting the WADI MAGHARA, Khenemsu was accompanied on his tours by Ameniseneb, Sitra, and Sebeko, also officials. A STELA erected by a subordinate, Harnakht, confirms the expedition and the unusual manner of travel, by boat. Khenemsu is also listed as Khentikhety-hotep in some records.

See also NATURAL RESOURCES.

Khensuhotep (fl. ca. 14th century B.C.E.) *author of the Maxims*
The *Maxims* were a religious literary text of the Eighteenth Dynasty (1550–1307 B.C.E.). Khensuhotep addressed his fellow Egyptians and urged them to remember that the gods honored silent prayer and decreed right behavior (MA'AT) in all creatures. The *Maxims* were popular throughout the Nile Valley.

Khentakawes (1) (fl. 25th century B.C.E.) *royal woman of the Fourth and Fifth Dynasties*
She was the daughter of Prince DJEDEFHOR', or MENKAURE, heirs to the throne of KHUFU (Cheops). Khentakawes married SHEPSESKHAF (r. 2472–2467 B.C.E.) and became the mother of SAHURÉ and KAKAI (Neferirkaré). She also may have been the mother of DJEDEFPTAH (Thamptis), who is listed in the TURIN CANON and mentioned by MANETHO, the Ptolemaic historian, as ruling Egypt for two years. Her daughter was KHAMA'AT, who married PTAHSHEPSES (1), the high priest of MEMPHIS. Khentakawes was honored with two tombs—one at GIZA and one at ABUSIR. Her tomb at Giza shows her with a royal BEARD and a URAEUS. She was possibly regent when Shepseskhaf died.

Khentakawes (2) (fl. 25th century B.C.E.) *royal woman of the Fifth Dynasty*
She was the consort of KAKAI (Neferirkaré) (r. 2446–2426 B.C.E.) and the mother of NEFEREFRÉ and NIUSERRÉ. Khentakawes was depicted as wearing the pharaonic symbol of the URAEUS and carrying a SCEPTER, perhaps serving as regent for a time.

Khentemsemti (fl. 19th century B.C.E.) *mining and royal treasury official of the Twelfth Dynasty*
He served AMENEMHET II (r. 1929–1892 B.C.E.) as a royal treasurer and a leader of expeditions to mines and quarries. Khentemsemti left an inscription about one such expedition on ELEPHANTINE Island at ASWAN.

Khentiamentiu   He was a divine being of Egypt, the forerunner of the god OSIRIS, dating to Predynastic Periods (before 3000 B.C.E.). Called "the Foremost of the Westerners," he was depicted as a JACKAL. The title indicates that Khentiamentiu was associated with the MORTUARY RITUALS as a guardian of the dead, who went to "the West." Normally the necropolis areas were located on the western shore of the Nile. Sometimes addressed as Ophis, Khentiamentiu was a warrior deity and the navigator for the sun's nightly voyage in TUAT, or the Underworld. His cultic shrines were in ABYDOS and ASSIUT, and he was sometimes associated with WEPWAWET, the wolf deity. His cult was popular in the First Dynasty (2920–2770 B.C.E.). The PYRAMID TEXTS of the Fourth Dynasty (2575–2465 B.C.E.) associated Khentiamentiu with Osiris. Soon after, Osiris became "the Foremost of the Westerners," and the Khentiamentiu cult disappeared.

Khentikus (Khentika) (fl. 24th and 23rd centuries B.C.E.) *vizier and royal judge of the Sixth Dynasty*
He served TETI (r. 2323–2291 B.C.E.) and PEPI I (r. 2289–2255 B.C.E.). His tomb near MEMPHIS declared his honors as a VIZIER and supreme judge of the court system. Khentikus, sometimes listed as Khentika, was depicted in tomb reliefs as passing judgment on five unworthy governors. Two condemned governors are already tied to poles in the scene, in preparation for physical punishment.

Khenut (fl. 24th century B.C.E.) *royal woman of the Fifth Dynasty*
She was a consort of UNIS (r. 2356–2323 B.C.E.). Khenut's tomb is located near Unis's mortuary temple in SAQQARA.

Kheper (Khepri; Kheperé)   He was a divine being of Egypt. A creator deity, Kheper was associated with the daily cycle of the sun and symbolized the sun at dawn. Having a cult center at HELIOPOLIS, Kheper was a manifestation of the god RÉ. He is depicted as a man with a SCARAB pushing the sun across the sky. In PETOSIRIS's tomb at TUNA EL-GEBEL, dating to the Ptolemaic Period (304–30 B.C.E.), Kheper is shown wearing an Atef CROWN. He was also mentioned in the PYRAMID TEXTS. Self-created, Kheper was associated with ATUM.

See also GODS AND GODDESSES; SOLAR CULTS.

khepesh (khopresh)   The sickle-shaped sword used by the Egyptians in military campaigns in the New Kingdom (1550–1070 B.C.E.), the weapon was HYKSOS in origin, introduced by the Asiatic invaders. This sickle-shaped sword was valuable, but not as valuable as the Hyksos chariot, which, eventually became Egypt's most valuable war machine.

khephresh   See CROWNS.

khert-neter   This term translates as "that which is beneath a god" and was used in ancient Egypt to denote a cemetery or necropolis. Most cemetery areas had particular patrons, deities who resided on overlooking cliffs and surveyed the tombs located in the region. MERESGER (1), a goddess of THEBES, is an example of such cliff-dwelling deities overlooking the *khert-neter*. Violation of such burial sites was considered sacrilege and brought about instant retaliation.

Kheruef (fl. 14th century B.C.E.) *palace official of the Eighteenth Dynasty*
He served as the royal steward of AMENHOTEP III (r. 1391–1353 B.C.E.). Kheruef's main duties were involved with the daily administrative affairs of Queen TIYE (1), Amenhotep III's dynamic and powerful consort. His tomb at DRA-ABU' EL-NAGA, on the western shore of THEBES, contains fine reliefs that display his life and honors. Amenhotep II is depicted in the reliefs, and there are scenes of Queen Tiye and AKHENATEN as a prince. A columned hall and painted scenes also grace Kheruef's tomb.

Khety I (Meryibré; Aktoy) (fl. 22nd century B.C.E.) *founder of the Ninth Dynasty*
He based his royal line at HERAKLEOPOLIS in 2134 B.C.E. The dynasty, combined with the Tenth, ruled a portion of Egypt until 2061 B.C.E. when MENTUHOTEP II united the Two Kingdoms again. Khety I gained considerable land after the fall of the Old Kingdom (2575–2134 B.C.E.), particularly north of ABYDOS. He was the son of Tefibi, a noble lord of ASSIUT, and he claimed to have descended from a princely line. He inscribed his name in ASWAN. His contemporaries described him as "cruel."

Khety II (Nebkauré) (fl. ca. 2100 B.C.E.) *ruler of the Ninth Dynasty*
He was the successor to KHETY I at HERAKLEOPOLIS. His mother had to serve as regent for his first four years of reign. Khety II is believed to be the ruler who invited "The ELOQUENT PEASANT," Khunianupu, to court. His name was inscribed at the WADI TIMULAT.

Khety III (Wah'karé) (fl. 22nd century B.C.E.) *third ruler of the Ninth Dynasty*
The date of his reign is unknown. Khety III is revered as the author of INSTRUCTIONS FOR MERIKARÉ, a didactic text that was addressed to his son. The *Instructions* are valuable for their historical perspective of the First Intermediate Period (2134–2040 B.C.E.) and for their portrayal of Khety III. He had witnessed the assault made on the city of THINIS by his allies at ASSIUT and sorely regretted the event.

During the assault a necropolis had been ravaged and desecrated, along with shrines and temples. The incident aroused the Theban royal line and set them on a military crusade that would destroy the Herakleopolitans. INYOTEF II of Thebes was a contemporary of Khety III, who also fought against invading Bedouins and Asiatics throughout his reign.

Khian (Swoserenré) (fl. 16th century B.C.E.) *one of the "Great Hyksos" rulers of the Fifteenth Dynasty (1640–1532 B.C.E.)*
He ruled from AVARIS in the eastern Delta on the Bubastite branch of the Nile, and he was a vigorous monarch, despite the fact that Upper Egypt, the southern domain, was in the control of THEBES. Khian's inscriptions are still visible all across Egypt and even in the Knossus of Crete. A granite lion form that was built into the wall of a house in Baghdad, Iraq, bears his name as well. He decorated shrines at GEBELEIN and BUBASTIS, and SCARABS and seal impressions of his name have been discovered in the Levant. A fragment of a vase with his titles was unearthed at Hattusas, modern Böghazköy, Turkey, the HITTITE capital.

Khnum The ancient Egyptian deity worshiped at ELEPHANTINE Island at ASWAN, he was a creator god revered as a ram. Khnum formed a triad with SATET and ANUKIS on Elephantine Island. His name meant "the Molder," and he used a potter's wheel to fashion the great cosmic egg and then all living creatures. THOTH aided him in this creative process by marking the number of years allotted to each. Khnum's cult dates to Predynastic Periods (before 3000 B.C.E.), and the centers of his worship were on the Elephantine (Abu), at BIGA, and at ESNA. Khnum was the deity of the first CATARACT of the Nile and the god of the inundations, associated with the goddesses MERIT (2) and HEKET. He was called "the Prince of the Two Lands" and "the Prince of the House of Life." Khnum brought the Nile to Egypt through two caverns in Aswan, where he was associated with Anukis and Satet.

Called also "the Soul of Ré," Khnum wore the horns of the oldest species of rams in Egypt (*Ovis longipes*). At ESNA, he had two different divine consorts, MENHET and NEITH (1). The reliefs at the Esna temple portray Khnum's creative powers. The FAMINE STELA at SEHEL ISLAND described prayers to Khnum in times of low Nile inundations. DJOSER (r. 2630–2611 B.C.E.) was honored by later generations for visiting the shrine of Khnum and ending a famine in his reign. The people of NUBIA (modern Sudan) incorporated Khnum into their cultic services and associated him with their deity Dedun. Khnum was portrayed as a robust man with a ram's head, wearing ivory horns, plumes, the SOLAR DISK, and the URAEUS.

Khnumhotep (1) (fl. 20th century B.C.E.) *remarkable nomarch of Beni Hasan in Middle Egypt*
He was a royal servant who founded a family in the Oryx NOME that served the Twelfth Dynasty. Khnumhotep accompanied AMENEMHET I (r. 1991–1962 B.C.E.) on his military campaigns, sailing with a fleet of 20 ships to put down rebellious outposts on the Nile. As a result of this faithful service, Khnumhotep was named the count of MENET-KHUFU and the head of the Oryx nome. Khnumhotep's sons, Nakht and Amenemhet, became court officials, and his daughter, Beket, married and gave birth to another Khnumhotep heir. Khnumhotep's tomb at BENI HASAN has exterior facades, three naves, and niches for statues.

Khnumhotep (2) (fl. 20th century B.C.E.) *grandson of Khnumhotep (1)*
He was the son of Beket, KHNUMHOTEP (1)'s daughter, and an official named Nehri. Khnumhotep succeeded his uncle Nakht as the ruler of the Oryx nome in the 19th year of the reign of AMENEMHET II (1929–1892 B.C.E.). He married the heiress of the Jackal nome, and his own son, another Nakht, inherited that territory. His other son, also named Khnumhotep, succeeded him as ruler of the Oryx nome. This Khnumhotep was buried with his ancestors in BENI HASAN, while his father's stela was found at WADI GASUS. Khnumhotep (2) claimed to be "the darling of his lord."

Khnumt (Khnumyt; Khnumet) (fl. 19th century B.C.E.) *royal woman of the Twelfth Dynasty*
She was probably the daughter of AMENEMHET II (r. 1929–1892 B.C.E.). Khnumt was buried during his reign at DASHUR. A cache of her royal jewels was found in the necropolis there, and the necklaces and crowns are remarkable for their beauty and craftsmanship. A trapdoor covered the entrance of her tomb, hiding it from robbers. A sandstone sarcophagus was in place in the tomb, but her mummified remains were badly damaged by robbers.

Khokha A site between SHEIKH ABD' EL-QURNA and DEIR EL-BAHRI, serving as a necropolis on the western side of the Nile at THEBES. Tombs dating to the Sixth

Dynasty (2323–2150 B.C.E.) were discovered in this necropolis, cut into the rocks. New Kingdom (1550–1070 B.C.E.) tombs were also built in Khokha. Several of the burial sites are beautifully painted and have fine reliefs.

Khons (1)   He was a moon deity, patron of childbirth, and member of the THEBAN triad with AMUN and MUT. His name was formed from *kh* for placenta, and *nsu* or *nsw* for ruler. He is usually depicted as a royal young man with the lock of youth, mummy wrappings, and the scepter of PTAH, or the CROOK and the FLAIL. His cult was popular throughout Egypt, and he is shown in reliefs at KARNAK, THEBES, MEDINET HABU, and the RAMESSEUM.

At KOM OMBO, Khons was honored as the son of SOBEK and HATHOR. There he was a lunar deity. At Karnak he was called Khons Neferhotep, "the Maker of Destinies." As Khons-Pa-Khart, he was "the Child" or "the Full Moon." Khons-Hunnu was "the Strong Youth," "the Bull of His Mother," a source of regeneration. Wearing the crescent and full-moon symbols on his head and the elaborate *menat* collar, Khons was the celestial chronographer, reckoning time. As Khons-pa-ari-Sekheru, the deity had authority over all evil spirits. In this capacity he was recorded in the BENTRESH STELA as an exorcist.

The Bentresh Stela dates to the reign of RAMESSES II (r. 1290–1224 B.C.E.) and is presently in LUXOR. This monument announces that Ramesses II sent a statue of Khons to a neighboring ruler to cure his daughter, who was suffering from demonic possession. The statue was Khons-the-Expeller-of-Demons. The god was also associated with RÉ in some periods and was then called Khons-ré. Khons personally designed the statue of his divine person that was taken to the sick or the possessed. The daughter was cured, and Khons was honored with a shrine. The ruler, however, had a vision almost four years later, indicating that Khons wished to return to Egypt. He was sent back to the Nile with a treasury of gifts.

Khons (2)   (fl. 13th century B.C.E.) *priestly official of the Nineteenth Dynasty*
He served in the reign of RAMESSES II (r. 1290–1224 B.C.E.) as the high priest of the cult of the deified TUTHMOSIS III. His tomb was discovered at KHOKHA on the western side of THEBES. Within the tomb the cults of Tuthmosis III and MONTU are depicted in reliefs and paintings. The ceiling of the tomb chamber also has birds, grapes, and textile designs. The arrival of the bark of the god Montu is elaborately portrayed.

Khufu (Cheops)   (d. 2528 B.C.E.) *second ruler of the Fourth Dynasty*
He reigned from 2551 B.C.E. until his death. He was the builder of the Great PYRAMID at GIZA. His name is

The Great Pyramid at Giza—Khufu's monument—the only surviving Wonder of the Ancient World *(Courtesy Steve Beikirch)*

a shortened version of *Khnum-khuefui,* "Khnum Protects Me." The Greeks listed him as Cheops. The son of SNEFRU and Queen HETEPHERES (1), Khufu ruled a unified country and used capable relatives as administrators. His Great Wife was MERITITES (1), who gave birth to Prince KEWAB and probably HETEPHERES (2). Another wife, Queen HENUTSEN, bore Prince Khufukhaf and probably KHAFRE (Chephren). There was another unidentified queen, possibly NEFERKAU, who gave birth to RA'DJEDEF.

Khufu's offspring included as well DJEDEFHOR, KHUMBAEF, MERYSANKH (2), MINKHAF, NEFERMA'AT, KHAME RERNEBTI (1), DjedefʼAha, and others. The royal family was actually divided into two political and clan groups, with rivalries and disputes that affected the dynasty after Khufu's demise. The reputation of Khufu was not good, as a result. Greek historians claimed they were informed of the details by Egyptian records and wrote ill of him. The raising of the Great Pyramid, which used CORVÉE labor, not slaves, was an almost overwhelming task. The Greeks related that Khufu's daughter had to sell herself in order to raise the necessary money to complete the project. The accusation is false, as Egypt did not have a currency until centuries later.

Khufu also dabbled in MAGIC, according to the legends, using a magician from MEIDUM, DJEDI, who sailed on the Nile in a barge full of women clad only in fishnets. The *TALE OF KHUFU AND THE MAGICIANS,* a Middle Kingdom (2040–1640 B.C.E.) papyrus, relates this exotic tale. The real Khufu was vigorous and active. He used the diorite quarries near ABU SIMBEL, fought campaigns in the SINAI, and initiated building projects around MEMPHIS. His name was found on seals of jars and vases in BEIT KHALLAF, north of ABYDOS, and the WESTCAR PAPYRUS details his reign. Only a small statuette was discovered as his portrait, now in the Egyptian Museum in Cairo.

His Great Pyramid in Giza was originally 753 square feet, rising 478 feet, and it is the only survivor of the Seven Wonders of the World. It took two decades of continuous labor, using corvée levies of workers in the land. Five boat pits were included in the complex on the south and east. The mortuary cult of Khufu was popular in Egypt, still observed in the nation during the Twenty-sixth Dynasty (664–525 B.C.E.) and even into the Roman Period in some areas.

Khunianupu *See* "The Eloquent Peasant" of Herakleopolis.

Khusebek (fl. 19th century B.C.E.) *military official of the Twelfth Dynasty*
He served Senwosret III (r. 1878–1841 B.C.E.) as a commander of troops. Khusebek accompanied Senwosret III on punitive campaigns in Syria and in Nubia (modern Sudan). His mortuary stela announces his career and honors, detailing the military efforts of his time. The stela was discovered at Abydos.

Khuy (fl. 23rd century B.C.E.) *father-in-law of Pepi I* (2289–2255 B.C.E.)
Khuy was a nomarch and the father of Ankhnesmery-Ré (1) and (2), who became Pepi I's consorts and the mothers of the heirs. His son, Djau, served as counselor and adviser for Pepi I and Pepi II.

king lists   These are historical monuments or documents that provide accounts of the rulers of Egypt in chronological order. Lists of the kings from the founding of Egypt to the current pharaoh became popular as demonstrations of the so-called unbreakable lines of rulers and their right to the throne.

These historical accounts of rulers sometimes omitted dynasties considered unworthy and glorified others. Pharaohs, such as Ramesses II (Ramesses the Great) (r. 1290–1224 B.C.E.), understood the use of monuments and declarations and built many such reminders of his rank and role throughout the Nile Valley. The following are some of the most well-known king lists.

Abydos Tablet   a list discovered in the corridors of the Hall of the Ancestors in the mortuary temple of Seti I (r. 1306–1290 B.C.E.) in Abydos. This list contains the names of the rulers from Aha (Menes) (r. 2920–? B.C.E.) to Seti I, a total of 76 rulers. There are reportedly intentional omissions in the Abydos Tablet, including the Second Intermediate Period rulers, Akhenaten, and other 'Amarna rulers. Ramesses II copied the list for his own temple. The Abydos Tablet is in the British Museum in London.

Karnak Tablet   a king list inscribed on the festival hall of Tuthmosis III at Karnak and using the *nesu* names, or royal names, of pharaohs from Aha (Menes) (r. 2920–? B.C.E.) to Tuthmosis III (1479–1425 B.C.E.). Based on earlier traditions, the list is not as accurate as

Seti I's at Abydos. Of particular interest, however, are the details of the Second Intermediate Period (1640–1550 B.C.E.) rulers, the Khetys or Aktoys, unseated by Mentuhotep II (r. 2061–2010 B.C.E.) when he united the Two Kingdoms. The Karnak Tablet is now in the Louvre in Paris.

Manetho's King List   the assembled record of Egyptian rulers compiled by Manetho, a historian of Sebennytos who wrote during the reign of Ptolemy I Soter (304–284 B.C.E.) and Ptolemy II Philadelphus (285–246 B.C.E.). This king list can be found in the *Chronography* of George Monk and the *Syncellus* of Tarassus, patriarch of Constantinople, who lived in the eighth century C.E. The oldest version is in the *Chronicle of Julius Africanus,* a Libyan of the third century C.E. This work, in turn, became part of the *Chronicle of Eusebius,* the bishop of Caesarea (264–340 C.E.).

Palermo Stone   a great stone slab, originally seven feet long and two feet high, now in five fragments. The largest fragment is in the Regional Archaeological Museum in Palermo, Italy. The stone is made of black diorite and is inscribed with annals of the various reigns. It dates to the Fifth Dynasty (2465–2323 B.C.E.). A secondary piece is in the Egyptian Museum in Cairo, and another is in the Petrie Museum at University College in London. Smaller versions of the Palermo Stone have been discovered in private tombs, mines, and quarries.

Saqqara Tablet   a monument found in the tomb of the royal scribe Thunery (Tenroy), probably dating to the reign of Ramesses II (1290–1224 B.C.E.). The tablet uses the *nesu* names (one of the royal names) of 47 rulers, starting in the Old Kingdom (2575–2134 B.C.E.). Originally 58 names were included. (11 names were damaged and lost over time). Reportedly, the list began with Anedjib, the fifth ruler of the First Dynasty (2920–2770 B.C.E.), and continued to the reign of Ramesses II. No rulers of the Second Intermediate Period (1640–1550 B.C.E.) were included. The Saqqara Tablet is now in the Egyptian Museum in Cairo.

Turin Canon   a document sometimes called the Turin Royal Papyrus, compiled in the reign of Ramesses II (1290–1224 B.C.E.). Done in the hieratic script, the Turin list begins with the dynasties of the gods and continues to Ramesses II. It is considered the most reliable of the king lists, but some of the names recorded in it are no longer decipherable. Originally in the possession of the king of Sardinia, the Turin Canon was sent to Turin, Italy, and was damaged in the process. The list is written in the hieratic style on a Ramessid Period papyrus. No predynastic rulers are in the list. The Royal Canon of Turin, as it is also called, was discovered by Bernardino Drovetti and is believed to be a copy of an earlier list. It is now in the Muzeo Egizio in Turin, Italy.

kites (1)   These were the names applied by the Egyptians to the goddesses Isis and Nephthys as part of the

Osirian cultic rituals. The goddesses lamented the death of OSIRIS, and their song of mourning was a popular aspect of the annual festivals of the god.

See also LAMENTATIONS OF ISIS AND NEPHTHYS.

kites (2)   They were Egyptian women who were hired or pressed into service during funerals to accompany and greet the coffins of the deceased when they were carried to the necropolises. Professional mourners, the *kites* wailed and evidenced their grief at each funeral. They are pictured in some renditions of the BOOK OF THE DEAD.

See also MUU DANCERS.

Kiya (fl. 14th century B.C.E.) *royal woman of the Eighteenth Dynasty, possibly a Mitanni princess*
She was a secondary consort of AKHENATEN (r. 1353–1335 B.C.E.). There is some indication that her origins were Mitanni and that she was named TADUKHIPA, being the daughter of King TUSHRATTA. It is also possible that she was a noble woman from AKHMIN. Kiya was held in high regard in Akhenaten's ninth regnal year, but she was out of favor by regnal year 11. She is recorded as having borne two sons and a daughter by Akhenaten, and she was portrayed on monuments in 'AMARNA.

After regnal year 11, however, she is no longer visible, and her name was removed from some reliefs. Kiya's COFFIN, gilded and inlaid in the RISHI PATTERN, was found in Queen TIYE's (1) tomb, apparently having served as a resting place for the remains of SMENKHARÉ (r. 1335–1333 B.C.E.). Canopic lids in Tiye's tomb had portraits of Kiya. Her mummy has not been identified.

Kleomenes (fl. fourth century B.C.E.) *Greek commissioned to build the city of Alexandria by Alexander III the Great (332–323 B.C.E.)*
A companion of ALEXANDER III THE GREAT, Kleomenes was charged with building the new capital of ALEXANDRIA in the Delta. Kleomenes worked with DEINOKRATES, the architect, and others, including Krateros of Olynthas, in starting the massive projects. Alexandria's building continued until the reign of PTOLEMY II PHILADELPHUS (285–246 B.C.E.).

knots   Considered magical elements by the Egyptians and used in specific ways for cultic ceremonies. AMULETS used knots as protective shields, and knotted emblems were worn daily. Elaborate golden knots were used on mummies in some periods. The exact cultic value of these designs and their placements varied according to regions and temple traditions.

Kom Aushim   A site in the FAIYUM region of the Nile, dating to the Middle Kingdom. The pharaohs of the Twelfth Dynasty (1991–1783 B.C.E.) used the area for royal retreats. However, no monuments from that dynasty are recognizable now. Kom Aushim was probably LETOPOLIS, a cult center of HORUS, called Hem by the Egyptians.

Kom Dara   This was a site in the necropolis near ASSIUT, with a vast tomb structure dating to the First Intermediate Period (2134–2040 B.C.E.). Massive, with vast outer walls, the tomb contains a sloping corridor leading to a subterranean chamber. No identification has been made as to the owner of the Kom Dara monument.

Kom el-Haten   A site on the western shore of THEBES, famed for the mortuary temple of AMENHOTEP III (r. 1391–1353 B.C.E.) and the seated figures of that pharaoh, called the COLOSSI OF MEMNON, the area was part of the vast necropolis serving Thebes, Egypt's New Kingdom (1550–1070 B.C.E.) capital. The temple no longer stands, having been used as a quarry for later dynasties and looted by the locals.

Kom el-Hisn   *See* IMU.

Kom Medinet Ghurob (Mi-Wer)   This was a site on the southeastern end of the FAIYUM, also called MI-WER in ancient records. TUTHMOSIS III (r. 1479–1425 B.C.E.) of the Eighteenth Dynasty established the site as a royal HAREM retreat and retirement villa. Two temples were erected on the site, now in ruins, as well as the royal harem residence. Kom Medinet Ghurob was used until the reign of RAMESSES V (1156–1151 B.C.E.). A central building with an enclosing wall, covering the area of three modern city blocks, composed this complex. Objects from the reign of Amenhotep III (1391–1353 B.C.E.) were found on the site. A head of Queen TIYE (1), fashioned out of wood, glass, and gesso, was discovered there. This head provides a remarkably individualistic portrait.

Kom Ombo   A site south of EDFU on the Nile that served as the cultic center for the deities HORUS the Elder and SOBEK, Kom Ombo was also a major center of Egyptian TRADE with the Red Sea and Nubian (modern Sudanese) cultures. Eighteenth Dynasty (1550–1307 B.C.E.) structures made Kom Ombo important, but there were also settlements from the Paleolithic Period in the area.

The temple of Haroeris (HORUS) and SOBEK was a double structure, with identical sections, the northern one for Haroeris and the southern one for Sobek. There was also a shrine to HATHOR on the site. The complex was dedicated as well to KHONS (1). Tasenetnofret, an obscure goddess called "the Good Sister," and Pnebtawy, called "the Lord of the Two Lands," were honored as well at Kom Ombo.

A double entrance is in the southwest, leading to a courtyard. Two HYPOSTYLE HALLS, offering halls, twin sanctuaries, magazines, vestibules, wells, and birth houses, called *MAMMISI,* compose the elements of the temple. The main temple is Ptolemaic in its present

Temple of Sobek and Haroeris (Horus) at Kom Ombo

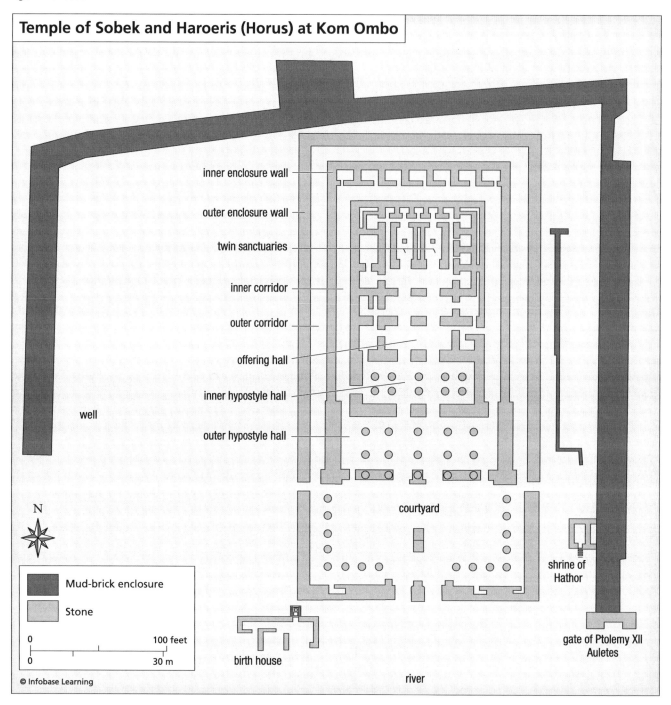

inner enclosure wall

outer enclosure wall

twin sanctuaries

inner corridor

outer corridor

offering hall

inner hypostyle hall

outer hypostyle hall

well

N

courtyard

Mud-brick enclosure

Stone

0   100 feet

0   30 m

© Infobase Learning

birth house

river

shrine of Hathor

gate of Ptolemy XII Auletes

form, with a gate fashioned by PTOLEMY XII Auletes (r. 80–58, 55–51 B.C.E.). Niches and crypts were also included, and mummies of CROCODILES were found, wearing golden earrings, manicures, and gilded nails. A NILOMETER was installed at Kom Ombo, and CALENDARS and portraits of the Ptolemies adorned the walls.

Konosso   A high-water island, dating to the Eighteenth Dynasty (1550–1307 B.C.E.), it was a staging point for TRADE and expeditions to NUBIA (modern Sudan). An inscription of TUTHMOSIS IV (r. 1401–1391 B.C.E.)

at Konosso gives an account of the site's purpose. The expeditions for TRADE were located in remote and wild territories, particularly in Nubia. The Egyptians, therefore, had to build garrisoned outposts that could serve as a refuge from attack and could hold necessary equipment and supplies. Expeditions and officials could retreat to Konosso in times of peril.

Koptos (Gebtu; Kabet; Qift)   This was a site south of QENA, called Gebtu or Kabet by the Egyptians and Koptos by the Greeks, serving as the capital of the fifth nome of Upper Egypt and as a center for trade expeditions to the Red Sea. Koptos was also the cult center of the god MIN (1). Min shared a temple with the goddess ISIS. Three pylons and a processional way that led to a gate erected by TUTHMOSIS III (r. 1479–1425 B.C.E.) were part of the temple design. HORUS was also honored in this temple, spanning Egypt's history. PTOLEMY II PHILA-DELPHUS (r. 285–246 B.C.E.) added to the temple, as did PTOLEMY IV PHILOPATOR (r. 221–205 B.C.E.). An original temple on the site had been erected and adorned by AMENEMHET I (r. 1991–1962 B.C.E.) and SENWOSRET I (r. 1971–1926 B.C.E.). A chapel of the god OSIRIS dates to the reign of Amasis (570–526 B.C.E.). A middle temple has additions made by OSORKON II (r. 883–855 B.C.E.). A temple that was discovered in the southern area of Koptos was refurbished by NECTANEBO II (r. 360–343 B.C.E.). CLEOPATRA VII (r. 51–30 B.C.E.) and PTOLEMY XV Caesarion (r. 44–30 B.C.E.) also constructed a small chapel on the site. This chapel was used as an oracle. Koptos also had gold mines and quarries, being located near the WADI HAMMAMAT.

Koptos Decree This was a document from the Sixth Dynasty, in the reign of PEPI I (2289–2255 B.C.E.). Found in the temple of MIN (1) at Koptos, the Decree grants immunity from taxes for all residents of the mortuary chapel for Pepi I's royal mother, Queen IPUT. This chapel was connected to Min's temple. The personnel of Queen Iput's (2) cult were also freed from the responsibility of paying for the travel of officials and the visit of any royal retinues. Such tax-exemption decrees were frequent in many periods, particularly for complexes concerned with mortuary cults.

Kula, el- A site on the western shore of the Nile, northwest of HIERAKONPOLIS and ELKAB. The remains of an Old Kingdom (2575–2134 B.C.E.) step PYRAMID were discovered there, without the usual complex structures. No identification of the pyramid has been possible to date.

Kurgus A site at the fifth cataract in NUBIA (modern Sudan), conquered by TUTHMOSIS I (r. 1504–1492 B.C.E.) and maintained by TUTHMOSIS III (r. 1479–1425 B.C.E.), Kurgus has a carved inscription designating it as Egypt's southern boundary. The city was involved in an overland TRADE route through WADI ALAKI. As the resources of Egypt's military and trade systems were stretched perilously thin at this southern outpost, fortifications were installed and units were assigned to keep supply lines open in an effort to stock and defend the site. When the New Kingdom fell in 1070 B.C.E., sites such as Kurgus were immediately occupied by the Nubians; the Egyptians were forced to retreat northward because of the lack of a central government.

Kuser A port on the Red Sea, also called Sewew, Kuser was located to the east of KOPTOS and was used extensively by the Egyptians. A shipbuilding industry prospered there, as Kuser was a staging point for maritime expeditions to PUNT in many eras of the nation's history, particularly in the New Kingdom (1550–1070 B.C.E.). This port was extremely valuable to the Egyptians. Queen-Pharaoh HATSHEPSUT (r. 1473–1458 B.C.E.) used Kuser and its services for her expedition to bring back myrrh trees and other products from Punt for her monument at DEIR EL-BAHRI.

Kush *See* NUBIA.

kyphi This was the Greek form of the Egyptian *kapet,* a popular incense or perfume of ancient Egypt, composed of many ingredients. The formulas varied considerably and were mentioned in medical texts. *Kyphi* was also used as a freshener for the air and clothes (even though the formulas included at times the excrement of animals). As a mouthwash it could be mixed with wine. *Kyphi* was sometimes used as incense in the Ptolemaic Period (304–30 B.C.E.), and formulas were discovered on the walls of the EDFU and PHILAE temples.

L

Lab'ayu (fl. 14th century B.C.E.) *prince of Canaan during the 'Amarna Period*
The prince's correspondence with AMENHOTEP III (r. 1391–1353 B.C.E.) demonstrates the role of vassal states in the vast EGYPTIAN EMPIRE of that historical period. Lab'ayu, whose capital was at Sechem, raided his neighbors in the hill country of northern Palestine, and Prince BIRIDIYA of AR-MEGIDDO wrote to Amenhotep III to complain about the problem. Lab'ayu was warned by Egyptian officials and sent word to Amenhotep III that he was innocent of all charges and loyal to the pharaoh. The Canaanite prince died in the reign of AKHENATEN (1353–1335 B.C.E.).

See also 'AMARNA LETTERS.

Labyrinth This is the Greek name given to the pyramid complex of AMENEMHET III (1844–1797 B.C.E.) at HAWARA, near the FAIYUM. The exact purpose of the complex has not been determined, but the name was bestowed upon the site because of the architectural complexity of the design. Shafts, corridors, and stone plugs were incorporated into the pyramid, and a central burial chamber was fashioned out of a single block of granite, weighing an estimated 110 tons. There are also shrines for NOME deities in the structure and 12 separate courts, facing one another, and demonstrating the architectural wonders of the site. An obvious burial complex, the Labyrinth has also been identified as an administrative or cultic center of the time.

Many believe the Labyrinth was discovered by Sir Flinders Petrie in the late 1800s, but Herodotus (484–420 B.C.E.), the Greek historian, had made note of it in his journey to Egypt more than 2,000 years earlier.

Herodotus reported that the Labyrinth contained 3,000 chambers, connected by corridors. When rediscovered, the structure was 1,000 feet in length and 800 feet wide. It was dedicated to the god Sobek and contained objects from the Eighteenth Dynasty (1550–1307 B.C.E.). Some scholars believe that the site still contains historical treasures.

ladder A mystical symbol associated with the cult of the god OSIRIS, called a *magat*. Used as an AMULET, the ladder honored the goddess NUT, the mother of OSIRIS. Models of the ladder were placed in tombs to invoke the aid of the deities. The ladder had been designed by the gods to stretch mystically when Osiris ascended into their domain. As an amulet, the ladder was believed to carry the deceased to the realms of paradise beyond the grave.

Ladice (fl. sixth century B.C.E.) *royal woman of the Twenty-sixth Dynasty*
The consort of AMASIS (r. 570–526 B.C.E.), Ladice was a Cyrenaica noble woman, possibly a member of the royal family of that state. Her marriage was undoubtedly part of a treaty between Egypt and CYRENE in North Africa.

Lady of the House of Books See SESHAT.

Lagus (fl. fourth and third centuries B.C.E.) *Greek military companion of Alexander III the Great and the father of Ptolemy I Soter*
Lagus served ALEXANDER III THE GREAT in campaigns and aided Ptolemy's career. He was married to ARSINOE (5), the mother of PTOLEMY I SOTER. The Ptolemaic royal

line (304–30 B.C.E.) was called the Lagide Dynasty in honor of Lagus's memory.

Lahun, el- A site in the FAIYUM region of Egypt, located south of CROCODILOPOLIS (Medinet el-Faiyum), the necropolis of KAHUN is located there as well. The river BAHR YUSEF (not of biblical origin, but honoring a local hero of Islam) enters the Faiyum in this area. El-Lahun was a regulating station for the Faiyum and the Bahr Yusef. In certain times of the year, corresponding to the modern month of January, the sluices were closed to drain the area and to clear the waterways and bridges.

Dominating the site is a pyramidal complex erected by SENWOSRET II (r. 1897–1878 B.C.E.). Made out of mud brick, the pyramid was erected on a rocky outcropping and had a stone casing. The MORTUARY TEMPLE of the complex was covered by red granite, and the surfaces were decorated with inscriptions. The burial chamber was lined with red granite slabs and contained a red granite SARCOPHAGUS. A subsidiary pyramid was erected nearby, enclosed within the main wall. Papyri from the period were discovered there, as well as medical instruments.

Lake of Fire This was a mysterious Underworld site designated in the mortuary relief called the *Book of Gates*. This text appears for the first time in the tomb of HOREMHAB (r. 1319–1307 B.C.E.). The Lake of Fire was located in "the Sacred Cavern of Sokar" and was the ultimate destination of damned souls. No one returned from the Lake of Fire, which burned in a sunless region.

Lake of Flowers The poetic name for one of the eternal realms of paradise awaiting the Egyptians beyond the grave, the site contained all the elements deemed inviting, such as fresh water, cool winds, and flowers. The Egyptians, surrounded by deserts in all eras, were quite precise about the necessary aspects of Amenti, the joyful existence prepared for the dead in the west. Other designations such as the LILY LAKE and the Fields of Food provided similar attributes.

lakes These were the water sources of Egypt beyond the boundaries of the Nile, part of the geographical composition of the Nile Valley. The scant rainfall, especially in Upper Egypt, made the land arid and devoid of any lake. The Delta and the FAIYUM areas of Lower Egypt, however, were graced with seven lakes in ancient times. They were QURUN (Birkat el-Qurun), NATRON, Manzilah, EDKU, Abukir, MAREOTIS, and Barullus. SIWA Oasis in the Western, or LIBYAN, DESERT was graced by Lake Zeytun.

Lamentations of Isis and Nephthys This is an ancient hieratic document from around 500 B.C.E. that was part of the Osirian cult. ISIS and NEPHTHYS wept over OSIRIS after he was slain by the god SET. The two goddesses also proclaimed Osiris's resurrection from the dead and his ascension into heaven. During the Late Period (712–332 B.C.E.), Osirian dramas were revived, and elaborate ceremonies were staged with the *Lamentations* as part of the rituals. Both the goddesses Isis and Nephthys were portrayed by priestesses during the ceremonies in which the hymn was sung, or the *Songs,* as they were also called, were read by a priest. These ceremonies were celebrated in the fourth month of the year, approximately December 21 on the modern calendar. The *Lamentations* were also called the *Festival Songs of the Two Weepers.* In time, the *Lamentations* were added to versions of the BOOK OF THE DEAD.

Land of the Bow This was a region of NUBIA (modern Sudan) controlled by Egypt from the Early Dynastic Period (2920–2575 B.C.E.) until the end of the New Kingdom (1070 B.C.E.). The area below the first cataract, also called WAWAT, attracted the Egyptians because of the local NATURAL RESOURCES and the advantageous trade routes. Associated with the concept of the NINE BOWS, the Land of the Bow was displayed in carvings on royal standards. Other lands of the east assumed that title in certain reigns. In some periods the Nine Bows were depicted on the inside of the pharaoh's shoes, so that he could tread on them in his daily rounds.

language and writing The writing systems of ancient Egypt were clearly visible to the world after the fall of the divine pharaohs and their dynastic reigns. But while the modern world presumed that the hieroglyphs contained a treasure trove of knowledge, no one understood the symbols or even recognized any element that would provide a clue to translators.

Then, in 1798, French emperor Napoleon Bonaparte (1769–1821) invaded Egypt in an effort to break English power in the Mediterranean. He brought with him thousands of French soldiers as well as a large contingent of archaeologists, artists, historians, and scholars. This small army spread out over Egypt, painting images of monuments, uncovering tombs, and looking for historical artifacts. The most important find made by this French scientific expedition was the ROSETTA STONE, discovered by an artillery officer, Lt. P. F. X. Bouchard, in the ruined Fort Julien at Rosetta, in the northern region of the Delta on the western channel of the Nile.

The Rosetta Stone was inscribed by the priests of Memphis on the occasion of an anniversary celebration of pharaoh PTOLEMY V EPIPHANUS (r. 205–108 B.C.E.). The stone contained 14 lines of hieroglyphs, 32 lines of demotic script, and 54 lines of Greek. When the French surrendered Egypt in the Treaty of Alexandria in 1801, the Rosetta Stone was passed to the British and was taken to London. Word had spread already about the stone, as the three languages inscribed reportedly repeated the same message. Specialists began working on the inscriptions, and, through the efforts of dedicated men such as French scholar Jean-François Champollion, the language of the ancient periods was revealed.

THE BIRTH OF HIEROGLYPHS

It was believed in the past that the hieroglyphs of Egypt were not developed until the later historical periods. It is now documented that Egypt crafted its writing system as early as the days of Sumeria, perhaps even earlier. Rock art dating to 3800 B.C.E., if not earlier, used hieroglyphic signs to portray SCORPION I (fl. ca. 3000 B.C.E.) of Dynasty 0. His tomb contained labels on grave goods that were clearly designated as gifts from various nomes, or provinces, of the Nile Valley. The hieroglyphs on these labels are distinct, which means they were in general use at the time.

The Greeks named the language signs hieroglyphs, meaning sacred carvings. Early Greek visitors saw such signs in temples and on tomb walls and assumed as a result that such glyphs pertained to spiritual matters. The hieroglyphs inscribed on tablets were used in varied

Hieroglyphs, the writing of ancient Egyptians, now known to be in use long before the unification of the Two Kingdoms, ca. 3000 B.C.E. *(Hulton Archive)*

forms throughout Egypt's history, the last known display being inscribed at PHILAE, dated 394 B.C.E.

The introduction of hieroglyphs was one of the most important developments in Egypt, as a tradition of literacy and recorded knowledge was thus begun. Probably less than 1 percent of the population was literate at any given time; however, the development of a script led to the establishment of EDUCATION standards and norms that were observed through the centuries by the vast armies of official scribes. In early times, the use of hieroglyphs was confined to a class of priests, and over the years the language in the oral form grew sophisticated and evolved, but the hieroglyphs remained comparatively traditional, protected against inroads by the priestly castes that trained the multitude of scribes.

HIEROGLYPHIC EGYPTIAN

Hieroglyphic Egyptian is basically a pictorial form, used by the early Egyptians to record an object or an event. The hieroglyph could be read as a picture, as a symbol of an image portrayed, or as a symbol for the sounds related to the image. In time the hieroglyphs were incorporated into art forms as well, inserted to specify particulars about the scene or event depicted.

Hieroglyphs were cut originally on cylindrical seals. These incised, roller-shaped stones (later replaced by handheld scarab seals) were rolled onto fresh clay jar stoppers. They were used to indicate ownership of an object (particularly royal ownership) and designated the official responsible for its care. Such cylinders and seals were found in the Predynastic Period (before 3000 B.C.E.) and First Dynasty (2920–2770 B.C.E.) tombs. Hieroglyphs accompanying the artistic renditions of the Early Dynastic Period (2920–2575 B.C.E.) began to conform to certain regulations. At the start of the Old Kingdom, a canon of hieroglyphs was firmly in place. From this period onward the hieroglyphic writing appeared on stone monuments and bas-reliefs or high reliefs. The hieroglyphs were also painted on wood or metal. They were incorporated into temple decorations and were also used in coffins, stelae, statues, tomb walls, and other monumental objects.

The obvious limitations of hieroglyphs for practical, day-to-day record keeping led to another, cursive, form called hieratic. In this form the hieroglyphs were simplified and rounded, in the same way that such writing would result from the use of a reed pen rather than a chisel on a stone surface.

THE HIERATIC STYLE

Although hieroglyphs continued to be used throughout pharaonic history, the cursive script called hieratic was introduced around 2868 B.C.E. to provide increased speed in writing, particularly for business and literary texts. The hieratic style was based on the hieroglyphs.

Certain sacred documents continued to be written in hieroglyphs, such as the Coffin Texts and the BOOK OF THE DEAD.

Originally, also, the hieratic style was written in columns. In time, the hieratic style adopted a grander, more distinguished appearance. Scribes working on important documents added flourishes to the letters and made an attempt to embellish the documents so they would command the same level of attention and respect as those prepared with hieroglyphs. The hieratic script became the standard style for business on the Nile.

In the Old Kingdom (2575–2134 B.C.E.) hieratic was barely distinguishable from hieroglyphic, but in the Middle Kingdom (2040–1640 B.C.E.) and New Kingdom (1550–1070 B.C.E.) the script developed unique qualities of its own. Hieratic was used until the Roman era, ca. 30 B.C.E., although Greek was the official language during the Ptolemaic Period (304–30 B.C.E.).

DEMOTIC SCRIPT

The demotic script, which can be translated as "popular script," evolved out of hieratic in the Twenty-sixth Dynasty era (664–525 B.C.E.). This style was used for almost all documents that were not of a religious nature or pertaining to the mortuary rituals. During the Ptolemaic Period (304–30 B.C.E.) demotic became popular, and various kinds of literature and scientific documents, as well as salutatory statements, used demotic, hence its inclusion in the Rosetta Stone memorial. The members of the Ptolemaic Dynasty preferred Greek, but the administration outside of the court found the demotic script timesaving and efficient. CLEOPATRA VII (r. 51–30 B.C.E.), the last ruler of Egypt, was the only member of the Ptolemaic Dynasty to speak, read, and write the ancient Egyptian language. All royal matters of the Ptolemies were noted in Greek.

LANGUAGE DEVELOPMENT

During the four millennia that Egyptian was spoken and written the language changed greatly, just as any language does. The linguistic stages of development follow.

Old Egyptian

Old Egyptian is the term used to designate the language of the Early Dynastic Period (2920–2575 B.C.E.) and the Old Kingdom (2575–2134 B.C.E.). Extant texts from this period are mostly official or religious, including the PYRAMID TEXTS, royal decrees, tomb inscriptions, and a few biographical documents. Old Egyptian was written in hieroglyphic.

Middle Egyptian

Middle Egyptian, the language of the First Intermediate Period (2134–2040 B.C.E.), was used through the New Kingdom and later. Middle Egyptian was written in hieroglyphic and in hieratic. Middle Egyptian is also called Classical Egyptian, and it is the language used on most monuments and on the famed Rosetta Stone.

Late Egyptian

Late Egyptian (ca. 1500–1000 B.C.E.) was written mainly in hieratic but also in hieroglyphic. Definite and indefinite articles were included, and phonetic changes entered the language.

Demotic Language

In the Twenty-sixth Dynasty (664–525 B.C.E.), demotic became the accepted language. The demotic language was written almost exclusively in the demotic script. During the Persian, Greek, and Roman periods, demotic script was used for legal, literary, and religious texts. Demotic is also included on the Rosetta Stone.

Coptic

Coptic is the last stage of the Egyptian language. After the conquest of Egypt by Alexander the Great, Greek replaced Egyptian as the official language of the country, although the population continued to speak Egyptian. Coptic developed to allow writing the Egyptian language in the Greek alphabet. The new writing system added a few letters from the demotic script to the Greek alphabet to represent Egyptian sounds the Greek language did not have. Coptic played an important role in the development of Christianity in Egypt, remaining the liturgical language of Egyptian Christians for centuries.

HOW TO READ HIEROGLYPHS

In the hieroglyphic writing only two classes of signs need to be distinguished: sense signs, or ideograms, and sound signs, or phonograms. The ideograms represent either the actual object depicted or some closely connected idea. Phonograms acquired sound values and were used for spelling. The vowels were not written in hieroglyphs, a factor which reflects the use of different vocalizations and context for words in the oral Egyptian language. The consonants remained consistent because the pronunciation of the word depended upon the context in which it appeared.

Hieroglyphic inscriptions consisted of rows of miniature pictures, arranged in vertical columns or horizontal lines. They normally read from right to left, although in some instances they were read in reverse. The signs that represented persons or animals normally faced the beginning of the inscription, a key as to the direction in which it should be read.

The alphabet is precise and includes specific characters for different sounds or objects. For each of the consonantal sounds there were one or more characters, and many single signs contained from two to four sounds. These signs, with or without phonetic value, were also used as determinatives. These were added at the ends of words to give them particular action or value. The decipherment of hieroglyphic writing was made possible with the discovery of the Rosetta Stone. Since that time, the study of Egypt's language has continued and evolved, enabling scholars to reassess previously known materials and to elaborate on the historical evidence concerning the people of the Nile.

Further reading: Adkins, Lesley, and Roy Adkins. *The Keys of Egypt: The Obsession to Decipher Egyptian Hieroglyphs.* New York: Harper Collins, 2000; Allen, James P. *Middle Egyptian: An Introduction to the Language and Culture of Hieroglyphs.* Cambridge: Cambridge University Press, 2010; Bertro, Maria Carmelo. *Hieroglyphics: The Writings of Ancient Egypt.* New York: Abbeville, 1996; David, Rosalie. *Handbook to Life in Ancient Egypt, Revised Edition.* New York: Facts On File, 2003; Kemp, Barry J. *Ancient Egypt: Anatomy of a Civilization.* London: Routledge, 1989; Scott, Henry Joseph, and Lenore Scott. *Egyptian Hieroglyphics.* London: Hippocrene, 1998.

Lansing Papyrus   This is a document now in the British Museum in London that appears to be related to the school and scribal systems of Egypt. The text of the papyrus praises scribes and extols the advantages of education and learning.

lapis lazuli   This is a semiprecious stone, a form of limestone, blue mineral lazurite, preferred by Egyptians over gold and silver. The stone, which could be opaque, dark, or greenish blue, was sometimes flecked with gold and was used in all eras, especially as amulets, small sculptures, and scarabs. The Egyptian name for lapis lazuli was *khesbedj*, representing vitality and youthfulness. Lapis lazuli originated in northeastern Afghanistan and was imported into Egypt. The goddess HATHOR was sometimes called the "Mistress of Lapis Lazuli."

See also NATURAL RESOURCES.

lapwing   *See* REKHET.

Lateran Obelisk   This is a monument belonging to TUTHMOSIS III (r. 1479–1425 B.C.E.) that was carved but not erected at KARNAK until the reign of TUTHMOSIS IV (1401–1391 B.C.E.). Tuthmosis IV had the unattended OBELISK raised and put in a place in the Karnak sacred precincts. The monument carries an inscription that attests to Tuthmosis IV's filial piety in performing that deed. The obelisk is now on display in the Vatican in Rome.

law   The documented laws of ancient Egypt provide a remarkable portrait of society in the Nile Valley. Egypt had local and national courts, which provided access to all classes of citizens. The laws were based on traditional moral values that endured. Furthermore, there seems to have been no distinction of rank or sex, which was unique in this time period. The legacy of such laws and court systems may well have contributed to the survival of Egypt while other civilizations collapsed.

Ancient Egyptian law was clearly governed by religious principles: Law was believed to have been handed down to mankind by the gods, and it was personified by the goddess MA'AT. She represented truth, righteousness, and justice and maintained the correct balance and order of the universe. By 3000 B.C.E. the Egyptian priest-astronomers had developed a philosophical outlook, also called MA'AT, that was based on the observations of the night sky, where the universe and the nightly procession of celestial bodies proclaimed order. *Ma'at* was the practice of moderation, cooperation, reverence, and duty. The priests taught that the order, beauty, and harmony of the universe had to be mirrored on earth if humans were to prosper.

The Egyptians had a very clear understanding of right and wrong. The NEGATIVE CONFESSIONS, which were part of the mortuary rituals, were precise in enumerating acts of evil and acts of good. This awareness did not always deter Egyptians from criminal activities, certainly, but the people were aware of required proper conduct and of penalties in the event they violated the law.

While it is certain that a legal system was in place, the laws that predicated the decisions of these courts remain difficult for scholars to assess today. A codified system of laws was published in the Late Period (712–332 B.C.E.), reportedly in eight volumes that have not been found. Some laws, or the result of the court decisions, however, have been recorded. For example, deserters from the battlefields were slain: Ramesses II (r. 1290–1224 B.C.E.) personally executed the commanders who had not speedily come to his aid during the battle of Kadesh, and the families of deserters or negligent commanders also suffered disgrace and the loss of assets. It is also known that former administrators charged and convicted for unlawful personal gain and abuse of the poor were exiled from Egypt for life, and their spouses, parents, cousins, and children had to leave the land as well. In addition, commoners who refused to appear at the site of monuments and join in the labor of the building processes were given punishments as well. (Commoners were required by corvée, the right of the ruler to demand annual periods of labor by the people, to build temples, pyramids, and other royal structures.) The families of those accused were also punished.

LAW IN EARLIER PERIODS

The people of the NILE remained close-knit in their NOME communities, even at the height of the empire, and they preferred to have their court cases and grievances settled under local jurisdiction. Each nome, or province, had a capital city, dating to Predynastic times. Lesser cities and towns within the nome functioned as part of a whole. In each town or village, however, there was a *seru*, a group of elders whose purpose it was to provide legal opinions and decisions on local events. The court, called the *djatjat* in the Old Kingdom (2575–2134 B.C.E.) and the KENBET thereafter, made legal and binding decisions and meted out the appropriate penalties. The *kenbet* was a factor on both the nome and high-court levels. This series of local and national courts followed a well-understood tradition of hearings and judgments.

Only during the periods of unrest or chaos, as in the two Intermediate Periods (First, 2134–2040 B.C.E.; Second, 1640–1550 B.C.E.), did such a custom prove disastrous. The popularity of "The ELOQUENT PEASANT," the tale of KHUNIANUPU, was due to the nation's genuine desire to have courts provide justice. Crimes involving capital punishment or those of treason, however, were not always within the jurisdiction of the local courts, and even the great *kenbet*, the supreme body of judgment, could not always render the ultimate decision on such matters, as they were reserved for the pharaohs.

The great *kenbets* in the capitals were under the supervision of the viziers of Egypt; in several periods there were two such offices, a VIZIER for Upper Egypt and another for Lower Egypt. This custom commemorated the unification of the nation in 3000 B.C.E. Petitions seeking judicial aid or relief could be made to the lower courts, and appeals of all lower court rulings could be made to the great *kenbet* by all citizens. Egyptians waited in line each day to give the judges their testimony or their petitions. The decisions concerning such matters were based on traditional legal practices, although there must have been written codes available for study.

There is some documentation available about court decisions and the officials involved during this time. Some cases were judged on the basis of precedence, while other cases were reserved for the pharaoh. In the Old Kingdom, a harem conspiracy was investigated by Weni, a high-ranking official serving PEPI I (r. 2289–2255 B.C.E.). Weni alone judged the queen who had tried to slay the pharaoh. The conclusions of Weni were never documented, but the queen disappeared soon after.

No distinction was allowed in the hearing of cases. Commoners and women were normally afforded the same opportunities as aristocrats in the courts. The poor were also to be safeguarded in their rights. "The Eloquent Peasant" was popular because he dared to admonish the judges again and again to give heed to the demands of the poor and not to be swayed by the mighty, the well connected, or the popular. The admonitions to the viziers of Egypt, as recorded in the Eighteenth Dynasty (1550–1307 B.C.E.) tomb of REKHMIRÉ, echo the same sort of vigilance required by all Egyptian officials. Some of the higher-ranking judges of ancient Egypt were called Attached to Nekhen, a title of honor that denoted the fact that their positions and roles were in the finest traditions of HIERAKONPOLIS, the original home of the first unifier of Egypt around 3000 B.C.E., NARMER. The title alluded to these judges' long and faithful tradition of service and their role in preserving customs and legal traditions of the past. Others were called the MAGNATES OF THE SOUTHERN TEN, and these officers of the government were esteemed for their services and for their rank in powerful Upper Egyptian nomes or capitals.

LAW IN LATER PERIODS

When Egypt acquired an empire in the New Kingdom era (1550–1070 B.C.E.), various governors were also assigned to foreign territories under Egyptian control, and these held judicial posts as part of their capacity. The viceroy of NUBIA, for example, made court decisions and enforced the law in his jurisdiction.

HOREMHAB (r. 1319–1307 B.C.E.), at the close of the Eighteenth Dynasty, set down a series of edicts concerning the law. He appears to be referring to past customs or documents in his decrees concerning compliances and punishments. The JUDICIAL PAPYRUS OF TURIN, dating to RAMESSES III (r. 1194–1163 B.C.E.), describes the uncovering of a legal plot. Ramesses III's assassination was the result of a harem conspiracy. After a scandalous delay and the interference of trusted administrative and judicial officials, the members of the conspiracy were tried and condemned to death or to mutilation and exile.

During the Ptolemaic Period (304–30 B.C.E.) the traditional court systems of Egypt applied only to native Egyptians. The Greeks in control of the Nile Valley were under the systems imported from their homelands. This double standard was accepted by the common people of Egypt as part of the foreign occupation. They turned toward their nomes and their traditions. Thus, the Egyptians learned how to survive the political and social changes of the world.

Further reading: David, Rosalie. *Handbook to Life in Ancient Egypt, Revised Edition.* New York: Facts On File, 2003; Kemp, Barry J. *Ancient Egypt: Anatomy of a Civilization.* London: Routledge, 1989; Tyldesley, Joyce. *Judgement of the Pharaoh: Crime and Punishment in Ancient Egypt.* London: Phoenix House, 2000; Versteed, Russ. *Law in Ancient Egypt.* Durham, N.C.: Carolina Academic Press, 2002.

Lay of the Harper   This is an unusual text discovered on tomb walls and other monuments of Egypt, reflecting upon death. Containing pessimistic views contrary to the accepted religious tenets concerning existence beyond the grave, the Lay of the Harper is solemn and foreboding. One version, found at THEBES and reportedly copied from the tomb of INYOTEF V (r. ca. 1640–1635 B.C.E.) of the Seventeenth Dynasty, is also called the Harper's Song. This text doubts the existence of an eternal paradise and encourages a hedonistic approach to earthly life that is contrary to the normal Egyptian concept of MA'AT.

legal system   *See* LAW.

Leontopolis (To-Remu; Taremu; Tell el-Mugdam)
This is a site known today as Tell el-Mugdam, in the Delta, that was the cultic center for the lion deity Mihas. Called To-Remu or Taremu by the Egyptians, Leontopolis was on the right bank of the Damietta branch of the Nile. The deities SHU and TEFNUT were also worshiped there in lion form. A temple was on the site at least by the Eighteenth Dynasty (1550–1307 B.C.E.). A lavish palace dating to the reign of RAMESSES III (1194–1163 B.C.E.) was found there also. The tomb of Queen KAROMANA (6), the mother of OSORKON IV (r. 713–712 B.C.E.), was also erected there. Nearby Mit Ya'ish contained the stela of OSORKON III (r. 777–749 B.C.E.) and Ptolemaic (304–30 B.C.E.), articles. The rulers of later dynasties usurped many of the original monuments in Leontopolis.

Letopolis   *See* KOM AUSHIM.

lettuce   A vegetable deemed sacred to the god MIN and endowed with magical properties, lettuce was used as a weapon against ghosts of the dead, along with honey. The vegetable could prick the dead and was used as a threat by a mother in a New Kingdom (1550–1070 B.C.E.) lullaby. Lettuce was also fed to the sacred animals in Min's shrines and cultic centers and was used in rituals honoring the god SET.

libraries   These were called "houses of the papyri" and normally part of the local PER-ANKH, or "House of Life." Education was a priority in every generation in ancient Egypt, and the schools were open to the qualified of all classes, although only a small percentage of the population was literate at any given time. The libraries were vast storehouses of accumulated knowledge and records. In the New Kingdom (1550–1070 B.C.E.) the pharaohs of the Middle Kingdom (2040–1640 B.C.E.) were much admired, indicating that the Egyptians had a profound realization of what had taken place in earlier times. Men like Prince KHA'EMWESET (1) of the Nineteenth Dynasty began studies of the past, surveying the necropolis sites of the first dynasties and recording their findings with meticulous care.

The priests of the *per-ankh* were required to recite or read copious documents and records of the various enterprises of the king. The levels of the Nile, the movement of the celestial bodies, and the biannual census were some of the subjects that could be summoned up from the libraries and from the lore of the priests. In all areas the libraries were actually archives, containing ancient texts and documents. The most famed library of Egypt, the LIBRARY OF ALEXANDRIA, was built during the

Ptolemaic Period (304–30 B.C.E.) and was burned in part during Julius CAESAR's campaign in ALEXANDRIA.

Library of Alexandria   A monument and ongoing educational institution founded in the reign of PTOLEMY I SOTER (304–284 B.C.E.), with a "daughter" library in the SERAPEUM (1) at SAQQARA. DEMETRIUS OF PHALERUM, a student of Aristotle, was expelled from Athens and arrived in ALEXANDRIA, visiting Ptolemy I. He recommended the construction of a great library and the pharaoh agreed instantly. A complex of buildings and gardens resulted, and in time this became a center of learning for the known world of that historical period. The original intent was to rescue Greek literary works and to provide a true center of learning. Within 200 years the Library of Alexandria had some 700,000 papyri. Visitors to Egypt were searched, and all books not yet in the library's possession were confiscated and placed in the collections.

The famous scholars of the time congregated at the Library of Alexandria, drawn by the vast collections, the largest in the world, and by the academic standards set by the institution. The Ptolemaic pharaohs maintained a policy of enriching the library, and their attitudes prompted the arrival of learned men from other nations. Herophilus, "the Father of Astronomy," was at the library, along with EUCLID, "the Father of Geometry." Other scholars included EATOSTHENES OF CYRENE, who calculated the circumference of the earth, CALLIMACHUS OF CYRENE, and AISTARCHUS OF SMOTHRACE. The sciences benefited from the studies at the Library, and various forms of literature, named Alexandrian in style, flourished.

The Library of Alexandria stood for approximately 300 years. It was partially burned in 48 B.C.E. when Julius CAESAR was attacked within the city and set fire to the ships in the harbor. It survived that damage but was probably again partially destroyed by Zenobia of Palmyra in 270 C.E. The major destruction took place in the occupation of Alexandria by Caliph Omar in 642 C.E.

The Egyptian government, working with the United Nations Educational, Scientific and Cultural Organization (UNESCO), began building a new Library of Alexandria in the 1990s. Located on the campus of the University of Alexandria, the new library cost approximately $200 million and opened in 2001.

Further reading: Canfora, Luciano. *The Vanished Library.* Berkeley: University of California Press, 1990; Casson, Lionel. *Libraries in the Ancient World.* New Haven, Conn.: Yale University Press, 2001; MacLeod, Roy. *The Library of Alexandria: Centre of Learning in the Ancient World.* London: B Tauris, 2000.

Libya (Tjehenu, Tjehemu)   This was the land bordering Egypt on the northwest, mentioned in papyri as far back as the Early Dynastic Period (2920–2575 B.C.E.) and providing the Nile Valley with two dynasties in the later eras. The Libyans, called the Tjehenu (or Tjehemu), were depicted on temple walls and portrayed as having the same characteristics as Egyptians. They were termed the *Hatiu-a,* "the Princes," perhaps because of their splendid attire. Bearded, light-skinned, and having red or fair hair and blue eyes, the Libyans were also identified as the Libu and MESHWESH, two major groups.

The Libyan areas that bordered the Delta were attacked by the early Egyptians in the Predynastic Period (before 3000 B.C.E.) as the southerners started moving north to unite the Two Kingdoms of the Nile Valley. DJER (r. ca. 2900 B.C.E.) recorded his campaign to rid the Delta of the Libyans. SNEFRU (r. 2575–2551 B.C.E.) used the same policy in dealing with them. The PALERMO STONE recorded his invasion of their territory. SAHURÉ (r. 2458–2446 B.C.E.) depicted an Egyptian goddess recording herds of cattle, sheep, and goats that he captured during his campaigns in the Fifth Dynasty in Libya. Members of the Libyan royal family were also brought to Egypt by Sahuré to serve as hostages.

During the Middle Kingdom (2040–1640 B.C.E.) such military campaigns against Libya were part of the Egyptians' ongoing policies. The Libyans were used as units of the pharaoh's army, either pressed into service or hired as mercenaries. SENWOSRET I (1991–1926 B.C.E.) still conducted assaults on Libya itself. When the Middle Kingdom collapsed, however, the Libyans became the aggressors. The HYKSOS, invaders who ruled in AVARIS in the eastern Delta, could not halt the Libyan incursions along the western border. The so-called WALL OF THE PRINCE, the forts erected both in the east and the west during the Middle Kingdom, failed to protect the Delta.

'AHMOSE (NEBPEHTIRÉ) (r. 1550–1525 B.C.E.) united Egypt and started the New Kingdom, routing the Hyksos and repelling the Libyans. His successor, AMENHOTEP I (r. 1525–1504 B.C.E.), had several military confrontations with the Libyans in the Western Desert. In the Nineteenth Dynasty, SETI I (r. 1306–1290 B.C.E.) met a combined force of Libu and Meshwesh in the Delta and banished them. His son and heir, RAMESSES II (r. 1290–1224 B.C.E.), met them again and vanquished them. His son, MERENPTAH (r. 1224–1214 B.C.E.), faced the Meshwesh, Ekwesh, and SEA PEOPLES and was victorious. RAMESSES III (r. 1194–1163 B.C.E.) was equally successful in his military campaigns against full-scale invasions of the Meshwesh and Sea Peoples. The result of this campaign was the capture of the Libyan clans, which were brought into Egypt. Some disappeared into the general population and some served in the Egyptian military or as an internal police force, similar to the Nubian MEDJAY. BUBASTIS (Tell Basta) and TANIS became the center of the Libyans from that time on, and the Twenty-second and Twenty-third Dynasties would emerge from their ranks in the Libyan Period, 945–712 B.C.E. Rulers such as SHOSHENQ I (r. 945–924 B.C.E.) brought a renaissance into Egypt in the arts and in military might. Ruling as contemporaries from TANIS and BUBASTIS, the Libyans could not maintain their domain as the Nubian kings moved on northern Egypt.

Libyan Desert (Western Desert)   An arid stretch of land on the western side of the Nile River, distinguished by its low hills, great dunes, and widely scattered oases, the Libyan Desert, harsher than the Arabian or Red Sea Desert on Egypt's eastern border, became part of the FAIYUM and benefited from reclamation efforts in some periods. The oases of SIWA, BAHARIA, FARAFRA, el-DAKHLA, and KHARGA were situated in this vast expanse, which became a TRADE route for Egypt. The Persian conqueror CAMBYSES (r. 525–522 B.C.E.) sent a vast military unit to the oasis of Siwa, famed for its shrine to the god AMUN. The military force entered the desert and was never seen again. Just recently, however, a group of Egyptians from HELWAN University discovered human remains, metal weapons, and fragments of textiles while on a geographical expedition in the Libyan Desert. Herodotus, the Greek historian, claimed that 50,000 Persians entered the wasteland with pack animals. The Egyptian Supreme Council of Antiquities has undertaken a mission to the region to determine the origin of the find.

Libyan Palette   A fragment of a palette discovered in ABYDOS that reflects the start of Egypt's historical period, dating to ca. 3000 B.C.E., the palette has two sides, both elaborately carved. One side has four panels, depicting bulls, donkeys, and sheep in a typical Naqada II design. The fourth panel depicts eight trees and two hieroglyphs forming Tjehenu, a people of Libya. On the other side a single panel has representations of seven fortified towns, an owl, a crested bird, a SCARAB, a reed hut, a bush, and a symbol of two raised arms. Symbols of animals crown the towns depicted, including falcons, a lion, and a scorpion. Destroying the towns, or the same town on several occasions, obviously in Libya, the animals represent Egypt's might.

See also MACEHEAD; PALETTE.

Lighthouse of Alexandria (Pharos)   This monument was called the Pharos, started by PTOLEMY I SOTER (r. 304–284 B.C.E.) in 279 B.C.E. and completed by PTOLEMY II PHILADELPHUS (r. 285–246 B.C.E.). Pharos is the name of the island containing the lighthouse, a Wonder of the Ancient World. The structure was 400 feet tall, and the light reflected from its mirrored fires could be seen some 25 miles out to sea, even at night. SOSTRATUS, who was brought to ALEXANDRIA from Cnidus, on the southwest coast of Asia Minor, designed the structure and aided in the construction.

The building had three separate tiers on a base, with square cross sections. The base was a square foundation 20 feet high, measuring 350 feet on either side and made of limestone, covered by marble. The first tier was 200–235 feet high, with an 80-foot terrace. The tier contained 300 chambers with windows and had parapet walls on the top. An inscription on this tier honors Sostratus, the Cnidian. The second tier was 115 feet high and octagonal in design. It was 55 feet across and faced with white marble. This tier also had a walled terrace. The third tier was 60 to 80 feet high, cylindrical in design, and fashioned out of brick, plastered to match the marble of the lower section. This tier was 30 feet in diameter at the top and had an open space surrounded by eight marble columns. A fire was burned in this cavity, reflected in a mirror to shine seaward. The dome covering the area was decorated with a 20-foot bronze image of the Greek god Poseidon, although some sources state that the statue depicted ALEXANDER III THE GREAT or the Greek god Helios.

The Egyptian government is now undertaking the task of building a duplicate of this wonder. In the Middle Ages, the lighthouse underwent alterations, as the Arabs placed a mosque at the beacon level. It was still standing in the twelfth century C.E., but falling into ruins. In 1477, the Mamaluk Sultan Qa'it Bay stripped the remains in order to build a fort for Alexandria.

Further reading: Clayton, Peter, and Martin Price, eds. *The Seven Wonders of the Ancient World.* New York: Routledge, 1990; Romer, John, and Elizabeth Romer. *Seven Wonders of the World: A History of the Modern Imagination.* New York: Seven Dials, 2001; Forster, E.M. *Alexandria: A History and a Guide Including "Pharos and Pharillon."* London: Marsilio, 1999.

Lily Lake   This was a name given to a paradise awaiting the dead in Amenti, the eternal resting place. This mortuary image of eternal bliss was the domain of Hrafhef, "HE-WHO-LOOKS-BEHIND-HIMSELF," the irritable deity who rowed worthy candidates to their repose.

linen   This is a material fashioned from flax, a plant cultivated in Egypt from ca. 5000 B.C.E. Flaxseeds were sown in mid-November and harvested four months later. The flax stems were sorted and bound together to dry, then rippled by large wooden combs. The flax was also soaked in water to soften the woody parts, which were removed when dried. A final combing produced waste products used for various purposes, such as lamp wicks. The final flax fibers became threads, and the youngest, greenest stems provided the fine varieties of materials, while the older, yellow stems produced fibers for quality linen. The fully mature plants were used for ropes and mats.

In the early settlements of Egypt, flax was hand spun to provide linens. The grasped spindle technique was adopted. The suspended spindle, with small weights and whorls, was also used. Middle Kingdom (2040–1640 B.C.E.) whorls were made from pottery or stone. The flax was spun counterclockwise. When two or more threads formed plied yarns they were spun in the opposite direction. The earliest linens produced in Egypt were plain, but various techniques were added in time. Looped patterns, warp ends, and other decorated touches were incorporated into the process, and in time the linen textures available were designed for climatic changes and rank. The linen ranged from the translucent gauze to coarse canvas. BYSSUS, called the "royal linen," a truly fine cloth, well made, was popular in Egypt.

"Linen of Yesterday" A poetic image employed by the ancient Egyptians to denote death and the changes that dying brings to humans, the phrase was included in the dirges sung by the *kites,* the professional women mourners at funerals. The mourners referred to the deceased as one who dressed in fine linen but who now sleeps in "the linen of yesterday." That image alluded to the fact that life upon the earth became yesterday to the dead. It was probably prompted by the custom of the commoners or the poor who gave used linens to the embalmers for the ritual preparation of each mummy. The poor could not afford new linens, so they wrapped their family corpses, called "Beloved Osirises," in those of "yesterday."

lion It was an ancient Egyptian theophany, or divine manifestation, associated with the gods RÉ, HORUS, and AKER. Called the *ma'au,* the lion was renowned for its courage and strength. The cult center for lion worship was established in LEONTOPOLIS in the Delta in the earliest periods. Several lion forms were worshiped in the temples, including Matit, Mehet, Mehos, and PAKHET, dating to the time of the First Dynasty (2920–2770 B.C.E.). The Akeru cult was involved in the worship of Ré. The Akeru, a pair of lions, guarded the sacred sites of the Ré cult and the "Gate of the Dawn," the mythical abode through which Ré passed each morning.

Lions of Sebua Called Sebel in some lists, they are a remarkable pair of stone figures erected by AMENHOTEP III (r. 1391–1353 B.C.E.) of the Eighteenth Dynasty at Sebua in southern NUBIA (modern Sudan). The lion figures were carried away by raiders of later eras when they invaded the territory and now are in the British Museum in London. During the 'Amarna Period, when AKHENATEN (Amenhotep IV; r. 1353–1335 B.C.E.), instituted the cult of ATEN, the inscriptions on the lions were destroyed, because of the religious nature of the words. TUT'ANKH AMUN (r. 1333–1323 B.C.E.) restored the reliefs when he returned the nation to the worship of AMUN at THEBES. He also added his own commemoratives.

Lisht, el- This was a site on the western shore, south of ABUSIR, that served as a necropolis for the city of ITJ-TAWY, the Twelfth Dynasty capital started by AMENEMHET I (r. 1991–1962 B.C.E.). The pyramids of Amenemhet I and SENWOSRET I (r. 1971–1926 B.C.E.) dominate the region, providing mortuary complexes on the elevated portion of the site. The pyramidal complex was called "Amun Is High and Beautiful." Two monuments discovered there are in the Metropolitan Museum in New York. The pyramid was built on a commanding position, and the complex functioned on two levels as royal family members and court officials were provided with tombs as part of the design. A causeway can still be seen, but the valley temple has disappeared. A great wall (*tenemos*) surrounded the area.

Amenemhet I's pyramid, also called "the Places of Amenemhet Shine," was covered originally with TUREH limestone and had an entrance on the north face. There was an offering chapel with a FALSE DOOR and a deep burial chamber included in the design. The pyramid of Amenemhet I was surrounded by royal tombs, containing family members and erected on adjoining lands. The pyramid complex of Senwosret I was called "the One Who Is Associated with Senwosret" and was erected in the southern area. Large and covered with Tureh limestone, the pyramid was surrounded by nine royal graves. The complex also contained 10 statues of the pharaoh.

There is no surviving evidence of a VALLEY TEMPLE in Senwosret I's complex, but a causeway survived, fashioned out of Tureh limestone and adorned with colorful reliefs. The pyramid is surrounded by two enclosure walls, the outer one made of brick, and the inner wall enclosing a MORTUARY TEMPLE and decorated with relief panels. Senwosret I's pyramid, named "Senwosret Surveys the Two Lands," and "Protected Are the Places of Senwosret," had a rubble and sand core. Irregular chambers were incorporated into the pyramid, and the entry was part of a chapel. Other tombs at el-Lisht include those of INTEFOKER, a high-ranking official, and SENWOSRET-ANKH, whose mastaba contained PYRAMID TEXTS and a star ceiling.

List of Offerings A mortuary document that specified the gifts to be presented to the deceased in tomb ceremonies, the *List* dates to the Old Kingdom (2575–2134 B.C.E.) and concerns private and royal tombs and sometimes includes presentations made by the pharaohs. Offerings of meat, drink, and incense were provided each day by the funerary priests contracted to perform the ceremonies. TOMB BALLS, containing wadded contracts made between the priests and the deceased or surviving relatives, were sometimes included in the grave sites as proof of the services rendered. The *List of Offerings* evolved over the centuries into a full LITURGY OF THE FUNERARY OFFERINGS, used in MORTUARY RITUALS.

Litanies of Sokar   This is a compilation of 100 lines addressed to the god SOKAR, a Memphite funerary deity. Discovered in the RHIND PAPYRUS, the litanies praised the deity, who was associated with PTAH and OSIRIS in mortuary traditions.

Litany of Osiris   A hymn recited to Osiris, the God of the Dead, the "Foremost of the Westerners" in many historical periods of Egypt, the litany was included in the ANI PAPYRUS, now in the British Museum in London.

Litany of Ré   This was a funerary text used in the tomb of TUTHMOSIS III (r. 1479–1425 B.C.E.). The highly stylized design of crude figures used in the reliefs on the walls of the tomb depict the deceased making his way through TUAT, or the Underworld, that led to eternal paradise. Remarkably executed, the figures depicting the stages of the litany demonstrate the metamorphosis of the afterlife and the harrowing endurance tests undergone by the deceased.

Litany of the Sun   This was a religious document displayed in the tomb of SETI I (r. 1306–1290 B.C.E.) and attributed to the cult of the god RÉ. Part of the established MORTUARY RITUALS of the New Kingdom (1550–1070 B.C.E.), the litany attests to the endurance of RÉ, even in the eras dominated by the deity AMUN at THEBES. In time the deity became Amun-Ré, incorporating the solar cult into the Theban theology.

literature   Ancient Egypt bequeathed to humankind a treasure trove of literary masterpieces as well as beautiful poems, lullabies, and love songs. Literature was a true form of cultural expression and art in ancient Egypt, both religious and secular in nature, that developed over time from the Early Dynastic Period (2920–2575 B.C.E.) to the Roman Period (after 30 B.C.E.). Traditionally didactic in nature, eventually it came to include tales, poems, songs, hymns, liturgies, prayers, and litanies.

DEVELOPMENTS

The earliest extant examples of hieroglyphic writing are found in religious contexts and date to the Old Kingdom (2575–2134 B.C.E.). Secular literature, which emerged as early as 2000 B.C.E, generally promoted the historical and military achievements of the kings and attempted to ensure their worldly success and continuation after death.

The people of the Nile had an intense interest in records, noting every act of the pharaohs, every natural event, and every speech made in the courts. No individual of standing or rank was buried in an undecorated tomb. The titles, positions, and accomplishments of such individuals were engraved on the walls of the burial sites, and sometimes on the sarcophagi, or coffins.

Great mortuary texts dominated grave sites, serving as a map for the deceased as he or she made the journey to paradise. Small armies of scribes were present at all court events, recording everything said or done. When the pharaohs campaigned in foreign lands, putting down rebellions or protecting Egyptian holdings, another army of scribes accompanied them. Scribes also copied documents from earlier ages as part of their training, preserving many documents and literary efforts. Some of these texts have been preserved on papyri or on OSTRACA, the boards and slates used by individual students.

During the Late Period (712–332 B.C.E.) and the Ptolemaic Period, few Egyptian literary works were forthcoming. The Ptolemaic Period produced remarkable masterpieces at Alexandria, but these were Greek in style and content. Around 195 B.C.E., ARISTOPHANES OF BYZANTIUM, the director of the LIBRARY OF ALEXANDRIA, was able to establish the Alexandrian Canon, a standard of excellence in all of the literary genres. Alexandrian poets impacted upon the literary works of the entire world of the time.

The literature of Egypt is so vast and covers so many centuries that it is normally accorded distinct categories, which follow.

RELIGIOUS TEXTS

Designed to bolster the state cult of the king, the oldest religious documents are the PYRAMID TEXTS, discovered on the walls of the various chambers of the pyramids of the rulers of the Fifth (2465–2323 B.C.E.) and Sixth Dynasties (2323–2150 B.C.E.). The texts delineate the magical spells that were designed to provide the king with an eternal bliss beyond the grave, where he would receive his rewards for service and be welcomed by the gods. The daily offerings to be made as part of the mortuary ritual in the pyramid were also listed.

Soon after, the nobles began to assume the same rights as the king as far as benefits beyond the grave were concerned, and they had Pyramid Texts placed in their coffins. These COFFIN TEXTS also contained spells and magical incantations to allow the dead to assume supernatural forms and to overcome whatever obstacles awaited them on their journey in the afterlife. The early forms of the BOOK OF THE DEAD date to this period, the First Intermediate Period (2134–2040 B.C.E.). The Book of the Dead underwent various changes over the centuries, remaining popular. The most complete versions date to the Ptolemaic Period (304–30 B.C.E.), and these contain as many as 150 separate spells. The coffin variety of the Book of the Dead was placed on PAPYRUS in the New Kingdom (1550–1070 B.C.E.).

Other religious texts, including the *Ritual of the Divine Cult,* the *Book of Gates,* and the *Destruction of Mankind,* all follow the same general pattern of magical incantations and descriptions of the various chambers or stages to be discovered in Tuat, or the Underworld. The elaborately beautiful hymns to the various deities were also popular. *OVERTHROWING APOPHIS* and other religious documents provide an insight into the religious aspects of Egyptian life. Especially graceful are the hymns to the gods AMUN and ATEN, which date to the New Kingdom (1550–1070 B.C.E.).

Magical papyri and mortuary stelae placed in ABYDOS as part of the great Osirian cult provide other information. The stelae announce the ranks, deeds, and general goodness of the owners. Letters were also written to the deceased, on the assumption that in the afterlife the individual had powers and could remedy situations on earth. The custom of informing the dead about contemporary issues remained popular in some areas of Egypt into modern times.

The mortuary regalia attracted not only the interest of native Egyptians but foreign residents as well. The Golden Mummies discovered in the BAHARIA OASIS in 2010 demonstrate the fact the Romans living in Egypt during the Roman Period adopted ancient Egyptian mortuary rituals for their own burials. Hundreds of Romans were mummified and buried with their family members, wearing golden masks and other gilded adornments.

SCIENTIFIC TEXTS

While the religious mortuary texts of Egypt dealt mainly with magic and divine intercession in human affairs, the nation also focused on the practical aspects of life. As a result, various sciences were undertaken, not in a speculative way but in order to facilitate the performance of daily activities. Medical texts reflected the practical aspects of Egyptian literature. Manuscripts from the New Kingdom, including the EBERS PAPYRUS and the EDWIN SMITH PAPYRUS, as well as others, display the anatomical knowledge and curative ability of the priests, who were regulated in their methods of diagnosis, treatment, and posttreatment.

Among mathematical texts discovered are the RHIND PAPYRUS. Another identifies agricultural crops, birds, animals, and geographical locations. Texts on astronomy, irrigation, geography, and husbandry were also found. Military texts abound, part of the record of events from the unification of Upper and Lower Egypt in 3000 B.C.E., with the exploits of the New Kingdom (1550–1070 B.C.E.) pharaohs described in detail. Travel records from that same period provide information about Egypt's relationships with other lands, and conditions in the world at the time. The *Report of WENAMUN*, composed at the end of the Twentieth Dynasty (ca. 1070 B.C.E.), is particularly enlightening. *The Tale of SINUHE THE SAILOR*, based on the death of AMENEMHET I (r. 1991–1962 B.C.E.), provides insight into the royal court intrigues and to the cultures of other nations during the Middle Kingdom.

LEGAL TEXTS

Legal documents consist mainly of wills or accounts of court events, although legal references in the ABBOTT PAPYRUS offer a view of social changes along the Nile, dealing with tomb robberies and their prosecution at the close of the New Kingdom. Wills placed in tombs, deeds of sale, census lists, and records of lawsuits have been discovered. The Edict of HOREMHAB (r. 1319–1307 B.C.E.) has provided information about the conditions in Egypt at the close of the Eighteenth Dynasty (1307 B.C.E.).

Texts concerning the government administration have been discovered as well. REKHMIRÉ, the VIZIER for TUTHMOSIS III (r. 1479–1425 B.C.E.), had the instructions of the king concerning his office, and the ideals of such a position, inscribed on his tomb walls at Thebes. Texts from the ELEPHANTINE, concerning the work of the viceroys of NUBIA (modern Sudan), date to many periods, as do the reports of officials on expeditions for the throne. Inscriptions of expeditions can be seen on cliffs in the various *wadis* and in the desert regions, announcing the mining and quarrying activities.

The WILBOUR PAPYRUS, now in the Brooklyn Museum, gives a recording of legal matters in the village of Neshi, in the FAIYUM. Other texts survive that attest to tax exemption for people working on particular monuments.

FANTASTIC TALES

The *TALE OF THE SHIPWRECKED SAILOR*, dating to the Middle Kingdom (2040–1640 B.C.E.), remained popular in Egypt. The story elaborates on mystical creatures and magical events and reads like a modern fantasy. The *TALE OF THE DOOMED PRINCE*, the *TALE OF TWO BROTHERS*, and the *TALE OF KHUFU AND THE MAGICIANS* all relate magical happenings and adventures rife with perils. The story concerning KHUFU (also known as Cheops) (r. 2551–2528 B.C.E.), the builder of the Great Pyramid at GIZA, has descriptions of idle hours spent on pleasure boats among harem maidens clothed in fishnets. The *Tale of Sinuhe the Sailor* (see SINUHE THE SAILOR) was later adapted into the stories of Sinbad the Sailor, whose adventures served as models for later works, such as *The Book of One Thousand and One Nights* (more commonly known as *Arabian Nights*). The oldest known version of the Cinderella fairy tale also originated on the Nile; the Egyptian story was recorded by the Greek historian Strabo (64/63 B.C.E.–24 C.E.) in his *Geographica*.

DIDACTIC TEXTS

The most popular and most enduring literature in ancient Egypt was in the didactic style. These writings were believed to be from the "TIME OF THE GODS" or written by the gods themselves. Entire generations of Egyptians, most unable to read or write, memorized these texts and recited them to their children.

Some of these texts bemoaned conditions in the land in times of dynastic weakness, while others maintained maxims and adages clearly meant to instruct. PTAH-HOTEP (2), a sage of the Fifth Dynasty (2465–2323 B.C.E.), and KAGEMNI, of the Third Dynasty (2649–2575 B.C.E.), were among the first to admonish royalty and commoner alike. KHETY III of the Ninth Dynasty gave his son MERIKARÉ instructions about the behavior of kings, as did AMENEMHET I (r. 1991–1962 B.C.E.) of the Twelfth Dynasty. Amenemhet I's discourse details the obligations of a ruler and the needs of his subjects. Also popular were the recorded words of "THE ELOQUENT PEASANT" OF HERAKLEOPOLIS from the First Intermediate Period (2134–2040 B.C.E.).

During the Ptolemaic Period (304–30 B.C.E.), a native Egyptian called Ankhsheshongy wrote *Instructions* based on the ancient style, despite the Greek influences around him. Written about 100 B.C.E., the *Instructions* became highly popular in the Nile Valley because the work brought the traditional forms of the past to life again.

Didactic literature remained a constant in Egypt, and many sages were honored in all eras by the Egyptians. Didactic literature was directly connected to the philosophical concept of *ma'at*. Considered the cosmic reflection of harmony, justice, order, and peace, *ma'at* was a social imperative that guided Egyptians in their daily life. The didactic sermons of the sages reminded Egyptians of each new generation of *ma'at*.

POETIC TEXTS

The religious and social events of the various historical periods were normally accompanied by music. The pleasures of music, feasting, and love became part of the rhythm of life on the Nile, eventually giving rise to love songs, which often told of lovesick swains separated from their sweethearts. Sycamore trees, birds, and the winds became messengers of love in the poetic texts, with the lovers pledging their hearts and vowing eternal affection. Love songs appear to have been recorded first in the Middle Kingdom; the late New Kingdom period provided many more. The songs capture the directness of the Egyptian people, as well as their sensitivity to the seasons, their easy affection, and their love of metaphor and conventional imagery. The hymn to SENWOSRET III (r. 1878–1841 B.C.E.) epitomizes this form of Egyptian literature.

The Egyptians also recited poetry about MEMPHIS, the NILE, and ghosts. One lullaby threatens any ghost who plans to harm a mother's child. She stands over her child and promises to throw garlic at the ghost or to destroy the ghost with what the ancient Egyptians believed was a traditional ghost-fighting weapon: lettuce.

TEMPLE TEXTS

A vast collection of hymns, prayers, litanies, and devotional recitations were inscribed on the walls and pillars of ancient Egyptian temples, now categorized as temple literature. Foundation deposits and other legal texts concerning the authorization of the temple as a site of worship were also displayed. The establishment of a cultic house of worship had to follow strict regulations provided by the various priesthoods and the government.

The various hymns and litanies were sung during services and during the processions in the streets of towns and cities. Temple musicians were also employed to provide inspirational performances in the services and processions, as the Egyptians enjoyed a great deal of sound accompanying any of their activities. In some eras, special religious hymns were composed in honor of pharaohs when these rulers visited regional shrines. Senwosret III (r. 1878–1841 B.C.E.), a truly popular and admired pharaoh, was serenaded with such hymns of praise in various temples.

Further reading: Cerny, Jaroslav. *Paper and Books in Ancient Egypt*. London: H. K. Levis, 1952; Davies, W. V. *Egyptian Hieroglyphs: Reading the Past*. London: British Museum Press, 1987; Fischer, Henry G. *Ancient Egyptian Calligraphy: A Beginner's Guide to Writing Hieroglyphs*. New York: Metropolitan Museum of Art, 1979; Foster, John. *Ancient Egyptian Literature: An Anthology*. Austin: University of Texas Press, 2001; Kaster, Joseph. *The Wisdom of Ancient Egypt*. New York: Michael O'Mara Books, 1993; Lichtheim, Miriam. *Ancient Egyptian Literature*. Berkeley, Calif.: University of California Press, 1975; Parkinson, R. B. *Reading Ancient Poetry: Among Other Histories*. London: Wiley-Blackwell, 2009; Simpson, William Kelly, ed. *The Literature of Ancient Egypt*. New Haven, Conn.: Yale University Press, 1973.

Liturgy of the Funerary Offerings   This is a list of the funerary gifts and rituals conducted by the priests involved in the mortuary cults of the ancient Egyptians. Evolving from the LIST OF OFFERINGS, which dates to the Old Kingdom (2575–2134 B.C.E.), the liturgy was devised to magically change meat, bread, and wine into divine spiritual substances, which were offered to the dead. This transmutation of offerings is documented in the tombs of the Fifth Dynasty (2465–2323 B.C.E.) but was probably part of Egypt's religious vision in use before that. More than 114 ceremonies were included in the liturgy.

The purification of the mummified remains, the incensing accompanied by magical incantations and prayers, were used to perform the rituals of the burial and restoration of the deceased in the liturgy. The priests were believed capable of revitalizing the senses and the various organs of the dead with the spells provided. These rituals were based on the resurrection of OSIRIS and on the basic creed that no life is obliterated at physical death but only transformed into forms that will accommodate the environment of eternity. The *Liturgy of the Funerary Offerings* was revised in several periods but remained popular throughout Egypt's history.

London Papyrus   This is a parchment or palimpsest dating to the Fourth Dynasty, being a copy of a document belonging to KHUFU (Cheops) (r. 2551–2528 B.C.E.). Several texts were originally written on this papyrus and then erased and rewritten. Scribes used papyri for practice as well as for permanent records or documents.

lotus   The symbol of rebirth or creation in Egypt, called the *sheshen,* the lotus was sacred to the god NEFERTEM and was a cosmological symbol of the god RÉ. The flower signified Ré's birth and power. The types of lotus native to Egypt were the *nymphaea,* the white, and *nymphaea cerula,* the blue. The lotus was also a symbol of Upper Egypt, as the papyrus epitomized Lower Egypt's domain. The *Lotus Offering* was a hymn popular in Edfu and in other shrines, honoring Ré's emergence from the primeval waters at the moment of creation. The flower was also used as bouquets and tributes at festivals and held at banquets by guests.

Loyalist Instruction   *See* SEHETEPIBRÉ.

Luxor   This is the modern Arabic name for Southern OPET, the area of THEBES in Upper Egypt that was dedicated to the god AMUN during the New Kingdom (1550–1070 B.C.E.). The modern name is derived from the Arabic *el-Aqsur,* the Castles, an obvious reference to the vast ruined complexes in the area.

One of the major structures in Luxor was a temple used for religious processions. Erected by AMENHOTEP III (r. 1391–1353 B.C.E.) of the Eighteenth Dynasty, the temple honored the Theban god Amun. The first PYLON of the Luxor temple and the colonnaded court of the temple were constructed by RAMESSES II (r. 1290–1224 B.C.E.) of the Nineteenth Dynasty. This section enclosed a sanctuary that was probably built by TUTHMOSIS III (r. 1479–1425 B.C.E.). Tuthmosis III personally directed the construction of the sanctuary during his reign in the Eighteenth Dynasty to accommodate the famous bark of Amun. The bark was part of the elaborate festival ceremonies and was refurbished periodically and protected in a safe storage area when not in use. AMENHOTEP III, a successor of Tuthmosis III, erected an actual temple on the site, beginning the complex.

Six colossal statues and two obelisks adorned the area leading to the second pylon, which was also built by Amenhotep III. The court of Ramesses II is located nearby, with colossal statues and double bud columns. In the same area, a colonnade and two rows of papyrus capital columns were fashioned, bordered by papyrus-bundle pillars in the same area. A transverse HYPOSTYLE HALL, with 32 more columns arranged in four rows of eight, opened onto the inner temple area. Additional hypostyle halls were surrounded by ritual chapels and led to the original sanctuary. Amenhotep III adorned the walls of the temple with reliefs depicting his birth and his royal parentage, an affectation used frequently

The great temple pylon gates of Luxor, flanked by an avenue of sphinxes *(Courtesy Steve Beikirch)*

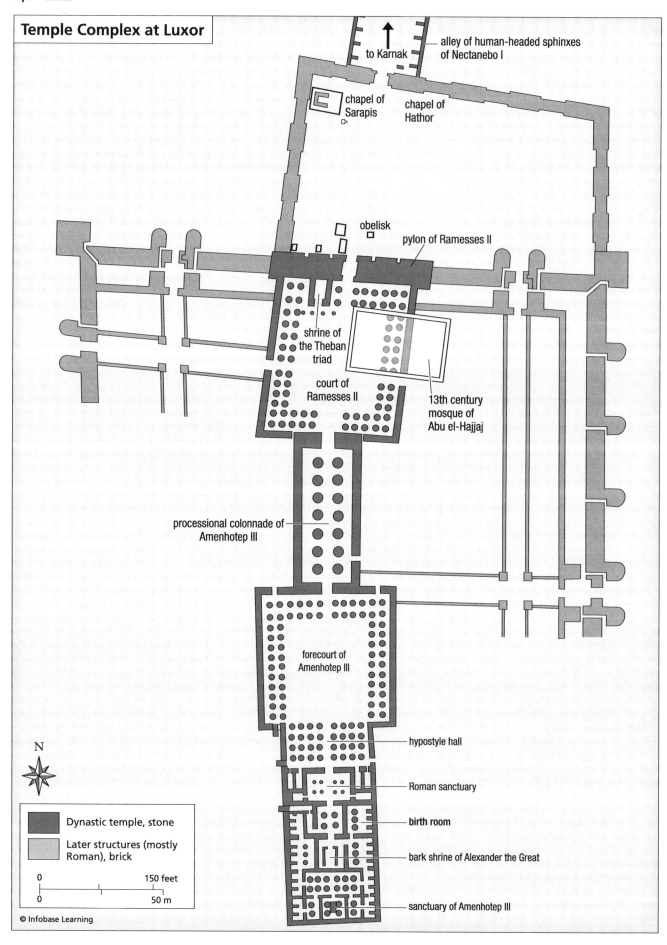

Temple Complex at Luxor

to Karnak

alley of human-headed sphinxes of Nectanebo I

chapel of Sarapis

chapel of Hathor

obelisk

pylon of Ramesses II

shrine of the Theban triad

court of Ramesses II

13th century mosque of Abu el-Hajjaj

processional colonnade of Amenhotep III

forecourt of Amenhotep III

hypostyle hall

Roman sanctuary

birth room

bark shrine of Alexander the Great

sanctuary of Amenhotep III

N

Dynastic temple, stone

Later structures (mostly Roman), brick

0   150 feet

0   50 m

© Infobase Learning

by the rulers of the New Kingdom. Tut'ankhamun (r. 1333– 1323 B.C.E.), newly converted to the worship of Amun after the fall of 'Amarna and Akhenaten's heretical cult of Aten, provided the temple with more reliefs, depicting the ceremonies being conducted in the sanctuary to honor Amun. It is not certain if these reliefs were actually the original ones of Amenhotep III or added to placate the priests of Amun and the Theban people. Horemhab, at the close of the Eighteenth Dynasty, attempted to use the same inscriptions to announce his own achievements and honors. Many statues and two red granite obelisks, one now in the Place de la Concorde in Paris, adorned the Luxor Temple. The barks of Mut, Khons (1), and other deities rested as well in the temple area, which was linked to the massive Karnak complex by a double row of sphinxes. The rulers of later eras, including the Late Period (712–332 B.C.E.) and the Ptolemaic Period (304–30 B.C.E.), added to Luxor temple, which also has an archway erected by the Romans.

The deity Amun was carried to the Luxor Temple once a year to visit his particular manifestation there. The god Amun adored at Luxor was a vibrant, ithyphallic form of the god, a patron of fertility and involved with the necropolis sites on the western shore of the Nile opposite Thebes. This same form of the deity was also worshipped in cultic rites at Medinet Habu and remained popular even in the periods of occupation by foreign armies.

The Feast of Opet, the annual celebration of this shrine, was an elaborate festival, complete with the sacrifice of animals and gala rituals. At this time the statues and barks of the Theban deities were carried in procession on the shoulders of the priests. The procession was led by dancers, singers, and musicians and cheered by the people, who came from miles around to celebrate the occasion. The barks were placed on great barges and floated on the Nile before returning to the temple precincts. A great sacrificial feast awaited the return of the deities, with acrobats, dancers, musicians, and throngs of adorers sounding the greeting.

The Greeks and Romans had a keen interest in Luxor temple, which was popular throughout all of the eras of occupation. Modern excavations, taking place as part of the restoration and preservation programs at Luxor, uncovered a trove of statues from the reign of Amenhotep III called "the Luxor Cachette." The statues, discovered recently in the temple and acclaimed as beautifully preserved works of art, were probably buried by the priests of Luxor during an invasion or some other political peril.

Further reading: Siliotti, Alberto. *Luxor, Karnak, and the Theban Temples.* Cairo: American University in Cairo Press, 2001; Strudwick, Nigel, and Helen M. Strudwick. *Thebes in Egypt: A Guide to the Tombs and Temples of Ancient Luxor.* Ithaca, N.Y.: Cornell University Press, 1999.

Lysimachus (d. ca. 280 B.C.E.) *king of Thrace in the reign of Ptolemy II Philadelphus*
Lysimachus's daughter, Arsinoe (1), became the queen of Egypt. In turn, Lysimachus married Arsinoe (2), Ptolemy's sister. After bearing him children, Arsinoe accused his son and heir, Agathocles (1), of attempting to murder the king. Lysimachus agreed to the execution of his own son, tearing apart his nation. Arsinoe did not benefit, however, as Lysimachus died in battle with Seleucus I, the Syrian king, before Arsinoe's son could inherit the throne of Thrace.

M

Ma'adi This is a site located south of Cairo dating to the Predynastic Period (ca. 3100 B.C.E.). Paleolithic settlements were discovered at Ma'adi, part of the stages called Naqada I and II. There were three necropolises found in the area, including one at Wadi Digla. Remains of oval and circular-shaped houses were found at this site. Posts stuck into the earth served as foundations, which were fashioned out of mud daub and wattle. Interior hearths, an advance of the time, were also discovered as part of the designs of these abodes. There is little indication, however, that roofs were included in the buildings. Windbreaks and sheltering walls formed the only protection for inhabitants. Demonstrations of agriculture and crafts are available at Ma'adi, as well as ancient copper processes.

Also found were wares imported from Palestine and donkey remains. Ma'adi served as an early trading post for Palestinian goods. The early Egyptians instituted trade with neighboring countries in the first dynastic periods and maintained a policy of exploring NATURAL RESOURCES as the civilization expanded on the Nile.

Ma'ahes (Mehos) An Egyptian lion deity also called Mehos and reportedly Nubian (modern Sudanese) in origin, the cult center of Ma'ahes was at LEONTOPOLIS, where the Egyptians addressed him as patron of the nation. He was depicted as a man wearing the *atef* CROWN or as a lion devouring Egypt's enemies. There were other lion cults, including the AKER. The lion was considered a symbol of strength, cunning, and royalty from the first eras of Nile habitation. The Aker assumed mortuary roles as well.

ma'at The name for the spiritual ideals and pervasive theme of social behavior for Egyptians of all historic periods, personified by the goddess MA'AT, *ma'at* is actually one of the earliest abstract terms recorded in human history. By 3000 B.C.E., *ma'at* had evolved into a single philosophy of life that was based on the observations of the night sky, where the universe and the nightly procession of celestial bodies proclaimed order. Such universal harmony appeared as a factor of existence that had to be mirrored on the earth if the Egyptians were to prosper and to serve as the divinely inspired "Gift of the Nile." *Ma'at* was the guiding principle for a national moral order and for human affairs, providing a lasting moral conviction.

As the cosmic reflection of harmony, justice, order, and peace, *ma'at* evolved as a social imperative by each new pharaoh ascending the throne. Each ruler proclaimed that he was mandated by the gods "to restore *ma'at*," no matter how illustrious the previous reign had been. *Ma'at* was the model for human behavior, in conformity with the will of the gods: the universal order evident in the heavens, cosmic balance upon the earth, the mirror of celestial beauty. *Ma'at* overcame the enemy of the nation, *isfet*, or chaos.

Awareness of the cosmic order was evident early in Egypt, as priest-astronomers charted the heavens and noted that the earth responded to the orbits of the stars and planets. The priests taught that human beings were commanded to reflect divine harmony by assuming the spirit of quietude, reasonable behavior, cooperation, and the recognition of the eternal qualities of existence as demonstrated by the earth and the sky. The NILE River in its annual inundations (flood conditions that impacted upon daily routines) had taught the Egyptians that cooperative efforts were necessary for survival and progress.

All Egyptians anticipated becoming part of the cosmos when they died, thus the responsibility for acting in accordance with its laws was reasonable. Strict adherence to *ma'at* allowed the Egyptians to feel secure with the world and with the divine plan for all creation. This concept of *ma'at* was as much a product of Egyptian ideas on cosmogony as of ethical awareness. Many Egyptians made a sincere effort in every historical period to achieve the reflection of celestial harmony, believing that *ma'at* was the essence of creation, evident in every new human life span and again in each hour upon the earth or in the sky.

Ma'at (Khama'at) An ancient goddess of Egypt worshipped as the personification of the spirit of cosmic harmony and social stability from the earliest eras in Egypt, she was depicted as a woman wearing an ostrich feather on her head, often displaying the wings of divinity. She maintained a vital role in the funerary rituals as well, taking part in the solemn weighing of human souls in Osiris's JUDGMENT HALLS of the Dead. The goddess was revered as the spirit of *ma'at*—the ideals that permeated Egyptian affairs.

During the reign of MENKAURÉ (2490–2472 B.C.E.), Ma'at was addressed as Khama'at. When Ma'at aided the god OSIRIS in judging the dead, she sometimes appeared as two identical goddesses. When she did, the arena of judgment was called "the Hall of Double Justice." Ma'at earned the respect of the other deities of Egypt because she embodied the nation's highest aspirations.

Ma'at Hornefruré (fl. 13th century B.C.E.) *royal woman of the Nineteenth Dynasty*
She was probably the daughter of the Hittite ruler HATTUSILIS III and Queen PEDUKHIPA. Ma'at Hornefruré was the consort of RAMESSES II (r. 1290–1224 B.C.E.), having married him as part of the alliance between Egypt and the Hittites in approximately the 34th year of his reign. Ramesses II sent a large procession, including troops, to welcome Ma'at Hornefruré to Egypt and prayed to the god SUTEKH for fair weather. A series of receptions and festivals celebrated her safe arrival. She became the ranking queen, or Great Wife, in time and then retired to MI-WER in the FAIYUM. A list of her personal belongings was found at this harem retreat. Her arrival was also recorded at ABU SIMBEL. It is probable that Ma'at Hornefruré was the inspiration for the Egyptian tale contained in the BENTRESH STELA. That romantic account appeared soon after her arrival on the Nile.

See also HITTITE ALLIANCE; KHONS (1).

Ma'atkaré (1) (fl. 11th century B.C.E.) *royal woman of the Twenty-first Dynasty*
She was the daughter of PINUDJEM (1) and HENUTTAWY and the granddaughter of RAMESSES XI (r. 1100–1070 B.C.E.). During the reign of PSUSENNES I (1040–992 B.C.E.) she became the GOD'S WIFE OF AMUN, or the Divine Adoratrice of Amun. She did not marry as the God's Wives adopted their successors, and she was called Ma'atkaré Mutemkhet in her divine role. The sister of Psusennes I, MASAHARTA, and MENKHEPERRESENB (2), Ma'atkaré appears to have died in childbirth.

A small mummy labeled Princess Moutemhet was found buried with her. Ma'atkaré's mummy clearly indicates that she had given birth just before dying. When the small mummy of Princess Moutemhet was unwrapped, however, it was found to be a small hamadryas baboon. Ma'atkaré's remains, buried within two coffins, were discovered at DEIR EL-BAHRI on the western shore of THEBES in 1881, in the great royal mummy cache.

Ma'atkaré (2) (fl. 10th century B.C.E.) *royal woman of the Twenty-second Dynasty*
She was the daughter of PSUSENNES II and Istemkhebe, who was the wife of Pindujem (2), the high priest of Amun in Thebes; she was also the consort of SHOSHENQ I (r. 945–924 B.C.E.). Shoshenq I had been a powerful leader of the MESHWESH, the major group of Libyans residing in Egypt, before taking the throne and founding his dynasty. Called the "Great Chief of the Meshwesh," he put aside Psusennes II's heirs to rule Egypt and to found a royal line that brought a certain renaissance to the Nile Valley and displayed a vigorous military policy. Ma'atkaré would have been a Libyan noblewoman.

Ma'atkaré (3) (fl. 10th century B.C.E.) *royal woman of the Twenty-second Dynasty*
She was probably the daughter of SHOSHENQ I and was the consort of OSORKON I (r. 924–909 B.C.E.), her brother. Her sons were SHOSHENQ II and TAKELOT II. She was probably the namesake of MA'ATKARÉ (2) and a Libyan.

Ma'atkaré (4) (fl. ninth century B.C.E.) *royal woman of the Twenty-second Dynasty*
She was the consort of OSORKON II (r. 883–855 B.C.E.) but was not the mother of the heir. She was probably a princess of the royal line and of Libyan descent.

Ma'atkaré (5) This was the throne name of Queen-Pharaoh HATSHEPSUT (r. 1473–1458 B.C.E.), also listed as Rema'atka.

ma'at kheru An ancient Egyptian phrase used to describe the deceased beings judged as pure of heart and worthy of the eternal paradise beyond the grave, the words meant "True of Voice," and they appeared in the renditions of the BOOK OF THE DEAD. In the JUDGMENT HALLS OF OSIRIS, ruled over by the god, souls were declared *ma'at kheru,* or could be deemed unworthy of paradise but of enough virtue to join the ever-moving retinue of Osiris. The souls of the damned as well as their physical remains were devoured by the demon AMEMAIT, obliterating them for all time, which was the ultimate horror for Egyptians.

macehead An early Egyptian weapon, attached to a shaft and highly decorated, maceheads serve as modern historical texts, as the surviving examples commemorate actual events that took place on the Nile. Certain examples of maceheads dating to NAGADA I (4000–3500 B.C.E.) have been discovered. These were disc-shaped and probably ritual objects, used in cultic ceremonies and not as weapons. Nagada II maceheads were pear-shaped and often elaborately decorated.

By the later Predynastic Periods, maceheads with PALETTES were included in MORTUARY RITUALS. HIERAKONPOLIS is the defining site for the discovery of such objects. The NARMER macehead and palettes were found there, as well as the SCORPION macehead and other cultic artistic wares. Such objects provide data concerning historical chronologies and events, as these mortuary decorations and items of daily use commemorated events experienced by the inhabitants of the Nile Valley.

Mafdet (Mefdet; Maftet) The feline goddess of Egypt who appeared as a CAT or as a lynx, she is mentioned in the PALERMO STONE, having aided the god RÉ by overthrowing his enemy, the evil serpent APOPHIS (1). Mafdet was normally depicted as a woman wearing a cat hide or a lynx skin. She was a patroness of the dead and protected the living from snakebites. Devotion to feline deities remained popular in Egypt throughout all historical periods.

Magas (fl. third century B.C.E.) *royal prince of the Ptolemaic Dynasty*
He was the son of PTOLEMY III EUERGETES I (r. 246–221 B.C.E.) and Queen BERENICE (3). Magas did not inherit the throne, which went to PTOLEMY IV PHILOPATOR (r. 221–205 B.C.E.). The prince was reportedly brutally murdered by Ptolemy IV as a result of being suspected of treason. Their mother, Queen Berenice, and an uncle died in the same royal purge.

magat A symbol of the spiritual ladder upon which the god OSIRIS ascended into heaven in cultic traditions, the *magat* was used in MORTUARY RITUALS and was deemed a powerful insignia for invoking the goddess NUT. She sponsored Osiris's ascent into heaven. The *magat* was also inscribed with images of the goddess Isis, denoting her role in the resurrection and ascension of Osiris. The deities of Egypt allowed a supernatural LADDER to descend from the heavens to aid Osiris in his ascension.

magic Called *heka* by the Egyptians, the performance of rituals in order to assume supernatural powers or to attain a desired end, magic was also called *sheta,* which meant "secret or unknown." *Shetau aktet* were unknown properties, and the *shetau neter* were the texts, rituals, and spells that produced results.

The god RÉ reportedly created *heka,* which allowed humans to call upon the gods and to have some control of their own destinies as mortals. Such magic was elevated to a divine status when used by the deities and was considered a simple form in the hands of human beings. Magic was a traditional part of religious rites in Egypt, viewed as the enabling force by which men and gods alike succeeded in their endeavors. Magic was the binding force between the earth and other worlds, the link between mortals and the divine.

Few Egyptians could have imagined life without magic because it provided them with a role in godly affairs and an opportunity to become one with the divine. The gods used magic, and the ANKH was the symbol of power that was held in the deities' hands in reliefs and statues. Magic as a gift from the god Ré was to be used for the benefit of all people. Its power allowed the rulers and the priests to act as intermediaries between the world and the supernatural realms.

Three basic elements were always involved in *heka*: the spell, the ritual, and in a related fashion, the magician. Spells were traditional but could also evolve and undergo changes during certain eras. They contained words that were viewed as powerful weapons in the hands of the learned of any age. Names were especially potent as magical elements. The Egyptians believed that all things came into existence by being named. The person or object thus vanished when its name was no longer evoked, hence the elaborate mortuary stelae, and the custom of later generations returning to the tombs of their ancestors to recite aloud the names and deeds of each person buried there.

Acts of destruction were related to magic, especially in tombs. The damage inflicted on certain hieroglyphic reliefs was designed to remove the magical ability of the objects. Names were struck from inscriptions to prevent their being remembered, thereby denying eternal existence. In the Old Kingdom tombs (2575–2134 B.C.E.) the hieroglyphs for animals and humans not buried on the site were frequently destroyed to keep them from resurrecting magically and harming the deceased, especially by devouring the food offerings made daily.

The Egyptians believed rituals to be part of all religious observances and set up an elaborate system of ceremonies for common usage even in death. Few texts survive, however, to explain these sorts of rituals. Egyptians also hoped to cast spells over enemies with words, gestures, and rites. AMULETS were common defenses against *heka* as they were believed to defend humans against the curses of foes or supernatural enemies.

Further reading: Bennett, James, and Vivianne Crowley. *Magic and Mysteries of Ancient Egypt.* New York: Sterling Publishing, 2001; David, Rosalie. *Cult of the Sun: Myth and Magic in Ancient Egypt.* New York: Barnes & Noble Books, 1998; El Mahdy, Christine. *Mummies, Myth and Magic in Ancient Egypt.* London: Thames & Hudson, 1991; Jacq, Christian, and Janet M. Davis, transl. *Magic and Mystery in Ancient Egypt.* Detroit: Souvenir Press, 2000; Wallis Budge, E. A. *Egyptian Magic.* New York: Carol Publishing Group, 1991; Wallis Budge, E. A. *Magic of Egypt: The Foundation of the Egyptian Religions: With the Magical Rituals and Spells Described.* New York: Holmes Publishing Group, 1995.

magical dream interpretation This was an aspect of Egyptian religious and cultic observances, and a part of *heka,* or magic, as practiced in Egypt. Dreams were considered important omens or prophetic signs. Papyri available in temple archives provided traditional views of the various elements of dreams, and certain priests were trained by the temples to provide interpretations for those who arrived in the precinct to have a prophetic dream in the very sanctuary of the god.

If a man saw himself with his mouth open while dreaming, he was told that the dread in his heart would be relieved by divine intervention. If a man saw his wife in his dream the omen was good, interpreted as meaning that all evils would retreat from him. Evils could also be foretold by dreams experienced in a temple setting. If a man dreamed he saw a dwarf, he was going to lose half of his natural life span. If he wrote on a papyrus in his dream he understood that the gods were beginning to tally his deeds for a final judgment. If a man died violently in his dream, however, he could be assured of living long after his father was entombed.

The interpretation of dreams was practiced by the Egyptians as part of a system prompted by an innate curiosity and concern about the future, and it was popular particularly in the later periods, when the nation was enduring instability and rapid change. The people used oracles also and consulted a calendar of lucky and unlucky days in order to ensure the successful outcome of their ventures.

See also CAIRO CALENDAR.

magical lullaby A charming song from ancient Egypt, crooned by mothers over their children's beds, the lullaby was intended to warn evil spirits and ghosts not to tarry or plan harm against the infants. Each mother sang about the items she possessed in order to wound the spirits of the dead. She carried LETTUCE to "prick" the ghosts, garlic to "bring them harm," and HONEY, which was considered "poison to the dead."

Magnates of the Southern Ten A title possessed by certain governors of the provinces of Upper Egypt, these were normally NOMARCHS, hereditary princes or nobles of ancient nome or provincial clans, who were entrusted with maintaining order and stability in their homelands on behalf of the ruling pharaohs. During the Ptolemaic Period (304–30 B.C.E.), the Magnates of the Southern Ten and other Egyptian legal systems were important to the native populations, as the Greeks established laws for themselves and their allies and allowed the nomes to maintain traditional forms for the Egyptian people.

Mahirpré (fl. 14th century B.C.E.) *remarkable official of the Eighteenth Dynasty*
He served TUTHMOSIS IV (r. 1401–1391 B.C.E.) and AMENHOTEP III (r. 1391–1353 B.C.E.), bearing the title of "fan-bearer," a court rank that denoted access to the pharaoh and a level of trust bestowed upon him by the ruler. Mahirpré was also called a "Child of the Nursery," or a veteran of the Kap, the palace school provided for royal sons and for individuals worthy of special educational facilities. This title denoted the fact that Mahirpré was raised with Tuthmosis IV and/or Amenhotep III in the royal apartments reserved for the children of the ruler. His name meant "Lion of the Battlefield."

Mahirpré was obviously of Nubian descent and was prominent. He died in his early 20s and was buried in the VALLEY OF THE KINGS with sumptuous funerary regalia, attesting to his status at court. His wooden SARCOPHAGUS was more than nine feet long, painted and embellished with gold leaf. Three anthropoid coffins were included in his tomb.

Mahirpré's mummified remains provide details about him as well. He was slightly built, with a dark brown complexion. A wig composed of corkscrew curls was glued to his skull. The skin on the soles of his feet is missing. The tomb of Mahirpré included an OSIRIS BED, a depiction fashioned of the deity out of barley and then planted. A beautifully illustrated BOOK OF THE DEAD was buried with Mahirpré, in which he is depicted with dark skin, denoting his racial ancestry.

Mahu (fl. 14th century B.C.E.) *police official of the Eighteenth Dynasty*
He served AKHENATEN (r. 1353–1335 B.C.E.) as a commander of police at 'AMARNA, the capital of the reign. Mahu may have been one of the MEDJAY, the Nubians (modern Sudanese) who served as mercenaries, ferocious warriors in battle, and as police in the nation's capital and in major Egyptian cities in times of peace. His tomb at the southern 'Amarna necropolis site was designed with a roughly cut cruciform chapel with two burial shafts. Some paintings in this tomb have survived.

Mai (Maiy) (fl. 14th century B.C.E.) *military official of the Eighteenth Dynasty*
He served AKHENATEN (r. 1353–1335 B.C.E.) as a military commander at 'AMARNA. Mai was a hereditary NOMARCH

aristocrat and also served as the overseer of the Royal Palace. His tomb was fashioned out of the cliffs overlooking 'Amarna. A magnificent carved portrait of Mai, seated with his wife, Werel, was also discovered in the tomb of RAMOSE (1) in THEBES.

Maia *See* MAYA.

Malik (fl. first century B.C.E.) *ruler of Nabataea, modern Jordan, in the reign of Cleopatra VII*
Malik's personal fisheries were given to CLEOPATRA VII (r. 51–30 B.C.E.) by Marc ANTONY. In 36 B.C.E., Cleopatra VII, leased the fisheries on the Red Sea to Malik for 200 talents per year, approximately $400,000. In 32 B.C.E., Malik refused to pay, and she roused the neighboring ruler, Herod, to launch punitive raids against the Nabataeans. Herod lost the battle of Qanawat in this campaign.

In retaliation, Malik's troops reportedly set fire to Cleopatra's galleys during the battle of ACTIUM, in which she was an ally of Marc Antony. Cleopatra and Marc Antony were subsequently defeated in this naval engagement by Octavian (AUGUSTUS) of Rome, and Egypt lost its independence.

Malkata A pleasure palace site on the western shore of the Nile at MEDINET HABU, south of THEBES, either erected by AMENHOTEP III (r. 1391–1353 B.C.E.) himself, or by Queen TIYE as a gift for the pharaoh's *heb-sed* (*see* SED). The original name for the site may have been Djarukha, "the Search for Evening" or "the Delight of Evening." Malkata is translated as "the Place Where Things Are Picked Up" in Arabic.

A miniature royal city, Malkata was founded as part of Amenhotep III's first *heb-sed* festival, commemorating his 30th regnal year. Several palace compounds composed the site, with administrative buildings, magazines, kitchens, and a temple to the deity AMUN. Residences for court officials were lavish, and all of the structures were vividly decorated. An artificial lake, the Habu (Birket Habu), and a harbor were constructed for the region, connected to the Nile and built within a matter of weeks. A T-shaped harbor remains visible in modern times. The ruler and his courtiers sailed on a barge dedicated to the god ATEN when he visited Malkata, which in time became his royal residence. He built a palace there for his harem and constructed others for Queen TIYE (1) and for AKHENATEN (Amenhotep IV), his heir.

All of the royal residences were elaborately painted and decorated by local artists. The entire complex, built out of sun-dried bricks, was linked to a nearby funerary temple by a causeway dedicated to the god Amun, who was honored in this shrine. The extravagant suites of the palace and temples were whitewashed and painted with scenes of daily life. Malkata was enlarged for the celebration of Amenhotep III's additional *heb-sed* festivals. A second lake was also fashioned on the eastern shore, and

the site covered more than 80 acres. Malkata was called "the House of Rejoicing Forever" during festivals.

Mallawi This was a site near el-Minya that served as a necropolis for that area in the Old Kingdom Period (2575–2134 B.C.E.). The cemetery is now called SHEIKH SAID. Some 90 graves were discovered there, dating to the early dynastic eras.

mammisi Birth houses used from the Late Period (712–332 B.C.E.) through the Roman Period in temple compounds and earlier in some regions of the Nile Valley, these structures were associated with religious celebrations and pageants concerning the births of deities and pharaohs. Originally the legends of supernatural births, such as the one claimed by Queen-Pharaoh HATSHEPSUT (r. 1473–1458 B.C.E.), were recorded on their stelae or on temple walls. In later eras the *mammisi* provided permanent stages for such mysteries. The Greeks named the buildings during their eras on the Nile, mainly in the Ptolemaic Period (304–30 B.C.E.), but the original structures were Egyptian in origin.

Mandet The sacred bark used by the god RÉ to ascend as the sun each morning, this mythological vessel had a counterpart, the MESEKET, which carried the deity back to earth each evening. The solar deities had several such miraculous vessels.
See also BARKS OF THE GODS.

Mandulis A god from NUBIA (modern Sudan), probably associated with the MEDJAY and other Nubians in the service of Egypt, Mandulis was adopted and worshipped as a god by the Egyptians, probably during the reign of TUTHMOSIS III (1479–1425 B.C.E.). The pharaohs of the Eighteenth Dynasty honored the Nubian gods as rewards for the loyalty of the mercenaries from the area below ASWAN.

Man E *See* "PRINCE UNKNOWN."

Manetho (fl. third century B.C.E.) *Egyptian historian of the Ptolemaic Period*
He served PTOLEMY II PHILADELPHUS (r. 285–246 B.C.E.). Manetho was born in SEBENNYTOS (Tjeb-Neter), now Samannud in the Delta. Manetho was a priest at HELIOPOLIS and started writing his history, *Aegypticae,* at the temple at Sebennytos. The three-volume work, in Greek, was dedicated to Ptolemy II. Only fragments of the *Aegypticae* have survived, but the work was extensively quoted by other writers of the period and is therefore known. Manetho discussed Egypt's dynasties, deities, and individuals of note. He listed some 30 dynasties, including personal and throne names of each ruler.

Manetho also wrote approximately seven other works, including *The Sacred Book, On Festivals, An Epit-*

ome of Physical Doctrine, On Ancient Ritual and Religion, On the Making of Kyphhi (incense), and *Criticisms of Herodotus.* He may have also written *The Book of Sophis.*

See also KING LISTS; MANETHO'S KING LIST.

Manethon (fl. third century B.C.E.) *religious counselor of the Ptolemaic Period*

He advised PTOLEMY I SOTER (304–284 B.C.E.). Ptolemy I was attempting to unite the Egyptian and Greek deities and religious practices to consolidate the people in acts of worship and cultic celebrations. Manethon, famed for his historical knowledge, was asked by Ptolemy I to assist in this process. With TIMOTHEUS, an Athenian, Manethon advised the adoption of SERAPIS (Osiris-Apis, or Osarapis) as the patron of the dynasty. The cult of Serapis contained the traditional aspects of Egyptian worship but provided the Greek citizens of the Nile Valley with familiar religious elements. The SERAPEUM (1) emerged as a result of this adoption. Manethon also compiled the sacred records of Egypt for the LIBRARY OF ALEXANDRIA.

Manetho's King List The work of the historian MANETHO from SEBENNYTOS, Egypt, who lived during the Ptolemaic Period (ca. 280 B.C.E.), Manetho's list, included in his work *Aegypticae,* divided Egypt into approximately 30 dynasties or royal lines of rulers. Scholars use Manetho's *Aegypticae* in conjunction with the TURIN CANON and other chronological records discovered in the various tombs and monuments of Egypt. Although it did not survive as a complete manuscript, it was excerpted enough by other ancient historians that it could be reconstructed.

See also KING LISTS.

Mansion of Isden A sacred site located on the mythological and cosmological Great PRIMEVAL MOUND, the site of creation, the Mansion of Isden is depicted in temple reliefs at EDFU. There is an accompanying text there that indicates that the first creation gods of Egypt discovered the mansion on the Primeval Mound. The Mansion of Isden was in ruins when the first gods arose in the acts of creation. The original purpose of the mansion is not known, but it remained a cultic site of importance in rituals throughout Egypt's historical periods.

"Man Who Tired of Life" See "DEBATE OF A MAN WITH HIS SOUL."

Mareotis An important lake in the Delta region of the Lower Kingdom of ancient Egypt now called Lake Maryet, the site was popular in the Ptolemaic Period (304–30 B.C.E.) as a vacation area and as an agricultural resource. Villas and plantations were maintained there with fruit trees, olive groves, and fields. Fresh water from the Canopic branch of the Nile fed the lake in all seasons. Lake Mareotis connected the great city of ALEXANDRIA to the Nile.

marriage This was the physical and emotional union undertaken by Egyptian men and women that appears to have conferred considerable social status, although a semi-legal aspect becomes clearly evident only in documents dating to the periods following the fall of the New Kingdom in 1070 B.C.E. There are no records of marriages taking place in temples or in government offices, but celebrations were held in conjunction with such unions. In general, ancient Egyptian marriages among commoners and lesser nobles appear to have been based on cohabitation.

Until the Twenty-sixth Dynasty (664–525 B.C.E.), prospective grooms normally sought permission for marriage from the intended bride's father, and in the Late Period (712–332 B.C.E.) the groom offered silver and cattle as a "bride price" to put an end to a father's claims on his daughter. These marriage contracts appear to have been drawn up to clarify a division of property in case of the dissolution of the union.

Royal marriages, recorded in almost every period, had religious and administrative aspects. Most of these unions were designed to promote the royal cult and were clearly based on the need to provide royal heirs who met the blood requirements for succession. The rulers of the first dynasties of Egypt married aristocratic Memphite women to augment their claims and to establish connections with the local noble families. These first rulers needed to bolster their claims to the throne, as they were from Upper Egypt and unknown to the Delta populations in the early eras.

Polygamy was an accepted part of royal life, designed to ensure heirs to the throne. Normally the son of a ruler (if there was one) married his sister or half sister and made her his "Great Wife," the ranking queen. He then took other wives to ensure legitimate heirs. Consanguinity was not a factor considered detrimental to such unions, either on a moral or genetic basis. In many instances the heir to the throne was not born of the sister-wife but of another member of the pharaoh's retinue of lesser queens, a process by which the possible negative genetic effects of such unions were allayed. In later years, rulers married foreign princesses as well, in politically expedient unions, conciliatory gestures to allies and buffer states. The Ptolemaic Period (304–30 B.C.E.) rulers married only Greek women, importing them from outside of Egypt or establishing unions within the royal families of Greek states.

There were ideals concerning marriage and the family, and many Egyptian sages, including one of the sons of KHUFU (r. 2551–2528 B.C.E.), counseled the people to marry and to raise up a patriotic and noble generation. In the case of Khufu's family, however, the presence of too many wives and offspring led to the probable murder of an heir and to division among the royal family. The various harems could be sources of intrigue and rivalry in some eras, as reported conspiracies and plots indicate.

Polygamy was not practiced by nonroyal Egyptians, including the noble classes, but marriages were arranged for political reasons among aristocrats, as evidenced by nome records. Family members, such as uncles, aunts, and cousins, did intermarry, and the extended nome families took care to keep their holdings secure by regulating unions among their offspring.

Not all of the marriages of ancient Egypt were successful, however, and in such cases divorce was an accepted remedy. Such dissolution of marriage required a certain open-mindedness concerning property rights and the economic survival of the ex-wife. In the dynasties following the fall of the New Kingdom, contracts become evident. These were possibly no more than mutually accepted guidelines for the division of property in the event of a divorce, but they could also have been legal expressions of the marriage union.

Many documents from the late periods appear to be true marriage contracts. In the case of divorce, the dowry provided by the groom at the time of marriage reverted to the wife for her support, or a single payment was given to her. In some instances the husband had to give one-third of the property acquired during the marriage, and in others the husband was obliged to provide alimony payments. The charge of adultery, if carried successfully against a wife, eliminated all legal obligations on the part of a husband.

See also FAMILY; WOMEN'S ROLE.

Masaharta (fl. 11th century B.C.E.) *temple official of the Twenty-first Dynasty (1070–945 B.C.E.)*
He was the son of PINUDJEM (1) and Istemkhebe. Masaharta followed his father as high priest of AMUN in Thebes, when Pinudjem took on the status of a second ruler on the Nile. He predeceased his father and was buried with his wife, Tajuheret, after years of controlling Upper Egypt from el-HIBA. Masaharta installed a set of SPHINXES at KARNAK and usurped a statue of AMENHOTEP II (r. 1427–1401 B.C.E.).

Both Masaharta and Tajuheret were buried in THEBES, and their mummified remains were discovered in the cache at DEIR EL-BAHRI in 1881. Masaharta's body was heavily packed and he also had a peculiar BEARD. He was buried in a cedar coffin. Tajuheret's face was heavily packed with linen, a piece of which protrudes from her mouth. Her mummified skin appears to have been damaged by insects.

Masara A valuable quarry site, the modern el-Masara, opposite ZAWIET EL-ARYAN, Masara was quarried extensively by AMENHOTEP I (r. 1525–1504 B.C.E.), who used the stone for his massive building programs, conducted early in the Eighteenth Dynasty. Limestone from Masara was transported to THEBES for the temple of PTAH and AMUN at Opet. The limestone from this quarry was particularly popular as a facing for monuments because of its lustrous beauty.

See also NATURAL RESOURCES.

Masara Stela This is a memorial dating to the reign of 'AHMOSE (NEBPEHTIRÉ) (1550–1525 B.C.E.), the founder of the New Kingdom. A QUARRY was opened at Masara on the eastern bank of the Nile by 'Ahmose, and the limestone quarried there was used for temples and shrines in Luxor and Heliopolis. An official named Neferperet erected a STELA that commemorated this quarrying activity. The monument states that captured oxen, taken from the HYKSOS, were used to drag the quarried stone from Masara to the banks of the Nile.

mastabas Low mud-brick structures with sloping walls used as tombs in the Predynastic Period (before 3000 B.C.E.) and in later eras. The name is from the Arabic word for mud benches. In the Early Dynastic Period (2920–2575 B.C.E.), mastabas were used for royal and private burials. The use of mastabas became necessary at that time because the simple trenches and shallow pits once used as grave sites no longer provided adequate protection for human remains that had been treated by the recently introduced mortuary processes. The increased use of mortuary regalia also complicated the burial requirements. These religious practices, along with the custom of celebrating commemorative services at the tomb, demanded a certain spaciousness of burial sites.

In the Old Kingdom (2575–2134 B.C.E.), mastabas served private individuals, and the walls of these tombs were extended and reinforced to meet the demands of more elaborate funerary rites. The Old Kingdom mastabas had burial chambers, storerooms, and chapels. Surviving mastabas from that historical period have been found in ABUSIR, ABYDOS, GIZA, MEIDUM, and SAQQARA. When separate burial chambers and chapels were incorporated into the designs, unbaked bricks were used for interior walls. These chambers were decorated at times and roofed with timber. The mastabas had embankments, faced with limestone.

FALSE DOORS were designed to serve as stelae on which the achievements, honors, and aspirations of the deceased could be proclaimed for future generations. The false doors, however, were sometimes actual entrances set into the walls and led to the SERDAB, the chamber in which the statue or statues of the deceased were normally placed. These chambers were also used in nonroyal tombs. The *serdab* was built with a slit in the wall so that the statues of the deceased placed within the chamber could view the funerary rituals being conducted in the chapel and could observe the gifts being offered in commemorative rites.

The actual burial chambers were placed at the end of long corridors or sometimes located deep in the ground behind shafts in the mastabas. Stone plugs, staircases, debris, and various traps were incorporated into the design in order to deter thieves and to protect the corpse and the funerary regalia. These burial chambers normally had vast storage areas and other compartments designed to hold tomb ritual materials.

The use of mastabas in ancient Egypt altered the mortuary processes in time. All of the bodies that were buried in shallow graves on the fringes of the desert, following the mortuary customs of the time, were preserved by the heat, the sand, and the lack of moisture in that harsh environment. Placing such corpses inside brick structures altered the natural preservation processes, and the priests were forced to devise the embalming processes to rectify the changes in preserving the dead. Mastabas were popular until the Twelfth Dynasty (1991–1783 B.C.E.) but continued in some areas until the Twenty-second Dynasty (945–712 B.C.E.).

Mastabat el-Fara'un This was Arabic for "Seat of the Pharaoh," given to the complex of PEPI I (r. 2289–2255 B.C.E.) at Memphis. Nearby, a monument of SHEP-SESKHAF (r. 2472–2467 B.C.E.) stands covered with Tureh limestone. Pepi I's mortuary temple contained an inner shrine of dressed stone blocks on a granite base. He died before completing his VALLEY TEMPLE, but the ruins of a causeway remain evident. The tomb is shaped in the form of an actual SARCOPHAGUS.

Matit She was a lion goddess whose cults were located in HIERAKONPOLIS and TANIS. The images of Matit were found on jars dating to the Early Dynastic Period (2920–2575 B.C.E.). In some historical periods Matit served as guardian of royal residences. Lion cults were popular in Egypt.

See also AKER.

Mau (1) (Mafdet) A feline deity sometimes called Mafdet in some regions of the nation, and worshiped in BUBASTIS and in the temple of NEITH (1) at SAIS, Mau aided the god RÉ in his nightly journey through TUAT, or the Underworld. CATS were mummified in her honor in various cities. She was associated with BASTET.

Mau (2) The spiritual being honored at BUBASTIS as a feline symbol of the goddess Bast, Mau resided in the PERSEA TREE and is associated with the traditions of recording pharaonic names on the leaves of the tree.

mau **(3)** This was the Egyptian cat, called *ma'au* when large in form. Sacred cats were worshiped and maintained in splendor in BUBASTIS and in SAIS.

Mau-Taui A guardian deity of the MORTUARY RITUALS and the JUDGMENT HALLS OF OSIRIS, serving as part of the deity Osiris's retinue, Mau-Taui aided Osiris in determining the worthiness of deceased Egyptians.

Maxims of Ani This is an Egyptian document dating to ca. 1000 B.C.E., but probably in its surviving form from the Nineteenth Dynasty (1307–1196 B.C.E.). Ani followed the usual didactic form in addressing his son about the responsibilities and obligations of life. The Egyptians revered didactic texts such as the *Maxims of Ani* as part of their LITERATURE in all eras of the nation's history. A complete version of the *Maxims* is in the Egyptian Museum of Cairo.

Maxims of Ptah-hotep One of the most popular and lasting didactic texts of Egypt, the *Maxims of Ptah-hotep* is believed to be authored by Ptah-hotep Tshefi, a member of a powerful Fifth Dynasty family. Ptah-hotep Tshefi is the grandson of PTAH-HOTEP (1), the VIZIER of IZEZI (Djedkaré) (r. 2388–2356 B.C.E.). The text was written in the reign of UNIS (r. 2356–2323 B.C.E.) or in the reign of Izezi. The *Maxims* have survived in 10 separate forms, including the PRISSE PAPYRUS in the Louvre in Paris, and in the British Museum in London. The text was also discovered in ostraca at DEIR EL-MEDINA, the community of workers of the VALLEY OF THE KINGS, on the western shore of the Nile at THEBES.

Ptah-hotep wrote about the spirit of MA'AT, the guiding principle of civic and social life in Egypt. This spirit was developed in the earliest eras, when the Egyptians noted the order, harmony, and beauty of the universe by watching the stars in the night sky. The people of the Nile believed that humans had to mirror the harmony, order, and beauty of that universe in order to survive. The spirit of *ma'at* called for cooperation, calm, service, and faith from the Egyptians and survived in practice over the centuries.

Later generations used the *Maxims* to instill the moral values of *ma'at* into their own historical periods. Especially concerned with the weak and the oppressed, Ptah-hotep exhorted his countrymen to conduct their affairs with quietude and righteousness. He urged them to be truthful and to treat one and all with kindness and respect.

The key element of didactic texts was the link that they formed with past ages and with the cults of the gods. They also built a bridge between the present era and "the time of the gods," the creation of all things on earth. This relationship was pivotal to Egyptian philosophy. Ceremonies in temples were not only events of the present but were believed to be simultaneously happening in the past.

Ptah-hotep urged his fellow citizens to remember that the waste of precious time was "an abomination," and that only trustworthy individuals should be counted as friends. He also preached that a moment of foolishness could destroy a lifetime of righteousness and urged caution in all of one's dealings. Ptah-hotep was buried in SAQQARA, and his maxims remained popular, even in the Graeco-Roman Period (332 B.C.E.–395 C.E.)

Maya (Maia) (fl. 14th century B.C.E.) *official of the Eighteenth Dynasty who saved the tomb of Tut'ankhamun*
Maya served TUT'ANKHAMUN (r. 1333–1323 B.C.E.) and HOREMHAB (r. 1319–1307 B.C.E.) as the overseer of the treasury. He was the official who protected Tut'ankhamun's tomb when Horemhab began destroying the 'AMARNA Period sites and burial places. Maya was sent by Horemhab to survey the temples of Egypt and to demolish 'AMARNA, the capital of AKHENATEN (r. 1353–1335 B.C.E.). Maya moved Akhenaten's mummy and other royal remains from that period to THEBES for reburial and protection. He then shielded the tomb of Tut'ankhamun, refusing to allow anyone to vandalize the site or the mummified remains.

Maya's tomb in SAQQARA, south of the causeway of the pyramid of UNIS, contained statues of him and his wife, MERIT, who was a chantress of the god AMUN. This tomb is exquisitely decorated and has beautifully painted chambers. The coffins in these chambers were made of wood, a rare material at the time.

Mayer B Papyrus A fragmentary text that is composed of the court records of the reigns of RAMESSES IX (1131–1112 B.C.E.) and RAMESSES XI (1100–1070 B.C.E.), the papyrus also concerns the robbery of the tomb of RAMESSES VI (r. 1151–1143 B.C.E.). A confession of a tomb robber makes the text vivid and historically revealing. Such robberies normally involved not only the perpetrators but officials and priests who made information about the royal tombs available and received a percentage of the profits. Egyptians condemned such acts not only as criminal but also as sacrilege.

See also TOMB ROBBERY TRIAL.

"May My Name Prosper" This was a mortuary phrase used by the ancient Egyptians and discovered in a document dating to the Sixth Dynasty (2323–2150 B.C.E.). The Egyptians believed that any nameless creature, including humans who were forgotten, was unable to exist in the afterlife. The gods and mankind had to know the name of the person in order for that man or woman to remain active and vitally sustained in the afterlife. The Egyptians thus asked their families and friends to make their names "prosper."

Those who could afford to hire priests to perform the mortuary rituals at the burial sites were ensured of continued remembrance. The royal cults provided hosts of priests to continue the daily rituals in the tomb complexes of the pharaohs and their families. Other Egyptians relied on the filial piety of their descendants. FESTIVALS were celebrated to bring families to the graves of their ancestors to continue the traditions of remembrance and praise.

"May the King Make an Offering" This was a phrase used in ancient Egypt, Hetep-di-nesu, translated as "An Offering Made by the King." The words normally opened the funerary texts written on stelae and on tomb walls of deceased Egyptians. They relate to the custom of the rulers providing a funerary offering to every important official, sometimes before his death. In time, the inscription was included in the mortuary formulas and concerned everyone, commoners as well as nobles. The funerary texts thus referred to an ancient tradition and implied that the ruler would provide spiritual offerings instead of the material ones brought to the gravesites in early eras.

See also LIST OF OFFERINGS; LITURGY OF THE FUNERARY OFFERINGS; MORTUARY RITUALS.

Mazeus (fl. fourth century B.C.E.) *Persian satrap who saved Egypt from destruction*
Serving DARIUS III CODOMAN (r. 335–332 B.C.E.), the Persian emperor who faced ALEXANDER III THE GREAT, Mazeus governed Egypt as a Persian province. He watched the disastrous defeats suffered by Darius III's military forces at the hands of the Greeks, and he decided to protect Egypt when Alexander and his army arrived on the Nile as victors. He welcomed them and opened the gates of the nation and cities to their company and thus spared the Egyptians and their cities. Mazeus was honored by Alexander for his wisdom and given a high office in the conqueror's government in Babylon.

Mazghuna This is a site south of DASHUR associated with the last rulers of the Twelfth Dynasty. The pyramidal forms of AMENEMHET IV (r. 1799–1787 B.C.E.) and Queen-Pharaoh SOBEKNEFERU (r. 1787–1783 B.C.E.) were discovered there. They were brother and sister, and they tried to revive their dynastic claims and halt the disintegration of Egypt and the start of the Second Intermediate Period, to no avail. The HYKSOS and other foreign contingents were already visible in the Delta, and the nome clans were instituting their own claims to land and power. The pyramidal tombs of these rulers are in ruins.

Medamud, Nag el- An Old Kingdom (2575–2134 B.C.E.) temple site, northeast of KARNAK at THEBES, the area was dedicated to the god MONTU and was maintained and refurbished by pharaohs of all eras. The Old Kingdom temple at Medamud had a sacred grove and was surrounded by a wall that contained a unique tunnel system, primeval mounds, and chambers. SENWOSRET III (r. 1878–1841 B.C.E.) also built a temple to the deity Montu at Medamud, and other additions discovered on the site were made by AMENHOTEP II (r. 1427–1401 B.C.E.) and some later rulers.

The local triad of Montu, Rattawy, and Harpocrates was worshipped at the temple. A processional way and giant statues of cobras made the Medamud temple distinct. There was a SACRED LAKE as well, and a shrine for the BULL symbols of Montu. The Greeks and Romans made additions in their own eras. PTOLEMY XII (r. 80–58, 55–51 B.C.E.) added three kiosks, and PTOLEMY VIII (r. 170–163, 145–116 B.C.E.) erected a HYPOSTYLE HALL. A second Montu temple was erected in the Ptolemaic Period.

Medes (Mada, Madai) They were a people living in Media Magna, now Azerbaijan, Kurdistan, and Kermanshah and once the ancient name of northwestern Iran. Also called Mada and Madai, the Medes were not known until the Assyrians entered their region in ca. 800 B.C.E. Media Magna was eventually conquered for the most part by the Assyrians in ca. 710 B.C.E. A Median monarchy arose at the same time, and by 625 B.C.E. the Median tribes of the region were united under Cyaxerxes and the capital was erected at Ecbatana (modern Hamadan). In 612 B.C.E., Cyaxerxes stormed Nineveh and put an end to the Assyrian Empire during the reign of PSAMMETICHUS I (664–610 B.C.E.) in Egypt, ending the threat to the Nile Valley.

In 550, Cyrus II of Persia conquered Media Magna, and Ecbatana became the new Persian capital. ALEXANDER III THE GREAT (r. 332–323 B.C.E.) conquered the Medes and Persians. Throughout this period the Medes dominated the Persian culture and revolted on several occasions, halting Persian assaults on Egypt. The Medes were Zoroastrians, remarkable astronomers, and learned occult masters, respected by other cultures for their lore. Members of one of the clans of the Medes, started by Magus, appear in the biblical Nativity narratives.

medicine *See* HEALTH AND DISEASE.

Medinet Habu (Djemet) A site on the western shore of the Nile at THEBES, once called Djemet, serving as a necropolis and monument depository. HATSHEPSUT (r. 1473–1458 B.C.E.) and TUTHMOSIS III (1479–1425 B.C.E.) erected a temple honoring the god AMUN at Medinet Habu. The dominating monument, however, is a fortified temple complex erected by RAMESSES III (1194–1163 B.C.E.), one of the most completely preserved shrines in Egypt. This temple is surrounded by a wall, complete with guardhouses and gateways, one fortified, and containing Ramessid reliefs. Other scenes and icons incor-

Medinet Habu, the *migdol* complex of Ramesses III at Thebes, used in later eras as a fortress *(Hulton Archive)*

porated into the temple are valuable historical texts of the era.

Called a MIGDOL, or Syrian-style fortress, Ramesses III's monument at Medinet Habu depicts Egypt's defeat of the SEA PEOPLES of the time. A pylon and pavilion gate open onto a courtyard with pillars. The royal residence was attached to this enclosure, which leads to a second court and a pillared complex containing a treasury and sanctuaries for the barks of Ramesses III and the gods Amun, KHONS (1), MONTU, and MUT. Two statues of the goddess SEKHMET guard the entrance. There is also a WINDOW OF APPEARANCE in this area, as well as a chapel honoring the ENNEAD and chapels of the gods RÉ, PTAH, SOKAR, and the deified Ramesses III. Other pylons and courts, and a SACRED LAKE, lead to vestibules and an elaborate HYPOSTYLE HALL. The sanctuary connected to this hall has a FALSE DOOR depicting Ramesses III as the deity Amun-Ré. A stairway leads to the roof, where solar ceremonies were conducted, and Osiride statues of Ramesses III grace some areas.

The original temple foundation dating to the Eighteenth Dynasty was actually started by TUTHMOSIS I (r. 1504–1492 B.C.E.) and was called "Splendor of the West" or "Amun is Splendid in Thrones." Hatshepsut directed much of the construction of the temple, but the dedication and opening of the site dates to the reign of Tuthmosis III. Four additional chapels in the complex were added during the Twenty-fifth (712–657 B.C.E.) and Twenty-sixth (664–525 B.C.E.) Dynasties. The mortuary cult of the GOD'S WIFE OF AMUN, or Divine Adoratrices of Amun, was also displayed in the complex. A columned forecourt honoring the Divine Adoratrice AMENIRDIS (1), a daughter of KASHTA (770–750 B.C.E.), and her burial site are part of the complex. The chapel of the Divine Adoratrices NITOCRIS (2) and SHEPENWEPET (1) is also in Medinet Habu.

The royal residence attached to the fortress was made out of mud brick and was decorated with stones and glazed tiles. Private apartments, vestibules, double staircases, and columned halls adjoined barracks, magazines, and workshops. The rulers of later historical periods refurbished and maintained Medinet Habu. In some troubled periods, the people of Thebes moved into the complex and kept it fortified and secure.

Medinet Habu Calendar

This was the most elaborate display of a calendar prior to the Ptolemaic Period (304–30 B.C.E.), a unique aspect of the MEDINET HABU temple erected by RAMESSES III (r. 1194–1163 B.C.E.) at THEBES. During the reign of Ramesses III the feasts honoring the deity AMUN were staged at Medinet Habu. The Medinet Habu Calendar was introduced during Ramesses III's 12th regnal year. The calendar lists all of the so-called feasts of heaven, celebrations honoring the Theban deity, Amun. Some of the feasts listed appear as newly established holidays designed to inspire the Egyptians of the era.

Medir (fl. 27th century B.C.E.) governor of the Third Dynasty

He served in the reign of DJOSER (2630–2611 B.C.E.). Medir was governor of certain territories in Upper Egypt. When the Nile failed to rise and inundate the land over a span of years, Djoser consulted with Medir, and with his vizier of Memphis, IMHOTEP, seeking remedies from them both. The two counselors advised that Djoser should visit ELEPHANTINE Island, because he had seen the god KHNUM in one of his dreams. Khnum's cult center was on the Elephantine. Djoser visited the shrine and made certain repairs and additions, and the Nile flooded the land soon after. This event was commemorated on the FAMINE STELA at SEHEL ISLAND in a later era.

Medjay

This was the name given to units of the Nubian (modern Sudanese) forces long in service in Egypt, particularly under KAMOSE of the Seventeenth Dynasty (ca. 1550 B.C.E.) when he began his efforts to oust the HYKSOS from the northwestern territories of the land. Kamose's father, TA'O II (Sekenenré; Djehuti'o) (d. 1555 B.C.E.), had started the war against the Hyksos ruler, APOPHIS. The Medjay, famed as warriors of cunning and stamina, served as scouts for the Egyptians on the marches or at the oases of the LIBYAN DESERT. In actual battle they formed light infantry units and rushed to the front lines, delighting in hand-to-hand combat and the slaughter of the enemy.

When 'AHMOSE (NEBPEHTIRÉ) (r. 1550–1525 B.C.E.), the brother of Kamose and the founder of the Eighteenth Dynasty and the New Kingdom (1550–1070 B.C.E.), assaulted the Hyksos capital of Avaris, the Medjay were again at his side. When the war ended successfully, the Medjay became the backbone of the newly formed state police in times of peace. Some of the members, men such as DEDU, distinguished themselves and were given high political and government posts. TUTHMOSIS III (r. 1479–1425 B.C.E.) built a temple to Dedun, the Nubian god who was probably patron of the Nubian troops. The Medjay are associated with the PAN-GRAVE people in southern Egypt and Lower Nubia. Indications are that these troops served as guardians of the viceroy of Kush and various FORTRESSES. The original Medjay forces are recorded as early as the Sixth Dynasty (2323–2150 B.C.E.) when they were used as mercenary troops.

See also BLEMMYES; MAHU.

Megabyzus (fl. fifth century B.C.E.) renowned general of Persia

He served ARTAXERXES I (r. 465–424 B.C.E.) in Egypt as the head of the forces occupying the Nile Valley. Megabyzus had started his career under XERXES I (r. 486–466 B.C.E.), becoming his brother-in-law. He aided the cabal that assassinated Xerxes I, however. Under Artaxerxes I, Megabyzus was sent to Egypt to put down the revolt of

INAROS, a native Egyptian who had slain General ACHAEMENES, Xerxes I's brother, in battle. After a series of skirmishes, Megabyzus forced Inaros to retreat to an island in the Nile. A traitor surrendered the rebel to the Persians, and Megabyzus promised Inaros's personal safety. The rebel was crucified, however, because the Persian queen mother, Amastris, would not allow the slayer of Achaemenes to live.

Megabyzus rebelled at the execution, which he believed broke his pledge and stained his honor. He went to Artaxerxes I's court and stated his views openly. For this and other openly critical remarks, Megabyzus was exiled to a small city on the Persian Gulf. There he pretended to have contracted leprosy and was soon returned to the court. The anger Megabyzus felt at having his sworn oath reviled kept him from marching against a second Egyptian rebel, ARMYRTAEUS, who declared the region of the far western Delta independent from Persian control.

Megiddo, Ar-   *See* AR-MEGIDDO, BATTLE OF

Mehen   A great serpent in the Egyptian cosmological traditions, associated with the solar cult of the god RÉ, Mehen was the protector of Ré, coiling around the solar bark of the deity as it traveled across the sky. Bearers carried Mehen and the bark on their journey. In some traditions, Mehen had two heads, one at each at each end, in order to destroy the enemies of Ré.

See also RELIGION AND COSMOLOGY; SOLAR CULT.

Mehu   (fl. 24th and 23rd centuries B.C.E.) *princely official of the Fifth and Sixth Dynasties*
Mehu served as VIZIER to UNIS (r. 2356–2323 B.C.E.) and TETI (r. 2323–2291 B.C.E.). He is recorded as being the son of Idut. Mehu was buried in a borrowed tomb at SAQQARA, near Unis's mortuary complex. A panel in the tomb depicts the original owner. MASTABA-shaped, the tomb had three chambers and a courtyard, with additional mudbrick masonry. A STELA was discovered, as well as reliefs, including one depicting the trapping of birds.

Mehurt (Mehturt; Mehueret)   A celestial being depicted in the form of a cow, this divine creature was associated with the cultic ceremonies of the god RÉ. The name of the being meant "Flooding Waters," and she represented the spiritual river of the heavens. Ré sailed his bark alongside her on his daily rounds. Mehurt was also considered part of the cult of ISIS. She was a protector of the dead when they appeared in the JUDGMENT HALLS OF OSIRIS beyond the grave.

Mehy   (fl. 14th century B.C.E.) *official of the Nineteenth Dynasty who incurred the wrath of Ramesses II*
He started his career in the reign of SETI I (1306–1290 B.C.E.). Mehy's rank and role remain a mystery. The

agents of RAMESSES II (r. 1290–1224 B.C.E.), the successor of Seti I, vandalized Mehy's reliefs in his tomb. Such reliefs would have provided details about his service to the pharaohs. It is obvious that Mehy was a warrior. He was normally depicted in princely trappings and appeared on Seti I's war reliefs. Some of the love songs of the era mention the fact that Mehy was a commoner by birth, and he was possibly a favorite of Seti I. In either case he earned the enmity of Ramesses II and was singled out for eternal disgrace by having his tomb portraits damaged.

Meidum   This site near the FAIYUM area served as a royal necropolis for the Third and Fourth Dynasties. A step PYRAMID at Meidum was probably started by HUNI (r. 2599–2575 B.C.E.) and completed by SNEFRU (r. 2575–2551 B.C.E.). This pyramid was erected on an earthen platform and was composed originally of eight layers. The structure collapsed some time later, possibly as late as the New Kingdom (1550–1070 B.C.E.). The outer casing, however, was damaged and collapsed during construction. The mummies of several individuals were discovered in the resulting debris. Interior passages and chambers led to a vertical shaft and a burial room, which was lined with limestone. The remains of a wooden coffin were discovered in this corbeled chamber, and a MORTUARY TEMPLE was also found on the east side of the pyramid, containing two rounded stelae. A causeway also led to a VALLEY TEMPLE.

A series of Fourth Dynasty (2575–2465 B.C.E.) MASTABA tombs surround the pyramid, some containing spectacular reliefs and statuary. The famous Meidum geese paintings were part of the reliefs in the tomb of NEFERMA'AT and his wife Atet. Nearby, the mastaba of Prince RAHOTEP and his wife NOFRET (1) contained a unique portrait style statue group. The paintings and statues are in the Egyptian Museum in Cairo. A Fifth Dynasty (2465–2323 B.C.E.) mummy was also found in Meidum.

Meir   This necropolis site was on the banks of the Nile, north of modern ASSIUT, the domain of the governor of CUSAE. The necropolis was used from the Sixth Dynasty (2323–2150 B.C.E.) to the Twelfth Dynasty (1991–1783 B.C.E.). Rock-cut tombs with burial shafts were uncovered at Meir. The Cusae officials and their families were entombed on the site. Cusae was once the capital of the fourteenth nome of Upper Egypt, and during the Second Intermediate Period (1640–1550 B.C.E.) was the southernmost holding of the HYKSOS. Beautiful reliefs and statues were recovered on this site.

mekes   An ancient Egyptian royal SCEPTER designed to be flat at one end, the *mekes* represented pharaonic powers in royal rites and was used by the rulers in many historical periods at formal court or temple ceremonies. The original cultic symbolism of the scepter is not known, and the ritual purpose is not clear.

See also ROYAL CULT

Meket-Aten (fl. 14th century B.C.E.) *royal woman of the Eighteenth Dynasty*
A princess, she was the daughter of AKHENATEN (r. 1353–1335 B.C.E.) and Queen NEFERTITI. Paintings depict her royal parents mourning her death at a young age. In the paintings a nurse is shown carrying a royal baby, leading to the assumption that Meket-Aten died in childbirth. Meket-Aten was buried at 'AMARNA, but her tomb and remains were vandalized. The Amarna necropolis suffered the same sort of destruction as the main capital buildings of Akhenaten at the hands of HOREMHAB (r. 1319–1307 B.C.E.) and the Amunite priests of THEBES. The surviving members of Akhenaten's reign did not fare much better after his death.

Meketré (fl. 21st century B.C.E.) *chancellor of the Eleventh Dynasty famous for his mortuary figures*
He served MENTUHOTEP II (r. 2061–2010 B.C.E.), as the chancellor and chief steward of Egypt during a period of war and reunification. Meketré also survived long enough to serve MENTUHOTEP III (r. 2010–1998 B.C.E.). His tomb at Deir el-Qurna, near DEIR EL-BAHRI, on the western shore of the Nile at THEBES, was designed to rest on the cliff. The tomb had a mud-brick wall and courtyard with limestone columns. The entrance leads 20 yards into the side of the cliff, where a chapel honors Meketré and his son, Inyotef.

The beautifully wrapped mummy of Wah, Meketré's estate manager, was discovered there also. Modern X rays revealed an elaborate funerary collar on Wah, necklaces, and two solid silver scarabs. The burial chamber of Meketré contained a cedar coffin with gilded inscriptions. Other relatives were buried in nearby shafts. A hidden chamber contained wooden replicas depicting daily life on Meketré's estate. Painted miniatures, including soldiers, ships, farmworkers, overseers, even cattle, were placed in the tomb with miniature gardens and buildings. A granary, bakery, spinning shop, and a workroom are depicted, as well as yachts. The buildings contained porticos, columns, and landscapes.

Mekhtemweskhet (1) (fl. 10th century B.C.E.) *royal woman of the Twenty-first Dynasty*
She was the consort of Shoshenq, a Libyan military commander at BUBASTIS, and the mother of OSOCHOR (r. 984–978 B.C.E.), SIAMUN (r. 978–959 B.C.E.), and SHOSHENQ I (r. 945–924 B.C.E.). She also had another son, Nimlot. Mekhtemweskhet was a Libyan noblewoman, a member of the ruling class of the MESHWESH, the Libyan ranking clan.

Mekhtemweskhet (2) (fl. seventh century B.C.E.) *royal woman of the Twenty-sixth Dynasty*
The consort of PSAMMETICHUS I (r. 664–610 B.C.E.), she was the daughter of HARSIESE, the high priest of HELIOPOLIS, and was probably the mother of NECHO II (r. 610–595 B.C.E.), Psammetichus I's heir. Mehtemweskhet's daughter was NITOCRIS (2), the GOD'S WIFE OF AMUN. Mekhtemweskhet was honored with a tomb chapel at KARNAK, along with Nitocris.

Mekhtemweskhet (3) (fl. seventh century B.C.E.) *royal woman of the Twenty-sixth Dynasty*
A consort of NECHO II (610–595 B.C.E.), she was probably the daughter of PSAMMETICHUS I and Queen MEKHTEMWESKHET (2). This Libyan queen was the mother of PSAMMETICHUS II.

Memmius, Lucius (fl. second century B.C.E.) *Roman official and scholar who arrived in Egypt in 112 B.C.E.*
His tour of the Nile Valley took place in the joint reign of PTOLEMY IX SOTER II (116–107, 88–81 B.C.E.) and CLEOPATRA (3). Memmius traveled to the FAIYUM region in Middle Egypt in order to study crocodiles at CROCODILOPOLIS. The royal court at ALEXANDRIA sent a letter to Faiyum officials, instructing them to assist Lucius Memmius in his efforts to see the LABYRINTH as well. The Labyrinth was the temple precinct of AMENEMHET III (r. 1844–1797 B.C.E.) at HAWARA in the Faiyum. The Egyptians were instructed to take "the greatest pains" in making Memmius satisfied at every turn.

Memnon   *See* COLOSSI OF MEMNON.

Memphis   This was the capital of ancient Egypt from the Early Dynastic Period (2920–2575 B.C.E.), continuing as a seat of political power even when the rulers maintained a capital in another area of the nation. Called Hiku-Ptah, or Hat-Ka-Ptah, "the Mansion of the Soul of PTAH," Memphis was located on the western side of the Nile, south of modern Cairo. The first capital of the first nome of Lower Egypt, Memphis was supposedly founded by AHA (Menes) (2920 B.C.E.). Legends state that this ruler altered the course of the Nile in order to clear the plain for his capital. This plain, on the western side of the Nile, was some four miles wide, and its western end sloped upward to the cliffs of the LIBYAN DESERT. The distinctive white walls of the capital were made of mud bricks overlaid with plaster and then painted. Memphis was thus called Ineb-hedj, "the White Walled." The original site is now covered by the modern village of Badrasheen and covers an archaeological field of three square miles.

In some eras Memphis was called "Ankh-Tawy," "the Life of the Two Lands." When the capital of Egypt was officially founded at HERAKLEOPOLIS, IT-TAWY, THEBES, or PER-RAMESSES in later historical periods, the affairs of state were conducted in part in Memphis, and most dynastic clans spent a portion of each year in residence there. The city remained great throughout the nation's various eras.

The modern name derives from the period of the Sixth Dynasty in the Old Kingdom, when PEPI I (r. 2289–2255 B.C.E.) built his beautiful pyramid in SAQ QARA. That mortuary monument was called Men-nefer-Maré "the Established and Beautiful Pyramid of Men-nefer-Maré." The name soon came to designate the surrounding area, including the city itself. It was called Men-nefer and then Menti. The Greeks, visiting the capital centuries later, translated the name as Memphis.

The temple of PTAH once dominated the capital, but only the precinct walls of that structure can be seen today in modern MIT RAHINAH. There are also remains of shrines dating to SETI I (r. 1306–1290 B.C.E.) of the Nineteenth Dynasty and RAMESSES II (r. 1290–1224 B.C.E.). MEREN PTAH (r. 1224–1214 B.C.E.) also built on the site. The necropolis area of Memphis was divided into six sections, including Saqqara, with its remarkable tombs of the Archaic Period and the Old Kingdom and earlier.

The palace of APRIES (r. 589–570 B.C.E.) has been uncovered in Memphis and has enclosure walls and courts still visible. Other archaeological discoveries at the site include a hypostyle hall and pylons, an embalming house for APIS bulls, elaborate figurines, the colossus of Ramesses II, and a temple. The Kom Fakhry necropolis of Memphis contains tombs from the First Intermediate Period (2134–2040 B.C.E.) and a Middle Kingdom (2040–1640 B.C.E.) settlement. The Persians ruled from Memphis during their historical period on the Nile (525–404 and 343–332 B.C.E.), and HERODOTUS, the Greek historian, praised the beauty of the city when he visited it. Memphis declined when ALEXANDRIA was founded in 332 B.C.E.

menat (1) A form of ancient Egyptian AMULET heavily weighted and used to counterbalance the heavy collars worn by the rulers and members of the aristocracy, the *menat* was attached to the back of such collars to keep them in place. As an amulet the *menat* was painted or carved with spells, prayers, and divine images. Made of stone, FAIENCE, or metal, it was worn with strands of beads when not used as a counterbalance.

menat (2) This was a fetish of virility, depicted on reliefs and statues of the god KHONS (1) and worn by Egyptians to foster fertility and health in women and virility in men. In this form the *menat* was fashioned out of glaze ware. The AMULET was also placed in the mummy wrappings of the deceased in mortuary rituals.

Mendes It was an ancient cult center on the site of modern el-Simballewein at TELL EL-RUB'A in the Delta, originally called Per-Ba'eb'djet. "The domain of the Ram Lord of BA'EB DJET," as Mendes was called in some

eras, the city was also the capital of the sixteenth nome of Lower Egypt. A goddess, HAT-MEHIT, was popular in Mendes and became the consort of Ba'eb-Djet. Their son was Harpocrates, a form of Horus. Old Kingdom (2575–2134 B.C.E.) tombs at Mendes denote the age of the site. A granite shrine was erected at Mendes by AMASIS (r. 570–526 B.C.E.). There are Ramessid Period (1307–1070 B.C.E.) ruins as well as Predynastic remains, indicating the continued occupation of Mendes. A cemetery of rams is present, and MASTABA tombs are located on the site. Mendes excavations are uncovering a vast collection of ruined structures and artifacts.

Menes *See* AHA.

Menet-Khufu The principal town of a region in the Oryx nome of Upper Egypt, associated with KHUFU (r. 2551–2528 B.C.E.), modern BENI HASAN is located nearby and is famed for its tombs. In ancient periods Menet-Khufu was called "the HORIZON of HORUS." The actual relationship between Khufu and the site is debatable. Many regions in the Nile Valley assumed the name of the reigning pharaoh as a demonstration of devotion and loyalty.

Menhet (fl. 15th century B.C.E.) *palace woman of the Eighteenth Dynasty, one of three Syrian sisters*
She was a lesser ranked consort or possibly a concubine of TUTHMOSIS III (1479–1425 B.C.E.). Menhet and her sisters, Merti and Menwi, were Syrians, the daughters of a chief, given to Tuthmosis III as tribute or as part of political pacts. Menhet and her sisters were buried in Valley of the Monkeys, Wadi Gabbenet el-Kurrub. Each of the sisters received the same exquisite funerary regalia and ritual mortuary offerings to ensure equal honors in death.

Menkauhor (d. 2388 B.C.E.) *seventh ruler of the Fifth Dynasty*
He reigned from 2396 B.C.E. until his death, succeeding NIUSERRÉ to the throne, and probably the son of Niuserré and Queen Khentikas. Menkauhor is recorded as having sent a mining expedition to the SINAI, perhaps to prepare his burial site. No pyramid has been identified as his, but he was probably buried in DASHUR. A cult honoring Menkauhor was also conducted in SAQQARA for many centuries. He probably erected a sun temple in ABUSIR.

Menkauré (Mycerinus) (d. 2472 B.C.E.) *fifth ruler of the Fourth Dynasty, the builder of the third pyramid at Giza*
The successor of KHAFRE, Menkauré ruled from 2490 B.C.E. until his death, and was called Mycerinus by the Greeks. He was Khafre's son, probably born to Queen KHAMERERNEBTY (2) or perhaps to Queen PERSENTI. His sons were Ka'auré, Khuenré, the chosen heir who died young, and SHEPSESKHAF, who succeeded him. His

daughter was KHENTAKAWES (1). Shepseskhaf possibly completed Menkauré's pyramid, the third one erected at GIZA, and it is known that he completed Menkauré's mortuary temple. He was recorded as being "pious," and his death was predicted by the ORACLE of BUTO.

His pyramid at Giza was designed smaller than the ones erected there by KHUFU and Khafre, but it was covered by costly ASWAN stone. A basalt SARCOPHAGUS was placed within the pyramid and contained fine panel decorations. Statues and other reliefs attest to the skill of the artisans of his historical period. In the Twenty-sixth Dynasty (664–525 B.C.E.) Menkauré's remains were placed into a new wooden coffin. His basalt SARCOPHAGUS was taken to Europe, but it reportedly went down in a shipwreck off the coast of Spain.

Menkhaf (fl. 26th century B.C.E.) *princely vizier of the Fourth Dynasty*
He was a son of KHUFU (Cheops) (r. 2551–2528 B.C.E.) and a lesser ranked wife. Menkhaf served as a VIZIER for his father but was not the designated heir. He was part of that dynasty's tradition of using only royal family members in positions of power or trust.

Menkheperresenb (1) (fl. 15th century B.C.E.) *architect and priestly official of the Eighteenth Dynasty*
He served TUTHMOSIS III (r. 1479–1425 B.C.E.) as the fourth prophet of AMUN and as a chief architect. He was also a nome aristocrat. Menkheperresenb was buried in KHOKHA on the western shore of THEBES, and his tomb contained scenes of everyday Egyptian life, temple workshops, and a portrait of Tuthmosis III. Menkheperresenb also controlled the royal residence at Thebes, called "the Gold and Silver Houses," a designation symbolizing the union of Upper and Lower Egypt under the pharaoh.

Menkheperresenb (2) (fl. 11th century B.C.E.) *high priest of Amun at Thebes in the Twenty-first Dynasty*
He served in this priestly capacity during the reign of PSUSENNES I (1040–992 B.C.E.). Menkheperresenb was the son of PINUDJEM (1) and Queen HENUTTAWY and the brother of Djedkhonsufankh. When his brother died, Menkheperresenb succeeded him in the temple office. He married Psusennes's daughter, Istemkhebe, who bore a daughter of the same name, as well as PSUSENNES II, PINUDJEM (2), and SMENDES II.

Unlike other members of his family, Menkheperresenb served as high priest of AMUN without assuming royal ceremonies and attire, but he did have his name recorded in a CARTOUCHE, a royal insignia. Menkheperresenb made his base of operations at el-HIBA and put down Theban revolts efficiently, exiling the leaders of these rebellions to the oases of the LIBYAN DESERT. He died in the last year of reign of Psusennes I and was buried in THEBES.

Menna (fl. 14th century B.C.E.) *treasury official of the Eighteenth Dynasty*
He served TUTHMOSIS IV (r. 1401–1391 B.C.E.) as a tax collector, estate inspector, and harvest collector. Menna was attached to the temple's assessment programs, visiting the various agricultural regions and tallying crops and tithes. His mortuary stela portrays him in the course of his duties. His tomb on the west bank of Thebes, at SHEIKH ABD' EL-QURNA, depicts his activities, including directing the punishment of errant officials who tried to avoid the tithes or duties imposed by the crown. His wife and daughter are portrayed as well in beautiful rural settings.

Menouthis This is a sunken city on the northern coast of Egypt, rediscovered with the cities of CANOPUS and Heraklion by divers. Menouthis was the wife of Canopus, a military aide of the Spartan king Menelaos, and was honored by having the city named after her. Canopus had visited Heraklion with Menelaos. He was stung by a viper while on this tour and died. Herodotus, the Greek historian who visited Egypt ca. 450 B.C.E., wrote about the cities and their naming.

When the city of ALEXANDRIA was founded by ALEXANDER III THE GREAT (r. 332–323 B.C.E.) in 331 B.C.E., as the new capital of Egypt, Heraklion lost its economic base. An earthquake and tidal wave destroyed all three cities sometime during the seventh or eighth century C.E. Statues, city grids, remains of temples, and tributes to the deities ISIS, OSIRIS, and SERAPIS are being recovered from Menouthis and the other sunken sites. Heraklion's remains are about four miles out at sea from the bay of Abu Qir, and artifacts and magnificent carved pieces are being lifted from their watery resting places. An elaborate museum area is planned by the Egyptian government to safeguard the relics being rescued from these ancient sites.

Mentjuhotep (ca. 16th century B.C.E.) *royal woman of the Seventeenth Dynasty*
She was a consort of TA'O I (Senakhtenré) (d. ca. 1540 B.C.E.). Mentjuhotep was buried at DRA-ABU' EL-NAGA in THEBES. Ta'o I ruled Thebes and most of Upper Egypt, while the Hyksos were in control of the northern domains. TA'O II (Sekenenré) (d. 1555 B.C.E.) would begin the crusade to force the HYKSOS out of the Nile Valley. Mentjuhotep was probably a lesser ranked consort, as TETISHERI was the Great Wife, or *hemet,* of the reign.

Mentuemhat (fl. seventh century B.C.E.) *"Prince of the City" of Thebes*
He was the fourth prophet of Amun at THEBES, called "the Prince of the City," and serving TAHARQA (r. 690–664 B.C.E.), TANUTAMUN (r. 664–657 B.C.E.), NECHO I (r. 672–664 B.C.E.), and PSAMMETICHUS I (664–610 B.C.E.), also ruling a part of Egypt in his lifetime. Mentuemhat witnessed the rise and fall of the Nubian Dynasty

and the Assyrian invasion of Egypt. ASSURBANIPAL, the Assyrian ruler, approved of Mentuemhat during his visit to Thebes as the conqueror of Egypt and allowed the Egyptian to remain in his position, impressed by the man's intellect and power.

Mentuemhat, however, defected to Taharqa, who had been forced to flee from Egypt and was regrouping to regain control. When Psammetichus I founded the Twenty-sixth Dynasty, Mentuemhat acknowledged his sovereignty. He also sponsored Princess NITOCRIS (2), the daughter of Psammetichus I, as the Divine Adoratrice of Amun or GOD'S WIFE OF AMUN. He ruled from ASWAN to HERMOPOLIS MAGNA and had three wives.

A black granite bust of Mentuemhat was discovered at KARNAK, and a standing statue depicts him as a robust, powerful man. Other private monuments display a high degree of artistic skills in the period. His tomb was erected at ASASIF in Thebes. This burial site is a rock-cut complex with outer courts and pylons. A single sloping passage leads to an incomplete chamber. The tomb is beautifully painted and the burial chamber is at the bottom of a shaft. There is a sun court, as well as side chapels, a portico, and a stairway. The ceiling decorations depict astronomical designs. Mentuemhat also erected a MORTUARY TEMPLE, with the separate chambers using differing style of decorations.

Mentuemzaf (Djed'ankhré) (fl. 17th or 18th century B.C.E.) *ruler of the Thirteenth Dynasty*
The actual dates of his reign are unknown. A monument honoring Mentuemzaf was discovered at DEIR EL-BAHRI, opposite Thebes. His son resided apparently at AVARIS, the seat of the growing power of the HYKSOS, or Asiatics, who were consolidating their hold on the eastern Delta. A second monument of Mentuemzaf was found in GEBELEIN.

Mentuhotep (fl. 20th century B.C.E.) *military official of the Twelfth Dynasty*
Serving SENWOSRET I (r. 1971–1926 B.C.E.) as a general of the armies, Mentuhotep led the Egyptian forces into NUBIA (modern Sudan), and there he erected a stela at WADI HALFA to commemorate the expedition. It is believed that Mentuhotep penetrated deeply into the area, seeking auspicious sites for forts and garrisoned TRADE centers and for stations in which the Egyptians could control Nubian traffic on the Nile. The next dynasty would promote the trade efforts of Mentuhotep.

Mentuhotep I (d. ca. 2134 B.C.E.) *ruler of Thebes of the Eleventh Dynasty*
He ruled Thebes from an unknown date until his death, in the era before Upper and Lower Egypt were unified. Mentuhotep I was listed on tomb fragments found in GEBELEIN and is recorded in the TURIN CANON. His consort was Sit-Sheryet, probably the mother of the heir, INYOTEF I (r. 2134–2118 B.C.E.). Documents from the period depict him as "the Son of HATHOR," the slayer of Nubians, Asiatics, and Libyans. Mentuhotep, as the heir of a Theban nomarchy, proclaimed pharaonic powers for himself and his line and established the patterns for reunification of Egypt under MENTUHOTEP II.

Mentuhotep II (Nebhepetré) (d. 2010 B.C.E.) *fourth ruler of the Eleventh Dynasty and the unifier of Upper and Lower Egypt*
Mentuhotep II was the son of INYOTEF III and Queen AOH, also called Yah. Assuming power in THEBES in 2061 B.C.E., he began the process of restoring Egypt after the chaotic First Intermediate Period (2134–2040 B.C.E.) and attacked the KHETY rulers and their allies. In 2040 B.C.E., Mentuhotep II's armies took the cities of ASSIUT and HERAKLEOPOLIS, putting an end to the Ninth and Tenth Dynasties and the First Intermediate Period.

He even led a force to DAKHLA Oasis in the LIBYAN DESERT to slay enemies seeking sanctuary there. This victory not only established the Eleventh Dynasty from Thebes as the rulers of a united Egypt but also ushered in the Middle Kingdom (2040–1640 B.C.E.). Mentuhotep consolidated Egypt's borders, fought the Libyans who had infiltrated the Delta, and campaigned against the Asiatics in the SINAI.

He is also recorded as having conducted expeditions in NUBIA (modern Sudan), where he levied tributes and promoted exploration of the area's NATURAL RESOURCES, including mines and quarries. Mentuhotep II had Nubians and Libyans in his army, who used their expertise and knowledge of the terrains involved in the various campaigns. His assault on Nubia started at ABU SIMBEL, and he cleared the Nile of foes all the way to the second cataract on the Nile. One of his chancellors, Khety, took a large fleet south to reopen trade as a result of these military actions. Mentuhotep II also used the services of BEBI, DAGI, and Ipy, talented men of the era who served as his viziers. Mentuhotep II built on the ELEPHANTINE Island, restoring temples there. He then restored and added to shrines and temples at DEIR EL-BAHRI, DENDEREH, ELKAB, ABYDOS, el-TOD, and ERMENT (Hermonthis).

Upon completing the unification of Egypt, Mentuhotep II was given the name Sank-ib-tawy, "He-Who-Makes-the-Heart-of-the-Two-Lands-to-Live." Administratively, Mentuhotep II set about centralizing power by receiving the resignations of local governors and NOMARCHS. He left many of them in place, but they owed their allegiance to him as a result. The defeated enemy leaders were pardoned when they supported his rule over the Two Kingdoms.

He married TEM (2), possibly the mother of MENTUHOTEP III; HENHENIT, who died in childbirth; and a group of lesser wives or concubines, including NEFERU (1), KHEMSIT, KAWIT (2), SADEH, AMUNET, NUBKHAS (1), INHAPI, and ASHAIT. He also had a rather vast harem of lesser wives and concubines.

DEIR EL-BAHRI was the site of the mortuary complex of Mentuhotep II, erected on the western shore of the Nile at Thebes, his clan home. The funerary temple is now almost destroyed but was originally designed with columned porticoes, terraces, and courtyards, where sycamore and tamarisk trees complemented the statues of the pharaoh. A sloping passage led to a burial chamber, made of blocks of sandstone and containing an alabaster sarcophagus. Mentuhotep's several wives and consorts, as well as members of his court, were buried in Deir el-Bahri. The site included BAB EL-HOSAN, the Gate of the Horse, where a shaft contained boat models.

His mortuary temple was designed to mirror the primeval mound and served as a model for later monuments erected on that site. Mentuhotep II was buried at the end of a long passage. The tomb was vandalized in later periods, and only his skull fragments and a piece of his jaw remain. A funerary monument depicting a seated Mentuhotep II and six queens was recovered. His sister Neferu (1), and a five-year-old child, MUYET, were also buried at Deir el-Bahri.

Mentuhotep II's Warriors

This is a remarkable collection of bodies discovered at DEIR EL-BAHRI, on the western shore of the Nile at THEBES, beside the mortuary complex of the ruler Mentuhotep II.

The ongoing attacks conducted by the Khetys (Aktoys) of the Ninth Dynasty against the rulers of Thebes, included a raid by the warriors of the Khety allies, the warriors of ASSIUT. They vandalized a cemetery and shrine while conducting their assaults. (Such an act was deemed sacrilege by all Egyptians.) In response, Mentuhotep II (r. 2061–2010 B.C.E.) summoned the military units of Upper Egypt and marched north to avenge the desecration. (According to legend, the "FOLLOWERS OF HORUS," the mythical warriors of the Theban domain, also marched north and destroyed Assiut and the Khetys and later united Egypt.) The warriors who died in battle were buried in Mentuhotep II's mortuary shrine at Deir el-Bahri and designated as Mentuhotep II's warriors. Almost 60 Egyptian soldiers were entombed with Mentuhotep II in ritual burial. They wore shrouds marked with the cartouche and seals of Mentuhotep II, identifying them as the pharaoh's comrades-in-arms who were destined to share rewards with him in paradise. The tomb was robbed during the Second Intermediate Period (1640–1550 B.C.E.) but then covered by a landslide, which effectively sealed it.

See also TOMB OF THE WARRIORS.

Mentuhotep II Unifies Egypt

CONTEXT

Following the initial unification of Upper and Lower Egypt ca. 2700 B.C.E., the newly united nation was ruled, for almost 400 years, by two royal dynasties. During this time Egypt's government became centralized and effective. Irrigation systems were put in place and the pyramids were constructed. The six succeeding dynasties ruled successfully for the next 500 years. Then, however, unrest and conflict among the priests and public officials of the ruling elite led to a decline in royal power. By the end of the Eighth Dynasty, ca. 2213 B.C.E., Egypt was led by a string of weak, ineffectual rulers.

The two royal families of the Ninth and Tenth Dynasties were usurpers from the city of Herakleopolis who ruled the northern domains but not the lands south of ABYDOS. Called the Khetys or the Aktoys, they established Herakleopolis as their capital and began their unstable rule. During the Eleventh Dynasty, the Khetys began a series of assaults on Thebes (modern Luxor), which had long been the bastion of the Inyotef kings of the Eleventh Dynasty and was now the royal domain of Mentuhotep II. The son of INYOTEF III and Queen AOH (also called Yah), Mentuhotep II would unify Upper and Lower Egypt for the second time in Egypt's history.

EVENT

In 2061 B.C.E., Mentuhotep II assumed power in Thebes. As ruler, Mentuhotep II remained alert of the Khety forces, especially when they started a new series of raids on southern lands, and he began to gather resources and establish border patrols. The situation came to a head when the warriors of ASSIUT, a city located south of HERMOPOLIS MAGNA, on the eastern side of the Nile, allied themselves to the Khetys and Herakleopolis. The Assiuts conducted several massive assaults on Theban territories.

During one such attack, the Assiut troops came across a large necropolis, or cemetery, at Thinis. Such precincts were deemed sacred to all Egyptians, housing as they did the remains of ancestors. (The dead, called "beloved Osirises" by the living, were believed to be able to involve themselves in the lives of their living family members.) The warriors of Assiut went on a rampage among the graves, vandalizing them and reducing the sacred site to rubble. This was sacrilege in the minds of all Egyptians, as they believed this act angered the gods and wounded the beloved dead.

When word of the damage reached the Khety ruler in Herakleopolis, he was reportedly shocked. Knowing that Mentuhotep II was a capable warrior of considerable piety, he understood that the Theban ruler would be compelled by his office and by his beliefs to avenge the sacrilege.

From Thebes, Mentuhotep II called to the armies of all of the Upper Egyptian towns and cities. At that time, the army of Egypt was composed of separate units from the nomes, or provinces. The nomarchs, the hereditary lords of each province, summoned their troops and set out for Thebes. These warriors marched under nome totems that declared the patronage of certain deities or were emblazoned with regional symbols. Once at the capital, the nomarchs held counsel with Mentuhotep II and they decided that their first target would be Assiut. No documentation is available describing the battle itself, but the city fell to the Thebans, who then headed for Herakleopolis. Within only a few weeks, Mentuhotep II was in control of the Khety domain, thus uniting the Upper and Lower Egyptian Kingdoms.

IMPACT

In 2040 B.C.E. Mentuhotep II's armies captured the cities of Assiut and Hierakonpolis and thus put an end to the Ninth and Tenth Dynasties. This victory not only established the Eleventh Dynasty from Thebes as the rulers of a united Egypt, but also ushered in the Middle Kingdom (2040–1640 B.C.E.), a period considered a golden age by later dynasties. Mentuhotep II consolidated Egypt's borders, fought the Libyans who had infiltrated the Delta, and campaigned against the Asiatics in the Sinai. Upon completing the unification of Egypt, Mentuhotep II was given the name Sank-ib-tawy, "He-Who-Makes-the-Heart-of-the-Two-Lands-to-Live." Administratively, Mentuhotep II set about centralizing power by receiving the resignations of certain local governors and nomarchs. Many he left in place, but they owed their allegiance to him as a result, and defeated enemy leaders were pardoned when they supported his rule over the Two Kingdoms.

In addition to unifying Egypt, Mentuhotep's victory indirectly contributed to a significant didactic text, *Instructions for Merikaré*, which has survived to the present day. Valuable for its historical perspective of the First Intermediate Period (2134–2040 B.C.E.), the text was reportedly written by KHETY III to his son, Merikaré. Khety III had witnessed the assault made on the city of Thinis by his allies of Assiut and sorely regretted the event. Describing that assault, which resulted in a general outrage in the land and a Theban military campaign that led to the ruin of the Khety line, the text clearly outlines the duties of a wise ruler and echoes the moral precepts of earlier dynasties on the Nile. In it, Khety III instruct his son and heir to imitate the great pharaohs of the past and to promote equal justice, compassion, and prudence in military campaigns, and expresses regret that such a devastation of Thinis had occurred in his name.

Further reading: Grajetzki, W. *The Middle Kingdom of Ancient Egypt: History, Archaeology and Society.* London: Duckworth, 2006; Parkinson, Richard. *Voices from Ancient Egypt: An Anthology of Middle Kingdom Writings.* London: British Museum Press, 2006.

Mentuhotep III (S'ankharé) (d. 1998 B.C.E.) *fifth ruler of the Eleventh Dynasty*

He reigned from 2010 B.C.E. until his death. Mentuhotep III was the son of MENTUHOTEP II and Queen TEM (2) or possibly NEFERU (1). He ascended the throne at an advanced age, and he is recorded on the ABYDOS and SAQQARA ruler lists and in the TURIN CANON. A veteran of his father's military campaigns, Mentuhotep III rebuilt fortresses in the eastern Delta and sent an expedition to PUNT. He also had wells dug along expedition routes and reopened the quarries at WADI HAMMAMAT.

His mortuary temple was built at DEIR EL-BAHRI, on the western shore at Thebes, but it was not completed. Mentuhotep also erected a temple to the god THOTH on a hill overlooking the Nile. The letters of an official named Hekanakhte, a mortuary priest in Thebes, provided considerable information about Mentuhotep III's reign. The heir, Mentuhotep IV, was born to Queen IMI. Another of his consorts was Queen AMUNET.

Mentuhotep IV (Nebtawyré) (d. 1991 B.C.E.) *sixth ruler of the Eleventh Dynasty*

He reigned from 1998 B.C.E. until his death. The son of MENTUHOTEP III and Queen IMI, he initiated expeditions to mines and quarries, and had an immense sarcophagus lid quarried in WADI HAMMAMAT and then sailed down the Nile to his tomb site. This mortuary monument was loaded onto a barge and carried north from the quarry with the aid of an army of 3,000 workers who were involved in the transportation.

Mentuhotep IV founded a harbor town (KUSER) on the Red Sea for the shipbuilding operations conducted by the Egyptians in preparation for journeys to PUNT. Kuser would become important to Egypt in the New Kingdom (1550–1070 B.C.E.) when expeditions to Punt were conducted regularly. Mentuhotep IV also mined at Wadi el-Hudi and elsewhere. AMENEMHET I, Mentuhotep's vizier, conducted many of the ongoing royal projects and usurped the throne.

Menyu   A god of ancient Egypt, called "the Lord of the Desert," Menyu was believed to be the son of ISIS and was revered in KOPTOS, worshipped as Neb-Semt, or desert deity. He was depicted in some periods as a warrior bull god. Menyu was also a deity of regeneration. He is listed on the PALERMO STONE.

Menzala   This is a lake in the Delta region of ancient Egypt. The lake is located near the Damietta branch of the Nile. Menzala is one of the few remaining bodies of water in the Delta, where the Nile had seven separate branches and the water levels of the lakes were higher.

Merenptah (Baenre'hotepirma'at) (d. 1214 B.C.E.) *fourth ruler of the Nineteenth Dynasty*

He reigned from 1224 B.C.E. until his death. Merenptah was the son of RAMESSES II and Queen ISETNOFRET (1). He was actually the 13th son designated as the royal heir. His older brothers died before they could receive the throne from their long reigning father (1290–1224 B.C.E.). Active militarily while a prince, Merenptah was apparently in his 50s when he became pharaoh.

A KARNAK inscription and the ATHRIBIS STELA give accounts of the difficulties he faced upon taking the throne. The Cairo Column also adds details. Merenptah faced a combined force of Libyans, Libu, Tekenu, and MESHWESH in the fifth year of his reign in the western Delta and defeated them. He then met the Libyans and a contingent of SEA PEOPLES, including the Meshwesh, Kehek, Sherden, Shekelesh, Lukka, Tursha, and Aka washa, repelling them. A major battle was fought at Per-yer in the Delta and then at "the Mount of the Horns of the Earth" in the Libyan Desert. Mauroy, a Libyan leader, fell in this battle, as Merenptah used chariots, infantry units, and archers to repel the enemy. More than 6,000 of the enemy died, and their families were taken captive.

Merenptah's chief consorts were ISETNOFRET (2) and TAKHAT (1). His sons were SETI II and probably AMENMESSES. He built a royal residence at MEMPHIS and restored temples elsewhere. He also aided the HIT-TITES, who were suffering from a severe famine. Seti II was made coruler before Merenptah died, probably in his early 70s. At his death he was corpulent, bald, and standing five feet seven inches tall. His tomb in the VAL-LEY OF THE KINGS on the western shore of THEBES was designed with five corridors and contained halls, side chambers, and annexes. This highly decorated tomb held a SARCOPHAGUS of red granite. The lid of the sar-cophagus depicted the BOOK OF THE GATES, a mortuary document. Another alabaster sarcophagus was also dis-covered on the site. The tomb had a trench dug in front of it to protect it from seasonal floods.

The mummy of Merenptah was found in the royal mummy cache in the tomb of AMENHOTEP II in 1898. Merenptah suffered from arthritis and calcification of the arteries. He had severe dental problems and evi-dence of prior fractures of the thigh bones. Merenptah's mummy was encrusted with salty nodules, probably caused by the embalming process.

Merenré I (Nemtyemzaf) (d. 2246 B.C.E.) *third ruler of the Sixth Dynasty*
He reigned from 2255 B.C.E. until his death. Merenré was the son of PEPI I and Queen ANKHNESMERY-RÉ (1). His wife was Queen NEITH (2) or Nit, who married PEPI II, and his daughter was Ipwet. Merenré I ruled only nine years, and he built a pyramid in SAQQARA but never finished the site. Merenré I also exploited the mines of SINAI, the quarries of NUBIA (modern Sudan), and the mines of ASWAN and HATNUB, and he visited ELEPHAN-TINE Island at ASWAN, appointing a governor for the region. He maintained as well the services of General WENI, who had been an official in the reign of Pepi I.

The Egyptians controlled the Nile down to the third cataract during Merenré I's reign. He cut five canals at the cataracts of the Nile and commissioned the local Nubians (modern Sudanese) to build ships for him out of timbers. A copper statue of Merenré I and Pepi I was found in HIERAKONPOLIS. A mummified body was dis-covered at Saqqara, but it was probably not his remains but evidence of a later burial. He was succeeded by his half brother, Pepi II.

Merenré (II) (Antiemdjaf) (fl. 22nd century B.C.E.) *shadowy ruler of the Sixth Dynasty*
He was reportedly the son of PEPI II (r. 2246–2152 B.C.E.) and Queen NEITH (2). Merenré II was devoted to a local deity, ANTI. He ruled only one year at the close of the dynasty with his consort, Queen NITOCRIS (1), as the dynasty was threatened by general unrest and the ambitions of powerful nomarchs who sought inde-pendence for their clans. When he died, Nitocris ruled alone. She is mentioned in the TURIN CANON. Her suc-cessor was possibly NEFERKURÉ, the son of Queen ANKHNES-PEPI and Pepi II.

Mereruka (fl. 23rd century B.C.E.) *chief justice and vizier of the Sixth Dynasty*
He served TETI (r. 2323–2291 B.C.E.) as VIZIER, chief jus-tice, and the supervisor of Teti's cult personnel. The son of the noble Nedjetempet, Mereruka married Princess SESHESHET, also called Idut. She was Teti's daughter. His son was Meryteti. Mereruka constructed the royal tomb of Teti as part of his duties as vizier.

Mereruka's own tomb in SAQQARA is a magnificent monument, shared by his royal wife and son. The tomb contains more than 30 chambers and was designed as a vast mastaba. A FALSE DOOR and a chapel with six pillars, including a statue of Mereruka, are part of the splendid architectural elements of the mastaba. There are painted scenes in corridors and in three of the chambers. A SERDAB was also part of the design. Scenes of gardening, fishing, fowling, hunting, harp playing, scribes, ban-quets, pets, and dwarves provide historical data of the period.

Meresger (1) (Meretseger) A cobra goddess of ancient Egypt's Theban necropolis, also called Mer-etseger, she was worshipped as "the Lady of Heaven" and the "Peak of the West" in Egyptian religious texts. Meresger was noted as a goddess who chastised the evil-doer. The Egyptians depicted her as a "Savage Lion" to all who performed sinful acts until they called upon her name for forgiveness. The goddess lived on the rocky spur of SHEIKH ABD' EL-QURNA, at the necropolis site of THEBES, where she was called "the Lover of Silence," an allusion to her mortuary role. She was popular through-out many eras of Egyptian history but declined in the Twenty-first Dynasty (1070–945 B.C.E.).

Meresger (2) (fl. 19th century B.C.E.) *royal woman of the Twelfth Dynasty*
She was a lesser ranked consort of SENWOSRET III (r. 1878–1841 B.C.E.), a ruler noted for his extensive HAREM. Meresger was not the mother of the heir.

Meri (fl. 20th century B.C.E.) *royal pyramid complex official of the Twelfth Dynasty at el-Lisht*
He served SENWOSRET I (r. 1971–1926 B.C.E.). Meri was the supervisor of the ruler's pyramid in el-LISHT, overseeing the construction of the mortuary complex. He also governed the pyramid territory. His funerary STELA, now in the Louvre in Paris, gives an account of his career and honors. The pyramidal complexes of the rulers demanded considerable attention and personnel. Small cities were erected at these sites to provide residences for priests and other attendants involved in the mortuary cults of the dead rulers, such cults lasting for decades, even centuries.

Merikaré (fl. 22nd century B.C.E.) *ruler of the Herakleopolitan Ninth Dynasty (2134–? B.C.E.)*
He was probably the son of KHETY III. The *INSTRUCTIONS FOR MERIKARÉ*, a didactic document attributed by scholars to his father, was written for him reportedly, although the authorship has not been proven. The text concerns the events of Khety III's reign, a period in which the Inyotefs were beginning their assaults on the Herakleopolitans. Khety III regrets many events that took place, and he speaks of the ideals and the spirit that the rulers and subjects should adopt in order to attain spiritual maturity.

Merikaré appears to have been middle-aged when Khety bequeathed him the Herakleopolitan throne. He faced growing tensions with THEBES in an uncertain political era of change, but he died before the armies of MENTUHOTEP II advanced upon his capital. ITY was his successor. Merikaré's mortuary pyramid was constructed near MEMPHIS.

Merimda Beni Salama This is a Predynastic site in the western Delta of Egypt, dating to ca. 4750 B.C.E., the first known settlement in the Nile Valley. Located 15 miles northwest of modern Cairo, Merimda had an estimated population of 16,000 in some historical periods, although the average was probably smaller. Graves found in the site contained mostly children, possibly the victims of a famine or an epidemic. Houses at Merimda were mostly windbreaks, or pole-framed structures with pitched roofs. Granaries and grid street patterns are evident. The Faiyum A culture pottery was discovered there, as well as stone MACEHEADS, polished black pottery, and fishing tools. The Merimda phase was contemporaneous with Upper Egypt's Badarian and Amratian phases.

Merit (1) (fl. 14th century B.C.E.) *noblewoman of the Eighteenth Dynasty*
She was the wife of MAYA, the treasurer for TUT'ANKHAMUN (r. 1333–1323 B.C.E.) and HOREMHAB (r. 1319–1307 B.C.E.). Maya protected the tomb of Tut'ankhamun when Horemhab set about destroying the surviving monuments of AKHENATEN (r. 1353–1335 B.C.E.) and the 'AMARNA Period. Also called Maia in some records, he built an elaborate tomb in SAQQARA. Merit is depicted in exquisite reliefs in the tomb with Maya, and the artistic splendor of her portraits and other scenes symbolize the high degree of skill evident in that period of Egyptian history.

Merit (2) She was an Egyptian divine being, called "the Goddess of the Inundation." Egypt was named Ta-Mera, or Ta-Merit, "the Land of the Inundation."

Meritites (1) (fl. 26th century B.C.E.) *royal woman of the Fourth Dynasty*
A consort of KHUFU (Cheops) (r. 2551–2528 B.C.E.), Meritites was the mother of Prince KEWAB and Princess HETEPHERES (2), Princess MERYSANKH (2), and Princess DJEDEFHOR and BAUFRÉ. She was buried in GIZA. The royal family of Khufu was divided between two factions, and Meritites' son Kewab, who was the rightful heir, was killed in a questionable manner. His successor represented the opposing side of the family and did not manage to keep the throne for long or to raise his own sons as heirs.

Meritites (2) (fl. 23rd century B.C.E.) *royal woman of the Sixth Dynasty*
She was the daughter probably of PEPI I (r. 2289–2255 B.C.E.). A small step PYRAMID, recording her as a queen, was discovered in SAQQARA. It is recorded that Meritites' pyramid became a pilgrimage site after her death.

merkhet This was an astral gauge used by the ancient Egyptians for architectural surveys and construction projects. Much like the modern plumb line, the *merkhet* provided relatively accurate measurements, something required for the construction of massive monuments that not only had to be based on secure foundations but were positioned according to astronomical configurations deemed appropriate.

Merneith (Merynit; Mereneith; Meryneith) (fl. ca. 29th century B.C.E.) *royal woman of the First Dynasty*
She was the consort of DJET or Wadji (date of reign unknown). Merneith bore Djet a daughter, also named Merneith, and a son, DEN, who would become the fourth ruler of the First Dynasty; clay seals bear her name as "the King's Mother." Queen Merneith served as regent for her son, who inherited the throne before reaching his majority. (The younger Merneith would later become

her brother's consort.) Merneith's mortuary complexes at ABYDOS and SAQQARA attest to her rank as a ruler in that period. The Abydos tomb follows the pharaonic style of that time and was surrounded by 41 other gravesites. These Egyptians, including artisans and craftsmen, possibly died as part of her mortuary ceremonies. Merneith died in the reign of Den. A STELA erected in her honor depicts her name entwined with the SEREKH (2) symbol, normally reserved for pharaohs. Merneith's coffin bore similar royal insignias. Her Abydos tomb was a brick lined pit with a wooden floor. Some 77 additional graves were discovered nearby. Her Saqqara tomb contained a boat pit.

Meroë A site on the eastern bank of the Nile in NUBIA (modern Sudan), north of modern Kabushiyah, it contains royal remains and unique monuments dating to the Twenty-fifth Dynasty (712–657 B.C.E.) and other historical periods. In the fifth century B.C.E., the great Kushite Empire was seated in Meroë. Vital and energetic, the people of Meroë remained powerful even in the Greco-Roman Period on the Nile. The necropolis of Meroë, Begarawiga, was filled with Kushite pyramids and royal burials. A temple to ISIS dates to the Napatan Period (ca. 1000–300 B.C.E.) at Meroë, and lavish palaces were erected there as well. A temple of AMUN was built in the second century B.C.E., as well as a temple of APEDEMAK, a Nubian lion deity.

Further reading: Priese, Karl-Heinz. *The Gold of Meroe.* New York: Metropolitan Museum of Art, 1993.

Mersa Matruh This was a site 185 miles west of ALEXANDRIA that served as a port of entry into Egypt. Pilgrims arriving to visit the oasis of SIWA during the Ptolemaic Period (304–30 B.C.E.) used the port and erected a city called Ammonia (later called Paraetonium). Modern Bates Island served as another trading port in the area. Siwa Oasis, called also Jupiter Ammon, was well known throughout the Mediterranean region, and many came from distant lands to worship AMUN in that vast desert site.

Meryamen (fl. 12th century B.C.E.) *prince of the Twentieth Dynasty*
A son of RAMESSES III (r. 1194–1163 B.C.E.), he was depicted as a Fan Bearer in reliefs, apparently not holding any other known official position. Meryamen was also portrayed on the walls of MEDINET HABU with 19 of his brothers, listed there as Ramesses-Meryamen.

Meryatum (1) (fl. 13th century B.C.E.) *royal woman of the Nineteenth Dynasty*
She was the daughter of RAMESSES II (r. 1290–1224 B.C.E.) and Queen NEFERTARI MERYMUT. She is depicted with her parents at the Queen's Temple at ABU SIMBEL. It is

believed that Meryatum accompanied her father on the occasion of the dedication of the Abu Simbel complex.

Meryatum (2) (fl. 13th century B.C.E.) *royal priest of Ré of the Nineteenth Dynasty*
The sixteenth son of RAMESSES II (r. 1290–1224 B.C.E.) and NEFERTARI, he served as the high priest of RÉ at HELIOPOLIS. Prince Meryatum is depicted at the Queen's Temple at ABU SIMBEL, and the temple of NUT at KARNAK bears his name. Meryatum officially visited the Egyptian turquoise mining operations in the SINAI.

Meryatum (3) (fl. 12th century B.C.E.) *royal priest of Ré of the Twentieth Dynasty*
The son of RAMESSES III (r. 1194–1163 B.C.E.), he served as the high priest of RÉ at Heliopolis. Meryatum outlived his father and was possibly buried at el-MATARRIYAH necropolis, in modern Cairo.

Meryet (1) (Merit; Mereret) (fl. 19th century B.C.E.) *royal woman of the Twelfth Dynasty*
She was the consort of SENWOSRET III (r. 1878–1841 B.C.E.). Meryet was buried in the mortuary complex of Senwosret III at DASHUR.

Meryet (2) (fl. 19th century B.C.E.) *royal woman of the Twelfth Dynasty*
She was a consort of AMENEMHET II (r. 1929–1892 B.C.E.). Little is known of her, as she was a lesser-ranked queen.

Merymose (fl. 14th century B.C.E.) *viceroy of the Eighteenth Dynasty, called the "King's Son of Kush"*
Serving AMENHOTEP III (r. 1391–1353 B.C.E.), he was the VICEROY of Kush, or the governor of NUBIA (modern Sudan). Merymose was responsible for trade routes and fortifications of the Egyptians south of Aswan. The region of Nubia was highly active during Merymose's term of office as the "King's Son of Kush," and he had to maintain garrisoned stations and navigable waterways along the Nile. His tomb at THEBES contained outstanding statuary.

Merynénefer (Qar) (fl. ca. 23rd century B.C.E.) *official of the pyramidal complexes of the Sixth Dynasty*
He was the overseer of the pyramidal complexes of KHUFU (Cheops) and MENKAURÉ (Mycerinus). Merynénefer was also a tenant of the pyramid complex of PEPI I and the inspector of priests in the pyramid of KHAFRE (Chephren). He served in several reigns. His tomb in GIZA is elaborate, with two FALSE DOORS and decorations. A portico displays pillars carved as the likenesses of Merynénefer, and there are statues of the deceased and his son and other male relatives. IDU, Merynénefer's father, was buried in an adjoining tomb in ABUSIR. He was the overseer of priests in the pyramidal complexes of Khufu and also Khafre (r. 2520–2494 B.C.E.). Elaborate paintings beautify this grave site.

Meryré (1) (fl. 14th century B.C.E.) *priestly official of the Eighteenth Dynasty*
He served AKHENATEN (Amenhotep IV; r. 1353–1335 B.C.E.) at 'AMARNA as the high priest of ATEN. Meryré held the position of the Great Seer of Aten when Akhenaten decided to share his powers with others near the end of his reign. Akhenaten's death resulted in the abandonment of 'Amarna and the end of Aten's cult. Meryré and his wife, Tener, disappeared and their beautifully adorned tomb at 'Amarna remained unfinished. Meryré reportedly was buried somewhere in 'Amarna, probably deposited in a secret cache in order to preserve his remains from the agents of HOREMHAB (r. 1319–1307 B.C.E.).

Many of the 'Amarna officials made arrangements to have their remains hidden when they died, as they witnessed the destruction turned loose on Akhenaten's capital after his death. The unused tomb of Meryré depicts him receiving decorations from the pharaoh and visiting Aten's temple. The paintings at this site record events and personalities of the 'Amarna Period and display the vivacious artistic styles of the era.

Meryré (2) (fl. 14th century B.C.E.) *official of the Eighteenth Dynasty at 'Amarna*
He served AKHENATEN (Amenhotep IV; r. 1353–1335 B.C.E.) as superintendent of Queen NEFERTITI's royal household. Meryré was the son of the high priest of ATEN, Meryré (1), and Tener. His unfinished tomb at 'Amarna depicts Akhenaten, Nefertiti, and SMENKHARÉ. Meryré (2) disappeared after Akhenaten's death, probably hiding to avoid the vengeance of HOREMHAB and other Amunites, who sought to obliterate all traces of the 'Amarna interlude. His burial site has not been identified.

Meryré (3) (fl. 13th century B.C.E.) *prince of the Nineteenth Dynasty*
He was the eleventh son of RAMESSES II (r. 1290–1224 B.C.E.). Meryré is depicted in a LUXOR temple relief as part of Ramesses II's KADESH military campaign. He is shown leading prisoners during that encounter, which took place in Ramesses II's fifth regnal year.

Merysankh (1) (fl. 26th century B.C.E.) *royal woman of the Third Dynasty*
She was a lesser consort of HUNI (r. 2599–2575 B.C.E.) and the mother of SNEFRU, the founder of the Fourth Dynasty. Probably a commoner by birth, she was reportedly deified in later dynasties.

Merysankh (2) (fl. 26th century B.C.E.) *royal woman of the Fourth Dynasty*
A daughter of KHUFU (r. 2551–2528 B.C.E.) and Queen MERITITES (1), Merysankh's life is not detailed.

Merysankh (3) (Meresankh; Mersyankh) (fl. 26th century B.C.E.) *royal woman of the Fourth Dynasty*
Merysankh was the daughter of Prince KEWAB and Queen HETEPHERES (2) and granddaughter of KHUFU and Queen MERITITES (1). She was the consort of KHAFRE (Chephren) (r. 2520–2494 B.C.E.). Merysankh was called "the King's Beloved Wife," "the Mistress of DENDEREH," "the Priestess of Bapefy," "the Priestess of THOTH," and "the Priestess of HATHOR." She inherited Prince Kewab's estate when he died and was at court when her mother, Hetepheres (2), married RA'DJEDEF (r. 2528–2520 B.C.E.). Marrying Khafre, Ra'djedef's successor, Merysankh became the mother of Prince Nebemakhet, Prince Khenterka, Prince Duwanera, and Princess Shepsetkau, along with other children.

She died suddenly in the reign of MENKAURÉ (2490–2472 B.C.E.), and her mother gave her the magnificent GIZA tomb that she had prepared for her own use. The MASTABA at Giza's eastern cemetery has a subterranean rock-cut chapel, a main chamber, false doors, and a shaft. Statues and reliefs within the tomb depict the royal family. Merysankh's embalming process was recorded as lasting a record 272 days. Her son Prince NEBEMAKHET is among those portrayed in reliefs.

Meryt-Amun (1) (Meryt-Aten) (fl. 14th century B.C.E.) *royal woman of the Eighteenth Dynasty*
She was the wife of SMENKHARÉ (r. 1335–1333 B.C.E.). Meryt-Amun was the daughter of AKHENATEN (Amenhotep IV) and Queen NEFERTITI. When Nefertiti left Akhenaten's palace in 'AMARNA and took up residence in a separate mansion, Hat-Aten, Meryt-Amun became queen in her place, even though she was married to Smenkharé. The death of Akhenaten in 1335 B.C.E. brought about Smenkharé's coronation. He had been Akhenaten's attendant for two years and had assumed many administrative duties.

Smenkharé and Meryt-Amun returned to THEBES to placate the priests of AMUN and the military faction led by General HOREMHAB. She was the mother of Merytaten-Tasherit and Merytaten the Younger. She died before Smenkharé.

Meryt-Amun (2) (fl. 15th century B.C.E.) *Royal woman of the Eighteenth Dynasty*
She was a daughter of TUTHMOSIS III and a consort of AMENHOTEP II (r. 1427–1401 B.C.E.). Meryt-Amun died at age 50 and was depicted as delicate, with brown wavy hair. She was buried at DEIR EL-BAHRI in two coffins, one fashioned out of cedar. PINUDJEM (1), the high priest of AMUN in the Twenty-first Dynasty, usurped Meryt-Amun's tomb for his daughter, Princess Entiu-nywas.

Meryt-Amun (3) (fl. 13th century B.C.E.) *royal woman of the Nineteenth Dynasty*
She was the eldest daughter of RAMESSES II (r. 1290–1224 B.C.E.) and Queen NEFERTARI MERYMUT. When Nefertari

Merymut died or retired to the harem palace near the FAIYUM, Meryt-Amun became a queen, ranking second to BINT-ANATH, her sister. A statue of Meryt-Amun, colossal in size and beautifully made, was unearthed recently at AKHMIN. The lips of the statue have retained the original red paint.

Meryt-Ré-Hatshepsut (fl. 15th century B.C.E.) *royal woman of the Eighteenth Dynasty*
She was the consort of TUTHMOSIS III (r. 1479–1425 B.C.E.). Meryt-Ré-Hatshepsut was not the first "Great Wife," or *hemet,* having been preceded by two others. She was, however, the mother of the heir, AMENHOTEP II. Meryt-Ré-Hatshepsut outlived Tuthmosis III and was honored in her son's reign. She was buried at THEBES, in the VALLEY OF THE QUEENS. The tomb designated as hers, however, does not appear to have been used. A quartzite, unfinished SARCOPHAGUS was found in that tomb. She was also the mother of Meryt-amun and Nebetiunet.

Meseket   This was a sacred bark used by the god RÉ in his nightly descent from the heavens. Ré rode on the MANDET in the morning to ascend into the sky on his appointed rounds. These sacred barks were accompanied by other divine beings and by the deceased souls who were not deemed worthy of eternal paradise but were allowed to survive in ETERNITY in the retinues of the gods.

See also BARKS OF THE GODS.

Mesentiu   The name of an ancient Egyptian group that originated in EDFU, a site south of THEBES, in Upper Egypt. The Mesentiu are featured in early accounts of the unification of the nation. They are part of "the Sons of HORUS." The Mesentiu were reportedly skilled in metallurgy and battle.

mesenty   This was an ancient Egyptian term that meant "the Lord of All Creation." Most cults assumed that title for their particular deities as part of the cosmogonic traditions fostered in the various cults, including AMUN and RÉ. From the earliest historical periods, however, PTAH was the true *mesenty.*

Meshwesh   They were a people dominating the region of modern LIBYA in many historical periods. Uniting with other Libyan groups and at times joined to the confederation known as the SEA PEOPLES, the Meshwesh at tempted many assaults on the western Delta. MERENPTAH (r. 1224–1214 B.C.E.) and RAMESSES III (r. 1194–1163 B.C.E.), among others, had to defeat such invasion forces.

With the fall of the New Kingdom in 1070 B.C.E., the Libyans began to enter the Nile Valley and the Meshwesh settled at BUBASTIS. Reportedly, HERIHOR of the Twenty-first Dynasty (1070–945 B.C.E.) belonged to a collateral family of the Meshwesh. The most famous of these Libyans was SHOSHENQ I (r. 945–924 B.C.E.), the founder of the Twenty-second Dynasty. The Libyans reinvigorated Egypt with their presence and served as military leaders of note and as administrators.

meska   This was a sacred symbol, fashioned out of the hide of a BULL and used as part of the costume of NOMARCHS and some PHARAOHS. The term "Bull of his Mother" was sometimes attached to the royal titles in ceremonies. The *meska* was a symbol of power and rebirth, as bulls were popular THEOPHANIES of the gods.

Meskhent (Meshkhent; Meskhenit)   She was an Egyptian goddess of childbirth, depicted as a birthing brick with a woman's head or as a woman with a brick on her head. Egyptian women sat on bricks designed to promote labor during childbirth. Meskhent assumed four forms and predicted the future of newborns. Meskhent is mentioned in the WESTCAR PAPYRUS, and she reportedly predicted the role of the first three pharaohs of the Fifth Dynasty (2465–2323 B.C.E.). She was associated with HATHOR in some eras.

In MORTUARY RITUALS, Meskhent was an attendant in the JUDGMENT HALLS OF OSIRIS, where she aided the deceased. She provided the magical powers so that the dead could be reborn in paradise. She was the divine sister of Anit and Tanenit. Her husband was SHAI, who represented destiny, fate, or luck.

Messuy (fl. 13th century B.C.E.) *governor of Kush in the Nineteenth Dynasty*
He served RAMESSES II (r. 1290–1224 B.C.E.) as VICEROY of Kush, the governor of the territories south of ASWAN in NUBIA (modern Sudan). In this role he was addressed as the "King's Son of Kush." Messuy constructed a temple at KALABASHAH, in a region called BEIT EL-WALI. A rock-cut shrine, the temple erected by Messuy was designed with columns and elaborate reliefs of the pharaoh. A causeway connected the temple to the Nile.

Mesthi-Imsety   *See* CANOPIC JARS; IMSETY.

mesu-heru   They were the guardians of the CANOPIC JARS, "the Four Sons of Horus." The jars contained the vital organs of the deceased, removed during the rituals of embalming. The preservation of internal organs ensured the purification of corpses and also protected parts of the body considered necessary to the deceased. The brain was removed and discarded, as the Egyptians did not equate thoughts, emotions, or ideals with the brain. They believed that the heart was the receptacle of such abilities.

See also CANOPIC JARS.

metals   *See* NATURAL RESOURCES.

Methen (Metjen) (fl. 27th century B.C.E.) *governor and biographer of the Third Dynasty, serving several pharaohs*
He served DJOSER (r. 2630–2611 B.C.E.) as a regional governor but was famous as well as a biographer. Methen started his career in the reign of SNEFRU (r. 2575–2551 B.C.E.) and rose in the ranks. He administered the Delta NOMES and the FAIYUM's eastern zone. Methen was buried in a brick MASTABA in SAQQARA, the royal necropolis, a sign of his rank. The tomb had a cruciform chapel and contained a small granite statue of Methen. His father was Anibesemonek.

Migdol (1)   This was a site in the SINAI, near TCHARU, where the Egyptians maintained a fortified tower with massive walls. When the Persian ruler CAMBYSES (r. 525–522 B.C.E.) attacked Egypt, he destroyed the site, which was later rebuilt. Tell el-Her, to the south, was also destroyed and rebuilt.

migdol **(2)**   This was a type of fortress, Syrian in design, heavily fortified. MEDINET HABU, the vast complex erected by RAMESSES III (r. 1194–1163 B.C.E.) was a *migdol*-style structure.

"Mighty Bull Appearing in Thebes"   An epithet used by TUTHMOSIS III (r. 1479–1425 B.C.E.) and other strong New Kingdom pharaohs, the title was usually preceded by the phrase "Life to HORUS." The two epithets were combined to notify the Egyptians that a human form of Horus had risen again in THEBES to protect the nation from all enemies. The BULL was always a symbol of strength and tenacity for the Egyptians and was used in several royal titles.

Miliku (fl. 14th century B.C.E.) *prince of Gaza (Gezer) and a vassal of Egypt*
He held the throne of his city-state in the reign of AKHENATEN (Amenhotep IV; r. 1353–1335 B.C.E.) and was mentioned in the 'AMARNA LETTERS, the correspondence concerning land disputes among the Egyptian vassal states and other pertinent topics of the era. Miliku was accused of land grabbing by other princes, and he wrote to Akhenaten asking for defenses against another vassal state. Akhenaten did send troops to Miliku, and slave women were given to Egypt in return for Egyptian goods.

military   *See* WARFARE.

Min (1) (Menu; Amsi; Khem)   An Egyptian fertility god, Min was depicted in the ithyphallic form and served as the patron of desert travels and guardian of harvests. He was worshipped in AKHMIN and KOPTOS from the earliest eras. Min was then the patron of hunters and nomads.

The god was normally shown as a man with an erect penis, wearing a plumed crown with a streamer. In some eras his statues resembled mummies. Originally such statues were painted blue-black, symbolizing divinity, and Min had a human head or a hawk's head. He held his phallus in his left hand. In that pose he was called "the God of the Lifted Hand."

The ancient deity of Koptos, a god called A'ahes or Rahes, was absorbed by the cult of Min early on. The temples of Min were round in design. LETTUCE was his symbol, and his festivals were joyous occasions. In time, Min was worshipped as Min-Horus. The PALERMO STONE gives an account of Min, and there were three colossal statues of the deity at Koptos. He was depicted on a bowl of KHA'SEKHEMWY, dating to ca. 2650 B.C.E. In some eras he was called Min-Isis-Horus.

Min (2) (fl. 15th century B.C.E.) *priestly official of the Eighteenth Dynasty*
Min served TUTHMOSIS III (r. 1479–1425 B.C.E.) as the mayor of THINIS and overseer of the priests of ANHUR. His most important position, however, was as archery instructor for AMENHOTEP II, Tuthmosis III's son and heir. A veteran of military campaigns, Min supervised the prince's military training and served as well as treasurer of Lower Egypt and judge. He was buried with honors in THEBES.

Minkhaf (fl. 26th century B.C.E.) *prince of the Fourth Dynasty*
A son of KHUFU (Cheops) (r. 2551–2528 B.C.E.), Minkhaf assumed powerful court roles, as this dynasty maintained a firm grip on the various government agencies, not sharing the offices with outsiders. He was not the heir to the throne.

Mirgissa   A site near the second cataract of the Nile, in NUBIA (modern Sudan), this was the largest of a series of fortified stations erected by SENWOSRET III (r. 1878–1841 B.C.E.) to protect Egyptian TRADE and to control traffic on the river. Troops were garrisoned at the site, and storage chambers were available for trade goods in transit. In some eras trade officials and governors took up residence there.

Mitannis   A powerful people who spoke the Hurrian language and invaded Mesopotamia and Syria, they emerged as a unified state during the Middle Kingdom (2040–1640 B.C.E.) or earlier, ruled by an Indo-Aryan royal line of kings. The Mitanni capital was Washukania or Washukanni, believed to be the modern Tell al-Fakhiriyeh in northern Syria. Coming from the Caspian Sea originally, the Mitanni had Indo-European connections and worshipped Indian deities. During their imperial period, they ruled from Assyria to the Levant.

The rise of the militaristic Eighteenth Dynasty (1550–1307 B.C.E.) brought Egypt into conflict with the Mitannis, who were expanding their own imperial domain. This expansion aided TUTHMOSIS I (r. 1504–1492 B.C.E.) and TUTHMOSIS III (r. 1479–1425 B.C.E.) in their successful campaigns, and the Mitannis suffered defeats at the hands of the Egyptians at Aleppo and CARCHEMISH. AMENHOTEP II (r. 1427–1401 B.C.E.) led an army into Mitanni domains, capturing KADESH on the Orontes River. TUTHMOSIS IV (r. 1401–1391 B.C.E.) asked ARTATAMA, the Mitanni king, for his daughter, to seal an alliance between the two states. Tuthmosis IV had to make this request seven times before the Mitanni princess arrived on the Nile. The Assyrians captured the Mitanni capital in the reign of the Assyrian king Adadnirari (1305–1274 B.C.E.), and made the state a vassal. Shalmanesser I (1273–1244 B.C.E.) annexed the Mitanni lands, ending the empire. Egypt's alliance with the Mitannis would prove costly in time, as Tuthmosis IV's preference for the Mitannis over the rising HITTITES would spark political and military problems for the Ramessids of the Nineteenth Dynasty (1307–1196 B.C.E.).

Mit Rahinah A temple site of the god PTAH, located near MEMPHIS, the shrine is half covered with water at the present time. A temple of Ptah dominated the site and contained an elaborate shrine and colossal statues of RAMESSES II (r. 1290–1224 B.C.E.). Stone blocks from the Old Kingdom (2575–2134 B.C.E.) and New Kingdom (1550–1070 B.C.E.) were salvaged from an older shrine. Ramesses II also erected a pylon in the western part of the temple and northern and southern gates.

A smaller temple at MIT RAHINAH included an embalming house of APIS, erected by SHOSHENQ I (r. 945–924 B.C.E.), with chapels added by SHABAKA (r. 712–698 B.C.E.) and AMASIS (r. 570–526 B.C.E.). This complex is west of the remains of an earlier temple dating to the reign of TUTHMOSIS IV (1401–1391 B.C.E.). At nearby Kom el-Rabi'a is a temple to HATHOR erected by Ramesses II and a temple to Ptah from the reign of MERENPTAH (1224–1214 B.C.E.). This has a palace compound as well. Tombs from the First Intermediate Period (2134–2040 B.C.E.) and the Middle Kingdom (2040–1640 B.C.E.) are at Mit Rahinah. There are also priest tombs nearby, built during the Twenty-second Dynasty (945–712 B.C.E.).

Mitry (fl. 24th century B.C.E.) *high-ranking legal official of the Fifth Dynasty (2465–2323 B.C.E.*
He served in the early periods of that royal line as a provincial administrator of royal territories. Mitry was also one of the MAGNATES OF THE SOUTHERN TEN, a high-ranking position as counselor and judge. His tomb in SAQQARA contained 11 wooden statues, extremely rare in ancient Egypt, life-sized portraits of the official and his wife.

Mi-wer This is a site near modern KOM MEDINET GHUROB in the FAIYUM region that served as a royal retirement estate for elderly or indisposed queens of the Eighteenth (1550–1307 B.C.E.), Nineteenth (1307–1196 B.C.E.), and Twentieth (1196–1070 B.C.E.) Dynasties. The complex at Mi-wer was started by TUTHMOSIS III (r. 1479–1425 B.C.E.) and was a vast estate with royal residences and educational institutions. RAMESSES II (r. 1290–1224 B.C.E.) used Mi-wer during his reign, and Queen NEFERTARI Merymut reportedly retired there after attending the dedication of her temple at ABU SIMBEL. The complex did not survive the end of the New Kingdom in 1070 B.C.E.

Mnevis A deity of Egypt, originally called *Mer-wer* or Nem-ur, "the Living Sun God," Mnevis was associated with RÉ, and called "the Soul of Ré." Mnevis was symbolized in rituals by a bull that was worshipped at HELIOPOLIS. This BULL was second in rank to APIS and was considered a true oracle. The mother cow giving birth to a Mnevis bull, which had to be entirely black and had to have tufts of hair on its body and tail, was believed to have been transformed into Hesat, a cow goddess. The Mnevis bull was so popular as part of the solar cult of Ré-Atum that AKHENATEN (r. 1353–1335 B.C.E.) declared that such animals should be buried at 'AMARNA (Akhetaten), his capital.

Most Mnevis bulls were interred in Heliopolis, in a necropolis under the modern site of Cairo's Arab el-Tawil. A stela of Prince 'Ahmose, believed to be the princely son of AMENHOTEP II (r. 1427–1401 B.C.E.), was discovered there. RAMESSES II (r. 1290–1224 B.C.E.) began the custom of erecting stone structures over rectangular pits, and each bull was buried in a large chamber decorated with reliefs. The pits were necessary because of the flat terrain of the area. MERENPTAH (r. 1224–1214 B.C.E.) buried a Mnevis bull during his reign, building a limestone sarcophagus for the internment. The various reliefs and sacred paintings portrayed the Mnevis bull with a sun disk and the uraeus on its horns. Mnevis was associated with OSIRIS in some historical periods and remained popular throughout the Late Period (712–332 B.C.E.).

Moalla, el- This is a necropolis south of THEBES, dating to the First Intermediate Period (2134–2040 B.C.E.). Two of the tombs at el-Moalla are famous for their decorations and paintings. These are the tombs of ANKHTIFY and SOBEK HOTEP. El-Moalla was a necropolis serving the area known as TOD. The Egyptians called it Hefat.

Moeris, Lake A vast water deposit in the FAIYUM region of Egypt, now represented by Birkat Qarun. During the Predynastic Period (before 3000 B.C.E.), the lake stood about 120 feet above sea level. The lake rose and sank periodically, and during the Middle Kingdom (2040–1640 B.C.E.) efforts were made to halt the silting of the channel that connected Lake Moeris to the Nile. Refurbished, the lake served as a flood route and as a reservoir. The area around the reduced Lake Moeris became popular in the Ptolemaic Period (304–30 B.C.E.).

Mokattem This was a site near modern Cairo used in many periods of Egyptian history as a source of fine quality limestone. DJOSER (r. 2630–2611 B.C.E.) used the QUARRY for the construction of the STEP PYRAMID in SAQQARA. Other pharaohs employed Mokattem's limestone in several eras. The stone was highly prized for its luster and stability.

See also NATURAL RESOURCES.

Momemphis A site in the Delta, probably at one time located near Terana on the Canopic branch of the Nile, Momemphis was the scene of a battle between AMASIS (r. 570–526 B.C.E.) and APRIES (r. 589–570 B.C.E.) for the throne of Egypt. Apries had been removed from power by the mutiny of his Egyptian troops. He fled from the Nile and returned with Greek mercenaries who did not support him with enthusiasm. Apries lost the battle and was taken prisoner. He was given to the Egyptian soldiers, who killed him.

mongoose See ICHNEUMON.

months They were the ancient Egyptian periods of 30 days each, incorporated into the calendar by the priests of early historical periods. The months were part of three seasons and are as follows:

Season of akhet—the inundation—winter
Thoth
Paopi
Athyr
Khoiak

Season of proyet or peret—the sowing—spring
Tybi (or Tobe)
Mekhir
Pnamenoth
Parmuthi

Season of shemu or shomu—the harvest—summer
Pakhons
Paoni
Epep
Mesore

The use of only 30 days in each month caused a gradual alteration between the true rotation of the earth and the seasons based on lunar calculation. The Egyptians attempted to remedy that situation by adding EPAGOMENAL DAYS at the end of the year.

Montu (Mont) He was a war deity dating to the Middle Kingdom (2040–1640 B.C.E.). The pharaohs of the Eleventh Dynasty (2040–1991 B.C.E.) were particularly dedicated to this god. Montu originated in THEBES and had two consorts, Tjenenyet and Ra'ttawy. He was normally depicted as a man with a hawk's head, adorned with plumes and a sun disk. The BUCHIS bulls were worshipped as theophanies of Montu. In the New Kingdom (1550–1070 B.C.E.), Montu was associated with the god RÉ and was addressed as Montu-Ré. The deity was originally part of the cult of HORUS at Thebes.

Montuhirkhopshef (1) (fl. 15th century B.C.E.) *royal official of the Eighteenth Dynasty famous for his tomb*
He served TUTHMOSIS III (r. 1479–1425 B.C.E.) and was a noble with ranks and titles. He was also related to the royal family. Montuhirkhopshef's tomb is famous at Thebes. The site contains a relief depicting the mortuary object called a *TEKENU.*

Montuhirkhopshef (2) (fl. 12th century B.C.E.) *prince of the Twentieth Dynasty*
He was the son of RAMESSES III (r. 1194–1163 B.C.E.) but not the heir to the throne. His wife was probably TAKHAT (2), who was buried in the tomb of AMENMESSES. Montuhirkhopshef may have been the father of RAMESSES IX (r. 1131–1112 B.C.E.). He was buried in Thebes, and his tomb in the VALLEY OF THE QUEENS depicts him making offerings.

Montuhirkhopshef (3) (fl. 12th century B.C.E.) *prince of the Twentieth Dynasty*
He was the son of RAMESSES IX (r. 1131–1112 B.C.E.) and probably Queen BAKETWEREL, but he was not the heir to the throne. Montuhirkhopshef was buried in the reign of RAMESSES X in a beautiful tomb containing his portraits.

mortuary rituals These were the ceremonies and elaborate processes evolving over the centuries in the burial of ancient Egyptians. Such rituals and traditions were maintained throughout the nation's history, changing as various material and spiritual needs became manifest. In the Predynastic Period (before 3000 B.C.E.), the Egyptians, following the customs of most primitive cultures of the area, buried their dead on the fringes of the settlement region, in this case the surrounding deserts. This custom was maintained for some time in Upper Egypt, but in Lower Egypt the people appear to have buried their dead under their houses as well.

Cemeteries in the MA'ADI cultural sequence (3400–3000 B.C.E.) contained human and animal graves. Unborn infant remains were found in graves inside the settlements. In the Badarian period (4500–4000 B.C.E.), the graves were oval or rectangular, roofed, and contained food offerings—the beginning of mortuary

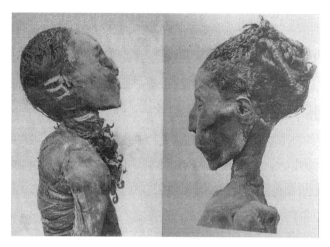

Mummy wigs, the human hair adornment found on Egyptian mummified remains, used by men and women and changing in style in the various historical eras *(Hulton Archive)*

regalias. The corpses of this period were covered with hides or reed mats, and some were positioned ritually and dusted with sacred powders. Rectangular stone palettes, used as part of the first grave offerings, were placed alongside the bodies, accompanied by ivory and stone objects introduced in the Badarian necropolis areas. In the Naqada II sites (3500–3000 B.C.E.) there is evidence of definite mortuary cults, as funerary pottery is evident. The graves were linked with wooden planks in some instances, plastered and painted, with niches designed to hold the ritual offerings provided at burials.

The corpses of the Predynastic Periods were normally placed in the graves on their left sides, in a fetal or sitting position. The religious texts of later eras continued to extort the dead to rise from their left sides and to turn to the right to receive offerings. The graves were also dug with reference to the Nile, so that the body faced the West, or Amenti, the western paradise of OSIRIS.

By the time Egypt was unified in ca. 3000 B.C.E., the people viewed the tomb as the instrument by which death could be overcome, not as a mere shelter for cast-off mortal remains. The grave thus became a place of transfiguration. The A'AKH, the transfigured spiritual being, emerged from the corpse as a result of religious ceremonies. The A'akh, the deceased, soared into the heavens as circumpolar stars, with the goddess NUT. As the PYRAMID TEXTS declared later: "Spirit to the sky, corpse into the earth." All of the dead were incorporated into cosmic realms, and the tombs were no longer shallow graves but the "houses of eternity."

The first dynasties of Egypt became sophisticated about death and the rituals of preparation. The need for a receptacle for the KA, the astral being that accompanied the mortal body throughout life, led the Egyptians to elaborate on burial processes and rituals. They began

to speak of death as "going to one's *ka.*" The dead were "those who have gone to their *kas.*" Through the intercession and guidance of these astral beings, the dead were believed to change from weak mortals into unique immortal spiritual beings, exchanging life on earth for the perfect existence in paradise.

The cult of Osiris also began to exert influence on the mortuary rituals and introduced the ideals of contemplating death as a "gateway into eternity." This deity, having assumed the cultic powers and rituals of older gods of the necropolis, or cemetery sites, offered human beings to prospects of salvation, resurrection, and eternal bliss. Osiris would remain popular throughout Egypt's history. His veneration added moral impetus to the daily lives of the people, common or noble, because he demanded, as did RÉ and the other deities, conformity to the will of the gods, a mirroring of cosmic order, and the practice of MA'AT, a spirit of quietude and cooperation throughout life. Osiris also served as the god of the dead, thus linking the living to those who had gone before them.

The impact of such philosophical and religious aspirations was great and lasting. The shallow graves, dug under the houses or in the fringe areas of the desert, were abandoned as a result of the new spiritual approach, and MASTABAS, the tombs made out of dried brick, were devised to provide not only a burial chamber but a place for offerings and rituals. Mastabas thus offered not only a safe receptacle for the corpse but served as abodes for the *ka,* and the *ba,* which accompanied it through eternity. The necropolis sites of the Early Dynastic Period (2920–2575 B.C.E.) were filled with mastabas that had upper, ground-level chambers, shafts, and hidden burial rooms. The mortuary ritual began to evolve at the same time, and offerings were provided and gifts laid in front of the deceased each day, especially when the corpse was of royal status.

The desert graves had provided a natural process for the preservation of the dead, something that the mastabas altered drastically. Corpses placed away from the drying sands, those stored in artificial graves, were exposed to the decaying processes of death. The commoners and the poor, however, conducted their burials in the traditional manner on the fringes of the desert and avoided such damage. The priests of the various religious cults providing funerary services and rituals discovered the damage that was being done to the corpses and instituted customs and processes to alter the decay, solely because the *ka* and the BA could not be deprived of the mortal remains if the deceased was to prosper in the afterlife. RESERVE HEADS (stone likenesses of the deceased) were placed just outside the tombs so that the spiritual entities of the deceased could recognize their own graves and return safely, and so that a head of the corpse would be available if the real one was damaged or stolen.

The elaborate mastabas erected in SAQQARA and in other necropolis sites and the cult of Osiris, the Lord of the Westerners, brought about new methods of preservation, and the priests began the long mortuary rituals to safeguard the precious remains. In the early stages the bodies were wrapped tightly in resin-soaked linen strips, which resulted only in the formation of a hardened shell in which the corpses eventually decayed. Such experiments continued throughout the Early Dynastic Period, a time in which the various advances in government, religion, and society were also taking place. Funerary stelae were also introduced at this time. The tombs of the rulers and queens were sometimes surrounded by the graves of servants as well, as courtiers may have been slain to accompany them into eternity. Such burials took place in the cemeteries around tombs, such as the tomb of MERNEITH (1), an important woman of the First Dynasty (2920–2770 B.C.E.). The custom was abandoned rather abruptly.

The embalming of the dead, a term taken from the Latin word which is translated as "to put into aromatic resins," was called *ut* by the Egyptians. The word *mummy* is from the Persian, meaning pitch or bitumen, which was used in embalming during the New Kingdom (1550–1070 B.C.E.) and probably earlier. In later eras corpses were coated or even filled with molten resin and then dipped in bitumen, a natural mixture of solid and semisolid hydrocarbons, such as asphalt, normally mixed with drying oil to form a paint-like substance.

In the beginning, however, the processes were different. Corpses dating to the Fourth Dynasty, those of queens HETEPHERES (2) and MERYSANKH (3), for example, show indications of having been embalmed with the old methods, which were cruder and less extensive. In order to accomplish the desired preservation, the early priests of Egypt turned to a natural resource readily available and tested in other ways: NATRON, called *net-jeryt* as it was found in the Natron Valley (or WADI NATRUN), near modern Cairo. That substance was also called *hesinen,* after the god of the valley, or *heshernen tesher,* when used in the red form. Natron is a mixture of sodium bicarbonate and sodium carbonate or sodium chloride. It absorbs moisture called hygroscopic, and is also antiseptic. The substance had been used as a cleansing agent from early eras on the Nile and then was used as a steeping substance that preserved corpses.

The priests washed and purified the bodies and then began to prepare the head of the corpse. The brain was sometimes left intact in the skull but more often, the priests inserted hooks into the nose, moving them in circular patterns until the ethmoid bones gave way and allowed an entrance into the central cavity. A narrow rod with a spoon tip scooped out the brains, which were discarded.

In some eras the brain was surgically removed from the bodies, a rather sophisticated operation because it involved the atlas vertebrae and entrance through the neck. Once cleared of brain matter, by use of the hook or by surgical means, the skull was packed with linens, spices, and Nile mud. On at least one occasion (as exemplified by a mummy available for modern forensic research) the head was packed with too much material and was swollen and split apart. The mouth was also cleansed and padded with oil-soaked linens, and the face was covered with a resinous paste. The eyes were sometimes filled with objects to maintain their shape and then covered with linen, one pad on each eyeball, and the lids closed over them. The corpse was then ready for the "Ethiopian Stone," a blade made out of obsidian.

Peculiarly enough, the mortuary priest who used the blade called the "Ethiopian Stone" and performed surgical procedures on the corpses being embalmed was reportedly shunned by his fellow priest and embalmers. He was trained to cut from the left side of the abdomen in order to expose the cavity there. Puncturing the diaphragm he pulled out all of the internal organs except the heart, an essential aspect of the embalming process in all ages. The mortuary spells and rituals demanded a union between the heart and the body. Care was taken to preserve the heart from injuries and to keep it in its rightful place. When a heart was accidentally moved or damaged, the priests stitched it carefully again. Mummies studied have shown evidence of such surgical care. All of the other organs in the abdomen (with the exception of the kidney, which was normally left intact and in place) were removed. The lungs were placed in a canopic jar protected by HAPI. The stomach was placed in a canopic jar protected by Duamutef, the intestines were given to the care of QEBEHSENNUF, and the liver placed in the jar assigned to IMSETY. These were the Sons of Horus, the designated patrons of the organs of the deceased.

Each period of ancient Egypt witnessed an alteration in the various organs preserved. The heart, for example, was preserved separately in some eras, and during the Ramessid dynasties the genitals were surgically removed and placed in a special casket in the shapes of the god Osiris. This was performed, perhaps, in commemoration of the god's loss of his own genitals as a result of the attacks by the god SET, or as a mystical ceremony. Throughout the nation's history, however, the CANOPIC JARS (so named by the Greeks of later eras) were under the protection of the MESU-HERU, the Four Sons of Horus. These jars and their contents, the organs soaked in resin, were stored near the SARCOPHAGUS in the special containers.

The reason that the priests cleansed the abdomens of the corpses so quickly was that decay and putrefaction started there instantly. With the organs removed, the cavity could be cleansed and purified, handled without infection, and embalmed with efficiency. The use of natron was involved in the next step of the process. The Greeks reported that the mummies of the ancient eras were soaked in a bath of natron. It has been established, however, that the liquid form of the crystals would not only hinder the drying process but would add to the bloating and decay. The bodies were thus buried in mounds of natron in its dry crystal form. When the natron bath had dried the corpse sufficiently, the nails were tied on and finger stalls placed on the corpse. The natron bath normally lasted 40 days or more, producing a darkened, withered corpse. The temporary padding in the cavities was removed and stored in containers for use in the afterlife.

The corpse was washed, purified, and dried, and then wads or pads of linen, packages of natron or sawdust, were used to fill the various empty portions of the remains. Aromatic resins were also used to make the corpse fragrant. The outer skin of the mummy, hardened by the natron, was massaged with milk, honey, and various ointments. The embalming incision made in the abdomen was closed and sealed with magical emblems and molten resin. The ears, nostrils, eyes, and mouth of the deceased were plugged with various wads of linen, and in the case of royal corpses the tongue was covered with gold. The eyes were pushed back with pads and closed, and the body was covered with molten resin.

The cosmetic preparations that were part of the final stages of embalming included the application of gold leaf, the painting of the face, and the restoration of the eyebrows. Wigs were placed on some corpses, and they were dressed in their robes of state and given their emblems of divine kingship. In some periods the bodies were painted, the priests using red ochre for male corpses and yellow for the women. Jewels and costly AMULETS were also placed on the arms and legs of the mummies.

The actual wrapping of the mummy in linen (called "yesterday's linen" in the case of the poor, who could only provide the embalmers with used cloth), took more than two weeks. This was an important aspect of the mortuary process, accompanied by incantations, hymns, and ritual ceremonies. In some instances the linens taken from shrines and temples were provided to the wealthy or aristocratic deceased, in the belief that such materials had special graces and magical powers. An individual mummy would require approximately 445 square yards of material.

Throughout the wrappings semiprecious stones and amulets were placed in strategic positions, each one guaranteed to protect a certain region of the human anatomy in the afterlife. The linen bandages on the outside of the mummy in later eras were often red in color. Later eras provided royal bodies with glass net coverings or beaded blankets. The mummy mask and the royal collars were placed on the mummies last. The mask, called a CARTONNAGE, developed from earlier periods. Linen sheets were glued together with resins or gum to shape masks to the contours of the heads of the corpses, then covered in stucco. These masks fitted the heads and shoulders of the deceased. Gilded and painted in an attempt to achieve a portrait, or at least a flattering depiction of the human being, the masks slowly evolved into a coffin for the entire body. The entire process took from 70 to 90 days, although one queen of the Old Kingdom was recorded as having been treated for 272 days. When it was ended, the body was placed within its coffin, and the funerary rituals could begin.

The funeral processions started from the valley temple of the ruler or from the embalming establishment early in the morning. Professional mourners, called KITES, were hired by the members of the deceased's family to wear the color of sorrow, blue-gray, and to appear with their faces daubed with dust and mud, signs of mourning. These professional women wailed loudly and pulled their hair to demonstrate the tragic sense of loss that the death of the person being honored caused to the nation. Servants of the deceased or poor relatives who owed the deceased respect headed the funeral procession. They carried flowers and trays of offerings, normally flowers and foods. Others brought clothes, furniture, and the personal items of the deceased, while the SHABTIS and funerary equipment were carried at the rear. The *shabtis* were small statues in the image of the deceased placed in the tomb to answer the commands of the gods for various work details or services. With these statues available, the deceased could rest in peace.

Boxes of linens and the clothes of the deceased were also carried to the tomb, along with the canopic jars, military weapons, writing implements, papyri, etc. The TEKENU was also carried in procession. This was a bundle designed to resemble a human form. Covered by animal skins and dragged on a sled to the place of sacrifice, the *tekenu* and the animals bringing it to the scene were ritually slain. The *tekenu* would have symbolized the actual courtiers and servants sacrificed in the mortuary rituals of the Early Dynastic Periods royal clans. The *sem,* or mortuary priests, followed next, dressed in a panther or leopard skin and wearing the traditional white linen robe of his calling. The *sem* priest would be accompanied by a retinue of other priests, such as the *ka* priests and others, the actual embalmers. The coffin and the mummy arrived on a boat, designed to be placed on a sled and carried across the terrain. When the coffin was to be sailed across the Nile to the necropolis sites of the western shore, two women mounted on either side. They and the kites imitated the goddesses ISIS and NEPHTHYS, who mourned the death of Osiris and sang the original LAMENTATIONS.

The family and friends of the deceased, an entire populace if the mummy was that of a ruler or queen, followed on land or on separate barges across the river.

The hearse boat used for the crossing had a shrine cabin adorned with flowers and with the palm symbols of resurrection. During the crossing the *sem* priest incensed the corpse and the females accompanying it. The professional mourners sometimes rode on top of the cabin as well, loudly proclaiming their grief to the neighborhood.

The procession landed on the opposite shore of the Nile and walked through the desert region to the site, where the *sem* priest directed the removal of the coffin so that it could be stood at its own tomb entrance for the rituals. In later eras a statue of the deceased was used in its place. A *ka* statue was often used in the same ceremony, an image of the deceased with upraised arms extending from the head. The priest touched the mouth of the statue or the coffin and supervised the cutting off of a leg of an ox, to be offered to the deceased as food. All the while the MUU DANCERS, persons who greeted the corpse at the tomb, performed with harpists, the *hery-heb* priests, and *ka* priests, while incensing ceremonies were conducted.

The mummy was then placed in a series of larger coffins and into the sarcophagus, which waited in the burial chamber inside. The sarcophagus was sealed, the canopic jars put carefully away, and the doors closed with fresh cement. Stones were sometimes put into place, and seals were impressed as a final protection. A festival followed this final closing of the tomb.

These rituals did not apply to all Egyptian burials. The poor conducted similar ceremonies on the desert fringes, sometimes using cliff sites for tombs. Another custom that originated in the Early Dynastic Period and remained popular throughout Egypt's history was the burial at ABYDOS, the city of the god of the dead, Osiris. Burial in Abydos assumed such importance, in fact, that various rulers had to designate certain areas of the city's necropolis as reserved and had to limit the number of interments allowed on the various sites.

Once the body was entombed, the mortuary rituals did not end. The royal cults were conducted every day, and those who could afford the services of mortuary priests were provided with ceremonies on a daily basis. The poor managed to conduct ceremonies on their own, this being part of the filial piety that was the ideal of the nation. A daily recitation of prayers and commemorations was based on the Egyptian belief that any nameless creatures, unknown to the gods or people, ceased to exist at all. Thus the name of the deceased had to be invoked on a daily basis in order for that person to be sustained even in eternity.

Documents dating to the Middle Kingdom (2040–1640 B.C.E.) indicate that members of the royal family and the nome aristocrats endowed mortuary priests for rituals to be conducted on a perpetual basis at their tombs, providing stipends and expense funds. Entire families or clans of priests conducted such services, particularly in the pyramidal complexes of the rulers.

Such pyramid rituals were paid by the state, as part of the royal cult. Mortuary offerings were brought every day. These gifts were listed first in the LIST OF OFFERINGS, started in the Old Kingdom, and evolved into the LITURGY OF THE FUNERARY OFFERINGS.

In return, the priests performing these rites were given estates, ranks, and honors that could not be turned over to other priests, except in the case of a son inheriting his father's priestly rank and position. A legal system emerged from these contracts, which protected the deceased against rivalry or disputes among the priests endowed to perform perpetual offerings. If a mortuary priest sued another for more rights or properties, he lost every rank and honor that he possessed. If a particular priest stopped the mortuary services that had been requested and paid for, his order instantly assumed all of his benefits and material goods.

A symbol of the contracts made by the mortuary priests and the deceased were the TOMB BALLS, discovered in ancient Egyptian burial chambers. Such balls, made or bits of papyrus and linen, were marked with the hieroglyph for "seal" or "contract." They are believed to be symbols of the contracts drawn up between the priests and the family of the deceased or the person himself. They were deposited by the priests as tokens of good faith, binding their agreements by placing them before the *ka* of the dead.

The daily mortuary liturgies that were performed each morning by the priests, in keeping with their contracts, involved a greeting of the deceased. The mummy, or in most cases a statue, was placed on a small stand. The Opening of the Mouth ceremony was then performed. This involved touching the lips of the deceased with a special instrument designed to emit magical properties, the UR-HEKA. The statue was then purified and given gifts of food and adornments. The *Liturgy of the Funerary Offerings* contained more than 114 separate ceremonies. The purpose of the ritual was to change meat, bread, and wine into divine, spiritual substances for the deceased and the gods. This transmutation of offerings was documented in tombs as far back as the Fifth Dynasty (2465–2323 B.C.E.). It was also believed that the ritual could revitalize the senses and the various organs of the deceased. All was based on the resurrection of Osiris and on the basic creed that no human life was obliterated at the moment of death but transformed into shapes that accommodated the eternal environment. The ritual of mortuary sacrifice followed, as food and drink were offered to the deceased. This followed the custom of the early eras, when the ruler was obliged to present such an offering for each citizen.

The mortuary rituals thus embraced all aspects of death among the Egyptian people. The preparation for the tomb, in keeping with spiritual aspirations and religious doctrines, provided each Egyptian with the necessary physical properties to ensure eternal bliss. The funerary rituals were conducted with great dignity and earnestness, in order to deliver the corpse to the ap pointed site, where transformations could take place. The mortuary ceremonies secured for the Egyptians a guarantee that they would not be forgotten.

Further reading: David, Rosalie, and Rick Archbold. *Conversations With Mummies: New Light on the Lives of Ancient Egyptians.* New York: HarperCollins, 2000; Hodel-Hoenes, Sigrid, and David Warburton, transl. *Life and Death in Ancient Egypt: Scenes from Private Tombs in New Kingdom Thebes.* Ithaca, N.Y.: Cornell Univ. Press, 2000; Hornung, Erik, and David Lorton, transl. *The Ancient Egyptian Books of the Afterlife.* Ithaca, N.Y.: Cornell Univ. Press, 1999; Perl, Lila, and Erika Weihs. *Mummies, Tombs, and Treasure: Secrets of Ancient Egypt.* New York: Clarion, 1990; Taylor, John H. *Death and the Afterlife in Ancient Egypt.* Chicago: Univ. of Chicago Press, 2001; Thomas, Thelma K. *Late Antique Egyptian Funerary Sculpture.* Princeton: Princeton Univ. Press, 1999.

mortuary temples   Religious structures used in pyramid and tomb complexes as part of the royal cults, these temples were not made for the mummified remains of

The golden mortuary mask of King Tut'ankhamun *(Hulton Archive)*

the deceased pharaohs but for the daily rituals of the royal funerary cultic ceremonies. By the era of the Third Dynasty (2649–2575 B.C.E.), the mortuary temple was joined to the tombs. These cultic shrines were linked to the pyramids and then to the VALLEY TEMPLES by causeways.

AMENHOTEP I (r. 1525–1504 B.C.E.) of the Eighteenth Dynasty was the first pharaoh to understand that such temples drew attention to the royal tomb and promoted robberies and the vandalism of mummies during the looting. The custom of erecting mortuary temples at a distance from the tombs was followed by Amenhotep I's successors. Royal mortuary cults, especially those associated with Amenhotep I and his mother, Queen 'AHMOSE NEFERTARI, both deified, lasted well into the next dynastic periods. The mortuary temples of the rulers of the New Kingdom (1550–1070 B.C.E.) and that of MENTUHOTEP II (r. 2061–2010 B.C.E.) have been examined by modern archaeologists and cataloged.

The mortuary temple of KHAFRE (r. 2520–2494 B.C.E.) at GIZA represents the typical architectural design of these structures. Connected to the pyramid or standing directly beside the monument, the temple also had a causeway linking it to the Nile. Two pillared halls led to an elaborate court of statues. These monuments were placed in separate chambers. Storerooms, shrines, and a chapel completed the temple design. A FALSE DOOR, an offering table, and other ritual materials were discovered in the chapel.

mummies   *See* MORTUARY RITUALS.

mummy caches   The deposits of royal and court mummies discovered in 1881 and 1898, and the deposit of priestly remains found in 1830, 1858, and 1891, these mummies, rewrapped and reburied because of vandalism and tomb robberies, were placed in secure sites in the Twenty-first Dynasty (1070–945 B.C.E.) or in later eras. The high priests of AMUN in THEBES undertook this task out of piety and respect for the pharaonic ancestors of Egypt.

The mummies discovered in a tomb in DEIR EL-BAHRI, on the western shore of Thebes in 1881, possibly were originally stored in the tomb of a queen. They were some of the greatest pharaohs of Egyptian history. An inscription declares that they were reburied there in "the twentieth day of the fourth day of winter in the tenth year of PINUDJEM (1), the High Priest of AMUN."

The cache contained the coffins and mummies of the official Nebseni, 'Ahmose-In-Hapi, Duathathor-HENUTTAWY, SETI I, TUTHMOSIS I, AMENHOTEP I, and TUTHMOSIS II.

Also discovered in the cache were the mummies of TUTHMOSIS III, RAMESSES II, RAMESSES III, RAMESSES IX, TA'O II (Sekenenré) (d. 1555 B.C.E.), SIAMUN (2), and 'AHMOSE and the remains of queens 'AHMOSE HETTINEHU, 'AHMOSE MERTAMON, 'AHMOSE NEFERTARI, 'Ahmose Sit-kamose, MA'ATKARÉ, NESKHONS, NODJMET, and TAWERET. The princes and princesses found in the cache include 'AHMOSE HETEMPET, 'AHMOSE SIPAIR, NESITANEBTISHRU (2), and SITAMUN (1). Also discovered were Djedptahaufankh, MASAHARTA, PINUDJEM I, PINUDJEM II, RAI, and anonymous remains.

The cache discovered in the tomb of AMENHOTEP II in 1898 was accompanied by an inscription that declares that these royal remains were placed there "on the sixth day of the fourth month of winter in the twelfth year of Pinudjem (1)." The mummies found there include, TUTHMOSIS IV, AMENHOTEP III, SETI II, MERENPTAH, SIPTAH, RAMESSES V, RAMESSES IV, and RAMESSES VI. The mummy of an unknown woman was also discovered in the cache. She was placed in a coffin bearing the name of SETHNAKHTE.

In TANIS, the mummies of PSUSENNES I, AMENEMOPET, OSORKON I, TAKELOT II, and SHOSHENQ II were found. BAB EL-GUSUS, near DEIR EL-BAHRI, contained the sarcophagi of 153 high priests and lesser personnel of the temple of Amun. This discovery was made in 1891. In 1830 some 60 mummies were found in the same area. An entire field of mummies from the Roman era of Egypt has been uncovered at BAHARIA OASIS, an area now called the VALLEY OF THE GILDED MUMMIES.

Mursilis I (d. ca. 1600 B.C.E.) *ruler of the Hittites*
He was the grandson and successor of Hattusilis, who was on the throne during the last decades of Egypt's Middle Kingdom (2040–1640 B.C.E.). Militarily active, Mursilis destroyed Aleppo, then an Amorite city, and ended the dynasty of Hammurabi at Babylon. His activities endangered Egypt's trade systems and caused alarms as the Nile rulers recognized the growing power of the HITTITES. Withdrawing to the capital, Hattusas, Mursilis was murdered by a brother-in-law.

Mursilis II (d. ca. 1306 B.C.E.) *ruler of the Hittites*
The son of SUPPILULIUMAS I, he reigned from ca. 1334 B.C.E. until his death. He was the brother of ZANNANZA, who had been invited to Egypt by Queen ANKHESENAMON and then murdered while nearing Egypt. As a result, Mursilis II had no affection for Egyptians. Mursilis II stabilized his empire by controlling Syria, a prize desired by the Ramessids. There were also confrontations between the Egyptians and HITTITES in the border areas at the close of the Eighteenth Dynasty and the beginning of SETI I's reign (1306–1290 B.C.E.), but the major battles and subsequent treaty would come in the reign of RAMESSES II (1290–1224 B.C.E.), Seti I's heir.

music Recreational and religious instruments were integrated into every aspect of Egyptian life. The god Ibi was considered the patron of such instruments, but other deities, such as HATHOR, were involved in the playing of music in all eras. Hymns and processional songs were part of all religious rituals, and the Egyptians enjoyed musical groups and bands at festivals and at celebrations. On certain feasts the queen and royal women, accompanied by musicians and dwarfs, danced and sang to the god and to the ruler.

In the Old Kingdom (2575–2134 B.C.E.) and probably in Predynastic Periods, flutes, including the double flutes, and clarinet-type instruments were played. Men played large portable versions of the harp, an instrument that evolved into immense and highly decorated pieces. The first harps were held in the hands or on the musician's lap, but later harps were freestanding and weighty. Trumpets appeared in the Old Kingdom as well.

Middle Kingdom (2040–1640 B.C.E.) harps were accompanied by the SISTRUM. Rattles, tambourines, clappers, and a type of guitar were played as well. Cymbals and castanets remained popular from the Old Kingdom onward. The lute and lyre appeared during the Second Intermediate Period (1640–1532 B.C.E.), the era of the HYKSOS domination, and were probably introduced by the Asiatics when they invaded the Nile region. New Kingdom (1550–1070 B.C.E.) tombs have reliefs depicting the use of such instruments. The angular and arched harps were in vogue during the empire, as well as the large and small drums and oboe pipe. Sistrums added a certain tonal variation to performances, especially in tombs, and the heads of MENAT (1) necklaces were struck to maintain certain tempos. Other instruments came into Egypt as a result of the various foreign invasions after the fall of the New Kingdom.

The musical tones achieved by the musicians were dependent upon the instrument used. Horns were adapted for royal or military purposes, and the Egyptians appear to have relished a clamorous noise on such occasions. In private gatherings, the music was soft and quite melodic. The sistrum and the CLAPPER were designed as instruments to be used in cultic ceremonies. The clapper denoted alterations in the rhythm of such rites, and the sistrum was sacred to the goddess Hathor and used in other rituals as well.

Mut A highly revered goddess of Egypt, whose name is translated as "Mother," she was normally portrayed as a handsome woman wearing a patterned sheath dress and the double crown. Her cult dates to the early eras, and she was honored as the consort of the god AMUN in THEBES. Before this union she was believed to have given birth to the deities and to humans with her tears.

Mut nurtured the pharaohs and was reported to have promised the rulers "Millions and Millions of Years and Jubilees." She was called "the Lady of Asheru," the name of her temple at KARNAK, "the Mighty and the Great." In Thebes, she was the self-created mother of the god KHONS (1). The VULTURE was her hieroglyph, and she was "the Mistress of the Double Crown of Egypt." At KHARGA OASIS, Mut was depicted with a lion's head. She was also hailed as "the Mistress of the House," marking her a patroness of children and motherhood.

In the earliest historical periods, Mut took the form of a cow at HELIOPOLIS, to carry the newly emerged Amun on her back. Also called "the Eye of Ré," Mut could be revered in all historical periods in this form. In time she became the guardian deity of the GOD'S WIFE OF AMUN or the Divine Adoratrices of Amun.

Mutemwiya (fl. 14th century B.C.E.) *royal woman of the Eighteenth Dynasty*
She was a secondary wife of TUTHMOSIS IV (r. 1401–1391 B.C.E.) and the mother of AMENHOTEP III (r. 1391–1353 B.C.E.). She is believed to have been a member of a powerful family of AKHMIN. When Tuthmosis died, Amenhotep III was young and Mutemwiya stood as regent. She was buried at THEBES.

Mutnodjmet (1) (fl. 14th century B.C.E.) *royal woman of the Eighteenth Dynasty*
She was the consort of HOREMHAB (r. 1319–1307 B.C.E.). Possibly the sister of Queen NEFERTITI, Mutnodjmet was depicted in the tomb of PANHESI, an official of the era, with her DWARF attendants. Maya's tomb also portrays her and her retinue. Her mummy was recovered in Horemhab's original tomb at MEMPHIS, and there is evidence that she had given birth, although Horemhab had no heirs.

Mutnodjmet died in her mid-40s, probably in childbirth. The newborn was buried with her. Mutnodjmet was buried in SAQQARA in the original tomb constructed by Horemhab before his coronation. AMENIA, Horemhab's first wife, a commoner, was also buried there. A black granite statue of Mutnodjmet, depicted with Horemhab, is in Turin.

Mutnodjmet (2) (fl. 10th century B.C.E.) *royal woman of the Twenty-first Dynasty*
The consort of PSUSENNES I (r. 1040–992 B.C.E.), Mutnodjmet was the mother of AMENEMOPE (r. 993–984 B.C.E.), SIAMUN (r. 978–959 B.C.E.), and Prince ANKHEFENMUT. The tomb built for Mutnodjmet was not used but served as a receptacle for the remains of Amenemope. Mutnodjmet was buried with Ankhefenmut in Psusennes I's tomb in TANIS.

Mutnofret (1) (fl. 15th century B.C.E.) *royal woman of the Eighteenth Dynasty*
She was the mother of TUTHMOSIS II (r. 1492–1479 B.C.E.). Serving possibly as a lesser-ranked consort of TUTHMOSIS I, Mutnofret appears to have possessed some royal standing in her own right. She was honored as the "King's Mother," after bearing Tuthmosis II.

Mutnofret (2) (fl. 13th century B.C.E.) *royal woman of the Nineteenth Dynasty*
She was a lesser-ranked consort of RAMESSES II (r. 1290–1224 B.C.E.). Mutnofret was depicted in the temple site at ABU SIMBEL.

Muu Dancers Ritual performers who served in mortuary ceremonies from the earliest times in Egypt, the Muu Dancers were viewed as delegates from the realms beyond the grave and were honored during their performances as demi-gods. They were also associated with the SOULS OF PE, the legendary rulers before the unification of Egypt, ca. 3000 B.C.E. These performers did not speak during their appearances but gestured to be understood. There were three types of Muu Dancers involved in funerals.

The first group met or intercepted the funerary processions in progress in order to give permission for entrance into the necropolis area. These performers wore high green crowns made of reeds, fashioned into cones. They also wore elaborate kilts. The second group stood as watchers in the Muu halls positioned in major necropolises and decorated as beautiful parks. BUTO, along with SAIS and HELIOPOLIS, were considered sites leading to paradise and had extensive Muu halls. The Muu Dancers who attended funerals being conducted in the designated halls were accompanied by small orchestras when they performed. These dancers were also crowned with reeds and wore kilts. They performed in pairs as the agents of the god OSIRIS.

The third group represented the Predynastic Period ancestors at Pe or Dep, a part of the city of Buto, in the central Delta, where they were called "the People of Pe." These dancers wore floral crowns of papyrus fronds or were bareheaded. Deemed sacred while performing, the Muu Dancers of this group also served as "the Souls of Pe," in royal ceremonies. At every funeral the chief priest or steward called to them: "Come! Oh Muu!" The Muu Dancers sang and performed ancient and intricate dances, sanctioned by their unique roles.

Muwatallis (Muwatallish) (d. ca. 1282 B.C.E.) *Hittite ruler in the reign of Ramesses II (1290–1224 B.C.E.)*
He was born ca. 1306 B.C.E., the son of MURSILIS II, and reigned from ca. 1306 B.C.E. until his death. When RAMESSES II reconquered Palestine and made the Orontes River the new Egyptian imperial frontier, Muwatallis was compelled to defend his realm. He fought Ramesses II at KADESH, modern Syria, near Lake Homs, and the outcome was indecisive, although both sides claimed victory. The tensions and campaigns continued throughout his reign. Muwatallis was succeeded on the Hittite throne by his son, Mursilis III (Urshi-Teshub). Hattusilis, another son of Muwatallis, revolted and took the throne.

Muyet (fl. 21st century B.C.E.) *very young royal female of the Eleventh Dynasty*

She was a member of the court in the reign of MENTUHOTEP II (2061–2010 B.C.E.). Muyet was only five years old when she died and was buried in a tomb provided for her in the vast mortuary complex at DEIR EL-BAHRI. She was buried with five necklaces of great beauty and value. Her limestone sarcophagus did not proclaim her actual status, and it is assumed that she was a princess of the line or an intended bride of the ruler.

Mycerinus *See* MENKAURÉ.

myrrh Called *anti* by the ancient Egyptians, the aromatic plant was brought to Egypt from PUNT. The trees were planted on temple grounds, and the gum resin product of the plant was used in rituals as incense and as a perfume for the gods, available in several forms. The great mortuary complexes at DEIR EL-BAHRI were adorned with myrrh trees when they were first constructed.

Mysteries of Osiris and Isis A series of so-called miracle plays staged at ABYDOS at certain times of the year, the mysteries were performed in conjunction with festivals honoring OSIRIS and ISIS and were popular in all historical periods. The plays depicted the life, death, mummification, resurrection, and celestial enthronement of Osiris, as well as the faithful services of Isis. Special chapels were erected for the mysteries at DENDEREH, ESNA, EDFU, and PHILAE. Similar productions were staged solely for Isis in some eras.

N

Nagada (Naqada) This is a site north of THEBES, sometimes called Ombos or Nukt, and a vital resource of the Predynastic Period of Egypt, dating to 4000–3000 B.C.E. The Predynastic necropolises of el-Ballas and Nukh depict the evolutionary patterns of this historical period, which is studied as Nagada I (Amratian), Nagada II (Gerzean), and Nagada III. More than 3,000 graves were discovered in this area.

The Nagada I culture is evidenced at the sites where warriors were buried in simple oval pits with maceheads, grave goods, and symbols of hierarchical authority. In use from 4000 to 3500 B.C.E., these sites contained examples of pottery advances, including red-polished and painted varieties. Statuettes, palettes, and metalwork show a social diversity in this region.

The Nagada II culture, from 3500 to 3200 B.C.E., is displayed in elaborate grave sites, including coffins, mortuary regalia, and multiple burials. New pottery forms are evident, and there are depictions of boats on the site. Copper, gold, and silver were used, and there is an increase of stonework evident.

The Nagada III culture, 3200–3000 B.C.E., shows elite burial sites and the rise of cities. The SCORPION MACEHEAD and other artistic treasures date to this period. Some 2,000 graves dating to the First Intermediate Period (2134–2040 B.C.E.) are also at Nagada, which is located across from KOPTOS and WADI HAMMAMAT. A tomb from the Early Dynastic Period (2920–2575 B.C.E.) is on the site as well. Jar sealings bearing the names of AHA (Menes) (2920 B.C.E.), NARMER (3000 B.C.E.), and NEITHOTEP were discovered there. A step PYRAMID was constructed at Tukh, with a trapezoidal nucleus and a thick base. No temple was erected with the pyramid. Vast amounts of pottery were found at Nagada, representing styles in use for some 1,500 years. These wares clearly define historical and artistic changes. Both the elite and commoners were buried at Nagada.

Nakare-Aba (fl. 22nd century B.C.E.) *ruler of the obscure Eighth Dynasty*
His pyramid was discovered in the southern SAQQARA complex of PEPI II. The dates of his actual reign are unknown, but his rule would have been brief, considering the era. Nothing else has been documented about him, as this dynasty ruled in the midst of unrest and political change and held only limited territories.

Nakhsebasteru (fl. sixth century B.C.E.) *royal woman of the Twenty-sixth Dynasty*
She was the consort of AMASIS (r. 570–526 B.C.E.) and second in rank to Queen LADICE, the Great Wife of the reign. Possibly a daughter of APRIES, who was overthrown by Amasis in a military coup, she was not the mother of the intended heir but added credence to Amasis's reign.

Nakht (1) (fl. 19th century B.C.E.) *mortuary official of the Twelfth Dynasty*
He served as the mayor of the mortuary complex of SENWOSRET III (r. 1878–1841 B.C.E.) at ABYDOS. The son of Khentikheti, Nakht, along with other members of his family, including Neferhor, Amenisoneb, and Sehetepibe, resided at the site called "Enduring Are the Places of Kha'kauré (Senwosret III) Justified in Abydos."

Nakht supervised the temple complex of the dead pharaoh, maintaining the royal cult ceremonies there and providing the required daily offerings and commemorations. This task was assumed by the family and fulfilled until the close of the Middle Kingdom Period with generations of caretakers and mortuary priests involved. The mayoral residence provided for Nakht was vast, with a columned hall, chambers, a courtyard, and a granary. Large towns developed at the mortuary structures of the rulers in order to sustain the vast number of priests and servants committed to the continuation of service in the royal cults.

See also MORTUARY RITUALS.

Nakht (2) (fl. 15th century B.C.E.) *priestly official and court astronomer of the Eighteenth Dynasty*
He served TUTHMOSIS IV (r. 1401–1391 B.C.E.) as a priest-astronomer and as the chief steward of the royal granaries and vineyards. Nakht charted astronomical changes that related to the agricultural seasons on the Nile. Such astronomical observances were vital to the inundation preparations each year, as the flooding Nile inundated entire regions of the valley and displaced countless numbers of Egyptians.

His tomb at SHEIKH ABD 'EL-QURNA in THEBES is noted for its paintings, although the structure is small. Tawi, Nakht's wife, was a chantress in the temple of AMUN, and she shared Nakht's tomb. The painting of the "Blind Harper" makes Nakht's tomb noteworthy. Other paintings depict banquets and daily routines. The eyes of Nakht in such portraits were scratched out, an act that the Egyptians believed would render him blind in the realms beyond the grave. This vandalism indicates Nakht's fall from power or the presence of a powerful enemy in the region.

Nakhthoreb (d. ca. 343 B.C.E.) *probably the last ruler of the Thirtieth Dynasty*
He was slain or deposed by the Persians, who started their second period of occupation on the Nile in 343 B.C.E. A magnificent SARCOPHAGUS intended for Nakhthoreb's burial was discovered in ALEXANDRIA. During his reign he erected a temple honoring OSIRIS and served APIS in the SERAPEUM territory at SAQQARA. The Persians ended this royal line but were fated to meet ALEXANDER III THE GREAT (r. 332–323 B.C.E.) and to lose Egypt and their other imperial domains forever.

Nakhtmin (1) (fl. 14th century B.C.E.) *military officer and possible prince of the Eighteenth Dynasty*
Nakhtmin may have been the son of AYA (2) (r. 1323–1319 B.C.E.) and Queen TEY. Aya, the successor of TUT'ANKHAMUN, married ANKHESENAMON, the young widow of Tut'ankhamun, but she disappeared soon after, and Tey, a commoner, assumed the role of Great Wife. Tey was married to Aya before his ascension.

Nakhtmin was a military general and was chosen by Aya as his heir but did not succeed him. He was put aside by HOREMHAB and not allowed to inherit the throne. Horemhab became the last pharaoh of the dynasty. A beautiful statue of a woman, dating to this period, has been identified as the wife of General Nakhtmin, presumably this official.

Nakhtmin (2) (fl. 13th century B.C.E.) *military official of the Nineteenth Dynasty*
Serving RAMESSES II (r. 1290–1224 B.C.E.), he was a noble of ABUSIR. Nakhtmin was the chief of military chariots and an ad hoc foreign ambassador. His TOMB, located in a cliff necropolis dating to the fifth century, is near Abusir. This tomb was designed as a multileveled gravesite. The structure had a large courtyard with nine roof supports and a limestone floor. Four small chambers were also discovered near the main hall. The walls were painted blue and green and depicted scenes from the *Book of the Gates,* a mortuary document.

names An aspect of Egyptian life with magical implications in all periods of the nation's history, names were essential to continued existence on the earth or beyond. Anyone without a name did not survive. The recitation of a name provided continued existence, especially to the dead. Thus, many annual festivals were held to honor ancestors and to recite their names aloud in rituals.

Priests were also contracted to perform rituals at the tomb sites that included the recitation of the names, ranks, and honors of the deceased. This reliance upon continued recognition on the earth for eternal survival was especially true for the royal Egyptians, who had a series of ROYAL NAMES with mystical powers.

See also VALLEY FESTIVAL.

Nanefer-ka-Ptah (fl. 13th century B.C.E.) *royal prince of the Nineteenth Dynasty*
A son of MERENPTAH (r. 1224–1214 B.C.E.), Nanefer-ka-Ptah was made famous by an Egyptian magical tale concerning the prince's discovery of the magical book of the god THOTH. He made a copy of the book, washed off the ink with beer, and then drank the brew. This allowed him to absorb the wisdom of the erased words. The Book of Thoth was supposedly a repository of vast amounts of occult and magical texts, revered by the priests. Nanefer-ka-Ptah's wife was Princess Ahura, and his son was Merab. The family was buried in KOPTOS.

See also MAGIC.

naos This was a Greek word that denoted a small shrine or sanctuary intended to house the image or symbols of a particular deity. In Egypt such shrines were made out of stone or wood and were not open to general worshippers. A *naos* was normally rectangular in shape and could be used for mortuary statues and the mummified remains of animals deemed as theophanies or symbols associated with the particular god. Only high-ranking priests of the cults could enter these sacred precincts.

Napata   This is a site below the third cataract of the Nile, in modern Dongola, in the Sudan, where the river makes dramatic loops in its progress. Napata is the site of a spectacular flat-topped mountain, called "the Holy Mount" or "the Table of Amun."

See also GEBEL BARKAL.

Narmer (fl. ca. 3000 B.C.E.) *one of the last Predynastic rulers associated with the unification of Upper and Lower Egypt*

Narmer is believed to have come from a royal family that at one time resided in HIERAKONPOLIS, a capital and shrine city of the god HORUS in the Predynastic Period of Egypt. He followed in the footstep of SCORPION I and others who tried to subdue the Delta. Scorpion I moved the capital of his reign to THINIS, and Narmer began his unification campaigns from that city.

A PALETTE discovered at Hierakonpolis depicts Narmer's efforts. A ceremonial MACEHEAD, also discovered in that city, depicts Narmer as capturing 120,000 men, 400 oxen, 1,422,000 goats, and the standards of the Delta nomes. After this victory, Narmer is believed to have married a Memphite female aristocrat in order to consolidate his gains. Queen NEITHOTEP was possibly that noble heiress. She is named in some lists as the mother of AHA (called Menes), the first ruler.

Narmer sent an expedition into the eastern desert, and his inscription was discovered on the rocks of WADI QASH, on the KOPTOS TRADE route. He was probably buried in SAQQARA or in the necropolis at TARKHAN. A cenotaph bearing his insignia was discovered in ABYDOS. The actual unification of Egypt was not accomplished until sometime around the close of the Second Dynasty (ca. 2640).

Narmer macehead   A symbolic weapon, dating to the unification of Egypt, ca. 3000 B.C.E., and signifying victory and power, the macehead of Narmer was found in HIERAKONPOLIS and now is in the Ashmolean Museum at Oxford. The Narmer macehead was probably used by the unifier of Upper and Lower Egypt in celebrations of the *heb-sed* ceremonies, the anniversary rituals popular in all historical eras as part of the state royal cults. Narmer is depicted in a tight cloak, wearing the red crown of Lower Egypt, a symbol of military victory over the northern territories. A woman, possibly NEITHOTEP, is shown being brought to Narmer in a palanquin as a tribute of the conquered Delta, although some scholars identify the figure as the ruler of the city of Buto.

Narmer Palette   A ceremonial vessel, also called Narmer's Victory Palette, that was discovered in HIERAKONPOLIS, the palette was designed for ceremonial use or for grinding antinomy, the popular cosmetic. Narmer is depicted wearing the war CROWN of Upper Egypt and the red wicker crown of Lower Egypt on this palette, signifying that he had conquered the territory in the north. Narmer is also shown as a BULL (a royal symbol), destroying a city with his horns and trampling the enemy troops under his hooves.

On the reverse side of the palette two fallen figures lie before him, probably representing the cities of SAIS and MEMPHIS. The god HORUS is shown coming to the king's aid by bringing prisoners to him. The palette, made of schist, is an important historical and artistic text and is now in the Ashmolean Museum at Oxford.

See also ART AND ARCHITECTURE.

Narmouthis (Narmonthis, Medinet Wadi)   This is a site on the southern edge of the FAIYUM, now modern Medinet Wadi. A temple dating to the Twelfth Dynasty was discovered at Narmouthis, erected in honor of the deities SOBEK and RENENUTET by AMENEMHET III (r. 1844–1797 B.C.E.). The temple is rectangular and contains HYPOSTYLE HALLS and papyrus COLUMNS, as well as a sanctuary with three chapels and a central shrine dedicated to Renenutet. The Twelfth Dynasty pharaohs were also honored there in deified forms.

The Ptolemaic Dynasty (304–30 B.C.E.) refurbished the temple at Narmouthis and added a processional way with lions and sphinxes, a kiosk, a portico, and transverse vestibule. Sandstone is the main material used throughout.

natron   A mildly antiseptic substance that has the ability to absorb moisture, it was used in all periods of ancient Egypt, associated especially with the processes of embalming and mummification. It was called *net-jeryt*, "Belonging to the God"; *besmen,* the name of a local god; or *besmen desher,* denoting a red variety of natron that was hygroscopic. It was found in WADI NATRUN, near modern Cairo, also called the Natron Valley, and in Upper and Lower Egyptian sites. Natron is a mixture of sodium bicarbonate and sodium carbonate or sodium chloride.

The substance was originally used as a detergent and as a tooth cleaner, and in some eras as a glaze for early craft wares. In time natron was used as the main preserving agent for mortuary rituals. The basic ingredient for embalming, natron was the steeping substance for drying corpses and preventing decay. It was used in its dry crystal form, and mummy linens were sometimes soaked in natron before wrapping. Natron was also formed into balls and chewed at certain religious ceremonies by the rulers or their priest representatives. When the substance was used in these rituals, natron represented the transformed state assumed by the dead in the paradise beyond the grave.

See also MORTUARY RITUALS.

Natron Lakes They were series of water deposits in the WADI NATRUN, near modern Cairo. The Wadi Natrun served as a source of NATRON, a major element in the embalming processes of MORTUARY RITUALS in all times of ancient Egypt.

natural resources The natural materials available to Egyptians in the Nile Valley and surrounding regions provided a vast array of metals, gems, and stones over the centuries. Nearby lands, easily controlled by Egyptian forces, especially in the period of the empire, held even greater resources, all of which were systematically mined or quarried by the various dynasties. These resources included.

agate a variety of chalcedony (silicon dioxide), colored in layers of red or brown, separated by graduated shades of white to gray. Agate was plentiful in Egypt from the earliest eras. It was called *ka* or *hedj* and was found in the deserts with jasper. Some agate was brought from PUNT and NUBIA (modern Sudan).

alabaster a lustrous white or cream-colored calcite (calcium carbonate), called *shés* by the Egyptians. Alabaster was quarried at HATNUB and at other eastern Nile sites. The stone was used in jewelry-making and in the construction of sarcophagi in tombs.

amethyst a translucent quartz (silicon dioxide) that is found in various shades of violet. Called

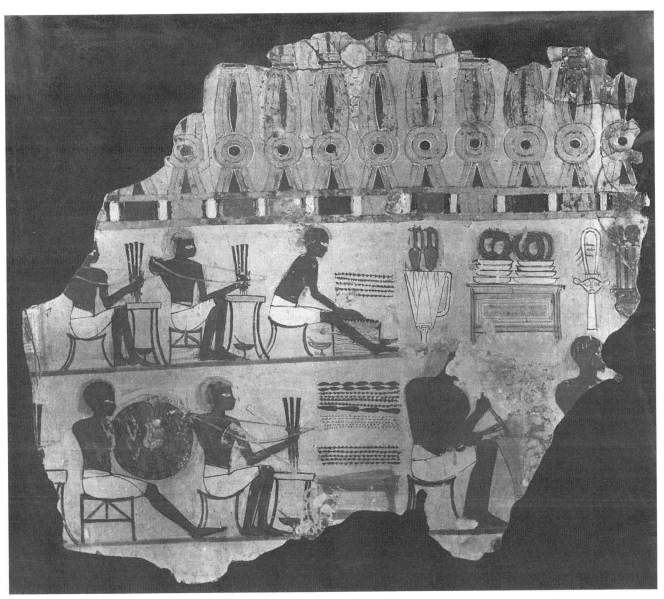

Skilled metalworkers displayed on a painted wall using pigments derived from the rich metals exploited in various mines, part of Egypt's rich natural resources *(Hulton Archive)*

Natural Resources of Ancient Egypt

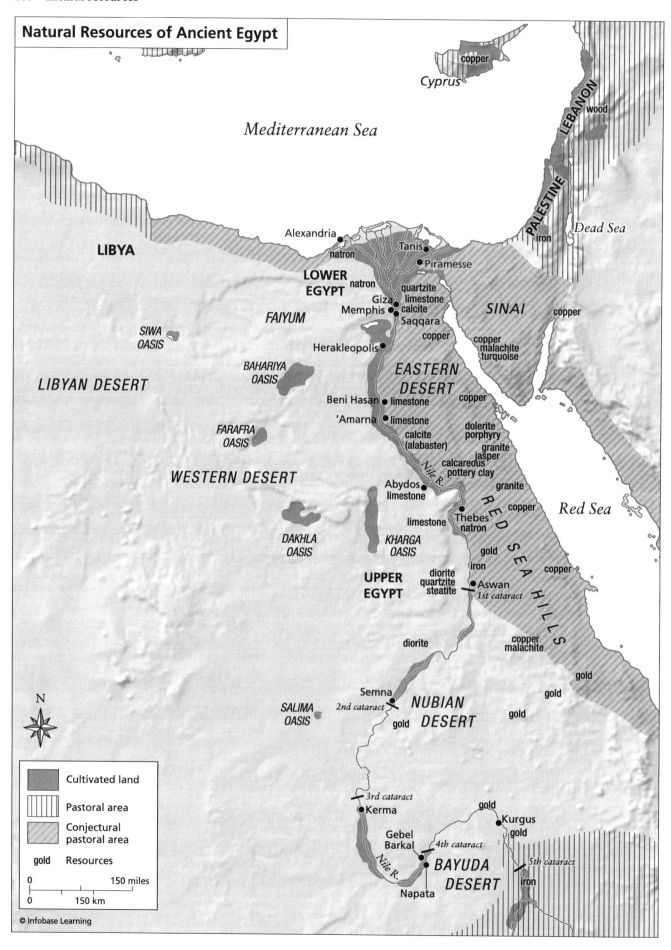

Mediterranean Sea

Cyprus copper

LEBANON wood

PALESTINE

Dead Sea

Alexandria iron

LIBYA natron Tanis

Piramesse

LOWER EGYPT natron

quartzite

limestone **SINAI** copper

Giza calcite

FAIYUM Memphis Saqqara

copper copper

SIWA OASIS malachite

turquoise

Herakleopolis

EASTERN DESERT

BAHARIYA OASIS

LIBYAN DESERT Beni Hasan limestone copper

'Amarna limestone

dolerite

FARAFRA OASIS calcite porphyry

(alabaster) granite

jasper

calcareous

pottery clay

WESTERN DESERT Abydos

limestone granite

Red Sea

copper

limestone Thebes

natron

DAKHLA OASIS *KHARGA OASIS*

gold

iron copper

UPPER EGYPT diorite

quartzite Aswan

steatite *1st cataract*

copper

N diorite malachite

gold

SALIMA OASIS Semna **NUBIAN** gold

2nd cataract **DESERT**

gold gold

3rd cataract gold

Kerma Kurgus

Gebel gold

Barkal *4th cataract*

BAYUDA *5th cataract*

Nile R. **DESERT** iron

Napata

	Cultivated land
	Pastoral area
	Conjectural pastoral area
gold	Resources

0 ___ 150 miles

0 ___ 150 km

© Infobase Learning

hesmen, the stone was quarried at Wadi el-Hudi near ASWAN in the Middle Kingdom Period (2040–1640 B.C.E.) and at a site northwest of ABU SIMBEL.

beryl   a translucent or transparent yellow-green stone formed by aluminum-beryllium silicate. Called *wadj en bakh,* the "green stone of the east," beryl was brought from the coast of the Red Sea during the Late Period.

carnelian   a translucent form of chalcedony that was available in colors from red-brown to orange. The stone was mined in the eastern and Nubian desert and was called *herset.* Carnelian was highly prized as rare and valuable and was used for heads, amulets, and inlays.

chalcedony   a translucent bluish-white type of quartz (silicon dioxide) called *herset hedji.* Chalcedony was mined in the eastern desert, the BAHARIA OASIS, and the FAIYUM. Some chalcedony was also found in Nubia and in the SINAI.

copper   a metal mined in the Wadi Maghara and in the Serabit el-Khadim of the Sinai region. Called *hemt,* copper was also found in meteorites and was then called *baa en pet.*

diorite   a hard igneous rock, speckled black or white. Found in ASWAN quarries, diorite was called *mentet* and was highly prized.

electrum   a metal popular in the New Kingdom Period (1550–1070 B.C.E.) although used in earlier times. Electrum was a naturally occurring combination of gold and silver. It was fashioned into the war helmets of the pharaohs. It was called *tjam (tchem),* or white gold, by the Egyptians; the Greeks called it electrum. The metal was highly prized, particularly because silver was scarce in Egypt. Electrum was mined in Nubia and was also used to plate obelisks.

faience   a decorative material fashioned out of fired quartz-paste with a glazed surface. The crushed quartz (silicon dioxide), mined at Aswan or in Nubia, was coated either blue or green. A substitute for turquoise, faience was used for many decorative objects.

feldspar   an orange semiprecious stone now called "Amazon Stone." When feldspar was a true green in color it was called *neshmet.* It was mined in the desert near the Red Sea or in the Libyan desert territories.

garnet   a translucent iron, or a silicate stone, mined near the Aswan area and in some desert regions. Garnet was called *hemaget* by the Egyptians and was used from the Badarian Period (ca. 5500 B.C.E.) through the New Kingdom Period.

gold   the favorite metal of the Egyptians, who started mining the substance as early as the First Dynasty (2920–2770 B.C.E.). Gold was mined in the eastern deserts, especially at WADI ABBAD near EDFU, and the Nubian (modern Sudanese) sites were the main sources. In later eras, other nations sent gold to Egypt as tribute. Gold was called *nub* or *nub nefer* when of the highest grade and *tcham (tjam)* when in the form of electrum.

hematite   an iron oxide that was opaque black or grayish black. The Egyptians called it *bia* and mined the substance in the eastern deserts and at Aswan and in the Sinai.

jasper   a quartz (silicon dioxide), available in green, yellow, and mottled shades, called *khenmet* or *mekhenmet.* Jasper was mined in the eastern deserts. The stone normally formed ISIS amulets and was used from the earliest eras.

limestone   an opaque calcium carbonate with varieties ranging from cream to yellow to pink to black. Found in the Nile hills from modern Cairo to ESNA, the stone was called *hedj* in the white form. White limestone was quarried in the TUREH area and was found as black in the eastern desert and pink in the desert near EDFU.

malachite   an opaque, emerald green copper carbonate found near the copper mines of Serabit el-Khadim and the WADI MAGHARA in the Sinai. Called *shesmet* or *wadj,* malachite was also found in Nubia and in the eastern desert.

marble   a crystalline limestone quarried in the eastern desert and used for statuary and stone vessels. Marble was called *ibhety* or *behet* by the Egyptians.

mica   a pearl-like potassium-aluminum silicate with iron and magnesium. Mica can be fashioned into thin sheets and was popular in the Middle Kingdom (2040–1640 B.C.E.). It was found in Nubia, and was called *pagt* or *irgeb.*

obsidian   a translucent volcanic glass that was probably quarried in Ethiopia (PUNT) or Nubia. Called *menu kem* when dark in color, obsidian was used for amulets and scarabs and for the eyes of statues.

olivine   a translucent magnesium-iron silicate found in many Egyptian regions. Called *perdjem,* olivine was used for beads and decorations.

onyx   with sardonyx, varieties of chalcedony, found in the eastern desert and other Nile Valley sites. Onyx beads were used in the Predynastic Period (before 3000 B.C.E.) and became popular in the Late Period (712–332 B.C.E.).

peridot   a transparent green or yellow-green variety of olivine that was probably brought into Egypt. No mining sites are noted. Peridot was called *perdjem* or *berget.*

porphyry   an igneous rock formation of various shades. The black variety was used in early eras, and the purple variety was popular as amulets and pendants.

quartz a hard, opaque silicon dioxide quarried in Nubia and near Aswan. Called *menu hedj* or *menu kem,* quartz was used for inlays, beads, and jewelry. Quartzite was found near HELIOPOLIS and at GEBEL EL-AHMAR.

rock crystal a hard, glasslike quartz of silicon dioxide found in the Nile Valley between the Faiyum and the BAHARIA OASIS and in the Sinai region. It was called *menu hedj,* when white.

silver a rare and highly prized metal in Egypt, called *hedj,* white gold. Silver was mined as electrum, called *tcham* or *tjam* in the WADI ALAKI, WADI MIAH, and in Nubia.

steatite a magnesium silicate, called soapstone. Steatite was found in the eastern desert from the WADI HAMMAMAT to the WADI HALFA and in Aswan. It was used extensively for scarabs and beads.

turquoise a stone treasured by the Egyptians, found beside copper deposits in the Wadi Maghara and Serabit el-Khadim in the Sinai. Called *mefkat,* turquoise was used in all eras, with the green variety preferred.

Naukratis (el-Nigrash; Kom Gi'eif) This is a site on the Canopic branch of the Nile in the western Delta, the modern Kom Gi'eif. The site originated in the Twenty-sixth Dynasty as the result of the trading privileges that PSAMMETICHUS I (r. 664–610 B.C.E.) gave Greek merchants, mostly Milesians, including permission to establish a trade center at Naukratis. AMASIS (r. 575–526 B.C.E.) granted these Greeks a series of trade monopolies during his reign, further enhancing Naukratis. The city was actually founded ca. 630 B.C.E., and the name of the site meant "ship power." Temples were erected to Greek deities and to the Egyptian gods AMUN and THOTH. Naukratis flourished until ALEXANDER III THE GREAT (r. 332–323 B.C.E.) founded the new capital of ALEXANDRIA.

Greek silver and Greek slaves were popular wares in Naukratis, and courtesans, taverns, and other amusements were plentiful. Coins minted in Naukratis aided in modernizing Egypt's financial system, and the Greeks conducted a large SCARAB industry in the city, becoming adept at producing a variety of fetish tokens and amulets. Recovered deity figures and pottery provide information about Greek imports and trade systems in the city.

See also TRADE AND EXCHANGE.

Nauri Decree A document issued by SETI I (r. 1306–1290 B.C.E.) in the fourth year of his reign, this decree was promulgated on behalf of the workers at Osiris's holy city of ABYDOS, where the king was in the process of constructing his great mortuary complex. The Nauri Decree incorporated prior legal codes, particularly the laws of HOREMHAB (r. 1319–1307 B.C.E.), serving as a charter for the temple and for its various estates, and it was designed to ensure the maintenance of the king's mortuary cult after his death. The workers were subject to a stern code of behavior while they built the tomb, with penalties for crimes clearly delineated.

The decree points to a troubled time during Seti I's reign that reflected earlier dynastic weaknesses. Normally, workers on the mortuary complexes of the rulers would not have required warnings or threats in order to regulate their behavior. Construction sites of early periods were deemed places of spirituality and dedication. In this period, however, conformity to the ideals of the nation had partially lessened and the impact of the mortuary rituals had declined. Severe physical punishments were included in this code. Certain crimes brought the punishment of 100 blows by a lash, the creation of five open wounds, the removal of a criminal's nose, or exile to the LIBYAN DESERT or beyond.

neb (1) An Egyptian symbol, it represents the act of obeisance or prostration performed by people before a ruler or the image of a deity.

neb (2) A hieroglyph translated as the word *all,* it was used on AMULETS and *ANKH* insignias to denote unity under the pharaoh and the gods.

Nebamun (1) (fl. 14th century B.C.E.) *Theban police official of the Eighteenth Dynasty, possibly a Medjay*
He served TUTHMOSIS IV (r. 1401–1391 B.C.E.) and AMENHOTEP III (r. 1391–1353 B.C.E.) as a commander of the Theban police force. Nebamun was probably a MEDJAY, a member of the mercenary unit that served the New Kingdom (1550–1070 B.C.E.) pharaohs in military campaigns. In times of peace the Medjay served as POLICE units in the capital and major cities. Nebamun was buried in THEBES. His STELA depicts Queen NEBETU'U (2), a lesser-ranked consort of TUTHMOSIS III (r. 1479–1425 B.C.E.).

Nebamun (2) (fl. 14th century B.C.E.) *official royal court sculptor of the Eighteenth Dynasty*
He served AMENHOTEP III (r. 1391–1353 B.C.E.) as a sculptor and was held in high esteem for his contributions to the ongoing building projects of the ruler. Nebamun's tomb was erected on the western shore of THEBES near DEIR EL-BAHRI and was shared with a fellow artist, IPUKI.

Nebamun (3) (fl. 13th century B.C.E.) *royal vizier of the Nineteenth Dynasty*
He served SETI I (r. 1306–1290 B.C.E.) as VIZIER, a demanding role as Seti I was revitalizing the nation and bringing stability to the land. Nebamun was buried on the western shore of THEBES with royal honors in gratitude for his loyalty and services to the throne.

Nebemakhet (fl. 25th century B.C.E.) *princely vizier of the Fourth Dynasty*
The son of KHAFRE (r. 2520–2494 B.C.E.) and Queen MERYSANKH (3), Nebemakhet did not succeed his father but became a priest for the royal cult. His tomb was built in the royal cemetery, and he is depicted in his mother's rock-cut tomb in GIZA. He is also recorded as serving for a time as vizier for MENKAURÉ (r. 2490–2472 B.C.E.). Nebemakhet's tomb is noted for paintings depicting jewelry workers of the era, already capable of using a variety of metals and gemstones.

Nebenteru (Ter) (fl. 13th century B.C.E.) *priestly official of the Nineteenth Dynasty*
He served both SETI I (r. 1306–1290 B.C.E.) and RAMESSES II (r. 1290–1224 B.C.E.) as high priest of AMUN. Nebenteru was a NOME aristocrat who was appointed high priest in the seventeenth year of Ramesses' reign. He was a descendant of the KHETY clan of the Ninth and Tenth Dynasties. Nebenteru's son, PASER (2), became vizier in the same period. In some lists Nebenteru is simply called Ter. He was the successor of NEBWENEF as high priest.

Neberu (fl. 15th century B.C.E.) *prince and military official of the Eighteenth Dynasty*
He served TUTHMOSIS III (r. 1479–1425 B.C.E.) as chief of the royal stables, a high-ranking post in this era of cavalry units, military campaigns, and imperial expansion. His tomb is in the VALLEY OF THE QUEENS on the western side of the NILE at THEBES. The portrait of him on the lid of his coffin bears a striking resemblance to Neberu's actual mummified remains.

Nebet (fl. 24th century B.C.E.) *royal woman of the Fifth Dynasty*
A consort of UNIS (r. 2356–2323 B.C.E.), she was buried with Queen KHENUT near the mortuary temple of Unis's pyramidal complex at SAQQARA. Nebet's MASTABA tomb was beautifully decorated and contains a painted scene depicting her in a seated position, smelling a lotus blossom.

Nebetku (fl. ca. 29th century B.C.E.) *court official of the First Dynasty*
Nebetku served DEN (reign uncertain) as a court steward. His tomb in the northern section of SAQQARA was altered twice during its construction, reflecting the emerging styles of the period. The tomb was designed as a pyramid originally but eventually became a MASTABA, indicating architectural aspirations that could not be accomplished at the time.

Nebetu'u (1) A goddess worshiped in ESNA, she was considered a form of the popular deity HATHOR. Nebetu'u was addressed as "the Mistress of the Territory." Her cult was not long-standing or well known in the Nile Valley.

Nebetu'u (2) (fl. 15th century B.C.E.) *royal woman of the Eighteenth Dynasty*
She was a lesser-ranked consort of TUTHMOSIS III (r. 1479–1425 B.C.E.). Nebetu'u died at a young age. She was depicted on a mortuary stela discovered in the tomb of an official of a later reign, NEBAMUN (1), perhaps denoting some sort of familial relationship. She was possibly the daughter of Prince Setum of the royal family.

Nebireyeraw (Swadjenré; Nebiryaw I) (fl. 17th century B.C.E.) *ruler of the Seventeenth Dynasty*
Nebireyeraw controlled THEBES and Upper Egypt and was a contemporary of the Hyksos ruler KHIAN, whose capital was at AVARIS. Nebireyeraw, also listed as Nebiryaw I, is noted for his stela at KARNAK. This monument commemorates the sale of a hereditary governorship at ELKAB (Nekheb) and deals with legal matters concerning the role of the vizier. The dates of his reign are uncertain, but he probably succeeded SOBE KEMSAF I.

Nebka (Zanakht; Neferkaure; Nebku; Sanakht; Zanakhte) (d. 2630 B.C.E.) *founder of the Third Dynasty of Egypt*
He ruled from 2649 B.C.E. until his death. The name Zanakht means "Strong Protection." A brother of his successor, DJOSER, Nebka had a reign that was militarily active. He exploited the SINAI, mining there for copper and turquoise, and his name was found inscribed at WADI MAGHARA. His royal seals were also found on ELEPHANTINE Island, and he was mentioned in a tomb at BEIT KHALLAF, north of ABYDOS.

Nebka was probably buried to the west of Djoser's STEP PYRAMID at the vast mortuary complex at SAQQARA. He was mentioned in the WESTCAR PAPYRUS, and his mortuary cult was popular for decades in the region.

Nebseni Papyrus This is an Egyptian mortuary text, older than the famed ANI PAPYRUS. Now in the British Museum, Nebseni's Papyrus is 76 feet long by one foot wide. It is a mortuary commemorative document, a revised version of the original, following the Theban changes of the later periods, called a RECENSION. The texts included in the papyrus are sometimes outlined in black. An address of the god HORUS to his father, the god OSIRIS, is included in the document. The papyrus was discovered in DEIR EL-BAHRI in 1881.

Nebt (fl. 21st century B.C.E.) *noblewoman and heiress of the Eleventh Dynasty*
Nebt was the heiress to the estates of the ELEPHANTINE Island at ASWAN. The mother of Princess NEFERU-KHAYET (2), who become a consort of MENTUHOTEP II (r. 2061–2010 B.C.E.), Nebt held a unique position in her own right. She was a patroness of the arts and retained librarians and scholars on her estates. Nebt held the rank

of NOME princess and was commemorated on a STELA erected in her territory.

Nebti Name   *See* ROYAL NAMES.

Nebt-Tawy (1) (fl. 13th century B.C.E.) *royal woman of the Nineteenth Dynasty*
A lesser-ranked consort of RAMESSES II (r. 1290–1224 B.C.E.), she was probably the mother of Nebt-Tawy (2). Nebt-Tawy was buried in the VALLEY OF THE QUEENS.

Nebt-Tawy (2) (fl. 13th century B.C.E.) *royal woman of the Nineteenth Dynasty*
She was the daughter of RAMESSES II (r. 1290–1224 B.C.E.) and probably Queen NEBT-TAWY (1). Nebt-Tawy was buried in the VALLEY OF THE QUEENS on the western shore of Thebes. She was interred in the tomb of an unknown royal woman named Tanedjemy.

Nebuchadnezzer (d. 562 B.C.E.) *Chaldean ruler of Babylon and a foe of Egypt*
He was the son of Nabopolassar and was born ca. 630 B.C.E. Nebuchadnezzer defeated NECHO II (r. 610–595 B.C.E.) of the Twenty-sixth Dynasty in the battle of CARCHEMISH in Syria. This defeat ended Egypt's involvement in that region. Nebuchadnezzer was a prince when he defeated Necho II and the Egyptian forces.

He succeeded his father and expanded his influence and dominance in the region until his death in 562 B.C.E. He is viewed as the greatest member of his dynasty, as Babylon flourished during his reign because of his military skills.

Nebusemekh   A character in an Egyptian short story that was discovered on a number of OSTRACA and dated to the Ramessid Period (1307–1070 B.C.E.). The tale concerns a meeting between the ghost Nebusemekh and the high priest of AMUN, Khomsehab, at Thebes. Nebusemekh relates his earthly status in the service of a ruler of the Seventeenth Dynasty, RAHOTEP (2) (ca. 1640 B.C.E.). This ruler supervised Nebusemekh's burial, but his tomb was eventually destroyed.

The tale is not complete in the ostraca, but Khomsehab appears to have found a new tomb site for Nebusemekh at DEIR EL-BAHRI, on the western shore of Thebes. The work is called a "ghost story" in modern collections, but it is not chilling or eerie. The Egyptians did not fear the spirits of the dead and made efforts to communicate with them in all historical periods.

See also ANCESTOR CULT LETTERS; LITERATURE.

Nebwawi (fl. 15th century B.C.E.) *priestly official of the Eighteenth Dynasty*
Nebwawi was the high priest of OSIRIS at ABYDOS in the reigns of TUTHMOSIS III (1479–1425 B.C.E.) and AMENHOTEP II (1427–1401 B.C.E.). He served HATSHEPSUT (r. 1473–1458 B.C.E.) in several capacities but managed to stay in favor with her successors. On occasion, Nebwawi was summoned to the court to serve as a counselor to the pharaohs, as his advice was valued. His mortuary STELA provides details of his life, and a statue was erected in THEBES in his honor. Another stela honoring Nebwawi was found in ABYDOS.

Nebwenef (fl. 13th century B.C.E.) *priestly official of the Nineteenth Dynasty*
He served in the reign of RAMESSES II (1290–1224 B.C.E.). Nebwenef was the high priest of AMUN and the first prophet of HATHOR and ANHUR, an exalted rank in the temple system. Priests were often required to assume positions beyond their original offices, especially if they were competent. His mortuary temple was built near Seti I, whom he had served at the beginning of his career. Nebwenef's tomb depicted Ramesses II and Queen NEFERTARI making the announcement of his appointment as high priest. Nebwenef retired at an advanced age and was succeeded in his office in the temple and in the royal court by NEBENTERU.

Nebyet (fl. 22nd century B.C.E.) *royal woman of the Eighth Dynasty*
The daughter of NEFERKU-HOR (reign uncertain), she was the wife of SHEMAY, the vizier of the reign. Documents from the ancient city of KOPTOS relate the power of Shemay and the marriage. Another text attests to the appointment of a new man named Kha'redni as her bodyguard. He was given the rank of commandant of soldiers. Shemay's power outlived the reign of Neferku-Hor.

Necho I (Nekau I) (d. 664 B.C.E.) *founder of the Twenty-sixth Dynasty*
He ruled from 672 B.C.E. until his death in SAIS and was called Nekau in some lists. Necho I was possibly a descendant of a Libyan prince of an earlier era and assumed royal titles for himself and his line. ASSURBANIPAL, the Assyrian king who invaded the territory ca. 667 B.C.E., found Necho I to be a cultured, realistic individual. As a result, Assurbanipal spared him and his son, PSAMMETICHUS I.

Necho I remained the ruler in SAIS even as TAHARQA (r. 690–664 B.C.E.) won Egypt's independence. When TANUTAMUN (r. 664–657 B.C.E.), the Nubian leader, began a campaign of his own to establish his rule in Egypt, Necho I became the Nubian's main target for revenge. When the two met in battle, Necho I was slain.

Necho II (Wehemibré) (d. 595 B.C.E.) *third ruler of the Twenty-sixth Dynasty*
He reigned from 610 B.C.E. until his death. The son of PSAMMETICHUS I and Queen MEKHTEMWESKHET (2), Necho II supported the Assyrians as buffers to the Per-

sian advances. He also sponsored military programs and refurbished the Egyptian navy with Greek mercenaries and vessels. Necho II even sent a fleet of hired Phoenicians to successfully circumnavigate Africa.

Necho II had military successes until ca. 605 B.C.E., when Prince NEBUCHADNEZZER, the heir to the throne of Babylon, defeated the Egyptians at CARCHEMISH. Necho II withdrew from his military interventions and built a grain TRADE system with Greece to spur the Nile Valley economy. He dug a canal, called the SWEET WATER CANAL, at WADI TIMULAT through the Pelusiac Nile, to link the Nile to the Red Sea. He also built Per-Temu-Tjeju, modern Tell el-Mashkuta, on the canal. Necho II also controlled all of the western OASES. Necho II was buried in a tomb in SAIS by his son and heir, PSAMMETICHUS II.

Nectanebo I (Kheperkaré) (d. 362 B.C.E.) *founder of the Thirtieth Dynasty*
He ruled from 380 B.C.E. until his death. Nectanebo I was a military commander from SEBENNYTOS, the son of General Djehor. Named Nakhtnebef at birth, he served HAKORIS (r. 393–380 B.C.E.) and NEPHRITES II (r. 380 B.C.E.) and assumed the throne when the latter died. He also married PTOLEMAIS (1), the daughter of the Greek General KHABRIAS, and a woman named Audjashu, who was his Great Wife.

Egypt was almost invaded by the Persian army during Nectanebo I's reign, led by PHARNABAZUS, the Persian satrap of the region, but the Nile armies proved victorious. Nectanebo I's son, TEOS, led a campaign in Syria and Palestine during this military action. Actually, the Persians and their Greek mercenaries had the advantage in this confrontation, but Pharnabazus and the Greek general Iphikrates quarreled and lost the campaign in the eastern Delta.

Nectanebo I built in KARNAK and PHILAE, revived the sacred animal cults, and constructed or refurbished monuments at EDFU, HERMOPOLIS MAGNA, and MENDES. A STELA discovered in ABYDOS depicts him offering to the gods MA'AT and THOTH. He also built an avenue of sphinxes at the temple of THEBES. A black granite stela from NAUKRATIS documents Nectanebo I's decree granting the temple of the goddess NEITH the right to collect one-tenth of all goods brought into the city from other countries. Nectanebo I also erected a black granite NAOS, a small shrine, to the goddess Neith (1) in DAMANHUR in the Delta. Teos served as coruler for the last three years of Nectanebo I's reign and buried his father in Sebennytos.

Nectanebo II (Senedjemibre'setepenahur) (d. 343 B.C.E.) *third ruler of the Thirtieth Dynasty*
He usurped the throne from his uncle TEOS, who was considered unfit by the royal family, and reigned from 360 B.C.E. until his death. Nectanebo II, who was named Nakhthoreb at birth, is believed to be the last native ruler of Egypt. He was the grandson of NECTANEBO I and a nephew of Teos. When Teos was on a military campaign, Nectanebo II's father, Tjahepimu, declared him the rightful ruler. The Spartan ruler AGESILAUS aided Nectanebo II in overthrowing Teos, who fled to the Persians.

ARTAXERXES III OCHUS attacked Egypt in 350 but was repulsed by Nectanebo II's armies. Nectanebo II then turned his attention to the Nile Valley and refurbished and rebuilt cities and temples. He rebuilt at BEHBEIT EL-HAGAR, ERMENT, BUBASTIS, and SAQQARA. He also built a gate at PHILAE. Nectanebo II was active in the bull cults of his era. He buried the sacred animals at Erment and rebuilt the BUCHEUM.

In 343, Artaxerxes III Ochus attacked Egypt again, defeating Nectanebo II at Pelusium. He fled to NUBIA but then returned to SEBENNYTOS. When he died he was to be buried at Sebennytos or at Rhakotis, the future city of ALEXANDRIA. A tomb prepared in SAIS was never used, but his black granite SARCOPHAGUS was later taken to Alexandria to be used as a public bath.

A legend developed about Nectanebo II after his death. It was stated that he went to Macedonia and attracted OLYMPIAS, the wife of King Philip, seducing her. ALEXANDER III THE GREAT was supposedly the offspring of that affair, thus making him eligible to rule Egypt as a true pharaoh.

Nefer (1) This was the hieroglyphic symbol for both "good" and "beautiful," in both the material and spiritual sense.

Nefer (2) This was an AMULET used by ancient Egyptians to promote happiness and good fortune. *Nefer* amulets were placed on the areas of the stomach and windpipes of mummies in order to protect these organs.

Neferefré (Ra'neferef) (d. 2416 B.C.E.) *ruler of the Fifth Dynasty*
The successor of SHEPSESKARÉ (Ini; 2426–2419 B.C.E.), Neferefré reigned from 2419 B.C.E. until his death. He was possibly the son of KAKAI (Neferirkaré) and Queen KHENTAKAWES (2). He is also listed in some records as a son of SAHURÉ. Neferefré built a sun temple at ABU GHUROB and sent an expedition to the SINAI. His unfinished pyramid at ABUSIR contained a cache of papyri and plaques. Wooden boats, statues of prisoners, and sculptures were also uncovered there. The papyri discovered dealt with cultic rituals and the personnel serving the pyramid.

Neferhent (1) (fl. 19th century B.C.E.) *royal woman of the Twelfth Dynasty*
She was a consort of SENWOSRET II (r. 1897–1878 B.C.E.). Her tomb in el-LAHUN contained two MACEHEADS, fash-

ioned out of granite and quartz. Neferhent was the mother of SIT-HATHOR YUNET.

Neferhent (2) (fl. 19th century B.C.E.) *royal woman of the Twelfth Dynasty*

She was a consort of SENWOSRET III (r. 1878–1841 B.C.E.) but was not the mother of the heir. Neferhent was buried in DASHUR in a MASTABA tomb in the vast royal complex of the reign.

Neferhetepes (fl. 26th century B.C.E.) *royal woman of the Fourth Dynasty*

She was the daughter of RA'DJEDEF (r. 2528–2520 B.C.E.) and possibly Queen HETEPHERES (2). Neferhetepes is believed to have been the mother of USERKHAF, the founder of the Fifth Dynasty. A beautiful bust of Neferhetepes is in the Louvre in Paris. She is recorded as having married a priest of Ré, "the Lord of Sokhebu," near ABU ROWASH. Neferhetepes was mentioned in the WESTCAR PAPYRUS. She was called "the King's Daughter of His Body, Prophetess of Ra'djedef."

Neferhetepes (2) (fl. 25th century B.C.E.) *royal woman of the Fifth Dynasty*

The daughter of KAKAI (Neferirkaré; r. 2446–2426 B.C.E.), she married an official named Ti. Neferhetepes's sons were allowed to inherit the rank of prince, despite their commoner father.

Neferhetepes (3) (fl. 25th century B.C.E.) *royal woman of the Fifth Dynasty*

She was a consort of USERKHAF (r. 2465–2458 B.C.E.) and probably his sister. Neferhetepes was possibly the mother of SAHURÉ. A tomb inscription depicts Neferhetepes as receiving offerings from the temple of PTAH.

Nefer-Horen-Ptah (fl. 24th century B.C.E.) *official of the Fifth Dynasty whose tomb has become famous because of its paintings*

He was buried in a small rock-cut site below the causeway of the burial complex of UNIS (r. 2356–2323 B.C.E.) in SAQQARA. Called the TOMB OF THE BIRDS, Nefer-Horen-Ptah's resting place was never completed or used. The structure, however, contains magnificent friezes depicting the capture and caging of the wild birds of the Nile Valley.

Neferhotep (1) (fl. ca. 18th century B.C.E.) *noted harpist in the late Twelfth or Thirteenth Dynasty*

Neferhotep's life and ability were memorialized on a small but beautifully carved mortuary stela that was donated by a friend, Nebsumenu. The stela was discovered in the tomb of a powerful courtier, Iki. Neferhotep is described on the monument as "True of Voice, Born of the Housewife Henu." The funerary monument depicts Neferhotep as a rather stout harpist enjoying bread, beer, meat and fowls, alabaster, and linen, all anticipated aspects of life beyond the grave.

See also MUSIC.

Neferhotep (2) (fl. 14th century B.C.E.) *official of the Eighteenth Dynasty*

He served both AYA (2) (r. 1323–1319 B.C.E.) and HOREMHAB (r. 1319–1307 B.C.E.) as the chief scribe of AMUN and superintendent of the royal domain. Neferhotep's tomb near DEIR EL-BAHRI on the western shore of THEBES is magnificently decorated and contains compelling images. He is greeted there as one "intent upon eternity, as you go to the land where all is changed."

Neferhotep (3) (fl. 13th century B.C.E.) *official of artisans at Deir el-Medina in the Nineteenth Dynasty*

Neferhotep was the chief workman at DEIR EL-MEDINA on the western shore of Thebes, in the reign of AMENMESSES, who usurped the throne in the reign of SETI II (r. 1214–1204 B.C.E.). Deir el-Medina was a community dedicated to providing the necropolis called the VALLEY OF THE KINGS with skilled artisans and craftsmen. During this period, the community was led by Neferhotep and prospered until his son, Paneb, threatened him.

Unable to control his son, who had some power in the court of Amenmesses, Neferhotep went before Vizier Amenmose, who judged the case. As a result, Amenmose was removed from office, and Paneb was given Neferhotep's position as chief worker at Deir el-Medina by Amenmesses. Paneb raped, stole, and took bribes until Amenmesses died and Seti II was restored to the throne. Paneb was then dismissed from Deir el-Medina.

Neferhotep I (Kha'sekhemré) (d. ca. 1730 B.C.E.) *ruler of the Thirteenth Dynasty*

He reigned from ca. 1741 B.C.E. until his death or possible retirement. Neferhotep I was the son of one Ha'ankhaf and the Lady Kemi. His father is portrayed in an ASWAN rock inscription as a priest, and his mother is described as "royal." Neferhotep I's consort was Queen SENEBSEN. He was the brother of SOBEKHOTEP IV and SAHATHOR (1). His cartouche was discovered in BYBLOS, modern Lebanon, and Prince Yantin of that city was a vassal of Egypt.

Neferhotep I ruled the entire Delta region, with the exception of XOIS and the HYKSOS territories of AVARIS. An Aswan inscription describes Neferhotep's search for a proper stone for a statue of OSIRIS. Such a statue was carved and taken to ABYDOS. Neferhotep I then closed the necropolis to more public burials and erected a STELA declaring his intent. People from all across Egypt brought their deceased loved ones to Abydos to inter them in the god Osiris's domain in order to provide them with eternal bliss. The crown finally had to control the number of individual burials in the area, and Neferhotep was one of several rulers who made such restrictions over the centuries. His portrait statue is in the museum in Bologna, Italy. He also participated in the Osirian Passion Plays. Neferhotep I's son was Wahnefer-Hotep, whose shabtis, miniature tomb figures believed to act as proxies for the deceased in the Underworld, were found in el-LISHT. Another son, Ha'ankhaf, died young. Records indicate that Neferhotep I was succeeded by SAHATHOR and then by SOBEKHOTEP IV.

Neferhotep III (Sekhemre'sankhtawy) (fl. 17th century B.C.E.) *one of the last rulers of the Thirteenth Dynasty*
His date of reign is unknown. A stela in KARNAK mentions his aid to the temples and shrines of Thebes. He is supposed to have worn the *khepresh,* the war CROWN made of ELECTRUM. This appears to be the first reference to that particular style of royal headdress. Neferhotep III conducted military campaigns against the HYKSOS, but the Asiatics were in full control of their Delta territories by that time.

Neferirkaré   *See* KAKAI.

Neferkara (fl. ca. 27th century B.C.E.) *obscure ruler of the Second Dynasty*
He was possibly the seventh in that line, but his date of reign is unknown. MANETHO, the Ptolemaic Period (304–30 B.C.E.) historian, states that Neferkara ruled for a quarter of a century. He is also on the Abydos KING LIST. The contemporary comment on Neferkara was that "the Nile flowed with honey for eleven days during his reign. . . ."

Neferkau (fl. 21st century B.C.E.) *royal woman of the Eleventh Dynasty*
She was probably a consort of INYOTEF II (r. 2118–2069 B.C.E.), who ruled only Thebes and Upper Egypt at the time. Neferkau's name was discovered on a shaft dug in the tomb of Inyotef II at el-TARIF, on the shore at THEBES.

Neferkhewet (fl. 15th century B.C.E.) *highly skilled artistic official of the Eighteenth Dynasty*
He served HATSHEPSUT (r. 1473–1458 B.C.E.) as royal architect. Her reign sponsored tremendous building projects in both the north and the south, and many talented individuals worked to provide splendid monuments throughout the Nile Valley. Neferkhewet's tomb on the western shore of THEBES provides documentation of his accomplishments and his honors as a servant of the court. Also honored are his wife, Ren-nefer, and his son, Amenenhet.

Neferku-Hor (Neterybau, Kapu-Yeby) (fl. 22nd century B.C.E.) *fourteenth ruler of the obscure Eighth Dynasty*
Neferku-Hor issued four decrees in one afternoon during his first year of rule, the dates of which are unknown. One decree lists the titles of his eldest daughter, NEBYET; a second orders the construction of a solar bark for the deity Horus-Min; and another provides honors for the house of SHEMAY, the vizier who married Nebyet. Shemay's family outlived Neferku-Hor.

Neferku-Min (Neferes) (fl. 22nd century B.C.E.) *obscure ruler of the Eighth Dynasty*
Listed in the TURIN CANON, Neferku-Min ruled less than two and one half years, but the dates of his reign are unknown.

Neferkuré (fl. 2150 B.C.E.) *founder of the Eighth Dynasty*
Neferkuré reportedly was a son or grandson of PEPI II and Queen ANKHNES-PEPI. He is listed in the TURIN CANON as having a reign of four years and two months, but the actual dates are not documented. Neferkuré built a small PYRAMID in SAQQARA. He also buried Queen Ankhnes-Pepi in a borrowed sarcophagus. His pyramid was named "enduring is the life of Neferkuré."

Neferma'at (fl. 26th century B.C.E.) *royal prince of the Fourth Dynasty*
He was the son of SNEFRU (r. 2575–2551 B.C.E.) and Princess NEFERT-KAU, Snefru's daughter, who became her father's consort. Neferma'at married Princess Itet or Atet, and their son was HEMIUNU, the vizier of KHUFU. Neferma'at was buried at MEIDUM. The famous Meidum Geese, the exquisitely painted fowls, were discovered in Princess Itet's tomb. Neferma'at also served as the vizier of Khufu and supervised the construction of the Great Pyramid at GIZA. The Fourth Dynasty maintained control by only using royal family members in positions of authority.

Neferperet (fl. 16th century B.C.E.) *building official of the Eighteenth Dynasty*
He served 'AHMOSE (NEBPEHTIRÉ) (r. 1550–1525 B.C.E.) as the superintendent of royal building projects. Neferperet directed the quarrying of stone at MASARA, south of modern Cairo. He also brought limestone to THEBES from HYKSOS ruins in the Delta. Used for the temples of PTAH and AMUN at OPET, the stone was carried on sledges. In an inscription on the walls of a Masara quarry, Neferperet announced that 'Ahmose opened the site in the 22nd year of his reign. He also describes himself as a hereditary prince and as a "Sole Companion of the King." Neferperet was buried in Thebes.

Neferrenpet (fl. 13th century B.C.E.) *vizier of the Nineteenth Dynasty*
He served RAMESSES II (r. 1290–1224 B.C.E.) as a treasury scribe and VIZIER. Neferrenpet's name and portrait were discovered in the Speos of HOREMHAB at GEBEL EL-SILSILEH. His tomb in THEBES depicts him as tallying pieces of jewelry. This relief is the last detailed account of the manufacture of jewelry in the New Kingdom Period

(1550–1070 B.C.E.), a time of exquisite workmanship, using a variety of metals and gemstones. Neferrenpet traveled throughout Egypt to maintain order in his role of vizier.

Nefer-rohu's Prophecy An Egyptian text attributed to a sage in the reign of SNEFRU (2575–2551 B.C.E.) but actually dating to the Twelfth Dynasty (1991–1783 B.C.E.), it is contained in the Leningrad Papyrus. Nefer-rohu, seeing the chaos engulfing Egypt at the end of the Old Kingdom, announced: "A king shall come from the south (Upper Egypt) . . . called Ameni. . . ." This prophecy was probably a propaganda device for AMENEMHET I (r. 1991–1962 B.C.E.), a usurper of the throne. He is described as a savior of Egypt and reportedly the son of a "Woman of Nubia."

Nefer-rohu also predicted the raising up of the WALL OF THE PRINCE, the series of fortresses on the eastern and western borders of the Delta, to defend Egypt from marauding nomadic tribes, especially in the northeast. The prophecy has also been found on tablets and ostraca, indicating that it was used in Egypt's educational system for centuries after it was first made public on the Nile. Nefer-rohu was a lector priest at BUBASTIS in the reign of Amenemhet I.

Nefersekheru (fl. 14th century B.C.E.) *court official of the Eighteenth Dynasty*
He served AMENHOTEP III (r. 1391–1353 B.C.E.) as a steward of the royal palaces. Amenhotep III had several royal residences in THEBES, including MALKATA, the great pleasure complex on the western shore. Malkata was a small city made of palaces and shrines and boasted a man-made lake. Nefersekheru was buried at Thebes. The royal families of that historical period used Thebes and MEMPHIS as capitals, but Amenhotep III preferred Thebes and his pleasure palaces there.

Nefert (Nofret; Nefertet) (fl. 19th century B.C.E.) *royal woman of the Twelfth Dynasty*
She was a consort of SENWOSRET II (r. 1878–1841 B.C.E.). Two black granite statues portraying Nefert have been discovered. One shows her wearing a headdress of the goddess HATHOR. She was the daughter of AMENEMHET II and was praised as "the ruler of all women." Nefert was buried in the royal cemetery complex at el-LAHUN.

Nefertari Merymut (fl. 13th century B.C.E.) *beloved royal woman of the Nineteenth Dynasty*
She was the consort of RAMESSES II (r. 1290–1224 B.C.E.) and his favorite wife. Nefertari Merymut is believed to have been the daughter of BAKENKHONSU or some other official of the court. She married Ramesses II when he was 15 and she died in the 24th year of his reign. A tomb fragment also connects Nefertari Merymut to the family of AYA (2) (1323–1319 B.C.E.), and she is believed to have

The monument honoring Queen Nefertari Merymut, the favorite consort of Ramesses II (r. 1290–1224 B.C.E.); this temple is at Abu Simbel. *(Courtesy Steve Beikirch)*

come from Thebes. Her brother, Amenmose, was the mayor of Thebes.

Nefertari Merymut was the mother of Princes Amenhirwonmef, Prehirwonmef, and Meryré, as well as Princesses Meryatum and Hentawi. None of her sons succeeded their father, as he outlived them, but they served in various capacities.

A temple in ABU SIMBEL honored Nefertari Merymut, who was deified while she lived. The temple was dedicated to the goddess HATHOR. Nefertari Merymut probably retired to the harem palace at MI-WER in the FAIYUM soon after the Abu Simbel temple was dedicated. While serving as the Great Wife, she took an active role in court affairs and corresponded with the families of foreign rulers. She was the constant companion of Ramesses II throughout their marriage, and he honored her in life and in death.

Her tomb in the VALLEY OF THE QUEENS at Thebes is one of the largest and most beautifully decorated sites in that necropolis. The tomb has an entry stairway and a central ramp. The interior is bi-level, and reliefs and paintings are elaborate and beautiful, depicting Nefertari Merymut in mortuary rituals and in daily routines of life. The burial chamber has pillars and annexes. The entire tomb is now being restored, having suffered considerable damage over the centuries.

Nefertem An Egyptian deity, called "the Lord of the Lotus Blossoms," and "the Protector of the Two Kingdoms," Nefertem was a sun god whose cult was established early in MEMPHIS. His name indicates that he was the personification of TEM (1) at HELIOPOLIS, the solar cult center. He was the son of PTAH and SEKHMET, forming the Memphite trinity. At HELIOPOLIS he was considered the son of BASTET, and in BUTO he was called the son of WADJET. Nefertem was portrayed as a young man wearing an open LOTUS flower crown with feathers and ornaments. The lotus was a symbol of creation and resurrection and played a role in the cosmogonic traditions of Egypt. In Heliopolis, Nefertem was depicted as the setting sun, and at other sites he was shown as a lion. The lotus was his symbol and perfumes were sacred to him. Nefertem was associated with RÉ in some cultic rituals.

Nefertiabet (fl. 26th century B.C.E.) *royal woman of the Fourth Dynasty*
She was a princess of the royal family, a daughter of KHUFU (r. 2551–2528 B.C.E.). Her mastaba at GIZA contains her portrait depicting her in the leopard skin of a priestess. A stela also commemorated Nefertiabet's service to Egypt in the cultic ceremonies maintained by the royal court.

Neferti's Prophecy   *See* NEFER-ROHU'S PROPHECY.

Nefertiti (fl. 14th century B.C.E.) *one of the most famous royal women of the Eighteenth Dynasty*
She was the consort of AKHENATEN (r. 1353–1335 B.C.E.) and a leading figure at 'AMARNA. Her name meant "the Beautiful Woman Has Come," and she is one of the most beloved and famous of all ancient Egyptians. Nefertiti's sculpted bust in the Egyptian Museum in Berlin is one of the best known of all Egyptian treasures. Little information is available concerning her origins, although there has been a great deal of speculation about her family ties. She may have been the daughter of AYA (2), the successor of TUT'ANKHAMUN. Her sister was possibly MUT-NODJMET (1), who married HOREMHAB, the last pharaoh of the dynasty.

In the fourth year of Akhenaten's reign, she appeared with him at the site of Akhetaten (el-'AMARNA), the city dedicated to the god ATEN. In the sixth year of Akhenaten's reign, Nefertiti's name was changed again to reflect the cult of Aten. Nefertiti lived with Akhenaten in 'Amarna, where he conducted religious ceremonies to Aten. They raised six daughters, but no sons. One of the daughters, Maketaten, died giving birth to a child, probably sired by her father, and the couple's grief was depicted in wall paintings. Nefertiti disappeared from the court after that. There is some evidence that she remained in 'Amarna, living in a villa called HAT-ATEN, but another daughter replaced her as the pharaoh's principal wife. SMENKHARÉ, who became Akhenaten's successor in 1335 B.C.E., reportedly assumed Nefertiti's religious name, leading to the speculation that Nefertiti actually played this role at the 'Amarna court. She was called Neferneferu-Aten, "the Exquisite Beauty of the Sun Disk."

A granite head and other unfinished portraits of Nefertiti have survived. In the Aten temple at KARNAK, Nefertiti is shown smiting Egypt's enemies. Her funerary regalia, along with the remains and effects of other 'Amarna royal family members, were removed from 'Amarna burial sites during the reign of Tut'ankhamun, but her mummified remains have not been identified. She outlived Akhenaten but probably did not have political power because she represented a period that was being reviled across Egypt. When Smenkharé died, Nefertiti reportedly served as a counselor for the young Tut'ankhamun during his brief reign. What happened to her after he died is not documented. She remains a symbol of Egypt's beauty and mystery.

Nefert-kau (fl. 26th century B.C.E.) *royal woman of the Fourth Dynasty*
She was both the daughter and consort of SNEFRU (r. 2575–2551 B.C.E.). Nefert-kau bore Snefru a son, Prince NEFERMA'AT, who served later pharaohs in the high offices of the court restricted to the royal family during this period. She was probably the daughter of Queen HETEPHERES (1).

Neferu (1) (fl. 21st century B.C.E.) *royal woman of the Eleventh Dynasty*
She was the sister and consort of MENTUHOTEP II (r. 2061–2010 B.C.E.), being the daughter of MENTUHOTEP I and Queen AOH (Yah). With Queen TEM (2), Neferu served as a *hemet*, or Great Wife. She was buried just north of the main DEIR EL-BAHRI complex of the pharaoh, and her gravesite was covered by HATSHEPSUT'S (1473–1458 B.C.E.) structures.

Neferu's tomb contained a chapel, sloping corridor, and a burial chamber. The walls were decorated with limestone and reliefs. The site became an ancient pilgrimage destination during the New Kingdom era. Hatshepsut's builders opened a passageway to Neferu's tomb chapel, which was visited by many devout Egyptians of the period.

Neferu (2) (fl. 20th century B.C.E.) *trade official of the Twelfth Dynasty*
Neferu served SENWOSRET I (r. 1971–1926 B.C.E.) as overseer of transportation and TRADE in NUBIA (modern Sudan), particularly in the region surrounding the fortress at BUHEN, south of the first cataract of the Nile. Buhen was fortified and served as an important garrison for protecting the expanding trade of the Middle Kingdom (2040–1640 B.C.E.) during Neferu's term of office. His mortuary STELA provides information about this historical period and is in the British Museum in London.

Neferu-Khayet (1) (fl. 21st century B.C.E.) *royal woman of the Eleventh Dynasty*
She was the consort of INYOTEF II (r. 2118–2069 B.C.E.) and the mother of INYOTEF III. Neferu-Khayet was the grandmother of MENTUHOTEP II, the unifier of Egypt in 2061 B.C.E. The Inyotef line ruled THEBES before Men-

tuhotep II marched on the Delta clans to end their powers. Neferu-Khayet was buried at Thebes.

Neferu-Khayet (2) (fl. 21st century B.C.E.) *royal woman and nome heiress of the Eleventh Dynasty*
She was a consort of MENTUHOTEP II (r. 2061–2010 B.C.E.) and a powerful nome aristocrat in her own right. Neferu-Khayet was the daughter of Princess NEBT, an heiress of ELEPHANTINE Island. A learned woman with considerable wealth, Neferu-Khayet maintained libraries and artworks as the Elephantine Island ranking woman.

Neferukheb (fl. 15th century B.C.E.) *royal woman of the Eighteenth Dynasty*
The daughter of TUTHMOSIS I (r. 1504–1492 B.C.E.) and Queen 'AHMOSE, Neferukheb was the elder sister of HATSHEPSUT, outranking her in the court. She died, however, before she could become politically powerful. Neferukheb was buried in THEBES.

Neferu-ptah (1) (fl. 19th century B.C.E.) *royal woman of the Twelfth Dynasty*
She was probably the sister of AMENEMHET III (r. 1844–1797 B.C.E.). Neferu-ptah was buried in a mud-brick pyramid in the HAWARA royal mortuary complex near the LABYRINTH. Her mortuary regalia, including jewelry and silver pieces, have been recovered, although her tomb was flooded and her sarcophagus was destroyed.

Neferu-ptah (2) (fl. 20th century B.C.E.) *royal woman of the Twelfth Dynasty*
She was the daughter of SENWOSRET I (r. 1971–1926 B.C.E.). An ivory wand bearing her name was discovered in Senwosret I's tomb. Neferu-ptah was buried near her father's pyramid at el-LISHT.

Neferu-Ré (fl. 15th century B.C.E.) *royal woman of the Eighteenth Dynasty*
She was the daughter of TUTHMOSIS II (r. 1492–1479 B.C.E.) and Queen-Pharaoh HATSHEPSUT (r. 1473–1458 B.C.E.) and possibly the consort of TUTHMOSIS III (r. 1479–1425 B.C.E.). Her most important role, however, was as the GOD'S WIFE OF AMUN, and she was educated to be a political partner to Hatshepsut when she assumed the throne as a female ruler.

SENENMUT, the powerful temple ally of Hatshepsut, and 'AHMOSE-PEN NEKHEBET were her official tutors. Senenmut was also named as her steward and as "Great Father Nurse." Six statues of Senenmut and Neferu-Ré have been discovered, as well as a statue of her as a young woman. A SINAI tablet refers to her as "King's Daughter, King's Wife." She reportedly gave birth to a son and heir, Amenemhet, but the child died in infancy.

Neferu-Ré aided Hatshepsut's reign and remained in the palace, even as Tuthmosis III was overshadowed by his stepmother and moved to MEMPHIS to maintain the great naval base there, called PERU-NEFER. Neferu-Ré died, however, in the 16th year of Hatshepsut's reign, weakening the queen-pharaoh.

Her tomb in a high cliff area on the western shore of Thebes contained a yellow quartzite sarcophagus but was never used. Neferu-Ré's body has not been found, but a CARTOUCHE was discovered near the site. She was depicted on the walls of a small temple as a God's Wife of Amun and was being trained as Hatshepsut's successor.

Nefret (fl. 20th century B.C.E.) *royal woman of the Twelfth Dynasty*
The mother of AMENEMHET I (r. 1991–1962 B.C.E.), Nefret was a commoner, supposedly of Nubian descent and from THEBES. When Amenemhet I usurped the throne upon the death of MENTUHOTEP IV, founding the Twelfth Dynasty, Nefret received the title of King's Mother. She was mentioned in NEFER-ROHU'S PROPHECY.

Nefrusheri (fl. 20th century B.C.E.) *royal woman of the Twelfth Dynasty*
She was the consort of SENWOSRET I (r. 1971–1926 B.C.E.) and the mother of AMENEMHET II. Nefrusheri was the daughter of AMENEMHET I and probably Queen NEFRU-SOBEK (2). She was buried in el-LISHT, having a small pyramid in Senwosret I's mortuary complex. A black granite statue was found in her tomb.

Nefru-Sobek (1) See SOBEKNEFERU.

Nefru-Sobek (2) (fl. 20th century B.C.E.) *royal woman of the Twelfth Dynasty*
She was a consort of AMENEMHET I (r. 1991–1962 B.C.E.), becoming queen when another favorite was involved in an ongoing HAREM plot, or when the older consort died. Another harem plot did succeed, taking the life of the pharaoh.
See also SINUHE THE SAILOR.

Nefru-Sobek (3) (fl. 20th century B.C.E.) *royal woman of the Twelfth Dynasty*
A daughter of SENWOSRET I (r. 1971–1926 B.C.E.), Nefru-Sobek was buried in el-LISHT. A granite bowl bearing her name was discovered in Senwosret I's tomb.

Nefrusy (Nefrussy) This was a site north of HERMOPOLIS MAGNA that was involved in the military campaigns of KAMOSE (r. 1555–1550 B.C.E.). The HYKSOS and their Asiatic allies maintained a garrison at Nefrusy. Kamose, who adapted the Hyksos CHARIOT and formed an effective Egyptian cavalry for his campaigns, attacked the garrison with a contingent of MEDJAY troops, the warriors of the south who were feared by the enemy. The defenders of Nefrusy were stunned by the arrival of Kamose's units and fled northward, relinquishing the outpost. This was one of the first military episodes undertaken by Kamose in his efforts to oust the Hyksos from Egypt. APOPHIS (2), the Hyksos king at AVARIS, died soon after this assault. Kamose did not live long enough to complete his efforts, a task that fell to his brother, 'AHMOSE (NEBPEHTIRÉ) (r. 1550–1525 B.C.E.).

Nefru-totenen (fl. 20th century B.C.E.) *royal woman of the Twelfth Dynasty*
The consort of AMENEMHET I (r. 1991–1962 B.C.E.), she was the mother of SENWOSRET I. Nefru-totenen was a commoner who probably married Amenemhet I before he usurped the throne. She was buried in a small pyramid at el-LISHT.

Negative Confessions   Part of the mortuary rituals of ancient Egypt now called the "Declarations of Innocence," this text was developed by the various priests of the temples to aid the deceased when in the presence of the FORTY-TWO JUDGES in the JUDGMENT HALLS OF OSIRIS. The confessions were to be recited to establish the moral virtue of the deceased and his or her right to eternal bliss. The Negative Confessions detail some of the ethical and moral concerns of the various eras of Egypt, expressing the aspirations and the acknowledgment of personal responsibility for actions. The confessions included

I have not stolen.
I have not plundered.
I have not slain people.
I have not committed a crime.
I have not stolen the property of a god.
I have not said lies.
I have not cursed.
I have not copulated with another man.
I have not copulated with another man's wife.
I have not caused anyone to weep.
I have not eaten my heart (indulged in despair).
I have not led anyone astray.
I have not gossiped.
I have not slandered.
I have not been contentious in affairs.
I have not caused terror.
I have not become heatedly angry.
I have not eavesdropped.
I have not made anyone angry.
I have not made anyone hungry.

Such confessions covered the scope of the average person's life in Egypt in all eras. The regulation of personal conduct was a constant theme in didactic LITERATURE on the Nile, including admonitions against petty acts and minor bad habits, which were consistently considered important to the social and spiritual well-being of the nation. The spirit of cooperation and quietude are also evident in the confessions. The length of the Negative Confessions varied, and in some periods each one of the affirmations was accompanied by an address to a particular judge.
See also MORTUARY RITUALS.

Nehah-ré   A serpentine being associated with the elaborate cultic traditions of the god RÉ, Nehah-ré attacked Ré on his nightly round through TUAT, or the Underworld, but failed to halt the divine travels. The serpent was slain each night, only to rise again to continue his deadly assaults.
See also APOPHIS (1).

Nehem-awit   She was a divine form of the goddess HATHOR, called "the Deliverer from Violence," "the Sweeper Away of the Oppressed," and "the One Who Serves the Deprived." Depicted as a woman wearing a solar or lunar disk crown, Nehem-awit was also associated with the musical instrument called the SISTRUM, or *seses*. She used the sistrum to repel evil spirits. Nehem-awit was sometimes shown wearing a sistrum crown or the pillar of Hathor on her head. The goddess was invoked by Egyptians of all eras as one who could repel curses and evil spirits.

Nehes   A divine being, a form of the sun god RÉ, his name was translated as "the Awakened One," "the Awakened," or "the Alert One." Nehes was a companion of Ré in the nightly journey through TUAT, or the Underworld, one of a retinue of spirits that guarded Ré's bark as the god visited waiting souls and restored the light of day.

Nehesy (1) (fl. 16th century B.C.E.) *obscure ruler of the Fourteenth Dynasty at Xois*
He was a contemporary of the HYKSOS Fifteenth Dynasty (1640–1532 B.C.E.) and ruled his small city at the same time that the last rulers of the Thirteenth Dynasty (ca. 1640 B.C.E.) and the Theban Seventeenth Dynasty (1640–1550 B.C.E.) were active. Nehesy, whose name meant "Nubian," was listed in the TURIN CANON. The dates of his reign are unknown.

He served as an official at XOIS and then assumed royal status locally. His name has been discovered in inscriptions at TELL EL-HABUA and at other eastern Delta sites, indicating some prominence in the region. Nehesy ruled only Xois but kept it out of the Hyksos domain.

Nehesy (2) (Nehsi) (fl. 15th century B.C.E.) *treasury and royal court official of the Eighteenth Dynasty*
Nehesy also served HATSHEPSUT (r. 1473–1458 B.C.E.) as chancellor. He served as well as the chief treasurer and as "the Guardian of the Royal Seal." Nehesy accompanied SENENMUT and Prince THUITY on an expedition to PUNT as part of Hatshepsut's TRADE ventures. He was

buried on the western shore of Thebes. His tomb had inscriptions concerning the reigns of Hatshepsut and Tuthmosis III. He was also honored with a shrine at GEBEL EL-SILSILEH in NUBIA (modern Sudan).

Nehi (fl. 15th century B.C.E.) *high-ranking official of the Eighteenth Dynasty*
Nehi served TUTHMOSIS III (r. 1479–1425 B.C.E.) as the viceroy of Kush, or NUBIA (modern Sudan). He was given the title of "King's Son of Kush," a rank that accompanied the office of the VICEROY of that territory in most historical periods. Nehi erected a victory STELA for Tuthmosis III at WADI HALFA. His residence was on the ELEPHANTINE Island at ASWAN, where he ruled over the regions of the south. Nehi brought tribute to the royal court each year, calling himself "a Servant Useful to His Lord, Filling His House with Gold." His governorship of Nubia extended as far south as the third cataract of the Nile.

Neith (1) (**Nit**) A goddess, sometimes called Nit by the Egyptians, whose cult dates to Predynastic Periods (before 3000 B.C.E.) on the Nile, she was the archer goddess of the Delta region, with a shrine at Basyun, on the Rosetta branch of the river. Another large temple dedicated to Neith was erected in SAIS, and she was popular in the FAIYUM and then in Upper Egypt.

A war goddess, Neith was depicted on an elaborate stela that dates to ca. 2900 B.C.E. in the reign of AHA, the first ruler, also called Menes. Aha reportedly erected Neith's temple at Sais. Her name seems to have originated from a term describing the weaving of flax or spells. Originally she was depicted as a cow goddess and was honored as the Mother Goddess of the Western Delta. She was also the patroness of the Libyans who ruled Egypt in the Twenty-second Dynasty (945–712 B.C.E.). Neith was depicted as a woman wearing the crown of Lower Egypt and holding bows and arrows.

Her hieroglyph name was believed to represent a loom shuttle, and the goddess became the patroness of weavers as well as hunting and warfare. In hymns she was addressed as "the Opener of the Ways." By the time of the Old Kingdom Period (2575–2134 B.C.E.), Neith was worshipped as the consort of the god SET and the mother of SOBEK. She was also associated with the goddess NUN, the symbol of primeval chaos. The PYRAMID TEXTS honor her as guarding OSIRIS and ISIS. She was also linked to the linen wrappings used in the mummification process.

Neith (2) (fl. 23rd century B.C.E.) *royal woman of the Sixth Dynasty*
She was a lesser-ranked queen of PEPI II (r. 2246–2152 B.C.E.). The daughter of PEPI I and ANKHNESMERY-RÉ (1), she was reportedly the widow of MERENRÉ I, Pepi II's predecessor. A pair of OBELISKS was recovered, bearing

her name, and her tomb in Pepi II's pyramidal complex in south SAQQARA was found to be quite elaborate. A wall that was designed with an entrance surrounds this gravesite. Vestibule walls are covered with reliefs at the opening of the tomb, leading to a colonnaded court with more reliefs. This court has square pillars and is a cult chamber with three niches, a SERDAB, and a FALSE DOOR. The actual burial chamber is decorated, and the ceiling is lined with star designs. The PYRAMID TEXTS of the epoch are on the walls, which also have the traditional palace facade design.

Neithotep (fl. 30th century B.C.E.) *royal woman of the First Dynasty*
She was probably the consort of NARMER and the mother of AHA, the Menes honored as the first pharaoh, ca. 2920 B.C.E. Her name meant the "goddess Neith is Content." Some scholars believe that Neithotep was the consort of Aha. Others believe that she is the woman depicted on the MACEHEAD of Narmer, the original heiress being presented to the unifier of Upper and Lower Egypt.

Neithotep was provided with a large tomb in ABYDOS by Aha. Her tomb is one of the earliest monuments in Egypt, designed as a brick mastaba with recessed panels on the exterior walls. The burial chamber was not subterranean but arranged at ground level. Objects bearing the names of Narmer and Aha were found in this tomb.

Neka-'ankh (fl. 25th century B.C.E.) *cultic official of the Fifth Dynasty*
He served as the mortuary priest for the pyramid of USERKHAF (r. 2465–2458 B.C.E.). Such priests performed cultic rituals for the deceased pharaohs, often residing in the actual pyramid complex. Neka'ankh's tomb was discovered in SAQQARA, and a part of it was removed and taken to the British Museum in London.

Nekau *See* NECHO I.

Nekauré (fl. 25th century B.C.E.) *prince of the Fourth Dynasty known for his last will and testament*
The son of KHAFRE (Chephren) (r. 2520–2494 B.C.E.), Nekauré was a mature adult when he died, and he inscribed a will on the walls of his tomb at Giza that announced that while "Living on His Two Feet, Without Ailing in Any Respect" he was stating his testament for his death. This phrase was the model for the modern term "Being of Sound Mind and Body." The will bequeathed 14 towns and two estates in the pyramidal complex of Khafre to his daughter, but her premature death made it revert to Nekauré again and eventually to his wife. Other properties were given to the mortuary priests in order to secure an endowment of his funerary cult. This will is a rare find, being the only document of its kind from that era in Egyptian history.

Nekheb *See* ELKAB.

Nekhebet This was the white VULTURE goddess, the patroness of Upper Egypt, whose name meant "She of Enkhab, or Nekheb," modern ELKAB. Nekhebet was part of the primeval cosmogonic traditions and symbolized nature and childbirth. In Upper Egypt she was honored as "the Lady of the Valley." Her cult dated to the earliest periods of Egyptian history. She was also depicted as a woman with a vulture headdress and a white CROWN. A long-stemmed flower, a water lily with a serpent entwined, was her symbol. 'ADJIB of the First Dynasty (2920–2770 B.C.E.) used her name in his royal titles. Then she was shown as a white vulture with wings outspread, holding the ANKH, the cross of life. She was also addressed as "the Great White Cow of Nekheb."

AMENHOTEP II (r. 1427–1401 B.C.E.) erected a temple to Nekhebet at Elkab. RAMESSES II (r. 1290–1224 B.C.E.) enlarged the shrine and added a PYLON. There are crypts under her temple that have elaborate reliefs and painted scenes. A SACRED LAKE was part of the architectural design. In the mortuary traditions, Nekhebet played a role in the saga of OSIRIS and inhabited the primeval abyss, NUN, the waters of chaos before creation. In this capacity she was revered as a patroness of nature and creation. Nekhebet was also revered as a consort of HAPI (1) in some eras.

Nekhebu (fl. 23rd century B.C.E.) *construction official of the Sixth Dynasty*
Nekhebu served PEPI I (r. 2289–2255 B.C.E.) as an architect and engineer and was involved in court-building projects. He also directed state-sponsored royal programs, including the construction of canals and temples. Nekhebu was revered throughout his life. Being close to the pharaoh, both he and his son were buried at GIZA.

Nekhen *See* HIERAKONPOLIS.

Nekonekh (fl. 25th century B.C.E.) *royal official of the Fifth Dynasty*
He served USERKHAF (r. 2465–2458 B.C.E.) in the royal court and was a nobleman, possibly related to the royal family. Nekonekh received many endowments of land and honors from the pharaoh, some dating originally to the reign of MENKAURÉ (r. 2490–2472 B.C.E.).

nemes A striped cloth headdress worn only by the pharaohs, in some historical periods, the *nemes*, which was distinguished by distending front panels, supported a full CROWN or simple URAEUS symbols. The *nemes* were fashioned out of stiff linens or leather.
See also DRESS.

Nemtyemzaf *See* MERENRÉ I.

Nenekhsekhmet (fl. 25th century B.C.E.) *medical official of the Fifth Dynasty*
He served SAHURÉ (r. 2438–2446 B.C.E.) as the chief physician of the court and held that high-ranked position for decades. Because of his service, he was given honors at his death. Sahuré provided two FALSE DOORS for Nenekhsekhmet's tomb, and in this burial site the ruler is depicted as praising the physician for his wisdom and age. Nenekhsekhmet's name is derived from his devotion as a medical man to the goddess SEKHMET.
See also HEALTH AND DISEASE.

Nenwif (fl. 15th century B.C.E.) *military official of the Eighteenth Dynasty*
Nenwif served TUTHMOSIS III (r. 1479–1425 B.C.E.) as a military commander and as the ranking officer of the newly formed cavalry units. In this capacity he accompanied Tuthmosis III on many of his prolonged and far-reaching campaigns. Nenwif was commemorated for his loyalty and skills on a mortuary stela at THEBES. His wife, Irenana, his son, Meru, and his daughter, Demiwedja, shared his mortuary honors. The names of the family members indicate possible MEDJAY origins, from Nubia (modern Sudan).
See also TUTHMOSIS III'S MILITARY CAMPAIGNS.

Neper He was an Egyptian grain deity dating to the early eras and associated with the annual harvests. Popular from the Predynastic Period, before ca. 3000 B.C.E., Neper was incorporated into the cult of OSIRIS soon after the unification of Upper and Lower Egypt. Many Osirian traditions and cultic rituals involved beds of grain and harvest observances, probably stemming from Neper's prior ceremonies.
See also OSIRIS BEDS; OSIRIS GARDENS.

Nephrites I (Baenre'merynetjeru) (d. 393 B.C.E.) *founder of the Twenty-ninth Dynasty*
He ruled from 399 B.C.E. until his death. Nephrites I's capital was at MENDES, but he controlled a good portion of the Nile Valley. He captured AMYRTAIOS of SAIS (r. 404–393 B.C.E.) and executed him at MEMPHIS. He also fought off ARTAXERXES III and the Persians. As ruler, he erected monuments throughout Egypt, refurbished existing sites, and also served as a patron of the APIS bull cult. Nephrites I was probably buried in Mendes. His SHABTI, the tomb figurine, was found in a sarcophagus there, and a tomb chapel on the site is believed to have been part of his mortuary complex. At his death, PSAMMETICHUS (4) vied with Nephrites I's son and heir and usurped the throne.

Nephrites II (fl. 380 B.C.E.) *deposed ruler of the Twenty-ninth Dynasty*
He inherited the throne in 380 B.C.E. from his father, HAKORIS, but was threatened by the rise of a new royal line. Nephrites ruled only four months, being deposed by NECTANEBO I (r. 380–362 B.C.E.).

Nephthys (Nebt-het)   The ancient Egyptian goddess, called the consort and female counterpart to SET, originally addressed as Nebt-het, she was the sister of ISIS, OSIRIS, and SET and tricked Osiris into siring her son, ANUBIS. When Osiris was slain, Nephthys aided Isis in finding his body and resurrecting him. She was part of the revered *LAMENTATIONS OF ISIS AND NEPHTHYS*.

Nephthys was a patroness of the dead and was associated as well with the cult of MIN. She was also a member of the ENNEAD of HELIOPOLIS. The goddess took the form of a kite, a bird displayed in funerary processions, and she was the patroness of HAPI, one of the CANOPIC JAR guardians. Her cult at Kom-Mer in Upper Egypt continued throughout all historical periods. She was called "the Lady of the Mansions" or "the Lady of the Books." She was also identified with the desert regions and was skilled in magic. Nephthys is depicted as a woman wearing the hieroglyph for "Castle" on her head.

Nesbenebded   *See* SMENDES (1).

Neser (Neres)   He was an ancient Egyptian fish deity whose cult dates to Predynastic Periods in Egypt, before the unification of Upper and Lower Egypt, ca. 3000 B.C.E. The god's rituals were popular in the Early Dynastic Period (2920–2575 B.C.E.) but then disappeared.

Neshi (fl. 16th century B.C.E.) *multitalented official of the Seventeenth Dynasty*
Neshi served KAMOSE (r. 1555–1550 B.C.E.) in a remarkable number of capacities. He was the treasurer of the court, the overseer of royal companions, and the overseer of ships, as well as the commander of the Egyptian fleet used by Kamose against the HYKSOS at AVARIS.

Neshi is recorded as being "the Vibrant One" on the KARNAK Stela that gives an account of Kamose's campaigns. He possibly served 'AHMOSE (NEBPEHTIRÉ) (r. 1550–1525 B.C.E.), the brother of Kamose and the founder of the Eighteenth Dynasty, or he was honored by the new pharaoh in retirement. Neshi received a plot of land in MEMPHIS from 'Ahmose. This land grant ended up as an element of a lawsuit by Neshi's descendant in the reign of RAMESSES II (1290–1224 B.C.E.).

Nesitanebetashru (1) (fl. ninth century B.C.E.) *royal woman of the Libyan Twenty-second Dynasty*
The consort of SHOSHENQ II (r. 883 B.C.E.), she was the mother of HARSIESE, the ill-fated prince of that royal line. Nesitanebetashru was a Libyan noble woman.

Nesitanebetashru (2) (fl. 11th century B.C.E.) *royal woman of the Theban branch of the Twenty-first Dynasty*
She was the daughter of PINUDJEM (2), the high priest of Amun, in the reign of PSUSENNES I (1040–992 B.C.E.) and his successors. She married Djeptahiufankh, another

Amunite priest, and remained in Thebes. Nesitanebetashru's mummy was discovered in the DEIR EL-BAHRI cache in 1881. Her remains are one of the finest mummies to survive over the centuries. Her body is lifelike, complete with artificial eyes made of stone and black pupils.

See also MORTUARY RITUALS.

Neskhonsu (fl. 11th century B.C.E.) *royal woman and God's Wife of Amun of the Twenty-first Dynasty*
She is recorded as being the wife of PINUDJEM (2), the high priest of AMUN at THEBES in the reign of PSUSENNES I (1040–992 B.C.E.) and his successors. Neskhonsu was installed as the GOD'S WIFE OF AMUN or the Divine Adoratrice of Amun, at Thebes. She was the niece of Pinudjem. A royal-style sarcophagus from her tomb provides an elaborate lists of her titles and privileges.

Neskhonsu was buried in the cliffs at DEIR EL-BAHRI on the western shore of Thebes. Her blue faience cup was also discovered there. Her SARCOPHAGUS was apparently usurped in a later historical period. She was beautifully depicted in her mortuary regalia as an aristocratic, elegant woman with long dark hair.

Nesnimu (fl. seventh century B.C.E.) *sage and official of the Twenty-sixth Dynasty*
He served PSAMMETICHUS I (r. 664–610 B.C.E.) as a valued counselor and as the mayor of various cities. Nesnimu started his career as a priest of the cult of Horus in EDFU but became well known for his wisdom and administrative skills. Psammetichus I appointed him as the mayor of eight separate Egyptian cities, one after another, and Nesnimu continued in these roles until his retirement.

Nessumontu (fl. 20th century B.C.E.) *military official of the Twelfth Dynasty*
He served AMENEMHET I (r. 1991–1962 B.C.E.) and SENWOSRET I (r. 1971–1926 B.C.E.) as a military commander. Nessumontu led an expedition against the Asiatic Bedouins in the SINAI, probably with Nubian (modern Sudanese) mercenary units. He was there to protect mines and QUARRIES, possibly reopening some sites. His mortuary stela, now in the Louvre in Paris, recounts his career.

See also NATURAL RESOURCES.

netcher   This was the ancient Egyptian name for the deity symbol used on totems and pennants. When a *netcher* was displayed on the FLAGSTAFF at the entrance to a temple or shrine, it denoted the presence of the deity in the structure. The *netcher* was visible when the pennants were flown by the wind. Flagstaffs and pennants were part of all religious buildings, dating to the displays of clan and NOME cult totems in the earliest periods in the Nile Valley.

Neterka (Chairés) (fl. 27th century B.C.E.) *obscure pharaoh of the Second Dynasty*
Neterka was reportedly the seventh ruler of his line. He was mentioned in the TURIN CANON. No other information has been documented about him.

neter nefer A title used by the pharaohs of Egypt to affirm their divine status, *neter* signified a deity. The use of the qualifying *nefer,* meaning good or beautiful, lessened the divine status to some extent, designating a human element that modified the godlike qualities on earth. This definition was acceptable to the Egyptians, who understood the role of the PHARAOH as being both human and divine while he lived. In many cases, however, the pharaohs were deified after death and in some instances even during their lifetime. RAMESSES II (r. 1290–1224 B.C.E.) was made a god at ABU SIMBEL before he died in 1224 B.C.E.

neterui An instrument used in the MORTUARY RITUALS of Egypt, called "the Opening of the Mouth," the *neterui,* used with the UR-HEKA in such ceremonies, was also placed in the mummy wrappings to secure the protection of the gods. It was a simple angle form made of stone or metal. The *neterui* was considered capable of summoning the gods for protection in the realms beyond the grave.

net spells They were magical formulas used by the Egyptians in mortuary rituals to provide mummies with needed protection on the last journey into *TUAT,* or the Underworld. They were included in the BOOK OF THE DEAD. These incantations allowed the deceased to avoid the snares of demons. Hraf-hef, called "HE-WHO-LOOKS-BEHIND-HIMSELF," the ferryman on the Lake of Eternity, could also be placated by the net spells. Hraf-hef was reportedly an irritable being who had to be cajoled into carrying the dead to the various paradises on the opposite shore.

Niankh-amun (fl. 24th century B.C.E.) *one of the Fifth Dynasty court officials buried in the tomb of the Two Brothers in Saqqara*
A royal manicurist in life, Niankh-amun shared his tomb with a fellow courtier named Khnumhotep. The tomb of the Two Brothers was an elaborate MASTABA located near the pyramid of UNIS (r. 2356–2323 B.C.E.). The families of both courtiers were also buried in the tomb.

Nibamon (Nibamun; Nebamon) (fl. 15th century B.C.E.) *military official of the Eighteenth Dynasty*
He served TUTHMOSIS III (r. 1479–1425 B.C.E.) as a steward and military officer. Nibamon was on the staff of a Queen NEBETU'U (2), a lesser-ranked consort of Tuthmosis III. He then entered military service and became a captain in the royal navy. For some time, Tuthmosis III was the commander of the main naval base near Memphis. Nibamon's mortuary stela, discovered in Thebes, contains details of his career.

Night of the Tear This was an ancient Egyptian FESTIVAL, called Qork en-Hatiu or Gerh-en-Hatiu to depict the tears of the goddess ISIS, shed as commemoratives of OSIRIS's death. Actually an agricultural or calendric festival, the celebration honored the annual inundations of the NILE River. The Night of the Tear was celebrated on the eleventh day of Paoni, considered by many scholars to be the modern June 17. The feast was also called the Night of the Drop. The rituals and celebrations of the Night of the Tear have continued over the centuries into modern times. Despite the fact that the Aswan High Dam has eliminated the flooding of the Nile, the Egyptians still salute the river on the elected day with flowers and candles prepared in small vessels that float on the surface of the Nile.

Nile This was the "Gift of the Gods" to Egypt, the world's longest river and the source of all life and abundance in the ancient Nile Valley. The Nile flows approximately 4,665 miles out of Africa's heart on a unique northward journey to the Mediterranean Sea and taps two separate climatic resources in order to come bounding into Egypt: the summer monsoons of Ethiopia and the Sudan, which feed the river with storm waters, and Central Africa's two annual rainy seasons, which nurture the Nile with gentle downpours and overflowing lakes.

The Nile flows from two sources. The White Nile rises from the deep pools of equatorial Africa, and the Blue Nile sweeps down from the Abyssinian highlands. These combine with many tributaries, including the Atbara, which joins the Nile at the fifth cataract, bringing vast quantities of affluvium and red mud.

The cataracts of the Nile, the progression of rocky, white-rapid regions, formed the southern border of ancient Egypt since the earliest historical periods. The first cataract at ASWAN demarcated the border of Egypt for centuries. The other cataracts provided rocky peaks upon which the Egyptians built a series of fortresses and garrisoned trading posts and towns to command traffic on the NILE in the area that is now Sudan.

Just above Aswan, at EDFU, the great Nile Valley begins. Limestone cliffs parallel the river for more than 400 miles, marching beside the shoreline, sometimes close to the water and sometimes swinging back toward the deserts. The cliffs reach heights of 800 feet in some areas, with mesas and plateaus glistening against the sky. The cliffs on the west stand like sentinels before the LIBYAN DESERT, and the eastern slopes withdraw into the Arabian or Red Sea Desert. This valley provided a true cultural and geographical shelter for the emerging people of the region.

The Delta of Lower Egypt is a watery fan of seven major tributaries emptying into the Mediterranean Sea: the Pelusiac, Tanite, Phatnitic (Damietta), Sebennytic, Bolbitinic (Rosetta), Mendesian, and Canopic branches. The waters of the BAHR YUSEF, a stream dedicated to Joseph (an Islamic hero and not the biblical patriarch), flow out of the Nile and into the FAIYUM, a natural depression alongside the river, about 65 miles south of modern Cairo, at ASSIUT. They are trapped in the depression and form a rich marshland region of wetlands and moist fields made available to the ancient Egyptian farmers. The site was also inhabited by CROCODILES, which were honored with a shrine.

The river's annual floods deposited a ribbon of fertile soil along its banks that enriched the farmlands and made agriculture the economic basis of the nation. In time, the Egyptians would use canals, irrigation ditches, and sophisticated hydraulic systems to reclaim lands and expand their agricultural base. When the Nile inundated the land the benefits were twofold. The river not only left rich deposits of mud and fertile silt but leached the soil of harmful salts as well. When the Nile began to recede at the end of the inundation, the Egyptians used dams and reservoirs to store water for the dry seasons of the year. The inundation of the river was gradual, heralded by the arrival of SOPDU, the Greek Sirius or the Dogstar, in the sky.

By July the first waters came rushing into the land, increasing every day until the fields and orchards were flooded. The inundation lasted through October, when the Nile receded again. It is estimated that Egypt received as much as 30 feet of mud as part of the inundation. For this reason the Egyptians called their land Khem, the Black Land. The deserts on either side of the river were called the Deshret, the Red Lands. The stark contrast between the two regions is still very much evident.

Along its banks the Nile sustained a variety of fish and fowl. Ducks, geese, water birds, and nesting birds could be caught in the marshes with clap nets or with throwing sticks. The Nile nurtured the sacred LOTUS, reeds, and the PAPYRUS plant, which scribes used to make papyri. The river was endless in its bounty, and the people sang its praises continually. Surviving hymns to the Nile reflect a true spirit of joy and celebration. The people of Egypt understood from the charts of the astronomer-priests when to anticipate the rising floods, taking appropriate steps to prepare for the inundation and conducting rituals to celebrate the religious significance of the event. Nile festivals remained popular in every historical period.

The river was always "the Father of Life" to the ancient Egyptians, or the "Mother of all Men" to some generations. The Nile was also the manifestation of the god HAPI (1), the divine spirit that unceasingly blessed the land with rich silt deposits from the continent's core.

The religious texts of ancient times link the Nile to a celestial stream that emptied out of the heavens on the Elephantine, or in the caves thought to be in that region. The annual flooding in Hapi's lands was thus called the "Libation," made in the honor of HORUS in the south and in honor of SET in the Delta.

The name for the river is Greek in origin, a version of the Semitic *Nakhl,* or "river." The Egyptians called the river Hep-Ur, Great Hapi, or "sweet water." Each generation addressed the Nile with its own special name and hymn of praise. The river was Egypt's life's blood, not only sustaining the people but imposing on them a sense of stewardship and a seasonal regimen, prompting the spirit of cooperation, called MA'AT, that was to become the hallmark of the nation for centuries.

Further reading: Midant-Reynes, Beatrix, and Ian Shaw, transl. *The Prehistory of Egypt.* London: Blackwell Publishers, 1999; Roberts, Timothy Roland. *Gift of the Nile: Chronicles of Ancient Egypt.* New York: Barnes & Noble Books, 1998.

Nile festivals   These were the celebrations of the river and the god HAPI (1), its divine manifestation in ancient Egypt, held throughout all historical periods. The NIGHT OF THE TEAR was the June holiday, dedicated to the goddess ISIS at the beginning of the annual inundation. It was believed that the goddess Isis shed tears over the body of her husband, OSIRIS, and these tears multiplied and caused the Nile to overflow its banks. The Night of the Tear honored Isis as the goddess of nurturing and mortuary powers, associating her with the basic life-giving function of the river.

The Night of the Dam or the Night of the Cutting of the Dam was celebrated when the inundation had reached its highest levels. Earthen dams were built to measure the height of the water, and then the upper levels were thinned and broken by boats. The ceremony signified the completion of the river's nurturing duties. The festival remained popular in all eras, and a version was performed in modern times at various sites in Egypt until the building of the dam at Aswan.

Nile level records   Inscriptions marking the heights of the various annual inundations of the Nile River were discovered on the rocks at SEMNA dating to the reign of AMENEMHET III of the Twelfth Dynasty (r. 1844–1797 B.C.E.). These records continued through the close of the Seventeenth Dynasty (1550 B.C.E.) and were part of the annual recording of the river's inundation levels, similar to the Nilometers.

Nilometers   Pillars or slabs were positioned at various strategic locations on the river to determine the height of the annual inundations or floods of the Nile. It was important for the Egyptians to determine the flow of the river each year, so they positioned the pillars far south of the first cataract at ASWAN to give early warning of any variation in the Nile's flood levels. Information concerning the projected flood levels was sent to the ruler and his administrators by messenger. The various regional governors were also informed so that any necessary preparations could be made for the event in their territories. Two such measuring devices were used in the Delta and at the first cataract in ancient times, and subsidiary pillars were positioned in the second and fourth cataracts during the period of the empire.

The pillars were inscribed with a scale cut into cubit measurements: 1 cubit equals 18–20.6 inches. Other measurements were inscribed on later pillars. The Nilometers not only provided information on the level of the floods but also allowed the priests and governors to determine the crops that would thrive as a result of the amount of silt being deposited. Prospective harvests were thus assessed and the tax bases of the crops determined in advance.

Nima'athap (Hapnima'at) (fl. 27th century B.C.E.) *royal woman of the Second and Third Dynasties*
She was the consort of KHA'SEKHEMWY (r. ca. 2640 B.C.E.) and the mother of DJOSER (r. 2630–2611 B.C.E.). Her titles included "Mother of the King's Children," and her name was found in Kha'sekhemwy's tomb. In Djoser's reign she bore the title "King's Mother." Nima'athap was deified after her death and worshipped as the ancestress of the Third Dynasty.

Nimlot (1) (Nemrot) (fl. 10th century B.C.E.) *Libyan chieftain of Bubastis*
He resided in Egypt in the region of the city of BUBASTIS and was the father of SHOSHENQ I (r. 945–924 B.C.E.). Called Nemrot in some lists, he was the husband of Princess Mehetemwashe. When Nimlot died, Shoshenq I, then a military commander, appealed to PSUSENNES II (r. 959–945 B.C.E.) for permission to establish a mortuary cult for his father and was allowed to make this filial gesture.

Nimlot (2) (fl. 10th century B.C.E.) *prince of the Libyan Twenty-second Dynasty*
He was the son of SHOSHENQ I (r. 945–924 B.C.E.) and Queen PENRESHNAS, the daughter of a Libyan noble. Nimlot served as a commander of the army and is recorded as being "a great chief of the foreigners, the Meshwesh." He contributed 60 BULLS to the shrine at HIERAKONPOLIS. As governor of Hierakonpolis, Nimlot controlled Middle Egypt and the nomes of Upper Egypt.

Nimlot (3) (fl. ninth century B.C.E.) *prince of the Libyan Twenty-second Dynasty*
He was the son of OSORKON II (883–855 B.C.E.), serving as a military commander at HERAKLEOPOLIS and then as high priest of AMUN in THEBES. His daughter, KARO-

MANA (5) Merymut, married TAKELOT II. His sons were Ptahwedjankhaf of Herakleopolis and Takelot. Nimlot restored order at Thebes after the rebellion prompted by HARSIESE.

Nimlot (4) (d. ca. 712 B.C.E.) *obscure ruler of the Twenty-third Dynasty*
He ruled from ca. 828 B.C.E. and then was reduced to the status of a vassal governor of his city-state. Nimlot ruled HERMOPOLIS only and joined the coalition started by TEFNAKHTE of SAIS and including OSORKON IV, PEFTJAU'ABAST of HERAKLEOPOLIS, and IUPUT of LEONTOPOLIS. The coalition faced PIANKHI (1), and his army of Nubians (modern Sudanese) at Herakleopolis and surrendered to his superior forces. Nimlot was allowed to remain the ruler of Hermopolis as a vassal of Piankhi after he surrendered to the Nubian ruler.

Nine Bows This was a term used to signify the enemies of Egypt in all eras, normally depicting the foreign nations already subdued. In one Ramessid (1307–1070 B.C.E.) relief the Nine Bows were portrayed as Libyans, NUBIANS, HITTITES, Syrians, Mesopotamians, Philistines, Dardanians, Lycians, Sardinians, and Silicians. The actual composition of the Nine Bows varied from one historical period to another, as nations rose and fell while Egypt endured. The enemies designated as the Nine Bows were sometimes depicted on the inner soles of the pharaoh's sandals so that he could tread upon their persons. They were also used on statues and reliefs that celebrated Egypt's military prowess.

Ninetjer (fl. 27th century B.C.E.) *third ruler of the Second Dynasty*
His capital was MEMPHIS, and he is listed on the PALERMO STONE and recorded as appearing "God-Like." The dates of his actual reign are unknown. Ninetjer erected a royal residence and conducted the APIS festivals. An alabaster statue of him has survived, and vases bearing his name were discovered in the STEP PYRAMID. He was possibly buried under the causeway of UNIS (r. 2356–2323 B.C.E.), which was built over the site at SAQQARA. His seals were found there.

Another tomb, near the grave site of HOTEP-SEKHEMWY in SAQQARA, has also been identified as his resting place. This burial site has corridors, storerooms, and three main galleries. The burial chamber collapsed, but Late Period (712–332 B.C.E.) coffins were discovered there in 1938. This tomb contained other passages and side chambers as well as a labyrinth. Ninetjer apparently put down a major rebellion in his thirteenth regnal year. His successor was possibly SENDJI, an obscure ruler listed as "the Fearful One."

Nineveh It was the capital of the ASSYRIAN or Agade nation situated on the eastern bank of the Tigris River near modern Mosul in northern Iraq. The city had seven and one half miles of defensive walls, erected on two mounds: Nebi Yunus and Kuyunjik. ASSURBANIPAL, an Assyrian king, built a palace and established a cuneiform library there. When he entered Egypt in the reign of TAHARQA (690–664 B.C.E.), ESSARHADDON, another Assyrian ruler, captured the queen, AMUN-DYEK'HET, and crown prince of the land, USHANAHURA, and took them back to Nineveh as slaves.

Nit   *See* NEITH (1).

Nitocris (1) (Nitigret) (fl. ca. 2153 B.C.E.) *fabled queen-pharaoh of the Sixth Dynasty*
HERODOTUS listed her and related a fable concerning her activities. Nitocris reportedly came to power after her brother, MERENRÉ II (r. ca. 2152 B.C.E.), was slain. In vengeance she supposedly invited hundreds of officials she believed responsible for her brother's death to a banquet in a subterranean chamber and then flooded it. She had a one-year reign and was listed in the TURIN CANON. Nitocris was the royal consort of Merenré II.

Nitocris (2) (fl. 7th century B.C.E.) *royal woman of the Twenty-sixth Dynasty*
She was the daughter of PSAMMETICHUS I (r. 664–610 B.C.E.), and Queen MEKHTEMWESKHET (2). Nitocris was "adopted" by SHEPENWEPET (2) and became a GOD'S WIFE OF AMUN, or a Divine Adoratrice of Amun, at Thebes. She lived into her 70s and in 595 B.C.E. "adopted" the daughter of PSAMMETICHUS II (595–589 B.C.E.). ANKHESNEFERIBRÉ thus became her successor. Nitocris was buried in a red granite SARCOPHAGUS in THEBES and was given a tomb chapel in KARNAK.

Niuserré (Izi) (d. 2392 B.C.E.) *sixth ruler of the Fifth Dynasty*
He reigned from 2416 B.C.E. until his death. Niuserré was probably the son of NEFEREFRÉ or KAKAI. His queens were KHENTIKUS, REPUTNEB, and NUB. He is also famed for his sun temple in ABU GHUROB, a structure made entirely of stone. Once called the Pyramid of Righa, the TEMPLE was designed with a large square base and a tapering platform, with an open court and ALTAR. This altar was fashioned out of a monolithic slab of travertine marble, surrounded by four adornments, carved with the hieroglyph of offering. Niuserré sent an expedition to the mines on the SINAI.

Nodjmet (fl. 11th century B.C.E.) *royal woman of the Twentieth Dynasty*
She was the wife of HERIHOR, the high priest of AMUN at THEBES, in the reign of RAMESSES XI (1100–1070 B.C.E.), and was depicted in reliefs in the temple of Khonsu at KARNAK. Her mummified remains, recovered in Thebes, had her heart within her body. Her hair was braided,

and she had artificial eyes and packed limbs and cheeks. Nodjmet's mummy reflects new embalming techniques introduced into the mortuary rituals in that era. She was discovered in an adzed coffin.

Nofret (1) (fl. 26th century B.C.E.) *royal woman of the Fourth Dynasty*
She was the wife of Prince RAHOTEP (1), a son of SNEFRU (r. 2575–2551 B.C.E.). A limestone statue of Nofret, one of a pair surviving as portraits of the couple, was found in their mastaba tomb in MEIDUM. The statue, realistic and lifelike, depicts a prosperous, amiable woman in the court dress of the time.

Nofret (2) (fl. 19th century B.C.E.) *royal woman of the Twelfth Dynasty*
A consort of SENWOSRET III (r. 1878–1841 B.C.E.), Nofret was buried in the pyramidal complex at el-LAHUN. A black quartzite statue of her survives.

nomarchs   The hereditary aristocracy of the Egyptian NOMES, or provinces, called the *heri-tep a'a*, these nobles raised their own armies, served as representatives of the pharaoh, and defended their borders. The nomarchs of ASSIUT and BENI HASAN were famed for their military prowess as well. In historical periods of weak rulers, the nomarchs became more independent and involved themselves in provincial feuds. Most nomarchs were hereditary princes or counts.

When 'AHMOSE (NEBPEHTIRÉ) (r. 1550–1525 B.C.E.) undertook the reorganization of Egypt after the expulsion of the HYKSOS (Asiatics), he punished the nomarchs that had served the foreigners. In time, 'Ahmose invited many such nome aristocrats to reside in the royal residence at Thebes, the capital. This deprived the nomarchs of their independence and made them hostages for the continued loyalty of their provinces.

The nomarchs were also called *djadjet*. They and their expanded families maintained their own lifestyles and traditions, even in eras of strong centralized rule. The cliff tombs of Assiut and Beni Hasan and other monuments testify to the continuing strength and dynamism of the nomes.

In the later eras of Egypt, the nomes assumed importance again as the people centered on their homelands and strengthened their territories. During the Ptolemaic Period (304–30 B.C.E.), for example, the legal systems of the nomes became paramount in maintaining judicial order, as the Ptolemies used one set of laws for the Greeks and Hellenized populations and another system for the native Egyptian populations. The Ptolemies relied upon the traditions of the nomes to clarify and conduct the legal requirements within the various provinces. The system proved effective, as the nomes carried on their normal court and council routines and proved stable in all instances. When the Romans occupied Egypt, the nation proved one of the most reliable provinces of the empire, as the nome system and the spirit of cooperation and joint projects were continued successfully.

nome This was a province or administrative region of ancient Egypt, called *sepat* or the *qah* in Egyptian and *nomos* by the Greeks. Some nomes date to Predynastic (before 3000 B.C.E.) times, and all were governed by a *heri-tep a'a,* or NOMARCH, a "Great Overlord," a hereditary title roughly equivalent to a prince or count. Such overlords were responsible for military levies demanded by the rulers and for taxes and tributes assessed for their territories. Each nome had a capital city and a cult center dedicated to the god of the region, as well as totems, but these changed in the course of Egyptian history. The total number of nomes varied over time and the nomes were finalized only in the Greco-Roman Period. A grid, called a *spat,* was used to designate the nomes.

The first recorded mention of such nomes dates to the reign of DJOSER (2630–2611 B.C.E.), although the armies marching with NARMER (ca. 3000 B.C.E.) carried totems depicting nome symbols. By the reign of NIUSERRÉ (2416–2392 B.C.E.), Egypt was divided into the 22 nomes in Upper Egypt and 20 nomes in Lower Egypt that prevailed for most of pharaonic Egypt's history.

Nubhotepti (fl. 17th century B.C.E.) *royal woman of the Thirteenth Dynasty*
She was called "the Child" in mortuary inscriptions. Nubhotepti was provided with a royal tomb at DASHUR, near the funerary complex of AWIBRÉ HOR. Her mummified remains indicate that she was 44 years of age or older when she died, and her portrayal as "the Child" remains a mystery.

Nubia This was the land composing modern Sudan below the first cataract of the Nile, called Ta-seti, WAWAT, and Kush in reference to specific regions over the various historical eras. The prehistoric period (ca. 6000–3100 B.C.E.) culture of the area was based at modern Khartoum. Nomadic cattle herders settled there, and evidence of pottery and other industries demonstrate a cultural development. From 4000 to 3100 B.C.E., the culture of Nubia was contemporaneous with Egypt's Nagada I and II.

The A Group of Nubia is evident ca. 3100–2800 B.C.E. in some areas. The rulers buried by this culture had elaborate tombs and funerary regalia. The A Group were enemies of southern Nubians and were colonized by the Egyptians. The C Group, prospering ca. 2100–1500 B.C.E., were linked to the B Group and resided in the area called Wawat by the Egyptians. They farmed, herded animals, and traded goods. During the Twelfth Dynasty (1991–1783 B.C.E.), the C Group was viewed as a threat, and the Egyptians began to fortify the second cataract installations.

The Kermeh culture in Nubia dates to ca. 1990–1550 B.C.E. Kermeh became an Egyptian colony under 'Ahmose (Nebpehtiré) (r. 1550–1525 B.C.E.), and many nobles of this culture were educated in Thebes as a result. The area was of vital concern to Egypt from the start of the dynastic period, and as early as the First Dynasty (2920–2770 B.C.E.) the Egyptian rulers were active to some extent in that region. AHA (Menes) (2920 B.C.E.) recorded the taking of two villages below GEBEL EL-SILSILEH during his reign, and the ruler DJER's name appears in a mutilated battle scene at WADI HALFA. Trade with Nubia was also considered essential to most dynastic ambitions and resulted in exploration and occupation of Nile sites, although the Egyptians did not penetrate deeply into the lands beyond the Nile shoreline.

The Egyptians representing throne interests exchanged pottery and stone for ivory, gold, ebony, ostrich feathers and eggs, leopard skins, copper, amethyst, carnelian, feldspar, oils, gum resins, cattle, dogs, and a variety of exotic wild animals. In time the Nubians manufactured additional goods in wood, leather, hide, and various types of metals, using these wares to trade as well, and accepting copper tools, jewelry, and amulets in exchange. The various Nubian cultures were also learning about the Egyptian cultic traditions and studying their architectural endeavors.

At the end of the Second Dynasty, KHA'SEKHEMWY (r. 2640 B.C.E.) led a military campaign into Nubia, starting colonies, fortifying the major mining sites, and building garrisons at the trading posts already in existence. The Egyptians maintained these posts but did not attempt to penetrate into the hinterland. The first such trading settlement known was at BUHEN, near the second cataract, founded as early as the Second Dynasty.

SNEFRU (r. 2575–2551 B.C.E.), the founder of the Fourth Dynasty, invaded Nubia and reported bringing back prisoners and cattle. The gold and copper mines of the region were probably being worked by then, and FORTRESSES and garrisoned positions were becoming more extensive. Nubians were already serving as mercenaries in the Egyptian army. General WENI, the commander of the military forces for PEPI I (r. 2289–2255 B.C.E.), attached various units of Nubian warriors to his forces when he conducted campaigns in the SINAI and Canaanite regions.

The extent of Egyptian activity in Nubia during the First Intermediate Period (2134–2040 B.C.E.) is in question to some extent, but MENTUHOTEP II (r. 2061–2010 B.C.E.) of the Eleventh Dynasty is credited with reconquering the original Egyptian holdings in Nubia after uniting Upper and Lower Egypt.

During the Middle Kingdom (2040–1640 B.C.E.), the QUARRIES and mining operations were reopened, and caravans from southern domains traded with the Egyptians at the fortresses maintained on the Nile. These fortresses stretched along the river from cataract to cataract, with each garrison positioned to send messages north or south in case the Nubians demonstrated widespread migrations or threatened the trade routes. In the Middle Kingdom the term Kush identified the lower territories of Nubia, a designation that was used throughout the New Kingdom as well.

When the Middle Kingdom collapsed, the Egyptians withdrew from Nubia, and the region around KERMEH became a capital for the people of Kush. The Kushites, however, were not able to assist the HYKSOS, or Asiatics, when the rulers of the Seventeenth Dynasty at Thebes began their northern assault in ca. 1560 B.C.E. KAMOSE, the last pharaoh of that line, and the older brother of 'AHMOSE, the founder of the New Kingdom, appears to have had a viceroy of Nubia. He may have taken possession of the former Egyptian territories before marching against APOPHIS (2), the Hyksos king, using the MEDJAY, the veteran Nubian troops in service to Thebes. When Kamose did go into battle he used these Nubians who had taken up residence in large numbers in the Egyptian Eastern Desert. The Medjay are believed to be the PAN-GRAVE people. The necropolis areas designated as pan-grave sites appear in southern Egypt at this time, as well as in Lower Nubia. The Medjay remains found below the first cataract probably belonged to those troops who served as an occupying force for the Egyptians there.

'Ahmose had viceroys of Nubia and rehabilitated the fortresses there. In time the Egyptians would control the Nile down to the fifth cataract. They did not venture far inland at any given point but were content to conduct extensive trading operations, along with their usual mining and quarrying systems.

During this period the Egyptians displayed little interest in the customs, religion, or national ideals of the Nubian people. Their god, DEDUN, received some royal patronage, as during the reign of TUTHMOSIS III (1479–1425 B.C.E.), but in general the region was viewed simply as an occupied territory and was extended none of the courtesies offered the Levantine city-states that were also part of the empire.

Nubia was administered by Egyptian officials according to accepted procedures. It was divided into an Upper Nubia and a Lower Nubia, each under the control of a governor. The northern province probably included the lands as far south as SEMNA, was called Wawat, and was administered at ANIBA. Upper Nubia was governed from AMARA West, at least during the Nineteenth Dynasty (1307–1196 B.C.E.). (Amara was founded by SETI I [r. 1306–1290 B.C.E.]. There are two settlements involved in Amara, on the eastern and western banks of the river.) Amara West was a vast FORTRESS complex with enclosing walls and defenses. The fortresses and garrisons were under a single commander, assisted by the usual assortment of Egyptian officials, scribes, bureaucrats, and agents.

Nubia was not occupied during the Third Intermediate Period (1070–712 B.C.E.), as the Egyptians were preoccupied with their own internal problems. During the reign of SHOSHENQ I (945–924 B.C.E.) of the Twenty-second Dynasty, Egypt traded with the Nubians, but few rulers could muster enough forces to control the traditional fortresses or trade stations. By 770–750 B.C.E., the Nubians had made inroads into the Theban nomes, and in 750 B.C.E., PIANKHI (1) led an army into Egypt to restore the Amunite temples and religious fervor.

The Twenty-fifth Dynasty (712–657 B.C.E.) was Nubian, but these rulers faced an Assyrian invasion and could not maintain their hold on the land. The MEROË culture then emerged, but lasted only until 350 C.E. This kingdom was relatively free of contact with others, being willing and able to do battle to halt the advances of conquerors. The Romans found them to be formidable foes at ASWAN in 24 B.C.E.

The Meroë culture included modern Sudan and established trade relationships with other cultures, both on the Nile and on the Red Sea. In time, after a revival of arts and architecture, a period of extensive pyramid construction was conducted at Meroë. The reliefs and artistic projects of this culture demonstrate skills and a thorough knowledge of the Egyptian canons. In time, Meroë was beset by tribal assaults and climatic changes, bringing about its collapse and the introduction of other influences.

Further reading: Burstein, Stanley Mayer, ed. *Ancient African Civilizations: Kush and Axum.* New York: Markus Wiener Publisher, 2001; Kendall, Timothy. *Kerma and the Kingdom of Kush, 2500–1500 B.C.: The Archaeological Discovery of an Ancient Nubian Empire.* Washington, D.C.: National Museum of African Art, Smithsonian Institution, 1999; Mann, Kenny. *Egypt, Kush, Aksun: Northeast Africa.* Silver Burdett Press, 1996; O'Connor, David. *Ancient Nubia: Egypt's Rival in Africa.* University Museum of Archaeology and Anthropology, 1994; Russman, Edna. *Nubian Kingdoms.* New York: Watts Franklin, 1999; Shinnie, Peter L. *Ancient Nubia.* New York: Routledge, 1995; Wallis Budge, E. A. *A History of Ethiopia: Nubia and Abyssinia.* ECA Associates, 1995.

Nubian Desert An arid stretch in northern Sudan, called also NUBIA or Kush by the Egyptians, the Arabic names are As-sahura or An-nubiya. South of Egypt, the desert stretches from the Nile to the Red Sea. It is a rugged region, with dunes, rocky areas, and uplands. The Nubian Desert was formed into a sandstone plateau with wadis and streams. The desert was always formidable, but trade caravans used the area in many historical periods.

Nubkhas (1) (fl. 21st century B.C.E.) *royal woman of the Eleventh Dynasty*
A consort of MENTUHOTEP II (r. 2061–2010 B.C.E.), Nubkhas was buried in DEIR EL-BAHRI near the great

mortuary complex of Mentuhotep II. Her tomb was surrounded with masonry and enclosed with boulders and rubble.

Nubkhas (2) (fl. 17th century B.C.E.) *royal woman of the Seventeenth Dynasty*
A lesser consort of SOBEKEMSAF I (r. ca. 1640 B.C.E.), Nubkhas was buried in the tomb of Sobekemsaf III at THEBES. Sobekemsaf I's burial site was vandalized by thieves, but Nubkhas's mummified remains were not disturbed because her burial chamber was separate and securely hidden.

Nubkheshed (1) (fl. 12th century B.C.E.) *royal woman of the Twentieth Dynasty*
She was a consort of RAMESSES V (r. 1156–1151 B.C.E.) and perhaps the mother of NUBKHESHED (2).

Nubkheshed (2) (fl. 12th century B.C.E.) *royal woman of the Twentieth Dynasty*
She was the consort of RAMESSES VI (r. 1151–1143 B.C.E.). Nubkheshed was the mother of RAMESSES VII and his brothers, including Prince Amenhirkhopshef. Nubkheshe also bore Princess Iset.

Nun The Egyptian god of the formless chaos or the watery abyss, which held the PRIMEVAL MOUND out of which the god ATUM (a form of RÉ) rose in cosmogonic traditions, Nun existed before the heaven and earth came into being. When the world was created, Nun moved to the edges of the universe, and there he signified the depths of the netherworld. He is depicted as a bearded individual on a solar bark.

As part of the OGDOAD of HELIOPOLIS, Nun was portrayed as a human with a head of a FROG or with the head of an ox, with ostrich feathers as a crown. One ancient relief shows Nun spitting out the northern and southern Niles. He could be found in deep wells or in caverns and was associated with the Nile inundation. He also had a role in the cults of PTAH and TATENEN.

Nut (Nuit) She was an ancient Egyptian goddess of the heavens, mentioned in the BOOK OF THE DEAD. The wife of GEB and his sister, NUT was separated from him by the command of ATUM. SHU raised her up so that Geb could not touch her, and a ban was placed on her bearing children. The EPAGOMENAL DAYS were the only periods in which Nut could conceive. The epagomenal days were added to the Egyptian calendar by the god THOTH, who played a game with the other deities so that he could aid Nut. During that time Nut gave birth to OSIRIS, HORUS (the Old), SET, ISIS, and NEPHTHYS.

Nut is depicted as a woman stretched over the horizons, with stars and celestial lights forming her garb. She was portrayed at times as a heavenly cow that ate the stars each morning and then gave birth to them at twilight. As a cow she carried the god RÉ on her back. When Nut was shown as a woman, she wore a round vase on her head, the hieroglyph of her name. Nut figures in many religious legends. In some of these traditions she is the cow that Ré mounted when he emerged from the abyss at the moment of creation. In the mortuary rituals she protected the deceased, who rose into her heavenly abode as stars.

Nut did not have a temple or a cult dedicated to her worship but there was a shrine honoring her in HELIOPOLIS. In some texts she was called Kha-bewes; "One with a Thousand Souls." Egyptians believed that souls went to Nut after death. She allowed them to dwell forever with the stars. The holiest of these souls became the polar stars, never setting and never changing.

Nwebhotep-Khred (Nubeti-Khred; Nubetepti-Khred) (fl. 18th century B.C.E.) *royal woman of the Twelfth Dynasty*
Her mummified remains were discovered in the tomb of AMENEMHET III (r. 1844–1797 B.C.E.) in the White Pyramid. This princess was buried beside AWIBRÉ HOR, an obscure ruler of the dynasty (date of reign unknown). She was wrapped in gilded plaster and wore a silver crown with a golden uraeus. Possibly the consort of Awibré, Nwebhotep-Khred was adorned with a collar, dagger, flagellum, scepters, and other funerary regalia.

Nykuhor (fl. 25th century B.C.E.) *royal official of the Fifth Dynasty*
He served USERKHAF (r. 2465–2428 B.C.E.) and his successors as a privy counselor and an inspector of scribes. A prince of the royal line, Nykuhor was married to Sekem-Hathor, a princess of the royal line. The dynasties of this era protected their status by maintaining complete control of government bureaus. Only those of the royal family could serve in a high-ranking office. Nykuhor and Sekem-Hathor were buried near Userkhaf in SAQQARA.

oases These lush, habitable depressions found in the LIBYAN DESERT of Egypt have been in use from Predynastic Period times (before 3000 B.C.E.) and served multiple purposes over the centuries. These were important sites in all historical periods because they served as links and outposts in the vast trade operations and bolstered military defenses. In some periods the oases were also places of exile for those banished from the lands by the various rulers.

Called *wehat* and *wake,* terms that denote a fertile region or garden, the oases connected the Nile Valley with Libya and the domains beyond the first cataract of the Nile. They also served as the residences of governors in some dynastic periods. The governors of the Old Kingdom (2575–2134 B.C.E.), for example, lived at Bahat in DAKHLA Oasis. During the expulsion of the HYKSOS, KAMOSE (r. 1555–1550 B.C.E.) of the Seventeenth Dynasty used the various oases as military garrisons and secret arms and personnel hiding places. From these remote sites he was able to campaign against the Asiatics with success because the enemy was not familiar with the terrain and was unable to track his units in the treacherous wilderness.

The major oases of Egypt were:

Baharia called the northern oasis, approximately 190 miles south of Cairo, located in the territory called the Black Desert. Baharia was a source of chalcedony in all eras. The tomb of Amenhotep Huy was discovered there. He was the governor of the region in the reign of AKHENATEN (r. 1353–1335 B.C.E.). Baharia was also famous for its wines, which were graded and classified when offered to consumers. New excavations at Baha-ria Oasis have uncovered a remarkable collection of graves, leading to a designation of part of the oasis as the VALLEY OF THE GILDED MUMMIES.

Dailah a small oasis located to the west of FARAFRA OASIS.

Dakhla called the Inner Oasis, or Tchesti, and located 213 miles southeast of FARAFRA OASIS, this site had historical significance. A cache of prehistoric rock art is available at Dakhla, dating to ancient times and demonstrating the existence of some of the earliest humans in the Nile Valley. The rock art in the wadi was made during times of floods and includes designs, hunting scenes, and figures of men and women with jewelry-clad arms. Goddesses and animals were also depicted here, in what is considered the greatest concentration of rock art in the world. The wadi in this region is called the "Wadi of the Pictures" as a result. Dakhla also contains the site called Deir el-Hagar. A temple dedicated to the god AMUN was discovered at Ain Birdiyeh. This temple and surrounding MASTABA tombs date to the Sixth Dynasty (2323–2150 B.C.E.).

Dunqul an oasis near the first cataract of the Nile, used in the reign of PEPI I (2289–2255 B.C.E.) by General WENI in his campaigns in Nubia (modern Sudan). The Dunqul Oasis is southwest of modern ASWAN, near Kurkur.

Farafra an oasis 213 miles northeast of DAKHLA Oasis in the area called the White Desert. The site was also named Ta-a het by the Egyptians. Farafra was a cattle-raising area from earliest times and offered lush pastures in the sea of desert sand.

Kharga   the Outer Oasis or the Southern Oasis, located 77 miles southwest of ASSIUT. Kharga Oasis was also called Uaht-rest. The site contains a temple dedicated to the deities HIBIS and Nadura. Considered a miniature jewel of nature because of the luxurious vegetation of the oasis, Kharga was dedicated to the god AMUN by DARIUS I (r. 521–486 B.C.E.), the Persian conqueror of Egypt.

Kurkur   an oasis situated to the west of ASWAN.

Siwa   the most famous of the oases, located 524 miles northwest of modern Cairo. In the Ptolemaic Period (304–30 B.C.E.) Siwa was known as Jupiter Ammon, named thus in honor of ALEXANDER III THE GREAT (r. 332–323 B.C.E.). The Macedonian ruler visited Siwa in order to be named a son of the deity Amun and a fitting ruler of Egypt. The oasis is northernmost in the Western Desert, closest to Libya, and it was always considered to be the richest of the sites, having many shrines and gilded objects of devotion.

The temple of AMUN, called Umm Ubayd, was the site of the famous oracle of Siwa, a major attraction for visitors and a vital part of Amunite rituals. Alexander the Great was hailed as a pharaoh by the oracle when he visited the oasis. Siwa is famous for wines and dates as well as for religious monuments. It is also noted as the destination of an ill-fated contingent of Persian soldiers sent by CAMBYSES (r. 525–522 B.C.E.) to loot the oasis temples and shrines. These troops disappeared without a trace, never returning to the Nile. Remains found in the area of Siwa on a recent expedition are now being studied as possible evidence of the Persian troop disappearance.

Oases Route   A caravan trail used by the Egyptians from the Old Kingdom Period (2575–2134 B.C.E.) for trading operations, the Oases Route started in THINIS, north of ABYDOS, on the west bank of the Nile, and led to NUBIA (modern Sudan). From Thinis, the Oases Route went also to KHARGA OASIS, where it linked up with the FORTY DAY ROUTE through Selima and then on to the DAKHLA and FARAFRA Oases. The rich agricultural areas of these oases and the Nubian territories beyond demanded control of the region. Dakhla Oasis and the surrounding districts were colonized in the Sixth Dynasty (2323–2150 B.C.E.), possibly earlier, in order to establish control over the lucrative trade enterprises.

obelisks   Unique stone monuments famed throughout the ages and vibrant symbols of ancient Egypt, obelisks are large upright stone beams with four sides and a tapering end carved into the form of a pyramidion. They were used as religious symbols and were called *tekenu* by the Egyptians. The obelisks were given their modern name by the Greeks, who believed that their shape resembled small spits.

An obelisk of the New Kingdom Period (1550–1070 B.C.E.) raised to catch the first rays of the dawn at Karnak, a form of the ritual *benben* (Courtesy Steve Beikirch)

Obelisks were considered sacred to the god RÉ and were used as well as emblems of other solar deities over the centuries. The ancient texts describe their particular role on the temple sites. According to the ancient traditions, obelisks came in pairs; two were in heaven and two were on the earth in every age.

HELIOPOLIS boasted obelisks from the early periods of the nation, and they were also raised at THEBES and at MEMPHIS. The temples of THOTH, AMUN, ISIS, KHNUM, OSIRIS, NEITH (1), PTAH, and other gods normally had obelisks as part of their designated design. During the New Kingdom Period (1550–1070 B.C.E.), the era of the vast Egyptian Empire, obelisks served as a favored architectural element of the great temples. The rulers of the New Kingdom used them to adorn Karnak and other religious sites at Thebes, and the Ramessid kings had obelisks fashioned for their new capital in the Delta.

The stone pillars were viewed as endowed with supernatural significance. They were inhabited by the gods or by the spirits of the deities from the instant that they were created and thus merited offerings and special ceremonies. TUTHMOSIS III (r. 1479–1425 B.C.E.) instituted such practices for the obelisks that he erected at KARNAK. A new feast and new liturgies were adopted for the offerings made to the god, as the obelisks were believed to have a genuine solar significance. They were positioned according to the traditional patterns in order to reflect the cultic aspirations. The natural daily manifestations of the dawn and the sunset were symbolized in mystical fashion by these pillars, and they had to conform to specifications as to height and location.

Most of the obelisks erected in ancient Egypt were of granite, quartzite, or basalt. At the ASWAN quarry, a favorite source of stone for obelisks during the imperial period, granite was heated by bonfires and then cooled by water until the stone split; wooden spikes drove passageways into the desired sections. Workmen cleared a path to the stone, marking the length, which was about 100 feet. Using tools made of hard stones, the workmen began to fashion the sides of the pillar, crawling in and around the obelisk to complete their section of the monument. Fires were also used when deemed necessary to make the stones expand. The formation of the obelisk was tedious and difficult, requiring laborers to continue chipping away at the stone until smooth sides were formed. Large boulders supported the stone being carved so that it would not crack as the workmen leveled the sides and completed the surface carving.

When the pillar was carved to satisfaction, ropes were slung around it and the stone was raised and placed on a heavy sledge. It took several thousand workmen to pull the sledge to the banks of the Nile. There, vessels waited to allow safe loading of the pillars. The unique aspect of this loading process is that the boats remained in dry dock until the pillars were safely on board. Then the vessel and the sacred cargo were slowly floated on water emptied into the dock. When the ship and the pillar were stabilized, the dock gates were opened and the vessel made its way out onto the Nile.

Nine galleys, each with more than 30 rowers, took the vessel and the obelisk to Thebes, where a ceremonial ritual and vast crowds awaited their arrival. A ramp was prepared in advance, and the pillar was pulled to the incline. The unique part of the ramp was a funnel-shaped hole, filled with sand. The obelisk was positioned over the hole and the sand was emptied, thus lowering the pillar into place. When the obelisk had been positioned on its base and fastened there, the ramp was removed and the priests and royal household arrived to take part in dedication rituals and in ceremonies in honor of the god of the stone.

Obelisks are characteristically Egyptian but have been honored by all civilizations since the fall of the New Kingdom. Few of the original pillars remain in Egypt as several capitals around the world boast at least one of these graceful emblems of faith, taken from the Nile. They remain insignias of another time and place and visions of a truly ancient artistry.

Ogdoad The eight gods worshipped in HERMOPOLIS MAGNA and first mentioned in the Middle Kingdom Period (2040–1640 B.C.E.) religious texts, these deities were believed to have been the first beings to emerge from the watery chaos at the time of creation. The Ogdoad was also believed to constitute the soul of the god Thoth. The male members of the Ogdoad, four in number, were always depicted as having frog heads. The four female divine consorts of these gods were always depicted as serpent-headed. The Ogdoad ruled on the earth and then were provided with powers beyond the grave. These deities were:

> **Amun and Amaunet** deities of hiddenness (added later and not part of the original eight).
>
> **Heh and Heket** deities of eternity, also listed as Huh and Hauhet.
>
> **Kek and Keket** deities of darkness, also listed as Kuk and Kauket.
>
> **Nun and Nunet** deities of primeval waters and chaos, associated with the Nile's inundations; also listed as Nun and Naunet.
>
> **Tenem and Tenemet** deities of the twilight.

The Ogdoad deities were believed responsible as well for the flow of the Nile and for the dawning of the sun each day. Amun and Amaunet were added to the Ogdoad in the PYRAMID TEXTS. They were proclaimed the first deities to arise from the primeval waters. The Ogdoad were thus a vital element of the moment of creation, remaining an important part of Egypt's cosmogonic system.

oils Substances used in Egyptian rituals and ceremonies, highly prized, and employed for cultic and royal observances, oils were also used in medical procedures, mummification, and as cosmetics bases. Tablets with shallow basins of alabaster have been found on many sites, an indication of a widespread use of such substances. A variety of these oils were available to the people of the Nile Valley in all eras.

The most popular was *hekenu,* a type of oil used to anoint the statues of the gods and to make the sanctuaries of the temples fragrant. Syrian balsam, *neck-enen* salve oils, cedar oils, and "Best Libyan" oils were also employed in ceremonies and in mummification processes. The daily rituals of anointing the pharaoh involved the highest grades of such substances.

See also DAILY ROYAL RITES; MORTUARY RITUALS.

Oil Tree *See* PAY LANDS.

Olympias (fl. fourth century B.C.E.) *royal woman of Macedonia*
She was the wife of King Philip II and the mother of ALEXANDER III THE GREAT (r. 332–323 B.C.E.). Olympias

was the daughter of Neoptolemus, the king of Epirus, and originally named Myrtale. Her name was probably changed when Philip II was victorious at the Olympic games in 356 B.C.E.

Philip II insulted Olympias when he also married Cleopatra, a noble Macedonian woman, and Olympias returned to Epirus in a rage. When she heard of her husband's assassination, however, she returned to be at Alexander's side. Cleopatra and her infant son were murdered upon Olympias's return to Pella, the Macedonian capital. Alexander, however, set out quickly to conquer Asia, and Olympias, feeling rejected, returned to Epirus once again.

Alexander's death in 332 B.C.E. led to an invitation to Olympias to act as regent for her grandson, ALEXANDER IV. She declined at first but then in 317 B.C.E. installed PHILIP III ARRHIDAEUS as the ruler. With the support of the military, Olympias put Philip, his wife, and his supporters to death. As a result, Olympias was condemned and slain.

The Egyptians took note of her death, remembering the popular tale that had circulated when Alexander the Great entered the Nile Valley. The Egyptians had spread the word that Olympias had been seduced by NECTANEBO II (r. 360–343 B.C.E.) during one of his visits to the region of Macedonia and had given birth to Alexander the Great as a result of their affair.

Omari, el- A site dating to the Predynastic Period (before 3000 B.C.E.), near TUREH in the southern suburb of modern Cairo, El-Omari was located at the WADI HAWI, or Wadi Haf, between Cairo and HELWAN. Two Predynastic cultures have been demonstrated there: A (contemporaneous with Amratian) and B (associated with Gerzean). The Omari culture dates to the Early Dynastic Period (2920–2575 B.C.E.).

Ombos A site south of KOPTOS on the western shore of the Nile. The Egyptians called the area Nubti, the Golden, because of the number of gold mines there. Ombos was inhabited from the Predynastic Period (before 3000 B.C.E.), and the god SET was the local patron. A temple discovered at Ombos once rivaled the DENDEREH shrine of HATHOR. This shrine was dedicated to the gods SOBEK and Haroeris. In the Ptolemaic Period (304–30 B.C.E.), Ombos was the capital of a separate nome, Ombites.

See also NATURAL RESOURCES.

On *See* HELIOPOLIS.

onions A favorite vegetable in all historical periods but used from the Twentieth Dynasty (1196–1070 B.C.E.) to the Twenty-second Dynasty (945–712 B.C.E.) as mummification substances, onions were placed in COFFINS and wrapped into the linens of the mummified remains.

Onions were also placed inside of mummies in their chest and pelvic cavities, stuffed into ears, and even used as artificial eyes in some eras.

See also MORTUARY RITUALS.

Onouphis *See* A'A NEFER.

Onouris *See* ANHUR.

"on the bricks" This was an ancient Egyptian term used to designate a woman in the act of giving birth. Expectant mothers who were nearing labor were placed on low stoops made of mud bricks to aid the process. These brick seats forced the women to assume a crouching position, thus aiding the birth. The goddess MESKHENT, a patron of childbearing, was depicted as a woman's head rising out of mud bricks.

Opet This was originally the name of the ancient goddess who was patroness of the southern district of THEBES, and then used to designate the entire area of the city that was used for a special shrine to the god AMUN. Opet was linked to the massive religious compound of KARNAK in LUXOR in annual observances and cultic ceremonies. The popular Feast of Opet was the first divine commemoration of each year from the start of the New Kingdom (1550 B.C.E.) and was held on the 18th day of the second month, which is calculated as mid-August on modern calendars. RAMESSES III (r. 1194–1163 B.C.E.) added to the splendor of the celebrations, which continued until mid-September.

The entire population took part, with Egyptians traveling from distant towns and cities to join in the festivities. Dancers, bands, singers, wrestlers, and other performers staged events around the religious processions. These observances date to the early historical periods in THEBES in various forms, but HATSHEPSUT (r. 1473–1458 B.C.E.) instituted the most famous version of the feast, and that form was maintained until the Twenty-fifth Dynasty (712–657 B.C.E.). During the celebrations the deity Amun and accompanying gods were carried in gilded sedans to great cedarwood barges that were moored at the Nile piers. These barges were large and plated in gold, with jeweled adornments. The barge of Amun was called "Mighty of Prow." Smaller portable shrines, called barks, were also paraded through the streets, accompanied by priests. ORACLE statues were taken on these shrines to the people, so that interviews could be offered personally.

oracles A deity's response to a query, delivered by a messenger of the divine, such as a statue of a god, the practice was widespread throughout ancient Egyptian historical periods and part of all major cult centers, even in the Libyan OASES, especially at SIWA. Oracles were always popular with the people, who had an innate curiosity about the future and daily affairs. They were used in conjunction with lucky and unlucky days.

On festival days, the statues of the gods were carried through the streets of the cities or floated on barges to the local shrines and necropolis regions. The people flocked to the processions, anxious for the statues to reach the STATIONS OF THE GODS that were erected on street corners. These stations were small stages, slightly elevated so that the people could view the statue of the deity on display. There the gods were asked questions about the future, and the devoted faithful, in turn, received ritualized and traditional responses.

The statue of the god moved on its pedestal or in its shrine in response to questions, or the entire shrine swayed to one side or another when the queries were posed to it. A movement in one direction indicated a negative response, and a movement in another direction provided a positive reply. In some cult centers the statues "spoke" to the faithful, as priests could be hidden within the shrine and could provide a muffled but audible response. Some of these priests offered sermons to the people as the of the "god" and repeated time-honored wisdom texts for the edification of the spectators.

The sacred BULLS of Egypt, the THEOPHANIES of some deities, were also used as oracles in their own temples. An animal was led into a vast hall crowded by faithful onlookers. The people posed their questions and the bull was loosed. Two doors opened onto chambers containing the bull's favorite food in order to elicit a response. One door signified a negative response to the question posed at the time and the other a positive reply. The bull entered one chamber or another, thus rendering its divine judgment on the matters under discussion.

The most famous oracle in Egypt was in Siwa Oasis, located 524 miles northwest of modern Cairo. The temple at Aghurmi in the Siwa Oasis had an ancient oracle site that was used by pilgrims. The temple of Umm Ubayd also had an oracle that welcomed visitors in all eras. ALEXANDER III THE GREAT (r. 332–323 B.C.E.), the Spartan general Lysander, the poet Pindar, and the Greek geographer Strabo all attended oracle ceremonies in Siwa.

Orbiney, Papyrus d'   A text of the Nineteenth Dynasty, dating to the reign of SETI I (r. 1306–1290 B.C.E.) and supposedly a copy of an earlier document, the papyrus contained the TALE OF TWO BROTHERS, the legend of good and evil, that dated to ancient historical periods. A memorandum from the workshop of a scribe named Ennana is also included. The PAPYRUS was purchased by Madame d'Orbiney of Italy, hence the name. She sold it to the British Museum in London.

Orion   This heavenly body was deemed significant to the ancient Egyptians, particularly in the early periods. Orion was deemed important when the cosmogonic,

or creation traditions that dominated Egyptian cultic practices, were being formulated by the priest astronomers on the Nile. The PYRAMID TEXTS, dating to the Fifth (2465–2323 B.C.E.) and Sixth (2323–2150 B.C.E.) Dynasties, recount the orbital path of Orion and the role of that heavenly body in the divine plan of the universe and of humans on the earth.

See also ASTRONOMY.

Osireion   The name given to the cenotaph of SETI I (r. 1306–1290 B.C.E.) at ABYDOS, erected to serve as his vast mortuary temple in OSIRIS's holy city, the structure was unfinished at the time of Seti I's death. His grandson MERENPTAH (r. 1224–1214 B.C.E.) completed it in his honor, and the temple stands as a remarkable example of Egyptian architectural and artistic advances. The custom of erecting cenotaphs, or false, secondary tombs, in the holy city of Abydos dates to the earliest eras on the Nile.

Seti I's temple reflected this tradition but added the elements of the artisans and builders of his era. The walls of this temple were covered with passages from the BOOK OF THE DEAD, the *Book of the Gates,* astronomical treatises, and other texts. A unique feature of the Osireion was an island that was surrounded by canals that held the water. The false SARCOPHAGUS of the pharaoh rested on the island.

A portico opened onto a shrine, leading to the first hypostyle hall that contained 12 pairs of papyrus columns and elaborate and beautiful reliefs. Seven chapels were also included in the design and led to a second hypostyle hall that had reliefs of nome standards. The

A view of the tomb of Seti I at Abydos, a cenotaph temple that honors the deity Osiris and eternity *(Courtesy Steve Beikirch)*

gods honored in this section include PTAH, RÉ-Harakhte, AMUN, Osiris, ISIS, HORUS, and PTAH-SOKAR. An Osirian chapel leads to a cultic ceremonial hall with two chambers. The Gallery of the King Lists is in this section, alongside a Corridor of Bulls, and a shrine for a SOKAR BOAT.

The original shrine on the site was possibly erected in the Old Kingdom (2575–2134 B.C.E.). Seti I's structure, built on the foundation, was made out of quartzite, sandstone, and granite. Merenptah (1224–1214 B.C.E.) added a long passage, decorated with scenes from the Book of the Dead.

Osiris One of the most popular and enduring deities of ancient Egypt, Osiris was a symbol of the eternal aspirations of the people and a god credited with civilizing the inhabitants of the Nile Valley. His cult dates to the Old Kingdom (2575–2134 B.C.E.), when he assumed the roles of other local deities, and continued into the Greco-Roman Period (after 332 B.C.E.). Osiris's earliest manifestation was Asar, a man-headed god of agriculture. ANDJETI was another fertility god who, united with Khentiamentiu of ABYDOS in agricultural celebrations, was absorbed into the Osirian cult in time. Possible DJED pillar symbols date to the First Dynasty (2920 B.C.E.) at HELWAN, and the cult is mentioned in the Fifth Dynasty (2465–2323 B.C.E.).

Osiris appears to have been part of the Heliopolitan pantheon and was mentioned in the PYRAMID TEXTS. His cult gained early acceptance at Abydos and at BUSIRIS. He was addressed as Wen-nefer, "the Beautiful," and then became Khentiamentiu, "the Foremost of the Westerners." Amenti, the West, always represented death and the grave to Egyptians and in time symbolized paradise and resurrection. Osiris was the Lord of Amenti in every historical period after his introduction to the Egyptian populace.

The traditions of Osiris were the basis for the god's cult, and a legendary account of his life is given in the Pyramid Texts. Osiris was slain by his brother deity, SET, and discovered by ISIS and NEPHTHYS. The goddess Isis, the wife of Osiris, stopped the corruption of his flesh and brought him back to life, but Set attacked the body again. A heavenly trial resulted, with Osiris accusing Set of the murderous acts before the gods. Osiris was praised as a patient endurer and ruler by the other gods during the trial, but they condemned Set as an evildoer.

The death of Osiris and his resurrection played an important part in the cult that became symbolic of the rulers of Egypt in time. The dead pharaohs of Egypt were considered embodiments of Osiris, having been equated with HORUS, Osiris's son, while on the throne. Other aspects of Osiris's cult included his dismemberment by Set and his reign in an ideal time before the start of the nation, 3000 B.C.E., referred to as "the Time of the Gods."

An Osiride pillar, a statue of Ramesses II (r. 1290–1224 B.C.E.) depicting him as Osiris in the realms beyond the grave *(Courtesy Thierry Ailleret)*

The earliest representation of Osiris dates to the Fifth Dynasty, when he was depicted as a man wearing a divine wig. In subsequent eras he kept his mortal appearance, but always in a mummified form, which was a symbol of his funerary role. In the Middle Kingdom (2040–1640 B.C.E.) Osiris was depicted wearing the white helmet of Upper Egypt, perhaps to designate the god's origins. In time he was normally portrayed wearing the *atef* CROWN, the elaborate plumed headdress. In his hands he carried the CROOK and FLAIL.

In the mortuary rituals, Osiris is the paramount judge of the deceased Egyptians, who had to appear in his Judgment Halls to face him and his companions, the FORTY-TWO JUDGES. The MORTUARY RITUALS in most eras revolved around this role of Osiris, and the BOOK OF THE DEAD offered various accounts of the ritual of weighing the hearts of the dead to judge their worthiness for eternal bliss.

The god, however, represented more than fertility and judgment. Most of his appeal was based on his embodiment of the cosmic harmony. The rising Nile was his insignia, and the moon's constant state of renewal symbolized his bestowal of eternal happiness in the lands beyond the grave. In this capacity he also be came the model of human endeavors and virtues, judging each and every individual at the moment of death and also demanding an accounting of human behavior and attitudes. This role distinguishes Osiris, particularly in view of the normal religious or moral concepts governing other nations on the early stages of human development.

In time, Abydos became the center of the cult of Osiris, and pilgrims made their way there for various celebrations. Families also arrived with the remains of their loved ones, seeking a small plot of land for a burial on the site. The deceased longed to be buried beside Osiris, and if such a burial was not possible, the relatives of the dead person placed a mortuary stela in the area of Abydos so that the individual could share in Osiris's bliss. Other cultic observances were conducted in the name of Osiris.

Further reading: Harris, Geraldine. *Isis and Osiris.* New York: NTC Publishing Group, 1997; Houston, Jean. *The Passion of Isis and Osiris: A Gateway to Transcendant Love.* New York: Ballantine Publishing Group, 1998; Schumann-Antelme, Ruth, and Jon Graham, trans. *Becoming Osiris: The Ancient Egyptian Death.* Rochester, Vt.: Inner Traditions International, 1998; Wallis Budge, E. A. *Osiris: The Egyptian Religion of Resurrection.* London: Kegan Paul, 2001.

Osiris beds Unique boxes used in tombs in many historical periods of Egypt's history, these "beds" were fashioned out of wood or pottery and made in the shape of mummified Osirises. They were normally hollow and filled with Nile mud and seeds of corn or grain. They were then wrapped in mummy linens. The seeds sprouted, representing the resurrection of Osiris and the return of the crops each year. The most famous Osiris bed was in the tomb of DJER (r. ca. 2900 B.C.E.), the second ruler of Egypt, whose ABYDOS tomb was identified as the actual grave of Osiris. KHENDJER (r. ca. 1740 B.C.E.) installed an elaborate Osiris bed in this tomb, depicting the god lying on a bier formed by the bodies of lions.

Osiris festivals These were the religious celebrations held throughout Egypt to honor the deity Osiris, especially in the cult center of ABYDOS. The seasonal cycles of life were mirrored in these feasts, as nature was personified in the death and resurrection of the god. The annual MYSTERIES OF OSIRIS AND ISIS, a form of passion play, was the most popular observance. A festival held in November, according to the modern calendar, was designed to "Behold the Beauty of the Lord." This was celebrated on the 17th to the 20th of Athyr (November 14–17) and was at times Egypt's most well attended observance.

Another festival, called "the Fall of the Nile," observed the receding waters of the rivers and was a time of mourning for Osiris. The Nile represented Osiris'

capacity to renew the earth and restore life to the nation. In modern May, on the 19th of Pakhons, the Egyptians returned to the river with small shrines containing metal (sometimes gold) vessels. They poured water into the Nile, crying out: "Osiris Is Found." Other shrines were cast adrift into the Nile. Mud and spices were also molded into shapes to honor Osiris's return.

This festival was similar to "the Night of the Tear" in modern June. The festival honoring an Osirian symbol, the *djed* or *djet* pillar, was held on the modern January 19. The pillars were raised up to welcome Osiris and the coming harvests. The pharaoh and his court participated in this festival. The queens and their retinues sang hymns for the occasion.

Osiris gardens Special plantings were placed inside of molds shaped like the mummified deity. These molds were filled with soil and fertilizers as well as grain seeds and Nile water. The Osiris gardens were tended during festivals honoring the god. They sprouted, demonstrating the powers of the deity, in much the same fashion as the OSIRIS BEDS.

Osiris mysteries These were the annual ceremonies conducted in honor of the god OSIRIS, sometimes called the Mysteries of Osiris and Isis, passion plays, or morality plays, and staged in ABYDOS at the beginning of each year. They are recorded as being observed in the Twelfth Dynasty (1991–1783 B.C.E.) but were probably performed for the general populace much earlier.

Dramas were staged in Abydos, with the leading roles assigned to high-ranking community leaders or to temple priests. The mysteries recounted the life, death, mummification, resurrection, and ascension of Osiris, and the dramas were part of a pageant that lasted for many days. Egyptians flocked to the celebrations. After the performances, a battle was staged between the FOLLOWERS OF HORUS and the FOLLOWERS OF SET. This was a time-honored rivalry with political as well as religious overtones. Part of the pageant was a procession in which a statue of Osiris, made out of electrum, gold, or some other precious material, was carried from the temple. An outdoor shrine was erected to receive the god and to allow the people to gaze upon "the Beautiful One." There again Osiris was depicted as rising from the dead and ascending to heavenly realms. Other mysteries honoring other deities were held in HELIOPOLIS, BUSIRIS, BUBASTIS, MEMPHIS, and THEBES. Some of these included processions and staged battles including dramas featuring WEPWAWET, the ancient wolf god.

Osiris's temple This was the major shrine of Osiris in ABYDOS, now called Kom el-Sultan by the Egyptians. There were many sites of worship dedicated to Osiris in the Nile Valley and beyond, but the god's main cultic temple was located in Abydos, the city dedicated to him. Only the ramparts of the temple are visible today. A limestone portico erected by RAMESSES II (r. 1290–1224 B.C.E.) is also evident. The temple, called the Osireion in some records, dates to the Third Dynasty (2649–2575 B.C.E.) or possibly earlier. This is older than the OSIREION erected by SETI I (r. 1306–1290 B.C.E.).

Osochor (Aa'kheperre setepenré; Osorkon the Elder) (d. 978 B.C.E.) *ruler of the Twenty-first Dynasty*
He reigned from 984 B.C.E. until his death. He succeeded AMENEMOPE at TANIS. Osochor was the son of a Libyan chief named SHOSHENQ and the Lady MEKHTEMWESKHET (1). No monuments are attributed to him. His son was SIAMUN (1).

Osorkon I (Sekhemkheperré setepenré) (d. 909 B.C.E.) *second ruler of the Twenty-second Dynasty*
He reigned from 924 B.C.E. at TANIS until his death. Osorkon I was the son and heir of SHOSHENQ I and the grandson of PSUSENNES II. His mother was either KAROMANA (1) or MA'ATKARE (2). He married Queen MA'ATKARÉ (3), and had another consort, TASEDKHONSU. His sons were SHOSHENQ II, TAKELOT I, and IUWELOT.

Osorkon I was militarily active, campaigning in the Levant and in Palestine. A statue of him was raised up in BYBLOS in modern Lebanon. In the early years of his reign, he was generous to Egypt's temples. He also developed a strong series of military units to control irrigation and development projects in the FAIYUM. KOPTOS and ABYDOS benefited as well from his patronage and he built temples at el-HIBA and Atfih.

When Iuput, his brother, retired as the high priest of Amun at THEBES, Osorkon I installed his son SHOSHENQ in that office and named him co-regent. Shoshenq, however, died before inheriting the throne and Osorkon I was succeeded by TAKELOT I. Osorkon I was buried in Tanis.

Osorkon II (Userma'atre Setepenamun) (d. 855 B.C.E.) *fifth ruler of the Twenty-second Dynasty*
He reigned from 883 B.C.E. until his death. Osorkon II was the son of TAKELOT I and Queen KAPES and the grandson of OSORKON I. His reign is considered by many to be the last true flowering of the dynasty. He allowed his cousin HARSIESE to assume the post of high priest of Amun in THEBES. Harsiese, the son of SHOSHENQ II, took a royal name and pharaonic titles, and Osorkon II's regal powers were thus reduced.

Marrying Queen KAROMANA (5) and Queen DJED-MUTESANKH, Osorkon II had four sons: SHOSHENQ, NIM-LOT (3) HARNAKHTE (2), and TAKELOT II. When Harsiese died, Osorkon appointed his son Nimlot as the successor in the Amunite priesthood in Thebes. Harnakhte was named the ranking prelate in TANIS. Shoshenq, the crown prince, did not live long enough to inherit the throne from his father.

Osorkon II embellished the temples at BUBASTIS and celebrated his *heb-sed (see* SED*)* at Bubastis in his 22nd regnal year. Temples were exempted from taxes during his reign. Osorkon II also built at MEMPHIS, Tanis, and Thebes, and he maintained a relative peace while watching the rise of Assyria. Records indicate that Osorkon II made a tribute to the Assyrian ruler Shalmanesser II (859–824 B.C.E.) to avoid battles and possible invasion.

When Osorkon II died, he was placed in a gigantic sarcophagus with a Ramessid Period lid in Tanis. The burial chamber was lined with granite. Prince Harnakhte was buried beside his father. There are some records that state that Harnakhte was too large for his sarcophagus, and as a result his mummy suffered the loss of its legs and feet. SHOSHENQ V was also buried with Osorkon II. Takelot II, Osorkon II's youngest son, succeeded him after a period of co-regency.

Osorkon III (d. 749 B.C.E.) *ruler of the Twenty-third Dynasty*
He reigned from 777 B.C.E. until his death. The son of TAKELOT II and Queen KAROMANA (5), he was made the high priest of Amun at THEBES while still a prince. His relative, HARSIESE, started a revolt that continued on and off for 12 years and forced Osorkon to take military action and to face banishment for a number of years. In one campaign, he burned the bodies of the rebels, an act that was condemned as sacrilege by the Egyptians. The BUBASTITE PORTAL in KARNAK describes some of his travails.

SHOSHENQ III usurped or inherited the throne and banished Osorkon from Thebes. In time, however, he was recalled and shared the prelature with IUPUT for two years. Osorkon III's younger brother, Bakenptah, served as high priest in HERAKLEOPOLIS. In 777 B.C.E., Osorkon III was crowned in Thebes and recognized by the Libyan Chiefs of Ma at MENDES. He was on the throne during the last 13 years of Shoshenq III's reign in Tanis. He married Queen KARAOTJET, the mother of SHEPENWEPET I, TAKELOT III, and RUDAMON. Shepenwepet I was made the GOD'S WIFE OF AMUN, or the Divine Adoratrice at Thebes. Takelot was put in charge of Herakleopolis and served as the high priest in Thebes. Takelot was then named co-regent and held this rank for six years before Osorkon III's death. Osorkon III was probably buried near MEDINET HABU.

Osorkon IV (Akheperré setepenamun) (fl. 713–712 B.C.E.) *ruler of the Twenty-second Dynasty*
He reigned only from 713 to 712 B.C.E. as the ruler of TANIS and BUBASTIS and the successor of SHOSHENQ IV. His mother was Queen KAROMANA (6). During his reign, the Nubian PIANKHI (1) (r. 750–712 B.C.E.) began his assault on Egypt. Osorkon IV joined a coalition of rulers and marched south under the leadership of TEFNAKHTE of SAIS. At HERAKLEOPOLIS the two armies clashed, and

Piankhi proved victorious. Osorkon IV was then made governor of Tanis by the Nubian (modern Sudanese) ruler. This arrangement did not survive the later invasions by the Nubian successors of Piankhi.

ostraca Fragments or slabs of stone or pottery used for writing or sketching by the ancient Egyptians, they were employed much like modern paper for memos and letters. Ostraca were often provided to students for practicing writing by copying literary texts. They are much more numerous in archaeological sites than papyri. The ostraca discovered by modern excavations of Egyptian sites bear copies of truly ancient texts, artistic renderings, examples of the use of the canon of art, and other information about local and national events.

Overthrowing Apophis This is an unusual document dating to the Ramessid Period (1307–1070 B.C.E.) but part of the religious mythology from ancient times in Egypt. Apophis was a serpent that assaulted the god RÉ on his journey through TUAT, or the Underworld, each night according to Heliopolitan religious traditions. In some eras Apophis was deemed a manifestation of the god SET and was halted in his evil each night by the prayers of the faithful. The ritual of overthrowing the serpent enemy of Ré included recitation of a list of the Apophis "secret" names, which when recited made him vulnerable. A selection of hymns to be sung on the occasion for his destruction were popular devotions, and many Egyptians made nightly vigils for this cause.

According to the ritual, the serpent had been previously annihilated, hacked to pieces, dismembered, and flung into the abyss by the prayers of the truly pious. This treatment of Apophis, however, did not deter him from making another attack upon Ré the following night, when he arose, fully reanimated. The Egyptians assembled in the temples to make images out of the serpent in wax. They spat upon the images, burned them, and mutilated them. Cloudy days or storms were signs that Apophis was gaining ground, and solar eclipses were interpreted as a sign of Ré's demise. The sun god emerged victorious each time, however, and the people continued their prayers and anthems.

Oxyrrhynchus (1) This is the modern city of el-Bahnasa, once called Harday. The capital of the nineteenth nome of Upper Egypt and located on the west bank of the BAHR YUSEF in the Faiyum, the site contained the mummified remains of dogs. OSIRIS was favored in this region, where more Greek papyri have been found than in any other site in Egypt. The elephant-snout fish, *Mormyrus kannume,* was revered there. The site was originally named Per-Mudjet.

oxyrrhynchus (2) This is the Nile fish believed to have eaten the phallus of the Egyptian god OSIRIS when SET dismembered him and cast his body parts into the river. Out of devotion to Osiris, some nomes declared that the fish was considered forbidden food. In some territories the fish was considered a delicacy because of the Osirian tradition.

P

paddle dolls These objects were unique mortuary accessories in the form of painted, flat wooden figures with elaborate hairdos composed of string, Nile mud, faience, or golden beads. The strings were interwoven with straw, copying the wigs fashionable in the Middle Kingdom (2040–1640 B.C.E.). Paddle dolls were discovered in some Eleventh Dynasty (2040–1991 B.C.E.) burial sites. Their role in the mortuary regalia is not understood, but it is possible that these dolls were provided as sexual companions for the deceased, as the paddle dolls were always feminine in form.

See also MORTUARY RITUALS.

pa duat This was a popular and often used tomb chamber that dates to early historical periods and served as residences for the patron deities of the gravesites. MENTUHOTEP II (r. 2061–2010 B.C.E.) had a *pa duat* designed into the upper court of his mortuary complex on the western shore of THEBES at DEIR-EL-BAHRI. Within the *pa duat,* priests dressed, anointed, and scented the images of the deity serving as the patron of the mortuary complex.

Pa'hemmetcher (fl. 12th century B.C.E.) *cavalry official of the Twentieth Dynasty*
He served RAMESSES III (r. 1194–1163 B.C.E.) as the Master of Horse. The Egyptian cavalry was an important element of the nation's military response, gaining a reputation in neighboring lands. Extensive breeding programs were instituted as well to insure ever-improved stocks. Pa'hemmetcher would have commanded cavalry units as well as the breeding programs. He was depicted in a shrine near ABU SIMBEL, honored there for his labors during Ramesses III's reign.

See also KAMOSE; WARFARE

Paheri (fl. 15th century B.C.E.) *mayoral official of the Eighteenth Dynasty*
He served TUTHMOSIS III (r. 1479–1425 B.C.E.) as the mayor of Nekheb (modern ELKAB), and Iuny (modern ESNA). Paheri had to concern himself with the agricultural activities in his district. His gravesite near modern Elkab was on the western shore of the Nile. Rock-cut and large, the tomb had animated low-relief paintings depicting agricultural scenes and contemporary figures. Paheri's charioteer, Khenmen, is shown caring for the horses being used. These steeds are called "the excellent team of the mayor beloved . . . about whom the mayor boasts to everyone." Paheri's wife, Henutreneheh, is also shown in the tomb. A statue of her was discovered there, and she is depicted as making offerings in a wall painting. Festival scenes in the tomb include a female harpist and a piper, as well as the required funerary images.

Paibek'khamon (fl. 12th century B.C.E.) *harem conspirator of the Twentieth Dynasty*
He was involved in the HAREM revolt directed at RAMESSES III (r. 1194–1163 B.C.E.). Paibek'khamon was the chief steward of the royal residence and plotted with TIYE (2), a lesser-ranked consort who wanted to place her son, Prince PENTAWERET, on the throne. Paibek'khamon carried messages to Queen Tiye's allies outside the palace. When the harem revolt was attempted, all of the plotters were arrested.

Paibek'khamon was judged guilty and was allowed to end his own life.

Pakhenti The religious shrine district south of THEBES (modern Luxor) dating to early historical periods, Pakhenti was associated with the cult of the god AMUN. Shrines were erected there for rituals celebrating Amunite festivals and holy days. Pakhenti was a small village beside OPET, the suburb of Thebes dedicated to Amun. The god Amun began as a local Theban cult and emerged as the most dominant deity of Egypt and Nubia (modern Sudan). The cult increased in power as the Theban warrior pharaohs credited Amun with their military victories and the growth of the empire.

See also LUXOR.

Pakhet A lioness deity, listed also as Pakht, and called "She Who Scratches." She was the patroness of the living and the dead in all eras. A shrine was erected by Queen-Pharaoh HATSHEPSUT (r. 1473–1458 B.C.E.) near Minya in the FAIYUM region, and SETI I (r. 1306–1290 B.C.E.) renovated this shrine. The goddess also appears in a burial chamber of Seti I, depicted with a lion head and an erect serpent, "spitting fire." Pakhet guarded the PERO, the royal residence, and cared for deceased Egyptians. Her shrine was adopted by the Greeks in the Ptolemaic Period (304–30 B.C.E.) and was renamed the SPEOS ARTEMIDOS, associating Pakhet with the Greek deity Artemis. Originally a desert huntress known for her ferocity against Egypt's enemies, Pakhet was depicted as a woman with a lion's head.

Palermo Stone The Palermo Stone is a document that is cited as a KING LIST but also has historical significance concerning the early eras of ancient Egypt. The stone is a fragment of diorite anfibolica and is considered a reliable source of information about certain pharaohs and their courts. It is 17 inches high and nine and three-quarters inches wide and was originally part of a six and one-half foot to seven-foot monument. The Palermo Stone, so named because it is in the Regional Archaeological Museum in Palermo, contains a king list from the Fifth Dynasty (2465–2323 B.C.E.). Smaller fragments are in the Egyptian Museum of Cairo and in the Petrie Museum of University College London. The Palermo Stone records Predynastic Period (before 3000 B.C.E.) rulers and dynastic pharaohs through KAKAI (r. 2446–2426 B.C.E.) Some 125 rulers are listed. The stone is inscribed on both sides and includes information about ceremonies, taxes, wars, and the inundation of the Nile.

The Palermo Stone also records a well-developed culture and a remarkable administrative government bureaucracy that functioned admirably from the first eras of Egypt. Written in archaic Egyptian, the document also gives insight into many aspects of life in the Nile Valley. These are annals of the reigns of the pharaohs of that period, day by day and year by year. Scholars have long recognized the implications of such records in regard to the function of future governments. The process of unification of the Two Kingdoms, Upper and Lower Egypt, is also made evident.

The document opens with accounts of the Predynastic Period rulers, providing names of unknown rulers leading to the First Dynasty. The other dynasties follow, with records of festivals, religious rituals, the building of ships, a military campaign in Nubia (modern Sudan), and even minute details, such as the installation of doors made from imported cedar wood in the palace. All of these recorded activities were preserved by a small army of trained scribes serving the courts and following the kings wherever they went to document their activities and royal roles. These scribes were much like the modern press corps found in the capitals of the world's nations. While the Palermo Stone does not authenticate the succession of some rulers, its day-to-day accounts provide portraits of an evolving people and the institutions that fostered growth and resilience.

palette A rectangular piece of wood or stone, called *mestha* by the Egyptians and used in daily routines, they were fashioned from eight to 16 inches long and two to three inches thick, with oval hollows at one end to accommodate ink, paint, or cosmetic pots. A groove cut out of the center, sloping at one end, held reeds. Some grooves had sliding corners, others used slats of wood glued across the grooves. Such palettes were normally inscribed with prayers to THOTH, the deity of wisdom. Several palettes were viewed as historical documents. Below are some of the more famous of these.

> **Ashmolean Palette** depicts animal groups, including a lute-playing fox and other fantastic beasts. It is now in the Ashmolean Museum at Oxford.
>
> **Battlefield Palette** show Libyans in a war with Egyptians, also depicts standards and groups of prisoners. The Herakleopolitan deity HORUS is portrayed with the lion and the vulture.
>
> **Bull Palette** depicts the bull (the symbol of royal power) goring northern prisoners. Standards are also displayed. The verso shows a conquered city with crenellated walls. It is now in the Louvre in Paris.
>
> **Hunter's Palette** depicts an expedition to hunt animals. Armed men, a shrine, and a BULL are also shown.
>
> **Libya Palette** depicts the irrigation and hydraulic systems of Egypt, vital to the agricultural base of the nation. This is also called the Cities Palette and is in the British Museum in London.
>
> **Narmer Palette** an elaborate instrument now in the Egyptian Museum of Cairo. NARMER is depicted on both sides of the palette and is called

nar, fish, and *mer,* a chisel. On the recto side he is wearing the red crown of the Delta, proclaiming victory in the north. A BULL, a depiction of Narmer, is shown destroying a city. Standards and the HORUS symbol add to the design. On the verso side, Narmer is shown in a kilt, wearing a false beard. He is carrying a MACEHEAD. A falcon accompanies his destruction of a city.

Ostrich Palette depicts Egyptians herding groups of animals. This is now in the Manchester Museum in England.

Scorpion Palette a large instrument used for grinding antimony. Hollow on one side, the palette was decorated with votive designs. SCORPION I, a ruler of a region before the unification in 3000 B.C.E., is depicted in animal forms destroying cities. Scorpion is portrayed as a falcon and a lion. Seven cities are shown being destroyed, or one city is shown being attacked seven times.

Pami (Userma'atre'setepenre'amun) (d. 773 B.C.E.) *ruler of the Twenty-second Dynasty*
He reigned from 783 B.C.E. until his death. His brother and successor was SHOSHENQ V. An obscure pharaoh, Pami was called "the cat." He ruled in TANIS.

pan-graves They are elaborate burial sites found throughout Upper Egypt, south of Cusae, and Upper NUBIA (modern Sudan) dating to the Seventeenth Dynasty of Thebes (1640–1550 B.C.E.). These graves are closely related to the MEDJAY units employed by KAMOSE when he began his assaults on the HYKSOS and their Asiatic allies, ca. 1555 B.C.E. They also reflect a period of migration by Nubians, during the Second Intermediate Period (1640–1550 B.C.E.).

The graves are between ten inches and six feet long and are usually shaped like a pan, shallow and oval or circular in design. The bodies placed inside were found clad in leather garments and bearing primitive jewelry. Pottery included in the graves dates to the C-Horizon (Nubian) variety—rough brown with patterns of oblique lines or undecorated. Painted skulls of horned animals were placed in nearby offertory pits, and the graves also held Egyptian axes and daggers. The pan-graves culture depicts cattle herders. The skulls, horns, and leather kilts reflect active nomadic lifestyles.

The pan-graves found in Lower Nubia date to the same period and were probably dug by immigrants to the region or by the Medjay, who settled in that territory as Egyptian allies or as an occupation force. Pan-graves pottery has also been found in ELKAB and QUBAN, an indication that the Medjay units garrisoned these positions for the Egyptians. There was some conflict between the Medjay and the local populations in Nubian districts in the past, and the troops would have been a reliable occupation force.

Panhesi (Panhey) (fl. 14th–12th centuries B.C.E.) *clan of public officials serving in the New Kingdom (1550–1070 B.C.E.).*
The first Panhesi was an official of the Eighteenth Dynasty, serving AKHENATEN (r. 1353–1335 B.C.E.). He was a member of the temple of ATEN during the 'AMARNA Period. His tomb portrays him as an elderly, heavyset man. The second Panhesi was an official of the Nineteenth Dynasty, serving RAMESSES II (r. 1290–1224 B.C.E.) as a scribe and director of the nation's gold stores. He was superintendent of the gold shipments from NUBIA. This Panhesi was buried in THEBES.

The last known Panhesi, an official of the Twentieth Dynasty, served Ramesses XI (r. 1100–1070 B.C.E.). He was the VICEROY of NUBIA, involved as well in military affairs. When a revolt against the high priest of AMUN took place in Thebes, Panhesi gathered up military units and marched to the area. There he put down the rebellion, dismissing the truant prelate. Returning to his administrative center on the ELEPHANTINE Island, Panhesi left one man in charge of the city. This man, HERIHOR, made himself high priest of Amun and began a process of divided rule in Egypt.

Panopolis This is a site northeast of AKHMIN, noted for a monument to the god MIN. The original chapel for Min dates to the reign of TUTHMOSIS III (1479–1425 B.C.E.). This was part of a complex erected originally by Nakhtmin, the first prophet of Min, in the reign of AHA (Menes; ca. 2920 B.C.E.). Reliefs in the structure portray Tuthmosis III making offerings before the god Min, AMUN, and other deities. PTOLEMY II PHILADELPHUS (r. 285–246 B.C.E.) is also portrayed there. Harma'kheru, the high priest of Min during Ptolemy II's reign, added to the shrine as part of the duties of his office.

papyrus A plant, *cyperus papyrus,* once common throughout the Nile Valley and now being reintroduced, the Egyptians called the plant *djet* or *tjufi.* The modern term is probably derived from *pa-p-ior,* which is translated as "that which is from the river." The ancient variety, *cyperus papyrus,* is a type of sedge, growing to a height of 25 feet, probably from eight to 10 feet in ancient periods. The plant was found throughout the Nile Valley, especially in the Delta region, and was the emblem of Lower Egypt.

A papyrus roll was called a *tchama* or a *djema.* The preparation of the papyrus by priests and scribes involved cutting the stem into thin strips, which were laid side by side perpendicularly, with a resin solution poured over the strips. A second layer of papyrus strips was then laid down horizontally and the two layers were pressed and allowed to dry. Immense rolls could be fashioned by joining the compressed sheets. One roll, now in the British Museum, measures 135 feet in length. The usual size was nine to 10 inches long and five to five and one-half inches wide. The rolls used in the temple or in state courts were 16 to 18 inches long.

Papyri were originally made for religious documents and texts, with sheets added to the rolls as needed. The sides of the papyrus are the *recto,* where the fibers run horizontally, and the *verso,* where the fibers run vertically. The *recto* was preferred, but the *verso* was used for documents as well, allowing two separate texts to be included on a single papyrus. Papyrus rolls were protected by the dry climate of Egypt. One roll discovered in modern times dates to ca. 3500 B.C.E.

The color of the papyrus varied from dark to a light brown. In the Ptolemaic Period (304–30 B.C.E.), the rolls were cream colored, yellow, or nearly white. Rolls were kept tightly secured by cords or strips of linen tied with knots. Papyri used for official functions sometimes had clay seals that designated their origin and contents. Papyri of importance were kept in wooden boxes.

The major papyri recovered from sites on the Nile include the following:

ABBOTT PAPYRUS
AMHERST PAPYRUS
ANASTASI PAPYRUS
ANI PAPYRUS
BEATTY PAPYRUS IV, CHESTER
BERLIN PAPYRI
EBERS PAPYRUS
GHUROB SHRINE PAPYRUS
HARRIS PAPYRUS
HEARST PAPYRUS
HUNEFER PAPYRUS
JUDICIAL PAPYRUS OF TURIN
KAHUN PAPYRUS
LANSING PAPYRUS
LONDON PAPYRUS
NEBSENI PAPYRUS
ORBINEY, PAPYRUS D'
PRISSE PAPYRUS
RAMESSEUM PAPYRI
RHIND PAPYRUS
SALLIER PAPYRI
SATIRICAL PAPYRUS
ST. PETERSBURG PAPYRUS
SMITH PAPYRUS, EDWIN
TURIN MINING PAPYRUS
VINDAB PAPYRUS 3873
WESTCAR PAPYRUS
WILBOUR PAPYRUS

papyrus scepter An amulet called the *wadj* or *uadj,* or the papyrus column, the papyrus scepter was believed to impart vigor, vitality, abundance, and virility to the wearer. Made of glazed ware and decorative stones, the amulet was shaped like a papyrus stem and bud. The robust growth of the papyrus represented the heartiness that was bestowed upon the wearer of the papyrus scepter.

See ROYAL CULT.

Par A divine form of the god AMUN, popular in THEBES as a fertility symbol, Par was called "the Lord of the Phallus." He was brought to the fields in various agricultural FESTIVALS to insure good harvests.

paradise This was the eternal abode available to the deceased Egyptians judged worthy of eternal bliss by the deity OSIRIS and the FORTY-TWO JUDGES of the JUDGMENT HALLS OF OSIRIS. The goddess MA'AT and the god THOTH aided in this determination. Such deceased Egyptians were denoted as *ma'at kheru,* "true of voice." The eternal paradises of the Egyptians always contained water, breezes, refreshments, and repose. Such edenic realms were called the Lake of Flowers, the Lake of Reeds, A'aru, Amenti, or Ma'ati. Ma'ati was the site beyond the grave where the deceased buried scepters of crystals containing flames of fire, symbols of the soul.

Paraetonium This was a harbor site on the Mediterranean Sea, west of ALEXANDRIA, the modern MERSA MATRUH. Ptolemaic (304–30 B.C.E.) in origin, Paraetonium was built near a fortress dating to RAMESSES II (r. 1290–1224 B.C.E.), now called Zawiyet Umm el-Rakham.

Parasites (fl. fifth century B.C.E.) *royal woman of Persia* She was the consort of DARIUS II (r. 423–405 B.C.E.). A noble woman, Parasites was recorded as politically ambitious and wealthy. She was Darius II's half sister. While he was only the son of ARTAXERXES I and a concubine, Parasites aided him in usurping the throne.

Paser (1) (fl. 15th century B.C.E.) *military official of the Eighteenth Dynasty*
Paser served AMENHOTEP II (r. 1427–1401 B.C.E.) as a troop commander of the nation's army. This role was an ongoing military command, as Amenhotep II was militarily active, maintaining the imperial gains of his father, TUTHMOSIS III. Paser was buried with honors at THEBES.

Paser (2) (fl. 13th century B.C.E.) *aristocratic and high-ranking official of the Nineteenth Dynasty*
He served SETI I (r. 1306–1290 B.C.E.) and RAMESSES II (r. 1290–1224 B.C.E.) as VIZIER. Paser's father was NEBENTERU, a high priest of AMUN, and his mother was an official of the GOD'S WIFE OF AMUN. He was a hereditary prince and count and the overseer of the city of THEBES. In his later years he succeeded his father as high priest of Amun and oversaw the building of Seti I's tomb. A statue of Paser is in the British Museum in London, and a SCARAB pectoral bearing his name was found on the mummy of an APIS bull in SAQQARA. Reliefs in his tomb

enumerate the duties of vizier, giving daily transactions in some instances.

Paser (3) (fl. 12th century B.C.E.) *official of the Twentieth Dynasty who brought grave robbers to justice*

Paser served as the mayor of THEBES for RAMESSES IX (r. 1132–1112 B.C.E.). In this capacity he investigated the rampant vandalism and desecration of necropolis sites, charging Prince PAWERO, the chief of necropolis sites, with criminal activity. Paser suffered harassment, threats, and abuse as a result, but he proved his accusations, bringing about Prince Pawero's fall. The AMHERST PAPYRUS and ABBOTT PAPYRUS document Paser's faithful service and the ordeals that he endured to put an end to the rampant tomb robberies and desecration of the dead.

See also TOMB ROBBERY TRIAL.

pat A social caste of ancient Egypt, associated with the god HORUS from early historical periods, the *pat* maintained hereditary titles, properties, and ranks and were considered true aristocrats, normally part of vast nome clans. The PYRAMID TEXTS of the Fifth and Sixth Dynasties (2465–2150 B.C.E.) depict the *pat* and Horus, their patron.

Patenemheb (fl. 14th century B.C.E.) *priestly official of the Eighteenth Dynasty*

He served AKHENATEN (r. 1353–1335 B.C.E.) and then HOREMHAB (r. 1319–1307 B.C.E.). Patenemheb was the high priest of RÉ who witnessed the rise of the cult of ATEN and the subsequent fall of 'AMARNA. He retained his rank during Akhenaten's reign because solar cults were not suppressed. When 'Amarna collapsed, Patenemheb received the patronage of Horemhab and aided in the restoration of the traditional temple rites in the Nile Valley.

Pawara (fl. 14th century B.C.E.) *Egyptian diplomat of the Eighteenth Dynasty who was murdered*

He served AKHENATEN (r. 1353–1335 B.C.E.) and was murdered while in Amurru, a vassal city-state on the Levantine coast ruled by King AZIRU. Pawara was the legate of Egypt when he was slain by Aziru's agents. Egypt was forced to evacuate Amurru as a result of the death. Akhenaten did not charge Aziru and did not retaliate for the death of his faithful servant. The Egyptian Empire was imperiled by such inactivity during the 'AMARNA Period.

Pawero (fl. 12th century B.C.E.) *prince and count of the Twentieth Dynasty, convicted of tomb robbery*

Pawero prospered during the reign of RAMESSES IX (1131–1112 B.C.E.) but was then brought to trial on charges of conspiracy and robbery. He was the chief of the necropolis police in THEBES during a period of increasing tomb vandalisms. PASER (3), the mayor of Thebes, accused Pawero of involvement in a ring of tomb invaders, and Pawero retaliated with threats and abuse. Paser, however, took the case to Ramesses IX, and Pawero was arrested. He and his gang of thieves were allied to high officials, thus causing a serious scandal.

The ABBOTT PAPYRUS and AMHERST PAPYRUS give accounts of the affair, in which lesser individuals confessed, implicating Pawero and others. A series of court hearings was held to express the criminal elements, and the convicted individuals received sentences of whippings, mutilations, exile, and even death. Sacrilege and blasphemy were part of such criminal activities, resulting in severe penalties for the guilty and their relatives.

Pay Lands   This is the original site where the gods came into being on the "FIRST OCCASION," the moment of creation according to cosmological traditions over the centuries. The deities associated with the PRIMEVAL MOUND formed the Pay Lands with their sacred utterings. These unique sites were called Djeba and Hareoty, the Blessed Islands, and were depicted in tomb reliefs in the temple of EDFU. PTAH, as Nefer-her, rose on the *Djeba*, and Ré's cosmological traditions involved a similar emergence. The falcon or hawk, the symbol of HORUS, was the lord of these abodes.

The traditions of Ré's cult denoted the Pay Lands as being associated with that deity's coming to his eternal mansion, called the Hinterland of WARET, the Island of Fury, the Mansion of Shooting, the Mansion of the Mystery, the House of Combat, and the Seat of the Two Gods. These sites were not geographically identified but maintained powerful connotations as spiritual domains of Ré.

In other traditions, the Pay Lands, called "the Place of the Ghosts" in some eras, were held to be gardens and marsh areas, sacred to the seats of several gods. The enemies of Egypt could not enter the Pay Lands because they were annihilated there. The Pay Lands were also eternal paradises commemorating creation. The Pay Lands revered throughout Egypt included the following:

Mound of the Radiant One
The Island of Ré
The Djed Pillar of the Earth
The High Hill
The Oil Tree Land
Behdet (Edfu)
He-Who-Is-Rich-in Kas
The Great Seat Where Enemies Are Slain
The Throne
The Praise of Ré
The Territory of Ré's Circuit
The Hinterland of Waret
The Island of Fury
The House of Combat
The Seat of the Two Gods

The Egyptian traditions normally designated specific spiritual realms as the source of their theological concepts and other sites as the destination of deceased humans. The Pay Lands thus added a mythological basis to the various cultic rituals and by their existence in the various traditions rooted the beliefs of each new generation in a quasi-historical reality. The custom of maintaining older traditions alongside newer revelations was bolstered by the celebration of such historical sites and events as the Pay Lands.

See also RELIGION AND COSMOLOGY.

Peak of the West This is the modern site of SHEIKH ABD 'EL-QURNA on the western shore of the Nile at THEBES. Identified as the peak of the west in a DEIR EL-MEDINA stela, the site was the home of the goddess MERESGER (1), called "the Lover of Silence" and "the Lady of Heaven." The Peak of the West is a spur of the hill that faces Thebes. The VALLEY OF THE KINGS and the VALLEY OF THE QUEENS are located beside this peak, which also serves as a backdrop to DEIR EL-BAHRI.

Pebatma (fl. eighth century B.C.E.) *royal Nubian woman of the Twenty-fifth Dynasty*
She was the consort of KASHTA (r. 770–750 B.C.E.) and the mother of PIANKHI (1), SHABAKA, ABAR, and, possibly, AMENIRDIS I, a Divine Adoratrice of Amun. Pebatma was queen of MEROË, in Kush, or NUBIA (modern Sudan), and she apparently did not accompany her husband or sons to Egypt. Meroë was a sumptuous Nubian city, steeped in pharaonic and Amunite traditions.

pectoral An elaborate form of necklace, fashioned out of FAIENCE, stones, or other materials and worn in all historical periods in Egypt, they were normally glazed, with blue-green designs popular in most eras. Most royal pectorals were decorated with golden images that honored the cultic traditions of the gods, with deities and religious symbols being incorporated into dazzling designs. Pectorals have been recovered in tombs and on mummified remains.

Pediese (fl. seventh century B.C.E.) *prince of the Twenty-sixth Dynasty, known for his elaborate tomb*
He was a son of PSAMMETICHUS I (r. 664–610 B.C.E.) and was buried with beautiful mortuary regalia and decorations. Pediese's tomb is located at the base of a deep shaft beside the STEP PYRAMID of DJOSER (r. 2630–2611 B.C.E.) in SAQQARA. Beautifully incised hieroglyphs on the walls of the tomb depict mortuary formulas and funerary spells to aid Pediese beyond the grave. Stars also decorate the ceiling. The prince's sarcophagus is massive and beautifully decorated. Djenhebu, Psammetichus I's chief physician and an admiral in the Egyptian navy, rested in another Twenty-sixth Dynasty tomb nearby.

Pedisamtawi (Potasimto) (fl. sixth century B.C.E.) *military commander of the Twenty-sixth Dynasty*
He served PSAMMETICHUS III (r. 526–525 B.C.E.) as an army general. Pedisamtawi led his troops to the temple of RAMESSES II at ABU SIMBEL and left an inscription there, written in Greek. He was on a campaign against rebels in NUBIA (modern Sudan) at the time.

Pedubaste (d. 803 B.C.E.) *founder of the Twenty-third Dynasty*
He reigned from 828 B.C.E. until his death, a contemporary of SHOSHENQ III (r. 835–783 B.C.E.) of the Twenty-second Dynasty. Pedubaste was at LEONTOPOLIS. He raised his son, Iuput, as his co-regent, but Iuput died before inheriting the throne. Pedubaste is commemorated in KARNAK inscriptions. He served as the high priest of Amun at THEBES in the reign of TAKELOT II and then fashioned his own dynasty. Pedubaste was succeeded by SHOSHENQ IV at Leontopolis.

Pedukhipa (fl. 13th century B.C.E.) *royal woman of the Hittites in the reign of Ramesses II*
She was the consort of the HITTITE ruler HATTUSILIS III. Pedukhipa wrote to Queen NEFERTARI, the beloved wife of RAMESSES II (r. 1290–1224 B.C.E.) and also received messages from the pharaoh, an indication of her political power. The letters were discovered in Böghazköy (modern Turkey), the site of Hattusas, the Hittite capital. Queen Pedukipa's daughter, probably MA'AT HORNEFRURÉ, married Ramesses II in the 34th year of his reign as a symbol of the alliance between Egypt and the Hittites.

Peftjau'abast (fl. 740–725 B.C.E.) *ruler of the Twenty-third Dynasty*
He reigned in HERAKLEOPOLIS 740–725 B.C.E. and married IRBAST'UDJEFRU, a niece of TAKELOT III and the daughter of RUDAMON. When PIANKHI (1) of NUBIA (modern Sudan) began to move northward to claim Egypt, Peftjau'abast joined a coalition of petty rulers and marched with them to halt the Nubian advance. Piankhi, however, crushed the Egyptians at HERAKLEOPOLIS. Peftjau'abast surrendered to Piankhi but remained in his city as a vassal governor.

Pega This was a site in ABYDOS that formed a gap in the mountains and was considered the starting point for souls on their way to eternal life. A well was dug near Pega and there the Egyptians deposited offerings for the dead. Such gifts were transported through the subterranean passages to Amenti, the netherworld.

See also MORTUARY RITUALS; PARADISE.

Pekassater (fl. eighth century B.C.E.) *royal Nubian woman of the Twenty-fifth Dynasty*
She was the consort of PIANKHI (1) (r. 750–712 B.C.E.) and the daughter of ALARA, the Nubian (modern Suda-

nese) king. Pekassater resided in NAPATA, the capital near the fourth cataract of the Nile. There is some indication that Queen Pekassater was buried at ABYDOS.

Pelusium A site on the most easterly mouth of the NILE, near Port Sa'id, the modern Tell Farama, the Egyptians called the city Sa'ine or Per Amun. Pelusium served as a barrier against enemies entering the Nile from Palestine. In 343 B.C.E., ARTAXERXES III OCHUS defeated NECTANEBO II at Pelusium, beginning the second Persian Period (343–332 B.C.E.) in Egypt.

Penne (Penno; Penni Pennuit) (fl. 12th century B.C.E.) *governor of the Twentieth Dynasty, a powerful "King's Son of Kush"*
He served RAMESSES IV (r. 1163–1156 B.C.E.) as the governor of NUBIA (modern Sudan) and was honored with the title of the "King's Son of Kush." Penne was also the mayor of ANIBA. His tomb in Aniba, south of ASWAN, contains reliefs that depict Penne being honored by Ramesses IV as "the Deputy of WAWAT," a district of Nubia. He was the superintendent of the quarries of the region. Penne erected a statue of the pharaoh and received two vessels of silver in return. His Aniba tomb is now on the west bank of the Aswan High Dam.

Penreshnas (fl. 10th century B.C.E.) *royal woman of the Twenty-second Dynasty*
A lesser ranked consort of SHOSHENQ I (r. 945–924 B.C.E.), she is commemorated as the daughter of a great chieftain of the period. Prince NIMLOT (2) was probably her son.

Pentaur, Poem of The Poem of Pentaur describes from the Egyptian perspective the battle of Kadesh, the defining campaign of RAMESSES II (Ramesses the Great) (r. 1290–1224 B.C.E.). The Poem of Pentaur was written by the vizier Pentaur or Pent-a-ur as a tribute to Ramesses II, copied by a scribe in a later era, and included in Papyrus Sallier III. Originally, the poetic version was inscribed on a wall at KARNAK, the great temple complex at THEBES (modern Luxor). An official version was also displayed elsewhere throughout the Nile Valley.

The battle of Kadesh was a famous confrontation between Ramesses II and the ruler MUWATALLIS of the HITTITES, taking place ca. 1285 B.C.E. on the Orontes River in modern Syria. The battle was recounted in 10 inscriptions, including bulletins, reliefs on temple walls, and a poetic form.

According to the poem, Ramesses II marched out of Egypt on the ninth day of the second month of summer, stopping at Tjel, an Egyptian outpost. He had the Regiment of Amun and three other major units with him, as well as the Sherden infantry, which comprised 20,000 men. Reaching Ramesses-Meryamen, an Egyptian fortress in the Valley of the Cedars in modern Leba-

non, Ramesses II saw no sign of the Hittites. Tricked by two "Shoshu," Hittite spies posing as local inhabitants, Ramesses II stretched his forces 30 miles into the enemy territory, divided his troops, and then made camp. When Muwatallis began a series of raids and ambushes, Ramesses II beat the Shoshu and received confirmation of the Hittite trap and his peril.

The Hittites reportedly had 3,500 chariots, each manned by three men, and an infantry of 18,000 to 19,000 with auxiliary units and escorts totaling 47,500. Apparently alarmed, Ramesses II sent for the Regiment of Ptah and purportedly scolded his officers for their laxity in assessing the situation. While this was happening, however, the Hittites broke through the Regiment of Ré, sealing the trap. Hundreds of Egyptians began to arrive at Ramesses II's camp in headlong flight, with the Hittite cavalry was close behind, followed by some 2,500 chariots. The Regiment of Amun was almost overwhelmed by the panicking soldiers and began to retreat northward.

According to the poem, Ramesses II, despite the chaos, began to fight his way through the enemy in order to reach his southern forces. With only his household troops, a few officers, and followers, and with the rabble of the defeated units standing by, he mounted his chariot and charged and broke through the east wing of the assembled force, allowing the Egyptians to escape the net that Muwatallis had cast and pushing the Hittites and their allies into the river, where they drowned. The brother of the Hittite king was also believed to have been killed in this charge.

Within the abandoned Egyptian camp, the enemy soldiers were looting, but they were surprised by a group of Ramesses II's soldiers and slain. Ramesses II gathered up his unit and held his position at the camp. The Hittite king, in turn, ordered his reserves of 1,000 chariots to attack, but Ramesses II and his unit were able to hold off the charge. The Regiment of Ptah soon after arrived, and the Hittite cavalry was driven into the city, took terrible losses, and eventually withdrew by the order of Muwatallis. Ramesses II did not capture Kadesh, and Muwatallis claimed a Hittite victory and the acquisition of the city of Apa (modern Damascus). Ramesses II also claimed victory and executed all of the Egyptians who had not rushed to his aid. This battle would not end the conflicts between Egypt and the Hittites. Almost two decades of confrontations finally led to the Egyptian–Hittite peace treaty.

The Poem of Pentaur recounts the battle in detail, with elegant and dramatic words depicting the valor and determination of Ramesses II, especially in the face of less-than-courageous demonstrations from his officers. Such dramatic images and praise were part of the divine cult, commemorating the heroism of the ruler and the sacrifices that he made for his people with the aid of the gods. The official versions were concise and formal in tone, another aspect of the royal cult. The battle of Kadesh was a stalemate between Egypt and the Hittites, but Ramesses II demonstrated his determination and vigor in the field. The men commanding the various reluctant forces reportedly were executed by Ramesses II personally.

Further reading: Healy, Mark. *The Warrior Pharaoh: Ramesses II and the Battle of Quadesh.* London: Osprey, 2000; Murname, William J. The *Road to Kadesh: A Historical Interpretation of the Battle Reliefs of King Sety I at Karnak.* Chicago: Oriental Institute of the University of Chicago, 1990.

Pentaweret (Pentaware) (fl. 12th century B.C.E.) *prince of the Twentieth Dynasty involved in a harem conspiracy*
He was the son of RAMESSES III (r. 1194–1163 B.C.E.) and a lesser-ranked consort, named TIYE (2). Queen Tiye entered into a harem conspiracy to assassinate Ramesses III and to put aside the heir, RAMESSES IV, in order to place her son on the throne. All of the plotters were arrested, including judicial officials, and all were punished with death, disfigurement, or exile. Pentaweret was to commit suicide as a result of his conviction in the trial conducted by the court. His death had led to conjectures that his remains are those of PRINCE UNKNOWN or Man E. Queen Tiye was believed to be one of the first to be executed.

Pepi I (Meryré) (d. 2255 B.C.E.) *second ruler of the Sixth Dynasty*
He reigned from 2289 B.C.E. until his death. Pepi I was the son and successor of TETI and Queen IPUT (1), who served as his regent in his first years. An unknown royal figure, USERKARÉ, possibly served as a co-regent before Pepi I inherited the throne.

Pepi I ruled with a certain vigor and was militarily innovative. He used General WENI to conduct campaigns in NUBIA and in the SINAI and Palestine with mercenary troops from Nubia (modern Sudan). Weni drove off the Sinai Bedouins and landed his troops on the Mediterranean coast, having transported them there on vessels. Pepi I's vessels were discovered in BYBLOS in modern Lebanon, and he sent an expedition to PUNT. During these campaigns Pepi I was called Neferja-hor or Nefersa-hor. He took the throne name Meryré or Mery-tawy soon after. His wives are listed as NEITH (2), IPUT (2), Yamtisy, WERET-IMTES (2), and Ujebten. Later in his reign he married two sisters, ANKHNESMERY-RÉ (1), and ANKHNESMERY-RÉ (2).

Pepi I built at ABYDOS, BUBASTIS, DENDEREH, ELEPHANTINE, and HIERAKONPOLIS. Copper statues fashioned as portraits of him and his son MERENRÉ I were found at Hierakonpolis. A HAREM conspiracy directed against him failed, but one of his older wives disappeared as a result. His sons, born to Ankhnesmery-Re (1) and (2) were Merenré I and Pepi II. His daughter was Neith (2).

Pepi I's pyramid in SAQQARA was called Men-nefer, "Pepi Is Established and Beautiful." The Greeks corrupted that name into MEMPHIS. The complex contains Pyramid Texts, popular at that time, and his burial chamber was discovered empty. The sarcophagus had disappeared, and only a canopic chest was found.

Pepi II (d. 2152 B.C.E.) *fourth ruler of the Sixth Dynasty, Egypt's longest-ruling pharaoh*
The pharaohs of the Sixth Dynasty (2323–2150 B.C.E.) ruled the Nile Valley during a troubled time. The Old Kingdom was coming to an end, and signs of unrest were everywhere. The founder of the dynasty, Teti (r. 2323–2291 B.C.E.), was reportedly murdered by his own bodyguards. An individual named Userkare then ruled for less than a year, followed by Pepi I (r. 2289–2255 B.C.E.), who took the throne name Meryré or Meryré-tawy. There was an attempt on his life, as well, an act that brought two noble-ranked sisters into his court to serve as his wives. Once married, the two women were both named Ankhensmery-Ré, a name that meant Pepi I was their life.

There were dedicated, loyal court officials, such as WENI, who served Pepi I and even judged the queen charged with the attempted assassination. Pepi I was vigorous, and he held the nation together until his death. His son Merenré I (r. 2255–2246 B.C.E.) ruled for a short period, followed by a small child, Pepi II. This child would astound Egypt and the world by ruling for 94 years. (There is an ongoing debate about the actual age of Pepi II; some scholars believe that his reign was shorter.)

BIOGRAPHY

The son of PEPI I and ANKHNESMERY-RÉ (2), Pepi II reigned from 2246 B.C.E. until his death. When he inherited the throne from his brother Merenré I, however, he was only a child and unable to rule the land. His mother served as his regent during his minority, and his uncle, the vizier Djau, maintained a stable government. They were aided by an assembly of Egyptian officials, including Harkhuf, the court trade official, who had served Pepi I. Harkhuf was appointed the overseer of foreign soldiers in the service of the throne and was also the governor of Nubian territories, a post that gave him unlimited authority.

Pepi II grew up in the palace with the rights and privileges of a pharaoh but was still under the care of his mother and uncle. While still a child, an expedition was conducted in his name by Harkhuf, who sent word that a dancing *deneg*, or DWARF, had been captured and was being brought back to MEMPHIS. Upon receiving the news, Pepi II dispatched detailed instructions on the care of the small captive, promising a reward to his official if the dwarf arrived safe and healthy. The letter stresses the importance of 24-hour care, lest the dwarf be drowned or injured. Harkhuf received the following communication from the boy-king:

Come north to the court immediately . . .
Thou shalt bring the dwarf with thee,
living, prosperous and healthy from
the land of the spirits, for the dances
of the god, to rejoice and gladden
the heart of the king of Upper and Lower
Egypt who lives forever. When he goes
Down with thee into the vessel, take care
lest he fall into the water. When he sleeps
at night, appoint excellent people, who
shall sleep beside him in his tent, inspect
ten times a night. My majesty desires to
see this dwarf more than the gifts of Sinai
and Punt. If thou arrivest at court, this
dwarf being with thee, alive, prosperous
and healthy, my majesty shall do for thee
a greater thing than that which was done
for the treasurer of the god, Burded, in
the time of Iseti, according to the heart's
desire of my majesty to see the dwarf.

—The tomb of Harkhuf at Abydos,
translated by James H. Breasted

Harkhuf did reach Pepi II's palace, and the dwarf was alive and healthy. During another expedition Harkhuf sailed to the third cataract of the Nile and included the text of Pepi II's message in the decorations of his own tomb in Abydos.

When he grew older, Pepi II was educated by priest tutors and probably studied at the KAP, a special educational setting for the royals of each dynasty. He married his half sister, NEITH (2), who would become his *hemet,* or Great Queen. He also married his niece, IPUT (2), Wedjebten, and probably ANKHNES-PEPI.

During his 94-year reign, the longest rule ever recorded in Egypt, Pepi II sent trading expeditions to Nubia and Punt and had a vast naval fleet at his disposal as he established trade routes. However, Pepi II failed to create a strong central government. During his reign, the royal court started to lose the true allegiance of the NOMARCHS (provincial aristocrats) and their people, and the nomarchs' power increased as the aging pharaoh's declined. Still, Pepi II was well liked, probably because he did not interfere with NOME affairs.

When Pepi II died, most of the people alive in the Nile Valley knew of no other pharaoh in their lifetime. Still popular, Pepi II was given a large state funeral. His pyramidal complex in southern SAQQARA has a large PYRAMID and three smaller ones. A MORTUARY TEMPLE, a causeway, and a VALLEY TEMPLE are also part of the complex design. The valley temple has rectangular columns, decorated and covered with carved limestone. The causeway, partially destroyed, has two granite doorways. The mortuary temple has passages and a vestibule. A central court has an 18-pillar colonnade, and the sanc-tuary is reached through a narrow antechamber that is decorated with scenes of sacrifices. A wall surrounds the complex, which is dominated by the pyramid called "Pepi Is Established and Alive." Constructed out of limestone blocks, the pyramid has an entrance at ground level on the north side. A small offering chapel leads to a rock-cut burial chapel and a star-decorated vestibule with PYRAMID TEXT reliefs. The extensive mortuary complex drained Egypt's treasury and set in motion a series of weaknesses that brought the Old Kingdom to an end. Pepi's son took the throne after his father but was unable to unite the people or establish strong central control.

HISTORICAL IMPACT

Two dynasties followed the reign of Pepi II, but they ruled only for a brief period and controlled a relatively small area. Pepi II's reign was perhaps too long, as his disabilities from age degraded his central control and ongoing efforts to serve the nation. Pepi, almost a recluse toward the end of his life, was not likely aware of the unrest and corruption taking place beyond the palace walls. Competent nomarchs began taking matters into their own hands to protect their regions, actions that lessened the authority of the pharaoh and his officials.

To compound the problems, Egypt faced a series of natural disasters, the greatest of which was the drying up of the Nile River in the Delta regions. Towns and farmlands became isolated in growing deserts with no access to water, and the Nile was soon no longer able to be used as a form of transportation and contact with other areas.

The literary works from this period, or written soon after, describe scenes of horror in the Nile Kingdom as Pepi II's rule proved unequal to the task of staving off social and political upheaval or providing a smooth and stable succession. Riots and chaos soon ensued, and, eventually, after attacking the city of Thebes (modern Luxor) in the Upper Kingdom, the Khety (Aktay) clan established the Ninth Dynasty.

Further reading: Breasted, James. *Ancient Records of Egypt: The First Through the Seventeenth Dynasties,* Vol. 1. Chicago: University of Illinois Press, 2001; Clayton, Peter. *Chronicle of the Pharaohs: The Reign-by-Reign Record of the Rulers and Dynasties of Ancient Egypt.* New York: Thames & Hudson, 1994; Wilkinson, Toby. *Early Dynastic Egypt.* London: Routledge, 1999.

Pepi-Nakht (fl. 23rd century B.C.E.) *noble official of the Sixth Dynasty*
He served in the reign of PEPI II (2246–2152 B.C.E.). Pepi-Nakht was the Old Kingdom equivalent of the VICEROY of Nubia (modern Sudan), serving as the governor of the lands below the first cataract. He was originally from the ELEPHANTINE. His cliff tomb at Aswan gives detailed information about his expeditions into Nubia to put

down a rebellion of local tribes there. He slew princes and nobles of the Nubian tribes and brought other chiefs back to MEMPHIS to pay homage to the pharaoh.

Pepi-Nakht also traveled to the Red Sea to bring back the body of an official slain in the coastal establishment (possibly KUSER), where the Egyptians had ships built for expeditions to PUNT. Kuser was the port used by the Egyptians in most eras. Pepi-Nakht bore the title of "Governor of Foreign Places." He was deified locally after his death and had a shrine at ASWAN.

See also DEIFICATION.

per-ankh An educational institution throughout Egypt, called "the House of Life," the *per-ankh* was erected in many districts and cities and was a depository for learned texts on a variety of subjects, particularly MEDICINE. The first reference to the *per-ankh* dates to the Old Kingdom (2575–2134 B.C.E.). The institution continued in other historical periods, flourishing in the Nineteenth Dynasty (1307–1196 B.C.E.) and later eras. Reportedly, two of the officials condemned in the harem plot against RAMESSES III (r. 1194–1163 B.C.E.) were from the *per-ankh*.

These institutions contained training services and resources in the various sciences. Most incorporated a *per-medjat,* a House of Books, as well. Clinics and sanatoria were attached to the *per-ankh* in ABYDOS, AKHMIN, 'AMARNA, EDFU, ESNA, KOPTOS, MEMPHIS, and THEBES. Priests in these institutions studied art, MAGIC, medicine, funerary rituals, sculpture, painting, the writing of sacred books, theological texts, mathematics, embalming, ASTRONOMY, and MAGICAL DREAM INTERPRETATION.

Major scholarly documents were maintained in these institutions and copied by scribes. The *per-ankh* also served as a workshop where sacred books were composed and written by the ranking scribes of the various periods. It is possible that many of the texts were not kept in the *per-ankh* but discussed there and debated. The members of the institution's staff, all scribes, were considered the learned men of their age. Many were ranking priests in the various temples or noted physicians and served the different rulers in many administrative capacities. The *per-ankh* probably existed only in important cities. Ruins of the House of Life were found at 'Amarna, and one was discovered at Abydos. Magical texts were part of the output of the institutions, as were the copies of the Book of the Dead.

Perdiccas (d. 321 B.C.E.) *Greek contemporary of Alexander the Great who tried to invade Egypt*
Perdiccas was the keeper of the royal seal and a trusted military companion of ALEXANDER III THE GREAT. He also aided Roxana, Alexander's widow, after the death of Alexander in 323 B.C.E. Perdiccas then established his own empire and led a Greek force into Egypt, hoping to take possession of the Nile Valley. PTOLEMY I SOTER (r. 304–284 B.C.E.) was satrap of the Nile at the time. The troops of Perdiccas were not committed to the necessary campaigns and feared such a rash move because of the inundation of the Nile River. As a consequence, Perdiccas was forced to withdraw and was subsequently murdered by his own mutinous officers.

perfume Lavish scents were used by the Egyptians and contained in beautiful bottles or vials. A perfume vial recovered in Egypt dates to 1000 B.C.E. Perfumes were part of religious rites, and the Egyptians invented a form of glass to hold the precious substance. Cones made of perfumed wax were also placed on the heads of guests at celebrations. As the warmth of the gathering melted the wax, the perfumes dripped down the head and provided lush scents. In the temples the idols of the gods were perfumed in daily rituals.

See also MYRRH.

Peribsen (Set; Sekhemib; Uaznes) (d. ca. 2600 B.C.E.) *fourth ruler of the Second Dynasty*
He reigned in an obscure and troubled historical period in Egypt and was originally named Set or Sekhemib. He changed it to Peribsen, erasing his original name on his funerary stela at ABYDOS. This name change possibly indicates a religious revolt that threatened him politically. Peribsen ruled Egypt for 17 years and was called "the Hope of All Hearts" and "Conqueror of Foreign Lands."

Peribsen's tomb in UMM EL-GA'AB was sunk into the desert and made of brick. The burial chamber had stone and copper vases, and storerooms were part of the design. The tomb, now called "the Middle Fort," had paneled walls and a chapel of brick. Two granite stelae were discovered there. His cult at ABYDOS and MEMPHIS was very popular and remained prominent for several hundred years. Peribsen's vases were found in SAQQARA. He was devoted to the god SET at OMBOS.

peristyle court An element of architectural design in Egyptian temples, peristyle courts were designed with a roofed colonnade on all four sides, resembling glades in the center of forests and adding a serene element of grandeur and natural beauty to shrines and divine residences. This style of architecture became famous throughout the world at the time.

per-nefer This was the ancient site of Egyptian mummification rituals, designated as "the House of Beauty." The royal funerary complexes of the PHARAOHS normally contained a chamber designated as the *per-nefer*. These were part of the VALLEY TEMPLES, and the royal remains were entombed within the confines of these chambers. Other sites were established for commoners who could not afford mummification at their tomb sites. The ritual and medical procedures at each *per-nefer* followed traditions and were regulated in all periods.

See also IBU.

pero (per-wer; per-a'a) The royal residence or palace. The word actually meant "the Great House" and designated not only the royal residence but the official government buildings in the palace complexes as well. Such centers were called "the Double House" or "the House of Gold and House of Silver," an allusion to Upper and Lower Egypt. The administration of the Two Kingdoms of Egypt, in the north and in the south, was conducted in their respective buildings.

These royal residences were normally made of bricks and thus perished over the centuries, but the ruins of some palaces, found at 'AMARNA, DEIR EL-BALLAS, PER-RAMESSES, etc., indicate the scope of the structures and the elaborate details given to the architectural and artistic adornments. In the reign of TUTHMOSIS III (1479–1425 B.C.E.) of the Eighteenth Dynasty, the term *pero* began to designate the ruler himself, and later pharaohs employed the word in cartouches.

Per-Ramesses (Pa-Ramesses; Peramesse; Pira messe)

A site in the Qantir district on the banks of the Pelusiac branch of the Nile, called "the Estate of Ramesses," the city was a suburban territory of the ancient capital of the HYKSOS, AVARIS. RAMESSES II (r. 1290–1224 B.C.E.) founded Per-Ramesses, although some aspects of the city date to RAMESSES I (r. 1307–1306 B.C.E.) as his royal line originated in the region of the Delta.

The formal name of the site, Per-Ramessé-se-Mery-Amun-'A-nakhtu, "the House of Ramesses, Beloved of Amun, Great of Victories," indicates the splendor and vitality of the new capital. A large palace, private residences, temples, military garrisons, a harbor, gardens, and a vineyard were designed for the city, which was the largest and costliest in Egypt. Processions, pageants, and festivals were held throughout the year. The original royal palace at Per-Ramesses is recorded as covering an area of four square miles. When the site was abandoned at the end of the Twentieth Dynasty (1070 B.C.E.) many monuments were transported to the nearby city of TANIS.

Persea Tree

This was the mythological tree of HELIOPOLIS that served varying functions associated with the feline enemy of APOPHIS. A fragrant cedar, the Persea Tree sheltered a divine cat being, called *mau*, dedicated to protecting the god RÉ.

When the serpent APOPHIS attacked Ré on his nightly journeys in TUAT, or the Underworld, the cat in the Persea Tree slew him. Trees were part of the cosmogonic traditions of Egypt and were deemed essential elements of the various paradises awaiting the deceased beyond the grave.

The Persea Tree that held the names of the rulers of Egypt, on a bas-relief from the Ramesseum; the goddess Sheshet (second from right) writes the name of Ramesses II (seated center) on the leaves of the tree. To his left sits the god Amun Ré and at far right is Thoth, the god of wisdom. *(Hulton Archive)*

Persen (fl. 25th century B.C.E.) *official of the Fifth Dynasty*

He served SAHURÉ (r. 2458–2446 B.C.E.) as an overseer of various royal projects and offices. An inscription from Persen's tomb depicts the honors he received from Queen NEFERHETEPES (3), the mother of Sahuré. She provided mortuary offerings at his tomb as a gesture of her appreciation for his services.

Persenti (fl. 26th century B.C.E.) *royal woman of the Fourth Dynasty*

Persenti was a lesser consort of KHAFRE (Chephren) (r. 2520–2494 B.C.E.). She was not the favorite and she was not the mother of the heir. Her son was NEKAURÉ. She was buried in the royal mortuary complex at GIZA.

Persia One of the major empires that competed with Egypt in the Late Period (712–332 B.C.E.), the Persian Empire was vast and well controlled, despite the rising power of the Greeks and the dominance of the MEDES in the Persian homeland. Cyrus the Great forged the true Persian Empire ca. 550 B.C.E.

The original Persians, members of the Indo-Europeans, were evident on the western Iranian plateau by 850 B.C.E. They were a nomadic people who claimed the name Parsa. By 600 B.C.E., they were on the southwestern Iranian plateau, dominated by the native Medes. The original capital of the Persians was Susa.

By 500 B.C.E., the Persian Empire extended from modern Pakistan in the Indus Valley to Thrace in the west and to Egypt in the south. The Persians ruled 1 million square miles of the earth at the height of their power. The raids of DARIUS I (r. 521–486 B.C.E.) into Thrace and Macedonia aroused a response that would result in the empire's destruction two centuries later. ALEXANDER III THE GREAT would bring about Persia's downfall in 332 B.C.E.

The first Persian to rule Egypt was CAMBYSES (r. 525–522 B.C.E.), who opened the Twenty-seventh Dynasty on the Nile. Cambyses was followed on the Persian throne by DARIUS I, XERXES I (r. 486–446 B.C.E.), ARTAXERXES I (r. 465–424 B.C.E.), and Darius II (r. 423–405 B.C.E.).

The Persians returned to rule as the Thirty-first Dynasty, or the Second Persian Period, in 343 B.C.E. This royal line, as were their predecessors, was plagued by profound internal problems in their homeland, with many emperors being slain. The rulers of Egypt during the Thirty-first Dynasty were ARTAXERXES III OCHUS (r. 343–338 B.C.E.), Artaxerxes IV ARSES (r. 338–336 B.C.E.), and DARIUS III CODOMAN (335–332 B.C.E.).

Per-Temu This was a site on the western edge of the Delta, the modern Tell el-Maskhuta, near Ismaliya and the Suez Canal. Originally a HYKSOS enclave, the site was used by NECHO II (r. 610–595 B.C.E.) to serve as a new city. Per-Temu was part of the WADI TIMULAT trade route.

pert-er-kheru This was an ancient Egyptian phrase meaning "from the mouth of the god," designating a moral or spiritual saying, normally those contained in the sacred texts from early periods. Adages, counsels, and the didactic literary works called "instructions," which had been handed down over the centuries, were incorporated into rituals. By repeating the *pert-er-kheru* over and over, the present was linked to the past and to the future.

Peru-Nefer It was the principal naval base of Egypt, located near MEMPHIS. Egypt had always maintained fleets of ships for Nile travel, opening the cataracts of the Nile River in order to reach Nubian (modern Sudanese) FORTRESSES and TRADE centers. In the Eighteenth Dynasty (1550–1307 B.C.E.) the need for such ships and the use of larger vessels for Mediterranean travel demanded an increase in naval training. As early as the Sixth Dynasty (2323–2150 B.C.E.) troops had been transported to Mediterranean campaign sites by boat.

The base of Peru-Nefer contained a ship dock and a repair complex for Nile and Mediterranean vessels employed in the trade and military campaigns of the historical period. TUTHMOSIS III (r. 1479–1425 B.C.E.) and AMENHOTEP II (r. 1427–1401 B.C.E.) served as com-

manders of the naval base before assuming the throne. Peru-Nefer declined at the end of the New Kingdom in 1070 B.C.E.

See also WARFARE.

Peryneb (fl. 24th century B.C.E.) *royal palace chamberlain of the Fifth Dynasty*
He served both IZEZI (r. 2388–2356 B.C.E.) and UNIS (r. 2356–2323 B.C.E.) as lord chamberlain of the royal household. Peryneb was the son of the VIZIER Shepses-ré, and he was buried near the pyramid of USERKHAF. His actual MASTABA is in the Metropolitan Museum in New York.

Pesuir (fl. 13th century B.C.E.) *honored viceroy of the Nineteenth Dynasty*
He served RAMESSES II (r. 1290–1224 B.C.E.) as viceroy of Kush, or NUBIA (modern Sudan). This office carried the title "King's Son of Kush." A sandstone statue of Pesuir was discovered in ABU SIMBEL, in the second hall of Ramesses II's temple. This rare honor attests to Pesuir's standing.

pet The ancient Egyptian word for the sky, which was also called *hreyet,* the *pet* was supported by four pillars, called PILLARS OF SHU, depicted in reliefs as mountains or as women with their arms outstretched. Many texts of Egyptian religious traditions allude to the four pillars, which were associated ritually to the solar bark of the god RÉ. The goddess NUT personified the sky also. The Egyptians believed that there was another *pet,* invisible to the living. This sky was over TUAT, the Underworld.

Pete'ese (fl. fifth century B.C.E.) *official petitioner of the Twenty-seventh Dynasty*
An elderly scribe, Pete'ese sent a petition to DARIUS I (r. 521–486 B.C.E.) describing the wrongs suffered by his family, dating all the way back to the reign of PSAMMETICHUS I (r. 664–610 B.C.E.) The petition, presenting a lurid tale of persecution, fraud, and imprisonment survived, but Darius I's response did not.

Petosiris (fl. third century B.C.E.) *priestly official of the early Ptolemaic Period, famed for his tomb decorations*
Petosiris probably served in the reign of PTOLEMY I SOTER (304–284 B.C.E.). He was the high priest of THOTH at HERMOPOLIS MAGNA. His tomb had a small temple at TUNA EL-GEBEL, Hermopolis Magna, and was called "the Great One of the Five Masters of the Works." An exquisite version of the BOOK OF THE DEAD was discovered there as well.

Petosiris's tomb-temple was fashioned in the Ptolemaic rectangular style, with a horned altar and a half-columned portico. His father, Seshu, and his brother, Djedthutefankh, were also buried with him. The tomb has a sanctuary with four square columns and a subterranean shaft and depicts the god Kheper. The wall reliefs indicate Greek influences. Petosiris's inner coffin was made of blackened pine, inlaid with glass.

petrified forests   These are two territories in which the trees have been petrified by natural causes over the centuries. One of the forests is located in the desert, east of modern Cairo, in the WADI LABBAB region. The second is east of MA'ADI, south of modern Cairo, in the Wadi el-Tih.

Peukestas   (fl. fourth century B.C.E.) *companion of Alexander the Great*
Called "the son of Markartatos," Peukestas was given a portion of Egypt by ALEXANDER III THE GREAT. A document called "the Order of Peukestas" was promulgated for this grant. This text was found in MEMPHIS and is reported by some as the earliest known Greek document in Egypt.

Phanes of Halicarnassus   (fl. sixth century B.C.E.) *Greek mercenary general who aided the Persian invasion of Egypt*
He was originally in the service of PSAMMETICHUS III (r. 526–525 B.C.E.) but defected and advised the Persian CAMBYSES (r. 525–522 B.C.E.) how to cross the eastern desert safely. Phanes counseled the Persians to hire Bedouin guides in order to use the sandy wastes efficiently. His sons had remained in Egypt when Phanes defected, and they were dragged in front of the Egyptians and mercenary troops amassed at the battle site so that Phanes and the Persians could see them just before the onset of the conflict. Phanes' two sons were both killed by having their throats slit, and their blood was drained into a large bowl. Wine was poured into the bowl, and the mercenary troops, outraged by Phanes' betrayal, sipped the blood to a man. Herodotus recorded this event in his *Histories,* Book Three.

pharaoh   It was the name of the rulers of Egypt, derived from the word *pero* or *pera'a,* which designated the royal residence. The term became associated with the ruler and was eventually used in cartouches and royal decrees. The roles of these rulers, along with their specific titles, evolved slowly after the unification of Upper and Lower Egypt c. 3000 B.C.E. Dynasties emerged after that unification, and a state cult was developed to define the powers of such pharaohs. In time the ruler was described in the tomb of REKHMIRÉ, serving TUTHMOSIS III (r. 1479–1425 B.C.E.) in the following terms: "He is a god by whose dealings one lives, the father and mother of all men, alone, by himself without an equal."

The pharaohs were officially titled *neter-nefer,* which gave them semidivine status. *Neter* meant god and *nefer* good and beautiful, an adjective that modified the godlike qualities and limited the pharaonic role and nature. The royal cults proclaimed this elevated status, beginning in the earliest dynastic periods, by announcing that the pharaohs were "the good god," the incarnation of HORUS, the son of RÉ. On earth they manifested the divine, and in death they would become OSIRIS. Through their association with these deities, the pharaohs assumed specific roles connected to the living, to the dead, and to natural processes. While on the throne, they were expected to serve as the supreme human, the heroic warrior, the champion of all rights, the dispenser of equal justice, and the defender of MA'AT and the nation.

Egypt belonged to each pharaoh, and the nation's ideals and destiny were physically present in his person. His enemies, therefore, were the enemies of the gods themselves and all things good in nature and in the divine order. This concept developed slowly, of course, and pharaohs came to the throne declaring that they were mandated by the gods "to restore *ma'at,*" no matter how illustrious their immediate predecessor had been. The semidivine nature of the pharaoh did not have a negative effect on the levels of service rendered by nobles or commoners, however. His role, stressed in the educational processes at all levels, inspired a remarkable devotion among civil servants, and each pharaoh attracted competent and faithful officials. The temple rituals added to the allure of the pharaoh and developed another contingent of loyal servants for the reign.

The rulers of Egypt were normally the sons and heirs of their immediate predecessors, either by "the Great Wife," the chief consort, or by a lesser-ranked wife. Some, including TUTHMOSIS III (r. 1479–1425 B.C.E.) of the Eighteenth Dynasty, were the offspring of the pharaoh and HAREM women. In the early dynasties the rulers married female aristocrats to establish connections to the local nobility of the Delta or MEMPHIS, the capital. In subsequent periods many married their sisters or half sisters, if available, and some, including AKHENATEN, took their own daughters as consorts. In the New Kingdom (1550–1070 B.C.E.) the rulers did not hesitate to name commoners as the Great Wife, and several married foreign princesses.

The rulers of the Early Dynastic Period (2920–2575 B.C.E.) were monarchs who were intent upon ruling a united land, although the actual process of unification was not completed until 2649 B.C.E. There is evidence that these early kings were motivated by certain ideals concerning their responsibilities to the people, ideals that were institutionalized in later eras. Like the gods who created the universe out of chaos, the pharaoh was responsible for the orderly conduct of human affairs. Upon ascending the throne, later pharaohs of Egypt claimed that they were restoring the spirit of *ma'at* in the land, cosmic order and harmony, the divine will.

Warfare was an essential aspect of the pharaoh's role from the beginning. The rulers of the Predynastic Periods, later deified as the SOULS OF PE and SOULS OF NEKHEN, had fought to establish unity, and the first dynastic rulers had to defend borders, put down rebellions, and organize the exploitation of NATURAL RESOURCES. A strong government was in place by the dynastic period, the nation being divided into provincial territories called nomes. Royal authority was imposed by an army of officials, who were responsible for the affairs of both Upper and Lower Egypt. The law was thus the expression of the ruler's will, and all matters, both religious and secular, were dependent upon his assent. The entire administration of Egypt, in fact, was but an extension of the ruler's power.

By the Third Dynasty, DJOSER (r. 2630–2611 B.C.E.) could command sufficient resources to construct his vast mortuary complex, a monumental symbol of the land's prosperity and centralization. The STEP PYRAMID, erected for him by IMHOTEP, the VIZIER of the reign, announced the powers of Djoser and reinforced the divine status of the rulers. Other Old Kingdom (2575–2134 B.C.E.) pharaohs continued to manifest their power with similar structures, culminating in the great pyramids at Giza.

In the First Intermediate Period (2134–2040 B.C.E.) the role of the pharaoh was eclipsed by the dissolution of central authority. Toward the end of the Old Kingdom certain powers were delegated to the nome aristocracy, and the custom of appointing only royal family members to high office was abandoned. The Seventh and Eighth Dynasties attempted to reinstate the royal cult, but these rulers could not stave off the collapse of those royal lines. In the Ninth and Tenth Dynasties, the KHETYS of HERAKLEOPOLIS assumed the role of pharaoh and began to work toward the reunification of Egypt, using the various nome armies as allies. The rise of the INYOTEFS of THEBES, however, during the Eleventh Dynasty, brought an end to the Khetys' designs. MENTUHOTEP II (r. 2061–2010 B.C.E.) captured Herakleopolis and reunited Upper and Lower Egypt.

The Middle Kingdom (2040–1640 B.C.E.) emerged from Mentuhotep II's victory over the northern rulers, and Egypt was again united under a central authority. When the Middle Kingdom collapsed in 1640 B.C.E., Egypt faced another period of turmoil and division. The Thirteenth through Sixteenth Dynasties vied for land and power, and the HYKSOS dominated the eastern Delta and then much of Lower Egypt. It is interesting that these Asiatic rulers, especially those among them called "the Great Hyksos," assumed the royal traditions of Egypt and embraced all of the titles and customs of their predecessors.

In THEBES, however, another royal line, the Seventeenth Dynasty, slowly amassed resources and forces and began the campaigns to expel the Hyksos. KAMOSE, the last king of this line, died in battle, and the assault on AVARIS, the Hyksos capital, was completed by 'AHMOSE (NEBPEHTIRÉ), who founded the New Kingdom (1550–1070 B.C.E.). This was the age of the Tuthmossids, followed by the Ramessids, Egypt's imperial period. Military activities characterized the period, and many of the kings were noted warriors. The prestige of the king was greatly enhanced as a result, and AMENHOTEP III and RAMESSES II had themselves deified. The New Kingdom, as did other dynastic eras in Egypt, drew to a close when the pharaohs were no longer able to assert their authority, and thereby galvanize the nation. The New Kingdom collapsed in 1070 B.C.E.

During the Third Intermediate Period (1070–712 B.C.E.), the role of the pharaoh was fractured, as competing crowned rulers or self-styled leaders issued their decrees from the Delta and Thebes. The rise of the Libyans in the Twenty-second Dynasty (945–712 B.C.E.) aided Egypt by providing military defenses and a cultural renaissance, but SHOSHENQ I (r. 945–924 B.C.E.) and his successors were clearly recognized as foreigners, and the dynasty was unable to approach the spiritual elements necessary for the revival of the true pharaoh of the past. This was evident to the Nubians (modern Sudanese), who watched a succession of city-states, petty rulers, and chaos in Egypt and entered the land to restore the periods of spiritual power and majesty. The Persians, entering the Nile Valley in 525 B.C.E., came with a sense of disdain concerning the cultic practices of Egypt and the various rulers competing for power.

ALEXANDER III THE GREAT, arriving in Egypt in 332 B.C.E., was one of the few occupying foreigners who appeared to embody the old ideals of the pharaohs, but his successors, the Ptolemies (304–30 B.C.E.), could not immerse themselves into the true spiritual concepts involved. They ruled only from ALEXANDRIA without impacting on the distant nomes. With the death of CLEOPATRA VII in 30 B.C.E., the pharaohs became faded monuments of the past.

Further reading: Berger, Melvin, and Gilda Berger. *Mummies of the Pharaohs: Exploring the Valley of the Kings.* Washington, D.C.: National Geographic Society, 2001; Clayton, Peter A. *Chronicle of the Pharaohs: The Reign-by-Reign Record of the Rulers and Dynasties of Ancient Egypt.* New York: Thames & Hudson, 1994; De Beler, Aude Gros. *Pharaohs.* Paris: La Maison de Molière, 2000; Muller, Hans Wolfgang, and Eberhard Thiem. *Gold of the Pharaohs.* Ithaca, N.Y.: Cornell University Press, 1999; Patridge, Robert B. *Faces of the Pharaohs: Royal Mummies and Coffins from Ancient Thebes.* New York: David Brown, 1996; Pickles, Dewayne E., and Arthur M. Schlesinger, ed. *Egyptian Kings and Queens and Classical Deities.* New York: Chelsea House, 1997; Quirke, Stephen. *Who Were the Pharaohs? A His-*

A limestone relief of Amenhotep III in his war chariot, discovered at Qurna *(Hulton Archive)*

tory of Their Names with a List of Cartouches. Mineola, N.Y.: Dover Publications, 1991; Tyldesley, Joyce A. *The Private Lives of the Pharaohs: Unlocking the Secrets of Egyptian Royalty.* New York: TV Books, 2001.

Pharbaites *See* HURBEIT.

Pharnabazus (fl. fourth century B.C.E.) *Persian satrap who commanded the Persian invasion of Egypt in 373 B.C.E.* This invasion took place in the reign of NECTANEBO I (380–362 B.C.E.). Pharnabazus's troops caused terrible damage to the Egyptian defenses but were repulsed. He also quarreled with the commander of the Greek mercenary army in his train. The Greeks, battle wise, tried to consolidate gains made by probing Egyptian weaknesses, but Pharnabazus overruled such activities, dooming the Persian cause. The Nile River served as well as a natural defense, inundating the Delta and destroying the Persian and Greek camps. The invading army withdrew from the scene.

Pharos *See* LIGHTHOUSE OF ALEXANDRIA.

Philae A religious site on an island at ASWAN, called "the Island in the Time of Ré," Philae comes from the Egyptian Paaleq or Pilak, meaning "the End" or "Remote Place." Philae's monuments, threatened by the Aswan High Dam, are now on Agilquiyya Island. The original site became active in the Thirtieth Dynasty. NECTANEBO I (r. 380–362 B.C.E.) erected a hall there as well as a kiosk. Several prominent temples distinguished Philae in time, dedicated to ISIS, Harendotus, IMHOTEP, and ARSENUPHIS.

The temple of Isis contains the hall of NECTANEBO II (r. 360–343 B.C.E.), eastern and western colonnades, a shrine to Imhotep, a gate from the reign of PTOLEMY II PHILADELPHUS (285–246 B.C.E.), and a second chapel. Two pylons are part of the design, as well as a *MAMMISI*, additional colonnades, and a quay.

PTOLEMY IV PHILOPATOR (r. 221–205 B.C.E.) and King ARKAMANI of MEROË, Nubia (modern Sudan), in a rare

The temple of Isis at Philae, now moved to higher ground to save it from the waters of the Aswan High Dam *(Courtesy Steve Beikirch)*

joint building program erected a temple dedicated to the deity Arsenuphis at Philae. Other Ptolemies added OBE-LISKS, a HYPOSTYLE HALL, a prenaos, a temple to HATHOR, and chapels. The last hieroglyphic inscription dates to 394 C.E., as the Romans added their own structures or adornments.

Philip III Arrhidaeus (d. 316 B.C.E.) *half brother of Alexander the Great and ruler of Egypt*
He reigned from 323 B.C.E. until he was murdered. PTOLEMY I SOTER served as Philip III's satrap in Egypt. Recorded by contemporaries as somewhat dimwitted, Philip III built a bark shrine for the god AMUN at KARNAK in THEBES and put a relief on the walls of the Karnak complex. Philip III married his half niece, ADEA-EURYDICE. He was murdered by OLYMPIAS, the queen mother of Alexander III the Great. ALEXANDER IV (r. 316–304 B.C.E.) succeeded him.

Phoenicians They were the people from modern Lebanon, so named by the Greeks, Phoinikes, "the red men." The Phoenicians were master traders and navigators, and they were well known for their inventions, including the popular *porphura,* a purple murex dye. They settled in the cities of Tyre and Sidon around 3000 B.C.E. and quickly began their trading and artistic crafts. Their alphabet was established by ca. 1000 B.C.E. in the city of Tyre.

By 900 B.C.E., the great Phoenician ships were sailing to Greece, Egypt, Assyria, and other lands concerned with the growing trade and commerce. The Phoenicians sought silver, tin, and copper and reportedly sailed to the present-day British Isles to visit the copper mines there. They exported chickens from India before 700 B.C.E., introducing them to the West. In 600 B.C.E. the Phoenicians circumnavigated Africa.

The cities of BYBLOS, Sidon, and Tyre were prospering in Phoenicia before 1000 B.C.E. The Phoenicians also founded Carthage in modern Tunisia and Goddir, modern Cadiz, in southern Spain. The Phoenicians were under the control of Persia's Cyrus I the Great ca. 540 B.C.E. and became part of the empire of ALEXANDER III THE GREAT in 332 B.C.E. From 300 B.C.E. until 150 B.C.E., the nation was part of the Seleucid empire.

Egypt conducted trade with Phoenicia in the Old Kingdom (2575–2134 B.C.E.) or perhaps earlier. During the New Kingdom (1550–1070 B.C.E.), under the imperial policies of the Tuthmossids and Ramessids, Phoenicia served as a vassal state. A statue of SHOSHENQ I (r. 945–924 B.C.E.) was placed in a Phoenician temple by the reigning prince of the time, ABIBAAL. Phoenicia continued trade networks with Egyptian dynasties after the fall of the Ramessids in 1070 B.C.E., and the land was heavily garrisoned by Egyptian troops. When CLEOPATRA VII (r. 51–30 B.C.E.) died, the Romans took control of Phoenicia.

phoenix This was a sacred symbol in Egypt, associated with the BENNU Bird, and with the ISHED and PERSEA Trees in cosmological traditions. Sometimes called "the BA of RÉ," the soul of the god Ré, the fabled bird was associated with Ré's cult at HELIOPOLIS. Originally the bird was depicted as a yellow wagtail, then as a gray heron. It was taught that the cry of the heron started all of the creative processes of the earth. The egg laid by the heron on the PRIMEVAL MOUND contained the god Ré. Herodotus, the Greek historian, described the symbol of the phoenix in use in his historical period as an eagle with red and gold plumage. Only one phoenix lived at a time. The phoenix symbolized rebirth and resurrection.

Piankhi (1) (Piye) (d. 712 B.C.E.) *Second ruler of the Nubian Twenty-fifth Dynasty*
He reigned over Egypt and Nubia (modern Sudan) from 750 B.C.E. until his death. He was the son of the Nubian ruler KASHTA and Queen PEBATMA. Piankhi entered Egypt in response to pleas from people suffering under the reign of TEFNAKHTE of SAIS in the Twenty-fourth Dynasty (r. 724–717 B.C.E.).

Piankhi claimed that his military campaign was justified by his desire to restore the faith of the people in the god AMUN. The great temple of Amun at NAPATA maintained the traditional tenets and rituals of the cult, but the Egyptians appeared to have become lax in their devotion. Piankhi sent an army into Egypt to rectify that lapse in Amunite fervor.

A stela of victory at the temple of Amun in Napata, reproduced at other major Egyptian sites, recounts the military campaigns conducted in his name. His army faced a coalition of Egyptian forces led by Tefnakhte of Sais. Other rulers allied with Tefnakhte were OSORKON IV of TANIS, PEFTJAU'ABAST of HERAKLEOPOLIS, NIMLOT (4) of HERMOPOLIS, and IUPUT (4) of LEONTOPOLIS. They marched to Herakleopolis and were defeated in a confrontation with Piankhi. Tefnakhte fled but was taken prisoner when the Nubians moved northward. Piankhi conducted two naval battles to defeat Tefnakhte in the Delta, and all of the local rulers surrendered. Piankhi returned to Thebes soon after to celebrate the Amunite Feast of OPET. He stayed several months and then returned to Napata.

Piankhi had married PEKASSATER, the daughter of Nubian king ALARA. While in Thebes, he had his sister, AMENIRDIS (1), adopted by SHEPENWEPET (1) as the GOD'S WIFE OF AMUN, or Divine Adoratrice of Amun. The Nubians ruled almost all of Egypt at the end of Piankhi's stay. His dynasty would bring about a renaissance of the arts in Egypt and would maintain a vigorous defense of the nation. Piankhi died at Napata and was buried in the royal necropolis at El-Kurru. Burial chambers for his favorite horses were erected around his tomb. Piankhi was succeeded by his brother SHABAKA.

Piankhi (2) (fl. 11th century B.C.E.) *priestly official of the Twenty-first Dynasty*
He served as the high priest of AMUN during the reign of RAMESSES XI (1100–1070 B.C.E.). A son-in-law of HERIHOR, Piankhi assumed the prelature of Amun without using royal titles or regalia, maintaining order in THEBES, and campaigning in NUBIA (modern Sudan) against rebels. His son, PINUDJEM (1), was married to HENUTTAWY, the daughter of SMENDES, and succeeded Piankhi as high priest of Amun. Piankhi died during the reign of RAMESSES XI.

"Pillar of His Mother"   The name given to a unique priestly caste associated with the cult of HORUS and ISIS in Egypt. The priests of this caste had to have the rank of prince in order to be inducted into this temple service. TUTHMOSIS III (r. 1479–1425 B.C.E.) was recorded as serving as a "Pillar of His Mother" when he was elevated to the rank of heir to the throne. The use of the term "Pillar" alluded to the strength in defending and protecting. "The Mother" referred to was probably Egypt, not the biological life giver.

Pillars of Shu   They were cosmological structures in Egyptian cults, four columns that supported the heavens, called PET. The Pillars of Shu stood at each corner of the rectangular formation of heaven and were guarded by the Sons of Horus, IMSETY, HAPI (2), DUAMUTEF, and QEBEHSENNUF. These supernatural beings also guarded the CANOPIC JARS of the deceased in tombs.

pillow amulet   This was a carved fetish in the form of the traditional wooden headrest of ancient Egypt. The Egyptians did not use pillows in the early pharaonic eras as such comforts were introduced later. An amulet used in mummified remains, this fetish assured that the head of the deceased would be resurrected safely beyond the grave.

Pinudjem (1) (fl. 11th century B.C.E.) *official and self-styled pharaoh of the Twenty-first Dynasty*
PINUDJEM served as high priest of AMUN at THEBES, and became a self-styled "pharaoh" in the reign of SMENDES (1070–1044 B.C.E.), assuming privileges and the attire of such god-kings. He was the son of PIANKHI (2) and inherited his father's temple rank in Thebes. Some years later, ca. 1054 B.C.E., Pinudjem assumed a royal name, Keper karé Setepenamun Kanakhhtemeryamun, and elevated himself to the rank of pharaoh. He usurped the KARNAK monuments of RAMESSES II as well. Pinudjem thus became Smendes' co-regent.

He supervised the reburial of royal mummies found violated in their tombs in Thebes while governing Upper Egypt as far south as Aswan, and he married Princess HENUTTAWY, the daughter of RAMESSES XI and Queen TANTAMUN (1). He also wed ISTEMKHEBE (1), who bore him MASAHARTA and Djedkhonsufankh. His other sons, PSUSENNES I and MENKHEPERRESENB (2), and daughters, MA'ATKARÉ (1) and Mutnodjmet, were the children of Henuttawy.

El-HIBA was the military fortress used by Pinudjem I. When he died in the seventh year of the reign of his son PSUSENNES I (1040–992 B.C.E.), he was buried on the western shore of Thebes in an unusual coffin of TUTHMOSIS I. His mummified remains were discovered in the DEIR EL-BAHRI cache in 1881, beautifully wrapped and encased in leather straps. His mummy reportedly has now disappeared, after being photographed in 1888.

Pinudjem (2) (fl. 11th century B.C.E.) *priestly official of the Twenty-first Dynasty*
He served as high priest of Amun in THEBES in the reign of PSUSENNES I (1040–992 B.C.E.). Pinudjem was probably the son of Menkheperresenb (2) and the grandson of Pinudjem (1). He married his niece NESKHONSU and his sister ISTEMKHEBE (3), who was the mother of PSUSENNES II.

Pinudjem faced a terrible scandal among the temple scribes and other officials when he took office although details of the affair are not known. He retired to a temple chamber to meditate upon the matter, and the god Amun revealed the true miscreants in the temple. Actually, a scribe named Tuthmosis uncovered the evildoers, inscribing his role on the wall of a chapel in KARNAK. Pinudjem, however, arrested the guilty. He was shown also making an offering to OSIRIS in a beautiful relief.

Neskhonsu died before Pinudjem, and she was buried in a cliff near DEIR EL-BAHRI at Thebes. Pinudjem was placed in the same tomb. Istemkhebe's mummy was so beautifully wrapped that it was left intact.

Piramesse   *See* PER-RAMESSES.

pirates *See* SEA PEOPLES, DEFEAT OF THE.

Pithom (1) This was a site near Ismaila, called Per-Atum or Per-Tum by the Egyptians. Located beside the canal leading from the Nile to the Red Sea, started in the Late Period (712–332 B.C.E.) and refurbished by DARIUS I (r. 521–486 B.C.E.), the area was once in the control of the Ramessids. RAMESSES II (r. 1290–1224 B.C.E.) built extensively on the site.

Pithom (2) This was a site in HELIOPOLIS, called the "Estate of Atum" and serving as a cultic center for the combined deities, RÉ-ATUM. HELIOPOLIS, originally called Iunu, the "pillar," or On, is now a suburb of modern Cairo. Pithom contained monuments and temples and was the source of cosmogonic traditions. Only a single OBELISK, a monument dating to the reign of SENWOSRET I (1971–1926 B.C.E.), remains at Pithom in Heliopolis.

plain of salt This was a natural deposit region near WADI NATRUN in the western Delta. Salt was recovered from this plain in all times of Egyptian history.

Pneb-tawy He was a divine being of ancient Egypt, called the son of HORUS the Elder. An obscure deity whose cult did not survive into later periods, Pneb-tawy was worshipped with his mother, the equally obscure goddess Taseunefer.

police They were the peacekeeping units serving the rulers of Egypt and normally assigned to specified territories. One of the oldest police groups was a border unit stationed in various forts or garrisons on the eastern, western, and southern frontiers of Egypt during every era. Members of the Bedouin tribes of the Sinai were part of the border patrol in some historical periods. The WALL OF THE PRINCE, instituted by AMENEMHET I (r. 1991–1962 B.C.E.) in the Twelfth Dynasty, aided the border units by providing them garrisons on the eastern and western borders. The string of fortresses below the first cataract dating to the same era also served to house these units.

A state police was developed after the Second Intermediate Period (1640–1550 B.C.E.) composed of the famed MEDJAY warriors. There had been other state units in the past, but this new police team maintained the capital and served the king personally. The backbone of the Medjay were Nubian (modern Sudanese) warriors who served KAMOSE (r. 1550 B.C.E.) and 'AHMOSE (NEB-PEHTIRÉ) (r. 1550–1525 B.C.E.) when they campaigned against the HYKSOS invaders and drove them out of Egypt. Starting with the New Kingdom (1550–1070 B.C.E.) 'Ahmose decreed that all foreigners have papers identifying their origins. Customhouses were also formed to tax imported items.

The TEMPLE police units were normally composed of initiated members of the various cults who were charged with maintaining the sanctity of the temple complexes. The regulations concerning sex, behavior, and attitude during and before all ritual ceremonies demanded vigilance, and the temples kept their own people available to insure order and a harmonious spirit.

Police units were stationed at the borders to watch over caravans and trading expeditions and to maintain order among the foreigners who came with their own goods to conduct business within Egyptian territory. Police also watched over the various necropolises of Egypt, particularly those having royal tombs. Mortuary complexes had to be guarded by priests and police, and the vast tombs of the Theban western shore had to be patrolled on a daily basis. Other units functioned under the direction of the nome chiefs in the various districts of Egypt. Still other units, mostly military, protected the workers in the quarry and mine sites in the desert area within Egypt's borders or in the surrounding territories, such as the SINAI.

Pompey (Gnaeus Pompeius Magnus) (d. 48 B.C.E.) *Roman general and enemy of Julius Caesar who was called Magnus (the Great)*
He was born in 106 B.C.E. and rose rapidly in Roman political circles, fighting for Sulla against Marius. Pompey put down Spartacus's slave rebellion and cleared the Mediterranean Sea of pirates. He also ended the war with Mithridates of Pontus.

Marrying Julia, the daughter of Julius CAESAR, Pompey joined the First Triumvirate of Caesar and Crassus, although the death of Julia caused an enmity between him and her father. In 55 B.C.E. he had PTOLEMY XII AULETES (80–58, 55–51 B.C.E.) restored to the throne of Egypt through the efforts of Gabinus. He also ruled Rome as consul while Caesar was in Gaul. Pompey was appointed the legal guardian of CLEOPATRA VII, the coruler of Egypt, in accordance with the will left by her father. He then entered into a civil war with Julius Caesar in 49 B.C.E. and was defeated by the latter at the battle of Pharsalus the following year. Fleeing to ALEXANDRIA, Pompey was murdered by Cleopatra VII's brother, PTOLEMY XIII (51–47 B.C.E.). His head was given to Caesar when he arrived in Alexandria.

posesh-khef This was a mortuary instrument of ancient Egypt, fashioned as a slightly forked tool. Made of horn or granite, the instrument was discovered in the tomb of MENTUHOTEP II (r. 2061–2010 B.C.E.) of the Eleventh Dynasty at DEIR EL-BAHRI. The *posesh-khef* was used in MORTUARY RITUALS to bring about resurrection and renewed life of certain organs of the deceased. Elaborate rites were performed on the deceased, whose mummified remains were stood upright. In later historical periods statues or cartonnage images received the mystical rites.

Potter, The (fl. ca. 130 B.C.E.) *mysterious prophet of Ptolemaic Egypt*
He became a public figure in the reign of PTOLEMY VIII EUERGETES II (170–163, 145–116 B.C.E.). The Potter was a devotee of the ancient Egyptian ways and announced an oracle prophecy concerning the return of "the Great Spirit," probably that of the goddess MA'AT, to MEMPHIS, Egypt's original capital.

When "the Great Spirit" returned to Memphis, according to the Potter, all evil would end and the foreigners would "drop like dead leaves from a dead branch." ALEXANDRIA, the Ptolemaic center, would return to its role as "a drying place by the sea for fishermen and their nets." The Potter's oracle was very popular among Egyptians because of their desire for independence but was proven unreliable by the course of events. The Ptolemaic royal line was not beloved by the Egyptians. These rulers were Greek in language, customs, and marriage, and they seldom left Alexandria to visit the various nomes.

Prehirwonmef (1) (fl. 13th century B.C.E.) *royal prince of the Nineteenth Dynasty*
He was the son of RAMESSES II (r. 1290–1224 B.C.E.) and Queen NEFERTARI, depicted in reliefs portraying the battle of KADESH in the fifth year of Ramesses II's reign. There with other princes, Prehirwonmef and his brothers were warned: "Keep yourselves clear of the battle." Reaching maturity, Prehirwonmef was in the military service but died at a young age and was buried in THEBES.

Prehirwonmef (2) (fl. 12th century B.C.E.) *royal prince of the Twentieth Dynasty*
He was a son of RAMESSES III (r. 1194–1163 B.C.E.) and served as a royal charioteer. Prehirwonmef was depicted with 19 of his brothers on the walls of MEDINET HABU. His tomb in the VALLEY OF THE QUEENS at Thebes has corridors and a square hall with a side chapel.

priests The numerous religious and temple attendants of Egypt, whose role remained constant in all historical periods, the priests kept the TEMPLE and sanctuary areas pure, conducted the cultic rituals and observances, and performed the great festival ceremonies for the public. Some served as well in specialized agencies, such as medicine or astronomy.

Soon after the unification of the kingdoms of Upper and Lower Egypt in 3000 B.C.E., the priests were in service in major religious centers throughout the nation. Cultic rituals had been conducted in all regions before the unification, but the centralization of the government allowed them to flourish and to influence the cultural development of the entire land. The priesthood was not viewed as a separate class, however, until the New Kingdom (1550–1070 B.C.E.).

HELIOPOLIS was an early center for the solar cult in honor of RÉ and ATUM, and many priests were engaged in the ongoing functions of the temples and shrines. The high priest of Heliopolis was called the "Great One of the Seers" and held many responsible positions in the Early Dynastic Period (2920–2575 B.C.E.) and Old Kingdom (2575–2134 B.C.E.) administrations. In some eras the head of the Heliopolitan cult was a member of the royal family, but most often the position was in the hands of a dedicated and talented commoner. The high priest of MEMPHIS, dedicated to the god PTAH, was sometimes called the "Great One Who Rules the Artificers," and many gifted men served in this capacity, including IMHOTEP, the builder of the STEP PYRAMID for DJOSER.

In the New Kingdom, the high priest of AMUN in THEBES held even greater powers. He was called the chief prophet of Amun. Other temples of Egypt came under his jurisdiction at this time, as Amun became the most powerful deity of the land. The Amunite priests were normally men dedicated to the service of their god and nation in an administrative capacity. MENKHEPERRESENB (1), a high-ranking Amunite during the reign of TUTHMOSIS III (1479–1425 B.C.E.), for example, was an architect and the head of the palace and the city of Thebes.

During the Third Intermediate Period (1070–712 B.C.E.) the priests of the temple of Amun at Thebes usurped the robes and ranks of the pharaohs while performing priestly and military duties because of ongoing rebellions in Upper Egypt. The self-proclaimed pharaohs ended with the collapse of the Twenty-first Dynasty (1070–945 B.C.E.), however, and the priesthoods remained traditional in their performances and services. The importance of such ministers of the gods faded during the Late Period (712–332 B.C.E.) but arose with the invasion of Egypt by the armies of ALEXANDER III THE GREAT (r. 332–323 B.C.E.).

The rulers of the ensuing Ptolemaic Period (304–30 B.C.E.) restored many of the priesthoods as tools for keeping the native population of the Nile Valley in check. Such rulers, however, worshipped the Greek pantheon of deities, making only the required devotions to the traditional gods of the Nile Valley on state occasions. The priests of Egypt, allowed to serve in peace, continued their own traditions and vied with one another and the imported foreign cults to provide the people with devotional events and inspirational celebrations. The traditions of these priesthoods, especially those involved in the mortuary rituals of the nation, flourished as the Greeks and then the Romans adopted the funerary customs of the land. Egyptian priests also went to other nations to spread the cults of the popular deities, such as ISIS and OSIRIS. These cults remained active during the Roman period in many cities of the world at the time.

Priests officiating in smaller temples were called *web* or *wab*. The *web* priest also served as a purificator during rituals and cultic rites. The *sem* priests were mortuary ritualists. The *hem-ka* priests performed funerary rites and the *hem-neter* assisted in the temples. The *kheri-heb* priest was the lector, the master of mortuary rituals for the royal clans, and was attended by the *heri-shesheta,* the head of mysteries (called *kheri-shesheta* in some sects). Other high-ranking priests of lesser temples were called *uab-aa amihru, ur hekau,* or *neter atef,* depending upon their role and their cult.

In the Old and Middle Kingdoms there were priestesses associated with the goddess cults, but during the New Kingdom their role was reduced to singing or to the various aspects of devotional groups. There is no evidence of temple prostitution in ancient Egypt, despite its existence in other contemporaneous societies.

In most periods the priests of Egypt were members of a family long connected to a particular cult or temple. Priests recruited new members from among their own clans, generation after generation. This meant that they did not live apart from their own people, and thus they maintained an awareness of the state of affairs in their communities.

Most priests in Egypt married and were succeeded by their children. Regulations concerning sex, however, were very stringent in every era, and priests were also obliged to fast before and after ceremonies and to maintain regularity in their own lifestyles and in their dress. Priests wore white linen in the temple and sandals, which were common only to the nobility or temple servants in each historical period. Leopard skins, pendants, and plaited hairpieces denoted their ranks and offices.

Temples were the center of each town or village, but they were not open to the public except on certain feast days. The priests alone entered the temples and worked in a series of chambers of increasing seclusion. The rank of the priest determined his access to interior sanctuaries. During their initial training periods, priests were taught quietude, modesty, and self-sacrifice. A spirit of dedication to the god and to the nation was also cultivated.

Priests served full-time or part-time, and for centuries the temples of Egypt mandated unity and honor among the people. Each morning the priests dressed, incensed, and anointed the statue of the god of the temple with oils. The interior shrine was then closed and sealed against intruders. At noon, purifying water was added to the holy fonts, and the sanctuaries were swept and washed again. At night more offerings were made, but the sanctuary was not opened. On certain days, in some eras several times a month, the god was carried on arks or ships into the streets or set sail on the Nile. There the oracles took place and the priests answered petitions.

"Primeval Island of Trampling" This was a mythical and cultic site in the cosmogonic traditions of Egypt. Associated with the moment of creation and the PRIME-VAL MOUND, the island was ruled by a being named AA. In time Aa and WA became associated with the cult of the deity RÉ. The exact purpose or history of this traditional site is not clear. Most temples made a reference to the Primeval Island of Trampling in their founding documents.

"Primeval Mound" It was the site of creation in Egypt's cosmological traditions, the first piece of land to emerge from the watery chaos of NUN and associated with the concept of the PAY LANDS. The temples of the various gods contained records of such sites, also called the High Dunes. EDFU had a particularly striking commemoration of the Primeval Mound, not only as a recorded tradition but also as an actual mound of earth used as a replica. Such islands offered the gods the sacred DJEBA, or perch, the seat of creation, and the call of the PHOENIX heard there brought them to life. Two divine lords, called the COMPANIONS OF THE DIVINE HEART and named WA and AA, guarded the Primeval Mound at Edfu.

The Primeval Mound assumed other forms and significances over the centuries as well. Called the "PRIMEVAL ISLAND OF TRAMPLING" in Edfu, the mound was viewed as the sacred domain of Horus the Elder. This island, along with the Island of Peace and the Island of Combat, was surrounded by the *wa-ret,* the primeval waters, and by darkness. Such sites were also honored as Ta-tenen, the Rising Lands. Most were associated with RÉ or with NEFERTEM, the lotus deity.

See also MANSION OF ISDEN.

Prince's Will *See* NEKAURÉ.

"Prince Unknown" (Man E) *(unknown) prince whose mummified remains date to an unknown era of Egypt*
This embalmed individual was discovered in DEIR EL-BAHRI in 1886 and is also called Man E in some lists. The mummy was placed in a plain white case, without inscriptions. The body of the prince was wrapped in sheepskin, a material considered unclean by religious standards in Egypt. The mummy was also covered in a white dough-like substance when discovered. When the corpse was recovered, the remains began to putrefy. Reburied in a yard, the body was cured of the damage done by the embalming processes.

The "Prince Unknown" died between the ages of 25 and 30. There are no wounds or marks on the remains, which had turned a dark mahogany color over the centuries. Some NATRON was packed between bandages and in pouches against the flesh. The arms and legs were twisted and the stomach distended. The facial features are also distorted in agony, as if from convulsion or pain. It is possible that the aristocratic individual was buried alive. The harem plot against RAMESSES III (r. 1194–1163 B.C.E.) claimed a prince PENTAWERET as a victim, and the mummy could be that usurper of the throne who was convicted and condemned to death. Pentaweret, however, was allowed to kill himself. Other possibilities are being explored. He may have been a foreign prince, possibly ZANNANZA of Babylon.

Prisse Papyrus A document dating to the reign of NIUSERRÉ (2416–2392 B.C.E.) in the Fifth Dynasty, the papyrus is now in the Louvre in Paris, with a second copy in the British Museum. The writings of the sage PTAH-HOTEP (2) are contained in this document.

proyet The second season of the year, also called *peret,* this period in the Egyptian calendar was composed of four months and was dedicated to "growth," as the name implies. *Proyet* was followed by *akhet,* the season of the inundation of the Nile, and by *shomu,* the harvest time.

Psammetichus I (Wahibré; Psamtik) (d. 610 B.C.E.)
second ruler of the Twenty-sixth Dynasty, reigning in Sais
Ruling from 664 B.C.E. until his death, he was the son of NECHO I, who had been put to death by TANUTAMUN (r. 664–657 B.C.E.) of the Twenty-fifth Dynasty for being a vassal of the ASSYRIANS. Psammetichus I fled to Nineveh, the Assyrian capital, when his father was slain, and he returned to Egypt with the Assyrian army of ASSURBANIPAL. He was called Nabu-shezibanni by Assurbanipal and was well liked by the Assyrians, as his father had been before him.

Psammetichus I assumed the throne of SAIS, eventually turning on and defeating the Assyrians and the Nubians who were trying to hold on to their Twenty-fifth Dynasty domain. He used the military might of Greek mercenaries in order to establish his own rule and to unify Egypt. By his ninth regnal year, he ruled over all areas of the nation, using oracles to win over some areas and brute force to subdue others.

His consort was MEKHTEMWESKHET (2), the daughter of HARSIESE, the high priest of HELIOPOLIS. His son was NECHO II, and his daughter was NITOCRIS (2). She was sent to THEBES, to be adopted by AMENIRDIS (2) as the GOD'S WIFE OF AMUN or a Divine Adoratrice of Amun. "The Adoption Stela of Nitocris" has survived to document this event.

Psammetichus I consolidated his control by building forts at NAUKRATIS and Daphne, in the eastern Delta, and on ELEPHANTINE Island. He also continued to employ Greek mercenaries, initiating Greek settlements of Ionians and Carians. Naukratis was possibly started as a result of his policies. Psammetichus I aided the Assyrians against the rising power of the Persians at Babylon and gained land on the Palestinian coast. He defeated Nabopolasser, the Mede, at Ashdod on the coast as well. When the Scythians threatened Egypt, Psammetichus I sent tribute and escaped their assaults.

He ruled from Sais and MEMPHIS and declared the goddess NEITH (1) as patroness of the dynasty. Egypt prospered under his leadership, as he restored the economy, trade, and the traditions of the past. When he died, he was buried in the temple of Neith at Sais.

See also PEDIESE.

Psammetichus II (Neferibré; Psamtik) (d. 589 B.C.E.)
fourth ruler of the Twenty-sixth Dynasty
He reigned from 595 B.C.E. until his death. He was the son of NECHO II and Queen MEKHTEMWESKHET (3). Militarily active, Psammetichus II conducted a major campaign in NUBIA (modern Sudan) in his third regnal year. His army was composed of Greek mercenaries, and he went as far south as Napata during his campaigns. This war was depicted on a wall of KARNAK to commemorate the campaigns. His Greek soldiers also left inscriptions at ABU SIMBEL.

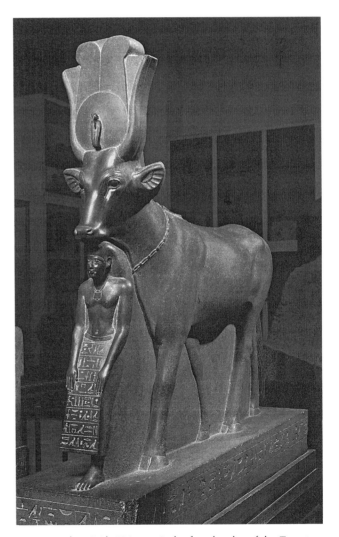

Psammetichus II (d. 589 B.C.E.), the fourth ruler of the Twenty-sixth Dynasty, depicted under the protection of the goddess Hathor, in the form of a sacred cow *(The Art Archive/ Egyptian Museum Cairo/Gianni Dagli Orti)*

A granite statue of Psammetichus II was erected at DAMANHUR in the Delta in a temple dedicated to HORUS. He also went to southern Palestine to encourage the various city-states of the area to band together and to fight against the rising power of the Babylonians.

Psammetichus II's consort was Queen TAKHAT (3), who was the mother of his son, APRIES, and his daughter, ANKHESNEFERIBRÉ. This daughter was sent to Thebes to be adopted as a GOD'S WIFE OF AMUN by NITOCRIS (2). When Psammetichus II died, he was buried in SAIS.

Psammetichus III (Ankhka-en-ré; Psamtik) (d. ca. 525 B.C.E.) *last ruler of the Twenty-sixth Dynasty*

He reigned only from 526 to 525 B.C.E. Within a year of his succession to the throne, Psammetichus III faced CAMBYSES (r. 525–522 B.C.E.) and the Persian army. At PELUSIUM, the Egyptians fought bravely but were forced to retreat. Psammetichus III fled, intent on raising an army. He was caught and taken in chains to Susa, the Persian capital at the time, where he died. Psammetichus III was allowed to live in comparative freedom in his first days in the Persian capital but then was suspected of treachery and executed.

Psammetichus (IV) (Usere'setepenptah) (fl. 393 B.C.E.) *usurper of the throne of the Twenty-ninth Dynasty*

He ruled only one year, 393 B.C.E. Setting aside the designated heir when NEPHRITES I died, he carried out his predecessor's policies. Psammetichus built in KARNAK and AKHMIN before being deposed by HAKORIS.

Psamtik (fl. sixth century B.C.E.) *official of the Twenty-sixth Dynasty*

Psamtik served AMASIS (r. 570–526 B.C.E.) as chief steward. His tomb in SAQQARA contained a beautifully carved statue depicting him being protected by the goddess HATHOR in the form of a cow, a traditional THEOPHANY for this deity.

Psusennes I ('Akheperre'setepenamun) (d. 992 B.C.E.) *ruler of the Twenty-first Dynasty*

He reigned from 1040 B.C.E. until his death. Psusennes I was the son of PINUDJEM I and Queen HENUTTAWY, and his name meant "the Star Appearing in the City." Psusennes I became the ruler in TANIS and refurbished the city, adding a temenos wall and a sanctuary of AMUN.

His queens were MUTNODJMET (2), WIAY, and TA'APENES. His sons were AMENEMOPE and Prince ANKHEFENMUT, who appears to have been disgraced in some unknown fashion. Psusennes I's daughter ISTEMKHEBE (2) was given in marriage to MENKHEPERRESENB (2), the high priest of Amun at Thebes.

This ruler also fostered a cult of MUT and KHONS and erected a temple for the goddess Mut. Psusennes I ruled for 48 years and took Amenemope as his co-regent. During his reign the Scythians stood poised to invade Egypt, and Psusennes offered a tribute and saved the nation.

When Psusennes died he was buried at TANIS, and his mummified remains, badly decomposed, evidence his advanced age. He had bad teeth and arthritis and was possibly crippled in his last years. The mummy of Psusennes I was discovered in Tanis, painted red, and his exquisite silver and gold (electrum) coffin was recovered. This magnificent piece was apparently made for MERENPTAH in the Ramessid Period. A pink granite sarcophagus held the remains, and Psusennes I's body was laid to rest with a mask of gold. His tomb also contained burial chambers for Queen Mutnodjmet, Prince Ankhefenmut (who had been removed from the succession), and General Wendjeba-en-Djed, a remarkable warrior who had served him well. Amenenope, the successor, was also buried in the tomb, as was SHOSHENQ III, who was interred there by OSORKON I, about a century later.

Psusennes II (Titkhepure'setepenré) (d. 945 B.C.E.) *seventh ruler of the Twenty-first Dynasty, reigning in Tanis*

He ruled from 959 B.C.E. until his death. The son of ISTEMKHEBE (3) and the high priest PINUDJEM (2), Psusennes rescued royal graves and mummies while in Thebes and continued supervising reburial operations from TANIS. His daughter became the wife of the Libyan military leader who succeeded Psusennes II as SHOSHENQ I. Psusennes II was buried in Tanis.

Ptah

The god of ancient Egypt in MEMPHIS, called Ptah-Sokar in a double form and Ptah-Sokar-Osiris in the triune style, Ptah dates to the earliest dynastic periods of Egypt and perhaps earlier. A sophisticated theology made Ptah somewhat obscure to the average Egyptian. The Memphite teachings concerning Ptah were discovered on a STELA, which explained the cosmogony and the cult of the region. According to these tenets, Ptah was the only true god, the creator, and all spiritual beings, divine or human, emanated from his will. The creation deities worshipped in other cities were supposed to have been devised by Ptah. This deity was also the source of the ethical and moral orders in the world, and he was called "the Lord of Truth" in all historical periods. He was deemed capable of bringing forth life with words, as the tongue announced what the god's heart experienced.

Memphis, the cult center of Ptah, was called Hiku-Ptah, or Hat-Ka-Ptah, the mansion of the soul of Ptah. Statues and reliefs depicting the god showed him as a man with very light skin, sometimes green, mummy wrappings, and an immense collar with the *menat*. Most depictions of Ptah were designed as pillars, emblems of justice. Called the First of the Gods, Ptah was a patron of the great architectural monuments of the Old Kingdom (2575–2134 B.C.E.).

As TATENEN he was revered as the creative urge, both for the world and for the individual works of art. Also called Hetepi and Khnemi, Ptah was associated with the chaos that existed before the moment of creation, and was then called Ptah-Nun. When associated with the Nile, the deity was worshipped as Ptah-Hapi; with the earth as Ptah-Tenen; and with the solar disk, called Ptah-Aten. The deity was also honored in the great complexes of AMUN in THEBES.

Ptah-hotep (1) (fl. 24th century B.C.E.) *vizier of the Fifth Dynasty*
Ptah-hotep served IZEZI (r. 2388–2356 B.C.E.) as VIZIER. He was buried alone in a tomb in SAQQARA, north of the STEP PYRAMID of DJOSER. His grandson was PTAH-HOTEP (2), the celebrated sage.

Ptah-hotep (2) (Tehefi) (fl. 24th century B.C.E.) *official and a famous sage of the Fifth Dynasty*
He served Unis (r. 2356–2323 B.C.E.) with his father, Akhethotep, as a VIZIER, but he was also esteemed as a popular sage in his era. The MAXIMS OF PTAH-HOTEP are found in the PRISSE PAPYRUS. One copy is in the Louvre in Paris, and a second copy is in the British Museum in London.

He exhorted his fellow Egyptians to conduct their affairs with quietude and righteousness. Ptah-hotep also urged them to be truthful and to treat their neighbors and fellow countrymen with kindness and tolerance. He was especially concerned with the weak and oppressed. Ptah-hotep's *Maxims* remained popular in all ages of Egypt's history as they provided demonstrations of the spirit of *ma'at,* the cohesive social and ethical standards that maintained order and stability.

He was buried in the mastaba of his father in SAQQARA. His tomb had pillared halls, corridors, and separate burial chambers. Ptah-hotep is depicted there wearing the panther skin of a high priest. Other paintings portray an entire day's activities, including children at play. An anonymous mummy shared Akhethotep's tomb as well.

Ptahshepses (1) (fl. 25th century B.C.E.) *official of the Fourth Dynasty*
He served SHEPSESKHAF (r. 2472–2467 B.C.E.) in varying court roles. Ptahshepses was raised in the royal palace and married KHAMA'AT, the daughter of Shepseskhaf. He was buried in SAQQARA, and the FALSE DOOR of his mastaba gives an account of his career.

Ptahshepses (2) (fl. 25th century B.C.E.) *official of the Fifth Dynasty*
He served SAHURÉ (r. 2458–2446 B.C.E.) as superintendent of royal works. Ptahshepses' mastaba was discovered in ABUSIR, near Sahuré's pyramidal complex. This tomb had an entryway, a colonnaded court with 20 pillars, a portico, and a hall with niches. Portraits of Ptahshepses and his wife are part of the decorations. Two officials in the 50th year of the reign of RAMESSES II (1290–1224 B.C.E.) entered this tomb and left graffiti on the walls.

Ptah-Sokar-Osiris figurines They were tomb images prized for magical powers and designs and used as SHABTIS. Fashioned normally out of wood, the figures were painted or gilded and then fastened to rectangular bases. These bases had two cavities, one in front and one at the side. The front cavity held a small piece of the deceased, which was then covered by the hawk-like SOKAR figure. The side cavity held written prayers. The god PTAH was the guardian of all created substance, and OSIRIS and Sokar were patrons of the deceased of Egypt.

Ptolemaeus *See* PTOLEMY, CLAUDIUS.

Ptolemaic script It was the hieroglyphic form (demotic) used in the Ptolemaic Period (304–30 B.C.E.), instituted by that dynasty. The form was characterized by letters or signs well shaped and placed in the epigraphic or inscription style.
See also LANGUAGE AND WRITING.

Ptolemais (1) (fl. fourth century B.C.E.) *royal woman of the Thirtieth Dynasty*
She was the consort of NECTANEBO I (r. 380–362 B.C.E.) and the daughter of an Athenian mercenary general named KHABRIAS, who was in Egypt serving Hakoris (r. 393–380 B.C.E.). Ptolemais probably married Nectanebo I when he was a general of Egypt's armies, known then as Nakhtnebef. She was the mother of TEOS.

Ptolemais (2) An ancient coastal city of Cyrenaica, now modern Libya, PTOLEMY III EUERGETES I (r. 246–221 B.C.E.) named the site when the area was taken by Egypt. Ptolemais served as a port for trading ships and flourished throughout many historical periods until the 14th century C.E.)

Ptolemy, Claudius (fl. second century C.E.) *Alexandrian astronomer and scholar*
Claudius Ptolemy, or Ptolemaeus, lived in Alexandria when the city was part of the Roman Empire. Few details of his life have survived. Ptolemy's most famous treatise was his study on astronomy, the *Almagest,* written in 13 books that covered the entire extent of knowledge of the heavens. The *Almagest* became the most widely accepted work on astronomy for the next millennium, even in the eras of Islam and the Byzantines. Ptolemy also had expertise in geography, including an extensive albeit inaccurate geographical guide to the ancient world.

Ptolemy I Soter (d. 284 B.C.E.) *founder of the Ptolemaic Period*

Ptolemy ruled from 304 B.C.E. until his death, establishing a unique Greek royal line on the Nile. He also firmly established Alexandria and was a vigorous military commander.

BIOGRAPHY

Ptolemy I was the son of Arsinoe, a Macedonian woman, and probably LAGUS, a Macedonian military companion of ALEXANDER III THE GREAT. According to some sources, Ptolemy may have been the illegitimate son of Alexander's father, Philip II of Macedon, meaning that he would have been a half brother to Alexander. As it was, Ptolemy knew, and was a friend of, Alexander from childhood and became one of the Macedonian king's most trusted bodyguards and generals. It is possible that Ptolemy was exiled briefly for advising Alexander to resist his father's plans to marry off PHILIP III ARRHIDAEUS (r. 323–316 B.C.E.), Alexander's intellectually challenged brother, to the daughter of a satrap in Caria; however, Ptolemy returned with the accession of Alexander to the Macedonian throne.

Ptolemy served with distinction in virtually all of Alexander's campaigns and was especially prominent in the later campaigns in India. Ptolemy's title of Soter, meaning "Savior," was bestowed upon him by the city of Rhodes when he relieved that small state (a Greek island off the coast of modern-day Turkey) during a siege. In the aftermath of Alexander's death in 323 B.C.E., Ptolemy took part in the division of the massive empire of the dead conqueror and received the post of satrap, or governor, of Egypt. He continued in that post for Philip III Arrhidaeus and ALEXANDER IV (r. 316–304 B.C.E.) of Macedon. He also ruled over parts of Libya and the adjacent Arabian regions; as such, he was a member of the so-called Diadochi (Successors), the generals who used the disintegration of Alexander's empire as a chance to establish themselves as rulers in their own right. When the body of Alexander the Great was being transported in a giant, mobile sarcophagus to Vergina, Macedonia's necropolis, Ptolemy along with units of the Egyptian army intercepted the funeral cortege at Damascus. Ptolemy I returned to Egypt, taking the body of Alexander the Great and the sarcophagus with him. The remains of Alexander were displayed at MEMPHIS to bolster Ptolemy I's claim before the Egyptian people that he was Alexander's rightful heir and should wield the authority to continue the Greek rule on the Nile. To tie himself even further to the legacy of Alexander, an elaborate tomb was completed in Alexandria by Ptolemy II, following Ptolemy I's designs. Reportedly, Cleopatra VII (r. 51–30 B.C.E.) took Julius Caesar to the tomb when he was in Alexandria.

Although Alexander the Great had been buried, the battle for control of his massive empire was far from over. A series of military confrontations took place between the survivors of Alexander's army, with Ptolemy fighting against all rivals and consolidating his hold on Egypt. Following a war against PERDICCAS, another heir to the empire of Alexander the Great, Ptolemy I controlled Egypt and Cyrenaica. In 304 B.C.E., resisting an attack by Antigonus, he assumed the title of pharaoh. He married EURYDICE, the daughter of King Antipater of Macedonia, having set aside the daughter of Nectanebo or some other ruler of the Thirtieth Dynasty. Later on, he also married Queen BERENICE (1).

Ptolemy I then joined generals LYSIMACHUS (360–281 B.C.E.) and Cassander (355–297 B.C.E.) against General ANTIGONUS I MONOPHTHALMUS (382–301 B.C.E.). This combined force marched on Antigonus's son, DEMETRIUS I POLIORCETES, at Gaza and defeated him. That campaign and victory set the seal upon Ptolemy I's claim of Egypt. He also fought at SALAMIS but lost, though ultimately he repelled Antigonus, who was killed at Ipsus in 301 B.C.E. Ptolemy I then added Palestine and southern Syria to his domains.

Ptolemy's efforts effectively created the Ptolemaic Dynasty that survived for the next three centuries. He assumed the title of pharaoh in 305 or 304 B.C.E. and embraced much of the religious tradition of Egypt in order to ease the transition of government and to establish a strong central government that could claim many of the luxuries of the older pharaonic dynasties.

Ptolemy set as his capital the great city of Alexandria that had been founded by Alexander the Great around 323 B.C.E. He began work on the great LIGHT-

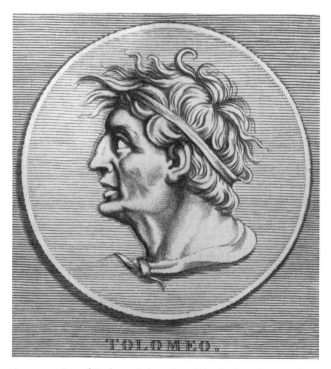

An engraving of Ptolemy I, founder of the Ptolemaic Period in Egypt, ca. 304–30 B.C.E. *(Hulton Archive)*

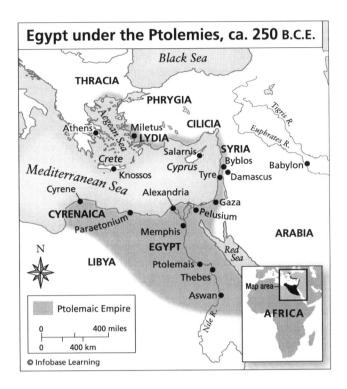

Egypt under the Ptolemies, ca. 250 B.C.E.

ancient land. CLEOPATRA VII (r. 51–30 B.C.E.) was the only Ptolemaic ruler able to read and write hieroglyphs. The Egyptians were allowed to live under their traditional laws and court system, and the Greeks were judged by their own legal codes. The Ptolemies conducted rituals of state in pharaonic robes and crowns, employing the traditional royal cult symbols. These rulers, however, did not marry Egyptian heiresses; rather, they imported their consorts from Greek and Macedonian families.

In Egypt, Ptolemy I built several structures that added to his legacy. In Tuna el-Gebel he built a shrine to THOTH, an Egyptian god of the moon and of wisdom. He also founded a museum at Alexandria, called "the Shrine of the Muses," to house sages and ancient papyri. (This would become the famed Library of Alexandria and research center.) He is also responsible for the plans for the lighthouse located at Pharos, the famed LIGHTHOUSE OF ALEXANDRIA, as well as for the construction of a mausoleum and a temple to Serapis. (Serapis was a deity introduced to Egypt during the reign of Ptolemy I.) A merging of the Egyptian gods Osiris and Apis, the god became the patron of the Ptolemies.

Ptolemy, careful to secure a clear Ptolemaic line, set aside Queen Eurydice, and disinherited her four children in favor of Berenice's three, particularly her son, Ptolemy II Philadelphus, who served as co-regent for a year. The Ptolemaic line ruled Egypt for almost 300 years.

Further reading: Chauveau, Michel, and David Lorton, transl. *Egypt in the Age of Cleopatra: History and Society under the Ptolemies.* Ithaca, N.Y.: Cornell University Press, 2000; Ellis, Walter M. *Ptolemy of Egypt.* New York: Routledge, 1994; Hölbl, Günther, and Tina Saavedra, transl. *A History of the Ptolemaic Empire.* New York: Routledge, 2000.

Ptolemy II Philadelphus (d. 246 B.C.E.) *second ruler of the Ptolemaic Period*
He reigned from 285 B.C.E. until his death and was the son of PTOLEMY I SOTER and Queen BERENICE (1). Ptolemy II married ARSINOE (1), the daughter of Lysimachus of Thrace, but exiled her to KOPTOS when his sister, another ARSINOE (2), returned to Egypt from Thrace. When he formally married his sister, he received the title Philadelphus, meaning "Brother-Sister Loving."

From 274 to 271 B.C.E., Ptolemy II had to defend Egypt from the Syrians, but he achieved power and lands from alliances with other Greek states. During his reign, ALEXANDRIA became a leading center for the arts and sciences. Ptolemy II also aided irrigation projects throughout the land. He celebrated a FESTIVAL every four years in honor of Ptolemy I Soter, whom he deified, and completed his great building projects, including the Library of Alexandria and the LIGHTHOUSE OF

HOUSE OF ALEXANDRIA (it was completed by his son), and in its time it became one of the Seven Wonders of the Ancient World. He also started the LIBRARY OF ALEXANDRIA, which became the greatest repository of knowledge in the ancient world and attracted the finest minds of the time. He supposedly gave his patronage to the great Greek scientist Euclid (fl. ca. 300 B.C.E.).

Ptolemy died in 284 B.C.E., having made arrangements for succession by naming as his heir PTOLEMY II PHILADELPHUS, his son born to Berenice. In the years before his death, Ptolemy authored a history of the campaigns of Alexander. The work is not extant, but it was noted for its detail and served as a major source for the Greek second century C.E. historian Arrian in his *Anabasis*, an account of the life and campaigns of Alexander the Great.

HISTORICAL IMPACT

Ptolemy I's reign provided Egypt with a relatively prosperous and stable foundation in a turbulent political period. The Egyptians did not actively oppose the Greek rulers, and only a few native sons started rebellions, all of which were short-lived. Rather than fight Ptolemy I's claim to power, the Egyptians largely resumed their lives up and down the Nile with their own religious practices and their own festivals and celebrations. The line of Ptolemy I certainly updated and modernized Egypt, but in the agricultural areas, and especially in the south, the Egyptians for the most part continued the ancient ways with very little interest in Alexandria or the line of Ptolemy I Soter.

The Ptolemaic line ruled Egypt but never immersed itself in the traditions and religious beliefs of that

A portrait of Ptolemy II, called Philadelphus, the second ruler of the Ptolemaic Period *(Hulton Archive)*

ALEXANDRIA. He added theaters, gardens, zoological displays, and gymnasiums to various sites as well.

Ptolemy II was called "the best paymaster, a freeman could have" by the Greek poet Theocrites. He even commissioned an expedition south into Africa's heartland to bring back elephants and other animals, as well as incense. He then sent a delegation to Rome and brought 70 Jewish scholars to Alexandria from Jerusalem to transcribe the Pentateuch accurately. A banquet reportedly lasted for seven nights upon the arrival of these scholars.

Ptolemy II was depicted in PHILAE offering incense and ointments to the gods. He erected a gate in the Philae temple. A stela was also mounted at Tell el-Maskhuta to commemorate his journey to Persia to reclaim religious masterpieces taken by past rulers of that nation. Ptolemy II also rebuilt a canal linking the Nile to the Gulf of Suez, a waterway renovated centuries later by Emperor Trajan. His children were PTOLEMY III EUERGETES, Lysimachus, and Berenice, who married Antiochus of Syria in 252. Ptolemy III Euergetes succeeded him.

See also CANAL OF NECHO II.

Ptolemy III Euergetes (d. 221 B.C.E.) *third ruler of the Ptolemaic Period*
He reigned from 246 B.C.E. until his death and was the son of PTOLEMY II PHILADELPHUS and Queen ARSINOE (2). BERENICE (3), the daughter of Magas, the king of Cyrene, was his consort. His sister, BERENICE (2), was slain in

Syria, and Ptolemy III invaded that land to avenge the murder. The Egyptian navy advanced against Seleucus III's forces in Thrace, across the Hellespont, capturing lands in Asia Minor. Ptolemy III led an army to Seleucia on the Tigris River but had to return to Egypt because of a low Nile inundation and famine. He faced an alliance of Seleucid Syria, Macedonia, and Rhodes but was joined by the ACHAEAN LEAGUE. A peace was organized in 242–241 B.C.E.

In Egypt, Ptolemy III colonized the FAIYUM and reformed the CALENDAR with the CANOPUS DECREE. He received the title Euergetes, meaning the Benefactor, as a result of these efforts. His campaigns in Syria took approximately five years, and Berenice stood as regent during his absence with success. During the remaining years of his reign, Ptolemy III built Minsha'a, near Sohag in Upper Egypt, as a sister city to Alexandria. Two offering tables, a limestone wall, and a pillar capital were found there. The site served as a trading center with NUBIA (modern Sudan) and the Red Sea.

He also constructed a temple in EDFU, restoring treasures stolen by the Persians centuries before. Ptolemy III built at the SERAPEUM, adding another library to accommodate an overflow of books, and borrowing more volumes to have them copied. Actually, the original manuscripts of Aeschylus, Sophocles, and Euripedes arrived in Alexandria on loan from Athens. Ptolemy III made copies and sent them back to Athens, keeping the originals. He forfeited an amount of silver, given in surety, as a result. During his reign, Ptolemy III and Queen Berenice were deified as "Benevolent Gods" by Egypt. The priests at Canopus declared their status in 238 B.C.E.

Ptolemy IV Philopator (d. 205 B.C.E.) *fourth ruler of the Ptolemaic Period*
He reigned from 221 B.C.E. until his death. The son of PTOLEMY III EUERGETES and Queen BERENICE (3), he was controlled by SOSIBIUS Alexander, a Greek counselor. Ptolemy IV is believed to have poisoned his mother and scalded his brother, MAGAS, to death. Because of his dissolute ways, Ptolemy IV could not maintain the loyalty of the various court officials.

Sensing this weakness, ANTIOCHUS III, the Seleucid king, threatened the Egyptian vassal territory of Caele Syria, some distance from Egypt's military defenses. Arabs in the region and defecting Egyptians joined Antiochus, but in 217 B.C.E., using phalanx maneuvers skillfully, the armies of Ptolemy IV defeated Antiochus at Raphia in southern Palestine. Ptolemy IV, however, did not follow up on his military advantage but made peace.

Called Philopator, "Lover of His Father," Ptolemy IV married his sister, ARSINOE (3), and she bore him PTOLEMY V EPIPHANES. In time, however, Ptolemy IV was controlled more and more by Sosibius and other counselors, including AGATHOCLES (2), and his sister, Agathoclea. They aided him in his excesses.

Native Egyptians in the Delta rebelled against him as a result, and by 205 B.C.E., the revolt was nationwide. Restoring order, Ptolemy IV refrained from all foreign interventions and began good relations with MEROË in Nubia (modern Sudan). A PHILAE inscription lists the cooperation between Ptolemy IV and King ARKAMANI of Meroë in building a temple for the Nubian deity ARSENUPHIS at Aswan. He also received ambassadors from Rome who were seeking grain. When Ptolemy IV died from his excesses, Sosibius and his confederates did not allow the news to be made public. To safeguard their own lives, they murdered Queen Arsinoe and installed Ptolemy V on the throne before announcing the royal death. Riots followed the announcements.

Ptolemy V Epiphanes (d. 180 B.C.E.) *fifth ruler of the Ptolemaic Period*
He reigned from 205 B.C.E. until his death. The son of PTOLEMY IV PHILOPATOR and Queen ARSINOE (3), Ptolemy V was only five years of age when the court counselor SOSIBIUS and his allies crowned him as king. These conspirators then murdered Queen Arsinoe. At the coronation, Sosibius issued writs of exile in the ruler's name against prominent Egyptians who opposed his powers. Sosibius, however, was soon forced to retire, and AGATHOCLES (2) became the young ruler's master.

General TLEPOLEMUS, the governor of Egypt's frontier city, PELUSIUM, did not intend to allow Queen Arsinoe's murderers to go unpunished. He rode into ALEXANDRIA with a small force and gathered the people of the city behind his impromptu army as he demanded that Ptolemy V be brought before the people. Agathocles had to allow the young ruler to appear in the arena, and there Tlepolemus accused the courtiers of murder. The Alexandrian people swept through the city when they heard the names of the criminals. Agathocles, Agathoclea, and their allies died at the hands of the outraged populace.

Freed of the courtiers, Ptolemy V Epiphanes was crowned again in MEMPHIS in a grand ceremony. Epiphanes meant "God Manifest." The event was accompanied by a decree remitting debts and taxes, releasing prisoners, benefiting temples, and pardoning rebels who had submitted. The nation rejoiced at the fall of the evil courtiers.

Ptolemy V eventually had to put down other revolts throughout Egypt, however. A battle with ANTIOCHUS III, the Syrian Seleucid king, was also fought in Ptolemy V's name in 201 B.C.E. Antiochus III continued to harass Egyptian lands until the Romans intervened in 194–193 B.C.E. Within Egypt Ptolemy V fought battles against rebels in 197 B.C.E. In order to quell the revolts in Upper Egypt, he invested the governor of Thebes with juridical powers. Peace was insured with Syria when Ptolemy

V married CLEOPATRA (1), the daughter of Antiochus III the Great. She bore him two sons, including PTOLEMY VI PHILOMETOR, and a daughter.

Ptolemy V also erected a stela on the ELEPHANTINE Island, at ASWAN, describing the famine and pious activities of the Old Kingdom pharaoh DJOSER (r. 2630–2611 B.C.E.). He slowly regained control of Upper Egypt and erected a temple of IMHOTEP, Djoser's gifted architect, at Philae. He also provided endowments for the cults of APIS, MNEVIS, and other animals, erecting a temple for Apis and equipping shrine and cult centers. Cleopatra poisoned Ptolemy V, and when he died, she stood as regent for Ptolemy VI Philometor.

Ptolemy VI Philometor (d. 145 B.C.E.) *sixth ruler of the Ptolemaic Period*
He reigned from 180 to 164 B.C.E. and then from 163 B.C.E. until his death. Ptolemy VI was the son of PTOLEMY V EPIPHANES and Queen CLEOPATRA (1), and when his father was poisoned, his mother stood as regent until her death in 176 B.C.E. Then two courtiers, Eulaeus and Lenaeus, became his self appointed guardians.

Ptolemy VI married his sister CLEOPATRA (2) and began to plan an invasion of Caele Syria. In 170 B.C.E., he raised up his brother, PTOLEMY VIII EUERGETES II, to rule with him and Cleopatra. The attempt to regain Caele Syria was unsuccessful, as ANTIOCHUS IV defeated the Egyptian forces and took PELUSIUM, the frontier city. Antiochus had other ambitions, but he withdrew when the Roman legate Papillius LAENAS and his legions persuaded him that any further assault would be met with a Roman response.

In 164 B.C.E., Ptolemy VI was expelled by his brother and fled to Rome, where he pleaded for aid. Ptolemy VIII was sent to Cyrenaica as a result but placed his case before the Roman Senate and received approval. He planned to return to Egypt but came face to face with his brother in a battle over Cyprus and lost. Ptolemy VIII was given Cyrenaica as part of the peace terms and the hand of one of Ptolemy VI's daughters in marriage.

In 155 B.C.E., the Seleucid Syrians tried to take Cyprus, but a rebel pretender arose to threaten the Seleucid throne. ALEXANDER BALAS, the rebel, was aided by Egypt and given the hand of CLEOPATRA THEA, Ptolemy VI's sister, in marriage. Cleopatra Thea appealed to Ptolemy VI to visit her because she was unhappy, and he went to Syria. Alexander Balas tried to assassinate him in order to take the Egyptian throne, and Ptolemy VI gave Cleopatra Thea to a new pretender to the Syrian throne, Demetrius II. The Syrians offered Ptolemy VI the throne, but he declined the honor. Alexander Balas was killed in a subsequent battle. During that confrontation Ptolemy VI also fell off his horse, fracturing his skull, and died.

He built the gate of the temple of PTAH at KARNAK, as well as figures at the entrance to the main temple of

HATHOR in PHILAE. He was also in the temple of KOM OMBO. His contemporaries described Ptolemy VI as pious and generous.

Ptolemy VII Neos Philopator (d. 145 B.C.E.) *seventh ruler of the Ptolemaic Period*

He reigned only during 145 B.C.E. The son of PTOLEMY VI PHILOMETOR, and Queen CLEOPATRA (2), he was called "the New Father Loving." Ptolemy VII served as a co-regent with his father as early as 147 B.C.E., and there is an indication that yet another brother shared the throne briefly. When Ptolemy VI died in Syria, the Egyptians asked PTOLEMY VIII EUERGETES II, Ptolemy VII's uncle, to take the throne. He married Cleopatra (3), Ptolemy VI's widow, and put Ptolemy VII aside. The young ruler was then executed.

Ptolemy VIII Euergetes II (Physkon) (d. 116 B.C.E.) *eighth ruler of the Ptolemaic Period*

He reigned from 170 to 163 B.C.E., and from 145 B.C.E. until his death. The son of PTOLEMY V EPIPHANES and probably Queen CLEOPATRA (1), he was called "Physcon," or Fatty. The Roman Scipio Africanus gave him that nickname. He ruled for a time with PTOLEMY VI PHILOMETOR and CLEOPATRA (2) and then tried to take control, expelling his brother. Rome settled the situation, and Ptolemy VIII was given Cyrenaica. At the death of Ptolemy VI, he put his nephew, Ptolemy VII, to death and married CLEOPATRA (2). He then married a niece, CLEOPATRA (3) and plotted against his first wife, who was popular.

As a result of court intrigue, Ptolemy VIII and Cleopatra (3) fled to Cyprus. There they sent for Memphites, a young son of Cleopatra (2), and murdered him. They cut up the body and delivered it to Cleopatra (2) as a birthday present. The couple returned to Egypt ca. 118 B.C.E. and sent Cleopatra (2) into exile. She died soon after, but Cleopatra (3) outlived her husband, who died in 116 B.C.E.

In 118 B.C.E., Ptolemy VIII issued the Amnesty Decree, an effort to put an end to the conflicts between the native Egyptians and the Greeks. He was considered a somewhat impetuous but magnanimous benefactor of Egyptian temples. At EDFU, he was depicted in the company of Egypt's protectors, the goddess BUTO and NEKHEBET, and his coronation festival was staged there. He is also depicted on a wall of Kom Ombo, and he erected a temple at Tod (Djerty), near ERMENT. Ptolemy VIII built two *MAMMISI* structures, one at Philae and a second temple of HORUS at Edfu.

Ptolemy IX Soter II (Lathyros) (d. 81 B.C.E.) *ninth ruler of the Ptolemaic Period*

He reigned from 116 to 107 B.C.E., and then from 88 B.C.E. until his death. The son of PTOLEMY VIII EUERGETES II and CLEOPATRA (3), he inherited the throne at a young age. His mother served as his regent, as he was called "Lathyros," or "Chickpea," at the start of his reign.

Ptolemy IX was accused of attempting to murder his mother, Queen Cleopatra (3), and was exiled to Cyprus while she was forced by the Roman Sulla to marry a younger son of PTOLEMY VII NEOS PHILOPATOR, PTOLEMY X ALEXANDER I, and continued to dominate Egypt. When Ptolemy X died in 88 B.C.E., Ptolemy IX returned to Egypt and remained on the throne to the age of 80. He received the name Soter, "the Savior," for his services. Ptolemy IX was depicted in KOM OMBO as sharing a boat with two gods amid plants, birds, and other deities.

Ptolemy X Alexander I (d. 88 B.C.E.) *tenth ruler of the Ptolemaic Period*

He reigned from 107 B.C.E. until his death. Ptolemy X was the son of Ptolemy VIII and CLEOPATRA (3). He was made the consort of Cleopatra (3) when his brother, Ptolemy IX, fled to CYPRUS. A degenerate, however, and normally ill, Ptolemy X bequeathed Egypt to Rome in his will before fleeing ALEXANDRIA. He died at sea and was replaced by Ptolemy XI.

Ptolemy XI Alexander II (d. 80 B.C.E.) *eleventh ruler of the Ptolemaic Period*

He married Cleopatra Berenice, who had followed her father, PTOLEMY IX SOTER II to the throne. Ptolemy XI ruled only one year in 80 B.C.E. Sulla, the ruler of Rome, had demanded that Ptolemy XI marry Cleopatra Berenice. He killed her within a year and was slain by an irate Alexandrian mob.

Ptolemy XII Neos Dionysius (Auletes) (d. 51 B.C.E.) *twelfth ruler of the Ptolemaic Period*

He reigned from 88 to 58 B.C.E. and from 55 B.C.E. until his death. The son of PTOLEMY IX SOTER II by a concubine, he was called Neos Dionysius, "the New Dionysius" or Nothos, "the Bastard." His lasting nickname was Auletes, "the Flute Player." He was the father of CLEOPATRA VII.

Ptolemy XII built at DENDEREH and EDFU and refurbished PHILAE. Much of his life had been spent in the court of Mithridates VI of Pontus at Sinope. When PTOLEMY XI ALEXANDER II died, he was recalled to Egypt. In 58 B.C.E., Ptolemy XII had to leave Egypt because of his unpopular rule. He was restored by the Roman general Gabinus through the intercession of POMPEY the Great in 55 B.C.E. RABIRIUS POSTUMOUS subsequently handled Ptolemy XII's affairs as a safeguard for Rome's interests. Ptolemy XII's will was deposited in Rome's public treasury and as a result, Pompey became the guardian of Egypt in 49 B.C.E. Ptolemy XII married his sister, CLEOPATRA (6) TRYPHAINA. More than 100 leading Alexandrian scholars went to Rome to protest Ptolemy XII's reinstatement and his reign. He was listed in the temple of KOM OMBO.

Ptolemy XIII (d. 47 B.C.E.) *coruler with Cleopatra VII and a victim of the war with Julius Caesar*

The son of PTOLEMY XII NEOS DIONYSIUS and possibly CLEOPATRA (6) TRYPHAINA, Ptolemy XIII had to share royal powers with his sister, starting their joint reign in 51 B.C.E. His court advisers, however, fostered his ambitions, and he forced CLEOPATRA VII to flee from ALEXANDRIA. POMPEY was named his guardian as a result. The war between Pompey and Julius CAESAR, however, interrupted this guardianship. When Pompey, fleeing from Caesar, landed in Egypt, he was slain by Ptolemy XIII's agents, hoping to have the victorious Caesar as an ally.

He was forced to join his army in the desert near Alexandria, however, when Caesar ruled in favor of Cleopatra VII's claims, joined in time by ARSINOE (4), his sister. Arsinoe complicated matters by murdering ACHILLAS, the military general who might have directed Egypt's forces with skill. Ptolemy XIII also faced additional armies when an ally of Caesar arrived with fresh troops. He died by drowning after an attempt to ambush Caesar failed. A shrine at KOM OMBO depicts him in various acts of worship. He also built in PHILAE.

Ptolemy XIV (d. 44 B.C.E.) *ruler of the Ptolemaic Period, sharing the throne with Cleopatra VII*

He was a coruler starting in 47 B.C.E. When PTOLEMY XIII died fighting the Romans, Ptolemy XIV, a younger brother of CLEOPATRA VII, was elevated to consort and co-regent status, a nominal position only, as Cleopatra VII was carrying Caesar's child. The assassination of Julius CAESAR alarmed Cleopatra VII, and she had Ptolemy XIV slain. No monuments from his brief reign survived.

Ptolemy XV Caesarion (Iwopaneftjer entynehem Setepenptah Irma'atenre' Sekhemankhamun) (d. 30 B.C.E.) *coruler of the Ptolemaic Period*

The son of CLEOPATRA VII and Julius CAESAR, Ptolemy XV started his reign in 44 B.C.E. Although he was only a child, he was raised to the throne to protect him. Ptolemy XIV, who had been coruler with Cleopatra VII, had been slain to make room for him.

Called Caesarion, his throne name meant "Heir of the Living God, the Chosen One of PTAH, Living the Rule of RÉ, the Living Image of AMUN." He was depicted with his mother on the wall of the temple of DENDEREH as being offered to the gods. The Roman Senate in 42 B.C.E. sponsored Ptolemy XV's elevation to the throne. He witnessed the disastrous battle of ACTIUM and the death of Cleopatra VII and Marc ANTONY and then was executed by the Romans, reportedly a death ordered by AUGUSTUS (Octavian) at the urging of Aeries Didymos, Ptolemy XV's former tutor.

Ptolemy Apion (d. 96 B.C.E.) *prince of the Ptolemaic Period*

He was the bastard son of PTOLEMY VIII EUERGETES II (170–163, 145–116 B.C.E.). Ptolemy became the governor of CYPRUS and ruled there until his death in 96 B.C.E.

Ptolemy Magas (fl. third century B.C.E.) *prince of the Ptolemaic Period*

He was the son of BERENICE (1) and stepson of PTOLEMY I SOTER (304–284 B.C.E.). When Ptolemy I married Berenice (1), Ptolemy Magas was made the governor of CYRENE. His daughter was BERENICE (3), and she married PTOLEMY III EUERGETES.

Ptolemy Philadelphos (fl. first century B.C.E.) *prince of the Ptolemaic Period*

He was the son of CLEOPATRA VII (51–30 B.C.E.) and Marc ANTONY. The youngest child of this pair, Ptolemy Philadelphos was made the ruler of Asia Minor and Syria. The deaths of his parents ended his powers.

Punt It was an unidentified land believed to have been located in eastern Sudan or Eritrea, and important in all eras of Egypt as a trade resource. The Egyptians reached Punt by going through the BITTER LAKES in the eastern Delta to the Red Sea or by going through the WADI HAMMAMAT on the KOPTOS Road to the city of KUSER on the Red Sea. Kuser was provided with shipbuilding facilities, and expeditionary fleets were outfitted for journeys to Punt in this city.

Punt offered ELECTRUM (a gold and silver mixture), gold, ivory, myrrh, incense, skins, boomerangs, cosmetics, spices, wild animals, resins, ebony, and aromatic gums in trade. Egypt's actual trade with Punt dates to the reign of SAHURÉ (2458–2446 B.C.E.), possibly earlier. In the Sixth Dynasty (2323–2150 B.C.E.) an Egyptian died while building a trading fleet on the Red Sea. Pepi II (2246–2152 B.C.E.) sent many expeditions to Punt, called "the land of the god." MYRRH, used as incense in religious festivals and rites, was imported in vast quantities and commonly tallied by scribes as a result of these trading ventures. Myrrh trees were also planted in the temple compounds.

In the Middle Kingdom, MENTUHOTEP II (r. 2061–2010 B.C.E.), SENWOSRET I (r. 1971–1926 B.C.E.), AMENEMHET II (r. 1929–1892 B.C.E.), and other pharaohs sent expeditions to Punt. In the New Kingdom (1550–1070 B.C.E.) such trade journeys were increased, and HATSHEPSUT (r. 1473–1458 B.C.E.) is well connected to this practice. Reliefs from her period depict the gathering of goods, the loading of vessels in Punt, return voyages, and the presentation of the trade wares in Thebes. Weights and measures are recorded as well.

TUTHMOSIS III (r. 1479–1425 B.C.E.), AMENHOTEP III (r. 1391–1353 B.C.E.), HOREMHAB (r. 1319–1307 B.C.E.), SETI

I (r. 1306–1290 B.C.E.), RAMESSES II (r. 1290–1224 B.C.E.);
and RAMESSES III (r. 1194–1163 B.C.E.) also sent expeditions to Punt during the New Kingdom period. A stela
in Amenhotep III's mortuary temple mentions Punt. The
HARRIS PAPYRUS from Ramesses II's historical period gives
a depiction of such expeditions. The royal and common
people of Punt came to visit Egypt and were also depicted
in reliefs. The illustrations in a temple in the reign of
Hatshepsut clearly portray a Puntite family that was
brought to Egypt on one of the expeditions of the time.

A chief is shown with his wife, two sons, and a
daughter. The wife of the chief is portrayed as having
pronounced curvature of the spine and folds of fat on
her arms and ankles. This condition has been diagnosed
as symptoms of various diseases of the African region.
These same reliefs depict Egyptian fleets sailing to and
from the fabled land, a convention that continued in the
Ramessid Period.

Pure Mound   A legendary site called Abaton in some
records, the Pure Mound was located on the island of
BIGA, near PHILAE. The PRIMEVAL MOUND and this site
were all considered the first true portions of the earth
that arose out of NUN, the original dark void or chaos at
the moment of creation.

Puyenré (fl. 15th century B.C.E.) *priestly official of the
Eighteenth Dynasty*
He served HATSHEPSUT (r. 1473–1458 B.C.E.) as a high-
ranking priest of the temple of AMUN. It is, however,
as an architect that he is principally remembered. He
created the beautiful shrine of MUT that Hatshepsut
erected, and he was consulted on other royal building
projects. Puyenré survived Hatshepsut and was accepted
by her successor, TUTHMOSIS III, whose KARNAK building projects were influenced by his designs. Puyenré was
buried with honors in Thebes. His tomb at QURNA has
reliefs portraying his work, including a session of tallying Asiatic spoils and tributes.

pylon   They are the majestic architectural entrance
forms adorning Egyptian temples, dating probably
to the Middle Kingdom (2040–1640 B.C.E.), possibly
earlier. The pyramid and sun temple of NIUSERRÉ (r.
2416–2392 B.C.E.) at ABUSIR and ABU GHUROB display
a form of pylon. The name pylon was taken from the
Greek word for gate. The Egyptian name was *bekhenet*.

The structure was composed of two battered towers
linked by a masonry bridge with cornices. The flat surface on the top was reserved for rituals honoring the god
RÉ. Most were built over a pile of rubble, but some had
interior chamber and stairs. The pylons were decorated
with reliefs and completed by flagstaffs. The pylon represented the AKHET (2), the religious symbol for the eternal
HORIZON. The divine patrons of the pylons were the goddesses ISIS and NEPHTHYS.

A pylon from the temple of Isis at Philae *(Courtesy Steve
Beikirch)*

pyramid   *See* PYRAMIDS, BUILDING OF THE GREAT (2575–
2465 B.C.E.)

pyramidion   *See* BENBEN.

pyramids, building of the great (2575–2465 B.C.E.)
No national or cultural symbol is as recognizable as the
great pyramids of Egypt, which were erected as tombs
for the pharaohs of the Fourth Dynasty (2575–2465
B.C.E.). The pyramids still stand today on the plateau of
GIZA, near modern Cairo; the Great Pyramid is the only
survivor of the Seven Wonders of the Ancient World.
While the pyramids are credited to individual pharaohs, they are products of the entire nation of Egypt,
as the men and women of the Nile Valley responded
to the call of the pharaohs to build these insignias of
resurrection.

CONTEXT
The pyramid, called *mr* by the Egyptians, was considered the place of ascent and point of departure for the
royal deceased on his/her journey to eternity. As such,
pyramids were given names to signify their special religious status as tombs of the pharoahs. Architecturally,
the pyramid represented the culmination of the mortuary structures developed during the Early Dynastic
Period (2920–2575 B.C.E.).

The pyramids were intended to be the burial places of the pharaohs and the nobles, safe havens in which their mummified remains could rest for eternity. Such tombs contained all of the material objects that they might need in the afterlife. Each pyramid was surrounded by smaller MASTABAS (brick tombs that resemble benches) in which the servants of the pharaoh would be buried so that pharaohs could have their faithful servants with them in the afterlife.

The mastabas, which were first used during the Early Dynastic Period (2920–2575 B.C.E.), were furnished with burial and offertory chambers. Some, such as those erected for the rulers and queens in SAQQARA and ABYDOS, were designed with facades with recessed and projecteing walls, after the design of the palaces of the era. These mastabas became known as "mansions for eternity." One such mastaba, that of an official in the reign of DEN in the First Dynasty (2920–2770 B.C.E.), a man named Nebtiu, started out resembling a pyramid but was then altered to its traditional form.

EVENT

By the Third Dynasty (2469–2575 B.C.E.), the pharaohs were secure in their roles and were largely uncontested by rivals seeking the throne. However, these rulers were acutely aware of the need to demonstrate their semidivine status and to inspire the people with insignias of power and artistry. Once such ruler, DJOSER (2630–2611 B.C.E.), asked his vizier IMHOTEP to design for him not only a tomb but an entire mortuary complex, a site that would proclaim to one and all that Djoser was a pharaoh who understood both his destiny on earth and beyond.

Imhotep had a series of mastabas placed one on top of another in a graduated design, forming the STEP PYRAMID at the necropolis of Saqqara. The Step Pyramid was originally 204 feet high, composed of six separate layers, or "steps," each one successively smaller in size. The base measured 358 feet by 411 feet. The layers of the pyramid were faced with limestone and were surrounded by a vast complex of buildings, replicas of those erected to celebrate SED FESTIVALS (anniversaries of reigns), as well as a wall that was carved in relief to resemble the royal palace facade. Because the Step Pyramid was the world's first large-scale structure to be built with stone, the architects were not aware that it was important to square the blocks with smooth, even sides; thus, the pyramid was unstable. Visitors can still see the cedar logs imported from Lebanon that were used to shore up the sides during construction.

The Step Pyramid contained a 90-foot shaft that led to underground chambers and passageways. The burial vault was 13 feet high and was encased entirely in granite, with a plug made of the same material to seal the entrance. The eastern section of the pyramid contained tombs of Djoser's queens and sons. Eleven shafts have been discovered, sunken to almost 100 feet. The enclosure around the pyramid contained shrines, altar chambers, courts, a *hed-sed* hall, storerooms, and the tombs of Djoser's courtiers. The site was actually a miniature city, with its own priests and liturgical schedules.

For his projects Imhotep would normally have had a regular workforce of laborers, stonecutters, and artisans, as such trained Egyptians made their living by building state and royal monuments. The size of this particular complex and pyramid, however, would have demanded the services of countless other Egyptians. Egypt did not have a monetary system until late in its history, and bartering and the payment of debts involved the exchange of goods, not coins. When the Nile flooded the land and river waters inundated the fields, plains, and orchards, depositing fertilizing silt and mud, the average Egyptians (most of whom were farmers) had to seek shelter and other ways of providing for themselves and their families. In return for their services Djoser ensured that those who labored on his pyramidal complex were fed, clothed, given medical care, and given gifts at the end of their days of service. This construction by the commoners on behalf of the pharaoh was called the system of corvée, or the right of the pharaoh to call upon his people to serve him on a particular undertaking. Excavations at Giza have uncovered the remains of a large complex designed to serve the needs of pyramid laborers. Bakeries, breweries, chapels, barracks, clinics, dining areas, and even tombs were incorporated into the site.

Other step pyramids were started soon after Djoser's reign. Some have been discovered at SEILA, Zawiyet el-Mayitin, El-KULA, EDFU, and on the ELEPHANTINE; they appear to be mostly tombs of nobles.

The first true or smooth-sided pyramid appeared in the reign of SNEFRU (2575–2551 B.C.E.), who was obsessed with the form. He erected two such tombs at DASHUR and then finished his father's pyramid at MEIDUM. The traditional pyramidal complex evolved from his father's tomb. Other true pyramids rose on the fringes of the desert area west of MEMPHIS, between Meidum and ABU ROWASH.

Snefru's son KHUFU (Cheops) (r. 2551–2528 B.C.E.) then constructed a pyramid at Giza that would become the first to perfect the pyramid's classical form. The centerpiece of Khufu's pyramidal complex was the pyramid built as a solar symbol, which stemmed from the ancient cult at HELIOPOLIS (ON), the ancient center of the sun god. The pyramid's four sides were designed to face the cardinal points of the earth, with the entrance normally on the north side, sometimes aboveground and sometimes level with the ground. An offertory shrine, a chapel for holding mortuary rites and rituals in commemoration of the royal cult, was built beside the pyramid. This building contained ceremonial chambers and the mandatory FALSE DOOR, through which the *ka* ("astral companion" or spirit) of the deceased ruler could escape.

Religious insignias and statues adorned the chambers, and the walls were inscribed and covered with reliefs.

A MORTUARY TEMPLE was constructed near the pyramid, with an elaborate entrance corridor and central court. Most of these temples have disappeared over the centuries, but when the pyramids were built they were lavish shrines, with offertory chambers, rooms containing ALTARS, storage rooms, and the traditional SERDAB. The *serdab* contained statues of the deceased pharaohs positioned so that their eyes could view through slits in the wall the daily ceremonies conducted in the deceased's name and memory. Nonroyal tombs also contained *serdabs*. A causeway led from this temple to a valley temple on the banks of the Nile or at a distance in the desert. The walls of the causeway were elaborately decorated, and originally they had stone roofs. VALLEY TEMPLES were the sites of initial funerary observances. They comprised various chambers designed to accommodate the priests involved in the obsequies.

Less elaborate pyramids and tombs were also built for queens and for favored nobles and certain members of the royal family. Workers constructed these near the main pyramid and brought solar barks or mortuary boats to the complex. Some, fashioned out of wood and gold, were buried by workers in deep pits in Fourth Dynasty pyramids. The pyramid of Khufu at Giza was provided with two boat pits. Walls surrounded this entire pyramidal complex, a traditional construction dating to the great limestone enclosure that surrounded the Step Pyramid in Saqqara. Workers placed private tombs and the burial places of lesser members of the royal clan or of the court just inside these walls.

The narrow corridor of stone leading into the interior of the Great Pyramid of Khufu at Giza *(Courtesy Steve Beikirch)*

The construction of true pyramids was an involved and lengthy process. For example, some estimate that the Great Pyramid of Khufu required the labor of thousands of workers over a 20-year period. Contrary to popular belief, the pyramids were not built by armies of slaves. It was not until later, during the Middle Kingdom (2040–1640 B.C.E.), when the great temple plantations arose and workers were needed to maintain the land holdings, that slaves were introduced into the economic system. Earlier, the commoner Egyptians bore the burden of erecting such monuments.

The first step involved in pyramid construction was the choice of a site by the architects and artists of the royal court, normally chosen because of the type of ground available. The desert fringes, with rocky cores and outcroppings, normally offered the firmest base for the weight of the construction. The site deemed appropriate would be leveled by workmen, who would then dig the foundation according to the design and architectural plan. The foundations of most pyramids contained foundation stelae and other commemorative inscriptions, much like the cornerstones of modern buildings. When the dedication rituals were completed, workmen began to dig for the subterranean level of the monument various chambers, corridors, and passageways.

The unfinished pyramid at ZAWIET EL-ARYAN has magnificent underground chambers and hallways. Workers installed stairways, passages, ramps, portcullises (stone slabs lowered into place to block halls at critical junctures, especially in the Fourth Dynasty pyramids), traps, and stone plugs beside the burial rooms and storage areas. Large ramps for lowering the granite or alabaster sarcophagi were also erected, sometimes with staircases on either side.

Once the site was chosen, construction of the pyramid itself would start. Some pyramids had solid stone cores, much like the mastaba levels of Imhotep's Step Pyramid, but others had walls filled with rubble, mud, and sand. Layers of masonry supported the walls, which workers encased in fine stone and then capped with the pyramidion (the uppermost piece of the pyramid). It is thought that workers built ramps to each level as the construction continued so that they could move the stones into place. As the pyramid grew in height, they would heighten the ramps. There is some debate about whether ramps were used. It is possible that workers built mounds that were attached to the sides or fashioned on the ascending levels. Workers removed such conveniences when the castings (the outer stones of the pyramid) were being added.

When the structure was completed, with the chambers painted and inscribed and the casing put into place, the funeral of the deceased commenced at the site. The sarcophagus was lowered into the burial chamber (some of which were made out of a single piece of stone), where rituals were also conducted. When the sarcophagus of

THE MAJOR PYRAMIDS OF EGYPT

Dynasty	Ruler	Location
Third	Djoser (2630–2611 B.C.E.)	northern Saqqara
	Sekhemkhet (2611–2601 B.C.E.)	northern Saqqara
	Kha'ba (2603–2599 B.C.E.)	Zawiet el-Aryan
Fourth	Snefru (2575–2551 B.C.E.)	Meidum
	Snefru	southern Dashur
	Snefru	northern Dashur
	Khufu (2551–2528 B.C.E.)	Giza
	Ra'djedef (2528–2520 B.C.E.)	Abu Rowash
	Khafre (2520–2494 B.C.E.)	Giza
	Menkauré (2490–2472 B.C.E.)	Giza
	Shepseskhaf (2472–2467 B.C.E.)	southern Saqqara
Fifth	Userkhaf (2465–2458 B.C.E.)	northern Saqqara
	Userkhaf	Abusir
	Sahuré (2458–2446 B.C.E.)	Abusir
	Kakai (2446–2426 B.C.E.)	Abusir
	Neferefré (2419–2416 B.C.E.)	Abusir
	Niuserré (2416–2392 B.C.E.)	Abusir
	Niuserré	Abu Ghurob
	Menkauhor (2396–2388 B.C.E.)	Dashur
	Menkauhor	Abusir (?)
	Izezi (2388–2356 B.C.E.)	southern Saqqara
	Unis (2356–2323 B.C.E.)	northern Saqqara
Sixth	Teti (2323–2291 B.C.E.)	northern Saqqara
	Pepi I (2289–2255 B.C.E.)	southern Saqqara
	Merenré (2255–2246 B.C.E.)	southern Saqqara
	Pepi II (2246–2152 B.C.E.)	southern Saqqara
Eighth	Qakaré Iby (date unknown)	southern Saqqara
Twelfth	Amenemhet I (1991–1962 B.C.E.)	el-Lisht
	Senwosret I (1971–1926 B.C.E.)	el-Lisht
	Amenemhet II (1929–1892 B.C.E.)	Dashur
	Senwosret II (1897–1878 B.C.E.)	el-Lahun
	Senwosret III (1878–1841 B.C.E.)	Dashur
	Amenemhet III (1841–1797 B.C.E.)	Dashur
	Amenemhet III	Hawara
	Sobekneferu (1787–1783 B.C.E.)	Mazghuna
Thirteenth	Khendjer (date unknown)	southern Saqqara

the ruler was in place, the burial chamber was sealed and plugged, and the corridors leading away from it were also blocked by various means. When the funeral cortege (procession) was outside, the entrance to the pyramid was sealed by moving stones into place to complete the wall and make the structure secure.

Khufu's Great Pyramid at Giza is the most outstanding example of a true pyramid. The base of the pyramid covers 13 acres, and a total of 2,300,000 yellow limestone stones were used in its construction. The pyramid was called the "Horizon of Khufu" and was positioned in keeping with the astronomical and religious traditions of the

era. Originally part of a vast complex, the pyramid now stands amid only two other great pyramids and various smaller tombs of queens and members of the royal family.

IMPACT

The Great Pyramid is the last surviving structure of the original Seven Wonders of the Ancient World and is the chief representative of the enormous achievement of Egyptian civilization. Collectively, the significance of this and the other surviving pyramids can be viewed from several perspectives, including the religious, architectural, and scientific.

The second monument at Giza, the burial complex of Khafre (Chephren) *(Courtesy Steve Beikirch)*

Religiously, the pyramids at Giza are distinct spiritual insignias, unique manifestations of the religious and cosmological traditions of the people of the Nile. For the Egyptians, the pyramid represented different levels of commitment and participation. Full-time work gangs—one of which called itself "the Drunkards of Menkauré," after Mycerinus (r. 2490–2472 B.C.E.), the builder of the third pyramid at Giza—labored all of their lives on a lasting monument, expecting to share in the joys of the afterlife with the pharaoh. The commoner Egyptians who responded to the pharaoh's call during the floodtime shared in the same expectation of eternal reward. Visible for miles, the pyramids represented not only a stage of resurrection but a symbol of a socially cohesive nation committed to a level of artistic achievement never seen before on earth.

For students of Egyptian history, the pyramids reveal the development of Egyptian spirituality and religious sentiment. Through the surviving stones, the inscriptions, the burial chambers, and even the positioning of the sites, Egyptologists have been able to study and assess the role of the gods; the teachings of death, judgment, and resurrection of the pharaohs; and the degree to which ancient Egyptians from the commoner to the pharaohs themselves embraced the belief in the afterlife. Other civilizations built immense mortuary sites and pursued forms of immortality in art and stone, but the scale and vision of the Egyptians earned them a truly historic place in the annals of human religious history.

Architecturally, the pyramids were among the foremost achievements in design and construction of ancient times. They represent the first large-scale building projects to be constructed in stone, and even today archaeologists debate exactly how they were completed. Beyond the mystery of their formation, the pyramids allow archaeologists and art historians to trace the development of construction techniques and the architectural priorities of different Egyptian artisans spanning several millennia. The achievement of the pyramids inspires architects today, from I. M. Pei's glass pyramid at the Louvre in Paris to the Luxor Hotel in Las Vegas, which provide ample evidence of the permanent influence of the pyramid form.

Connected closely to the architectural impact of the pyramids was the scientific achievement of their construction. Experiments and research continue in the hope of duplicating the different logistical methods that might have been used in their physical creation. Beyond moving and installing the enormous blocks of stone, the Egyptians needed to master the basics of mathematics and geometry and even rudimentary physics. It is unlikely that the Egyptian architects understood the concept of the mathematical constant *pi,* but they were proficient in precise measurements of cubits (a unit of length) through the use of the royal cubit rod, the half circle, and the plumb level for vertical surfaces. At the same time, Egyptian engineers bequeathed scientific principles of the right angle, triangles, and other forms of measurement.

The scientific knowledge was also applied to the practical demands of choosing sites for pyramids, including detailed surveys of the environment, to determine where the ground could withstand the colossal weight of the pyramidal structure. Then there was the question of hauling millions of tons of stone to the pyramid sites, including the barges that carried stones from the quarries along the Nile from as far away as Aswan. Little wonder that in the ancient world the pyramids were viewed as unequaled masterpieces in engineering and Egyptians were given a reputation for great scientific prowess.

Finally, the pyramids retain of lasting historical significance. For 4,000 years, those living in and visiting Egypt have marveled at the building of the pyramids and the fact that such colossal feats of engineering were undertaken to house the remains of dead kings. That sense of awe has not been lost in the modern era. For the student of ancient Egypt, the pyramids are a gateway to understanding the whole of ancient Egyptian life.

Further reading: Hawass, Zahi A. *The Pyramids of Ancient Egypt.* New York: Carnegie Museum of Natural History, 1998; Isler, Martin, and Dieter Arnold. *Sticks, Stones, and Shadows: Building the Egyptian Pyramids.* Norman: University of Oklahoma, 2001; Lawton, Ian, and Chris Ogilvie-Herald. *Giza: The Truth: The People, Politics, and History Behind the World's Most Famous Archaeological Site.* Montpelier, Vt.: Invisible Cities Press, 2001; Siliotti, Alberto. *Guide to Pyramids of Egypt.* New York: Barnes & Noble Books, 1997; Verner, Miroslav, and Steven Rendall, transl. *The Pyramids: The Mystery, Culture, and Science of Egypt's Great Monuments.* New York: Grove Press, 2001.

Pyramid Texts The oldest surviving examples of religious literature in Egypt, these texts were actually inscriptions on the walls of the royal pyramids of the Fifth and Sixth Dynasties (2465–2323 B.C.E. and 2323–2150 B.C.E.). The priests of HELIOPOLIS wrote the texts that appear in the tomb of UNIS (r. 2356–2323 B.C.E.) and those of other pharaohs and their queens. Unis's Pyramid Texts served as the standard for other inscriptions. Funerary formulas, spells, incantations, and magical phrases that enabled the pharaoh to become the sun and a star were included. The texts provided the traditional forms called the "sun-ladder," which could be used to ascend into the heavens. They were discontinued when the pharaohs abandoned the construction of the pyramids. As the tombs were smaller at the close of the Old Kingdom (2134 B.C.E.), COFFIN TEXTS repeated the formulas in confined spaces.

See also CANNIBAL HYMN; TOMB TEXTS.

pyramid workers Groups of skilled artisans and builders who served as the builders of the pyramids of the Old Kingdom (2575–2134 B.C.E.), these groups are now called "gangs," and they left inscriptions detailing their work. The gangs used colorful names such as "Friends of KHUFU" and the "DRUNKARDS of MENKAURÉ." Some gangs existed for more than six decades. Their support facilities, residence, and necropolis areas are being uncovered in modern excavations.

See also DEIR EL-MEDINA; GIZA; SERVANTS OF THE PLACE OF TRUTH.

Pythagoras (d. ca. 500 B.C.E.) *famous Greek mathematician who visited Egypt*
He was on the Nile in the reign of AMASIS (570–526 B.C.E.). Pythagoras went to MEMPHIS, HELIOPOLIS, and then to THEBES. He remained in the region for more than two decades, earning the respect of the local priests and eventually being allowed to take part in sacrifices to the gods.

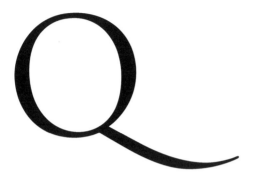

Qa'a (Qa'a hedjet Bieneches) (d. 2760 B.C.E.) *last ruler of the First Dynasty*
He reigned ca. 2770 B.C.E. until his death. His name meant "His Arm Is Raised," and MANETHO, the Ptolemaic Period historian, listed him as Bieneches. Few details of his reign have survived, but he is recorded in the KING LISTS of SAQQARA, ABYDOS, and Turin. Stone vessels bearing his name were found in the pyramidal complex of DJOSER (r. 2630–2611 B.C.E.). Qa'a was possibly the son of SEMERKHET.

He was probably buried at ABYDOS, where two stelae were discovered on the east side of the tomb. The Abydos gravesite was a deep pit with a burial chamber and magazine roofed with timber. Some 26 graves surround his Abydos resting place. A tomb in Saqqara was once assigned to Qa'a, but it now is considered to be the grave of a noble named MENKHAF. Four Saqqara funerary complexes date to Qa'a's reign, and stelae of Qa'a's officials have been discovered there.

Qakaré Iby (fl. ca. 2100 B.C.E.) *ruler of the brief Eighth Dynasty*
All that remains from his undocumented reign is a small pyramid in southern SAQQARA, bearing his name, which translates as "Strong Is the Soul of Ré." The Pyramid Texts, popular in earlier dynasties, adorn Qakaré Iby's pyramid.

Qantir A modern village adjoining Khataneh in the eastern Delta, once possibly the site of PER-RAMESSES, the site served as the capital of the Ramessids (1307–1196, 1196–1070 B.C.E.), near BUBASTIS (Zagazig). The site was abandoned for TANIS in the Twenty-first Dynasty (1070–945 B.C.E.), and stones, monuments, and other pieces were taken to Bubastis in the Twenty-second Dynasty (945–712 B.C.E.).

Qar (fl. ca. 2200 B.C.E.) *official of the Sixth Dynasty*
He served as a judge and VIZIER. Qar's tomb in ABUSIR is a vast complex, containing the burials of several generations of his family. Painted reliefs depict many aspects of that historical period and FALSE DOORS are part of the design. The tomb has an open court with side chambers.

Qarta (fl. 23rd century B.C.E.) *priestly official of the Sixth Dynasty*
He served PEPI I (r. 2289–2255 B.C.E.) as chancellor. Qarta was a priest and a noted librarian and archivist. He was buried in the necropolis reserved for esteemed nobles in SAQQARA, honored by his grave near Pepi I.

Qarun, Lake A body of water in the northwestern edge of the FAIYUM, also called Berket el Kurun, or Qarun Pond, the present lake is only a vestigial reminder of the original body of water that was once subject to inundation by the Nile. By the New Kingdom (1550–1070 B.C.E.), the lake no longer exchanged water with the river. Now it is a marshland, growing saltier, but still supporting a variety of fish and migratory birds.

Qasr el-Saghah A site in the western area of the FAIYUM, located at the base of a limestone cliff, Twelfth (1991–1783 B.C.E.) and Thirteenth (1783–1640 B.C.E.) Dynasty tombs were discovered there. A workman's town was active in QASR WA'-L-SAIYAD, which also had a military garrison. The remains of this town include a terrace and stairway. "PAN-GRAVES" were also uncovered there.

Qasr Qarun This is a site on the western extremity of Lake QARUN, also recorded as Dionysius Qasr Qarun and serving as a staging place for caravans to BAHARIA OASIS in the LIBYAN DESERT. A temple to the god SOBEK, dated to the Ptolemaic Period (304–30 B.C.E.), dominates the region. The temple has corridors, chambers, tunnels, and spiral staircases. Oracular secret niches are part of the design. There was once a roof chapel on the structure as well.

Qasr wa'-l-Saiyad It is a site on the Nile, south of ABYDOS, where First Intermediate Period (2134–2040 B.C.E.) tombs have been found. These are rock-cut chambers for the local NOMARCHS of the territory. Vast and elaborately decorated with reliefs, the tombs belonged to the nomarchs Idu Seneni, Tjauti, and others.

Qaw el-Kebir A site on the Nile south of ASSIUT, called Tjebu or Djenga by the Egyptians and Antaiopolis by the Greeks, Qaw el-Kebir is a Twelfth Dynasty (1991–1783 B.C.E.) necropolis that was refurbished by later dynasties. PTOLEMY IV PHILOPATOR (221–205 B.C.E.) constructed a temple on the site, and PTOLEMY VI PHILOMETOR (180–164, 163–145 B.C.E.) restored the structure.

Qebehsennuf He was a divine being, the son of HORUS, associated with mortuary rituals. The Four Sons of Horus served as guardians of the organs of the deceased, removed from the body during embalming processes and placed in CANOPIC JARS. Qebehsennuf guarded the intestines of the deceased. The canopic jars holding such organs were designed with hawk heads.

See also PILLARS OF SHU.

Qebhet A goddess considered the personification of "cool water," therefore a patroness and symbol of the eternal paradises awaiting the dead beyond the grave, she was a daughter of ANUBIS, although originally a serpent deity. In some eras, Qebhet was associated with regional NILE and SOLAR CULTS. Her popularity was confined to a few nomes or provinces.

Qebhui He was an Egyptian deity, the lord of the north wind. The god was usually depicted as a four-headed ram with four wings or a man with four ram heads.

Qedeshet A Syrian goddess introduced into Egypt during the Eighteenth Dynasty (1550–1307 B.C.E.), Qedeshet became part of the Min-Reshef triad in Upper Egypt. She was depicted as a naked woman holding snakes and flowers and standing on a lion.

Qift *See* KOPTOS.

Quarrel of Apophis and Sekenenré It is a text that dates to the Ramessid Period (1307–1070 B.C.E.) and deals with the opening events of the Theban assaults on the HYKSOS holdings in the Delta. The document, incomplete in its surviving form, demonstrates the Egyptian bias toward the Hyksos and does not clearly explain the reasons for the war that ensued.

Sekenenré, also known as TA'O II (d. 1555 B.C.E.), the ruler of THEBES and Upper Egypt, received a message from APOPHIS (r. ca. 1585–1553 B.C.E.), the Hyksos, or Asiatic, ruler at AVARIS in the Delta. The messenger related Apophis's complaint that the snoring hippopotami in the sacred pool at Thebes were keeping the Hyksos ruler awake at night. Considering the fact that Apophis's royal residence was about 400 miles to the northeast, the Thebans, upon hearing the complaint, were "stupefied." It was obvious to Ta'o II and his courtiers that Apophis was either out of his mind or acting in a belligerent fashion. The text ends abruptly, so the actual discussion and response are not provided.

Ta'o II began a campaign to oust the Hyksos, who ruled Lower Egypt as far south as CUSAE. He was brutally slain, however, and his son, KAMOSE, replaced him as the ruler of Thebes. Kamose actually carried on the military confrontations against the Hyksos and was approaching Avaris when he too died. Apophis was already deceased. 'AHMOSE (NEBPEHTIRÉ) (r. 1550–1525 B.C.E.), Kamose's brother, would be the one to actually oust the Asiatics from Egypt and start the New Kingdom (1550–1070 B.C.E.).

quarries They were the geological conformations of ancient Egypt, especially in its southern regions, and characterized by limestone cliffs. Limestone, favored by the Egyptians for the casings of pyramids, was abundant at various sites throughout the Nile Valley. Granite was found in Aswan in two varieties: the red, called Syenite by the Greeks (after Syene, Greek for Aswan), and the black. Basalt, calcite, diorite, obsidian, porphyry, quartzite, and serpentine were among the minerals quarried. A variety of semiprecious stones were also mined.

The quarry sites of the Nile Valley included

el-Tureh (Tura), a site opposite Giza, where fine limestone was extracted

Gebel el-Ahmar, northeast of modern Cairo, which yielded quartzite

Bersha, near el-Tureh (Tura), known for limestone

Gebel el-Silsileh, north of Aswan, a source of sandstone

Hatnub, near 'Amarna, quarried for alabaster

Ibhet, south of Aswan, contained black granite, with red granite available from other quarries in the territory

Gebelein, south of Luxor, offering beige limestone

Qurna, a source of dolomitic limestone near Thebes

Wadi Hammamat, containing graywacke, near Koptos

Aswan, which offered sandstone (quartzite) and granite and served as the southern boundary

Nubia, an important source of hard stones and minerals, modern Sudan

Western Desert, providing diorite gneiss and possibly carnelian, west of the Nile

Wadi el-Hudi, yielding amethyst, south of Thebes

Quarry Map   *See* BEKHEN QUARRY MAP.

Quban (Contra-Pselkis)   It was a fortress located opposite el-DAKKA and occupying a strategic position just south of the first cataract of the Nile in NUBIA (modern Sudan). Three circular walls with rounded bastions protected the fortress at Quban. SENWOSRET I (r. 1971–1926 B.C.E.) probably originated the first defense elements here. Quban's fortress was refurbished by the rulers of the Ramessid Period (1307–1070 B.C.E.) when they garrisoned Egyptian holdings in northern Nubia. AMENEMHET III (r. 1844–1797 B.C.E.), TUTHMOSIS III (r. 1479–1425 B.C.E.), and RAMESSES II (r. 1290–1224 B.C.E.) made major renovations on the site.

Qubbet el-Hawwa   A site on the bluff at ASWAN, overlooking the Nile, called "the Dome of the Wind," it is a necropolis containing tombs from the Old Kingdom (2575–2134 B.C.E.) and the Middle Kingdom (2040–1640 B.C.E.). Some military and trade expedition leaders were buried at Qubbet el-Hawwa, including HARKHUF, PEPI-NAKHT, and SARENPUT.

queens   The royal consorts of the rulers of ancient Egypt who derived their rank and powers from their husbands, these women were themselves often the daughters of rulers, but they could be aristocrats or even commoners. In some instances women of the harem, or lesser wives, attained the rank of queen by giving birth to an heir. In the CARTOUCHES of royal Egyptian women, the designations "King's Daughter," "King's Wife," or "King's Mother" were carefully applied. Though many princesses of the royal line did not marry their brothers, or half brothers, the firstborn royal daughter often did in order to safeguard the throne.

As queens, royal wives administered the palace and the harems and had some say in state affairs of the nation or the capital. Queen mothers, whether royal or commoner, those who had given birth to an heir, were elevated in the reigns of their sons and given additional honors. They were distinguished by wearing the golden vulture crown at state affairs.

In some periods the rulers married their daughters also. AKHENATEN, for example, married several of his daughters, and RAMESSES II made his daughters consorts after their mothers died or retired. AMENHOTEP

Nefertiti, the queen of Akhenaten, whose name means "the Beautiful Woman Has Come" *(Hulton Archive)*

III was encouraged by Queen TIYE (1) to marry their daughters, Princesses SITAMUN (2) and ISET (3), probably in the hope of increasing the number of heirs to the throne.

Some queens were from foreign lands. KIYA, the wife of Akhenaten, was believed to be a MITANNI princess, and MA'AT HORNEFRURÉ, wife of Ramesses II, was probably the HITTITE princess mentioned in the BENTRESH STELA. TUTHMOSIS III had three Syrian wives, daughters of chieftains, who were buried in separate tombs and provided with duplicate funerary regalia. Amenhotep III married a princess from Babylon.

Egyptian princesses were not given in marriage to cement foreign alliances, no matter how persistent the requests, until the late eras of Egypt, when foreign groups held the throne. To enhance his prestige, one Asiatic ruler wrote that he would accept any Egyptian woman of high birth as his bride, knowing that he could pass her off as a princess to his own people. Those princesses who did not marry heirs to the throne wed officials or remained at court unmarried.

There were queens who usurped the throne or held political power temporarily as regents for their minor sons. Regents include MERNEITH of the First Dynasty (2920–2770 B.C.E.), believed to have been the wife of DJET and the mother of DEN, and ANKHNESMERY-RÉ (2) of the Sixth Dynasty (2323–2150 B.C.E.), who served as co-regent with her brother, the vizier DJAU, for PEPI II. In the New Kingdom (1550–1070 B.C.E.) two female regents assumed the throne themselves: HATSHEPSUT of the Eighteenth Dynasty (1550–1307 B.C.E.) and TWOSRET of the Nineteenth Dynasty (1307–1196 B.C.E.). A woman ruler, NITOCRIS (1), ended the Sixth Dynasty, according to some lists, and another, SOBEKNEFERU, closed the Twelfth Dynasty (1991–1783 B.C.E.).

The queens, whether in command of Egypt or serving as a consort to the pharaohs, remain fascinating facets of Egyptian history for the modern world. Some of them left an imprint on their own times, and others stand as exotic examples of feminine charms on the Nile.

In the Early Dynastic Period (2920–2575 B.C.E.), Merneith, probably only a regent, had two mortuary complexes built at ABYDOS and SAQQARA, using the royal insignias. NEITHOTEP, the possible mother of AHA, the first ruler of Egypt, was honored with similar mortuary monuments, one containing the seals of the fabled NARMER.

In the Old Kingdom (2575–2134 B.C.E.), the two queens named HETEPHERES left relics of their existence: one in tomb furnishings that had to be moved because of grave robberies, the second as a witness to royal dynastic feuds. The KHAMERERNEBTY queens have left their own mark. The second Queen Khamerernebty is commemorated by a beautiful statue that depicts her beside the ruler KHAFRE in a remarkable display of equality and femininity. KHENTAKAWES (1), the wife of SHEPSESKHAF, is called the "Mother of the Fifth Dynasty." Two sisters named Ankhnesmery-Ré, given to Pepi I in marriage, bore him heirs, and one served as regent for her son, Pepi II.

In the Middle Kingdom (2040–1640 B.C.E.), a bevy of women accompanied MENTUHOTEP II in his tomb at DEIR EL-BAHRI, and on the sarcophagi of many of them the world is told that the inhabitant was "the Sole Favorite of the King." The mother of AMENEMHET I (Nofret), a usurper, was honored by her son when he had cemented his claims to the throne. Sobekneferu, the last ruler of the Twelfth Dynasty, was a woman who maintained her reign for only four years.

As the New Kingdom (1550–1070 B.C.E.) is better documented, this period of Egyptian history provides a roster of famous women. TETISHERI, the commoner wife of TA'O I (Senakhtenré; Djehuti'o) (d. ca. 1540 B.C.E.) of the Seventeenth Dynasty, was the grandmother of 'AHMOSE (NEBPEHTIRÉ), the founder of the New Kingdom, and she lived to an old age with him and Queen AH'HOTEP (1). 'Ahmose was married to 'AHMOSE NEFERTARI, who gained prominence by appearing with the pharaoh at public functions and by having her name mentioned in public records. She was deified after her death with her son, AMENHOTEP I.

Hatshepsut, the daughter of TUTHMOSIS I, claimed the throne after serving as the regent for Tuthmosis III and ruled Egypt, building a temple at DEIR EL-BAHRI and sending expeditions to PUNT and other sites in continued trade. TIYE, the commoner wife of Amenhotep III, appeared in public records and in foreign correspondence. NEFERTITI, the commoner wife of Akhenaten, stands unrivaled as an example of grace and loveliness from that age. Kiya, probably the foreign-born second wife of Akhenaten, is depicted with her own exotic charms.

In the Ramessid Period women such as NEFERTARI MERYMUT, whose loveliness graces shrines on the Nile, including the temple built in her honor at ABU SIMBEL, speak of a cultured era. Twosret, who served as a regent for a time, took the throne with her foreign vizier, BAY, at her side.

During the Third Intermediate Period (1070–712 B.C.E.) and the Late Period (712–332 B.C.E.), the queens of Egypt did not have the powers of their sisters in the past. Another sort of woman, serving as the GOD'S WIFE OF AMUN at THEBES (modern Luxor), had considerable political and religious powers instead, serving as the spokespersons for their royal families in the capital.

The arrival of the Ptolemaic Period (304–30 B.C.E.), however, brought women of vigor and intellect to the courts. They were Greeks, not Egyptians, as no native women were the mothers of the Ptolemaic rulers. Their exploits and adventures were varied, and many of these queens suffered at the hands of their relatives. CLEOPATRA VII (r. 51–30 B.C.E.) was the last sole ruler of Egypt, and she was notorious throughout the ancient world of her time as a brilliant, enchanting, and politically astute individual who held her own in the company of the leading men of the times.

queen's titles The queens of Egypt of primary rank were called the *hemet* (the Great Wife). If they were able to bear the pharaoh's heirs, they received the additional title of "Mother of the King" and wore the VULTURE headdress of NEKHEBET, the goddess protector of Upper Egypt. Other titles bestowed upon them were "Mistress of the Two Lands," "Mistress of Upper and Lower Egypt," "For Whom the Sun Rises," and "Great of Favors."

The title of "the GOD'S WIFE OF AMUN" began in the reign of 'AHMOSE (NEBPEHTIRÉ) (1550–1525 B.C.E.), founder of the New Kingdom, when Queen 'AHMOSE NEFERTARI received that rank in exchange for privileges offered to her. The role, also called the Divine Adoratrices of Amun in some eras, evolved over the centuries into a religious office of considerable power.

Quernet Murai   A necropolis site on the eastern hill of DEIR EL-MEDINA on the western shore of the Nile. Tombs from the Eighteenth Dynasty (1550–1307 B.C.E.) and the Ramessid Period (1307–1070 B.C.E.) were excavated there. The tombs discovered were constructed for the Servants of the Place of Truth, the workers in the royal tombs of the VALLEY OF THE KINGS. Such workers, particularly those of rank within the Deir el-Medina complex, were lavishly decorated. Details about the actual labors of the workers as well as some biographical details have been found in these tombs.

Qurna   *See* SHEIKH ABD' EL-QURNA.

Qus (Gesa; Apollinopolis Parva)   A site north of THEBES, on the western bank of the Nile, involved in the vast trade expeditions of Egypt. The Egyptians called the site Gesa, and the Greeks named it Apollinopolis Parva. Qus served as departure point for expeditions to the WADI HAMMAMAT and the Red Sea. Two PYLONS from the Ptolemaic Period (304–30 B.C.E.) dedicated to Haroeris and HEKET remain there.

R

Ra'djedef (Djedef-ré) (d. 2520 B.C.E.) *third ruler of the Fourth Dynasty*

The builder of the "Lost Pyramid" at ABU ROWASH, this pharaoh was a son of KHUFU (Cheops) and a lesser queen. He succeeded Khufu in 2528 B.C.E., becoming the heir upon the death of Prince Kewab, who died while on a trade expedition beyond Egypt's borders. In the past, Ra'djedef was believed to have killed Kewab, usurping the throne. It was also believed that Ra'djedef was assassinated before he could complete his mortuary pyramid, as the structure was discovered in a ruined condition. He was recorded as marrying HETEPHERES (2), his half sister and the widow of Prince Kewab. She was the mother as well of Kewab's daughter, MERYSANKH (3), who married Ra'djedef's successor, KHAFRE (Chephren). Hetepheres (2) bore Ra'djedef a daughter, NEFERHETEPES (1). He also married Khentetka and had three sons, Setka, Baka, and Harnit. They are all listed in Ra'djedef's unfinished pyramid in ABU ROWASH, but none inherited the throne.

Ra'djedef chose the royal name "Son of Ré," indicating a religious revolt of some sort, and was mentioned in the TURIN CANON. He also abandoned the GIZA plateau, building his mortuary complex in Abu Rowash, near the Third Dynasty (2649–2575 B.C.E.) necropolis to the north. This unfinished complex was designed with Ra'djedef's MORTUARY TEMPLE, called "Ra'djedef Is a *Seh-edu* Star." The mortuary temple was started on the east side of the pyramid. A large boat pit was built on the southern end.

Some 20 statues were discovered on the site, now in a ruined condition. Red quartzite and other fine stones were used throughout the complex. A SPHINX was also found on the site, the first use of that symbol in royal tombs. Ra'djedef's pyramid was ransacked as a quarry by later pharaohs, and he remains a mysterious individual.

Some scholars now credit Ra'djedef with the transformation of the Sphinx into a memorial for Khufu. The face on the Sphinx has long been thought to have been that of KHAFRE (r. 2520–2494 B.C.E.) but is now believed to be that of Khufu. An ongoing debate about this monument continues, including about the information available in the INVENTORY STELA, which dates to the reign of Khufu (or is a copy of an earlier document) and details the presence of the Sphinx long before the pyramids were built on the Giza plateau.

Rahotep (1) (fl. 26th century B.C.E.) *prince of the Fourth Dynasty, famed for his mortuary statue*

A son of SNEFRU (r. 2575–2551 B.C.E.), Rahotep was married to Princess NOFRET (1) and buried with her in a mastaba tomb near the pyramid of MEIDUM. Rahotep served as the high priest of the god RÉ at HELIOPOLIS. He also served as the director of expeditions and as the chief of royal building. There is a possibility that Rahotep was the son of HUNI (r. 2599–2575 B.C.E.), buried in Snefru's reign. A remarkable portrait statue of Rahotep was discovered at Meidum. Nofret was also depicted by another remarkable statue in the tomb. These limestone portrayals were fashioned with inlaid eyes and depict individuals of vitality and charm.

See also ART AND ARCHITECTURE.

Rahotep (2) (Wah'ankh) (d. ca. 1630 B.C.E.) *ruler, or possibly the founder, of the Seventeenth Dynasty*

He was also called Rahotep Wah'ankh and is mentioned in reliefs in the tomb of AMENMESSES of the Nineteenth

Dynasty in the VALLEY OF THE KINGS. Rahotep restored the temples of MIN and OSIRIS at KOPTOS and ABYDOS. His pyramid was erected at DRA-ABU' EL-NAGA, the oldest section of the necropolis of Thebes.

Rai (fl. 16th century B.C.E.) *court woman of the Eighteenth Dynasty*
She served in the reign of 'AHMOSE (NEBPEHTIRÉ) (1550–1525 B.C.E.), as a wet nurse of Queen 'AHMOSE-NEFERTARI. Rai was buried in Thebes in a newly made coffin of sycamore wood. Her original coffin was used to bury Princess 'AHMOSE-IN-HAPI. Rai's remains were discovered at DEIR EL-BAHRI in 1881. Her mummy clearly shows that she was a graceful and delicate woman with abundant masses of hair, woven into braids.

See also MORTUARY RITUALS.

Raia (fl. 14th century B.C.E.) *royal woman of the Nineteenth Dynasty, the mother-in-law of Seti I*
Raia's daughter, Queen TUYA, probably married Seti I (r. 1306–1290 B.C.E.) before he became pharaoh. Raia's husband, Ruia, was a lieutenant of charioteers in the army of Ramesses I before he was asked by HOREMHAB to found a new royal line. She was buried in Thebes.

Ramesses (fl. 13th century B.C.E.) *prince of the Nineteenth Dynasty*
He was the son of RAMESSES II (r. 1290–1224 B.C.E.) and Queen ISETNOFRET (1) and campaigned with his father in NUBIA, serving as a charioteer. A general and the appointed heir to the throne from Ramesses II's regnal years of 40–50, Prince Ramesses died before inheriting. He followed AMENHIRKHOPSHEF (2) in the line of succession. Prince Ramesses was depicted at ABU SIMBEL. He denoted funerary items for the APIS bulls and conducted inquiries into a legal matter concerning the mortuary temple of TUTHMOSIS I.

Ramesses I (Menpehtiré) (d. 1306 B.C.E.) *founder of the Nineteenth Dynasty*
He reigned only from 1307 B.C.E. until his death the following year. Chosen as the successor to the throne by HOREMHAB, Ramesses I served for a time as co-regent while Horemhab lived and then began his own royal line. The son of an Egyptian military commander, a commoner named Seti, Ramesses I was born in AVARIS, the former capital of the HYKSOS in the eastern Delta. Joining the army, Ramesses I fought at the side of Horemhab and became a commander of troops, superintendent of cavalry troops, a royal envoy, superintendent of "the Mouths of the Nile," the branches of the river in the Delta, and a full general.

In time, Ramesses I served as Horemhab's VIZIER and high priest of AMUN, a rank that placed him in command of all the cults and temples of the nation. When Horemhab died childless, Ramesses I was installed as the deputy of the throne, becoming the heir. His wife SITRÉ was the mother of SETI I. As Ramesses I was quite elderly when he succeeded Horemhab, Seti I was already a military commander.

The name Ramesses was translated as "Ré Fashioned Him," and his throne name, Menpehtiré, was translated as "Enduring Is the Might of Ré." In his first months of power, Ramesses I restored the great temple of KARNAK in THEBES, completing the second PYLON and a vestibule. He also added a colonnaded hall. Ramesses I named Seti I as his co-regent and died only 16 months after his coronation.

At WADI HALFA, a stela bears his name and commemorates his temple offerings. Ramesses I conducted a Nubian campaign, probably led by Seti I in his name. His tomb was prepared in the VALLEY OF THE KINGS but was not completed. It has a double row of stairs, a burial chamber, and three annexes. Portraits of the goddess MA'AT decorate the entrance. The burial chamber contains a yellow granite sarcophagus with figures of the goddess Isis on the ends. Paintings were used instead of cut reliefs as tomb adornments.

The mummified remains of Ramesses I were missing for centuries. The remains were probably stolen from the tomb and in 1860 bought by an agent of the Niagara Museum and Daredevil Hall of Fame in Ontario, Canada. Put on display in a glass case, Ramesses I remained in the museum for 130 years. A Canadian businessman then bought the contents of the museum, and Ramesses I went on display at the Michael C. Carlos Museum at Emory University. On October 24, 2003, the mummy was returned to Egypt and laid in state in the Museum of Egyptian Antiquities until 2004, when it was moved to the Luxor Museum. (LUXOR is a modern city on the site of THEBES, the ancient capital.) There forensic studies identified the remains as Ramesses I.

Ramesses II (Ramesses the Great; Userma'atre'setepenré) (d. 1224 B.C.E.) *third ruler of the Nineteenth Dynasty, called "the Great"*
Ramesses II reigned from 1290 B.C.E. until his death. He was one of the longest-reigning pharaohs of Egypt.

BIOGRAPHY

The son of SETI I and Queen TUYA, Ramesses II was introduced early to the military careers of his family. His grandfather, RAMESSES I, and his great-grandfather, Seti, had been commanders in the field. Ramesses II accompanied his father in a Libyan campaign when he was a teenager. He also went to war in the Mediterranean and Palestine regions.

He became the co-regent in the seventh year of the reign of Seti I, who reportedly said, "Crown Him as king that I may see his beauty while I live with him." His throne name meant "Strong in Right Is RÉ." He also con-

Ramesses II depicted in a colossal statue in the Luxor temple
(*Courtesy Steve Beikirch*)

ducted a Nubian campaign at age 22, during which he was accompanied by two of his own sons.

In Egypt, he aided Seti I in vast restoration programs up and down the Nile. Together they built a new palace at PER-RAMESSES, the new capital of Egypt founded by Ramesses I in the eastern Delta. Wells, QUARRIES, and mines were also reopened. The new city was erected near or on the site of the former HYKSOS capital of Avaris. Ramesses I was from this region in the Delta and believed it was a better geographic location for the main royal city. THEBES (modern Luxor) and MEMPHIS, the oldest capital, remained administrative centers controlled by trusted officials. When Seti I died, Ramesses II resided at his funeral, a required obligation for an heir.

Inheriting the throne, Ramesses II completed his father's buildings and began to restore the empire. He made promotions among his aides, refurbished temples and shrines, and campaigned on the borders of the land.

The building of Per-Ramesses remained a priority, as was the completion of Seti's temples at Abydos. At Per-Ramesses, Ramesses II enlarged the royal residence, adding doorways, balconies, throne rooms, and chambers. These new areas were decorated with faience tiles and statues. He also built ABU SIMBEL, south of ASWAN, and temples in DERR in NUBIA (modern Sudan), and in ABYDOS. KARNAK and the RAMESSEUM were also among his architectural projects. In his 21st regnal year, he repelled the SEA PEOPLES and the Assyrians.

He then began a war with the Hittites that would last for decades. In his fourth regnal year, Ramesses II campaigned and won possession of the city of Kadesh, a vassal state that his father had lost to the Hittites. This warrior nation was a threat to Egypt, and the young pharaoh was eager to start a conflict that would demonstrate Egypt's might. In the following year, the battle of KADESH, a military campaign commemorated in the Poem of PENTAUR (or Pentauret) on the walls of KARNAK and in the SALLIER PAPYRUS III, took place. Ramesses II almost perished in that confrontation when he was ambushed by the enemy. Both sides declared victory after the battle, but it was a military stalemate. The Hittite king Muwatallis II died soon after, and the Hittites became involved in a struggle over the succession in Hattusas, their capital.

This particular campaign led to a temporary truce but then continued in a series of three phases. After pushing the Egyptian domain to Beirut (modern Lebanon), Ramesses II again met the enemy in battle at Kadesh; both sides claimed victory. Later he battled to recover Palestine, which had been encouraged to revolt. Lastly, Ramesses II conquered Hittite lands far from Egypt and deep inside the enemy's empire, leading the Hittites to ask for a treaty. As events had transpired, the rise of the Assyrian Empire was enough to concern both the Egyptians and the Hittites. The Assyrians were termed "the Mad Dogs" by their contemporaries and were the most feared of the newly rising empires of the Near East because of their ruthless tactics, their willing destruction of enemy territory, and the infamous treatment of prisoners and conquered people. In time, the Assyrians would invade the Nile Valley. In this historical period, however, they were still only a perceived strategic threat.

An alliance was formed between the Egyptians and Hittites, and copies of the treaty have been recovered. One version, written in cuneiform on a silver tablet, was discovered in the ruins of Hattusas, in modern Turkey. A second version, in hieroglyphs, survived at Karnak. The royal families of the allies formed a close relationship, with the Hittite queen Pudukhipa sending gifts and letters to Queen Nefertari-Merymut, Ramesses II's *hemet*, or Great Wife.

Ramesses II's wives and consorts were many, numbering 200 in some periods of his reign. His favorite was Nefertari-Merymut, who probably married him before he became a royal prince. She bore him children and was honored in a temple at ABU SIMBEL. When she retired to the harem villa at MIWER in the FAIYUM, ISETNOFRET (1) became the leading queen. When Isetnofret retired or died, MERYT-AMUN (3), Nefertari's daughter, became *hemet*. In Ramesses' 34th regnal year, she was joined by a Hittite princess, who arrived in Egypt as a symbol of the Egyptian-Hittite alliance. It is probable that she was given the name MA'AT HORNEFERURÉ. She became a Great Wife and assumed many duties of the court. BINTANET, the daughter of Isetnofret, also assumed that role in time, as did NEBET-TAWY (1). These women governed the lesser queens and the concubines within the *pero*, or palace.

Ramesses had more than 100 sons and numerous daughters. His sons were named in order of birth as heirs to the throne. Twelve of these princes did not outlive their father, resulting in the succession of prince Merenptah, Ramesses' 13th son, to crown prince. Some of the sons who have been identified over the centuries are Montuhirkhopshef (or Montuhirwenemuf), Neben-Kharru, Mery-Amun, Amun-wia, Seti, Setep-en-Ré, Mery-ré, Hor-her-wenemuf, Amenhotep, Itamun, Mery-Atum-Ramesses, and KHA'EMWESET (1). The most famous of Ramesses II's successors, Kha'emweset is considered the world's first Egyptologist. He served as the High Priest of Ptah but was revered as a sage and as a great magician whose reputation endured until the Ptolemaic Period (304–30 B.C.E.).

A unique mega-tomb, the largest burial site in the VALLEY OF THE KINGS at Thebes, was erected as the grave of Ramesses II's royal sons. Uncovered in 2006, this tomb, KV5, has pillared halls and T-shaped corridors. Some 67 chambers with wall paintings have also been discovered thus far, and another level of the structure promises additional chambers.

Ramesses II was possibly deified at the celebration of his first *heb-sed*, or at the commemoration of his coronation. Ramesses II married a daughter of the Hittite ruler HATTUSILIS III, probably MA'AT HORNEFRURÉ, in 1257 B.C.E. Statues and other monuments honored him throughout Egypt. When he died, MERENPTAH, his 13th son and heir, placed him in a tomb in the Valley of the Kings at Thebes. This large tomb is long and was highly decorated, with the end chambers at an angle to the entrance corridors. His mummified remains, however, had to be removed to keep them safe from robbers. His original tomb was possibly flooded before he died, as two such monuments bear his name in the Valley of the Kings.

Wrapped in floral garlands, Ramesses II's remains were discovered in the mummy cache in DEIR EL-BAHRI in 1881. He had red hair, possibly the result of the mummification process, and his body was contained in a cedarwood coffin. The mummy shows that he suffered from smallpox at one time. He had a patrician nose and was six feet in height. His face had jutting eyebrows, thick lashes, a strong jaw, and round ears. His genital organs had been removed and placed in a statue of the god OSIRIS, probably as an act of reverence for the deity SET, the patron of his family's original home. His muscles were atrophied from age, and he suffered from arteriosclerosis. The remains were eventually put on display at the Cairo Museum.

HISTORICAL IMPACT

Ramesses II, called "the Great," provided Egypt with decades of prosperity and splendors. The so-called Hittite Alliance, signed in 1280 B.C.E. by Ramesses II and Hattusilis III, is recognized as the oldest known international agreement. This Hittite-Egyptian treaty was a remarkable pact, one of the first in recorded history to contain pertinent clauses. (An extradition clause was included in the treaty, the first such clause in history.)

His successors were not able to remain on the throne long enough to continue the labors that he began, and few of them possessed his energy or vision. However, within a century, another Ramesses, RAMESSES III, would take the throne and serve Egypt as a "shield of the nation," as Ramesses II had acted throughout his life.

Further reading: Healy, Mark. *The Warrior Pharaoh: Ramesses II and the Battle of Quadesh.* London: Osprey Publishing, 2000; Kitchen, K. A. *Ramesside Inscriptions: Ramesses II, His Contemporaries.* London: Blackwell, 2000; Menu, Bernadette. *Ramesses II: Great of the Pharaoh.* New York: Harry N. Abrams, 1999; Montet, Pierre. *Everyday Life in the Days of Ramesses the Great.* Philadelphia: University of Pennsylvania, 1998; Tyldesley, Joyce A. *Ramesses: Egypt's Greatest Pharaoh.* New York: Penguin, 2001.

Ramesses II Cycle   This was a text found on a STELA in the temple of KHONS (1) at THEBES. The text is an account of "Princess Bekhen," a fanciful tale prompted by the marriage of RAMESSES II (r. 1290–1224 B.C.E.) to the daughter of the HITTITE ruler HATTUSILIS III in 1257 B.C.E. The tale involves demons and the god KHONS and was popular for several centuries in Egypt.

See also BENTRESH STELA.

Ramesses II's Colossal Statue   This is a figure found in the ruins of ancient MEMPHIS, now in an enclosed shelter there. Originally more than 12.8 meters high, the statue was carved out of limestone. Beautifully fashioned, the statue depicts Ramesses II in his royal regalia. The figure is damaged and is displayed in a prone position rather than standing erect.

Ramesses III (Userma'atre'meryamun) (d. 1163 B.C.E.) *second ruler of the Twentieth Dynasty*
He reigned from 1194 B.C.E. until his untimely death. RAMESSES III was the last great pharaoh of Egypt's New

Kingdom and the last true warrior-king. His throne name meant "Powerful to the Jubilee of Ré, beloved of Amun."

BIOGRAPHY

The son of SETHNAKHTE, the founder of the royal line, and Queen TIYE-MERENISET, Ramesses III served as coruler before inheriting the throne. He was militarily active from the start of his reign, and was of a mature age when he was crowned and faced unrest in the land. In his fifth regnal year, Ramesses III faced a confederacy of Libyans, led by the MESHWESH, the most powerful tribe of that area. Ramesses III used mercenary troops to defeat the enemy, and the campaign lasted seven years as the Libyans plundered Delta territories. Ramesses III is recorded as slaying 12,535 of the enemy forces, with collected heads, hands, or phalli used as markers for the count.

In his eighth regnal year, Ramesses III conducted a northern war against the Sea Peoples. These Asia Minor nomads had destroyed the HITTITE holdings and other city-states. Enemy warriors, with their families in tow, faced the Egyptians in southern Palestine and in the Delta. Ramesses III organized defensive operations and repelled the attacks of the Sea Peoples both on land and sea. Specifically, he moved defensive units to the eastern border and fortified the Nile branches in the Delta. His operation also included a clever tactic of trapping attacking Sea Peoples in the Nile. By allowing the Sea Peoples to enter only certain Nile channels and then moving floating islands and debris behind them, Ramesses III trapped entire contingents, which allowed his naval units to annihilate those of the Sea Peoples. On land, the Sea Peoples' forces were met by the Egyptian cavalry. Those captured by Ramesses were compelled either to join his army or live as slaves (see SEA PEOPLES, DEFEAT OF THE). Some of the Sea Peoples, such as the Sherden Pirates, were welcomed into the Egyptian navy because of their skills. Ramesses III's defenses and his naval assaults saved the Nile Valley from these foreign invaders.

The Second Libyan War followed in Ramesses III's 11th regnal year. The Meshwesh invaded the Nile Valley, reaching the outskirts of HELIOPOLIS. The Libyans entered a canal there, called the WATERS OF RÉ, and found the Egyptians waiting. The Libyan king KEPER and his son, Meshesher, died in the battle, and 2,175 Libyans perished as well. Ramesses III chased the enemy 11 miles into the desert and captured 2,052 Libyans, including women and children.

Soon after, Ramesses III invaded Syrian cities that had been devastated by the Sea Peoples. He led his troops against five such settlements and then captured two Hittite fortresses. He also conducted a Nubian campaign, listing 124 sites in the records on MEDINET HABU of his battles. While he was campaigning, Ramesses III was supervising the building of Medinet Habu at Thebes. The structure was started in his sixth regnal year and completed in the 12th. This lavish complex contained architectural and artistic innovations, as well as Asiatic and Nubian metals and displays. The dedication of Medinet Habu signaled the end of Ramesses III's wars, as Egypt had entered a period of peace.

He thus turned his attention to the nation, reopening the granite QUARRIES at ASWAN and the mines of the SINAI. He also sent an expedition to PUNT. Temples across Egypt were repaired and refurbished. PER-RAMESSES, which had been closed in the political chaos, also reopened, and Ramesses built a new royal residence. He began construction in ABYDOS, ASSIUT, ATHRIBIS, ELKAB, HELIOPOLIS, HERMOPOLIS, MEMPHIS, Per-Ramesses, THINIS, and Thebes.

His Great Wife, or *hemet,* was ISET (2) (Iset Takemdjert), recorded as being the daughter of a foreign ruler. Other consorts were TITI and TIY. His sons included KHA'EMWESET II, AMENHIRKHOPSHEF, Preherwenemef, Sethirkhopshef, Meryamun, Meryatum, MONTUHIRKHOPSHEF, and RAMESSES IV, VI, and VIII. The ranking daughter of Ramesses III was Titi.

In the 32nd year of Ramesses III's reign, Queen TIYE (2), who wanted to place her son PENTAWERET on the throne, plotted the death of Ramesses, who was attacked while at Medinet Habu, his great fortress and residence. All of the conspirators and accomplices were apprehended and condemned for the attack and for the reported use of magic, something forbidden when involved with the royal family. The attack may have been successful, as Ramesses III died shortly after the capture of the conspirators, though it is not certain if his death was brought on by the assassination attempt or by unrelated causes. He was buried in the VALLEY OF THE KINGS in a tomb now called the Tomb of the Harpers. This grave site has 10 chambers and three passages.

Buried in a carapace, Ramesses III was moved to DEIR EL-BAHRI in later eras and was discovered in the mummy cache in 1881. The tomb, KV11, is one of the largest in the Valley of the Kings. His mummy was packed in resins and placed in a sarcophagus of pink granite. A well room and magazines are part of the design. A pillared hall is decorated with the text of the *BOOK OF THE GATES,* a mortuary document. Other mortuary texts were used in the burial chamber, as well, including the *Book of the Earth.* Ramesses III was buried with a collection of bronze SHABTIS.

HISTORICAL IMPACT

The second pharaoh of the Twentieth Dynasty, Ramesses III is remembered as the last of the great warrior-pharaohs of the New Kingdom. His reign coincided with severe upheavals elsewhere in the Mediterranean that affected Egypt, including the invasion of the Sea Peoples and the Libyans. While these events were confronted energetically by Ramesses, the resources and troops needed to confront these crises also hastened the decline and ultimate end of the New Kingdom.

Beyond his military achievements, Ramesses III began to refurbish Egyptian temples and cities. Though the vast scale of his construction efforts could be seen at Karnak, Per-Ramesses, and other sites, his masterpiece was Medinet Habu, a Migdol-style fortress of Syrian influence in design. This towering structure served as a place of repose for Ramesses III, and an upper story was designed to accommodate members of the court. The Great Harris Papyrus (or Papyrus Harris I), a valuable statement of his reign's achievements, was commissioned by his son and successor, RAMESSES IV.

As the last great pharaohs of his dynasty, Ramesses III represented a terminal phase in the dynastic history of the New Kingdom. Had he lived, he might have been able to complete the restabilization of Egypt.

Further reading: Cline, Eric, and David O'Connor. *Ramesses III: The Life and Times of Egypt's Last Hero.* Ann Arbor: University of Michigan Press, 2010; Redford, Susan. *The Harem Conspiracy: The Murder of Ramesses III.* DeKalb, Il.: Northern Illinois University Press, 2008.

Ramesses IV (Heqama'atre'setepenamun) (d. 1156 B.C.E.) *third ruler of the Twentieth Dynasty*

He reigned from 1163 B.C.E. until his death. The son of RAMESSES III and probably Queen ISET (2), he buried his father and placed the HARRIS PAPYRUS I in the tomb during the MORTUARY RITUALS. The HAREM conspirators, who had plotted the death of his father, met their final ends during his reign.

Young when crowned, Ramesses IV proclaimed a general amnesty and was active in refurbishing sites in the Nile Valley. He built in THEBES, ABYDOS, HELIOPOLIS, KARNAK, EDFU, EL-TOD, ESNA, BUHEN, GARF HUSSEIN, MEDAMUD, ERMENT, and KOPTOS. He also sent expeditions to the WADI HAMMAMAT and to the SINAI and reopened QUARRIES to aid in constructing temples at DEIR EL-BAHRI, at THEBES. His viceroy, Hori, governed NUBIA (modern Sudan) in this historical period.

Marrying Queen Isetnofret, Ramesses IV prayed to the gods for a long reign to better serve Egypt but that ambition was not to be fulfilled. A second consort was Queen TENTOPET, or Duatentapet, and his sons were RAMESSES V and AMENHIRKHOPSHEF. Dying young, possibly of smallpox, Ramesses IV was buried in the VALLEY OF THE KINGS. His tomb was designed with steps leading to three corridors and to a chamber that was decorated with inscriptions from the BOOK OF THE DEAD. The burial chamber is square with an astronomical ceiling and a granite sarcophagus. Painted reliefs serve as decorations.

Ramesses IV's mummified corpse was moved to the tomb of AMENHOTEP II in THEBES and was recovered there. In his embalmed state of preservation, Ramesses

IV is clean-shaven and bald, and his mummy was stuffed with lichen in his chest and abdomen. His eyes had been filled with two onions to retain their shape during the mortuary rituals.

Ramesses V (Userma'atre'sekhepenré) (d. 1151 B.C.E.) *fourth ruler of the Twentieth Dynasty*

He reigned from 1156 B.C.E. until his death. He was the son of RAMESSES IV and Queen TENTOPET. Ramesses V reopened the mines at GEBEL EL-SILSILEH and the SINAI and built at HELIOPOLIS and at the Nubian (modern Sudanese) fortress of BUHEN. The WILBOUR PAPYRUS dates to his reign, and he is recorded also as marrying Queen NUBKHESHED (1).

Ramesses V's reign was troubled by a lethal epidemic of smallpox and by conditions approaching a civil war. As many as six members of the royal family died of smallpox, and Ramesses V's mummy carries scars from the disease. He may have died from smallpox or have been a victim of the political unrest of the period. The fragmentary hieratic papyrus of Turin indicates that he was buried in year two of his successor, RAMESSES VI. Whether he was held prisoner and died in captivity or died and was kept in an embalmed state as a corpse for years, Ramesses V was put to rest in the VALLEY OF THE KINGS and then finally reburied in the tomb of AMENHOTEP II. His chest and abdomen were filled with sawdust, an unusual mummification material. His head also displays a major wound, inflicted before or shortly after his death, adding to the mystery.

The tomb of Ramesses V was designed with an entrance passage, a well room, and a pillared hall, decorated with paintings. His burial chamber has a ceiling depicting the goddess NUT and reliefs from the *Book of Days* and the *Book of the Heavens*. The mask from his anthropoid COFFIN was recovered.

Ramesses VI (Nebma'atre'meryamun) (d. 1143 B.C.E.) *fifth ruler of the Twentieth Dynasty*

He reigned from 1151 B.C.E. until his death, possibly a usurper of the throne of his nephew, RAMESSES V. Ramesses VI was reportedly the son of RAMESSES III and Queen ISET. He also married a Queen NUBKHESED (2), perhaps the widow of Ramesses V. His son was RAMESSES VII, and his daughter, ISET, became a GOD'S WIFE OF AMUN at Thebes. His other sons were Panebenkemyt and Amenhirkhopshef.

Ramesses VI sent an expedition to the SINAI, and he was the last of his royal line to work the turquoise mines there. He left statues and a KARNAK relief. When he died, he was buried in the tomb of Ramesses V, blocking the original tomb on the site, that of TUT'ANKHAMUN, thus saving it from plunderers. This tomb extends into the cliff and is one of the most beautifully decorated sites in the VALLEY OF THE KINGS. An astronomical ceiling design, with royal VULTURE symbols, is displayed, and long corridors and vaults depicting the goddess NUT are evident. Robbers invaded his tomb during the next dynastic period, and the mummy of Ramesses VI was hacked to pieces, damaging his head and trunk. The priests of later dynasties had to pin his remains to a board in order to transfer them to the tomb of AMENHO-TEP II for security. His remains contained the head of an unknown woman.

Ramesses VII (Userma'atre'meryamun) (d. 1136 B.C.E.) *sixth ruler of the Twentieth Dynasty*

He reigned from 1143 B.C.E. until his death. Ramesses VII was the son of RAMESSES VI and probably Queen NUBKHESED (2), also called Itames. He married Isetnofret and had a son who died as an infant. He built additions or refurbished temples at MEMPHIS, KARNAK, and ELKAB. His only true monument, however, is his tomb in the VALLEY OF THE KINGS on the western shore of the Nile at Thebes. He was proclaimed on a stela, however, and a SCARAB that was discovered bears his CARTOUCHE.

His tomb in the Valley of the Kings is small but beautifully decorated, with corridors and a burial chamber. Ramesses VII's granite SARCOPHAGUS was fashioned in the shape of a cartouche but was smashed by robbers. His body was never found, but his tomb had an entrance passageway and a painted burial chamber. A rock hollow was part of the design, covered by a stone block and decorated.

Ramesses VIII (Userma'atre'ankhenamun) (d. 1131 B.C.E.) *seventh ruler of the Twentieth Dynasty*

He reigned from 1136 B.C.E. until his death. He was a son of RAMESSES III and probably Queen ISET. The last surviving son of Ramesses III, he was pictured in MEDINET HABU as Prince Sethirkhopshef. When he died, Ramesses VIII was buried secretly in Thebes, where his empty SAR-COPHAGUS was found. Little is known of his reign.

Ramesses IX (Neferkare'setenré) (d. 1112 B.C.E.) *eighth ruler of the Twentieth Dynasty*

He reigned from 1131 B.C.E. until his death. Ramesses IX was a grandson of RAMESSES III, the son of Prince Montuhirkhopshef and Princess Takhat. Coming to the throne after his uncle, he provided Egypt with a brief but stable period. His wife was probably Queen BAKETWEREL, and RAMESSES X was probably his son. The tomb robberies and the subsequent trials took place in his reign. Another son, Nebma'atré, became the high priest of HELIOPOLIS. He also had a son named Montuhirkhopshef.

Two documents concerning trade and economics depict Ramesses IX's reign. The true power of Egypt was already in the hands of the priests of AMUN, and inflation and other problems were causing unrest in the Nile Valley. Ramesses IX, who was the last pharaoh of Egypt to rule over NUBIA (modern Sudan) was bur-

ied in the VALLEY OF THE KINGS on the western shore of Thebes. His tomb was designed with three decorated corridors and three square-shaped halls, including one for offerings and containing four squared pillars. The burial chamber was decorated with scenes from the *Book of the Caverns* and depicted the goddess NUT, surrounded by solar barks and stars. Ramesses IX's mummified remains were discovered in the cache of DEIR EL-BAHRI in a coffin belonging to Princess NESKHONSU, the wife of PINUDJEM II.

Ramesses X (Khenerma'atre'setepenré) (d. 1000 B.C.E.) *ninth ruler of the Twentieth Dynasty*

He reigned from 1112 B.C.E. until his death. He was probably the son of RAMESSES IX and Queen BAKETWEREL. He married Queen TIYE (3) and his son was RAMESSES XI. Little is known of his reign, but the Libyans had invaded Thebes and the workers in the area were not receiving their normal rations. His tomb in the VALLEY OF THE KINGS at Thebes has been identified but not explored. No mummy has ever been found.

Ramesses XI (Menma'atre'setepenptah) (d. 1070 B.C.E.) *last ruler of the Twentieth Dynasty and the New Kingdom*

He reigned from 1100 B.C.E. until his death. Ramesses XI was the son of RAMESSES X and Queen TIYE, and married Queen TANUTAMUN. They had two daughters, HENUT-TAWY and another Tanutamun. He also had a second consort, possibly Baketwerel.

The state of Egypt was perilous at the time, as the *Report of WENAMUN*, a literary work of the reign, indicates. Thebes was in a state of constant revolt, and Ramesses XI was a recluse. Local Thebans used MEDI-NET HABU, Ramesses III's temple, as a fortress because of the riots and unrest. Hundreds died in the Theban revolt. The viceroy of Nubia, PANHESI, took control of the city but was ousted by HERIHOR, who became the high priest of Amun and commander of Upper Egypt. He died before Ramesses XI, who built a tomb in the VALLEY OF THE KINGS at Thebes but did not use it. This tomb was unfinished, but elaborate, with pillared halls, a shaft, and a burial chamber. The mummy of Ramesses XI has never been found.

Ramessesnakht (fl. 12th century B.C.E.) *priestly official of the Twentieth Dynasty*

He served RAMESSES IV (r. 1163–1156 B.C.E.) as the high priest of AMUN in THEBES. He may have held this office in earlier reigns as well. Ramessesnakht led an expeditionary force of 8,000 Egyptians to the QUARRIES of WADI HAMMAMAT. He brought back stone materials for Ramesses IV's building programs. He also assumed many high ranks and put his sons, Nesamon and Amenhotep, in high offices. He was related to the mayor of Thebes. Ramessesnakht's usurpation of power aided the decline of the New Kingdom.

Ramesses-Nebweben (fl. 13th century B.C.E.) *prince of the Nineteenth Dynasty*

He was a son of RAMESSES II (r. 1290–1224 B.C.E.). Ramesses-Nebweben was buried in the FAIYUM, near the retirement center of the HAREM at MI-WER. He was a hunchback and spent most of his life at the harem retreat, dying at a young age.

Ramesseum This was the temple built by RAMESSES II (r. 1290–1224 B.C.E.) at THEBES. Called "the Temple of the Million Years," the structure was part of Ramesses II's mortuary cult. The temple was dedicated to the deified Ramesses II and to the god AMUN, called "the United With Eternity." The site was named the Memnomium, or the Tomb of Ozymandias, by the Greeks.

The structure was surrounded by a brick wall and superimposed on a temple constructed originally by SETI I. Pylons depicted Ramesses II's battle of KADESH and his Syrian victories. The Ramesseum had a HYPOSTYLE HALL, courts, and a throne room. A colossal statue of Ramesses II, more than 55 feet tall, was discovered in the first court. An astronomical chamber was also found on the site, composing a second hypostyle hall.

In the southeast, a temple dedicated to Seti I and Queen TUYA, the royal parents of Ramesses II, was

Ramesseum columns, part of the elaborate hypostyle hall in the funerary monument of Ramesses II *(Courtesy Thierry Ailleret)*

erected, and an avenue of sphinxes surrounded various buildings. There were also chambers that served as sanctuaries for the assorted solar barks. A royal residence was part of the design. The Twenty-second (945–712 B.C.E.) and Twenty-third (828–712 B.C.E.) Dynasties used the storage areas of the Ramesseum as a burial site. A papyrus discovered on the site contained a version of "The Tale of the ELOQUENT PEASANT," and medical texts concerning the treatment of stiffening limbs were also found.

In the reign of Ramesses IX (1131–1112 B.C.E.), priests serving the Ramesseum were caught removing golden objects from this shrine. An accomplice, a gardener named Kar, confessed how quantities of golden decorations were taken. He also named his confederates, many of whom were in the priesthood. They were severely punished, as their crimes included not only theft but sacrilege in desecrating a religious site.

Ramesseum Papyri A series of documents discovered in the great temple built by RAMESSES II (r. 1290–1224 B.C.E.) at Thebes, the first was discovered during an expedition to the site during 1895–1896 and is now in the Berlin Museum. "The Tale of the ELOQUENT PEASANT" was contained in this papyrus. The Ramesseum Papyrus IV dates to 1900 B.C.E. and contained magicomedical material. The text called Papyrus V is purely medical, concerned with "stiffening of the limbs," the condition of arthritis. Another text describes various illnesses being treated in Kahun.

Ram of Mendes He was a divine being in Egypt, BA'EB DJET, called "the Ram of Tjet" or "the Soul Lord of Tjet." This cult was founded in the Second Dynasty (2770–2649 B.C.E.) and prospered in BUBASTIS. The word BA was translated in this cult as "soul" or "ram." In time the Ram of Mendes was believed to embody the souls of the deities RÉ, SHU, GEB, and OSIRIS. The Ram's consort was Hatmehit, a dolphin goddess. PTOLEMY II PHILADELPHUS (r. 285–246 B.C.E.) aided the cult of the Ram of Mendes.

Ramose (1) (fl. 14th century B.C.E.) *vizier of the Eighteenth Dynasty*

He served in this high office for AMENHOTEP III (r. 1391–1353 B.C.E.) and AKHENATEN (r. 1353–1335 B.C.E.). A trusted courtier, Ramose's career spanned the traditional and the 'AMARNA periods, although he died before 'Amarna became Egypt's capital in Akhenaten's reign. Ramose was a relative of the famed AMENHOTEP, SON OF HAPU. Ramose accepted the cult of ATEN.

His tomb in SHEIKH ABD 'EL-QURNA, on the western shore of Thebes, contains traditional and 'Amarna-style reliefs. They depict Aten rituals, as well as the usual scenes, and include a portrait of Amenhotep, son of Hapu, always recognized by his long flowing hair. The tomb was unfinished and not used, and Ramose's remains have never been discovered.

Ramose (2) (fl. 13th century B.C.E.) *official of the Nineteenth Dynasty*
He served as a scribe and administrator for RAMESSES II (r. 1290–1224 B.C.E.). Ramose was a temple official, belonging to a family that held high positions since the reign of TUTHMOSIS IV of the Eighteenth Dynasty. He served as a scribe in the temple treasury, as accountant for the Cattle of Amun, and as a chief administrator for the House of the Seal Bearer. His tomb in 'AMARNA was cruciform in shape with a transverse galley and a burial shaft. It was unfinished but contained statue remnants and painted scenes.

Ramose (3) (fl. 15th century B.C.E.) *official of the Eighteenth Dynasty*
He served HATSHEPSUT (r. 1473–1458 B.C.E.). His wife was HATNOFER, and he was buried with her at Thebes. Ramose was the father of SENENMUT, the tutor of Neferu-Ré.

Ra'neferef *See* NEFEREFRÉ.

Ranofer (fl. ca. 24th century B.C.E.) *priestly official of the Fifth Dynasty*
He served several pharaohs as a prophet of the gods PTAH and SOKAR. His famous statues are in the Egyptian Museum in Cairo. Life-sized and fashioned out of painted limestone, the statues were found in his SAQQARA tomb and vividly display the artistic skills of the era.

Raphia This is a site in southwestern Palestine, near modern Gaza, where PTOLEMY IV PHILOPATOR (r. 221–205 B.C.E.) defeated ANTIOCHUS III of Syria. Both sides used elephant cavalries in this battle. The Egyptians proved triumphant by using the heavier African elephant in the engagement, which was decisive for the long-term survival of Ptolemaic Egypt.

rastau This was the name given to small passages built into pyramids and tombs, extending some distance in the Great PYRAMID at GIZA, erected by KHUFU (Cheops) (r. 2551–2528 B.C.E.). They were once believed to be vents for air circulation, but recent explorations of these passages by small robots indicate that they do not appear to reach the outer walls. The passages may have had a spiritual purpose, serving as an entrance to the realms beyond the grave.

Rawer (fl. 25th century B.C.E.) *priestly official of the Fifth Dynasty*
He served KAKAI (Neferirkaré) (r. 2446–2426 B.C.E.) as a priest of MIN and as a ritual master. Rawer was termed an indicator of the secret words of the gods, believed to have great magical powers. His tomb, southwest of the Great SPHINX in SAQQARA, contained a STELA that records

that this priest was accidentally struck by Kakai during a religious ceremony but sustained no injuries. This site is a vast complex of 20 alcoves and 25 wall corridors. A portrait of Rawer was included in the decorations, depicting him in a loincloth, with a pyramidal apron and a badge across his chest and shoulders.

Ré He was the major solar deity of the ancient Egyptians, whose cult at HELIOPOLIS, or HERMOPOLIS MAGNA, developed in the Early Dynastic Period. Ré was the most popular solar deity of Egypt, and his cult incorporated many of the attributes and mythology of various other temples. Ré appeared on the ancient pyramidal stone in the Phoenix Hall at Heliopolis, as a symbol of rebirth and regeneration. Ré's cult concerned itself with material benefits: health, children, virility, and the destiny of the nation. Representing the sun, the cult was rooted in the nurturing aspects of nature and light.

The sun was called Khepri at dawn, Ré at noon, and ATUM at night. As Atum the god was depicted as a human with a double crown upon his head. As Khepri he took the form of the sacred beetle. As Ré the god was depicted as a man with the head of a falcon (or hawk), surmounted by the cobra and the URAEUS. He was also identified with HORUS, then called Ré-Horakhty, Ré-Horus. In this form he was the horizon dweller. At dawn Ré came across the sky in his SOLAR BOAT, called the "Boat of Millions of Years," accompanied by lesser divinities of his train.

The god Ré appeared in the form of Atum in the creation myths taught at Heliopolis. PTAH is supposed to have shaped the egg out of which Ré arose. In the other cosmogonic or creation tales of Egypt, Ré was depicted as rising as a LOTUS flower from the waters of the abyss. In turn he begat GEB, the earth, and NUT, the sky. Of these were born OSIRIS, SET, ISIS, and NEPHTHYS. The waxing and waning of the moon was the monthly restoration of the EYE OF RÉ by the god Thoth. This eye, alongside the EYE OF HORUS, became one of the holiest symbols of ancient Egypt.

Ré was the Living King, as OSIRIS was the Dead King. During the Old Kingdom the concept of the kings assuming the powers of Ré took root. The kings became the physical sons of the deity, a concept that would remain constant throughout Egyptian history. Even ALEXANDER III THE GREAT after he conquered Egypt with his Greek armies journeyed to the oasis of SIWA in the LIBYAN DESERT to be adopted as a son of the god Ré and be given the powers of the true kings of the Nile. During the New Kingdom the god AMUN was united to Ré to become the most powerful deity in Egypt.

Ré, Eye of A pendant considered powerful and used as a sign of divine protection, the goddess ISIS was associated with the Eye of Ré in one cultic tradition, and the deities BUTO and HATHOR assumed that mystical form.

The Eye of Ré was considered a spiritual entity that perfected the will of the god Ré.

rebels of Egypt

They were a select group of native Egyptians who tried to unite their fellow countrymen in revolts against foreign occupiers of the Nile Valley. In all of these rebellions the Egyptians failed to support these self-proclaimed leaders. Most of the rebels were from THEBES, the traditional area for the rise of warrior princes over the centuries. NARMER, MENTUHOTEP II, and 'AHMOSE (NEBPEHTIRÉ) had risen in their turns to march northward and to cleanse the land of alien stain. There were no such warriors in Egypt in the later eras, and no clans were able to amass armies in Upper Egypt to repel foreign intruders. Still, certain individuals began rebellions that were short-lived but reflected the ancient spirit of the Nile Valley.

AMYRTAIOS, who ruled a small area of the Delta in the reign of ARTAXERXES I (465–424 B.C.E.), survived the Persian assault on INAROS, a prince of HELIOPOLIS. Inaros killed a royal prince of Persia in a battle and was hunted down and captured by General MEGABYZUS. He was then crucified at the command of the slain prince's royal mother. Amyrtaios was not pursued during the Inaros episode and remained in control of his small domain.

The third rebel against the Persians was KHABABASH, reportedly the successor to NECTANEBO II (r. 360–343 B.C.E.). He was not successful, but his leadership and his desire for a free Egypt was repeatedly commemorated over the years by the Egyptians and by PTOLEMY I SOTER (r. 304–284 B.C.E.) on the SATRAP STELA.

Four rebels raised a call to arms during the Ptolemaic Dynasty, the line of Greeks who claimed Egypt following the death of ALEXANDER III THE GREAT in 323 B.C.E. CHARONNOPHIS and HOR-WEN-NEFER, Thebans, each started rebellions in the reign of PTOLEMY IV PHILOPATER (221–205 B.C.E.) but were easily defeated.

In the reign of PTOLEMY V EPIPHANES (205–180 B.C.E.), two other rebels tried to gain the support of the Egyptians. Probably their fellow countrymen recognized the fact that the Greeks would not allow the Ptolemaic line to fall, and an independent Egypt faced enemies, including the Seleucids and the growing power called Rome. ANKHWENNOFRÉ led a small group for a time but failed. HARONOPHIS faced the Greeks and also met defeat.

recensions

An evolving form of mortuary and religious LITERATURE in Egypt that demonstrates the advances made in the burial rites and semimagical rituals concerning the dead, these works are variations of the BOOK OF THE DEAD. Written in hieroglyphs, the recensions demonstrated the ongoing changes made in such literature concerning death and the realms beyond the grave. They are divided into three historical categories.

On (Heliopolis) Recensions—the Heliopolitan form that developed ca. 3300 B.C.E., probably variations of even earlier texts. This form was discovered in Old Kingdom (2575–2134 B.C.E.) tombs, copied on coffins and sarcophagi.

Theban Recensions—the variations started in the first half of the Eighteenth Dynasty (1550–1307 B.C.E.), written in hieroglyphs on papyri and divided into titled chapters. Vignettes were also added to personalize the texts. Illustrations were then included, making it necessary to abbreviate or omit some chapters. The original Theban Recensions contained 180 chapters, although no extant papyrus has all of them. These reproduced the historical traditions of the priests at HELIOPOLIS, HERAKLEOPOLIS, ABYDOS, and THEBES. Internal references link the Theban version to the First Dynasty reign of "Semti," probably SEMERKHET. Other references date to the reign of MENKAURÉ (2490–2472 B.C.E.) in the Fourth Dynasty. A later form of the Theban Recensions was started in the Twentieth Dynasty (1196–1070 B.C.E.).

Saite Recensions—a series of recensions started during the Twenty-fourth Dynasty (724–712 B.C.E.) or perhaps later and popular only in the area of SAIS in the Delta.

Redji (Redyzet) (fl. 27th century B.C.E.) *royal woman of the Third Dynasty*

She was probably a daughter of DJOSER (r. 2630–2611 B.C.E.). A statue of Princess Redji was discovered in SAQQARA and is now in the Turin Museum. Shown elaborately dressed in a pose, Redji's statue demonstrates the growing artistic skills of that early period.

Reed Fields

A sacred designation for the deceased Egyptians, fulfilling the requirements of all paradises, having water, cool breezes, and fertile tracts, the Reed Fields were sometimes depicted as a group of verdant islands. All of the mortal occupations and recreations were revived there. The dead had to perform agricultural labors, tasks assigned to the SHABTI figurines that accompanied the deceased. The BOOK OF THE DEAD used symbols of bound reeds to illustrate the Reed Fields.

See also PARADISE.

Re'emkuy (fl. 24th century B.C.E.) *royal prince of the Fifth Dynasty*

He was the eldest son of IZEZI (r. 2388–2356 B.C.E.) and the designated heir. Prince Re'emkuy served as a chief lector priest, a scribe of the Sacred Writings, and as a "Servant of the Throne." He was also listed as a "Sole Companion of the King." Dying at a young age, Prince Re'emkuy was buried in the SAQQARA tomb of a judge, Neferiryetnes. The reliefs and decorations of the MAS-

TABA were changed to provide the prince with a suitable resting place.

Rehu-er-djersenb (fl. 20th century B.C.E.) *official of the Twelfth Dynasty, famous for his tomb reliefs*
He served AMENEMHET I (r. 1991–1962 B.C.E.) as chancellor. He was buried in a large mastaba in el-LISHT, near Amenemhet I's pyramidal complex. The walls of Rehu-er-djersenb's tomb contain elaborate reliefs, including one depicting him hunting in the Nile marshes. An ABYDOS STELA lists Rehu-er-djesenb's prominent family, 23 in number. This stela was discovered in 1912.

rekhet A hieroglyph in the form of a lapwing bird, sometimes listed as *rekhyt,* the hieroglyph symbolized an entire caste of Egyptians in the era of unification (ca. 3000 B.C.E.). This caste was depicted on the SCORPION macehead and on other objects from the unification. The *rekhet* caste revolted in the Delta during the reign of DJOSER (2630–2611 B.C.E.) and had to be routed. Djoser is depicted in the STEP PYRAMID as crushing them as enemies of a true Egypt. *Rekhet* birds were winged and crested and used in temple rituals. With other symbols they represented the power of the pharaohs. The bird is depicted as a crested plover (*Vanellus vanellus*).

Rekhmiré (fl. 15th century B.C.E.) *vizier of the Eighteenth Dynasty*
He served TUTHMOSIS III (r. 1479–1425 B.C.E.). Rekhmiré was the son of Neferuhen, a priest of Amun; the grandson of A'AMETJU, the VIZIER for HATSHEPSUT (r. 1473–1458 B.C.E.); and the nephew of Useramun, or Woser, who was Tuthmosis III's vizier in the early years of his reign. Tuthmosis III reportedly said of Rekhmiré: "There was nothing he did not know." After Tuthmosis III's death, Rekhmiré was also vizier for AMENHOTEP II (r. 1427–1401 B.C.E.) but fell out of favor.

Rekhmiré's tomb, in the cliff areas of the western shore of THEBES, was never used. The burial chamber was incomplete and one wall was empty of reliefs. The figures of Rekhmiré in other parts of the tomb were damaged. The tomb, however, was decorated with illustrations of the daily activities and offices of the vizier and recorded the personal views of Tuthmosis III concerning the ideals and aspirations that are appropriate to the office of vizier. The depiction of the ceremonies for the installation of a vizier is complete, and there are other scenes portraying tributes, trade, and daily life, as well as funerary rites. Rekhmiré's wife, Meryt, is also depicted.

Rekh-nesu This was the term for the companion of the pharaoh, also recorded as *Rekh-neset*. The *Rekh-nesu* was "One Whom the King Knows," originally a title given to counselors who conducted the affairs of state. In time it was bestowed as an honor on an outstanding official. The title gave such an individual rank, status, and supposed free access to the pharaohs.

religion and cosmogony The ancient Egyptians had no word or single hieroglyph to denote religion as it is viewed in the modern age. Their spiritual ideals permeated every aspect of their lives to the point that such traditions and practices were considered a natural element of existence. The Greeks and other visitors described the Egyptians as the most religious people on earth. Ancient Egyptians showed an intense devotion and ardor in the midst of a vast pantheon of competing deities and numerous priestly factions.

RELIGION

Predynastic cultural sequences give evidence of one of the earliest inclinations of Egyptian religion—the belief in an afterlife. Animals were carefully buried alongside humans in the prehistoric eras, and the color green, representing resurrection and regeneration, figured prominently in grave rites. Fertility goddesses from the NAGADA I and II cultural sequences attest to the rudiments of cultic practices. A young male fertility god was also evident, as were indications of the emerging rites of various deities, including NEITH, MIN, and HORUS. AMULETS, slate palettes, block figures with religious associations, and the Horus and SET symbols were also found.

With the unification of Egypt in the Early Dynastic Period, the various local deities assumed regional importance. Horus became the patron of the kings, alongside Set, in the eastern DELTA. PTAH became the principal deity of MEMPHIS, the first capital, and the cult of RÉ flourished at HELIOPOLIS. SOKAR was evident in royal ceremonies, according to the PALERMO STONE and other documents from that era. NEKHEBET and WADJET had already been designated as the patrons of Upper and Lower Egypt. WEPWAWET, THOTH, ANUBIS, and the APIS bull were accepted as part of the Egyptian pantheon.

The royal cult was a special aspect of religion from the early period, associated with Horus and OSIRIS. The concept of the king as intermediary between the divine and the human was firmly in place by the time of the Old Kingdom (2575–2134 B.C.E.). From the Fifth Dynasty pharaohs were addressed "the son of 'Ré." Dead rulers were identified with Osiris.

FESTIVALS and rituals played a significant part in the early cultic practices in Egypt. Every festival celebrated a sacred or mythical time of cosmogonic importance (honoring the SOULS OF PE and SOULS OF NEKHEN, for example) and upheld religious teachings and time-honored beliefs. Such festivals renewed the awareness of the divine and symbolized the powers of renewal and the sense of the "other" in human affairs.

From the Early Dynastic period a tendency to henotheism is evident in Egypt, especially in hymns and didactic literature. Creation was explained in complex cosmogonic texts, and the presence of several, conflicting explanations of how the world began did not present a problem for Egyptians.

Egyptians did not demand a system of logical development of their religion. All that was necessary were the observances of the cultic rites and the festivals so that the people could mirror the divine order as interpreted by the priests. While the cults and celebrations represented regional or national preoccupation with particular deities, the individual Egyptians were quite free to worship a god according to their own inclinations. The people exercised free will in this regard, which led to an awareness of social and religious obligations, especially in the observance of the spirit of MA'AT.

Surrounded by a variety of gods, Egyptians still maintained belief in one supreme deity who was self-existent, immortal, invisible, omniscient, and the maker of heaven and earth and the Underworld, TUAT. The various gods assumed the supreme rank as the sole deity when addressed by their particular worshiper.

Ré was credited with having announced that all men were the equal recipients of sunlight, air, water, and harvests. Ré also instructed all men to live as brothers and to think on the West, AMENTI, the symbol of the grave and the afterlife. Amun was believed capable of nurturing and protecting each Egyptian as an individual while he also sustained the creatures of the field and the river and led the nation's military and cultural advances.

Religious beliefs were not codified in doctrines, tenets, or theologies. Few Egyptians explored the mystical or esoteric aspects of theology. The celebrations were sufficient, because they provided a profound sense of the spiritual and aroused an emotional response on the part of adorers. Hymns to the gods, processions, and cultic celebrations provided a continuing infusion of spiritual idealism into the daily life of the people.

In the First Intermediate Period (2134–2040 B.C.E.) following the fall of the Old Kingdom, the local or regional gods reassumed importance because of the lack of a centralized government. The god of the capital region usually assumed leadership over the other gods and assimilated their cults. Although Ré, Horus, Osiris, and Isis held universal sway, and Ptah remained popular, other deities began to assume rank. MONTU of HERMONTHIS, Amun of THEBES, SOBEK in the FAIYUM, and other local deities drew worshipers. The COFFIN TEXTS emerged at this time, making available to nonroyal personages the mortuary rites once exclusive to the kings.

When MENTUHOTEP II put an end to the Herakleopolitan royal line in 2040 B.C.E., ushering in the Middle Kingdom, the religious life of Egypt was altered. Mentuhotep and his successors strengthened the solar cult, which had implications for the royal cults as well, the king being the model of the creator god on earth. Also during the Middle Kingdom ABYDOS became the focal point of the Osirian Mysteries, and pilgrims flocked to the city. Osiris was identified with the dead pharaoh, the ruler of the realm of the dead. Those judged as righteous by Osiris and his Underworld companions were entitled to paradise.

The Second Intermediate Period (1640–1550 B.C.E.) did not have a tremendous impact on the religious life of the nation because the HYKSOS, who dominated the Delta regions, and the Thebans, who controlled Upper Egypt, stayed constant in their observances. To enhance their legitimacy the Hyksos and their Asiatic allies were quick to assume the cultic observances of the previous kings. When 'AHMOSE ousted the Hyksos, ushering in the New Kingdom (1550–1070 B.C.E.), the royal cult again predominated, but alongside it Amun, the god of Thebes, assumed importance. The brief 'AMARNA Period, in which AKHENATEN tried to erase the Amunite cult and replace it with that of the god ATEN, was too short-lived to have had lasting impact. Akhenaten, Aten, and the temporary capital at el-'Amarna were obliterated by later kings. HOREMHAB (r. 1319–1307 B.C.E.) went so far as to date his reign, which followed the 'Amarna episode, from the close of AMENHOTEP III's reign, so as to eradicate all traces of Akhenaten and his three successors.

The Ramessid kings upheld the royal cult and the established pantheon. PER-RAMESSES, the new capital in the eastern Delta, was a great conglomeration of temples and stages for cultic festivals. Until the New Kingdom collapsed in 1070 B.C.E., the spiritual traditions were maintained, and later eras saw again the same religious patterns along the Nile. During the Third Intermediate Period and the Late Period, religious fervor in the Nile Valley remained constant but was dependent upon NOME enthusiasm rather than state-operated cultic observances. The Ptolemaic Period stressed Greek heritage but allowed the native Egyptians to maintain their traditional forms of worship and even tried to unite the Greek and Egyptian factions by forming new deities that were a combination of the traditions of both nations.

One last aspect of Egyptian religion that needs to be understood is the use of animal figures or animal heads in the portrayals of the divine beings of Egypt. The various depictions of such creatures in the ruins of the temples and shrines have given rise to exotic interpretations and to esoteric explanations of those images. The current understanding of the use of such animals is that these creatures were viewed as THEOPHANIES, images that were devised to represent the gods in different manifestations or forms. The Egyptians lived close to nature, surrounded by animals, birds, insects, serpents, and fish. Some of these were used as representations of the local nome gods before the unification of Upper and Lower Egypt in 3000 B.C.E. Serving as the local fetish or totem, they disappeared or were absorbed into the cults of the various gods in time. The Egyptians did not worship animals or serpents but relied upon their familiar forms to demonstrate what they believed to be spiritual truths.

COSMOGONY

Cosmogony was the body of creation traditions of Egypt, legends that assumed political and religious significance in each new age of the nation. The number and variety of these myths provide insight into the development of Egyptian spiritual values and clearly delineate the evolution of certain divine cults.

To begin with, the ancient people of the Nile did not concern themselves with doctrinal or theological purity and precision, but they did adhere to a logical progression in matters of religious significance. Spiritual consciousness and a harmonious unity, both in the individual and in the nation, were elements that kept Egyptians secure and stable. Their religious aspirations were cultic in nature, dependent upon ritual and celebration, upon renewed manifestations of ideals and values. Dogmas or doctrines did not concern the common individuals specifically. In fact, the Egyptians were uncomfortable with spiritual concepts that demanded complex logical and reasonable development. It was enough for them to see the deity, to hear his or her concerns for the land, and to mirror the cosmic harmony that their astronomical abilities had gleaned for them in the sky.

There were basic systems of creation theology in all times of Egypt's development. They were found at Heliopolis, HERMOPOLIS MAGNA, Memphis, and Thebes. Other local temples provided their own cosmogonic information, but the four major ones provided the framework for spiritual evolution in Egypt.

The basic tenets of these cosmological systems were twofold: (1) The universe was once a primordial ocean called NUN or Nu; (2) A primeval hill arose to bring life out of chaos and darkness. The cosmogonic tenets of the city of Heliopolis are available in the PYRAMID TEXTS of the Old Kingdom but are scant and appear to make reference to what was common knowledge of the time. In this creation story the god ATUM emerges from the watery chaos called Nun. Atum made his first appearance on the hill that became the great temple at Heliopolis. By 2300 B.C.E. the god Atum was identified with Ré, becoming Ré-Atum, symbolized by the BENBEN or a SCARAB. Ré-Atum began making the other divine beings of Egypt through masturbation. SHU, his son, was then spit out of his mouth, and Ré-Atum vomited out TEFNUT.

Shu was the god of the air, and Tefnut was his consort, also considered to represent moisture and order in the material world. Both of these deities were associated with the legends concerning the Eye of Ré-Atum. This Eye was responsible for the birth of human beings and was the symbol of the sun. Atum lost Shu and Tef-

nut, and when he found them again, his tears became humans. Shu and Tefnut gave birth to GEB, the earth, and NUT, the sky. They, in turn, gave birth to ISIS, Osiris, NEPHTHYS, and Set. All of these divine beings, with Ré-Atum, formed the ENNEAD (the nine) of Heliopolis. In some eras the Ennead also included Horus.

In the city of Hermopolis Magna, the cosmogonic decrees held that the original gods were formed as an OGDOAD (octet). These were NUN, the primeval ocean, and his consort Naunet (the male depicted as a frog-headed man and the woman as having a serpent's head); HEH and Hauhet representing darkness; Kuk and Kauket (or Nia and Niat, representing nonentity); and Amun and his consort AMAUNET representing concealment. This Ogdoad was responsible for the "Golden Age" before humans in the Nile Valley. Amun became popular because of his role in stirring up the waters and the darkness to cause life. The original appearance of the god took on great significance in temple lore, and the original sites associated with Amun's creation were called PRIMEVAL MOUNDS. The Hermopolitan cosmogony included the appearance of a cosmic egg laid by a celestial GOOSE or an IBIS. A popular tradition from this time was that of the LOTUS, which brought the god Ré to the world. The Ogdoad of Hermopolis concerned themselves with the rising of the sun and the inundation of the Nile, both vital to Egypt's prosperity.

The Memphite creation story was very old and complex; PTAH was the creator of the entire world according to the Memphite priests. The Ennead of Heliopolis and other divinities were only manifestations of Ptah's creative powers. Ptah was the Heart and the Tongue, the seat of the intellect and the weapon of creative power. As Atum spat out the gods in other creation tales, he did so at Ptah's command, the result of the will of Ptah. Sia was the power of understanding, and Hu was the creative force of Ptah's words. This cosmogonic theory was sophisticated and demanded a considerable amount of metaphysical awareness, something that defeated the cult from the beginning. Ptah was the creative principle, fashioning not only the world and human beings but moral and ethical order. Ptah had not only made the other gods but had instituted the formulas for their worship, offerings, rituals, and ceremonies. Ptah made the cities and the men and women who inhabited them, and he set the standards for personal and national behavior. In time Ptah was joined with Osiris, to extend his reign even into the afterlife, as he was also united with Sokar.

The Theban cosmogony was late in arriving on the scene, coming into fullness in the New Kingdom (1550–1070 B.C.E.). The priests of Amun, understanding the need for a creation story that would provide their deity with rank and privileges above the other gods of Egypt, used the original concept of Amun as the air divinity of Hermopolis Magna. Thebes became the first Primeval

Mound, the original PAY LAND, the place of "the Appearance of the watery chaos and the creation of all life." Amun created himself in Thebes, and all the other gods were merely manifestations of him. He was Ptah, the lotus, the Ogdoad. Amun then became TATENEN, the Primeval Mound of Memphis. Thebes also assumed Osiris into its domain, claiming that the god was born in the New Kingdom capital.

Further reading: David, Rosalie. *Religion and Magic in Ancient Egypt.* New York: Penguin, 2003; Pinch, Geraldine. *Egyptian Mythology: A Guide to the Gods, Goddesses, and Traditions of Ancient Egypt.* Oxford, U.K.: Oxford University Press, 2003; Redford, Donald. *The Ancient Gods Speak: A Guide to Egyptian Religion.* Oxford, U.K.: Oxford University Press, 2002; Wallis-Budge, E. A. *From Fetish to God in Ancient Egypt.* New York: Dover Books, 1988; Wilkinson, Richard. *The Ancient Gods Speak: A Guide to Egyptian Religion.* London: Thames & Hudson, 2003.

Re'neb (Kakau, Nubnefer) (d. 2649 B.C.E.) *second ruler of the Second Dynasty*
He was the successor of HOTEPSEKHEMWY, the founder of the line, who ruled from 2700 B.C.E. until his death. He is called Kakau or Nubnefer in some king lists and is denoted as Kaichan by MANETHO. His name meant "Ré Is the Lord," and he may have been a usurper. His seals were in SAQQARA and on a TRADE route near ERMENT. Re'neb is given credit for aiding the APIS bull cult in MEMPHIS and the MNEVIS cult at HELIOPOLIS. He is also credited with introducing the sacred ram cult of MENDES. His SEREKH was discovered on a granite stela in ABYDOS. His tomb is believed to have been situated under the causeway of UNIS's funerary complex in SAQQARA.

Renenet (Renenutet) An Egyptian goddess of good fortune, she was considered an incarnation of ISIS as the patroness of harvests. She was also worshipped as the celestial cobra that nursed the pharaohs. A temple dedicated to Renenet was erected in the FAIYUM during the Middle Kingdom (2040–1640 B.C.E.). She was also associated with the cults of HATHOR and other goddesses concerning harvests, fate, happiness, and childbirth.

Renpet (1) A goddess of the Egyptian year, and the Egyptian word for year, Renpet was very popular in the late periods of Egypt. She was depicted as a woman wearing various symbols of crops and harvests. In some eras she was associated with the solar cult of SOPDU, called Sirius, the Dog Star, by the Greeks. Sopdu signaled the coming inundation of the Nile each year.

***renpet* (2)** The Egyptian hieroglyphic sign denoting the regnal year of a PHARAOH, the *renpet* sign appears to have been introduced in the reign of DJET, the third ruler of the First Dynasty (2920–2770 B.C.E.). Such a sign allowed significant annual events to be recorded accurately for each reign. The PALERMO STONE contains the *renpet* hieroglyph as a separation symbol to compartmentalize information about the reigns of the pharaohs.

See also KING LISTS.

Report of Wenamun A text that dates to the Twentieth Dynasty, the *Report of Wenamun* was discovered in Papyrus Moscow 120. Wenamun was recorded in this work as serving in the reign of RAMESSES XI (r. 1100–1070 B.C.E.), the last ruler of the New Kingdom. (When he died, Egypt was divided between two priest aristocrats.) The *Report of Wenamun,* credited to Wenamun, was formerly considered an important document of that historical period, demonstrating the fallen status of Egypt. In this age, however, a more sophisticated view of the document brings to light the possibility that the report was a satire, a literary form pioneered and appreciated by the ancient Egyptians.

Report of Wenamun has historical interest as it depicts Egyptian life and the loss of prestige and military power. It was written at a time when the nation was no longer a leader in the region, and the ruler was a recluse, kept in ignorance by officials. The report also details customs, traditions, and the political realities of the time.

Wenamun, possibly a fictitious character, was sent by RAMESSES XI on an expedition for timber to the Mediterranean coast, a vital resource rare in Egypt in that era. On his return home he reported his trials and tribulations to the court. Wenamun, as he demonstrates his annoyances, arrogance, and rudeness, clearly demonstrates the fact that he was not the best agent for the expedition.

Another character—a priest of Amun, SMENDES, who would divide Egypt with another ally—also figures in the text. He has authority over Wenamun and his approval apparently was necessary, which was an indication that Ramesses XI was not in charge of the nation, even while still on the throne. Smendes approves of the journey for timber, and Wenamun makes his way to Byblos in Phoenicia (modern Lebanon). On his way to Tyre, another Phoenician city, Wenamun is robbed of 36 deben. Upon reaching Tyre, Wenamun demands that the prince of that city repay him for his loss. When his demand goes unheeded, Wenamun sails on to Byblos, where he is received by Prince Tjekerbaal.

Berating this prince also, Wenamun finds 30 deben belonging to the ruler and "confiscates" the funds, planning to hold the coins until he receives his original deben. At the same time, Wenamun announces to everyone that the god Amun is the only true deity in the world, the master of land and sea, ships, animals, humans, and more.

Prince Tjekerbaal, beside himself at Wenamun's stern belief in Amun, demands to see the royal commission given to Wenamun by Ramesses XI. Smendes had kept the commission, however, leaving Ramesses XI unable to provide it. Then Tjekerbaal recalls a former ambassador from Egypt, the famed Kha'emweset, known for his courtesies and skills. This former ambassador is buried in Byblos, but Wenamun refuses to visit Kha'emweset's tomb. Instead, he pitches his tent on the harbor beach of Byblos and complains to everyone passing by. The harbor master soon visits him to order him off the beach because of complaints.

In order to put an end to Wenamun's visit, Tjekerbaal loads his ship with the needed wood and sends him off on his return voyage. Meanwhile, the owners of the deben "confiscated" by Wenamun demand that he be imprisoned for theft. Tjekerbaal grants these individuals permission to set sail after Wenamun and to do whatever they like with him. Wenamun arrives back in Egypt safely, however, and he makes his report to Ramesses XI. What the pharaoh thought of the report is unknown.

reptile charmer This was an occupation of the ancient Egyptians and one that is still in demand on the modern Nile. One such noted reptile charmer served at DEIR EL-MEDINA, the settlement of the workers in the tombs of the VALLEY OF THE KINGS. Others lived in villages and served entire areas. Still others were stationed at mines and quarries.

The reptile charmers normally conducted themselves as priests, physicians, scribes, or laborers but were on call when venomous snakes or scorpions posed a threat to the local populations. They were required to be on hand at all construction sites. These charmers were adept at handling the deadly reptiles, and many had been stung enough times to have built levels of immunity in their systems

Repyt A lioness deity of Egypt, popular in many historical periods, her temple at ATHRIBIS was once the same size as the temple of HATHOR in DENDEREH. This shrine was erected in the Ptolemaic Period (304–30 B.C.E.). PTOLEMY IX SOTER II (116–107, 88–81 B.C.E.) added to this temple.

reserve heads Ancient Egyptian busts created as portraits of the deceased, the heads frequently had broken ears and marks of scoring. It is believed that the damaged ears were the accidental results of the breaking of the molds, which were made out of linen and thin plaster. The damage could have taken place at that instant. For some reason the heads were not repaired or restored. Reserve heads were placed outside of the TOMBS, although some were found in the burial chambers or at the bottom of grave shafts. They date to the Fourth Dynasty (2575–2465 B.C.E.), used mostly in GIZA, ABUSIR, SAQQARA, and DASHUR. More than 30 such heads, exquisitely portraying the deceased, have survived over the centuries. They were used as spare heads if the corpses needed replacements, and they identified the graves for wandering *kas*, or astral spirits set free in the grave.

Restoration Stela This monument dating to the reign of TUT'ANKHAMUN (1333–1323 B.C.E.), describes the ruined state of Egypt as a result of the reign of AKHENATEN (1353–1335 B.C.E.) at 'AMARNA. Both the chaos in Egypt's temples and the precarious positions of the armed forces abroad are depicted in this stela.

resurrection It was the continuing Egyptian belief that souls never died but achieved renewed existence in eternity when mortal remains were prepared and placed in appropriate tomb sites. Every religious ceremony conducted in connection with the funerary and mortuary rites was designed to foster that belief. In the cult of OSIRIS an important aspect was the god's resurrection and ascension into heaven, with the promise that all mortals could share in his eternal bliss after being judged by him beyond the grave. This concept of resurrection had a positive and profound element in Egyptian life. The people of the Nile Valley held firmly to the belief that souls renewed their existence in eternity, where death could not touch them again. Funerary rituals and texts reassured the Egyptians of the transitory nature of life and death, events that the individual could survive.

Ret She was an ancient Egyptian goddess, considered the consort of RÉ and the mother of all the gods. Called Re-et in some lists, she was considered the female sun. She was worshipped in HELIOPOLIS and was depicted normally as a woman wearing horns and a SOLAR DISK.

Rhind Papyrus This is a mathematical text copied by a Theban scribe, probably during the reign of APOPHIS (ca. 1585–1553 B.C.E.), the HYKSOS contemporary of the Seventeenth Dynasty (1640–1550 B.C.E.). The papyrus deals with fractions, calculus, and other mathematical processes known at the time. The Rhind Papyrus also contains material concerning science and wisdom literature. It is possible that the present form resulted from yet another copy made by a scribe in the reign of AMENHOTEP I (1525–1504 B.C.E.). Sometimes called the 'Ahmose Papyrus, it was purchased by Alexander Henry Rhind in 1858, hence the name.

Rib-Hadda (Rib-Addi) (fl. 14th century B.C.E.) *ruler of ancient Byblos, now a city in modern Lebanon*
Rib-Hadda was in power during the reign of AKHENATEN (1353–1335 B.C.E.), serving as an ally of Egypt. This king wrote to Akhenaten, warning him about ABDIASHIRTA of Amurru, a city-state in the region. Rib-Hadda was being

attacked by Abdiashirta and was begging Akhenaten for troops and grain. He suffered exile from BYBLOS when no Egyptian aid was forthcoming.

See also 'AMARNA LETTERS.

rishi pattern This is a term for the feathered design used on the SARCOPHAGI of the Seventeenth (1640–1550 B.C.E.) and the Eighteenth (1550–1307 B.C.E.) Dynasties. The pattern imitated the wings of the god HORUS, thus enfolding the deceased in the sarcophagus within the protective power of the deity. Theban tombs from these dynastic periods have the rishi pattern evident on the sarcophagus.

rising sun A sacred symbol in Egypt, associated with the HORIZON, the rising sun was displayed in an AMULET that was deemed powerful in conveying life and RESURRECTION beyond the grave. The symbol of Harmachis, Hor on the Horizon, was the amulet that depicted a sun rising between two mountains of hills. It was popular in MORTUARY RITUALS.

Rite of the House of Morning This was a solemn ceremony conducted each day in ancient Egyptian palaces. The pharaoh's rising was a great event. Priests and courtiers attended him, ready to assist in bathing and dressing. He washed in water from the local temple lake to symbolize his primordial rebirth, and the water represented the chaotic abyss of the god NUN. The king was then anointed, robed, invested with the royal insignias, and praised by priests wearing the masks of the gods HORUS and THOTH. If the king was not in residence at the time, a substitute official or a member of the royal family was given similar honors in his stead. In some eras the king also chewed bits of natron, another symbol of rebirth and resurrection.

See also DAILY ROYAL RITES.

rituals They were the often elaborate ceremonies conducted throughout all of the historical periods of Egypt as religious, magical, or state displays of power and belief. Such ceremonies depicted events taking place in the affairs of humans and the gods. In Egypt, rituals and beliefs were so closely bound that one could not exist without the other.

The temple of the deity was considered not as a material structure but as a HORIZON, the place where the deity reigned, opening onto the land of glorious light beyond the dawn. FESTIVALS and rituals celebrated the sacred cultic traditions, cosmic or historical, of the time when the sacred was manifested. Rituals were religious renewals, the demonstrations of the divine.

River of Heaven A waterway called the Celestial Stream, the Celestial River, or the Spiritual Nile, the River of Heaven was the counterpart of the actual Nile and was believed to enter the earthly sphere on the ELEPHANTINE Island, at ASWAN. The River of Heaven was depicted in the mortuary texts and was associated with the god RÉ's nightly sojourn. This Nile flowed through TUAT, the land beyond the grave.

Roau (Ro-an, Roen, Ra-an) (fl. 15th century B.C.E.) *priestly official of the Eighteenth Dynasty*
He served TUTHMOSIS III (r. 1479–1425 B.C.E.) as the chief steward of AMUN. Roau was in charge of the mortuary complex of Queen AH'HOTEP (I), the mother of 'AHMOSE (NEBPEHTIRÉ), the founder of the New Kingdom (1550–1070 B.C.E.) and the Eighteenth Dynasty. Queen Ah'hotep's cult was still active in the reign of Tuthmosis III, and he erected a shrine in her honor. Tuthmosis III donated a tomb to Roau as a reward for his services.

Rodis (Rhodopis) (fl. seventh or sixth century B.C.E.) *Greek woman living in Naukratis, Egypt, called one of the most beautiful women of the world*
NAUKRATIS, founded in the Twenty-sixth Dynasty (664–525 B.C.E.), was the residence of Greek merchants and traders on the Canopic branch of the Nile. Rodis, a resident of the city, was heralded in legend as one of the most beautiful women of all time. As a result of her charms she was the center of attention and had Greek and Egyptian suitors.

Rome One of the most powerful of the ancient states, Rome emerged from a small, rural community in Italy to conquer most of the Mediterranean world and to bring to an end the long pharaonic history of Egypt in 30 B.C.E.

The first significant involvement of Rome in the affairs of Egypt occurred in 170 B.C.E. when the strife between Egypt and Syria (under King ANTIOCHUS IV) ended with both sides appealing to the Romans to decide who should be the rightful claimant to the throne. The two candidates were PTOLEMY VIII EUERGETES II (the favorite of the Egyptians) and PTOLEMY VI PHILOMETOR (the nephew and favorite of Antiochus IV). The Roman Senate decided to split the rule of the country, so that Philometor reigned in MEMPHIS and Euergetes controlled ALEXANDRIA. This state of affairs proved unsatisfactory to the Egyptians, who wasted no time upon Antiochus's departure back to Syria to rise up against Philometor. Antiochus responded by marching on Egypt with an army. The Egyptians appealed once more to Rome.

The Roman Senate dispatched a three-man commission to Egypt, and in 168 there occurred the famous encounter between Antiochus IV and Papillius Laenas at Eleusis just outside of Alexandria. Laenas gave Antiochus the terms of the Senate: the Syrians must depart Egypt or there would be war. Laenas then used a stick to draw a circle in the sand around Antiochus's feet and demanded an answer before he set foot out of the ring.

The Syrian agreed to the Senate's demands, and Ptolemy VI was installed as ruler of all Egypt; Ptolemy VIII was made king of Cyrenaica.

Rome now stood as the supreme arbiter of Egyptian affairs. Thus, when PTOLEMY XII NEOS DIONYSIUS was driven from Egypt in 58 B.C.E. he fled to Rome. After paying extensive bribes and cultivating the political favor of Julius CAESAR, Ptolemy XII returned to Egypt and was reinstated with the assistance of three Roman legions. The remainder of his reign was as a virtual client of Rome, and Ptolemy left provision in his will for the Romans to have oversight over the transition of power to his children, CLEOPATRA VII and PTOLEMY XIII.

The bitter political struggle between Cleopatra and her brother went largely unnoticed by the Romans owing to their own civil war. In 48 B.C.E., however, following the defeat of POMPEY the Great by Julius Caesar at the battle of Pharsalus, Pompey fled to Egypt and what he hoped would be the sanctuary of the court of Ptolemy. The Roman general was immediately assassinated by a cabal of Egyptian courtiers, and his head was given as a gift to Caesar upon the dictator's arrival in Alexandria.

Caesar decided the dispute between Ptolemy and Cleopatra in favor of the queen, and Ptolemy died in the fighting that followed. In a famous romance, Caesar and Cleopatra became lovers and produced PTOLEMY XV CAESARION. Following Caesar's assassination in 44 B.C.E., Cleopatra established a relationship with Marc ANTONY. Their political and personal alliance culminated in the war with Caesar's nephew, Octavian (the future AUGUSTUS) and the battle of ACTIUM in 31 B.C.E. The defeat of the Egyptian fleet and army opened the door for the Roman conquest of Egypt. Cleopatra committed suicide in famed fashion by stinging herself with an asp, and Marc Antony died on his own sword. Octavian, the future Augustus, entered Alexandria on August 1, 30 B.C.E. Henceforth, until the Arab conquest in 641 C.E., Egypt remained a territory of the Roman Empire and then the Byzantine Empire.

romis This was an Egyptian term for "true humans," also called *piromis*. These were the intellectual or artistic members of the Egyptian society, as contrasted with the alien or peasant classes of the various nomes or provinces.

See also SOCIAL EVOLUTION IN EGYPT.

ropes Essential tools and elements in Egyptian life, termed cordage in some instances, strings, twine, cable, or ropes were fashioned by twisting or braiding fibers into a line that could be tied or used to bear weights or stresses. Most Egyptian ropes were S-twisted to the right. Three S-twisted strands formed a Z-twisted cord. They were made from the papyrus plant (*Cyperus papyrus*), halfa grass (*Desmostachya bipinnata*), the dom palm (*Hyphaene thebaica*), and the date palm (*Phoenix dactilifera*), along with others. The halfa grass was most common. These ropes were used in the construction of the spirit boat discovered in the pyramid pits of KHUFU (Cheops) (r. 2551–2528 B.C.E.). The Egyptians were masters at rope making.

Roset This was a site near ABYDOS in Upper Egypt deemed a holy place by Egyptians. Cliffs were prominent in the territory, and at Roset there is a cave that was considered to be one of the entrances to TUAT, the land beyond the grave. The proximity of Roset to ABYDOS, the city of the god OSIRIS, may have caused the spiritual designation.

Rosetta Stone One of the most famous archaeological discoveries in the world, the Rosetta Stone opened the door to modern deciphering of the ancient Egyptian hieroglyphs. It was discovered in 1799 by a French artillery officer, Lt. P. F. X. Bouchard, a member of Napoleon Bonaparte's army, in the ruined Fort Julien at Rosetta during the French invasion of Egypt. This town of Rosetta, as it is known in the West (Rashid is its Egyptian name), was in the northern region of the Delta on the western channel of the Nile. The inscriptions discovered on the Rosetta Stone were originally created by the priests of MEMPHIS during the reign of PTOLEMY V EPIPHANES (205–180 B.C.E.), commemorating the ruler's accession and patronage.

When the French surrendered Egypt in the Treaty of Alexandria in 1801, the stone passed to the British under Article 16 and was put on display in the British Museum in London. Following the efforts of several scholars in previous historical periods, work began on deciphering the ancient hieroglyphs. The Jesuit Athanasius Kircher (1602–1680 C.E.) made contributions in deciphering; Abbé Jean-Jacques Barthélemy identified some cartouches of the ancient pharaohs in 1761. (A cartouche is an ellipse found in reliefs, paintings, sculptures, and papyri that encircles certain royal names).

The Rosetta Stone is a portion of a large black basalt stone STELA, measuring three feet nine inches by two feet and a half inch. The stone is inscribed with 14 lines of hieroglyphs, 32 lines of demotic script, and 54 lines of Greek.

In 1822, Jean-François Champollion of France and Thomas Young of England started the last phases of decipherment of the Rosetta Stone. Young, recognizing the cartouche form, decided that the names of Ptolemy and Cleopatra could be written in symbols with phonetic values that would correspond to their names in Greek. He managed to assign accurately the correct values to six signs with partially correct values for three more. Young also recognized the direction in which the texts should be read by ascertaining the direction in which birds in the inscriptions were facing.

The Rosetta Stone is associated closely with Champollion (1796–1832), who dedicated his life to its study. A linguist and a scholar of Asian matters, Champollion knew ancient languages, including Coptic, which is related to hieroglyphs. Because of his knowledge of the biblical languages, he was able to determine the exact methods in which the hieroglyphs were to be translated. In 1821 Champollion took up the task and published memoirs on the decipherment of both the hieroglyphs and the hieratic form of the Egyptian language. He recognized that some signs were alphabetical, some syllabic, and some determinative. He also established the fact that the royal names of the pharaohs were depicted within the form of the cartouche. Aware that pharaohs wrote their names in cartouches, when Champollion saw that the Greek inscription mentioned the name Ptolemy, he knew that the cartouche in the hieroglyphic text had to be Ptolemy. With the letters of Ptolemy's name established, Champollion was able to use the established letters to translate other names. Adding to his work was a discovery of a Greek inscription on the base of an obelisk on the island of Philae by Egyptologist Giovanni Battista Belzoni (1778–1823), which Champollion used to decipher the name Cleopatra.

Champollion's work inspired many Egyptologists, and a presentation of his findings was made to the Académie des Inscriptions et Belles-Lettres. The report became known as the "Letter to M. Dacier" and was well received. In 1824 Champollion wrote *Précis du système hiéroglyphique des anciens Égyptiens* (Precise hieroglyphic system of the ancient Egyptians). The recognition of his labors and successes brought him the support of King Charles X of France (r. 1757–1836) and Duke Leopold II of Tuscany (r. 1747–1792), who organized the Franco-Tuscan expedition to the Nile. Champollion, accompanied by his pupil Ippolito Rosellini (1800–1843), set sail for Egypt in June 1828. They confirmed his discoveries in the field, establishing practices and methods for future studies. Champollion, having returned to France, died of a stroke in 1832.

Roy (1) (fl. 15th century B.C.E.) *financial official of the Eighteenth Dynasty*
He served TUTHMOSIS III (r. 1479–1425 B.C.E.) as chief treasurer. An inscription cut into the rocks of SERABIT EL-KHADIM, dating to Tuthmosis III's 25th regnal year, depicts the pharaoh making a libation to HATHOR with Roy attending him. An inscription of eight lines praises Tuthmosis III, and another eight lines of hieroglyphs depict Roy as having been appointed a commander of the army sent to bring back malachite stone. There is a reference to "the sea," indicating the Mediterranean or Red Sea.

See also NATURAL RESOURCES.

Roy (2) (fl. 13th century B.C.E.) *temple official of the Nineteenth Dynasty*
He served MERENPTAH (r. 1224–1214 B.C.E.) as the high priest of AMUN. The title became hereditary during Roy's tenure. He had inherited the office from BAKENKHONSU, and both apparently were members of the AMENEMOPET clan.

royal cults   The royal cults resulted from the DEIFICATION of the pharaohs of Egypt, as well as courtiers and certain queens, during their reigns or after their burials. Such deified individuals were considered intermediaries between the world of humans and the gods. AMENHOTEP I (r. 1525–1504 B.C.E.), for example, and his mother, 'AHMOSE-NEFERTARI, were deified and honored with shrines and temples.

The royal cults were particularly important when associated with mortuary complexes of deceased rulers, many remaining active for centuries after their institution. Such cults were centered at PYRAMIDS or tomb sites and were maintained by vast retinues. At times small cities were erected to house the priests and workers involved in the ongoing ceremonies and celebrations. The Ptolemaic Period (304–30 B.C.E.) continued the practice.

Royal List   *See* KING LISTS.

royal names   They were the titles employed by the rulers of Egypt from the earliest eras, containing magical and spiritual connotations. The titles were elaborately designed with five elements that denoted the connection of the pharaoh to the gods, to their divine purposes, and to their roles in the nation. The royal names included the following:

  Horus name—the first one used, symbolizing the role of the pharaoh as the representative of the god HORUS on earth. The name was normally written in a *SEREKH* and established the pharaoh's right to rule the land.
  Nebti **name**—called the Two Goddesses or Two Ladies title and linking the pharaoh to the patronesses of Upper and Lower Egypt, WADJET and NEKHEBET, the cobra and the vulture. This was a sign of unification for Egypt. The pharaohs also wore the *URAEUS*, the royal symbol of the cobra and the VULTURE, the goddesses protecting the Upper and Lower Kingdoms.
  Golden Horus name—called the *Bik nub*, the depiction of a hawk on a golden symbol, representing the concept that the pharaoh was made of gold. His flesh was actually "the gold of the gods," the earthly manifestation of the divine.
  Nesut-Bit **name**—also called the Sedge and the Bee, the Suten-Bat, a title symbolizing the unity

of Upper and Lower Egypt under the pharaoh's rule. The north and south combined to provide the pharaoh with a *prenomen* or a cartouche name. This was the most important and the most frequently used title. In some inscriptions the appearance of this name alone designated the particular pharaoh. The BEE was the symbol of the Delta and Lower Egypt, and the sedge represented Upper Egypt.

Son of Ré name—called the Si-Ré and depicted by the hieroglyphs of the pintail duck and a disk, the duck meaning "son" of the god Ré, the disk. This was the pharaoh's actual birth name normally.

Royal Wadi   This was the name given to the desert road from 'AMARNA, the capital of AKHENATEN (r. 1353–1335 B.C.E.) to the TOMBS of royal family members and court officials in the cliff areas of the region. These tombs were ransacked following Akhenaten's demise and the abandonment of 'Amarna. The remains of the royal family members were brought to THEBES, and parts of their mortuary regalia were used in the tomb of TUT'ANKHAMUN (r. 1333–1323 B.C.E.).

Ruaben   (fl. 27th century B.C.E.) *noble of the Second Dynasty*
He served in the reign of NINETJER (ca. 2680 B.C.E.). Ruaben's tomb was constructed in SAQQARA. Stone fragments bearing his name were discovered in the massive gravesite, and it is possible that Ruaben was buried in the funerary complex of Ninetjer, whose remains and burial chamber have not yet been found.

Rudamon   (d. ca. 712 B.C.E.) *ruler of the Twenty-third Dynasty*
He reigned at LEONTOPOLIS from ca. 747 B.C.E. until defeated by PIANKHI (r. 750–712 B.C.E.) of the Twenty-fifth Dynasty, the Nubian who invaded Egypt. Rudamon was the son of OSORKON III and Queen TENTSAI. He succeeded TAKELOT III, his brother, and his heir was IUPUT II. Rudamon built at KARNAK and MEDINET HABU. His daughter, IRBAST'UDJEFRU, married PEFTJAU'ABAST.

Rudamon joined the coalition of rulers that tried to defend the land against the armies of Piankhi. The Egyptians were routed by Piankhi's Nubians and had to surrender. Rudamon was allowed to remain in Leontopolis as a vassal governor.

Rudjek   (fl. 26th century B.C.E.) *royal mortuary official of the Fourth Dynasty*
Rudjek served KHUFU (Cheops) (r. 2551–2528 B.C.E.) as counselor and as the head of the priests who took care of the royal mortuary complex in GIZA, the site of the Great PYRAMID of Khufu and those of his successors. Rudjek described himself as a "friend" of Khufu.

Ruia   (fl. 14th century B.C.E.) *father-in-law of Seti I*
Ruia was the father of Queen TUYA, the consort of SETI I (r. 1306–1290 B.C.E.). Tuya, a commoner, had married Seti I before his father, RAMESSES I, was designated by HOREMHAB as heir. Seti I thus became the second ruler of the Nineteenth Dynasty. Ruia was a commander of CHARIOTS in the Egyptian army, a force strengthened by Horemhab and expanded by Ramesses I and his successors. Ruia and his wife, Raia, were buried in THEBES.

S

sa This was the hieroglyph for protection, duplicated in metals and woods to form AMULETS in ancient Egypt. Formed as a life preserver, the *sa* was worn around the neck and was a rolled mat design, shaped like an ANKH, or ansate cross. The gods Bes and Tawaret were honored with this symbol. By the Middle Kingdom (2040–1640 B.C.E.) the *sa* was used as jewelry, and in the New Kingdom (1550–1070 B.C.E.) the sign appeared in other designs as well.

sa-ankh Called "the fluid of life" or "water of life," also *sa-en-ankh,* a divine substance derived from the gods RÉ and HORUS, the *sa-ankh* was reserved at temples and used in ceremonies held to honor the role of the PHARAOH. The ruler became the counterpart of RÉ, the earthly manifestation of the deity, by partaking of "the water of life." The *sa-ankh* was also given to pharaohs in the early morning rituals of waking.

See also DAILY ROYAL RITES; RITE OF THE HOUSE OF MORNING.

Sabef (fl. 28th century B.C.E.) *official and royal companion of the First Dynasty*
He served QA'A (r. ca. 2770–2760 B.C.E.) in the royal residence and as a royal counselor. His funerary STELA in ABYDOS described his honorary status as a "companion," a title that indicated he had free access to the pharaoh.

See also "FRIEND OF THE KING."

Sabni (fl. 22nd century B.C.E.) *prince and governor of the Sixth Dynasty*
He served PEPI II (r. 2246–2152 B.C.E.) as the governor of ASWAN and was called "the overseer of southern lands." Sabni was an hereditary prince of ELEPHANTINE Island and worked with Prince Mekhu, his father. Sabni directed the QUARRY operations for two obelisks, obligated to carve and transport them to HELIOPOLIS. With an official named HEKAIB, Sabni also undertook the punitive expeditions to retrieve the remains of slain Egyptians in NUBIA (modern Sudan). When he reached the remains of Mekhu, his father, and brought them back to Egypt, Sabni was met by a group of priests, embalmers, and mourners sent by Pepi II. Sabni and Mekhu were buried in Qubbet el-Hawwa, "the Dome of the Wind," a necropolis site at ASWAN. Their tomb has painted scenes, FALSE DOORS representing each deceased, OBELISKS, offering tables, and reliefs.

Sabu, Ibebi (fl. 24th century B.C.E.) *official of the Fifth and Sixth Dynasties*
He served UNIS (r. 2356–2323 B.C.E.) and TETI (r. 2323–2291 B.C.E.) in several capacities. Sabu was a counselor and master of ceremonies for Unis, receiving the title of "companion," and then became the high priest of PTAH in Teti's reign. Ibebi Sabu conducted Teti's coronation rites. His mastaba in SAQQARA contains an account of his honors and Teti's ascent to the throne.

Sabu, Thety (fl. 23rd century B.C.E.) *priestly official of the Sixth Dynasty*
He served TETI (r. 2323–2291 B.C.E.) as the high priest of PTAH. He was the son of IBEBI SABU. Thety Sabu was so talented that he became the sole high priest. Prior to his term of office it was believed necessary to install at least two individuals as prelates to manage ceremonies and the vast estates of Ptah. Thety Sabu conducted this office alone. His tomb was in SAQQARA and contained a FALSE DOOR that is now in the Egyptian Museum in Cairo.

Sacred Book of the Temple This was a text copied onto a monumental inscription, pertaining to the shrines and sacred sites in Egypt. The list of holy places contained the names, standing structures, and mythical sites associated with the deities of the land. Most temples and cult centers had copies of the inscription and used it as a reference.

See also FOUNDATION DEPOSITS.

sacred lake It was an architectural feature of the larger temples of Egypt, reproductions of the primordial waters of *nunu* that existed before the moment of creation. Rectangular in design normally, the lakes were reserved for certain rituals and used as well for cleansing. The larger sacred lakes served as receptacles for the barks of the gods at festivals. KARNAK and other major temples contained such lakes, all man-made. When the pharaoh was in residence, the water from the local sacred lake was used to baptize him in the morning rising rituals.

The sacred lakes were in use throughout all of the historical periods of Egypt. Also called *she netjeri,* the divine pool, the lakes were stone lined and at times were fashioned with elaborate staircases. They also served as sanctuaries for sacred birds, CROCODILES, or HIPPOPOTAMI. Certain three-sided lakes were used in Osirian monuments. A few were circular or shaped as horseshoes. The sacred temple lake at Thebes figured in the dispute between the HYKSOS ruler APOPHIS (r. 1585–1553 B.C.E.) and TA'O II (Sekenenré; Djehuti'o) (d. 1555 B.C.E.).

See also QUARREL OF APOPHIS AND SEKENENRÉ.

Sadeh (fl. 21st century B.C.E.) *court woman of the Eleventh Dynasty*
She was a concubine of MENTUHOTEP II (r. 2061–2010 B.C.E.). In her tomb in the royal complex at DEIR EL-BAHRI on the western shore of THEBES, she is listed as "the Sole Favorite of the King." This title was an honorary designation shared by all of the women buried there, indicating that they were lesser-ranked consorts or concubines. Sadeh was possibly the daughter of Queen ASHAIT, another "Sole Favorite of the King" buried in the complex.

"saff" tombs This was the name given to the tombs constructed in the EL-TARIF district on the western shore of THEBES (modern LUXOR). The name is derived from the Arabic for "row," indicating similar tombs constructed in a line. Dating to the Eleventh Dynasty (2040–1991 B.C.E.), the "saff" tombs were blended forms of MASTABAS and PYRAMIDS as well as rock-cut sites placed on cliffs. Pillars opening onto sunken forecourts were part of the design, and the tomb doors opened onto corridors and burial chambers. Most "saff" tombs were topped with PYRAMIDIONS.

Sages of Mehweret Ancient divine beings in Egypt, revered from the earliest times as the mentors of the god THOTH, the sages reportedly dictated their accumulated wisdom to Thoth, an act inscribed on the walls of the temple of EDFU. The Sages of Mehweret came from the dawn of time, and their admonitions provided Egypt with the basis for the steadily evolving moral code.

See also "TIME OF THE GODS."

sah This was the ancient Egyptian concept of the spiritual body of an individual being released from the material bonds of the flesh. Also called *sashu,* this spiritual essence was released from the body during mummification processes and the funerary rituals. Glorified in its new state, the *sah* was empowered by prayers and litanies to experience spiritual bliss.

See also A'AKH.

Sahara Mousteria *See* BIR TARFAWI; EGYPT.

Sahathor (1) (fl. ca. 1730 B.C.E.) *obscure ruler of the Thirteenth Dynasty*
His reign is not well documented, but he was the successor of his brother, NEFERHOTEP I, with whom he may have had a brief coregency.

Sahathor (2) (fl. 19th century B.C.E.) *treasury official of the Twelfth Dynasty*
He served in the reign of AMENEMHET II (1929–1892 B.C.E.) as an assistant treasurer and expedition leader. Sahathor conducted a mining expedition and brought gold and turquoise to court from NUBIA (modern Sudan). He also conducted an expedition to bring rare plants to the pharaoh. His ABYDOS tomb carries accounts of his exploits as well as reports of his promotions and court favors. A stylish statue of Sahathor was also inscribed in a niche in his tomb.

See also NATURAL RESOURCES.

Sahuré (d. 2446 B.C.E.) *second ruler of the Fifth Dynasty*
He reigned from 2458 B.C.E. until his death. Sahuré was the successor of USERKHAF and possibly the son of Queen KHENTAKAWES (1). A builder and innovator, Sahuré started sending fleets of ships along the coast of Palestine and conducted expeditions to PUNT. He exploited the mines in the SINAI territory and quarried diorite stone at ABU SIMBEL near ASWAN. Mentioned in the PALERMO STONE, Sahuré campaigned against the Libyans and made raids on Syrian-held lands. His name meant "He Who Comes to RÉ."

Sahuré began the royal cemetery at ABUSIR south of SAQQARA. He erected a pyramidal complex there, complete with a valley temple, causeway, and mortuary temple. It was designed with colonnaded courts and reliefs depicting his military campaigns and is considered a model of Fifth Dynasty funerary architecture, using not only basic building materials from the local region but fine limestone from the TUREH (Tura) QUARRY as well. Sahuré's desert hunting expeditions and his naval fleet are depicted on the pyramid. The scenes are in low relief and were once painted.

His mortuary temple had rainspouts shaped as lion heads, forerunner of the Gothic gargoyles. Copper-lined bases and lead plugs were also discovered in the complex, as were red granite palm columns. His pyramid was called Sekhet-Ré, "the Field of Ré." A second pyramid was built in the eastern complex, possibly for an unknown consort. In the later eras, Sahuré's complex was used as a sanctuary for the goddess SEKHMET. Sahure was succeeded on the throne by his brother KAKAI.

St. Petersburg Papyrus   *See TALE OF THE SHIPWRECKED SAILOR.*

Sais (Zau, Sai, Sa-el-Hagar)   It is a site on the right bank of the Rosetta or Canopic branch of the Nile in the Delta region. Called Zau or Sai by the Egyptians, Sais is the modern Sa-el-Hagar. The city was the cult center of the goddess NEITH (1) and the capital of the Twenty-sixth Dynasty (664–525 B.C.E.). The rulers of the Twenty-fourth Dynasty (724–712 B.C.E.) also resided in Sais, which served as the capital of PSAMMETICHUS I (r. 664–610 B.C.E.). No monuments remain, however, as the city was looted by later dynasties and by the Persians. The burial sites of the Twenty-sixth Dynasty are still evident in the territory, some having yielded exquisite objects of the mortuary regalia of the Necho-Psammetichus royal line.

sakieh (sakia)   It was an Egyptian waterwheel designed to take water out of the Nile for use in agricultural projects. Oxen or humans powered the *sakieh*, which was used side by side with the later *shaduf*, the irrigation tool introduced by the HYKSOS.

See also AGRICULTURE; FAIYUM.

Salamis   This was the principal coastal city of Cyprus, where a naval battle took place between PTOLEMY I SOTER (r. 304–284 B.C.E.) and DEMETRIUS I POLIORCETES of Macedonia and his allies in 306 B.C.E. The Egyptians were defeated in the battle. At the time of the engagement, Salamis was an important Egyptian TRADE center. The battle also took place early in the reign of Ptolemy I, at a time when the former generals of ALEXANDER III THE GREAT struggled for supremacy in the Mediterranean world.

See also DIADOCHE.

Sal Island   It is an eight-mile-long site south of the third cataract of the Nile in NUBIA (modern Sudan). A famous summit there was called Gebel Adou. 'AHMOSE (NEBPEHTIRÉ) (r. 1550–1525 B.C.E.) fortified an Egyptian

outpost there, and a temple was erected on the island by AMENHOTEP I (r. 1525–1504 B.C.E.). The site served as an outpost of Egyptian TRADE activities. SETI I (r. 1306–1290 B.C.E.) put down a rebellion on Sal Island, at Sha'at, defeating the Irem, a local warrior people. The island became the administrative base of the VICEROY of Nubia in Seti I's reign.

Salitis (Sharek; Sharlek)   (fl. ca. 1640 B.C.E.) *Asiatic who founded the Fifteenth Dynasty, called the Great Hyksos* He started his line in MEMPHIS and then moved his capital to AVARIS on the eastern side of the Bubastis branch of the Nile in the Delta. Salitis is believed to have held the Avaris throne for about 19 years. He ruled the entire Delta and Egypt as far south as GEBELEIN. He is called "Sultan" in some lists, and his Asian name was Sharek or Sharlek. Salitis and his successors in Avaris were called the Great Hyksos because of their dominance. Salitis had an alliance with the KERMEH culture in NUBIA (modern Sudan), and his seals were found there. He was a contemporary of INYOTEF IV of Thebes, whose line held Upper Egypt. Salitis fortified Avaris against possible assaults by the Thebans.

Sallier Papyri   This is collection of ancient Egyptian texts purchased by one M. Sallier from an Egyptian sailor. These papyri contained accounts of the campaigns of RAMESSES II (r. 1290–1224 B.C.E.) and the confrontations of TA'O II (Sekenenré; Djehuti'o) (d. 1555 B.C.E.) of the Seventeenth Dynasty (1640–1550 B.C.E.) with APOPHIS (1585–1553 B.C.E.) of the Fifteenth Dynasty, starting the war against the Hyksos. Also included is a copy of the Poem of PENTAUR, the account of Ramesses II's battle of KADESH. The *SATIRE ON TRADES* is part of the accounts and literary texts.

The Sallier Papyri are in the British Museum in London. Papyrus IV, for example, dating to the 56th regnal year of Ramesses II, is long and composed over an earlier text, with exercises, notes, and memorabilia on the verso. A CALENDAR of lucky and unlucky days is part of the material in this papyrus.

See also QUARREL OF APOPHIS AND SEKENENRÉ.

Salt Papyrus   This is an Egyptian account from the Nineteenth Dynasty (1307–1196 B.C.E.), discovered in DEIR EL-MEDINA. A petition from a worker named Amenakhte is included in this document. He wrote about another worker, Paneb, and his numerous crimes, expecting some sort of redress in the local court system.

See also "THE ELOQUENT PEASANT" OF HERAKLEOPOLIS."; LAW.

Samto-wetefnakht   (fl. seventh century B.C.E.) *trade and mayoral official of the Twenty-sixth Dynasty* He served PSAMMETICHUS I (r. 664–610 B.C.E.) as the mayor of HERAKLEOPOLIS and as "the master of shipping." His family had a firm grip on the Nile TRADE. When NITOCRIS (2), the princess of the royal house, sailed to Thebes to be adopted as the GOD'S WIFE OF AMUN, or Divine Adoratrice of Amun, she traveled on one of Samto-wetefnakht's ships.

Sanakhte   *See* NEBKA.

Sanctuary of Ptah   It was a site at Thebes, on the western shore between DEIR EL-MEDINA and the VALLEY OF THE QUEENS, dedicated to the god PTAH. Small shrines and votive stelae honoring Ptah were erected in this district by the pharaohs of the Nineteenth Dynasty (1307–1196 B.C.E.) and the Twentieth Dynasty (1196–1070 B.C.E.).

Saqqara   A site west of MEMPHIS on the edge of the LIBYAN DESERT, Saqqara was part of the necropolis area of the capital. The site contains important historical and archaeological monuments, including the STEP PYRAMID of Third Dynasty ruler DJOSER (r. 2630–2611 B.C.E.), and extends from ABU ROWASH to MEIDUM. This necropolis was named after the god Sokar of Memphis, a deity of the dead. (It has also been proposed that the name is derived from the Beni Saqqar, a local Bedouin tribe.) Holding 4,000 years of building projects by the Egyptians, Saqqara is one of the oldest and most elaborately structured areas in the Nile Valley.

SITE DESCRIPTION

Designed as a miniature city, the sacred burial place of Saqqara holds temples, tombs, and underground galleries. It is dominated by the Step Pyramid, which is enclosed in a mile-long wall that stood more than 30 feet high. The Step Pyramid was designed by IMHOTEP, the VIZIER of Djoser, as an advanced mastaba tomb, with six separate mastaba tombs placed one on top of another to form a pyramid. The six tiers rose almost 200 feet on a 500-foot base, hence the tomb's name.

Mastaba tombs were elongated pits covered by a formation that resembles a bench, or *mastaba*, the Arabic word for bench. While providing a distinguished tomb appearance, the masataba burials horrified the mortuary priests when they opened a few tombs to study the condition of the remains. Burials of commoners in the desert sands assured that the corpse would be preserved. (The heat and the sand dehydrated the human flesh and protected it.) The mastaba tomb conditions, however, corrupted the buried remains quickly. Once this was recognized, mortuary rituals were changed and the mummification processes were soon introduced.

Saqqara was used as a burial ground from Early Dynastic times. Archaeologists discovered hieroglyphs depicting the name of NARMER—the unifier of the Two Kingdoms (Upper and Lower Egypt) and the father of AHA (Menes), the founder of the First Dynasty (2920–2770 B.C.E.)—in a chamber under the Step Pyramid. A mastaba-style tomb, dating to the reign of Aha, was also uncovered. On the eastern edge of Saqqara, near ABUSIR, a line of noble mastabas dating to the First Dynasty have been excavated. They were made of sun-dried bricks and decorated in the palace facade style, a popular style at the time also found at ABYDOS that imitated the buttresses and columns of mud-brick royal palaces. These mastabas had chambers and a core. The first cult-of-the-dead design appeared on these tombs at the close of the First Dynasty. Tombs from the Second Dynasty (2770–2649 B.C.E.) were found to the west of the original tombs. Pharaohs were buried at Saqqara at the beginning of the Second Dynasty.

The Third Dynasty Step Pyramid opened an entirely new era in the mortuary rituals and in the mortuary monuments of ancient Egypt, marking the first step toward the immense pyramids that became a hallmark of the next centuries and enduring symbols of ancient Egypt. All of the pharaohs of the Old Kingdom (2575–2134 B.C.E.) had tombs positioned north of the Step Pyramid. The necropolis for the mummified remains of sacred APIS bulls, called SERAPEUM (1), were also located there. Other tombs have been discovered as well, including the Fifth Dynasty pyramid of Unis (r. 2356–2323 B.C.E.) and Twenty-seventh Dynasty Persian shaft tombs; some date to as late as the Greco-Roman times.

CONSTRUCTION

The Step Pyramid is the oldest stone structure of its size in the world. Six different plans were used in its construction. The Step Pyramid was surrounded by *temenos* walls, a colonnaded entrance, *heb-sed* courts for rituals, chapels, magazines for provisions, and offering temples. The compound held buildings requested by Djoser or believed by Imhotep to be proper for the pharaoh's reign. The Step Pyramid was also provided with a SERDAB, an underground chamber that contained a statue of Djoser. Constructed at the statue's eye level was a slot so that Djoser could watch ceremonies in his honor.

The pyramid complex of SEKHEMKHET (r. 2611–2601 B.C.E.) of the Third Dynasty is located southwest of the Step Pyramid. It includes an unfinished step pyramid, containing an unused alabaster sarcophagus. A wooden sarcophagus holding the remains of a small child was discovered there as well. A few other surviving traces of enclosure walls at the western side of the Saqqara necropolis, including the so-called Great Enclosure (currently being investigated by a team from the Royal Museum of Scotland), suggest that additional Third Dynasty rulers probably began to erect similar monuments.

Some tombs from the Fourth Dynasty (2575–2465 B.C.E.) are located in the southern section of Saqqara, including the tomb of SHEPSESKHAF (r. 2472–2467 B.C.E.), now called MASTABA EL-FARA'UN. This tomb is fashioned

The complex at Saqqara of the Step Pyramid of Djoser, a pharaoh of the Third Dynasty; mortuary structures and storage areas surround the pyramid, using the palace facade design. *(Courtesy Steve Beikirch)*

in the shape of a giant sarcophagus, with corridors, ramps, and a separate chamber. The mortuary temple has terraces and pillared halls.

Yet another complex in Saqqara belongs to Fifth Dynasty (2465–2323 B.C.E.) founder USERKHAF (r. 2465–2458 B.C.E.). The pyramid, located in the northeast corner of Djoser's complex of the Step Pyramid, was called "Pure Are the Places of Userkhaf." Modern names for the tomb include the "Scratched Pyramid" and "El-Harem el-Mekharbesh." It was constructed out of limestone, faced with higher quality Tureh stone. Only ruins remain, surrounded by a *temenos* wall, a paved causeway, and a portico with red granite columns. The mastaba of AKHETHOTEP and PTAH-HOTEP (2) is located close by.

The pyramidal complex of IZEZI (Djedkaré) (r. 2388–2356 B.C.E.), located in the southern part next to the tomb of Pepi I, bears Izezi's name, and the pyramid was called "Izezi Is Beautiful." A vestibule opens into a passage that leads to a burial chamber and antechamber; the limestone slab roof is pitched at an angle. Within the burial chamber, a black basalt sarcophagus and fragments of a mummy were also discovered. The mortuary temple of Izezi was destroyed by the Eighteenth Dynasty (1550–1307 B.C.E.) burial sites. This temple had beautiful reliefs and statues of animals. A smaller queen's pyramid is part of the complex.

The pyramidal complex of Unis includes a long causeway leading to the mortuary temple and to a valley temple. This complex was fashioned out of limestone slabs and is designed to follow the general terrain. Carved scenes of daily life decorate the causeway, and the ceiling was starred. The mortuary temple has a granite gateway and inscriptions. The floors are alabaster, with limestone walls and granite columns. A partial inscription of the mortuary temple states that Prince KHA'EMWESET (1), a son of RAMESSES II (r. 1290–1224 B.C.E.), restored the site in the Nineteenth Dynasty (1307–1196 B.C.E.). The pyramid of Unis, called "Beautiful Are the Places of Unis," was also fashioned out of limestone and encased in Tureh stone. A limestone plug originally sealed the pyramid at ground level. A corridor leads to a vestibule and portcullises, connected to another corridor and antechamber and a burial chamber. A black granite SARCOPHAGUS was discovered in this chamber, which had alabaster and limestone walls that were painted blue and inscribed with the PYRAMID TEXTS. The valley temple of Unis is now partially hidden by a modern access road. This complex is also believed to have covered earlier gravesites. Near Unis's pyramid the graves of his family were erected as well. The tombs of queens KHENUT and NEBET were erected north of the funerary temple. A relief depicts Khenut in a seated position, smelling a LOTUS. Unis's daughter, Idut, was buried nearby in a tomb originally fashioned for the viceroy of the reign, Ihuy. Other sites, including the Tomb of the Birds, are also in the area.

Also near these complexes are tombs of prominent Egyptian officials of several historical periods. NIANKH-AMUN and Khnumhotep were buried in a mastaba called the "Tomb of the Hairdressers" or the "Tomb of the Two Brothers." MERERUKA's mastaba, shared with his wife and son, and the tomb of KAGEMNI are near the pyramid of TETI (2323–2291 B.C.E.). Beyond that is the Street of Tombs and the mastaba of Ti.

The pyramidal complex of Teti of the Sixth Dynasty (2323–2150 B.C.E.) overlooks the scene on the edge of the plateau of Saqqara. The pyramid of Teti was called "the Place of Teti, Son of Ré, Is Enduring Forever." The structure was faced with limestone, and the entrance was blocked by a chapel that was added later and by a sloping passage. The burial chamber contained a wooden sarcophagus and the ceiling was painted blue and decorated with stars. The walls were inscribed with the Pyramid Texts. A mortuary temple contained niches and a small sanctuary and was set against the face of the pyramid. Teti's cult flourished for centuries at this complex. The small pyramids of Queens IPUT (1) and KAWIT (1) are located beside his pyramid.

In the southern section of Saqqara, the pyramidal complex of PEPI I (r. 2289–2255 B.C.E.) is in ruins. The pyramid collapsed, destroying a black basalt sarcophagus. A rose granite canopic chest was also destroyed, along with alabaster jars. The Pyramid Texts used as decorations are particularly beautiful in surviving corridors and in the burial chamber, which is painted green.

The pyramid of MERENRÉ I (r. 2255–2246 B.C.E.) is located nearby, and the unfinished pyramid shows ancient signs of vandalism. A black basalt sarcophagus contained a mummy, but it was not Merenré I. Limestone statues of prisoners taken by Merenré I's military campaigns, or from earlier battles, were discovered there.

ARCHAEOLOGY

Saqqara became one of the most important archaeological sites in all of Egypt. With its wide-ranging tombs and architecture it is a crucial place of study for the entire religious and political history of Egypt.

The scientists who accompanied Napoleon Bonaparte (1769–1821) on his campaign to Egypt in 1798—the same experts who discovered the Rosetta Stone and visited thousands of sites in the Nile Valley—also arrived at Saqqara. Their work was cursory, but the descriptions they included in their records inspired generations of later archaeologists. They also placed Saqqara on the map as a place worth visiting, which, unfortunately, encouraged looting of the site.

The first serious effort at excavation was undertaken by the German archaeologist Karl Lepsius, starting in 1842. He was followed in 1851 by Auguste Mariette, from France, who discovered the Serapeum, the necropolis erected for the burial of the sacred Apis bulls in Saqqara. In 1905, the British Egyptologist James Edward Quibell was named chief inspector at Saqqara and established regular schedules and a scientific approach to excavations. Quibell was succeeded by Cecil Mallaby Firth, who supervised the work around the Djoser pyramid for several decades in the early 20th century until his death in 1931. He was assisted from 1926 by the remarkable French archaeologist Jean-Philippe Lauer, who labored at Saqqara for the next 75 years until his death in 2001.

In 1935, the British Egyptologist Walter Bryan Emery became supervisor. He remained at Saqqara until 1939, when the start of World War II interrupted the work. After the war, he returned to Egypt and served at Saqqara from 1953 to 1956 and then again in 1964, at which time he made the important discovery of the sacred animals necropolis, which included the mummified remains of thousands of animals, including baboons, dogs, cats, and birds.

The later half of the 20th century witnessed numerous teams of international archaeologists working across the entire Saqqara site, including teams from Australia, France, Poland, and the Netherlands. Dutch archaeologists have worked at the site since 1975. Among the most significant of recent finds are the discovery by Zakaria Goneim of the unfinished step pyramid of Sekhemkhet, and the excavation of New Kingdom tombs by a team from Cairo University in the area near the Monastery of Apa Jeremias.

In 2010 tombs of various queens were opened, including that of Queen Behenu, possibly a consort of Pepi I (r. 2289–2255 B.C.E.); the walls of her tomb were covered with Pyramid Texts. The site at Saqqara was looted in 2011 during the overthrow of Hosni Mubarak. Once the teams are able to return to their excavations they will assess the amount of damage and potential loss.

Saqqara Table This is a royal relief discovered in the tomb of TJUENEROY, or Thuneroi, a scribe in the court of Ramesses II (r. 1290–1224 B.C.E.). The cartouches of 57 or 58 rulers of Egypt were inscribed in TJUENEROY's tomb, all listed as pharaohs honored by RAMESSES II.

See also KING LISTS.

sarcophagus They are the stone receptacles for the mummified remains of ancient Egyptians, from the Greek term meaning "eater of flesh." The Greek term supposedly referred to a type of limestone that was believed to dissolve human remains. Stone sarcophagi used in the Fifth Dynasty (2465–2323 B.C.E.) had intricate patterns resembling the facades of the palaces of the time, and these patterns sometimes included

A rendering of a sarcophagus and accompanying regalia in a tomb at Thebes *(Hulton Archive)*

painted replicas of the same colored materials. These sarcophagi were so heavy and large that they had to be placed inside the burial chambers before funerals because of the labor involved in setting them in place. It is believed that the sarcophagus constructed for KHUFU (Cheops) (r. 2551–2528 B.C.E.) was actually incorporated into the pyramid in the process of constructing that monument.

Stone sarcophagi became rare by the Middle Kingdom (2040–1640 B.C.E.) and were used exclusively for royal or noble burials. Their decorations were austere, but some, such as the ones discovered in DEIR EL-BAHRI at Thebes, in the mortuary complex of MENTUHOTEP II (r. 2061–2010 B.C.E.), were discovered with painted reliefs. The New Kingdom (1550–1070 B.C.E.) form of the sarcophagus was either rectangular or anthropoid. The sarcophagi used for nonroyal persons as early as the Eighteenth Dynasty and in the Ramessid Dynasties sometimes represented the deceased in daily attire. The royal sarcophagi were rectangular, carved with the figures of deities and embellished with bands of religious texts.

At the start of the Nineteenth Dynasty in 1307 B.C.E., the custom developed of carving the form of the king in high relief on the outer lid. The inner and outer surfaces were painted with mortuary texts. Sometimes a picture of the goddess NUT, the sky deity, lined the interior. With the close of the New Kingdom in 1070 B.C.E., the sarcophagi lost popularity until after 650 B.C.E., when the royal families again adopted their use. They continued to hold the remains of the pharaohs during the Ptolemaic Period (304–30 B.C.E.) and even in later eras.

See also COFFINS; MORTUARY RITUALS.

Sardinians   *See* SEA PEOPLES, DEFEAT OF THE.

Sarenput (fl. 20th century B.C.E.) *military official of the Twelfth Dynasty*
He served SENWOSRET I (r. 1971–1926 B.C.E.) and AMEN-EMHET II (r. 1929–1892 B.C.E.) as a mayor and then as a commander of a southern frontier garrison. He also served as the chief priest of the cults of the gods KHNUM

and SATET. Sarenput was buried at ASWAN in an elaborate tomb. The reliefs in his tomb depict him at a sports event, fishing on the Nile, and walking with his favorite DOG.

Satet (Satis) She was an Egyptian goddess hailed as the "Mistress of the ELEPHANTINE." Originally a goddess of the hunt, Satet became patroness of the Nile River's inundations and was associated with the first cataract of the Nile, south of ASWAN. SENWOSRET III (r. 1878–1841 B.C.E.) built a canal in her honor.

Satet's cult dates to ca. 2900 B.C.E. on Elephantine Island. Her temple started as a rock niche there, assuming magnificence over the centuries. Also called "She Who Runs Like an Arrow," Satet was a consort of the god KHNUM and the mother of ANUKIS. She was worshipped as the patroness of the southern frontier, the one who "spread the life-giving waters of the Nile." Upper Egypt was sometimes called Ta-Satet, "the Land of Satet."

Also associated with protecting the Egyptians in war, Satet carried arrows to slay the nation's enemies. The PYRAMID TEXTS list her as the purificator of the deceased, and her name was found in the SAQQARA necropolis. She was portrayed as a woman wearing the white crown of Upper Egypt and carrying a bow and arrows or an *ankh*. In some depictions, the white crown on her head had antelope horns extending on either side. She was also shown wearing the vulture headdress, normally reserved to queens who had given birth to heirs. Satet's original home was Sehel Island. She may originally have been a Nubian goddess.

Satire on Trades A Middle Kingdom (2040–1640 B.C.E.) literary text also called "the Instruction of Dua-Khety" (or Duaf), the text was discovered in the SALLIER PAPYRUS II, ANASTASI PAPYRUS VII, and on OSTRACA and boards. The satire stresses the disadvantages of being stone workers, farmers, carpenters, etc., especially when compared to the life of a SCRIBE, which is called "the path of the god," a way of attaining honor, knowledge, and rank. The *Satire on Trades* is also listed as the "Hymn of Praise of Learning." It is attributed to one Achtoes, composed for his son, Pepi. The extant versions may be based on earlier renditions, and the work mentions a pre-Middle Kingdom text that was used as a copying exercise.

See also LITERATURE.

Satirical Papyrus This is a document dating to the Twentieth Dynasty (1196–1070 B.C.E.), a collection of artistic works satirizing the state of the nation during the reigns of the last Ramessid kings. Charming animals demonstrate the peculiar reversal of roles taking place in that particular era. A mouse is being shown pampered and served by cats. A baby mouse is depicted in the arms of a loving cat nurse. As the social order of the nation eroded, the satirical drawings served as a warning and as an incisive commentary on the breakdown of society. The Satirical Papyrus is now in the Egyptian Museum in Cairo.

Satkamose (fl. 16th century B.C.E.) *royal woman of the Eighteenth Dynasty*
She was a consort of AMENHOTEP I (r. 1525–1504 B.C.E.) but a secondary queen, as AH'HOTEP (2) was the Great Wife. Satkamose did not give birth to the heir. She was possibly the royal daughter of TA'O II (Sekenenré; Djehuti'o) (d. 1555 B.C.E.) and Queen AH'HOTEP (1).

Satrap Stela This monument was erected by PTOLEMY I SOTER (r. 304–284 B.C.E.) in 311 B.C.E. to announce his role in freeing Egypt from the Persian domination. Ptolemy I linked his own name to a native Egyptian, KHABABASH, who led a doomed insurrection against the Persians in 338. Ptolemy I was the satrap, or governor, of Egypt when he erected the STELA, serving ALEXANDER III THE GREAT's successors. In time he would assume the throne in his own right.

See also REBELS OF EGYPT.

sboyet This was the ancient Egyptian term for literature as an instructional or reforming instrument. Didactic texts come under this description, the instructions, adages, or admonitions of sages in the various historical periods. Such writings played an important role in the moral and social development of the nation. The *sboyet* were revered and copied by the scribes of each new generation on the Nile, never considered irrelevant.

See also "TIME OF THE GODS."

scarab It is the form of a beetle, *Scarabeus sacer* or *Scarabeus harabas*, and associated with the cult of the god RÉ. The beetle pushes a ball of dung into a hole and lays eggs in the matter, thus providing its young with security and food. This action was revered as Ré's movement across the sky. The first flight of newly hatched scarab beetles also mirrored Ré's rising. The scarab personified Khepri as well, the aspect of Re seen at dawn.

Called *kheprar*, the scarab had no wings or legs in the early depictions, which date as early as the Old Kingdom (2575–2134 B.C.E.), but then became more stylized and detailed. Scarabs were fashioned out of stone-glazed earthenware, stones, and gems. When made of blue faience, they were used as amulets and attached to the torso wrappings of mummies. They also formed an amulet of the heart and were composed of large basalt designs during the New Kingdom (1550–1070 B.C.E.). Winged scarabs were also popular in mortuary rituals.

During the reign of TUTHMOSIS III (1479–1425 B.C.E.), the ruler's cartouche was carved into the backs of scarabs. AMENHOTEP III (r. 1391–1353 B.C.E.) also used large scarabs as commemoratives of his marriage to Queen

TIYE (1). The scarab became one of the most popular symbols and was used in pendants, decorative designs, and jewelry, while retaining its cultic significance and mortuary connotations. Another plainer version was also used, called scaraboids.

scepter This was an ancient Egyptian royal insignia, depicting the time-honored traditions in each new reign. Called the *hekat* when formed as a shepherd's CROOK, the scepter represented the early agricultural beginnings of the land and designated the PHARAOH as the shepherd of humans, called "the flocks of god." When the scepter was in the form of a *waset,* a carved emblem, it represented the god SET and formed another insignia of ruling. Yet another type of scepter was the *SEKHEM,* attributed to the god OSIRIS and kept at ABYDOS. This scepter had a golden face at the top and denoted Osiris's powers.

School Boy Texts They were written materials used in the teaching institutions of Egypt as exercises in copying. Found on OSTRACA and in some surviving papyri, these texts were traditional, maintaining the tone and style of the original documents from the past. They were designed to acquaint students of each new generation with didactic literature and with the literary compositions of earlier eras. Most urged the young Egyptian males to become scribes.

science and technology A pragmatic people who nonetheless celebrated a bevy of deities and a god-pharaoh, the Egyptians did not delve into scientific studies unless such endeavors provided practical results or alleviated a need or crisis. They used science and technology only as necessary pursuits, used to perpetuate their civilization on the Nile.

MEDICINE

Medicine made Egypt famous throughout the world. Originally medicine in the Nile Valley was a combination of magical spells, amulets, and the use of animal wastes, but priest-physicians from certain temple cults began studying the human body in order to alleviate the illnesses and physical disabilities that they saw afflicting the people. These priests were not connected to mortuary rituals or mummification at the *PER-NEFER,* the House of Beauty, where mummification rituals took place. Their cultic knowledge and training was quite distinct from the practice of medicine, and they were somewhat isolated in Egyptian society as a result.

IMHOTEP, who built the STEP PYRAMID for DJOSER (r. 2630–2611 B.C.E.), pioneered the science. He wrote a book about symptoms, diagnoses, and treatments and included a unique section on how the physician could determine whether he was qualified to undertake such care. The work became the standard for apprentice phy-

sicians. Imhotep's work was used as a reference for later physicians but has never been discovered by archaeologists. Others followed and the *PER-ANKH,* the House of Life, became research centers throughout the land. A wide-ranging pharmaceutical program, trauma care, and surgery resulted from their efforts.

Rulers across the world in all eras requested the gift of a priest-physician from the various pharaohs. These physicians were also in service at every royal construction site, accompanying royal trade expeditions and the military forces on campaigns. When the Greeks visited Egypt and later accompanied ALEXANDER THE GREAT (r. 332–323 B.C.E.) into the Nile Valley in 332 B.C.E., they were amazed by the medical knowledge available in Egypt. The EDWIN SMITH PAPYRUS and other surviving papyri indicate the systematized programs adapted in medicine over the early decades and then through the various historical periods.

MATHEMATICS

The Egyptians were not interested in mathematics as a science until the Ptolemaic Period (304–30 B.C.E.). However, in the early eras, the builders of the pyramids, monuments, temples, and fortresses used mathematics to manage their projects. The RHIND PAPYRUS, dating to the Seventeenth Dynasty (1640–1550 B.C.E.), was written by a scribe at THEBES. The papyrus contains notations regarding fractions, calculus, and other forms of math. Certainly the architects and builders of the pharaohs had to have knowledge of such concepts, including such measurements as right angles.

In addition, the Nile River demanded calculations every year. When the Nile flooded, inspectors at Aswan's Nilometer—a large structure that had pools and measuring poles—analyzed the water levels so that some prediction could be made about the height of the river when it passed certain areas to the north. Measuring the rise in the water level at ASWAN, the inspectors had to make calculations concerning the elevations of cities, monuments, and farmlands northward. They also had to calculate how high the water would be when it reached each geographic location. Some would see heavy inundations because of their location, while others would see milder floods. Messengers carrying word of what each location could expect boarded small ships and sped northward so that each vital region could prepare properly.

NATURAL SCIENCES AND EXPLORATION
Astronomy

Like other early civilizations, the Egyptians studied the night skies and charted the movement of stars and planets. The priest-astronomers noted the beauty, order, and harmony of the celestial bodies and taught the people of the Nile Valley that societies on the earth had to mirror the heavens if they were to survive. This philosophical system, called MA'AT, guided Egypt throughout its historical periods.

On the practical side, astronomy was used to fashion a concept of time and season. Ancient Egyptians quickly realized that the appearance in the night sky of Sirius, the Dog Star, which they called Sopdu, signaled the coming floods of the Nile across the land. Preparations began immediately to direct the flooding where possible and to evacuate the areas that would be inundated. The Egyptian CALENDAR also evolved from this nightly study, as did the Sothic Cycle, which did not always coincide with the solar cycle. In addition to a calendar, the Egyptians developed maps and illustrations of heavenly beings, with symbols representing the various divine personages involved. The maps eventually adorned the ceilings of tombs.

NAKHT (2), a trusted court astronomer serving TUTHMOSIS IV (r. 1401–1391 B.C.E.), was also the chief steward of granaries and vineyards and combined his experience in an innovative chart. Noticing the clear signals evident in the movement of the stars and planets, he carefully developed a method by which the changes would give advance warnings to begin inundation trenches and sluices to capture as much Nile water as possible, providing the time needed for such labor.

Geology

The bureaucratic and expedition leaders who went across the Nile Valley into NUBIA (modern Sudan, below Aswan) and the Sinai Peninsula in search of necessary resources probably had years of experience rather than scholarly study. They trekked across wastelands in search of precious stones and vital minerals and in time were able to collect what they needed. The Egyptians learned from their observations and from probing into the surfaces of various regions. The great deposits of limestone, granite, quartz, sandstone, and other needed materials were quickly identified, and a geological map that identified such repositories was developed and in use during the New Kingdom (1550–1070 B.C.E.). Gold mines were opened, and precious stones were harvested with systematic processes according to the personnel available at the time.

BUILDING TECHNIQUES AND MATERIALS
Dams, Canals, and Water Control

The channels of the Nile in the DELTA region in Lower Egypt framed robust tracts of lands for crops; the FAIYUM, in the central part of the country, offered an endless array of grains, and the plains served large herds of animals. In order to sustain this agricultural success, hydraulic power was applied for irrigation and water resource areas were maintained. The BAHR YUSUF, a stream that flowed out of the Nile and into the Faiyum, was dammed early on so that the Nile water would enter the Faiyum but have no exit route.

Water wheels, called the SHADUF, and the use of dikes and trenches made organized irrigation possible as the river water could be lifted from the main flow and fed into a tapestry of low ditches that fed the crops on either side. An example of the Egyptian ability to direct Nile waters is MALKATA, the pleasure palace of AMENHOTEP III (r. 1391–1353 B.C.E.). This palace was built on the western shore of the Nile, near Medinet Habu, south of Thebes (modern Luxor) as a gift for Amenhotep III on the occasion of his *heb-sed*, his royal anniversary of coronation. A miniature royal city, Malkata was provided with an artificial lake. The western shore site included a harbor that was constructed in a T-shape and filled with river water that was then blocked from exiting. The harbor, completed in just two weeks, is still visible on the site. Malkata became "the House of Eternal Rejoicing."

Egyptians had been working to control the course of the Nile River since the beginning of their history. When AHA (Menes) founded Egypt in 2920 B.C.E., he set up a series of dams and cleared a vast portion of flat land of Nile water to create MEMPHIS, the first capital of the Upper and Lower Kingdoms, as Egypt was called. Later, in Nubia, SENWOSRET III (r. 1878–1841 B.C.E.) faced the cataracts of the Nile. These cataracts had vast rapids that destroyed any boats trying to navigate there. Senwosret III's military units built large passageways for ships alongside the cataracts. These passageways were canals into which the Nile was allowed to pass, thus giving the ships an alternate route past the cataracts. The garrisoned troops at the various fortresses positioned at the cataracts maintained the canals for emergencies. The pharaohs following Senwosret III refurbished the canals when they started their own campaigns.

Boats and Boat Building

In order to maintain their remarkable building projects, the Egyptians had to be able to move massive stone components, sometimes from long distances. They did not have the wheel until the HYKSOS introduced the chariot and other inventions around 1660 B.C.E. On land the Egyptians used sledges and manpower. On the water they used barges and other vessels.

When archaeologists discovered the boat of KHUFU (Cheops) (r. 2551–2528 B.C.E.) in a vast stone structure buried beside the Great Pyramid in 1954, they were able to study the ingenious methods by which ships of all size were constructed in the Nile Valley. Only wood and fiber ropes held the vessel secure. Khufu's boat, actually part of his mortuary ritual, is 14 stories high, and constructed out of precious woods. In the holy city of ABYDOS, the sacred necropolis of Egypt, an astounding number of such boats were discovered buried in a field.

Kuser, on the Red Sea, became a ship-building center, where vessels were made and equipped for expeditions to a land called PUNT, which has not yet been identified but is believed to have been modern Ethiopia. In time, Egypt had a large navy, with the main facility at PERU-NEFER, near Memphis. TUTHMOSIS III (r. 1479–1425 B.C.E.), while set aside by Hatshepsut, served as the commander of the naval base.

Stonemasonry

Maintaining the momentum in building projects, the Egyptians invented the obelisk—the slender, towering pieces of rock crowned by the cultic insignia called the BENBEN. Obelisks were cut out of great formations of stone by workers who sat for weeks using stone wedges to wear down the stone. The obelisks were not blocks of stone mounted one on top of the other but towered as a single insignia.

The columns of Karnak and Thebes, and the chapels, statues, and pylons, were all fashioned out of stone. The walls of such religious enclaves were inscribed with religious glyphs or with accounts of pharaonic events. The stonemasons of Egypt were frequently involved in creating monuments or tombs. DEIR EL-MEDINA, a village on the western shore of the Nile at Thebes, housed such builders, artisans, and laborers. They were the driving force behind the amazing tombs in the VALLEY OF THE KINGS and the VALLEY OF THE QUEENS.

Metallurgy and Metals

The artistry of metallurgy was also practiced by the Egyptians, who discovered early on that their sacred symbols, set in gold and jewels, could be used in the growing trade efforts. The number of products exported grew with each passing decade. For centuries the royals of the Nile wore magnificent gold collars, necklaces, and bracelets. Tombs still hold fragments of grave goods made of precious metals that attest to the powers of the metalworkers on the Nile. Certainly the golden mask of TUT'ANKHAMUN (r. 1333–1323 B.C.E.) is world renowned, as are many other gold and silver funerary pieces. Museums around the world display similar relics of long-dead pharaohs and queens.

See also ASTRONOMY; BOATS; HEALTH AND DISEASE.

Further reading: Boyer, Carl B. History of Mathematics. Princeton: Princeton University Press, 1985; Clagett, Marshall. Ancient Egyptian Science: A Source Book. Volume 3: Ancient Egyptian Mathematics. Philadelphia: American Philosophical Society, 1999; David, Rosalie. Handbook to Life in Ancient Egypt, Revised Edition. New York: Facts On File, 2003; Gillings, Richard J. Mathematics in the Time of the Pharaohs. Cambridge: MIT Press, 1972; Kemp, Barry J. Ancient Egypt: Anatomy of a Civilization. London: Routledge, 1989; Nicholson, Paul T., and Ian Shaw, eds. Ancient Egyptian Materials and Technology. Cambridge: Cambridge University Press, 2000; Peet, Thomas Eric. The Rhind Mathematical Papyrus, British Museum 10057 and 10058. London: Hodder & Stoughton, 1923; Robins, R. Gay, and Charles C. D. Shute. The Rhind Mathematical Papyrus: An Ancient Egyptian Text. London: British Museum, 1987; Rossi, Corinna. Architecture and Mathematics in Ancient Egypt. Cambridge: Cambridge University Press, 2007; Scheel, Bernd. Egyptian Metalworking and Tools. Haverfordwest: Shire Publications, 1989.

scorpion A venomous arachnid symbolizing the goddess SELKET and associated with the cult of OSIRIS-ISIS-HORUS. Seven giant scorpions accompanied the goddess Isis as her guardians. One stung the infant Horus, according to cultic traditions. The Egyptians believed that scorpions killed only men, out of reverence for Isis.

Scorpion I (Pe; Zekhen; Ip) (fl. ca. 31st century B.C.E.) *ruler of the so-called Dynasty 0 of Egypt*
Scorpion I was an Upper Egyptian ruler who waged war in the southern and northern regions of Egypt, thus beginning the process of its unification as early as ca. 3050 B.C.E. He reportedly unified Upper Egypt and the areas north to around modern Cairo. After his campaigns Scorpion I made the city of THINIS (also known as This) his capital and started the Thinite dynasty that would bring NARMER (fl. ca. 3000 B.C.E.) to power.

BIOGRAPHY

Scorpion I was the first of two kings of Upper Egypt, his name possibly referring to Selket, the scorpion goddess of Egypt. Although originally residing and holding court in HIERAKONPOLIS, where he was called Ip, Scorpion I ultimately made his capital Thinis, possibly in a logistical move to prepare for a northern march to the Delta. In addition to Hierakonpolis and Thinis, his name has also been found in TUREH, in TARKHAN, and in Cairo suburbs.

Once considered a legendary figure of the Predynastic Period, which the Egyptians called "the Time of the Gods," Scorpion I was determined to have been a historical figure chiefly through the excavation of a tomb, U-j, at Abydos. Despite the fact that it had been looted, this tomb is considered a strong candidate for his final resting place. Verification was provided in 2008 when Dr. John Darnell of Yale University studied the graffiti carved into rock formations in the southern Egyptian desert to the west of the Nile and found that these crude hieroglyphs describe Scorpion I as victorious in battle, perhaps commemorating an actual event or providing an allegorical account of good vanquishing evil in his reign.

Although not much is known about Scorpion I, the Scorpion MACEHEAD, which is housed at the Ashmolean Museum at Oxford University in England, serves as a historical text. Maceheads were early Egyptian weapons, though it is believed the Scorpion Macehead was only used for ceremonial purposes, as it was too large to be employed in battle. Highly decorated, this macehead depicts Scorpion I as a king with the white CROWN of Upper Egypt. He wears a kilt and a belted loincloth to which a bull's tail, a symbol of strength, is attached. Scorpion I is shown digging a canal with a hoe. Before him a man fills a basket with earth, while others water a potted palm. Fashioned out of limestone, the Scorpion Macehead was found at Hierakonpolis. Another artifact, the Scorpion Palette—a large instrument used for grinding antimony—is also viewed as a historical document. On it Scorpion I is portrayed as a falcon and a lion, either destroying seven cities in the Delta or destroying one city seven times.

Scorpion's U-j. tomb in Abydos was fashioned in the MASTABA style, as a raised mound in a form resembling a bench. Dug deep into the earth, it contains 12 separate chambers. No remains were found in the burial chamber (although Scorpion I was reportedly buried there at one time), but a vast number of elaborate grave goods were in the tomb upon discovery. Archaeologists discovered some wine jars, and an ivory crook, the symbol of the ruler, was also found. Narrow doors were included in the tomb's architectural design, apparently to allow the spirit of Scorpion I to wander freely within the enclosure. The palace facade style, an architectural design, was used on the outer part of the tomb. (Rulers following Scorpion I continued using this design in their own tombs.) The tomb contained boxes and objects carved of ivory. Seven of the boxes contained linens. The hieroglyphs on the labels and tags of the grave goods name many of the cities and towns in Egypt during Scorpion I's reign as well as note the foreign countries taking part in trade and tribute. Tablets discovered in the site indicate the number of linens and oils delivered to Scorpion, as well as taxes and the names of institutions of the period. These tablets indicate Scorpion I's power, which was recognized by the NOMARCHS, the leaders of provinces.

In addition to his tomb, archaeologists have discovered the remains of a temple dedicated to Scorpion I. Acacia poles were part of its design, standing five feet tall. A hall with 10-foot-high ceilings was also part of the structure, made with cedar wood walls daubed in red plaster. Archaeologists found niches and a sacred enclosure within. This temple was the first in the hypostyle design that would be used in all eras of Egyptian history.

HISTORICAL IMPACT

Scorpion I laid the framework for the rise of the First Dynasty when he made the city of Thinis his capital. Thinis would become home to the early unifiers of Egypt and a Thinite royal dynasty that would dominate for centuries.

The objects found in Scorpion I's tomb caused archaeologists to reevaluate what they had previously believed about early Egyptian culture. The wine jars discovered in Scorpion I's tomb in Abydos, the royal necropolis from the earliest eras, were among the first indications of ancient wine consumption. Archaeologists found wine residue lining these jars, along with herbs and other natural additives. The crook found is also of note. A derivation of the herding backgrounds of the first Egyptians, this symbol carried by Scorpion would also be carried by the pharaohs of the Nile Valley in the many dynasties to come. The most significant discovery linked to Scorpion I, however, was hieroglyphics. Once found, archaeologists realized that the oldest known Egyptian writing dates to Scorpion I's reign. Some believe, in fact, that Scorpion's Delta conquests prompted the use of hieroglyphs on account of the need to create written records. Regardless, the hieroglyphs discovered in Scorpion I's tomb indicate that writing was commonplace in Egypt much earlier than was formerly believed; the Egyptians were as advanced as, and may have even preceded, the Sumerian culture in the use of written language symbols.

Further reading: Midant-Reynes, Beatrix. *The Prehistory of Egypt: From the First Egyptians to the First Pharaohs.* London: Wiley-Blackwell, 2000; Wenke, Robert J. *The Ancient Egyptian State: The Origins of Egyptian Culture (c. 8000–2000 BC).* Cambridge: Cambridge University Press, 2009; Wilkinson, Toby. *Early Dynastic Egypt.* London: Routledge, 1999.

scribe It was the profession of the literate elite of ancient Egypt who assumed a variety of functions in the various historical periods in government and religious institutions. Some scribes achieved high rank and honors, and the profession was highly esteemed. In one ancient document the life of a scribe is called "the path of the god." Literacy was the prerequisite for any higher secular or religious office.

Scribes were exclusively men and were recruited from all classes of society, as literacy and loyalty were the two basic qualifications. They were educated by priests and encouraged to develop their skills in specialized record keeping or in temple and government affairs. Scribes were assigned to government or estate offices or to the various agencies of temples after receiving training in reading, writing, and the basic tenets of law, temple lore, and administrative procedures. They had to have command of nearly 800 hieroglyphs of Middle Egyptian, and the additional signs when they were added to the language in the Ramessid Period (1307–1070 B.C.E.).

Scribes were normally attached to the various temples they served, but in the New Kingdom (1550–1070 B.C.E.), when the religious complexes grew larger and more sophisticated, lay scribes were hired. Scribes were also required to have knowledge of the classic texts and mathematics. Initially they performed routine tasks, normally recordkeeping.

The best-known symbol of the scribe was his kit or palette, which contained slates, inks, smoothing stones for papyri, and reed brushes, which were kept firm by chewing the end of the fibers. The kits, regular cases with indentations on one side for small cakes of ink, were attached to a cord. The ink was fashioned out of lampblack or any carbonized material, mixed with gum and water by the scribe. Brushes were held in the center cavity of a box, which had small pieces of wood glued across the opening or a sliding cover to keep them in place. Brushes could be fine or heavy depending on their use and age.

In the larger temples, scribes worked as archivists or as librarians. They kept the census, recorded tax assessments, measured the rise of the Nile, and generally maintained the vast religious and government correspondence. Some accompanied military expeditions or local government officials to the mines and quarries, to record the annual findings there. Many important inscriptions and documents of the military exploits of the New Kingdom, especially those of TUTHMOSIS III (r. 1479–1425 B.C.E.) and RAMESSES II (r. 1290–1224 B.C.E.), were the work of scribes. They remained powerful even in the Roman Period, after 30 B.C.E.

Sea Peoples   *See* SEA PEOPLES, DEFEAT OF THE.

Sea Peoples, defeat of the (1186 B.C.E.)   The Sea Peoples were a confederation of various clans who were active as pirates and marauders in the Ramessid Period, the Ninteenth Dynasty (1307–1196 B.C.E.), and the Twentieth Dynasty (1196–1070 B.C.E.). RAMESSES II (r. 1290–1224 B.C.E.) sought a pact with the HITTITE ruler HATTUSILIS III in defense against these wide-ranging attackers, and MERENPTAH (r. 1224–1214 B.C.E.) also faced one contingent of them during his reign. During the reign of RAMESSES III (r. 1194–1163 B.C.E.), however, the Sea Peoples were joined by even more dangerous allies as they began a march on the Mediterranean world that would take countless lives and demolish capitals and territories that had flourished for centuries.

CONTEXT

According to records on the walls of MEDINET HABU at THEBES, the Sea Peoples were actually both a naval and land force. The boats of the Sea Peoples' flotilla were not only filled with veteran warriors but with entire families; these plunderers were accompanied by their wives and children wherever they went. The Sea Peoples included the Ekwesh, believed to be Greek Achaeans; Teresh, Anatolian sailors, possibly the Tyrrhenians; and Lukka, an Anatolian coastal people. Sailing with them were the Sherdana, probably a group of Sardinians; Shekelesh, identified as members of the Sicilian Siculi; Peleset, from Crete; and others not identified with certainty, including possibly the Kizzuwatna, Arzawa, Zakala, Alasiya, Tjeker, and Denyen. The MESHWESH, Libyans who were active in Egypt's

Delta, are also also listed on the walls of Medinet Habu.

The earliest Sea Peoples groups had fortified cities and worked in copper mines. Displaced by larger groups, the Sea Peoples turned to the nomadic life of traveling marauders, conquering CYPRUS and blockading Syrian ports. They began their first campaigns near their homelands, where the Mycenaean Greeks repulsed them. Later, having developed new tactics, the Sea Peoples attacked other nations, including the Hittites.

One of these Sea Peoples' groups, the Sherden Pirates, was on the Mediterranean coast during the New Kingdom (1550–1070 B.C.E.) and the Nineteenth Dynasty when they began raiding the Egyptian Delta with deadly force. A stela from TANIS stated, "None were able to stand before them."

EVENT

In Ramesses III's eighth regnal year, the Sea Peoples, including the Sherden Pirates, attacked Cilicia, CARCHEMISH, Palestine, Arzawa, CYPRUS, Amurru, and the HITTITES, and arrived in the Delta region with the Libyans as part of their armada. These marauders came by sea in ships, as well as by land in wooden carts with solid wheels, which contained their posessions and families and which were drawn across the deserts by humpback cattle. The Sea Peoples wore kilts and headdresses of feathers or pleated stiffened cloths. They carried spears, short swords, and round shields.

Ramesses III first encountered the Sea Peoples when they sought the safety of the Egyptian Nile after crop failures in the eastern Mediterranean region pushed them westward. In order to repel land and sea assaults, Ramesses III positioned his military units on the eastern border and then fortified the Nile branches in the Delta. By allowing the Sea Peoples to enter only certain Nile channels and then moving floating islands and debris behind them, Ramesses III trapped entire contingents, which allowed his naval units to annihilate those of the Sea Peoples. On land, the Sea Peoples' forces were met by the Egyptian cavalry.

The battles raged on, and the Sea Peoples faced devastating losses. Many were taken prisoner by Ramesses III's units, and eventually the invasion collapsed, as innumerable Sea Peoples perished. When the fighting ended, Ramesses III began to round up the survivors. As many of the Sea Peoples were able seamen and skilled navigators, Ramesses III recruited such persons into the Egyptian navy. Others he took as prisoners or made them slaves. Two groups of Sea Peoples were given special treatment, however. Carrying round shields and large swords, some of these buccaneers were employed as Ramesses III's personal guards, for which they received land grants in repayment. A second group, the Peleset, were moved into a vassal state in Palestine.

IMPACT

Although not much is known about the origins and eventual destinations of the Sea Peoples, they were famous in the ancient world. They plagued the eastern Mediterranean and created a power vacuum. Even after Ramesses III's victory, they were never truly subdued, fighting both for and against the Egyptians in subsequent years. The Peleset, who were sent to Palestine, were likey later known as the Philistines recorded in the Old Testament of the Bible, who destroyed the Hittite Empire.

Egypt withstood the assaults of the Sea Peoples, but the cost to the Nile Valley was lasting and damaging. Although Ramesses III was a valiant "shield of the nation" (a title by which the pharaohs of the Middle Kingdom were known), his resources were taxed far beyond their limit, and records suggest he did not hold the affection or respect of the Egyptians of his era. His administration may have held foreigners in positions of trust, a condition indicating he possibly lost the loyal devotion of the families of officials and faithful servants. Later a victim of a harem assassination plot, Ramesses III lived just long enough to convene a judicial procedure against the conspirators. The Sea Peoples were also known to have destroyed the great trading port of Ugarit, which Egyptian merchants and travelers often visited to trade.

The Ramessid Dynasty in place after Ramesses III's death was also affected by the lack of resources and plagued by a smallpox epidemic, familial treacheries, and a lack of resources. Although Egypt was successful in repelling the attacks of the Sea Peoples, the incursions probably hastened the slow decline of the imperial era of Egypt.

Further reading: Dothan, Trude, and Moshe Dothan. *People of the Sea: The Search for the Philistines.* N.Y.: Scribners, 1992; Oren, Eliezer. *The Sea Peoples and Their World: A Reassessment.* Philadelphia: University of Pennsylvania Press, 2000.

seasons   The designation of certain times of the year in Egypt, appearing in their written form in the Early Dynastic Period (2920–2575 B.C.E.), there were three seasons of the year, composed of four months each, with 30 days in each month. The symbol for the entire year was a sprouted bud, and the word for year was *renpet.* The year began in the season of AKHET, the time of the inundation of the Nile, starting approximately the third week of July according to modern calculations. *Akhet* was followed by PROYET (or *peret*), the time of sowing. The last season, SHOMU (or *shemu*), was the time of the harvest. Each season had its own festivals and cultic observations.

Seat of the First Occasion   This was the Egyptian term for a TEMPLE as the original site of the first creation and the designated god's entrance into the world. Each temple was deemed the actual location upon which the deity appeared for the first time and was celebrated annually as the cosmogonic source of life.

seb   This was a FESTIVAL in Egypt associated in many instances with harvests. The entire royal court attended celebrations in the fields for the festival, held near their residences or at certain designated sites. The festivals ended with the ruler and his retinue sailing on the Nile or on one of the SACRED LAKES of a temple.

See also SED.

Sebennytos (Tjebnutjer; Samannub)   This was a site on the left bank of the Damietta branch of the Nile, called Tjebnutjer by the Egyptians and now modern Samannub. MANETHO, the Ptolemaic Period historian, was a native of Sebennytos. A temple of a local deity was discovered on the site, and blocks bearing the name of NECTANEBO II (r. 360–343 B.C.E.) and Ptolemaic rulers were discovered there.

An ALTAR from the reign of AMENEMHET I (1991–1962 B.C.E.) and an Old Kingdom (2575–2134 B.C.E.) FALSE DOOR were found on the site. A shrine dating to NEPHRITES I (r. 399–393 B.C.E.), a statue from the reign of PSAMMETICHUS I (664–610 B.C.E.), and a sculptured piece from NECTANEBO I (r. 380–362 B.C.E.) were recovered as well.

Sebni   *See* SABNI.

Sebu'a, el-   A site at the Wadi es-Sebu'a, in NUBIA (modern Sudan), where RAMESSES II (r. 1290–1224 B.C.E.) built a temple dedicated to the gods AMUN and RÉ-Harakhte, this temple was noted for its SPHINX-lined entrance and colossal figures of the pharaoh. Six human-headed sphinxes formed the decoration for the second court, where four hawk-headed sphinxes were positioned. Another PYLON opened to a third court. Storage rooms were built on an underground level for this temple.

sed (heb-sed)   This was an ancient Egyptian FESTIVAL dating to Predynastic times (before 3000 B.C.E.) and remaining popular throughout Egypt's history. Also called the *heb-sed* (*see* SED) in some eras, this festival, a symbolic recreation of the ruler's physical and magical powers, demonstrated a ruler's vigor after three decades. The *heb-sed* was usually celebrated in the 30th year of the ruler's reign and every three years to 10 years thereafter. Details of the *sed* are obscure because the FESTIVAL changed over the centuries. The hieroglyph for *sed* is an image of an open-sided pavilion with a column and two thrones.

It is believed that the *sed* festival became a substitute for the traditional and archaic custom of slaying the pharaoh, sparing his life, and allowing him a ceremonial foretaste of his rule in the afterlife. During the ceremony the pharaoh visited the shrines of the various gods, dressed in a short garment that completely enveloped his torso and arms. The ruler performed the rite of "going around the wall," danced, and jumped in order to demonstrate his rejuvenation.

The festival also included ritual battles between the FOLLOWERS OF HORUS and the FOLLOWERS OF SET and the herding of oxen and cattle around the royal residence. At the close of the ceremony, the ruler was attired in jubilee clothing and distributed honors and gifts to higher-ranked subjects. The *sed* ceremony ended at a temple lake, where the ruler mounted a barge. The festival lasted two or more months in some eras, uniting the Egyptians to the gods. Some pharaohs, such as Pepi II (r. 2246–2152 B.C.E.) and Ramesses II (r. 1290–1224 B.C.E.), lived long enough to celebrate more than one festival, and others anticipated their 30 years of reign, celebrating one or more *sed* festivals without actually achieving the proper number of years of rule.

The *heb-sed* festival was was depicted in the STEP PYRAMID of DJOSER (r. 2630–2611 B.C.E.) in SAQQARA, in the southern tomb area. Djoser was portrayed running a race, being crowned, sitting on the throne of Lower Egypt and then on the throne of Upper Egypt, and dispensing gifts to the local priesthoods.

sedge A particular hieroglyphic symbol of the plant, serving as the insignia of Upper Egypt and joined with the BEE symbol of the Delta in Lower Egypt to reflect a united land. The Two Kingdoms of Egypt were thus portrayed by the sedge and the bee and were used separately or in a combined form. The sedge became part of the royal names of the pharaohs in time.

Sefer-t A mythological creature associated with the PYRAMID TEXTS and the MORTUARY RITUALS of the Fifth Dynasty (2465–2323 B.C.E.), the Sefer-t was a winged lion with magical powers. The Pyramid Texts depict the creature as a friend of Unis (r. 2356–2323 B.C.E.) in the afterlife.

See also CANNIBAL HYMN.

Segerseni (fl. 20th century B.C.E.) *rebel from Nubia (modern Sudan) who opposed the Twelfth Dynasty*
He opposed AMENEMHET I (r. 1991–1962 B.C.E.) when he founded that royal line upon the death of MENTUHOTEP IV. Segerseni wanted to stop Amenemhet I and fought repeated, intense campaigns before he was defeated. Later, Segerseni's allies fought the armies of Egypt on ELEPHANTINE Island before being routed.

Sehel Island A site between the first and second cataracts of the Nile, south of ASWAN, ancient fortifications, a canal, and inscriptions were discovered there. The canal dates to the Middle Kingdom (2040–1640 B.C.E.) or perhaps earlier, and TUTHMOSIS I (r. 1504–1492 B.C.E.) cleared the waterway for his Nubian campaigns. The

FAMINE STELA, erected on Sehel Island in the Ptolemaic Period (304–30 B.C.E.), commemorates a visit by DJOSER (r. 2630–2611 B.C.E.) to the shrine of KHNUM.

Sehetepibré (Sehetepibré-ankh) (fl. 19th century B.C.E.) *financial official and esteemed sage of the Twelfth Dynasty*
He served SENWOSRET III (r. 1878–1841 B.C.E.) and AMENEMHET III (r. 1844–1797 B.C.E.) as a court treasurer. Sehetepibré is famous for his *Loyalist Instruction,* in which he advised his fellow Egyptians to obey the pharaoh in all things. Such behavior, he suggested, led to high offices and honors. The *Loyalist Instruction* was inscribed on an ABYDOS stela and is now in the Louvre in Paris, having been inscribed with a poem dedicated to Amenemhet III.

This official had to take tours of the natural resource sites to tally potential assets of the various regions. Sehetepibré and his father, Tay, who also served as treasurer, left an inscription on a rock at ASWAN. The relief that records their presence on the scene was carved onto a cliff across from the ELEPHANTINE Island.

See also NATURAL RESOURCES.

Seila This was a site bordering the FAIYUM territory of Egypt, south of el-LISHT. A PYRAMID was erected on a desert spur at Seila. This pyramid, probably built by HUNI (r. 2599–2575 B.C.E.), was constructed out of limestone blocks. The pyramid was designed with four steps and was 99 square feet at the base.

Sekenenré *See* TA'O II.

Seker *See* SOKAR.

Sekhaen-Ré (d. ca. 1520 B.C.E.) *fifth ruler of the lesser Hyksos Sixteenth Dynasty*
This dynasty was contemporary with the Great HYKSOS of the Fifteenth Dynasty at AVARIS. No monuments survive from the reign of Sekhaen-Ré.

sekhem (1) This was the Egyptian term for the vital force of a human being that serves as a companion in eternity but is distinct from the KA and the BA. The term translates literally as "to have mastery over something."

sekhem (2) This was the Egyptian term for the powers of a deity, normally written with additives. Osiris was described as *sekhem-o,* having great power. Osiris's *sekhem* SCEPTER was kept in the god's shrine at ABYDOS to demonstrate his magical attributes. This scepter had a golden face at the top. Two crown feathers and two cobras protected the face. The scepter was inlaid with blue faience or with stones and was beribboned.

sekhem (3) This was the Egyptian term for royal acts that aided or restored MA'AT in the land. These were physical acts in comparison to HEKA, ritual symbols. The military campaigns of the pharaohs and the establishment of just laws and traditions were all acts of *sekhem*, because they insured the security and honor of Egypt. Each PHARAOH declared that he was commanded by the gods to restore *ma'at*. The double CROWN of Egypt, called *pschent* by the Greeks, was originally named *pa-sekhemty* as it displayed the double powers of the rulers of the Two Kingdoms, Upper and Lower Egypt.

sekhem (4)   They were the magical powers involved in the MORTUARY RITUALS. Such powers were infused into the mummy of the deceased through rituals and incantations. The BOOK OF THE DEAD was a repository of *sekhem*, and mortuary priests were initiated into the ceremonies that imparted such powers to the deceased. This form of *sekhem* involved overcoming the obstacles facing the dead in the journey to the paradise beyond the grave.

See also HEKA; MAGIC; PRIESTS.

Sekhem-kha (fl. 28th century B.C.E.) *nobleman whose Saqqara tomb became famous*
Sekhem-kha's tomb was designated at one time as the resting place of DJET of the First Dynasty (2920–2770 B.C.E.). The tomb contains a burial chamber in which 300 bulls' heads, fashioned out of clay and equipped with actual horns, are on display. A symbol of royalty, such a tomb decoration is unusual for a nobleman. Sekhem-kha probably served Djet or DEN, Djet's successor.

Sekhemkharé (fl. 25th century B.C.E.) *princely vizier of the Fourth Dynasty*
A royal prince, he was the son of KHAFRE (Chephren) (r. 2520–2494 B.C.E.). He did not inherit the throne but served as VIZIER for the pharaohs of his royal line. Sekhemkharé also counseled the early rulers of the Fifth Dynasty (2465–2323 B.C.E.). In that dynasty the royal power was maintained by a policy of allowing only members of the royal family to hold the highest offices, and outsiders were relegated to minor roles in the court or government.

Sekhemkhet (Djoserti) (d. 2061 B.C.E.) *third ruler of the Third Dynasty*
He reigned from 2611 B.C.E. until his death. His name meant "Powerful in Body." Sekhemkhet was the successor of DJOSER. His name was inscribed on a cliff near WADI MAGHARA, indicating some military or expeditionary campaigns for the NATURAL RESOURCES of the territory, the turquoise mines of the SINAI.

Sekhemkhet built a pyramid at SAQQARA, southwest of the STEP PYRAMID. This tomb was designed by IMHOTEP, the architect of the Step Pyramid, but was never completed. The masonry wall of the tomb was 27 feet deep, and the platform was 1700 feet on the north-south axis and 600 feet wide. An unused single black SARCOPHAGUS of alabaster was discovered in the pyramid, and a wooden coffin was also found. The sarcophagus was T-shaped and sealed but empty. A cache of funerary regalia was also discovered in the pyramid. This treasure trove held amulets, bracelets, a golden tube, and seals honoring Sekhemkhet's name.

Sekhemré-Wahkhau Rahotep (fl. ca. 1640 B.C.E.) *reportedly the founder of the Seventeenth Dynasty*
He ruled from 1640–? B.C.E., at Thebes, and he maintained peaceful relations with the HYKSOS, who ruled the Delta at the same time. Sekhemré-Wahkhau Rehotep's territory included the southern nomes of Egypt.

Sekhmet   She was a powerful war goddess of Egypt, the destroyer of pharaoh's enemies, called "She Who Is Powerful." Sekhmet was a lioness deity, the consort of PTAH and the mother of NEFERTEM and Imhotep in MEMPHIS. A daughter of the god RÉ, Sekhmet struck at evildoers and spread plagues. She also healed the righteous. Her clergymen were physicians and magicians.

Sekhmet had a popular role among the rulers of Egypt, as she was believed to bring about the conception of the pharaohs. In the form of a cobra she was called MEHEN, and she possibly came from NUBIA (modern Sudan) in the early eras. She was also called the "EYE OF RÉ."

Her statues normally depicted her as a woman with a lion's head, and at times she wore a sun disk on her head. In this form she was a warrior manifestation of the sun, causing flames to devour the enemies of Egypt. In some eras, the gates of Sekhmet's temples were opened as a signal of the onset of a military campaign. AMENEMHET III (r. 1844–1797 B.C.E.) included 700 statues of Sekhmet in his mortuary temple in DASHUR. She was also portrayed on the wall of the temple of SAHURÉ (r. 2458–2446 B.C.E.) at ABUSIR. This portrait acquired a widespread reputation for its miraculous cures.

Seleucus I Nicator (d. ca. 281 B.C.E.) *general and ally of Egypt*
He had been a governor in the service of ALEXANDER III THE GREAT (r. 332–323 B.C.E.) and took control of Babylon when Alexander died. Seleucus I Nicator allied himself with PTOLEMY I SOTER (r. 304–284 B.C.E.) to defeat Antigonus at Ipsus and to secure their holdings. He proved an unreliable agent of Ptolemy I, however, and was murdered.

Selket (Serqset)   The scorpion goddess of Egypt associated with the OSIRIS-ISIS-HORUS cult, Selket was worshipped as early as the First Dynasty (2920–2770 B.C.E.), possibly even earlier. She was originally part of the cult of NUN, the deity of the dark water abyss. In the PYRA-

MID TEXTS, Selket was invoked in the mortuary rituals and was declared the protectoress of QEBEHSENNUF, the guardian of the CANOPIC JARS holding human intestines. She also guarded the royal coffin and the canopic chests. A strikingly beautiful statue of Selket, fashioned out of gold and depicting a young woman with a scorpion on her head, was discovered in the tomb of TUT'ANKHAMUN (r. 1333–1323 B.C.E.). Selket also protected the goddess ISIS and the child HORUS, and her spells cured stings and bites.

Semerkhet (Semempses) (fl. ca. 2700 B.C.E.) *sixth ruler of the First Dynasty*
His actual date of reign is undocumented. His name meant "Thoughtful Friend." MANETHO, the Ptolemaic Period (304–30 B.C.E.) historian, listed Semerkhet as Semempses. He was mentioned in the PALERMO STONE but not on the Saqqara KING LIST. Possibly a usurper, he erased the name of his predecessor on jubilee vases. Many disasters apparently took place during his reign.

He was buried in ABYDOS, but no Saqqara tomb has been discovered. A STELA of black quartz with ivory labels was found in his tomb. An ebony plaque of the SOKAR BOAT was also found in his tomb. In some lists he is identified as the son of 'ADJIB and Queen TARSET. Semerkhet's son and heir was Qasemktet.

Semna This was an important military site at the second cataract in NUBIA (modern Sudan), where the Egyptians erected a FORTRESS and a temple complex. Semna marked the southern border of Egypt throughout much of the Middle Kingdom (2040–1640 B.C.E.). A STELA made of red granite discovered on the site records that SENWOSRET III (r. 1878–1841 B.C.E.) made the original foundation of the fortress of Semna. This fortress had served as a trading settlement in previous eras. A second stela, discovered in the temple complex, dedicated the shrine to the Nubian god DEDUN. KHNUM was also venerated at Semna.

Semna's fortress overlooked the Semna Gorge and was opposite the fortress of Kemna. In time another fortress, called Semna South, was erected in the region. Yet another fortress, URONARTI, was also built nearby. Detailed reports were sent to THEBES, called the Semna Dispatches, about tracking operations. The MEDJAY, some of whom were in the service of the Egyptians as Nubian mercenaries, were in the territory. Senwosret III campaigned at Semna in his 12th regnal year. This region of Nubia had been conquered by SENWOSRET I (r. 1971–1926 B.C.E.) earlier in the dynasty.

Senakhtenré *See* TA'O I.

Se'n Ba Stela A commemorative monument discovered in ABYDOS in a chamber adjoining the cenotaph of DJER (r. ca. 2900 B.C.E.), the second ruler of the First Dynasty, the stela demonstrates the prolonged use of writing in Egypt, starting at an earlier time than previously believed. Considered one of the most beautiful stone monuments of the period, the Se'n Ba Stela set the standard for later hieroglyphic commemoratives.

Sendjemib This was a clan dating to the Old Kingdom Period of Egypt and known for faithful service to the rulers of the nation. Inti Sendjemib served IZEZI (r. 2388–2356 B.C.E.) as an administrator. He also had a lake drained and formed for Izezi's personal use. Inti Sendjemib's son, Mehi, built a tomb at GIZA for his father and carried on the tradition of courtly service.

Sendji (Sened) (fl. ca. 2750 B.C.E.) *ruler of the Second Dynasty*
His name meant "the Fearful One." Sendji was included in some KING LISTS, and a Fourth Dynasty (2575–2465 B.C.E.) noble named Shery inscribed a document in his tomb stating that he was the overseer of the *ka* of Sendji's tomb. It is believed that Sendji was buried under one of the galleries of the STEP PYRAMID at SAQQARA.

No monuments have been discovered from Sendji's reign, but his cult was observed for many centuries. A bronze statue was made of him in the Twenty-sixth Dynasty (664–525 B.C.E.). His name was also found on a stone fragment in the mortuary temple of KHAFRE (Chephren) (r. 2520–2494 B.C.E.) in Giza.

Senebtisy (fl. 20th century B.C.E.) *royal woman of the Twelfth Dynasty*
She was possibly the consort of AMENEMHET I (r. 1991–1962 B.C.E.). Her tomb at el-LISHT was one of many vandalized and robbed by local thieves of the era. Her mummified remains, however, had been interred in three gilded coffins and were untouched. Senebtisy's remains were adorned with fine jewelry pieces that were recovered. In some records Senebtisy is listed as the daughter of the VIZIER Senuseret, serving possibly as a lesser-ranked wife of Amenemhet I.

Senedjim (fl. 13th century B.C.E.) *artisan official of the Nineteenth Dynasty*
He served RAMESSES II (r. 1290–1224 B.C.E.) as a supervisor of the workers in the tombs of the VALLEY OF THE KINGS. These were the SERVANTS OF THE PLACE OF TRUTH, who lived in DEIR EL-MEDINA. Senedjim resided in Deir el-Medina and was buried there, as these workers were allowed to fashion elaborate tombs for themselves and their families.

Senenmen (Sen Men; Sonimen) (fl. 15th century B.C.E.) *expeditionary official of the Eighteenth Dynasty*
He served TUTHMOSIS II (r. 1492–1479 B.C.E.) and was originally identified as the brother of SENENMUT but now is considered an unrelated fellow official of the powerful favorite. Senenmen was the leader of an expedition to

PUNT, accompanied by Senenmut, Nehesy, and THUITY, all ranking officials of the court.

Senenmut (fl. 15th century B.C.E.) *favorite court official of the Eighteenth Dynasty*
He served as a chief counselor of HATSHEPSUT (r. 1473–1458 B.C.E.) and as tutor to Princess NEFERU-RÉ. Ten surviving statues depict him with Neferu-Ré. He also provided needed support and counsel to the queen-pharaoh. Senenmut came from ERMENT, possibly, and he was the son of Ramose and Hatnofer. His sisters were 'A' Ahotep and Nofrethor. His brothers were also active in the court, including a Senenmen, Minhotep, and Hatnufer.

Senenmut started his career in an earlier era and earned many titles in the temple of AMUN by the reign of TUTHMOSIS II (1492–1479 B.C.E.). He was the Prophet of the Bark of Amun; Overseer of the Prophets of MONTU in Erment; Chief Steward of Amun, Overseer of the Granaries, Storehouses, Fields, Cattle, and Slaves; Controller of the Hall of Amun; Overseer of the Works of Amun; and Overseer of All of the Works of the King in the Temple of Amun. Senenmut was also honored for his architectural skills. He was involved in the various building projects of Hatshepsut, including the temple of DEIR EL-BAHRI on the western shore of the Nile at Thebes and the KARNAK temple. A statue depicts him as a master architect.

He amassed more than 80 titles as an official and administrator in the royal court and worked with HAPUSENEB and other supporters of Hatshepsut's reign. Many legends concerning Senenmut have arisen over the years. The many titles and favors bestowed upon him have given rise to much speculation. What is known is the fact that Senenmut dared to attempt to link his own tomb with that of the queen-pharaoh. This or some other transgression brought about his fall from power. He never occupied the tomb that he constructed and never used the red quartzite sarcophagus prepared for him. A statue in the shrine of Tuthmosis III (r. 1479–1425 B.C.E.) at Deir el-Bahri, however, called Djeser-Akhet, reportedly was given to Senenmut. A shrine at GEBEL EL-SILSILEH depicts Senenmut making offerings to the local deity and an ASWAN inscription also credits him with quarrying OBELISKS for Hatshepsut.

His sudden death or disappearance in the 19th year of Hatshepsut's reign left the queen-pharaoh vulnerable. A mummified horse was discovered in Senenmut's tomb. He had fashioned two tombs actually, one in SHEIKH ABD' EL-QURNA and the uncompleted one at Deir el-Bahri.

Senheb (fl. 24th century B.C.E.) *dwarf textile official of the Sixth Dynasty*
He was a DWARF who supervised the royal textile works and was honored for his skills and knowledge. Senheb married a princess and raised two normal sized children. Buried in GIZA, Senheb was honored with a statue depicting him, his wife, and their two children.

Senisonbe (Seniseb) (fl. 15th century B.C.E.) *royal woman of the Eighteenth Dynasty*
She was the mother of TUTHMOSIS I (r. 1504–1492 B.C.E.), having royal lineage from a collateral side of the royal family of 'AHMOSE (NEBPEHTIRÉ) (r. 1550–1525 B.C.E.). She was probably married to another royal personage. Senisonbe received many honors in Tuthmosis I's reign.

Sennacherib (d. 681 B.C.E.) *Assyrian king and enemy of Egypt*
He ruled from ca. 704 B.C.E. until his death and was a contemporary of SHABAKA (r. 712–698 B.C.E.). A series of confrontations between the Egyptians and the ASSYRIANS took place in Palestine. In 701 B.C.E., Sennacherib met the Egyptian army and was defeated, ending his plans for occupying Egypt.

See also ASSYRIANS.

Sennufer (fl. 15th century B.C.E.) *nome prince and official of the Eighteenth Dynasty*
He served AMENHOTEP II (r. 1427–1401 B.C.E.) as mayor of THEBES. He probably held the rank of "Royal Seal Bearer" for TUTHMOSIS III (r. 1479–1425 B.C.E.), and he was also the supervisor of the gardens of AMUN's temple. Sennufer was a hereditary prince of his NOME.

Sennufer's tomb at SHEIKH ABD' EL-QURNA on the western bank of the Nile at Thebes is elaborately painted with scenes depicting his career. His wife, Senetney, was listed as "the King's nurse." There is some indication that Sennufer's tomb was originally prepared for TUTHMOSIS II (r. 1492–1479 B.C.E.) but was abandoned by the ruler. CANOPIC JARS and other funerary regalia were discovered in the tomb. The antechamber depicts an arbor of vines and grapes and religious scenes. Family portraits also decorate the walls. The actual burial chamber was subterranean.

Sennuwy (Sennuity) (fl. 20th century B.C.E.) *royal woman of the Twelfth Dynasty, known for her beautiful portrait statue*
She was the wife of Prince HEPZEFA, in the reign of SENWOSRET I (1971–1926 B.C.E.). Her statue was discovered in the fortress of KERMEH at the third cataract of the Nile in NUBIA (modern Sudan). Prince Hepzefa was perhaps commander of the fort territory. The statue of Sennuwy depicts a beautiful young woman and is considered one of the finest examples of Egyptian sculpture from the Middle Kingdom.

See also ART AND ARCHITECTURE.

Senwosret I (Kheperkaré) (d. 1926 B.C.E.) *second ruler of the Twelfth Dynasty*
He reigned from 1971 B.C.E. until his death. The son of AMENEMHET I and Queen NEFRU-TOTENEN, he served as co-regent with his father for 10 years before ascending the throne. As a prince, Senwosret I began his Nubian

and Libyan campaigns. Amenemhet I was assassinated while Senwosret I was campaigning in Libya, beyond the WADI NATRUN. The event is an element of the popular tale known as *SINUHE THE SAILOR*, as the character Sinuhe was supposedly a servant of Senwosret I's consort, Queen NEFRUSHERI, daughter of Amenemhet I. Senwosret I raced back to Egypt to crush the HAREM conspiracy responsible for the murder and to punish the intended usurpers. The capital at the time was at ITJ-TAWY, a site on the border between Upper and Lower Egypt.

Militarily active, Senwosret I campaigned in NUBIA (modern Sudan) all the way to the third cataract and also founded the great fortress of BUHEN. He used quarries and mines and controlled the oases of the LIBYAN DESERT and the resources in the SINAI. He built KERMEH fortress in Nubia and regulated operations at the mines of WADI HALFA as well as regional diorite quarries. Copper was mined in Wadi Hudi, and red granite was taken from a quarry south of ASWAN.

Senwosret I was not interested in wholesale conquest and limited his campaigns to the defense of Egypt's borders and to the exploitation of available resources. He also promoted trade with Crete and other Aegean isles and with Palestine and Syria. Within Egypt, he was a prolific builder, refurbishing the temple of Ré-Atum in HELIOPOLIS. The famed WHITE CHAPEL dates to his reign, and he is credited with establishing the core of the KARNAK complex itself. He also erected two obelisks there.

Senwosret I was active in restoring the FAIYUM region, adding to the irrigational monuments there. He founded a temple to SEKHMET-Hathor at IMU, now called Kom el-Hisn, the Mound of the Fort, in the Delta. The temple was rectangular and contained a bark chapel and pillars. He is also credited with building 35 separate religious structures from the Faiyum to the Delta.

A stone stela made for a temple in Heliopolis and dating to Senwosret I's reign was copied by a scribe serving AMENHOTEP III (r. 1391–1353 B.C.E.). Five hundred years old when copied, the stela vanished. The copy indicates a text in the form of a poem, actually serving as a temple inscription commemorating an addition built by Senwosret I, given with other elaborate donations.

The *INSTRUCTIONS OF AMENEMHET I* date also to his reign. His father was supposed to have dictated the instructions, a text that warns of the perils of a weak monarch. This work is also called *Amenemhet's Instructions* or the *Testament of Amenemhet*.

Senwosret I's son and heir was AMENEMHET II, who served as his co-regent. His daughters were ITEKUYET, NEFRU-SOBEK (2), NEFERU-PTAH (2), and Nenseddjedet. They were buried with Senwosret I and Queen NEFRUSHERI in el-LISHT, where a pyramidal complex was constructed. The pyramid was filled with rubble with a limestone covering. Smaller pyramids served as gravesites for the family members. The great pyramid was called "Senwosret Surveys the Two Lands."

Senwosret II (Kha'kheperré) (d. 1878 B.C.E.) *fourth ruler of the Twelfth Dynasty*

He reigned from 1897 B.C.E. until his death. Senwosret II was the son of AMENEMHET II and probably Queen MERYET (2). He served as co-regent before his father died, and he married NEFERT. Senwosret II was the patron of the FAIYUM territory of Egypt, starting a vast reclamation of the region and restoring thousands of acres of marshlands. He also campaigned in NUBIA (modern Sudan), making that domain a province of Egypt. He constructed a series of FORTRESSES on the Nile and built an 80-foot wall at ELKAB and another wall at ANIBA. Senwosret II, seeing the growing independent minds of the nomarchs, the landed nobility of Egypt, broke their power with stern measures and taxes. He received tribute from Syria and other lands and maintained a strong military presence at mines and quarries.

His son and heir was SENWOSRET III, born to Queen WERERET. He also married Queen NEFERHENT (1). His daughters were SIT-HATHOR, SIT-HATHOR YUNET, Itkayt,

A column from the White Chapel, built at Karnak by Senwosret I of the Twelfth Dynasty; the hieroglyphs depict the pharaoh honoring the god Min with battle treasures. *(Courtesy Thierry Ailleret)*

and Neferet. Senwosret II was one of Egypt's tallest pharaohs, standing six feet, six inches tall and depicted in reliefs and statues. He was buried in a pyramid complex (KAHUN) at LAHUN called "Contented Is Senwosret," or Het-Hotep-Senwosret, "the House of Peace of Senwosret." This complex was erected on a rocky spur at Lahun, at the mouth of the Faiyum. The pyramid was surrounded by family mastaba tombs and was covered in limestone. RAMESSES II (r. 1290–1224 B.C.E.) plundered the complex to use the materials for his own projects.

Senwosret III (Kha'kauré) (d. 1841 B.C.E.) *fifth ruler of the Twelfth Dynasty*

The son and heir of SENWOSRET II and Queen WERERET, Senwosret III, also known as Kha'kauré, reigned from 1878 B.C.E. until his death. Having served as co-regent with his father, Senwosret III ruled Egypt for almost four decades, maintaining strong border defenses and expanding the cultivation area of the FAIYUM by some 17,000 acres. He was honored by the Egyptians as the true "Shield of the Nation."

BIOGRAPHY

While still a prince, Senwosret III supervised the measurements of the Nile waters and refurbished the instruments and facilities for calculations of oncoming floods. Such duties won him the support of the NOMARCHS, the aristocrats of the various provinces, such as the official DJEHUTIHOTEP, the "Great Lord of the Hare Nome." Coming to the throne well educated and militarily experienced, he started his campaigns in NUBIA (modern Sudan) in his sixth regnal year and reopened the canal at the first cataract of the Nile, at SEHEL ISLAND, in order to facilitate the movement of Egyptian units to the southern Nubian sites. The records at Sehel state that Senwosret III erected a chapel to the Nubian patron goddess of the region, Anuket, there. He also strengthened the fortresses in the territory and added new defensive structures, including SEMNA, URONARTI, MIRGISSA, and Askut. The Sehel canal was called "Beautiful Are the Ways of Kha'kauré."

In his eighth regnal year Senwosret III studied the rapids of the Nile, using his trained troops to find ways to allow Egyptian ships to sail freely to any destination. While campaigning in his ninth regnal year Senwosret III went as far south as Semna, at the second cataract of the Nile. There he erected a stela, announcing that he had extended Egypt's boundary farther south than any of his ancestors. A NILOMETER at Dal Island, some 60 miles south of Semna, dates to this period in his reign. He became the patron deity of Nubia after his death, having erected a fortress at Uronarti.

Senwosret III's campaigns in Palestine were also vigorous, and he was claimed in inscriptions to be "Egypt's shield" and "the throat-slitter of the Asiat-

An oil portrait of Senwosret III, the great Middle Kingdom Period warrior pharaoh, displaying the sacred scarab *(M. Bunson)*

ics." He was much loved for his monuments and temple donations as well, erecting statues in BIGA and ELEPHANTINE Island, as well as HIERAKONPOLIS. At ERMENT he added to the temple of MONTU and refurbished that deity's shrine at MEDAMUD. He also added to the temple of OSIRIS in ABYDOS. Senwosret III erected six statues and a stela at DEIR EL-BAHRI. Records also indicate that he brought great treasures of semiprecious stones to Egypt from the SINAI and founded the Royal Cemetery in Abydos.

As an administrator, Senwosret III regulated the nome hereditary aristocrats and instituted a new court system. He divided the government into three vizierates: Upper Egypt, Lower Egypt, and Nubia. He also removed the nome governors who had amassed hereditary powers.

Senwosret III's *hemet,* or Great Wife, was NEFERHENT (2). His lesser queens were MERESGER (2), MERYET (1), NOFRET, Khemetnefer-Sheri, SOBEK-SHEDTY-NEFERU, SITWERET, and possibly SIT HATHOR-YUNET. Senwosret's son and heir was AMENEMHET III, born to Queen Neferhent. His daughters were Menut, SENTSENEB, Meryt, and Sihathor. Amenemhet III served as co-regent before Senwosret III died.

Senwosret III was deified in the temple of Amada in Nubia. A cycle of hymns was written for him while he lived, as he was greatly loved by the people of the Nile. The portraits found of Senwosret III depict a stern, grim individual with a vigorous face.

DASHUR was the site of Senwosret III's burial complex, and another Abydos complex has also been discovered. The Dashur burial site contained a pyramid that was made out of mud brick, lined with limestone. The burial chamber within the pyramid was lined with red granite, with a sarcophagus of the same vivid stone. Seven mastabas surround the ruined monument. Archaeologists recovered from this complex a cache of jewelry, and three cedar boats also were found. The queens and family members were buried in subterranean levels. The Abydos tomb had cult rituals celebrated there for two centuries.

HISTORICAL IMPACT

A warrior and an astute administrator, Senwosret III is one of the most famous pharaohs of the Middle Kingdom. Called the "Shield of the Nation" and reigning for almost four decades, his service to the nation remained the standard of pharaonic achievements for centuries after his death; Senwosret III was one of the few kings who was deified and honored with a cult during his lifetime.

Senwosret III abolished the power of the provincial nobility when he removed the nome governors who had amassed hereditary powers and thus ended their threat to the throne. He also strengthened the annexation and colonization of Nubia, where he became the patron deity after his death. Senwosret III's military campaigns resulted in an era of peace and economic prosperity. His royal line, following in the paths of earlier pharaohs, restored stone quarries and mines. In Senwosret III's time, the name Kush, for Nubia, became popular, designating the more southern territories of that land, and Egypt exploited the natural resources of that region, especially the gold mines.

Beginning his studies before he was pharaoh, Senwosret III understood the importance of the Nile's waters and spent part of his reign repairing or building Egyptian strongholds along the Nile in Nubia. Vast fortresses, such as the famous Buhen Fortress, guarded each explored Nile cataract, and traffic on the Nile was strictly controlled by trade officials. He also built a Nilometer at Dal Island, south of Semna, in order to have advance warning about the rise of the river during the periods of inundation.

Further reading: Arnold, Dieter. *The Pyramid Complex of Senwosret III at Dahshur: Architectural Studies.* New York: Metropolitan Museum of Art Series, 2002; Wegner, Josef. "The Nature and Chronology of the Senwosret III–Amenemhat III Regnal Succession," *Journal of Near Eastern Studies* 55, Vol. 4 (1996), pp. 249–279.

Senwosret-ankh (fl. 20th century B.C.E.) *royal building official for rulers of the Twelfth Dynasty*
He served AMENEMHET I (r. 1991–1962 B.C.E.) and SENWOSRET I (r. 1971–1926 B.C.E.) as the high priest of PTAH at MEMPHIS. He was also the royal builder for the pharaohs. Senwosret-ankh's mastaba at el-LISHT is ruined, but the original burial was at the end of a deep shaft. Having a starred ceiling, the chamber is decorated with the PYRAMID TEXTS. His sarcophagus was fashioned out of stone blocks set into a floor cavity.

sepat This was the Egyptian name for a NOME or province, used as well to describe the symbols of such entities. These symbols, normally representing a local deity or animal theophany, were carried on poles and served as totems. The *sepat* was always placed just below the totem and was formed by a depiction of a plot, crossed and semi-crossed by the lines of canals. Below the *sepat* was another titular figure associated with the nome.

Sept He was a deity of the twentieth nome of Egypt, called "the Lord of the East," "the Smiter of the Mentiu," or "Sept of the Tusks." He became HORUS the Elder, Per-Sept, in the Eastern Desert regions, especially in the WADI TIMULAT, modern Saft al-Hannah.

Serabit el-Khadim This was a mining territory in the SINAI, operated by the Egyptians from the Old Kingdom (2575–2134 B.C.E.) to the Ptolemaic Period (304–30 B.C.E.). General WENI started the military campaigns for control of the mines at Serabit el-Khadim under PEPI I (r. 2289–2255 B.C.E.). The Twelfth Dynasty (1991–1783 B.C.E.) especially exploited the natural resources in the area. Those pharaohs designated Serabit el-Khadim as "the Eyes Are in Festival." Copper was sought there, as well as semiprecious stones. A rock-cut chapel dedicated to HATHOR, "the Lady of Turquoise," dates to the Twelfth Dynasty at Serabit el-Khadim. Expeditions to the region included the escorts of army units.

See also NATURAL RESOURCES.

Serapeum (1) This was a necropolis erected for the burials of the sacred APIS bulls in SAQQARA. Also called the "House of Oserapis," the term Serapeum refers to the ground-level part of the structure, and great vaults, corridors, and chapels were part of the design. SERAPIS was a deity formed in the reign of PTOLEMY I SOTER (304–284 B.C.E.) as an effort to link Greek traditions to the older Egyptian cultic ceremonies. The name Serapeum dates to the Ptolemaic Period also, as the Greek rulers wanted to cement the cult of Serapis and to unite both Greeks and native Egyptians in worship.

The Apis bull cult was started probably by AHA (Menes) in ca. 2900 B.C.E., and it is mentioned in the PALERMO STONE. The bulls were buried in the temple of PTAH near MIT RAHINAH originally. In the New Kingdom

(1550–1070 B.C.E.), the monumental interment of the bulls was standardized, and more than 60 mummified Apis have been recovered.

KHA'EMWESET (1), the son of RAMESSES II (r. 1290–1224 B.C.E.), was involved in establishing the original bull burial site that became the Serapeum in Saqqara. The lower chamber walls of the monument were then covered in gold leaf. Other pharaohs, including PSAMMETICHUS I (r. 664–610 B.C.E.), added galleries. Priests danced at the funerals of the Apis bulls, and immense CANOPIC JARS were part of the mortuary regalia. In time a transverse gallery was added with vaults. A pink granite sarcophagus with black markings was found there. In the Ramessid gallery, founded by Ramesses II, an untouched Apis bull and human remains were discovered. Some 24 monolithic SARCOPHAGI, measuring from 10 to 13 feet in height and from 13 to 16 feet in length, were recovered.

Serapeum (2)   This was a second necropolis for APIS bulls, dedicated to SERAPIS and erected in ALEXANDRIA, the capital founded by ALEXANDER III THE GREAT (r. 332–323 B.C.E.). PTOLEMY I SOTER (r. 304–284 B.C.E.) fostered the cult of Serapis and chose the Greek Parmeniscus to design a proper temple for the site. Serapis was worshipped in this temple and burial site as late as 391 C.E.

Serapis   A deity introduced into Egypt in the reign of PTOLEMY I SOTER (r. 304–284 B.C.E.), a Greek version of Osiris-Hapi, the god became the patron of the Ptolemies. He was usually depicted as an old man, with a cerberus at his side. His name was given to the necropolis of the APIS bulls in SAQQARA, but his cult was popular only in ALEXANDRIA and MEMPHIS. In some ceremonies Serapis formed a trinity with the gods ISIS and HORUS. A statue dating to Roman times shows Serapis as a father deity.

serdab   A chamber in Egyptian TOMBS designed to hold statues of the deceased, the word is Arabic for "cellar." Large statues of prominent dead Egyptians were positioned in the *serdab* so that the deceased could witness the ritual ceremonies being conducted as part of the ongoing cultic observances. Each *serdab* was connected to the rituals conducted in the mortuary-offering chamber by a small window, or slits constructed at the eye level of the statues. The *serdab* and window thus provided the dead with access to the ceremonies being held for their repose. The slits or small windows of the *serdab* were called "the Eyes of the *ka* House." Some tombs of the royal deceased contained four *serdab* chambers, each containing a portrait sculpture.

serekh (1)   This was a large building erected in the Early Dynastic Period (2920–2575 B.C.E.), having an elaborate paneled facade, with two square towers and intricately recessed doorways. Constructed of costly wooden materials, the *serekh* served as the royal residence, the PERO, or palace. The royal tombs in ABYDOS and the STEP PYRAMID in SAQQARA used the *serekh* design.

serekh (2)   This was an Egyptian symbol serving the names of the earliest rulers. DJET, or Wadj, the third pharaoh of the First Dynasty (2920–2770 B.C.E.), adopted the *serekh* design as his personal symbol of power. The *serekh* appears on a STELA from his reign and denotes his royal status. The ruler's name was inscribed above the *serekh* symbol in a rectangle, topped by the Horus sign. This device was the first cartouche form.

Servants of the Place of Truth   Also called the Servitors of the Place of Truth, the name assumed by workers who labored in the necropolis of the VALLEY OF THE KINGS at THEBES, these artisans and workmen lived in DEIR EL-MEDINA, which dates to the reign of AMENHOTEP I (1525–1504 B.C.E.). The servants designed, constructed, and decorated the royal tombs. They were provided with residences and monthly rations.

During the reign of RAMESSES III (1194–1163 B.C.E.), 60 such servants were supervised by a man named Amenakht, who complained that rations were not being delivered to Deir el-Medina. The workers assembled at the mortuary temple of TUTHMOSIS III of a previous dynasty and started a strike. They marched on the RAMESSEUM, and violence ensued until VIZIER Ta put a halt to the affair. These protests took place in the year of the hyena.

The servants were allowed to fashion tombs for themselves and their families, and many exquisite examples of these tombs have survived. The affairs of the workers at Deir el-Medina worsened as the last Ramessid Dynasty declined after the death of Ramesses III in 1163 B.C.E.

Seshat (Sefkhet-Abut)   She was a goddess of Egypt serving as the patroness of learning, called "the Lady of Books." The patroness of writing also, Seshat was a consort of the god THOTH and she was associated with the PERSEA TREE. This unique symbol, and "the Tree of Heaven," were the receptacles of historical records. Seshat wrote the name of each ruler upon the Persea's leaves when he was crowned. Seshat also served as "the Keeper of Memories," inscribing human and divine deeds on other leaves of the Persea Tree.

Also called Sefkhet-Abut, Seshat was "the Mistress of Architects." HATSHEPSUT (r. 1473–1458 B.C.E.) offered Seshat tallies of the goods brought from PUNT to Egypt. The goddess was normally depicted as a woman wearing a leopard skin and carrying writing reeds, a scribe's palette, or plumes. In time, Seshat became a protectoress of the LIBRARY OF ALEXANDRIA in the Ptolemaic Dynasty (304–30 B.C.E.).

See also GODS AND GODDESSES.

Sesheshet (Idut; Hor-watet-khet) (fl. 23rd century B.C.E.) *royal woman of the Sixth Dynasty*
She was a daughter of TETI (r. 2323–2291 B.C.E.). Sesheshet married MERERUKA, a prominent vizier of the time, and she was commemorated with a statue, depicting her as a *KA,* entering the world through a FALSE DOOR. Mereruka's tomb at Saqqara is well known for its elaborate reliefs and statues. There are 32 chambers in this tomb. Sesheshet bore a son, Meri-Teti.

Seshi (Mayebre) (d. ca. 1635 B.C.E.) *ruler of the Asiatic Fifteenth Dynasty, the Great Hyksos*
He ruled from the HYKSOS capital of AVARIS and was a contemporary of the Seventeenth Dynasty of Thebes. His throne name meant "Just in the Heart of Ré." Seshi's seals and SCARABS were found throughout Lower Egypt and as far south as the third cataract of the Nile in NUBIA (modern Sudan). He was the successor of SALITIS, the founder of the dynasty.

Set (Seth; Sutekh) An Egyptian deity, also recorded as Seth, which meant "instigator of confusion," he was the son of GEB and NUT and the brother of OSIRIS, ISIS, and NEPHTHYS. The Greeks associated him with Typhon, and Set was regarded as both good and bad.

First recorded in NAGADA, Set was worshipped in the Predynastic Period, before 3000 B.C.E. In the Osirian tradition he murdered OSIRIS, fought HORUS, and was judged by the other deities. Set was exiled to the outer perimeters of the universe. He was a defender of RÉ, however, and he became the patron of the HYKSOS of AVARIS.

KOM OMBO was a major cult center of Set as he was given Upper Egypt by GEB and then lost it to HORUS. In the PYRAMID TEXTS he is called both evil and good, becoming evil during the Third Intermediate Period (1070–712 B.C.E.). In some eras he was associated with the slaying of APOPHIS, the wicked serpent that made nightly attempts to destroy the god Ré. During the Ramessid Period (1307–1070 B.C.E.) he was viewed as the god of foreign lands and was supposedly married to the goddess Nephthys. As a love god he was often invoked by the use of chants, AMULETS, and charms.

He is best known, however, for his part in the Osirian cult. Set murdered Osiris and set his coffin adrift. When Isis found the body and restored it, Set cut the flesh to pieces and hid them. Isis found all of Osiris except for his phallus and brought about his resurrection. Horus, the son of Osiris, then set about seeking revenge and Osiris pleaded a case against Set before the gods.

Cult centers for Set were located along caravan routes and in the western oases. He was elevated to a national god when RAMESSES II (r. 1290–1224 B.C.E.) honored him at the new capital, PER-RAMESSES, in the eastern Delta. In time, the dominant Osirian cult led to the decline of the Set cult. Set had his own following, a group that fought mock battles with the Followers of Horus at festivals. The Set advocates always lost.

See also FOLLOWERS OF SET.

Set Animal *See* TYPHONEAN ANIMAL.

Setau (fl. 13th century B.C.E.) *viceroyal official of the Nineteenth Dynasty*
He served RAMESSES II (r. 1290–1224 B.C.E.) as the governor of NUBIA, the region below ASWAN (modern Sudan). A mortuary stela commemorates Setau's career and honors. He began his service to the crown as a scribe and then became a steward of the temple of AMUN and ultimately the viceroy of Nubia. Setau was the official who rebuilt part of the Ramessid temple in ABU SIMBEL after the earthquake that took place in the 31st year of Ramesses II's reign.

Sethirkhopshef (1) (fl. 13th century B.C.E.) *prince of the Nineteenth Dynasty*
He was an heir of RAMESSES II (r. 1290–1224 B.C.E.) who died before taking the throne. He signed a letter to HATTUSILIS III, the ruler of the HITTITES, congratulating him on the peace treaty forged between the Hittites and Egypt. Sethirkhopshef was buried in the VALLEY OF THE QUEENS. He died in Ramesses II's 21st regnal year. There is some indication that he was originally named Amenhirkhopshef.

Sethirkhopshef (2) (fl. 12th century B.C.E.) *princely victim of smallpox in the Twentieth Dynasty*
A son of RAMESSES III (r. 1194–1163 B.C.E.), he was a charioteer of the royal stables but died during a smallpox epidemic. Sethirkhopshef was buried in THEBES. His tomb has corridors leading to a square chamber and a burial site. Ramesses III is depicted in the reliefs of the tomb as introducing Sethirkhopshef to the deities of Egypt's world beyond the grave. Sethirkhopshef was buried in the VALLEY OF THE QUEENS.

Sethnakhte (Userkha'ure'meryamun) (d. 1194 B.C.E.) *founder of the Twentieth Dynasty*
He ruled from 1196 B.C.E. until his death. Little is known of his background but it is possible that he was a grandson of RAMESSES II (r. 1290–1224 B.C.E.). Sethnakhte was elderly when he founded the dynasty. He was married to TIYE-MERENISET and had a son, RAMESSES III.

Sethnakhte took the throne of Egypt "to clear the land of traitors," a reference to the reign of TWOSRET (1198–1196 B.C.E.), the queen who usurped power at the close of the Nineteenth Dynasty with the help of an official named BAY, also called Irsu. He was assuming the throne to welcome back "the ready faces which had been turned away." These were officials and servants who had fled the court during Twosret's reign.

Restoring order, Sethnakhte opened temples and started his own tomb. He was unable to complete it, however, and was placed in the usurped tomb of Twosret. Some scenes and reliefs were altered for his burial while Twosret's cartouches were covered with plaster. Sethnakhte's coffin was found in the mummy cache in the tomb of AMENHOTEP II at Thebes. The unidentified mummy discovered in Sethnakhte's tomb may be his royal remains. A granite sarcophagus was found there in ruins.

Seti (fl. 13th century B.C.E.) *prince of the Nineteenth Dynasty*
He was a son of RAMESSES II (r. 1290–1224 B.C.E.), the ninth heir to the throne. His mother was Queen NEFERTARI-Merymut. He served as a court priest and as a military commander. Temple reliefs at LUXOR temple show him leading prisoners to his father in the battle of KADESH. Seti died before he could inherit the throne.

Seti I (Menma'atré; Meryen-Ptah) (d. 1290 B.C.E.)
second ruler of the Nineteenth Dynasty
He reigned from 1306 B.C.E. until his death. Seti I's reign was heralded as a "Repeating of Births," a term denoting divine inspiration and used originally in the Twelfth Dynasty (1991–1783 B.C.E.). He was the son of RAMESSES I and Queen SITRÉ.

A commoner at birth, Seti I was raised in the military commands of Egypt and came to the throne as a tough campaigner bent on restoring Egypt's empire. He marched out of Tjel, a border FORTRESS, with three divisions and overran Palestine, Syria, and the surrounding territories. Seti I reoccupied strategic forts and garrisons on the Mediterranean coast and returned to Egypt with prisoners and treasures. In the KARNAK temple at THEBES (modern Luxor), Seti I had reliefs inscribed on the entire north wall to commemorate this campaign. He is depicted marching to Palestine and conducting battles. In subsequent campaigns he advanced on the Amorite coastlands, captured the region of the Orontes River, and confronted the HITTITES. He received the whole of Palestine and the Syrian coastal regions as a result of his military efforts.

Seti I also met a Libyan invasion of the Delta with equal vigor, and he fought two battles to rid the northern area of the invaders. He led campaigns in NUBIA (modern Sudan), founding AMARA and SHAAT-ER-REQAL between the second and third cataracts. A site on SAL ISLAND, Shatt became the administrative base for the viceroy of Nubia, an individual named Amenemope. The Nubian campaigns were conducted by Seti I to put down a revolt by the Irem people. Seti I plundered the region as a result.

In Egypt he restarted reclamation of the natural resources, digging wells in strategic places to benefit miners and quarry workers. He administered the land from MEMPHIS, AVARIS, and THEBES and restored

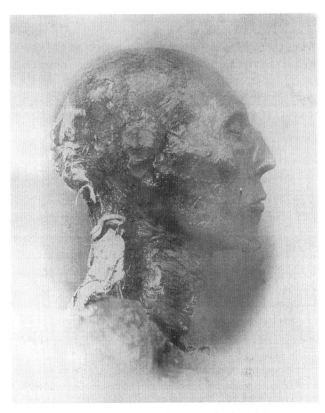

The mummified head of Seti I, the second ruler of the Nineteenth Dynasty, noted as a handsome warrior pharaoh *(Hulton Archive)*

temples damaged in the 'AMARNA Period. At Karnak, Seti I completed his father's plan to convert the area between the second and third pylons into a vast HYPOSTYLE HALL. His son, RAMESSES II, was coruler at the time, and he aided his father in the Karnak building. The vast hall arose with the roof supported by 134 sandstone columns, inscribed with reliefs. Seti I also built a temple in ABYDOS, called "the House of Millions of Years of Menma'atré, Joyful in the Heart of Abydos." He died before completing the cenotaph, now called the OSIREION, and Ramesses II finished the temple, endowing it for continued rituals.

Seti I's tomb in the VALLEY OF THE KINGS at Thebes is the largest one constructed there, dug some 300 feet into the cliffs. Passages and elaborate columns were designed with painted reliefs, some using "the sun and shadow" style. An alabaster coffin was inscribed with the text of the *Book of the Gates*. An astronomical ceiling and more than 700 SHABTIS figures, made of stone, wood, and faience, were discovered in the tomb.

Seti I's mummified remains were found in the cache at DEIR EL-BAHRI in 1881. He was a handsome elderly man, with good teeth and his heart still in his body. His wife was Queen TUYA, and he had two sons. The eldest died young, leaving the throne to Ramesses II. His daughters, HENUTMIRÉ and TIA (1), survived him.

Seti II (Userkheprure'setepenré) (d. 1204 B.C.E.) *fifth ruler of the Nineteenth Dynasty*

He reigned from 1214 B.C.E. until his death. Seti II was the son of MERENPTAH and Queen ISETNOFRET (2) and he married TAKHAT (1), a daughter of RAMESSES II. He also married TWOSRET and possibly Tia'a. Seti II was the victim of a court plot and his throne was usurped temporarily by a relative, AMENMESSES, who ruled only a brief time. Seti II regained the throne and began building at KARNAK. He erected a sandstone station of the gods and colossal statues before he died. He had two sons, Seti-Merenptah, who predeceased him, and Ramesses-Siptah.

Seti II's tomb in the VALLEY OF THE KINGS contained short passageways and a burial chamber with four pillars. He was buried in a red granite sarcophagus but was moved to the tomb of AMENHOTEP II, where he was discovered in the cache of royal mummies. His remains displayed cropped hair, good teeth, and an arthritic hip.

Setka (fl. 26th century B.C.E.) *prince of the Fourth Dynasty*

He was the son of RA'DJEDEF (r. 2528–2520 B.C.E.) and probably Queen Khentetka. Presumably the heir to Ra'djedef's throne, Setka was put aside for KHAFRE, who was crowned as the successor. Setka belonged to one side of KHUFU's family and was possibly viewed as a usurper. Nothing is known of Setka after Ra'djedef's death. A statue of the prince, seated as a scribe, was found in Ra'djedef's pyramid in ABU ROWASH.

Setna Khamwas He was a remarkable fictional character obviously based on the son of RAMESSES II, Setna Khamwas, a prince of the Nineteenth Dynasty. This fictional prince was the hero of an Egyptian ghost story discovered in a papyrus dating to the Ptolemaic Period (340–30 B.C.E.). He supposedly sought the "Book of Thoth," the legendary repository of occult knowledge, and found it in the tomb of another fictional character, Prince Neferkaptah, in the Memphis necropolis.

When the book was recovered, Neferkaptah appeared to Setna Khamwas with his wife and son, Ihwey. Setna had to play a board game with Neferkaptah in order to earn ownership of the book. Defeated three times and pounded into the ground, Setna was freed by spells uttered by his brother, Inaros. Setna dreamed of a female demon named Tabubna as a result.

He and Prince Neferkaptah held lengthy discussions about the "Book of Thoth." Neferkaptah had hunted for it during his lifetime and had found it at the bottom of the Nile near KOPTOS. The text was in separate boxes, guarded by reptiles. Setna realized that such knowledge was dangerous and better left hidden.

Set-Qesu He was an ancient Egyptian demon depicted in scenes of the JUDGMENT HALLS OF OSIRIS in mortuary works. Called "the crusher of bones," Set-Qesu carried out any punishments decreed by Osiris and his fellow judges against the unworthy deceased.

See also FORTY-TWO JUDGES.

Seven Hathors Divine beings who played the role of the Greek Fates in Egypt, they could tell the future and knew the moment of death for each Egyptian. Because a person's destiny depended upon the hour of his or her birth or death and the luck or ill-fortune connected with it, the Seven Hathors were believed to exchange any prince born under unfavorable auspices with a more fortunate child, thus protecting the dynasty and the nation. The Egyptians were greatly concerned with the lucky or unlucky fate of individuals.

See also TREE OF HEAVEN.

Sewew The Egyptian name for the coastal area on the Red Sea, Sewew was opposite KOPTOS on the WADI GASUS and was the region of KUSER, the active expeditionary port. The Egyptians used the regional resources of Sewew to maintain elaborate shipbuilding programs for expeditions to PUNT and other trade enterprises.

See also TRADE AND EXCHANGE.

Sha'at-er-Reqal It was a site on SAL ISLAND in Nubia (modern Sudan), where SETI I (r. 1306–1290 B.C.E.) fought the Irem people and founded a new administrative base for the VICEROY of Nubia. Amenemope, the viceroy in that era, erected two stelae to commemorate Seti I's victory. It contains rock inscriptions dating to the reign of MENTUHOTEP II (2061–2010 B.C.E.). The inscriptions concern Mentuhotep II and his mother, Queen AOH, the consort of INYOTEF III of Thebes. The Shaat-er-Reqal text commemorates the campaign conducted by the pharaoh against WAWAT, a northern region of Nubia.

Shabaka (Neferkaré) (d. 698 B.C.E.) *founder of the Nubian Twenty-fifth Dynasty, which ruled all of Egypt and Nubia*

He reigned from 712 B.C.E. until his death. Shabaka was the son of the Nubian ruler KASHTA and Queen PEBATMA and was originally called Sabacon. He ruled all of Egypt and NUBIA, succeeding PIANKHI (1). In his first years he had to put down rebels in Nubia and in the Delta. Shabaka captured BAKENRENEF (r. 717–712 B.C.E.) of the Twenty-fourth Dynasty at SAIS and burned him to death.

He ruled in MEMPHIS, making that ancient site the capital again, and restored the SERAPEUM in SAQQARA. Shebaka built at KARNAK and MEDINET HABU. He also aided the temple sites in THEBES, MEMPHIS, ABYDOS, DENDERAH, ESNA, and EDFU. Shabaka encouraged the Palestinians in their revolt against Syria. He urged the

Shabaka (d. 698 B.C.E.), the founder of the Nubian Twenty-fifth Dynasty, in a bust at the Louvre *(Erich Lessing / Art Resource, NY)*

Egyptians to return to the worship of AMUN and the other deities.

He had two daughters and two sons, Haremakhet and Tanutamun. Haremakhet was made high priest of Amun in Thebes. Shabaka was buried at el-Kurru, south of GEBEL BARKAL between the third and fourth cataracts of the Nile in Nubia. He was succeeded on the throne of Egypt by SHEBITKU, the son of Piankhi.

Shabaka Stone This was a religious monument also called the Stela of MEMPHIS, one of the most important religious texts of the Late Period. The stone dates to the reign of SHABAKA (712–698 B.C.E.). He found a sacred papyrus concerning spiritual and creation themes being eaten by worms in a Memphis temple and had the text transferred to a basalt slab. The stone represents the doctrines of the temple of PTAH. With the decline of Egypt, the Shabaka Stone was eventually lost, becoming a farmer's millstone. It was recovered in the area of the former capital.

shabtis (shawabtis; ushabtis) The ancient miniature tomb figures of Egypt, called "the Answerer," these figures were part of the mortuary regalia, placed in TOMBS to act as proxies or substitutes for the deceased in TUAT, the land beyond the grave. It was believed that the *shabtis* would perform any and all labors demanded of the deceased in the afterlife. SETI I (r. 1306–1290 B.C.E.) had 700 *shabtis* in his tomb sites.

These mortuary substitute figures were fashioned out of wood and then out of faience, metals, clay, or stone. Nobles and royals kept one figure in the tomb for each day of the year, plus one overseer *shabti*. The figures were usually inscribed with prayers urging the *shabtis* to assume all obligations assigned to the deceased. There is an undocumented connection between the PERSEA TREE and the *shabti* in Egyptian traditions. The tree was called a *shawab*. In some eras, the *shabtis* were buried in individual boxes with vaulted lids. Scribe *shabtis* were found in some tombs.

shaduf An ancient Egyptian irrigation device still in use on the Nile, introduced into the land by the HYKSOS, or Asiatic, invaders of the Second Intermediate Period (1640–1550 B.C.E.), the *shaduf* is a simple wooden instrument consisting of a pole with a bucket on one end and a weight on the other. The *shaduf* enabled a farmer, working alone, to raise water from the Nile and to deposit it in the appropriate canal or irrigation ditch. The use of the device after the Hyksos period increased Egypt's agricultural output. Scholars estimate that the *shaduf* increased cultivation by 10 percent. The device was just one of the many contributions made by the Hyksos during their occupation of the eastern Delta.

Shai She was an Egyptian goddess who determined the fate of individuals and events, associated with mortuary rituals and the JUDGMENT HALLS OF OSIRIS. Shai was part of the cult of RENENET, the goddess of fortune. Shai had powers over the living and the dead, and her name is translated as "what is ordained." Considered the guardian of *shay*, fate, Shai was one of the attendants of the scales upon which the goddess MA'AT weighed the hearts of the deceased Egyptians in judgment.

The *shabtis* discovered in the burial chamber of King Tut'ankhamun and now in the Egyptian Museum in Cairo *(S. M. Bunson)*

Shalmaneser III (d. ca. 828 B.C.E.) *Assyrian ruler who tried to conquer Egypt*
He made attempts to begin an assault on the Nile Valley in the reigns of OSORKON II (883–855 B.C.E.) and TAKELOT II (860–835 B.C.E.). Shalamneser III was the son of Ashurnasirpal (d. 859 B.C.E.), who assumed the Assyrian throne in Kalakh, now Nimrod (near modern Mosul) in Iran. Shalmaneser III reigned over the Assyrian empire from 858 B.C.E. until his death. He was militarily active and faced Egyptian cohorts on several occasions, as the Egyptians were part of confederations of Mediterranean countries determined to halt Assyrian advances. Shalmaneser III was victorious at the battle of Qarqar on the Orontes River but was delayed as a result and died before he could enter the Nile Valley.

Shat en Sebau This was the ancient text called the *Book of the Pylons,* a mortuary work that was a version of THE BOOK OF THE DEAD. The journey through TUAT, the Underworld, was the central theme of this mortuary text.

See also TOMB TEXTS.

Shawab *See* PERSEA TREE.

Shebitku (Djedkauré) (d. 690 B.C.E.) *ruler of the Nubian Twenty-fifth Dynasty*
He was the successor of his uncle, SHABAKA, and reigned 698–690 B.C.E. He was the son of PIANKHI (1) and Queen PEKASSATER. Shebitku married AMENIRDIS (1), a GOD'S WIFE OF AMUN, or Divine Adoratrice of Amun, who retired from that office. His sister, SHEPENWEPET (2), took her place as the God's Wife at Thebes.

Shebitku sided with the Palestinians and Phoenicians (modern Lebanese) in their revolt against the Assyrians. He faced the Assyrian King SENNACHERIB (r. 704–681 B.C.E.) in battle as a result but kept Egypt secure. He left no major monuments but did build at MEDINET HABU. When he died, his remains were taken to Napata, in NUBIA (modern Sudan). He was followed on the throne by his brother, TAHARQA.

shebyu This was a collar worn as an insignia of honor. Originally the collar was associated with the cult of OSIRIS as a symbol of union with RÉ and transformation in the afterlife. The pharaohs wore a *shebyu* of intricate design, and others wore modified versions. The collar was fashioned out of solid gold rings strung on five or more cords, with a clasp covered in gold and bearing the cartouche of the royal hieroglyphs or a spiritual admonition. Smaller gold beads were strung on 14 smaller cords, sometimes tipped with metal bell-shaped ornaments. The dead pharaohs were depicted wearing the *shebyu,* although some wore it in life.

See also AMULETS; MORTUARY RITUALS.

Shed (Hor-Shed) He was an Egyptian deity called "the Savior," the patron of deserts and the hunt. His cult originated in THINIS, and he was depicted as a young prince, wearing the lock of youth. Shed hunted serpents, scorpions, and crocodiles, thus serving as a pest controller. The god often appeared in a chariot drawn by two horses. He was sometimes called Hor-Shed, "the lord of deserts and heaven."

See also GODS AND GODDESSES.

She-dou (fl. ca. 23rd century B.C.E.) *priest of the Old Kingdom*
She-dou's tomb was discovered on the GIZA plateau. He described himself as a "servant of the goddess NEITH." Four painted statues of She-dou were found in his tomb near the pyramids. He is depicted as wearing a white kilt and a wide collar with blue, yellow, and white stones.

Shedsunefertum (fl. 10th century B.C.E.) *official of the Twenty-second Dynasty*
He served SHOSHENQ I (r. 945–924 B.C.E.) as high priest of PTAH. Shedsunefertum was married to a princess of the Twenty-first Dynasty. The cult of Ptah, one of the earliest in Egypt, was popular throughout the historical periods of Egypt, and the priests of Ptah exerted considerable influence in the court.

Sheikh Abd' el-Qurna (Quru) It was a site on the western bank of the Nile at THEBES, used as a necropolis area. Actually a long hill, Sheikh Abd' el-Qurna contained Middle Kingdom (2040–1640 B.C.E.) and New Kingdom (1550–1070 B.C.E.) tombs. The largest Theban necropolis, the site is northwest of the RAMESSEUM and is divided into three sections. The most famous tombs belonged to dynastic officials, including NAKHT (2), a steward for TUTHMOSIS IV (r. 1401–1391 B.C.E.). Nakht was also an astronomer of AMUN. His small tomb has a painted vestibule and a famous relief of a banquet scene, including the figure of a blind harpist.

The tomb of 'Amethu, the VIZIER of TUTHMOSIS III (r. 1479–1425 B.C.E.) is also on this site, designed as a T-shaped enclosure halfway up the cliff. The tomb has a portico and a corridor. The tomb of Ramose is the burial site of the vizier serving AMENHOTEP III (r. 1391–1353 B.C.E.) and AKHENATEN (r. 1353–1335 B.C.E.). The tomb combines the traditional and 'AMARNA styles and depicts Akhenaten and Queen NEFERTITI in reliefs. Unfinished, the site has a HYPOSTYLE HALL with 32 columns and an inner hall with eight columns and a shrine. SETI I (r. 1306–1290 B.C.E.) erected a temple on the site, honoring his father and several deities. A colonnaded court and solar cult chambers were part of this shrine, with a vestibule, sanctuary, and a bark of AMUN. The tomb of REKHMIRÉ, a vizier of TUTHMOSIS III (r. 1479–1425 B.C.E.) and AMENHOTEP II (r. 1427–1401 B.C.E.) is also at Quru. Unfinished, the site has valuable historical reliefs and texts concerning the duties of the vizier. PUNT figures are depicted in a hall near the entrance.

Sheikh el-Beled   *See* KA'APER STATUE.

Sheikh Said   This was a site south of el-BERSHA in central Egypt. The region served as an Old Kingdom (2575–2134 B.C.E.) necropolis for the local populace. NOMARCH tombs were discovered in Sheikh Said, which also served the territory of HATNUB.

Shemay (fl. 22nd century B.C.E.) *official of the Eighth Dynasty*
Shemay served as the VIZIER for Upper Egypt. His son, Idy, was the governor of the seven southernmost nomes. The father and son had to deal with the rising Ninth Dynasty and the Inyotef line in Thebes.

Shemay probably served NEFERKU-HOR, listed in some records as the 14th ruler of the dynasty (date unknown). He married NEBYET, a daughter of Neferku-Hor, and became a governor and then vizier.

shena   An addition made to the *PERO,* or royal residence, in the Twelfth Dynasty (1991–1783 B.C.E.) era and repeated as an architectural design element in later historical periods, the *shena* was a structure designed to offer court servants housing and kitchen areas. The *khenty,* a similar structure designed to serve high-ranking officials, was also initiated in this dynastic period.

shendyt   A kilt-like skirt worn by pharaohs and, in a modified form, by officials and commoners, the *shendyt* underwent fashionable changes, particularly in the New Kingdom (1550–1070 B.C.E.), forming a distinctive angular style. A central tab design was also used as a decoration.
See also DRESS.

shennu   It was the cartouche used by the pharaohs to display their hieroglyphic royal names. The original symbol associated with this CARTOUCHE design was the *shen,* an insignia portraying the sun's orbit. This was a long circle, elongating into an oval frame. The eternal powers of the god RÉ were thus displayed, representing the patronage of that deity in each dynasty.

Shepenwepet (1) (fl. eighth century B.C.E.) *princess of the Twenty-third Dynasty and a God's Wife of Amun*
She was the daughter of OSORKON III (r. 777–749 B.C.E.) and Queen KARAOTJET and was given titles of religious power as the God's Wife of Amun, a Divine Adoratrice of Amun. Shepenwepet was also called the Consort of Hor, the Prophetess of Amun, and the Seeress of Montu. She "adopted" her successor, AMENIRDIS (1), the sister of Piankhi (1) (750–712 B.C.E.). Her tomb chapel was erected in KARNAK.

Shepenwepet (2) (fl. seventh century B.C.E.) *princess of the Twenty-fifth Dynasty and a God's Wife of Amun*
She was the sister of SHEBITKU (r. 698–690 B.C.E.) and was "adopted" by AMENIRDIS to be eligible for this role. In the reign of TAHARQA (690–664 B.C.E.), Shepenwepet "adopted" Amenirdis (2) but was forced in 656 B.C.E. by PSAMMATICHUS I (r. 664–610 B.C.E.) to place his daughter, NITOCRIS (2), into the office, bypassing Amenirdis (2). Shepenwepet had a tomb at KARNAK.

Shepseskaré (Ini) (d. 2419 B.C.E.) *fourth ruler of the Fifth Dynasty*
He reigned from 2426 B.C.E. until his death. He is also listed as Ini. Shepseskaré was the successor of KAKAI (Neferirkaré). He is not well known and his reign was brief. Seal impressions bearing his name were found in ABUSIR, where he started but did not complete a pyramidal tomb.

Shepseskhaf (d. 2467 B.C.E.) *last ruler of the Fourth Dynasty*
He reigned from 2472 B.C.E. until his death, the son of MENKAURÉ. Shepseskhaf completed his father's monuments and reportedly feuded with the priests of various temples over doctrines. He also married BUNEFER and had a son, Djedefptah, who is sometimes listed as Thamptis. His sister was Khentakawes. Khama'at was his daughter, who married Ptahshepses, the high priest of Memphis. Shepseskhaf erected a tomb in southern SAQQARA, called MASTABAT EL-FARA'UN, "the Pharaoh's Bench." Rectangular in design, this mastaba was unfinished and was never used.

Sherden Pirates   *See* SEA PEOPLES, DEFEAT OF.

Shere (fl. 25th century B.C.E.) *mortuary complex official of the Fourth Dynasty*
He served as a mortuary priest for the tombs of SENDJI and PERIBSEN of the Second Dynasty (2700–2649 B.C.E.), whose royal mortuary cults were still active. A slab from Shere's tomb was reportedly recovered and taken to England in the reign of King Charles II.

Sheshi (1) (Mayebré) (d. ca. 1600 B.C.E.) *second ruler of the Asiatic Fifteenth Dynasty, the Great Hyksos*
He ruled from the capital of AVARIS in the Delta region, a contemporary of the Seventeenth Dynasty of Thebes. His throne name was translated as "Just Is the Heart of RÉ." Sheshi's seals were found throughout Lower Egypt as far south as the third cataract of the Nile in Nubia (modern Sudan). He was a successor of SALITIS, the founder of the dynasty, and he was listed in the TURIN CANON.

Sheshi (2)   *See* ANKH-MA-HOR.

Sheshmu An ancient Egyptian deity associated with the olive and grape presses, he played a singular role in the inscription of the pyramidal tombs of UNIS (r. 2356–2323 B.C.E.) at SAQQARA. Sheshmu is recorded in the CANNIBAL HYMN discovered in that tomb, as pressing the gods of Egypt, cooking them along with ancestors of the pharaoh, and then presenting them to Unis. No shrine or cultic monuments to Sheshmu have survived.

Shesmetet She was a lioness goddess dating to the Early Dynastic Period (2920–2575 B.C.E.), a form of the deity BASTET. She was popular especially in the reign of DJOSER (2630–2611 B.C.E.), and her girdle served as a powerful talisman.

sheta This was the ancient Egyptian word for a mystery or a hidden secret. All matter was supposed to contain *shetau akhet*, truly hidden powers. A *shetai* was a hidden god, or something completely incomprehensible. The ISIS cult was particularly *shetai*, noted for its mysteries. The hieroglyphs describing such enigmatic spiritual matters can be translated only by using phonetic values as clarifiers.

Shipwrecked Sailor *See* TALE OF THE SHIPWRECKED SAILOR.

shomu (shemu) A season of the Egyptian calendar, it was celebrated following *akhet* and *proyet* each year. Shomu was the time of harvests, comprising four months of 30 days each.

Shoshenq I (Hedjkheperre'setepenré) (d. 924 B.C.E.)
founder of the Libyan Twenty-second Dynasty
He ruled from 945 B.C.E. until his death. Shoshenq I was the son of the Libyan leader NIMLOT (1), and the nephew of OSORKOR (r. 984–978 B.C.E.), and was based in BUBASTIS. Called "the Great Chief of the MESHWESH," the Libyans residing in Egypt's Delta, he served PSUSENNES II (r. 959–945 B.C.E.) and married the ruler's daughter, MA'ATKARÉ (2).

Having served as the commander of Egypt's military forces, Shoshenq I united THEBES and TANIS, the capital. He fought in Canaan and took the city of Jerusalem. At Ar-Megiddo he erected a stela and renewed ties with Babylon. In Egypt, he built in KARNAK and reopened the quarries at GEBEL EL-SILSILEH. The BUBASTITE PORTAL at Karnak records his military exploits. He also erected a cenotaph for his father at ABYDOS. He is probably the Shishas of the Old Testament.

Having three sons, IUPUT, NIMLOT (2), and Djedptahaufankh, Shoshenq I used them politically. He made Iuput the high priest of AMUN and the governor of Upper Egypt. Nimlot was made commander of HERAKLEOPOLIS, and Djedptahaufankh became third prophet of Amun. A second consort, KAROMANA (1), was the mother of Shoshenq I's heir, OSORKON I. (However, some records indicate MAATKARE (2) was actually Osorkon's mother.) A daughter, Ta'apenes, was married to the Edomite prince Hadad, who had been given refuge in Egypt. Another consort of Shoshenq I was Queen PENRESHNAS, a Libyan aristocrat.

Shoshenq I was buried in TANIS. His coffin, made of silver and decorated with a hawk's head, was discovered in an antechamber of the tomb of Psusennes I. The mummy within his coffin was undisturbed but destroyed by dampness. A calcite canopic chest was also recovered.

Shoshenq II (Hegakheperre'setepenré) (d. 883 B.C.E.)
fourth ruler of the Twenty-second Dynasty, reigning only one year
He was the son of OSORKON I and Queen MA'ATKARÉ (3) and possibly the high priest of Amun at Thebes, for a time, called Shoshenq Meryamun. Osorkon I made him coruler of Egypt, but Shoshenq II died suddenly of an infected head wound. He was survived by his son, HARSIESE, and his wife, Queen NESITANEBETASHRU (1). Shoshenq II was buried in TANIS but was moved to the tomb of Psussenes I when his own resting place flooded. He had two sarcophagi, one dating to the Thirteenth Dynasty (1783–1640 B.C.E.).

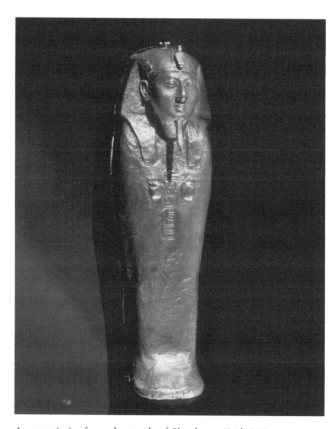

A canopic jar from the tomb of Shoshenq II (d. 883 B.C.E.), the fourth ruler of the Twenty-second Dynasty, in the Cairo Museum *(Werner Forman / Art Resource, NY)*

Shoshenq III (Userma'atre'setepenré) (d. 783 B.C.E.)
seventh ruler of the Twenty-second Dynasty, a usurper
He reigned from 835 B.C.E. until his death, having usurped the throne upon the death of TAKELOT II, putting aside the heir, Prince OSORKON. Shoshenq III was probably the son of OSORKON II (r. 883–855 B.C.E.) and Queen KAROMANA (4). He married Lady TENTAMOPET.

In his sixth regnal year, Shoshenq III witnessed the rise of HARSIESE, the son of SHOSHENQ II, as the high priest of AMUN in THEBES. Harsiese began a series of revolts in Thebes, as PEDUBASTE I of the Twenty-third Dynasty assumed the throne and ruled at LEONTOPOLIS (828–803 B.C.E.). Egypt was divided between TANIS and Leontopolis. Shoshenq III built in MEMPHIS and MENDES and celebrated his *heb-sed* (see SED) at the temple of AMUN in Tanis. His vassal cities included BUSIRIS, BUTO, and SAIS. He also named Prince Osorkon to the office of high priest of Amun in Thebes.

His sons were Bakennefi, who died young, PAMI, who was his successor, and possibly SHOSHENQ V. Shoshenq III was buried at Tanis near the temple of Amun. His seal has been discovered on a statuette and on CANOPIC JARS.

Shoshenq IV (Userma'atre'meryamun) (d. 797 B.C.E.)
second ruler of the Twenty-third Dynasty
He reigned from ca. 803 B.C.E. until his death. He succeeded PEDUBASTE, the founder of the dynasty in LEONTOPOLIS. Little is known of his reign.

Shoshenq V (Akhepruré) (d. 735 B.C.E.) *ninth ruler of the Twenty-second Dynasty in Tanis*
He reigned from 773 B.C.E. until his death. Shoshenq V was probably the brother of PAMI and a son of SHOSHENQ III and Queen TENTAMOPET. There was a dispute over his coronation, but he ruled many decades in TANIS. There he built a temple and a *heb-sed* (see SED) chapel. His son and heir was OSORKON IV.

Shu
He was an Egyptian deity of the air, the patron of light and atmosphere. At the command of ATUM, Shu lifted NUT from the embrace of the earth god GEB and transformed her into the sky. A solar deity, Shu was depicted as a man carrying a SCEPTER, an ANKH or a MA'AT feather. He wore a SOLAR DISK on his head.

The consort of TEFNUT, Shu was also part of lion cults. The four pillars of heaven were his symbols. He was worshiped at HELIOPOLIS and at LEONTOPOLIS. Shu was called "He Who Rises Up." He was a member of the ENNEAD in Heliopolis and was also associated with the cult of RÉ, protecting that deity from the serpent APOPHIS. Shu was the personification of divine intelligence in Egypt.

See also PILLARS OF SHU.

Shunet el-Zabib
A double walled FORTRESS called "the Storehouse of Dates" and located on the northern boundary of ABYDOS at Umm el-Ga'ab, this necropolis area dates to the Early Dynastic Period (2920–2575 B.C.E.). The funerary enclosure of KHA'SEKHEMWY (r. ca. 2649 B.C.E.) was made of mud brick and erected on the site. It is revered as the oldest standing monumental structure in the world and is part of Shunet el-Zabib. The walls of the entire structure are vast. Cenotaphs have been discovered, as well as a series of boat pits.

Shuta (fl. 14th century B.C.E.) *Military official of the Eighteenth Dynasty in the 'Amarna Period*
He served as a military commander in the reign of AKHENATEN (1353–1335 B.C.E.). Some records indicate that he was the grandfather or great grandfather of RAMESSES I (r. 1307–1306 B.C.E.). He was mentioned in the 'AMARNA LETTERS, the correspondence of Akhenaten's period, actually accused by BIRYAWAZA, the prince of Damascus, of unjustly demanding land grants for Egypt. Shuta and other commanders were being forced to vacate certain vassal states during Akhenaten's reign as the empire collapsed.

Siamun (1) (Netjerkheperre'setepenamun) (d. 959 B.C.E.) *sixth ruler of the Twenty-first Dynasty*
He reigned in TANIS from 978 B.C.E. until his death. Siamun was the successor of OSORKOR (Osorkon the Elder) and the son of PSUSENNES I and Queen MUTNODJMET (2). He erected monuments in Tanis, including additions to the temple of HORUS and the temple of AMUN. A block inscribed with his name announced that Siamun added to the monuments of PER-RAMESSES and to the temple at MEMPHIS. A small bronze SPHINX, bearing his features and inlaid with gold, was discovered at Memphis.

Siamun campaigned against the Philistines and reportedly sent his daughter to the harem of Solomon. In Egypt he transferred vulnerable mummies to secure tomb sites. He also welcomed Prince Hadad of Edom, who was fleeing attacks in his city. Hadad married a daughter of Siamun and had a son, Genubath. Siamun may have been a member of the Theban branch of this royal line.

Siamun (2) (fl. 16th century B.C.E.) *prince of the Eighteenth Dynasty*
He was probably the son of 'AHMOSE (NEBPEHTIRÉ) (r. 1550–1525 B.C.E.). The remains of this prince were discovered in the DEIR EL-BAHRI cache in 1881. His mummy was severely damaged, and his bones were found in an oblong bundle in a cedar coffin. The inscriptions on the coffin of Siamun identify the remains of the prince.

Sihathor (fl. 19th century B.C.E.) *mining official of the Twelfth Dynasty*
He served AMENEMHET II (r. 1929–1892 B.C.E.) as supervisor of the mines of Egypt in the SINAI and in the region below the cataracts of the Nile. Sihathor was considered

an expert on turquoise, the stone prized by the Egyptians and favored by the goddess HATHOR. He took part in the construction of the pyramid of Amenemhet II at DASHUR and supervised the building of 10 statues for the mortuary complex of the pharaoh. Sihathor's mortuary STELA, which gives an account of his career and his era, is in the British Museum in London.

See also NATURAL RESOURCES.

Silsileh   *See* GEBEL EL-SILSILEH.

Simonthu (fl. 20th century B.C.E.) *harem and court official of the Twelfth Dynasty*
He served AMENEMHET II (r. 1929–1892 B.C.E.) as "the chief of works" for the court and a royal scribe. Simonthu appears to have held administrative duties in the king's own HAREM. His mortuary stela, now in the British Museum in London, gives an account of his life.

Sinai   This is the peninsula on Egypt's eastern border, called Shibh Jazirat Sina in Arabic and the triangular link between Africa and Asia. The Sinai comprises 23,500 square miles, bounded by the Gulf of Suez, the Gulf of Aqaba, and the Negev Desert. The Mediterranean and Red Seas also serve as boundaries.

The Sinai was always part of the life of ancient Egypt, serving as a resource for minerals and stones and as a barrier against nomadic tribes and foreign armies in most historical periods. The Sinai attracted the Egyptians in the earliest eras, possessing copper, malachite, turquoise, and several other types of precious and semiprecious stones used in decorative arts. The Predynastic Period (before 3000 B.C.E.) graves found in Egypt contained turquoise articles, indicating that the early inhabitants of the Nile Valley mined the stones or traded with the Sinai BEDOUINS for the items.

The mines and quarries founded by the Egyptians in the Sinai date to the Early Dynastic Period (2920–2575 B.C.E.), and Old Kingdom (2575–2134 B.C.E.) rulers also exploited the area. Expeditions and military campaigns were conducted to insure that the Egyptian use of the area could continue without hindrance. The Bedouins in the Sinai revolted against the continued presence of the Egyptians in the reign of SNEFRU (2575–2551 B.C.E.), and these nomadic people were confronted and defeated by Egyptian military units in a series of Sinai campaigns.

PEPI I (r. 2289–2255 B.C.E.) mandated his military commander, General WENI, to conduct major campaigns in the Sinai, and as a result, the Egyptians chased one Bedouin tribe all the way to Mount Carmel to punish them for hindering Egyptian activities in their original homeland. When the Old Kingdom collapsed, however, the Asiatics, the name for the dwellers in the Sinai and in the eastern territories, entered the Nile Valley and caused severe social and political problems.

The rise of MENTUHOTEP II (r. 2061–2010 B.C.E.) and the union of the Two Kingdoms in Egypt put an end to Asiatic incursions and renewed Egypt's presence in the Sinai minefields and quarries. AMENEMHET I (1991–1962 B.C.E.), the founder of the Twelfth Dynasty, assumed the same military posture, erecting a series of fortresses on the borders of Egypt and the Sinai. The great copper mines of the Sinai region were in full operation at this time.

The collapse of the Middle Kingdom and the rise of the Hyksos in the Second Intermediate Period brought an invasion of Asiatics from the Sinai, particularly the HYKSOS, who ruled the Delta region and extended Egypt's borders to the northern Sinai and even to parts of Palestine. They were driven out of Egypt by the armies of 'AHMOSE (NEBPEHTIRÉ) (r. 1550–1525 B.C.E.), the founder of the New Kingdom.

The New Kingdom (1550–1070 B.C.E.) rulers used the Sinai quarries and mines extensively. HATSHEPSUT (r. 1473–1458 B.C.E.) left inscriptions in the region, mementos of the mining expeditions conducted in her name. In the Nineteenth Dynasty, RAMESSES II (r. 1290–1224 B.C.E.) erected a temple at the copper mines. These mines and quarries did not remain in Egypt's hands after the reign of RAMESSES III (1194–1163 B.C.E.).

Sporadic quarrying and mining operations were conducted by the various rulers of the Third Intermediate Period (1070–712 B.C.E.) in the Sinai, but they did not sustain operations in the region. During the Late Period (712–332 B.C.E.), only a few expeditions were supported. The Ptolemaic Period (304–30 B.C.E.) accelerated the operations in the Sinai to a degree, and the Romans, gaining control of Egypt after the death of CLEOPATRA VII in 30 B.C.E., institutionalized Sinai resource sites and carried out vigorous control of the traditional and historical operations.

Further reading: Greenwood, Ned H. *The Sinai: A Physical Geography.* Austin: University of Texas Press, 1997; Saadeldin, Mursi, and Ayman Aaher, Mursi Saad El Din, ed. *Sinai.* New York: New York University Press, 1998; Siliotti, Alberto. *Sinai.* Cairo: American University in Cairo Press, 2001.

Sinai Inscriptions   These are hieroglyphic records discovered on the rock walls of WADI MAGHARA in the SINAI Peninsula. One dates to the reign of SNEFRU (2575–2551 B.C.E.), giving an account of his exploits and campaigns against the local BEDOUINS, the Bedu or Bedwi, and his use of the copper mines of the area.

SAHURÉ (r. 2458–2446 B.C.E.) of the Fifth Dynasty is also depicted smiting the Bedouins on the Sinai. MENKAUHOR (r. 2396–2388 B.C.E.) sent smaller expeditions into the region, as did IZEZI (Djedkaré) (r. 2388–2356 B.C.E.) during his reign. A STELA was erected as a marker by this expedition. PEPI I (r. 2289–2255 B.C.E.) is also depicted smiting the Bedouins on a stela that announces his jubilee. Queen ANKHNESMERY-RÉ (2) erected a similar stone to commemorate an expedition during her regency for PEPI II (r. 2246–2152 B.C.E.). This malachite stone was discovered on a terraced region of the Sinai. Later rulers, including AMENEMHET II (r. 1929–1892 B.C.E.) left other inscriptions.

Sinuhe the Sailor He is one of the most interesting literary characters of the ancient world, preserved in the BERLIN PAPYRI and in an inscription in a Twentieth Dynasty (1196–1070 B.C.E.) tomb. The character is the hero of a tale concerning the reign of SENWOSRET I (1971–1926 B.C.E.), who came to the throne when his father, AMENEMHET I, was assassinated by a HAREM plot. Senwosret I was in Libya, campaigning there with Sinuhe, who served as an official of Amenemhet I's harem and was possibly involved in some way in the harem plot. He intended to travel south but ended up in Palestine, Lebanon, and other lands. Sinuhe was invited to Syria by a nobleman and married his daughter. Becoming a patriarch there he defends the lands and has adventures.

Sinuhe means "son of the sycamore," a tree popular in myths and in Egyptian love poetry. His adventures served as models for later works, particularly the Arabian Nights tales and the character of the modern Sinbad the Sailor. The tale provides considerable detail about the Middle Kingdom period, including the court of Senwosret I, who invited him to return to Egypt. Sinuhe was welcomed with gifts and a pardon. The pharaoh also erected a fine tomb for Sinuhe.

Siptah (Akhenre'setepenré; Ramesses-Siptah; Meryenptah) (d. 1198 B.C.E.) *seventh ruler of the Nineteenth Dynasty*
He reigned from 1204 B.C.E. until his death. He was listed as "King's Son," and his mother was Queen TIA (2). He was originally called Ramesses-Siptah, the son of SETI II. Forensic studies indicate that Siptah was possibly a victim of poliomyelitis, appearing clubfooted. Siptah was reportedly placed on the throne by BAY, with Queen TWOSRET serving as his regent because of his young age. He conducted campaigns in NUBIA (modern Sudan) in his first regnal year, and inscriptions concerning him were found in a temple in WADI HALFA. He also built a mortuary temple north of the RAMESSEUM in THEBES (modern Luxor).

Siptah died young and was buried in the VALLEY OF THE KINGS with Queen Tia. His mummified remains were stuffed with dry lichen, and his cheeks padded by strips of linen. His tomb was designed long and straight, with decorated corridors, a square antechamber, and a burial place with four pillars. A red granite sarcophagus was in the burial room. Siptah was moved in a later era, because of tomb robberies, and his mummy was discovered with other royal remains in the tomb of AMENHOTEP II.

Sirenput (1) (fl. 20th century B.C.E.) *military governor of the Twelfth Dynasty*
He served SENWOSRET I (r. 1971–1926 B.C.E.) as a military commander and as the governor of the south. He was a noble from ASWAN who also served as the overseer of the priests of KHNUM and SATET. His tomb in Aswan has a doorway leading to a columned courtyard with scenes of paradise as decorations. The tomb also has square pillars, a long passage, and a statue recess. A large figure of Sirenput was discovered. He was also portrayed with his dogs and family members.

Sirenput (2) (Nubkaré-nakht) (fl. 20th century B.C.E.) *military governor of the Twelfth Dynasty*
He served AMENEMHET II (r. 1929–1892 B.C.E.) as the governor of the south and a military commander. Sirenput was the son of Satet-hotep. His tomb is on the western bank of the Nile at ASWAN and contains elaborate paintings, a six-pillared hall, a recessed corridor, and statues. He is depicted on four pillars discovered in rear chambers. Portraits of his family and vivid scenes of birds and animals were also completed. An Osiride statue of Sirenput was found in the tomb as well.

Sirius *See* SOPDU.

Sisatet (fl. 19th century B.C.E.) *financial official of the Twelfth Dynasty*
He served SENWOSRET III (r. 1878–1841 B.C.E.) as a royal treasurer. Sisatet was the son of an official named Ameni and his mother was Sitamene. Sisatet accompanied IKHERNOFRET, a relative, to ABYDOS, where a stela was erected. He succeeded Ikhernofret as treasurer after serving in that agency throughout his career.

sistrum Called the *seses* or *shesheset* by the ancient Egyptians, it was a musical instrument that was popular in the cult of the goddess HATHOR. The sistrum was formed as a stick-like wooden or metal object, with a frame and small metal disks that rattled when the instrument was shaken by a hand. Designed with a broad band of copper, bent almost double, the sistrum had wires inserted through holes drilled into the band, containing the disks. When shaken, the sistrum makes a shimmering sound. The head of Hathor was often depicted on the instrument or the horns of a cow were incorporated into its design. The sistrum was a favored instrument in cultic rites in Egypt's temples and shrines and was used in religious processions. The sistrum took the form of a cartouche and was honored for this coincidence. When the sistrum was used by the goddess NEHEM-AWIT, a divine form of Hathor, evil spirits fled from the sound. Some of these sistrums were later fashioned out of FAIENCE.

See also MUSIC.

Sistrum Mansion   A site in the seventh nome of Upper Egypt, the Sistrum Mansion was a royal estate, also called "Kheperkere, the Justified Is Mighty." The structure was erected by SENWOSRET I (r. 1971–1926 B.C.E.) and was dedicated to a local goddess who was depicted in the form of a sistrum, a popular musical instrument that was always fashioned with a human head at the base. In time, the sistrum became the symbol of the goddess Hathor at Dendera. During the Greco-Roman Period (332 B.C.E.–395 C.E.) the sistrum was still venerated. The shrine of Hathor was then called "Diospora Parva."

See also MUSIC.

Sitamun (1)   (fl. 16th century B.C.E.) *royal woman of the Eighteenth Dynasty*
She was a daughter of 'AHMOSE (NEBPEHTIRÉ) (r. 1550–1525 B.C.E.) and Queen 'AHMOSE NEFERTARI, who died young and was buried in a sycamore coffin. Her original tomb was vandalized and her remains were hacked to bits by robbers looking for jewels or gold in her mummy wrappings. Sitamun was among the mummies found in the royal cache in DEIR EL-BAHRI in 1881.

Sitamun (2)   (fl. 14th century B.C.E.) *royal woman of the Eighteenth Dynasty*
The daughter of AMENHOTEP III (r. 1391–1353 B.C.E.) and Queen TIYE (1), Sitamun married her father and bore him two sons. She reportedly had a suite in Amenhotep III's tomb, and her furniture was deposited in the tomb of her grandfather, TUTHMOSIS IV. Sitamun was buried at THEBES.

Sit-Hathor   (fl. 20th century B.C.E.) *royal woman of the Twelfth Dynasty*
She was the consort of AMENEMHET I (r. 1991–1962 B.C.E.) and the mother of Princess Nenseb-Djebet and Princess DEDYET (2). Sit-Hathor was buried in the royal mortuary complex at el-LISHT.

Sit-Hathor Meryt (Sit-Hathor Horneryt)   (fl. 19th century B.C.E.) *royal woman of the Twelfth Dynasty*
She was probably the daughter of AMENEMHET II (r. 1929–1892 B.C.E.) and was buried in the royal mortuary complex at DASHUR. Her mummy was disturbed, but some of her beautiful jewelry survived the robbery. Sit-Hathor Meryt's SARCOPHAGUS was carved out of sandstone.

Sit-Hathor Yunet   (fl. 19th century B.C.E.) *royal woman of the Twelfth Dynasty*
She was reportedly the daughter of SENWOSRET II (r. 1897–1878 B.C.E.) and Queen NEFERHENT (1). The sister of Senwosret III, she was possibly his consort. Sit-Hathor Yunet was buried in DASHUR, and her jewels and mortuary regalia survived tomb robberies. Many displays of affection from royal family members were discovered in her gravesite. The cartouches of Senwosret II and AMENEMHET III were also in her tomb.

Sitiah   (fl. 15th century B.C.E.) *royal woman of the Eighteenth Dynasty*
She was a consort of TUTHMOSIS III (r. 1479–1425 B.C.E.) and held the rank of Great Wife. Sitiah received this rank upon the death of NEFERU-RÉ, as late as Tuthmosis III's 22nd regnal year. A commoner, and the daughter of the royal nurse Ipu, she either did not live long or retired to the harem villa at MI-WER in the FAIYUM at a young age. She bore no heirs. Sitiah was replaced by MERYT-RÉ-HATSHEPSUT.

Sit-Kamose   (fl. 16th century B.C.E.) *royal woman of the Eighteenth Dynasty*
She was a princess of Thebes in the reign of 'AHMOSE I (1550–1525 B.C.E.), or possibly KAMOSE (r. 1555–1550 B.C.E.) of the Seventeenth Dynasty. Her mummified remains were discovered at DEIR EL-BAHRI in 1881. The priests of the Twenty-first Dynasty (1070–945 B.C.E.) placed them there after finding her tomb vandalized. A large woman, Sit-Kamose's mummy was packed with linens. She was placed in a sycamore coffin and garlanded with flowers.

Sitré   (fl. 14th century B.C.E.) *royal woman of the Nineteenth Dynasty*
She was the consort of RAMESSES I (r. 1307–1306 B.C.E.), an elderly commoner when Ramesses I founded the Nineteenth Dynasty. Sitré was the mother of SETI I and a military woman, having moved with Ramesses I during his career and having supported him as he rose in rank. She died in the reign of Seti I, much honored by the court. She was buried in the first tomb in the VALLEY OF THE QUEENS, and her gravesite had a hall and an unfinished burial chamber. Paintings on the walls depict her making offerings to the gods of Egypt.

Siwa   One of the oases in the LIBYAN DESERT, the most honored of the fertile islands, Siwa is situated west of ALEXANDRIA in the Delta area and served as a famous religious destination for centuries. ORACLES at the temple of AMUN drew countless pilgrims, and the religious houses there were well endowed. ALEXANDER III THE GREAT visited the temple of the oracle in 331 B.C.E., and was crowned there as the son of AMUN, a true pharaoh. This temple was originally stolid and plain. During the Ptolemaic Dynasty (304–30 B.C.E.), however, half columns, courts, antechambers, and a sanctuary were added or refurbished. In an earlier era, AMASIS (r. 570–526 B.C.E.) had dedicated new additions.

A second temple dedicated to Amun, called Umm 'Ubayda, was located near the rock of Aghurmi at Siwa. Another site, Ain el-Gubah, called "the Spring of the Sun," is ancient in origin. A necropolis served Siwa at

Gebel el-Mawta, or Qarat el-Mussaberin, the "Ridge of Mummies."

CAMBYSES (r. 525–522 B.C.E.), the Persian conqueror, sent a rather large force to Siwa Oasis, having heard of the wealth of the region, known for wines and dates as well as religious ceremonies. This Persian army marched into the desert and disappeared. The entire force was lost and this disappearance remained a mystery. Recent excavations in the area, however, may have uncovered the Persian soldiers and their equipment. In the Greco-Roman era, Siwa Oasis was named Jupiter Ammon.

sma-tawy (sema-tawy) This was the symbol of the unified Upper and Lower Egypt. The insignia was fashioned out of the signs of the Two Kingdoms, the entwined PAPYRUS and LOTUS. The *sma-tawy* appeared on thrones, sacred barks, or in the decorations in palaces and temples.

Smendes (1) (Nesbenebded; Hedjkheperre'setepenré)
(d. 1044 b.c.e.) *founder of the Twenty-first Dynasty*
He reigned from 1070 B.C.E. until his death. Smendes had served RAMESSES XI (r. 1100–1070 B.C.E.), the last ruler of the Twentieth Dynasty, and took the throne when the Ramessid line ended. In order to consolidate his claims, Smendes married Princess TANTAMUN (2), the daughter of Ramesses XI. Smendes is derived from Nesbenebded, his commoner name. He was a native of Djedet in the Delta.

Smendes established his capital in TANIS, as HERI-HOR, the high priest of Amun in Thebes, played the role of co-regent. In Smendes's 16th regnal year, PINUDJEM (1), the new high priest of Amun, openly displayed pharaonic titles and rituals. Smendes's sons were PSUSENNES I and Amenemnisu, and his daughter was HENUTTAWY. He resided at MEMPHIS and constructed the enclosing wall in KARNAK and LUXOR. An inscription attesting to his reign was discovered at GEBELEIN. He was buried in TANIS.

Smendes (2) (fl. 11th century B.C.E.) *priestly official of the Twenty-first Dynasty*
He served as high priest of Amun during the reign of PSUSENNES I (1040–992 B.C.E.). The son of MENKHE PER-RESENB (2) and ISTEMKHEBE (2), he was elderly when he succeeded his father in the role of high priest. Smendes served two years and was succeeded by his son, PINUD-JEM (2).

Smenkharé (Ankhepruré) (d. 1333 B.C.E.) *eleventh ruler of the Eighteenth Dynasty*
He reigned at 'AMARNA and THEBES from 1335 B.C.E. until his death at a young age. Married to Queen Meryt-amun, who had replaced her mother, NEFERTITI, as the consort of AKHENATEN, Smenkharé was depicted as Akhenaten's companion before that ruler died, serving for a time as co-regent. He also took the religious title of Nefertiti, Nefer-Nefru-Aten, leading to speculation that Smenkharé was actually Nefertiti.

When Smenkharé assumed the throne upon the death of Akhenaten, he bowed to pressure from the various priesthoods and the military and returned to Thebes. He ruled from that capital for two years. He was reportedly buried in BIBAN EL-MOLUK, near Thebes, and his funerary regalia was used in the tomb of TUT'ANKHAMUN. A tomb was also prepared for Smenkharé at 'Amarna. His tomb in the VALLEY OF THE KINGS had an undecorated coffin and a shrine for Queen TIYE. His sarcophagus was originally made for a woman and then altered. No mummy has been identified as his remains.

Smith Papyrus, Edwin It is an Eighteenth Dynasty (1550–1307 B.C.E.) text, which may have been a copy of a papyrus that originated in the Third Dynasty (2649–2575 B.C.E.). Concerned with the medical practices of the priest-physicians of Egypt, the document contains 48 separate sections that discuss symptoms of diseases, diagnostic traditions, and treatments—all aspects of ancient Egyptian medicine. The medical procedures seem remarkably modern in objective analysis of a medical problem and the method by which symptoms could be alleviated. The Edwin Smith Papyrus is one of the texts that have enabled modern scholars to assess medical knowledge in pharaonic Egypt.

Snefru (d. 2551 B.C.E.) *founder of the Fourth Dynasty*
He ruled from 2575 B.C.E. until his death. Snefru was probably the son of HUNI and MERYSANKH (1). His name meant "He of Beauty," and he was one of Egypt's early great pharaohs. The PALERMO STONE gives accounts of his campaigns in LIBYA, NUBIA (modern Sudan), and the SINAI. The WESTCAR PAPYRUS calls him an amiable ruler who liked amusements. He was made a god in the SINAI, where an inscription at WADI MAGHARA depicts his concern for the area's turquoise mines. He also built a fleet of 40 ships to trade with Phoenicia (modern Lebanon) for their prized wood. Snefru established trade enterprises with other Mediterranean city-states as well.

During his reign the cultural and artistic standards of Egypt were stabilized. Snefru devised the use of the CARTOUCHE for displaying royal names, as earlier rulers had used a circular shell. In Egyptian records, he was called "the Beneficent Ruler."

In his Nubian campaigns, Snefru boasted that he brought back "7,000 captives and 200,000 oxen and sheep." He used Nubian MEDJAY as well as the BLEMMYES to aid his control of the copper, turquoise, and malachite mines of the Sinai.

Snefru married HETEPHERES (1) and had sons and daughters. His son Neferma'at died young. Another son, Rahotep, called Kanefer as well, served as his vizier. His heir was KHUFU. Prince Snefrukhaf is also listed as a son of Snefru, as is Prince Snefru-seneb.

Snefru perfected the pyramid form during his reign. Three pyramids, possibly four, are believed to be the work of Snefru, who pioneered this type of tomb. The MEIDUM pyramid, the two at DASHUR, and possibly one at SEILA, west of Meidum, on the crest of Gebel el-Rus, are all credited to Snefru's reign. The rubble fragments at Seila contain Snefru's titles as well as statues, tables, and stelae. At Meidum there was a Hall of NOMES. The rulers of the Twelfth Dynasty (1991–1783 B.C.E.) deified Snefru and made his achievements their standards, also electing to be buried near him at Dashur. He had cultic shrines at ABYDOS, the ELEPHANTINE, EDFU, EL-KULA, Seila, KOM OMBO, and elsewhere.

Sobek

A deity originally called Msuh and associated with CROCODILES, Sobek, depicted either as a man with a crocodile's head or as a crocodile, was the patron deity of the Thirteenth Dynasty (1783–1640 B.C.E.). Many kings of that line bore his name in their royal titles. Sobek was mentioned in the PYRAMID TEXTS as a son of the goddess NEITH (1). He was considered to be one of the beings that emerged from the watery chaos at the moment that the world began. The FAIYUM and the city of CROCODILOPOLIS were his sacred abodes, and a temple was built for him on the banks of the Nile in Upper Egypt, in KOM OMBO. Sobek was also associated with AHA, the first king of Egypt. The god was equated in some nomes with SET, and there crocodiles were ritually slaughtered. In other regions, crocodiles were venerated. Crocodilopolis (Medinet el-Faiyum) was his main center, but he also had temples at GEBEL EL-SILSILEH and GEBELEIN. In the New Kingdom (1550–1070 B.C.E.), Sobek was associated with the god AMUN and was also worshipped as Sobek-Ré

Sobekemsaf I (Sekhemré-wadjka'u) (fl. ca. 1650 B.C.E.) second ruler of the Seventeenth Dynasty

He reigned ca. 1640 B.C.E., but the actual dates are undocumented. Sobekemsaf I ruled in THEBES, as a contemporary of the HYKSOS Fifteenth and Sixteenth Dynasties (1640–1532 B.C.E.) in the Delta, and he built in ABYDOS, KARNAK, TOD, and on ELEPHANTINE Island during his reign. He also led an expedition to NUBIA (modern Sudan). Sobekemsaf's tomb was vandalized in the reign of RAMESSES IX (1131–1112 B.C.E.). A heart SCARAB belonging to Sobekemsaf, fashioned out of green jasper and with a human rather than an insect head, was recovered. The remains of his consort, Queen NUBKHAS (2), disappeared from the tomb, probably a victim of robbers.

Sobekemsaf II (Sekhemré-shedtawy) (fl. ca. 1570 B.C.E.) fourth ruler of the Seventeenth Dynasty in Thebes

He reigned ca. 1570 B.C.E. Sobekemsaf II built at KARNAK and ABYDOS and was remembered as a "great" ruler, whose monuments stand even to this day. He was a contemporary of the Hyksos Dynasties, the Fifteenth and Sixteenth in the Delta (1640–1532 B.C.E.). Sobekemsaf's tomb was mentioned in the ABBOTT PAPYRUS.

Sobekhirkhab (fl. 19th century B.C.E.) mining official of the Twelfth Dynasty

He served in the reign of AMENEMHET III (1844–1797 B.C.E.) as a superintendent of Egyptian mining operations at SERABIT EL-KHADIM in the SINAI. Sobekhirkhab erected a STELA on the walls of the reservoir near the mines, a source of much needed water. On the monument he states that he opened the mines and returned with all his men healthy. The stela also honors the goddess HATHOR, patroness of such operations.

Sobekhotep (fl. 14th century B.C.E.) chancellor of Egypt in the Eighteenth Dynasty

He served TUTHMOSIS IV (r. 1401–1391 B.C.E.) as CHANCELLOR and as the mayor of the "Southern Lake," the FAIYUM region. The territory was also called the Southern Channel or the Channel of Sobek. His tomb in THEBES contains paintings of various local industries.

Sobekhotep I (Kha'ankhré) (fl. ca. 1750 B.C.E.) ruler of the obscure Thirteenth Dynasty

He reigned ca. 1750 B.C.E. Cylinder seals and scarabs bearing his royal name have been discovered. The Papyrus Bulaq 18 dates to his reign.

Sobekhotep II (Sekhemré-khutawy) (fl. ca. 1730 B.C.E.) ruler of the obscure Thirteenth Dynasty

The dates of his reign are unknown. Sobekhotep II left monuments in MEDAMUD and DEIR EL-BAHRI. He also had Nile floods recorded at SEMNA, where his statue was found. Listed in the TURIN CANON, Sobekhotep II is mentioned in reliefs at Nag Hammadi, the ELEPHANTINE, and BUBASTIS.

Sobekhotep III (Sekhemré-swadjtawy) (fl. ca. 1745 B.C.E.) ruler of the obscure Thirteenth Dynasty

The dates of his reign are unknown. Sobekhotep III was the son of a Theban prince, Mentuhotep, and the Lady Auhetabu. He married ANA (1) and had two daughters, Ankhetitak and Fent Ankhet. Papyri dating to his reign provide details about the administration of the court of Thebes and his control of NUBIA (modern Sudan). He issued decrees and established three ministries. Sobekhotep III built a temple gate with a colonnade for MONTU at MEDAMUD and had statues at the third cataract of the NILE in Nubia.

Sobekhotep IV (Kha'neferré) (fl. ca. 1730 B.C.E.) ruler of the obscure Thirteenth Dynasty

He possibly reigned from ca. 1730 to 1720 B.C.E. and was the brother of NEFERHOTEP I and SAHATHOR (1). Colossal statues of him have survived in TANIS, made of red granite. Sobekhotep IV campaigned in NUBIA (modern Sudan). He also had to put down rebellions inside Egypt's borders. During his reign, the HYKSOS took over the territory of AVARIS in the Delta.

Sobekhotep V (Kha'hotepré) (fl. ca. 1720 B.C.E.) *ruler of the obscure Thirteenth Dynasty*
He possibly reigned 1720–1715 B.C.E. Sobekhotep V was the son of SOBEKHOTEP IV. Little documentation of his reign survives, but he left a stela in KARNAK.

Sobek-khu-Za'a (fl. 19th century B.C.E.) *military official of the Twelfth Dynasty*
He served in the reigns of SENWOSRET III (1878–1841 B.C.E.) and AMENEMHET III (1844–1797 B.C.E.) as superintendent of the Nile's measurements, and then as the commander of the pharaoh's personal troops. He was also a governor.

Sobek-khu-Za'a was a prince and count of a nome. He left a stela at ABYDOS that provides a dramatic account of one of his campaigns in Syria and he fought as well in Nubia (modern Sudan). During Amenemhet III's reign, Sobek-khu-Za'a was named one of the guardians of the royal NILOMETERS. He was 66 years old at the time.

Sobekneferu (Nefru-Sobek) (d. 1783 B.C.E.) *last ruler of the Twelfth Dynasty, reigning as a queen-pharaoh*
She ruled Egypt from 1787 B.C.E. until her death. She was a daughter of AMENEMHET III and the half sister of AMENEMHET IV. Her name meant "the beauty of Sobek." Sobekneferu was listed in the TURIN CANON and in the SAQQARA KING LIST.

She was a co-regent with her father and married to her brother, Amenemhet IV. When he died in 1787 B.C.E., she assumed the throne, ruling from ITJ-TAWY, the dynastic capital. Sobekneferu completed Amenemhet III's mortuary temple at HAWARA and possibly resided at times during the year at Shedet (CROCODILOPOLIS) in the FAIYUM.

Three headless statues of her were found at TELL EL-DAB'A, and a monument at the second cataract honored her reign. Cylinder seals with her *serekh* and statuary fragments have also been found. Her torso is in the Louvre in Paris. Sobekneferu is believed to have built a pyramid at MAZGHUNA, near DASHUR, but did not use it. She and Amenemhet IV were possibly buried somewhere nearby.

social evolution in Egypt Ongoing traditions dominated life in the Nile Valley from the earliest eras until the end of the nation's independence and the beginning of Roman domination. Several social factors, such as the divine status of the rulers and the foundation of society based on clan structures in the NOMES, fluctuated and were dimmed or revived over the centuries. The moral order and the imperatives of spiritual beliefs, later systematized in the concept of *ma'at,* however, remained constant, providing stability in times of peace and a certain resiliency in eras of chaos.

PREDYNASTIC PERIOD

The first inhabitants of the Nile Valley were herdsmen and farmers who left the desert area when the monsoons failed and the area became an arid wasteland. They settled in the Delta and the region of Upper Egypt in the south. The Nile River was the dominating factor of life from the Predynastic Periods before 3000 B.C.E., as the first inhabitants entered the Nile Valley. The Nile's annual inundation made human existence possible but only as a cooperative venture of shared responsibilities based on seasonal demands. The Nile Valley, surrounded by inhospitable desert wastes, made the Egyptians aware of their blessings.

The river and the annual inundations also turned their attentions and energies inward, fostering a sense of human destiny and stimulating artistic and architectural activities that cut across social caste levels. The dominant cultic forms of worship that developed during this time, especially that of the god Ré, stressed a basic equality of humans in existence on earth and in the spiritual world beyond the grave. The caste system of the clans was firmly in place, but commoners, or simple farmers, knew their own value and their destinies in eternal realms. The temple hierarchies were also being formed.

EARLY DYNASTIC PERIOD

When the regions of Upper and Lower Egypt were united by Narmer around 3000 B.C.E., the dynastic patterns of rule evolved slowly as nome clans took power with the imperative of unity becoming dominant. The act of unity, in fact, sparked the birth of Egypt, a coming into being that focused energies and set in motion creative forces in all walks of life. Literacy was dominant and vital as most male children attended classes. A bureaucracy—based on earlier nome and clan administrative traditions—arose and the compelling pantheon of deities was already in place, worshipped at cultic bases throughout the Nile Valley.

The ruler was supreme after the unification, although some areas of Egypt had to be persuaded or militarily compelled to become part of the new society, a process that took decades. By the end of the First Dynasty (2920–2770 B.C.E.) the rulers could wear the Double Crown, representing Upper and Lower Egypt, with actual authority and with the consent of the people.

During the First and Second Dynasties (2770–2649 B.C.E.), in fact, the civilizing elements of government, art, literacy, cultic religion, and a sense of unique destiny arose as natural elements of life on the Nile. This

A relief depicting the daily labors, recreation, and ceremonial events on the Nile in the Middle Kingdom Period (2040–1640 B.C.E.) *(Hulton Archive)*

remarkable sense of awareness spurred the Egyptians of all economic and political levels toward advancement.

The pharaoh DJOSER (r. 2630–2611 B.C.E.) was a critical force in this era and demonstrates the unique social foundations in place. He was a "living god," embodying the religious mandates and serving as the supreme judge of all. He had enough power as well to marshal the resources of the earth and human labor to embark on a massive construction program that drew on the loyalty and fervor of the people. Workers came from far and wide to raise up the STEP PYRAMID at SAQQARA, joining in a holy union with the pharaoh and proclaiming their belief in the divine system on earth and in the paradises waiting beyond the grave.

Djoser's vizier and architect, IMHOTEP, demonstrates yet another social uniqueness of Egypt. Imhotep was not divine and had not inherited a throne, but he had brought artistic vision, wisdom, and fidelity to his various offices and stood beside the pharaoh as a beloved "companion." This paradoxical aspect of Egypt would continue throughout all of the dynasties. The ruler was a god, but he did not deter the wise, the talented, or the dedicated from achieving rank and power. What was necessary for the individual Egyptian in any historical period to rise in rank and honors as public servants or as faithful members of villages was dedication, loyalty, conformity to accepted traditions, and a commitment to *ma'at,* the guiding principle of life in the Nile Valley.

THE OLD KINGDOM PERIOD

The NOMARCHS, the aristocratic clan families that controlled hereditary ranks and estates, were powerful in the Old Kingdom (2575–2134 B.C.E.), and commoners looked to them to control regional matters and to maintain stability and peace. The commoners were assured of equal justice in the nation's courts and of their right to appeal to higher authorities in cases of juridical incompetence or malice.

Men and women married, raised families, bequeathed their holdings to their heirs, and went to their tombs assured of paradise in a spiritual form. When the ruler called for laborers for the great monuments, the people responded with enthusiasm because this was part of their pact with the gods and with Egypt. When the ruler declared that an enemy was threatening Egypt, the people knew that such a foe had to be evil and deserving of punishment. They marched to war behind their nomarchs and clan totems to free Egypt from menace.

The Old Kingdom nurtured the traditions of previous generations and brought them to full flower. Egypt was prosperous, protected by the gods, and in the service of the anointed ruler on the throne. The individual Egyptians could attend schools, follow in the trade of their fathers, or invent new ways of making a living. All Egyptians, however, stood at the tombs of their ancestors to keep their memories alive. They also worshipped the gods and practiced henotheism, the art of believing in one god while not denying the presence of an entire pantheon of deities.

Men and women set dowry arrangements and took up cohabitation as marriage. The wife was the sole mistress of the house, the one who set the discipline, and might become one of the matriarchs of the village or city neighborhood. The men performed their labors and met with others to settle disputes in council. Many marriages were love-matches, especially among the common classes, and most were monogamous. The mandate of the historical period was the obligation of the people to raise up "stout sons" for Egypt.

During the Fourth (2575–2465 B.C.E.), Fifth (2465–2323 B.C.E.), and Sixth (2323–2150 B.C.E.) Dynasties, the nation prospered, and irrigation, AGRICULTURE, and religious factors of life were aided by vast building projects and improvements. During this period the supremacy of the pharaoh was stressed, and in many reigns only members of the royal families held positions of power. The commoners were estranged to some extent, and the various nomarchs began to assume powers. There were still commoners of wisdom and valor, such as KAGEMNI and MERERUKA, serving TETI (r. 2323–2291 B.C.E.), but the government was becoming decentralized. The nomarchs, however, served as loyal, capable representatives of the pharaoh, and remarkable individuals appear in this era. The governing officials of some areas, such as NUBIA (modern Sudan), had to raise armies, garrison outposts, levy taxes, conduct trade, and perform quarrying or mining operations. A vast army of dedicated assistants made such labors possible.

THE FIRST INTERMEDIATE PERIOD

All of this prosperity and determined service came to an end in the 94-year reign of PEPI II (2246–2152 B.C.E.). His successors, including a queen-pharaoh, NITOCRIS (1), could not stem the tide of decline, and thus chaos, an element of existence most feared by the Egyptians, descended on the Nile. The First Intermediate Period (2134–2040 B.C.E.) witnessed the collapse of the monarchy and the steady rise of the nomarchs and industrious commoners. The literature of the era demonstrates confusion, a profound sense of loss, and despair.

The rulers of the Ninth (2134–? B.C.E.) and Tenth (?–2040 B.C.E.) Dynasties tried to regroup, but the Egyptian people did not respond until an act of sacrilege so alarmed everyone that the Thebans of Upper Egypt raised an army and retook all of the nation. In the battles for land and power, a group from the north assaulted THINIS, the original area of NARMER. Ancient grave sites were destroyed, an act that was shockingly depraved in the minds of the Egyptians. During this era, however, "THE ELOQUENT PEASANT" OF HERAKLEOPOLIS, abused by a local nomarch, took his case to the pharaoh and became a popular sage when he triumphed legally.

MENTUHOTEP II (r. 2061–2010 B.C.E.) assumed the mantle of moral outrage that resulted from the desecration of Thinis tombs and marched on the remaining rulers of the Tenth Dynasty, ending the disunity and the chaos. Egyptians applauded this campaign because Egypt could not survive as two entities in one valley. The Nile and the gods, in their view, demanded a united people.

THE MIDDLE KINGDOM PERIOD

The Middle Kingdom (2040–1640 B.C.E.) was a time of rejuvenation, military expansion, monuments, religious fervor, and artistic vitality, because the nation was one, and ma'at, the order of the cosmos, had been restored. The Mentuhoteps, the Amenemhets, and the Senwosrets came to the throne with the ability to inspire their people. Focusing on the FAIYUM and other internal needs of the nation, these pharaohs also reined in the nomarchs and consolidated the powers of government in their own divine persons. A true golden age arose in Egypt, and individual citizens could look back at "The Eloquent Peasant" who had spoken for all commoners in the previous era. Women served as regents for infant nomarchs, held property, and bequeathed their estates. Another queen-pharaoh, Sobekneferu, ended this historical period.

THE SECOND INTERMEDIATE PERIOD

The Middle Kingdom came to an end because of the growing presence of eastern Asiatics in the land. A sage of the period lamented the signs of the "desert," the BEDOUINS from the east, in the Nile Valley. Actually, the Second Intermediate Period (1640–1550 B.C.E.) was a time of political rather than social upheavals. The people watched the HYKSOS, the dominant Asiatics, assume power and erect a capital, but the viziers and other officials maintained order in the north while the Thebans controlled Upper Egypt.

Rival dynasties emerged in the Delta, but the Hyksos maintained a firm grip on their holdings and were careful to uphold ancient traditions alongside their alien architecture and art. They also opened eastern borders, and many groups in the Levant deemed themselves Egyptians as a result. In the south, Nubians entered Egypt to serve under the Theban rulers of the Seventeenth Dynasty (1640–1550 B.C.E.), who would rise up to restore a united land.

TA'O II (Sekenenré; Djehuti'o) (r. ca. 1560 B.C.E.) and his son, KAMOSE (r. 1555–1550 B.C.E.), led the campaign to oust the Hyksos. They faced complacent Egyptians who prospered under the Asiatic rulers and had no compelling reason to see Egypt united under Thebans as a consequence. 'AHMOSE (NEBPEHTIRÉ) (r. 1550–1525 B.C.E.) came to the throne after his brother, Kamose, and within a decade he was on the march north. TETISHERI, AH'HOTEP (1), and 'AHMOSE-NEFER-TARI were queens of Thebes during the period. They were able to attract the allegiance of the people and to lead the nation into the famed era of the New Kingdom (1550–1070 B.C.E.). The Tuthmosid and Ramessid dynasties provided the leadership for Egypt's empire in this period, and the average citizen of the Nile assumed new imperatives as a result.

THE NEW KINGDOM PERIOD

The role of the divine pharaoh, a truly Egyptian god-king, signaled the restoration of MA'AT throughout the land. The people knew that military campaigns conducted by such rulers not only expanded the nation's holdings as an empire but kept Egypt secure. The rise of the cult of Amun at Thebes revived the nation spiritually, and the nomes remained cooperative, sending their ablest young men into the service of the gods or the pharaoh. Educational institutions thrived; ART AND ARCHITECTURE and medicine prospered; and the standing armies patrolled entire regions. Such armies no longer depended upon the cooperation of nomarchs but remained on duty and prepared for far-flung campaigns in the empire. Conscription became part of the commoners' lives at the same time.

Commoners who were not educated tilled the soil and celebrated an extraordinary number of religious festivals throughout the year. Women had increased legal rights and served in the temples of Egypt as chantresses, with some becoming part of the "harem" of Amun.

At the same time, Egyptians became rather sophisticated and cosmopolitan. Foreigners, who had come to Egypt as a result of trade or conquest, were not viewed with disdain by the average person but accepted on their own terms. The traditional caste system imposed by the nomes disintegrated as well, and a definite middle class of traders, craftsmen, and artisans arose in this era.

Golden tableware that dates to the Nineteenth Dynasty (Hulton Archive)

The period of 'AMARNA and the reign of AKHENATEN (1353–1335 B.C.E.) proved disastrous for the average Egyptian and the empire. The people remembered TUTHMOSIS I (r. 1504–1492 B.C.E.) and TUTHMOSIS III (r. 1479–1425 B.C.E.) and had thrilled at the sight of AMENHOTEP II (r. 1427–1401 B.C.E.). The new ruler, however, Akhenaten, was a solitary man, who closed the traditional temples of the old gods and made ATEN the deity of the land. The Egyptians did not accept him.

The coronation of HOREMHAB (r. 1319–1307 B.C.E.) came as a relief, and the rise of the Ramessids rejuvenated the land. SETI I (r. 1306–1290 B.C.E.), RAMESSES II (r. 1290–1224 B.C.E.), and RAMESSES III (r. 1194–1163 B.C.E.) stood as true pharaohs for the people, and the decline of their era filled most with a sense of dread. Famines, droughts, lawlessness, and suffering followed, and one year was called "the Year of the Hyena" because of the miseries inflicted upon the land.

THE THIRD INTERMEDIATE PERIOD

The collapse of the Ramessids in 1070 B.C.E. opened the Third Intermediate Period that lasted until 712 B.C.E. The rulers of the Twenty-first Dynasty and the Amunite priests of Thebes maintained familial ties but separate spheres of authority. This was not a time of calm or dedication. These priests and rulers were reduced to usurping the monuments and mortuary regalias of previous pharaohs. Thebes rioted, and nomes withdrew their support in critical ventures. Nubia and the eastern empire were lost to Egypt, and the people experienced no sense of unity or destined powers.

The loss of FESTIVALS and rituals altered the social fabric of Egypt in the same era. Even the cultic ceremonies celebrated in this era could only mimic the splendors of past rites. Cultic experiences were vital to the Egyptians, who did not want to delve into the theological or esoteric lore. Seeing the image of the god, marching through temple courts and singing the popular hymns of the day, was enough to inspire the average man or woman on the Nile. HERIHOR and other Amunite leaders began a renaissance, but the dynasty could not sustain power.

The true renaissance came with the Libyans of the Twenty-second Dynasty (945–712 B.C.E.). The Egyptians for the most part accepted the rule of this foreign clan, the descendants of the MESHWESH Libyans who had fought for a place in the Nile Valley during the New Kingdom era. SHOSHENQ I (r. 945–924 B.C.E.) appeared as a new warrior pharaoh, expanding the nation's realms. He refurbished temples and restored a certain level of piety in the land. At his death, however, the dynasty was splintered by the Twenty-third (828–712 B.C.E.), Twenty-fourth (724–712 B.C.E.), and Twenty-fifth (770–712 B.C.E.) Dynasties.

THE LATE PERIOD

These doomed royal lines had limited authority and no following among their fellow Egyptians who watched the Nubians gain power. PIANKHI (r. 750–712 B.C.E.) proclaimed the Twenty-fifth Dynasty the bearer of Amun and the restorer. He soon controlled all of Egypt, as the people supported his religious revival and were subdued by his barbaric cruelty. Those Egyptians who opposed him and his Nubian forces ended up as slaves, a new policy in the nation.

This Nubian line was interrupted by a brief occupation of the Nile Valley by the Assyrians, led by ESSARHADDON. TAHARQA (r. 690–664 B.C.E.) fled to Nubia and then fought to regain his throne. There was no massive uprising of the Egyptians to aid him in his quest because the battle had nothing to do with good versus evil or the restoration of *ma'at*. The people understood that this was a contest between Assyrians and Nubians, played out on the banks of the Nile. The mayor of Thebes at the time, MENTUEMHAT, represented his fellow countrymen as the foreign armies swept across the land. A ranking priest of Amun at Thebes and called "the Prince of the City," Mentuemhat watched events unfold but maintained his routines and his obligations. He appeared so able, so competent, that the Assyrians withdrew from Thebes, leaving him in charge of the area.

Remarkably, no Egyptian rebellion arose to eject the foreign occupiers. The population of that era did not possess the same spirit as their ancestors. They retreated, instead, aware of the impact of alien intruders and yet unmoved by the march of invading forces. A spirit of renewed nationalism was developing in the nomes, however, and a cultured revival was evident in the far-flung regions that did have direct contact with the political seats of power. They equated all of the dynastic forces at war within the land as enemies, the spawn of SET, and sought peace and the old ways within their nomes.

This was a peculiar social reaction, but it was deeply rooted in the traditions of Egypt. The native people feared chaos, recognizing it as the root of destruction in any human endeavor. The Egyptians appear to have had a growing sense of the inevitable in this historical period. Egypt was no longer safe, no longer protected by the deserts or shielded by warrior pharaohs. The clans could only protect their traditions and their spiritual lore by defending their limited resources and domains.

The Twenty-sixth Dynasty at SAIS offered the nation a shrewd royal line of administrators and militarily active rulers. The Persians, led by CAMBYSES (r. 525–522 B.C.E.), put an end to this native dynasty by taking control of Egypt as the Twenty-seventh Dynasty (525–404 B.C.E.). By 404 B.C.E., the Twenty-eighth Dynasty displayed the only resistance force of the era. The Twenty-ninth (393–380 B.C.E.) and Thirtieth (380–343 B.C.E.) Dynasties followed, providing competent rulers but mandated by realities that dragged Egypt into vast international struggles. The people watched as the resources and armies of the Nile were squandered in defense of foreign treaties and alliances that offered Egypt little promise. One ruler of the era, TEOS (r. 365–360 B.C.E.), robbed Egypt's temples to pay for his military campaigns beyond the nation's borders.

THE GRECO-ROMAN PERIOD

When the Persians returned in 343 B.C.E., the Egyptian people offered no resistance. ARTAXERXES III OCHUS led a large Persian force into the Nile Valley, and only one man, KHABABASH, led a short-lived revolt. The arrival of ALEXANDER III THE GREAT in 332 B.C.E. brought joy to the Egyptians, and they greeted him as a true liberator. The Persians had been cruel taskmasters for the most part, but they had also held Egypt's historical glories in disdain. This attitude had a chilling effect on the native people. The artistic, architectural, and agricultural achievements of Egypt drew such conquerors to the Nile, but they arrived with alien attitudes and even contempt.

Egypt was also a conglomeration of peoples in that era. Many groups had come to the land, and races mingled easily in all areas. The bureaucracy and the temples continued to function with stability because the Egyptians refused to surrender to chaos even during cruel occupations. The pattern of enduring and protecting the unseen traditions and spiritual modes of the past became the paramount activity of men and women in all areas of the land. Their ancestors had watched foreign armies come and go, while the pyramids and the temples survived and flourished. In their own eras, they were the protectors of the past.

Alexander the Great's retinue taught the native peoples that their ancestors were wise in adopting their own defensive modes. The young conqueror was crowned as a true pharaoh, but those who followed him had no intention of reviving the past on the Nile. The Ptolemaic Period (304–30 B.C.E.) was another time in which the rulers and the average citizens had little or no impact upon one another.

In ALEXANDRIA, the new capital, the Ptolemies ruled as Hellenes, transporting Greek scholars, ideals, and even queens to the Nile to support their rule. Positions of power and trust rested in the hands of Greeks or Hellenized Egyptians, and the nation became involved in Mediterranean affairs. In religious matters, the Greeks upheld the old traditions but introduced Greek deities and concepts. Even the royal cults of the rulers assumed the rigid and formalized Hellenic styles.

The Egyptians were also isolated to the traditional courts and laws of the nation. Ptolemaic law was directed toward the Greeks, while the juridical system traditional to the Nile Valley was maintained at local levels. The people seldom saw Greeks or Ptolemaic representatives, and their private lives went on with stability

and calm. The pattern had been set, and it would prove successful when the Ptolemies gave way to Rome.

Octavius, who became AUGUSTUS and first emperor of Rome, understood the potential and the achievements of the Egyptians and took possession of the Nile Valley. For the empire, Egypt became the "bread basket" from which emperors fed their imperial subjects and also the strategic gateway to the Red Sea and the spices and trade of the east. While inhabitants of one of the most important provinces in the empire, Egyptians went on with their lives and lived as they always had, dependent upon the abundance of the Nile.

Sohag *See* ATHRIBIS.

Sokar (Seker) An ancient Egyptian god of the Memphite necropolis from Predynastic times, he was actually a spirit guardian of the tombs but was elevated in rank after 3000 B.C.E. He was united with PTAH and depicted as having come from that deity's heart and mind as a force of creation. When the cult of OSIRIS developed a triune deity, Osiris-Ptah-Sokar emerged. That trinity is called Osiris-Sokar-Asar in some lists.

Sokar's theophany was the hawk, and his shrine and sacred bark date to the period before the First Dynasty. He is represented in reliefs as a pygmy with a large head and heavy limbs, wearing a beetle on his head and standing on a cabinet, with hawks in attendance. Sokar represented darkness and decay. The dead remained with Sokar until RÉ's light awakened them. The feast of Sokar was celebrated in the fourth year of the Second Dynasty (2770–2649 B.C.E.) and is noted in the PALERMO STONE. One of his litanies was included in the RHIND PAPYRUS, and he was the patron of the necropolis district of MEMPHIS. In the New Kingdom Period (1550–1070 B.C.E.) Sokar regained popularity. In his statues the god was fashioned as a hollow mummy, containing copies of the BOOK OF THE DEAD or corn kernels. He was called "He Who Is Upon His Sand," a reference to his desert origins.

Sokar Boat (Seker Boat) It was the Hennu, a bark mentioned in the BOOK OF THE DEAD. The vessel was designed with a high brow, terminating in the head of a horned animal, usually a gazelle or oryx. The Sokar Boat had three oars. In the center was a funerary chest with a cover surmounted by the head of a hawk. The chest stood upon a base with curving ends, and the entire structure rested upon a sledge with runners. The PYRAMID TEXTS depict the Sokar Boat, and sanctuaries were erected for such vessels in Lower Egypt.

Soknoknonneus He was a mysterious crocodile deity popular in the Faiyum region in the later eras of Egypt. A temple to Soknoknonneus was reportedly erected in the FAIYUM but has now vanished. He was originally called Soknopaiou-Mesos and was revered as a form of SOBEK.

solar boat   They were crafts meant to convey the kings to paradise and to carry deities. Examples of such vessels were buried in great pits beside the pyramids. The god RÉ's bark, used in his daily travels, was also a solar boat. Such vessels became elegant symbols of Egypt's cultic rituals.

See also BARKS OF THE GODS; SUN BOAT.

solar cult   It was the state religion of Egypt, which can be traced to Predynastic Periods (before 3000 B.C.E.) and was adapted over the centuries to merge with new beliefs. RÉ, the sun god, accompanied by HORUS, the sky god, constituted the basis of the cult, which emerged in HELIOPOLIS. Other Egyptian deities were also drawn into the solar religion: THOTH, ISIS, HATHOR, and WADJET. In time OSIRIS was linked to the cult as well. The rulers of the Fourth (2575–2465 B.C.E.) and Fifth (2465–2323 B.C.E.) Dynasties particularly revered the cult and erected many sun temples in that epoch. From the reign of RA'DJEDEF (2528–2520 B.C.E.) the rulers declared themselves "the Sons of Ré," and the solar disk, emblem of the sun, became the symbol of these pharaohs.

The social implications of the cult were evident in the PYRAMID TEXTS, which date to the Fifth and Sixth Dynasties. In them Ré calls all Egyptian men and women to justice, equality, and the understanding that death awaits them all in time. Even in the New Kingdom Period (1550–1070 B.C.E.), the Ramessids bore names meaning "Ré fashioned him."

solar disk   A sacred symbol of Egypt, representing the sun and in some eras called the ATEN, this disk was normally depicted as resting on the Djet or Tjet tree of the god OSIRIS. ISIS and NEPHTHYS are also portrayed in cultic symbols as saluting the solar disk, and BABOONS, representing the god THOTH, were believed to praise the solar disk's rising.

Soleb   A site in NUBIA (modern Sudan), in the territory of the third cataract of the Nile. AMENHOTEP III (r. 1391–1353 B.C.E.) erected a temple there, and Soleb served as the capital of Kush, or Nubia, during his reign. The temple was dedicated to the god AMUN but also presented Amenhotep III as a deified ruler.

Sonebi (fl. 20th century B.C.E.) *aristocrat of the Twelfth Dynasty*
He served in the reigns of AMENEMHET I (1991–1962 B.C.E.) and SENWOSRET I (1971–1926 B.C.E.). Sonebi was a prince of the fourteenth nome, the son of Ukhotep of MEIR. His tomb, located in Meir, contained cellars, MENATS (2), SISTRUMS, and other mortuary symbols. The tomb, reflecting Sonebi's rank and office of provincial

governor, contains elaborate paintings and reliefs, as well as hymns to HATHOR.

Song of the Harper   *See* LAY OF THE HARPER.

Son of Ré Name   *See* ROYAL NAMES.

Sons of Horus   *See* CANOPIC JARS.

Sopdu (Sopdet)   He was an ancient Egyptian god and the star known to the Greeks as Sirius, Sothis, or the Dogstar, Alpha Canis Majoris. The appearance of Sopdu signaled the beginning of AKHET, the SEASON of inundation of the Nile. Sopdu was also a divinity of the eastern desert and the god of the four corners of the earth, with HORUS, SET, and THOTH. When associated with Horus, the god was "the Sharp Horus." The star was sometimes represented in a feminine form and then was associated with the goddess HATHOR. His consort was Sopdet.

Sopdu's name meant "to prepare," and he was represented by a zodiacal light on a tall cone. He probably was eastern in origin and was transformed into the husband of Sah (Orion). Sopdu was mentioned in the PYRAMID TEXTS. The god was also depicted on an Abydos ivory tablet, owned by DJER of the First Dynasty (2920–2770 B.C.E.).

See also SOTHIC CYCLE.

Sosibius (fl. third century B.C.E.) *courtier involved in murder and a deadly cabal*
He served PTOLEMY IV PHILOPATOR (r. 221–205 B.C.E.), and when that ruler died, Sosibius and fellow courtiers, including one AGATHOCLES (2), murdered Queen ARSINOE (3) to remove her influence. Sosibius thus became the guardian of the heir, PTOLEMY V EPIPHANES, who was placed on the throne at the age of five. He remained guardian until he retired in 202 B.C.E. When the people of ALEXANDRIA, led by General TLEPOLEMUS, avenged the death of Arsinoe (3), Sosibius may have been slain with his fellow conspirators.

Sostratus of Cnidus (fl. third century B.C.E.) *Greek architect who designed the Lighthouse of Alexandria, the Pharos*
He was asked to design the monument by Ptolemy I Soter (r. 304–284 B.C.E.), who knew of Sostratus's reputation and achievements. Sostratus was honored with a plaque on one of the tiers of the LIGHTHOUSE OF ALEXANDRIA, a Wonder of the Ancient World.

Sothic Cycle   It was a method of measuring time in ancient Egypt, associated with the rising of SOPDU (Sirius). For the Egyptian the solar year measured 365 days and six hours. These additional hours added up to a discrepancy of a quarter day per year, an error that was corrected after a period of 1,460 years, termed the Sothic

Cycle. Such cycles had termination dates of 1317, 2773, 4323 B.C.E., etc. The synchronization of time was possible in the interims by calculating years from the cycle dates.

See also CALENDAR; SOTHIC RISING.

Sothic Rising The term defining the star and goddess Sopdet, who gave birth to the morning star and personified Sirius, or SOPDU. The Sothic rising coincided with the start of the solar year once every 1,460 or 1,456 years. The time between such risings was called the Sothic Cycle. The actual accounts of the Sothic Risings in ancient Egyptian documents enabled scholars to designate dates for the dynasties and to establish chronologies.

Sothis See SOPDU.

soul bird It was a human-headed bird, representing BA, or soul, that was placed on the SHABTI figures found in tombs in Egypt. The shabti was placed in the gravesite to perform any required labors in Amenti, the land beyond death. The soul birds appeared as part of the SHABTI figures in the Nineteenth Dynasty. The BA, or soul, was represented in various versions of the BOOK OF THE DEAD from earliest times.

soul houses They were elaborate mortuary miniatures placed in the tombs of the Middle Kingdom Period (2040–1640 B.C.E.). Also called the house of the KA, these miniatures were models of Egyptian residences, some two-storied with double staircases. Made of pottery and sometimes highly detailed, the soul houses were placed in the forecourts of tombs as offerings to the kas of the deceased, the astral companions. They served as the ka's residence in death.

Souls of Nekhen The title given to the Predynastic rulers of HIERAKONPOLIS, who were believed to have attained celestial status beyond the grave, the Souls of Nekhen were guardians of Upper Egypt, as their counterparts, the SOULS OF PE, served as patrons of Lower Egypt in BUTO. The Souls of Nekhen were thought to accompany the PHARAOH during certain commemorative ceremonies, such as the heb-sed (see SED), and were prominent at coronations, when priests donned special garb and stood as representatives of these archaic rulers.

The CROWNS of Egypt could not be presented to a pharaoh without permission by the Souls of Nekhen and Pe. MORTUARY RITUALS were also conducted on their behalf and they had their own ritual centers in the capital. One such soul was depicted on a statue of AMENHOTEP III (r. 1391–1353 B.C.E.), dressed as an Egyptian wolf or wild DOG. The Souls of Nekhen and the Souls of Pe were mentioned in the PALERMO STONE.

Souls of Pe The title of the Predynastic rulers of Pe or BUTO, a site south of TANIS, in the Delta, believed to have become celestial beings in the afterlife, they were the guardians of Lower Egypt, as the SOULS OF NEKHEN protected Upper Egypt. The Souls of Pe were thought to greet each new PHARAOH during coronation rituals and were called upon to guard the land in each new reign. MORTUARY RITUALS were conducted on their behalf, and the Souls of Pe had their own cultic shrines in the capitals of Egypt. They were mentioned in the PALERMO STONE and were always depicted with the heads of HAWKS.

Speos Anubis This was a shrine erected at DEIR EL-BAHRI on the western shore of THEBES to honor the deity of the dead. This mortuary god received daily offerings at the speos.

Speos Artemidos This was the Greek name for the rock chapel dedicated to the goddess PAKHET or Pakht at BENI HASAN. The chapel was erected by HATSHEPSUT (r. 1473–1458 B.C.E.) and TUTHMOSIS III (r. 1479–1425 B.C.E.) and refurbished by SETI I (r. 1306–1290 B.C.E.), who inserted his own CARTOUCHE into the decorations. The speos had a portico with four pillars cut into the rock, along with narrow chambers and a deeper sanctuary. The shrine appears to have been erected on the site of a previous structure of the goddess's cult. The Greeks associated Pakhet with their own Artemis, hence the name. The site is now called the Stable of Antar, named after a warrior poet of modern Islam.

Speos of Hathor This was the title of a shrine erected at DEIR EL-BAHRI, on the western shore of the Nile in THEBES. The goddess HATHOR was honored at this shrine, and only royal princesses could serve as priestesses in ceremonies. Offerings made to Hathor during rituals included miniature cows, platters of blue and white faience, and strings of faience scarabs. Flowers and fruit were also dedicated to Hathor in elaborate services.

sphinx It was the form of a recumbent lion with the head of a royal personage, appearing in Egypt in the Old Kingdom (2575–2134 B.C.E.). Originally called hu, or "the hewn object," the sphinx became Hun-Harmakhu, "the hewn Harmachis (Horemakhet)." This divine being was also addressed as "Horus on the Horizon" and as Sheshep-ankh, "the living image" of the god Atum. Modern Egyptians herald the sphinx as Abu Hol, "the Father of Terror."

The Great Sphinx, on the GIZA plateau, measures approximately 70 feet from base to crown and reportedly bears the face of KHAFRE (r. 2520–2494 B.C.E.). Measuring some 150 feet in length, the Great Sphinx is a crouching lion with outstretched paws and a human head, clad in the nemes, the striped head covering reserved for pharaohs in the early eras. The actual stone of the figure dates to 5000–7000 years ago geologically, according to some scientists, and may have been an original rock formation carved to resemble the sphinx form. The Great Sphinx was also supposed to hold the repository of ancient Egyptian wisdom, including the lost Book of THOTH. Modern repairs and excavations have revealed no such treasures.

The INVENTORY STELA, now in the Egyptian Museum in Cairo, describes the construction of the Great Sphinx. Another stela, erected between the paws of the sphinx by TUTHMOSIS IV (r. 1401–1391 B.C.E.), gives an account of his act of clearing the area of sand and of restoring the sphinx itself. The stela, 11 feet, 10 inches tall and seven feet, two inches wide, was placed at the site to commemorate Tuthmosis IV's dream. He was on a hunting expedition on the plateau as a prince and rested beside the sphinx. To his amazement, he heard the figure complain about its state of disrepair. Tuthmosis IV was promised the throne of Egypt if he cleared away the sand and rubble, even though he was not the heir at the time. He fulfilled the command of the sphinx and became pharaoh.

The actual portrait of Khafre on the face of the sphinx is debatable, as new investigations indicate that KHUFU (Cheops) (r. 2551–2528 B.C.E.) is the one depicted. Some scholars believe that Khufu's son, RA'DJEDEF (r. 2528–2520 B.C.E.), had the face created on the sphinx, which possibly resembled a lion in earlier times.

Other noted sphinx figures include the Alabaster Sphinx, said to weigh 80 tons and discovered in the ruins of the city of MEMPHIS, the oldest capital of Egypt. The face on this particular sphinx is believed to be that of AMENEMHET II (r. 1929–1892 B.C.E.).

The Sphinxes of TANIS are unique versions of this form dating to the Twelfth Dynasty. They were created for AMENEMHET III (r. 1844–1797 B.C.E.) out of black granite. Their faces are framed by the manes of lions rather than the striped *nemes*. Remarkably striking, these forms were unique to Tanis but were used by later pharaohs. HATSHEPSUT (r. 1473–1458 B.C.E.) was depicted as a Tanis sphinx. Smaller versions of the sphinx were used to form annexes between temples in THEBES (modern LUXOR). In some instances these sphinxes were ram-headed, then called *criosphinx*. Such figures lined the avenue between shrines in Thebes.

Further reading: Hawass, Zahi A. *The Secrets of the Sphinx: Restoration Past and Present.* Cairo: American University in Cairo Press, 1999.

"Sponge-cake Shrine"   An unusual bark receptacle erected by TUTHMOSIS III (r. 1479–1425 B.C.E.) at KARNAK, this religious monument was built alongside the WHITE CHAPEL of SENWOSRET I (r. 1971–1926 B.C.E.) and the Ala-baster Shrine of AMENHOTEP I (r. 1525–1504 B.C.E.) and TUTHMOSIS I (r. 1504–1492 B.C.E.) in that great temple site at Thebes. Tuthmosis III's shrine was made of calcite and had reliefs depicting that pharaoh making offerings to the deity AMUN-RÉ. The modern name for the monument refers to the deterioration evident. The calcite blocks used in the original construction have become severely pitted, giving the structure the appearance of sponge cake.

stations of the gods   They were the shrines erected in Egypt's major cities to provide resting places for the arks or barks of the various deities when they were paraded through the streets during festivals. Highly decorated, these stations provided spectacles for the participating worshippers.

At each station, the bearers of the god's vehicle rested while the cultic priests purified and incensed the entire parade. ORACLES were also conducted at these stations. In the major cities of Egypt, the arks or barks of the ranking deities were carried through the streets from five to 10 times each month as part of the liturgical CALENDAR and the cultic observances.

stela   This is the Greek word for a pillar or vertical tablet inscribed or decorated with reliefs. Such monuments were called *wadj* or *aha* by the Egyptians and were used as mortuary or historical commemoratives. Stelae were made of wood in the early eras, but as that material became scarce and the skills of the artisans increased, stones were used. They were normally rounded at one end, but a stela could be made in any style.

In the tombs, the mortuary stelae were placed in prominent positions. In most cases the stelae were incorporated into the false door of the tomb. Others were freestanding pillars or tablets set into the tomb walls, listing the achievements of the inhabitant of the gravesite. Stelae were used to designate boundaries, as in the city of 'AMARNA, or to specify particular roles of temples and shrines. They have provided the world with detailed information about the historical periods of ancient Egypt.

Stela of Donation   This is a memorial tablet dating to the reign of 'AHMOSE (NEBPEHTIRÉ) (r. 1550–1525 B.C.E.) and concerning the honors bestowed upon Queen 'AHMOSE-NEFERTARI, his beloved consort. The stela announces that the queen has resumed her honorary role as the second prophet of AMUN, a prominent priestly role at Thebes. Instead, she was endowed with the title and estate of the GOD'S WIFE OF AMUN. 'Ahmose-Nefertari is depicted with Prince 'AHMOSE-SIPAIR, who possibly served as co-regent with 'Ahmose but died before he could inherit the throne. AMENHOTEP I, the eventual heir, shared a mortuary cult with 'Ahmose-Nefertari, and they were deified posthumously.

Step Pyramid   It was the tomb of DJOSER (r. 2630–2611 B.C.E.) erected in SAQQARA and called the first free-standing stone structure known on earth. Designed by IMHOTEP, Djoser's VIZIER and architect, the pyramid was conceived as a MASTABA tomb, but six separate mastaba forms were placed one on top of another, diminishing in size to form a pyramid. In its final form, with six tiers, the Step Pyramid rose almost 200 feet on a base of nearly 500 feet from north to south and close to 400 feet from east to west. The nucleus of the structure was faced with Tureh limestone.

The original mastabas were 26 feet, each side facing a cardinal point measuring 207 feet. When completed, the sides of each tier were extended by 14 feet and faced a second time with limestone. Other mastabas were formed above the original and enlarged to form the step pattern until the six layers were intact.

A great shaft was designed within the Step Pyramid, 23 feet square and descending 90 feet into the earth. The burial chamber at the bottom is encased in granite. A cylindrical granite plug sealed the room, and a hole at the northern end of the underground chamber allowed the body of Djoser to be lowered into place. The granite plug used to seal the chamber weighed three tons. The shaft was then sealed with rubble. Other shafts, 11 in number, were designed for the tombs of Djoser's royal family members. Adjoining subterranean passages and chambers were adorned with fine reliefs and with blue faience tiles designed to resemble the matted curtains of the royal residences at MEMPHIS. Mazes were also incorporated into the design as a defense against tomb robbers.

The Step Pyramid stands as the centerpiece of a vast mortuary complex in Saqqara, enclosed by a wall 33 feet high and more than a mile in length. The wall was made of limestone and contained 211 bastions and 14 doors, all carved to resemble the facade of the royal palace. The main entrance at the southeast corner leads to a hall 175 feet long, decorated with engaged columns. A vestibule with eight columns connects to this hall. Another court held the sacred stones carried by the pharaohs in the *heb-sed* rituals and three shrines.

A special chamber was designed to honor the patroness of Lower Egypt, with statues of cobras and appropriate reliefs. That chamber led to a chapel, which contained a false tomb, complete with a shaft, glazed tiles, and inscriptions, followed by another court, all called the House of the South, containing proto-Doric columns, engaged. The House of the North, with similar design, had engaged papyrus COLUMNS. A room of special interest incorporated into the complex was the *serdab*, the slitted chamber which contained a statue of Djoser, positioned so that he could witness the mortuary rituals being conducted in his honor by the priests of the royal cult and also view the rising of the North Star. The statue was the first life-sized representation of a human being in Egypt.

Two other buildings represented the Upper and Lower Kingdoms in the complex. Some 30,000 vases, made of alabaster, granite, diorite, and other stones, were found on the site as well. Saqqara was a miniature city of 400 rooms, galleries, and halls, where priests and custodians served for decades. Modern excavations are unearthing new chambers, monuments, and tombs. Dur-

The Step Pyramid, the first pyramidal monument ever erected in Egypt; built at Saqqara for Djoser, the Step Pyramid was the creation of the priest official Imhotep. *(Courtesy Steve Beikirch)*

ing the Saite Dynasty, the Twenty Sixth (664–525 B.C.E.), a gallery was excavated in the Great South Court and revealed chambers.

Strato (fl. third century B.C.E.) *Greek scientist and royal tutor*

He arrived in Alexandria in the reign of PTOLEMY I SOTER (304–284 B.C.E.) to tutor the heir to the Egyptian throne, PTOLEMY II PHILADELPHUS. Strato was considered the leading physicist at the Athens Lyceum and was revered. He, in turn, invited PHILETAS OF COS and ZENODOTUS of Ephesus to Alexandria, adding to that city's reputation as an academic center.

sun boat It was a divine vehicle depicted in an early cosmogonic myth, the mode by which the god RÉ, or the sun itself, traveled through the sky into the realms of night. The sun deity, whether personified as Ré or in his original form, was thought to travel across the sky on this vessel. Sometimes the boat or bark was shown as a double raft. On his journey, Ré was accompanied by the circumpolar stars or by his own double. Sometimes he rowed the boat himself, sometimes he moved by magic. *Heka*, MAGIC, accompanied the sun in most myths.

The ENNEAD of Heliopolis was composed of gods who also accompanied the sun in its daily journey. The SOULS OF NEKHEN and the SOULS OF PE were mentioned in some myths as riding in the vessel daily. In some early depictions, the boat was a double serpent, its two heads forming the prow and the bow. The sun boat had many adventures during the day, and at night it faced all the terrors of the darkness, when the dead rose up to the vessel through the waters. When the sun was associated with the cult of Ré, the boats were given specific names.

sun's well This was the name given to a pool in the sacred precincts of HELIOPOLIS (originally the city of On and now a suburb of modern Cairo). Associated with the deity RÉ, the sun's well was viewed as a site of the original creation. The god Ré rose as a LOTUS of the sun's well.

Suppiluliumas I (d. ca. 1325 B.C.E.) *ruler of the Hittites and a threat to Egypt*

He ruled the HITTITE Empire in the reigns of AMENHOTEP III (1391–1353 B.C.E.) and AKHENATEN (1353–1335 B.C.E.). Suppiluliumas I fought Egypt's allies, the MITANNIS, in Syria. He also destroyed the city-state of KADESH, taking the royal family of that city and its court as prisoners. He exchanged gifts with Amenhotep III and Akhenaten, growing powerful during their reigns. Suppiluliumas's son, Prince ZANNANZA, was sent to Egypt to become the consort of Queen ANKHESENAMON, the widow of TUT'ANKHAMUN (r. 1333–1323 B.C.E.), but he was slain at the borders. The Hittites began a series of reprisal attacks as a result, and Suppiluliumas I died of a plague brought to his capital by Egyptian prisoners of war.

Sutekh A very ancient deity of Egypt, called "the Lord of Egypt." His cult dates to the First Dynasty (2920–2770 B.C.E.), perhaps earlier, at OMBOS, near NAGADA. Sutekh was originally depicted as a donkey-like creature but evolved over the decades into a beautiful recumbent canine. Considered a form of the god SET, Sutekh was popular with RAMESSES II (r. 1290–1224 B.C.E.), who beseeched the god for good weather during the visit of a HITTITE delegation to Egypt.

Sweet Water Canal A manmade waterway started probably the Middle Kingdom Period (2040–1640 B.C.E.). The canal linked the Nile River at BUBASTIS to the WADI TIMULAT and the BITTER LAKES. During the reign of NECHO I, the Sweet Water Canal led eventually to the Red Sea.

sycamore This was a sacred tree of Egypt, *Ficus sycomonus,* viewed as a divine natural element in all eras. The fig of the tree was relished and its shade was prized. The souls of the dead also enjoyed the benefits of the sycamore, coming to roost in the tree as birds. Twin sycamores stood on the horizon of eternity, guarding the sun. The mortuary complex of MENTUHOTEP II (r. 2061–2010 B.C.E.) at DEIR EL-BAHRI, on the western shore of the Nile in Thebes, was designed with a sycamore grove. The sycamore grew at the edge of the desert near MEMPHIS in the Early Dynastic Period (2920–2575 B.C.E.) and was venerated as an abode of the goddess HATHOR, "the Lady of the Sycamore." Some religious texts indicate a legend or myth had developed concerning the tree. The tree was also involved in the cults of RÉ, MUT, and ISIS.

Syrene *See* ASWAN.

Syrian Wars This is the name given to a series of confrontations and actual battles conducted by the Ptolemaic rulers and the kings of the Seleucid Empire. The first war involved PTOLEMY II PHILADELPHUS (r. 285–246 B.C.E.), who conquered Phoenicia, Anatolia, and the Cyclades, all Seleucid territories. The war took place between 274 and 271 B.C.E.

Ptolemy II lost Phoenicia and Anatolia to the Seleucid king ANTIOCHUS II (THEOS) in a war that was conducted from 260–253 B.C.E. From 245–241 B.C.E., Ptolemy II saw Egypt's sea power destroyed, and the Seleucids suffered losses as well.

PTOLEMY IV PHILOPATOR (r. 221–205 B.C.E.) was involved in another campaign in 219–216 B.C.E. and won the battle of RAPHIA, capturing southern Syria and Palestine (Coele Syria). In 202–200 B.C.E., the Seleucids once again fought to regain Palestine, confronting PTOLEMY V EPIPHANES (r. 205–180 B.C.E.).

T

Ta'a (fl. 12th century B.C.E.) *courageous official of the Twentieth Dynasty*

He served RAMESSES III (r. 1194–1163 B.C.E.) as VIZIER. Ta'a is mentioned in the records of the royal jubilee of the reign. His successors would rebel against Ramesses III and be captured at ATHRIBIS, but he was a loyal servant of the pharaoh. He sailed north after gathering religious articles from Thebes, taking them to PER-RAMESSES, the alternate capital at the time. He visited Egyptian cities while en route. During the strike of tomb workers at DEIR EL-MEDINA, Ta'a distributed rations to the people in order to avert disaster. His courage and wisdom delayed the unrest that struck Thebes.

See also TOMB WORKERS' REVOLT.

Ta'apenes (fl. 10th century B.C.E.) *royal woman of the Twenty-first Dynasty*

She was the consort of PSUSENNES I (r. 1040–992 B.C.E.), a lower-ranked queen, as MUTNODJMET (2) was the Great Wife, or *hemet*. Some records indicate that Ta'apenes's sister was sent to Jerusalem to serve at the court there.

Tabiry (fl. eighth century B.C.E.) *royal woman of the Nubian Twenty-fifth Dynasty*

She was the consort of PIANKHI (r. 750–712 B.C.E.) and the daughter of the Nubian ruler ALARA and Queen Kasaga. Tabiry was possibly the mother of SHABAKA and SHEPENWEPET (2). It is not known if Tabiry accompanied Piankhi on his military campaigns in Egypt. Her daughter, SHEPENWEPET (2), became a GOD'S WIFE OF AMUN, or Divine Adoratrice of Amun, during Piankhi's reign.

Tadukhipa (fl. 14th century B.C.E.) *royal woman of the Eighteenth Dynasty, a Mitanni princess*

She was a consort of AMENHOTEP III (r. 1391–1353 B.C.E.) and a MITANNI royal princess, given to Amenhotep III to cement the ties between Egypt and her homeland. Tadukhipa was also a niece of the MITANNI princess Khirgipa, who had entered Amenhotep III's HAREM earlier. Tadukhipa arrived shortly before Amenhotep III died or perhaps soon after. She is mentioned in a letter written by Queen TIYE (1), Amenhotep III's widow, as having married AKHENATEN. As a result, some scholars believe that Tadukhipa was Queen KIYA of Akhenaten's court.

See also 'AMARNA.

Taharqa (Khure' nefertem; Tarku; Tirhaka) (d. 664 B.C.E.) *ruler of the Nubian Twenty-fifth Dynasty*

He reigned from 690 B.C.E. until forced to abandon Egypt. He was the son of PIANKHI and the cousin of SHEBITKU, whom he succeeded. His mother, ABAR, came from NUBIA (modern Sudan) to visit and to bless his marriage to Queen AMUN-DYEK'HET. They had two sons, Nesishutef nut, who was made the second prophet of Amun, and USHANAHURU, who was ill-fated. Taharqa's daughter, AMENIRDIS (2), was adopted by SHEPENWEPET (2) and installed as a GOD'S WIFE OF AMUN at THEBES.

In 674 B.C.E., Taharqa met the Assyrian king ESSARHADDON and his army at Ashkelon, defeating the enemy and raising a STELA to celebrate the victory. He also built extensively, making additions to the temples of AMUN and MONTU at KARNAK and to MEDINET HABU and MEMPHIS. One of his structures at Karnak was erected between a SACRED LAKE and the outer wall. He built

Taharqa (d. 664 B.C.E.), ruler of the Twenty-fifth Dynasty, depicted under the protection of the god Amun in the form of a ram (© The Trustees of the British Museum / Art Resource)

two colossal *uraei* at Luxor as well and a small shrine of Amun at the third cataract of the Nile.

In 680 B.C.E., Essarhaddon once again attacked Egypt and took the capital of Memphis and the royal court. Taharqa fled south, leaving Queen Amun-dyek'het and Prince Ushanahuru to face the enemy. They were taken prisoner by Essarhaddon and sent to Nineveh, Assyria. Two years later, Taharqa marched with an army to retake Egypt, and Essarhaddon died before they met. Taharqa massacred the Assyrian garrison in Egypt when he returned. ASSURBANIPAL, Essarhaddon's successor, defeated Taharqa. TANUTAMUN, Taharqa's cousin, was installed as co-regent and successor and Taharqa returned to Nubia. He was buried at Nuri in Nubia. His pyramidal tomb was small but designed with three chambers.

Tait An Egyptian goddess who served as the patroness of the city of AKHMIN and was associated with the cults of ISIS and OSIRIS, Tait was the guardian of linen, was used in the mortuary rituals, and was depicted as a beautiful woman carrying a chest of linen. When associated with the cults of Osiris and Isis, she was called Isis-Tait. Tait aided Isis in wrapping the body of the god Osiris after he was slain by SET.

Takelot I (Userma'atre'setepenamun) (d. ca. 883 B.C.E.) *ruler of the Twenty-second Dynasty*
He reigned from 909 B.C.E. until his death. The son of OSORKON I and Queen KAROMANA (2) or Queen TASEDKONSU, Takelot I was not the original heir. A brother, SHOSHENQ II, died before he could inherit the throne, and Takelot I became regent. He married Queen

KAPES, the mother of OSORKON II. Thebes revolted during Takelot I's reign, and he sent his brother, IUWELOT, there to become the high priest of Amun, followed by SMENDES III. He left no monuments and was succeeded by Osorkon II. Takelot I was interred in TANIS in a gold coffin and in a sarcophagus usurped from the Twelfth Dynasty and placed in the tomb of Smendes.

Takelot II (Hedjkheperre'setepenré) (d. 835 B.C.E.) *ruler of the Twenty-second Dynasty*
He reigned from 860 B.C.E. until his death. Takelot II was the son of OSORKON II and Queen KAROMANA (4) but not the original heir. A brother, Shoshenq, did not live long enough to inherit the throne. NIMLOT, the high priest of Thebes, was his half brother. Takelot II married Nimlot's daughter, KAROMANA (5) Merymut, who was the mother of OSORKON III.

During his reign, Takelot faced a Theban revolt led by HARSIESE. He sent his son, Prince OSORKON, to THEBES to put down the rebellion that raged for a decade. A truce was finally drawn up but a second revolt began soon after. The rebellion was recorded on the walls of KARNAK at Thebes. Takelot was buried in the TANIS tomb of his father.

Takelot III (fl. ca. 749 B.C.E.) *ruler of the obscure Twenty-third Dynasty at Leontopolis*
The dates of his reign are unknown. He was the son of OSORKON III and Queen KARAOTJET so probably inherited the throne ca. 749 B.C.E. In that time of turmoil, Takelot III was named to the throne of SHOSHENQ V at TANIS and also held sway over HERAKLEOPOLIS. He ruled only two years, however, and during that time appointed his sister SHEPENWEPET (1) the GOD'S WIFE OF AMUN at Thebes. RUDAMON, his brother, succeeded him. Takelot III's family was buried at DEIR EL-BAHRI in Thebes, interred on a terrace of HATSHEPSUT's shrine. His tomb has not been discovered.

Takhat (1) (fl. 13th century B.C.E.) *royal woman of the Nineteenth Dynasty and the mother of a usurper*
She was probably a lesser-ranked consort of MERENPTAH (r. 1224–1214 B.C.E.). Takhat was also the mother of AMENMESSES, who usurped the throne from SETI II (r. 1214–1204 B.C.E.). She was probably a daughter of RAMESSES II. Takhat was buried in the tomb of Amenmesses. Some records list her as a consort of SETI II and as the mother of Amenmesses and Seti-Merenptah. She was reportedly depicted on a statue of Seti II at KARNAK.

Takhat (2) (fl. 12th century B.C.E.) *Royal woman of the Twentieth Dynasty*
She was the wife of Prince Montuhirkhopshef, a son of RAMESSES III (1194–1163 B.C.E.). Takhat was the mother of RAMESSES IX.

Takhat (3) (fl. sixth century B.C.E.) *Royal woman of the Twenty-sixth Dynasty*
She was a consort of PSAMMETICHUS II (r. 595–589 B.C.E.). Takhat may have been the mother of APRIES.

Takheredeneset (fl. sixth century B.C.E.) *royal woman of the Twenty-sixth Dynasty*
She was the mother of AMASIS (r. 570–526 B.C.E.). A commoner by birth, Takheredeneset watched her son's military career, and perhaps aided him, as he usurped the throne from Apries in 570 B.C.E., after the Egyptian army revolted over foreign battles. It is also possible that she died before this occurred.

talatat They were small stone blocks used in the 'AMARNA Period, in the reign of AKHENATEN (1353–1335 B.C.E.) in his capital. The name of the stone is taken from the Arabic for "hand breaths" or may be a variation of the Italian *tagliata,* or "cut stonework." The *talatat* blocks were fashioned out of sandstone and normally had beautiful decorative reliefs. When Akhenaten died and 'Amarna was abandoned, the *talatat* blocks were removed from the original site and used by successive rulers for their own construction projects. They have been identified at such sites as KARNAK and HERMOPOLIS MAGNA.

Tale of Khufu and the Magicians A series of literary texts found in the WESTCAR PAPYRUS and sometimes called *King Cheops and the Magicians.* The tale in this cycle records the stories told by KHUFU (Cheops) (2551–2528 B.C.E.) at his court. Delightful images of pharaohs sailing in gilded barges with beautiful maidens cast only in fishnets and details of magical spells compose the stories. The important element of the tale, however, is a prediction about the births of the first three pharaohs of the next dynasty, the Fifth (2465–2323 B.C.E.).
See also LITERATURE.

Tale of Mohor *See* TRAVELS OF AN EGYPTIAN.

Tale of Prince Setna A literary text discovered in the Ptolemaic Period (304–30 B.C.E.) but concerning a supposed son of RAMESSES II (r. 1290–1224 B.C.E.) of the Nineteenth Dynasty. Prince Setna sees a woman named Tabubna, the daughter of a Bastite priest. Losing his heart to her, Setna enters into a life of servitude and eventual horror. Tabubna has cast a spell on him and forces him to undertake torments and bear shame, eventually killing his own children. At the end of the tale Setna wakes up and discovers that he was only dreaming. He is safe and free of his devouring love for Tabubna.
See also LITERATURE.

Tale of Sinuhe *See* SINUHE THE SAILOR.

Tale of the Doomed Prince It is an Egyptian literary work dating to the New Kingdom Period (1550–1070 B.C.E.) and found in the HARRIS PAPYRUS 500 from the reign of RAMESSES IV (1163–1156 B.C.E.). This is a story of an Egyptian prince among the MITANNIS. He finds true love with a princess of that land but faces three fates. Love and loyalty are the main elements of the tale, but the resolution is missing, leaving the reader pondering the prince's final destiny. The tale is incomplete in extant form.
See also LITERATURE.

Tale of the Eloquent Peasant *See* "THE ELOQUENT PEASANT" OF HERAKLEOPOLIS.

Tale of the Shepherds It is a fragmented text now in a papyrus in the Egyptian Museum, in Berlin. Also called the *Tale of the Herders,* the work relates how shepherds discover a goddess in a shrub along the Nile. The goddess alarms the shepherds, who run to the local chieftain and inform him of their encounter. The chieftain returns with them to the scene, where he chants spells that force the goddess to leave the shelter of the shrub. She then "came forth, terrible in appearance." What happens at this point is unknown as the ending of the tale has been lost.
See also LITERATURE.

Tale of the Shipwrecked Sailor Discovered in a papyrus from the Middle Kingdom (2040–1640 B.C.E.), it is the story of an expedition returning by sea from the southern domains of Egypt or possibly from a trade expedition. A sailor recounts the adventures that took place when his boat was damaged and sank during a storm. He alone survived the ordeal, swimming to an island. A gigantic snake ruled the island, the only survivor of its species after an attack by comets or a falling star. The serpent counseled the sailor and inspired in him patience and valor. When a ship came within sight of the island, the serpent restored him to his fellowmen, with gifts of ointments, myrrh, animals, and other precious objects that the sailor delivered to the pharaoh.

The papyrus upon which the tale was copied is in the Hermitage collection in St. Petersburg, Russia. It is noted for its detailed account of the voyages undertaken in the areas of the Red and Mediterranean Seas, especially the trips to PUNT. The tale was written by a scribe, Amen-a'a, the son of one Amenti.
See also LITERATURE.

Tale of Two Brothers It is a text found in the Papyrus D'ORBINEY in the British Museum in London. Considered one of the finest examples of Egyptian narrative literature and dated to the Nineteenth Dynasty (1307–1196 B.C.E.), the story is an account of the adventures of two Egyptian deities. Anup, believed to represent ANUBIS, and Bata (or Batu), a Predynastic god, are caught in a triangle when Anup's wife tries to seduce Bata and fails. In revenge she claims that he assaulted her. Anup sets out to kill Bata, who flees.

The god SHU, seeing that evil is taking place, separates the two with a stream filled with CROCODILES, and there, Bata explains what really happened. Anup, ashamed, goes home to kill his wife and to throw her to the DOGS. Bata goes on a journey and has many adventures, siring a future ruler of Egypt. His journey is religious in nature and much beloved by the Egyptians for its didactic overtones. The tale was reported to be in the library of SETI II (r. 1214–1204 B.C.E.).

Tale of Wenamun See REPORT OF WENAMUN; LITERATURE.

Tamara (Ta-Mera) This was the Egyptian word for "the Land of the Inundation" and the name for Egypt used by the native population.

Tanis This is the modern Sa'el Hagar, located in the western Delta on an enormous mound at Lake MENZALA, an important port. The site was once sacred to the god SET and was a NOME capital. The Egyptians called it Djanet, Djárnet, or Dj'ane. Tanis became important during the Twenty-first Dynasty (1070–945 B.C.E.) and the Twenty-second Dynasty (945–712 B.C.E.), but the HYKSOS were also in the region during the Second Intermediate Period (1640–1550 B.C.E.) and a shrine on the site contains the seals of RAMESSES II (r. 1290–1224 B.C.E.).

The great temple of AMUN in Tanis contains six royal tombs, three of them found intact. The main portion of the tomb and 15 obelisks date to Ramesses II, and the gate of the shrine to the reign of SHOSHENQ III (835–783 B.C.E.).

Another temple on the site was erected in the Thirtieth Dynasty (380–343 B.C.E.). This shrine had a lake on the northeastern corner and was made out of granite with palmiform columns. A limestone gate erected by PTOLEMY I SOTER (r. 304–284 B.C.E.) was also discovered. Attached to this Amun complex was a temple dedicated to the god HORUS, with additional chapels for the deities MUT, KHONS (1), and ASTARTE (Ishtar), who was a Canaanite goddess.

Royal tombs designed with deep chambers were uncovered as well in the area of Tanis. OSORKON II (r. 883–855 B.C.E.) was buried in a chamber of granite, with adjoining limestone rooms. TAKELOT II (r. 860–835 B.C.E.) was also discovered in this tomb, which had Osirian decorations. The tomb of PSUSENNES I (r. 1040–992 B.C.E.) contained his royal remains and those of PSUSENNES II (r. 959–945 B.C.E.), AMENEMOPE (r. 993–984 B.C.E.), and SHOSHENQ II (r. 883 B.C.E.). An unidentified mummy was also found there.

An obelisk at the ruins of the city of Tanis *(Courtesy Library of Congress)*

The remains of Psusennes I were discovered buried in a pink granite sarcophagus with a mask of gold, all probably usurped from earlier burial sites. A silver coffin was discovered as well inside the sarcophagus and the remains of SHOSHENQ III (r. 835–783 B.C.E.) had been deposited there.

Tanis Sphinxes They are figures made for AMEN-EMHET III (r. 1844–1797 B.C.E.) in conjunction with the local cult rituals conducted in the FAIYUM and other regions. This SPHINX form is a recumbent LION with outstretched paws, a human face, and a large leonine mane. The ears of the Tanis Sphinxes were large. This type of sphinx was brought to Tanis during the Ramessid Period (1307–1070 B.C.E.) and remains associated with that site. HATSHEPSUT (r. 1473–1458 B.C.E.) was memorialized as a Tanis sphinx.

Tanis Stela A monument erected by PTOLEMY II PHILADELPHUS (r. 285–246 B.C.E.), the stela depicts him and his consort ARSINOE (2). The ruler wears the red and white crowns of Egypt and carries a SCEPTER. Arsinoe is shown wearing the red crown with Isis plumes, the horns of HATHOR, and the horns of AMUN. She carries a scepter and an *ankh*, an ansate cross that symbolized life.

Tanqur This is a site in NUBIA (modern Sudan), located about 75 miles above the second cataract of the Nile. An inscription erected there in the reign of TUTHMOSIS I (1504–1492 B.C.E.) depicts that pharaoh's hand-to-hand battle with a local chief during a military campaign. This expedition, which ultimately continued on to Tombos, took place in Tuthmosis I's second regnal year. The viceroy of Nubia serving Tuthmosis I erected the monument to commemorate the event. Tanqur has dangerous outcroppings, making travel on that part of the Nile perilous.

Tantamani *See* TANUTAMUN.

Tantamun (1) (fl. 11th century B.C.E.) *royal woman of the Twentieth Dynasty*
She was the consort of RAMESSES XI (r. 1100–1070 B.C.E.) and the mother of Princess Tantamun and Princess HENUTTAWY. Princess Tantamun would become the consort of SMENDES (r. 1070–1044 B.C.E.).

Tanutamun (Bakaré; Tantamani) (d. ca. 655 B.C.E.) *fourth ruler of the Nubian Twenty-fifth Dynasty*
He reigned from 664 B.C.E. until 657 B.C.E. He then retired from Egypt and possibly ruled for a time in NUBIA (modern Sudan). Tanutamun was a nephew of TAHARQA, who had suffered defeat at the hands of the ASSYRIANS. When ASSURBANIPAL attacked Egypt and looted THEBES, Tanutamun retired to Nubia. He had won back Thebes, ASWAN, and MEMPHIS prior to Assur-

banipal's invasion. In that campaign he put NECHO I to death in 664 B.C.E. and forced PSAMMETICHUS I to flee to Assyria.

A stela inscribed in GEBEL BARKAL depicts Tanutamun's coronation at Napata in 664 B.C.E. Called "the Dream Stela," this monument also details Tanutamun's dream of two snakes. He believed this vision symbolized that he would rule both Upper and Lower Egypt. Tanutamun was buried at Nuri, the royal necropolis in Nubia.

Ta'o I (Senakhtenré; Djehuti'o) (d. ca. 1540 B.C.E.) *ruler of the Seventeenth Dynasty, at Thebes*
The dates of his reign are not known. Ta'o I apparently usurped the throne of Thebes from INYOTEF VII and was possibly related to INYOTEF V. Ta'o ruled contemporaneously with the HYKSOS but maintained control of Upper Egypt as far south as ASWAN.

His queen was a commoner, TETISHERI, who outlived him and directed the course of Theban affairs for decades. He also married a Queen MENTJUHOTEP. Ta'o I and Tetisheri resided at DEIR EL-BALLAS, north of Thebes. His children included TA'O II (Sekenenré; Djehuti'o) (d. 1555 B.C.E.) and Princess AH'HOTEP (1). Ta'o I, called the Elder, was the third ruler of a second group of the Seventeenth Dynasty. He was buried in Thebes.

Ta'o II (Sekenenré; Djehuti'o) (d. 1555 B.C.E.) *second to the last ruler of the Seventeenth Dynasty at Thebes*
Called also "the Brave," Ta'o II ruled from an unknown date until ca. 1555 B.C.E. as a contemporary of the HYKSOS, who ruled at AVARIS. The son of TA'O I (Senakhtenré; Djehuti'o) (d. ca. 1540 B.C.E.) and Queen TETISHERI, Ta'o II married Queen Ah'hotep (I), who bore him two sons, KAMOSE and 'AHMOSE, and many daughters. He also had lesser consorts, 'AHMOSE-IN-HAPI and HENUTEMPET.

Around 1554 B.C.E., Ta'o II received a message from the HYKSOS king APOPHIS (r. 1585–1553 B.C.E.), complaining that the sacred hippopotami in the temple pool at Thebes kept him awake at night. The message, contained in the SALLIER PAPYRUS II and called the QUARREL OF APOPHIS AND SEKENENRÉ (Ta'o II), was obviously a calculated insult. Apophis's residence at AVARIS was more than 400 miles to the north, which meant that the announcement was politically nuanced, perhaps a provocation.

Ta'o II responded instantly by starting military campaigns against the Hyksos holdings. He met a violent death, probably at the hands of enemy attackers during this campaign. His mummified remains, buried originally in DRA-ABU' EL-NAGA, and then placed in the royal mummy cache at DEIR EL-BAHRI, clearly demonstrate the ferocity of the attackers.

Ta'o II suffered five major wounds, including two axe cuts that caused a skull fracture, a blow to the bridge of his nose, a blow to the left cheek, and another to the right side of his head. His ribs and vertebrae were also damaged. His attackers used axes, spears, and possibly arrows. Ta'o II must have been assaulted while asleep, as the arms and hands bore no wounds. His mummified remains indicate that Ta'o II was slender and muscular, with long black curly hair and a healthy set of teeth. He was buried in a large anthropoid coffin with the *rishi* design. These remains, however, still carry a terrible odor of decay, indicating that he died some distance from Thebes and thus the mortuary rituals were delayed too long to purify the corpse. Tao II's sons, KAMOSE and 'AHMOSE (NEBPEHTIRÉ), continued the war against the Hyksos, eventually ousting them from Egypt.

Tarif, el- This was a site on the western shore of the Nile, the northernmost necropolis of THEBES. Large and filled with monuments, Tarif was connected to the mortuary complex of MENTUHOTEP II (r. 2061–2010 B.C.E.). The site was constructed in a rock court and contained "SAFF" TOMBS, taken from the Arabic for "row." Tombs from the Eleventh Dynasty, as well as the Old Kingdom Period (2575–2134 B.C.E.) MASTABAS, were found there. The three most impressive tombs belong to INYOTEF I (r. 2134–2118 B.C.E.) at Saff el-Dawaba, INYOTEF II (r. 2118–2069 B.C.E.) at Saff el Kisasiya, and INYOTEF III (r. 2069–2061 B.C.E.) at Saff el-Bagar. These tombs had doors and pillared facades.

Tarkhan This was a site in the FAIYUM region of the Nile, located on the western bank in an area called the lower valley. The necropolis there dates to the Old Kingdom Period (2575–2134 B.C.E.). Predynastic tombs were also built in Tarkhan, where mortuary regalia and the names of various rulers, including NARMER, were unearthed.

Tarset (fl. 28th century B.C.E.) *royal woman of the First Dynasty*
She was the consort of 'ADJIB (ca. 2700 B.C.E.). The ranking queen, Tarset was also the mother of SEMERKHET, the heir. She was probably the ranking heiress of the Memphis clans, married to 'Adjib to consolidate his political claims to the throne.

Tasedkhonsu (fl. 10th century B.C.E.) *royal woman of the Libyan Twenty-second Dynasty*
She was the consort of OSORKON I (r. 924–909 B.C.E.). The ranking queen, or *hemet*, Tasedkhonsu was the mother of TAKELOT I, SMENDES III, and Prince IUWELOT.

Tatenen (Tenen; Ta-tonen) He was an earth deity of Egypt, also called Tenen, or Ta-tonen. Tatenen was believed to have emerged from the watery abyss as "the Lord of Creation" and was worshipped in MEMPHIS. His name meant "the Risen Land," and he was also called "the Revered One." Tatenen always carried two staffs that he brought into the world to repel the serpent from

the great PRIMEVAL MOUND. He also carried a mace, called "the Great White of the Earth Makers," the cultic origin unknown, and the weapon was dedicated to his son, the falcon. This mace had magical powers and in some historical periods was worshipped as a separate deity. The famous DJED pillar was brought into the world by Tatenen, as well as another amulet called "the Similitude of the Front of the God." Tatenen became associated with the cult of PTAH and his *djed* pillar became a popular symbol of OSIRIS.

Tawaret (Taueret; Thueris) Also called Thueris by the Greeks, she was the patroness of childbirth in ancient Egypt. Tawaret was normally depicted as a HIPPOPOTAMUS, sometimes dressed in the robes of a queen and wearing a lion's mane and a CROWN. Her head had the shape of a CROCODILE's snout and she had the feet of a lion.

Tawaret was also shown as a hippopotamus with the head of a lion. In this form she carried daggers that she used to smite the spiritual and physical enemies of Egypt. Tawaret carried the SA AMULET. Her cult center was at Thebes and she remained popular during celebrations at OPET (modern LUXOR), where a Beautiful Feast of Tawaret was conducted each year.

Tcharu (Tharu) This was an Egyptian fortified city near modern El-Qantara, bordering the SINAI Peninsula. The site was located on the WAY OF HORUS, a military highway used by the Egyptians. Tcharu was renamed Sile by the Greeks during the Ptolemaic Period. The city was an outpost on the military road that led through the BITTER LAKES and Arish to Gaza in Palestine. A canal dating to the reign of Necho II was fortified when it was built, and Tcharu had protected wells and compounds to defend it from BEDOUIN or Asiatic attacks.

Tchay (Tchoy) (fl. 13th century B.C.E.) *court official of the Nineteenth Dynasty*
He served MERENPTAH (r. 1224–1214 B.C.E.) as a royal scribe of dispatches. His tomb on the western shore of Thebes was discovered at KHOKHA and celebrated for its size and decorations. Tchay's tomb contains reliefs of the *Book of the Gates*, a mortuary text, and portraits of AMENHOTEP I (r. 1525–1504 B.C.E.) and Queen 'AHMOSE-NEFERTARI. These royals had been deified during the Eighteenth Dynasty. Other reliefs depict a tree goddess, scenes of the celebration of the festival of SOKAR, BABOONS adoring the rising sun, and a SOLAR BOAT. Portraits of Tchay and his family were included.

Teachings of Tuaf This was a text used in Egyptian schools in the New Kingdom Period (1550–1070 B.C.E.). The text was copied by students and used to inspire SCRIBES. It appears to be a version of the *SATIRE ON TRADES*. Texts from older eras remained ever popular and were used in educational and religious settings in all historical periods.

See also LITERATURE.

Tebtynis   This was a site in the FAIYUM region of Egypt, the modern Omm el-Borigat. Tebtynis was a cult center of the god SOBEK and contained a temple honoring that deity. The temple dates to the Middle Kingdom Period (2040–1640 B.C.E.) and was designed with a square tank-like lake in the main courtyard. CROCODILES, the THEOPHANIES of SOBEK, were probably maintained in this lake. Reliefs dating to the Ptolemaic Period (304–30 B.C.E.) were discovered in a vestibule of the temple. The shrine was enclosed by a mud-brick wall. A treasure trove of papyri was discovered at Tebtynis.

Tefibi (fl. ca. 21st century B.C.E.) *aristocrat of the Ninth Dynasty who was accused of sacrilege*
He served in the reign of KHETY III (date of reign unknown) and was a nobleman of ASSIUT. Tefibi joined Khety III in plundering tombs in the ABYDOS region while on a campaign against the Thebans. This act of sacrilege brought the ruler and Tefibi shame and prompted the Thebans to begin the reunification of Egypt, ending the Khety rule. Tefibi's tomb in Assiut was shared by his sons, KHETY I and II, and is located in a cliff overlooking the area. He was a disciple of the wolf or JACKAL deity WEPWAWET.

Tefnakhte (Shepsesré) (d. 717 B.C.E.) *founder of the short-lived Twenty-fourth Dynasty at Sais*
He ruled from 724 B.C.E. until his death. Tefnakhte held the areas called "the Four Chiefs of Ma," Libyan enclaves. These were SEBENNYTOS, BUSIRIS, MENDES, and Pi-Sopd. He was allied with OSORKON II and IUPUT II of TANIS and LEONTOPOLIS when the Nubians (modern Sudanese) began their invasion of Egypt. When PIANKHI entered Egypt with his Nubian troops, Tefnakhte went to HERAKLEOPOLIS to defeat him. Piankhi easily routed the Egyptian coalition forces, however, and Osorkon II and other allies surrendered.

Tefnakhte fled to MEMPHIS and was captured there and exiled to a remote area of the Delta. He swore allegiance to Piankhi, but in 720 or 719 B.C.E. he declared himself sole ruler of Egypt. A STELA from his era shows him worshiping the goddess NEITH (1). Tefnakhte was succeeded on the throne by his son BAKENRENEF (Bocchoris) in 717 B.C.E.

Tefnut (Tefent)   She was an ancient Egyptian goddess, honored as the twin sister and consort of SHU. Originally she was the consort of a god named Tefen, but his cult disappeared. As Tefen's wife, she was called Tefent. Tefnut personified moisture, rain, and dew and also had a place in solar cults. She was associated with PTAH at HELIOPOLIS. Tefnut served as a means by which Ptah brought life into the world.

In historical periods, Tefnut was associated with the goddess MA'AT and represented the space between heaven and earth. With Ma'at, Tefnut was sometimes viewed as a spiritual force rather than a divine being. She was depicted as a lioness or as a woman with a lion's head. Tefnut supported the sky with Shu and received the newly risen sun each morning.

tekenu   A mortuary symbol made of reeds and fashioned to represent a human being with or without a head, the *tekenu* was placed on a sled and pulled by oxen to funerals. There the oxen were slain and the *tekenu* burned. The ritual dates to the earliest eras of Egypt and may have commemorated the ceremonies in which courtiers, prisoners of war, and other individuals were sacrificed to accompany royal persons to the grave. The *tekenu* assumed any guilt assigned to the deceased and purified the newly departed for ETERNITY.

See also MORTUARY RITUALS.

Tell el-Dab'a   It was a site in the eastern Delta, part of the HYKSOS encampment at AVARIS during the Second Intermediate Period (1640–1550 B.C.E.) and settled as early as the Thirteenth Dynasty by the Asiatics. Hyksos-style residences, tombs, and statues have been found at Tell el-Dab'a, along with hundreds of artifacts from the period of Hyksos domination.

Tell el-Habua   It was a fortified site in the eastern Delta, east of TELL EL-DAB'A. The area was populated and given defensive structures during the Middle Kingdom Period (2040–1640 B.C.E.), possibly serving as a component of the fortifications called the WALL OF THE PRINCE.

Tell el-Mugdam   *See* LEONTOPOLIS.

Tell el-Rub'a   It was a site northwest of modern El-Simbelawein in the Delta. The Egyptians called the area Per-banebdjedet, "the Domains of the Ram Lord." It was historically listed as MENDES and a popular gathering place for rituals of Mendes' cult. Tell el-Rub'a was a site in the eastern Delta, north of el-LISHT. The HYKSOS occupied the territory during the Second Intermediate Period (1640–1550 B.C.E.). Pottery from Palestine, Syria, and Crete were discovered there. The Hyksos traded extensively and did not maintain eastern borders during their period of occupation of the Delta.

Tell Ibrahim Awad   This was a site in the eastern Nile Delta containing five temples that date to the Predynastic Period (ca. 3000 B.C.E.). These temples held some 1,000 ritual objects, but little is known of the titular deities worshipped there. A ceramic baboon found on the site links the area to the god THOTH, but no documentation confirms this. The five temples were uncovered under a Middle Kingdom Period (2040–1640 B.C.E.) shrine. A tomb dating to the First Dynasty (2920–2770 B.C.E.) and containing funerary objects was also constructed on the site. An adjacent settlement, also Predynastic, has been unearthed as well in the area.

Tem (1) He was a solar deity of Egypt, the offspring of NUN, primeval chaos. He was also called Ré-tem and was associated with the cult of RÉ, depicting the setting sun. His name probably translated as "to be complete."

Tem (2) (fl. 21st century B.C.E.) *royal woman of the Eleventh Dynasty*
She was the ranking consort of MENTUHOTEP II (r. 2061–2010 B.C.E.). The mother of MENTUHOTEP III, Tem died young or retired and was replaced by NEFERU (1). Tem's tomb at DEIR EL-BAHRI, on the western shore of THEBES, is large and beautiful. Alabaster slabs form her resting place, positioned on a sandstone base.

Temeh This was a region in NUBIA (modern Sudan) cited in the inscriptions of HARKHUF at ABYDOS. Harkhuf served PEPI II (r. 2246–2152 B.C.E.) as an expedition leader. He was made famous when he brought a dancing DWARF to Pepi II, who was quite young at the time.

temple models They were miniature stone shrines serving as cultic insignias of the gods. One such model was discovered at TELL-EL YAHUDIYEH, dating to the reign of SETI I (1306–1290 B.C.E.) of the Nineteenth Dynasty. Temple models were fashioned with PYLONS, statues, halls, and even OBELISKS, and were placed in shrines as tributes to the deities. The models were inscribed with the name of the donor and were called the "holy of holies." Others were blocks built out of stone, with holes that were fashioned to allow the devotees to insert obelisks, walls, pylons, statues, and other traditional temple adornments.

temple rituals They were the cultic ceremonies conducted at ancient Egyptian shrines and temples over the centuries. Normally the rites began with the offering of incense at the noon hour, although in some eras the rites began early in the morning, especially if attended by the king personally. The INCENSE offered in the morning was myrrh when that substance was available. At night the incense was of a type called *kyphi*. The censer used in the ceremony was a bronze pan, which contained pellets burning in a heated dish or bowl.

The priests dressed and cleaned the god's statue and shrine each day. Most statues of the gods were clothed in colors deemed appropriate to their particular cult or region. Food was then offered to the god. The trays of

A temple kiosk, a unique shrine form used at Philae in the Ptolemaic Period (304–30 B.C.E.) *(Courtesy Steve Beikirch)*

vegetables, meat, fruits, breads, cakes, etc., were taken the next day to the various mortuary complexes in the region or to the tombs of the deceased Egyptians who had contracted with priests to conduct daily rituals on their behalf.

When the god's meal ended, the temple was swept, scrubbed, and then closed. The floors of the temple were normally sanded and washed every day by lesser-ranked priests. At night the god was again saluted and offered gifts and tributes, but the sanctuary, the chamber in which the image of the god rested, was not opened a second time. It was enough for the priests to recite the prayers and hymns in front of his shrine.

When the god was taken out of the temple for a procession or a visit to another temple, the queen or ranking woman of the area escorted or greeted the statue. SISTRUMS, drums, horns, and other musical instruments accompanied the god and were played during cultic ceremonies.

See also MUSIC.

temples They were the gathering place for Egyptian cultic rites, religious structures considered the "HORIZON" of a divine being, the point at which the god came into existence during the creation. Temples had links to the past, and the rituals conducted within their courts were formulas handed down through many generations. The temple was also a mirror of the universe and a representation of the PRIMEVAL MOUND where creation began.

Originally, temples were crude huts that were surrounded by short walls or enclosures. The emblems of the gods, the totems, were placed on a pole in front of the gateway, and early temples also had two poles, bearing flags and insignias. When the Egyptians learned to

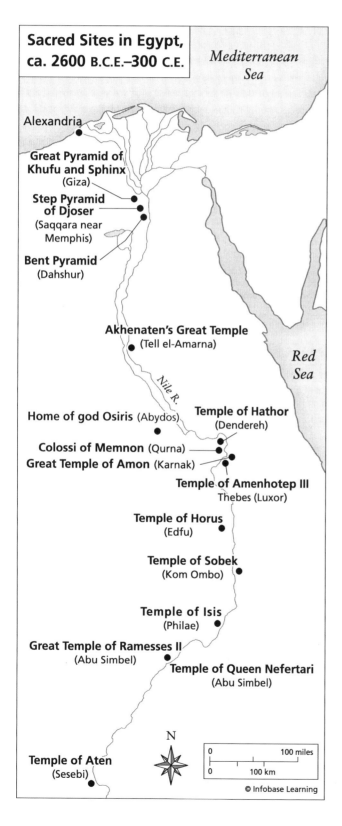

Sacred Sites in Egypt, ca. 2600 B.C.E.–300 C.E.

Mediterranean Sea

Alexandria

Great Pyramid of Khufu and Sphinx (Giza)

Step Pyramid of Djoser (Saqqara near Memphis)

Bent Pyramid (Dahshur)

Nile R.

Akhenaten's Great Temple (Tell el-Amarna)

Red Sea

Home of god Osiris (Abydos)

Temple of Hathor (Dendereh)

Colossi of Memnon (Qurna)

Great Temple of Amon (Karnak)

Temple of Amenhotep III Thebes (Luxor)

Temple of Horus (Edfu)

Temple of Sobek (Kom Ombo)

Temple of Isis (Philae)

Great Temple of Ramesses II (Abu Simbel)

Temple of Queen Nefertari (Abu Simbel)

N

0   100 miles
0   100 km

Temple of Aten (Sesebi)

© Infobase Learning

batter (or gently slope) walls and to raise up enormous structures of stone, the temples became great monuments of cultic ceremonies. Temples and tombs were the only buildings in ancient Egypt to be made of durable materials because of their importance in society. Some temples were created as boxlike shrines, with central courts for statues; at times they were elaborately columned, particularly the massive temples of the various state gods. Still others evolved out of shrines originally made for the barks of the gods.

The basic plan of the Egyptian temple, decreed by the gods themselves, did not vary much in any given area. Most temples had a brick enclosure wall, then a PYLON, the slightly battered or slanted gateway fitted with grooves for the mandatory flagstaffs. The pylons of the larger temples had doors originally made of wood, but in the later eras these were fashioned out of bronze or gold. Before the pylon was the forecourt or reception area. When the temple was opened for the occasional public ceremony, the people would enter through this court. In the early eras such courts were simple squares; in time they became great colonnades.

Other vestibules, colonnades, courts, and chambers opened onto the front entrance, usually leading backward at a slight incline. The HYPOSTYLE HALLS that dominated the major shrines such as KARNAK were not inclined but part of the entrance structures. These opened onto the smaller rooms, which were never opened to the public and never used as stages for major cultic rituals. Each new section of the temple was elevated higher from the ground so that its rooms became smaller, dimmer, and more mysterious. Such chambers were part of an avenue of rooms that led steadily upward to the higher, smaller, and darker sanctuaries, restricted to the initiated. The holy of holies, the single room representing the Primeval Mound, was at the rear, remote, shadowy, and secure against the curiosity of the common worshippers. Few Egyptians saw such sacred chambers. The gods were hidden there from man throughout Egypt's history.

Egyptian worshippers did not feel compelled in any era to enter the secret rooms or to gaze upon the images of the gods. They welcomed the mysterious manifestations of the divine being as they witnessed them in the cultic rites and in the architecture of the temple. The use of aquatic plant designs in the columns and lower wall reliefs alluded to the watery abyss out of which the universe was created. The river, the sun, and the verdant earth were all represented in the chambers and courts, making the temple precinct a complete microcosm.

Some alterations in temple architecture were made over the centuries, but the designs conformed to the original general plan. The shrines of the Early Dynastic Period (2920–2575 B.C.E.) had three contiguous chambers leading to the sanctuary and hidden shrine of the god. During the Old Kingdom Period (2575–2134 B.C.E.)

ELEMENTS OF THE EGYPTIAN TEMPLES

The basic elements or designs that were used in the construction and maintenance of all cultic temples on the Nile in all historic periods were all regimented from the earliest eras. Each element served a particular purpose in the cultic events constructed on the site, and each demonstrated the consistent power of the traditions of Egyptian history. These elements were

landing stage—a small dock on the banks of the Nile that allowed the barks of the gods to moor at the temple site. The landing stage could also include an avenue of sphinxes that connected the dock to the temple or, at times, linked one temple to another.

flagstaff—called *senut* and normally displayed in pairs before a temple to inform the people of the particular deity in residence in the temple. Flagstaffs, tall and made of cedar, were considered a vital aspect of any temple facade.

pylons—made to front the gates or to serve as entrances to different sections of the temple. Slightly battered, or set at an angle, the pylons formed the symbol of the horizon of each temple. Statues and obelisks, as well as flagstaffs, adorned such pylons.

enclosing walls—mud-brick barriers used to protect the sacred precincts of temples. These enclosed the actual complex of the cultic structures, including groves, lakes, and gardens.

forecourts—areas adjoining the pylons at the main entrances or at the openings of each new section of the temple. These forecourts often contained columns and statues.

hypostyle halls—large areas that served as naves or corridors linking parts of the temple. Heavily columned, the hypostyle halls could be roofed or open to air. Some of these halls sheltered barks of the gods. The columns represented the forests that were plentiful on the Nile in the early eras of settlement.

sanctuaries—small, reserved chambers that were positioned within the core of the temple. Most sanctuaries had three auxiliary chapels and were reserved to high-ranking priests. The image of the temple deity reposed there.

Typical columned corridors leading to the Djeseru-Djeseru, the sanctuaries of temples dating to the New Kingdom Period (1550–1070 B.C.E.) *(Courtesy Steve Beikirch)*

the number of such chambers was increased to five. By the New Kingdom Period, the era of Karnak and other vast complexes, the temples could hold any number of chambers. The central shrines in the New Kingdom Period (1550–1070 B.C.E.) were box-like, carved out of granite blocks that weighed 50 or more tons. These temples also contained magazines, storerooms, work chambers for the priests and scribes, administrative bureaus, and a brick-lined pit for the barks of the god. The larger temples also contained sacred lakes.

When a new temple was dedicated, ritual and cultic celebrations were staged on the site, attended by the king or his representative. All of the deities of the past were depicted by priests wearing masks, or by tokens of the divine beings in attendance. Every god of Egypt thus took part in the consecration of the new shrine, as the gods had manifested themselves at the beginning of the world. There were also particular deities who were involved in the creation of new temples and were thus invoked on that solemn occasion. Rituals were held every day in the existing temples of Egypt, and the priests followed a traditional pattern of worship and service, with the accent on cleansing and purification.

Further reading: Arnold, Dieter. *Temples of Ancient Egypt.* Ithaca, N.Y.: Cornell University Press, 1997; Arnold, Dieter. *Temples of the Last Pharaohs.* Oxford, U.K.: Oxford University Press, 1999; Shafer, B. E., ed. *Temples of Ancient Egypt.* Ithaca, N.Y.: Cornell University Press, 1999; Wilkinson, Richard H. *The Complete Temples of Ancient Egypt.* New York: Thames & Hudson, 2000.

Teo (fl. 15th century B.C.E.) *royal woman of the Eighteenth Dynasty*
A consort of AMENHOTEP II (r. 1427–1401 B.C.E.), she was not the ranking queen but was the mother of TUTHMOSIS IV (r. 1401–1391 B.C.E.). He was not the original heir but survived to take the throne after a mystical episode at the Great SPHINX at GIZA. Teo was honored in Tuthmosis IV's reign.

Teos (Irma'atenré; Tachos; Zedhor) (fl. ca. 365 B.C.E.) *second ruler of the Thirtieth Dynasty*
He reigned from 365 to 360 B.C.E. He was the co-regent of NECTANEBO I and was the son of Queen UDJASHU. Teos started his rule by invading Palestine with the aid of King AGESILAUS of Sparta, but they quarreled and failed in their efforts. Teos taxed the Egyptian temples to finance his military campaigns, making powerful enemies and causing a general uproar.

His cousin, NECTANEBO II, realizing the damage being done to the royal line, started a battle for the throne, aided by King Agesilaus and the Spartan allies of Egypt. Teos was forced to abdicate the throne and to retire in disgrace for his sacrilege and abuse of sacred funds.

Terenuthis   This was a site in the Delta near the WADI NATRUN and the Rosetta branch of the Nile, the modern Kom Abu Billo. The city was the cult center for the goddess RENENET but was also dedicated to HATHOR, "the Mistress of Turquoise."

A temple dating to the Ptolemaic Period (304–30 B.C.E.) was erected to honor Hathor. This temple also served as a burial place for sacred cows and was started by PTOLEMY I SOTER (r. 304–284 B.C.E.) and completed by PTOLEMY II PHILADELPHUS (r. 285–246 B.C.E.). The shrine was noted for its exquisite reliefs. The nearby necropolis area serving Terenuthis contained tombs dating to the Sixth Dynasty (2323–2150 B.C.E.) through the Roman Period. During the New Kingdom Period (1550–1070 B.C.E.), the coffins were fashioned to depict the deceased reclining and had carefully formed lids.

Teti (1) (fl. 25th century B.C.E.) *mortuary complex official of the Fourth Dynasty*
He served as the superintendent of the Great Pyramid of KHUFU (Cheops) (r. 2551–2528 B.C.E.) at GIZA during the reign of one of that pharaoh's successors. He is listed in his tomb as a "royal kinsman." Teti also served as a priest in the temples of HATHOR and NEITH (1). His mortuary regalia is in the British Museum in London.

Teti (2) (fl. 16th century B.C.E.) *aristocratic official of the Seventeenth Dynasty charged with treason*
He was a count of KOPTOS, charged with treason by INYOTEF VII (r. ca. 1570 B.C.E.) of THEBES. Teti was collaborating with the HYKSOS, contemporaries of the Seventeenth Dynasty, who ruled the Delta regions. The KOPTOS DECREE, attributed to Inyotef VII, announces the charges against Teti and the loss of his titles, lands, and assets. An individual named Neinemhet received the count's rank and estate.

Teti (Seheptawy) (d. 2291 B.C.E.) *founder of the Sixth Dynasty*
He ruled from 2323 B.C.E. until his death. The circumstances of his coming to power are not documented, but Teti married IPUT, the daughter of UNIS, the last pharaoh of the Fifth Dynasty. Court officials remained at their posts when Unis died and served Teti.

Possibly a physician, Teti wrote texts that were available to MANETHO in the Ptolemaic Period (304–30 B.C.E.). He was the first to promote the HATHOR cult at DENDEREH, and he is listed in the TURIN CANON. Teti commanded a census in Egypt every one or two years, and he fostered trade with BYBLOS in modern Lebanon and with PUNT and NUBIA (modern Sudan). Devoted to OSIRIS in his original form KHENTIAMENTIU, Teti issued a decree exempting Abydos, the deity's cult center, from taxes.

Teti was married to KAWIT (1) and WERET-IMTES (1). His son and heir was PEPI I, and he gave his daughter, SESHESHET, to vizier MERERUKA. Reportedly, the members of his own royal bodyguard assassinated Teti. They were possibly allies of USERKARÉ, who succeeded him on the throne.

Teti's pyramid, called "the Prison" in modern times, was erected in SAQQARA and was inscribed with the PYRAMID TEXTS. A SISTRUM was discovered in the pyramid as well as a statue of Teti, fashioned out of black and pink mottled granite. Pyramids for his queens were also part of the mortuary complex. Nobles of his reign built tombs nearby. These officials included KAGEMNI and Mereruka. Teti's pyramid was designed with burial shafts and his remains indicate a hasty embalming.

Tetiky (fl. 16th century B.C.E.) *urban official of the Eighteenth Dynasty*
Serving in the reign of 'AHMOSE (NEBPEHTIRÉ) (r. 1550–1525 B.C.E.), Tetiky was the mayor of THEBES (modern Luxor). He was also involved in the vast building programs instituted by 'Ahmose to establish Thebes as the capital of Egypt and the chief residence of his dynasty. The designation of Thebes as the capital of the nation involved massive building projects and the development of burial complexes on the western shore.

Tetisheri (fl. 16th century B.C.E.) *royal woman of the Seventeenth and Eighteenth Dynasties, called "the Mother of the New Kingdom"*
She was the consort of TA'O I (Senakhtenré; Djehuti'o) (d. ca. 1540 B.C.E.) at THEBES and the mother of TA'O II (Sekenenré; Djehuti'o) (d. 1555 B.C.E.) and AH'HOTEP (1).

Her grandsons were KAMOSE and 'AHMOSE (NEBPEHTIRÉ), founder of the Eighteenth Dynasty and the New Kingdom (1550–1070 B.C.E.).

A commoner, Tetisheri was the daughter of a judge named Tjenna and Lady Neferu. When Ta'o I died, Tetisheri installed her son and daughter on the throne and aided the military efforts to oust the HYKSOS. She maintained her leadership at the palace at DEIR EL-BALLAS, north of Thebes, and lived to see Egypt free of the Asiatics, reaching the age of 70. Decrees were issued by 'Ahmose (Nebpehtiré) (r. 1550–1525 B.C.E.) concerning her service to the nation.

A Theban tomb complex was erected for her, as well as a cenotaph at ABYDOS, and estates and companies of priests ensured continuing mortuary rituals on her behalf. A statue of her is in the British Museum, but it is now regarded as having been made long after her death. Tetisheri is shown wearing the VULTURE headdress reserved for the royal mothers of the heirs to the throne in this monument. Her mummified remains were discovered in a coffin dating to the reign of RAMESSES I (r. 1307–1306 B.C.E.), indicating her reburial, probably in the Twenty-first Dynasty (1070–945 B.C.E.).

Tety *See* KHA'BA.

Tey (fl. 30th century B.C.E.) *royal woman of the First Dynasty*

A consort of AHA (r. 2920–? B.C.E.), she was depicted in a temple relief in the shrine of the god MIN in PANOPOLIS, near AKHMIN. Tey was buried in ABYDOS.

Thales (d. ca. 545 B.C.E.) *Ionian Greek philosopher of Miletus who visited Egypt ca. 580 B.C.E.*

Thales studied NAUKRATIS and other Egyptian cities and expounded on his theories about water being the essence of all matter. He also predicted an eclipse of the sun on May 28, 585 B.C.E., and he was listed as one of the legendary Seven Wise Men, or Sages, of Greece. While in Egypt, he measured a PYRAMID by contrasting the length of its shadow with that of his walking stick's shadow and then calculating the ratio. Thales also studied the NILE floods and pursued astronomical and geometric gains made on the Nile. None of his writings have survived. He was welcomed to Egypt by APRIES (r. 589–570 B.C.E.).

Thaneni (fl. 15th century B.C.E.) *court official in charge of military inscriptions in the Eighteenth Dynasty*

Thaneni served TUTHMOSIS III (r. 1479–1425 B.C.E.) as a royal SCRIBE and had the role of supervisor of the KARNAK inscriptions of Tuthmosis III's annals. These detailed his military campaigns and other events on the walls of the temple. Thaneni's tomb at Thebes announced his career and honors.

Tharu *See* TCHARU.

Theban Book of Recension *See* BOOK OF THE DEAD; RECENSIONS.

Thebes An extensive metropolitan area that is now called Luxor, the city of Thebes was located in Upper (southern) Egypt on the east bank of the Nile, east of the great temple complex of KARNAK. Thebes was the capital of Egypt during the MENTUHOTEP era of the Eleventh Dynasty (2040–1991 B.C.E.) and during much of the New Kingdom (1550–1070 B.C.E.). When the Ramessid Dynasty (1307–1196 B.C.E.) built a new capital, Per-Ramesses, in the Delta, Thebes remained a powerful religious center of the deity Amun. The site was originally called Waset or Uast, in honor of a religious symbol, the Was scepter. The Greeks named the city Thebes and also called it Diospolis Magna, the "Great City of the Gods." Homer celebrated it as the "City of 100 Gates" and other foreign visitors sang its praises.

Modern Luxor is a large commercial and tourist city with a population of approximately 490,000; it is the seat of the Luxor Governorate.

HISTORY

There is evidence that Thebes was occupied in the Old Kingdom (2575–2134 B.C.E.) and perhaps even earlier. At that time the city was a minor trading post, but the local clans kept the area secure when the First Intermediate Period (2134–2040 B.C.E.) brought chaos to the rest of the nation. The Theban lands of that dynasty declared their independence and gave rise to a succession of princes who waged war to unite the Egyptian NOMES (provinces). Mentuhotep II reunited Upper and Lower Egypt and ruled from Thebes.

It is believed that Thebes served as a joint capital in that era, but the rulers appear to have taken up residence in a number of locations throughout the year. The Twelfth Dynasty, started by another Theban, AMENEMHET I (r. 1991–1962 B.C.E.), established a new capital on the border between Upper and Lower Egypt. Governors resided in Thebes, ruling over the southern territories for the throne.

During the Second Intermediate Period (1640–1550 B.C.E.), when the HYKSOS dominated the Delta territories, the Thebans again stood firm, denying these Asiatic invaders access to most of the southern domains. In the early days there was a truce between the two forces: The Thebans took their herds into the Delta to graze there without incident, and the Hyksos were allowed to sail past Thebes to trade below the cataracts with the Nubians. The truce ended with an insulting message sent by APOPHIS, the Hyksos ruler, to TA'O II (Sekenenré) (d. 1555 B.C.E.), the ruler of Thebes. The Theban armies began to march on the Hyksos strongholds as a result. When Ta'o II died in battle or in an ambush, his son KAMOSE (r. 1555–1550 B.C.E.) entered the war and rolled back the Hyksos forces. He died before taking AVARIS, the Hyksos capital, and was succeeded by his brother, 'AHMOSE, who evicted the Asiatics with campaigns on land and sea. He even sent his armies against the temporary stronghold of the Hyksos at Sharuhen in Palestine, once again chasing the Asiatics all the way to Syria.

As a result of this victory, the god AMUN received considerable support from the ruling clan, especially at Karnak, and the city became the deity's cult center. The shrines, temples, and buildings erected in Thebes gave it a reputation for splendor and beauty that lasted for centuries. All other cities were judged in comparison to Thebes. The Tuthmossids of the Eighteenth Dynasty (1550–1307 B.C.E.) lavished care and wealth upon Thebes, making it again the nation's capital, although MEMPHIS remained an administrative center of government and a temporary residence of the royal clan. During the reign of AKHENATEN (r. 1353–1335 B.C.E.), Thebes was abandoned for 'AMARNA, to the north. His death, however, signaled a return to Thebes and a resumption of the building projects and adornment of the temples, shrines, and royal residences. When the Ramessids came to power in 1307 B.C.E., they built a new capital, Per-Ramesses, reportedly on the site of Avaris, their clan home. Thebes, however, remained popular not only as a residence during certain months of the year but as the site of the royal burial grounds. The deity Amun remained powerful as well, and the rulers continued to adorn the temples and shrines of the god throughout Egyptian history. The rulers of the Third Intermediate Period (1070–712 B.C.E.), the Late Period (712–332 B.C.E.), and the Ptolemaic Period (304–30 B.C.E.) did not reside solely in Thebes, but the city received benefices from these dynasties. The Romans continued to lavish shrines and adornments on the site.

POPULATION

The population of Thebes varied widely throughout its history, growing rapidly with the rise of the city as a capital and then declining as Egypt's power centers moved elsewhere. Established in the Old Kingdom (2575–2134 B.C.E.) as a trading site, the city grew slowly in size with its designation as Waset, the capital of a nome and its subsequent presence as one of the government centers in the time of Mentuhotep II and the Eleventh Dynasty. With the Twelfth Dynasty, governors were appointed in Thebes, but it is likely that the population did not decrease significantly because of administrative needs and the development of the city's economic life through trade along the Nile.

Scholars believe that at its height in the New Kingdom Thebes had one of the largest populations in the ancient world, perhaps as high as 65,000 or more. This population held steady throughout the New Kingdom and likely averaged around 50,000.

Luxor temple, offering a magnificent display of the New Kingdom Period (1550–1070 B.C.E.) architectural achievement and Amunite fervor *(Courtesy Thierry Ailleret)*

Thebes was able to avoid a sharp decline when the Ramessid Dynasty moved the new capital to Per-Ramesses, in the Delta, because it was by then the chief religious center for the cult of Amun. This meant that Egyptians continued to travel to the city as pilgrims, and the priests remained a strong presence in the city.

Like Memphis, Thebes eventually declined on account of the general deterioration of the dynasties. Both cities were entirely eclipsed from the fourth century B.C.E. by Alexandria, the new political and economic capital of Egypt. The religious significance of the area remained well into the time of the Romans, but its population had entered into irreversible decline.

ECONOMY

The Theban economy developed from a small trading center to the economic pillar of the kingdom as its political significance increased. Early on, Theban merchants traded with ASWAN in Nubia, bringing minerals, pottery, and animals into the city. Once Thebes became the capital of Egypt in the New Kingdom, its economic strength grew considerably as merchants came from across the Egyptian Empire and beyond. It had one of the largest ports in all of Egypt from the time of Mentuhotep. Ships brought grain, fruit, vegetables, and many other products from Nubia in the south and Palestine and beyond in the northeast. The area around Thebes was known as a cattle center, with grazing plains and ranches.

Much of the city's economic importance stemmed from its political position. As the capital first of a nome and then of all Egypt, it benefited from the need for palaces, the presence of the governing class, and the laborers needed to construct and maintain the buildings and monuments. Furthermore, Thebes was a religious pilgrimage site from the time of the New Kingdom. The cult of Amun had existed even prior to this time period, but it reached its zenith during the New Kingdom and then retained some of its significance even after the political decline of the city. The building and maintenance of the enormous religious complex at Karnak led to great commercial and architectural activity that contributed to the city's wealth. Thebes's economy served the material and spiritual needs of the large number of priests and pilgrims who made their way to the cult center dedicated to Amun.

Thebes was an active trading center as late as the Ptolemaic Period, in which time it was used as a gateway to the products of Upper Egypt, Nubia, and the upper Nile regions.

SIGNIFICANCE

Called the "City of 100 Gates," Thebes highlighted the vigor, devotion, and artistic vision of the ancient Egyptians. Great palaces, administrative buildings, trade centers, shrines, and chapels provided Thebes with a vibrant and stable economy. As the royal residences, schools, medical clinics, and government buildings were built out of bricks that did not survive over the centuries, the religious structures and those related to mortuary rituals are the monuments that today intrigue modern visitors from across the world.

Some of the most lavish monuments remain at the site, including the temples at OPET (now Luxor) and Karnak on the Nile's east bank, and the Valley of the Kings and the Valley of the Queens on the west bank. The temple at Opet was connected to the popular Opet festival during which the sacred bark of Amun was carried to Opet. Thebes also used the western shore of the Nile as a necropolis, or burial center. The Valley of the Kings holds the tombs of Ramesses II, III, and IV, and the temple of Seti I, and archaeologists continue to map, excavate, and repair the site. Popular as a tourist destination, the Valley of the Kings also contains the tomb of TUT'ANKHAMUN (1333–1323 B.C.E.).

Further reading: Hawass, Zahi. *The Lost Tombs of Thebes: Life in Paradise.* London: Thames & Hudson, 2009; Livraga, Giorgio. *Thebes.* Trans. Julian Scott. Boston: New Acropolis, 1986; Manniche, Lise. *City of the Dead: Thebes in Egypt.* Chicago, 1987; Strudwick, Nigel, and Helen M. Strudwick. *Thebes in Egypt: A Guide to the Tombs and Temples of Ancient Luxor.* Ithaca, N.Y.: Cornell University Press, 1999.

Theocritus (d. 250 B.C.E.) *Greek creator of pastoral poetry who visited Alexandria*
He was a poet from Syracuse who arrived in ALEXANDRIA during the reign of PTOLEMY II PHILADELPHUS (285–246 B.C.E.). Theocritus was on the island of Cos when he wrote to Ptolemy II, asking him to be his patron. In Alexandria, he became a master of poetry, writing the *Idylls,* which was copied by later Latins, and other revered works. The *Idylls* depicts Alexandrian women at a festival.

theophanies They were the various images of animals or reptiles used by Egyptians to represent certain aspects of the nation's deities. Particular strengths or abilities were shown in such images to define attributes of the gods. Some theophanies date to Predynastic Periods (before 3000 B.C.E.), and others evolved over the centuries. It was believed that animals, even serpents or reptiles, represented nature in a manner unknown to humans. Their species existed in modes of creation beyond the human awareness. Theophanies thus represented "the otherness" of earth's creatures and their roles in the ongoing spans of life, called in some eras "the living images of the gods."

Theshen (fl. 25th century B.C.E.) *counselor of the Fifth Dynasty*
He served SAHURÉ (r. 2458–2446 B.C.E.) as treasurer, counselor, and companion. Theshen was the son of

Zezemoneki and Lady Nubhotep. His tomb, a gift from his father, was prepared for him when he was very young. He added adornments to the various chambers as he prospered.

Thethi (fl. 22nd century B.C.E.) *court official of the Eleventh Dynasty in Thebes*
He served in the reigns of INYOTEF I (2134–2118 B.C.E.) and INYOTEF II (2118–2069 B.C.E.). Thethi was the royal treasurer and a favored courtier during both reigns. The Inyotefs ruled only Thebes and Upper Egypt at that time. Thethi's STELA, the first recorded document of that dynasty, depicts the funeral of Inyotef I and the ascension of Inyotef II to the throne. Thethi prepared Inyotef I's tomb at THEBES. He was buried near Inyotef I.

Thinis (Girga) A site in Upper Egypt just north of ABYDOS, called Girga in modern times, Thinis was the home of the early unifiers of Egypt, ca. 3000 B.C.E. The Thinite royal dynasties of the earlier periods dominated for centuries. A brick MASTABA tomb near the site contained vases and jars with the seals of KHUFU (Cheops) (r. 2551–2528 B.C.E.). This mastaba is at BEIT KHALLAF.

At the end of the First Intermediate Period (2134–2040 B.C.E.) a battle was fought at Thinis between the Tenth and Eleventh Dynasties. The KHETYS of the Tenth Dynasty (ca. 2000 B.C.E.) and the Thebans of the Eleventh Dynasty (2134–2040 B.C.E.) engaged in military activities there. Prince Herunefer of Thebes died in the confrontation. Khety raids on Thinis and Abydos and the eventual destruction of ancient gravesites, viewed as a sacrilege, led to MENTUHOTEP II's unification of Egypt ca. 2040 B.C.E. and his destruction of the Khetys.

See also INSTRUCTIONS FOR MERIKARÉ.

Thinite Period This is a term used to designate the earliest dynastic eras, dating to 2920 B.C.E., dated as well from 3150 to 2700 B.C.E. in some lists. The unifiers of Egypt marched on the Delta from THINIS (modern Girga) near ABYDOS. They were the so-called FOLLOWERS OF HORUS, a militaristic people led by NARMER (ca. 3000 B.C.E.), one of the last Predynastic rulers associated with the unification of Upper and Lower Egypt. The Nagada II, or Gerzean, artistic period demonstrates the advances of the Thinite nome of Upper Egypt during the early period.

HIERAKONPOLIS, a site in Upper Egypt, between Esna and Edfu, located across the Nile from Elkab, is part of this artistic era. PALETTES and MACEHEADS depict the unification of the Two Kingdoms by Narmer and his predecessors. Architecturally Hierakonpolis displayed political centralization and advances in construction. The PALERMO STONE cites the era's achievements, and funerary regalia from tombs supplement the documentation.

See also ART AND ARCHITECTURE.

Thoth The ancient god of learning and wisdom, also called Djehuti, he was created from the seed of HORUS or sprang from the head of SET, depending upon which cultic tradition was preferred. He was called "the Master of the Healing Arts," "the Beautiful of Night," "the Lord of Heavens," and "the Silent Being" and was also worshipped as "the Excellent Scribe" and "Great of Magic."

Thoth was usually depicted as a man with the head of an IBIS, and his THEOPHANIES were the ibis and the BABOON. He was also considered a moon deity and was sometimes shown carrying a SCEPTER and an ANKH. Thoth was also honored as a scribe deity at HERMOPOLIS MAGNA and then assigned greater prominence, assuming the head of a dog-headed ape.

As the patron of the dead, Thoth wears an ATEF crown; as the new moon, A'AH, he is depicted in mummified form. Thoth is credited with inventing the number and the orbits of celestial bodies as the secretary of the gods OSIRIS and RÉ. In his astronomical role he was addressed as "the Governor of the Years," "the White Disk," and "the Bull Among the Stars of Heaven."

Thoth was also a protector of priest-physicians and was associated in some temples with the inundation of the Nile. His great cultic festival was celebrated on the New Year, and he was considered skilled in magic and became the patron of all scribes throughout the nation. Thoth appears in the HORUS legends and was depicted in every age as the god who "loved truth and hated abomination."

He is credited with providing the EPAGOMENAL DAYS in the Egyptian calendar and with the healing of the EYE OF HORUS. Many cultic centers honored Thoth, and he was particularly well served by the Tuthmossid rulers of the Eighteenth Dynasty (1550–1307 B.C.E.)

Thoth, Book of This was a mysterious text, described as contained in 42 papyri and considered a treasury of occult lore, now lost to the world. The document was reportedly dictated by the god Thoth to priests and scribes and maintained as sacred secrets to be kept hidden from uninitiated eyes.

Two of the sections of the *Book of Thoth* contained hymns to the god. Four were dedicated to astronomical lore, containing a list of fixed stars, an account of solar and lunar eclipses, and sections concerning the rising of the sun and moon. The skilled astronomers of Egypt had to memorize these texts. Ten rolls of the book dealt with religious matters, supplemented by 10 more rolls dealing with priestly concerns, including obligations and regulations of the various cults. The major thrust of the *Book of Thoth* was philosophical, with scientific and medical texts.

No longer in existence, or at least not yet discovered, the *Book of Thoth* was supposed to be kept "inside an iron box, inside a bronze box, covered by a sycamore box, over an ebony or ivory box over a silver box. . . ." The *Book of Thoth* was supposedly hidden in an area of the Nile near KOPTOS. Because of its occult nature, the work has been prominent in esoteric explanations of Egyptian cultic practices, even though the actual texts have never been available for modern studies.

See also SETNA KHAMWAS (2).

Thuity (fl. 15th century B.C.E.) *noble official of the Eighteenth Dynasty*
Serving HATSHEPSUT (r. 1473–1458 B.C.E.) and possibly TUTHMOSIS I (r. 1504–1492 B.C.E.) and TUTHMOSIS II (r. 1492–1479 B.C.E.), Thuity was "the Overseer of the Double Gold and Silver House," the royal residence. He was the successor to INENI in many positions. A hereditary prince and count, Thuity started his court career as a scribe and steward. He led an expedition to PUNT and then supervised many of Hatshepsut's building projects. Thuity held titles in the government and in the temple. He was also associated with the great barge called "Beginning of the River-User-het-Amun." Thuity was buried at THEBES.

Thunany (fl. 15th century B.C.E.) *royal military scribe of ancient Egypt*
He accompanied TUTHMOSIS III (r. 1479–1425 B.C.E.) on his vast military campaigns. Such scribes were part of Tuthmosis III's military exploits, recording marches, battles, and even botanical specimens encountered during the trek of the armies. Thunany and others could authenticate such campaigns as eyewitnesses. Their testimony was used as the basis for the inscriptions and historical records. Thunany was buried in Thebes, and his tomb contains strong images of his adventures.

Thuré (fl. 15th century B.C.E.) *military commander and viceroy of the Eighteenth Dynasty*
He served TUTHMOSIS I (r. 1504–1492 B.C.E.) in various capacities. Thuré was in control of BUHEN, the Egyptian FORTRESS at WADI HALFA in NUBIA (modern Sudan). He rebuilt that Middle Kingdom (2040–1640 B.C.E.) structure and instituted advanced Egyptian defenses. Thuré also became the VICEROY of Nubia, called "the King's Son of Kush."

As viceroy, Thuré directed the digging of wells, the refurbishing of forts and TRADE centers, and police operation. He was provided with an elite team of soldiers called "the Brave Ones," who crossed 110 miles of desert to protect a series of wells. As a result, Thuré knew the area and the customs of the local populations. Thuré advised Tuthmosis I during his campaign to KURGUS at the fourth cataract. He had started his career in the reign of AMENHOTEP I (1525–1504 B.C.E.) and provided decades of loyal service to the pharaohs of this historical period.

Thuthotep (fl. 19th century B.C.E.) *princely governor of the Twelfth Dynasty*
He served in the reigns of AMENEMHET II (1929–1892 B.C.E.), SENWOSRET II (1897–1878 B.C.E.), and SENWOS-RET III (1878–1841 B.C.E.) as the governor of HERMOPOLIS (Khemenu) nome, called the Hare province. Thuthotep's father was Prince Kei, or Key, whose father, Nehri, lived to such an advanced age that he stepped aside and allowed Thuthotep to take succession.

The tomb of Thuthotep at el-BERSHA, famous for its decorations, contains a unique painting depicting the delivery of a colossal statue. The relief shows more than 170 warriors from Thuthotep's nome pulling the statue in four double rows. The colossus was quarried at HAT-NUB and sent to HERMOPOLIS where it was erected in its designated place. The statue is believed to have weighed 60 tons, standing more than 22 feet high. Thuthotep was the official overseeing the safe delivery of the colossus. Priests, soldiers, and other nome officials were involved as well.

Thuya See YUYA AND THUYA.

Ti (fl. 25th century B.C.E.) *royal barber and overseer of the Fifth Dynasty*
Ti served KAKAI (r. 2446–2426 B.C.E.) as a royal barber and overseer of royal lands. He married Princess NEFER-HETEPES (2), Kakai's daughter, and their sons inherited the rank of prince. Ti served also as the steward of the funerary complexes of dynastic rulers. His elaborate MASTABA was discovered in SAQQARA, and the entrance to his tomb has a pillared vestibule and an open pillared court. Stairs descend to a subterranean passage that leads to an antechamber and burial room. Princess Neferhetepes was buried with Ti. The tomb has vivid reliefs, including a scene depicting a hippo hunt. A SERDAB, agricultural paintings, and a FALSE DOOR add to the tomb's splendor. A painted limestone statue of Ti, six foot five inches in size, was also recovered.

Tia (1) (fl. 13th century B.C.E.) *royal woman of the Nineteenth Dynasty*
She was the daughter of SETI I (r. 1306–1290 B.C.E.) and Queen TUYA, and the sister of RAMESSES II (r. 1290–1224 B.C.E.). Tia married an official, also named Tia, the son of a scribe, Amenwhosu, and they had a daughter, Mutma'atnefer. The tomb of Tia in MEMPHIS was fashioned out of limestone and contained magnificent reliefs. The site was designed with a porch and a court, two tomb chapels, a shrine, and an exterior PYRAMID.

Tia (2) (fl. 13th century B.C.E.) *royal woman of the Nineteenth Dynasty*
She was the consort of the usurper AMENMESSES (r. ca. 1214 B.C.E.) and the mother of SIPTAH (r. 1204–1198 B.C.E.). Tia may have been a widowed consort of MERENPTAH (r. 1224–1214 B.C.E.).

"Time of the Gods" This was a romantic Egyptian term used to designate the Predynastic Periods before

3000 B.C.E. The term also referred to the reigns of certain deities, particularly solar gods and goddesses. These deities were believed to have abandoned their earthly powers to reside in the heavens. The "Time of the Gods" added specific dignity and authority to older traditions or rites, providing them with divine origins. As the various cults evolved over the centuries, the original purposes and customs prevailed because they came into existence in the "Time of the Gods."

Timotheus (fl. third century B.C.E.) *Athenian priest historian who was summoned to Alexandria*
He was from a priestly family in Athens and was requested by PTOLEMY I SOTER (r. 304–284 B.C.E.) to come to ALEXANDRIA to assist in uniting the Egyptian and Greek pantheons of the gods. Timotheus arrived in the new capital and began work with MANETHON, who was also an adviser. His family had ties to the rites of the Greek gods Demeter and Persephone, and he was also familiar with the shrines and oracles at Eleusis and Delphi. Using Timotheus's advice, Ptolemy I established the cult of SERAPIS, the Egyptian Osiris-Apis, and made the deity the patron of the Ptolemaic Dynasty.

Timsah (Timseh) This was a lake in the eastern Delta of Egypt, adjacent to the site chosen for the modern Suez Canal.

Titi (fl. 12th century B.C.E.) *royal woman of the Twentieth Dynasty*
She was a consort of RAMESSES III (r. 1194–1163 B.C.E.). Titi was buried in the VALLEY OF THE QUEENS on the western shore of Thebes. Her tomb, cruciform in shape, is small but elaborately decorated.

Tiye (1) (fl. 14th century B.C.E.) *powerful royal woman of the Eighteenth Dynasty*
The consort of AMENHOTEP III (r. 1391–1353 B.C.E.), Tiye held considerable power during her husband's reign. She was the daughter of YUYA, a commoner priest of AKHMIN, and Thuya, a servant of Queen MUTEMWIYA. Tiye probably married Amenhotep III when she was 12 years old. Intelligent, hardworking, and aware of the needs of the empire, Tiye held administrative posts to assist her somewhat indolent spouse. Her name appeared on official acts and even on the announcement of Amenhotep III's marriage to a foreign princess.

Giving birth to Tuthmosis, the original heir who did not survive long enough to become co-regent, and to AKHENATEN, Tiye also had several daughters, BAKETAMUN, SITAMUN (2), HENNUTTANEB, Nebtiah, and Iset.

Amenhotep III erected a pleasure complex in MALKATA on the western shore of Thebes, including a palace for Tiye. He then retired to the complex, allowing Tiye to conduct the imperial affairs and to direct royal officials.

Tiye was even mentioned by foreign kings in their correspondence. She was widowed at the age of 48 and joined Akhenaten in 'AMARNA.

Many portraits were made of Tiye, who was depicted as having a high forehead, prominent cheekbones, wide-set, heavy-lidded eyes, and a pouting lower lip. She was buried at Thebes, and a controversy has developed over her tomb and mummified remains.

Tiye (2) (fl. 12th century B.C.E.) *royal woman of the Twentieth Dynasty who plotted a royal assassination*
She was a low-ranked consort of RAMESSES III (r. 1194–1163 B.C.E.) of the Twentieth Dynasty. She plotted his assassination with accomplices and was caught and condemned. Tiye was the mother of Prince PENTAWERET and tried to slay Ramesses III and to overthrow RAMESSES IV, the heir. She enlisted the aid of many court officials and military commanders as she arranged the murders.

The plotters struck while Ramesses III celebrated the first day of the 32nd year of his reign. Discovered and investigated, Tiye and her HAREM cohorts managed to corrupt the judges and officials studying her case. The matter was finally decided in court. Tiye disappeared immediately afterward and was probably executed. Pentaweret reportedly was allowed to commit suicide.

Tiye (3) (Tyte) (fl. 11th century B.C.E.) *royal woman of the Twentieth Dynasty*
She was the consort of RAMESSES (r. 1112–1100 B.C.E.) and the mother of RAMESSES XI and Princess BAKETWEREL II. Also listed as Tyte, she was a daughter of RAMESSES IX.

Tiye-Mereniset (fl. 12th century B.C.E.) *royal woman of the Twentieth Dynasty*
She was the consort of SETHNAKHTE (r. 1196–1194 B.C.E.), the founder of that royal line. Her name meant "Tiye, Beloved of Isis." She married Sethnakhte before he became the ruler of Egypt, and she was the mother of RAMESSES III.

Tjel This was a site on the border of Egypt, modern Tell Abu Seifa, and one of the frontier outposts. Tjel was heavily fortified and had a series of wells
See also TCHARU; WALL OF THE PRINCE.

Tjemehu A people depicted in ancient Egyptian texts as a blond or red-headed and fair-skinned strain of Libyans, the Tjemehu lived in the western desert and took part in invasions and campaigns during the New Kingdom Period (1550–1070 B.C.E.) and in later historical periods.

Tjet (Djet) He was an unusual deity of Egypt, worshipped in BUSIRIS and MENDES, the personification of the popular amulet associated with the god OSIRIS and representing that deity's spinal cord or backbone. Tjet was depicted in the ANI PAPYRUS. Figures of the deity were made of gold, crystal, porcelain, or gilded wood. Tjet appeared in the miracle plays conducted by the Osirian cult priests at ABYDOS.

Tjueneroy (fl. 13th century B.C.E.) *building official of the Nineteenth Dynasty*
He served RAMESSES II (r. 1290–1224 B.C.E.) as a director of royal monuments. Tjueneroy conducted his duties in MEMPHIS and in PER-RAMESSES, the new capital of the dynasty. He was the author of a valuable king list.

Tlepolemus (fl. second century B.C.E.) *general of the Ptolemaic Period who brought down a palace cabal*
Tlepolemus was a military official in the reign of PTOLEMY V Epiphanes (205–180 B.C.E.) who altered the course of history by opposing palace conspirators. He was the governor of Pelusium on Egypt's eastern frontier when he heard that Queen ARSINOE (3), the mother of young Ptolemy V, had been murdered. A courtier named AGATHOCLES (2) was responsible. SOSIBIUS, an official who was part of the original plot, had served as guardian of Ptolemy V and had retired. Agathocles became the royal guardian in his place, an event that enraged Tlepolemus and started him marching toward ALEXANDRIA with an army.

In the streets of Alexandria, the people witnessed the arrival of Tlepolemus and his forces and joined them at the palace. Agathocles, seeing the mob and Tlepolemus, resigned hastily and fled the scene. The boy ruler was taken to a stadium, and there, Tlepolemus announced the crimes. Ptolemy V agreed to the mob's demand for Agathocles' blood and the elevation of Tlepolemus to the role of guardian. Agathocles was slain by the angry Alexandrians, and his sister and other family members were also torn to pieces. Tlepolemus took charge of Ptolemy V's future. He was dismissed from the guardianship a short time later.

Tod This was a site on the eastern banks of the Nile south of Thebes, serving as a cultic center for the god MONTU. SENWOSRET I (r. 1971–1926 B.C.E.) erected a temple to that deity at Tod. Artifacts bearing the seals of AMENEMHET II (r. 1929–1892 B.C.E.) were also discovered on the site, including cylinders and cuneiform inscriptions. The temple was obviously built on the foundation of an earlier shrine, dating to the Old Kingdom Period (2575–2134 B.C.E.). Tod remained an active center even in the Roman Period, after 30 B.C.E.

PTOLEMY VIII EUERGETES II (r. 170–163, 145–116 B.C.E.) added a SACRED LAKE to the temple in his era as well. The temple approach was designed with an avenue of SPHINX figures and a way station for the sacred bark

of Montu. TUTHMOSIS III (r. 1479–1425 B.C.E.) presented the station to the complex. The nearby necropolis of el-MOALLA served Tod.

See also TOD TREASURES.

Tod Treasures They are a collection of silver vessels discovered in the temple of MONTU at TOD, south of Thebes. These date to the reign of AMENEMHET II (1929–1892 B.C.E.) and are of Asiatic design. Secured inside four bronze boxes, the Treasures of Tod include silver cups of Aegean and Levantine design, Babylonian cylinder seals, and lapis amulets. They were objects placed in the foundation of the Montu temple.

tomb The evolving grave sites and structures erected by the Egyptians for their mortuary rituals and for the internment of their dead, the early tombs of the Egyptians, in both the north and south, were dug out of the soil on the fringes of the deserts. Several such burial sites have been discovered, and one entire setting is now in the British Museum. The bodies were laid in the ground with pottery, personal items, and weapons, following the customs of other primitive peoples throughout the world. In time, however, the funerary offerings and the regalia accompanying the corpses demanded larger receptacles, as the MORTUARY RITUALS became more sophisticated. The Egyptians began building MASTABAS, tombs made out of dried bricks, with shafts and burial chambers dug into the ground. The main level of the mastaba contained a room for ceremonies and then an additional room, a *SERDAB*, used to position a statue of the deceased so that his spirit could witness the services being offered in his name. The STEP PYRAMID at SAQQARA started the phase of royal pyramids, but these vast complexes, some the size of small cities, were reserved only for royalty and their immediate associates. Commoners and the lesser nobles of the land continued to build their tombs at the edge of the desert, although cliff tombs were popular in many nomes. Others built mastabas in the desert, and these were accompanied by cenotaphs, false tombs constructed for religious purposes, to honor a particular god or region. Such cenotaphs were discovered in the necropolis areas of ABYDOS and at GEBEL el-SILSILEH.

Temples were used in conjunction with tombs eventually, and it became evident that such sites were vulnerable to robbers. AMENHOTEP I (r. 1525–1504 B.C.E.) decided to use the cliffs in the VALLEY OF THE KINGS on the western shore of THEBES as his burial site. Others in the dynasty imitated him, and the VALLEY OF THE QUEENS was also opened for the royal women and princes. The tombs of these individuals were maintained by mortuary priests, contracted and supported by the will of the deceased or by royal decree. The priests performed daily rituals of offerings and prayers at these

The elaborate paintings in the Valley of the Kings site depicting Ramesses II (r. 1290–1224 B.C.E.) in his glorified eternal role (*Courtesy Steve Beikirch*)

sites, and entire families continued in service at the tombs as hereditary priests.

tomb balls Clay documents discovered in ancient Egyptian tombs, all marked with the hieroglyph for "contract" or "seal," these balls are believed to have represented the contracts drawn up on behalf of the deceased and his or her family with the mortuary PRIESTS. Such priests were commissioned to continue daily MORTUARY RITUALS at the tombs. Some of the tomb balls contained bits of papyrus and linen. These balls were probably deposited in the tombs of the deceased by the mortuary priests as symbols of the contracts drawn up for future services.

Tomb of the Birds This is a burial site located in the causeway of the pyramidal complex of UNIS (r. 2356–2323 B.C.E.) in SAQQARA. The MASTABA belonged to NEFER-HOREN-PTAH, a Fifth Dynasty official. The Tomb of the Birds contains agricultural scenes and depictions of caged birds in vivid settings.

Tomb of the Warriors It is a burial site at DEIR EL-BAHRI, on the western shore in Thebes, that dates to the reign of MENTUHOTEP II (2061–2010 B.C.E.). The remains of 60 soldiers who died in the service of Mentuhotep II's reunification campaigns were buried in this rock-cut crypt. The bodies were not mummified but were preserved by elements within their tomb. They were buried close to Mentuhotep II's royal mortuary complex, a high honor. These soldiers may have performed a service of valor or may have been part of an elite military unit used by Mentuhotep II with success.

See also MENTUHOTEP II'S WARRIORS.

Tombos An island at the third cataract of the Nile in NUBIA (modern Sudan). TUTHMOSIS I (r. 1504–1492 B.C.E.) made Tombos the center of his Nubian military campaigns in the second year of his reign. He garrisoned the island, erecting a fortress called "None-Face-Him-among-the-Nine-Bows-Together." A STELA was also erected to commemorate Tuthmosis I's victories over the local population and to proclaim his Asiatic campaigns on the Euphrates River. This stela was engraved on a rock in the area.

Tomb Robbery Trial It was a judicial investigation that was conducted in the reign of RAMESSES IX (1131–1112 B.C.E.) and reflected the decline of the Egyptian government of that historical period. The actual trial came about as a result of the investigations demanded by PASER (3), the mayor of Thebes, over vandalized tombs. He suffered abuse and harassment as a result of his insistence, especially from Prince PAWERO, who was the head of the necropolis sites and necropolis police of that era. Investigations continued, and eventually the involvement of higher-ranked officials was uncovered, including Prince Pawero, who was indicted and tried for his duplicity and sacrilege. The ABBOTT PAPYRUS gives some details about the investigation and about the tombs searched for desecration and vandalism.

tomb texts The various mortuary documents inscribed or painted on the tomb walls in various eras of Egyptian history. Some, compiled as the BOOK OF THE DEAD, were included in the funerary regalia or were reproduced in tomb reliefs. The most popular texts used as burial chamber decorations included

Am Duat originally called "the Book of the Hidden Room" or "that which is in Tuat" (or the Underworld). Stick figures, starkly black and stylized, portray the 12 sections on the tomb walls. The Twelve Hours of the Night compose another version of the Am Duat. The tomb of TUTHMOSIS III (r. 1479–1425 B.C.E.) is decorated with the Am Duat, also listed as Amduat or Am Tuat.

Book of Gates the illustrations first used in the tomb of HOREMHAB (r. 1319–1307 B.C.E.) and depicting the twelve parts of TUAT, or the Underworld, complete with fierce guardians, a lake of fire, and the secret caverns of the deity SOKAR.

Book of Caverns a variation on the traditional BOOK OF THE DEAD texts, depicting vast caverns that formed TUAT.

Book of the Earth a text that appeared first in the reign of RAMESSES III (1194–1163 B.C.E.).

A papyrus tomb text in a copy of the Book of the Dead depicting a deceased couple, Ani and his wife, worshiping Osiris *(Hulton Archive)*

A false door in a tomb from the Old Kingdom Period (2575–2134 B.C.E.) that depicts the deceased returning from Tuat, the land beyond the grave *(S. M. Bunson)*

Represented in four sections, the mortuary document displayed the rising of RÉ as the sun of NUN, the primordial chaos.

Book of the Heavens   a tomb text appearing in the reign of RAMESSES IV (1163–1156 B.C.E.). The 12 hours of eternal night and the passage of the god RÉ are depicted in this mortuary document.

Litany of Ré   a text that offers praise to the deity and lists the 75 forms assumed by RÉ as the supreme solar deity and Underworld traveler.

Tomb Workers' Revolt   A small rebellion that took place during the reign of RAMESSES III (1196–1163 B.C.E.). THE SERVANTS OF THE PLACE OF TRUTH, DEIR EL-MEDINA, labored solely for the ruler and were dependent upon rations and goods provided. In Ramesses III's 29th year, these laborers elected a man named Amennakht to represent them in negotiations for better conditions.

The workers had not received rations for more than a month and had suffered as a consequence. They began to assemble at the mortuary temple of TUTHMOSIS III to register their plight. On the following day they assembled at the RAMESSEUM nearby and complained again. Officials listened but did not provide rations. Violence, punishments, and quarrels developed, continuing the drastic situation. A VIZIER named Ta'a tried to alleviate the situation but was not successful. The PAPYRUS that records these events ends abruptly without giving a resolution.

Tract of Ré   A sacred region of Egypt, stretching from HELIOPOLIS to AVARIS, a site in the eastern Delta near modern QANTIR on the Pelusiac branch of the Nile. This entire area was the homeland of the Ramessids and once served as a capital setting for the HYKSOS. Many monuments were erected on this sacred tract.

trade and exchange   The system of exchanging goods with local communities and foreign markets was essential to the economy of ancient Egypt. Trade practices are documented for Dynasty 0, the era before the founding of the First Dynasty in 2920 B.C.E., and continued until the fall of Egypt some 3,000 years later, when Rome directed all activities.

The rulers of Dynasty 0 resided in HIERAKONPOLIS at least 800 years before the founding of the First Dynasty. Hierakonpolis was in Upper Egypt, between ESNA and EDFU, and was originally called Nekhen. The first documented ruler of Hierakonpolis was SCORPION I. He conquered surrounding sites and areas and then moved his capital to THINIS. NARMER, the famous warrior who invaded the DELTA, was a Thinite and a descendant of Dynasty 0. Recent excavations in Hierakonpolis have uncovered breweries, royal graves, and primitive mortuary temples, indicating the history and age of the site. When Scorpion I came to power he inherited administrative traditions and a thriving trade system. Labels on the grave goods in his tomb clearly display the names of sites up and down the Nile. Other products reflect the influence of foreign cultures, indicating that contact had been made with other lands. The NARMER PALETTE, for example, with its depiction of monsters and entwined long-necked serpents, is distinctly Mesopotamian in design. Knife handles from the same period demonstrate further Mesopotamian influences, probably brought about by an exchange of trade goods and artistic values. Mesopotamian cylinder seals were found in NAGADA II sites. It is possible that trade was not the basis for the appearance of such goods in Egypt; there are some who theorize that such products were brought into Egypt by migrant Mesopotamians entering the Nile Valley.

The early communities on the Nile traded with one another, strictly through barter, sharing products and processes in an effort to establish solid economic bases. By 3500 B.C.E., however, trade with NUBIA (modern Sudan) was active, as well as with Mesopotamia and other cultures.

The Nile Valley was a virtual storehouse of NATURAL RESOURCES, and the lush farming lands gave Egypt the reputation of being "the bread basket of the world" in ancient eras. Over time the pursuit of available assets became imperative and progressed into a determined three-pronged effort that was sustained in most dynastic eras: Egypt's pharaohs safeguarded Egypt's agricultural base as a rich source of commercially valued goods, sought out all other natural resources available, and garrisoned regions in which they conducted trade or gathered additional resources.

EARLY DYNASTIC AND OLD KINGDOM PERIODS (2920–2134 B.C.E.)

Evidence of Egyptian trade missions to Phoenicia (modern Lebanon) dates to the reign of 'ADJIB of the First

Dynasty (ca. 2800 B.C.E.). Phoenicia was popular for its cedarwood and oils. Syrian-style pottery has also been found in tombs from this period. Such trade was probably conducted by sea, as the Asiatic BEDOUINS in the SINAI made land-based caravans dangerous.

During the Old Kingdom Period (2575–2134 B.C.E.), a site called Serabit el-Khadim in the Sinai was used as a mine for precious turquoise, a stone considered sacred to the goddess HATHOR. (Hathor was called the "Lady of the Turquoise.") The Egyptians brought gifts to placate the local Bedouin peoples and to open a trade center, but the local tribes were vigorous in attacking the mine. A general named WENI, who served PEPI I (r. 2289–2255 B.C.E.) in many capacities, took an army of Egyptians and mercenaries into the Sinai, including the fierce MEDJAY warriors from Nubia, and fought the Bedouin. The Medjay would remain part of Egyptian history for centuries. Copper was also mined at Serabit el-Khadim, and the sites were garrisoned and fortified after the defeat of the Bedouin, who were then labeled "Troglydites" by the Egyptians. Wells were dug and a rock-cut chapel was created in honor of Hathor.

Egypt traded with the Libyans by the Early Dynastic Period (2920–2575 B.C.E.), probably for olive oil. The rulers also fought to maintain Egypt's western borders and to subjugate the Libyans, called the Hatiu-a in that period.

Nubia also was an early trading partner. DJER (r. ca. 2900 B.C.E.), the second king of the First Dynasty, is reported to have taken part in a battle at WADI HALFA, where two villages were subdued. KHA'SEKHEMWY, who actually completed the unification of Egypt during his reign (ca. 2650 B.C.E.), conducted punitive campaigns there as well, probably to safeguard the trade centers being operated in the region. Ebony and ivory from the Nubian area were items prized by the Egyptians, who gave the Nubians copper tools, jewelry, and amulets in return. Some local Nubian chiefs appear to have served as trade agents for the Egyptians, no doubt for a percentage of all goods brought to the centers by the outlying peoples. These chiefs grew wealthy, as the Nubian gravesites indicate. The Egyptians established a trading settlement at BUHEN, at the second cataract, in the Second Dynasty, probably to provide a center for the caravans arriving from the interior regions. By the Sixth Dynasty (2323–2150 B.C.E.), the Egyptians were fortifying trade centers on the Nile deep within Nubia. Groups of Nubians moved to these fortified sites, seeking the protection of the garrisons. Some groups, however, remained hostile. In the same era, two princes, Mekhu and his son SABNI, of the ELEPHANTINE Island at ASWAN, conducted trade journeys. Prince Mekhu was slain by Nubians, and Prince Sabni, with the official HEKAIB, recovered his remains. Mekhu was buried on Elephantine Island with honors.

The adventures of the Egyptian royal governor HARKHUF in the same dynasty are well documented.

Harkhuf was called the "King's Son of Kush," the title of the viceroy of Nubia. He brought back incense, ebony, oils, panther skins, elephant tusks, and a marvelous dancing DWARF, who was the delight of the boy ruler PEPI II (r. 2246–2152 B.C.E.). Another expedition leader serving Pepi II, like Harkhuf, had to put down a rebellion by the Nubians. His name was PEPI-NAKHT, and he traveled to the Red Sea to bring back the body of an Egyptian diplomat who was slain while on a trade mission. The Egyptians had already recognized the exotic lands on the Red Sea and had established a shipbuilding center for future sea expeditions.

In an earlier dynasty, Prince KEWAB, the son and heir of KHUFU (Cheops) (r. 2551–2528 B.C.E.), the builder of the Great PYRAMID on the GIZA plateau, had died while possibly on a foreign trade expedition. His death was recorded as taking place while away from Egypt. The collapse of the Old Kingdom reduced activities in foreign trade efforts, but the nation would later pursue such advantages again.

MIDDLE KINGDOM (2040–1640 B.C.E.)

In the Middle Kingdom Period, after MENTUHOTEP II had reunited Egypt in 2040 B.C.E., the trading centers began to flourish once more. Expeditions were sent to PUNT in almost every reign, and a shipbuilding operation center on the Red Sea was begun to facilitate them. Contact had been made with Punt as early as the Fifth Dynasty (2465–2323 B.C.E.), as reported by the PALERMO STONE. In the Middle Kingdom Period the Egyptians had contact with many of the Mediterranean nations, perhaps even Crete, called Kheftiu by the Nile people. Minoan pottery was discovered in Middle Kingdom tombs. In Nubia the major forts were refurbished and new ones erected at critical junctures along the Nile, to facilitate trade and the extraction of natural resources. Egypt conducted trade in the Mediterranean region, and a special relationship was developed with BYBLOS in Phoenicia, where considerable Egyptian influence is obvious.

The pharaohs of the Twelfth Dynasty, particularly SENWOSRET III (r. 1878–1841 B.C.E.), were vigorous in protecting mines, quarries, and trade centers. The oases of Egypt were used as rest stops for caravans coming up from the Nubian south, and canals were built or refurbished alongside the cataracts of the Nile in order to allow ships to bypass the treacherous series of rapids on the river. It was the responsibility of the viceroys of Kush (Nubia) to put down rebellions, clear caravan trade routes, and repair the canals. Great fortresses were built at the cataracts to protect the border and serve as rest stops and transfer terminals for trade expeditions.

NEW KINGDOM (1550–1070 B.C.E.)

The New Kingdom Period (1550–1070 B.C.E.) was the period in which the armies of the Nile marched to the Euphrates and to the fifth cataract, just above modern

Khartoum, Sudan. The expeditions to Punt are well documented in this era also, especially those sent by HATSHEPSUT (r. 1473–1458 B.C.E.).

The exact location of Punt remains unknown, but many scholars believe it was Ethiopia. Expeditions started at Kaptos and went to Kuser, on the Red Sea, to board ships for the voyages. When 'AHMOSE (NEB-PEHTIRÉ) (r. 1550–1525 B.C.E.) founded the Eighteenth Dynasty, he fortified Sal Island, at the third cataract of the Nile in modern Sudan. A summit, called Gebel Adau, on the eight-mile-long island was known as the "Table of the God AMUN." Sal Island became a vital trade center, and later pharaohs established temples of Amun there and in other locations. Priests of the cult of Amun served the traders and, in time, the Nubians, who became fervent in their devotion to the deity. Several New Kingdom pharaohs, including SETI I (r. 1306–1290 B.C.E.), had to conduct punitive campaigns in the area, as the Irem, a warrior people, tried to stop the trade activities. Tombs and other sites were opened as well.

Egyptians were much taken with luxury goods in this period, and the tributes coming from exotic lands (either vassal or client states or allies) increased their appetite for foreign items. This trend also affected the design of monuments, which now favored unique additions such as myrrh trees. Hatshepsut (r. 1473–1458 B.C.E.) sent an expedition to Punt to bring the trees to her great temple at DEIR EL-BAHRI, which also used Nubian and Sinai products.

In Egypt itself, trade centers and ports were opened to provide more outlets for the growing contacts. A port was opened to serve HELIOPOLIS (called On by the Egyptians and now a suburb of modern Cairo). The mines of Egypt were kept in repair and regularly inspected. RAMESSES V (r. 1156–1151 B.C.E.) established a map of such holdings, now known as the TURIN MINING PAPYRUS. This document is considered the world's oldest geographical map. The Fawakir gold mines and the Wadi Hammamat are detailed. The great trade routes out of Nubia were also protected, such as the 40-day route, a pathway that made travel for the caravans simpler and more secure.

The Libyans fought against Egypt on several occasions, especially in the Nineteenth Dynasty and Twentieth Dynasty, joined by a roving group of brigands called the SEA PEOPLES, but the region was exploited and trade was continued. The Libyan trade, as well as the trade with other regions, appears to have been officially regulated in this period with tolls and tariffs. The kings sent out expeditions and fleets regularly, and many officials led the commercial ventures, some coming from the bureau established for foreign trade. Caravans moved through the Libyan Desert area oases, and pack trains were sent into the northern Mediterranean domains.

It is believed that Egypt conducted trade in this era with Cyprus, Crete, Cilicia, Ionia, the Aegean islands, and perhaps even with mainland Greece. Syria remained a popular destination for trading fleets and caravans, where Syrian products were joined with those coming from the regions of the Persian Gulf. The Egyptians received wood, wines, oils, resins, silver, copper, and cattle in exchange for gold (which they had in vaster amounts than any other country), linens, papyrus paper, leather goods, and grains. Money was not in use in Egypt at this time, but a fixed media of exchange was instituted so that trade goods could be valued consistently and fairly. Gold, silver, copper, and even grain were used as bartering values.

Tributes and foreign trade declined after the reign of RAMESSES III (1194–1163 B.C.E.). Expeditions to the mining regions of the Sinai ended after Ramesses V (r. 1156–1151 B.C.E.), but no drastic end to trade is evident after HERIHOR and SMENDES usurped the throne and power in 1070 B.C.E. Egypt was an established trading partner with the world around it, and that tradition was maintained in good times and bad.

THIRD INTERMEDIATE PERIOD (1070–712 B.C.E.)

During the Third Intermediate Period (1070–712 B.C.E.), trade appears to have continued in the hands of newly appointed bureaucrats and independent adventurers. Trade was necessary to Egypt's economy and was a factor of stability as the land splintered into rival city-states. When the Twenty-fifth Dynasty (770–657 B.C.E.) arose out of Nubia, trade with the southern domain flourished, but Mediterranean trade systems were not abandoned by that or succeeding royal lines.

In order to bolster trade, PSAMMATICHUS I (r. 664–610 B.C.E.) opened the city of NAUKRATIS in the DELTA on the Canopic branch of the Nile. Greek traders and merchants resided in the new city, receiving trade rights that gave them an advantage in the world markets. Founded ca. 630 B.C.E., Naukratis meant "ship power" and reflected the maritime efforts involved in trade at the time. Greek silver and Greek slaves were brought to Egypt, revitalizing the nation's trade and allowing more exports to reach new markets. In return for the imports, Egyptians exported grain and manufactured artistic wares.

TRADE INTERRUPTED

The Persian occupation of Egypt from 525 to 404 B.C.E. and from 343 to 332 B.C.E. interrupted the trade processes. The victories of Macedonian king ALEXANDER THE GREAT (r. 332–323 B.C.E.) ended the Persian Empire and introduced the Ptolemaic Period. During this era (304–30 B.C.E.), the Faiyum and other agricultural regions were protected. PARAETONIUM, a harbor on the Mediterranean Sea, west of the city of ALEXANDRIA, flourished. The site was constructed on a ruined fortress from the reign of Ramesses II. The founding of Alexandria by Alexander the Great heightened the trade capabilities and profits of Egypt, and Egyptian trade reached new heights, maintained by the dynasty until the suicide of Egyptian queen CLEOPATRA VII (r. 51–30 B.C.E.). The Romans, who made Egypt a province with a special status, understood the value of the trade processes, employed protective measures, and regulated such commerce out of Alexandria.

Further reading: David, Rosalie. *Handbook to Life in Ancient Egypt, Revised Edition.* New York: Facts On File, 2003; Kemp, Barry J. *Ancient Egypt: Anatomy of a Civilization.* London: Routledge, 1989; Mark, Samuel. *From Egypt to Mesopotamia: A Study of Predynastic Trade Routes.* Austin: Texas Monthly Press, 1997; Price, Betsy. *Ancient Economic Thought.* London: Routledge, 1997; Zingarelli, Andrea Paula. *Trade and Market in New Kingdom Egypt: Internal Socio-economic Processes and Transformations.* London: British Archaeological Reports, 2010.

Travels of an Egyptian (The Tale of Mohor)   It is a literary text dating to the last periods of the Nineteenth Dynasty (1307–1196 B.C.E.). This text is believed to be an actual journal of a tour, serving as a geographical exercise for students. An official depicts his travels through Syria and Palestine, including assaults and hardships. It has been compared to the REPORT OF WENAMUN of a later era.

Tree of Heaven   A plant that grew in the mythical paradises of the Egyptians. Associated with the cult of HATHOR, the tree was a resting place for the SEVEN HATHORS, who supplied the deceased Egyptians with celestial food beyond the grave.

See also PERSEA TREE.

Troja   *See* TUREH.

Tschesertep   A serpent demon mentioned in a magical formula in the PYRAMID TEXTS, the creature was one of the many enemies of the human soul that had to be conquered in order to reach the bliss of paradise beyond the grave. Such serpents were also the enemies of the god RÉ and assaulted him on his journeys through TUAT, or the Underworld, each night.

See also APOPHIS.

Tuat (Duat)   This was the realm of the dead in Egyptian cultic traditions formed by OSIRIS's body as a circular valley. Tuat was the destination of the deceased after being judged in the halls of the god Osiris that were in the sixth section of the abode. The soul of the dead had to undertake a journey in order to reach Tuat, following the example of the god RÉ, who made the same perilous journey each night. The souls of Egyptians waited in the first section of Tuat for Ré to waken them and the souls of foreigners were in the

fifth division. The damned and the demons watched Ré pass as well, and they wailed when he abandoned them. There were many levels, similar to Dantes' vision of the underworld.

Osiris was also present in Tuat and he brought rebirth to the dead. Ré sailed through Tuat and then to the paradise. The mortuary text used in the tombs describes Osiris as "He Who Is in Tuat." The Seven Arits, supernatural beings who could also number as many as 12, guarded the gates. There were also 12 circles that had to be descended by all making the journey. Upon nearing paradise, the dead were bathed in and then absorbed by a radiant light.

Tudhaliyas IV (Tudkhaliash) (d. ca. 1220 B.C.E.) *king of the Hittites and an ally of Egypt*
He was in power during the reign of RAMESSES II (1290–1224 B.C.E.). The son of Khatusilis, Tudhaliyas IV ruled from ca. 1250 to 1220 B.C.E. Tudhaliyas IV maintained peace with Egypt during his reign, despite occasional clashes over control of vassal city-states. The ASSYRIANS threatened the HITTITES in the east, and small western states were making raids and incursions upon the region.

Tumas   It was a site on the Nile located some 150 miles south of ASWAN in NUBIA (modern Sudan). PEPI I (r. 2289–2255 B.C.E.) celebrated a victory over the Nubians at Tumas, probably a battle won by General WENI in the ruler's name. An inscription on the local rocks commemorated the event.

Tuna el-Gebel   A site in the desert west of HERMOPOLIS (modern el-Ashmunien), serving as the northwest boundary of the capital of AKHENATEN (r. 1353–1335 B.C.E.) at 'AMARNA, Tuna el-Gebel was a necropolis, sacred to the god THOTH. The site was popular in the later historical periods of Egypt. A STELA depicting Akhenaten, Queen NEFERTITI, and three daughters was discovered at Tuna el-Gebel. Persian papyri from the Second Persian Period (343–332 B.C.E.) were also found, as well as many tombs, containing mummified IBISES and dog-headed BABOONS. The tomb of PETOSIRIS, serving PHILIP III ARRHIDAEUS (r. 333–316 B.C.E.) is a treasure on the site. This tomb was built as a temple, with a columned vestibule, pillars, cultic chambers, and elaborate reliefs. An ancient waterworks with a deep shaft and catacombs are also located in Tuna el-Gebel.

Tureh, el- (Tura; Trozia; Troja)   A limestone QUARRY that was part of the MOKATTEM Hills in the southern region of modern Cairo, Tureh was used for limestone as early as the Old Kingdom Period (2575–2134 B.C.E.). A Sixth Dynasty (2323–2150 B.C.E.) inscription mentions a sarcophagus fashioned out of Tureh limestone by order of a pharaoh. The Tureh Inscription, dated to the reign of AMENEMHET III (1844–1797 B.C.E.), designates the reopening of the quarry for temple projects. Tureh limestone was prized for its fine quality.

Turin, Judicial Papyrus of   See JUDICIAL PAPYRUS OF TURIN.

Turin Canon   This is the finest chronological list of Egyptian rulers, preserved on a papyrus in the Egyptian Museum of Turin. The papyrus is composed of 12 pages, formed as a roll, and the list begins with AHA (Menes) and ends with RAMESSES II (r. 1290–1224 B.C.E.). Written in the hieratic style, the document was first assessed by Champollion le Jeune. The king of Sardinia owned the Turin papyrus and donated it to the museum. Sent in a crate, the papyrus arrived in crumpled fragments but was reconstructed into the existing document. The 12 pages each contain 26 to 30 names of Egypt's rulers.

Turin Mining Papyrus   This is a document dated to the reign of RAMESSES IV (1163–1156 B.C.E.) and considered the world's earliest geological map. Now in Turin, Italy, the Turin Mining Papyrus depicts the WADI HAMMAMAT and the Fawakir gold mines in use in that era. Ramesses IV sent expeditions there during his reign.

Tushratta (fl. 14th century B.C.E.) *last independent ruler of the Mitanni Empire*
He was in power in the reign of AMENHOTEP III (1391–1353 B.C.E.). Tushratta, an ally of Egypt, sent Amenhotep III a statue of the goddess Ishtar in order to heal the pharaoh from an illness. Tushratta also asked for a sign of Amenhotep's good will, preferring gold, which he wrote was "as plentiful as dust" in Egypt.

Tut'ankhamun (Nebkhepruré) (d. 1323 B.C.E.) *twelfth ruler of the Eighteenth Dynasty from 1333 B.C.E. until his untimely death, and the most famous pharaoh of Egypt*
The death of Amenhotep IV, known more commonly as AKHENATEN (r. 1353–1335 B.C.E.), signaled a drastic change in ancient Egypt. This pharaoh, known as the "heretic," had ruled from a new capital, 'AMARNA, which honored the god Aten. The people of Egypt refused to follow Akhenaten in the worship of this deity, and Akhenaten isolated himself from the people and closed the temples of the ancient gods. Akhenaten's son and heir, SMENKHARÉ, took the throne but ruled only to 1333 B.C.E., when he died. His death brought Tut'ankhamun, only a child, to the throne of Egypt.

BIOGRAPHY

For many years, Tut'ankhamun's father was believed to be Akhenaten, and in February of 2010, the renowned Egypt archaeologist Dr. Zahi Hawass confirmed through DNA testing Akhenaten's parenthood of Tut'ankhamun. During this same DNA testing, a then-unidentified body was confirmed to be that of Queen Tiye, the *hemet,* or

Great Wife, of Amenhotep III (r. 1391–1353 B.C.E.). Thus, Queen Tiye was proven to be the mother of Akhenaten and grandmother of Tut'ankhamun. Furthermore, another unidentified female body through DNA testing was confirmed to be Tut'ankhamun's mother. A name has yet determined for this woman, though in addition to being Tut'ankhamun's mother, she was also Akhenaten's full sister and wife.

As the successor of Smenkharé, Tut'ankhamun was only eight years old at the time of his succession. He reigned from 1333 B.C.E. until his untimely death in 1323 B.C.E. Tut'ankhamun was married to ANKHESENAMON, the third daughter of NEFERTITI and Akhenaten, and for a time the young couple remained at 'Amarna. Later, they moved to MEMPHIS and refurbished the apartments of AMENHOTEP III at THEBES for their use. Nefertiti joined the young couple in Thebes but did not remain in the court for long. Until this point Tut'ankhamun had been called Tut'ankhaten, but he had abandoned his Aten name by his fourth regnal year. The change signaled that he had sworn allegiance to the popular god Amun.

The RESTORATION STELA, which dates to this period, gives an account of Tut'ankhamun's efforts to stabilize the government and to restore the temples and cultic rites of the old gods of Egypt after the 'Amarna Period. He even subsidized new priests, as well as palace staff, from his own pocket. It is believed that AYA (2) was one of his counselors at the time, and he probably suggested the reform measures. Tut'ankhamun also moved some of the bodies of the royal family from 'Amarna to Thebes, as evidenced by a cache of royal jewelry apparently stolen during the reburial and then hidden in the royal Wadi area.

With the help of veteran counselors and advisors, such as the military leader HOREMHAB, the young royal couple planned to promote the restoration of the god Amun and the traditions of the Nile Valley. Tut'ankhamun also worked to restore the prestige of the pharaoh. It is possible that he conducted military campaigns: A portrait was discovered on a chest in his tomb in the VALLEY OF THE KINGS that depicts him as riding in a war chariot, wearing a blue war helmet and charging Egypt's enemies. (Blue was the color of helmets commonly worn for battle.)

Tut'ankhamun renovated temples and shrines and attended festivals and religious celebrations and processions. He is also credited with a mortuary temple in the area of MEDINET HABU. He had designed colossal statues of himself for this shrine, but they were usurped by his successors. Tut'ankhamun died suddenly in 1323 B.C.E., some 10 years after being crowned. His body was given to the priests of the *per-nefer,* the "House of Beauty," who used mortuary processes and rituals to mummify the remains. The "Servants of the Place of Truth," the architects, artists, and laborers of Deir el-Medina in charge of building the pharaoh's tomb in the Valley of the Kings, assembled grave offerings. The objects buried with the royalty at 'Amarna were hastily brought to Thebes, as Tut'ankhamun had not lived long enough to accumulate the vast treasures of other pharaohs. It is believed that the magnificent articles discovered in his tomb were originally those of Akhenaten and other 'Amarna residents. For example, while the now-famous golden facemask is a portrait of Tut'ankhamun, it was probably borrowed from Akhenaten's riches. (A separate portrait facial piece of Tut'ankhamun was likely created and attached to the mask of Akenaten.) Because Tut'ankhamun died at such a young age and so suddenly, leaving limited time to bring a sarcophagus from a quarry, it is believed that the sarcophagus of his burial was also borrowed from Akhenaten's tomb in 'Amarna. Tut'ankhamun's decorated COFFINS also carry signs of having alterations in decorations. (Many scholars believe Tut'ankhamun's canopic coffinettes were originally intended for Smenkharé.) Furthermore, the small statues in the tomb resemble a feminine form, suggesting that they were taken from Nefertiti's tomb. Because tomb treasures were taken from the 'Amarna necropolis and put into Tut'ankhamun's tomb, many believe Horemhab, who was attempting to erase 'Amarna from history, would have vandalized the tomb of Tut'ankhamun had Tut'ankhamun's treasurer, MAYA, not intervened to protect it.

The walls of Tut'ankhamun's tomb also lack the extensive decorations normally included in the tombs of pharaohs. The painting alongside his sarcophagus depicts Aya burying Tut'ankhamun with the mortuary rituals. The two figures are overly large, the size of which saved wall artists from having to add yards of hieroglyphs or other mortuary designs in the tomb that would serve as his resting place. Another tomb, located beside his grave site, was recently opened and contained articles that indicate that some mortuary rituals were conducted there. Two mummified fetuses of what are believed to be his children, born prematurely, were found in coffins sealed with Tut'ankhamun's name.

After his death, Queen Ankhesenamon made the extraordinary offer of herself and the throne of Egypt to the Hittite king SUPPILULIUMAS I. The HITTITE prince sent to marry Ankhesenamon as a result of her invitation was slain at Egypt's border, however, probably by Horemhab's men. She married Aya and then disappeared.

The cause of Tut'ankhamun's death has long been the subject of discussion among Egyptologists. Many thought that he had been assassinated, as his remains showed an apparent blow to the head, but this head wound was determined to be suffered postmortem. Based on a CT scan taken in 2005, it is now believed that the young king had broken the tibia in his left leg a short time before his death. The leg became infected, and there was also the apparent presence of necrotiz-ing bacteria that was destroying the soft tissue and bone in his foot. DNA studies revealed the presence of malaria tropica, the fatal form of malaria that attacks the brain. Based on these studies, the conclusion is that Tut'ankhamun died from malaria. These efforts, led by Dr. Zahi Hawass, put to rest the conspiracy theories about his death that have been so popular over the decades. The evidence gathered from forensic studies indicate that the king also suffered from a cleft palette, a clubfoot, scoliosis, and curvature of the spine. These afflictions, consistent in part with the genetic defects that were the result of the inbreeding among the members of the 'Amarna dynasty, would have made his daily life a struggle.

The long-undiscovered tomb of King Tut'ankhamun was found in 1922 by the English Egyptologists Howard Carter (1874–1939) and George Herbert, the fifth Earl of Carnarvon (1866–1923). The discovery caused a global eruption in interest in ancient Egypt and made Tut'ankhamun the most famous pharaoh in Egyptian history. While the contents of the tomb traveled the world on a series of exhibits, King Tut'ankhamun's mummy remained in his tomb in the Valley of the Kings. In 2007, on the 85th anniversary of the tomb's discovery, the mummy was placed on display in his underground tomb at Luxor (modern-day Thebes) in a climate-controlled glass enclosure.

HISTORICAL IMPACT

The life and death of Tut'ankhamun and his stunning tomb treasures have become part of the modern consciousness. People throughout the world know Tut'ankhamun's name and have heard of the golden mask and the other priceless relics buried with him. The discovery of his tomb, and the wealth of his funeral regalia, renewed interest in ancient Egypt and the pharaohs of the Nile Valley. Today thousands of people visit the museum in Cairo where his grave goods are on display.

It is historical irony that a young king who died at the age of 19 and served for barely a decade at the end of a declining dynasty should become the best known and arguably the most beloved of all the pharaohs. His popularity was the result of his tomb being found almost entirely intact, making the find the most important in all of Egyptology. For that alone, King Tut, as he is known to the modern world, was given a place of prominence in the history of Egypt.

The reign of Tut'ankhamun also marked the formal end of the failed religious reform of his father, Akhenaten. Thus, the 'Amarna Period was brought to a close, and the young king brought a return to the worship of Amun and the traditional religious system that had been in place in Egypt for thousands of years.

Further reading: El Mahdy, Christine. *Tutankhamun: The Life and Death of the Boy-King.* New York: St. Martin's

Press, 2000; Hawass, Zahi. *Tutankhamun: The Golden King and the Great Pharaohs*. New York: National Geographic, 2008; James, T. G. Henry, Araldo de Luca, and Elisabetta Ferrero. *Tutankhamun*. New York: Friedman/Fairfax, 2000; Reeves, C. N., and Nicholas Reeves. *The Complete Tutankhamun: The King, the Tomb, the Royal Treasure*. New York: Thames & Hudson, 1995.

Tuthmosis (fl. 14th century B.C.E.) *prince of the Eighteenth Dynasty*

He was the ranking son and heir of AMENHOTEP III (r. 1391–1353 B.C.E.) and Queen TIYE (1). Tuthmosis was made the high priest of PTAH at MEMPHIS and the supervisor of all priests throughout Egypt. He initiated the rites for the burial of the APIS bull in Memphis and then died suddenly before he could inherit the throne. Amenhotep IV (AKHENATEN) became the heir. Tuthmosis fashioned a unique sarcophagus for his cat. He was depicted in a relief of the historical period and remained popular, as the Apis rituals continued for centuries.

Tuthmosis I (Akheperkaré) (d. 1492 B.C.E.) *third ruler of the Eighteenth Dynasty and the founder of the Egyptian Empire*

He reigned from 1504 B.C.E. until his death. Not the heir to the throne of Amenhotep I, TUTHMOSIS I was probably a prince of a collateral line or an heir of the Theban nome aristocracy. His mother, SENISONBE, is identified only as "King's Mother," but she reportedly had political power of her own.

Tuthmosis I married 'AHMOSE (1), a possible sister of Amenhotep I, and was named heir when the king died childless. 'Ahmose bore Tuthmosis two daughters, NEFERUKHEB and HATSHEPSUT, and two sons, WADJMOSE and AMENMOSE. These two sons were militarily active but predeceased their father. TUTHMOSIS II, born to MUTNOFRET (1), a lesser-ranked royal woman and perhaps a nome heiress, became the heir.

Assuming the throne, Tuthmosis I began many building projects, including the extension of the great temple of AMUN at KARNAK. Aided by INENI, the famed architect of the era, Tuthmosis I added pylons, courts, and statues to the shrine, setting the standard for the eventual magnificence of the temple. He also led a military campaign into NUBIA (modern Sudan) in his second regnal year, fighting the local warrior clans and penetrating beyond the second cataract. Some records indicate that Tuthmosis battled the chief of the Nubians there. A hand-to-hand combat cost the Nubian his life and his territory. Tuthmosis returned to Thebes with the body of the chief hanging from the prow of his ship. After defeating the local inhabitants, Tuthmosis started a new series of FORTRESSES on the Nile and named a new viceroy of Nubia to handle the affairs below the cataracts. He also cleared the ancient canals at the various cataracts.

His greatest military exploits, however, were conducted in the lands beyond the eastern borders of Egypt. Like others of his line, he smarted over the recent domination of the HYKSOS, or Asiatics, in the Delta region of Egypt. He felt that the Egyptians needed to avenge themselves for the shame and led an army against several Asiatic territories in order to subdue tribes and to create buffer states and vassals. Tuthmosis I managed to reach the Euphrates River near CARCHEMISH in modern Syria, erecting a stela there to commemorate his victory. His exploits allowed him to boast that he had enlarged the boundaries of Egypt to match the circuit of the sun. He made the Euphrates Egypt's new border. Tuthmosis I also fought the MITANNI chariot corps.

At Karnak, to commemorate his victories and to bolster his popularity, he had a HYPOSTYLE HALL built entirely of cedarwood columns and added a copper and gold door, OBELISKS, and FLAGSTAFFS tipped with ELECTRUM. The tomb of Tuthmosis I was also begun early in his reign. Ineni supervised the preparation in secret, placing it high in the cliffs overlooking the western shore of Thebes. The ruler's mortuary temple, quite magnificent in design, was located near MEDINET HABU. Tuthmosis I was so popular that his mortuary cult continued into the Nineteenth Dynasty (1307–1196 B.C.E.). He brought Egypt renewed vigor and a sense of continuity and stability. Above all, his military campaigns healed the wounds of the Thebans and set the pattern of empire.

The mummified remains identified as those of Tuthmosis I were found with a cache of bodies in DEIR EL-BAHRI, reburied there when later dynasties discovered the original royal tombs had been vandalized. The corpse of the ruler was bald, showing signs of arthritis and poor teeth. Tuthmosis I had a narrow face and an arched nose. There have been questions as to the true identity of the corpse over the years, with some scholars holding the opinion that it is not Tuthmosis I because of the apparent age discrepancies.

Tuthmosis II (Akheperneré) (d. 1479 B.C.E.) *fourth ruler of the Eighteenth Dynasty*

He reigned from 1492 B.C.E. until his death. The son of TUTHMOSIS I and MUTNOFRET (1), a lesser-ranked wife and possibly a sister of Queen 'AHMOSE, the wife of TUTHMOSIS I, Tuthmosis II was not ambitious or entirely healthy. There has been considerable doubt about the military capacities of this heir to the throne. Frail and sickly, he was overshadowed by HATSHEPSUT, his queen, throughout his reign. However, it is recorded that he conducted at least one campaign against the Asiatics. One fragmented document states that he even entered Syria with his army and conducted another campaign in NUBIA. This campaign, however, is recorded in another place as having been accomplished by others in his name. He is supposed to have come to the area to view the trophies of victory. There he also began to take Nubian princes to be raised as Egyptians.

Tuthmosis II added to the KARNAK shrine but left no other monuments to his reign except a funerary chapel. He had a daughter, NEFERU-RÉ, the offspring of Hatshepsut, and a son, TUTHMOSIS III, from a HAREM woman named ISET (1). This son was declared his heir before Tuthmosis II died at the age of 29 or 30.

His mummified remains give evidence of a systemic illness, possibly from tooth decay, an affliction quite common in that period. He was heavyset, without the characteristic Tuthmossid muscular build, but his facial features resembled those of his warrior father. No tomb has been discovered, but his mummy was found in the cache of royal remains at DEIR EL-BAHRI.

Tuthmosis III (Menkheperré) (d. 1425 B.C.E.) *fifth ruler of the Eighteenth Dynasty, called "the Napoleon of Egypt"*

Tuthmosis III reigned from 1479 B.C.E. until his death. He was the son of TUTHMOSIS II and ISET (1), a HAREM woman, and was named heir before his father's death. On later monuments Tuthmosis III inscribed an account of the miraculous event that he claimed took place when he was named the heir to the throne. The god AMUN supposedly forced the priests bearing his sacred ark into the ceremonial chamber to kneel at a certain point. The ark was saluting a novice of the temple, Prince Tuthmosis, who at the time was serving a type of novitiate in a separate cult reserved for the princes of Egypt. The bearers of the sacred ark prostrated themselves in front of the prince, and Tuthmosis III rose up as the heir to the throne.

BIOGRAPHY

Although Tuthmosis III was named heir, he was too young to rule at the time of the death of his father, Tuthmosis II, so HATSHEPSUT, Tuthmosis II's queen, was named regent. She allowed Tuthmosis's coronation and perhaps married him to her daughter, NEFERU-RÉ. Two years later, however, with the help of her courtiers and the priests of Amun, led by HAPUSENEB and SENENMUT, she took the throne in her own name, adopted masculine attire, and became queen-pharaoh. Tuthmosis III was allowed to wear the robes and crowns of a king, but he was relegated to the background, serving as the commander of the great naval base of Peru-Nefer near MEMPHIS. That situation continued until ca. 1469 B.C.E., when Neferu-Ré and Senenmut died, leaving Hatshepsut vulnerable. Hatshepsut was herself becoming increasingly ill, further contributing to her increasing vulnerability.

Tuthmosis III had conducted some military campaigns during Hatshepsut's reign, and he had spent a great deal of time preparing the land and naval forces of Egypt for his own expeditions. Thus, with Hatshep-

sut ill or possibly already dead, Tuthmosis III, now the sole pharaoh, began his true reign by leading a vast army out of Egypt to attack the king of KADESH, a northern Mediterranean region, and its allies. Territories throughout western Asia joined in the revolt, and Tuthmosis III had to combat them in order to reestablish Egyptian suzerainty over the region. He led some regiments on land routes while sending troops and supplies by ship to the Palestinian coast to meet him; the combined forces would face the Asiatic army at the fortress of AR-MEGIDDO, located on Mount Carmel (now in modern Israel). The Asiatics expected that he would attack them directly, and they waited in force on the main road to Mount Carmel, some distance from the fortress. Tuthmosis III, however, changed the direction his troops were marching at Aruna, some distance from the Asiatic position, and took his troops single file over Mount Carmel in order to surprise the enemy from behind. The Egyptian cavalry also moved over the narrow mountain trail, arriving at the Kina River intact. The cavalry units, much feared in this era, sent the Asiatics in panic-stricken flight into the fortress of Ar-Megiddo.

With the Asiatics inside the fortress, Tuthmosis III laid siege, building a wall around the outer defenses, the first such documented siege in history. He left a token force there while he raided the lands of the neighboring rulers and chieftains. The campaign lasted only a few months; those in Ar-Megiddo were ultimately left no choice but to surrender. For the Asiatics the defeat was a disaster and a catastrophe, and today the fortress is remembered for the horrors endured there.

On his return to Thebes, Tuthmosis III stopped with his troops to harvest the crops of the Asiatics, and Egypt was subsequently flooded with treasure, tribute, and dignitaries from every land and city-state in the region as a result of its newly gained imperial status. He also instituted the policy of bringing the young aristocratic men and women of each of his conquered lands (including those from his Kadesh victory) to Thebes, where they were trained in Egyptian customs and culture. When they were old enough, these young people, now intimately familiar with all aspects of Egyptian life, returned to their homelands as vassal rulers. Tuthmosis III regulated the internal affairs in the nation as well, setting the standards for viziers and court officials and using their talents to launch building projects.

Tuthmosis III spent 20 years on military campaigns both on land, along the Mediterranean coast, and at sea, sailing south to the cataracts of the Nile below Aswan, in the region of Nubia (modern Sudan). His campaigns were often undertaken by the MEDJAY, the Nubian berserker warriors, who also served as scouts. On campaigns, Tuthmosis also brought a small unit of faithful scribes, who kept records of every event. On one expedition, records were made of local flora and reproduced on a wall of Karnak, now called the Botanical Wall. Another one of his generals, named Amenhotep, recorded the event that took place when Tuthmosis III spotted a herd of elephants and decided to hunt them. One elephant charged Tuthmosis's chariot, but Amenhotep moved in and cut the elephant's tusk, allowing the pharaoh to escape from harm.

Tuthmosis was probably married to Neferu-Ré. The only child of Tuthmosis II and Hatshepsut, she was her mother's staunchest ally. Hatshepsut had groomed Neferu-Ré to become the "God's Wife of Amun" a rank and dedication open only to royal women and part of the Amun cult. A recently discovered portrait relief of Neferu-Ré shows her in this role, which would have led to her receiving the throne from her mother. She reportedly bore Tuthmosis III a son while serving as the *hemet,* or Great Wife. She died suddenly, possibly from malaria. After the death of the young *hemet,* Tuthmosis married SITIAH, a short-lived queen. MERYT-RÉ-HATSHEPSUT then became the Great Wife, and they had a son, AMENHOTEP II, and several daughters. Tuthmosis III also had other wives, including Queen NEBETU'U (2), as well as some from other kingdoms sent as tributes or as symbols of vassalage.

Tuthmosis III was one of Egypt's greatest generals. He conquered lands from the fifth cataract of the Nile to the Euphrates River, where he raised a stela. In Egypt he raised up another stela, known as "Hymn of Victory." This is a monument of black granite discovered in KAR-NAK and now in the Egyptian Museum in Cairo. The hieroglyphs on the stela give praise to the god Amun for the pharaoh's victories and commemorate his having reached the Euphrates River. Military records of his reign were recorded almost every year of his life. Some of his exploits, such as taking the city of Joppa, became part of Arabian folklore that is repeated today in the tale of Ali Baba.

Tuthmosis III died in the 55th year of his reign and was buried in a tomb in the VALLEY OF THE KINGS. His tomb (KV34) was discovered by Victor Loret in 1898 and is recognized as one of the most notable of the royal tombs because of the remarkable presence of a complete funerary text, the AM DUAT, the New Kingdom version of the BOOK OF THE DEAD. His mummified remains, damaged from vandalism and later reburied in DEIR EL-BAHRI, give evidence of his having been five feet tall and of medium build. His statues depict a handsome face, lynx eyes, and a hawk-like nose.

HISTORICAL IMPACT

Tuthmosis III ruled Egypt for nearly 54 years, and his reign represented one of the greatest and most stable eras in the long history of ancient Egypt. He earned the title of the "Napoleon of Egypt" for his immense achievements in the battlefield and presided over a massive construction program that reflected the vitality of his reign and the zenith of the Eighteenth Dynasty.

Through his 17 military campaigns, he extended the Egyptian Empire to the largest area in its history. By the time of his death, the empire stretched from Syria to Nubia, and he was the first pharaoh since Tuthmosis I (r. ca. 1525–1512 B.C.E.) to march on the Euphrates River, as part of his campaign against the Mitannis. Egypt extended into the Near East and became one of the great powers in the ancient world, ranking in international prestige among such Near Eastern civilizations as the later Assyrians, Babylonians, and Persians. More than 300 cities were captured by Tuthmosis III's army. Some princes and ranking aristocrats of conquered foreign lands (including Nubia) were not only educated in Egypt but were brought to the Kap, the palace academy for members of the royal family.

Reflecting Tuthmosis III's success was the enormous building program undertaken by the pharaoh. During his 10th regnal year, the monuments of Hatshepsut began to show signs of vandalism and desecration. Her obelisk at Karnak was plastered over (which ironically actually protected the inscriptions over the centuries), and her figure in reliefs was also scratched away. It is possible that Tuthmosis III sanctioned the destruction; however, some believe that Tuthmosis III's allies started removing Hatshepsut from the public memory in order to preserve the tradition of patrilineal rule in the land. Regardless, the demolition of the woman ruler's monuments and the construction boom were related to Egypt's new economic prosperity. Tuthmosis III built more than 50 temples and commissioned tombs for his nobles. In this sense, he built on the achievements of Hatshepsut, but his era brought the art and architecture of the Nile Valley to unprecedented heights of achievement and innovation.

See also TUTHMOSIS III'S MILITARY CAMPAIGNS.

Further reading: Cline, Eric. *Thutmose III: A New Biography.* Ann Arbor: University of Michigan Press, 2006; Gabriel, Richard. *Thutmose III: The Military Biography of Egypt's Greatest Warrior King.* Dulles, Va.: Potomac Books, 2009.

Tuthmosis III's Hymn of Victory   It is a monument of black granite discovered in KARNAK and now in the Egyptian Museum in Cairo. The hieroglyphs on the STELA give praise to the god Amun for the pharaoh's victories and commemorate his having reached the Euphrates River.

Tuthmosis III's Instructions to His Vizier   This is a recorded tomb text, addressed to REKHMIRÉ, an official of Tuthmosis's reign and discovered on the tomb of this VIZIER at THEBES. The instructions are considered remarkable for their detailed description of the functions of government and the standards necessary for the proper administration of national affairs at all levels.

Tuthmosis III's Military Campaigns Tuthmosis III's Military Campaigns is a document recorded at KAR-NAK by a scribe named Thaneni and compiled of the records made during Tuthmosis III's activities beyond the borders of Egypt. The document details a series of military campaigns. During these campaigns, Tuthmosis III captured 119 cities from northern Palestine and Judaea and conquered 248 cities in northern Syria as far to the east as Chaboras. These campaigns have earned him the title "Napoleon of Egypt." Tuthmosis took 17 towns and districts on this campaign. In another record 115 towns and districts are named, and on yet another list, recorded on a pylon in AMUN's temple, the names of 400 towns, districts, and regions are cited.

The first campaign was at AR-MEGIDDO, the fortress at Mount Carmel, undertaken in the 22nd to 23rd regnal year. The military venture was prompted by a revolt started by the king of KADESH. He and his allies waited on the road in front of the mountains, and Tuthmosis III, despite the arguments of his advisers, took his army up and over Mount Carmel, single file for 40 miles.

Coming out of the pass, Tuthmosis III camped north of Ar-Megiddo in the dark, using the banks of the Kina stream. He waited there until his entire force was prepared for battle. The enemy below saw the Egyptian chariots and knew that their line of retreat was interdicted. One by one they dropped their weapons and ran toward Ar-Megiddo for safety. The southern wing of Tuthmosis III's army was on the hill at the brook, and the northern wing was northwest of the fortress. They raced forward as the enemy threatened to enter Ar-Megiddo, some having to climb up clotheslines to reach safety.

Tuthmosis III's troops stopped to gather up the abandoned treasures of the foe, and Kadesh escaped. The pharaoh laid siege to Ar-Megiddo. He erected a wall called "Menkheperre-Is-the-Surrounder-of-the-Asiatics" and then left a small force to maintain a siege. The Egyptians took Tyre in Phoenicia (modern Lebanon) and other cities before Tuthmosis III returned to Thebes to celebrate the Feast of OPET.

In his 24th regnal year, Tuthmosis made an elaborate march through Palestine and Syria. There he was assured of the loyalty of the local rulers. Tributes were sent by the Assyrians and other conquered domains. The following year Tuthmosis made a second inspection tour, harvesting crops and gathering botanical specimens. Other similar campaigns followed.

In his 29th regnal year, Tuthmosis III led his forces to Tripoli in southern Phoenicia. Some cities in the area of modern Syria and Lebanon were revolting against Egyptian rule. After defeating these local forces the Egyptians feasted on fruits and grain harvests from the local areas, and Phoenician vessels were taken. The troops of Tuthmosis III returned to Egypt by water. They

Tuthmosis III, the "Napoleon of Egypt," in the Egyptian Museum in Cairo *(S. M. Bunson)*

carried gold, lead, copper, jewels, slaves, wines, incense, and oils to the Nile.

The following year's campaign was undertaken when Tuthmosis III sailed with his army to Simyra, near Kadesh. The king of Kadesh was still in rebellion, which aroused the Phoenicians and others. Once again the Egyptians harvested crops and brought back treasures from Phoenicia.

In his 31st regnal year, Tuthmosis III returned to Phoenicia, where he put down a revolt and received tribute and the homage of the Syrians. He also garrisoned and stocked forts and outposts. The harbor of Phoenicia served as bases for inland raids and punitive assaults.

The 33rd regnal year was the time of Tuthmosis III's greatest Asiatic campaign, his conquest of the area of the Euphrates River. Tuthmosis III crushed Kadesh and subdued other coastal cities before moving into the Euphrates area. He brought boats and rafts with his troops in order to move his units across the river. There he fought at CARCHEMISH and entered the lands of the Naharin, allies of the Syrians. The MITANNIS defended the city of Carchemish but were defeated. At the Euphrates, Tuthmosis erected a stela beside that of TUTHMOSIS I, his grandfather. Babylonian ambassadors approached him at this time, offering tributes. The HIT-TITES also offered gifts.

On the way back to the Phoenician coast, Tuthmosis III hunted elephants and was almost killed by a charging bull. General AMENEMHAB saved the pharaoh by hacking at the elephant's trunk and taking Tuthmosis III to a hiding place in the rocks on the riverbank.

In his 34th regnal year, Tuthmosis conducted an inspection tour and received tribute from CYPRUS. In the next year he returned to the Phoenician coast to defeat rebels at a site listed as Araina. Prisoners, horses, chariots, armor, gold, silver, jewelry, wild goats, and wood were brought back to the Nile. He conducted punitive campaigns also in his 36th and 37th regnal years, and returned to Phoenicia in the 38th regnal year. Cities near the Litany River were in revolt, and punitive raids and battles subdued them. Cyprus and Syria sent tributes, and Tuthmosis III replenished his local garrisons.

During the following year Tuthmosis III conducted campaigns against the BEDOUINS on Egypt's northeastern frontier. He supplied his troops in Phoenician forts and defeated a group called the Shasu. In his 40th and 41st regnal years, he received tributes from Cyprus, Kush (the Egyptian name for NUBIA, modern Sudan), and from the Syrians and Hittites.

His last campaign was conducted in his 42nd regnal year, when he was 70 years old. Tuthmosis III entered the field yet another time against the city of Kadesh. He marched to the Orontes River, where that city and Tunip were well defended. Tunip leaders set out a mare to disturb the Egyptian cavalry, but General Amenemhab stalked the animal and slit her belly, making her unappealing to the Egyptian stallions and adding to the bloodlust of the horses in the battle.

Tuthmosis III's Nubian Annals   Recorded at KARNAK, they recall Tuthmosis's expedition through the first cataract, where he cleared the ancient canal. Tuthmosis took 17 towns and districts on this campaign. In another record 115 towns and districts are named, and on yet another list, recorded on a pylon in AMUN's temple, the names of 400 towns, districts, and regions are cited.

Tuthmosis IV (Menkheprure) (d. 1391 B.C.E.) *eighth ruler of the Eighteenth Dynasty, associated with the Great Sphinx at Giza*
He reigned from 1401 B.C.E. until his death. The son of AMENHOTEP II and Queen TEO, Tuthmosis IV saw military duty at the naval station of PER-NEFER near MEMPHIS as a prince. He also led an armed tour of Syria and Palestine and received the title of "Conqueror of Syria" for his efforts. Tuthmosis IV fought in Nubia as a young man and proved himself courageous.

When he took the throne of Egypt he was faced with rebellions in Syria and in the lands below the cataracts. He was politically involved in the growing rivalry between the emerging state of Hatti, the HITTITES, and the MITANNI Empire and sided with the Mitannis, a choice that would plague the Nineteenth Dynasty. Tuthmosis IV married a Mitanni princess to seal the alliance. When Assyria threatened the Mitannis, Tuthmosis IV sent them gold to help pay for their defense.

Peace brought Egypt prosperity, however, and Tuthmosis IV restored and embellished many buildings, including an obelisk of TUTHMOSIS III at KARNAK. That pillar had been lying on its side for three decades; Tuthmosis IV raised it and added an inscription at its base. He erected as well a small mortuary temple and a station for the bark of the god AMUN. As a prince, he had also restored the Great SPHINX at GIZA, and a legend evolved out of that event. Not the designated heir, Tuthmosis IV rested beside the Great Sphinx while on a hunting trip. He heard the Sphinx complain about its pitiful condition. Tuthmosis IV was told that if he restored the Great Sphinx he would become pharaoh. He refurbished the site and left a stela between the paws of the Great Sphinx to commemorate the dream and the work accomplished.

His wife was Queen MUTEMWIYA, considered by some to have been a MITANNI princess. His heir was AMENHOTEP III. Tuthmosis IV died at an early age, wasted from some illness, possibly dental infections. His tomb on Thebes's western shore was a great complex of underground passages, stairways, and chambers, and he had a yellow quartzite sarcophagus. His burial chamber was not decorated, but painted scenes were used in other rooms. The mummy of a royal prince, standing erect against the wall, was also discovered in the tomb. The burial hall was designed with pillars and a sunken crypt with a granite SARCOPHAGUS.

His mummified remains show that he had well-manicured fingernails, pierced ears, and a full head of hair. Tuthmosis IV's feet were broken off by tomb robbers who were looking for golden amulets and jewels in his mummy wrappings. His remains were found in the cache in the tomb of AMENHOTEP II.

Tutu (fl. 14th century B.C.E.) *diplomatic official of the Eighteenth Dynasty*
He served AKHENATEN (Amenhotep IV) (r. 1353–1335 B.C.E.) as a chamberlain, minister of protocol, and diplomat. Tutu served at 'AMARNA and was mentioned in the correspondence of the era. His tomb in 'Amarna was unfinished, but it was designed elaborately and contained reliefs of Akhenaten. Rock-cut, the tomb appears as a MASTABA. The mortuary displays depict Tutu's honors, court scenes, and religious rites.

Tuya (fl. 13th century B.C.E.) *royal woman of the Nineteenth Dynasty*
She was the consort of SETI I (r. 1306–1290 B.C.E.) and the mother of RAMESSES II (1290–1224 B.C.E.). A commoner, Tuya was the daughter of a military commander of chariots, RAIA, and his wife, also named Raia. She married Seti I before he came to the throne and bore a son who died young. Tuya was also the mother of Princesses TIA (1) and HENUTMIRE. She outlived Seti I and was honored by Ramesses II. Statues of Tuya were uncovered at ABU SIMBEL, PER-RAMESSES, and at the RAMESSEUM. She died in the 22nd or 23rd regnal year of Ramesses II.

Her tomb in the VALLEY OF THE QUEENS in THEBES was a great sepulcher with a stairway to subterranean levels. A vestibule, annexes, and a burial chamber compose the structure of the tomb. The sarcophagus in the burial chamber was fashioned out of pink granite.

Twin Souls   They were two deities who were believed to have met in TUAT, or the Underworld. The Twin Souls are RÉ and OSIRIS in their supernatural forms, merging to replenish their life forces. The Twin Souls of Ré and Osiris joined every night while Ré was journeying through Tuat. After a battle with the evil serpent APOPHIS (1), Ré was considered renewed by his association with Osiris.

Two Companions of the Sacred Heart   Divine beings associated with the cosmological traditions and with the cult of the god RÉ, the companions resided on the original PRIMEVAL MOUND, the point of creation, and they accompanied Ré in that instant. They were depicted with reverence on the walls of the temple at EDFU in Upper Egypt. Their names were WA and AA.

Two Dog Palette   This is a Predynastic carving presented to the temple of HORUS at HIERAKONPOLIS, ca. 3000 B.C.E. The palette is now in the Ashmolean Museum of Oxford.

Two Fingers   This was a cultic symbol depicting the index and medius fingers and used as an amulet for both living and dead. The fingers represent the divine digits of the god HORUS when he ascended to the heavens on a LADDER. Horus aided OSIRIS in the ascent of the ladder by offering him his fingers as support.

Two Ladies   This was the name given to two goddesses of Egypt: NEKHEBET and WADJET, or BUTO. Shown as a VULTURE and a cobra, the goddesses were the patronesses of Upper and Lower Egypt and the protectors of the pharaoh. Their images were used in the royal crowns, forming the symbol of the URAEUS.

Twosret (Sitrémeritamun) (d. ca. 1196 B.C.E.) *queen-pharaoh of the Nineteenth Dynasty*
She ruled from 1198 B.C.E. until her death. The widow of SETI II, having been a secondary wife, and the mother of Seti-Merenptah, Twosret served as the regent for the heir, SIPTAH. He disappeared after five or six years, and she ruled in her own right, assisted by her counselor, BAY, who was a foreigner who had usurped power. Her reign did not last long, because she had no popular support, and the later Ramessids struck her name from the royal rolls.

Twosret built a handsome tomb in the VALLEY OF THE KINGS, but SETHNAKHTE, the founder of the Twentieth Dynasty, usurped it. Several reliefs remain, as well as seals of her reign and a sandstone stela. The mummy of Twosret was apparently destroyed by Sethnakhte when he took her tomb for his own burial. There are no portraits of Twosret. She may have been a daughter of MERENPTAH. She was actually involved in resource sites in the SINAI and in Palestine, and she built at HELIOPOLIS and at THEBES. A small cache of jewels was discovered in her tomb.

Typhonean Animal   This is the name given to the creature called the SET Animal in Egypt. The creature was depicted as a recumbent canine with the ears of a donkey and an elongated tail. The Typhonean neck was long and decorated with golden rings. A pectoral found at DASHUR displayed this creature.

U

Uadj *See* DJET.

Uadjet *See* WADJET.

Uat-Ur (Wadj-Wer) This was the Egyptian name for the Mediterranean Sea, translating as the "Great Green." The Mediterranean was depicted in reliefs and paintings as a man with breasts for nurturing. The skin of the Uat-Ur figures in such displays was covered in a wave design, representing the vast sea. Uat-Ur was often portrayed with the NILE River, HAPI (1). The Mediterranean Sea was part of the Egyptian transportation system in early eras. Naval forces were designed for use in the transportation of troops or for the TRADE expeditions that set out on the Mediterranean from various Delta sites.

Uben This was the Egyptian name of the spiritual beings deemed responsible for each new dawn on the Nile. They brought the brightness of day, welcoming the rising sun as special agents of light. The dog-faced BABOON, the Hedjwereu, "the Great One," was depicted as greeting the sun in reliefs and paintings. Temples, particularly those dedicated to the god THOTH, kept baboons to welcome the dawn and these spiritual beings each day.

Udimu *See* DEN.

Udjaharresnet (fl. sixth century B.C.E.) *official in the Persian Twenty-seventh Dynasty*
Udjaharresnet served CAMBYSES (r. 525–522 B.C.E.) and DARIUS I (r. 521–486 B.C.E.) as CHANCELLOR and chief physician. He erected a STELA commemorating the arrival of Cambyses, the Persian conqueror who founded

the alien dynasty. Udjaharresnet had served Egypt in his youth as a commander of ships and as a physician. During the reign of Darius I, he was directed to refurbish and restore the *PER-ANKH,* the research and educational institution of Egypt. This official was buried in a shaft at ABUSIR.

Ukh-hotep (fl. 20th century B.C.E.) *priestly official of the Twelfth Dynasty*
Ukh-hotep served SENWOSRET I (r. 1971–1926 B.C.E.) as the hereditary ruler of ASSIUT and as the superintendent of the prophets in the Assiut temples. He was associated with the cult of HATHOR. The son of another Ukh-hotep and Lady Mersi, Ukh-hotep was buried at MEIR, near MALLAWI. His tomb was large and contained elaborate reliefs, as well as a registry of his family, a false door, and a statue niche. A third Ukh-hotep also served Senwosret I.

Umm el-Ga'ab This was the necropolis of the city of ABYDOS, called "the Mother of Pots" by modern local residents. This was one of Egypt's earliest cemeteries, used by the rulers of the First Dynasty (2920–2770 B.C.E.). Second Dynasty (2770–2649 B.C.E.) monuments, associated with PERIBSEN and KHA'SEKHEMWY, were also found on the site, called "Peger" in some records. Some Predynastic graves are also at Umm el-Ga'ab.

The superstructures of the royal tombs have been destroyed over the centuries, exposing the remains of brick-lined burial pits. The rulers deposited stelae and clay sealings in these chambers as well as ivory figurines and mortuary furniture. The tomb of DJER, the second ruler of the First Dynasty, was declared the resting place of the deity OSIRIS. As a result, the tomb received many honors and votive offerings, particularly during the New Kingdom Period (1550–1070 B.C.E.). A tomb dating to the Twenty-first Dynasty (1070–945 B.C.E.) was erected for Psusennes, the son of the high priest of AMUN, MENKHEPERRESENB (2), at Umm el-Ga'ab. The tomb has a chapel, burial shaft, and mortuary stela. The site is famous for the sounds made by the finely grained sands of the region. This sand makes aeolian melodies when blown over the ruins and the dunes by the wind. The Egyptians believed the sounds originated in the tombs.

Unfinished Pyramid *See* ZAWIET EL-ARYAN.

Unis (Weni; Wenis) (d. 2323 B.C.E.) *ninth ruler of the Fifth Dynasty*

Reigning 2356–2323 B.C.E., Unis was possibly a son of IZEZI (Djedkaré), inheriting the throne when the original heir, Remkuy, died. The TURIN CANON lists Unis, whose reign was prosperous.

He married Queen NEBET and KHENUT. Unis did not have an heir, but his daughter, IPUT (1), married TETI, who founded the Sixth Dynasty. Unis conducted trade with BYBLOS, in Phoenicia (modern Lebanon), and NUBIA (modern Sudan), and he sent an expedition to Nubia that was recorded on the Elephantine Island. This expedition returned to Egypt with a giraffe, a rare sight in Egypt at the time. He also fought a battle with the BEDOUINS in the SINAI Peninsula.

Queen Nebet, the mother of Prince Unis-ankh, and Queen Khenut were buried in Unis's mortuary complex in SAQQARA. This pyramidal structure is in the northern part of the Saqqara necropolis and was restored centuries later by KHA'EMWESET (1), a son of RAMESSES II (r. 1290–1224 B.C.E.). The pyramid had a rubble core and was designed with a long causeway that led to the VALLEY TEMPLE, a MORTUARY TEMPLE, and two boat pits. The PYRAMID TEXTS serve as reliefs in this tomb and offer vigorous images, including the CANNIBAL HYMN. The site has burial shafts and a multichambered chapel. Prince Unis-ankh and Princess Iput were buried there.

Unu He was the hare deity of Egypt called "the Springer-up." The hare was considered a form of the god RÉ and was worshipped at HERMOPOLIS. His consort was WENUT, a goddess of THEBES. Some of the gods and goddesses of the nation were associated with nature and with animal, THEOPHANIES, used as symbols of special virtues or strength.

uraeus The insignia of the rulers of ancient Egypt, worn on CROWNS and headdresses to denote rank, the uraeus was composed of symbols of the cobra and the VULTURE, sometimes the cobra alone. The reptile represented WADJET, the protectoress of Lower Egypt and the vulture was NEKHEBET, the vulture goddess who served Upper Egypt. Wadjet was always shown with its hood extended, threatening the enemies of Egypt as the serpent threatened the foes of the god RÉ. The cobra was sometimes depicted in the cults of the deities HORUS and OSIRIS.

ur-heka This was the instrument traditionally used in MORTUARY RITUALS by the attending priest during the ceremony of the Opening of the Mouth, the ceremony restoring the human senses of the deceased in the eternal realms, and in other cultic rites. This instrument ensured that the deceased would have control of his or her vital senses beyond the grave. AMULETS and other funerary pieces included spells that safeguarded the integrity of the human form while undergoing the transformations of death.

Ur-hiya (fl. 13th century B.C.E.) *military official of the Nineteenth Dynasty*

He served SETI I (r. 1306–1290 B.C.E.) as a military commander. Ur-hiya was apparently a Canaanite or Hurrian who had risen through the ranks of the army, probably coming to Seti I's attention before he took the throne. The presence of aliens in Egypt's military forces was unique to the New Kingdom Period (1550–1070 B.C.E.), although mercenary units were used in some campaigns in the earliest dynasties. Each foreigner on the Nile was given the opportunity to serve his adopted land by performing military or state duties to prove his worth. Such aliens were not treated as mercenaries but considered as citizens of the Nile.

Uronarti This was a site near the second cataract of the Nile in NUBIA (modern Sudan), where SENWOSRET III (1878–1841 B.C.E.) erected a FORTRESS to control traffic on the river. Uronarti fortress, large, fortified, and garrisoned, was built on an island south of the strategic stronghold of SEMNA. Triangular in design, Uronarti also served AMENHOTEP I (r. 1525–1504 B.C.E.) during the New Kingdom Period conquest of Nubia.

Userhet (1) (fl. 15th century B.C.E.) *officials of the Eighteenth Dynasty*

He served AMENHOTEP II (r. 1427–1401 B.C.E.) as a royal SCRIBE. Userhet also carried the rank of a "Child of the Nursery," belonging to the KAP. The Kap was a term used to indicate that Userhet was raised and educated with the royal children in the palace. Userhet's tomb at KHOKHA on the western shore of the Nile at Thebes has scenes of everyday life. A STELA and a statue of Userhet were found in the tomb.

Userhet (2) (fl. 14th century B.C.E.) *official of the Eighteenth Dynasty*

Userhet served AMENHOTEP III (r. 1391–1353 B.C.E.) as a royal scribe and as a tutor for AKHENATEN, the heir to the throne. He was buried on the western shore of Thebes, in a small cruciform tomb that carried descriptions of his honors and years of dedicated service to the throne.

Userhet (3) (fl. 13th century B.C.E.) *temple official of the Nineteenth Dynasty*
Userhet served as a high priest of the cult of TUTHMOSIS I during the reign of RAMESSES II (1290–1224 B.C.E.). The cult of Tuthmosis I remained popular following his death in 1492 B.C.E. Userhet was one of the many priests who maintained the MORTUARY RITUALS and schedules of offerings in the resting place of this great military pharaoh.

The tomb of Userhet at KHOKHA, on the western shore of Thebes, contains scenes of the endless tributes paid daily to the memory of Tuthmosis I. Other scenes depict Userhet and his family in their own mortuary ceremonies and in eternal paradises in TUAT, or the Underworld.

Userhet-amun This was the name of the Egyptian bark presented to KARNAK by 'AHMOSE (NEBPEHTIRÉ) (r. 1550–1525 B.C.E.) to celebrate Egypt's expulsion of the HYKSOS and their allies, and the unification of the Two Kingdoms. The bark was called "Mighty of Brow Is AMUN." Such barks of the gods of Egypt were sometimes large enough to be used as true vessels on water. Others were designed to be carried in street processions as miniature representations. The bark presented to Karnak by 'Ahmose started the custom among the pharaohs of commemorating events or favors with such demonstrations of piety and fervor.

Userkaré (fl. 24th century B.C.E.) *obscure ruler of the Sixth Dynasty*
He was the successor to TETI (r. 2323–2291 B.C.E.). Userkaré's name was translated as "the *ka* of Ré is Powerful." He was listed in the TURIN CANON and at ABYDOS. Possibly a usurper, he ruled only three years. It is conceivable that he was a nominal ruler, overseeing Queen Iput's regency for the true heir, PEPI I. He started a tomb in an area south of ASSIUT, and this construction is documented. His name was also discovered at QAW EL-KEBIR.

Userkhaf (d. 2458 B.C.E.) *founder of the Fifth Dynasty*
He reigned from 2465 B.C.E. until his death. Userkhaf was probably the son of Princess NEFERHETEPES (1), the daughter of RA'DJEDEF (r. 2528–2520 B.C.E.) and possibly HETEPHERES (2). The WESTCAR PAPYRUS foretold his coming, associating him with the legends of Princess KHENTAKAWES. His father may have been Sa'khebu, a priest of RÉ. He reigned a comparatively short time but he was a vigorous monarch, stressing the traditions of *ma'at*. His throne name, Iry-ma'at, meant "He who puts *MA'AT* into practice." Userkhaf is listed in the TURIN CANON and at ABYDOS.

Userkhaf enlarged a temple of MONTU at Tod, south of Thebes. He also started trade with the city-state in the Aegean. He married Khentakawes, a daughter of MEN KAURÉ, and she was reportedly the mother of SAHURÉ, Userkhaf's heir.

His MORTUARY TEMPLE was erected in the northeast corner of the STEP PYRAMID in SAQQARA and was called "Pure are the places of Userkhaf." Built of limestone and faced with Tureh stone, the tomb pyramid had a MORTUARY TEMPLE on the southern side. Temple reliefs depict birds, and a pink granite head of Userkhaf was uncovered in the courtyard. The site was surrounded by a wall and had a paved causeway and a portico with red granite columns. A queen's pyramid and a subsidiary pyramid were erected on the western side of the mortuary temple.

Userkhaf also built a solar temple at ABU GHUROB, made of mud brick and faced with limestone. A wall encloses this monument, and an obelisk with a *BENBEN* was fashioned on a podium as part of the design. The shrine contained a sun altar and a causeway to the VALLEY TEMPLE. Another head of Userkhaf, made of schist, was discovered here. In the southern section, a bark of RÉ was fashioned out of bricks.

ushabtis See SHABTIS.

Ushanahuru (fl. seventh century B.C.E.) *prince of the Twenty-fifth Dynasty*
He was the son of TAHARQA (r. 690–664 B.C.E.) and Queen AMUN-DYEK'HET and was at MEMPHIS with the queen when the ASSYRIANS, led by ESSARHADDON, entered the capital. Taharqa fled south to NUBIA, abandoning his queen and heir. Both Amun-dyek'het and Ushanahuru were taken to NINEVEH and made slaves. They were never seen again in Egypt.

V

Valley Festival This was a unique celebration held annually on the western shore of THEBES, and also called "the Beautiful Feast of the Valley." The celebration had its origin in the Middle Kingdom Period (2040–1640 B.C.E.) rituals, probably beginning as a festival honoring the goddess HATHOR. It was normally held in the second month of *shomu*, the time of harvest on the Nile, corresponding to the modern month of May or June.

The sacred barks of AMUN, MUT, and KHONS (1), the Theban triad, were taken across the Nile to the necropolis area during the celebration, docking at DEIR EL-BAHRI. The living Egyptians visited the tombs of their dead, and priests blessed the gravesites. Processions, music, flowers, and incense marked the spirit of the festival. Families spent the night beside the tombs of their ancestors, serenaded while they held picnics and entertained by wandering bands of temple musicians and chanters.

Valley of the Gilded Mummies This is a Greco-Roman (304 B.C.E.–336 C.E.) necropolis at BAHARIA OASIS, containing 100 identified burial sites. Several thousand mummies appear to have been buried on the site. The remains being recovered in the graves of the valley have elaborately gilded CARTONNAGE masks and most were buried in groups. Some were covered in gold entirely, while other mummies had painted scenes and designs on their plain cartonnage. Still others were buried in ceramic anthropoid coffins.

Tombs containing the remains have entrance chambers and separate burial compartments. The entrance chambers were also used as sites for mortuary rituals. Some burial rooms have niches and shafts. These tombs are located near the Temple of ALEXANDER III THE GREAT (r. 332–323 B.C.E.) at Baharia. The necropolis was in use until the fourth century C.E.

Valley of the Kings Now called Biban el-Muluk in Arabic, the Valley of the Kings is one of the most significant burial sites in the world, dating to the New Kingdom Period (1550–1070 B.C.E.) of Egypt. The Valley of the Kings is located on the western shore of the Nile opposite THEBES (modern Luxor). The main area is a dried river valley that is dominated by a high peak, naturally shaped as a pyramid, and contains the tombs of the most celebrated pharaohs of Egypt.

SITE DESCRIPTION

The Eighteenth Dynasty (1550–1307 B.C.E.), founded after 'AHMOSE (NEBPEHTIRÉ) (r. 1550–1525 B.C.E.) ousted the HYKSOS, or Asiatics, from the Delta, began to fashion elaborate mortuary complexes on the western shore of the Nile at Thebes. 'Ahmose's heir, AMENHOTEP I (r. 1525–1504 B.C.E.), seeing the extent of robberies and vandalism of royal resting places, separated his burial site from his MORTUARY TEMPLE in order to protect his remains. His successor, TUTHMOSIS I (r. 1504–1492 B.C.E.), following Amenhotep I's example, was the first ruler to have his royal tomb carved out of the expanse of the Valley of the Kings.

This sacred Valley of the Kings necropolis was remote and easily guarded. It is located at the base of a peak called SHEIKH ABD' EL-QURNA, which is sacred to the goddess MERESGER, called "the Lady of the Peak," and "the Lover of Silence." Meresger was described as haunting evildoers until they reformed. Then she became a powerful divine patron, and was, in earlier histori-

Valley of the Kings

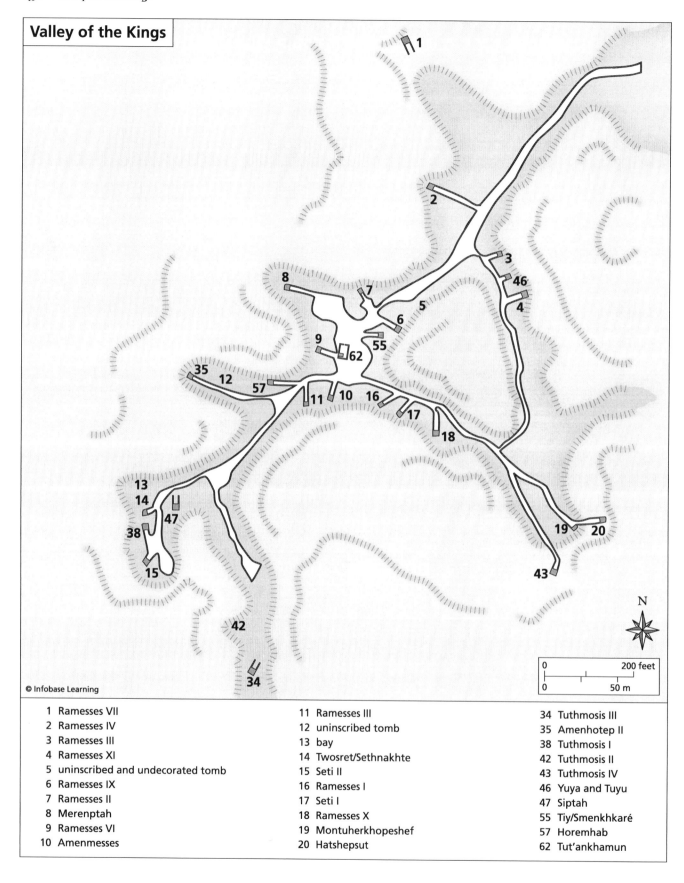

© Infobase Learning

0   200 feet
0   50 m

1 Ramesses VII	11 Ramesses III	34 Tuthmosis III
2 Ramesses IV	12 uninscribed tomb	35 Amenhotep II
3 Ramesses III	13 bay	38 Tuthmosis I
4 Ramesses XI	14 Twosret/Sethnakhte	42 Tuthmosis II
5 uninscribed and undecorated tomb	15 Seti II	43 Tuthmosis IV
6 Ramesses IX	16 Ramesses I	46 Yuya and Tuyu
7 Ramesses II	17 Seti I	47 Siptah
8 Merenptah	18 Ramesses X	55 Tiy/Smenkhkaré
9 Ramesses VI	19 Montuherkhopeshef	57 Horemhab
10 Amenmesses	20 Hatshepsut	62 Tut'ankhamun

cal periods, associated with the cult of the goddess of HATHOR. The Valley of the Kings was also known as "the Place of Truth." The necropolis is actually composed of two distinct areas: the western valley, originally called "the Necropolis of the Monkeys," which contains four royal tombs, including that of AYA (r. 1323–1319 B.C.E.) and AMENHOTEP III (r. 1391–1353); and two burial sites (of two sisters, Syrian princesses sent to Egypt to be lesser wives of TUTHMOSIS III). The main section is most of the eastern valley, which contains the tombs of the pharaohs. Because the eastern valley is located on a dried river that has been flooded over the centuries, there has been severe damage to some of the tombs. The western valley leads to a natural amphitheater surrounded by towering walls, with bays and ravines. Both valleys are separated from Thebes and the Nile by the Theban massif, a dominating mountain range of the region.

The general plan of the royal tombs in the Valley of the Kings developed early in the Eighteenth Dynasty. Most tombs contained a central passage leading to a series of sloping corridors, halls, shafts, and burial chambers. Some were dug straight into the rock, while others angled, probably because of natural barriers. The angle of descent was often quite steep.

In the Nineteenth Dynasty (1307–1196 B.C.E.), the tombs were not as inclined and were straighter in design. Passages were blocked or sealed, and wooden doors were installed. False burial chambers protected the deeper passages that led to the actual resting places of the pharaohs. By the Twentieth Dynasty (1196–1070 B.C.E.), the tombs were smaller and simpler because of the short reigns of the rulers and the lack of resources.

CONSTRUCTION

The workers in the Valley of the Kings were all specialists in their fields of expertise. Laborers dug the core of the tomb out of the solid mountains. (The entire region was a series of peaks, gullies, and ravines that formed adaptable tomb sites.) Once the walls were defined, workers came with smoothing instruments and a type of plaster. Behind these workers came teams of artists who sketched out the decorative elements. The larger tombs are beautifully decorated throughout. Certain elements of the BOOK OF THE DEAD, the mortuary ritual text, were placed on walls as reliefs, inscribed on coffins, or placed in parchment form with the deceased to guide him or her on the perilous journey to TAUT, the Underworld. Such mortuary texts could be translated into wonderful designs in royal burial chambers, and the artists were given specific texts chosen by the particular pharaohs to illustrate.

The decoration of these tombs was normally religious in nature, and sections of the sites were named after the various stages of the god Ré's journey through Tuat. Pillars, reliefs, paintings, and statuary graced each chamber and corridor. Magazines, or storage rooms,

were also included in the designs. The deceased pharaoh was also depicted in the embrace of various deities, illustrating the glories awaiting him beyond the grave. These specialized artists, called the "Servants of the Place of Truth," spent their entire lives in such labors, educating their sons in the same artistry. When the tomb was prepared, priests and officials began to place the deceased's favorite pieces of furniture, crowns, statues, and symbols of the reign in the tomb. (The workers left the tomb at this stage.)

The basic design of the tombs contained a series of corridors leading to chambers and hidden sanctuaries. Chapels with angled corridors offering access to other rooms were sometimes included, as were shafts and dead ends to protect the tomb from robbers. Some of the larger tombs had pillared chambers, vents for the travel of the KA, the astral companions of the deceased.

The deepest of the tombs found in the Valley of the Kings is one built for HATSHEPSUT, although it was never used. The largest single tomb, and the finest, is that of Seti I. His actual burial chamber measures more than 1,000 square feet. One of the most spectacular tombs in the Valley of the Kings is that of TUT'ANKHAMUN, discovered in 1922. Another site that drew world attention is the tomb erected by RAMESSES II (r. 1290–1224 B.C.E.) for his royal sons. Named KV5, this massive site has been undergoing recent excavations and contains more than 100 chambers thus far. A hall containing 16 pillars, descending stairways, offering chapels, magnificent reliefs, and passages link the tomb with the actual burial site of Ramesses II.

ARCHAEOLOGY

Archaeologists, visitors and tourists, writers, and grave robbers have been fascinated by the Valley of the Kings for literally hundreds of years. Serious scientific interest has been constant since the early 19th century, and the site gained world fame with the discovery in 1922 of the tomb of Tut'ankhamun. Excavations have focused on the royal tombs that have been discovered over the last two centuries. The tombs are designated KV (Kings' Valley) and numbered in order of their discovery from KV1, which has been open since antiquity, to KV63, which was discovered in 2005 by Dr. Otto Schaden.

The military expedition of Napoleon in 1799 brought French scientists to Egypt, and some of these scientists made their way to the Valley of the Kings. In 1817 the Italian adventurer and archaeologist Giovanni Belzoni (1778–1823) discovered several tombs, including the tomb of Seti I (KV17), although his assumption that he had unearthed all of the tombs proved to be inaccurate. This was confirmed by the remarkable work of English archaeologist and Egyptologist Howard Carter (1874–1939), who found several additional tombs.

Further work was achieved under the direction of the American Egyptologist Theodore Davis (1837–1915), who served in the Valley of the Kings from 1902 to 1914. His excavations led to the discovery of some 30 tombs, including KV55 (the 'Amarna cache) and KV57 (the tomb of Horemhab). Thinking that he had discovered the tomb of King Tut'ankhamun himself, KV54 turned out to be only the embalming tomb of the boy king. Like Belzoni, Davis was mistaken in his belief that all of the tombs had been found. This was proven in 1922 with the discovery of KV62, the actual tomb of Tut, by Howard Carter. That one discovery created an international stir and placed Egypt and Egyptian archaeology on the international map.

In 1978 the British archaeologist John Romer began the Theban Mapping Project, with the objective of mapping out comprehensively the whole of the Valley of the Kings. The project has been ongoing and uses the most modern of technology to provide three-dimensional imaging. It is under the direction of American Egyptologist Dr. Kent Weeks. In 1979 the Valley of the Kings was designated a World Heritage Site.

In 2005 another chamber was discovered, termed KV63, located beside the famous burial site of King Tut'ankhamun. The official announcement was made in 2006, and the credit was given to a team of American archaeologists from the University of Memphis led by Dr. Otto Schaden. Initially thought to be a royal tomb, excavations and study determined the chamber to be a staging chamber for the process of mummification. This was followed in 2008 with the discovery of two possible additional tomb entrances.

Further reading: Baines, John, and Jaromir Malik. *Cultural Atlas of Ancient Egypt.* New York: Facts On File, 2000; Bierbrier, M. L. *The Tomb-Builders of the Pharaohs.* Cairo: American University in Cairo Press, 1993; Bongioanni, Alessandro. *Luxor and the Valley of the Kings.* New York: White Star, 2004; Davis, Theodore M. *The Tomb of Siphtah with the Tomb of Queen Tiyi.* London: Gerald Duckworth & Co., 2001; Davis, Theodore M. *The Tombs of Harmhabi and Touatânkhamanou.* London: Duckworth Publishing, 2001; Reeves, Nicholas. *Valley of the Kings: The Decline of a Royal Necropolis.* London: Keegan Paul, 1990; Reeves, Nicholas, and Richard H. Wilkinson. *The Complete Valley of the Kings.* London: Thames & Hudson, 2008; Romer, John. *Valley of the Kings.* New York: Henry Holt, 1981; Siliotti, Alberto. *Guide to the Valley of the Kings.* New York: Barnes and Noble, 1997; Strudwick, Nigel, and Helen Strudwick. *Thebes in Egypt.* Ithaca, N.Y.: Cornell University, 1999; Weeks, Kent R. *KV 5: A Preliminary Report on the Excavation of the Tomb of the Sons of Ramesses II in the Valley of the Kings.* Cairo: American University Press, 2000; Weeks, Kent. *The Treasures of Luxor and the Valley of the Kings.* New York: White Star, 2005; Weeks, Kent. *Valley of the Kings: The Tombs and the Funerary Temples of Thebes West.* New York: White Star, 2002; Wilkinson, Richard H. *Valley of the Sun Kings: New Explorations in the Tombs of the Pharaohs.* Tucson: University of Arizona Egyptian Expedition, 1994.

Valley of the Queens This was the royal necropolis of the New Kingdom Period (1550–1070 B.C.E.), located southwest of MEDINET HABU on the western shore of the Nile at THEBES. The site was called Ta-set-neferu, "the Place of the Royal Children," in the ancient periods and is now called Biban el-Harim, "the Doors of the Women," or Biban el-Melikat, "the Doors of the Daughters," in Arabic. The queens, princes, and princesses of the New Kingdom were buried here. The necropolis is believed to contain 70 tombs. Located in an arid wadi, the site was developed first on the southern hill and then on the northwest side.

The most famous tomb of the Valley of the Queens was built for Queen NEFERTARI MERYMUT, the Great Wife of RAMESSES II (r. 1290–1224 B.C.E.). This site has columned chambers, stairs, ramps, and an offering hall with shelves and a burial chamber with four pillars and three annexes. Elaborately decorated with polychrome reliefs, the tomb depicts Queen Nefertari Merymut in the usual funerary scenes but also portrays her in everyday scenes of mortal life. The BENNU (phoenix) and the AKER lions are also displayed. "The Great Wives" of the New Kingdom all have tombs in this necropolis.

The tombs of the royal sons of the New Kingdom Period include the resting place of AMENHIRKHOPSHEF (1), the son of RAMESSES III (r. 1194–1163 B.C.E.). This tomb has a ramp, three chambers, and two annexes, all painted with scenes and cultic symbols. A vestibule was part of the design.

The tomb of KHA'EMWESET (2), another prince of the dynasty and also a son of RAMESSES III, is in the Valley of the Queens as well. This is designed with three chambers, two annexes, and a ramp. The walls are covered with painted reliefs.

Some officials of the Eighteenth Dynasty (1550–1307 B.C.E.) were given the honor of having small pit tombs in the Valley of the Queens. Other princesses and princes were also provided with similar pit tombs.

valley temples They were an element of royal mortuary complexes, designed to complement and mirror the PYRAMID mortuary vestibule. In use in the Old Kingdom Period (2575–2134 B.C.E.), the valley temples were erected on the banks of the Nile, not far from the pyramid sites that were located in the desert. The mortuary temple was normally erected beside the pyramid and was connected to the VALLEY TEMPLE by a gigantic causeway, covered and elaborately decorated. Both temples had T-shaped entrance halls.

There is evidence that the valley temple had a specific mortuary function in some reigns. Actual embalming rituals were conducted on the deceased rulers in these temples. Special chambers were part of the valley temple design, providing the arenas for the various stages of the preparation and the wrapping of the pharaoh's human remains. The priests associated with this detailed process took up residence in the valley temple for the duration of the embalming process. When the valley temple was used for mortuary preparation, it was called PER-NEFER, "the House of Beauty," or WABT, "the Place of Purification."

viceroy   This was an office of the Egyptian royal government, originally given to hereditary princes and counts of the various nomes or provinces and then bestowed upon commoners who displayed integrity, administrative skills, and loyalty. These officers also governed territories outside of Egypt, such as the domain called Kush, the Egyptian NUBIA (modern Sudan). The VICEROY of Kush was given an honorary title of "the King's Son of Kush," denoting his rank and favor. 'AHMOSE (NEBPEHTIRÉ) (r. 1550–1525 B.C.E.) established this position as Egypt put down rebellions south of ASWAN and reopened FORTRESSES and TRADE centers on the Nile. In the reign of TUTHMOSIS III (1479–1425 B.C.E.), the viceroy of Kush governed from Mi'am, 140 miles south of the first cataract of the Nile. Many of the viceroys of Nubia had to maintain standing armies and had to possess certain military skills. They were used to halt rebellions or to delay invasions until the regular army units could get to the scene. The viceroy of Nubia served on the ELEPHANTINE Island at Aswan in many eras. Certain governors of the northlands were also appointed during the New Kingdom Period (1550–1070 B.C.E.) in order to maintain control of the Egyptian areas in Palestine, Phoenicia, modern Lebanon, and Syria during the time of the empire.

See also NOMARCHS; VIZIER; ADMINISTRATION.

Victory Stela   This monument was erected by PIANKHI (r. 750–712 B.C.E.), the Nubian warrior of the Twenty-fifth Dynasty. Now in the Egyptian Museum in Cairo, this stela commemorates Piankhi's conquest of Egypt and his victory over the native Egyptians who opposed him. These were petty rulers of the Twenty-third (828–712 B.C.E.) and Twenty-fourth (724–712 B.C.E.) Dynasties who had limited domains in SAIS, HERAKLEOPOLIS, HERMOPOLIS, TANIS, and Thebes. Piankhi's Nubian armies swept northward, defeating the Egyptians. He celebrated the feast of OPET at THEBES as a result of his swift campaign. The stela commemorates his victories and contains a reproach concerning the ruler NIMLOT (4) of the Twenty-third Dynasty at Hermopolis. Nimlot is scolded for mistreating his horses.

Vidaranag (fl. fifth century B.C.E.) *Persian military commander of the Elephantine Island*
Vidaranag commanded the Persian troops at ASWAN in the reign of DARIUS II (423–405 B.C.E.). The satrap, or provincial governor, of Egypt, ARSAMIS, was away from Egypt when the priests of the god KHNUM complained to Vidaranag and bribed him to destroy the local Jewish temple. Vidaranag was punished for his misuse of his office.

Vindab Papyrus 3873   This is a document in the Vienna Kunsthistoriche Museum, dating to the second century B.C.E., the Late Period, and Ptolemaic Period of Egyptian history. The papyrus is inscribed in the hieratic and demotic styles and contains a description of a burial of a sacred APIS bull in SAQQARA.

vizier   This was the highest nonroyal office in ancient Egypt, called a *djat* or *tjat*, served as the prime minister of the nation in all periods. In the Old Kingdom Period of Egypt the viziers were normally kinsmen of the ruler, members of the royal clan, and thus trusted with the affairs of the court. An exception to this tradition, however, was the best-known vizier of the Old Kingdom, a commoner named IMHOTEP, who was revered as a high priest and as a physician. He built the STEP PYRAMID for DJOSER (r. 2630–2611 B.C.E.) of the Third Dynasty. Gradually the office was divided, with one vizier serving as the director of affairs for Lower Egypt and the other governing the territories of Upper Egypt. The vizier of Upper Egypt ruled from the ELEPHANTINE to ASSIUT, and the other governed all the lands above Assiut.

Viziers heard all domestic territorial disputes, maintained a cattle and herd census, controlled the reservoirs and the food supply, supervised industries and conservation programs, and were required to repair all dikes. The biannual census of the population came under their purview, as did the records of rainfall and the varying levels of the Nile during its inundation. All government documents used in ancient Egypt had to have the seal of the vizier in order to be considered authentic and binding. Tax records, storehouse receipts, crop assessments, and other necessary agricultural statistics were kept in the offices of these viziers.

Members of the royal family normally served as assistants to the viziers in every era. The office was considered an excellent training ground for the young princes of each royal line, although many queens and princesses also received extensive training and undertook a period of service with the vizier and his staff. Queen-Pharaoh HATSHEPSUT (r. 1473–1458 B.C.E.) and TIYE (1), the consort of AMENHOTE III (r. 1391–1353 B.C.E.), are New Kingdom Period examples of royal women involved in the day-to-day administration of the nation.

If the capital was in the south, at THEBES, the vizier of Upper Egypt lived there and served also as mayor of the city. Normally, the vizier was assisted in his duties by the mayor of the western shore, because the vast necropolis sites and the artisans' villages there demanded supervision. The viziers of Upper and Lower Egypt saw the ruler on a daily basis or communicated with him frequently. Both served as the chief justices of the Egyptian courts and listened to appeals or decisions from the NOME justices. Other state officials, such as the treasurer, CHANCELLOR, keeper of the seal, etc., served under the viziers in a tight-knit and efficient bureaucracy. 'AHMOSE (NEBPEHTIRÉ) (r. 1550–1525 B.C.E.) of the Eighteenth Dynasty established the viceroyalty of Nubia in order to maintain order in the rapidly expanding territories below the cataracts. This viceroy was called "the King's Son of Kush."

The most famous vizier of the New Kingdom was REKHMIRÉ, who served TUTHMOSIS III (r. 1479–1425 B.C.E.). The able official was buried at Thebes, and on his tomb walls he gave an account of Tuthmosis III's instructions concerning the duties and obligations of a righteous vizier. The commands or instructions are remarkable for their detailed description of the workings of all levels of government. They include a description of the vizier's palace office, the type of reports deemed necessary to maintain communications with other government bureaus, and 30 separate activities that were part of his position. Again and again stress is placed on service to the oppressed or the weak, a theme that dates back to the sages of the Old Kingdom Period and "THE ELOQUENT PEASANT" of the Tenth Dynasty. Normally the viziers of Egypt were remarkable men, astute, well-trained, and dedicated to the service of rich and poor alike, in an ideal expression of the spirit of MA'AT, the ethical and moral principal guiding the nation. The role of vizier was maintained to some degree in the later historical periods of Egypt.

Votaresses of Karnak   They were a religious group composed of high-ranking Egyptian women in the reign of 'AHMOSE (NEBPEHTIRÉ) (r. 1550–1525 B.C.E.). 'Ahmose's queen, 'AHMOSE-NEFERTARI, held the rank of "GOD'S WIFE OF AMUN" and gathered women to perform temple services. The "HAREM" of Amun and "the Divine Adoratrices of Amun" were started as a result. The Votaresses of Karnak appear to have served separately for a time, then were absorbed into other religious offices.

vulture   The Egyptian variety of this bird was associated with NEKHEBET, the patroness of Upper Egypt. Named *nerau* by the Egyptians, the vulture was called "Pharaoh's chicken" (*Neophron percnopterus*). The bird usually grows to more than two feet long and is white with black flight feathers. It has a slender beak, a bare face, and a cascading mane of feather. The Egyptian vulture ranges in northern and eastern Africa, as well as southern Europe, and in the Middle East, even to Afghanistan and India. Other vulture species were present in Egypt, but only this species was associated with Nekhebet.

W

wabt This was the site of embalming, located either in the VALLEY TEMPLES of the pyramids in the royal mortuary complexes or in the institutions provided for this essential aspect of the funerary preparations. Also called *wabet,* the "house of purification," or PER-NEFER, "the House of Beauty," the sites were governed by the rituals of purification and preparation for the actual chemical processes of embalming.

See also MORTUARY RITUALS.

wadi An Arabic term for a gully or dried riverbed, used in the modern designation of sites, the major wadi locations in ancient Egypt include

> **Wadi Abbad** a site east of Edfu in Upper Egypt, where gold mining operations were conducted in the New Kingdom Period (1550–1070 B.C.E.). SETI I (r. 1306–1290 B.C.E.) erected residential compounds and wells for workers there, as well as a temple. The gold mine in the site was given to the temple of Abydos in a special decree.
>
> **Wadi Abul Suffian** a Nagada Predynastic cultural site at HIERAKONPOLIS. Black tipped and polished red ware was discovered there, as well as feline pottery masks, straw-tempered vessels, and a cylinder vessel. The skeletal remains of four humans and a cow were buried on the site.
>
> **Wadi Alaki** a site near QUBAN at the second cataract of the Nile in NUBIA (modern Sudan), favored for its gold resources. Wadi Alaki underwent repairs and restoration in the reign of RAMESSES II (1290–1224 B.C.E.), and other pharaohs of the Nineteenth Dynasty also restored the area.

Ramesses II dug a well on the site to aid the workers. He also reopened shafts of previous mines to further enhance the output.

> **Wadi es-Sebua** a site south of ASWAN in NUBIA, which was excavated and moved to save it from rising waters caused by the Aswan High Dam. RAMESSES II (r. 1290–1224 B.C.E.) erected a temple there honoring RÉ and his own deified person. An avenue of SPHINXES was part of the temple design, as well as rock-cut interiors, courts, vestibules, a sanctuary, engaged statues, and two colossi of Ramesses II.
>
> **Wadi Garawi** a site south of HOLWAN, in the southern suburb of modern Cairo. The remains of a dam used in quarrying processes for the area's stone resources were uncovered there. A stone-cutter's settlement ruins were also removed from the site.
>
> **Wadi Gasus** a site on the coast of the Red Sea near KOPTOS, called the area of SEWEW by the Egyptians. An Eighteenth Dynasty (1550–1307 B.C.E.) stela was found at Wadi Gasus, as well as a text from the Middle Kingdom Period (2040–1640 B.C.E.). This site was used in all historical periods as a starting point for expeditions to PUNT. The Egyptians lost some officials in the region, victims of hostile attacks, but the wadi and other important sites in the area were kept guarded by Egyptian military units in the New Kingdom Period (1550–1070 B.C.E.).
>
> **Wadi Halfa** a site south of ABU SIMBEL, near the second cataract of the Nile in NUBIA (modern Sudan), considered a strategic defensive posi-

tion in many eras. Inscriptions in the area commemorate the Nubian campaigns of SENWOSRET I (r. 1971–1926 B.C.E.). A temple was erected there originally by TUTHMOSIS III (r. 1479–1425 B.C.E.) and contains later data concerning the reign of SIPTAH (1204–1198 B.C.E.) on its pillars. Another inscription, on a Nineteenth Dynasty (1307–1196 B.C.E.) stela, commemorated the temple, which was dedicated to the god HORUS.

Wadi Hammamat an important roadway, beginning in KOPTOS, where the Nile swerved closest to the Red Sea, and then stretching to the Red Sea operations of Egyptian TRADE groups. An important quarry was also located near the beginning of the wadi. Inscriptions excavated in the region date to the Eleventh Dynasty (2134–1991 B.C.E.) and relate that 3,000 men entered the Wadi Hammamat to transport a SARCOPHAGUS lid. Way stations were erected on this roadway and patrols were rotated for safe travel. Greywacke granite was quarried at Wadi Hammamat and Bir Fawakhir and a temple dedicated to MIN was also found nearby.

Wadi Hawi a site southeast of ASWAN, noted for the mining of amethyst during the Middle Kingdom Period (2040–1640 B.C.E.). SENWOSRET I (r. 1971–1926 B.C.E.) also mined there.

Wadi Kubbaniya a site near ASWAN that contained prehistoric artifacts. These objects date to the Late Paleolithic Period 21,000–12,000 B.C.E. Hunter-gatherers assembled where, close to the water source caused by the annual inundation of the Nile.

Wadi Labbab a site near modern Cairo where a PETRIFIED FOREST has stood for centuries.

Wadi Maghara a site in the western SINAI Peninsula, near modern Abu Zuneima, popular for the mines and NATURAL RESOURCES exploited early in Egypt's history. Inscriptions from the Fourth (2575–2465 B.C.E.), Fifth (2465–2323 B.C.E.), and Sixth (2323–2150 B.C.E.) Dynasties were uncovered at Wadi Maghara. Inscriptions dating to the reign of AMENEMHET III (1844–1797 B.C.E.) were also discovered on the site. Copper, turquoise, and malachite mines were operated there. *See also* SINAI; SINAI INSCRIPTIONS.

Wadi Matuka (Murgassi) a site on the western side of the Nile in NUBIA (modern Sudan), located on a rocky cliff high above the river. A defensive bastion was erected there by the Egyptians, and HATSHEPSUT (r. 1473–1458 B.C.E.) also built a temple on the site.

Wadi Mi'ah a site near EDFU in Upper Egypt, that leads to gold mines some 35 miles inland from the river, at BARRAMIYEH, Wadi Mi'ah leads as well to Mersa Alam on the Red Sea. SETI I (r.

1306–1290 B.C.E.) dug and repaired wells for miners there and erected a rock temple. GEBEL EL-ZEBARA, another gold mine region nearby, also benefited from Seti I's patronage.

Wadi Murgassi *See* WADI MATUKA.

Wadi Nasb an area of the western SINAI Peninsula noted for copper, turquoise, and malachite mines. Snefru (r. 2575–2551 B.C.E.) left an inscription on the site. These mines were associated with the operations of Wadi Maghara.

Wadi Natrun an OASIS on the western edge of the Delta, serving as a main source of NATRON, the popular substance associated with embalming in Egypt and used on a daily basis as a detergent. "THE ELOQUENT PEASANT," KHUNIANUPU, of the First Intermediate Period (2134–2040 B.C.E.), began his travels and quest in this wadi.

Wadi Qash a site near KOPTOS on the main TRADE route to the Red Sea. Inscriptions from Predynastic and Early (2920–2575 B.C.E.) Periods were discovered there.

Wadi Qena a road leading from Qena to the Red Sea. Close by is a site of ruins called Umm Digal, "the Mother of Columns." Marble columns still stand in the area, dating to the Ptolemaic Period (304–30 B.C.E.) or the later Roman Period.

Wadi Qubannet el-Qirud a site in the LIBYAN DESERT, near DEIR EL-BAHRI, called the Valley of the Tombs of the Monkeys. The three Syrian lesser-ranked wives of TUTHMOSIS III (r. 1479–1425 B.C.E.) were buried there in identical tombs with sumptuous mortuary regalia.

Wadi Sidri a site in the SINAI Peninsula near modern Abu Zuneima. The turquoise mines of the area were exploited by the Egyptians in several eras.

Wadi Timulat a fertile depression north of BUBASTIS in the eastern Delta, used by the ancient Egyptians as a path to the Red Sea. The wadi led to the BBITTER LAKES, which in turn opened onto the Red Sea. The route was called the SWEET WATER CANAL by the Egyptians and was used by the Late Period (712–332 B.C.E.) rulers to open a canal.

Wadj *See* DJET.

wadjet The symbol of "the EYE OF RÉ" or "the EYE OF HORUS," powerful AMULETS of strength and protection, the *wadjet* depicted the sun and moon, vital elements in Nile mythology. The *wadjet* was worn by the living and by the dead in the mummy wrappings of the deceased. The amulet was fashioned out of blue or green faience, sometimes with semiprecious stones in golden settings.

Wadjet (Uadjet) A cobra deity serving as the patron goddess of ancient Egypt, the protectress of the northern territories, Lower Egypt, called Buto in Greek texts, Wadjet was associated at times with the goddess HATHOR. NEKHEBET was her sister goddess, the patroness of Upper Egypt. Wadjet was also associated with the Osirian cult and was believed to have helped the goddess ISIS keep watch over the infant deity HORUS on CHEMMIS in the Delta. Wadjet arranged the reeds and foliage to hide the divine mother and son from all enemies so that Horus could mature to strike down his father's assassin, SET. Wadjet was depicted as a cobra or as a woman. As a woman holding the crown of Lower Egypt, with an entwined papyrus SCEPTER and serpent, she was included in the coronation ceremonies of the rulers. The goddess offered the crown to each new ruler in the rituals, and her image was used in the royal symbol, the URAEUS.

Wadjkaré (fl. 22nd century B.C.E.) *ruler of the brief Eighth Dynasty*
He is an obscure ruler, as the only surviving documentation of his reign is a royal exemption decree issued by him. His name was translated as "Prosperous Is the Soul of RÉ."

Wadjmose (fl. 15th century B.C.E.) *prince of the Eighteenth Dynasty*
He was the son of TUTHMOSIS I (r. 1504–1492 B.C.E.), and Queen 'AHMOSE. A brother of Queen-Pharaoh HATSHEPSUT, Wadjmose died before he could inherit the throne. Wadjmose was buried on the western shore of THEBES, south of the RAMESSEUM. His tomb contained a small chapel and three shrines.

Wall of the Prince This was a series of FORTRESSES erected by AMENEMHET I (r. 1991–1962 B.C.E.) to defend the eastern borders of Egypt. A corresponding series of fortresses was placed in strategic locations on the western border as well, and all of these military outposts were heavily garrisoned to stop the encroaching tribes attempting to enter the Delta. The pharaohs of the Twelfth Dynasty (1991–1783 B.C.E.) maintained these fortresses, and the New Kingdom Period (1550–1070 B.C.E.) rulers restored them periodically. The Wall of the Prince was mentioned by Neferti, or Nefer-rohu, in his prophetic writings honoring AMENEMHET I (r. 1991–1962 B.C.E.). There are indications that the original series of fortresses were built by MENTUHOTEP III (r. 2010–1998 B.C.E.) and reconstructed by Amenemhet I and his successors.
See also NEFER-ROHU'S PROPHECY.

Wapuat *See* WEPWAWET.

waret This was the ancient Egyptian name for the watery abyss from which RÉ rose from the moment of creation. Egyptians feared darkness and chaos as the destroyers of humanity and remembered the cosmological traditions concerning the act of creation. The PRIME-VAL MOUND, the life-giving island in the center of *waret*, remained the symbol of existence in all historical periods.
See also NUN.

warfare The military power of ancient Egypt kept enemies at bay for centuries. No sensible ruler of a city-state or nation wanted to face the Egyptian army at the height of its fighting prowess. For the Egyptians, warfare had a religious component to it, for they viewed the pharaohs of Egypt to be semidivine beings. Thus, an enemy that attacked Egypt was defying the gods themselves. The pharaoh was seen as the "shield of the people," and this title was passed on to the royal heirs who themselves took part in battles from a young age.

PREDYNASTIC PERIOD

In the earliest periods, the pharaohs and military units had a definitive role in maintaining the sovereignty of the territory and in obtaining natural resources and new lands. When AHA (Menes) started Egypt as a nation in 2920 B.C.E., he inherited a strong military as well as administrative and religious traditions. SCORPION I (ca. 3000 B.C.E.) had made war against other regions in the desert and on the Nile. Beginning his series of conquests to promote the unification of the land, he was also the heir to the efforts of the undocumented kings of Dynasty 0 at HIERANKOPOLIS and then at THINIS. (NARMER, who defeated the rulers of Lower Egypt in the Nile DELTA region, came out of Thinis.)

Warfare must have been a continuing process throughout the Predynastic Period, as conflicting groups carved out their territories and established the perimeters of their influence. The totems of many of the Upper Egyptian NOMES, or provinces, were depicted in documents about Narmer, indicating that these warrior groups were already established to some extent and used as military units.

EARLY DYNASTIC PERIOD

The early rulers of Egypt did not preside over a united land in the First Dynasty (2920–2770 B.C.E.). There is evidence of resistance on the part of various regions. Aha recorded adding territories in the south (probably the area between GEBEL EL-SILSILEH and ASWAN). DJER (r. ca. 2900 B.C.E.) recorded a campaign against the Asiatics in the Eastern Desert. PERIBSEN, during the Second Dynasty (2770–2649 B.C.E.), made raids into Palestine, probably exploratory expeditions or raids for cattle and other loot. KHA'SEKHEMWY (r. 2649 B.C.E.), the last pharaoh of the Second Dynasty, probably secured Egypt's unification, indicating continual or at least sporadic warfare on the Nile up to that era. It is possible that the first settlement at BUHEN, in NUBIA (modern Sudan), was made in his reign, as Kha'sekhemwy and his successors had started to penetrate the territories below the first cataract of the Nile.

OLD KINGDOM

The rulers of the Old Kingdom were militarily active. The Egyptian interest in the SINAI territory led them to conduct punitive expeditions against the local BEDOUINS, the Asiatic nomads who resented Egyptian efforts to set up mines and quarries there. In the reign of SNEFRU at the start of the Fourth Dynasty (2575–2465 B.C.E.), Egypt had a large fleet of naval vessels as well, supposedly sent to the Levant on trading expeditions.

BUHEN, at the second cataract of the Nile in Nubia, became a base for southern trade and was fortified with stone walls and a dry moat. All of the rulers of Snefru's dynasty, including the pyramid builders of GIZA, are represented at Buhen by seals. SNOFRU is said to have conducted a massive raid in the vicinity of Buhen, and it is probable that other Nubian settlements were begun in this period.

The rulers of the Fifth Dynasty continued the warfare. In that period the Egyptian army is recorded as having started the campaigns in Palestine and other Mediterranean coastal regions. UNIS, the last ruler of the Fifth Dynasty, claimed to have made five expeditions into Syria. The Canaan reliefs from the Sixth Dynasty depict assaults on Palestinian walled cities. In addition to the pharaoh, they also portray an aristocrat named WENI.

During the reign of PEPI I (r. 2289–2255 B.C.E.) the Egyptians had a turquoise mine at SERABIT EL-KHADIM in the Sinai. The Bedouins defended their natural resources by repeatedly attacking the mine. General Weni, who served Pepi I, marched with an army into the Sinai against the Bedouins, accompanied by a force of MEDJAY, from Nubia. These fierce warriors would remain a vital part of Egyptian military campaigns. (In peacetime, they served as the capital police force.) Weni garrisoned the mines and put up fortifications and barracks. He used both land and sea, marching some units north to the Sinai and using ships to transfer other units and needed

A relief depicting Ramesses II (r. 1290–1224 B.C.E.) in battle array, displayed on a Karnak wall *(Hulton Archive)*

supplies. Later Weni proved just as innovative while campaigning in Nubia, as he built a canal beside the cataracts so that warships could be diverted safely from the rapids.

Weni, as commander of the royal armies, levied troops from the local NOMES when any military campaign seemed imminent. NOMARCHS were responsible for a certain number of troops, to be supplemented by Nubian mercenaries under command of caravan leaders or trade supervisors. Many of these troops were veterans of militia training or active duty in previous campaigns. The basic unit of the army at the time was the battalion, although its exact size and functions are not documented. The militia-levy system had its obvious drawbacks. Troops brought from the various nomes held allegiance only to their own leaders. The extra levies used as support for the militias were even less nationalistically oriented. For this reason there must have been some core units of the Egyptian army that were maintained as a regular force. There is evidence of so-called household units at the time. Weni's position was that of commander of troops, but he also performed other tasks for the ruler. Some generals served as caravan leaders as the expansion of trade warranted a military presence in remote regions. These positions appear to have been hereditary, the beginnings of a military caste. Ordinance and other logistical and provisionary departments were already functioning, and there were reserves and supplies mandated for the military units.

Men like Weni used Nubian mercenaries, particularly when he served as the governor of Upper Egypt, but trade was the key to Egypt's relationship with Nubia. The Egyptian royal governor HARKHUF and his famous expedition for the child ruler PEPI II (r. 2246–2152 B.C.E.) indicate a limited role in Nubia, mostly economic, not military. Buhen and the other forts were no longer invested with troops, and Nubia was comparatively free of Egyptian forces.

The soldiers of the Old Kingdom were depicted as wearing skullcaps and carrying clan or nome totems. They used maces with wooden heads or pear-shaped stone heads. Bows and arrows were standard gear, with square-tipped flint arrowheads and leather quivers. Some shields, made of hides, were in use but not generally. Most of the troops were barefoot, dressed in simple kilts, or naked.

FIRST INTERMEDIATE PERIOD

With the collapse of the Old Kingdom in 2134 B.C.E., military activities in Egypt were confined once again to the regions within the nation's borders. The KHETY clan of HERAKLEOPOLIS moved against their northern and western neighbors to carve out a new royal realm. These rulers of the Ninth and Tenth Dynasties (2134–2040 B.C.E.) were vigorous warriors, aided by nome allies. They could not penetrate into Upper Egypt because

of the Theban resistance, and eventually the Thebans attacked their southern outposts and began marching on their capital. Nubian troops were employed in the battles in the place of the ruler. In 2040 B.C.E., the armies of the Theban ruler MENTUHOTEP II took Herakleopolis, and the internal wars of Egypt were coming to a close.

The campaigns of Mentuhotep II in this restoration of unity took on a mythical quality that remained popular for centuries. As the ruler of THEBES (modern Luxor), Mentuhotep II had repelled the attacks by the Khety clan. However, when the warriors of Assiut, allies of the Khety clan, attacked an Upper Egypt necropolis, or cemetery, and vandalized graves, their act scandalized the entire nation. Mentuhotep II called out the FOLLOWERS OF HORUS, the famed warriors of the south, and marched on the Khetys and their allies. Some 82 of MENTUHOTEP II's WARRIORS who died in the act of vengeance were embalmed and mummified on the battlefield by the mortuary priests who accompanied the army. These bodies bore the seals and cartouche (royal insignia) of Mentuhotep II and were buried on the site of his mortuary temple at DEIR EL-BAHRI, across the Nile from Thebes.

THE MIDDLE KINGDOM

Mentuhotep II's conquest of Herakleopolis started the Middle Kingdom. The land was united, but there were standing armies in some nomes, and aristocrats did not hesitate to use their forces to exact vengeance or to consolidate holdings. Such nobles were free to act on their own behalf as long as they provided the required number of troops to the royal campaigns. However, the petty feuds between the nomes were ended in the Twelfth Dynasty.

There was a standing royal army in this period, composed of conscripts, led by a minister of war and a commander in chief of the army, or an official who worked in that capacity. Frontier units were on duty at the borders, and troops accompanied many of the mining and quarrying expeditions.

Mentuhotep and his successors continued vigorous campaigns against Libya and the Sinai and are reported as having expanded their operations even into Syrian lands. The rulers of the Twelfth Dynasty (1991–1783 B.C.E.), the Amenemhets, started their reigns with military campaigns. AMENEMHET I (r. 1991–1962 B.C.E.) was a usurper and was skilled in military affairs, having served in martial and administrative affairs for the last Mentuhotep. Upon staking his claims, he took an armada of ships up and down the Nile to discourage any rebellions from nome clans. He also erected a series of garrisoned fortresses on the northern borders, called the WALL OF THE PRINCE. When Amenemhet I died, his son and heir, SENWOSRET I, was on a campaign in Libya, having a small unit of bodyguards with him.

A vast army of scribes and administrators served the military forces of Egypt in this period. The frontier fortifications were manned, and there were even "shock troops" used in campaigns. There are some indications that professional soldiers were in the ranks of the Egyptian army at this time, called "the Brave" or "the Valiant." Officers could be denoted in reliefs by the feathers that they wore in their caps.

In Nubia the Middle Kingdom had considerable impact. The Mentuhoteps continued their raids, and the Amenemhets made a policy of fortifying trade settlements as part of their dynastic goals. Senwosret I (1971–1926 B.C.E.) erected several fortresses and kept them fully staffed with troops. Ikkur, ANIBA, and QUBAN date to this era, and the region around Buhen was more stiffly fortified. The Twelfth Dynasty rulers may have erected fortresses as far south as SEMNA.

The name Kush came into being around this time, to designate a region of Nubia that had its capital at KERMEH. During the last part of the Old Kingdom and the First Intermediate Period, the Nubians had built a relatively strong state in the area. SENWOSRET III completed the pacification of Kush and established the southern borders of Egypt as far south as Semna and URONARTI.

The military gear of the Middle Kingdom was much the same as that of the Old Kingdom, although troops now carried axes and copper blades, bound to wooden hafts with leather thongs. A long bronze spear became popular, and the soldiers wore leather shirts and kilts.

THE SECOND INTERMEDIATE PERIOD

There was warfare throughout much of Egypt during the period following the collapse of the Middle Kingdom in 1640 B.C.E. Asiatics began to consolidate their holdings after having penetrated Egypt, and established their own domains. The HYKSOS, as these Asiatics were called, introduced horses into the Nile Valley, using the animals to pull chariots and to carry loads. The horses of that era were not actually heavy enough to carry the weight of a man for long distances, something that the Egyptians remedied quickly.

After a brief period of tolerance, the Thebans began to assault the southern outposts of the Hyksos, as TA'O II (Sekenenré) (r. ca. 1560 B.C.E.) began a full-scale war to oust the aliens from the Nile. When he died, his son KAMOSE took the field in his place. Under his command the Egyptians fielded cavalry units, having lightened the Hyksos chariot and also having trained special units for such tactics. He also commanded an unusual fighting force, called the MEDJAY, a group of Nubians who had allied themselves with Egypt's cause. The Medjay served as scouts for the main units and then as light infantry. Kamose used the LIBYAN DESERT oases as effective hiding places in his assaults on the Hyksos, and he was within striking distance of AVARIS, the Hyksos capital, when he died or was slain in battle.

THE NEW KINGDOM

'AHMOSE (NEBPEHTIRÉ) (r. 1550–1525 B.C.E.), his younger brother, took up the cause and surrounded Avaris, using both land and sea forces. The Hyksos were forced to withdraw from Egypt, and the New Kingdom began. Egypt's army was no longer a confederation of nome levies but a first-class military force. The ruler was the commander in chief, but the vizier and another administrative series of units handled the logistical and reserve affairs. Apparently the senior officers of the army could debate campaign events with the ruler while on tours, and others were consulted for their experience.

The army was organized into divisions in the New Kingdom, both chariot forces and infantry. Each division numbered approximately 5,000 men. These divisions carried the names of the principal deities of the nation. When Egypt was not at war, the army served as a reserve force, stationed in both Upper and Lower Egypt.

The chariot force was divided into squadrons of 25 men each, and the infantry contained two types of soldiers, the veterans and the conscripts of the campaign. The kings had their own elite corps, serving as bodyguards and special shock troops. There were alien mercenary units in the army in this period as well. Some, like the SHERDEN PIRATES, were pressed into service after capture, and others, like the Libyans and Nubians, were long-established units of mercenaries. A definite officer corps existed, with the lowest grade commanding 50 men and the highest, led by the "standard-bearers," in charge of as many as 250 men. The troop commander was in charge of several brigades or commanded entire fortresses. Above this level were the various administrative officer staffs. In many instances the princes of Egypt led units into action, as in the case of two of Ramesses II's sons, who went to war in Nubia while still lads.

Pack animals were used for the various supplies, but boats were important in this period as well. A great naval station was located at PERU-NEFER, near Memphis. AMENHOTEP II, the son of TUTHMOSIS III (r. 1479–1425 B.C.E.), commanded that depot and a shipbuilding site while still a prince. Ox-drawn carts were also used in the field.

The pharaohs of the New Kingdom started with the war against the Hyksos and continued campaigns throughout that period. 'Ahmose's successor, AMENHOTEP I, maintained the military structures, but it was TUTHMOSIS I (r. 1504–1492 B.C.E.) who took the armies of Egypt to the Euphrates River and began the empire. His grandson, Tuthmosis III, fought at AR-MEGIDDO and then conducted 20 more campaigns in order to put down rebellions among the occupied or vassal states of the Mediterranean region. Tuthmosis III also took hostages from the royal families of conquered states and cities and trained them in Egypt so that they were ready to rule in their own time as allies.

Tuthmosis III was one of the greatest warrior-kings of Egypt; he expanded the empire founded by his grandfather, Tuthmosis I, until it stretched from modern Sudan to the Euphrates River. *(Hulton Archive)*

In Nubia, meanwhile, tribes had risen again, and 'Ahmose I and his successors had to campaign there. Under Tuthmosis I the Egyptian fleet made its way south and established a fort at Tombos, which enabled the Egyptians to assault the regions easily. Tuthmosis I went as far as the fourth cataract. When he withdrew to Egypt, the body of the king of the warring tribe hung upside down on the prow of his ship. The interest in Nubia was mostly economic, and Egypt did little to respect the ways of the Nubians.

HOREMHAB, the last ruler of the Eighteenth Dynasty (1319–1307 B.C.E.), was a trained military commander. He conducted campaigns to maintain the empire, which had diminished during the 'AMARNA Period and with the fall of the MITANNIS, Egypt's allies. Before he died he placed RAMESSES I, a military comrade-in-arms, on the throne, and the Ramessids began their military exploits.

The Ramessids, experts in campaigns and enthusiastic about the empire, warred constantly to maintain a balance of power. They faced the mighty HITTITES, and in the battle of KADESH both the Egyptians and Hittites escaped disaster narrowly. An alliance was the result of the conflict, which divided lands between them. The great military leader of Egypt in this period was RAMESSES II (1290–1224 B.C.E.). His son, MERENPTAH, had to fight the Sea Peoples and the Libyans, and conducted his campaigns with cunning and fervor. The last great warrior pharaoh of this era was RAMESSES III (1194–1163 B.C.E.), who maintained Egypt's military prowess, which gave way eventually to dynastic weakness and the avarice of the priests of AMUN, which brought an end to the New Kingdom.

THE THIRD INTERMEDIATE PERIOD

The military activities of Egypt after the fall of the New Kingdom and the rise of the Twenty-first Dynasty (1070–945 B.C.E.) were confined to the efforts of the crown and the high priests of Amun, working together, to put down the rebellions taking place in Upper Egypt. These Amunite priests resided at el-HIBA, a fortified site. The rise of the Twenty-second Dynasty (945–712 B.C.E.), founded by SHOSHENQ I, a Libyan, started new military expansion, especially in Canaan and Palestine. The Twenty-third Dynasty (ca. 828–712 B.C.E.) was a period of small city-states, with no national military agenda. The Twenty-fourth Dynasty (745–712 B.C.E.) at Sais was equally inactive, eventually attacked by the Twenty-fifth Dynasty (770–712 B.C.E.) of Nubia, modern Sudan. PIANKHI (1) (r. 750–712 B.C.E.), the son of KASHTA, the dynastic founder, ruled in Thebes and Nubia and northward, gaining control of Egypt by 712 B.C.E.

THE LATE PERIOD

In the Twenty-fifth Dynasty (712–657 B.C.E.), the Assyrians invaded Egypt, destroying the reign of TAHARQA (690–664 B.C.E.). The Twenty-sixth Dynasty (664–525 B.C.E.) fostered Hellenic alliances and conducted revolts within the ranks of vassal states.

Egypt also conducted campaigns in Palestine, Nubia, and Syria. APRIES (r. 589–570 B.C.E.) involved Egypt in a Libyan war as well, and he lost his throne and his life as a result. His royal line was destroyed by the Persian invasion led by CAMBYSES (r. 525–522 B.C.E.) and the founding of the Twenty-seventh Dynasty (525–404 B.C.E.).

AMYRTAIOS (r. 404–393 B.C.E.) led a revolt and instituted the Twenty-eighth Dynasty, but the line ended at his death. The Twenty-ninth Dynasty (393–380 B.C.E.) found itself involved in affairs of the entire region, and Greek mercenaries fought Egypt. Usurpation was another source of conflict in this period, and HAKORIS fought battles on the side of the Greeks in their battles against the Persians. NECTANEBO I, who founded the

Thirtieth Dynasty (380–343 B.C.E.), put the successors of Hakoris aside.

The Second Persian Period (343–332 B.C.E.) brought the Thirty-first Dynasty to Egypt, but the Persians ruled through satraps, who had to put down rebellions. The Persians ended with DARIUS III CODOMAN, who was defeated by ALEXANDER III THE GREAT (332–323 B.C.E.).

GRECO-ROMAN PERIOD

At the death of Alexander the Great, PTOLEMY I SOTER (r. 304–284 B.C.E.) declared himself the ruler of Egypt and engaged the Nile Valley's armies in a series of campaigns. His successors fought among themselves and involved Egypt in Hellenic military campaigns. The Seleucids also attacked Egypt until the powerful Romans began to adopt a protective stance concerning the Ptolemaic reigns. Defeating CLEOPATRA VII in 30 B.C.E., AUGUSTUS (Octavian) made Egypt a part of the Roman Empire.

Further reading: Carman, John, and Anthony Harding, eds. *Ancient Warfare: Archaeological Perspectives.* London: Sutton Publishing, 2000; Ferrill, Arthur. *The Origins of War: From the Stone Age to Alexander the Great (History & Warfare).* Boulder, Colo.: Westview Press, 1997; Hasel, Michael. *Domination and Resistance: Egyptian Military Activity in the Southern Levant, Ca. 1300–1185 B.C.* Boston: Brill Academic Publishers, 1998; Kern, Paul Bentley. *Ancient Siege Warfare.* Bloomington, Ind.: Indiana University Press, 1999; Morkot, Robert. *A to Z of Ancient Egyptian Warfare.* Lanham, Md.: Scarecrow, 2003; Morkot, Robert. *Historical Dictionary of Ancient Egyptian Warfare.* Lanham, Md.: Scarecrow, 2003; Partridge, Robert B. *Fighting Pharaohs: Weapons and Warfare.* Bradford, Mass.: Pear Tree Publishing, 2009; Shaw, Ian. *Egyptian Warfare and Weapons.* London: Shire Publications, 1999; Spalinger, Anthony. *War and Ancient Egypt.* London: Wiley-Blackwell, 2005.

Waset *See* THEBES.

Waters of Ré This was the branch of the Nile that began at HELIOPOLIS and flowed to the northeast to enrich the agricultural area of the Delta. During the Nineteenth Dynasty (1307–1196 B.C.E.), the same branch of the Nile was called the "Waters of Avaris," as the Ramessids of that royal line erected their great capital on the site of the HYKSOS capital of AVARIS. That part of the river became "the Waters of HORUS" at el-Qantara and then emptied into the Mediterranean Sea near Sinu, the PELUSIUM of the Ptolemaic Period (304–30 B.C.E.).

Waty (fl. 26th century B.C.E.) *official of the Fourth Dynasty*
Waty served KHAFRE (r. 2520–2494 B.C.E.) as a court musician. The mummified remains of Waty were so beautifully embalmed and wrapped that his features were distinguishable beneath the linens. The embalming preserved Waty's flesh so carefully that a callus is still evident on one foot. His sarcophagus was uncovered in a tomb in SAQQARA.

Wawat This was the area between ASWAN and the first cataract of the Nile, in Kush or NUBIA (modern Sudan). The region was continually under military assaults by the Egyptians, as the local inhabitants rebelled and became independent during eras of dynastic weakness. ANIBA was the capital of Wawat, called Mi'am in some periods. Aniba was well fortified by the Egyptians and contained storage areas for military wares and TRADE surpluses. The VICEROY of Nubia resided in Wawat during some historical periods. The people of Wawat were paying tribute as early as the Sixth Dynasty (2323–2150 B.C.E.), perhaps even earlier.

Wayheset (fl. 10th century B.C.E.) *official of the Twenty-second Dynasty*
Wayheset served SHOSHENQ I (r. 945–924 B.C.E.) as a military emissary. He was sent to the DAKHLA Oasis, where Egyptians were rebelling against Libyan domination of the land. The revolt was short-lived and confined to the area of the oasis. Wayheset thus freed Shoshenq I to begin his military campaigns in Palestine without distractions.

Way of Horus Sometimes called the Royal Road, this was an ancient Egyptian road of strategic importance that linked the eastern modern border town of El-Qantas to Gaza in southern Palestine and beyond. The road was kept under guard by the Egyptians to protect the caravans that traveled it, and garrisons were built at various locations to repel nomad and BEDOUIN attacks. The road ran directly across the Isthmus of Suez, also secured by a series of fortified wells dug by the Egyptians to accommodate caravans and military forces on the move.

See also DEIR EL-BALAH.

Way of the Sea A route used by TUTHMOSIS III (r. 1479–1425 B.C.E.) and AMENHOTEP II (r. 1427–1401 B.C.E.) along the coastal plains and valleys of Palestine on several of their military campaigns. Amenhotep II attacked Palestine from this route, going to Sharon Plain, Upper Galilee, and Jezreel.

See also TUTHMOSIS III'S MILITARY CAMPAIGNS.

Wedjebten (fl. 22nd century B.C.E.) *royal woman of the sixth dynasty*
She was a lesser-ranked consort of PEPI II (r. 2246–2152 B.C.E.). Wbjeten was buried in Pepi II's mortuary complex in southern SAQQARA. Wedjebten was not the mother of Pepi II's heir.

Wegaf (Khutawyré) (d. 1779 B.C.E.) *founder of the Thirteenth Dynasty*
Wegaf started an obscure royal line, reigning 1783–1779 B.C.E. He was a disciple of the deity OSIRIS and erected four stelae to form a sacred area, *ta djeser,* in ABYDOS, around the tomb of DJER, believed to be the actual resting place of Osiris. He also built at UMM EL-GA'AB in Abydos. Little else is known of his reign in a turbulent period of Egyptian history.

weights and measures They were the official designations used in ancient Egypt for architectural projects and for determining the values of bartered materials. Length was measured in royal cubit, 20 inches; palmwidth, 3 inches; and finger-width, 3/4 inch. The *khet* was the measurement of 110 square cubits or 2/3 of an acre.

The liquid measurements the Egyptians used were the *hekat,* which were made up of *kin* or pints and served as the equivalent of just over a modern gallon. The *khar* measured 17 gallons. Measurements of weights included the *deden,* equal to two modern pounds and divided into ten *gite* or twelve *shat.*

In the construction of the PYRAMIDS, the *seked* was the determined slope of the monument, while the *pesu* was the measurement of the beer and bread served to the workers from a single unit of grain.

Wenamun *See* REPORT OF WENAMUN.

Wendjebaendjeb (fl. 11th century B.C.E.) *general and military commander of the Twenty-first Dynasty*
He served PSUSENNES I (r. 1040–992 B.C.E.), also holding several religious offices in the royal court in TANIS. A tomb was prepared for Wendjebaendjeb in Psusennes I's own mortuary complex near the temple of AMUN in Tanis. He was buried in a granite sarcophagus from the Nineteenth Dynasty (1307–1196 B.C.E.), usurped for his use. It has also been reported that the sarcophagus belonged originally to Queen MUTNODJMET (1), the consort of HOREMHAB (r. 1319–1307 B.C.E.) of the Eighteenth Dynasty.

Weneg (Wadjnes) (fl. 27th century B.C.E.) *obscure ruler of the Second Dynasty*
He was reportedly the successor to NINETJER. At ABYDOS and SAQQARA he was called Wadjnes. Vases bearing his seals were found in the pyramid complex of DJOSER (r. 2630–2611 B.C.E.) in Saqqara. No tomb has been identified for Weneg.

Weni (Unis, Wenis) (fl. 23rd century B.C.E.) *military official serving Pepi I*
Weni was a commander and expedition leader for PEPI I (r. 2289–2255 B.C.E.). An innovative, energetic individual, Weni used mercenary troops to further Egypt's domains. His tomb in ABYDOS contained a limestone stela that provided biographical details and insights into this Old Kingdom Period. Weni was an aristocrat who assumed court offices after serving apprentice roles in the reign of Pepi's father, TETI (2323–2291 B.C.E.). Fulfilling duties as the warden or governor of various royal sites, Weni was also asked to investigate a harem conspiracy led by a minor consort, Queen WERET-IMTES (2). The fate of the royal lady was not disclosed on the stela.

Weni then led a large army of Egyptians and Nubian mercenaries (the first ever recorded in Egyptian texts) to battle against "Asiatic Sand-dwellers," obviously BEDOUINS of the SINAI. He speaks of a site called "Gazelle's head," unknown today. Weni, however, moved half of his troops by ship and half of them by land, thus catching the enemy between two separate forces. The ferried units landed behind the enemy position.

This commander also led expeditions to NUBIA (modern Sudan), where he dug canals at the northern cataracts of the Nile and built naval vessels out of acacia wood. The ships and barges carried granite blocks for Pepi's pyramid. Weni's tomb also contained a song about the army returning in safety after defeating Egypt's enemies.

Wenis *See* WENI.

Wenut She was a rabbit or hare goddess of Egypt, serving as a patroness of THEBES. She was the consort of UNU, the hare god, and she was depicted in the totems of the Theban nome and as part of the *was* SCEPTER.

Wepemnofret (fl. 26th century B.C.E.) *royal prince of the Fourth Dynasty*
Wepemnofret was the son of KHUFU (Cheops) (r. 2551–2528 B.C.E.) and an unnamed queen. He was not the heir. A stela belonging to Wepemnofret was found in a MASTABA of the Great Western Cemetery near the Great PYRAMID at GIZA. The stela was set into the walls of the tomb.

Wepwawet (Wapuat) The wolf deity of Egypt, depicted as well as a JACKAL, he became part of the cult of ANUBIS but remained popular in some nomes. Wepwawet was a friend of OSIRIS and was revered as "the Opener of the Ways," a reference to the roads of TUAT, or the realms beyond the grave. In some traditions Wepwawet piloted the sun boat of the god RÉ as it traveled through the chambers of the night. He also aided the dead on their journeys to paradise. The cult centers for Wepwawet were at ASSIUT and in some NOMES. The gods HORUS and SET joined Wepwawet at Assiut, where the three roamed the hills as wolves.

Wereret (Weret) (fl. 19th century B.C.E.) *royal woman of the Twelfth Dynasty*
The consort of SENWOSRET II (r. 1897–1878 B.C.E.), Wereret was the daughter of AMENEMHET II and probably

the mother of SENWOSRET III. She is mentioned in the KAHUN PAPYRUS, and a fragment of her statue was discovered on ELEPHANTINE Island. Wereret was buried near the pyramid of Senwosret III at DASHUR in a limestone MASTABA containing a red granite sarcophagus. An intact jewelry cache was found in a tomb wall, and 50 large pieces and 7,000 beads were uncovered intact. This large collection of pieces included rings, bracelets, amulets, scarabs, and two god lions. A portion of Wereret's mummified remains that were vandalized by tomb robbers was recovered.

Weret (Wer) An ancient Egyptian god of the sky, referred to as "the Great One" in hymns and litanies, he was identified with the cults of THOTH and HORUS in various regions. The sun and the moon were traditionally held to be his eyes, and on moonless nights he was thought to be blind. In this blinded state Weret was the protector of priest-physicians who treated diseases of the eyes and the patron of blind musicians. In some reliefs he was depicted as a harp-playing god.

Weret-Imtes (1) (Weretyamtes) (fl. 24th century B.C.E.) *royal woman of the Sixth Dynasty*
She was a lesser-ranked wife of TETI (r. 2323–2291 B.C.E.) and probably the mother of WERET-IMTES (2).

Weret-Imtes (2) (fl. 23rd century B.C.E.) *royal woman of the Sixth Dynasty*
She was a lesser-ranked consort of PEPI I (r. 2289–2255 B.C.E.) who was charged with a harem revolt on behalf of her son. She appears to have conspired to eliminate Pepi I from the throne, by exiling him or murdering him. An official named WENI, a military genius of that historical period, was called upon to investigate the accused royal woman alone. Weret-Imtes was obviously punished, along with her son, but no record was given as to the exact requirements of fulfilling justice in this matter. Penalties for those who attacked the sacred person of the pharaoh normally included death, disfigurement, and/or exile into the desert wastes.

Wersu (Worsu) (fl. 15th century B.C.E.) *mining official of the Eighteenth Dynasty*
Wersu served in the reign of AMENHOTEP II (1427–1401 B.C.E.) as the superintendent of the gold-mining operations in the southern domains and may have served as viceroy of NUBIA as well. Statues of him and his wife were discovered in KOPTOS.

Westcar Papyrus This is a document treasured for historical details about the Fourth Dynasty, particularly the reign of KHUFU (Cheops) (2551–2528 B.C.E.), the builder of the Great PYRAMID. The TALE OF KHUFU AND THE MAGICIANS and a prophecy concerning SAHURÉ (r. 2458–2446 B.C.E.), KAKAI (Neferirkaré; r. 2446–2426 B.C.E.), and USERKHAF (r. 2465–2458 B.C.E.) are contained in this papyrus. The papyrus is now in Berlin, Germany.

Western Waters (Western River) This was a term used to denote the Canopic branch of the Nile in the Delta. The Western Waters irrigated an area noted for vineyards and fine wines. In some historical periods the rulers of Egypt built residences in this lush region.

Westptah (fl. 25th century B.C.E.) *beloved vizier of the Fifth Dynasty*
Westptah served in the reigns of SAHURÉ (2458–2446 B.C.E.) and KAKAI (Neferirkaré; 2446–2426 B.C.E.). He began his career during the reign of Sahuré and later became VIZIER of Egypt under Kakai. A noted architect and the chief justice of the nation, Westptah fell ill while attending the ruler. The court physician was summoned but could not save the aged official. When Westptah died, Kakai was supposedly inconsolable. He arranged for the ritual purification of the body in his presence and then commanded that an ebony coffin be made for Westptah. The vizier's son, Mernuterseteni, was ordered by the pharaoh to bury his father with specific tomb endowments and rituals. Westptah was given a grave site next to the pyramid of Sahuré in return for his services to the nation. The tomb contained a touching description of these honors.

White Chapel A small but exquisite structure at KARNAK in THEBES, erected by SENWOSRET I (r. 1971–1926 B.C.E.), the chapel has now been restored in Karnak and is a masterpiece of Egyptian architecture of the Middle Kingdom Period (2040–1640 B.C.E.), an era considered by later generations of Egyptians as the golden age of the nation. The carved wall reliefs depict Senwosret I being embraced by PTAH, AMUN, ATUM, and HORUS, each god placed at the cardinal points of the earth.

Wiay (fl. 11th century B.C.E.) *royal woman of the Twenty-first Dynasty*
Wiay was the second-ranked consort of PSUSENNES I (r. 1040–992 B.C.E.) after Queen MUTNODJMET (2). She was the mother of ISTEMKHEBE (2), who married MENKHEPER-RESENB (2), the high priest of AMUN in Thebes.

Widia (fl. 14th century B.C.E.) *prince of the city-state of Ashkelon on the coastal plain of modern Israel*
A vassal of Egypt, Prince Widia wrote to AKHENATEN (r. 1353–1335 B.C.E.) to express his loyalty. The Egyptian imperial holdings were in a state of unrest during the 'AMARNA Period, and Widia's city was relatively close to the Egyptian command post at Gaza. Ashkelon revolted and was retaken by RAMESSES II (r. 1290–1224 B.C.E.).

Wilbour Papyrus A long document dating to the fourth year of the reign of RAMESSES V (1156–1151

B.C.E.), this text concerns legal matters in a village named Neshi, south of Memphis in the FAIYUM area. Fields are listed in this papyrus, depicting the dominance of the temple's holding in the region. The text also records types of grain harvested. The Wilbour Papyrus is in the Brooklyn Museum, New York.

Window of Appearance   An architectural innovation popular in the New Kingdom Period (1550–1070 B.C.E.) and made famous by AKHENATEN (r. 1353–1335 B.C.E.) at 'AMARNA, this window was actually a stage set into the walls of the palace, where he could stand before the people. From this elevated position the ruler dispensed honors to officials. Akhenaten and Queen NEFERTITI were depicted in the 'Amarna Window of Appearance, honoring the faithful servants of their reign, including HOREMHAB (r. 1319–1307 B.C.E.). The tomb of NEBWENEF in Thebes depicts RAMESSES II (r. 1290–1224 B.C.E.) and Queen NEFERTARI at a Window of Appearance. The Window of Appearance symbolizes the HORIZON.

Woman of Tell Halif   (fl. 3300–3000 B.C.E.) *Egyptian woman buried in the Negev Desert, dating to the Early Bronze IB Period*
Part of the emerging Egyptian culture, the Woman of Tell Halif and her gravesite represent an Egyptian presence in the Negev region. A potsherd discovered in the grave is ingrained with the *SEREKH,* or royal sign of NARMER, the unifier of Upper and Lower Kingdoms on the Nile.

women's role   It was a social position varying over the centuries and subject to the various nomes and epochs. Some women achieved lasting fame, while the majority served in positions related to their homes and families.

Royal women and those of nonroyal status seldom had records attesting to their duties or rights, and in almost every case (with the exception of the queen-pharaohs) they were considered for the most part in terms of their relationships to the surrounding males. Even the mortuary stelae, the tablets erected for women as gravesite commemoratives, equated them normally with their husbands, fathers, or sons. In the tombs women were portrayed in secondary positions if they were shown at all. In some historical periods women were portrayed the same size as their husbands, but in most instances they were smaller and placed in a peripheral area.

The royal women were the best documented, but even they are only cursorily mentioned in dynastic records. In the nomes, however, many women, such as Princess NEBT, did maintain their own estates and hold high ranks personally or as regents for their minor sons. In times of building, for example, women were subject to the corvée, the service given to the pharaoh at pyramid or temple sites. Women went with the men to the building sites and did the cooking, weaving, or nursing. They received honors as a result.

Khamerernebty, the consort of Menkauré of the Old Kingdom Period, in a strikingly intimate pose *(Hulton Archive)*

Legally, the women of ancient Egypt were the equals of men, and they are mentioned frequently in regulations concerning the proper attitudes of officials. Some didactic literature warns young men against frivolous or flirtatious women, but there is also a text that admonishes young men to think about the travails and sufferings that their mothers endured for their sake. Women depicted in the mortuary reliefs and paintings are shown conducting the normal household tasks, although women of higher status no doubt had household servants to do these chores.

Women are presented in most tomb scenes as young and beautiful, whether they are the wives or mothers of the men buried there. Such idealization was part of the mortuary or funerary art and did not represent the actual age or physical condition of the women portrayed.

No women were recorded as having excelled in the various arts. No government positions were held by women, except as regents for the royal heirs or nome heirs, and even in the temples the roles of women were normally peripheral. The early priestesses were relegated to the role of songstresses or chantresses in the

New Kingdom Period (1550–1070 B.C.E.). In the Eighteenth Dynasty, queens held the rank of "GOD'S WIFE OF AMUN," a role that would evolve into a politically powerful role in later generations, restricted to princesses of the various dynasties.

At the same time, however, women bought and bartered items in the marketplace, sold real estate, oversaw doctor's treatments, piloted boats, and served as court-appointed executrixes of estates. They normally married only with their consent, unless they were NOME heiresses or members of the royal families. They testified as valid witnesses in court, drew up wills, and filed for divorce. In a divorce proceeding, the woman kept her dowry and was usually awarded one-third of the joint property. In the Late Period (712–332 B.C.E.) couples made prenuptial agreements. Higher-ranked women were comparatively literate and quite equal to men before the law. Daughters received shares of all inheritances and maintained personal properties.

Further reading: Arnold, Dorothea. *The Royal Women of Amarna: Images of Beauty in Ancient Egypt.* New Haven, Conn.: Yale University Press, 1996; Hawass, Zahi A. *Silent Images: Women in Pharaonic Egypt.* New York: Harry Abrams, 2000; Rowlandson, Jane, and Roger S. Bagnall, eds. *Women and Society in Greek and Roman Egypt.* Cambridge, U.K.: Cambridge University Press, 1998; Tyldesley, Joyce A. *Daughters of Isis: Women of Ancient Egypt.* London: Penguin, 1995.

Woser (fl. 15th century B.C.E.) *vizier of the Eighteenth Dynasty*
He served TUTHMOSIS III (r. 1479–1425 B.C.E.). Woser was the uncle of the famed REKHMIRÉ, who followed him in that office. Two tombs at THEBES and a shrine at GEBEL EL-SILSILEH commemorated Woser. The latter shrine had a single chamber with a statue niche at one end.

"writing from the god himself" This was a term used to denote any text that dated to the early historical periods of the nation. Such a text, having been preserved over the centuries, was deemed sacred and viewed as divine inspiration. Because of its age, the text was revered and carefully observed.

writing materials *See* SCRIBE.

X

Xerxes I (d. 466 B.C.E.) *Persian king of Egypt of the Twenty-seventh Dynasty*

Xerxes I reigned over Egypt from 486 B.C.E. until his death, but he never visited the Nile personally. He was the son of DARIUS I and Queen Atossa, and he completed the city of Persepolis, a site that his father had begun as a capital. He also put down rebellions in the Persian Empire.

The Egyptians recorded Xerxes as a "criminal" after he crushed a revolt on the Nile in his second year, using the military units and commanders on the Nile. Xerxes also forced the Egyptian fleet to punish the Greeks at SALAMIS and instituted his son ACHAEMENES as satrap of Egypt. Xerxes was murdered with his son Crown Prince Darius in his own court and was succeeded by ARTAXERXES I, his son by Queen AMESTRIS.

See also MEGABYZUS.

Xois A site in the Delta (the modern Sakha) that served as the capital of the Thirteenth Dynasty (1783–1640 B.C.E.). The Xoite rulers were limited in their powers, as the HYKSOS surrounded them and other cities raised up their own royal lines. The rulers of Xois were named in the TURIN CANON and listed by MANETHO. They were probably eliminated during the Second Intermediate Period (1640–1550 B.C.E.) and certainly removed from power when 'AHMOSE (NEBPEHTIRÉ) (r. 1550–1525 B.C.E.) ousted the Hyksos and reunited the nation.

The city of Xois was overrun by Libyan invaders from the west in the reign of RAMESSES III (1194–1163 B.C.E.). He mounted a large military force and repelled the MESHWESH, the dominating Libyan clan, and their allies from the area in order to free the city and safeguard the entire Delta.

Xerxes I (d. 466 B.C.E.), Persian emperor and king of Egypt in the Twenty-seventh Dynasty *(© The Art Gallery Collection / Alamy)*

Yakoba'am (fl. 16th century B.C.E.) *ruler of the Hyksos Sixteenth Dynasty*
He was a founder of a line of HYKSOS kings (ca. 1640–1532 B.C.E.), a minor Asiatic group serving as contemporaries, or possibly as vassals of the Great Hyksos of the Fifteenth Dynasty at AVARIS. SCARABS bearing Yakoba'am's name were discovered in northern Egypt and in Palestine.

Yam This was a region of NUBIA (modern Sudan) south of ASWAN. As early as the Sixth Dynasty (2323–2150 B.C.E.), the Egyptians were trading with this area. An official of that dynasty named HARKHUF, who served PEPI II (r. 2246–2152 B.C.E.), was reported as having visited Yam.

Yanhamu (fl. 14th century B.C.E.) *Egyptian governor of Palestine in the 'Amarna Period*
He served in the reign of AKHENATEN (1353–1335 B.C.E.). Yanhamu was probably a Canaanite appointed to the office by Akhenaten. His correspondence was discovered in the 'AMARNA LETTERS, as he reported events to the Egyptian capital and relayed the growing elements of unrest in the region. Yanamu reported that he received a letter from Mut-ba'la, the prince of Pella, a former site in modern Jordan. The vassal was protesting his innocence in the ongoing territorial disputes in the area. Yanhamu and other dignitaries of Egypt's imperial holdings were not supplied with sufficient troops or provisions during this reign, resulting in a loss of vassal states and conquered domains.

Yaqub-Hor (Mer-user-ré) (fl. 16th century B.C.E.) *ruler of the Fifteenth Dynasty, called the Great Hyksos*
Yaqub-Hor was the successor of either Sheshi or SALITIS and reportedly reigned 18 years. Few details about his reign have survived.

Yerdjet A people of NUBIA (modern Sudan), residing near the second cataract of the Nile, the Yerdjet began paying tribute to Egypt as early as the Sixth Dynasty (2323–2150 B.C.E.). Many nomadic groups migrated to the Nile area to be protected by the Egyptian garrisons. Others, having established residence long before, had to accept the occupation of their lands.

Yewelot (fl. 10th century B.C.E.) *royal prince of the Twenty-second Dynasty*
He was the son of OSORKON I (r. 924–909 B.C.E.) and probably Queen KAROMANA (2). Yewelot served as the high priest of AMUN at THEBES. He wrote a decree concerning the distribution of his property, and this document provides details of the period.

Yuia *See* YUYA.

Yuny (fl. 13th century B.C.E.) *aristocratic official of the Nineteenth Dynasty*
Yuny served RAMESSES II (r. 1290–1224 B.C.E.) as the chief scribe of the court. His tomb at DEIR EL-DURUNKA, south of ASSIUT, has reliefs that depict Yuny as a hereditary prince and count in his nome. A life-sized statue of him was found in his tomb.

Yuti (fl. 14th century B.C.E.) *sculptor of the Eighteenth Dynasty*
Yuti served AKHENATEN (r. 1353–1335 B.C.E.) as one of the royal sculptors of 'AMARNA, the capital. A panel in the tomb of Huya, another official of 'Amarna, depicts Yuti painting a statue of BAKETAMUN, the sister of Akhenaten, who assumed the name Baketaten while living with her brother. Yuti is shown painting with his left hand.

Yuya and Thuya (Yuia and Tuiya) (fl. 14th century B.C.E.) *officials in the Eighteenth Dynasty, the parents of Queen Tiye*

Tiye (1) was the consort of AMENHOTE III (r. 1391–1353 B.C.E.). Yuya was the Master of Horse for the royal cavalry, a general officer of chariot units. He and Thuya were not Egyptians but came from the Hurrian region of modern Syria. He also served as prophet of the god MIN and as a supervisor of the oxen of Min in AKHMIN. Thuya was the supervisor of the harem of Mi'am and the harem of AMUN. She was also the mistress of robes in the temple of Min.

Their tomb was elaborately prepared, and their mummies were beautifully embalmed. An OSIRIS BED was included in their funerary regalia. This gravesite was in the VALLEY OF THE KINGS, a unique privilege, and it contained one of the most lavish displays of mortuary furnishings ever uncovered. Both beautifully embalmed mummies were in gilded frameworks. Yuya was called "the god's father," a court title of respect.

Z

Zanakht *See* NEBKA.

Zannanza (fl. 14th century B.C.E.) *ill-fated prince of the Hittites*
The son of the Hittite king SUPPILULIUMAS I (d. ca. 1325 B.C.E.), he was sent to Egypt in response to the marriage offer made by Queen ANKHESENA-MON, the daughter of AKHENATEN and the widow of TUT'ANKHAMUN (r. 1333–1323 B.C.E.). Ankhesenamon offered her throne to the HITTITES if they would send a prince to wed her. Prince Zannanza made the journey but was killed at the border, probably by command of HOREMHAB (r. 1319–1307 B.C.E.), then a general of the armies. This event impacted on Egypt's relations with the Hittites in future reigns and brought about the death of Suppiluliumas I.

Zawiet el-Amwat It was a site on the eastern shore of the Nile, north of BENI HASAN, that served as an early necropolis. The site was called "the Place of the Dead." A step pyramid from the Third Dynasty (2649–2575 B.C.E.), trapezoid in design and covered with masonry, was discovered there. There are also 19 tombs on the site associated with HEBENU (modern Kom el-Ahmar) in the Oryx nome. Six of these tombs date to the Old Kingdom Period (2575–2134 B.C.E.). Also present is the Eighteenth Dynasty (1550–1307 B.C.E.) tomb of Nefersekheru.

Zawiet el-Aryan This is a site south of GIZA, on the edge of the desert, containing two pyramids and a tomb dating probably to the Third Dynasty (2649–2575 B.C.E.). The northern pyramidal monument, now listed as "the Unfinished Pyramid," may have been built by NEBKA (r. 2649–2630 B.C.E.), and it is called "Nebka is a Star." The lavish decorations of the monument, however, lead to a belief that it was actually constructed in a later reign. The substructure and enclosing wall were started and then abandoned. The second monument is called the Layer Pyramid and was built out of small stone blocks. The tomb nearby contained eight stone bowls inscribed with seals of KHA'BA (r. 2603–2599 B.C.E.), and it is believed that this was his mortuary monument.

Zenodotus (fl. ca. 280 B.C.E.) *first director of the Library of Alexandria*
He was appointed director of the LIBRARY OF ALEXANDRIA for life by PTOLEMY I SOTER (r. 304–284 B.C.E.). Zenodotus was from Ephesus, in modern Turkey, and he was invited to Egypt where he became the tutor to PTOLEMY II PHILADELPHUS.

Zenon (fl. third century B.C.E.) *Carian Greek serving Egypt in the Ptolemaic Period*
He served PTOLEMY II PHILADELPHUS (r. 285–246 B.C.E.). Zenon was an assistant to the treasurer Apollonius, who was the finance minister for the throne and who also maintained a vast estate at a site in the FAIYUM region. Zenon lived beside the Faiyum and managed Apollonius's estates in the region. A document concerning a complex irrigation system in use in this area has survived; it indicates that dikes and canals provided water to the fields.

Although he was based near the Faiyum, Zenon also traveled to ALEXANDRIA, Palestine, and Syria. His archives, depicting his historical period in Egypt in detail, have survived.

Zerukha This was the site called MALKATA on the western shore of THEBES. AMENHOTEP III (r. 1391–1353 B.C.E.) built his vast pleasure palaces and shrines at Malkata, and an artificial lake was created on the site.

APPENDIX: HOW TO STUDY ANCIENT EGYPT

Many students of ancient Egypt find their area of research truly rewarding. A unique civilization that once ruled from the modern city of Khartoum in the Sudan to the Euphrates River, its vestiges convey the impression that the ancient Egyptians understood their destiny on Earth. They also seem to have looked forward to enjoying themselves beyond the grave, a fact that colored and shaped their generally optimistic outlook on life.

The history of ancient Egypt as an independent nation ended in 30 B.C.E. with the suicide of Cleopatra VII. Egypt went on to become a prized province of the Roman Empire and remained vigorous because of its natural resources and magnificent cities. When Rome collapsed in the fifth century, however, interest in pharaonic Egypt waned. Year after year the deserts on either side of that fertile strip of land gradually reclaimed the sites of ancient Egypt. Entire temples, such as Abu Simbel and Karnak, were buried under the sands, with their treasures hidden away from thieves or plunderers. The people of the Nile Valley and the outside world forgot about the gods and the pharaohs, although a few continued to be tantalized by ancient legends.

Since the 19th century, however, the study of ancient Egypt's art, documents, temples, tombs, and other monuments and sites has evolved into a unique and popular field of archaeology. Men and women of many nations have dedicated their lives to this field and, in the process, have recovered, restored, and revealed centuries of splendor on the Nile River.

There are several ways of learning about the history of ancient Egypt, and the student will appreciate the wide number of disciplines that are involved. The field most associated with ancient Egypt is archaeology, and Egyptology is tied closely to the archaeological study of Egypt's past. Connected to archaeological study are the fields of art history and the historical study of religion, literature, war, and even science and engineering. Linguistic studies are also crucial to deciphering the hiero-glyphs and other scripts of ancient Egypt that are found on the temple walls or carved on artifacts. The study of language was vital in opening up ancient Egypt to the rest of the world, as demonstrated by the translation of the Rosetta Stone, which was discovered during Napoleon Bonaparte's campaign in Egypt at the end of the 18th century. The different academic disciplines look at the same evidence and artifacts—such as temples, pyramids, mummies, graves, papyri, and stelae—but see them through the lenses of their specializations. Scholars from multiple disciplines work together at each site to develop a comprehensive picture of the purpose and details of life at the site, and how it fit into wider Egypt at the time.

EGYPTOLOGY AND HISTORIOGRAPHY IN THE ANCIENT WORLD

Egyptian and Classical sources remain a vital area of study for historians and archaeologists engaged in expanding knowledge of ancient Egypt. The works of these writers and early historians provide crucial details about events and their sequence, the personalities of those who reigned, and the context in which they ruled. The study of these sources is a key starting point for any investigation into ancient Egypt, and any credible Egyptologist will rely on them extensively for research and fieldwork.

Egyptian Sources

The first Egyptologist was a royal prince of Egypt, a son of Ramesses II (Ramesses the Great) (r. 1290–1224 B.C.E.) and heir to the throne after the deaths of his three older brothers. His name was Kha'emweset, and he served as the high priest of the temple of the god Ptah in Heliopolis (On). The great monuments of Egypt were already relics of the past in Kha'emweset's era. He studied them and directed workers to repair and restore such works of art and devotion. Kha'emweset did not outlive his royal father.

While ancient Egyptians did not write a history of the nation, they did keep copious day-to-day records of activities and events in the courts of the pharaoh. During the Predynastic Period (before 3000 B.C.E.), groups of scribes resided in the palaces of what is now known as Dynasty 0. Fragments of the Palermo Stone—a stela 17 inches high and 9 ¾ inches wide and so named because pieces are in the Regional Archaeological Museum in Palermo, Italy—provide dynasty-by-dynasty and Predynastic Period data. Smaller fragments are in the Museum of Egyptian Antiquities in Cairo, Egypt, and in the Petrie Museum of University College in London. On the Palermo Stone, rulers kept records of when they performed religious ceremonies and presided over festivals, announced the level of Nile waters expected in the annual flood, gave an account of taxes collected, or recorded when an heir to the throne was born. The names of the rulers are not included with these events, but a king list catalogs the rulers from the First Dynasty through the Fifth Dynasty. Other king lists, such as those of Ramesses II and Manetho and the one at Abydos, are found in tombs with the cartouches of dead kings, engraved on the walls, or preserved on papyri. These are valuable to Egyptologists for determining the chronologies of kings, family genealogies, and patterns of succession.

Classical Accounts

Diodorus Siculus (fl. first century B.C.E.)   Diodorus Siculus, one of the foremost historians of Greece, visited Egypt ca. 60–59 B.C.E. He wrote the *Bibliotheca historica,* a history of the world from the beginning to the time of Julius Caesar. The history was contained in 40 volumes and included compilations of lost authors. Egyptian history was the basis of part of the work, and continual events as well as accounts of the Nile myths and mummification processes were detailed. His visit to the Nile Valley was much encouraged by the Ptolemies. Scholars today recognize that he borrowed extensively from Hectaeus for his history, but he also did original research on religious ceremonies, temples, events, and the Nile River. He memorably expressed his belief that Egyptians were so devout that the common people would resort to cannibalism in times of famine rather than consume sacred animals.

Hectaeus of Aldera (fl. ca. 300 B.C.E.)   Hectaeus was a Greek historian who in the reign of Ptolemy I Soter (r. 304–284 B.C.E.) authored a history of Egypt. Hectaeus traveled on the Nile and spent time at Thebes (modern Luxor). There he visited the Ramasseum of Ramesses II (r. 1290–1224 B.C.E.). The historian called Ramesses II by the name Ozymandias in a famous lament. Diodorus Siculus reportedly borrowed extensively from the work of Hectaeus.

Herodotus (d. c. 430 B.C.E.)   Herodotus, a Greek historian, is regarded as the "Father of History." His famous nine-volume work, *The Histories,* includes details about Egyptian life and customs in the second book. He toured the Nile Valley around 450 B.C.E., visiting cities and going as far south as Aswan and the Elephantine Island, the gateway to Nubia (modern Sudan). Herodotus talked to the priests of the various deity cults who, reportedly, spent hours explaining their deities, rituals, and devotions. Herodotus focused his research on Egyptian temples, rituals, and mummification processes. He described the Egyptians as the most religious human beings in the world.

Herodotus has been critiqued harshly by scholars for his tendency to incorporate myths and fanciful tales in his historical accounts. For these reasons, he has been dubbed by his critics the "Father of Lies." Nevertheless, where his claims regarding Egypt are concerned, modern archaeology has confirmed at least some of his observations.

Josephus, Flavius (ca. 37–ca. 100)   Flavius Josephus is the most famous Jewish historical writer of the Roman imperial era. He is best known as the author of two very useful and important histories of his own people, *Jewish Antiquities* and *The Jewish War. Antiquities* covered Jewish history from the earliest times to 66 and the start of the rebellion. Organized into 20 books, it was completed in 93 or 94. His *Jewish War* was actually two books in one, the first a brief chronicle of events from about 170 B.C.E. to 66 C.E. and the second a long, precise analysis of the war from 66 to 73. In his *Antiquities,* Josephus covered a number of aspects of Egyptian history as they related to the early history of the Jewish people, including the role of Abraham (such as the claim that Abraham taught the Egyptians science) and Moses. Josephus also was important in being perhaps the first ancient writer to mention the Egyptian historian Manetho, referring to him in his polemic *Contra Apionem* (Against Apion). While hostile to Manetho, Josephus copied Manetho's king lists, helping to preserve the chronology of Egypt's rulers.

Manetho (fl. third century B.C.E.)   Manetho was an Egyptian historian of the Ptolemaic Period. A priest at Heliopolis (On), now a suburb of modern Cairo, he served in the reign of Ptolemy II Philadelphus (r. 285–246 B.C.E.). Manetho's history of Egypt, *Aegypticae,* written in Greek, is only found in fragments, but he was quoted extensively by his contemporaries. Extracts of his work are also preserved in the writings of Flavius Josephus. His work listed some 30 dynasties over the centuries, and he appears to have researched the rise of the Hyksos invaders in the Second Intermediate Period (1640–1550 B.C.E.), calling them the Hikau-Khoswet, the "Horse Princes." Manetho was a prolific author, writing seven other books. The Ptolemies promoted historical perspectives as part of their wider effort to attach their own Greek heritage to the much older history of Egyptian pharaonic rule. Manetho remains the most comprehensive ancient source for the sequence of rulers and dynasties.

Plutarch (before 50–after 120) A Greek historian, writer, and one of the most popular and widely read authors of the ancient world, Plutarch is best known for the *Moralia,* 78 separate compositions that include dialogues concerning the intelligence of animals and works of moral philosophy on Aristotle, Plato, Epicureanism, Stoicism, and atheism. He is also well known for the *Lives,* 23 paired biographies of Greek and Roman historical figures, which are notable for their vivid, anecdotal narrative style and historical detail. Plutarch wrote about Egypt, especially in his *Moralia,* where he included aspects of Egyptian religion and biographies of Alexander the Great and Cleopatra VII. His description of Isis and Horus influenced subsequent images of the Egyptian deities. It is unclear where he found his source material. He made at least one visit to Egypt and also clearly relied on large amounts of available sources, including those by Herodotus, Diodorus Siculus, and Manetho. He likewise found the Egyptian priests a useful source especially as Egyptian deities were popular in some regions of the Hellenistic world, including parts of Asia Minor and Rome. While his writings include numerous small errors, Plutarch is still much read by Egyptologists.

Strabo (fl. late first century B.C.E.) A famed geographer, the Greek Strabo was also one of the foremost travelers in the Roman world. He visited numerous countries and provinces and was a friend of Aelius Gallus, the prefect of Egypt, an association that afforded him the opportunity to study Egypt in some detail. Strabo wrote the vast historical work *Historical Sketches* in 43 books, which covered the history of Rome from 146 B.C.E. probably to the fall of Egypt in 30 B.C.E. Unlike his 17 books on geography, *Geographia,* which are extant in their entirety (minus book seven, which is in existence only as an epitome), none of the 42 volumes of *Historical Sketches* have survived

Strabo focused the 17th book of his *Geographia* on Egypt. He described the Nile and various sites, as well as the Nilometer. Strabo left a vivid account of Egyptian festivals even as he noted one of the most significant realities of the Egyptian sites: Inexorably, they were being buried beneath the encroaching sands of the desert. Nevertheless, he left an invaluable record for future archaeologists, so much so that 19th-century Egyptologist François Auguste Ferdinand Mariette relied on Strabo in his rediscovery of the remarkable sarcophagi of the Apis bulls at Saqqara in 1851.

MODERN EGYPTOLOGY

The historians of the ancient world wrote about Egypt, but after the Arab conquest of Egypt in the seventh century there was little interest in Egypt's ancient past. This situation changed dramatically in 1798 when Napoleon Bonaparte invaded Egypt as part of his wider campaign to destroy Britain's overseas empire. He brought with him thousands of soldiers, but he was also accompanied by a group of archaeologists, artists, geologists, and scholars. A confrontation with Lord Nelson and the British navy stranded Napoleon in Egypt for a time, and the French artists and scholars set out across Egypt and uncovered spectacular art and architecture. They painted what they saw, sketching tombs and temples and trying to solve the riddle of the ancient Egyptian hieroglyphs.

Napoleon's experts studied the flora and fauna of Egypt, measured the Great Pyramid at Giza, and wandered through the Valley of the Kings at Thebes (modern Luxor). Upon returning to Europe these findings were collected in the *Description de l'Égypte,* which was published in many volumes. The magnificent renderings of the splendors of the Nile Valley caused a lasting stir throughout Europe.

The most valued artifact recovered was the Rosetta Stone, a slab of black basalt on which are engraved ancient hieroglyphs alongside Greek text and a cursive script from the Late Period. It held the answers to the written language of ancient Egypt. This valuable artifact was ceded by Napoleon to the British in the Treaty of Alexandria in 1801 and taken to the British Museum in London. As scholars realized that this stone was the key to understanding the hieroglyphs of ancient Egypt, many began competing to decipher the messages on the basalt slab.

With the discovery of the Rosetta Stone, a new era had begun. Europe was suddenly made aware of ancient Egypt, and the deciphering of the hieroglyphs helped launch the field of modern Egyptology. Explorers from Europe (such as the German Karl Lepsius) mapped out the sites and helped make the first preliminary excavations. The labors of the first Egyptologists paved the way for the gradual professionalization of the field. Formal digs, the use of scientific methods, and the careful preservation of the artifacts discovered on the sites all helped define the field of archaeology today. Much as today, scholars from different countries (such as England, France, and Italy) made contributions to the field, assisted by the dynasty of Muhammad Ali (whose members ruled Egypt as the nominal representatives of the Ottoman Turks), who decided to open Egypt to the West. Excavation projects survived the political upheaval of the late 19th and early 20th centuries and the achievement of Egyptian independence in 1923.

Notable in the history of Egyptology has been the Supreme Council of Antiquities, which was established in 1859 under the title Department of Antiquities. Its one purpose has been to provide some element of control and order over the many archaeological digs being conducted across Egypt and to prevent the looting of the country's artifacts. The early heads of the department were Europeans, but over time Egyptians assumed the directorship, and they represented Egypt's commitment to safeguard the past. The department holds the exclusive authority to grant permission to dig or restore Egyptian archaeological sites and monuments. Non-Egyptian archaeologists must report their findings to the council, and failure to do so has led to the expulsion of some archaeologists from the country. The council is also actively engaged in recovering stolen artifacts and returning them to Egypt. This has included an effort to bring back famous pieces to Egypt, including the Rosetta Stone and a bust of Nefertiti. The importance of Egyptian artifacts is obvious. It is estimated that 78 percent of the world's ancient artifacts are in Egypt, and the country remains an active center for archaeological work. One of the most remarkable in recent years, for example, is the Theban Mapping Project, which began in 1978 and is working toward a comprehensive database of Thebes. New discoveries are made every month in other parts of Egypt, from new tombs and mummies to carvings in distant spots in the deserts on both sides of the Nile.

Notable Historians and Archaeologists
Giovanni Belzoni (1778–1823) Giovanni Belzoni, an Italian from Venice, gave up a circus career to help construct irrigation equipment in Cairo in 1814. He was hired by the antiquities collector Henry Salt, the British consul general of Egypt, and, while famed as a flamboyant character, he proved a hardworking explorer of Egyptian antiquities.

Belzoni earned lasting fame for his work in removing the massive bust of Ramesses II from the Ramesseum and supervising its transport to England. (It is currently housed in the British Museum as one of the museum's greatest possessions.) He later opened the tomb of Seti I, made investigations at the temple of Edfu and the temple at Abu Simbel, excavated at Karnak, and became one of the first Western visitors in the second pyramid of Giza and the oasis of Bahariya. After his return to England, he authored several books on his discoveries, including *Narrative of the Operations and Recent Discoveries within the Pyramids, Temples, Tombs and Excavations in Egypt and Nubia.*

Belzoni used his skills as a showman to promote the romance and mystery of ancient Egypt to the English and hence across Europe. He made a model of the tomb of Seti I, which was staged with great flourish at the Egyptian Hall in Piccadilly, London; in 1822 he had a similar exhibition in Paris. He died in Africa while on a new set of adventures and travels.

Howard Carter (1874–1939) Howard Carter was an English archaeologist who earned international fame for his discovery in 1922 of the tomb of Tut'ankhamun. Arriving in Egypt at the age of 17 with the support of the Egypt Exploration Fund, he served under such notable archaeologists as Flinders Petrie and Gaston Maspero.

In 1899 he was named the first chief inspector for the British government's Egyptian antiquities department. In this post he was in charge of various excavations in Thebes but resigned in 1905 after a controversy involving local Egyptian authorities and French tourists.

In 1908 Carter was hired by English aristocrat George Herbert, more widely known as Lord Carnarvon, to supervise his planned excavations in Egypt, which included digs in the Valley of the Kings. Carter brought a level of professionalism and exacting research to the projects that climaxed dramatically on November 26, 1922, with the discovery of King Tut'ankhamun's tomb. The tomb chamber was penetrated on February 16, 1923, and the world sat in astonishment at the sheer scale of the treasures. Carter became overnight the most famous archaeologist in history. He undertook a tour of the United States in 1924, during which he delivered a series of wildly popular lectures. The full excavation of the tomb was not completed until 1932; Carter died seven years later in London, England.

Jean-François Champollion (1790–1832) Jean-François Champollion, a Frenchman versed in ancient languages, including Coptic, and trained at the Collège de France in Paris, pieced together the fragments of languages displayed on the Rosetta Stone. Some scholars believe that Egyptology began on September 22, 1822, the day Champollion announced his findings to the Paris Acadèmie des Inscriptions et Belles-Lettres. His announcement became famous as the "Lettre à M. Dosier." In 1824 Champollion issued *Précis du système hiéroglyphique des anciens Égyptiens* (The hieroglyphic system of the ancient Egyptians). Aided by King Charles of France and Duke Leopold of Tuscany, Champollion went to Egypt in 1828. He was accompanied by Ipolito Rosellini (1800–1843), who published *The Monuments of Ancient Egypt and Nubia.*

Amelia Edwards (1891–1892) Amelia Edwards was an English journalist, traveler, and Egyptologist. She visited Egypt with friends in 1873 and fell in love with the country. Her tour included a journey to Khartoum in modern Sudan. A popular author and illustrator, she founded the Egyptian Exploration Fund and established a chair in Egyptology at University College, London, naming Flinders Petrie as the first scholar to hold the chair.

Zahi Hawass (1947–   ) Zahi Hawass is the secretary general of Egypt's Supreme Council of Antiquities. He is one of the most important modern figures in preserving the abundant antiquities of ancient Egypt while making the wider world better aware of their significance. Hawass has also been active in encouraging governments and museums around the world to return ancient Egyptian artifacts to their rightful home in Egypt.

A native of Damietta, Egypt, he earned a doctorate in Egyptology from the University of Pennsylvania (where he was a Fulbright fellow). He then taught at the American University in Cairo and the University of California, Los Angeles (UCLA). Returning to Egypt, he was appointed chief inspector of antiquities for the Giza Pyramids and then named in 2002 the secretary general of Egypt's Supreme Council of Antiquities. In 2009 he was appointed vice minister of culture by then-president Hosni Mubarak. During the upheaval in Egypt in early 2011, he was appointed minister of antiquities, a new post in the Egyptian cabinet, but he resigned in early March 2011. He was soon renamed to the post by Prime Minister Essam Sharaf. Hawass subsequently retired in July 2011 after it was made clear to him by Egyptian authorities that he would not be allowed to remain in his position owing to the political changes in the country. His blog is widely read by archaeologists, both professional and amateur, all over the world.

François Auguste Ferdinand Mariette (1821–1881) François Auguste Ferdinand Mariette was a French explorer, archaeologist, and Egyptologist best known for his extensive work in preserving the great antiquities of Egypt through the first of the Egyptian museums. Skilled in hieroglyphs (he taught himself most of what he learned) and Egyptian history, he was sent in 1850 by the Louvre Museum in Paris to Cairo to purchase Coptic, Arabic, and Syriac manuscripts. His first major discovery was at Saqqara, where he found a vast treasury of statues and remains. These were excavated over the next several years, despite the hostility of other European archaeologists. Within a short time, he was sending antiquities to France, but he also took part in the agreement between the Louvre and the Egyptian authorities to allow half of the discovered pieces to remain in Egyptian hands.

In 1858 Mariette was named to the new post of conservator of Egyptian monuments by Ismail Pasha (the Ottoman governor of Egypt) and starting in 1863 worked to establish a museum in Cairo to house the increasing number of antiquities and to help prevent the booming business in illegal trafficking of statues, Egyptian art, and mummified remains. He gave the rest of his life to archaeology and excavations and left his mark on a host of sites throughout Egypt, including Memphis, Meidum, Abydos, Thebes, Dendera, Edfu, Karnak, and even parts of the Sudan and the area around the Great Sphinx at Giza.

Such was the esteem granted to him and his work by the Egyptian authorities that he was given a host of honors in his lifetime, including the Ottoman rank of pasha. He was buried in a sarcophagus that was given a place of honor in the garden of the Egyptian Museum. In an interesting side story, in 1869 he was commissioned by the Ismail pasha to compose the plot for an opera. It eventually was used as the plot of the famed opera *Aida* by Giuseppe Verdi.

Gaston Maspero (1846–1916)   Gaston Maspero was a French Egyptologist and the successor to Auguste Mariette as head of the Egyptian antiquities office in Cairo, a position of great importance in preserving the archaeological legacy of Egypt. A native of Paris, he studied at the École Normale, where he met Auguste Mariette, for whom he accomplished the remarkable feat of translating several hieroglyphic texts. After work in Peru, he went to Egypt in 1880 as head of an archaeological expedition and succeeded Mariette in 1881. In this position Maspero continued the legacy of excavations, especially at Deir el-Bahri, Saqqara, Luxor, and Giza, including the site surrounding the Great Sphinx. He also introduced the innovation of charging the growing number of tourists to visit the sites of ancient Egypt and worked to curb the rampant problems of stolen and plundered antiquities being sold to treasure seekers.

In 1886 he left Egypt to teach in Paris, but he returned to the post in 1899. He oversaw the continued growth and development of the Egyptian Museum (then called the Bulak Museum). Among the young and promising staff members was Howard Carter, who helped discover the tomb of Tut'ankhamun. His writings included the monumental *Histoire ancienne des peuples de l'Orient classique* (History of the Ancient Peoples of the Classic East) and *Études de mythologie et d'archéologie Égyptiennes* (Studies of Egyptian mythology and archaeology).

William Matthew Flinders Petrie (1854–1942) William Matthew Flinders Petrie was an English archaeologist who was responsible for establishing many of the key methods and practices of Egyptology. For his achievement, he has been called the "Father of Modern Egyptology." After early training in archaeology (including a study of Stonehenge), he arrived in Egypt in 1880 and performed the first major archaeological study of the Giza plateau. His work there remains the foundation for almost all of the studies that followed.

Returning to England, he met Amelia Edwards, who subsequently became one of his greatest supporters and who helped secure his post as chair in Egyptology that she established at University College in London. He returned to Egypt in 1884 and made excavations at Tanis and Faiyum. He went to Palestine in 1890 but returned to Egypt the next year to work at the temple of Aten at 'Amarna. In 1896 he made the immensely important discovery of the Merneptah, or "Israel," stela at Luxor that includes the first mention of Israel in any Egyptian text. Starting in 1926, he focused chiefly on Palestine. He retired to Jerusalem in 1933 with his wife, taking residence at the British School of Archaeology. He died in Jerusalem.

Petrie left a lasting legacy for Egyptologists by his great stress on detailed and accurate research and study of sites and remains; he also helped to train many of the Egyptologists who followed him and who helped bring Egyptian archaeological studies into the modern era. One of his most famous students was Howard Carter, who discovered the tomb of Tut'ankhamun.

John Gardner Wilkinson (d. 1875) John Gardner Wilkinson was born in England, went to Egypt in 1821, and remained there for 12 years. He excavated at Karnak in modern Luxor and sailed on the Nile all the way to the fourth cataract in modern Sudan. He also mapped 'Amarna. Wilkinson provided leadership in the first stages of British efforts in Egyptology.

GUIDANCE FOR THE STUDENT

The ancient Egyptians maintained and fostered a vibrant civilization for more than 3,000 years, and studying this civilization can be immensely rewarding. The best starting place for research are the primary documents that were for so long a riddle to scholars—until the discovery of the Rosetta Stone unlocked the secrets of hieroglyphs. From here, the student can progress to the museums, collections, and traveling exhibits around the world that house artifacts of ancient Egypt, and to the secondary sources, the scholarly literature on the subject written over the centuries.

Primary Documents

Egyptian primary sources are more complicated for the student of ancient Egypt than those of other cultures and civilizations because of the sheer length of Egyptian history and the many different kinds of materials available. Still, the translations of hieroglyphs and the preservation of so many of the original decrees and writings of the ancient Egyptians offer a treasury of knowledge that should not be missed. There are several types of documentation, including papyri, stelae, wall reliefs, and crafts. These historical documents have been steadily recovered and translated by teams of archaeologists and Egyptologists.

The ancient crafts open the door to the history of Egypt, starting in the ancient city of Hierakonpolis, the first residence of Scorpion I (ca. 3000 B.C.E.). He was the warrior-king who started the unification of Egypt, followed by Narmer and then by Aha (Menes), who founded the nation and the capital of Memphis in 2920 B.C.E. Several palettes (flat stone receptacles possibly used for cosmetics) and maceheads (cylindrical coverings that were attached to a wooden or metal staff and served as early weapons) fashioned in Hierakonpolis document the unification of Egypt and are thus considered historic documents. The most famous palette is the Narmer Palette, which depicts Narmer after his victory in the Delta.

The documents made of papyrus in the Nile Valley hold within them biographies of individuals, announcements of events, or records of judicial affairs, but in many cases also reveal personalities, politics, religious beliefs, and scientific data. The beginnings of the great medical profession in Egypt are clearly documented in some papyri, which sometimes refer to other, older papyri lost over the centuries. The Great Harris Papyrus carefully details the reign and achievements of Ramesses III (r. 1194–1163 B.C.E.), including his possible assassination by plotters in his own harem. Papyri accounts that describe the chaos and tragedies in the two Intermediate Periods (2134–2040 B.C.E. and 1640–1550 B.C.E.) were considered in the past to be somewhat embellished. New studies, however, indicate that events described in the first episode, when a channel of the Nile dried up, leaving prosperous communities stranded in arid wildernesses, were accurate. Panicked, the Egyptian commoners blamed the hereditary princes and lords of their nomes, or provinces, and attacked them. The papyri portray a national tragedy in clear and vivid images.

Another source of documentation is the relief, or inscription, installed in the walls of a temple or tomb. Every official, public servant, or court figure had his appointments, titles, and experiences inscribed on his tomb wall. The most informative reliefs and inscriptions made at the beginning of the New Kingdom (1550–1070 B.C.E.) were discovered in the tombs of 'Ahmose Pen-Nekheket and 'Ahmose, son of Ta'o II. These Egyptians were serving in the army of 'Ahmose (Nebpehtiré) (r. 1550–1525 B.C.E.), the Theban who routed the Hyksos, chasing them out of Egypt and all the way to modern Syria. Their tombs' walls clearly describe 'Ahmose's campaigns. The Book of the Dead, painted in glowing images or in simple figures, decorated the walls of royal burials. This book served as the guide for the deceased into Tuat, or the Underworld, and it clearly displayed the terrors that awaited the unworthy. For Egyptologists it reveals the fundamental beliefs of the Egyptians concerning eternity.

It was a stela, a smooth standing stone with a rounded head, that opened the door to understanding the Egyptian hieroglyphs. The Rosetta Stone, worn and partially broken, carried the announcement of Ptolemy V Epiphanes (r. 205–180 B.C.E.) in hieroglyphs and demotic script. The message was also inscribed in Greek, which made it possible for Jean-François Champollion and others to take on the task of translating the words and understanding the ancient Egyptian language.

Students are assisted considerably in becoming familiar with primary documents through the work of such scholars as Sir E. A. Wallis Budge (1857–1934) and James Henry Breasted (1865–1935), both of whom wrote volumes about the language of Egypt and the occult, spiritual, and ritual aspects of ancient Egyptian life. Breasted also copied hieroglyphs and made translations of ancient proclamations in tombs, temples, and stelae. Their work aided the understanding of the profound spiritual treasury of the people of the Nile.

The study of primary documents raises the question as to whether a student should take the time to master the hieroglyphs. The answer depends on how much time one plans to devote to the study of ancient Egypt, or even if one is thinking of becoming an Egyptologist. Just as the serious study of ancient Rome or Greece demands a passing familiarity with Latin or Greek, so too should someone committed to the professional study of ancient Egypt consider mastering the hieroglyphs. Fortunately, today there are a number of guidebooks for learning hieroglyphs, so the task is simpler than in the past. The time taken to study ancient Egyptian language will be beneficial in unlocking further the minds and literary styles of the ancient Egyptian people. Put simply, the greater access one has to the writings, culture, and personalities of the people of the past, the deeper one's knowledge will become.

Museums and Exhibits

Local museums and displays in cities across the world have Egyptian sections that house stunning artifacts, some of displays even including portions of actual temples, statues, stelae, or tombs recovered from the past. These displays can help deepen our understanding of history by allowing us to discover firsthand what ancient Egyptians cherished. Among the greatest museums for studying Ancient Egypt are:

The National Museums in Berlin: http://www.smb.spk-berlin.de/smb/sammlungen/details.php?lang=en&objectId=2

The British Museum: http://www.britishmuseum.org/

Egyptian Museum: http://egyptsites.wordpress.com/2009/03/01/cairo-museum-of-egyptian-antiquities/

The Louvre Museum: http://www.louvre.fr/

Luxor Museum: http://www.touregypt.net/luxormuseum.htm

The Metropolitan Museum of Art: http://www.metmuseum.org/works_of_art/egyptian_art

The Oriental Institute of the University of Chicago: http://oi.uchicago.edu/museum/

The Petrie Museum of Egyptian Archaeology: http://www.ucl.ac.uk/museums/petrie

Vatican Museums: http://mv.vatican.va/3_EN/pages/MEZ/MEZ_Main.html

Secondary Sources

The study of secondary sources—histories, architectural studies, and biographies—brings its own set of requirements. There are literally thousands of new books every decade on the topic of ancient Egypt. Many are now considered classics in the field, while new volumes examine some specific aspects of Egyptian civilization, a particular dynasty or pharaoh, or the full scope of Egyptian history from a perspective never examined before. Choosing which books to read or buy can be daunting.

A general history of ancient Egypt will set the stage for anyone interested in delving into the history of the Nile civilization. Quite a few of these general histories are listed in the Selected Bibliography at the end of this encyclopedia. Certain periods, naturally, will become the focus of one's studies, as each individual learning about a world long past will be drawn to particular aspects. Readers will find suggested further reading lists at the end of major entries throughout the encyclopedia. Look at these as starting points for additional study.

Journals present the latest documentation about sites or persons of note. There are several respected journals, including *KMT: A Modern Journal of Ancient Egypt* and *Journal of Egyptian Archaeology*. The Internet is also an especially valuable tool today. There are literally thousands of reference points on the Web for conducting research on ancient Egypt. Naturally, some sites are better and more reliable than others, and opinions differ on the value of some over others. This brings up Wikipedia. Initially disdained by most academics, Wikipedia at this point is too omnipresent in searches to dismiss, but it is still worthwhile to make several suggestions regarding its use.

Wikipedia is edited by the users of the site, meaning that nonexperts have as much access to the creation and editing of entries as professionally trained scholars with many years of experience. Entries may include inaccurate information and reflect biases, and therefore the student must use any material from this source with the same care that he or she would any other Internet site. A very good discussion of these points can be found at the Laurence McKinley Gould Library at Carleton College in Minnesota on a site page titled "Using Wikipedia" (http://apps.carleton.edu/campus/library/for_faculty/faculty_find/wikipedia/).

There are many more sites than Wikipedia to assist in the study of Egyptian history. The following are a few that the average student might find useful. These are general, accessible, maintained, and offer a helpful series of pages regarding Egyptian history, culture, and religion. There are others, and it is expected that this list will continue to grow:

The British Museum: http://www.ancientegypt.co.uk

The Ancient Egyptian Site: http://www.ancient-egypt.org/

The Oriental Institute of the University of Chicago: http://oi.uchicago.edu/OI/MUS/ED/TRC/EGYPT/egypthome.html

The Institute of Egyptian Art and Archaeology: http://www.memphis.edu/egypt/

Internet Ancient History Sourcebook: http://www.fordham.edu/halsall/ancient/asbook04.html

Ancient Egypt Online: http://www.ancientegyptonline.org

GLOSSARY

a'akh   a spirit freed from the bonds of the flesh.

A'amu   the name given to the Asiatics, particularly the Hyksos.

A'aru   a paradise beyond the grave.

a'asha   the word for the jackal, also *auau* or *sab*.

Abaton   the Pure Mound of creation.

Abu   the name of the elephant, ivory, and Elephantine Island.

Achaean League   a confederation of Greek city-states and allies that achieved considerable prominence in the reign of Ptolemy II Philadelphus (r. 285–246 B.C.E.).

afnet   the head covering of gods and pharaohs.

Aigyptos   the Greek word that gave rise to the modern name of Egypt; it was derived from the term *Hiku-Ptah*, which denoted the city of Memphis as "the Mansion of the Soul of Ptah."

akhet (1)   the season of inundation.

akhet (2)   the symbol of the horizon.

Akh-iker-en-Ré   ancestors, termed "the excellent departed ones in Ré."

Alashya   the Egyptian name for Cyprus.

alchemy   a term derived from the ancient Egyptian skill in the working of precious metals; the word is derived from the Arabic *al-kimia,* the art of Khemet, Khem, or Kamt, which means the Black Land—Egypt.

Amenti   the mythological domain of the dead described as located spiritually in the West, considered the residence of the god Osiris; it was a luxurious paradise of lakes, trees, and flowers and was an abode of peace for all eternity for those deemed worthy of such rewards.

ames   the name for the scepter in the form of a club or mace that was used as a royal insignia in most eras; the kings maintained the insignias of ancient times and incorporated them into the newer rituals of office.

Anatolians   a people living in the lands now called Turkey; the Anatolians built many ancient cities, including Hacilar, which dates to 5400 B.C.E.

ankh   the ansate cross, the symbol of life.

Ankh-tawy or Ankh-taui   a name for old Memphis, "the Life of the Two Lands."

"appearing"   a term for the dawning of a god or the coronation or emergence of a ruler as a manifestation of a deity; the term was considered appropriate for use in the titles of barks and buildings.

aser   the name for the tamarisk tree connected to cultic traditions and to several deities who recorded personages and events.

Aswan Nilometer   a station in the temple of the goddess Satet on the Elephantine Island that served as an observation point for the rise and fall of the Nile each year; the Nilometer was actually a tubular structure with 90 steps, steeply graded and marked to allow the measurement of the river's inundation each year.

Atbara (Astaboras)   a tributary of the Nile River that enters the Nile at the fifth cataract, in Nubia (modern Sudan), bringing vast quantities of alluvium and red mud to the Nile Valley.

aut   the ancient Egyptian name for the funerary offerings for the deceased, when such offerings could be afforded by the family, or contracted before death; the priesthood maintained special groups of trained officials who offered goods to the deceased as part of mortuary rituals.

auta   the name for the cobra, the goddess Wadjet; in a striking position with a full hood displayed, this symbol was represented on the crowns of the kings in the form of the Uraeus.

awet   the ancient crook and flail, the royal symbol of the pharaohs, adopted from the god Osiris and the ancient shepherd deity Andjeti; the crook denoted the pharaoh's role as the guardian of the people of the Nile.

ba   the human or divine soul.

ba'a en pet   copper from heaven, a meteorite.

ba'ankh   the term for a "living soul," one that has reached paradise; the god Osiris was sometimes referred to as a *ba'ankh* in rituals because of his powers in the realm beyond the grave and his role as the judge of the dead.

bain-a'abtiu   souls transformed into baboons to greet the dawn.

Bakhau the mythical "Land of the Sunrise."

bay a surveying instrument used by the ancient Egyptians for determining Nile sites and for architectural planning; it gave the builders an accurate sighting on the horizon and charted the terrain, important elements in the construction of temples and shrines.

bekhenet the pylon style of gates.

Bedawi the Bedouins of the Sinai, also called *badu* or *bedwi*.

benben the pyramidal rays of the sun as a symbol.

Bennu the phoenix-like sacred bird.

berget the stone peridot.

bia the resource called hematite.

bik the falcon.

Biya the word for the ancient bee kings of the Delta region and Lower Egypt; the Bee King was called "the honey man" in some eras and was depicted wearing a red basket crown called the *deshret,* which was combined with the *hedjet,* or white war helmet of Upper Egypt, when the Two Kingdoms were united, ca. 3000 B.C.E.

booza the name of beer, also called *heneket.*

byssus the name given to fine linen products developed in certain regions in Egypt, especially in Akhmin; originally believed to be of cotton, the byssus products have been found to contain quality linen.

cenotaphs the mortuary complexes or simple tombs built to provide a probable religiously motivated burial site that remained empty; the cenotaphs contained no bodies but were ceremonial in nature.

clapper a musical instrument of Egypt, also used as a warning or signal in religious rituals, normally fashioned out of bone, metal, or wood; it was held in both hands and was fastened together, and one part was struck against the other to produce a sharp sound.

Council of Ten a unit of government for the territory of Upper Egypt, working with "the Officials of Nekhen"; this council, which had a counterpart in the Delta area of Lower Egypt, handled nome affairs and served as the crown's liaison to the *djadjet,* an assembly of nomarchs, or hereditary lords of the provinces.

crook a royal symbol, the *awet,* carried by the rulers of ancient Egypt, representing the early shepherds, the scepter had magical powers and represented traditions of the past and the government; the crook was carried with the flail, called the *nekhakha,* which represented Osiris and Min.

deben an Egyptian unit of weight, equivalent to 32 ounces or 91 grams.

desheru "the Red Ones," the Followers of Set.

deshret the red basket crown of the Delta Bee Kings.

Deshret the term for the desert lands.

djeba the reed perch used at the moment of creation.

djed a pillar associated with Osiris.

Djeseru-Djeseru the sanctuary, or Holy of Holies.

erpati hati'o the term for the nobility of the nomes, or provinces, of the nation; in some eras women inherited the rights and rank of this class.

Geswaret the name of the mythical creation site, called "the Island of Trampling."

hat the physical human heart.

heb the Egyptian term for festival.

heb-sed the royal festival commemorating three decades of rule.

hedj (1) the word for agate, also called *ka.*

hedj (2) the word for limestone.

hedj (3) the color white.

Hedjerew "the Great White One," a sacred baboon.

hedjet the white war helmet of Upper Egypt.

heka (1) the word for magical power.

heka (2) the crook carried by a pharaoh.

heker an Egyptian decoration.

hemaget the name for garnet.

hemet the word for wife, used in all social groups, royal, aristocratic, or commoner.

hemt the name for copper.

herset the name given to carnelian.

herset-hedji the name for chalcedony.

Heru-Shemsu the Followers of Horus.

hes used with purification, the name for baptism.

hesmen the name for amethyst.

Hiku-Ptah the mansion of the soul of Ptah, Memphis.

"Horus-in-the-Nest" a term used in all historical periods to designate the heirs or crown princes of each dynasty when they were proclaimed in public rituals as future rulers.

ibhety the name given to marble.

ibu the site of mortuary embalming.

Ikhemu-Seku "the Stars that Never Fail" (polar stars).

Ikhemu-Weredu "the Never Resting Stars" (planets in orbit).

Ineb-Hedj "the White Walled," Memphis.

Intiu a word used to designate the inhabitants of the Nile Valley in the Predynastic Period (before 3000 B.C.E.); the name was one of reverence, translated as "Pillar People."

irgeb the name for mica.

Iset "the Seat," associated with the goddess Isis.

isfet the word for chaos or disorder, a state abhorred by the people of the Nile Valley; *ma'at,* the social imperative of the nation, opposed *isfet* and its manifestations.

iunu the word for pillar.

ka the astral being that accompanies humans on earth and in eternity.

kapet the name for incense.

kenbet a court system of Egypt.

kenken-ur a term used to designate the "Great Cackler," the mythological cosmic layer of the cosmic egg, the Goose-goddess, Ser-t; the term was associated as well with the earth deity, Geb, who sired Osiris, Isis, Set, and Nephthys; his wife was Nut, the sky.

ketj the color yellow.

khaibit the spiritual essence freed at death.

khat an altar or table of offerings.

khatru the name of the mongoose.

khay a term meaning "to shine forth," used to describe the appearance of the pharaoh at temple ceremonies and state affairs; the word was also used to depict the sun at the dawn of creation and was associated with the concepts of horizons and the use of the royal "window of appearances."

khem the color black.

Khemet Egypt, the Black Land.

khenmet the name for jasper.

khepesh (khopresh) the sickle-shaped sword, Hyksos in origin, used by the Egyptians in military campaigns in the New Kingdom (1550–1070 B.C.E.).

khephresh the military crown, fashioned out of electrum.

khesbed the color blue.

khesbedj the name for lapis lazuli.

kite a weight unit equivalent to one-tenth of a *deben,* 3.33 ounces or 9.1 grams.

kohl the Arabic term for the ancient Egyptian cosmetic used to adorn eyes.

Kush the Egyptian word for Nubia (modern Sudan).

Layer Pyramid the modern name given to the monument erected at Zawiet el-Aryan at Giza by Kha'ba (r. 2603–2599 B.C.E.).

ma'at the system of individual serenity and common service.

ma'at kheru "True of Voice," the dead worthy of paradise.

ma'au a large cat.

magat the ladder of Osiris.

Mandet the morning bark of Ré.

Manu the mythological mountain site, called "the Land of Sunset."

mat the name for gravesite.

mat-en-Abu the name of the Aswan granite.

mefkat the name for turquoise.

mekes the royal scepter, flat at one end.

mekhemnet the name for jasper.

menat the counterweight amulet of fertility.

mentet the name for diorite.

menu-hedj the name for quartz.

menu-kem the name for obsidian.

merkhet an astral survey guide.

meska the hide of a bull, a royal symbol.

Mesu-betesht the Followers of Horus.

mesut a word for evening, actually meaning "the Time of Birth."

miw or *mau* also *mut,* the cat or kitten.

Mut-netjier "the Mother of the Gods," a term applied to Isis.

muu a dwarf, also called *nem* or *hua.*

neb an act of prostration or obeisance.

nefer a term meaning good and beautiful.

Nehet the sycamore tree.

nekhakha the flail used in royal rites.

nerau Egyptian vulture.

neshmet the name of feldspar.

netcher   a deity symbol used on temple flags.

neter   a word for a deity, translated as "power" or "strength," as well as "renewal" or "renovation."

neterit   the word for a sacred domain or a divine site, a building or a town dedicated to a particular deity or group of gods.

neter nefer   the name for the pharaoh.

noon meal   a repast called "time to perfume the mouth" by the ancient Egyptians.

nub   the name for gold; *nub nefer* if high grade.

nuheh   the word for eternity, also *shennu*.

nunu (nunn-nu)   the name for the great watery abyss that existed before the creation, this primeval chaos was the oldest entity in the world; it was the personification of *nunu*.

pa duat   a tomb chamber for the patron deity.

pat   an ancient Egyptian caste, associated with Horus.

Patuit-Taui   the name of the First Occasion, creation.

per-ankh   "the House of Life," an educational institution.

perdjem   the name for olivine.

Per-Hay   "the House of Rejoicing," at Thebes.

Per-khenret   the word for harem.

Per-Medjat   the House of Books, a library.

per-nefer   "the House of Beauty," an embalming site.

pero or *pero a'a*   the Great House, the palace.

Pert-er-Kheru   a term for "from the mouth of the god," denoting any ancient text or document or saying.

pet   the word for sky.

Piromis   true humans, artists or intellectuals.

posesh-khef   the mortuary forked instrument used to instill resurrection in the corpse.

proyet   the season of growing.

qas   the word for an embalmed body that has been wrapped in linen for burial.

Qau   the name for the ancient road leading to the porphyry quarries in the northeastern desert area in the Sinai.

Rastau   a term used in early Egyptian historical periods to designate part of the necropolis of Saqqara near Memphis.

rekhet   the lapwing bird symbol, denoting a caste of the ancient historical periods.

Rekh-nesu   a court title meaning "One Whom the King Knows."

ren   the word for name.

renpet   the regnal years of a ruler.

sia   the word for wisdom in Egypt, associated with magic and with *hu*, the word for creativity; it was part of the creation of the world, embodied in *heka*, pure magic.

speos   the Greek word for ancient Egyptian shrines dedicated to particular deities.

Tamara (Ta-Mera)   the word for "the Land of the Inundation" and the name for Egypt used by the native population.

sa-ankh   "the Waters of Life," meaning ritual waters.

sah   an individual free from the flesh.

seb   a festival.

sebi   the word for circumcision.

sed   an ancient royal feast.

sekhem   the vital force of a human being that serves as a companion in eternity but is distinct from the *ka* and *ba*; translated literally as "to have mastery over something."

senut   the term for flagstaffs at temple entrances.

sepat   the name for a nome, or province, and a nome totem.

seshed   a type of royal crown.

shabti   the figure placed in the tomb to answer a divine summons.

Shemau   the name for the Upper Kingdom, the southern portion of Egypt.

shen, shennu   "that which encircles," a circle that evolved into a cartouche.

shena   the part of the palace reserved for servants and the kitchens.

shes   the word for alabaster.

sheshen   the name for the lotus.

sheshmet   the word for malachite.

sheta   a hidden mystery, secret lore.

shomu (shemu)   a season of the Egyptian calendar for harvests, comprising four months of 30 days each, celebrated following *akhet* and *proyet* each year.

shoy   the term for fate, also called *shai*.

Shub   the Persea Tree, a cedar tree in Heliopolis.

sma-tawy   the symbol of the unified Upper and Lower Kingdoms.

Swenet   "the Southern Gate," a term for Aswan.

Ta-Meht   a word meaning Lower Egypt.

Ta-Resu   a word meaning Upper Egypt.

Ta-set a'a   the "Great Place," the Valley of the Kings.

Ta-set-neferu   the "Place of the Royal Children," the Valley of the Queens.

Ta-Seti   a section of Nubia, "the Land of the Bow."

Ta-she   an area of the Faiyum, the Land of the Lakes.

thet   an amulet called the Girdle of Isis.

tjam   a word for electrum or white gold.

tjehenet   the word for faience, translated as brilliant.

Tuat   the term for the Underworld, also called Duat.

uatch   the term for the green stone amulet.

Uat-ur   "the Great Green," the Mediterranean Sea.

Uben   the spirits that bring the dawn.

uraeus   the cobra and vulture, a royal symbol.

ur-heka   a mortuary instrument used to open the mouth of the corpse.

wadj   the color green.

wadj-en-Bakh   "the Green Stone of the East," beryl.

wadjet   the symbol of the Eye of Ré.

waret   the abyss from which Ré arose.

wedjau   an amulet of a god.

Wepet-renpet   the New Year.

wereret   the double crown of the pharaohs.

Zent   a dead bird, an omen of misfortune.

SELECT BIBLIOGRAPHY

The following is a suggested reading list of Egyptian studies and histories. The selected books are in English or English translation.

Adams, Barbara. *Egyptian Mummies*. Ayelsbury: Shire Publications, 1984.

Adkins, Lesley and Roy. *The Keys of Egypt: The Obsession to Decipher Egyptian Hieroglyphs*. New York: Harper Collins, 2000.

Aldred, Cyril. *Egypt to the End of the Old Kingdom*. London: Thames & Hudson, 1965.

———. *The Egyptians*. London: Thames & Hudson, 1961; 2nd ed., 1984.

———. *Egyptian Art in the Days of the Pharaohs, 3100–320 B.C.* New York: Thames & Hudson, 1985.

Allen, James P. *Middle Egyptian: An Introduction to the Language and Culture of Hieroglyphs*. Cambridge, Eng.: Cambridge University Press, 2000.

———. *Religion and Philosophy in Ancient Egypt*. New Haven, Conn.: Yale University Press, 1989.

Allen, Thomas G. *The Egyptian Book of the Dead: Documents in the Oriental Institute Museum at the University of Chicago*. Chicago: University of Chicago Press, 1960.

Allen, Troy. *The Ancient Egyptian Family: Kinship and Social Structure*. London: Routledge, 2008.

Andrews, Carol. *Egyptian Mummies*. London: British Museum Press, 1984.

Antelme, Ruth, and Stephane Rossini. *Becoming Osiris: The Ancient Egyptian Death Experience*. Rochester, Vt.: Inner Traditions International Ltd., 1998.

Armour, Robert. *Gods and Myths of Ancient Egypt*. Cairo: American University in Cairo Press, 1986.

Arnold, Dieter. *Temples of Ancient Egypt*. Ithaca, N.Y.: Cornell University Press, 1997.

———. *Temples of the Last Pharaohs*. Oxford, U.K.: Oxford University Press, 1999.

Arnold, Dorothea, Christiane Ziegler, and James P. Allen, eds. *Egyptian Art in the Age of the Pyramids*. New Haven, Conn.: Yale University Press, 1999.

Ashby, Muata Abhaya. *The Hymns of Amun: Ancient Egyptian Mystical Psychology*. New York: Cruzian Mystic, 1997.

Assman, Jan, and Anthony Alcock, transl. *Egyptian Solar Religion in the New Kingdom: RE, Amun and the Crisis of Polytheism*. New York: Routledge, 1995.

Baines, John, and Jaromír Málek. *Atlas of Ancient Egypt*. Oxford, U.K.: Phaidon, 1980.

Bennett, James, and Vivianne Crowley. *Magic and Mysteries of Ancient Egypt*. New York: Sterling Publishing, 2001.

Berbrier, Morris. *Tomb Builders of the Pharaohs*. New York: Charles Scribner's Sons, 1984.

Bertro, Maria Carmelo. *Hieroglyphics: The Writings of Ancient Egypt*. New York: Abbeville, 1996.

Blackman, Aylward M. *Gods, Priests and Men: Studies in the Religion of Pharaonic Egypt*. 2d ed. London: Kegan Paul International, 1995.

Bowman, Alan. *Egypt after the Pharaohs, 332 B.C.–A.D. 642*. Berkeley: University of California Press, 1986.

Borghouts, Joris F., "Akhu and Hekau: Two Basic Notions of Ancient Egyptian Magic, and the Concept of Divine Creative Word," in Alessandro Roccati and Alberto Siliotti, eds., *Magic in Egypt in the Time of the Pharaohs: International Study Conference, Milan 29–31 October 1985*. Milan: Rassegna Internazionale di Cinematografia Archeologica Arte e Natura Libri, 1987, pp. 29–46.

———. "The Edition of Magical Papyri in Turin: A Progress Report," in Alessandro Roccati and Alberto Siliotti, eds., *Magic in Egypt in the Time of the Pharaohs: International Study Conference, Milan 29–31 October 1985*. Milan: Rassegna Internazionale di Cinematografia Archeologica Arte e Natura Libri, 1987, pp. 257–269.

Bowman, Alan K. *Egypt After the Pharaohs: 332 B.C.–A.D. 642 from Alexander to the Arab Conquest*. Berkeley: University of California Press, 1996.

Breasted, James H. *Ancient Records of Egypt,* 4 vols. Chicago: University of Chicago Press, 1906.

———. *The Dawn of Conscience*. New York: Scribner's, 1933; repr. 1968.

———. *Development of Religion and Thought in Ancient Egypt: Lectures Delivered on the Morse Foundation at Union Theological Seminary*. New York: Scribner's, 1912; repr., Harpers & Brothers, 1959.

———. *A History of Egypt: From the Earliest Times to the Persian Conquest*. New York: Simon and Schuster, 1999.

Brier, Bob. *Ancient Egyptian Magic*. New York: Morrow, 1980.

Brown, Dale, ed. *Egypt: Land of the Pharaohs*. Alexandria, Va.: Time-Life Books, 1992.

Budge, E. A. Wallis. *From Fetish to God in Ancient Egypt*. London: Oxford University Press, 1934; repr. 1972.

———. *Egyptian Magic*. New York: University Books, 1958.

———. *The Egyptian Sudan: Its History and Monuments,* 2 vols. 1907. Reprint, London: Kegan Paul, 1986.

———. *The Mummy: Handbook of Egyptian Funerary Archaeology*. 1893. Reprint, London: KPI, 1987.

Caminos, Ricardo A., "Magic for the Dead," in A. Roccati and A. Siliotti, eds., *Magic in Egypt in the Time of the Pharaohs: International Study Conference, Milan 29–31*

October 1985. Milan: Rassegna Internazionale di Cinematografia Archeologica Arte e Natura Libri, 1987, pp. 147–159.

Cerny, Jaroslav. *Ancient Egyptian Religion.* London: Hutchinson's University Library, 1957.

Chauvreau, Michel. *Egypt in the Age of Cleopatra.* Ithaca, N.Y., and London: Cornell University Press, 1997.

Clark, R. T. Rundle. *Myth and Symbol in Ancient Egypt.* London: Thames & Hudson, 1959.

Clayton, Peter A. *Chronicle of the Pharaohs.* London: Thames & Hudson, 1994.

Cline, Eric H., and David Kevin O'Connor. *Amenhotep III: Perspectives on His Reign.* Ann Arbor, Mich.: University of Michigan Press, 2001.

Cohen, R., and R. Westbrook, eds. *Amarna Diplomacy: The Beginnings of International Relations.* Baltimore: Johns Hopkins University Press, 2000.

Cottrell, Leonard. *Life Under the Pharaohs.* London: Evans Brothers, 1955; London: Pan, 1957; New York: Holt, Rinehart, 1960.

———. *Egypt.* London: Vane, 1966.

Cruz-Uribe, Eugene, and George R. Hughes, "A Strike Pa pyrus from the Reign of Amasis," *Serapis* 5 (1979): 21–26.

David, A. Rosalie. *The Ancient Egyptians: Religious Beliefs and Practices.* London: Routledge & Kegan Paul, 1982.

———. *Cult of the Sun: Myth and Magic in Ancient Egypt.* London: Dent, 1980.

———. *The Egyptian Kingdoms.* 1975. Reprint, Oxford, U.K.: Elsevier, 1988.

———. *Handbook to Life in Ancient Egypt.* New York: Facts On File, 1998.

Davies, W. V. *Egyptian Hieroglyphs.* London: British Museum, 1987.

Dawson, Warren R., "The Number 'Seven' in Egyptian Texts," *Aegyptus* 8 (1927): 97–107.

———. "Notes on Egyptian Magic," *Aegyptus* 11 (1931): 23–28.

De Beler, Aude Gros. *Pharaohs.* Paris: La Maison de Molière, 2000.

Diodorus Siculus. *Diodorus on Egypt.* London: MacFarland & Co. 1985.

Donadoni, Sergio, and Anna Maria Donadoni Roveri. *Egyptian Civilization,* 3 vols. Milan: 1987–1989.

Dodson, Aidan. *Monarchs of the Nile.* London: Rubicon Press, 1995.

Dodson, Aidan, and Dyan Hilton. *The Complete Royal Families of Ancient Egypt.* London: Thames & Hudson, 2004.

Drioton, Éienne. *Religions of the Ancient East.* London: Burns and Oates, 1959.

Dzierzykary-Rogalski, Tadeusz, "The Magic Procedure of Breaking Bones in Ancient Egypt (Dakhleh Oasis)," *Africana-Bulletin* 30 (1981): 221–224.

El-Daly, Okasha. *Egyptology: The Missing Millennium.* London: UCL Press, 2005.

Ellis, Normandi, Gary Roberston, and Robert Kelley. *Awakening Osiris: The Egyptian Book of the Dead.* New York: Phanes, 1991.

El Mahdy, Christine. *Tutankhamun: The Life and Death of the Boy-King.* New York: St. Martin's Press, 2000.

Emery, W. B. *Archaic Egypt.* Harmondsworth, U.K.: Penguin, 1987.

Empereur, Jean-Yves. *Alexandria Rediscovered.* New York: George Braziller, 1998.

Engelbach, Reginald. *Introduction to Egyptian Archaeology, with Special Reference to the Egyptian Museum, Cairo.* 1946. Reprint, Cairo: Government Printing Office, 1961.

Englund, Gertie, ed. *The Religion of the Ancient Egyptians: Cognitive Structures and Popular Expressions.* Uppsala: S. Academie Ubsaliensis, 1989.

Erman, Adolf. *Life in Ancient Egypt.* New York: Blom, 1969.

Evans, Humphrey. *The Mystery of the Pyramids.* New York: Crowell, 1979.

Eyre, C. J., "An Accounts Papyrus from Thebes," *JEA* 66 (1980): 108–119.

Faulkner, Raymond O. *The Ancient Egyptian Book of the Dead.* London: British Museum Publications, 1985.

Fazzini, Richard, James F. Romano, and Madeleine E. Cody. *Art for Eternity: Masterworks from Ancient Egypt.* New York: Scala Books, 1999.

Fedden, Robin. *Egypt: Land of the Valley.* London: Murray, 1977.

Filer, Joyce. *Disease.* Austin: University of Texas Press, 1996.

Finegan, Jack. *Archaeological History of the Ancient Middle East.* New York: Dorset Press, 1986.

Fischer, Henry G. *Women of the Old Kingdom and of the Heracleopolitan Period.* New York: Metropolitan Museum of Art, 1989.

Fletcher, J. *Chronicle of a Pharaoh: The Intimate Life of Amenhotep III.* Oxford, U.K.: Oxford University Press, 2000.

Forbes, R. J. *Studies in Ancient Technology,* 7 vols. Leiden: Brill, 1955–1963.

Frankfort, Henri. *Ancient Egyptian Religion: An Interpretation.* New York: Columbia University Press, 1948.

Frankfurter, David. *Religion in Roman Egypt.* Princeton, N.J.: Princeton University Press, 2000.

Gahlin, Lucia. *Egypt: Gods, Myths and Religion.* New York: Lorenz, 2001.

Gardiner, Alan H. "Magic (Egyptian)," in James Hastings, ed., *Encyclopedia of Religion and Ethics.* Edinburgh: T&T Clark, 1915; repr. New York: Scribner's, 1922, Vol. 8, pp. 262–269.

———. "Ramesside Texts Relating to the Taxation and Transport of Corn," *JEA* 27 (1941): 19–73.

Ghalioungui, Paul. *The Physicians of Pharaonic Egypt.* Deutsches Archaologisches Institut, Abteilung Kairo, Sonderschrift 10. Mainz am Rhein: Verlag Philipp von Zabern, 1983.

Goedicke, Hans. *Studies in the Hekanakhte Papers.* Baltimore: Halgo, 1984.

———. "Unity and Diversity in the Oldest Religion of Ancient Egypt," in Hans Goedicke, Hans and J. J. M. Roberts, eds., *Unity and Diversity: Essays in the History Literature and Religion of the Ancient Near East.* Baltimore: Johns Hopkins University Press, 1975, pp. 201–217.

Goelet, Ogden, ed.; Raymond, Faulkner, transl. *The Egyptian Book of the Dead: The Book of Going Forth by Day.* New York: Chronicle Books, 2000.

Grafton, Elliot Smith. *The Royal Mummies.* Cairo: Cairo Museum Press, 1909.

Grant, Michael. *Cleopatra.* London: Phoenix Press, 2000.

Greenblatt, Miriam. *Hatshepsut and Ancient Egypt.* New York: Marshall Cavendish, 2000.

Griffiths, J. Gwyn. *Plutarch's De Iside et Osiride.* Swansea: University of Wales Press, 1970.

———. "The Religion of Ancient Egypt," in Geoffret Parrinder, ed., *Man and His Gods: Encyclopedia of the World's Religions.* London: Hamlyn, 1971, pp. 112–123.

Grimal, Nicolas. *A History of Ancient Egypt.* Cambridge, U.K.: Blackwell, 1995.

Hardy, Eduard Rochie. *The Large Estates of Byzantine Egypt.* New York: Columbia University Press, 1931.

Hare, Tom. *Remembering Osiris: Number, Gender, and the World in Ancient Egyptian Representational Systems.* Stanford, Calif.: Stanford University Press, 1999.

Harris, James, and Edward Wente. *An X-Ray Atlas of the Royal Mummies.* Chicago: University of Chicago Press, 1980.

Harris, James, ed. *The Legacy of Egypt,* 2nd ed. Oxford, U.K.: Clarendon, 1971.

Hart, George. *Pharaohs and Pyramids: A Guide Through Old Kingdom Egypt.* London: Herbert Press, 1991.

Hawass, Zahi A. *The Pyramids of Ancient Egypt.* New York: Carnegie Museum of Natural History, 1998.

———. *Silent Images: Women in Pharaonic Egypt.* New York: Harry N. Abrams, Inc., 2000.

———. *The Secrets of the Sphinx: Restoration Past and Present.* Cairo: American University in Cairo Press, 1999.

Hawass, Zahi, and Farouk Hosni. *The Mysteries of Abu Simbel: Ramesses II and the Temples of the Rising Sun.* Cairo: American University in Cairo Press, 2001.

Hayes, William C., "Daily Life in Ancient Egypt," *National Geographic Magazine* 80 (1941): 419–515. Repr. in *Everyday Life in Ancient Times.* Washington, D.C.: National Geographic Society, 1951.

Healy, Mark. *The Warrior Pharaoh: Ramesses II and the Battle of Quadesh.* London: Osprey, 2000.

Herodotus. *Books I–IX.* A. D. Godley, transl. 4 vols. Cambridge, Mass.: Harvard University Press, 1920–1925; repr. 1946.

Hickmann, Hans. *Music Under the Pharaohs.* Cairo: Egyptian State Tourist Administration, 1959.

Hobson, Christine. *The World of the Pharaohs: A Complete Guide to Ancient Egypt.* New York: Thames & Hudson, 1987.

Hodel-Hoenes, Sigrid, and David Warburton, transl. *Life and Death in Ancient Egypt: Scenes from Private Tombs in New Kingdom Thebes.* Ithaca, N.Y.: Cornell University Press, 2000.

Hodges, Henry. *Technology in the Ancient World.* London: Penguin, 1970.

Hoffmeier, J. K. *"Sacred" in the Vocabulary of Ancient Egypt: The Term Dsr, with Special Reference to Dynasties IX–XX.* Freiburg: Schweiz Götingen, 1985.

Holbl, Gunther, and Tina Saavedra, transl. *A History of the Ptolemaic Empire.* New York: Routledge, 2000.

Hornung, Erik, and John Baines, transl. *Conceptions of God in Ancient Egypt: The One and the Many.* Ithaca, N.Y.: Cornell University Press, 1982.

Hornung, Erik, and David Lorton, transl. *History of Ancient Egypt: An Introduction.* Ithaca, N.Y.: Cornell University Press, 1999.

———. *The Ancient Egyptian Books of the Afterlife.* Ithaca: Cornell University Press, 1999.

Isler, Martin, and Dieter Arnold. *Sticks, Stones, and Shadows: Building the Egyptian Pyramids.* Norman: University of Oklahoma, 2001.

Jacq, Christian. *Egyptian Magic.* Warminster: Aris and Philips, 1985.

Jacq, Christian, and Janet M. Davis, transl. *Magic and Mystery in Ancient Egypt.* Detroit, Mich.: Souvenir Press, 2000.

James, T. G. H. *Ancient Egypt: The Land and Its Legacy.* London: British Museum, 1988.

———. *The Archaeology of Ancient Egypt.* London: Bodley Head, 1972.

———. *An Introduction to Ancient Egypt.* London: British Museum, 1979.

———. *The British Museum Concise Introduction to Ancient Egypt.* Ann Arbor, Mich.: University of Michigan Press, 2005.

———. *Pharaoh's People: Scenes From Life in Imperial Egypt.* London: Bodley Head, 1984.

———. *Ancient Egypt: The Land and Its Legacy.* London: British Museum, 1988.

James, T. G. Henry, Araldo de Luca, and Elisabetta Ferrero. *Tutankhamun.* New York: Friedman/Fairfax, 2000.

Janssen, Jac J. *Commodity Prices from the Ramessid Period: An Economic Study of the Village of Necropolis Workmen at Thebes.* Leiden: Brill, 1975.

———. "Prolegomena to the Study of Egypt's Economic History During the New Kingdom," *SÄK* 3 (1975): 127–185.

Johnson, Allan Ch., and Louis C. West. *Byzantine Egypt: Economic Studies.* Amsterdam: Hakkert, 1949; repr., 1967.

Johnson, Paul. *The Civilization of Ancient Egypt.* London: Weidenfeld and Nicolson, 1978.

Jordan, Paul. *Egypt the Black Land.* Oxford, U.K.: Phaidon, 1976.

Kákosy, László, "Some Problems of the Magical Healing Statues," in Alessandro Roccati and Alberto Siliotti, eds., *Magic in Egypt in the Time of the Pharaohs: International Study Conference, Milan 29–31 October 1985.* Milan: Rassegna Internazionale di Cinematografia Archeologica Arte e Natura Libri, 1987, pp. 171–186.

Kamil, Jill. *The Ancient Egyptians: How They Lived and Worked.* 1976. Reprint, Cairo: American University in Cairo, 1984.

Kaster, Joseph. *The Literature and Mythology of Ancient Egypt.* London: Penguin, 1985.

———. *The Wisdom of Ancient Egypt.* New York: Barnes and Noble, 1993.

Kemp, Barry J. *Ancient Egypt: Anatomy of a Civilization.* London: Routledge, 1989.

Kitchen, Kenneth A. *The Third Intermediate Period in Egypt (1100–650 B.C.),* 2d ed., rev. Warminster, U.K.: Aris and Phillips, Ltd., 1986.

Kong, S. *The Books of Thoth: The Adventure that Unveiled the Mysteries of Ancient Egypt.* Victoria, B.C., Canada: Evergreen Press Property Ltd., 1998.

Kuhrt, Amélie. *The Ancient Near East,* Vol. II. London: Routledge, 1995.

Lesko, Barbara. *The Great Goddesses of Egypt.* Norman: University of Oklahoma Press, 1999.

———. *The Remarkable Women of Ancient Egypt.* Berkeley, Calif.: Scribe, 1978.

———. *Women's Earliest Records from Ancient Egypt and Western Asia.* Atlanta, Ga.: Scholar's Press, 1989.

Lewis, Naphtali. *Life in Egypt Under Roman Rule.* Oxford, U.K.: Clarendon, 1983.

Lexova, I. *Ancient Egyptian Dances.* Mineola, N.Y.: Dover Publications, Inc., 2000.

Lichtheim, Miriam. *Ancient Egyptian Literature.* Berkeley: University of California Press, 1975.

Lindsay, Jack. *Daily Life in Roman Egypt.* London: Müller, 1963.

———. *The Origins of Alchemy in Graeco-Roman Egypt.* London: Müller, 1970.

Lucas, A. *Ancient Egyptian Materials and Industries.* 1962. Reprint, London: Histories and Mysteries of Man, 1989.

Lürker, Manfred. *The Gods and Symbols of Ancient Egypt: An Illustrated Dictionary,* transl. Barbara Cummings. New York: Thames & Hudson, 1980.

Lutz, Henry F., "Egyptian Song and Music," *University of California Chronicle* 27 (1925): 134–152.

MacLennan, Hugh. *Oxyrhynchus: Economical and Social Study.* 1935. Reprint, Princeton, N.J.: Princeton University Press, 1968.

MacLeod, Roy. *The Library of Alexandria: Centre of Learning in the Ancient World.* London: B. Tauris, 2000.

McDonald, John. *The Tomb of Nefertari.* Los Angeles: Getty Conservation Institute, 1996.

Malek, Jaromir. *Egyptian Art.* New York: Phaidon Press, 1999.

———. *In the Shadow of the Pyramids: Egypt During the Old Kingdom.* London: Orbis, 1986.

El Mallakh, Kamal, and Robert Bianchi. *Treasures of the Nile: Art of Temples and Tombs of Egypt.* New York: Newsweek, 1980.

Manetho. Transl. W. G. Waddell. Cambridge, Mass.: Harvard University Press, 1940; repr., 1948.

Manley, Deborah. *The Nile, A Traveller's Anthology.* London: Cossell, 1991.

Manniche, Lise. *Music and Musicians in Ancient Egypt.* London: British Museum, 1991.

Martin, Geoffrey. *The Hidden Tombs of Memphis.* London: Thames & Hudson, 1991.

Maspero, Gaston C., and Emile Brugsch, Nicholas Reeves, and G. Raggett, trans. *Royal Tombs of Deir el-Bahri.* New York: Routledge, 1993.

Mazar, Amihai. *Archaeology of the Land of the Bible.* New York: Doubleday, 1990.

Menu, Bernadette. *Ramesses II, Greatest of the Pharaohs.* New York: Abrams, 1998.

Mertz, Barbara. *Red Land, Black Land: The World of the Ancient Egyptians.* New York: Coward-McCann, 1966.

———. *Temples, Tombs and Hieroglyphs: A Popular History of Ancient Egypt.* London: Gollancz, 1964.

Midant-Reynes, Beatrix, and Ian Shaw, transl. *The Prehistory of Egypt: From the First Egyptians to the First Pharaohs.* London: Wiley-Blackwell, 2000.

Moens, M-F., and W. Wetterstrom, "The Agricultural Economy of an Old Kingdom Town in Egypt's Western Delta: Insight from the Plant Remains," *JNES* 47 (1988): 159–173.

Montet, Pierre. *Lives of the Pharaohs.* New York: World, 1968.

Montserrat, Dominic. *Akhenaten: History, Fantasy and Ancient Egypt.* New York: Routledge, 2000.

Morenz, Siegfried. *Egyptian Religion.* London: Methuen, 1973.

Moret, Alexandre. *The Nile and Egyptian Civilization.* London: Kegan Paul, 1927.

Moret, Alexandre M., and Georges Davy. *From Tribe to Empire: Social Organization Among Primitives and in the Ancient East.* London: Kegan Paul, 1926.

Morkot, R. *Ancient Egypt and the Middle East.* London: Dorling Kindersley, 2001.

Murphy, Edwin, trans. *Diodorus On Egypt.* London: McFarland, 1985.

Murray, Margaret A. *The Splendor That was Egypt: A General Survey of Egyptian Culture and Civilization.* London: Sidgewick and Jackson, 1949.

Mysliwiec, Karol, and David Lorton, trans. *The Twilight of Ancient Egypt: 1st Millennium B.C.* Ithaca, N.Y.: Cornell University Press, 2000.

Needler, Winifred, "A Statuette of the Egyptian Sixth Dynasty, About 2400 B.C.," *Bulletin of the Royal Ontario Museum of Archaeology, University of Toronto* 18 (1952): 9–12.

Newby, P. H. *The Egypt Story: Its Art, Its Monuments, Its People, Its History.* Cairo: American University in Cairo, 1985.

Nicholson, Paul T., and Ian Shaw. *Ancient Egyptian Materials and Technology.* Cambridge: Cambridge University Press, 2000.

Nims, Charles F. *Thebes of the Pharaohs: Pattern for Every City.* London: Elek, 1965; Toronto: Ryerson, 1965.

Nunn, John F. *Ancient Egyptian Medicine.* Norman: University of Oklahoma Press, 1996.

O'Clery, Helen. *The Pegasus Book of Egypt.* London: Dolson, 1968.

O'Connor, D., and E. Cline, eds. *Amenhotep III, Perspectives on His Reign.* Ann Arbor: University of Michigan Press, 1998.

Oakes, Lorna. *Ancient Egypt: An Illustrated Reference to the Myths, Religions, Pyramids and Temples of the Land of the Pharaohs.* New York: Barnes & Noble, 2003.

Peck, William, Karl Butzer, I. E. S. Edwards, Barbara Mertz, William Kelly Simpson, Virginia Lee Davis, Edna Russman, and Anthony J. Spalinger. *Ancient Egypt: Discovering its Splendors*. Washington, D.C.: National Geographic Society, 1978.

Petrie, W. M. F. *Egyptian Decorative Art*. 1895. Reprint, London: Methuen, 1978.

———. *Social Life in Ancient Egypt*. 1923. Reprint, New York: Cooper Square, 1970.

Pickles, Dewayne E., and Arthur M. Schlesinger, ed. *Egyptian Kings and Queens and Classical Deities*. New York: Chelsea House, 1997.

Pomeroy, Sarah B. *Women in Hellenistic Egypt: From Alexander to Cleopatra*. New York: Schocken, 1984.

Quirke, Stephen. *Ancient Egyptian Religion*. London: BM, 1992.

———. *The Cult of Ra: Sun-Worship in Ancient Egypt*. New York: Thames & Hudson, 2001.

Quirke, Stephen, and A. J. Spencer. *The British Museum Book of Ancient Egypt*. London: British Museum, 1992.

Raven, Maarten, "Charms for Protection During the Epagomenal Days," in *Essays on Ancient Egypt in Honour of Herman te Velde*. Egyptological Memoirs 1 (1997): 275 ff.

Ray, Jay D., "A Consideration of Papyrus Kahun 13," *JEA* 59 (1973): 222–223.

Redford, Donald. *Akhenaten*. Princeton, N.J.: Princeton University Press, 1987.

Reeves, C. N., and Nicholas Reeves. *The Complete Tutankhamun: The King, the Tomb, the Royal Treasure*. New York: Thames & Hudson, 1995.

Reeves, Nicholas and Richard Wilkinson. *The Complete Valley of the Kings*. London: Thames & Hudson, 1996.

Reymond, E. A. E., "Fragment of a Temple Account Roll," *JEA* 60 (1974): 189–199.

Ritner, Robert K. *The Mechanics of Ancient Egyptian Magical Practice*. Chicago: Oriental Institute, 1993.

Robichon, Clement, and Alexandre Varille. *Eternal Egypt*. London: Duckworth, 1955.

Robins, Gay. *The Art of Ancient Egypt*. Cambridge, Mass.: Harvard University Press, 2000.

———. "Some Images of Women in New Kingdom Art and Literature," in B. Lesko, ed., *Women's Earliest Records from Ancient Egypt and Western Asia*. Atlanta, Ga.: Scholar's Press, 1989, pp. 105–116.

———. *Women in Ancient Egypt*. London: British Museum Press, 1993.

Roccati, Alessandro, and Alberto Siliotti, eds., *Magic in Egypt in the Time of the Pharaohs: International Study Conference, Milan 29–31 October 1985*. Milan: Rassegna Internazionale di Cinematografia Archeologica Arte e Natura Libri, 1987, pp. 257–269.

Romer, John. *Romer's Egypt: A New Light on the Civilization of Ancient Egypt*. London: Michael Joseph, 1982.

———. *Valley of the Kings*. New York: Henry Holt, 1994.

Rowlandson, Jane, and Roger Bagnall, eds. *Women and Society in Greek and Roman Egypt: A Sourcebook*. Cambridge: Cambridge University Press, 1998.

Ruffle, John. *The Egyptians: An Introduction to Egyptian Archaeology*. Ithaca, N.Y.: Cornell University Press, 1977.

Saleh, Mohammed, and Hourig Sourouzian. *Egyptian Museum, Cairo: Official Catalogue*. Mainz am Rhein: Verlag Phillip von Zabern, 1987.

Sameh, Waly el-Dine. *Daily Life in Ancient Egypt*. Trans. Michael Bullock. London: McGraw Hill, 1964.

Samson, Julia. *Nefertiti and Cleopatra: Queen-Monarchs in Ancient Egypt*. London: Rubicon, 1985 and 1990.

Sauneron, Serge, and David Lorton, transl. *The Priests of Ancient Egypt: New Edition*. Ithaca, N.Y.: Cornell University Press, 2000.

Scott, Henry Joseph, and Lenore Scott. *Egyptian Hieroglyphics*. London: Hippocrene, 1998.

Scott, Nora E. *The Home Life of the Ancient Egyptians*. New York: Metropolitan Museum of Art, 1947.

Seleem, Ramses. *Illustrated Egyptian Book of the Dead*. New York: Sterling Publishers, 2001.

Sewell, Barbara. *Egypt Under the Pharaohs*. London: Evans Brothers, 1968.

Shafer, Byron R., ed. *Religion in Ancient Egypt: Gods, Myths, and Personal Practice*. Ithaca, N.Y.: Cornell University Press, 1993.

———. *Temples of Ancient Egypt*. Ithaca, N.Y.: Cornell University Press, 1999.

Shaw, Ian, ed. *The Oxford History of Ancient Egypt*. Oxford, U.K.: Oxford University Press, 2000.

Shaw, Ian, and Paul Nicholson. *The Dictionary of Ancient Egypt*. London: Abrams, 1995.

Shorter, Alan W. *Everyday Life in Ancient Egypt*. London: Sampson Low, Marston, 1932.

Siliotti, Alberto. *Abu Simbel and the Nubian Temples*. Cairo: American University in Cairo Press, 2001.

———. *Luxor, Karnak, and the Theban Temples*. Cairo: American University in Cairo Press, 2001.

Silverman, David P., ed. *Ancient Egypt*. Oxford, U.K.: Oxford University Press, 1997.

Silverman, David, ed. *Ancient Egypt*. New York: Oxford University Press, 1997.

Simpson, William K. *Papyrus Reisner, 3: The Records of a Building Project in the Early Twelfth Dynasty*. Boston: Museum of Fine Arts, 1969.

———. *Papyrus Reisner, 4: Personnel Accounts of the Early Twelfth Dynasty*. Boston: MFA, 1986.

Simpson, William K., and Whitney M. Davis, eds. *Studies in Ancient Egypt, the Aegean, and the Sudan*. Boston: Museum of Fine Arts, 1981.

Singer, Charles, E. J. Holmyard, and A. R. Hall. *A History of Technology, 1: From Early Times to the Fall of the Ancient Empires*. Oxford, U.K.: Clarendon, 1956.

Smith, Grafton Elliot. *The Ancient Egyptians and the Origin of Civilization*. London: Harper, 1923.

Smith, Harry S., and Rosalind Hall, eds. *Ancient Centres of Egyptian Civilization*. London: Egyptian Education Bureau, 1983.

Smith, William Stevenson, and William Kelly Simpson. *The Art and Architecture of Ancient Egypt*. New Haven, Conn.: Yale University Press, 1999.

Snell, Daniel. *Life in the Ancient Near East.* New Haven, Conn.: Yale University Press, 1997.

Spencer, Jeffrey. *Death in Ancient Egypt.* Harmondsworth, U.K.: Penguin, 1982.

Stevenson, Smith, W., rev. by W. Simpson. *Art and Architecture of Ancient Egypt.* New Haven, Conn.: Yale University Press, 1998.

Stewart, Desmond. *The Pyramids and Sphinx.* New York: Newsweek Books, 1971.

Stierlin, Henri. *The Cultural History of the Pharaohs.* London: Aurum, 1983.

Strouhal, Eugen. *Life in Ancient Egypt.* Cambridge, U.K.: University Press, 1992.

Strudwick, Nigel, and Helen M. Strudwick. *Thebes in Egypt: A Guide to the Tombs and Temples of Ancient Luxor.* Ithaca, N.Y.: Cornell University Press, 1999.

Szpakowska, Kasia. *Daily Life in Ancient Egypt.* London: Wiley-Blackwell, 2007.

Taylor, John H. *Death and the Afterlife in Ancient Egypt.* Chicago: University of Chicago Press, 2001.

———. *Egyptian Coffins.* Shire Egyptology, 11. Aylesbury, U.K.: Shire Publications, 1989.

Thomas, Angela P. *Egyptian Gods and Myths.* Aylesbury, U.K.: Shire Publications, 1986.

Tierney, Tom. *Ancient Egyptian Fashions.* Mineola, N.Y.: Dover, 1999.

Tobin, Vincent A. *Theological Principles of Egyptian Religion.* New York: Peter Lang, 1989.

Trigger, Bruce G. *Early Civilizations: Ancient Egypt in Context.* Cairo: The American University in Cairo Press, 1993.

———. "The Mainlines to Socio-Economic Development in Dynastic Egypt to the End of the Old Kingdom," in Lech Krzyzanik and Michal Kabusiewicz, eds., *Origin and Early Development of Food-Producing Cultures in North-Eastern Africa.* Poznan: Polska Akademia Nauk, 1984, pp. 101–108.

Trigger, Bruce, Barry Kemp, David O'Connor, and Alan Lloyd. *Ancient Egypt: A Social History.* Cambridge, U.K.: University Press, 1983.

Tyldesley, Joyce A. *Daughters of Isis: Women of Ancient Egypt.* London: Penguin, 1995.

———. *Hatchepsut: The Female Pharaoh.* London: Penguin, 1998.

———. *Ramesses: Egypt's Greatest Pharaoh.* New York: Penguin, 2001.

Verner, Miroslav, and Steven Rendall, transl. *The Pyramids: The Mystery, Culture, and Science of Egypt's Great Monuments.* New York: Grove Press, 2001.

Vleeming, Sven P. *Papyrus Reinhardt: An Egyptian Land List From the Tenth Century* B.C. Berlin: Akademie Verlag, 1993.

Walker, Susan, and Peter Higgs, eds. *Cleopatra of Egypt: From History to Myth.* Princeton, N.J.: Princeton University Press, 2001.

Ward, William A. *Essays on Feminine Titles of the Middle Kingdom and Related Subjects.* Beirut: American University, 1986.

———. "Some Aspects of Private Land Ownership and Inheritance in Ancient Egypt, ca. 2500–1000 B.C.," in Tarif Khalidi, ed., *Land Tenure and Social Transformation in the Middle East.* Beirut: American University, 1984, pp. 63–77.

———. *The Spirit of Ancient Egypt.* Beirut: Khayats, 1965.

Watterson, Barbara. *Gods of Ancient Egypt.* Stroud, U.K.: Sutton Publishing, 1999.

———. *Women in Ancient Egypt.* Stroud, U.K.: Sutton, 1991.

Weeks, Kent. *The Lost Tomb.* New York: William Morrow, 1998.

Weigall, Arthur. *The Life and Times of Akhnaton.* New York: Cooper Square Press, 2000.

Wellesz, Egon, ed. *Ancient and Oriental Music.* Oxford, U.K.: University Press, 1957.

Wenig, Steffen. *The Woman in Egyptian Art.* Leipzig: Edition Leipzig, 1969.

White, Jon E. Manchip. *Ancient Egypt: Its Culture and History.* London: Allen and Unwin, 1970.

———. *Everyday Life in Ancient Egypt.* New York: Putnam, 1963.

Wilkinson, John Gardiner. *The Manners and Customs of the Ancient Egyptians,* 3 vols. London: John Murray, 1878.

Wilkinson, R. H. *The Complete Gods and Goddesses of Ancient Egypt.* London: Thames & Hudson, 2003.

———. *The Complete Temples of Ancient Egypt.* New York: Thames & Hudson, 2000.

Wilkinson, Richard H., and Richard Wilk. *Symbol & Magic in Egyptian Art.* New York: Thames & Hudson, 1999.

Wilkinson, Toby A. H. *Early Dynastic Egypt.* New York: Routledge, 1999.

Williams, Bruce. *Excavations Between Abu Simbel and the Sudan Frontier, Part Seven: 25th Dynasty and Napatan Remains at Qustul Cemeteries W and V.* Chicago: Oriental Institute, 1990.

Wilson, John A. *The Burden of Egypt: An Interpretation of Ancient Egyptian Culture.* Chicago: University of Chicago Press, 1951.

———. *Egypt: The Kingdom of the "Two Lands,"* in *At the Dawn of History: A Background to Biblical History.* Edited by E. A. Speiser. London: Allen, 1964, pp. 267–347.

Winlock, H. E. *Excavations of Deir El-Bahri, 1911–1931.* London: Kegan Paul International Limited, 2000.

Yoyotte, Jean. *Treasures of the Pharaohs: The Early Period; The New Kingdom; The Late Period.* Geneva: Editions d'Art Albert Seira, 1968.

INDEX